Best Jobs for the 21st Century

Fifth Edition

Part of JIST's Best Jobs® Series

Michael Farr and Laurence Shatkin, Ph.D.

Also in JIST's *Best Jobs* Series

- 200 Best Jobs for College Graduates
- 300 Best Jobs Without a Four-Year Degree
- 200 Best Jobs Through Apprenticeships
- 50 Best Jobs for Your Personality
- 40 Best Fields for Your Career
- 225 Best Jobs for Baby Boomers
- 250 Best-Paying Jobs
- 150 Best Jobs for Your Skills

- 175 Best Jobs Not Behind a Desk
- 150 Best Jobs Through Military Training
- 150 Best Jobs for a Better World
- 200 Best Jobs for Introverts
- 10 Best College Majors for Your Personality
- 150 Best Low-Stress Jobs
- 150 Best Recession-Proof Jobs

JIST *Works*
America's Career Publisher®

Best Jobs for the 21st Century, Fifth Edition

© 2009 by JIST Publishing

Published by JIST Works, an imprint of JIST Publishing

7321 Shadeland Station, Suite 200

Indianapolis, IN 46256-3923

Phone: 800-648-JIST Fax: 877-454-7839

E-mail: info@jist.com Web site: www.jist.com

Some Other Books by the Authors

Michael Farr

The Quick Resume & Cover Letter Book

Same-Day Resume

Overnight Career Choice

100 Fastest-Growing Careers

Top 100 Careers Without a Four-Year Degree

Laurence Shatkin

Quick Guide to College Majors and Careers

90-Minute College Major Matcher

Your $100,000 Career Plan

New Guide for Occupational Exploration

150 Best Recession-Proof Jobs

Quantity discounts are available for JIST products. Have future editions of JIST books automatically delivered to you on publication through our convenient standing order program. Please call 800-648-JIST or visit www.jist.com for a free catalog and more information.

Visit www.jist.com for information on JIST, free job search information, tables of contents and sample pages, and ordering information on our many products.

Acquisitions Editor: Susan Pines

Development Editors: Aaron Black, Stephanie Koutek

Cover and Interior Designer: Aleata Halbig

Cover Image: Creatas Images, Fotosearch

Interior Layout: Aleata Halbig

Proofreaders: Jovana San Nicolas-Shirley, Jeanne Clark

Indexer: Joy Dean Lee

Printed in the United States of America

11 10 09 08   9 8 7 6 5 4 3 2 1

Library of Congress Cataloging-in-Publication Data

Farr, Michael.

Best jobs for the 21st century / Michael Farr and Laurence Shatkin. -- 5th ed.

    p. cm. -- (JIST's best jobs series)

Includes index.

ISBN 978-1-59357-536-6 (alk. paper)

1. Vocational guidance. 2. Occupations--Forecasting. I. Shatkin, Laurence. II. Title.

HF5381.15.F37 2009

331.702--dc22

2008046425

We have been careful to provide accurate information throughout this book, but it is possible that errors and omissions have been introduced. Please consider this in making any career plans or other important decisions. Trust your own judgment above all else and in all things.

Trademarks: All brand names and product names used in this book are trade names, service marks, trademarks, or registered trademarks of their respective owners.

ISBN 978-1-59357-536-6

This Is a Big Book, But It Is Very Easy to Use

This book is designed to help you explore career options in a variety of interesting ways. The nice thing about it is that you don't have to read it all. Instead, we designed it to allow you to browse and find information that most interests you.

The table of contents will give you a good idea of what's inside and how to use the book, so we suggest you start there. Part I of the book is made up of interesting lists that will help you explore jobs based on pay, interests, education level, personality type, and many other criteria. Part II provides descriptions for each job included in the book. Just find a job that interests you in one of the lists in Part I and look up its description in Part II. Simple.

How We Selected the Best Jobs for the 21st Century

Deciding on the "best" job is a choice that only you can make, but objective criteria can help you identify jobs that are, for example, better paying than other jobs with similar duties. Here is an explanation of the process we used to determine which jobs to include in this book.

We sorted 727 major jobs from highest to lowest in terms of earnings, growth rate through 2016, and number of annual openings. We then assigned a number to their relative position on each list. The job position numbers on the three lists were then combined, and jobs with the lowest total scores were put on top, followed by jobs with higher total scores on down the list. We included the 500 jobs with the lowest total scores in the book. The first list in Part I is called "The 500 Best Jobs Overall," and it contains the 500 jobs with the best scores in order of their combined scores on all three measures (earnings, growth rate, and openings). You can find descriptions for all 500 best jobs in Part II.

We are not suggesting that the 500 jobs with the best overall scores for earnings, growth, and number of openings are all good ones for you to consider—some will not be. But the 500 jobs that met our criteria present such a wide range of jobs that you are likely to find one or more that will interest you. The jobs that met our "best jobs" criteria are also more likely than average to have higher pay, faster projected growth, and a larger number of openings than other jobs at similar levels of education and training.

Some Things You Can Do with This Book

- ❋ Identify more-interesting or better-paying jobs that don't require additional training or education.
- ❋ Develop long-term plans that may require additional training, education, or experience.
- ❋ Explore and select a college major or a training or educational program that relates to a career objective.
- ❋ Find reliable earnings information to negotiate pay.
- ❋ Prepare for interviews and the job search.

These are a few of the many ways you can use this book. We hope you find it as interesting to browse as we did to put together. We have tried to make it easy to use and as interesting as occupational information can be.

When you are done with this book, pass it along or tell someone else about it. We wish you well in your career and in your life.

Credits and Acknowledgments: While the authors created this book, it is based on the work of many others. The occupational information is based on data obtained from the U.S. Department of Labor and the U.S. Census Bureau. These sources provide the most authoritative occupational information available. The noneconomic job-related information is from the O*NET database, which was developed by researchers and developers under the direction of the U.S. Department of Labor. They, in turn, were assisted by thousands of employers who provided details on the nature of work in the many thousands of job samplings used in the database's development. We used the most recent version of the O*NET database, release 13. We appreciate and thank the staff of the U.S. Department of Labor for their efforts and expertise in providing such a rich source of data. The taxonomy of college majors (the Classification of Instructional Programs) is from the U.S. Department of Education.

Table of Contents

Summary of Major Sections

Introduction. A short overview to help you better understand and use the book. *Starts on page 1.*

Part I: The Best Jobs Lists. Very useful for exploring career options! Lists are arranged into easy-to-use groups. The first group of lists presents the best overall jobs—jobs with the highest earnings, projected growth, and number of openings. More specialized lists follow, presenting the best jobs for workers age 16–24, workers 55 and over, part-time workers, self-employed workers, women, and men. Other lists present the best jobs at various levels of education, by interest, and by personality type. The column starting at right presents all the list titles within the groups. *Starts on page 15.*

Part II: The Job Descriptions. Provides complete descriptions of the 500 jobs that met our criteria for high pay, fast growth, or large number of openings. Each description contains information on earnings, projected growth, job duties, skills, related job titles, education and training required, related knowledge and courses, and many other details. *Starts on page 145.*

Detailed Table of Contents

Introduction

We kept this introduction short to encourage you to actually read it. For this reason, we don't provide many details on the technical issues involved in creating the job lists or descriptions. Instead, we give you short explanations to help you understand and use the information the book provides for career exploration or planning. We think this brief and user-oriented approach makes sense for most people who will use this book.

Who This Book Is For and What It Covers

We created this book to help students and adults explore their career, education, training, and life options. Employers, educators, program planners, career counselors, and others will also find this book to be of value.

To create it, we started with 949 major jobs at all levels of training and education. From these, we selected those with the highest earnings, projected growth rate, and number of job openings. Part I contains lists that rank the jobs according to many criteria, including earnings, growth, openings, education level, and interest area. Part II contains job descriptions for all of the jobs.

We think you will find many of the job lists in Part I interesting and useful for identifying career options to consider. The job descriptions are also packed with useful information.

Where the Information Comes From

The information we used in creating this book comes from three major government sources:

⁂ **The U.S. Department of Labor:** We used several data sources to construct the information we put into this book. We started with the jobs included in the U.S. Department of Labor's O*NET database. The O*NET includes information on about 950 occupations and is now the primary source of detailed information on occupations. The Labor Department updates the O*NET on a regular basis, and we used the most recent one available, version 13. Because we also wanted to include earnings, growth, number of openings—information not included in the O*NET—we used sources at the U.S. Department of Labor's Bureau of Labor Statistics (BLS). The Occupational Employment Statistics survey provided the most reliable figures on earnings we could obtain, and the Employment Projections program provided the nation's best figures on job growth and openings. These two BLS programs use a slightly different system of job titles than the O*NET does, but we were able to link the BLS data to most of the O*NET job titles we used to develop this book.

⊛ **The U.S. Census Bureau:** Data on the demographic characteristics of workers came from the Current Population Survey (CPS), conducted by the U.S. Census Bureau. This includes our information about the proportion of workers in each job who are men and women, are self-employed, or work part time. As with the BLS data, we had to match slightly different sets of job titles, but we were able to identify CPS data for almost all the O*NET jobs.

⊛ **The U.S. Department of Education:** We used the Classification of Instructional Programs, a system developed by the U.S. Department of Education, to cross-reference the education or training programs related to each job.

Of course, information in a database format can be boring and even confusing, so we did many things to help make the data useful and present it to you in a form that is easy to understand.

How the 500 Best Jobs Were Selected

The "This Is a Big Book, But It Is Very Easy to Use" section at the beginning of this book gives a brief description of how we selected the jobs we include in this book. Here are a few more details:

1. We began by creating our own database of information from the O*NET, the Census Bureau, and other sources to include the information we wanted. This database covered 949 job titles at all levels of education and training.

2. We eliminated 222 jobs that lacked information or did not meet our standards for good jobs.

3. We ranked the remaining 727 jobs three times, based on these major criteria: median annual earnings, projected growth through 2016, and number of job openings projected per year.

4. We then added the three numerical rankings for each job to calculate its overall score.

5. To emphasize jobs that tend to pay more, are likely to grow more rapidly, and have more job openings, we selected the 500 job titles with the best total overall scores.

For example, the job with the best combined score for earnings, growth, and number of job openings is Computer Software Engineers, Applications, so this job is listed first even though it is not the best-paying job (which is a tie among 11 jobs, such as Surgeons and Chief Executives), the fastest-growing job (which is Network Systems and Data Communications Analysts), or the job with the most openings (which is Office Clerks, General).

Understand the Limits of the Data in This Book

In this book, we use the most reliable and up-to-date information available on earnings, projected growth, number of openings, and other topics. The earnings data came from the U.S. Department of Labor's Bureau of Labor Statistics. As you look at the figures, keep in mind that they are estimates. They give you a general idea about the number of workers employed, annual earnings, rate of job growth, and annual job openings.

Understand that a problem with such data is that it describes an average. Just as there is no precisely average person, there is no such thing as a statistically average example of a particular job. We say this because data, while helpful, can also be misleading.

Take, for example, the yearly earnings information in this book. This is highly reliable data obtained from a very large U.S. working population sample by the Bureau of Labor Statistics. It tells us the average annual pay received as of May 2007 by people in various job titles. (Actually, it is the median annual pay, which means that half earned more and half less.)

This sounds great, except that half of all people in that occupation earned less than that amount. For example, people who are new to the occupation or with only a few years of work experience often earn much less than the median amount. People who live in rural areas or who work for smaller employers typically earn less than those who do similar work in cities (where the cost of living is higher) or for bigger employers. People in certain areas of the country earn less than those in others. Other factors also influence how much you are likely to earn in a given job in your area. For example, Aircraft Mechanics and Service Technicians in the Detroit–Livonia–Dearborn, Michigan, metropolitan division have median earnings of $56,740, probably because Northwest Airlines has a hub in Detroit and its mechanics are unionized. By comparison, the Allentown–Bethlehem–Easton, Pennsylvania, metropolitan area has no major airline hub and only a small aircraft service facility with nonunionized workers. Aircraft Mechanics and Service Technicians there earn a median of only $31,540.

Beginning wages vary greatly, too, depending not only on location and size of employer, but also on what skills and educational credentials a new hire brings to the job.

Also keep in mind that the figures for job growth and number of openings are projections by labor economists—their best guesses about what we can expect between now and

2016. Those projections are not guarantees. A catastrophic economic downturn, war, or technological breakthrough could change the actual outcome.

Finally, don't forget that the job market consists of both job openings and job *seekers*. The figures on job growth and openings don't tell you how many people will be competing with you to be hired. The Department of Labor does not publish figures on the supply of job candidates, so we are unable to tell you about the level of competition you can expect. Competition is an important issue that you should research for any tentative career goal. The *Occupational Outlook Handbook* provides informative statements for many occupations. You should speak to people who educate or train tomorrow's workers; they probably have a good idea of how many graduates find rewarding employment and how quickly. People in the workforce can provide insights into this issue as well. Use your critical thinking skills to evaluate what people tell you. For example, educators or trainers may be trying to recruit you, whereas people in the workforce may be trying to discourage you from competing. Get a variety of opinions to balance out possible biases.

So, in reviewing the information in this book, please understand the limitations of the data. You need to use common sense in career decision making as in most other things in life. We hope that, by using that approach, you find the information helpful and interesting.

Data Complexities

For those of you who like details, we present some of the complexities inherent in our sources of information and what we did to make sense of them here. You don't need to know these things to use the book, so jump to the next section of the introduction if details bore you.

We selected the jobs on the basis of economic data, and we include information on earnings, projected growth, and number of job openings for each job throughout this book. We think this information is important to most people, but getting it for each job is not a simple task.

Earnings

The employment security agency of each state gathers information on earnings for various jobs and forwards it to the U.S. Bureau of Labor Statistics (BLS). This information is organized in standardized ways by a BLS program called Occupational Employment Statistics, or OES. To keep the earnings for the various jobs and regions comparable, the OES screens out certain types of earnings and includes others, so the OES earnings we use in this book represent straight-time gross pay exclusive of premium pay. More specifically, the OES earnings include each job's base rate; cost-of-living allowances; guaranteed pay; hazardous-duty pay; incentive pay, including commissions and production bonuses; on-call pay; and tips. The OES earnings do not include back pay, jury duty pay, overtime pay, severance pay, shift differentials, nonproduction bonuses, or tuition reimbursements.

Also, self-employed workers are not included in the estimates, and they can be a significant segment in certain occupations. When data on annual earnings for an occupation is highly unreliable, OES does not report a figure, which meant that we reluctantly had to exclude a few occupations, such as Hunters and Trappers, from this book.

For each job, we report three figures related to earnings:

⊛ The Annual Earnings figure shows the median earnings (half earn more, half earn less).

⊛ The Beginning Wage figure shows the 10th percentile earnings (the figure that exceeds the earnings of the lowest 10 percent of the workers). This is a rough approximation of what a beginning worker may be offered.

⊛ The Earnings Growth Potential figure represents the ratio between the 10th percentile and the median. In a job for which this figure is high, you have great potential for increasing your earnings as you gain experience and skills. When the figure is low, it means you will probably need to move on to another occupation to improve your earnings substantially. For the 500 jobs in this book, the earnings growth potential ranges from a high of 71.0% for Judges, Magistrate Judges, and Magistrates to a low of 10.5% for Postal Service Clerks. Because the percentage figures would be hard to interpret, we use verbal tags to indicate the level of Earnings Growth Potential: "very low" when the percentage is less than 25, "low" for 25%–35%, "medium" for 35%–40%, "high" for 40%–50%, and "very high" for any figure higher than 50%. For the highest-paying jobs, those for which BLS reports the median earnings as "more than $145,600," we are unable to calculate a figure for Earnings Growth Potential.

The median earnings for all workers in all occupations were $31,410 in May 2007. The 500 jobs in this book were chosen partly on the basis of good earnings, so their average is a respectable $43,865. (This is a weighted average, which means that jobs with larger workforces are given greater weight in the computation. It also is based on the assumption that a job with income reported as "more than $145,600" pays exactly $145,600, so the actual average is somewhat higher.)

The beginning (that is, 10th percentile) wage for all occupations in May 2007 was $16,060. For the 500 jobs in this book, the weighted average is $26,932.

The earnings data from the OES survey is reported under a system of job titles called the Standard Occupational Classification system, or SOC. Most of these jobs can be cross-referenced to the O*NET job titles we use in this book, so we can attach earnings information to most job titles and descriptions. But a small number of the O*NET jobs simply do not have earnings data available for them from the sources we used and, therefore, were not included. In some other cases, an SOC title cross-references to more than one O*NET job title. For example, the O*NET has separate information for Accountants and for Auditors, but the BLS reports earnings for a single SOC occupation called Accountants and Auditors. Therefore you may notice that the salary we report for Accountants ($57,060) is identical to the salary we report for Auditors. In reality, there probably is a difference, but this is the best information available.

Projected Growth and Number of Job Openings

This information comes from the Office of Occupational Statistics and Employment Projections, a program within the Bureau of Labor Statistics (BLS) that develops information about projected trends in the nation's labor market for the next ten years. The most recent projections available cover the years from 2006 to 2016. The projections are based on information about people moving into and out of occupations. The BLS uses data from various sources in projecting the growth and number of openings for each job title—some data comes from the Census Bureau's Current Population Survey and some comes from an Occupational Employment Statistics (OES) survey. The BLS economists assumed a steady economy unaffected by a major war, depression, or other upheaval. They also assumed that recessions may occur during the decade covered by these projections, as would be consistent with the pattern of business cycles we have experienced for several decades. However, because their projections cover 10 years, the figures for job growth and openings are intended to provide an average of both the good times and the bad times.

Like the earnings figures, the figures on projected growth and job openings are reported according to the Standard Occupation Classification (SOC) classification. So again, we had to exclude a few jobs from this book because this information is not available for them. As with earnings, some of the SOC jobs crosswalk to more than one O*NET job. To continue the example we used earlier, the Department of Labor reports growth (17.7%) and openings (134,463) for one SOC occupation called Accountants and Auditors, but in this book, we report these figures separately for the O*NET occupation Accountants and for the O*NET occupation Auditors. When you see that Accountants has a 17.7% projected growth rate and 134,463 projected job openings and Auditors has the same two numbers, you should realize that the 17.7% rate of projected growth represents the *average* of these two occupations—one may actually experience higher growth than the other—and that these two occupations will *share* the 134,463 projected openings.

The Department of Labor provides a single figure (22.9%) for the projected growth of 38 postsecondary teaching jobs and also provides a single figure (237,478) for the projected annual job openings for these 38 jobs. Because these college-teaching jobs are related to very different interests—from engineering to art to forestry to social work—and because separate *earnings* figures are available for each of the 38 jobs, we thought you'd appreciate having these jobs appear separately in the lists in this book. If the trends of the last several years continue, none of these jobs can be expected to grow or take on workers at a faster rate than the other 37. Therefore, in preparing the Part I lists and the Part II descriptions, we assumed that all of these college-teaching jobs share the same rate of projected job growth, 22.9%, and we computed a figure for their projected job openings by dividing the total (237,478) into 38 parts, each of which is proportional in size to the current workforce of the job.

While salary figures are fairly straightforward, you may not know what to make of job-growth figures. For example, is projected growth of 15% good or bad? Keep in mind that the average (mean) growth projected for all occupations by the BLS is 10.4%. One-quarter of the SOC occupations have a growth projection of 3.2% or lower. Growth of 11.6% is the median, meaning that half of the occupations have more, half less. Only one-quarter of the occupations have growth projected at more than 17.4%.

Because the jobs in this book were selected as "best" partly on the basis of job growth, their mean growth is 12.3%, which compares favorably to the mean for all jobs. Among these 500 jobs, the job ranked 125th by projected growth has a figure of 19.7%, the job ranked 250th (the median) has a projected growth of 12.8%, and the job ranked 375th has a projected growth of 9.8%.

The number of job openings for the 500 best jobs is slightly lower than the national average for all occupations. The BLS projects an average of about 35,000 job openings per year for the 750 occupations that it studies, but for the 500 occupations included in this book, the average is about 34,000 openings. The job ranked 125th for job openings has a figure of about 35,000 annual openings, the job ranked 250th (the median) has about 14,300 openings projected, and the job ranked 375th has about 6,600 openings projected.

However, keep in mind that figures for job openings depend on how BLS defines an occupation. For example, consider the college teaching jobs. The Office of Occupational Statistics and Employment Projections recognizes one occupation called Teachers, Postsecondary, and projects 237,478 annual job openings for this occupation. As explained earlier in this introduction, we divided this huge occupation into 38 separate occupations, following the practice of O*NET and of the OES program. The "average" number of openings for all occupations changes substantially, depending on whether you deal with college teachers as one or 38 occupations. So it follows that, because the way BLS defines occupations is somewhat arbitrary, any "average" figure for job openings is also somewhat arbitrary.

Perhaps you're wondering why we present figures on both job growth *and* number of openings. Aren't these two ways of saying the same thing? Actually, you need to know both. Consider the occupation Makeup Artists, Theatrical and Performance, which is projected to grow at the astounding rate of 39.8%. There should be lots of opportunities in such a fast-growing job, right? Not exactly. This is a tiny occupation, with only about 2,100 people currently employed. So, even though it is growing rapidly, it will not create many new jobs (about 400 per year). Now consider Team Assemblers. Because of the decline of domestic manufacturing, this occupation is hardly growing at all—it's growing at the glacial rate of 0.1%. Nevertheless, this is a huge occupation that employs over 1.25 million workers. So, even though its growth rate is unimpressive, it is expected to take on over 260,000 new workers each year as existing workers move on to other jobs, retire, or die. That's why we base our selection of the best jobs on both of these economic indicators and why you should pay attention to both when you scan our lists of best jobs.

Other Job Characteristics

Like the figures for earnings, some of the other figures used to create the lists of jobs in this book are shared by more than one job title. Usually this is the case for occupations that are so small that the Bureau of Labor Statistics (BLS) does not release separate statistics for them. For example, the occupation Cardiovascular Technologists and Technicians has a total workforce of only about 45,000 workers, so the BLS does not report a specific figure for the percentage of women workers. In this case, we had to use the figure that the BLS reports for a group of occupations it calls Diagnostic Related Technologists and Technicians. We relied on this same figure for four other jobs: Diagnostic Medical Sonographers, Nuclear Medicine Technologists, Radiologic Technicians, and Radiologic Technologists. You may notice similar figure-sharing among related jobs where we list the percentages of workers in specific age brackets.

Information in the Job Descriptions

We used a variety of government and other sources to compile the job descriptions we provide in Part II. Details on these various sources are mentioned later in this introduction in the section "Part II: The Job Descriptions."

Part I: The Best Jobs Lists

There are 69 separate lists in Part I of this book—look in the table of contents for a complete list of the lists. The lists are not difficult to understand, because they have clear titles and are organized into groupings of related lists.

Depending on your situation, some of the job lists in Part I will interest you more than others. For example, if you are young, you may be interested to learn the highest-paying jobs that employ high percentages of workers age 16–24. Other lists show jobs within interest groupings, by personality type, by level of education, and in other ways that you might find helpful in exploring your career options.

Whatever your situation, we suggest you use the lists that make sense for you to help explore career options. Following are the names of each group of lists along with short comments on each group. You will find additional information in a brief introduction provided at the beginning of each group of lists in Part I.

Here is an overview of each major group of lists you will find in Part I.

Best Jobs Overall: Lists of Jobs with the Highest Pay, Fastest Growth, and Most Openings

Four lists are in this group, and they are the ones that most people want to see first. The first list presents all 500 job titles in order of their combined scores for earnings, growth, and number of job openings. Three more lists in this group present the 100 jobs with the highest earnings, the 100 jobs projected to grow most rapidly, and the 100 jobs with the most openings.

Best Jobs Lists by Demographic

This group of lists presents interesting information for a variety of types of people based on data from the U.S. Census Bureau. The lists are arranged into groups for workers age 16–24, workers age 55 and older, part-time workers, self-employed workers, women, and men. We created five lists for each group, basing the last four on the information in the first list:

* Jobs having the highest percentage of people of each type
* 25 jobs with the best combined scores for earnings, growth, and number of openings
* 25 jobs with the highest earnings
* 25 jobs with the highest growth rates
* 25 jobs with the largest number of openings

Best Jobs Lists Based on Levels of Education and Experience

We created separate lists for each level of education and training as defined by the U.S. Department of Labor. We put each of the 500 job titles into one of the lists based on the education and training required for entry. Jobs within these lists are presented in order of their total combined scores for earnings, growth, and number of openings. The lists include jobs in these groupings:

* Short-term on-the-job training
* Moderate-term on-the-job training
* Long-term on-the-job training
* Work experience in a related job
* Postsecondary vocational training
* Associate degree
* Bachelor's degree
* Work experience plus degree
* Master's degree
* Doctoral degree
* First professional degree

Best Jobs Lists Based on Interests

These lists organize the 500 jobs into groups based on interests. Within each list, jobs are presented in order of their total scores for earnings, growth, and number of openings. Here are the 16 interest areas used in these lists: Agriculture and Natural Resources; Architecture and Construction; Arts and Communication; Business and Administration; Education and Training; Finance and Insurance; Government and Public Administration; Health Science; Hospitality, Tourism, and Recreation; Human Service; Information Technology; Law and Public Safety; Manufacturing; Retail and Wholesale Sales and Service; Scientific Research, Engineering, and Mathematics; Transportation, Distribution, and Logistics. These interest areas are based on the 16 U.S. Department of Education career clusters.

Best Jobs Lists Based on Personality Types

These lists organize the 500 jobs into six personality types, which are described in the introduction to the lists: Realistic, Investigative, Artistic, Social, Enterprising, and Conventional. The jobs within each list are presented in order of their total scores for earnings, growth, and number of openings.

Bonus Lists: Jobs with the Greatest Changes in Outlook Since the Previous Edition

These two lists show the jobs that have had the greatest revisions to their job-growth projections since the previous edition of this book. One lists the 25 jobs with the greatest increase in job-growth projection, and the other lists the 25 jobs with the greatest decrease.

Part II: The Job Descriptions

This part of the book provides a brief but information-packed description for the jobs that met our criteria for this book. The descriptions in Part II are presented in alphabetical order by job title. This makes it easy to look up any job you find in Part I that you want to learn more about.

We used the most current information from a variety of government sources to create the descriptions. We designed the descriptions to be easy to understand, and the sample that follows—with an explanation of each of its component parts—will help you better understand and use the descriptions.

- **Job Title:** This is the job title for the job as defined by the U.S. Department of Labor and used in its O*NET database.
- **Data Elements:** The information on education, earnings, growth, annual openings, percentage of self-employed workers, and percentage of part-time workers comes from various government databases, as we explained earlier in this introduction.

Job Title →

Administrative Services Managers

Data Elements →

- ❋ Education/Training Required: Work experience plus degree
- ❋ Annual Earnings: $70,990
- ❋ Beginning Wage: $36,000
- ❋ Earnings Growth Potential: High
- ❋ Growth: 11.7%
- ❋ Annual Job Openings: 19,513
- ❋ Self-Employed: 0.6%
- ❋ Part-Time: 4.7%

Summary Description and Tasks →

Plan, direct, or coordinate supportive services of an organization, such as recordkeeping, mail distribution, telephone operator/receptionist, and other office support services. May oversee facilities planning and maintenance and custodial operations. Monitor the facility to ensure that it remains safe, secure, and well-maintained. Direct or coordinate the supportive services department of a business, agency, or organization. Set goals and deadlines for the department. Prepare and review operational reports and schedules to ensure accuracy and efficiency. Analyze internal processes and recommend and implement procedural or policy changes to improve operations such as supply changes or the disposal of records. Acquire, distribute, and store supplies. Plan, administer, and control budgets for contracts, equipment, and supplies. Oversee construction and renovation projects to improve efficiency and to ensure that facilities meet environmental, health, and security standards and comply with government regulations. Hire and terminate clerical and administrative personnel. Oversee the maintenance and repair of machinery, equipment, and electrical and mechanical systems. Manage leasing of facility space. Participate in architectural and engineering planning and design, including space and installation management. Conduct classes to teach procedures to staff. Dispose of, or oversee the disposal of, surplus or unclaimed property.

Personality Type →

Personality Type: Enterprising. These occupations frequently involve starting up and carrying out projects and can involve leading people and making many decisions. They sometimes require risk taking and often deal with business.

GOE Information →

GOE—Interest Area/Cluster: 04. Business and Administration. **Work Group:** 04.02. Managerial Work in Business Detail. **Other Jobs in This Work Group:** First-Line Supervisors/Managers of Housekeeping and Janitorial Workers; First-Line Supervisors/Managers of Office and Administrative Support Workers; Meeting and Convention Planners.

Skills—Management of Financial Resources: Determining how money will be spent to get the work done and accounting for these expenditures. **Management of Personnel Resources:** Motivating, developing, and directing people as they work; identifying the best people for the job. **Programming:** Writing computer programs for various purposes. **Service Orientation:** Actively looking for ways to help people. **Coordination:** Adjusting actions in relation to others' actions. **Monitoring:** Assessing how well one is doing when learning or doing something. **Writing:** Communicating effectively with others in writing as indicated by the needs of the audience. **Speaking:** Talking to others to effectively convey information.

← **Skills**

Education and Training Programs: Business Administration and Management, General; Business/Commerce, General; Medical/Health Management and Clinical Assistant/Specialist Training; Public Administration; Purchasing, Procurement/Acquisitions, and Contracts Management; Transportation/Transportation Management. **Related Knowledge/Courses—Personnel and Human Resources:** Principles and procedures for personnel recruitment; selection; training; compensation and benefits; labor relations and negotiation; and personnel information systems. **Clerical Practices:** Administrative and clerical procedures and systems such as word-processing systems, filing and records management systems, stenography and transcription, forms, design principles, and other office procedures and terminology. **Economics and Accounting:** Economic and accounting principles and practices, the financial markets, banking, and the analysis and reporting of financial data. **Administration and Management:** Principles and processes involved in business and organizational planning, coordination, and execution. This includes strategic planning, resource allocation, manpower modeling, leadership techniques, and production methods. **Customer and Personal Service:** Principles and processes for providing customer and personal services, including needs assessment techniques, quality service standards, alternative delivery systems, and customer satisfaction evaluation techniques. **Law and Government:** Laws, legal codes, court procedures, precedents, government regulations, executive orders, agency rules, and the democratic political process.

← **Education/ Training Program(s)**

← **Related Knowledge/ Courses**

Work Environment: Indoors; more often standing than sitting.

← **Work Environment**

* **Summary Description and Tasks:** The first part of each job description provides a summary of the occupation in bold type. It is followed by a listing of tasks that are generally performed by people who work in the job. This information comes from the O*NET database; where necessary, we edited the tasks to keep them from exceeding 2,200 characters.

* **Personality Type:** The O*NET database assigns each job to its most closely related personality type. Our job descriptions include the name of the related personality type. You can find more information on the personality types as well as a brief definition of each type in the introduction to the lists of jobs based on personality types in Part I.

* **GOE Information:** This information cross-references the Guide for Occupational Exploration (or the GOE), a system developed by the U.S. Department of Labor that organizes jobs based on interests. We use the groups from the *New Guide for Occupational Exploration*, Fourth Edition, as published by JIST. That book uses a set of interest areas based on the 16 career clusters developed by the U.S. Department of Education and used in a variety of career information systems. Here we include the major interest area the job fits into, its more specific work group, and a list of O*NET job titles that are in this same GOE work group. This information will help you identify other job titles that have similar interests or require similar skills. You can find more information on the GOE and its interest areas in the introduction to the lists of jobs based on interests in Part I.

* **Skills:** The O*NET database provides data on 35 skills, so we decided to list only those that were most important for each job rather than list pages of unhelpful details. For each job, we identified any skill with a rating for level of mastery that was higher than the average rating for this skill for all jobs and a rating for importance that was higher than very low. We order the skills by the amount by which their ratings exceed the average rating for all occupations, from highest to lowest. If there are more than eight such skills, we include only those eight with the highest ratings. If no skill has a rating higher than the average for all jobs, we say "None met the criteria." Each listed skill is followed by a brief description of that skill.

* **Education/Training Program(s):** This part of the job description provides the name of the educational or training program or programs for the job. It will help you identify sources of formal or informal training for a job that interests you. To get this information, we used a crosswalk created by the National Crosswalk Service Center to connect information in the Classification of Instructional Programs (CIP) to the O*NET job titles we use in this book. We made various changes to connect the O*NET job titles to the education or training programs related to them and also modified the names of some education and training programs so they would be more easily understood. In 22 cases, we abbreviated the listing of related programs for the sake of space; such entries end with "others."

⊛ **Related Knowledge/Courses:** This entry can help you understand the most important knowledge areas that are required for a job and the types of courses or programs you will likely need to take to prepare for it. For each job, we identified the highest-rated knowledge area in the O*NET database, so every job has at least one listed. We identified any additional knowledge area with a rating that was higher than the average rating for that knowledge area for all jobs. We listed as many as six knowledge areas in descending order.

⊛ **Work Environment:** We included any work condition with a rating that exceeds the midpoint of the rating scale. The order does not indicate any condition's frequency on the job. Consider whether you like these conditions and whether any of these conditions would make you uncomfortable. Keep in mind that when hazards are present (for example, contaminants), protective equipment and procedures are provided to keep you safe.

Getting all the information we used in the job descriptions was not a simple process, and it is not always perfect. Even so, we used the best and most recent sources of data we could find, and we think that our efforts will be helpful to many people.

Sources of Additional Information

Hundreds of sources of career information exist, so here are a few we consider most helpful in getting additional information on the jobs listed in this book.

Print References

⊛ *O*NET Dictionary of Occupational Titles:* Revised on a regular basis, this book provides good descriptions for all jobs listed in the U.S. Department of Labor's O*NET database. There are 950 job descriptions at all levels of education and training, plus lists of related job titles in other major career information sources, educational programs, and other information. Published by JIST.

⊛ *New Guide for Occupational Exploration:* The new edition of the *GOE* is cross-referenced in the descriptions in Part II. The *New GOE* provides helpful information to consider about each of the interest areas and work groups, descriptions of all O*NET jobs within each GOE group, and many other features useful for exploring career options. This most recent edition is published by JIST.

⊛ *Enhanced Occupational Outlook Handbook:* Updated regularly, this book provides thorough descriptions for 270 major jobs in the current *Occupational Outlook Handbook,* brief descriptions for the O*NET jobs that are related to each, brief descriptions of thousands of more-specialized jobs from the *Dictionary of Occupational Titles,* and other information. Published by JIST.

Internet Resources

⊛ **The U.S. Department of Labor Bureau of Labor Statistics Web site:** The Department of Labor Bureau of Labor Statistics Web site (www.bls.gov) provides a lot of career information, including links to other Web pages that provide information on the jobs covered in this book. This Web site is a bit formal and, well, confusing, but it will take you to the major sources of government career information if you explore its options.

⊛ **O*NET site:** Go to http://online.onetcenter.org for a variety of information on the O*NET database, including links to sites that provide detailed information on the O*NET job titles presented in Part II of this book.

⊛ **CareerOneStop:** This site (www.careeronestop.org) is operated by the Minnesota Department of Labor on behalf of the U.S. Department of Labor and provides access to state and local information about occupations. It also can identify a one-stop career center near you that can help you find local job openings and providers of education and training.

Thanks

Thanks for reading this introduction. You are surely a more thorough person than those who jumped into the book without reading it, and you will probably get more out of the book as a result. We wish you a satisfying career and, more important, a good life.

PART I

The Best Jobs Lists

This part contains a lot of interesting lists, and it's a good place for you to start using the book. Here are some suggestions for using the lists to explore career options:

⚜ The table of contents at the beginning of this book presents a complete listing of the list titles in this section. You can browse the lists or use the table of contents to find those that interest you most.

⚜ We gave the lists clear titles, so most require little explanation. We provide comments for each group of lists.

⚜ As you review the lists of jobs, one or more of the jobs may appeal to you enough that you want to seek additional information. As this happens, mark that job (or, if someone else will be using this book, write it on a separate sheet of paper) so that you can look up the description of the job in Part II.

⚜ Keep in mind that all jobs in these lists meet our basic criteria for being included in this book, as explained in the introduction. All lists, therefore, contain jobs that have high pay, high growth, or large numbers of openings. These measures are easily quantified and are often presented in lists of best jobs in the newspapers and other media. Although earnings, growth, and openings are important, you also should consider other factors in your career planning, such as location, liking the people you work with, and having opportunities to be creative. Many other factors that may help define the ideal job for you are difficult or impossible to quantify and thus aren't used in this book, so you will need to consider the importance of these issues yourself.

⚜ All data used to create these lists comes from the U.S. Department of Labor and the Census Bureau. The earnings figures are based on the average annual pay received by full-time workers. Because the earnings represent the national averages, actual pay rates can vary greatly by location, amount of previous work experience, and other factors.

Some Details on the Lists

The sources of the information we used in constructing these lists are presented in this book's introduction. Here are some additional details on how we created the lists:

⊛ Some jobs have the same scores for one or more data elements. For example, in the category of fastest-growing, two jobs (Court Reporters and Surgical Technologists) are expected to grow at the same rate, 24.5 percent. Therefore we ordered these two jobs alphabetically, and their order in relation to each other has no other significance. Avoiding these ties was impossible, so understand that the difference of several positions on a list may not mean as much as it seems.

⊛ Likewise, it is unwise to place too much emphasis on small differences in outlook information: projections for job growth and job openings. For example, Refuse and Recyclable Material Collectors are projected to have 37,785 job openings per year, whereas 37,731 openings are projected for Helpers—Carpenters. This is a difference of only 54 jobs spread over the entire United States, and of course, it is only a projection. Before 2007, the Bureau of Labor Statistics rounded these projections to the nearest 1,000 and would have assigned these two occupations the same figure (38,000), which would have given Helpers—Carpenters the higher rank on the basis of alphabetical ordering. So, again, keep in mind that small differences of position on a list aren't very significant.

Best Jobs Overall: Lists of Jobs with the Highest Pay, Fastest Growth, and Most Openings

The four lists that follow are this book's premier lists. They are the lists that are most often mentioned in the media and the ones that most readers want to see.

To create these lists, we started with a database of 949 jobs, eliminated 222 that lacked information or did not meet our standards for good jobs, and ranked the remaining 727 major jobs according to a combination of their earnings, growth, and openings. We then selected the 500 jobs with the best total scores for use in this book. (The process for ranking the jobs is explained in more detail in the introduction.)

The first list presents all 500 best jobs according to these combined rankings for pay, growth, and number of openings. Three additional lists present the 100 jobs with the top scores in each of three measures: annual earnings, projected percentage growth through 2016, and number of annual openings. Descriptions for all the jobs in these lists are included in Part II.

The 500 Best Jobs Overall—Jobs with the Best Combination of Pay, Growth, and Openings

This list arranges all 500 jobs that were selected for this book in order of their overall scores for pay, growth, and number of openings, as explained in the introduction. The job with the best overall score was Computer Software Engineers, Applications. Other jobs follow in order of their total scores for pay, growth, and openings. These 500 jobs are the ones we use throughout this book: in the other lists in Part I and in the descriptions found in Part II.

As you look over the list, remember that jobs near the top of the list are not necessarily "good" jobs—nor are jobs toward the end of the list necessarily "bad" ones for you to consider. Their positions in the list are simply a result of each one's total score based on pay, growth, and number of openings. This means, for example, that some jobs with low pay and modest growth but a high number of openings appear higher on the list than some jobs with higher pay and modest growth but a low number of openings. A "right" job for you could be anywhere on this list.

The 500 Best Jobs Overall

Job	Annual Earnings	Percent Growth	Annual Openings
1. Computer Software Engineers, Applications	$83,130	44.6%	58,690
2. Computer Systems Analysts	$73,090	29.0%	63,166
3. Computer Software Engineers, Systems Software	$89,070	28.2%	33,139
4. Management Analysts	$71,150	21.9%	125,669
5. Registered Nurses	$60,010	23.5%	233,499
6. Sales Agents, Financial Services	$68,430	24.8%	47,750
7. Sales Agents, Securities and Commodities	$68,430	24.8%	47,750
8. Network Systems and Data Communications Analysts	$68,220	53.4%	35,086
9. Financial Analysts	$70,400	33.8%	29,317
10. Computer Security Specialists	$64,690	27.0%	37,010
11. Network and Computer Systems Administrators	$64,690	27.0%	37,010
12. Health Specialties Teachers, Postsecondary	$80,700	22.9%	19,617
13. Personal Financial Advisors	$67,660	41.0%	17,114
14. Anesthesiologists	$145,600+	14.2%	38,027
15. Family and General Practitioners	$145,600+	14.2%	38,027
16. Internists, General	$145,600+	14.2%	38,027
17. Obstetricians and Gynecologists	$145,600+	14.2%	38,027
18. Psychiatrists	$145,600+	14.2%	38,027
19. Surgeons	$145,600+	14.2%	38,027
20. Computer and Information Systems Managers	$108,070	16.4%	30,887
21. Pediatricians, General	$140,690	14.2%	38,027
22. Pharmacists	$100,480	21.7%	16,358
23. Construction Managers	$76,230	15.7%	44,158
24. Financial Managers, Branch or Department	$95,310	12.6%	57,589
25. Treasurers and Controllers	$95,310	12.6%	57,589
26. Medical and Health Services Managers	$76,990	16.4%	31,877
27. Accountants	$57,060	17.7%	134,463
28. Auditors	$57,060	17.7%	134,463
29. Market Research Analysts	$60,300	20.1%	45,015

(continued)

(continued)

The 500 Best Jobs Overall

Job	Annual Earnings	Percent Growth	Annual Openings
30. Physical Therapists	$69,760	27.1%	12,072
31. Marketing Managers	$104,400	14.4%	20,189
32. Social and Community Service Managers	$54,530	24.7%	23,788
33. Lawyers	$106,120	11.0%	49,445
34. Dental Hygienists	$64,740	30.1%	10,433
35. Physician Assistants	$78,450	27.0%	7,147
36. Cost Estimators	$54,920	18.5%	38,379
37. Biological Science Teachers, Postsecondary	$71,780	22.9%	9,039
38. Business Teachers, Postsecondary	$64,900	22.9%	11,643
39. Civil Engineers	$71,710	18.0%	15,979
40. Database Administrators	$67,250	28.6%	8,258
41. Sales Representatives, Wholesale and Manufacturing, Technical and Scientific Products	$68,270	12.4%	43,469
42. Instructional Coordinators	$55,270	22.5%	21,294
43. Industrial Engineers	$71,430	20.3%	11,272
44. Multi-Media Artists and Animators	$54,550	25.8%	13,182
45. Veterinarians	$75,230	35.0%	5,301
46. Public Relations Specialists	$49,800	17.6%	51,216
47. Education Administrators, Postsecondary	$75,780	14.2%	17,121
48. Sales Managers	$94,910	10.2%	36,392
49. Occupational Therapists	$63,790	23.1%	8,338
50. Training and Development Specialists	$49,630	18.3%	35,862
51. Art, Drama, and Music Teachers, Postsecondary	$55,190	22.9%	12,707
52. Computer Systems Engineers/Architects	$71,510	15.1%	14,374
53. Network Designers	$71,510	15.1%	14,374
54. Software Quality Assurance Engineers and Testers	$71,510	15.1%	14,374
55. Web Administrators	$71,510	15.1%	14,374
56. Web Developers	$71,510	15.1%	14,374
57. Engineering Teachers, Postsecondary	$79,510	22.9%	5,565
58. Environmental Engineers	$72,350	25.4%	5,003
59. Medical Scientists, Except Epidemiologists	$64,200	20.2%	10,596
60. Surveyors	$51,630	23.7%	14,305
61. Architects, Except Landscape and Naval	$67,620	17.7%	11,324
62. Elementary School Teachers, Except Special Education	$47,330	13.6%	181,612
63. Vocational Education Teachers, Postsecondary	$45,850	22.9%	19,313
64. Compensation, Benefits, and Job Analysis Specialists	$52,180	18.4%	18,761
65. Criminal Investigators and Special Agents	$59,930	17.3%	14,746

The 500 Best Jobs Overall

Job	Annual Earnings	Percent Growth	Annual Openings
66. English Language and Literature Teachers, Postsecondary	$54,000	22.9%	10,475
67. Immigration and Customs Inspectors	$59,930	17.3%	14,746
68. Police Detectives	$59,930	17.3%	14,746
69. Police Identification and Records Officers	$59,930	17.3%	14,746
70. Administrative Services Managers	$70,990	11.7%	19,513
71. Education Teachers, Postsecondary	$54,220	22.9%	9,359
72. Environmental Scientists and Specialists, Including Health	$58,380	25.1%	6,961
73. Mathematical Science Teachers, Postsecondary	$58,560	22.9%	7,663
74. Self-Enrichment Education Teachers	$34,580	23.1%	64,449
75. Paralegals and Legal Assistants	$44,990	22.2%	22,756
76. Logisticians	$64,250	17.3%	9,671
77. Medical and Public Health Social Workers	$44,670	24.2%	16,429
78. Actuaries	$85,690	23.7%	3,245
79. Special Education Teachers, Preschool, Kindergarten, and Elementary School	$48,350	19.6%	20,049
80. Employment Interviewers	$44,380	18.4%	33,588
81. Personnel Recruiters	$44,380	18.4%	33,588
82. Loan Officers	$53,000	11.5%	54,237
83. Educational, Vocational, and School Counselors	$49,450	12.6%	54,025
84. Nursing Instructors and Teachers, Postsecondary	$57,500	22.9%	7,337
85. Computer Science Teachers, Postsecondary	$62,020	22.9%	5,820
86. Public Relations Managers	$86,470	16.9%	5,781
87. Executive Secretaries and Administrative Assistants	$38,640	14.8%	235,314
88. Advertising Sales Agents	$42,820	20.3%	29,233
89. Mental Health Counselors	$36,000	30.0%	24,103
90. Customer Service Representatives	$29,040	24.8%	600,937
91. Property, Real Estate, and Community Association Managers	$43,670	15.1%	49,916
92. Technical Writers	$60,390	19.5%	7,498
93. General and Operations Managers	$88,700	1.5%	112,072
94. First-Line Supervisors/Managers of Construction Trades and Extraction Workers	$55,950	9.1%	82,923
95. Substance Abuse and Behavioral Disorder Counselors	$35,580	34.3%	20,821
96. Insurance Sales Agents	$44,110	12.9%	64,162
97. Clergy	$40,460	18.9%	35,092
98. Health Educators	$42,920	26.2%	13,707
99. Psychology Teachers, Postsecondary	$60,610	22.9%	5,261

(continued)

(continued)

The 500 Best Jobs Overall

Job	Annual Earnings	Percent Growth	Annual Openings
100. Computer Support Specialists	$42,400	12.9%	97,334
101. Education Administrators, Elementary and Secondary School	$80,580	7.6%	27,143
102. Kindergarten Teachers, Except Special Education	$45,120	16.3%	27,603
103. Middle School Teachers, Except Special and Vocational Education	$47,900	11.2%	75,270
104. Computer and Information Scientists, Research	$97,970	21.5%	2,901
105. Child, Family, and School Social Workers	$38,620	19.1%	35,402
106. Clinical Psychologists	$62,210	15.8%	8,309
107. Counseling Psychologists	$62,210	15.8%	8,309
108. School Psychologists	$62,210	15.8%	8,309
109. Law Teachers, Postsecondary	$87,730	22.9%	2,169
110. Bill and Account Collectors	$29,990	22.9%	118,709
111. Mental Health and Substance Abuse Social Workers	$36,640	29.9%	17,289
112. Copy Writers	$50,660	12.8%	24,023
113. Correctional Officers and Jailers	$36,970	16.9%	56,579
114. Poets, Lyricists, and Creative Writers	$50,660	12.8%	24,023
115. Medical Assistants	$27,430	35.4%	92,977
116. Real Estate Brokers	$58,860	11.1%	18,689
117. Economics Teachers, Postsecondary	$75,300	22.9%	2,208
118. Construction and Building Inspectors	$48,330	18.2%	12,606
119. Chemistry Teachers, Postsecondary	$63,870	22.9%	3,405
120. Social and Human Service Assistants	$26,630	33.6%	80,142
121. Sales Representatives, Wholesale and Manufacturing, Except Technical and Scientific Products	$50,750	8.4%	156,215
122. Surgical Technologists	$37,540	24.5%	15,365
123. Dental Assistants	$31,550	29.2%	29,482
124. Agricultural Sciences Teachers, Postsecondary	$78,460	22.9%	1,840
125. Licensed Practical and Licensed Vocational Nurses	$37,940	14.0%	70,610
126. Airline Pilots, Copilots, and Flight Engineers	$145,600+	12.9%	4,073
127. Police Patrol Officers	$49,630	10.8%	37,842
128. Sheriffs and Deputy Sheriffs	$49,630	10.8%	37,842
129. Training and Development Managers	$84,340	15.6%	3,759
130. Radiologic Technicians	$50,260	15.1%	12,836
131. Radiologic Technologists	$50,260	15.1%	12,836
132. Physics Teachers, Postsecondary	$70,090	22.9%	2,155
133. Geoscientists, Except Hydrologists and Geographers	$75,800	21.9%	2,471

The 500 Best Jobs Overall

Job	Annual Earnings	Percent Growth	Annual Openings
134. History Teachers, Postsecondary	$59,160	22.9%	3,570
135. Pharmacy Technicians	$26,720	32.0%	54,453
136. Compensation and Benefits Managers	$81,410	12.0%	6,121
137. Fitness Trainers and Aerobics Instructors	$27,680	26.8%	51,235
138. Communications Teachers, Postsecondary	$54,720	22.9%	4,074
139. Foreign Language and Literature Teachers, Postsecondary	$53,610	22.9%	4,317
140. First-Line Supervisors/Managers of Non-Retail Sales Workers	$67,020	3.7%	48,883
141. Automotive Master Mechanics	$34,170	14.3%	97,350
142. Automotive Specialty Technicians	$34,170	14.3%	97,350
143. Pipe Fitters and Steamfitters	$44,090	10.6%	68,643
144. Plumbers	$44,090	10.6%	68,643
145. Environmental Science and Protection Technicians, Including Health	$39,370	28.0%	8,404
146. Chief Executives	$145,600+	2.0%	21,209
147. Physical Therapist Assistants	$44,130	32.4%	5,957
148. First-Line Supervisors/Managers of Landscaping, Lawn Service, and Groundskeeping Workers	$38,720	17.6%	18,956
149. Political Science Teachers, Postsecondary	$63,100	22.9%	2,435
150. Atmospheric, Earth, Marine, and Space Sciences Teachers, Postsecondary	$73,280	22.9%	1,553
151. Radiation Therapists	$70,010	24.8%	1,461
152. Adult Literacy, Remedial Education, and GED Teachers and Instructors	$44,710	14.2%	17,340
153. Marriage and Family Therapists	$43,600	29.8%	5,953
154. Philosophy and Religion Teachers, Postsecondary	$56,380	22.9%	3,120
155. Sociology Teachers, Postsecondary	$58,160	22.9%	2,774
156. Dentists, General	$137,630	9.2%	7,106
157. First-Line Supervisors/Managers of Police and Detectives	$72,620	9.2%	9,373
158. Biomedical Engineers	$75,440	21.1%	1,804
159. Rehabilitation Counselors	$29,630	23.0%	32,081
160. Directors—Stage, Motion Pictures, Television, and Radio	$61,090	11.1%	8,992
161. Producers	$61,090	11.1%	8,992
162. Program Directors	$61,090	11.1%	8,992
163. Talent Directors	$61,090	11.1%	8,992
164. Technical Directors/Managers	$61,090	11.1%	8,992
165. Flight Attendants	$61,120	10.6%	10,773
166. Respiratory Therapists	$50,070	22.6%	5,563

(continued)

(continued)

The 500 Best Jobs Overall

Job	Annual Earnings	Percent Growth	Annual Openings
167. Art Directors	$72,320	9.0%	9,719
168. Special Education Teachers, Middle School	$48,940	15.8%	8,846
169. Speech-Language Pathologists	$60,690	10.6%	11,160
170. Preschool Teachers, Except Special Education	$23,130	26.3%	78,172
171. Aerospace Engineers	$90,930	10.2%	6,498
172. Medical and Clinical Laboratory Technologists	$51,720	12.4%	11,457
173. Real Estate Sales Agents	$40,600	10.6%	61,232
174. Construction Carpenters	$37,660	10.3%	223,225
175. Rough Carpenters	$37,660	10.3%	223,225
176. Interior Designers	$43,970	19.5%	8,434
177. Legal Secretaries	$38,810	11.7%	38,682
178. Education Administrators, Preschool and Child Care Center/Program	$38,580	23.5%	8,113
179. First-Line Supervisors/Managers of Personal Service Workers	$33,900	15.5%	37,555
180. Secondary School Teachers, Except Special and Vocational Education	$49,420	5.6%	93,166
181. Claims Examiners, Property and Casualty Insurance	$53,560	8.9%	22,024
182. Insurance Adjusters, Examiners, and Investigators	$53,560	8.9%	22,024
183. Meeting and Convention Planners	$43,530	19.9%	8,318
184. Bookkeeping, Accounting, and Auditing Clerks	$31,560	12.5%	286,854
185. Diagnostic Medical Sonographers	$59,860	19.1%	3,211
186. Truck Drivers, Heavy and Tractor-Trailer	$36,220	10.4%	279,032
187. Recreation and Fitness Studies Teachers, Postsecondary	$52,170	22.9%	3,010
188. Natural Sciences Managers	$104,040	11.4%	3,661
189. First-Line Supervisors/Managers of Mechanics, Installers, and Repairers	$55,380	7.3%	24,361
190. Forensic Science Technicians	$47,680	30.7%	3,074
191. Roofers	$33,240	14.3%	38,398
192. Engineering Managers	$111,020	7.3%	7,404
193. Architecture Teachers, Postsecondary	$68,540	22.9%	1,044
194. Electricians	$44,780	7.4%	79,083
195. Brokerage Clerks	$37,360	20.0%	10,826
196. Forest Fire Fighters	$43,170	12.1%	18,887
197. Medical Secretaries	$28,950	16.7%	60,659
198. Municipal Fire Fighters	$43,170	12.1%	18,887
199. Biological Technicians	$37,810	16.0%	15,374

The 500 Best Jobs Overall

Job	Annual Earnings	Percent Growth	Annual Openings
200. Sales Engineers	$80,270	8.5%	7,371
201. First-Line Supervisors/Managers of Office and Administrative Support Workers	$44,650	5.8%	138,420
202. First-Line Supervisors/Managers of Transportation and Material-Moving Machine and Vehicle Operators	$49,850	10.2%	16,580
203. Medical Records and Health Information Technicians	$29,290	17.8%	39,048
204. Hydrologists	$68,140	24.3%	687
205. Chemists	$63,490	9.1%	9,024
206. Biochemists and Biophysicists	$79,270	15.9%	1,637
207. Cardiovascular Technologists and Technicians	$44,940	25.5%	3,550
208. Chiropractors	$65,890	14.4%	3,179
209. Nursing Aides, Orderlies, and Attendants	$23,160	18.2%	321,036
210. Painters, Construction and Maintenance	$32,080	11.8%	101,140
211. Graduate Teaching Assistants	$28,060	22.9%	20,601
212. Gaming Supervisors	$42,980	23.4%	4,602
213. Interpreters and Translators	$37,490	23.6%	6,630
214. Directors, Religious Activities and Education	$35,370	19.7%	11,463
215. Probation Officers and Correctional Treatment Specialists	$44,510	10.9%	18,335
216. Bus and Truck Mechanics and Diesel Engine Specialists	$38,640	11.5%	25,428
217. Anthropology and Archeology Teachers, Postsecondary	$64,530	22.9%	910
218. Receptionists and Information Clerks	$23,710	17.2%	334,124
219. Appraisers, Real Estate	$46,130	16.9%	6,493
220. Assessors	$46,130	16.9%	6,493
221. Veterinary Technologists and Technicians	$27,970	41.0%	14,674
222. Storage and Distribution Managers	$76,310	8.3%	6,994
223. Transportation Managers	$76,310	8.3%	6,994
224. Environmental Science Teachers, Postsecondary	$64,850	22.9%	769
225. Automotive Body and Related Repairers	$35,690	11.6%	37,469
226. Mates—Ship, Boat, and Barge	$57,210	17.9%	2,665
227. Pilots, Ship	$57,210	17.9%	2,665
228. Ship and Boat Captains	$57,210	17.9%	2,665
229. Operations Research Analysts	$66,950	10.6%	5,727
230. Area, Ethnic, and Cultural Studies Teachers, Postsecondary	$59,150	22.9%	1,252
231. Landscaping and Groundskeeping Workers	$22,240	18.1%	307,138
232. Mechanical Engineers	$72,300	4.2%	12,394
233. Gaming Managers	$64,410	24.4%	549
234. Criminal Justice and Law Enforcement Teachers, Postsecondary	$51,060	22.9%	1,911

(continued)

The 500 Best Jobs Overall

Job	Annual Earnings	Percent Growth	Annual Openings
235. Massage Therapists	$34,870	20.3%	9,193
236. Occupational Therapist Assistants	$45,050	25.4%	2,634
237. Computer Programmers	$68,080	–4.1%	27,937
238. Social Work Teachers, Postsecondary	$56,240	22.9%	1,292
239. Geography Teachers, Postsecondary	$61,310	22.9%	697
240. Industrial-Organizational Psychologists	$80,820	21.3%	118
241. Security Guards	$22,570	16.9%	222,085
242. Cargo and Freight Agents	$37,060	16.5%	9,967
243. Cartographers and Photogrammetrists	$49,970	20.3%	2,823
244. Forest Fire Fighting and Prevention Supervisors	$65,040	11.5%	3,771
245. Municipal Fire Fighting and Prevention Supervisors	$65,040	11.5%	3,771
246. Court Reporters	$45,330	24.5%	2,620
247. First-Line Supervisors/Managers of Helpers, Laborers, and Material Movers, Hand	$40,640	12.5%	13,877
248. First-Line Supervisors/Managers of Housekeeping and Janitorial Workers	$32,850	12.7%	30,613
249. Food Service Managers	$44,570	5.0%	59,302
250. Maintenance and Repair Workers, General	$32,570	10.1%	165,502
251. Tile and Marble Setters	$38,720	15.4%	9,066
252. Electrical Engineers	$79,240	6.3%	6,806
253. Forestry and Conservation Science Teachers, Postsecondary	$63,790	22.9%	454
254. Graphic Designers	$41,280	9.8%	26,968
255. Operating Engineers and Other Construction Equipment Operators	$38,130	8.4%	55,468
256. Aircraft Mechanics and Service Technicians	$49,010	10.6%	9,708
257. Landscape Architects	$57,580	16.4%	2,342
258. Home Economics Teachers, Postsecondary	$58,170	22.9%	820
259. Coaches and Scouts	$27,840	14.6%	51,100
260. Cement Masons and Concrete Finishers	$33,840	11.4%	34,625
261. Bus Drivers, Transit and Intercity	$33,160	12.5%	27,100
262. Emergency Medical Technicians and Paramedics	$28,400	19.2%	19,513
263. Private Detectives and Investigators	$37,640	18.2%	7,329
264. First-Line Supervisors/Managers of Correctional Officers	$55,720	12.5%	4,180
265. Brickmasons and Blockmasons	$44,070	9.7%	17,569
266. Audio and Video Equipment Technicians	$36,050	24.2%	4,681
267. Mobile Heavy Equipment Mechanics, Except Engines	$41,450	12.3%	11,037

The 500 Best Jobs Overall

Job	Annual Earnings	Percent Growth	Annual Openings
268. Optometrists	$93,800	11.3%	1,789
269. Industrial Machinery Mechanics	$42,350	9.0%	23,361
270. Library Science Teachers, Postsecondary	$56,810	22.9%	702
271. Office Clerks, General	$24,460	12.6%	765,803
272. Industrial Production Managers	$80,560	−5.9%	14,889
273. First-Line Supervisors/Managers of Food Preparation and Serving Workers	$28,040	11.3%	154,175
274. Purchasing Managers	$85,440	3.4%	7,243
275. Aircraft Structure, Surfaces, Rigging, and Systems Assemblers	$45,420	12.8%	6,550
276. Mapping Technicians	$33,640	19.4%	8,299
277. Surveying Technicians	$33,640	19.4%	8,299
278. Music Composers and Arrangers	$40,150	12.9%	8,597
279. Music Directors	$40,150	12.9%	8,597
280. Police, Fire, and Ambulance Dispatchers	$32,660	13.6%	17,628
281. Heating and Air Conditioning Mechanics and Installers	$38,360	8.7%	29,719
282. Refrigeration Mechanics and Installers	$38,360	8.7%	29,719
283. Medical and Clinical Laboratory Technicians	$34,270	15.0%	10,866
284. Construction Laborers	$27,310	10.9%	257,407
285. Water and Liquid Waste Treatment Plant and System Operators	$37,090	13.8%	9,575
286. Agents and Business Managers of Artists, Performers, and Athletes	$66,440	9.6%	3,940
287. Librarians	$50,970	3.6%	18,945
288. Special Education Teachers, Secondary School	$49,640	8.5%	10,601
289. Human Resources Assistants, Except Payroll and Timekeeping	$34,970	11.3%	18,647
290. Urban and Regional Planners	$57,970	14.5%	1,967
291. Environmental Engineering Technicians	$40,690	24.8%	2,162
292. Tellers	$22,920	13.5%	146,077
293. Nuclear Medicine Technologists	$64,670	14.8%	1,290
294. Aviation Inspectors	$51,440	16.4%	2,122
295. Freight and Cargo Inspectors	$51,440	16.4%	2,122
296. Transportation Vehicle, Equipment and Systems Inspectors, Except Aviation	$51,440	16.4%	2,122
297. Budget Analysts	$63,440	7.1%	6,423
298. Security and Fire Alarm Systems Installers	$35,390	20.2%	5,729
299. Athletes and Sports Competitors	$38,440	19.2%	4,293

(continued)

(continued)

The 500 Best Jobs Overall

Job	Annual Earnings	Percent Growth	Annual Openings
300. Purchasing Agents, Except Wholesale, Retail, and Farm Products	$52,460	0.1%	22,349
301. Demonstrators and Product Promoters	$22,570	18.0%	32,779
302. Funeral Directors	$50,370	12.5%	3,939
303. Production, Planning, and Expediting Clerks	$39,690	4.2%	52,735
304. Electronics Engineers, Except Computer	$83,340	3.7%	5,699
305. Sheet Metal Workers	$39,210	6.7%	31,677
306. Curators	$46,000	23.3%	1,416
307. Aquacultural Managers	$53,720	1.1%	18,101
308. Crop and Livestock Managers	$53,720	1.1%	18,101
309. Nursery and Greenhouse Managers	$53,720	1.1%	18,101
310. Medical Transcriptionists	$31,250	13.5%	18,080
311. Financial Examiners	$66,670	10.7%	2,449
312. First-Line Supervisors/Managers of Production and Operating Workers	$48,670	–4.8%	46,144
313. Coroners	$48,400	4.9%	15,841
314. Environmental Compliance Inspectors	$48,400	4.9%	15,841
315. Equal Opportunity Representatives and Officers	$48,400	4.9%	15,841
316. Government Property Inspectors and Investigators	$48,400	4.9%	15,841
317. Licensing Examiners and Inspectors	$48,400	4.9%	15,841
318. Transportation Security Screeners	$28,240	12.6%	29,298
319. First-Line Supervisors/Managers of Retail Sales Workers	$34,470	4.2%	221,241
320. Skin Care Specialists	$27,190	34.3%	6,643
321. Commercial Pilots	$61,640	13.2%	1,425
322. Air Traffic Controllers	$112,930	10.2%	1,213
323. Statisticians	$69,900	8.5%	3,433
324. Sailors and Marine Oilers	$32,570	15.7%	8,600
325. Editors	$48,320	2.3%	20,193
326. Telecommunications Equipment Installers and Repairers, Except Line Installers	$54,070	2.5%	13,541
327. Drywall and Ceiling Tile Installers	$36,520	7.3%	30,945
328. Computer Hardware Engineers	$91,860	4.6%	3,572
329. Lodging Managers	$44,240	12.2%	5,529
330. Electrical Engineering Technicians	$52,140	3.6%	12,583
331. Electronics Engineering Technicians	$52,140	3.6%	12,583
332. Elevator Installers and Repairers	$68,000	8.8%	2,850
333. Tire Repairers and Changers	$21,880	20.2%	18,829

The 500 Best Jobs Overall

Job	Annual Earnings	Percent Growth	Annual Openings
334. Cooks, Restaurant	$21,220	11.5%	238,542
335. Medical Equipment Repairers	$40,320	21.7%	2,351
336. Boilermakers	$50,700	14.0%	2,333
337. Survey Researchers	$36,820	15.9%	4,959
338. Hairdressers, Hairstylists, and Cosmetologists	$22,210	12.4%	73,030
339. Recreation Workers	$21,220	12.7%	61,454
340. Architectural Drafters	$43,310	6.1%	16,238
341. Civil Drafters	$43,310	6.1%	16,238
342. Athletic Trainers	$38,360	24.3%	1,669
343. Telecommunications Line Installers and Repairers	$47,220	4.6%	14,719
344. Advertising and Promotions Managers	$78,250	6.2%	2,955
345. Chemical Engineers	$81,500	7.9%	2,111
346. Insurance Underwriters	$54,530	6.3%	6,880
347. Motorboat Mechanics	$34,210	19.0%	4,326
348. Industrial Engineering Technicians	$47,490	9.9%	6,172
349. Civil Engineering Technicians	$42,580	10.2%	7,499
350. Highway Maintenance Workers	$32,600	8.9%	24,774
351. Electrical Power-Line Installers and Repairers	$52,570	7.2%	6,401
352. Railroad Conductors and Yardmasters	$58,650	9.1%	3,235
353. Tour Guides and Escorts	$22,110	21.2%	15,027
354. Film and Video Editors	$47,870	12.7%	2,707
355. Helpers—Installation, Maintenance, and Repair Workers	$22,920	11.8%	52,058
356. Wholesale and Retail Buyers, Except Farm Products	$46,960	−0.1%	19,847
357. Prosthodontists	$145,600+	10.7%	54
358. Solderers and Brazers	$32,270	5.1%	61,125
359. Welders, Cutters, and Welder Fitters	$32,270	5.1%	61,125
360. Atmospheric and Space Scientists	$78,390	10.6%	735
361. Commercial and Industrial Designers	$56,550	7.2%	4,777
362. Ship Engineers	$56,090	14.1%	1,102
363. Interviewers, Except Eligibility and Loan	$27,320	9.5%	54,060
364. Helpers—Carpenters	$24,340	11.7%	37,731
365. Locksmiths and Safe Repairers	$33,230	22.1%	3,545
366. Podiatrists	$110,510	9.5%	648
367. Occupational Health and Safety Specialists	$60,140	8.1%	3,440
368. Marine Architects	$76,200	10.9%	495
369. Marine Engineers	$76,200	10.9%	495
370. Cooks, Institution and Cafeteria	$21,340	10.8%	111,898

(continued)

(continued)

The 500 Best Jobs Overall

Job	Annual Earnings	Percent Growth	Annual Openings
371. Mechanical Drafters	$44,740	5.2%	10,902
372. Microbiologists	$60,680	11.2%	1,306
373. Orthodontists	$145,600+	9.2%	479
374. Teacher Assistants	$21,580	10.4%	193,986
375. Truck Drivers, Light or Delivery Services	$26,380	8.4%	154,330
376. Helpers—Pipelayers, Plumbers, Pipefitters, and Steamfitters	$25,350	11.9%	29,332
377. Epidemiologists	$60,010	13.6%	503
378. Mathematicians	$90,870	10.2%	473
379. Oral and Maxillofacial Surgeons	$145,600+	9.1%	400
380. Economists	$80,220	7.5%	1,555
381. Bus Drivers, School	$25,860	9.3%	59,809
382. Dietitians and Nutritionists	$49,010	8.6%	4,996
383. Physicists	$96,850	6.8%	1,302
384. Postal Service Mail Carriers	$44,500	1.0%	16,710
385. Judges, Magistrate Judges, and Magistrates	$107,230	5.1%	1,567
386. Billing, Cost, and Rate Clerks	$29,970	4.4%	81,885
387. Billing, Posting, and Calculating Machine Operators	$29,970	4.4%	81,885
388. Statement Clerks	$29,970	4.4%	81,885
389. Set and Exhibit Designers	$43,220	17.8%	1,402
390. Animal Trainers	$26,190	22.7%	6,713
391. Fire-Prevention and Protection Engineers	$69,580	9.6%	1,105
392. Industrial Safety and Health Engineers	$69,580	9.6%	1,105
393. Product Safety Engineers	$69,580	9.6%	1,105
394. Tapers	$42,050	7.1%	9,026
395. Materials Scientists	$76,160	8.7%	1,039
396. Anthropologists	$53,080	15.0%	446
397. Archeologists	$53,080	15.0%	446
398. Electrical and Electronics Repairers, Commercial and Industrial Equipment	$47,110	6.8%	6,607
399. Glaziers	$35,230	11.9%	6,416
400. Computer, Automated Teller, and Office Machine Repairers	$37,100	3.0%	22,330
401. Nuclear Engineers	$94,420	7.2%	1,046
402. Court Clerks	$32,330	8.8%	16,163
403. License Clerks	$32,330	8.8%	16,163
404. Municipal Clerks	$32,330	8.8%	16,163
405. Refuse and Recyclable Material Collectors	$29,420	7.4%	37,785

The 500 Best Jobs Overall

Job	Annual Earnings	Percent Growth	Annual Openings
406. Helpers—Brickmasons, Blockmasons, Stonemasons, and Tile and Marble Setters	$26,260	11.0%	22,500
407. Reinforcing Iron and Rebar Workers	$37,890	11.5%	4,502
408. Mining and Geological Engineers, Including Mining Safety Engineers	$74,330	10.0%	456
409. Camera Operators, Television, Video, and Motion Picture	$41,850	11.5%	3,496
410. Insurance Appraisers, Auto Damage	$51,500	12.5%	1,030
411. Nuclear Power Reactor Operators	$70,410	10.6%	233
412. Orthotists and Prosthetists	$60,520	11.8%	295
413. Chefs and Head Cooks	$37,160	7.6%	9,401
414. Automotive Glass Installers and Repairers	$31,470	18.7%	3,457
415. Aircraft Cargo Handling Supervisors	$37,760	23.3%	523
416. Emergency Management Specialists	$48,380	12.3%	1,538
417. Makeup Artists, Theatrical and Performance	$35,250	39.8%	392
418. Residential Advisors	$23,050	18.5%	8,053
419. Pest Control Workers	$29,030	15.5%	6,006
420. Petroleum Engineers	$103,960	5.2%	1,016
421. Medical Equipment Preparers	$27,040	14.2%	8,363
422. Pesticide Handlers, Sprayers, and Applicators, Vegetation	$28,560	14.0%	7,443
423. Machinists	$35,230	–3.1%	39,505
424. Secretaries, Except Legal, Medical, and Executive	$28,220	1.2%	239,630
425. Tree Trimmers and Pruners	$29,800	11.1%	9,621
426. Shipping, Receiving, and Traffic Clerks	$26,990	3.7%	138,967
427. Farmers and Ranchers	$33,360	–8.5%	129,552
428. Library Technicians	$27,680	8.5%	29,075
429. Gaming Surveillance Officers and Gaming Investigators	$27,440	33.6%	2,124
430. Photographers	$27,720	10.3%	16,100
431. Slaughterers and Meat Packers	$22,500	12.7%	15,511
432. Dispatchers, Except Police, Fire, and Ambulance	$33,140	1.5%	29,793
433. City and Regional Planning Aides	$35,870	12.4%	3,571
434. Physical Therapist Aides	$22,990	24.4%	4,092
435. Social Science Research Assistants	$35,870	12.4%	3,571
436. Audiologists	$59,440	9.8%	980
437. Eligibility Interviewers, Government Programs	$39,110	3.1%	11,337
438. Fine Artists, Including Painters, Sculptors, and Illustrators	$42,070	9.9%	3,830
439. Bakers	$22,590	10.0%	31,442
440. Materials Engineers	$77,170	4.0%	1,390

(continued)

(continued)

The 500 Best Jobs Overall

Job	Annual Earnings	Percent Growth	Annual Openings
441. Structural Iron and Steel Workers	$42,130	6.0%	6,969
442. Fashion Designers	$62,810	5.0%	1,968
443. Occupational Health and Safety Technicians	$44,020	14.6%	886
444. Recreational Vehicle Service Technicians	$31,760	18.2%	2,442
445. Electrical Drafters	$49,250	4.1%	4,786
446. Electronic Drafters	$49,250	4.1%	4,786
447. Food Scientists and Technologists	$57,870	10.3%	663
448. Insurance Claims Clerks	$32,040	−1.3%	42,246
449. Insurance Policy Processing Clerks	$32,040	−1.3%	42,246
450. Payroll and Timekeeping Clerks	$33,810	3.1%	18,544
451. Subway and Streetcar Operators	$50,520	12.1%	587
452. Millwrights	$46,090	5.8%	4,758
453. Sociologists	$61,140	10.0%	403
454. Loan Interviewers and Clerks	$31,680	−0.9%	40,217
455. Vocational Education Teachers, Secondary School	$50,090	−4.6%	7,639
456. Zoologists and Wildlife Biologists	$55,100	8.7%	1,444
457. Geological Sample Test Technicians	$50,950	8.6%	1,895
458. Geophysical Data Technicians	$50,950	8.6%	1,895
459. Aerospace Engineering and Operations Technicians	$54,930	10.4%	707
460. Nuclear Equipment Operation Technicians	$66,140	6.7%	1,021
461. Nuclear Monitoring Technicians	$66,140	6.7%	1,021
462. Political Scientists	$91,580	5.3%	318
463. Archivists	$43,110	14.4%	795
464. Astronomers	$99,020	5.6%	128
465. Mechanical Engineering Technicians	$47,280	6.4%	3,710
466. Commercial Divers	$41,610	17.7%	248
467. Food Batchmakers	$23,730	10.9%	15,704
468. Embalmers	$36,800	14.3%	1,660
469. Helpers—Electricians	$24,880	6.8%	35,109
470. Agricultural Engineers	$67,710	8.6%	225
471. Fire Inspectors	$50,830	11.0%	644
472. Fire Investigators	$50,830	11.0%	644
473. Insulation Workers, Mechanical	$36,570	8.6%	5,787
474. Inspectors, Testers, Sorters, Samplers, and Weighers	$30,310	−7.0%	75,361
475. Industrial Truck and Tractor Operators	$28,010	−2.0%	89,547
476. Pipelayers	$31,280	8.7%	8,902

The 500 Best Jobs Overall

Job	Annual Earnings	Percent Growth	Annual Openings
477. Meat, Poultry, and Fish Cutters and Trimmers	$21,050	10.9%	17,920
478. Team Assemblers	$24,630	0.1%	264,135
479. Museum Technicians and Conservators	$35,350	15.9%	1,341
480. Credit Analysts	$54,580	1.9%	3,180
481. Soil and Plant Scientists	$58,000	8.4%	850
482. Laborers and Freight, Stock, and Material Movers, Hand	$21,900	2.1%	630,487
483. Reservation and Transportation Ticket Agents and Travel Clerks	$29,820	1.1%	30,754
484. Maintenance Workers, Machinery	$35,590	−1.1%	15,055
485. Excavating and Loading Machine and Dragline Operators	$34,050	8.3%	6,562
486. Bailiffs	$36,900	11.2%	2,223
487. Parts Salespersons	$28,130	−2.2%	52,414
488. Tax Examiners, Collectors, and Revenue Agents	$46,920	2.1%	4,465
489. Umpires, Referees, and Other Sports Officials	$24,770	16.0%	4,461
490. Arbitrators, Mediators, and Conciliators	$48,840	10.6%	546
491. Correspondence Clerks	$29,500	12.0%	4,334
492. Merchandise Displayers and Window Trimmers	$24,830	10.7%	9,103
493. Motorcycle Mechanics	$30,300	12.5%	3,564
494. Plasterers and Stucco Masons	$36,430	8.1%	4,509
495. Broadcast Technicians	$32,230	12.1%	2,955
496. Ambulance Drivers and Attendants, Except Emergency Medical Technicians	$21,140	21.7%	3,703
497. Structural Metal Fabricators and Fitters	$31,030	−0.2%	20,746
498. Chemical Technicians	$40,740	5.8%	4,010
499. Concierges	$25,540	14.1%	4,893
500. Hazardous Materials Removal Workers	$36,330	11.2%	1,933

Jobs 6 and 7 share 47,750 openings. Jobs 10 and 11 share 37,010 openings. Jobs 14, 15, 16, 17, 18, 19, and 21 share 38,027 openings. Jobs 24 and 25 share 57,589 openings. Jobs 27 and 28 share 134,463 openings. Jobs 52, 53, 54, 55, and 56 share 14,374 openings. Jobs 65, 67, 68, and 69 share 14,746 openings. Jobs 80 and 81 share 33,588 openings. Jobs 106, 107, and 108 share 8,309 openings. Jobs 112 and 114 share 24,023 openings. Jobs 127 and 128 share 37,842 openings. Jobs 130 and 131 share 12,836 openings. Jobs 141 and 142 share 97,350 openings. Jobs 143 and 144 share 68,643 openings. Jobs 160, 161, 162, 163, and 164 share 8,992 openings. Jobs 174 and 175 share 223,225 openings. Jobs 181 and 182 share 22,024 openings. Jobs 196 and 198 share 18,887 openings. Jobs 219 and 220 share 6,493 openings. Jobs 222 and 223 share 6,994 openings. Jobs 226, 227, and 228 share 2,665 openings. Jobs 244 and 245 share 3,771 openings. Jobs 276 and 277 share 8,299 openings. Jobs 278 and 279 share 8,597 openings. Jobs 281 and 282 share 29,719 openings. Jobs 294, 295, and 296 share 2,122 openings. Jobs 307, 308, and 309 share 18,101 openings. Jobs 313, 314, 315, 316, and 317 share 15,841 openings. Jobs 330 and 331 share 12,583 openings. Jobs 340 and 341 share 16,238 openings. Jobs 358 and 359 share 61,125 openings. Jobs 368 and 369 share 495 openings. Jobs 386, 387, and 388 share 81,885 openings. Jobs 391, 392, and 393 share 1,105 openings. Jobs 396 and 397 share 446 openings. Jobs 402, 403, and 404 share 16,163 openings. Jobs 433 and 435 share 3,571 openings. Jobs 445 and 446 share 4,786 openings. Jobs 448 and 449 share 42,246 openings. Jobs 457 and 458 share 1,895 openings. Jobs 460 and 461 share 1,021 openings. Jobs 471 and 472 share 644 openings.

The 100 Best-Paying Jobs

We sorted all 500 jobs based on their annual median earnings from highest to lowest. *Median earnings* means that half of all workers in each of these jobs earn more than that amount and half earn less. We then selected the 100 jobs with the highest earnings to create the list that follows.

It shouldn't be a big surprise to learn that most of the highest-paying jobs require advanced levels of education, training, or experience. For example, most of the 20 jobs with the highest earnings require a doctoral or professional degree, and others, such as Chief Executives and Engineering Managers, require extensive training and experience beyond the bachelor's degree. Although the top 20 jobs may not appeal to you for various reasons, you are likely to find others that will among the top 100 jobs with the highest earnings.

Keep in mind that the earnings reflect the national average for all workers in the occupation. This is an important consideration, because starting pay in the job is usually much less than the pay that workers can earn with several years of experience. (You can see figures for starting pay in the Part II job descriptions.) Earnings also vary significantly by region of the country, so actual pay in your area could be substantially different.

The 100 Best-Paying Jobs	
Job	Annual Earnings
1. Airline Pilots, Copilots, and Flight Engineers	$145,600+
2. Anesthesiologists	$145,600+
3. Chief Executives	$145,600+
4. Family and General Practitioners	$145,600+
5. Internists, General	$145,600+
6. Obstetricians and Gynecologists	$145,600+
7. Oral and Maxillofacial Surgeons	$145,600+
8. Orthodontists	$145,600+
9. Prosthodontists	$145,600+
10. Psychiatrists	$145,600+
11. Surgeons	$145,600+
12. Pediatricians, General	$140,690
13. Dentists, General	$137,630
14. Air Traffic Controllers	$112,930
15. Engineering Managers	$111,020
16. Podiatrists	$110,510
17. Computer and Information Systems Managers	$108,070
18. Judges, Magistrate Judges, and Magistrates	$107,230
19. Lawyers	$106,120
20. Marketing Managers	$104,400

The 100 Best-Paying Jobs

Job	Annual Earnings
21. Natural Sciences Managers	$104,040
22. Petroleum Engineers	$103,960
23. Pharmacists	$100,480
24. Astronomers	$99,020
25. Computer and Information Scientists, Research	$97,970
26. Physicists	$96,850
27. Financial Managers, Branch or Department	$95,310
28. Treasurers and Controllers	$95,310
29. Sales Managers	$94,910
30. Nuclear Engineers	$94,420
31. Optometrists	$93,800
32. Computer Hardware Engineers	$91,860
33. Political Scientists	$91,580
34. Aerospace Engineers	$90,930
35. Mathematicians	$90,870
36. Computer Software Engineers, Systems Software	$89,070
37. General and Operations Managers	$88,700
38. Law Teachers, Postsecondary	$87,730
39. Public Relations Managers	$86,470
40. Actuaries	$85,690
41. Purchasing Managers	$85,440
42. Training and Development Managers	$84,340
43. Electronics Engineers, Except Computer	$83,340
44. Computer Software Engineers, Applications	$83,130
45. Chemical Engineers	$81,500
46. Compensation and Benefits Managers	$81,410
47. Industrial-Organizational Psychologists	$80,820
48. Health Specialties Teachers, Postsecondary	$80,700
49. Education Administrators, Elementary and Secondary School	$80,580
50. Industrial Production Managers	$80,560
51. Sales Engineers	$80,270
52. Economists	$80,220
53. Engineering Teachers, Postsecondary	$79,510
54. Biochemists and Biophysicists	$79,270
55. Electrical Engineers	$79,240
56. Agricultural Sciences Teachers, Postsecondary	$78,460
57. Physician Assistants	$78,450
58. Atmospheric and Space Scientists	$78,390

(continued)

(continued)

The 100 Best-Paying Jobs

Job	Annual Earnings
59. Advertising and Promotions Managers	$78,250
60. Materials Engineers	$77,170
61. Medical and Health Services Managers	$76,990
62. Storage and Distribution Managers	$76,310
63. Transportation Managers	$76,310
64. Construction Managers	$76,230
65. Marine Architects	$76,200
66. Marine Engineers	$76,200
67. Materials Scientists	$76,160
68. Geoscientists, Except Hydrologists and Geographers	$75,800
69. Education Administrators, Postsecondary	$75,780
70. Biomedical Engineers	$75,440
71. Economics Teachers, Postsecondary	$75,300
72. Veterinarians	$75,230
73. Mining and Geological Engineers, Including Mining Safety Engineers	$74,330
74. Atmospheric, Earth, Marine, and Space Sciences Teachers, Postsecondary	$73,280
75. Computer Systems Analysts	$73,090
76. First-Line Supervisors/Managers of Police and Detectives	$72,620
77. Environmental Engineers	$72,350
78. Art Directors	$72,320
79. Mechanical Engineers	$72,300
80. Biological Science Teachers, Postsecondary	$71,780
81. Civil Engineers	$71,710
82. Computer Systems Engineers/Architects	$71,510
83. Network Designers	$71,510
84. Software Quality Assurance Engineers and Testers	$71,510
85. Web Administrators	$71,510
86. Web Developers	$71,510
87. Industrial Engineers	$71,430
88. Management Analysts	$71,150
89. Administrative Services Managers	$70,990
90. Nuclear Power Reactor Operators	$70,410
91. Financial Analysts	$70,400
92. Physics Teachers, Postsecondary	$70,090
93. Radiation Therapists	$70,010
94. Statisticians	$69,900
95. Physical Therapists	$69,760

The 100 Best-Paying Jobs

Job	Annual Earnings
96. Fire-Prevention and Protection Engineers	$69,580
97. Industrial Safety and Health Engineers	$69,580
98. Product Safety Engineers	$69,580
99. Architecture Teachers, Postsecondary	$68,540
100. Sales Agents, Financial Services	$68,430

The 100 Fastest-Growing Jobs

We created this list by sorting all 500 best jobs by their projected growth over the ten-year period from 2006 to 2016. Growth rates are one measure to consider in exploring career options, as jobs with higher growth rates tend to provide more job opportunities.

Jobs in the computer and medical fields dominate the 20 fastest-growing jobs. Network Systems and Data Communications Analysts is the job with the highest growth rate—the number employed is projected to grow by half from 2006 to 2016. You can find a wide range of rapidly growing jobs in a variety of fields and at different levels of training and education among the jobs in this list.

The 100 Fastest-Growing Jobs

Job	Percent Growth
1. Network Systems and Data Communications Analysts	53.4%
2. Computer Software Engineers, Applications	44.6%
3. Personal Financial Advisors	41.0%
4. Veterinary Technologists and Technicians	41.0%
5. Makeup Artists, Theatrical and Performance	39.8%
6. Medical Assistants	35.4%
7. Veterinarians	35.0%
8. Skin Care Specialists	34.3%
9. Substance Abuse and Behavioral Disorder Counselors	34.3%
10. Financial Analysts	33.8%
11. Gaming Surveillance Officers and Gaming Investigators	33.6%
12. Social and Human Service Assistants	33.6%
13. Physical Therapist Assistants	32.4%
14. Pharmacy Technicians	32.0%
15. Forensic Science Technicians	30.7%
16. Dental Hygienists	30.1%
17. Mental Health Counselors	30.0%

(continued)

(continued)

The 100 Fastest-Growing Jobs

Job	Percent Growth
18. Mental Health and Substance Abuse Social Workers	29.9%
19. Marriage and Family Therapists	29.8%
20. Dental Assistants	29.2%
21. Computer Systems Analysts	29.0%
22. Database Administrators	28.6%
23. Computer Software Engineers, Systems Software	28.2%
24. Environmental Science and Protection Technicians, Including Health	28.0%
25. Physical Therapists	27.1%
26. Computer Security Specialists	27.0%
27. Network and Computer Systems Administrators	27.0%
28. Physician Assistants	27.0%
29. Fitness Trainers and Aerobics Instructors	26.8%
30. Preschool Teachers, Except Special Education	26.3%
31. Health Educators	26.2%
32. Multi-Media Artists and Animators	25.8%
33. Cardiovascular Technologists and Technicians	25.5%
34. Environmental Engineers	25.4%
35. Occupational Therapist Assistants	25.4%
36. Environmental Scientists and Specialists, Including Health	25.1%
37. Customer Service Representatives	24.8%
38. Environmental Engineering Technicians	24.8%
39. Radiation Therapists	24.8%
40. Sales Agents, Financial Services	24.8%
41. Sales Agents, Securities and Commodities	24.8%
42. Social and Community Service Managers	24.7%
43. Court Reporters	24.5%
44. Surgical Technologists	24.5%
45. Gaming Managers	24.4%
46. Physical Therapist Aides	24.4%
47. Athletic Trainers	24.3%
48. Hydrologists	24.3%
49. Audio and Video Equipment Technicians	24.2%
50. Medical and Public Health Social Workers	24.2%
51. Actuaries	23.7%
52. Surveyors	23.7%
53. Interpreters and Translators	23.6%
54. Education Administrators, Preschool and Child Care Center/Program	23.5%
55. Registered Nurses	23.5%

The 100 Fastest-Growing Jobs

Job	Percent Growth
56. Gaming Supervisors	23.4%
57. Aircraft Cargo Handling Supervisors	23.3%
58. Curators	23.3%
59. Occupational Therapists	23.1%
60. Self-Enrichment Education Teachers	23.1%
61. Rehabilitation Counselors	23.0%
62. Agricultural Sciences Teachers, Postsecondary	22.9%
63. Anthropology and Archeology Teachers, Postsecondary	22.9%
64. Architecture Teachers, Postsecondary	22.9%
65. Area, Ethnic, and Cultural Studies Teachers, Postsecondary	22.9%
66. Art, Drama, and Music Teachers, Postsecondary	22.9%
67. Atmospheric, Earth, Marine, and Space Sciences Teachers, Postsecondary	22.9%
68. Bill and Account Collectors	22.9%
69. Biological Science Teachers, Postsecondary	22.9%
70. Business Teachers, Postsecondary	22.9%
71. Chemistry Teachers, Postsecondary	22.9%
72. Communications Teachers, Postsecondary	22.9%
73. Computer Science Teachers, Postsecondary	22.9%
74. Criminal Justice and Law Enforcement Teachers, Postsecondary	22.9%
75. Economics Teachers, Postsecondary	22.9%
76. Education Teachers, Postsecondary	22.9%
77. Engineering Teachers, Postsecondary	22.9%
78. English Language and Literature Teachers, Postsecondary	22.9%
79. Environmental Science Teachers, Postsecondary	22.9%
80. Foreign Language and Literature Teachers, Postsecondary	22.9%
81. Forestry and Conservation Science Teachers, Postsecondary	22.9%
82. Geography Teachers, Postsecondary	22.9%
83. Graduate Teaching Assistants	22.9%
84. Health Specialties Teachers, Postsecondary	22.9%
85. History Teachers, Postsecondary	22.9%
86. Home Economics Teachers, Postsecondary	22.9%
87. Law Teachers, Postsecondary	22.9%
88. Library Science Teachers, Postsecondary	22.9%
89. Mathematical Science Teachers, Postsecondary	22.9%
90. Nursing Instructors and Teachers, Postsecondary	22.9%
91. Philosophy and Religion Teachers, Postsecondary	22.9%
92. Physics Teachers, Postsecondary	22.9%
93. Political Science Teachers, Postsecondary	22.9%

(continued)

(continued)

The 100 Fastest-Growing Jobs

Job	Percent Growth
94. Psychology Teachers, Postsecondary	22.9%
95. Recreation and Fitness Studies Teachers, Postsecondary	22.9%
96. Social Work Teachers, Postsecondary	22.9%
97. Sociology Teachers, Postsecondary	22.9%
98. Vocational Education Teachers, Postsecondary	22.9%
99. Animal Trainers	22.7%
100. Respiratory Therapists	22.6%

The 100 Jobs with the Most Openings

We created this list by sorting all 500 best jobs by the number of job openings that each is expected to have per year. Jobs that employ lots of people are also likely to have more job openings in a given year. Many of these occupations, such as Construction Laborers, are not among the highest-paying jobs. But jobs with large numbers of openings often provide easier entry for new workers, make it easier to move from one position to another, or are attractive for other reasons. Some of these jobs may also appeal to people re-entering the labor market, part-time workers, and workers who want to move from one employer to another. And some of these jobs pay quite well, offer good benefits, or have other advantages.

The 100 Jobs with the Most Openings

Job	Annual Openings
1. Office Clerks, General	765,803
2. Laborers and Freight, Stock, and Material Movers, Hand	630,487
3. Customer Service Representatives	600,937
4. Receptionists and Information Clerks	334,124
5. Nursing Aides, Orderlies, and Attendants	321,036
6. Landscaping and Groundskeeping Workers	307,138
7. Bookkeeping, Accounting, and Auditing Clerks	286,854
8. Truck Drivers, Heavy and Tractor-Trailer	279,032
9. Team Assemblers	264,135
10. Construction Laborers	257,407
11. Secretaries, Except Legal, Medical, and Executive	239,630
12. Cooks, Restaurant	238,542
13. Executive Secretaries and Administrative Assistants	235,314
14. Registered Nurses	233,499
15. Construction Carpenters	223,225
16. Rough Carpenters	223,225

The 100 Jobs with the Most Openings

Job	Annual Openings
17. Security Guards	222,085
18. First-Line Supervisors/Managers of Retail Sales Workers	221,241
19. Teacher Assistants	193,986
20. Elementary School Teachers, Except Special Education	181,612
21. Maintenance and Repair Workers, General	165,502
22. Sales Representatives, Wholesale and Manufacturing, Except Technical and Scientific Products	156,215
23. Truck Drivers, Light or Delivery Services	154,330
24. First-Line Supervisors/Managers of Food Preparation and Serving Workers	154,175
25. Tellers	146,077
26. Shipping, Receiving, and Traffic Clerks	138,967
27. First-Line Supervisors/Managers of Office and Administrative Support Workers	138,420
28. Accountants	134,463
29. Auditors	134,463
30. Farmers and Ranchers	129,552
31. Management Analysts	125,669
32. Bill and Account Collectors	118,709
33. General and Operations Managers	112,072
34. Cooks, Institution and Cafeteria	111,898
35. Painters, Construction and Maintenance	101,140
36. Automotive Master Mechanics	97,350
37. Automotive Specialty Technicians	97,350
38. Computer Support Specialists	97,334
39. Secondary School Teachers, Except Special and Vocational Education	93,166
40. Medical Assistants	92,977
41. Industrial Truck and Tractor Operators	89,547
42. First-Line Supervisors/Managers of Construction Trades and Extraction Workers	82,923
43. Billing, Cost, and Rate Clerks	81,885
44. Billing, Posting, and Calculating Machine Operators	81,885
45. Statement Clerks	81,885
46. Social and Human Service Assistants	80,142
47. Electricians	79,083
48. Preschool Teachers, Except Special Education	78,172
49. Inspectors, Testers, Sorters, Samplers, and Weighers	75,361
50. Middle School Teachers, Except Special and Vocational Education	75,270
51. Hairdressers, Hairstylists, and Cosmetologists	73,030
52. Licensed Practical and Licensed Vocational Nurses	70,610

(continued)

The 100 Jobs with the Most Openings

Job	Annual Openings
53. Pipe Fitters and Steamfitters	68,643
54. Plumbers	68,643
55. Self-Enrichment Education Teachers	64,449
56. Insurance Sales Agents	64,162
57. Computer Systems Analysts	63,166
58. Recreation Workers	61,454
59. Real Estate Sales Agents	61,232
60. Solderers and Brazers	61,125
61. Welders, Cutters, and Welder Fitters	61,125
62. Medical Secretaries	60,659
63. Bus Drivers, School	59,809
64. Food Service Managers	59,302
65. Computer Software Engineers, Applications	58,690
66. Financial Managers, Branch or Department	57,589
67. Treasurers and Controllers	57,589
68. Correctional Officers and Jailers	56,579
69. Operating Engineers and Other Construction Equipment Operators	55,468
70. Pharmacy Technicians	54,453
71. Loan Officers	54,237
72. Interviewers, Except Eligibility and Loan	54,060
73. Educational, Vocational, and School Counselors	54,025
74. Production, Planning, and Expediting Clerks	52,735
75. Parts Salespersons	52,414
76. Helpers—Installation, Maintenance, and Repair Workers	52,058
77. Fitness Trainers and Aerobics Instructors	51,235
78. Public Relations Specialists	51,216
79. Coaches and Scouts	51,100
80. Property, Real Estate, and Community Association Managers	49,916
81. Lawyers	49,445
82. First-Line Supervisors/Managers of Non-Retail Sales Workers	48,883
83. Sales Agents, Financial Services	47,750
84. Sales Agents, Securities and Commodities	47,750
85. First-Line Supervisors/Managers of Production and Operating Workers	46,144
86. Market Research Analysts	45,015
87. Construction Managers	44,158
88. Sales Representatives, Wholesale and Manufacturing, Technical and Scientific Products	43,469
89. Insurance Claims Clerks	42,246

The 100 Jobs with the Most Openings

Job	Annual Openings
90. Insurance Policy Processing Clerks	42,246
91. Loan Interviewers and Clerks	40,217
92. Machinists	39,505
93. Medical Records and Health Information Technicians	39,048
94. Legal Secretaries	38,682
95. Roofers	38,398
96. Cost Estimators	38,379
97. Anesthesiologists	38,027
98. Family and General Practitioners	38,027
99. Internists, General	38,027
100. Obstetricians and Gynecologists	38,027

Jobs 15 and 16 share 223,225 openings. Jobs 28 and 29 share 134,463 openings. Jobs 36 and 37 share 97,350 openings. Jobs 43, 44, and 45 share 81,885 openings. Jobs 53 and 54 share 68,643 openings. Jobs 60 and 61 share 61,125 openings. Jobs 66 and 67 share 57,589 openings. Jobs 83 and 84 share 47,750 openings. Jobs 89 and 90 share 42,246 openings. Jobs 97, 98, 99, and 100 share 38,027 openings with each other and with three jobs not included in this list.

Best Jobs Lists by Demographic

We decided that it would be interesting to include lists in this section that show what sorts of jobs different types of people are most likely to have. For example, what jobs have the highest percentage of men or young workers? We're not saying that men or young people should consider these jobs over others based solely on this information, but it is interesting information to know.

In some cases, the lists can give you ideas for jobs to consider that you might otherwise overlook. For example, perhaps women should consider some jobs that traditionally have high percentages of men in them. Or older workers might consider some jobs typically held by young people. Although these aren't obvious ways of using these lists, the lists may give you some good ideas of jobs to consider. The lists may also help you identify jobs that work well for others in your situation—for example, jobs with plentiful opportunities for part-time work, if that's something you want to do.

All lists in this section were created through a similar process. We began with the 500 best jobs and sorted those jobs in order of the primary criterion for each set of lists. Next, we sorted those jobs in order of the primary criterion for each set of lists and produced a list of jobs with a high percentage of workers who fit the criterion, ordered from highest to lowest percentage. For example, when we sorted the 500 jobs based on the percentage of workers age 16 to 24, we set the cutoff point at 20% and produced a list of 43 jobs, ranging from a high of 66.4% to a low of 20.2%. For other criteria, such as number of part-time workers or female workers, we used other cutoff points. From this initial list of jobs with a high percentage of each type of worker, we created four more-specialized lists:

 ❋ 25 Best Jobs Overall (the subset of jobs that have the highest combined scores for earnings, growth rate, and number of openings)
 ❋ 25 Best-Paying Jobs
 ❋ 25 Fastest-Growing Jobs
 ❋ 25 Jobs with the Most Openings

Again, each of these four lists includes only jobs that have high percentages of different types of workers. The same basic process was used to create all the lists in this section. The lists are very interesting, and we hope you find them helpful.

Best Jobs with the Highest Percentage of Workers Age 16–24

From our list of 500 jobs used in this book (or, to be precise, the 491 for which we had information about the age of workers), this list contains jobs with the highest percentage (more than 20%) of workers age 16 to 24, presented in order of the percentage of these young workers in each job. Younger workers are found in all jobs, but jobs with higher percentages of younger workers may present more opportunities for initial entry or upward mobility. Many jobs with the highest percentages of younger workers are those that don't require extensive training or education, but there is a wide variety of jobs in different fields among these jobs.

Best Jobs with the Highest Percentage of Workers Age 16–24

Job	Percent Age 16–24
1. Transportation Security Screeners	66.4%
2. Helpers—Brickmasons, Blockmasons, Stonemasons, and Tile and Marble Setters	41.2%
3. Helpers—Carpenters	41.2%
4. Helpers—Electricians	41.2%
5. Helpers—Pipelayers, Plumbers, Pipefitters, and Steamfitters	41.2%
6. Recreational Vehicle Service Technicians	39.9%
7. Tire Repairers and Changers	39.9%
8. Athletes and Sports Competitors	34.5%
9. Coaches and Scouts	34.5%
10. Umpires, Referees, and Other Sports Officials	34.5%
11. Residential Advisors	34.0%
12. Tellers	33.8%
13. Helpers—Installation, Maintenance, and Repair Workers	33.6%
14. Cooks, Institution and Cafeteria	33.1%
15. Cooks, Restaurant	33.1%

Best Jobs with the Highest Percentage of Workers Age 16–24

Job	Percent Age 16–24
16. Library Technicians	32.5%
17. Laborers and Freight, Stock, and Material Movers, Hand	30.3%
18. Fitness Trainers and Aerobics Instructors	30.2%
19. Recreation Workers	30.2%
20. City and Regional Planning Aides	28.0%
21. Environmental Science and Protection Technicians, Including Health	28.0%
22. Forensic Science Technicians	28.0%
23. Social Science Research Assistants	28.0%
24. Tour Guides and Escorts	27.4%
25. Embalmers	26.6%
26. Ambulance Drivers and Attendants, Except Emergency Medical Technicians	26.4%
27. Plasterers and Stucco Masons	25.9%
28. Landscaping and Groundskeeping Workers	25.5%
29. Pesticide Handlers, Sprayers, and Applicators, Vegetation	25.5%
30. Tree Trimmers and Pruners	25.5%
31. Pharmacy Technicians	24.7%
32. Surgical Technologists	24.7%
33. Veterinary Technologists and Technicians	24.7%
34. Receptionists and Information Clerks	24.5%
35. Animal Trainers	23.8%
36. Construction Laborers	23.7%
37. Customer Service Representatives	22.8%
38. Hazardous Materials Removal Workers	22.6%
39. Roofers	22.4%
40. First-Line Supervisors/Managers of Food Preparation and Serving Workers	21.4%
41. Interviewers, Except Eligibility and Loan	20.9%
42. Sailors and Marine Oilers	20.8%
43. Concierges	20.2%

The jobs in the following four lists are derived from the preceding list of the jobs with the highest percentage of workers age 16–24.

Best Jobs Overall with a High Percentage of Workers Age 16–24

Job	Percent Age 16–24	Annual Earnings	Percent Growth	Annual Openings
1. Forensic Science Technicians	28.0%	$47,680	30.7%	3,074
2. Environmental Science and Protection Technicians, Including Health	28.0%	$39,370	28.0%	8,404
3. Athletes and Sports Competitors	34.5%	$38,440	19.2%	4,293
4. Embalmers	26.6%	$36,800	14.3%	1,660
5. Surgical Technologists	24.7%	$37,540	24.5%	15,365
6. Plasterers and Stucco Masons	25.9%	$36,430	8.1%	4,509
7. City and Regional Planning Aides	28.0%	$35,870	12.4%	3,571
8. Hazardous Materials Removal Workers	22.6%	$36,330	11.2%	1,933
9. Social Science Research Assistants	28.0%	$35,870	12.4%	3,571
10. Roofers	22.4%	$33,240	14.3%	38,398
11. Sailors and Marine Oilers	20.8%	$32,570	15.7%	8,600
12. Recreational Vehicle Service Technicians	39.9%	$31,760	18.2%	2,442
13. Tree Trimmers and Pruners	25.5%	$29,800	11.1%	9,621
14. Customer Service Representatives	22.8%	$29,040	24.8%	600,937
15. Pesticide Handlers, Sprayers, and Applicators, Vegetation	25.5%	$28,560	14.0%	7,443
16. Transportation Security Screeners	66.4%	$28,240	12.6%	29,298
17. First-Line Supervisors/Managers of Food Preparation and Serving Workers	21.4%	$28,040	11.3%	154,175
18. Veterinary Technologists and Technicians	24.7%	$27,970	41.0%	14,674
19. Coaches and Scouts	34.5%	$27,840	14.6%	51,100
20. Fitness Trainers and Aerobics Instructors	30.2%	$27,680	26.8%	51,235
21. Library Technicians	32.5%	$27,680	8.5%	29,075
22. Interviewers, Except Eligibility and Loan	20.9%	$27,320	9.5%	54,060
23. Construction Laborers	23.7%	$27,310	10.9%	257,407
24. Pharmacy Technicians	24.7%	$26,720	32.0%	54,453
25. Helpers—Brickmasons, Blockmasons, Stonemasons, and Tile and Marble Setters	41.2%	$26,260	11.0%	22,500

Best-Paying Jobs with a High Percentage of Workers Age 16–24

Job	Percent Age 16–24	Annual Earnings
1. Forensic Science Technicians	28.0%	$47,680
2. Environmental Science and Protection Technicians, Including Health	28.0%	$39,370
3. Athletes and Sports Competitors	34.5%	$38,440

Best-Paying Jobs with a High Percentage of Workers Age 16–24

Job	Percent Age 16–24	Annual Earnings
4. Surgical Technologists	24.7%	$37,540
5. Embalmers	26.6%	$36,800
6. Plasterers and Stucco Masons	25.9%	$36,430
7. Hazardous Materials Removal Workers	22.6%	$36,330
8. City and Regional Planning Aides	28.0%	$35,870
9. Social Science Research Assistants	28.0%	$35,870
10. Roofers	22.4%	$33,240
11. Sailors and Marine Oilers	20.8%	$32,570
12. Recreational Vehicle Service Technicians	39.9%	$31,760
13. Tree Trimmers and Pruners	25.5%	$29,800
14. Customer Service Representatives	22.8%	$29,040
15. Pesticide Handlers, Sprayers, and Applicators, Vegetation	25.5%	$28,560
16. Transportation Security Screeners	66.4%	$28,240
17. First-Line Supervisors/Managers of Food Preparation and Serving Workers	21.4%	$28,040
18. Veterinary Technologists and Technicians	24.7%	$27,970
19. Coaches and Scouts	34.5%	$27,840
20. Fitness Trainers and Aerobics Instructors	30.2%	$27,680
21. Library Technicians	32.5%	$27,680
22. Interviewers, Except Eligibility and Loan	20.9%	$27,320
23. Construction Laborers	23.7%	$27,310
24. Pharmacy Technicians	24.7%	$26,720
25. Helpers—Brickmasons, Blockmasons, Stonemasons, and Tile and Marble Setters	41.2%	$26,260

Fastest-Growing Jobs with a High Percentage of Workers Age 16–24

Job	Percent Age 16–24	Percent Growth
1. Veterinary Technologists and Technicians	24.7%	41.0%
2. Pharmacy Technicians	24.7%	32.0%
3. Forensic Science Technicians	28.0%	30.7%
4. Environmental Science and Protection Technicians, Including Health	28.0%	28.0%
5. Fitness Trainers and Aerobics Instructors	30.2%	26.8%
6. Customer Service Representatives	22.8%	24.8%
7. Surgical Technologists	24.7%	24.5%
8. Animal Trainers	23.8%	22.7%

(continued)

(continued)

Fastest-Growing Jobs with a High Percentage of Workers Age 16–24

Job	Percent Age 16–24	Percent Growth
9. Ambulance Drivers and Attendants, Except Emergency Medical Technicians	26.4%	21.7%
10. Tour Guides and Escorts	27.4%	21.2%
11. Tire Repairers and Changers	39.9%	20.2%
12. Athletes and Sports Competitors	34.5%	19.2%
13. Residential Advisors	34.0%	18.5%
14. Recreational Vehicle Service Technicians	39.9%	18.2%
15. Landscaping and Groundskeeping Workers	25.5%	18.1%
16. Receptionists and Information Clerks	24.5%	17.2%
17. Umpires, Referees, and Other Sports Officials	34.5%	16.0%
18. Sailors and Marine Oilers	20.8%	15.7%
19. Coaches and Scouts	34.5%	14.6%
20. Embalmers	26.6%	14.3%
21. Roofers	22.4%	14.3%
22. Concierges	20.2%	14.1%
23. Pesticide Handlers, Sprayers, and Applicators, Vegetation	25.5%	14.0%
24. Tellers	33.8%	13.5%
25. Recreation Workers	30.2%	12.7%

Jobs with the Most Openings with a High Percentage of Workers Age 16–24

Job	Percent Age 16–24	Annual Openings
1. Laborers and Freight, Stock, and Material Movers, Hand	30.3%	630,487
2. Customer Service Representatives	22.8%	600,937
3. Receptionists and Information Clerks	24.5%	334,124
4. Landscaping and Groundskeeping Workers	25.5%	307,138
5. Construction Laborers	23.7%	257,407
6. Cooks, Restaurant	33.1%	238,542
7. First-Line Supervisors/Managers of Food Preparation and Serving Workers	21.4%	154,175
8. Tellers	33.8%	146,077
9. Cooks, Institution and Cafeteria	33.1%	111,898
10. Recreation Workers	30.2%	61,454
11. Pharmacy Technicians	24.7%	54,453

Jobs with the Most Openings with a High Percentage of Workers Age 16–24

Job	Percent Age 16–24	Annual Openings
12. Interviewers, Except Eligibility and Loan	20.9%	54,060
13. Helpers—Installation, Maintenance, and Repair Workers	33.6%	52,058
14. Fitness Trainers and Aerobics Instructors	30.2%	51,235
15. Coaches and Scouts	34.5%	51,100
16. Roofers	22.4%	38,398
17. Helpers—Carpenters	41.2%	37,731
18. Helpers—Electricians	41.2%	35,109
19. Helpers—Pipelayers, Plumbers, Pipefitters, and Steamfitters	41.2%	29,332
20. Transportation Security Screeners	66.4%	29,298
21. Library Technicians	32.5%	29,075
22. Helpers—Brickmasons, Blockmasons, Stonemasons, and Tile and Marble Setters	41.2%	22,500
23. Tire Repairers and Changers	39.9%	18,829
24. Surgical Technologists	24.7%	15,365
25. Tour Guides and Escorts	27.4%	15,027

Best Jobs with a High Percentage of Workers Age 55 and Over

Older workers don't change careers as often as younger ones do, and on average, they tend to have been in their jobs for quite some time. Many of the jobs with the highest percentages of workers age 55 and over—and those with the highest earnings—require considerable preparation, either through experience or through education and training. These are not the sort of jobs most younger workers could easily get. That should not come as a big surprise, as many of these folks have been in the workforce for a long time and therefore have lots of experience.

But go down the list of the jobs with the highest percentage (more than 20%) of older workers, and you will find a variety of jobs that many older workers could more easily enter if they were changing careers. Some would make good "retirement" jobs, particularly if they allowed for part-time work or self-employment.

Best Jobs with the Highest Percentage of Workers Age 55 and Over

Job	Percent Age 55 and Over
1. Farmers and Ranchers	52.3%
2. Marine Architects	44.3%
3. Marine Engineers	44.3%
4. Clergy	42.0%
5. Librarians	39.0%
6. Bus Drivers, School	38.2%
7. Bus Drivers, Transit and Intercity	38.2%
8. Demonstrators and Product Promoters	38.2%
9. Sociologists	37.8%
10. Property, Real Estate, and Community Association Managers	35.2%
11. Clinical Psychologists	35.0%
12. Counseling Psychologists	35.0%
13. Industrial-Organizational Psychologists	35.0%
14. School Psychologists	35.0%
15. Real Estate Brokers	34.5%
16. Real Estate Sales Agents	34.5%
17. Aquacultural Managers	33.9%
18. Crop and Livestock Managers	33.9%
19. Nursery and Greenhouse Managers	33.9%
20. Art Directors	33.9%
21. Fine Artists, Including Painters, Sculptors, and Illustrators	33.9%
22. Multi-Media Artists and Animators	33.9%
23. Astronomers	33.3%
24. Copy Writers	33.3%
25. Physicists	33.3%
26. Poets, Lyricists, and Creative Writers	33.3%
27. Archivists	32.5%
28. Curators	32.5%
29. Museum Technicians and Conservators	32.5%
30. Lodging Managers	31.6%
31. Chief Executives	31.5%
32. Funeral Directors	31.0%
33. Natural Sciences Managers	30.9%
34. Private Detectives and Investigators	30.4%
35. Court Clerks	30.4%
36. Instructional Coordinators	30.4%

Best Jobs with the Highest Percentage of Workers Age 55 and Over

Job	Percent Age 55 and Over
37. License Clerks	30.4%
38. Municipal Clerks	30.4%
39. Management Analysts	30.1%
40. Cost Estimators	29.9%
41. Education Administrators, Elementary and Secondary School	28.7%
42. Education Administrators, Postsecondary	28.7%
43. Education Administrators, Preschool and Child Care Center/Program	28.7%
44. Appraisers, Real Estate	28.6%
45. Assessors	28.6%
46. Veterinarians	28.4%
47. Medical Equipment Repairers	28.3%
48. Bookkeeping, Accounting, and Auditing Clerks	28.2%
49. Aviation Inspectors	28.1%
50. Freight and Cargo Inspectors	28.1%
51. Transportation Vehicle, Equipment and Systems Inspectors, Except Aviation	28.1%
52. Arbitrators, Mediators, and Conciliators	27.8%
53. Judges, Magistrate Judges, and Magistrates	27.8%
54. Lawyers	27.8%
55. Directors, Religious Activities and Education	27.7%
56. Tour Guides and Escorts	27.7%
57. Dentists, General	27.4%
58. Oral and Maxillofacial Surgeons	27.4%
59. Orthodontists	27.4%
60. Prosthodontists	27.4%
61. Music Composers and Arrangers	27.3%
62. Music Directors	27.3%
63. Anesthesiologists	27.2%
64. Family and General Practitioners	27.2%
65. Internists, General	27.2%
66. Obstetricians and Gynecologists	27.2%
67. Pediatricians, General	27.2%
68. Psychiatrists	27.2%
69. Surgeons	27.2%
70. Insurance Sales Agents	27.1%
71. Administrative Services Managers	27.1%
72. Coroners	27.0%

(continued)

(continued)

Best Jobs with the Highest Percentage of Workers Age 55 and Over

Job	Percent Age 55 and Over
73. Environmental Compliance Inspectors	27.0%
74. Equal Opportunity Representatives and Officers	27.0%
75. Government Property Inspectors and Investigators	27.0%
76. Licensing Examiners and Inspectors	27.0%
77. Gaming Supervisors	26.9%
78. Construction and Building Inspectors	26.8%
79. Medical Records and Health Information Technicians	26.1%
80. Electrical and Electronics Repairers, Commercial and Industrial Equipment	26.0%
81. Petroleum Engineers	25.8%
82. First-Line Supervisors/Managers of Housekeeping and Janitorial Workers	25.7%
83. Audiologists	25.6%
84. Nuclear Engineers	25.5%
85. Executive Secretaries and Administrative Assistants	25.5%
86. Legal Secretaries	25.5%
87. Medical Secretaries	25.5%
88. Secretaries, Except Legal, Medical, and Executive	25.5%
89. Engineering Managers	25.5%
90. Educational, Vocational, and School Counselors	25.3%
91. Marriage and Family Therapists	25.3%
92. Mental Health Counselors	25.3%
93. Rehabilitation Counselors	25.3%
94. Substance Abuse and Behavioral Disorder Counselors	25.3%
95. Maintenance and Repair Workers, General	25.3%
96. Social and Community Service Managers	25.3%
97. Millwrights	25.2%
98. Ship Engineers	25.0%
99. Gaming Surveillance Officers and Gaming Investigators	24.9%
100. Security Guards	24.9%
101. Materials Engineers	24.7%
102. Medical and Health Services Managers	24.7%
103. Optometrists	24.6%
104. Chemical Engineers	24.3%
105. Purchasing Managers	24.3%
106. Postal Service Mail Carriers	24.2%
107. Cartographers and Photogrammetrists	24.2%
108. Surveyors	24.2%

Best Jobs with the Highest Percentage of Workers Age 55 and Over

Job	Percent Age 55 and Over
109. Purchasing Agents, Except Wholesale, Retail, and Farm Products	23.8%
110. Correspondence Clerks	23.7%
111. Nuclear Equipment Operation Technicians	23.5%
112. Nuclear Monitoring Technicians	23.5%
113. Architects, Except Landscape and Naval	23.4%
114. Landscape Architects	23.4%
115. Flight Attendants	23.2%
116. Budget Analysts	23.0%
117. Payroll and Timekeeping Clerks	22.9%
118. Structural Metal Fabricators and Fitters	22.7%
119. Geological Sample Test Technicians	22.6%
120. Geophysical Data Technicians	22.6%
121. Environmental Scientists and Specialists, Including Health	22.6%
122. Geoscientists, Except Hydrologists and Geographers	22.6%
123. Hydrologists	22.6%
124. Truck Drivers, Heavy and Tractor-Trailer	22.5%
125. Truck Drivers, Light or Delivery Services	22.5%
126. Pharmacists	22.5%
127. Emergency Management Specialists	22.5%
128. Technical Writers	22.4%
129. Airline Pilots, Copilots, and Flight Engineers	22.4%
130. Commercial Pilots	22.4%
131. Personal Financial Advisors	22.3%
132. Secondary School Teachers, Except Special and Vocational Education	22.2%
133. Vocational Education Teachers, Secondary School	22.2%
134. Animal Trainers	22.2%
135. Economists	22.1%
136. Adult Literacy, Remedial Education, and GED Teachers and Instructors	22.1%
137. Self-Enrichment Education Teachers	22.1%
138. Elementary School Teachers, Except Special Education	22.0%
139. Middle School Teachers, Except Special and Vocational Education	22.0%
140. Licensed Practical and Licensed Vocational Nurses	22.0%
141. Interviewers, Except Eligibility and Loan	22.0%
142. First-Line Supervisors/Managers of Mechanics, Installers, and Repairers	22.0%
143. Gaming Managers	22.0%
144. Human Resources Assistants, Except Payroll and Timekeeping	21.9%
145. Maintenance Workers, Machinery	21.7%

(continued)

(continued)

Best Jobs with the Highest Percentage of Workers Age 55 and Over

Job	Percent Age 55 and Over
146. Fire Inspectors	21.6%
147. Fire Investigators	21.6%
148. Industrial Machinery Mechanics	21.6%
149. Tax Examiners, Collectors, and Revenue Agents	21.5%
150. First-Line Supervisors/Managers of Personal Service Workers	21.4%
151. Machinists	21.4%
152. Embalmers	21.4%
153. Concierges	21.3%
154. Electrical Engineers	21.3%
155. Electronics Engineers, Except Computer	21.3%
156. Anthropologists	21.2%
157. Archeologists	21.2%
158. Political Scientists	21.2%
159. Eligibility Interviewers, Government Programs	21.1%
160. Construction Managers	21.1%
161. First-Line Supervisors/Managers of Non-Retail Sales Workers	21.0%
162. Sales Representatives, Wholesale and Manufacturing, Except Technical and Scientific Products	21.0%
163. Sales Representatives, Wholesale and Manufacturing, Technical and Scientific Products	21.0%
164. Registered Nurses	21.0%
165. Railroad Conductors and Yardmasters	21.0%
166. Urban and Regional Planners	20.9%
167. Photographers	20.8%
168. Fire-Prevention and Protection Engineers	20.8%
169. Industrial Engineers	20.8%
170. Industrial Safety and Health Engineers	20.8%
171. Product Safety Engineers	20.8%
172. Industrial Production Managers	20.6%
173. Civil Engineers	20.6%
174. First-Line Supervisors/Managers of Office and Administrative Support Workers	20.5%
175. Billing, Cost, and Rate Clerks	20.3%
176. Billing, Posting, and Calculating Machine Operators	20.3%
177. Statement Clerks	20.3%
178. Agents and Business Managers of Artists, Performers, and Athletes	20.3%
179. First-Line Supervisors/Managers of Retail Sales Workers	20.1%

The jobs in the following four lists are derived from the preceding list of the jobs with the highest percentage of workers age 55 and over.

Best Jobs Overall with a High Percentage of Workers Age 55 and Over

Job	Percent Age 55 and Over	Annual Earnings	Percent Growth	Annual Openings
1. Management Analysts	30.1%	$71,150	21.9%	125,669
2. Registered Nurses	21.0%	$60,010	23.5%	233,499
3. Anesthesiologists	27.2%	$145,600+	14.2%	38,027
4. Family and General Practitioners	27.2%	$145,600+	14.2%	38,027
5. Internists, General	27.2%	$145,600+	14.2%	38,027
6. Obstetricians and Gynecologists	27.2%	$145,600+	14.2%	38,027
7. Psychiatrists	27.2%	$145,600+	14.2%	38,027
8. Surgeons	27.2%	$145,600+	14.2%	38,027
9. Pediatricians, General	27.2%	$140,690	14.2%	38,027
10. Pharmacists	22.5%	$100,480	21.7%	16,358
11. Construction Managers	21.1%	$76,230	15.7%	44,158
12. Medical and Health Services Managers	24.7%	$76,990	16.4%	31,877
13. Personal Financial Advisors	22.3%	$67,660	41.0%	17,114
14. Lawyers	27.8%	$106,120	11.0%	49,445
15. Social and Community Service Managers	25.3%	$54,530	24.7%	23,788
16. Cost Estimators	29.9%	$54,920	18.5%	38,379
17. Instructional Coordinators	30.4%	$55,270	22.5%	21,294
18. Civil Engineers	20.6%	$71,710	18.0%	15,979
19. Veterinarians	28.4%	$75,230	35.0%	5,301
20. Industrial Engineers	20.8%	$71,430	20.3%	11,272
21. Sales Representatives, Wholesale and Manufacturing, Technical and Scientific Products	21.0%	$68,270	12.4%	43,469
22. Education Administrators, Postsecondary	28.7%	$75,780	14.2%	17,121
23. Multi-Media Artists and Animators	33.9%	$54,550	25.8%	13,182
24. Architects, Except Landscape and Naval	23.4%	$67,620	17.7%	11,324
25. Surveyors	24.2%	$51,630	23.7%	14,305

Jobs 3, 4, 5, 6, 7, 8, and 9 share 38,027 openings.

Best-Paying Jobs with a High Percentage of Workers Age 55 and Over

Job	Percent Age 55 and Over	Annual Earnings
1. Airline Pilots, Copilots, and Flight Engineers	22.4%	$145,600+
2. Anesthesiologists	27.2%	$145,600+
3. Chief Executives	31.5%	$145,600+
4. Family and General Practitioners	27.2%	$145,600+
5. Internists, General	27.2%	$145,600+
6. Obstetricians and Gynecologists	27.2%	$145,600+
7. Oral and Maxillofacial Surgeons	27.4%	$145,600+
8. Orthodontists	27.4%	$145,600+
9. Prosthodontists	27.4%	$145,600+
10. Psychiatrists	27.2%	$145,600+
11. Surgeons	27.2%	$145,600+
12. Pediatricians, General	27.2%	$140,690
13. Dentists, General	27.4%	$137,630
14. Engineering Managers	25.5%	$111,020
15. Judges, Magistrate Judges, and Magistrates	27.8%	$107,230
16. Lawyers	27.8%	$106,120
17. Natural Sciences Managers	30.9%	$104,040
18. Petroleum Engineers	25.8%	$103,960
19. Pharmacists	22.5%	$100,480
20. Astronomers	33.3%	$99,020
21. Physicists	33.3%	$96,850
22. Nuclear Engineers	25.5%	$94,420
23. Optometrists	24.6%	$93,800
24. Political Scientists	21.2%	$91,580
25. Purchasing Managers	24.3%	$85,440

Fastest-Growing Jobs with a High Percentage of Workers Age 55 and Over

Job	Percent Age 55 and Over	Percent Growth
1. Personal Financial Advisors	22.3%	41.0%
2. Veterinarians	28.4%	35.0%
3. Substance Abuse and Behavioral Disorder Counselors	25.3%	34.3%
4. Gaming Surveillance Officers and Gaming Investigators	24.9%	33.6%

Fastest-Growing Jobs with a High Percentage of Workers Age 55 and Over

Job	Percent Age 55 and Over	Percent Growth
5. Mental Health Counselors	25.3%	30.0%
6. Marriage and Family Therapists	25.3%	29.8%
7. Multi-Media Artists and Animators	33.9%	25.8%
8. Environmental Scientists and Specialists, Including Health	22.6%	25.1%
9. Social and Community Service Managers	25.3%	24.7%
10. Gaming Managers	22.0%	24.4%
11. Hydrologists	22.6%	24.3%
12. Surveyors	24.2%	23.7%
13. Education Administrators, Preschool and Child Care Center/Program	28.7%	23.5%
14. Registered Nurses	21.0%	23.5%
15. Gaming Supervisors	26.9%	23.4%
16. Curators	32.5%	23.3%
17. Self-Enrichment Education Teachers	22.1%	23.1%
18. Rehabilitation Counselors	25.3%	23.0%
19. Animal Trainers	22.2%	22.7%
20. Instructional Coordinators	30.4%	22.5%
21. Geoscientists, Except Hydrologists and Geographers	22.6%	21.9%
22. Management Analysts	30.1%	21.9%
23. Medical Equipment Repairers	28.3%	21.7%
24. Pharmacists	22.5%	21.7%
25. Industrial-Organizational Psychologists	35.0%	21.3%

Jobs with the Most Openings with a High Percentage of Workers Age 55 and Over

Job	Percent Age 55 and Over	Annual Openings
1. Bookkeeping, Accounting, and Auditing Clerks	28.2%	286,854
2. Truck Drivers, Heavy and Tractor-Trailer	22.5%	279,032
3. Secretaries, Except Legal, Medical, and Executive	25.5%	239,630
4. Executive Secretaries and Administrative Assistants	25.5%	235,314
5. Registered Nurses	21.0%	233,499
6. Security Guards	24.9%	222,085

(continued)

(continued)

Jobs with the Most Openings with a High Percentage of Workers Age 55 and Over

Job	Percent Age 55 and Over	Annual Openings
7. First-Line Supervisors/Managers of Retail Sales Workers	20.1%	221,241
8. Elementary School Teachers, Except Special Education	22.0%	181,612
9. Maintenance and Repair Workers, General	25.3%	165,502
10. Sales Representatives, Wholesale and Manufacturing, Except Technical and Scientific Products	21.0%	156,215
11. Truck Drivers, Light or Delivery Services	22.5%	154,330
12. First-Line Supervisors/Managers of Office and Administrative Support Workers	20.5%	138,420
13. Farmers and Ranchers	52.3%	129,552
14. Management Analysts	30.1%	125,669
15. Secondary School Teachers, Except Special and Vocational Education	22.2%	93,166
16. Billing, Cost, and Rate Clerks	20.3%	81,885
17. Billing, Posting, and Calculating Machine Operators	20.3%	81,885
18. Statement Clerks	20.3%	81,885
19. Middle School Teachers, Except Special and Vocational Education	22.0%	75,270
20. Licensed Practical and Licensed Vocational Nurses	22.0%	70,610
21. Self-Enrichment Education Teachers	22.1%	64,449
22. Insurance Sales Agents	27.1%	64,162
23. Real Estate Sales Agents	34.5%	61,232
24. Medical Secretaries	25.5%	60,659
25. Bus Drivers, School	38.2%	59,809

Jobs 16, 17, and 18 share 81,885 openings.

Best Jobs with a High Percentage of Part-Time Workers

Look over the list of the jobs with high percentages (more than 25%) of part-time workers, and you will find some interesting things. For example, the list is dominated by postsecondary teaching jobs; many college teachers are part-timers, often referred to as adjunct faculty. You'll note that all of these jobs are estimated to have 27.8% part-time workers. In reality, there are probably different percentages of part-timers in these jobs, but separate figures are not available. Many of the other jobs on the list involve providing services at times when most other people are not working. Some are in the field of health care.

Some part-time workers may want the freedom of time that this work arrangement can provide, but others may do so because they can't find full-time employment in these areas. These folks may work in other full- or part-time jobs to make ends meet. If you want to work part time now or in the future, these lists will help you identify jobs that are more likely to provide that opportunity. If you want full-time work, the lists may also help you identify jobs for which such opportunities are more difficult to find. In either case, it's good information to know in advance.

Note: The earnings estimates in the following lists are based on a survey of both part-time and full-time workers. On average, part-time workers earn about 10 percent less per hour than full-time workers.

Jobs with the Highest Percentage of Part-Time Workers

Job	Percent Part-Time Workers
1. Library Technicians	65.0%
2. Dental Hygienists	58.7%
3. Demonstrators and Product Promoters	56.1%
4. Transportation Security Screeners	55.3%
5. Massage Therapists	42.9%
6. Adult Literacy, Remedial Education, and GED Teachers and Instructors	41.3%
7. Self-Enrichment Education Teachers	41.3%
8. Athletes and Sports Competitors	39.1%
9. Coaches and Scouts	39.1%
10. Umpires, Referees, and Other Sports Officials	39.1%
11. Fitness Trainers and Aerobics Instructors	38.2%
12. Recreation Workers	38.2%
13. Teacher Assistants	38.0%
14. Music Composers and Arrangers	37.0%
15. Music Directors	37.0%
16. Dental Assistants	35.7%
17. Bus Drivers, School	34.1%
18. Bus Drivers, Transit and Intercity	34.1%
19. Receptionists and Information Clerks	31.7%
20. Hairdressers, Hairstylists, and Cosmetologists	31.1%
21. Cooks, Institution and Cafeteria	29.9%
22. Cooks, Restaurant	29.9%
23. Occupational Therapists	29.8%
24. Tour Guides and Escorts	29.0%
25. Interpreters and Translators	28.5%

(continued)

(continued)

Jobs with the Highest Percentage of Part-Time Workers

Job	Percent Part-Time Workers
26. Audiologists	28.3%
27. Agricultural Sciences Teachers, Postsecondary	27.8%
28. Anthropology and Archeology Teachers, Postsecondary	27.8%
29. Architecture Teachers, Postsecondary	27.8%
30. Area, Ethnic, and Cultural Studies Teachers, Postsecondary	27.8%
31. Art, Drama, and Music Teachers, Postsecondary	27.8%
32. Atmospheric, Earth, Marine, and Space Sciences Teachers, Postsecondary	27.8%
33. Biological Science Teachers, Postsecondary	27.8%
34. Business Teachers, Postsecondary	27.8%
35. Chemistry Teachers, Postsecondary	27.8%
36. Communications Teachers, Postsecondary	27.8%
37. Computer Science Teachers, Postsecondary	27.8%
38. Criminal Justice and Law Enforcement Teachers, Postsecondary	27.8%
39. Economics Teachers, Postsecondary	27.8%
40. Education Teachers, Postsecondary	27.8%
41. Engineering Teachers, Postsecondary	27.8%
42. English Language and Literature Teachers, Postsecondary	27.8%
43. Environmental Science Teachers, Postsecondary	27.8%
44. Foreign Language and Literature Teachers, Postsecondary	27.8%
45. Forestry and Conservation Science Teachers, Postsecondary	27.8%
46. Geography Teachers, Postsecondary	27.8%
47. Graduate Teaching Assistants	27.8%
48. Health Specialties Teachers, Postsecondary	27.8%
49. History Teachers, Postsecondary	27.8%
50. Home Economics Teachers, Postsecondary	27.8%
51. Law Teachers, Postsecondary	27.8%
52. Library Science Teachers, Postsecondary	27.8%
53. Mathematical Science Teachers, Postsecondary	27.8%
54. Nursing Instructors and Teachers, Postsecondary	27.8%
55. Philosophy and Religion Teachers, Postsecondary	27.8%
56. Physics Teachers, Postsecondary	27.8%
57. Political Science Teachers, Postsecondary	27.8%
58. Psychology Teachers, Postsecondary	27.8%
59. Recreation and Fitness Studies Teachers, Postsecondary	27.8%
60. Social Work Teachers, Postsecondary	27.8%
61. Sociology Teachers, Postsecondary	27.8%

Jobs with the Highest Percentage of Part-Time Workers

Job	Percent Part-Time Workers
62. Vocational Education Teachers, Postsecondary	27.8%
63. Physical Therapist Aides	27.1%
64. Physical Therapist Assistants	27.1%
65. Tellers	27.1%
66. Dietitians and Nutritionists	27.0%
67. Makeup Artists, Theatrical and Performance	26.3%
68. Skin Care Specialists	26.3%
69. Office Clerks, General	26.0%
70. Dentists, General	25.9%
71. Oral and Maxillofacial Surgeons	25.9%
72. Orthodontists	25.9%
73. Prosthodontists	25.9%
74. Directors, Religious Activities and Education	25.2%
75. Kindergarten Teachers, Except Special Education	25.1%
76. Preschool Teachers, Except Special Education	25.1%

The jobs in the following four lists are derived from the preceding list of the jobs with the highest percentage of part-time workers.

Best Jobs Overall with a High Percentage of Part-Time Workers

Job	Percent Part-Time Workers	Annual Earnings	Percent Growth	Annual Openings
1. Health Specialties Teachers, Postsecondary	27.8%	$80,700	22.9%	19,617
2. Dental Hygienists	58.7%	$64,740	30.1%	10,433
3. Business Teachers, Postsecondary	27.8%	$64,900	22.9%	11,643
4. Biological Science Teachers, Postsecondary	27.8%	$71,780	22.9%	9,039
5. Engineering Teachers, Postsecondary	27.8%	$79,510	22.9%	5,565
6. Occupational Therapists	29.8%	$63,790	23.1%	8,338
7. Art, Drama, and Music Teachers, Postsecondary	27.8%	$55,190	22.9%	12,707
8. Self-Enrichment Education Teachers	41.3%	$34,580	23.1%	64,449
9. Law Teachers, Postsecondary	27.8%	$87,730	22.9%	2,169
10. Computer Science Teachers, Postsecondary	27.8%	$62,020	22.9%	5,820
11. Dental Assistants	35.7%	$31,550	29.2%	29,482
12. Mathematical Science Teachers, Postsecondary	27.8%	$58,560	22.9%	7,663

(continued)

(continued)

Best Jobs Overall with a High Percentage of Part-Time Workers

Job	Percent Part-Time Workers	Annual Earnings	Percent Growth	Annual Openings
13. Vocational Education Teachers, Postsecondary	27.8%	$45,850	22.9%	19,313
14. Economics Teachers, Postsecondary	27.8%	$75,300	22.9%	2,208
15. English Language and Literature Teachers, Postsecondary	27.8%	$54,000	22.9%	10,475
16. Fitness Trainers and Aerobics Instructors	38.2%	$27,680	26.8%	51,235
17. Education Teachers, Postsecondary	27.8%	$54,220	22.9%	9,359
18. Nursing Instructors and Teachers, Postsecondary	27.8%	$57,500	22.9%	7,337
19. Psychology Teachers, Postsecondary	27.8%	$60,610	22.9%	5,261
20. Agricultural Sciences Teachers, Postsecondary	27.8%	$78,460	22.9%	1,840
21. Preschool Teachers, Except Special Education	25.1%	$23,130	26.3%	78,172
22. Chemistry Teachers, Postsecondary	27.8%	$63,870	22.9%	3,405
23. Physics Teachers, Postsecondary	27.8%	$70,090	22.9%	2,155
24. Atmospheric, Earth, Marine, and Space Sciences Teachers, Postsecondary	27.8%	$73,280	22.9%	1,553
25. History Teachers, Postsecondary	27.8%	$59,160	22.9%	3,570

Best-Paying Jobs with a High Percentage of Part-Time Workers

Job	Percent Part-Time Workers	Annual Earnings
1. Oral and Maxillofacial Surgeons	25.9%	$145,600+
2. Orthodontists	25.9%	$145,600+
3. Prosthodontists	25.9%	$145,600+
4. Dentists, General	25.9%	$137,630
5. Law Teachers, Postsecondary	27.8%	$87,730
6. Health Specialties Teachers, Postsecondary	27.8%	$80,700
7. Engineering Teachers, Postsecondary	27.8%	$79,510
8. Agricultural Sciences Teachers, Postsecondary	27.8%	$78,460
9. Economics Teachers, Postsecondary	27.8%	$75,300
10. Atmospheric, Earth, Marine, and Space Sciences Teachers, Postsecondary	27.8%	$73,280
11. Biological Science Teachers, Postsecondary	27.8%	$71,780
12. Physics Teachers, Postsecondary	27.8%	$70,090
13. Architecture Teachers, Postsecondary	27.8%	$68,540
14. Business Teachers, Postsecondary	27.8%	$64,900

Best-Paying Jobs with a High Percentage of Part-Time Workers

Job	Percent Part-Time Workers	Annual Earnings
15. Environmental Science Teachers, Postsecondary	27.8%	$64,850
16. Dental Hygienists	58.7%	$64,740
17. Anthropology and Archeology Teachers, Postsecondary	27.8%	$64,530
18. Chemistry Teachers, Postsecondary	27.8%	$63,870
19. Forestry and Conservation Science Teachers, Postsecondary	27.8%	$63,790
20. Occupational Therapists	29.8%	$63,790
21. Political Science Teachers, Postsecondary	27.8%	$63,100
22. Computer Science Teachers, Postsecondary	27.8%	$62,020
23. Geography Teachers, Postsecondary	27.8%	$61,310
24. Psychology Teachers, Postsecondary	27.8%	$60,610
25. Audiologists	28.3%	$59,440

Fastest-Growing Jobs with a High Percentage of Part-Time Workers

Job	Percent Part-Time Workers	Percent Growth
1. Makeup Artists, Theatrical and Performance	26.3%	39.8%
2. Skin Care Specialists	26.3%	34.3%
3. Physical Therapist Assistants	27.1%	32.4%
4. Dental Hygienists	58.7%	30.1%
5. Dental Assistants	35.7%	29.2%
6. Fitness Trainers and Aerobics Instructors	38.2%	26.8%
7. Preschool Teachers, Except Special Education	25.1%	26.3%
8. Physical Therapist Aides	27.1%	24.4%
9. Interpreters and Translators	28.5%	23.6%
10. Occupational Therapists	29.8%	23.1%
11. Self-Enrichment Education Teachers	41.3%	23.1%
12. Agricultural Sciences Teachers, Postsecondary	27.8%	22.9%
13. Anthropology and Archeology Teachers, Postsecondary	27.8%	22.9%
14. Architecture Teachers, Postsecondary	27.8%	22.9%
15. Area, Ethnic, and Cultural Studies Teachers, Postsecondary	27.8%	22.9%
16. Art, Drama, and Music Teachers, Postsecondary	27.8%	22.9%
17. Atmospheric, Earth, Marine, and Space Sciences Teachers, Postsecondary	27.8%	22.9%
18. Biological Science Teachers, Postsecondary	27.8%	22.9%
19. Business Teachers, Postsecondary	27.8%	22.9%

(continued)

(continued)

Fastest-Growing Jobs with a High Percentage of Part-Time Workers

Job	Percent Part-Time Workers	Percent Growth
20. Chemistry Teachers, Postsecondary	27.8%	22.9%
21. Communications Teachers, Postsecondary	27.8%	22.9%
22. Computer Science Teachers, Postsecondary	27.8%	22.9%
23. Criminal Justice and Law Enforcement Teachers, Postsecondary	27.8%	22.9%
24. Economics Teachers, Postsecondary	27.8%	22.9%
25. Education Teachers, Postsecondary	27.8%	22.9%

Jobs with the Most Openings with a High Percentage of Part-Time Workers

Job	Percent Part-Time Workers	Annual Openings
1. Office Clerks, General	26.0%	765,803
2. Receptionists and Information Clerks	31.7%	334,124
3. Cooks, Restaurant	29.9%	238,542
4. Teacher Assistants	38.0%	193,986
5. Tellers	27.1%	146,077
6. Cooks, Institution and Cafeteria	29.9%	111,898
7. Preschool Teachers, Except Special Education	25.1%	78,172
8. Hairdressers, Hairstylists, and Cosmetologists	31.1%	73,030
9. Self-Enrichment Education Teachers	41.3%	64,449
10. Recreation Workers	38.2%	61,454
11. Bus Drivers, School	34.1%	59,809
12. Fitness Trainers and Aerobics Instructors	38.2%	51,235
13. Coaches and Scouts	39.1%	51,100
14. Demonstrators and Product Promoters	56.1%	32,779
15. Dental Assistants	35.7%	29,482
16. Transportation Security Screeners	55.3%	29,298
17. Library Technicians	65.0%	29,075
18. Kindergarten Teachers, Except Special Education	25.1%	27,603
19. Bus Drivers, Transit and Intercity	34.1%	27,100
20. Graduate Teaching Assistants	27.8%	20,601
21. Health Specialties Teachers, Postsecondary	27.8%	19,617
22. Vocational Education Teachers, Postsecondary	27.8%	19,313

Jobs with the Most Openings with a High Percentage of Part-Time Workers

Job	Percent Part-Time Workers	Annual Openings
23. Adult Literacy, Remedial Education, and GED Teachers and Instructors	41.3%	17,340
24. Tour Guides and Escorts	29.0%	15,027
25. Art, Drama, and Music Teachers, Postsecondary	27.8%	12,707

Best Jobs with a High Percentage of Self-Employed Workers

About 8% of all working people are self-employed. Although you may think of the self-employed as having similar jobs, they actually work in an enormous range of situations, fields, and work environments that you may not have considered.

Among the self-employed are people who own small or large businesses, as many real estate brokers and funeral directors do; professionals who own their own practices, as many lawyers, psychologists, and medical doctors do; people working on a contract basis for one or more employers, as many editors do; people running home consulting or other businesses; and people in many other situations. They may go to the same worksite every day, as most attorneys do; visit multiple employers during the course of a week, as many models do; or do most of their work from home, as many craft artists do. Some work part time, others full time.

The point is that there is an enormous range of situations. One of them could make sense for you now or in the future.

The following list contains jobs in which more than 30% of the workers are self-employed.

Jobs with the Highest Percentage of Self-Employed Workers

Job	Percent Self-Employed Workers
1. Farmers and Ranchers	100.0%
2. Multi-Media Artists and Animators	69.7%
3. Copy Writers	65.9%
4. Poets, Lyricists, and Creative Writers	65.9%
5. Massage Therapists	64.0%
6. Real Estate Brokers	63.5%

(continued)

(continued)

Jobs with the Highest Percentage of Self-Employed Workers

Job	Percent Self-Employed Workers
7. Fine Artists, Including Painters, Sculptors, and Illustrators	62.6%
8. Real Estate Sales Agents	60.2%
9. Art Directors	59.0%
10. Animal Trainers	56.9%
11. Construction Managers	56.3%
12. Agents and Business Managers of Artists, Performers, and Athletes	55.8%
13. Photographers	54.3%
14. Lodging Managers	53.0%
15. Chiropractors	51.7%
16. Prosthodontists	51.3%
17. Property, Real Estate, and Community Association Managers	50.9%
18. First-Line Supervisors/Managers of Non-Retail Sales Workers	45.4%
19. Food Service Managers	44.8%
20. Music Composers and Arrangers	44.7%
21. Music Directors	44.7%
22. Hairdressers, Hairstylists, and Cosmetologists	44.5%
23. First-Line Supervisors/Managers of Landscaping, Lawn Service, and Groundskeeping Workers	44.1%
24. Orthodontists	43.3%
25. Painters, Construction and Maintenance	42.2%
26. Makeup Artists, Theatrical and Performance	39.7%
27. Industrial-Organizational Psychologists	39.3%
28. Skin Care Specialists	38.9%
29. First-Line Supervisors/Managers of Personal Service Workers	38.6%
30. Dentists, General	36.6%
31. Clinical Psychologists	34.2%
32. Counseling Psychologists	34.2%
33. First-Line Supervisors/Managers of Retail Sales Workers	34.2%
34. School Psychologists	34.2%
35. Tile and Marble Setters	33.8%
36. Appraisers, Real Estate	32.7%
37. Assessors	32.7%
38. Construction Carpenters	31.8%
39. Rough Carpenters	31.8%
40. Personal Financial Advisors	30.9%
41. First-Line Supervisors/Managers of Housekeeping and Janitorial Workers	30.7%
42. Oral and Maxillofacial Surgeons	30.6%

The jobs in the following four lists are derived from the preceding list of jobs with the highest percentage of self-employed workers. Where the following lists give earnings estimates, keep in mind that these figures are based on a survey that *doesn't include self-employed workers*. The median earnings for self-employed workers in these occupations may be significantly higher or lower.

Best Jobs Overall with a High Percentage of Self-Employed Workers

Job	Percent Self-Employed Workers	Annual Earnings	Percent Growth	Annual Openings
1. Personal Financial Advisors	30.9%	$67,660	41.0%	17,114
2. Construction Managers	56.3%	$76,230	15.7%	44,158
3. Multi-Media Artists and Animators	69.7%	$54,550	25.8%	13,182
4. Clinical Psychologists	34.2%	$62,210	15.8%	8,309
5. Counseling Psychologists	34.2%	$62,210	15.8%	8,309
6. Property, Real Estate, and Community Association Managers	50.9%	$43,670	15.1%	49,916
7. School Psychologists	34.2%	$62,210	15.8%	8,309
8. Copy Writers	65.9%	$50,660	12.8%	24,023
9. First-Line Supervisors/Managers of Landscaping, Lawn Service, and Groundskeeping Workers	44.1%	$38,720	17.6%	18,956
10. Industrial-Organizational Psychologists	39.3%	$80,820	21.3%	118
11. Poets, Lyricists, and Creative Writers	65.9%	$50,660	12.8%	24,023
12. Real Estate Brokers	63.5%	$58,860	11.1%	18,689
13. Appraisers, Real Estate	32.7%	$46,130	16.9%	6,493
14. Assessors	32.7%	$46,130	16.9%	6,493
15. First-Line Supervisors/Managers of Non-Retail Sales Workers	45.4%	$67,020	3.7%	48,883
16. Construction Carpenters	31.8%	$37,660	10.3%	223,225
17. Real Estate Sales Agents	60.2%	$40,600	10.6%	61,232
18. Rough Carpenters	31.8%	$37,660	10.3%	223,225
19. First-Line Supervisors/Managers of Personal Service Workers	38.6%	$33,900	15.5%	37,555
20. Massage Therapists	64.0%	$34,870	20.3%	9,193
21. Art Directors	59.0%	$72,320	9.0%	9,719
22. Chiropractors	51.7%	$65,890	14.4%	3,179
23. Tile and Marble Setters	33.8%	$38,720	15.4%	9,066
24. Dentists, General	36.6%	$137,630	9.2%	7,106
25. Food Service Managers	44.8%	$44,570	5.0%	59,302

Jobs 4, 5, and 7 share 8,309 openings. Jobs 8 and 11 share 24,023 openings. Jobs 13 and 14 share 6,493 openings. Jobs 16 and 18 share 223,225 openings.

Best-Paying Jobs with a High Percentage of Self-Employed Workers

Job	Percent Self-Employed Workers	Annual Earnings
1. Oral and Maxillofacial Surgeons	30.6%	$145,600+
2. Orthodontists	43.3%	$145,600+
3. Prosthodontists	51.3%	$145,600+
4. Dentists, General	36.6%	$137,630
5. Industrial-Organizational Psychologists	39.3%	$80,820
6. Construction Managers	56.3%	$76,230
7. Art Directors	59.0%	$72,320
8. Personal Financial Advisors	30.9%	$67,660
9. First-Line Supervisors/Managers of Non-Retail Sales Workers	45.4%	$67,020
10. Agents and Business Managers of Artists, Performers, and Athletes	55.8%	$66,440
11. Chiropractors	51.7%	$65,890
12. Clinical Psychologists	34.2%	$62,210
13. Counseling Psychologists	34.2%	$62,210
14. School Psychologists	34.2%	$62,210
15. Real Estate Brokers	63.5%	$58,860
16. Multi-Media Artists and Animators	69.7%	$54,550
17. Copy Writers	65.9%	$50,660
18. Poets, Lyricists, and Creative Writers	65.9%	$50,660
19. Appraisers, Real Estate	32.7%	$46,130
20. Assessors	32.7%	$46,130
21. Food Service Managers	44.8%	$44,570
22. Lodging Managers	53.0%	$44,240
23. Property, Real Estate, and Community Association Managers	50.9%	$43,670
24. Fine Artists, Including Painters, Sculptors, and Illustrators	62.6%	$42,070
25. Real Estate Sales Agents	60.2%	$40,600

Fastest-Growing Jobs with a High Percentage of Self-Employed Workers

Job	Percent Self-Employed Workers	Percent Growth
1. Personal Financial Advisors	30.9%	41.0%
2. Makeup Artists, Theatrical and Performance	39.7%	39.8%
3. Skin Care Specialists	38.9%	34.3%
4. Multi-Media Artists and Animators	69.7%	25.8%
5. Animal Trainers	56.9%	22.7%

Fastest-Growing Jobs with a High Percentage of Self-Employed Workers

Job	Percent Self-Employed Workers	Percent Growth
6. Industrial-Organizational Psychologists	39.3%	21.3%
7. Massage Therapists	64.0%	20.3%
8. First-Line Supervisors/Managers of Landscaping, Lawn Service, and Groundskeeping Workers	44.1%	17.6%
9. Appraisers, Real Estate	32.7%	16.9%
10. Assessors	32.7%	16.9%
11. Clinical Psychologists	34.2%	15.8%
12. Counseling Psychologists	34.2%	15.8%
13. School Psychologists	34.2%	15.8%
14. Construction Managers	56.3%	15.7%
15. First-Line Supervisors/Managers of Personal Service Workers	38.6%	15.5%
16. Tile and Marble Setters	33.8%	15.4%
17. Property, Real Estate, and Community Association Managers	50.9%	15.1%
18. Chiropractors	51.7%	14.4%
19. Music Composers and Arrangers	44.7%	12.9%
20. Music Directors	44.7%	12.9%
21. Copy Writers	65.9%	12.8%
22. Poets, Lyricists, and Creative Writers	65.9%	12.8%
23. First-Line Supervisors/Managers of Housekeeping and Janitorial Workers	30.7%	12.7%
24. Hairdressers, Hairstylists, and Cosmetologists	44.5%	12.4%
25. Lodging Managers	53.0%	12.2%

Jobs with the Most Openings with a High Percentage of Self-Employed Workers

Job	Percent Self-Employed Workers	Annual Openings
1. Construction Carpenters	31.8%	223,225
2. Rough Carpenters	31.8%	223,225
3. First-Line Supervisors/Managers of Retail Sales Workers	34.2%	221,241
4. Farmers and Ranchers	100.0%	129,552
5. Painters, Construction and Maintenance	42.2%	101,140
6. Hairdressers, Hairstylists, and Cosmetologists	44.5%	73,030
7. Real Estate Sales Agents	60.2%	61,232

(continued)

(continued)

Job	Percent Self-Employed Workers	Annual Openings
8. Food Service Managers	44.8%	59,302
9. Property, Real Estate, and Community Association Managers	50.9%	49,916
10. First-Line Supervisors/Managers of Non-Retail Sales Workers	45.4%	48,883
11. Construction Managers	56.3%	44,158
12. First-Line Supervisors/Managers of Personal Service Workers	38.6%	37,555
13. First-Line Supervisors/Managers of Housekeeping and Janitorial Workers	30.7%	30,613
14. Copy Writers	65.9%	24,023
15. Poets, Lyricists, and Creative Writers	65.9%	24,023
16. First-Line Supervisors/Managers of Landscaping, Lawn Service, and Groundskeeping Workers	44.1%	18,956
17. Real Estate Brokers	63.5%	18,689
18. Personal Financial Advisors	30.9%	17,114
19. Photographers	54.3%	16,100
20. Multi-Media Artists and Animators	69.7%	13,182
21. Art Directors	59.0%	9,719
22. Massage Therapists	64.0%	9,193
23. Tile and Marble Setters	33.8%	9,066
24. Music Composers and Arrangers	44.7%	8,597
25. Music Directors	44.7%	8,597

Jobs with the Most Openings with a High Percentage of Self-Employed Workers

Jobs 1 and 2 share 223,225 openings. Jobs 14 and 15 share 24,023 openings. Jobs 24 and 25 share 8,597 openings.

Best Jobs Employing a High Percentage of Women

To create the lists that follow, we sorted the 500 best jobs according to the percentages of women and men in the workforce. (Actually, it was the 371 jobs for which we had this information.) We knew we would create some controversy when we first included the best jobs lists with high percentages (more than 70%) of men and women in earlier editions. But these lists aren't meant to restrict women or men from considering job options; our reason for including these lists is exactly the opposite. We hope the lists help people see possibilities that they might not otherwise have considered.

The fact is that jobs with high percentages of women or high percentages of men offer good opportunities for both men and women if they want to do one of these jobs. So we suggest that women browse the lists of jobs that employ high percentages of men and that men browse the lists of jobs with high percentages of women. There are jobs in both sets of lists that pay well, and women or men who are interested in them and who have or can obtain the necessary education and training should consider them.

An interesting and unfortunate tidbit to bring up at your next party is that the average earnings for the jobs with the highest percentage of women is $35,552, compared to average earnings of $56,029 for the jobs with the highest percentage of men. (The calculations assumed that the five male-dominated jobs paying "more than $145,600" had earnings of exactly $145,600, which means that the actual average is probably higher than $56,029.) But earnings don't tell the whole story. We computed the average growth and job openings of the jobs with the highest percentage of women and found statistics of 14.3% growth and 59,608 openings, compared to 10.2% growth and 29,421 openings for the jobs with the highest percentage of men. This discrepancy reinforces the idea that men have had more problems than women in adapting to an economy dominated by service and information-based jobs. Many women may simply be better prepared, possessing more appropriate skills for the jobs that are now growing rapidly and have more job openings.

Best Jobs Employing the Highest Percentage of Women

Job	Percent Women
1. Kindergarten Teachers, Except Special Education	97.7%
2. Preschool Teachers, Except Special Education	97.7%
3. Executive Secretaries and Administrative Assistants	97.3%
4. Legal Secretaries	97.3%
5. Medical Secretaries	97.3%
6. Secretaries, Except Legal, Medical, and Executive	97.3%
7. Dental Hygienists	97.1%
8. Dental Assistants	96.1%
9. Dietitians and Nutritionists	95.3%
10. Licensed Practical and Licensed Vocational Nurses	93.4%
11. Occupational Therapists	92.9%
12. Receptionists and Information Clerks	92.4%
13. Registered Nurses	92.3%
14. Hairdressers, Hairstylists, and Cosmetologists	92.0%
15. Speech-Language Pathologists	92.0%
16. Payroll and Timekeeping Clerks	91.4%
17. Bookkeeping, Accounting, and Auditing Clerks	91.3%
18. Teacher Assistants	90.9%
19. Human Resources Assistants, Except Payroll and Timekeeping	89.3%
20. Athletic Trainers	89.0%

(continued)

(continued)

Best Jobs Employing the Highest Percentage of Women

Job	Percent Women
21. Billing, Cost, and Rate Clerks	89.0%
22. Billing, Posting, and Calculating Machine Operators	89.0%
23. Medical Assistants	89.0%
24. Medical Equipment Preparers	89.0%
25. Medical Transcriptionists	89.0%
26. Occupational Health and Safety Specialists	89.0%
27. Occupational Health and Safety Technicians	89.0%
28. Orthotists and Prosthetists	89.0%
29. Statement Clerks	89.0%
30. Nursing Aides, Orderlies, and Attendants	88.7%
31. Occupational Therapist Assistants	88.7%
32. Physical Therapist Aides	88.7%
33. Physical Therapist Assistants	88.7%
34. Tellers	87.3%
35. Insurance Claims Clerks	86.9%
36. Insurance Policy Processing Clerks	86.9%
37. Medical Records and Health Information Technicians	86.6%
38. Paralegals and Legal Assistants	86.4%
39. Demonstrators and Product Promoters	85.9%
40. Special Education Teachers, Middle School	85.3%
41. Special Education Teachers, Preschool, Kindergarten, and Elementary School	85.3%
42. Special Education Teachers, Secondary School	85.3%
43. Makeup Artists, Theatrical and Performance	85.1%
44. Skin Care Specialists	85.1%
45. Librarians	84.9%
46. Office Clerks, General	84.5%
47. Eligibility Interviewers, Government Programs	82.7%
48. Elementary School Teachers, Except Special Education	82.2%
49. Middle School Teachers, Except Special and Vocational Education	82.2%
50. Massage Therapists	82.0%
51. Pharmacy Technicians	81.8%
52. Surgical Technologists	81.8%
53. Veterinary Technologists and Technicians	81.8%
54. Court Clerks	81.4%
55. License Clerks	81.4%
56. Municipal Clerks	81.4%
57. Child, Family, and School Social Workers	80.1%

Best Jobs Employing the Highest Percentage of Women

Job	Percent Women
58. Medical and Public Health Social Workers	80.1%
59. Mental Health and Substance Abuse Social Workers	80.1%
60. Interviewers, Except Eligibility and Loan	79.4%
61. Loan Interviewers and Clerks	77.0%
62. Audiologists	76.7%
63. Court Reporters	75.3%
64. Flight Attendants	74.5%
65. Compensation and Benefits Managers	72.7%
66. Training and Development Managers	72.7%
67. Bill and Account Collectors	72.2%
68. Cardiovascular Technologists and Technicians	72.0%
69. Diagnostic Medical Sonographers	72.0%
70. Medical and Clinical Laboratory Technicians	72.0%
71. Medical and Clinical Laboratory Technologists	72.0%
72. Nuclear Medicine Technologists	72.0%
73. Radiologic Technicians	72.0%
74. Radiologic Technologists	72.0%
75. Insurance Underwriters	71.9%
76. Medical and Health Services Managers	71.2%
77. Compensation, Benefits, and Job Analysis Specialists	70.9%
78. Employment Interviewers	70.9%
79. Personnel Recruiters	70.9%
80. Training and Development Specialists	70.9%

The jobs in the following four lists are derived from the preceding list of the jobs employing the highest percentage of women. Keep in mind that the earnings estimates in the following lists are based on a survey of *all* workers, not just women. On average, women earn about 75 percent of the earnings of men in the same occupation. The earnings differences for the occupations in the following lists may be significantly higher or lower.

Best Jobs Overall Employing a High Percentage of Women

Job	Percent Women	Annual Earnings	Percent Growth	Annual Openings
1. Registered Nurses	92.3%	$60,010	23.5%	233,499
2. Dental Hygienists	97.1%	$64,740	30.1%	10,433
3. Medical and Health Services Managers	71.2%	$76,990	16.4%	31,877

(continued)

(continued)

Best Jobs Overall Employing a High Percentage of Women

Job	Percent Women	Annual Earnings	Percent Growth	Annual Openings
4. Training and Development Specialists	70.9%	$49,630	18.3%	35,862
5. Compensation, Benefits, and Job Analysis Specialists	70.9%	$52,180	18.4%	18,761
6. Elementary School Teachers, Except Special Education	82.2%	$47,330	13.6%	181,612
7. Medical Assistants	89.0%	$27,430	35.4%	92,977
8. Special Education Teachers, Preschool, Kindergarten, and Elementary School	85.3%	$48,350	19.6%	20,049
9. Executive Secretaries and Administrative Assistants	97.3%	$38,640	14.8%	235,314
10. Occupational Therapists	92.9%	$63,790	23.1%	8,338
11. Paralegals and Legal Assistants	86.4%	$44,990	22.2%	22,756
12. Employment Interviewers	70.9%	$44,380	18.4%	33,588
13. Personnel Recruiters	70.9%	$44,380	18.4%	33,588
14. Bill and Account Collectors	72.2%	$29,990	22.9%	118,709
15. Child, Family, and School Social Workers	80.1%	$38,620	19.1%	35,402
16. Medical and Public Health Social Workers	80.1%	$44,670	24.2%	16,429
17. Mental Health and Substance Abuse Social Workers	80.1%	$36,640	29.9%	17,289
18. Pharmacy Technicians	81.8%	$26,720	32.0%	54,453
19. Kindergarten Teachers, Except Special Education	97.7%	$45,120	16.3%	27,603
20. Dental Assistants	96.1%	$31,550	29.2%	29,482
21. Middle School Teachers, Except Special and Vocational Education	82.2%	$47,900	11.2%	75,270
22. Preschool Teachers, Except Special Education	97.7%	$23,130	26.3%	78,172
23. Surgical Technologists	81.8%	$37,540	24.5%	15,365
24. Physical Therapist Assistants	88.7%	$44,130	32.4%	5,957
25. Licensed Practical and Licensed Vocational Nurses	93.4%	$37,940	14.0%	70,610

Jobs 12 and 13 share 33,588 openings.

Best-Paying Jobs Employing a High Percentage of Women

Job	Percent Women	Annual Earnings
1. Training and Development Managers	72.7%	$84,340
2. Compensation and Benefits Managers	72.7%	$81,410
3. Medical and Health Services Managers	71.2%	$76,990
4. Dental Hygienists	97.1%	$64,740
5. Nuclear Medicine Technologists	72.0%	$64,670
6. Occupational Therapists	92.9%	$63,790
7. Flight Attendants	74.5%	$61,120
8. Speech-Language Pathologists	92.0%	$60,690
9. Orthotists and Prosthetists	89.0%	$60,520
10. Occupational Health and Safety Specialists	89.0%	$60,140
11. Registered Nurses	92.3%	$60,010
12. Diagnostic Medical Sonographers	72.0%	$59,860
13. Audiologists	76.7%	$59,440
14. Insurance Underwriters	71.9%	$54,530
15. Compensation, Benefits, and Job Analysis Specialists	70.9%	$52,180
16. Medical and Clinical Laboratory Technologists	72.0%	$51,720
17. Librarians	84.9%	$50,970
18. Radiologic Technicians	72.0%	$50,260
19. Radiologic Technologists	72.0%	$50,260
20. Special Education Teachers, Secondary School	85.3%	$49,640
21. Training and Development Specialists	70.9%	$49,630
22. Dietitians and Nutritionists	95.3%	$49,010
23. Special Education Teachers, Middle School	85.3%	$48,940
24. Special Education Teachers, Preschool, Kindergarten, and Elementary School	85.3%	$48,350
25. Middle School Teachers, Except Special and Vocational Education	82.2%	$47,900

Fastest-Growing Jobs Employing a High Percentage of Women

Job	Percent Women	Percent Growth
1. Veterinary Technologists and Technicians	81.8%	41.0%
2. Makeup Artists, Theatrical and Performance	85.1%	39.8%
3. Medical Assistants	89.0%	35.4%
4. Skin Care Specialists	85.1%	34.3%

(continued)

(continued)

Fastest-Growing Jobs Employing a High Percentage of Women

Job	Percent Women	Percent Growth
5. Physical Therapist Assistants	88.7%	32.4%
6. Pharmacy Technicians	81.8%	32.0%
7. Dental Hygienists	97.1%	30.1%
8. Mental Health and Substance Abuse Social Workers	80.1%	29.9%
9. Dental Assistants	96.1%	29.2%
10. Preschool Teachers, Except Special Education	97.7%	26.3%
11. Cardiovascular Technologists and Technicians	72.0%	25.5%
12. Occupational Therapist Assistants	88.7%	25.4%
13. Court Reporters	75.3%	24.5%
14. Surgical Technologists	81.8%	24.5%
15. Physical Therapist Aides	88.7%	24.4%
16. Athletic Trainers	89.0%	24.3%
17. Medical and Public Health Social Workers	80.1%	24.2%
18. Registered Nurses	92.3%	23.5%
19. Occupational Therapists	92.9%	23.1%
20. Bill and Account Collectors	72.2%	22.9%
21. Paralegals and Legal Assistants	86.4%	22.2%
22. Massage Therapists	82.0%	20.3%
23. Special Education Teachers, Preschool, Kindergarten, and Elementary School	85.3%	19.6%
24. Child, Family, and School Social Workers	80.1%	19.1%
25. Diagnostic Medical Sonographers	72.0%	19.1%

Jobs with the Most Openings Employing a High Percentage of Women

Job	Percent Women	Annual Openings
1. Office Clerks, General	84.5%	765,803
2. Receptionists and Information Clerks	92.4%	334,124
3. Nursing Aides, Orderlies, and Attendants	88.7%	321,036
4. Bookkeeping, Accounting, and Auditing Clerks	91.3%	286,854
5. Secretaries, Except Legal, Medical, and Executive	97.3%	239,630
6. Executive Secretaries and Administrative Assistants	97.3%	235,314
7. Registered Nurses	92.3%	233,499
8. Teacher Assistants	90.9%	193,986
9. Elementary School Teachers, Except Special Education	82.2%	181,612

Jobs with the Most Openings Employing a High Percentage of Women

Job	Percent Women	Annual Openings
10. Tellers	87.3%	146,077
11. Bill and Account Collectors	72.2%	118,709
12. Medical Assistants	89.0%	92,977
13. Billing, Cost, and Rate Clerks	89.0%	81,885
14. Billing, Posting, and Calculating Machine Operators	89.0%	81,885
15. Statement Clerks	89.0%	81,885
16. Preschool Teachers, Except Special Education	97.7%	78,172
17. Middle School Teachers, Except Special and Vocational Education	82.2%	75,270
18. Hairdressers, Hairstylists, and Cosmetologists	92.0%	73,030
19. Licensed Practical and Licensed Vocational Nurses	93.4%	70,610
20. Medical Secretaries	97.3%	60,659
21. Pharmacy Technicians	81.8%	54,453
22. Interviewers, Except Eligibility and Loan	79.4%	54,060
23. Insurance Claims Clerks	86.9%	42,246
24. Insurance Policy Processing Clerks	86.9%	42,246
25. Loan Interviewers and Clerks	77.0%	40,217

Jobs 13, 14, and 15 share 81,885 openings. Jobs 23 and 24 share 42,246 openings.

Best Jobs Employing a High Percentage of Men

If you haven't already read the intro to the previous group of lists, "Best Jobs Employing a High Percentage of Women," consider doing so. Much of the content there applies to these lists as well.

We didn't include these groups of lists with the assumption that men should consider only jobs with high percentages of men or that women should consider only jobs with high percentages of women. Instead, these lists are here because we think they are interesting and perhaps helpful in considering nontraditional career options. For example, some men would do very well in and enjoy some of the jobs with high percentages of women but may not have considered seriously. Similarly, some women would very much enjoy and do well in some jobs that traditionally have been held by high percentages of men. We hope that these lists help you consider options that you simply didn't seriously consider because of gender stereotypes.

In the jobs on the following lists, more than 70% of the workers are men, but increasing numbers of women are entering many of these jobs.

Best Jobs Employing the Highest Percentage of Men

Job	Percent Men
1. Excavating and Loading Machine and Dragline Operators	99.8%
2. Bus and Truck Mechanics and Diesel Engine Specialists	99.5%
3. Railroad Conductors and Yardmasters	99.3%
4. Drywall and Ceiling Tile Installers	99.2%
5. Tapers	99.2%
6. Brickmasons and Blockmasons	99.1%
7. Pipe Fitters and Steamfitters	98.8%
8. Pipelayers	98.8%
9. Plumbers	98.8%
10. Plasterers and Stucco Masons	98.7%
11. Elevator Installers and Repairers	98.6%
12. Heating and Air Conditioning Mechanics and Installers	98.6%
13. Refrigeration Mechanics and Installers	98.6%
14. Ship Engineers	98.5%
15. Mobile Heavy Equipment Mechanics, Except Engines	98.4%
16. Structural Iron and Steel Workers	98.4%
17. Tire Repairers and Changers	98.4%
18. Cement Masons and Concrete Finishers	98.3%
19. Automotive Master Mechanics	98.2%
20. Automotive Specialty Technicians	98.2%
21. Motorboat Mechanics	98.2%
22. Motorcycle Mechanics	98.2%
23. Recreational Vehicle Service Technicians	98.2%
24. Automotive Body and Related Repairers	98.1%
25. Construction Carpenters	98.1%
26. Rough Carpenters	98.1%
27. Millwrights	98.0%
28. Tile and Marble Setters	97.7%
29. Reinforcing Iron and Rebar Workers	97.6%
30. Roofers	97.6%
31. Electricians	97.4%
32. Industrial Machinery Mechanics	97.4%
33. Pest Control Workers	97.4%
34. Mapping Technicians	97.3%
35. Operating Engineers and Other Construction Equipment Operators	97.3%
36. Surveying Technicians	97.3%
37. First-Line Supervisors/Managers of Construction Trades and Extraction Workers	97.1%

Best Jobs Employing the Highest Percentage of Men

Job	Percent Men
38. Mates—Ship, Boat, and Barge	97.1%
39. Pilots, Ship	97.1%
40. Ship and Boat Captains	97.1%
41. Automotive Glass Installers and Repairers	96.9%
42. Boilermakers	96.8%
43. Helpers—Brickmasons, Blockmasons, Stonemasons, and Tile and Marble Setters	96.8%
44. Helpers—Carpenters	96.8%
45. Helpers—Electricians	96.8%
46. Helpers—Pipelayers, Plumbers, Pipefitters, and Steamfitters	96.8%
47. Fire Inspectors	96.7%
48. Fire Investigators	96.7%
49. Forest Fire Fighters	96.7%
50. Municipal Fire Fighters	96.7%
51. Electrical Power-Line Installers and Repairers	96.5%
52. Construction Laborers	96.4%
53. Sheet Metal Workers	96.4%
54. Helpers—Installation, Maintenance, and Repair Workers	95.9%
55. Insulation Workers, Mechanical	95.9%
56. Maintenance and Repair Workers, General	95.9%
57. Maintenance Workers, Machinery	95.9%
58. Commercial Divers	95.8%
59. Locksmiths and Safe Repairers	95.8%
60. Glaziers	95.6%
61. Aircraft Mechanics and Service Technicians	95.5%
62. Electrical and Electronics Repairers, Commercial and Industrial Equipment	95.5%
63. Security and Fire Alarm Systems Installers	95.5%
64. Truck Drivers, Heavy and Tractor-Trailer	95.5%
65. Truck Drivers, Light or Delivery Services	95.5%
66. Highway Maintenance Workers	95.4%
67. Water and Liquid Waste Treatment Plant and System Operators	95.4%
68. Marine Architects	94.9%
69. Marine Engineers	94.9%
70. Airline Pilots, Copilots, and Flight Engineers	94.8%
71. Commercial Pilots	94.8%
72. Sailors and Marine Oilers	94.5%
73. First-Line Supervisors/Managers of Mechanics, Installers, and Repairers	94.3%

(continued)

(continued)

Best Jobs Employing the Highest Percentage of Men

Job	Percent Men
74. Mechanical Engineers	94.2%
75. Solderers and Brazers	94.2%
76. Welders, Cutters, and Welder Fitters	94.2%
77. Telecommunications Line Installers and Repairers	94.0%
78. First-Line Supervisors/Managers of Landscaping, Lawn Service, and Groundskeeping Workers	93.8%
79. Construction Managers	93.7%
80. Industrial Truck and Tractor Operators	93.7%
81. Mining and Geological Engineers, Including Mining Safety Engineers	93.7%
82. Petroleum Engineers	93.7%
83. Machinists	93.2%
84. Electrical Engineers	92.9%
85. Electronics Engineers, Except Computer	92.9%
86. Nuclear Power Reactor Operators	92.6%
87. Landscaping and Groundskeeping Workers	92.5%
88. Painters, Construction and Maintenance	92.5%
89. Pesticide Handlers, Sprayers, and Applicators, Vegetation	92.5%
90. Tree Trimmers and Pruners	92.5%
91. Medical Equipment Repairers	92.3%
92. Nuclear Engineers	91.6%
93. Construction and Building Inspectors	91.5%
94. Refuse and Recyclable Material Collectors	91.3%
95. Subway and Streetcar Operators	91.1%
96. Hazardous Materials Removal Workers	90.8%
97. Engineering Managers	90.5%
98. Agricultural Engineers	89.6%
99. Environmental Engineers	89.6%
100. Product Safety Engineers	89.6%
101. Computer Hardware Engineers	89.2%
102. Storage and Distribution Managers	88.3%
103. Transportation Managers	88.3%
104. Materials Engineers	88.0%
105. Parts Salespersons	88.0%
106. First-Line Supervisors/Managers of Correctional Officers	87.5%
107. First-Line Supervisors/Managers of Police and Detectives	87.5%
108. Forest Fire Fighting and Prevention Supervisors	87.5%
109. Municipal Fire Fighting and Prevention Supervisors	87.5%

Best Jobs Employing the Highest Percentage of Men

Job	Percent Men
110. Atmospheric and Space Scientists	87.1%
111. Civil Engineers	86.8%
112. Aerospace Engineers	86.7%
113. Telecommunications Equipment Installers and Repairers, Except Line Installers	86.5%
114. Audio and Video Equipment Technicians	86.4%
115. Broadcast Technicians	86.4%
116. Computer, Automated Teller, and Office Machine Repairers	86.3%
117. Biomedical Engineers	86.2%
118. Astronomers	86.1%
119. Physicists	86.1%
120. Chemical Engineers	85.7%
121. Police Patrol Officers	85.7%
122. Sheriffs and Deputy Sheriffs	85.7%
123. Fire-Prevention and Protection Engineers	85.1%
124. Industrial Engineers	85.1%
125. Industrial Safety and Health Engineers	85.1%
126. Clergy	84.5%
127. Concierges	84.3%
128. Podiatrists	84.3%
129. Ambulance Drivers and Attendants, Except Emergency Medical Technicians	83.9%
130. Aviation Inspectors	83.8%
131. Freight and Cargo Inspectors	83.8%
132. Transportation Vehicle, Equipment and Systems Inspectors, Except Aviation	83.8%
133. Industrial Production Managers	82.8%
134. Laborers and Freight, Stock, and Material Movers, Hand	82.7%
135. Cost Estimators	82.6%
136. Cartographers and Photogrammetrists	82.0%
137. Surveyors	82.0%
138. Aircraft Cargo Handling Supervisors	81.9%
139. First-Line Supervisors/Managers of Helpers, Laborers, and Material Movers, Hand	81.9%
140. First-Line Supervisors/Managers of Transportation and Material-Moving Machine and Vehicle Operators	81.9%
141. Air Traffic Controllers	81.6%
142. Computer Security Specialists	81.6%
143. Network and Computer Systems Administrators	81.6%
144. Camera Operators, Television, Video, and Motion Picture	81.1%

(continued)

(continued)

Best Jobs Employing the Highest Percentage of Men

Job	Percent Men
145. Film and Video Editors	81.1%
146. Aquacultural Managers	80.7%
147. Crop and Livestock Managers	80.7%
148. Nursery and Greenhouse Managers	80.7%
149. Aerospace Engineering and Operations Technicians	79.8%
150. Civil Engineering Technicians	79.8%
151. Electrical Engineering Technicians	79.8%
152. Electronics Engineering Technicians	79.8%
153. Environmental Engineering Technicians	79.8%
154. Industrial Engineering Technicians	79.8%
155. Mechanical Engineering Technicians	79.8%
156. Chefs and Head Cooks	79.6%
157. First-Line Supervisors/Managers of Production and Operating Workers	79.1%
158. Funeral Directors	78.5%
159. Architectural Drafters	78.4%
160. Civil Drafters	78.4%
161. Electrical Drafters	78.4%
162. Electronic Drafters	78.4%
163. Mechanical Drafters	78.4%
164. Chiropractors	78.2%
165. Geological Sample Test Technicians	78.1%
166. Geophysical Data Technicians	78.1%
167. Computer Software Engineers, Applications	78.1%
168. Computer Software Engineers, Systems Software	78.1%
169. Computer Systems Analysts	78.1%
170. Embalmers	78.0%
171. Meat, Poultry, and Fish Cutters and Trimmers	77.7%
172. Slaughterers and Meat Packers	77.7%
173. Transportation Security Screeners	77.6%
174. Dentists, General	77.5%
175. Environmental Scientists and Specialists, Including Health	77.5%
176. Geoscientists, Except Hydrologists and Geographers	77.5%
177. Hydrologists	77.5%
178. Oral and Maxillofacial Surgeons	77.5%
179. Orthodontists	77.5%
180. Prosthodontists	77.5%

Best Jobs Employing the Highest Percentage of Men

Job	Percent Men
181. Chief Executives	76.2%
182. Criminal Investigators and Special Agents	76.0%
183. Immigration and Customs Inspectors	76.0%
184. Police Detectives	76.0%
185. Police Identification and Records Officers	76.0%
186. Architects, Except Landscape and Naval	75.6%
187. Landscape Architects	75.6%
188. Network Systems and Data Communications Analysts	75.4%
189. Gaming Surveillance Officers and Gaming Investigators	75.3%
190. Security Guards	75.3%
191. First-Line Supervisors/Managers of Non-Retail Sales Workers	74.5%
192. Farmers and Ranchers	74.4%
193. Computer Programmers	74.0%
194. Food Scientists and Technologists	73.9%
195. Soil and Plant Scientists	73.9%
196. Cargo and Freight Agents	73.1%
197. Computer Systems Engineers/Architects	73.0%
198. Network Designers	73.0%
199. Software Quality Assurance Engineers and Testers	73.0%
200. Web Administrators	73.0%
201. Web Developers	73.0%
202. Sales Representatives, Wholesale and Manufacturing, Except Technical and Scientific Products	72.8%
203. Sales Representatives, Wholesale and Manufacturing, Technical and Scientific Products	72.8%
204. Optometrists	72.4%
205. Chemical Technicians	71.9%
206. Sales Agents, Financial Services	71.3%
207. Sales Agents, Securities and Commodities	71.3%
208. Bailiffs	70.9%
209. Correctional Officers and Jailers	70.9%
210. General and Operations Managers	70.1%

The jobs in the following four lists are derived from the preceding list of the jobs employing the highest percentage of men. Keep in mind that the earnings estimates in the following lists are based on a survey of *all* workers, not just men. On average, men earn about 133% of the earnings of women in the same occupation. The earnings differences for the occupations in the following lists may be significantly higher or lower.

Best Jobs Overall Employing a High Percentage of Men

Job	Percent Men	Annual Earnings	Percent Growth	Annual Openings
1. Computer Software Engineers, Applications	78.1%	$83,130	44.6%	58,690
2. Computer Systems Analysts	78.1%	$73,090	29.0%	63,166
3. Computer Software Engineers, Systems Software	78.1%	$89,070	28.2%	33,139
4. Sales Agents, Financial Services	71.3%	$68,430	24.8%	47,750
5. Sales Agents, Securities and Commodities	71.3%	$68,430	24.8%	47,750
6. Network Systems and Data Communications Analysts	75.4%	$68,220	53.4%	35,086
7. Computer Security Specialists	81.6%	$64,690	27.0%	37,010
8. Network and Computer Systems Administrators	81.6%	$64,690	27.0%	37,010
9. Construction Managers	93.7%	$76,230	15.7%	44,158
10. Civil Engineers	86.8%	$71,710	18.0%	15,979
11. Cost Estimators	82.6%	$54,920	18.5%	38,379
12. Industrial Engineers	85.1%	$71,430	20.3%	11,272
13. Sales Representatives, Wholesale and Manufacturing, Technical and Scientific Products	72.8%	$68,270	12.4%	43,469
14. Environmental Engineers	89.6%	$72,350	25.4%	5,003
15. Computer Systems Engineers/Architects	73.0%	$71,510	15.1%	14,374
16. Network Designers	73.0%	$71,510	15.1%	14,374
17. Software Quality Assurance Engineers and Testers	73.0%	$71,510	15.1%	14,374
18. Web Administrators	73.0%	$71,510	15.1%	14,374
19. Web Developers	73.0%	$71,510	15.1%	14,374
20. Criminal Investigators and Special Agents	76.0%	$59,930	17.3%	14,746
21. Immigration and Customs Inspectors	76.0%	$59,930	17.3%	14,746
22. Police Detectives	76.0%	$59,930	17.3%	14,746
23. Police Identification and Records Officers	76.0%	$59,930	17.3%	14,746
24. Architects, Except Landscape and Naval	75.6%	$67,620	17.7%	11,324
25. Surveyors	82.0%	$51,630	23.7%	14,305

Jobs 4 and 5 share 47,750 openings. Jobs 7 and 8 share 37,010 openings. Jobs 15, 16, 17, 18, and 19 share 14,374 openings. Jobs 20, 21, 22, and 23 share 14,746 openings.

Best-Paying Jobs Employing a High Percentage of Men

Job	Percent Men	Annual Earnings
1. Airline Pilots, Copilots, and Flight Engineers	94.8%	$145,600+
2. Chief Executives	76.2%	$145,600+
3. Oral and Maxillofacial Surgeons	77.5%	$145,600+

Best-Paying Jobs Employing a High Percentage of Men

Job	Percent Men	Annual Earnings
4. Orthodontists	77.5%	$145,600+
5. Prosthodontists	77.5%	$145,600+
6. Dentists, General	77.5%	$137,630
7. Air Traffic Controllers	81.6%	$112,930
8. Engineering Managers	90.5%	$111,020
9. Podiatrists	84.3%	$110,510
10. Petroleum Engineers	93.7%	$103,960
11. Astronomers	86.1%	$99,020
12. Physicists	86.1%	$96,850
13. Nuclear Engineers	91.6%	$94,420
14. Optometrists	72.4%	$93,800
15. Computer Hardware Engineers	89.2%	$91,860
16. Aerospace Engineers	86.7%	$90,930
17. Computer Software Engineers, Systems Software	78.1%	$89,070
18. General and Operations Managers	70.1%	$88,700
19. Electronics Engineers, Except Computer	92.9%	$83,340
20. Computer Software Engineers, Applications	78.1%	$83,130
21. Chemical Engineers	85.7%	$81,500
22. Industrial Production Managers	82.8%	$80,560
23. Electrical Engineers	92.9%	$79,240
24. Atmospheric and Space Scientists	87.1%	$78,390
25. Materials Engineers	88.0%	$77,170

Fastest-Growing Jobs Employing a High Percentage of Men

Job	Percent Men	Percent Growth
1. Network Systems and Data Communications Analysts	75.4%	53.4%
2. Computer Software Engineers, Applications	78.1%	44.6%
3. Gaming Surveillance Officers and Gaming Investigators	75.3%	33.6%
4. Computer Systems Analysts	78.1%	29.0%
5. Computer Software Engineers, Systems Software	78.1%	28.2%
6. Computer Security Specialists	81.6%	27.0%
7. Network and Computer Systems Administrators	81.6%	27.0%
8. Environmental Engineers	89.6%	25.4%
9. Environmental Scientists and Specialists, Including Health	77.5%	25.1%

(continued)

(continued)

Fastest-Growing Jobs Employing a High Percentage of Men

Job	Percent Men	Percent Growth
10. Environmental Engineering Technicians	79.8%	24.8%
11. Sales Agents, Financial Services	71.3%	24.8%
12. Sales Agents, Securities and Commodities	71.3%	24.8%
13. Hydrologists	77.5%	24.3%
14. Audio and Video Equipment Technicians	86.4%	24.2%
15. Surveyors	82.0%	23.7%
16. Aircraft Cargo Handling Supervisors	81.9%	23.3%
17. Locksmiths and Safe Repairers	95.8%	22.1%
18. Geoscientists, Except Hydrologists and Geographers	77.5%	21.9%
19. Ambulance Drivers and Attendants, Except Emergency Medical Technicians	83.9%	21.7%
20. Medical Equipment Repairers	92.3%	21.7%
21. Biomedical Engineers	86.2%	21.1%
22. Cartographers and Photogrammetrists	82.0%	20.3%
23. Industrial Engineers	85.1%	20.3%
24. Security and Fire Alarm Systems Installers	95.5%	20.2%
25. Tire Repairers and Changers	98.4%	20.2%

Jobs with the Most Openings Employing a High Percentage of Men

Job	Percent Men	Annual Openings
1. Laborers and Freight, Stock, and Material Movers, Hand	82.7%	630,487
2. Landscaping and Groundskeeping Workers	92.5%	307,138
3. Truck Drivers, Heavy and Tractor-Trailer	95.5%	279,032
4. Construction Laborers	96.4%	257,407
5. Construction Carpenters	98.1%	223,225
6. Rough Carpenters	98.1%	223,225
7. Security Guards	75.3%	222,085
8. Maintenance and Repair Workers, General	95.9%	165,502
9. Sales Representatives, Wholesale and Manufacturing, Except Technical and Scientific Products	72.8%	156,215
10. Truck Drivers, Light or Delivery Services	95.5%	154,330
11. Farmers and Ranchers	74.4%	129,552
12. General and Operations Managers	70.1%	112,072
13. Painters, Construction and Maintenance	92.5%	101,140

Jobs with the Most Openings Employing a High Percentage of Men

Job	Percent Men	Annual Openings
14. Automotive Master Mechanics	98.2%	97,350
15. Automotive Specialty Technicians	98.2%	97,350
16. Industrial Truck and Tractor Operators	93.7%	89,547
17. First-Line Supervisors/Managers of Construction Trades and Extraction Workers	97.1%	82,923
18. Electricians	97.4%	79,083
19. Pipe Fitters and Steamfitters	98.8%	68,643
20. Plumbers	98.8%	68,643
21. Computer Systems Analysts	78.1%	63,166
22. Solderers and Brazers	94.2%	61,125
23. Welders, Cutters, and Welder Fitters	94.2%	61,125
24. Computer Software Engineers, Applications	78.1%	58,690
25. Correctional Officers and Jailers	70.9%	56,579

Jobs 5 and 6 share 223,225 openings. Jobs 14 and 15 share 97,350 openings. Jobs 19 and 20 share 68,643 openings. Jobs 22 and 23 share 61,125 openings.

Best Jobs Lists Based on Levels of Education and Experience

The lists in this section organize the 500 best jobs into groups based on the education or training typically required for entry. Unlike in many of the previous sections, here we don't include separate lists for highest pay, growth, or number of openings. Instead, we provide one list that includes all the occupations in our database that fit into each of the education levels and that ranks them by their total combined score for earnings, growth, and number of openings.

These lists can help you identify a job with higher earnings or upward mobility that requires a similar level of education to the job you now hold. For example, you will find jobs within the same level of education that require similar skills, yet one pays significantly better than the other, is projected to grow more rapidly, or has significantly more job openings per year. This information can help you leverage your present skills and experience into jobs that might provide better long-term career opportunities.

You can also use these lists to explore possible job options if you were to get additional training, education, or work experience. For example, you can use these lists to identify occupations that offer high potential and then look into the education or training required to get the jobs that interest you most.

The lists can also help you when you plan your education. For example, you might be thinking about vocational training but you aren't sure what kind of work you want to do. The lists show that Brokerage Clerks need moderate-term on-the-job training and earn $37,360, while Automotive Glass Installers and Repairers need long-term on-the-job training and only earn an average of $31,470. If you want higher earnings with less training, this information might make a difference in your choice.

The Education Levels

A clear relationship exists between education and earnings—the more education or training you have, the more you are likely to earn. The lists that follow arrange all 21 jobs that met our criteria for inclusion in this book (see the introduction) by level of education, training, and work experience. These are the levels typically required for a new entrant to begin work in each occupation.

We included on each list all the occupations in our database that fit into each of the education levels. We then arranged these occupations based on each of their total scores for earnings, growth, and number of openings.

The following definitions are used by the federal government to classify jobs based on the minimum level of education or training typically required for entry into a job. We use these definitions to construct the lists in this section. Use the training and education level descriptions as guidelines that can help you understand what is generally required, but understand that you will need to learn more about specific requirements before you make a decision on one career over another.

- **Short-term on-the-job training:** It is possible to work in these occupations and achieve an average level of performance within a few days or weeks through on-the-job training.
- **Moderate-term on-the-job training:** Occupations requiring this type of training can be performed adequately after a one- to twelve-month period of combined on-the-job and informal training. Typically, untrained workers observe experienced workers performing tasks and are gradually moved into progressively more difficult assignments.
- **Long-term on-the-job training:** This training requires more than 12 months of on-the-job training or combined work experience and formal classroom instruction. This includes occupations that use formal apprenticeships for training workers that may take up to four years. It also includes intensive occupation-specific, employer-sponsored training, such as police academies. Furthermore, it includes occupations that require natural talent that must be developed over many years.
- **Work experience in a related occupation:** This type of job requires experience in a related occupation. For example, police detectives are selected based on their experience as police patrol officers.
- **Postsecondary vocational training:** This requirement can vary from training that involves a few months to usually less than one year. In a few instances, as many as four years of training may be required.

- ✸ **Associate degree:** This degree usually requires two years of full-time academic work beyond high school.
- ✸ **Bachelor's degree:** This degree requires approximately four to five years of full-time academic work beyond high school.
- ✸ **Work experience plus degree:** Jobs in this category are often management-related and require some experience in a related nonmanagerial position.
- ✸ **Master's degree:** Completion of a master's degree usually requires one to two years of full-time study beyond the bachelor's degree.
- ✸ **Doctoral degree:** This degree normally requires two or more years of full-time academic work beyond the bachelor's degree.
- ✸ **First professional degree:** This type of degree normally requires a minimum of two years of education beyond the bachelor's degree and frequently requires three years.

Another Warning About the Data

We warned you in the introduction to use caution in interpreting the data we use, and we want to do it again here. The occupational data we use is the most accurate available anywhere, but it has its limitations. The education or training requirements for entry into a job are those typically required as a minimum, but some people working in those jobs may have considerably more or different credentials. For example, although a bachelor's degree is considered the usual requirement for Construction Managers, more than one-third of the people working in this occupation have no formal education beyond high school. On the other hand, Fitness Trainers and Aerobics Instructors usually need to have completed only postsecondary vocational training, but over half of these workers are college graduates.

Similarly, you need to be cautious about assuming that more education or training always leads to higher income. It is true that people with jobs that require long-term on-the-job training typically earn more than people with jobs that require short-term on-the-job training. (For the jobs in this book, the average annual difference is $16,856.) However, some people with short-term on-the-job training earn more than the average for the highest-paying occupations listed in this book; furthermore, some people with long-term on-the-job training earn much less than the average shown in this book—this is particularly true of people just beginning in these careers.

So as you browse the following lists, please use them as a way to be encouraged rather than discouraged. Education and training are very important for success in the labor market of the future, but so are ability, drive, initiative, and—yes—luck.

Having said this, we encourage you to get as much education and training as you can. You used to be able to get your schooling and then close the schoolbooks forever, but this isn't a good attitude to have now. You will probably need to continue learning new things throughout your working life. This can be done by going back to school, which is a good thing for many people. But other workers may learn through workshops, adult education programs, certification programs, employer training, professional conferences, Internet training, or reading related books and magazines. Upgrading your computer skills—and other technical skills—is particularly important in our rapidly changing workplace, and you avoid doing so at your peril.

Best Jobs Requiring Short-Term On-the-Job Training

Job	Annual Earnings	Percent Growth	Annual Openings
1. Bill and Account Collectors	$29,990	22.9%	118,709
2. Office Clerks, General	$24,460	12.6%	765,803
3. Receptionists and Information Clerks	$23,710	17.2%	334,124
4. Landscaping and Groundskeeping Workers	$22,240	18.1%	307,138
5. Human Resources Assistants, Except Payroll and Timekeeping	$34,970	11.3%	18,647
6. Sailors and Marine Oilers	$32,570	15.7%	8,600
7. Security Guards	$22,570	16.9%	222,085
8. Transportation Security Screeners	$28,240	12.6%	29,298
9. Tellers	$22,920	13.5%	146,077
10. Interviewers, Except Eligibility and Loan	$27,320	9.5%	54,060
11. Truck Drivers, Light or Delivery Services	$26,380	8.4%	154,330
12. Helpers—Pipelayers, Plumbers, Pipefitters, and Steamfitters	$25,350	11.9%	29,332
13. Court Clerks	$32,330	8.8%	16,163
14. License Clerks	$32,330	8.8%	16,163
15. Municipal Clerks	$32,330	8.8%	16,163
16. Helpers—Carpenters	$24,340	11.7%	37,731
17. Loan Interviewers and Clerks	$31,680	–0.9%	40,217
18. Refuse and Recyclable Material Collectors	$29,420	7.4%	37,785
19. Helpers—Installation, Maintenance, and Repair Workers	$22,920	11.8%	52,058
20. Shipping, Receiving, and Traffic Clerks	$26,990	3.7%	138,967
21. Medical Equipment Preparers	$27,040	14.2%	8,363
22. Correspondence Clerks	$29,500	12.0%	4,334
23. Tire Repairers and Changers	$21,880	20.2%	18,829
24. Tree Trimmers and Pruners	$29,800	11.1%	9,621
25. Helpers—Brickmasons, Blockmasons, Stonemasons, and Tile and Marble Setters	$26,260	11.0%	22,500
26. Postal Service Mail Carriers	$44,500	1.0%	16,710
27. Reservation and Transportation Ticket Agents and Travel Clerks	$29,820	1.1%	30,754
28. Industrial Truck and Tractor Operators	$28,010	–2.0%	89,547
29. Teacher Assistants	$21,580	10.4%	193,986
30. Physical Therapist Aides	$22,990	24.4%	4,092

Best Jobs Requiring Short-Term On-the-Job Training

Job	Annual Earnings	Percent Growth	Annual Openings
31. Residential Advisors	$23,050	18.5%	8,053
32. Laborers and Freight, Stock, and Material Movers, Hand	$21,900	2.1%	630,487
33. Helpers—Electricians	$24,880	6.8%	35,109
34. Food Batchmakers	$23,730	10.9%	15,704
35. Meat, Poultry, and Fish Cutters and Trimmers	$21,050	10.9%	17,920

Jobs 13, 14, and 15 share 16,163 openings.

Best Jobs Requiring Moderate-Term On-the-Job Training

Job	Annual Earnings	Percent Growth	Annual Openings
1. Correctional Officers and Jailers	$36,970	16.9%	56,579
2. Advertising Sales Agents	$42,820	20.3%	29,233
3. Customer Service Representatives	$29,040	24.8%	600,937
4. Truck Drivers, Heavy and Tractor-Trailer	$36,220	10.4%	279,032
5. Medical Assistants	$27,430	35.4%	92,977
6. Bookkeeping, Accounting, and Auditing Clerks	$31,560	12.5%	286,854
7. Brokerage Clerks	$37,360	20.0%	10,826
8. Social and Human Service Assistants	$26,630	33.6%	80,142
9. Painters, Construction and Maintenance	$32,080	11.8%	101,140
10. Roofers	$33,240	14.3%	38,398
11. Dental Assistants	$31,550	29.2%	29,482
12. Cargo and Freight Agents	$37,060	16.5%	9,967
13. Operating Engineers and Other Construction Equipment Operators	$38,130	8.4%	55,468
14. Maintenance and Repair Workers, General	$32,570	10.1%	165,502
15. Pharmacy Technicians	$26,720	32.0%	54,453
16. Cement Masons and Concrete Finishers	$33,840	11.4%	34,625
17. Medical Secretaries	$28,950	16.7%	60,659
18. Production, Planning, and Expediting Clerks	$39,690	4.2%	52,735
19. Aircraft Structure, Surfaces, Rigging, and Systems Assemblers	$45,420	12.8%	6,550
20. Mapping Technicians	$33,640	19.4%	8,299
21. Surveying Technicians	$33,640	19.4%	8,299
22. Bus Drivers, Transit and Intercity	$33,160	12.5%	27,100

(continued)

(continued)

Best Jobs Requiring Moderate-Term On-the-Job Training

Job	Annual Earnings	Percent Growth	Annual Openings
23. Police, Fire, and Ambulance Dispatchers	$32,660	13.6%	17,628
24. Construction Laborers	$27,310	10.9%	257,407
25. Drywall and Ceiling Tile Installers	$36,520	7.3%	30,945
26. Locksmiths and Safe Repairers	$33,230	22.1%	3,545
27. Subway and Streetcar Operators	$50,520	12.1%	587
28. Tapers	$42,050	7.1%	9,026
29. Billing, Cost, and Rate Clerks	$29,970	4.4%	81,885
30. Billing, Posting, and Calculating Machine Operators	$29,970	4.4%	81,885
31. Statement Clerks	$29,970	4.4%	81,885
32. Railroad Conductors and Yardmasters	$58,650	9.1%	3,235
33. Eligibility Interviewers, Government Programs	$39,110	3.1%	11,337
34. Demonstrators and Product Promoters	$22,570	18.0%	32,779
35. Bailiffs	$36,900	11.2%	2,223
36. Highway Maintenance Workers	$32,600	8.9%	24,774
37. Cooks, Institution and Cafeteria	$21,340	10.8%	111,898
38. Secretaries, Except Legal, Medical, and Executive	$28,220	1.2%	239,630
39. Hazardous Materials Removal Workers	$36,330	11.2%	1,933
40. Payroll and Timekeeping Clerks	$33,810	3.1%	18,544
41. Animal Trainers	$26,190	22.7%	6,713
42. Bus Drivers, School	$25,860	9.3%	59,809
43. Dispatchers, Except Police, Fire, and Ambulance	$33,140	1.5%	29,793
44. Gaming Surveillance Officers and Gaming Investigators	$27,440	33.6%	2,124
45. Insulation Workers, Mechanical	$36,570	8.6%	5,787
46. Tour Guides and Escorts	$22,110	21.2%	15,027
47. Excavating and Loading Machine and Dragline Operators	$34,050	8.3%	6,562
48. Insurance Claims Clerks	$32,040	−1.3%	42,246
49. Insurance Policy Processing Clerks	$32,040	−1.3%	42,246
50. Maintenance Workers, Machinery	$35,590	−1.1%	15,055
51. Inspectors, Testers, Sorters, Samplers, and Weighers	$30,310	−7.0%	75,361
52. Pest Control Workers	$29,030	15.5%	6,006
53. Pesticide Handlers, Sprayers, and Applicators, Vegetation	$28,560	14.0%	7,443
54. Team Assemblers	$24,630	0.1%	264,135
55. Slaughterers and Meat Packers	$22,500	12.7%	15,511
56. Pipelayers	$31,280	8.7%	8,902
57. Ambulance Drivers and Attendants, Except Emergency Medical Technicians	$21,140	21.7%	3,703
58. Structural Metal Fabricators and Fitters	$31,030	−0.2%	20,746

Best Jobs Requiring Moderate-Term On-the-Job Training

Job	Annual Earnings	Percent Growth	Annual Openings
59. Parts Salespersons	$28,130	–2.2%	52,414
60. Concierges	$25,540	14.1%	4,893
61. Merchandise Displayers and Window Trimmers	$24,830	10.7%	9,103

Jobs 20 and 21 share 8,299 openings. Jobs 29, 30, and 31 share 81,885 openings. Jobs 48 and 49 share 42,246 openings.

Best Jobs Requiring Long-Term On-the-Job Training

Job	Annual Earnings	Percent Growth	Annual Openings
1. Police Patrol Officers	$49,630	10.8%	37,842
2. Sheriffs and Deputy Sheriffs	$49,630	10.8%	37,842
3. Pipe Fitters and Steamfitters	$44,090	10.6%	68,643
4. Plumbers	$44,090	10.6%	68,643
5. Flight Attendants	$61,120	10.6%	10,773
6. Talent Directors	$61,090	11.1%	8,992
7. Technical Directors/Managers	$61,090	11.1%	8,992
8. Forest Fire Fighters	$43,170	12.1%	18,887
9. Municipal Fire Fighters	$43,170	12.1%	18,887
10. Claims Examiners, Property and Casualty Insurance	$53,560	8.9%	22,024
11. Insurance Adjusters, Examiners, and Investigators	$53,560	8.9%	22,024
12. Construction Carpenters	$37,660	10.3%	223,225
13. Rough Carpenters	$37,660	10.3%	223,225
14. Coaches and Scouts	$27,840	14.6%	51,100
15. Electricians	$44,780	7.4%	79,083
16. Automotive Body and Related Repairers	$35,690	11.6%	37,469
17. Boilermakers	$50,700	14.0%	2,333
18. Cooks, Restaurant	$21,220	11.5%	238,542
19. Mobile Heavy Equipment Mechanics, Except Engines	$41,450	12.3%	11,037
20. Tile and Marble Setters	$38,720	15.4%	9,066
21. Industrial Machinery Mechanics	$42,350	9.0%	23,361
22. Interpreters and Translators	$37,490	23.6%	6,630
23. Purchasing Agents, Except Wholesale, Retail, and Farm Products	$52,460	0.1%	22,349
24. Nuclear Power Reactor Operators	$70,410	10.6%	233
25. Brickmasons and Blockmasons	$44,070	9.7%	17,569
26. Athletes and Sports Competitors	$38,440	19.2%	4,293

(continued)

(continued)

Best Jobs Requiring Long-Term On-the-Job Training

Job	Annual Earnings	Percent Growth	Annual Openings
27. Water and Liquid Waste Treatment Plant and System Operators	$37,090	13.8%	9,575
28. Audio and Video Equipment Technicians	$36,050	24.2%	4,681
29. Air Traffic Controllers	$112,930	10.2%	1,213
30. Environmental Compliance Inspectors	$48,400	4.9%	15,841
31. Equal Opportunity Representatives and Officers	$48,400	4.9%	15,841
32. Government Property Inspectors and Investigators	$48,400	4.9%	15,841
33. Licensing Examiners and Inspectors	$48,400	4.9%	15,841
34. Heating and Air Conditioning Mechanics and Installers	$38,360	8.7%	29,719
35. Refrigeration Mechanics and Installers	$38,360	8.7%	29,719
36. Sheet Metal Workers	$39,210	6.7%	31,677
37. Electrical Power-Line Installers and Repairers	$52,570	7.2%	6,401
38. Elevator Installers and Repairers	$68,000	8.8%	2,850
39. Wholesale and Retail Buyers, Except Farm Products	$46,960	−0.1%	19,847
40. Motorboat Mechanics	$34,210	19.0%	4,326
41. Reinforcing Iron and Rebar Workers	$37,890	11.5%	4,502
42. Glaziers	$35,230	11.9%	6,416
43. Telecommunications Line Installers and Repairers	$47,220	4.6%	14,719
44. Bakers	$22,590	10.0%	31,442
45. Automotive Glass Installers and Repairers	$31,470	18.7%	3,457
46. Photographers	$27,720	10.3%	16,100
47. Umpires, Referees, and Other Sports Officials	$24,770	16.0%	4,461
48. Farmers and Ranchers	$33,360	−8.5%	129,552
49. Recreational Vehicle Service Technicians	$31,760	18.2%	2,442
50. Machinists	$35,230	−3.1%	39,505
51. Millwrights	$46,090	5.8%	4,758
52. Fine Artists, Including Painters, Sculptors, and Illustrators	$42,070	9.9%	3,830
53. Structural Iron and Steel Workers	$42,130	6.0%	6,969
54. Motorcycle Mechanics	$30,300	12.5%	3,564
55. Plasterers and Stucco Masons	$36,430	8.1%	4,509

Jobs 1 and 2 share 37,842 openings. Jobs 3 and 4 share 68,643 openings. Jobs 6 and 7 share 8,992 openings with each other and with three other jobs not included in this list. Jobs 8 and 9 share 18,887 openings. Jobs 10 and 11 share 22,024 openings. Jobs 12 and 13 share 223,225 openings. Jobs 30, 31, 32, and 33 share 15,841 openings with each other and with another job not included in this list. Jobs 34 and 35 share 29,719 openings.

Best Jobs Requiring Work Experience in a Related Job

Job	Annual Earnings	Percent Growth	Annual Openings
1. Sales Representatives, Wholesale and Manufacturing, Technical and Scientific Products	$68,270	12.4%	43,469
2. Criminal Investigators and Special Agents	$59,930	17.3%	14,746
3. Immigration and Customs Inspectors	$59,930	17.3%	14,746
4. Police Detectives	$59,930	17.3%	14,746
5. Police Identification and Records Officers	$59,930	17.3%	14,746
6. Vocational Education Teachers, Postsecondary	$45,850	22.9%	19,313
7. Self-Enrichment Education Teachers	$34,580	23.1%	64,449
8. Gaming Managers	$64,410	24.4%	549
9. Mates—Ship, Boat, and Barge	$57,210	17.9%	2,665
10. Pilots, Ship	$57,210	17.9%	2,665
11. Ship and Boat Captains	$57,210	17.9%	2,665
12. Executive Secretaries and Administrative Assistants	$38,640	14.8%	235,314
13. First-Line Supervisors/Managers of Construction Trades and Extraction Workers	$55,950	9.1%	82,923
14. First-Line Supervisors/Managers of Non-Retail Sales Workers	$67,020	3.7%	48,883
15. Real Estate Brokers	$58,860	11.1%	18,689
16. Construction and Building Inspectors	$48,330	18.2%	12,606
17. First-Line Supervisors/Managers of Landscaping, Lawn Service, and Groundskeeping Workers	$38,720	17.6%	18,956
18. First-Line Supervisors/Managers of Police and Detectives	$72,620	9.2%	9,373
19. Sales Representatives, Wholesale and Manufacturing, Except Technical and Scientific Products	$50,750	8.4%	156,215
20. Industrial Production Managers	$80,560	–5.9%	14,889
21. Forest Fire Fighting and Prevention Supervisors	$65,040	11.5%	3,771
22. Municipal Fire Fighting and Prevention Supervisors	$65,040	11.5%	3,771
23. Storage and Distribution Managers	$76,310	8.3%	6,994
24. Transportation Managers	$76,310	8.3%	6,994
25. Gaming Supervisors	$42,980	23.4%	4,602
26. First-Line Supervisors/Managers of Mechanics, Installers, and Repairers	$55,380	7.3%	24,361
27. First-Line Supervisors/Managers of Correctional Officers	$55,720	12.5%	4,180
28. First-Line Supervisors/Managers of Personal Service Workers	$33,900	15.5%	37,555
29. Private Detectives and Investigators	$37,640	18.2%	7,329
30. Aviation Inspectors	$51,440	16.4%	2,122
31. Freight and Cargo Inspectors	$51,440	16.4%	2,122

(continued)

(continued)

Best Jobs Requiring Work Experience in a Related Job

Job	Annual Earnings	Percent Growth	Annual Openings
32. Transportation Vehicle, Equipment and Systems Inspectors, Except Aviation	$51,440	16.4%	2,122
33. First-Line Supervisors/Managers of Transportation and Material-Moving Machine and Vehicle Operators	$49,850	10.2%	16,580
34. First-Line Supervisors/Managers of Office and Administrative Support Workers	$44,650	5.8%	138,420
35. First-Line Supervisors/Managers of Food Preparation and Serving Workers	$28,040	11.3%	154,175
36. First-Line Supervisors/Managers of Housekeeping and Janitorial Workers	$32,850	12.7%	30,613
37. Ship Engineers	$56,090	14.1%	1,102
38. First-Line Supervisors/Managers of Helpers, Laborers, and Material Movers, Hand	$40,640	12.5%	13,877
39. First-Line Supervisors/Managers of Production and Operating Workers	$48,670	−4.8%	46,144
40. Food Service Managers	$44,570	5.0%	59,302
41. Aircraft Cargo Handling Supervisors	$37,760	23.3%	523
42. First-Line Supervisors/Managers of Retail Sales Workers	$34,470	4.2%	221,241
43. Coroners	$48,400	4.9%	15,841
44. Lodging Managers	$44,240	12.2%	5,529
45. Emergency Management Specialists	$48,380	12.3%	1,538
46. Fire Inspectors	$50,830	11.0%	644
47. Fire Investigators	$50,830	11.0%	644
48. Chefs and Head Cooks	$37,160	7.6%	9,401

Jobs 2, 3, 4, and 5 share 14,746 openings. Jobs 9, 10, and 11 share 2,665 openings. Jobs 21 and 22 share 3,771 openings. Jobs 23 and 24 share 6,994 openings. Jobs 30, 31, and 32 share 2,122 openings. Job 43 shares 15,841 openings with four other jobs not included in this list. Jobs 46 and 47 share 644 openings.

Best Jobs Requiring Postsecondary Vocational Training

Job	Annual Earnings	Percent Growth	Annual Openings
1. Automotive Master Mechanics	$34,170	14.3%	97,350
2. Automotive Specialty Technicians	$34,170	14.3%	97,350
3. Licensed Practical and Licensed Vocational Nurses	$37,940	14.0%	70,610
4. Surgical Technologists	$37,540	24.5%	15,365

Best Jobs Requiring Postsecondary Vocational Training

Job	Annual Earnings	Percent Growth	Annual Openings
5. Preschool Teachers, Except Special Education	$23,130	26.3%	78,172
6. Court Reporters	$45,330	24.5%	2,620
7. Fitness Trainers and Aerobics Instructors	$27,680	26.8%	51,235
8. Nursing Aides, Orderlies, and Attendants	$23,160	18.2%	321,036
9. Real Estate Sales Agents	$40,600	10.6%	61,232
10. Bus and Truck Mechanics and Diesel Engine Specialists	$38,640	11.5%	25,428
11. Aircraft Mechanics and Service Technicians	$49,010	10.6%	9,708
12. Commercial Pilots	$61,640	13.2%	1,425
13. Emergency Medical Technicians and Paramedics	$28,400	19.2%	19,513
14. Massage Therapists	$34,870	20.3%	9,193
15. Architectural Drafters	$43,310	6.1%	16,238
16. Civil Drafters	$43,310	6.1%	16,238
17. Insurance Appraisers, Auto Damage	$51,500	12.5%	1,030
18. Security and Fire Alarm Systems Installers	$35,390	20.2%	5,729
19. Makeup Artists, Theatrical and Performance	$35,250	39.8%	392
20. Telecommunications Equipment Installers and Repairers, Except Line Installers	$54,070	2.5%	13,541
21. Electrical and Electronics Repairers, Commercial and Industrial Equipment	$47,110	6.8%	6,607
22. Skin Care Specialists	$27,190	34.3%	6,643
23. Mechanical Drafters	$44,740	5.2%	10,902
24. Commercial Divers	$41,610	17.7%	248
25. Hairdressers, Hairstylists, and Cosmetologists	$22,210	12.4%	73,030
26. Medical Transcriptionists	$31,250	13.5%	18,080
27. Camera Operators, Television, Video, and Motion Picture	$41,850	11.5%	3,496
28. Electrical Drafters	$49,250	4.1%	4,786
29. Electronic Drafters	$49,250	4.1%	4,786
30. Embalmers	$36,800	14.3%	1,660
31. Solderers and Brazers	$32,270	5.1%	61,125
32. Welders, Cutters, and Welder Fitters	$32,270	5.1%	61,125
33. Computer, Automated Teller, and Office Machine Repairers	$37,100	3.0%	22,330
34. Library Technicians	$27,680	8.5%	29,075

Jobs 1 and 2 share 97,350 openings. Jobs 15 and 16 share 16,238 openings. Jobs 28 and 29 share 4,786 openings. Jobs 31 and 32 share 61,125 openings.

Best Jobs Requiring an Associate Degree

Job	Annual Earnings	Percent Growth	Annual Openings
1. Registered Nurses	$60,010	23.5%	233,499
2. Dental Hygienists	$64,740	30.1%	10,433
3. Software Quality Assurance Engineers and Testers	$71,510	15.1%	14,374
4. Paralegals and Legal Assistants	$44,990	22.2%	22,756
5. Radiologic Technicians	$50,260	15.1%	12,836
6. Radiologic Technologists	$50,260	15.1%	12,836
7. Radiation Therapists	$70,010	24.8%	1,461
8. Physical Therapist Assistants	$44,130	32.4%	5,957
9. Veterinary Technologists and Technicians	$27,970	41.0%	14,674
10. Respiratory Therapists	$50,070	22.6%	5,563
11. Diagnostic Medical Sonographers	$59,860	19.1%	3,211
12. Computer Support Specialists	$42,400	12.9%	97,334
13. Environmental Science and Protection Technicians, Including Health	$39,370	28.0%	8,404
14. Interior Designers	$43,970	19.5%	8,434
15. Cardiovascular Technologists and Technicians	$44,940	25.5%	3,550
16. Medical Records and Health Information Technicians	$29,290	17.8%	39,048
17. Occupational Therapist Assistants	$45,050	25.4%	2,634
18. Electrical Engineering Technicians	$52,140	3.6%	12,583
19. Electronics Engineering Technicians	$52,140	3.6%	12,583
20. Funeral Directors	$50,370	12.5%	3,939
21. Nuclear Medicine Technologists	$64,670	14.8%	1,290
22. Legal Secretaries	$38,810	11.7%	38,682
23. Industrial Engineering Technicians	$47,490	9.9%	6,172
24. Environmental Engineering Technicians	$40,690	24.8%	2,162
25. Medical and Clinical Laboratory Technicians	$34,270	15.0%	10,866
26. Civil Engineering Technicians	$42,580	10.2%	7,499
27. Medical Equipment Repairers	$40,320	21.7%	2,351
28. Nuclear Equipment Operation Technicians	$66,140	6.7%	1,021
29. Nuclear Monitoring Technicians	$66,140	6.7%	1,021
30. Fashion Designers	$62,810	5.0%	1,968
31. Aerospace Engineering and Operations Technicians	$54,930	10.4%	707
32. Geological Sample Test Technicians	$50,950	8.6%	1,895
33. Geophysical Data Technicians	$50,950	8.6%	1,895
34. Mechanical Engineering Technicians	$47,280	6.4%	3,710
35. City and Regional Planning Aides	$35,870	12.4%	3,571

Best Jobs Requiring an Associate Degree

Job	Annual Earnings	Percent Growth	Annual Openings
36. Social Science Research Assistants	$35,870	12.4%	3,571
37. Chemical Technicians	$40,740	5.8%	4,010
38. Broadcast Technicians	$32,230	12.1%	2,955

Job 3 shares 14,374 openings with four other jobs not included in this list. Jobs 5 and 6 share 12,836 openings. Jobs 18 and 19 share 12,583 openings. Jobs 28 and 29 share 1,021 openings. Jobs 32 and 33 share 1,895 openings. Jobs 35 and 36 share 3,571 openings.

Best Jobs Requiring a Bachelor's Degree

Job	Annual Earnings	Percent Growth	Annual Openings
1. Computer Software Engineers, Applications	$83,130	44.6%	58,690
2. Computer Systems Analysts	$73,090	29.0%	63,166
3. Computer Software Engineers, Systems Software	$89,070	28.2%	33,139
4. Network Systems and Data Communications Analysts	$68,220	53.4%	35,086
5. Financial Analysts	$70,400	33.8%	29,317
6. Sales Agents, Financial Services	$68,430	24.8%	47,750
7. Sales Agents, Securities and Commodities	$68,430	24.8%	47,750
8. Computer Security Specialists	$64,690	27.0%	37,010
9. Network and Computer Systems Administrators	$64,690	27.0%	37,010
10. Construction Managers	$76,230	15.7%	44,158
11. Personal Financial Advisors	$67,660	41.0%	17,114
12. Market Research Analysts	$60,300	20.1%	45,015
13. Accountants	$57,060	17.7%	134,463
14. Auditors	$57,060	17.7%	134,463
15. Civil Engineers	$71,710	18.0%	15,979
16. Environmental Engineers	$72,350	25.4%	5,003
17. Industrial Engineers	$71,430	20.3%	11,272
18. Cost Estimators	$54,920	18.5%	38,379
19. Database Administrators	$67,250	28.6%	8,258
20. Social and Community Service Managers	$54,530	24.7%	23,788
21. Computer Systems Engineers/Architects	$71,510	15.1%	14,374
22. Network Designers	$71,510	15.1%	14,374
23. Web Administrators	$71,510	15.1%	14,374
24. Web Developers	$71,510	15.1%	14,374
25. Public Relations Specialists	$49,800	17.6%	51,216
26. Multi-Media Artists and Animators	$54,550	25.8%	13,182

(continued)

(continued)

Best Jobs Requiring a Bachelor's Degree

Job	Annual Earnings	Percent Growth	Annual Openings
27. Biomedical Engineers	$75,440	21.1%	1,804
28. Architects, Except Landscape and Naval	$67,620	17.7%	11,324
29. Compensation, Benefits, and Job Analysis Specialists	$52,180	18.4%	18,761
30. Surveyors	$51,630	23.7%	14,305
31. Airline Pilots, Copilots, and Flight Engineers	$145,600+	12.9%	4,073
32. Substance Abuse and Behavioral Disorder Counselors	$35,580	34.3%	20,821
33. Special Education Teachers, Preschool, Kindergarten, and Elementary School	$48,350	19.6%	20,049
34. Technical Writers	$60,390	19.5%	7,498
35. Elementary School Teachers, Except Special Education	$47,330	13.6%	181,612
36. Loan Officers	$53,000	11.5%	54,237
37. Logisticians	$64,250	17.3%	9,671
38. Employment Interviewers	$44,380	18.4%	33,588
39. Personnel Recruiters	$44,380	18.4%	33,588
40. Aerospace Engineers	$90,930	10.2%	6,498
41. Medical and Public Health Social Workers	$44,670	24.2%	16,429
42. Child, Family, and School Social Workers	$38,620	19.1%	35,402
43. Middle School Teachers, Except Special and Vocational Education	$47,900	11.2%	75,270
44. Health Educators	$42,920	26.2%	13,707
45. Insurance Sales Agents	$44,110	12.9%	64,162
46. Property, Real Estate, and Community Association Managers	$43,670	15.1%	49,916
47. Kindergarten Teachers, Except Special Education	$45,120	16.3%	27,603
48. Copy Writers	$50,660	12.8%	24,023
49. Poets, Lyricists, and Creative Writers	$50,660	12.8%	24,023
50. Graduate Teaching Assistants	$28,060	22.9%	20,601
51. Sales Engineers	$80,270	8.5%	7,371
52. Forensic Science Technicians	$47,680	30.7%	3,074
53. Computer Programmers	$68,080	–4.1%	27,937
54. Electrical Engineers	$79,240	6.3%	6,806
55. Mechanical Engineers	$72,300	4.2%	12,394
56. Cartographers and Photogrammetrists	$49,970	20.3%	2,823
57. Secondary School Teachers, Except Special and Vocational Education	$49,420	5.6%	93,166
58. Recreation Workers	$21,220	12.7%	61,454
59. Electronics Engineers, Except Computer	$83,340	3.7%	5,699
60. Computer Hardware Engineers	$91,860	4.6%	3,572

Best Jobs Requiring a Bachelor's Degree

Job	Annual Earnings	Percent Growth	Annual Openings
61. Meeting and Convention Planners	$43,530	19.9%	8,318
62. Adult Literacy, Remedial Education, and GED Teachers and Instructors	$44,710	14.2%	17,340
63. Directors, Religious Activities and Education	$35,370	19.7%	11,463
64. Landscape Architects	$57,580	16.4%	2,342
65. Special Education Teachers, Middle School	$48,940	15.8%	8,846
66. Medical and Clinical Laboratory Technologists	$51,720	12.4%	11,457
67. Chemical Engineers	$81,500	7.9%	2,111
68. Chemists	$63,490	9.1%	9,024
69. Atmospheric and Space Scientists	$78,390	10.6%	735
70. Marine Architects	$76,200	10.9%	495
71. Marine Engineers	$76,200	10.9%	495
72. Biological Technicians	$37,810	16.0%	15,374
73. Nuclear Engineers	$94,420	7.2%	1,046
74. Appraisers, Real Estate	$46,130	16.9%	6,493
75. Assessors	$46,130	16.9%	6,493
76. Probation Officers and Correctional Treatment Specialists	$44,510	10.9%	18,335
77. Materials Scientists	$76,160	8.7%	1,039
78. Financial Examiners	$66,670	10.7%	2,449
79. Petroleum Engineers	$103,960	5.2%	1,016
80. Mining and Geological Engineers, Including Mining Safety Engineers	$74,330	10.0%	456
81. Fire-Prevention and Protection Engineers	$69,580	9.6%	1,105
82. Industrial Safety and Health Engineers	$69,580	9.6%	1,105
83. Product Safety Engineers	$69,580	9.6%	1,105
84. Graphic Designers	$41,280	9.8%	26,968
85. Athletic Trainers	$38,360	24.3%	1,669
86. Materials Engineers	$77,170	4.0%	1,390
87. Budget Analysts	$63,440	7.1%	6,423
88. Editors	$48,320	2.3%	20,193
89. Special Education Teachers, Secondary School	$49,640	8.5%	10,601
90. Occupational Health and Safety Specialists	$60,140	8.1%	3,440
91. Orthotists and Prosthetists	$60,520	11.8%	295
92. Insurance Underwriters	$54,530	6.3%	6,880
93. Set and Exhibit Designers	$43,220	17.8%	1,402
94. Survey Researchers	$36,820	15.9%	4,959
95. Commercial and Industrial Designers	$56,550	7.2%	4,777

(continued)

(continued)

Best Jobs Requiring a Bachelor's Degree

Job	Annual Earnings	Percent Growth	Annual Openings
96. Film and Video Editors	$47,870	12.7%	2,707
97. Agricultural Engineers	$67,710	8.6%	225
98. Food Scientists and Technologists	$57,870	10.3%	663
99. Zoologists and Wildlife Biologists	$55,100	8.7%	1,444
100. Dietitians and Nutritionists	$49,010	8.6%	4,996
101. Soil and Plant Scientists	$58,000	8.4%	850
102. Museum Technicians and Conservators	$35,350	15.9%	1,341
103. Credit Analysts	$54,580	1.9%	3,180
104. Occupational Health and Safety Technicians	$44,020	14.6%	886
105. Tax Examiners, Collectors, and Revenue Agents	$46,920	2.1%	4,465

Jobs 6 and 7 share 47,750 openings. Jobs 8 and 9 share 37,010 openings. Jobs 13 and 14 share 134,463 openings. Jobs 21, 22, 23, and 24 share 14,374 openings with another job not included in this list. Jobs 38 and 39 share 33,588 openings. Jobs 48 and 49 share 24,023 openings. Jobs 70 and 71 share 495 openings. Jobs 74 and 75 share 6,493 openings. Jobs 81, 82, and 83 share 1,105 openings.

Best Jobs Requiring Work Experience Plus Degree

Job	Annual Earnings	Percent Growth	Annual Openings
1. Computer and Information Systems Managers	$108,070	16.4%	30,887
2. Financial Managers, Branch or Department	$95,310	12.6%	57,589
3. Treasurers and Controllers	$95,310	12.6%	57,589
4. Management Analysts	$71,150	21.9%	125,669
5. Marketing Managers	$104,400	14.4%	20,189
6. Medical and Health Services Managers	$76,990	16.4%	31,877
7. Sales Managers	$94,910	10.2%	36,392
8. Chief Executives	$145,600+	2.0%	21,209
9. Training and Development Specialists	$49,630	18.3%	35,862
10. General and Operations Managers	$88,700	1.5%	112,072
11. Public Relations Managers	$86,470	16.9%	5,781
12. Actuaries	$85,690	23.7%	3,245
13. Education Administrators, Postsecondary	$75,780	14.2%	17,121
14. Administrative Services Managers	$70,990	11.7%	19,513
15. Education Administrators, Elementary and Secondary School	$80,580	7.6%	27,143
16. Training and Development Managers	$84,340	15.6%	3,759
17. Engineering Managers	$111,020	7.3%	7,404

Best Jobs Requiring Work Experience Plus Degree

Job	Annual Earnings	Percent Growth	Annual Openings
18. Natural Sciences Managers	$104,040	11.4%	3,661
19. Compensation and Benefits Managers	$81,410	12.0%	6,121
20. Directors—Stage, Motion Pictures, Television, and Radio	$61,090	11.1%	8,992
21. Education Administrators, Preschool and Child Care Center/Program	$38,580	23.5%	8,113
22. Producers	$61,090	11.1%	8,992
23. Program Directors	$61,090	11.1%	8,992
24. Art Directors	$72,320	9.0%	9,719
25. Music Composers and Arrangers	$40,150	12.9%	8,597
26. Music Directors	$40,150	12.9%	8,597
27. Judges, Magistrate Judges, and Magistrates	$107,230	5.1%	1,567
28. Purchasing Managers	$85,440	3.4%	7,243
29. Aquacultural Managers	$53,720	1.1%	18,101
30. Crop and Livestock Managers	$53,720	1.1%	18,101
31. Nursery and Greenhouse Managers	$53,720	1.1%	18,101
32. Agents and Business Managers of Artists, Performers, and Athletes	$66,440	9.6%	3,940
33. Advertising and Promotions Managers	$78,250	6.2%	2,955
34. Arbitrators, Mediators, and Conciliators	$48,840	10.6%	546
35. Vocational Education Teachers, Secondary School	$50,090	–4.6%	7,639

Jobs 2 and 3 share 57,589 openings. Jobs 20, 22, and 23 share 8,992 openings with each other and with two other jobs not included in this list. Jobs 25 and 26 share 8,597 openings. Jobs 29, 30, and 31 share 18,101 openings.

Best Jobs Requiring a Master's Degree

Job	Annual Earnings	Percent Growth	Annual Openings
1. Physical Therapists	$69,760	27.1%	12,072
2. Physician Assistants	$78,450	27.0%	7,147
3. Occupational Therapists	$63,790	23.1%	8,338
4. Mental Health Counselors	$36,000	30.0%	24,103
5. Environmental Scientists and Specialists, Including Health	$58,380	25.1%	6,961
6. Instructional Coordinators	$55,270	22.5%	21,294
7. Geoscientists, Except Hydrologists and Geographers	$75,800	21.9%	2,471
8. Mental Health and Substance Abuse Social Workers	$36,640	29.9%	17,289
9. Hydrologists	$68,140	24.3%	687

(continued)

(continued)

Best Jobs Requiring a Master's Degree

Job	Annual Earnings	Percent Growth	Annual Openings
10. Marriage and Family Therapists	$43,600	29.8%	5,953
11. Clergy	$40,460	18.9%	35,092
12. Rehabilitation Counselors	$29,630	23.0%	32,081
13. Educational, Vocational, and School Counselors	$49,450	12.6%	54,025
14. Industrial-Organizational Psychologists	$80,820	21.3%	118
15. Speech-Language Pathologists	$60,690	10.6%	11,160
16. Operations Research Analysts	$66,950	10.6%	5,727
17. Statisticians	$69,900	8.5%	3,433
18. Economists	$80,220	7.5%	1,555
19. Curators	$46,000	23.3%	1,416
20. Urban and Regional Planners	$57,970	14.5%	1,967
21. Librarians	$50,970	3.6%	18,945
22. Political Scientists	$91,580	5.3%	318
23. Epidemiologists	$60,010	13.6%	503
24. Anthropologists	$53,080	15.0%	446
25. Archeologists	$53,080	15.0%	446
26. Sociologists	$61,140	10.0%	403
27. Archivists	$43,110	14.4%	795

Jobs 24 and 25 share 446 openings.

Best Jobs Requiring a Doctoral Degree

Job	Annual Earnings	Percent Growth	Annual Openings
1. Health Specialties Teachers, Postsecondary	$80,700	22.9%	19,617
2. Business Teachers, Postsecondary	$64,900	22.9%	11,643
3. Biological Science Teachers, Postsecondary	$71,780	22.9%	9,039
4. Engineering Teachers, Postsecondary	$79,510	22.9%	5,565
5. Economics Teachers, Postsecondary	$75,300	22.9%	2,208
6. Agricultural Sciences Teachers, Postsecondary	$78,460	22.9%	1,840
7. Chemistry Teachers, Postsecondary	$63,870	22.9%	3,405
8. Computer Science Teachers, Postsecondary	$62,020	22.9%	5,820
9. Physics Teachers, Postsecondary	$70,090	22.9%	2,155
10. Art, Drama, and Music Teachers, Postsecondary	$55,190	22.9%	12,707

Best Jobs Requiring a Doctoral Degree

Job	Annual Earnings	Percent Growth	Annual Openings
11. Atmospheric, Earth, Marine, and Space Sciences Teachers, Postsecondary	$73,280	22.9%	1,553
12. Mathematical Science Teachers, Postsecondary	$58,560	22.9%	7,663
13. Psychology Teachers, Postsecondary	$60,610	22.9%	5,261
14. Political Science Teachers, Postsecondary	$63,100	22.9%	2,435
15. Education Teachers, Postsecondary	$54,220	22.9%	9,359
16. English Language and Literature Teachers, Postsecondary	$54,000	22.9%	10,475
17. Nursing Instructors and Teachers, Postsecondary	$57,500	22.9%	7,337
18. History Teachers, Postsecondary	$59,160	22.9%	3,570
19. Architecture Teachers, Postsecondary	$68,540	22.9%	1,044
20. Anthropology and Archeology Teachers, Postsecondary	$64,530	22.9%	910
21. Environmental Science Teachers, Postsecondary	$64,850	22.9%	769
22. Communications Teachers, Postsecondary	$54,720	22.9%	4,074
23. Medical Scientists, Except Epidemiologists	$64,200	20.2%	10,596
24. Philosophy and Religion Teachers, Postsecondary	$56,380	22.9%	3,120
25. Sociology Teachers, Postsecondary	$58,160	22.9%	2,774
26. Computer and Information Scientists, Research	$97,970	21.5%	2,901
27. Foreign Language and Literature Teachers, Postsecondary	$53,610	22.9%	4,317
28. Forestry and Conservation Science Teachers, Postsecondary	$63,790	22.9%	454
29. Area, Ethnic, and Cultural Studies Teachers, Postsecondary	$59,150	22.9%	1,252
30. Recreation and Fitness Studies Teachers, Postsecondary	$52,170	22.9%	3,010
31. Clinical Psychologists	$62,210	15.8%	8,309
32. Counseling Psychologists	$62,210	15.8%	8,309
33. Geography Teachers, Postsecondary	$61,310	22.9%	697
34. School Psychologists	$62,210	15.8%	8,309
35. Home Economics Teachers, Postsecondary	$58,170	22.9%	820
36. Social Work Teachers, Postsecondary	$56,240	22.9%	1,292
37. Criminal Justice and Law Enforcement Teachers, Postsecondary	$51,060	22.9%	1,911
38. Biochemists and Biophysicists	$79,270	15.9%	1,637
39. Library Science Teachers, Postsecondary	$56,810	22.9%	702
40. Physicists	$96,850	6.8%	1,302
41. Mathematicians	$90,870	10.2%	473
42. Astronomers	$99,020	5.6%	128
43. Microbiologists	$60,680	11.2%	1,306

Jobs 31, 32, and 34 share 8,309 openings.

Best Jobs Requiring a First Professional Degree

Job	Annual Earnings	Percent Growth	Annual Openings
1. Anesthesiologists	$145,600+	14.2%	38,027
2. Family and General Practitioners	$145,600+	14.2%	38,027
3. Internists, General	$145,600+	14.2%	38,027
4. Obstetricians and Gynecologists	$145,600+	14.2%	38,027
5. Psychiatrists	$145,600+	14.2%	38,027
6. Surgeons	$145,600+	14.2%	38,027
7. Pediatricians, General	$140,690	14.2%	38,027
8. Pharmacists	$100,480	21.7%	16,358
9. Lawyers	$106,120	11.0%	49,445
10. Veterinarians	$75,230	35.0%	5,301
11. Law Teachers, Postsecondary	$87,730	22.9%	2,169
12. Chiropractors	$65,890	14.4%	3,179
13. Prosthodontists	$145,600+	10.7%	54
14. Orthodontists	$145,600+	9.2%	479
15. Dentists, General	$137,630	9.2%	7,106
16. Oral and Maxillofacial Surgeons	$145,600+	9.1%	400
17. Optometrists	$93,800	11.3%	1,789
18. Podiatrists	$110,510	9.5%	648
19. Audiologists	$59,440	9.8%	980

Jobs 1, 2, 3, 4, 5, 6, and 7 share 38,027 openings.

Best Jobs Lists Based on Interests

This group of lists organizes the 500 best jobs into 16 interest areas. You can use these lists to identify jobs quickly based on your interests. Within each interest area, jobs are listed by combined score for earnings, job growth, and job openings, from highest to lowest.

Find the interest area or areas that appeal to you most and review the jobs in those areas. When you find jobs you want to explore in more detail, look up their descriptions in Part II. You can also review interest areas in which you've had past experience, education, or training to see whether other jobs in those areas would meet your current requirements.

Note: The 16 interest areas used in these lists are those used in the *New Guide for Occupational Exploration,* Fourth Edition, published by JIST. The original GOE was developed by the U.S. Department of Labor as an intuitive way to assist in career exploration. The 16 interest areas used in the *New GOE* are based on the 16 career clusters that the U.S. Department of Education's Office of Vocational and Adult Education developed in 1999 and that many states now use to organize their career-oriented programs and career information.

Descriptions for the 16 Interest Areas

Brief descriptions follow for the 16 interest areas we use in the lists. The descriptions are from the *New Guide for Occupational Exploration,* Fourth Edition. Some of them refer to jobs (as examples) that aren't included in this book.

Also note that we put each of the 500 best jobs into only one interest area list, the one it fit into best. However, many jobs could be included in more than one list, so consider reviewing several interest areas to find jobs that you might otherwise overlook.

⊛ **Agriculture and Natural Resources:** *An interest in working with plants, animals, forests, or mineral resources for agriculture, horticulture, conservation, extraction, and other purposes.* You can satisfy this interest by working in farming, landscaping, forestry, fishing, mining, and related fields. You may like doing physical work outdoors, such as on a farm or ranch, in a forest, or on a drilling rig. If you have a scientific curiosity, you could study plants and animals or analyze biological or rock samples in a lab. If you have management ability, you could own, operate, or manage a fish hatchery, a landscaping business, or a greenhouse.

⊛ **Architecture and Construction:** *An interest in designing, assembling, and maintaining components of buildings and other structures.* You may want to be part of the team of architects, drafters, and others who design buildings and render plans. If construction interests you, you might find fulfillment in the many building projects that are being undertaken at all times. If you like to organize and plan, you can find careers in managing these projects. Or you can play a more direct role in putting up and finishing buildings by doing jobs such as plumbing, carpentry, masonry, painting, or roofing, either as a skilled craftsworker or as a helper. You can prepare the building site by operating heavy equipment or installing, maintaining, and repairing vital building equipment and systems such as electricity and heating.

⊛ **Arts and Communication:** *An interest in creatively expressing feelings or ideas, in communicating news or information, or in performing.* You can satisfy this interest in creative, verbal, or performing activities. For example, if you enjoy literature, perhaps writing or editing would appeal to you. Journalism and public relations are other fields for people who like to use their writing or speaking skills. Do you prefer to work in the performing arts? If so, you could direct or perform in drama, music, or dance. If you especially enjoy the visual arts, you could create paintings, sculpture, or ceramics or design products or visual displays. A flair for technology might lead you to specialize in photography, broadcast production, or dispatching.

⊛ **Business and Administration:** *An interest in making a business organization or function run smoothly.* You can satisfy this interest by working in a position of leadership or by specializing in a function that contributes to the overall effort in a business, a nonprofit organization, or a government agency. If you especially enjoy working with people, you may find fulfillment from working in human resources. An interest in numbers may lead you to consider accounting, finance, budgeting, billing, or financial record-keeping. A job as an administrative assistant may interest you if you like a variety of tasks in a busy environment. If you are good with details and word processing, you may enjoy a job as a secretary or data-entry clerk. Or perhaps you would do well as the manager of a business.

❋ **Education and Training:** *An interest in helping people learn.* You can satisfy this interest by teaching students, who may be preschoolers, retirees, or any age in between. You may specialize in a particular academic field or work with learners of a particular age, with a particular interest, or with a particular learning problem. Working in a library or museum may give you an opportunity to expand people's understanding of the world.

❋ **Finance and Insurance:** *An interest in helping businesses and people be assured of a financially secure future.* You can satisfy this interest by working in a financial or insurance business in a leadership or support role. If you like gathering and analyzing information, you may find fulfillment as an insurance adjuster or financial analyst. Or you may deal with information at the clerical level as a banking or insurance clerk or in person-to-person situations providing customer service. Another way to interact with people is to sell financial or insurance services that will meet their needs.

❋ **Government and Public Administration:** *An interest in helping a government agency serve the needs of the public.* You can satisfy this interest by working in a position of leadership or by specializing in a function that contributes to the role of government. You may help protect the public by working as an inspector or examiner to enforce standards. If you enjoy using clerical skills, you could work as a clerk in a law court or government office. Or perhaps you prefer the top-down perspective of a government executive or urban planner.

❋ **Health Science:** *An interest in helping people and animals be healthy.* You can satisfy this interest by working on a health-care team as a doctor, therapist, or nurse. You might specialize in one of the many different parts of the body (such as the teeth or eyes) or in one of the many different types of care. Or you may want to be a generalist who deals with the whole patient. If you like technology, you might find satisfaction working with X rays or new diagnostic methods. You might work with relatively healthy people, helping them to eat better. If you enjoy working with animals, you might care for them and keep them healthy.

❋ **Hospitality, Tourism, and Recreation:** *An interest in catering to the personal wishes and needs of others so that they can enjoy a clean environment, good food and drink, comfortable lodging away from home, and recreation.* You can satisfy this interest by providing services for the convenience, care, and pampering of others in hotels, restaurants, airplanes, beauty parlors, and so on. You may want to use your love of cooking as a chef. If you like working with people, you may want to provide personal services by being a travel guide, a flight attendant, a concierge, a hairdresser, or a waiter. You may want to work in cleaning and building services if you like a clean environment. If you enjoy sports or games, you could work for an athletic team or casino.

❋ **Human Service:** *An interest in improving people's social, mental, emotional, or spiritual well-being.* You can satisfy this interest as a counselor, social worker, or religious worker who helps people sort out their complicated lives or solve personal problems. You may work as a caretaker for very young people or the elderly. Or you may interview people to help identify the social services they need.

❋ **Information Technology:** *An interest in designing, developing, managing, and supporting information systems.* You can satisfy this interest by working with hardware, software, multimedia, or integrated systems. If you like to use your organizational skills, you might work as a systems or database administrator. Or you can solve complex problems as a software engineer or systems analyst. If you enjoy getting your hands on hardware, you might find work servicing computers, peripherals, and information-intense machines such as cash registers and ATMs.

❋ **Law and Public Safety:** *An interest in upholding people's rights or in protecting people and property by using authority, inspecting, or investigating.* You can satisfy this interest by working in law, law enforcement, fire fighting, the military, and related fields. For example, if you enjoy mental challenge and intrigue, you could investigate crimes or fires for a living. If you enjoy working with verbal skills and research skills, you may want to defend citizens in court or research deeds, wills, and other legal documents. If you want to help people in critical situations, you may want to fight fires, work as a police officer, or become a paramedic. Or, if you want more routine work in public safety, perhaps a job in guarding, patrolling, or inspecting would appeal to you. If you have management ability, you could seek a leadership position in law enforcement and the protective services. Work in the military gives you a chance to use technical and leadership skills while serving your country.

❋ **Manufacturing:** *An interest in processing materials into intermediate or final products or maintaining and repairing products by using machines or hand tools.* You can satisfy this interest by working in one of many industries that mass-produce goods or by working for a utility that distributes electrical power or other resources. You might enjoy manual work, using your hands or hand tools in highly skilled jobs such as assembling engines or electronic equipment. If you enjoy making machines run efficiently or fixing them when they break down, you could seek a job installing or repairing such devices as copiers, aircraft engines, cars, or watches. Perhaps you prefer to set up or operate machines that are used to manufacture products made of food, glass, or paper. You could enjoy cutting and grinding metal and plastic parts to desired shapes and measurements. Or you may want to operate equipment in systems that provide water and process wastewater. You may like inspecting, sorting, counting, or weighing products. Another option is to work with your hands and machinery to move boxes and freight in a warehouse. If leadership appeals to you, you could manage people engaged in production and repair.

❋ **Retail and Wholesale Sales and Service:** *An interest in bringing others to a particular point of view by personal persuasion and by sales and promotional techniques.* You can satisfy this interest in various jobs that involve persuasion and selling. If you like using knowledge of science, you may enjoy selling pharmaceutical, medical, or electronic products or services. Real estate offers several kinds of sales jobs as well. If you like speaking on the phone, you could work as a telemarketer. Or you may enjoy selling apparel and other merchandise in a retail setting. If you prefer to help people, you may want a job in customer service.

⊛ **Scientific Research, Engineering, and Mathematics:** *An interest in discovering, collecting, and analyzing information about the natural world; in applying scientific research findings to problems in medicine, the life sciences, human behavior, and the natural sciences; in imagining and manipulating quantitative data; and in applying technology to manufacturing, transportation, and other economic activities.* You can satisfy this interest by working with the knowledge and processes of the sciences. You may enjoy researching and developing new knowledge in mathematics, or perhaps solving problems in the physical, life, or social sciences would appeal to you. You may want to study engineering and help create new machines, processes, and structures. If you want to work with scientific equipment and procedures, you could seek a job in a research or testing laboratory.

⊛ **Transportation, Distribution, and Logistics:** *An interest in operations that move people or materials.* You can satisfy this interest by managing a transportation service, by helping vehicles keep on their assigned schedules and routes, or by driving or piloting a vehicle. If you enjoy taking responsibility, perhaps managing a rail line would appeal to you. If you work well with details and can take pressure on the job, you might consider being an air traffic controller. Or would you rather get out on the highway, on the water, or up in the air? If so, you could drive a truck from state to state, be employed on a ship, or fly a crop duster over a cornfield. If you prefer to stay closer to home, you could drive a delivery van, taxi, or school bus. You can use your physical strength to load freight and arrange it so that it gets to its destination in one piece.

Best Jobs for People Interested in Agriculture and Natural Resources

Job	Annual Earnings	Percent Growth	Annual Openings
1. Environmental Engineers	$72,350	25.4%	5,003
2. First-Line Supervisors/Managers of Construction Trades and Extraction Workers	$55,950	9.1%	82,923
3. First-Line Supervisors/Managers of Landscaping, Lawn Service, and Groundskeeping Workers	$38,720	17.6%	18,956
4. Environmental Science and Protection Technicians, Including Health	$39,370	28.0%	8,404
5. Landscaping and Groundskeeping Workers	$22,240	18.1%	307,138
6. Mining and Geological Engineers, Including Mining Safety Engineers	$74,330	10.0%	456
7. Aquacultural Managers	$53,720	1.1%	18,101
8. Crop and Livestock Managers	$53,720	1.1%	18,101
9. Nursery and Greenhouse Managers	$53,720	1.1%	18,101
10. Food Scientists and Technologists	$57,870	10.3%	663
11. Tree Trimmers and Pruners	$29,800	11.1%	9,621
12. Petroleum Engineers	$103,960	5.2%	1,016
13. Zoologists and Wildlife Biologists	$55,100	8.7%	1,444

Best Jobs for People Interested in Agriculture and Natural Resources

Job	Annual Earnings	Percent Growth	Annual Openings
14. Pest Control Workers	$29,030	15.5%	6,006
15. Pesticide Handlers, Sprayers, and Applicators, Vegetation	$28,560	14.0%	7,443
16. Agricultural Engineers	$67,710	8.6%	225
17. Geological Sample Test Technicians	$50,950	8.6%	1,895
18. Geophysical Data Technicians	$50,950	8.6%	1,895
19. Soil and Plant Scientists	$58,000	8.4%	850
20. Farmers and Ranchers	$33,360	–8.5%	129,552
21. Excavating and Loading Machine and Dragline Operators	$34,050	8.3%	6,562

Jobs 7, 8, and 9 share 18,101 openings. Jobs 17 and 18 share 1,895 openings.

Best Jobs for People Interested in Architecture and Construction

Job	Annual Earnings	Percent Growth	Annual Openings
1. Construction Managers	$76,230	15.7%	44,158
2. Architects, Except Landscape and Naval	$67,620	17.7%	11,324
3. Surveyors	$51,630	23.7%	14,305
4. Pipe Fitters and Steamfitters	$44,090	10.6%	68,643
5. Plumbers	$44,090	10.6%	68,643
6. Construction Carpenters	$37,660	10.3%	223,225
7. Rough Carpenters	$37,660	10.3%	223,225
8. Electricians	$44,780	7.4%	79,083
9. Landscape Architects	$57,580	16.4%	2,342
10. Painters, Construction and Maintenance	$32,080	11.8%	101,140
11. Roofers	$33,240	14.3%	38,398
12. Tile and Marble Setters	$38,720	15.4%	9,066
13. Boilermakers	$50,700	14.0%	2,333
14. Construction Laborers	$27,310	10.9%	257,407
15. Brickmasons and Blockmasons	$44,070	9.7%	17,569
16. Cement Masons and Concrete Finishers	$33,840	11.4%	34,625
17. Maintenance and Repair Workers, General	$32,570	10.1%	165,502
18. Operating Engineers and Other Construction Equipment Operators	$38,130	8.4%	55,468
19. Commercial Divers	$41,610	17.7%	248
20. Helpers—Installation, Maintenance, and Repair Workers	$22,920	11.8%	52,058
21. Heating and Air Conditioning Mechanics and Installers	$38,360	8.7%	29,719

(continued)

(continued)

Best Jobs for People Interested in Architecture and Construction

Job	Annual Earnings	Percent Growth	Annual Openings
22. Refrigeration Mechanics and Installers	$38,360	8.7%	29,719
23. Elevator Installers and Repairers	$68,000	8.8%	2,850
24. Helpers—Carpenters	$24,340	11.7%	37,731
25. Security and Fire Alarm Systems Installers	$35,390	20.2%	5,729
26. Helpers—Pipelayers, Plumbers, Pipefitters, and Steamfitters	$25,350	11.9%	29,332
27. Sheet Metal Workers	$39,210	6.7%	31,677
28. Glaziers	$35,230	11.9%	6,416
29. Electrical Power-Line Installers and Repairers	$52,570	7.2%	6,401
30. Telecommunications Equipment Installers and Repairers, Except Line Installers	$54,070	2.5%	13,541
31. Architectural Drafters	$43,310	6.1%	16,238
32. Civil Drafters	$43,310	6.1%	16,238
33. Reinforcing Iron and Rebar Workers	$37,890	11.5%	4,502
34. Telecommunications Line Installers and Repairers	$47,220	4.6%	14,719
35. Drywall and Ceiling Tile Installers	$36,520	7.3%	30,945
36. Helpers—Brickmasons, Blockmasons, Stonemasons, and Tile and Marble Setters	$26,260	11.0%	22,500
37. Highway Maintenance Workers	$32,600	8.9%	24,774
38. Tapers	$42,050	7.1%	9,026
39. Hazardous Materials Removal Workers	$36,330	11.2%	1,933
40. Structural Iron and Steel Workers	$42,130	6.0%	6,969
41. Helpers—Electricians	$24,880	6.8%	35,109
42. Insulation Workers, Mechanical	$36,570	8.6%	5,787
43. Pipelayers	$31,280	8.7%	8,902
44. Plasterers and Stucco Masons	$36,430	8.1%	4,509

Jobs 4 and 5 share 68,643 openings. Jobs 6 and 7 share 223,225 openings. Jobs 21 and 22 share 29,719 openings. Jobs 31 and 32 share 16,238 openings.

Best Jobs for People Interested in Arts and Communication

Job	Annual Earnings	Percent Growth	Annual Openings
1. Multi-Media Artists and Animators	$54,550	25.8%	13,182
2. Public Relations Specialists	$49,800	17.6%	51,216
3. Copy Writers	$50,660	12.8%	24,023

Best Jobs for People Interested in Arts and Communication

Job	Annual Earnings	Percent Growth	Annual Openings
4. Poets, Lyricists, and Creative Writers	$50,660	12.8%	24,023
5. Public Relations Managers	$86,470	16.9%	5,781
6. Directors—Stage, Motion Pictures, Television, and Radio	$61,090	11.1%	8,992
7. Producers	$61,090	11.1%	8,992
8. Program Directors	$61,090	11.1%	8,992
9. Talent Directors	$61,090	11.1%	8,992
10. Technical Directors/Managers	$61,090	11.1%	8,992
11. Technical Writers	$60,390	19.5%	7,498
12. Art Directors	$72,320	9.0%	9,719
13. Interior Designers	$43,970	19.5%	8,434
14. Police, Fire, and Ambulance Dispatchers	$32,660	13.6%	17,628
15. Interpreters and Translators	$37,490	23.6%	6,630
16. Music Composers and Arrangers	$40,150	12.9%	8,597
17. Music Directors	$40,150	12.9%	8,597
18. Graphic Designers	$41,280	9.8%	26,968
19. Audio and Video Equipment Technicians	$36,050	24.2%	4,681
20. Editors	$48,320	2.3%	20,193
21. Agents and Business Managers of Artists, Performers, and Athletes	$66,440	9.6%	3,940
22. Air Traffic Controllers	$112,930	10.2%	1,213
23. Set and Exhibit Designers	$43,220	17.8%	1,402
24. Film and Video Editors	$47,870	12.7%	2,707
25. Makeup Artists, Theatrical and Performance	$35,250	39.8%	392
26. Dispatchers, Except Police, Fire, and Ambulance	$33,140	1.5%	29,793
27. Photographers	$27,720	10.3%	16,100
28. Commercial and Industrial Designers	$56,550	7.2%	4,777
29. Camera Operators, Television, Video, and Motion Picture	$41,850	11.5%	3,496
30. Fashion Designers	$62,810	5.0%	1,968
31. Merchandise Displayers and Window Trimmers	$24,830	10.7%	9,103
32. Fine Artists, Including Painters, Sculptors, and Illustrators	$42,070	9.9%	3,830
33. Broadcast Technicians	$32,230	12.1%	2,955

Jobs 3 and 4 share 24,023 openings. Jobs 6, 7, 8, 9, and 10 share 8,992 openings. Jobs 16 and 17 share 8,597 openings.

Best Jobs for People Interested in Business and Administration

Job	Annual Earnings	Percent Growth	Annual Openings
1. Management Analysts	$71,150	21.9%	125,669
2. Accountants	$57,060	17.7%	134,463
3. Auditors	$57,060	17.7%	134,463
4. Training and Development Specialists	$49,630	18.3%	35,862
5. Employment Interviewers	$44,380	18.4%	33,588
6. Executive Secretaries and Administrative Assistants	$38,640	14.8%	235,314
7. Personnel Recruiters	$44,380	18.4%	33,588
8. Compensation, Benefits, and Job Analysis Specialists	$52,180	18.4%	18,761
9. Bookkeeping, Accounting, and Auditing Clerks	$31,560	12.5%	286,854
10. General and Operations Managers	$88,700	1.5%	112,072
11. Logisticians	$64,250	17.3%	9,671
12. First-Line Supervisors/Managers of Office and Administrative Support Workers	$44,650	5.8%	138,420
13. Administrative Services Managers	$70,990	11.7%	19,513
14. Meeting and Convention Planners	$43,530	19.9%	8,318
15. Training and Development Managers	$84,340	15.6%	3,759
16. Brokerage Clerks	$37,360	20.0%	10,826
17. Office Clerks, General	$24,460	12.6%	765,803
18. Compensation and Benefits Managers	$81,410	12.0%	6,121
19. Chief Executives	$145,600+	2.0%	21,209
20. Legal Secretaries	$38,810	11.7%	38,682
21. Medical Secretaries	$28,950	16.7%	60,659
22. First-Line Supervisors/Managers of Housekeeping and Janitorial Workers	$32,850	12.7%	30,613
23. Operations Research Analysts	$66,950	10.6%	5,727
24. Budget Analysts	$63,440	7.1%	6,423
25. Production, Planning, and Expediting Clerks	$39,690	4.2%	52,735
26. Billing, Cost, and Rate Clerks	$29,970	4.4%	81,885
27. Billing, Posting, and Calculating Machine Operators	$29,970	4.4%	81,885
28. Statement Clerks	$29,970	4.4%	81,885
29. Industrial Engineering Technicians	$47,490	9.9%	6,172
30. Human Resources Assistants, Except Payroll and Timekeeping	$34,970	11.3%	18,647
31. Shipping, Receiving, and Traffic Clerks	$26,990	3.7%	138,967
32. Secretaries, Except Legal, Medical, and Executive	$28,220	1.2%	239,630
33. Correspondence Clerks	$29,500	12.0%	4,334
34. Payroll and Timekeeping Clerks	$33,810	3.1%	18,544

Jobs 2 and 3 share 134,463 openings. Jobs 5 and 7 share 33,588 openings. Jobs 26, 27, and 28 share 81,885 openings.

Best Jobs for People Interested in Education and Training

Job	Annual Earnings	Percent Growth	Annual Openings
1. Health Specialties Teachers, Postsecondary	$80,700	22.9%	19,617
2. Business Teachers, Postsecondary	$64,900	22.9%	11,643
3. Biological Science Teachers, Postsecondary	$71,780	22.9%	9,039
4. Engineering Teachers, Postsecondary	$79,510	22.9%	5,565
5. Law Teachers, Postsecondary	$87,730	22.9%	2,169
6. Computer Science Teachers, Postsecondary	$62,020	22.9%	5,820
7. Economics Teachers, Postsecondary	$75,300	22.9%	2,208
8. Agricultural Sciences Teachers, Postsecondary	$78,460	22.9%	1,840
9. Art, Drama, and Music Teachers, Postsecondary	$55,190	22.9%	12,707
10. Mathematical Science Teachers, Postsecondary	$58,560	22.9%	7,663
11. Chemistry Teachers, Postsecondary	$63,870	22.9%	3,405
12. Psychology Teachers, Postsecondary	$60,610	22.9%	5,261
13. Physics Teachers, Postsecondary	$70,090	22.9%	2,155
14. Atmospheric, Earth, Marine, and Space Sciences Teachers, Postsecondary	$73,280	22.9%	1,553
15. Nursing Instructors and Teachers, Postsecondary	$57,500	22.9%	7,337
16. Education Teachers, Postsecondary	$54,220	22.9%	9,359
17. English Language and Literature Teachers, Postsecondary	$54,000	22.9%	10,475
18. History Teachers, Postsecondary	$59,160	22.9%	3,570
19. Preschool Teachers, Except Special Education	$23,130	26.3%	78,172
20. Fitness Trainers and Aerobics Instructors	$27,680	26.8%	51,235
21. Political Science Teachers, Postsecondary	$63,100	22.9%	2,435
22. Self-Enrichment Education Teachers	$34,580	23.1%	64,449
23. Architecture Teachers, Postsecondary	$68,540	22.9%	1,044
24. Education Administrators, Elementary and Secondary School	$80,580	7.6%	27,143
25. Vocational Education Teachers, Postsecondary	$45,850	22.9%	19,313
26. Sociology Teachers, Postsecondary	$58,160	22.9%	2,774
27. Education Administrators, Postsecondary	$75,780	14.2%	17,121
28. Philosophy and Religion Teachers, Postsecondary	$56,380	22.9%	3,120
29. Anthropology and Archeology Teachers, Postsecondary	$64,530	22.9%	910
30. Communications Teachers, Postsecondary	$54,720	22.9%	4,074
31. Health Educators	$42,920	26.2%	13,707
32. Graduate Teaching Assistants	$28,060	22.9%	20,601
33. Environmental Science Teachers, Postsecondary	$64,850	22.9%	769
34. Foreign Language and Literature Teachers, Postsecondary	$53,610	22.9%	4,317
35. Area, Ethnic, and Cultural Studies Teachers, Postsecondary	$59,150	22.9%	1,252
36. Forestry and Conservation Science Teachers, Postsecondary	$63,790	22.9%	454

(continued)

(continued)

Best Jobs for People Interested in Education and Training

Job	Annual Earnings	Percent Growth	Annual Openings
37. Recreation and Fitness Studies Teachers, Postsecondary	$52,170	22.9%	3,010
38. Education Administrators, Preschool and Child Care Center/Program	$38,580	23.5%	8,113
39. Geography Teachers, Postsecondary	$61,310	22.9%	697
40. Instructional Coordinators	$55,270	22.5%	21,294
41. Home Economics Teachers, Postsecondary	$58,170	22.9%	820
42. Social Work Teachers, Postsecondary	$56,240	22.9%	1,292
43. Criminal Justice and Law Enforcement Teachers, Postsecondary	$51,060	22.9%	1,911
44. Library Science Teachers, Postsecondary	$56,810	22.9%	702
45. Elementary School Teachers, Except Special Education	$47,330	13.6%	181,612
46. Educational, Vocational, and School Counselors	$49,450	12.6%	54,025
47. Curators	$46,000	23.3%	1,416
48. Special Education Teachers, Preschool, Kindergarten, and Elementary School	$48,350	19.6%	20,049
49. Middle School Teachers, Except Special and Vocational Education	$47,900	11.2%	75,270
50. Secondary School Teachers, Except Special and Vocational Education	$49,420	5.6%	93,166
51. Kindergarten Teachers, Except Special Education	$45,120	16.3%	27,603
52. Librarians	$50,970	3.6%	18,945
53. Teacher Assistants	$21,580	10.4%	193,986
54. Adult Literacy, Remedial Education, and GED Teachers and Instructors	$44,710	14.2%	17,340
55. Special Education Teachers, Middle School	$48,940	15.8%	8,846
56. Special Education Teachers, Secondary School	$49,640	8.5%	10,601
57. Library Technicians	$27,680	8.5%	29,075
58. Vocational Education Teachers, Secondary School	$50,090	−4.6%	7,639
59. Museum Technicians and Conservators	$35,350	15.9%	1,341
60. Archivists	$43,110	14.4%	795

Best Jobs for People Interested in Finance and Insurance

Job	Annual Earnings	Percent Growth	Annual Openings
1. Sales Agents, Financial Services	$68,430	24.8%	47,750
2. Sales Agents, Securities and Commodities	$68,430	24.8%	47,750

Best Jobs for People Interested in Finance and Insurance

Job	Annual Earnings	Percent Growth	Annual Openings
3. Financial Managers, Branch or Department	$95,310	12.6%	57,589
4. Treasurers and Controllers	$95,310	12.6%	57,589
5. Financial Analysts	$70,400	33.8%	29,317
6. Market Research Analysts	$60,300	20.1%	45,015
7. Personal Financial Advisors	$67,660	41.0%	17,114
8. Cost Estimators	$54,920	18.5%	38,379
9. Bill and Account Collectors	$29,990	22.9%	118,709
10. Insurance Sales Agents	$44,110	12.9%	64,162
11. Loan Officers	$53,000	11.5%	54,237
12. Tellers	$22,920	13.5%	146,077
13. Appraisers, Real Estate	$46,130	16.9%	6,493
14. Assessors	$46,130	16.9%	6,493
15. Claims Examiners, Property and Casualty Insurance	$53,560	8.9%	22,024
16. Insurance Adjusters, Examiners, and Investigators	$53,560	8.9%	22,024
17. Insurance Underwriters	$54,530	6.3%	6,880
18. Survey Researchers	$36,820	15.9%	4,959
19. Credit Analysts	$54,580	1.9%	3,180
20. Insurance Claims Clerks	$32,040	−1.3%	42,246
21. Insurance Policy Processing Clerks	$32,040	−1.3%	42,246
22. Insurance Appraisers, Auto Damage	$51,500	12.5%	1,030
23. Loan Interviewers and Clerks	$31,680	−0.9%	40,217

Jobs 1 and 2 share 47,750 openings. Jobs 3 and 4 share 57,589 openings. Jobs 13 and 14 share 6,493 openings. Jobs 15 and 16 share 22,024 openings. Jobs 20 and 21 share 42,246 openings.

Best Jobs for People Interested in Government and Public Administration

Job	Annual Earnings	Percent Growth	Annual Openings
1. Social and Community Service Managers	$54,530	24.7%	23,788
2. Immigration and Customs Inspectors	$59,930	17.3%	14,746
3. Aviation Inspectors	$51,440	16.4%	2,122
4. Construction and Building Inspectors	$48,330	18.2%	12,606
5. Financial Examiners	$66,670	10.7%	2,449
6. Freight and Cargo Inspectors	$51,440	16.4%	2,122
7. Transportation Vehicle, Equipment and Systems Inspectors, Except Aviation	$51,440	16.4%	2,122

(continued)

(continued)

Best Jobs for People Interested in Government and Public Administration

Job	Annual Earnings	Percent Growth	Annual Openings
8. Occupational Health and Safety Specialists	$60,140	8.1%	3,440
9. Court Reporters	$45,330	24.5%	2,620
10. Urban and Regional Planners	$57,970	14.5%	1,967
11. Environmental Compliance Inspectors	$48,400	4.9%	15,841
12. Equal Opportunity Representatives and Officers	$48,400	4.9%	15,841
13. Government Property Inspectors and Investigators	$48,400	4.9%	15,841
14. Licensing Examiners and Inspectors	$48,400	4.9%	15,841
15. Court Clerks	$32,330	8.8%	16,163
16. License Clerks	$32,330	8.8%	16,163
17. Municipal Clerks	$32,330	8.8%	16,163
18. Nuclear Monitoring Technicians	$66,140	6.7%	1,021
19. City and Regional Planning Aides	$35,870	12.4%	3,571
20. Fire Inspectors	$50,830	11.0%	644
21. Occupational Health and Safety Technicians	$44,020	14.6%	886
22. Tax Examiners, Collectors, and Revenue Agents	$46,920	2.1%	4,465

Job 2 shares 14,746 openings with another job not included in this list. Jobs 3, 6, and 7 share 2,122 openings. Job 11, 12, 13, and 14 share 15,841 openings with each other and with another job not included in this list. Jobs 15, 16, and 17 share 16,163 openings. Job 18 shares 1,021 openings with another job not included in this list. Job 19 shares 3,571 openings with another job not included in this list. Job 20 shares 644 openings with another job not included in this list.

Best Jobs for People Interested in Health Science

Job	Annual Earnings	Percent Growth	Annual Openings
1. Anesthesiologists	$145,600+	14.2%	38,027
2. Family and General Practitioners	$145,600+	14.2%	38,027
3. Internists, General	$145,600+	14.2%	38,027
4. Obstetricians and Gynecologists	$145,600+	14.2%	38,027
5. Psychiatrists	$145,600+	14.2%	38,027
6. Surgeons	$145,600+	14.2%	38,027
7. Registered Nurses	$60,010	23.5%	233,499
8. Pediatricians, General	$140,690	14.2%	38,027
9. Pharmacists	$100,480	21.7%	16,358
10. Physical Therapists	$69,760	27.1%	12,072
11. Medical Assistants	$27,430	35.4%	92,977
12. Dental Hygienists	$64,740	30.1%	10,433

Best Jobs for People Interested in Health Science

Job	Annual Earnings	Percent Growth	Annual Openings
13. Medical and Health Services Managers	$76,990	16.4%	31,877
14. Physician Assistants	$78,450	27.0%	7,147
15. Veterinarians	$75,230	35.0%	5,301
16. Pharmacy Technicians	$26,720	32.0%	54,453
17. Dental Assistants	$31,550	29.2%	29,482
18. Veterinary Technologists and Technicians	$27,970	41.0%	14,674
19. Occupational Therapists	$63,790	23.1%	8,338
20. Surgical Technologists	$37,540	24.5%	15,365
21. Physical Therapist Assistants	$44,130	32.4%	5,957
22. Medical Records and Health Information Technicians	$29,290	17.8%	39,048
23. Nursing Aides, Orderlies, and Attendants	$23,160	18.2%	321,036
24. Radiation Therapists	$70,010	24.8%	1,461
25. Radiologic Technicians	$50,260	15.1%	12,836
26. Radiologic Technologists	$50,260	15.1%	12,836
27. Licensed Practical and Licensed Vocational Nurses	$37,940	14.0%	70,610
28. Biological Technicians	$37,810	16.0%	15,374
29. Cardiovascular Technologists and Technicians	$44,940	25.5%	3,550
30. Respiratory Therapists	$50,070	22.6%	5,563
31. Occupational Therapist Assistants	$45,050	25.4%	2,634
32. Diagnostic Medical Sonographers	$59,860	19.1%	3,211
33. Chiropractors	$65,890	14.4%	3,179
34. Massage Therapists	$34,870	20.3%	9,193
35. Dentists, General	$137,630	9.2%	7,106
36. Medical and Clinical Laboratory Technologists	$51,720	12.4%	11,457
37. Speech-Language Pathologists	$60,690	10.6%	11,160
38. Athletic Trainers	$38,360	24.3%	1,669
39. Medical and Clinical Laboratory Technicians	$34,270	15.0%	10,866
40. Nuclear Medicine Technologists	$64,670	14.8%	1,290
41. Prosthodontists	$145,600+	10.7%	54
42. Orthodontists	$145,600+	9.2%	479
43. Optometrists	$93,800	11.3%	1,789
44. Animal Trainers	$26,190	22.7%	6,713
45. Medical Transcriptionists	$31,250	13.5%	18,080
46. Oral and Maxillofacial Surgeons	$145,600+	9.1%	400
47. Coroners	$48,400	4.9%	15,841
48. Physical Therapist Aides	$22,990	24.4%	4,092
49. Podiatrists	$110,510	9.5%	648

(continued)

(continued)

Best Jobs for People Interested in Health Science

Job	Annual Earnings	Percent Growth	Annual Openings
50. Medical Equipment Preparers	$27,040	14.2%	8,363
51. Embalmers	$36,800	14.3%	1,660
52. Orthotists and Prosthetists	$60,520	11.8%	295
53. Dietitians and Nutritionists	$49,010	8.6%	4,996
54. Audiologists	$59,440	9.8%	980

Jobs 1, 2, 3, 4, 5, 6 and 8 share 38,027 openings. Jobs 25 and 26 share 12,836 openings. Job 47 shares 15,841 openings with four other jobs not included in this list.

Best Jobs for People Interested in Hospitality, Tourism, and Recreation

Job	Annual Earnings	Percent Growth	Annual Openings
1. Gaming Managers	$64,410	24.4%	549
2. First-Line Supervisors/Managers of Personal Service Workers	$33,900	15.5%	37,555
3. Gaming Supervisors	$42,980	23.4%	4,602
4. Coaches and Scouts	$27,840	14.6%	51,100
5. First-Line Supervisors/Managers of Food Preparation and Serving Workers	$28,040	11.3%	154,175
6. Skin Care Specialists	$27,190	34.3%	6,643
7. Food Service Managers	$44,570	5.0%	59,302
8. Athletes and Sports Competitors	$38,440	19.2%	4,293
9. Flight Attendants	$61,120	10.6%	10,773
10. Hairdressers, Hairstylists, and Cosmetologists	$22,210	12.4%	73,030
11. Lodging Managers	$44,240	12.2%	5,529
12. Tour Guides and Escorts	$22,110	21.2%	15,027
13. Cooks, Restaurant	$21,220	11.5%	238,542
14. Recreation Workers	$21,220	12.7%	61,454
15. Cooks, Institution and Cafeteria	$21,340	10.8%	111,898
16. Chefs and Head Cooks	$37,160	7.6%	9,401
17. Concierges	$25,540	14.1%	4,893
18. Reservation and Transportation Ticket Agents and Travel Clerks	$29,820	1.1%	30,754
19. Umpires, Referees, and Other Sports Officials	$24,770	16.0%	4,461

Best Jobs for People Interested in Human Service

Job	Annual Earnings	Percent Growth	Annual Openings
1. Social and Human Service Assistants	$26,630	33.6%	80,142
2. Medical and Public Health Social Workers	$44,670	24.2%	16,429
3. Mental Health Counselors	$36,000	30.0%	24,103
4. Substance Abuse and Behavioral Disorder Counselors	$35,580	34.3%	20,821
5. Child, Family, and School Social Workers	$38,620	19.1%	35,402
6. Clergy	$40,460	18.9%	35,092
7. Mental Health and Substance Abuse Social Workers	$36,640	29.9%	17,289
8. Rehabilitation Counselors	$29,630	23.0%	32,081
9. Clinical Psychologists	$62,210	15.8%	8,309
10. Counseling Psychologists	$62,210	15.8%	8,309
11. Marriage and Family Therapists	$43,600	29.8%	5,953
12. Probation Officers and Correctional Treatment Specialists	$44,510	10.9%	18,335
13. Directors, Religious Activities and Education	$35,370	19.7%	11,463
14. Interviewers, Except Eligibility and Loan	$27,320	9.5%	54,060
15. Eligibility Interviewers, Government Programs	$39,110	3.1%	11,337
16. Residential Advisors	$23,050	18.5%	8,053

Jobs 9 and 10 share 8,309 openings with each other and with another job not included in this list.

Best Jobs for People Interested in Information Technology

Job	Annual Earnings	Percent Growth	Annual Openings
1. Computer Software Engineers, Applications	$83,130	44.6%	58,690
2. Computer Systems Analysts	$73,090	29.0%	63,166
3. Computer Software Engineers, Systems Software	$89,070	28.2%	33,139
4. Computer and Information Systems Managers	$108,070	16.4%	30,887
5. Network Systems and Data Communications Analysts	$68,220	53.4%	35,086
6. Computer Security Specialists	$64,690	27.0%	37,010
7. Network and Computer Systems Administrators	$64,690	27.0%	37,010
8. Computer and Information Scientists, Research	$97,970	21.5%	2,901
9. Computer Systems Engineers/Architects	$71,510	15.1%	14,374
10. Network Designers	$71,510	15.1%	14,374
11. Software Quality Assurance Engineers and Testers	$71,510	15.1%	14,374
12. Web Administrators	$71,510	15.1%	14,374
13. Web Developers	$71,510	15.1%	14,374

(continued)

(continued)

Best Jobs for People Interested in Information Technology

Job	Annual Earnings	Percent Growth	Annual Openings
14. Computer Support Specialists	$42,400	12.9%	97,334
15. Database Administrators	$67,250	28.6%	8,258
16. Computer Programmers	$68,080	–4.1%	27,937
17. Computer, Automated Teller, and Office Machine Repairers	$37,100	3.0%	22,330

Jobs 6 and 7 share 37,010 openings. Jobs 9, 10, 11, 12, and 13 share 14,374 openings.

Best Jobs for People Interested in Law and Public Safety

Job	Annual Earnings	Percent Growth	Annual Openings
1. Criminal Investigators and Special Agents	$59,930	17.3%	14,746
2. Police Detectives	$59,930	17.3%	14,746
3. Police Identification and Records Officers	$59,930	17.3%	14,746
4. Lawyers	$106,120	11.0%	49,445
5. Paralegals and Legal Assistants	$44,990	22.2%	22,756
6. Correctional Officers and Jailers	$36,970	16.9%	56,579
7. Emergency Medical Technicians and Paramedics	$28,400	19.2%	19,513
8. Security Guards	$22,570	16.9%	222,085
9. Forensic Science Technicians	$47,680	30.7%	3,074
10. Police Patrol Officers	$49,630	10.8%	37,842
11. Sheriffs and Deputy Sheriffs	$49,630	10.8%	37,842
12. First-Line Supervisors/Managers of Correctional Officers	$55,720	12.5%	4,180
13. Forest Fire Fighting and Prevention Supervisors	$65,040	11.5%	3,771
14. Municipal Fire Fighting and Prevention Supervisors	$65,040	11.5%	3,771
15. Private Detectives and Investigators	$37,640	18.2%	7,329
16. Forest Fire Fighters	$43,170	12.1%	18,887
17. Municipal Fire Fighters	$43,170	12.1%	18,887
18. Transportation Security Screeners	$28,240	12.6%	29,298
19. First-Line Supervisors/Managers of Police and Detectives	$72,620	9.2%	9,373
20. Gaming Surveillance Officers and Gaming Investigators	$27,440	33.6%	2,124
21. Judges, Magistrate Judges, and Magistrates	$107,230	5.1%	1,567
22. Emergency Management Specialists	$48,380	12.3%	1,538

Best Jobs for People Interested in Law and Public Safety

Job	Annual Earnings	Percent Growth	Annual Openings
23. Fire Investigators	$50,830	11.0%	644
24. Bailiffs	$36,900	11.2%	2,223
25. Arbitrators, Mediators, and Conciliators	$48,840	10.6%	546

Jobs 1, 2, and 3 share 14,746 openings with each other and with another job not included in this list. Jobs 10 and 11 share 37,842 openings. Jobs 13 and 14 share 3,771 openings. Jobs 16 and 17 share 18,887 openings. Job 23 shares 644 openings with another job not included in this list.

Best Jobs for People Interested in Manufacturing

Job	Annual Earnings	Percent Growth	Annual Openings
1. Automotive Master Mechanics	$34,170	14.3%	97,350
2. Automotive Specialty Technicians	$34,170	14.3%	97,350
3. Automotive Body and Related Repairers	$35,690	11.6%	37,469
4. First-Line Supervisors/Managers of Mechanics, Installers, and Repairers	$55,380	7.3%	24,361
5. Bus and Truck Mechanics and Diesel Engine Specialists	$38,640	11.5%	25,428
6. Aircraft Structure, Surfaces, Rigging, and Systems Assemblers	$45,420	12.8%	6,550
7. First-Line Supervisors/Managers of Helpers, Laborers, and Material Movers, Hand	$40,640	12.5%	13,877
8. Industrial Machinery Mechanics	$42,350	9.0%	23,361
9. Ship Engineers	$56,090	14.1%	1,102
10. First-Line Supervisors/Managers of Production and Operating Workers	$48,670	–4.8%	46,144
11. Aircraft Mechanics and Service Technicians	$49,010	10.6%	9,708
12. Medical Equipment Repairers	$40,320	21.7%	2,351
13. Mobile Heavy Equipment Mechanics, Except Engines	$41,450	12.3%	11,037
14. Water and Liquid Waste Treatment Plant and System Operators	$37,090	13.8%	9,575
15. Motorboat Mechanics	$34,210	19.0%	4,326
16. Locksmiths and Safe Repairers	$33,230	22.1%	3,545
17. Tire Repairers and Changers	$21,880	20.2%	18,829
18. Solderers and Brazers	$32,270	5.1%	61,125
19. Welders, Cutters, and Welder Fitters	$32,270	5.1%	61,125
20. Industrial Production Managers	$80,560	–5.9%	14,889

(continued)

(continued)

Best Jobs for People Interested in Manufacturing

Job	Annual Earnings	Percent Growth	Annual Openings
21. Nuclear Power Reactor Operators	$70,410	10.6%	233
22. Electrical and Electronics Repairers, Commercial and Industrial Equipment	$47,110	6.8%	6,607
23. Machinists	$35,230	–3.1%	39,505
24. Team Assemblers	$24,630	0.1%	264,135
25. Automotive Glass Installers and Repairers	$31,470	18.7%	3,457
26. Millwrights	$46,090	5.8%	4,758
27. Refuse and Recyclable Material Collectors	$29,420	7.4%	37,785
28. Recreational Vehicle Service Technicians	$31,760	18.2%	2,442
29. Slaughterers and Meat Packers	$22,500	12.7%	15,511
30. Bakers	$22,590	10.0%	31,442
31. Industrial Truck and Tractor Operators	$28,010	–2.0%	89,547
32. Food Batchmakers	$23,730	10.9%	15,704
33. Inspectors, Testers, Sorters, Samplers, and Weighers	$30,310	–7.0%	75,361
34. Maintenance Workers, Machinery	$35,590	–1.1%	15,055
35. Meat, Poultry, and Fish Cutters and Trimmers	$21,050	10.9%	17,920
36. Motorcycle Mechanics	$30,300	12.5%	3,564
37. Structural Metal Fabricators and Fitters	$31,030	–0.2%	20,746

Jobs 1 and 2 share 97,350 openings. Jobs 18 and 19 share 61,125 openings.

Best Jobs for People Interested in Retail and Wholesale Sales and Service

Job	Annual Earnings	Percent Growth	Annual Openings
1. Customer Service Representatives	$29,040	24.8%	600,937
2. Marketing Managers	$104,400	14.4%	20,189
3. Sales Managers	$94,910	10.2%	36,392
4. Sales Representatives, Wholesale and Manufacturing, Technical and Scientific Products	$68,270	12.4%	43,469
5. Property, Real Estate, and Community Association Managers	$43,670	15.1%	49,916
6. Receptionists and Information Clerks	$23,710	17.2%	334,124
7. Sales Representatives, Wholesale and Manufacturing, Except Technical and Scientific Products	$50,750	8.4%	156,215
8. Advertising Sales Agents	$42,820	20.3%	29,233

Best Jobs for People Interested in Retail and Wholesale Sales and Service

Job	Annual Earnings	Percent Growth	Annual Openings
9. Real Estate Sales Agents	$40,600	10.6%	61,232
10. First-Line Supervisors/Managers of Non-Retail Sales Workers	$67,020	3.7%	48,883
11. Real Estate Brokers	$58,860	11.1%	18,689
12. Sales Engineers	$80,270	8.5%	7,371
13. Demonstrators and Product Promoters	$22,570	18.0%	32,779
14. First-Line Supervisors/Managers of Retail Sales Workers	$34,470	4.2%	221,241
15. Funeral Directors	$50,370	12.5%	3,939
16. Purchasing Managers	$85,440	3.4%	7,243
17. Advertising and Promotions Managers	$78,250	6.2%	2,955
18. Purchasing Agents, Except Wholesale, Retail, and Farm Products	$52,460	0.1%	22,349
19. Parts Salespersons	$28,130	−2.2%	52,414
20. Wholesale and Retail Buyers, Except Farm Products	$46,960	−0.1%	19,847

Best Jobs for People Interested in Scientific Research, Engineering, and Mathematics

Job	Annual Earnings	Percent Growth	Annual Openings
1. Civil Engineers	$71,710	18.0%	15,979
2. Industrial Engineers	$71,430	20.3%	11,272
3. Actuaries	$85,690	23.7%	3,245
4. Natural Sciences Managers	$104,040	11.4%	3,661
5. Aerospace Engineers	$90,930	10.2%	6,498
6. Medical Scientists, Except Epidemiologists	$64,200	20.2%	10,596
7. Engineering Managers	$111,020	7.3%	7,404
8. Environmental Scientists and Specialists, Including Health	$58,380	25.1%	6,961
9. Geoscientists, Except Hydrologists and Geographers	$75,800	21.9%	2,471
10. School Psychologists	$62,210	15.8%	8,309
11. Biochemists and Biophysicists	$79,270	15.9%	1,637
12. Biomedical Engineers	$75,440	21.1%	1,804
13. Electrical Engineers	$79,240	6.3%	6,806
14. Industrial-Organizational Psychologists	$80,820	21.3%	118
15. Chemists	$63,490	9.1%	9,024
16. Mapping Technicians	$33,640	19.4%	8,299

(continued)

(continued)

Best Jobs for People Interested in Scientific Research, Engineering, and Mathematics

Job	Annual Earnings	Percent Growth	Annual Openings
17. Surveying Technicians	$33,640	19.4%	8,299
18. Computer Hardware Engineers	$91,860	4.6%	3,572
19. Mechanical Engineers	$72,300	4.2%	12,394
20. Chemical Engineers	$81,500	7.9%	2,111
21. Hydrologists	$68,140	24.3%	687
22. Cartographers and Photogrammetrists	$49,970	20.3%	2,823
23. Physicists	$96,850	6.8%	1,302
24. Electronics Engineers, Except Computer	$83,340	3.7%	5,699
25. Environmental Engineering Technicians	$40,690	24.8%	2,162
26. Atmospheric and Space Scientists	$78,390	10.6%	735
27. Economists	$80,220	7.5%	1,555
28. Mathematicians	$90,870	10.2%	473
29. Nuclear Engineers	$94,420	7.2%	1,046
30. Statisticians	$69,900	8.5%	3,433
31. Civil Engineering Technicians	$42,580	10.2%	7,499
32. Marine Architects	$76,200	10.9%	495
33. Marine Engineers	$76,200	10.9%	495
34. Microbiologists	$60,680	11.2%	1,306
35. Fire-Prevention and Protection Engineers	$69,580	9.6%	1,105
36. Industrial Safety and Health Engineers	$69,580	9.6%	1,105
37. Product Safety Engineers	$69,580	9.6%	1,105
38. Materials Scientists	$76,160	8.7%	1,039
39. Social Science Research Assistants	$35,870	12.4%	3,571
40. Electrical Engineering Technicians	$52,140	3.6%	12,583
41. Electronics Engineering Technicians	$52,140	3.6%	12,583
42. Astronomers	$99,020	5.6%	128
43. Epidemiologists	$60,010	13.6%	503
44. Mechanical Drafters	$44,740	5.2%	10,902
45. Materials Engineers	$77,170	4.0%	1,390
46. Political Scientists	$91,580	5.3%	318
47. Anthropologists	$53,080	15.0%	446
48. Archeologists	$53,080	15.0%	446
49. Aerospace Engineering and Operations Technicians	$54,930	10.4%	707
50. Mechanical Engineering Technicians	$47,280	6.4%	3,710
51. Electrical Drafters	$49,250	4.1%	4,786
52. Electronic Drafters	$49,250	4.1%	4,786

Best Jobs for People Interested in Scientific Research, Engineering, and Mathematics

Job	Annual Earnings	Percent Growth	Annual Openings
53. Chemical Technicians	$40,740	5.8%	4,010
54. Nuclear Equipment Operation Technicians	$66,140	6.7%	1,021
55. Sociologists	$61,140	10.0%	403

Job 10 shares 8,309 openings with another job not included in this list. Jobs 16 and 17 share 8,299 openings. Jobs 32 and 33 share 495 openings. Jobs 35, 36, and 37 share 1,105 openings. Job 39 shares 3,571 openings with another job not included in this list. Jobs 40 and 41 share 12,583 openings. Jobs 47 and 48 share 446 openings. Jobs 51 and 52 share 4,786 openings. Job 54 shares 1,021 openings with another job not included in this list.

Best Jobs for People Interested in Transportation, Distribution, and Logistics

Job	Annual Earnings	Percent Growth	Annual Openings
1. Airline Pilots, Copilots, and Flight Engineers	$145,600+	12.9%	4,073
2. Mates—Ship, Boat, and Barge	$57,210	17.9%	2,665
3. Pilots, Ship	$57,210	17.9%	2,665
4. Ship and Boat Captains	$57,210	17.9%	2,665
5. Cargo and Freight Agents	$37,060	16.5%	9,967
6. Truck Drivers, Heavy and Tractor-Trailer	$36,220	10.4%	279,032
7. Storage and Distribution Managers	$76,310	8.3%	6,994
8. Transportation Managers	$76,310	8.3%	6,994
9. Bus Drivers, Transit and Intercity	$33,160	12.5%	27,100
10. Commercial Pilots	$61,640	13.2%	1,425
11. First-Line Supervisors/Managers of Transportation and Material-Moving Machine and Vehicle Operators	$49,850	10.2%	16,580
12. Sailors and Marine Oilers	$32,570	15.7%	8,600
13. Aircraft Cargo Handling Supervisors	$37,760	23.3%	523
14. Railroad Conductors and Yardmasters	$58,650	9.1%	3,235
15. Ambulance Drivers and Attendants, Except Emergency Medical Technicians	$21,140	21.7%	3,703
16. Bus Drivers, School	$25,860	9.3%	59,809
17. Truck Drivers, Light or Delivery Services	$26,380	8.4%	154,330
18. Postal Service Mail Carriers	$44,500	1.0%	16,710
19. Laborers and Freight, Stock, and Material Movers, Hand	$21,900	2.1%	630,487
20. Subway and Streetcar Operators	$50,520	12.1%	587

Jobs 2, 3, and 4 share 2,665 openings. Jobs 7 and 8 share 6,994 openings.

Best Jobs Lists Based on Personality Types

These lists organize the 500 best jobs into groups matching six personality types. The personality types are Realistic, Investigative, Artistic, Social, Enterprising, and Conventional. This system was developed by John Holland and is used in the *Self-Directed Search (SDS)* and other career assessment inventories and information systems.

If you have used one of these career inventories or systems, the lists will help you identify jobs that most closely match these personality types. Even if you have not used one of these systems, the concept of personality types and the jobs that are related to them can help you identify jobs that suit the type of person you are.

As we did for the education levels, we have created only one list for each personality type. We've ranked the jobs within each personality type based on each one's total combined score for earnings, growth, and annual job openings. Each job is listed in its primary personality type, but you should be aware that most also are linked to one or two secondary personality types. Consider reviewing the jobs for more than one personality type so you don't overlook possible jobs that would interest you.

Descriptions of the Six Personality Types

Following are brief descriptions for each of the six personality types used in the lists. Select the two or three descriptions that most closely describe you and then use the lists to identify jobs that best fit these personality types.

- **Realistic:** These occupations frequently involve work activities that include practical, hands-on problems and solutions. They often deal with plants; animals; and real-world materials such as wood, tools, and machinery. Many of the occupations require working outside and don't involve a lot of paperwork or working closely with others.

- **Investigative:** These occupations frequently involve working with ideas and require an extensive amount of thinking. These occupations can involve searching for facts and figuring out problems mentally.

- **Artistic:** These occupations frequently involve working with forms, designs, and patterns. They often require self-expression, and the work can be done without following a clear set of rules.

- **Social:** These occupations frequently involve working with, communicating with, and teaching people. These occupations often involve helping or providing service to others.

- **Enterprising:** These occupations frequently involve starting up and carrying out projects. These occupations can involve leading people and making many decisions. They sometimes require risk taking and often deal with business.

- **Conventional:** These occupations frequently involve following set procedures and routines. These occupations can include working with data and details more than with ideas. Usually there is a clear line of authority to follow.

Best Jobs for People with a Realistic Personality Type

Job	Annual Earnings	Percent Growth	Annual Openings
1. Civil Engineers	$71,710	18.0%	15,979
2. Surveyors	$51,630	23.7%	14,305
3. Computer Support Specialists	$42,400	12.9%	97,334
4. Construction and Building Inspectors	$48,330	18.2%	12,606
5. Correctional Officers and Jailers	$36,970	16.9%	56,579
6. Radiologic Technicians	$50,260	15.1%	12,836
7. Radiologic Technologists	$50,260	15.1%	12,836
8. Surgical Technologists	$37,540	24.5%	15,365
9. Police Patrol Officers	$49,630	10.8%	37,842
10. Automotive Master Mechanics	$34,170	14.3%	97,350
11. Automotive Specialty Technicians	$34,170	14.3%	97,350
12. Pipe Fitters and Steamfitters	$44,090	10.6%	68,643
13. Plumbers	$44,090	10.6%	68,643
14. Cardiovascular Technologists and Technicians	$44,940	25.5%	3,550
15. Pilots, Ship	$57,210	17.9%	2,665
16. Forest Fire Fighters	$43,170	12.1%	18,887
17. Municipal Fire Fighters	$43,170	12.1%	18,887
18. Cartographers and Photogrammetrists	$49,970	20.3%	2,823
19. Biological Technicians	$37,810	16.0%	15,374
20. Airline Pilots, Copilots, and Flight Engineers	$145,600+	12.9%	4,073
21. Landscaping and Groundskeeping Workers	$22,240	18.1%	307,138
22. Construction Carpenters	$37,660	10.3%	223,225
23. Rough Carpenters	$37,660	10.3%	223,225
24. Roofers	$33,240	14.3%	38,398
25. Electricians	$44,780	7.4%	79,083
26. Security Guards	$22,570	16.9%	222,085
27. Truck Drivers, Heavy and Tractor-Trailer	$36,220	10.4%	279,032
28. Aviation Inspectors	$51,440	16.4%	2,122
29. Freight and Cargo Inspectors	$51,440	16.4%	2,122
30. Transportation Vehicle, Equipment and Systems Inspectors, Except Aviation	$51,440	16.4%	2,122
31. Bus and Truck Mechanics and Diesel Engine Specialists	$38,640	11.5%	25,428
32. Tile and Marble Setters	$38,720	15.4%	9,066
33. Aircraft Structure, Surfaces, Rigging, and Systems Assemblers	$45,420	12.8%	6,550
34. Athletes and Sports Competitors	$38,440	19.2%	4,293
35. Environmental Engineering Technicians	$40,690	24.8%	2,162
36. Automotive Body and Related Repairers	$35,690	11.6%	37,469

(continued)

(continued)

Best Jobs for People with a Realistic Personality Type

Job	Annual Earnings	Percent Growth	Annual Openings
37. Veterinary Technologists and Technicians	$27,970	41.0%	14,674
38. Painters, Construction and Maintenance	$32,080	11.8%	101,140
39. Mobile Heavy Equipment Mechanics, Except Engines	$41,450	12.3%	11,037
40. Audio and Video Equipment Technicians	$36,050	24.2%	4,681
41. Medical Equipment Repairers	$40,320	21.7%	2,351
42. Aircraft Mechanics and Service Technicians	$49,010	10.6%	9,708
43. Boilermakers	$50,700	14.0%	2,333
44. Commercial Pilots	$61,640	13.2%	1,425
45. Ship Engineers	$56,090	14.1%	1,102
46. Brickmasons and Blockmasons	$44,070	9.7%	17,569
47. Security and Fire Alarm Systems Installers	$35,390	20.2%	5,729
48. Surveying Technicians	$33,640	19.4%	8,299
49. Industrial Machinery Mechanics	$42,350	9.0%	23,361
50. Operating Engineers and Other Construction Equipment Operators	$38,130	8.4%	55,468
51. Bus Drivers, Transit and Intercity	$33,160	12.5%	27,100
52. Water and Liquid Waste Treatment Plant and System Operators	$37,090	13.8%	9,575
53. Cement Masons and Concrete Finishers	$33,840	11.4%	34,625
54. Medical and Clinical Laboratory Technicians	$34,270	15.0%	10,866
55. Construction Laborers	$27,310	10.9%	257,407
56. Heating and Air Conditioning Mechanics and Installers	$38,360	8.7%	29,719
57. Maintenance and Repair Workers, General	$32,570	10.1%	165,502
58. Refrigeration Mechanics and Installers	$38,360	8.7%	29,719
59. Tire Repairers and Changers	$21,880	20.2%	18,829
60. Motorboat Mechanics	$34,210	19.0%	4,326
61. Sheet Metal Workers	$39,210	6.7%	31,677
62. Transportation Security Screeners	$28,240	12.6%	29,298
63. Telecommunications Equipment Installers and Repairers, Except Line Installers	$54,070	2.5%	13,541
64. Cooks, Restaurant	$21,220	11.5%	238,542
65. Sailors and Marine Oilers	$32,570	15.7%	8,600
66. Commercial Divers	$41,610	17.7%	248
67. Electrical Engineering Technicians	$52,140	3.6%	12,583
68. Electronics Engineering Technicians	$52,140	3.6%	12,583
69. Locksmiths and Safe Repairers	$33,230	22.1%	3,545
70. Animal Trainers	$26,190	22.7%	6,713

Best Jobs for People with a Realistic Personality Type

Job	Annual Earnings	Percent Growth	Annual Openings
71. Subway and Streetcar Operators	$50,520	12.1%	587
72. Civil Drafters	$43,310	6.1%	16,238
73. Electrical Power-Line Installers and Repairers	$52,570	7.2%	6,401
74. Elevator Installers and Repairers	$68,000	8.8%	2,850
75. Civil Engineering Technicians	$42,580	10.2%	7,499
76. Helpers—Installation, Maintenance, and Repair Workers	$22,920	11.8%	52,058
77. Telecommunications Line Installers and Repairers	$47,220	4.6%	14,719
78. Drywall and Ceiling Tile Installers	$36,520	7.3%	30,945
79. Helpers—Carpenters	$24,340	11.7%	37,731
80. Nuclear Power Reactor Operators	$70,410	10.6%	233
81. Helpers—Pipelayers, Plumbers, Pipefitters, and Steamfitters	$25,350	11.9%	29,332
82. Camera Operators, Television, Video, and Motion Picture	$41,850	11.5%	3,496
83. Cooks, Institution and Cafeteria	$21,340	10.8%	111,898
84. Reinforcing Iron and Rebar Workers	$37,890	11.5%	4,502
85. Aerospace Engineering and Operations Technicians	$54,930	10.4%	707
86. Oral and Maxillofacial Surgeons	$145,600+	9.1%	400
87. Automotive Glass Installers and Repairers	$31,470	18.7%	3,457
88. Mechanical Drafters	$44,740	5.2%	10,902
89. Truck Drivers, Light or Delivery Services	$26,380	8.4%	154,330
90. Electrical and Electronics Repairers, Commercial and Industrial Equipment	$47,110	6.8%	6,607
91. Glaziers	$35,230	11.9%	6,416
92. Pest Control Workers	$29,030	15.5%	6,006
93. Embalmers	$36,800	14.3%	1,660
94. Gaming Surveillance Officers and Gaming Investigators	$27,440	33.6%	2,124
95. Highway Maintenance Workers	$32,600	8.9%	24,774
96. Recreational Vehicle Service Technicians	$31,760	18.2%	2,442
97. Bus Drivers, School	$25,860	9.3%	59,809
98. Tapers	$42,050	7.1%	9,026
99. Farmers and Ranchers	$33,360	−8.5%	129,552
100. Pesticide Handlers, Sprayers, and Applicators, Vegetation	$28,560	14.0%	7,443
101. Helpers—Brickmasons, Blockmasons, Stonemasons, and Tile and Marble Setters	$26,260	11.0%	22,500
102. Medical Equipment Preparers	$27,040	14.2%	8,363
103. Slaughterers and Meat Packers	$22,500	12.7%	15,511
104. Museum Technicians and Conservators	$35,350	15.9%	1,341
105. Solderers and Brazers	$32,270	5.1%	61,125

(continued)

(continued)

Best Jobs for People with a Realistic Personality Type

Job	Annual Earnings	Percent Growth	Annual Openings
106. Welders, Cutters, and Welder Fitters	$32,270	5.1%	61,125
107. Computer, Automated Teller, and Office Machine Repairers	$37,100	3.0%	22,330
108. Machinists	$35,230	–3.1%	39,505
109. Refuse and Recyclable Material Collectors	$29,420	7.4%	37,785
110. Geological Sample Test Technicians	$50,950	8.6%	1,895
111. Electrical Drafters	$49,250	4.1%	4,786
112. Millwrights	$46,090	5.8%	4,758
113. Ambulance Drivers and Attendants, Except Emergency Medical Technicians	$21,140	21.7%	3,703
114. Nuclear Equipment Operation Technicians	$66,140	6.7%	1,021
115. Nuclear Monitoring Technicians	$66,140	6.7%	1,021
116. Mechanical Engineering Technicians	$47,280	6.4%	3,710
117. Structural Iron and Steel Workers	$42,130	6.0%	6,969
118. Umpires, Referees, and Other Sports Officials	$24,770	16.0%	4,461
119. Bakers	$22,590	10.0%	31,442
120. Tree Trimmers and Pruners	$29,800	11.1%	9,621
121. Food Batchmakers	$23,730	10.9%	15,704
122. Team Assemblers	$24,630	0.1%	264,135
123. Bailiffs	$36,900	11.2%	2,223
124. Laborers and Freight, Stock, and Material Movers, Hand	$21,900	2.1%	630,487
125. Industrial Truck and Tractor Operators	$28,010	–2.0%	89,547
126. Insulation Workers, Mechanical	$36,570	8.6%	5,787
127. Meat, Poultry, and Fish Cutters and Trimmers	$21,050	10.9%	17,920
128. Motorcycle Mechanics	$30,300	12.5%	3,564
129. Broadcast Technicians	$32,230	12.1%	2,955
130. Helpers—Electricians	$24,880	6.8%	35,109
131. Hazardous Materials Removal Workers	$36,330	11.2%	1,933
132. Maintenance Workers, Machinery	$35,590	–1.1%	15,055
133. Plasterers and Stucco Masons	$36,430	8.1%	4,509
134. Excavating and Loading Machine and Dragline Operators	$34,050	8.3%	6,562
135. Pipelayers	$31,280	8.7%	8,902
136. Structural Metal Fabricators and Fitters	$31,030	–0.2%	20,746

Jobs 6 and 7 share 12,836 openings. Job 9 shares 37,842 openings with another job not included in this list. Jobs 10 and 11 share 97,350 openings. Jobs 12 and 13 share 68,643 openings. Job 15 shares 2,665 openings with two other jobs not included in this list. Jobs 16 and 17 share 18,887 openings. Jobs 22 and 23 share 223,225 openings. Jobs 28, 29, and 30 share 2,122 openings. Job 48 shares 8,299 openings with another job not included in this list. Jobs 56 and 58 share 29,719 openings. Jobs 67 and 68 share 12,583 openings. Job 72 shares 16,238 openings with another job not included in this list. Jobs 105 and 106 share 61,125 openings. Job 110 shares 1,895 openings with another job not included in this list. Job 111 shares 4,786 openings with another job not included in this list. Jobs 114 and 115 share 1,021 openings.

Best Jobs for People with an Investigative Personality Type

Job	Annual Earnings	Percent Growth	Annual Openings
1. Computer Software Engineers, Applications	$83,130	44.6%	58,690
2. Anesthesiologists	$145,600+	14.2%	38,027
3. Family and General Practitioners	$145,600+	14.2%	38,027
4. Internists, General	$145,600+	14.2%	38,027
5. Obstetricians and Gynecologists	$145,600+	14.2%	38,027
6. Psychiatrists	$145,600+	14.2%	38,027
7. Surgeons	$145,600+	14.2%	38,027
8. Computer Software Engineers, Systems Software	$89,070	28.2%	33,139
9. Pharmacists	$100,480	21.7%	16,358
10. Pediatricians, General	$140,690	14.2%	38,027
11. Computer Systems Analysts	$73,090	29.0%	63,166
12. Management Analysts	$71,150	21.9%	125,669
13. Network Systems and Data Communications Analysts	$68,220	53.4%	35,086
14. Computer and Information Scientists, Research	$97,970	21.5%	2,901
15. Engineering Teachers, Postsecondary	$79,510	22.9%	5,565
16. Network and Computer Systems Administrators	$64,690	27.0%	37,010
17. Veterinarians	$75,230	35.0%	5,301
18. Industrial Engineers	$71,430	20.3%	11,272
19. Environmental Engineers	$72,350	25.4%	5,003
20. Computer Systems Engineers/Architects	$71,510	15.1%	14,374
21. Market Research Analysts	$60,300	20.1%	45,015
22. Software Quality Assurance Engineers and Testers	$71,510	15.1%	14,374
23. Geoscientists, Except Hydrologists and Geographers	$75,800	21.9%	2,471
24. Dentists, General	$137,630	9.2%	7,106
25. Medical Scientists, Except Epidemiologists	$64,200	20.2%	10,596
26. Aerospace Engineers	$90,930	10.2%	6,498
27. Biochemists and Biophysicists	$79,270	15.9%	1,637
28. Biomedical Engineers	$75,440	21.1%	1,804
29. Environmental Scientists and Specialists, Including Health	$58,380	25.1%	6,961
30. Optometrists	$93,800	11.3%	1,789
31. Clinical Psychologists	$62,210	15.8%	8,309
32. School Psychologists	$62,210	15.8%	8,309
33. Environmental Science and Protection Technicians, Including Health	$39,370	28.0%	8,404
34. Industrial-Organizational Psychologists	$80,820	21.3%	118
35. Forensic Science Technicians	$47,680	30.7%	3,074
36. Hydrologists	$68,140	24.3%	687

(continued)

(continued)

Best Jobs for People with an Investigative Personality Type

Job	Annual Earnings	Percent Growth	Annual Openings
37. Diagnostic Medical Sonographers	$59,860	19.1%	3,211
38. Prosthodontists	$145,600+	10.7%	54
39. Electrical Engineers	$79,240	6.3%	6,806
40. Operations Research Analysts	$66,950	10.6%	5,727
41. Orthodontists	$145,600+	9.2%	479
42. Medical and Clinical Laboratory Technologists	$51,720	12.4%	11,457
43. Computer Hardware Engineers	$91,860	4.6%	3,572
44. Podiatrists	$110,510	9.5%	648
45. Electronics Engineers, Except Computer	$83,340	3.7%	5,699
46. Chemical Engineers	$81,500	7.9%	2,111
47. Mechanical Engineers	$72,300	4.2%	12,394
48. Nuclear Medicine Technologists	$64,670	14.8%	1,290
49. Physicists	$96,850	6.8%	1,302
50. Atmospheric and Space Scientists	$78,390	10.6%	735
51. Chemists	$63,490	9.1%	9,024
52. Survey Researchers	$36,820	15.9%	4,959
53. Mathematicians	$90,870	10.2%	473
54. Nuclear Engineers	$94,420	7.2%	1,046
55. Economists	$80,220	7.5%	1,555
56. Marine Architects	$76,200	10.9%	495
57. Marine Engineers	$76,200	10.9%	495
58. Urban and Regional Planners	$57,970	14.5%	1,967
59. Computer Programmers	$68,080	–4.1%	27,937
60. Petroleum Engineers	$103,960	5.2%	1,016
61. Microbiologists	$60,680	11.2%	1,306
62. Materials Scientists	$76,160	8.7%	1,039
63. Fire-Prevention and Protection Engineers	$69,580	9.6%	1,105
64. Industrial Safety and Health Engineers	$69,580	9.6%	1,105
65. Product Safety Engineers	$69,580	9.6%	1,105
66. Industrial Engineering Technicians	$47,490	9.9%	6,172
67. Materials Engineers	$77,170	4.0%	1,390
68. Mining and Geological Engineers, Including Mining Safety Engineers	$74,330	10.0%	456
69. Astronomers	$99,020	5.6%	128
70. Coroners	$48,400	4.9%	15,841
71. Occupational Health and Safety Specialists	$60,140	8.1%	3,440
72. Epidemiologists	$60,010	13.6%	503

Best Jobs for People with an Investigative Personality Type

Job	Annual Earnings	Percent Growth	Annual Openings
73. Political Scientists	$91,580	5.3%	318
74. Anthropologists	$53,080	15.0%	446
75. Archeologists	$53,080	15.0%	446
76. Dietitians and Nutritionists	$49,010	8.6%	4,996
77. Audiologists	$59,440	9.8%	980
78. Food Scientists and Technologists	$57,870	10.3%	663
79. Zoologists and Wildlife Biologists	$55,100	8.7%	1,444
80. Fire Investigators	$50,830	11.0%	644
81. Sociologists	$61,140	10.0%	403
82. Chemical Technicians	$40,740	5.8%	4,010
83. Agricultural Engineers	$67,710	8.6%	225
84. Soil and Plant Scientists	$58,000	8.4%	850

Jobs 2, 3, 4, 5, 6, 7, and 10 share 38,027 openings. Job 16 shares 37,010 openings with another job not included in this list. Jobs 20 and 22 share 14,374 openings with three other jobs not included in this list. Jobs 31 and 32 share 8,309 openings with each other and with another job not included in this list. Jobs 56 and 57 share 495 openings. Jobs 63, 64, and 65 share 1,105 openings. Job 70 shares 15,841 openings with four other jobs not included in this list. Jobs 74 and 75 share 446 openings. Job 80 shares 644 openings with another job not included in this list.

Best Jobs for People with an Artistic Personality Type

Job	Annual Earnings	Percent Growth	Annual Openings
1. Multi-Media Artists and Animators	$54,550	25.8%	13,182
2. Architects, Except Landscape and Naval	$67,620	17.7%	11,324
3. Poets, Lyricists, and Creative Writers	$50,660	12.8%	24,023
4. Technical Writers	$60,390	19.5%	7,498
5. Art Directors	$72,320	9.0%	9,719
6. Interior Designers	$43,970	19.5%	8,434
7. Landscape Architects	$57,580	16.4%	2,342
8. Graphic Designers	$41,280	9.8%	26,968
9. Editors	$48,320	2.3%	20,193
10. Hairdressers, Hairstylists, and Cosmetologists	$22,210	12.4%	73,030
11. Interpreters and Translators	$37,490	23.6%	6,630
12. Music Composers and Arrangers	$40,150	12.9%	8,597
13. Music Directors	$40,150	12.9%	8,597
14. Architectural Drafters	$43,310	6.1%	16,238
15. Film and Video Editors	$47,870	12.7%	2,707

(continued)

(continued)

Best Jobs for People with an Artistic Personality Type

Job	Annual Earnings	Percent Growth	Annual Openings
16. Set and Exhibit Designers	$43,220	17.8%	1,402
17. Commercial and Industrial Designers	$56,550	7.2%	4,777
18. Photographers	$27,720	10.3%	16,100
19. Makeup Artists, Theatrical and Performance	$35,250	39.8%	392
20. Fashion Designers	$62,810	5.0%	1,968
21. Merchandise Displayers and Window Trimmers	$24,830	10.7%	9,103
22. Fine Artists, Including Painters, Sculptors, and Illustrators	$42,070	9.9%	3,830

Job 3 shares 24,023 openings with another job not included in this list. Jobs 12 and 13 share 8,597 openings. Job 14 shares 16,238 openings with another job not included in this list.

Best Jobs for People with a Social Personality Type

Job	Annual Earnings	Percent Growth	Annual Openings
1. Registered Nurses	$60,010	23.5%	233,499
2. Health Specialties Teachers, Postsecondary	$80,700	22.9%	19,617
3. Physical Therapists	$69,760	27.1%	12,072
4. Dental Hygienists	$64,740	30.1%	10,433
5. Physician Assistants	$78,450	27.0%	7,147
6. Business Teachers, Postsecondary	$64,900	22.9%	11,643
7. Biological Science Teachers, Postsecondary	$71,780	22.9%	9,039
8. Occupational Therapists	$63,790	23.1%	8,338
9. Medical Assistants	$27,430	35.4%	92,977
10. Art, Drama, and Music Teachers, Postsecondary	$55,190	22.9%	12,707
11. Law Teachers, Postsecondary	$87,730	22.9%	2,169
12. Mental Health Counselors	$36,000	30.0%	24,103
13. Substance Abuse and Behavioral Disorder Counselors	$35,580	34.3%	20,821
14. Economics Teachers, Postsecondary	$75,300	22.9%	2,208
15. Agricultural Sciences Teachers, Postsecondary	$78,460	22.9%	1,840
16. Computer Science Teachers, Postsecondary	$62,020	22.9%	5,820
17. Radiation Therapists	$70,010	24.8%	1,461
18. Mathematical Science Teachers, Postsecondary	$58,560	22.9%	7,663
19. Preschool Teachers, Except Special Education	$23,130	26.3%	78,172
20. Chemistry Teachers, Postsecondary	$63,870	22.9%	3,405
21. English Language and Literature Teachers, Postsecondary	$54,000	22.9%	10,475

Best Jobs for People with a Social Personality Type

Job	Annual Earnings	Percent Growth	Annual Openings
22. Fitness Trainers and Aerobics Instructors	$27,680	26.8%	51,235
23. Physics Teachers, Postsecondary	$70,090	22.9%	2,155
24. Education Teachers, Postsecondary	$54,220	22.9%	9,359
25. Atmospheric, Earth, Marine, and Space Sciences Teachers, Postsecondary	$73,280	22.9%	1,553
26. Psychology Teachers, Postsecondary	$60,610	22.9%	5,261
27. Self-Enrichment Education Teachers	$34,580	23.1%	64,449
28. Vocational Education Teachers, Postsecondary	$45,850	22.9%	19,313
29. Mental Health and Substance Abuse Social Workers	$36,640	29.9%	17,289
30. Nursing Instructors and Teachers, Postsecondary	$57,500	22.9%	7,337
31. Medical and Public Health Social Workers	$44,670	24.2%	16,429
32. Health Educators	$42,920	26.2%	13,707
33. Political Science Teachers, Postsecondary	$63,100	22.9%	2,435
34. History Teachers, Postsecondary	$59,160	22.9%	3,570
35. Architecture Teachers, Postsecondary	$68,540	22.9%	1,044
36. Instructional Coordinators	$55,270	22.5%	21,294
37. Rehabilitation Counselors	$29,630	23.0%	32,081
38. Physical Therapist Assistants	$44,130	32.4%	5,957
39. Anthropology and Archeology Teachers, Postsecondary	$64,530	22.9%	910
40. Environmental Science Teachers, Postsecondary	$64,850	22.9%	769
41. Sociology Teachers, Postsecondary	$58,160	22.9%	2,774
42. Communications Teachers, Postsecondary	$54,720	22.9%	4,074
43. Philosophy and Religion Teachers, Postsecondary	$56,380	22.9%	3,120
44. Foreign Language and Literature Teachers, Postsecondary	$53,610	22.9%	4,317
45. Graduate Teaching Assistants	$28,060	22.9%	20,601
46. Marriage and Family Therapists	$43,600	29.8%	5,953
47. Training and Development Specialists	$49,630	18.3%	35,862
48. Forestry and Conservation Science Teachers, Postsecondary	$63,790	22.9%	454
49. Area, Ethnic, and Cultural Studies Teachers, Postsecondary	$59,150	22.9%	1,252
50. Geography Teachers, Postsecondary	$61,310	22.9%	697
51. Recreation and Fitness Studies Teachers, Postsecondary	$52,170	22.9%	3,010
52. Education Administrators, Preschool and Child Care Center/Program	$38,580	23.5%	8,113
53. Elementary School Teachers, Except Special Education	$47,330	13.6%	181,612
54. Counseling Psychologists	$62,210	15.8%	8,309
55. Home Economics Teachers, Postsecondary	$58,170	22.9%	820
56. Educational, Vocational, and School Counselors	$49,450	12.6%	54,025

(continued)

(continued)

Best Jobs for People with a Social Personality Type

Job	Annual Earnings	Percent Growth	Annual Openings
57. Social Work Teachers, Postsecondary	$56,240	22.9%	1,292
58. Special Education Teachers, Preschool, Kindergarten, and Elementary School	$48,350	19.6%	20,049
59. Criminal Justice and Law Enforcement Teachers, Postsecondary	$51,060	22.9%	1,911
60. Occupational Therapist Assistants	$45,050	25.4%	2,634
61. Secondary School Teachers, Except Special and Vocational Education	$49,420	5.6%	93,166
62. Library Science Teachers, Postsecondary	$56,810	22.9%	702
63. Middle School Teachers, Except Special and Vocational Education	$47,900	11.2%	75,270
64. Kindergarten Teachers, Except Special Education	$45,120	16.3%	27,603
65. Speech-Language Pathologists	$60,690	10.6%	11,160
66. Child, Family, and School Social Workers	$38,620	19.1%	35,402
67. Clergy	$40,460	18.9%	35,092
68. Chiropractors	$65,890	14.4%	3,179
69. Nursing Aides, Orderlies, and Attendants	$23,160	18.2%	321,036
70. Licensed Practical and Licensed Vocational Nurses	$37,940	14.0%	70,610
71. Respiratory Therapists	$50,070	22.6%	5,563
72. Adult Literacy, Remedial Education, and GED Teachers and Instructors	$44,710	14.2%	17,340
73. Athletic Trainers	$38,360	24.3%	1,669
74. Physical Therapist Aides	$22,990	24.4%	4,092
75. Coaches and Scouts	$27,840	14.6%	51,100
76. Special Education Teachers, Middle School	$48,940	15.8%	8,846
77. Emergency Medical Technicians and Paramedics	$28,400	19.2%	19,513
78. Equal Opportunity Representatives and Officers	$48,400	4.9%	15,841
79. Probation Officers and Correctional Treatment Specialists	$44,510	10.9%	18,335
80. Special Education Teachers, Secondary School	$49,640	8.5%	10,601
81. Teacher Assistants	$21,580	10.4%	193,986
82. Recreation Workers	$21,220	12.7%	61,454
83. Massage Therapists	$34,870	20.3%	9,193
84. Tour Guides and Escorts	$22,110	21.2%	15,027
85. Vocational Education Teachers, Secondary School	$50,090	–4.6%	7,639
86. Eligibility Interviewers, Government Programs	$39,110	3.1%	11,337
87. Orthotists and Prosthetists	$60,520	11.8%	295
88. Residential Advisors	$23,050	18.5%	8,053

Best Jobs for People with a Social Personality Type

Job	Annual Earnings	Percent Growth	Annual Openings
89. Emergency Management Specialists	$48,380	12.3%	1,538
90. Concierges	$25,540	14.1%	4,893
91. Arbitrators, Mediators, and Conciliators	$48,840	10.6%	546

Job 54 shares 8,309 openings with two other jobs not included in this list. Job 78 shares 15,841 openings with four other jobs not included in this list.

Best Jobs for People with an Enterprising Personality Type

Job	Annual Earnings	Percent Growth	Annual Openings
1. Sales Agents, Financial Services	$68,430	24.8%	47,750
2. Sales Agents, Securities and Commodities	$68,430	24.8%	47,750
3. Financial Managers, Branch or Department	$95,310	12.6%	57,589
4. Computer and Information Systems Managers	$108,070	16.4%	30,887
5. Construction Managers	$76,230	15.7%	44,158
6. Medical and Health Services Managers	$76,990	16.4%	31,877
7. Lawyers	$106,120	11.0%	49,445
8. Marketing Managers	$104,400	14.4%	20,189
9. Personal Financial Advisors	$67,660	41.0%	17,114
10. Customer Service Representatives	$29,040	24.8%	600,937
11. Sales Representatives, Wholesale and Manufacturing, Technical and Scientific Products	$68,270	12.4%	43,469
12. Public Relations Specialists	$49,800	17.6%	51,216
13. Social and Community Service Managers	$54,530	24.7%	23,788
14. Sales Managers	$94,910	10.2%	36,392
15. General and Operations Managers	$88,700	1.5%	112,072
16. Education Administrators, Postsecondary	$75,780	14.2%	17,121
17. Employment Interviewers	$44,380	18.4%	33,588
18. Personnel Recruiters	$44,380	18.4%	33,588
19. Public Relations Managers	$86,470	16.9%	5,781
20. Administrative Services Managers	$70,990	11.7%	19,513
21. Logisticians	$64,250	17.3%	9,671
22. Insurance Sales Agents	$44,110	12.9%	64,162
23. Criminal Investigators and Special Agents	$59,930	17.3%	14,746
24. Police Detectives	$59,930	17.3%	14,746
25. Advertising Sales Agents	$42,820	20.3%	29,233

(continued)

(continued)

Best Jobs for People with an Enterprising Personality Type

Job	Annual Earnings	Percent Growth	Annual Openings
26. Property, Real Estate, and Community Association Managers	$43,670	15.1%	49,916
27. Chief Executives	$145,600+	2.0%	21,209
28. Education Administrators, Elementary and Secondary School	$80,580	7.6%	27,143
29. First-Line Supervisors/Managers of Construction Trades and Extraction Workers	$55,950	9.1%	82,923
30. Training and Development Managers	$84,340	15.6%	3,759
31. Copy Writers	$50,660	12.8%	24,023
32. First-Line Supervisors/Managers of Non-Retail Sales Workers	$67,020	3.7%	48,883
33. Compensation and Benefits Managers	$81,410	12.0%	6,121
34. Gaming Managers	$64,410	24.4%	549
35. Demonstrators and Product Promoters	$22,570	18.0%	32,779
36. Natural Sciences Managers	$104,040	11.4%	3,661
37. Real Estate Brokers	$58,860	11.1%	18,689
38. First-Line Supervisors/Managers of Landscaping, Lawn Service, and Groundskeeping Workers	$38,720	17.6%	18,956
39. First-Line Supervisors/Managers of Personal Service Workers	$33,900	15.5%	37,555
40. Engineering Managers	$111,020	7.3%	7,404
41. Sheriffs and Deputy Sheriffs	$49,630	10.8%	37,842
42. First-Line Supervisors/Managers of Food Preparation and Serving Workers	$28,040	11.3%	154,175
43. Real Estate Sales Agents	$40,600	10.6%	61,232
44. Directors—Stage, Motion Pictures, Television, and Radio	$61,090	11.1%	8,992
45. First-Line Supervisors/Managers of Police and Detectives	$72,620	9.2%	9,373
46. Producers	$61,090	11.1%	8,992
47. Program Directors	$61,090	11.1%	8,992
48. Talent Directors	$61,090	11.1%	8,992
49. Technical Directors/Managers	$61,090	11.1%	8,992
50. Directors, Religious Activities and Education	$35,370	19.7%	11,463
51. First-Line Supervisors/Managers of Office and Administrative Support Workers	$44,650	5.8%	138,420
52. Meeting and Convention Planners	$43,530	19.9%	8,318
53. Flight Attendants	$61,120	10.6%	10,773
54. Mates—Ship, Boat, and Barge	$57,210	17.9%	2,665
55. Sales Engineers	$80,270	8.5%	7,371
56. Ship and Boat Captains	$57,210	17.9%	2,665
57. Air Traffic Controllers	$112,930	10.2%	1,213

Best Jobs for People with an Enterprising Personality Type

Job	Annual Earnings	Percent Growth	Annual Openings
58. First-Line Supervisors/Managers of Housekeeping and Janitorial Workers	$32,850	12.7%	30,613
59. Food Service Managers	$44,570	5.0%	59,302
60. Industrial Production Managers	$80,560	–5.9%	14,889
61. Gaming Supervisors	$42,980	23.4%	4,602
62. Storage and Distribution Managers	$76,310	8.3%	6,994
63. Transportation Managers	$76,310	8.3%	6,994
64. First-Line Supervisors/Managers of Mechanics, Installers, and Repairers	$55,380	7.3%	24,361
65. Forest Fire Fighting and Prevention Supervisors	$65,040	11.5%	3,771
66. Municipal Fire Fighting and Prevention Supervisors	$65,040	11.5%	3,771
67. Appraisers, Real Estate	$46,130	16.9%	6,493
68. Purchasing Managers	$85,440	3.4%	7,243
69. Skin Care Specialists	$27,190	34.3%	6,643
70. Private Detectives and Investigators	$37,640	18.2%	7,329
71. Curators	$46,000	23.3%	1,416
72. First-Line Supervisors/Managers of Correctional Officers	$55,720	12.5%	4,180
73. First-Line Supervisors/Managers of Retail Sales Workers	$34,470	4.2%	221,241
74. First-Line Supervisors/Managers of Helpers, Laborers, and Material Movers, Hand	$40,640	12.5%	13,877
75. First-Line Supervisors/Managers of Transportation and Material-Moving Machine and Vehicle Operators	$49,850	10.2%	16,580
76. Judges, Magistrate Judges, and Magistrates	$107,230	5.1%	1,567
77. First-Line Supervisors/Managers of Production and Operating Workers	$48,670	–4.8%	46,144
78. Agents and Business Managers of Artists, Performers, and Athletes	$66,440	9.6%	3,940
79. Funeral Directors	$50,370	12.5%	3,939
80. Financial Examiners	$66,670	10.7%	2,449
81. Advertising and Promotions Managers	$78,250	6.2%	2,955
82. Aircraft Cargo Handling Supervisors	$37,760	23.3%	523
83. Aquacultural Managers	$53,720	1.1%	18,101
84. Crop and Livestock Managers	$53,720	1.1%	18,101
85. Nursery and Greenhouse Managers	$53,720	1.1%	18,101
86. Lodging Managers	$44,240	12.2%	5,529
87. Parts Salespersons	$28,130	–2.2%	52,414

(continued)

(continued)

Best Jobs for People with an Enterprising Personality Type

Job	Annual Earnings	Percent Growth	Annual Openings
88. Wholesale and Retail Buyers, Except Farm Products	$46,960	–0.1%	19,847
89. Railroad Conductors and Yardmasters	$58,650	9.1%	3,235
90. Chefs and Head Cooks	$37,160	7.6%	9,401

Jobs 1 and 2 share 47,750 openings. Job 3 shares 57,589 openings with another job not included in this list. Jobs 17 and 18 share 33,588 openings. Jobs 23 and 24 share 14,746 openings with each other and with two other jobs not included in this list. Job 31 shares 24,023 openings with another job not included in this list. Job 41 shares 37,842 openings with another job not included in this list. Jobs 44, 46, 47, 48, and 49 share 8,992 openings. Jobs 54 and 56 share 2,665 openings with each other and with another job not included in this list. Jobs 62 and 63 share 6,994 openings. Jobs 65 and 66 share 3,771 openings. Job 67 shares 6,493 openings with another job not included in this list. Jobs 83, 84, and 85 share 18,101 openings.

Best Jobs for People with a Conventional Personality Type

Job	Annual Earnings	Percent Growth	Annual Openings
1. Accountants	$57,060	17.7%	134,463
2. Auditors	$57,060	17.7%	134,463
3. Financial Analysts	$70,400	33.8%	29,317
4. Computer Security Specialists	$64,690	27.0%	37,010
5. Treasurers and Controllers	$95,310	12.6%	57,589
6. Cost Estimators	$54,920	18.5%	38,379
7. Database Administrators	$67,250	28.6%	8,258
8. Executive Secretaries and Administrative Assistants	$38,640	14.8%	235,314
9. Compensation, Benefits, and Job Analysis Specialists	$52,180	18.4%	18,761
10. Actuaries	$85,690	23.7%	3,245
11. Paralegals and Legal Assistants	$44,990	22.2%	22,756
12. Bill and Account Collectors	$29,990	22.9%	118,709
13. Immigration and Customs Inspectors	$59,930	17.3%	14,746
14. Loan Officers	$53,000	11.5%	54,237
15. Network Designers	$71,510	15.1%	14,374
16. Police Identification and Records Officers	$59,930	17.3%	14,746
17. Web Administrators	$71,510	15.1%	14,374
18. Web Developers	$71,510	15.1%	14,374
19. Sales Representatives, Wholesale and Manufacturing, Except Technical and Scientific Products	$50,750	8.4%	156,215
20. Social and Human Service Assistants	$26,630	33.6%	80,142
21. Dental Assistants	$31,550	29.2%	29,482

Best Jobs for People with a Conventional Personality Type

Job	Annual Earnings	Percent Growth	Annual Openings
22. Bookkeeping, Accounting, and Auditing Clerks	$31,560	12.5%	286,854
23. Pharmacy Technicians	$26,720	32.0%	54,453
24. Receptionists and Information Clerks	$23,710	17.2%	334,124
25. Claims Examiners, Property and Casualty Insurance	$53,560	8.9%	22,024
26. Insurance Adjusters, Examiners, and Investigators	$53,560	8.9%	22,024
27. Legal Secretaries	$38,810	11.7%	38,682
28. Medical Secretaries	$28,950	16.7%	60,659
29. Medical Records and Health Information Technicians	$29,290	17.8%	39,048
30. Office Clerks, General	$24,460	12.6%	765,803
31. Brokerage Clerks	$37,360	20.0%	10,826
32. Court Reporters	$45,330	24.5%	2,620
33. Tellers	$22,920	13.5%	146,077
34. Assessors	$46,130	16.9%	6,493
35. Mapping Technicians	$33,640	19.4%	8,299
36. Production, Planning, and Expediting Clerks	$39,690	4.2%	52,735
37. Cargo and Freight Agents	$37,060	16.5%	9,967
38. Police, Fire, and Ambulance Dispatchers	$32,660	13.6%	17,628
39. Budget Analysts	$63,440	7.1%	6,423
40. Statisticians	$69,900	8.5%	3,433
41. Librarians	$50,970	3.6%	18,945
42. Human Resources Assistants, Except Payroll and Timekeeping	$34,970	11.3%	18,647
43. Purchasing Agents, Except Wholesale, Retail, and Farm Products	$52,460	0.1%	22,349
44. Insurance Appraisers, Auto Damage	$51,500	12.5%	1,030
45. Billing, Cost, and Rate Clerks	$29,970	4.4%	81,885
46. Billing, Posting, and Calculating Machine Operators	$29,970	4.4%	81,885
47. Insurance Underwriters	$54,530	6.3%	6,880
48. Medical Transcriptionists	$31,250	13.5%	18,080
49. Statement Clerks	$29,970	4.4%	81,885
50. Environmental Compliance Inspectors	$48,400	4.9%	15,841
51. Government Property Inspectors and Investigators	$48,400	4.9%	15,841
52. Licensing Examiners and Inspectors	$48,400	4.9%	15,841
53. Interviewers, Except Eligibility and Loan	$27,320	9.5%	54,060
54. Occupational Health and Safety Technicians	$44,020	14.6%	886
55. Archivists	$43,110	14.4%	795
56. Secretaries, Except Legal, Medical, and Executive	$28,220	1.2%	239,630

(continued)

(continued)

Best Jobs for People with a Conventional Personality Type			
Job	Annual Earnings	Percent Growth	Annual Openings
57. Court Clerks	$32,330	8.8%	16,163
58. License Clerks	$32,330	8.8%	16,163
59. Municipal Clerks	$32,330	8.8%	16,163
60. Shipping, Receiving, and Traffic Clerks	$26,990	3.7%	138,967
61. Fire Inspectors	$50,830	11.0%	644
62. City and Regional Planning Aides	$35,870	12.4%	3,571
63. Geophysical Data Technicians	$50,950	8.6%	1,895
64. Social Science Research Assistants	$35,870	12.4%	3,571
65. Dispatchers, Except Police, Fire, and Ambulance	$33,140	1.5%	29,793
66. Insurance Claims Clerks	$32,040	−1.3%	42,246
67. Insurance Policy Processing Clerks	$32,040	−1.3%	42,246
68. Inspectors, Testers, Sorters, Samplers, and Weighers	$30,310	−7.0%	75,361
69. Postal Service Mail Carriers	$44,500	1.0%	16,710
70. Credit Analysts	$54,580	1.9%	3,180
71. Electronic Drafters	$49,250	4.1%	4,786
72. Library Technicians	$27,680	8.5%	29,075
73. Loan Interviewers and Clerks	$31,680	−0.9%	40,217
74. Payroll and Timekeeping Clerks	$33,810	3.1%	18,544
75. Tax Examiners, Collectors, and Revenue Agents	$46,920	2.1%	4,465
76. Reservation and Transportation Ticket Agents and Travel Clerks	$29,820	1.1%	30,754
77. Correspondence Clerks	$29,500	12.0%	4,334

Jobs 1 and 2 share 134,463 openings. Job 4 shares 37,010 openings with another job not included in this list. Job 5 shares 57,589 openings with another job not included in this list. Jobs 13 and 16 share 14,746 openings with each other and with two other jobs not included in this list. Jobs 15, 17, and 18 share 14,374 openings with each other and with two other jobs not included in this list. Jobs 25 and 26 share 22,024 openings. Job 34 shares 6,493 openings with another job not included in this list. Job 35 shares 8,299 openings with another job not included in this list. Jobs 45, 46, and 49 share 81,885 openings. Jobs 50, 51, and 52 share 15,841 openings with each other and with two other jobs not included in this list. Jobs 57, 58, and 59 share 16,163 openings. Job 61 shares 644 openings with another job not included in this list. Jobs 62 and 64 share 3,571 openings. Job 63 shares 1,895 openings with another job not included in this list. Jobs 66 and 67 share 42,246 openings. Job 71 shares 4,786 openings with another job not included in this list.

Bonus Lists: Jobs with the Greatest Changes in Outlook Since the Previous Edition

The previous edition of this book, which came out in 2006, used job-growth figures from the Bureau of Labor Statistics (BLS) that were projected for the period from 2002 to 2012.

Since that edition was prepared, BLS has updated its projections twice, based on the latest economic data and improvements to their forecasting models. Some jobs now are expected to have much better job growth than was previously projected; for other jobs, expectations for job growth have been scaled back.

We thought you might be interested in seeing which 25 jobs had the greatest *increases* and greatest *decreases* in job-growth projection, so we compiled the following two lists. We based the lists on those 342 jobs that were included in the best 500 jobs in both editions.

Jobs with the Greatest Increase in Job-Growth Projection

Job	Projected Job Growth 2002–2012	Projected Job Growth 2006–2016	Change in Forecast
1. Financial Analysts	18.7%	33.8%	15.1%
2. Farmers and Ranchers	–20.6%	–8.5%	12.1%
3. Gaming Managers	12.4%	24.4%	12.0%
4. Forensic Science Technicians	18.9%	30.7%	11.8%
5. Court Reporters	12.7%	24.5%	11.8%
6. Sales Agents, Financial Services	13.0%	24.8%	11.8%
7. Sales Agents, Securities and Commodities	13.0%	24.8%	11.8%
8. Substance Abuse and Behavioral Disorder Counselors	23.3%	34.3%	11.0%
9. Civil Engineers	8.0%	18.0%	10.0%
10. Multi-Media Artists and Animators	15.8%	25.8%	10.0%
11. Veterinarians	25.1%	35.0%	9.9%
12. Industrial Engineers	10.6%	20.3%	9.7%
13. Bookkeeping, Accounting, and Auditing Clerks	3.0%	12.5%	9.5%
14. Actuaries	14.9%	23.7%	8.8%
15. Real Estate Brokers	2.4%	11.1%	8.7%
16. Aviation Inspectors	7.7%	16.4%	8.7%
17. Gaming Supervisors	15.7%	23.4%	7.7%
18. Marriage and Family Therapists	22.4%	29.8%	7.4%
19. Advertising Sales Agents	13.4%	20.3%	6.9%
20. Medical Equipment Repairers	14.8%	21.7%	6.9%
21. Prosthodontists	4.1%	10.7%	6.6%
22. Personal Financial Advisors	34.6%	41.0%	6.4%
23. Curators	17.0%	23.3%	6.3%
24. Executive Secretaries and Administrative Assistants	8.7%	14.8%	6.1%
25. First-Line Supervisors/Managers of Personal Service Workers	9.4%	15.5%	6.1%

Jobs with the Greatest Decrease in Job-Growth Projection

Job	Projected Job Growth 2002–2012	Projected Job Growth 2006–2016	Change in Forecast
1. Hazardous Materials Removal Workers	43.1%	11.2%	–31.9%
2. Medical Records and Health Information Technicians	46.8%	17.8%	–29.0%
3. Medical Assistants	58.9%	35.4%	–23.5%
4. Physical Therapist Aides	46.4%	24.4%	–22.0%
5. Physician Assistants	48.9%	27.0%	–21.9%
6. Special Education Teachers, Secondary School	30.0%	8.5%	–21.5%
7. Sales Managers	30.5%	10.2%	–20.3%
8. Computer and Information Systems Managers	36.1%	16.4%	–19.7%
9. Audiologists	29.0%	9.8%	–19.2%
10. Epidemiologists	32.5%	13.6%	–18.9%
11. Advertising and Promotions Managers	25.0%	6.2%	–18.8%
12. Computer Programmers	14.6%	–4.1%	–18.7%
13. Interviewers, Except Eligibility and Loan	28.0%	9.5%	–18.5%
14. Agents and Business Managers of Artists, Performers, and Athletes	27.8%	9.6%	–18.2%
15. Survey Researchers	33.6%	15.9%	–17.7%
16. Fitness Trainers and Aerobics Instructors	44.5%	26.8%	–17.7%
17. Computer Support Specialists	30.3%	12.9%	–17.4%
18. Computer Software Engineers, Systems Software	45.5%	28.2%	–17.3%
19. Self-Enrichment Education Teachers	40.1%	23.1%	–17.0%
20. General and Operations Managers	18.4%	1.5%	–16.9%
21. Credit Analysts	18.7%	1.9%	–16.8%
22. Speech-Language Pathologists	27.2%	10.6%	–16.6%
23. Electricians	23.4%	7.4%	–16.0%
24. Emergency Management Specialists	28.2%	12.3%	–15.9%
25. Database Administrators	44.2%	28.6%	–15.6%

PART II

The Job Descriptions

This part of the book provides descriptions for all the jobs included in the lists in Part I. The introduction gives more details on how to use and interpret the job descriptions, but here is some additional information:

* Job descriptions are arranged in alphabetical order by job title. This approach allows you to quickly find a description if you know its correct title from one of the lists in Part I.

* If you are using this section to browse for interesting options, we suggest you begin with the table of contents. Part I features many interesting lists that will help you identify job titles to explore in more detail. If you have not browsed the lists in Part I, consider spending some time there. The lists are interesting and will help you identify job titles you can find described in the material that follows. The job titles in Part II are also listed in the table of contents.

Accountants

- ❋ Education/Training Required: Bachelor's degree
- ❋ Annual Earnings: $57,060
- ❋ Beginning Wage: $35,570
- ❋ Earnings Growth Potential: Medium
- ❋ Growth: 17.7%
- ❋ Annual Job Openings: 134,463
- ❋ Self-Employed: 9.5%
- ❋ Part-Time: 9.3%

The job openings listed here are shared with Auditors.

Analyze financial information and prepare financial reports to determine or maintain record of assets, liabilities, profit and loss, tax liability, or other financial activities within an organization. Prepare, examine, or analyze accounting records, financial statements, or other financial reports to assess accuracy, completeness, and conformance to reporting and procedural standards. Compute taxes owed and prepare tax returns, ensuring compliance with payment, reporting, or other tax requirements. Analyze business operations, trends, costs, revenues, financial commitments, and obligations to project future revenues and expenses or to provide advice. Report to management regarding the finances of establishment. Establish tables of accounts and assign entries to proper accounts. Develop, maintain, and analyze budgets, preparing periodic reports that compare budgeted costs to actual costs. Develop, implement, modify, and document recordkeeping and accounting systems, making use of current computer technology. Prepare forms and manuals for accounting and bookkeeping personnel and direct their work activities. Survey operations to ascertain accounting needs and to recommend, develop, or maintain solutions to business and financial problems. Work as Internal Revenue Service (IRS) agents. Advise management about issues such as resource utilization, tax strategies, and the assumptions underlying budget forecasts. Provide internal and external auditing services for businesses or individuals. Advise clients in areas such as compensation, employee health-care benefits, the design of accounting or data processing systems, or long-range tax or estate plans. Investigate bankruptcies and other complex financial transactions and prepare reports summarizing the findings. Represent clients before taxing authorities and provide support during litigation involving financial issues. Appraise, evaluate, and inventory real property and equipment, recording information such as the description, value, and location of property.

Maintain or examine the records of government agencies. Serve as bankruptcy trustees or business valuators.

Personality Type: Conventional. These occupations frequently involve following set procedures and routines and can include working with data and details more than with ideas. Usually there is a clear line of authority to follow.

GOE—Interest Area/Cluster: 04. Business and Administration. **Work Group:** 04.05. Accounting, Auditing, and Analytical Support. **Other Jobs in This Work Group:** Accountants and Auditors; Auditors; Budget Analysts; Industrial Engineering Technicians; Logisticians; Management Analysts; Operations Research Analysts.

Skills—Management of Financial Resources: Determining how money will be spent to get the work done and accounting for these expenditures. **Systems Analysis:** Determining how a system should work and how changes will affect outcomes. **Systems Evaluation:** Looking at many indicators of system performance and taking into account their accuracy. **Operations Analysis:** Analyzing needs and product requirements to create a design. **Judgment and Decision Making:** Weighing the relative costs and benefits of a potential action. **Programming:** Writing computer programs for various purposes. **Mathematics:** Using mathematics to solve problems. **Time Management:** Managing one's own time and the time of others.

Education and Training Programs: Accounting; Accounting and Business/Management; Accounting and Computer Science; Accounting and Finance. **Related Knowledge/Courses—Economics and Accounting:** Economic and accounting principles and practices, the financial markets, banking, and the analysis and reporting of financial data. **Clerical Practices:** Administrative and clerical procedures and systems such as word-processing systems, filing and records management systems, stenography and transcription, forms, design principles, and other office procedures and terminology. **Mathematics:** Numbers and their operations and interrelationships, including arithmetic, algebra, geometry, calculus, and statistics and their applications. **Law and Government:** Laws, legal codes, court procedures, precedents, government regulations, executive orders, agency rules, and the democratic political process. **Computers and Electronics:** Electric circuit boards, processors, chips, and computer hardware and software, including applications and programming. **Personnel and Human Resources:** Principles and procedures for personnel recruitment; selection; training; compensation and benefits; labor relations and negotiation; and personnel information systems.

Work Environment: Indoors; sitting.

Actuaries

* Education/Training Required: Work experience plus degree
* Annual Earnings: $85,690
* Beginning Wage: $48,750
* Earnings Growth Potential: High
* Growth: 23.7%
* Annual Job Openings: 3,245
* Self-Employed: 0.0%
* Part-Time: 5.9%

Analyze statistical data, such as mortality, accident, sickness, disability, and retirement rates, and construct probability tables to forecast risk and liability for payment of future benefits. May ascertain premium rates required and cash reserves necessary to ensure payment of future benefits. Ascertain premium rates required and cash reserves and liabilities necessary to ensure payment of future benefits. Analyze statistical information to estimate mortality, accident, sickness, disability, and retirement rates. Design, review, and help administer insurance, annuity, and pension plans, determining financial soundness and calculating premiums. Collaborate with programmers, underwriters, accountants, claims experts, and senior management to help companies develop plans for new lines of business or for improving existing business. Determine or help determine company policy and explain complex technical matters to company executives, government officials, shareholders, policyholders, or the public. Testify before public agencies on proposed legislation affecting businesses. Provide advice to clients on a contract basis, working as a consultant. Testify in court as expert witness or to provide legal evidence on matters such as the value of potential lifetime earnings of a person who is disabled or killed in an accident. Construct probability tables for events such as fires, natural disasters, and unemployment, based on analysis of statistical data and other pertinent information. Determine policy contract provisions for each type of insurance. Manage credit and help price corporate security offerings. Provide expertise to help financial institutions manage risks and maximize returns associated with investment products or credit offerings. Determine equitable basis for distributing surplus earnings under participating insurance and annuity contracts in mutual companies. Explain changes in contract provisions to customers.

Personality Type: Conventional. These occupations frequently involve following set procedures and routines and can include working with data and details more than with ideas. Usually there is a clear line of authority to follow.

GOE—Interest Area/Cluster: 15. Scientific Research, Engineering, and Mathematics. **Work Group:** 15.06. Mathematics and Data Analysis. **Other Jobs in This Work Group:** Mathematical Technicians; Mathematicians; Social Science Research Assistants; Statistical Assistants; Statisticians.

Skills—Programming: Writing computer programs for various purposes. **Mathematics:** Using mathematics to solve problems. **Operations Analysis:** Analyzing needs and product requirements to create a design. **Complex Problem Solving:** Identifying complex problems, reviewing the options, and implementing solutions. **Active Learning:** Working with new material or information to grasp its implications. **Quality Control Analysis:** Evaluating the quality or performance of products, services, or processes. **Troubleshooting:** Determining what is causing an operating error and deciding what to do about it. **Critical Thinking:** Using logic and analysis to identify the strengths and weaknesses of different approaches.

Education and Training Program: Actuarial Science. **Related Knowledge/Courses—Mathematics:** Numbers and their operations and interrelationships, including arithmetic, algebra, geometry, calculus, and statistics and their applications. **Economics and Accounting:** Economic and accounting principles and practices, the financial markets, banking, and the analysis and reporting of financial data. **Sales and Marketing:** Principles and methods involved in showing, promoting, and selling products or services. This includes marketing strategies and tactics, product demonstration and sales techniques, and sales control systems. **Computers and Electronics:** Electric circuit boards, processors, chips, and computer hardware and software, including applications and programming. **Personnel and Human Resources:** Principles and procedures for personnel recruitment; selection; training; compensation and benefits; labor relations and negotiation; and personnel information systems. **Law and Government:** Laws, legal codes, court procedures, precedents, government regulations, executive orders, agency rules, and the democratic political process.

Work Environment: Indoors; sitting; using hands on objects, tools, or controls; repetitive motions.

Administrative Services Managers

* Education/Training Required: Work experience plus degree
* Annual Earnings: $70,990
* Beginning Wage: $36,000
* Earnings Growth Potential: High
* Growth: 11.7%
* Annual Job Openings: 19,513
* Self-Employed: 0.6%
* Part-Time: 4.7%

Plan, direct, or coordinate supportive services of an organization, such as recordkeeping, mail distribution, telephone operator/receptionist, and other office support services. May oversee facilities planning and maintenance and custodial operations. Monitor the facility to ensure that it remains safe, secure, and well-maintained. Direct or coordinate the supportive services department of a business, agency, or organization. Set goals and deadlines for the department. Prepare and review operational reports and schedules to ensure accuracy and efficiency. Analyze internal processes and recommend and implement procedural or policy changes to improve operations such as supply changes or the disposal of records. Acquire, distribute, and store supplies. Plan, administer, and control budgets for contracts, equipment, and supplies. Oversee construction and renovation projects to improve efficiency and to ensure that facilities meet environmental, health, and security standards and comply with government regulations. Hire and terminate clerical and administrative personnel. Oversee the maintenance and repair of machinery, equipment, and electrical and mechanical systems. Manage leasing of facility space. Participate in architectural and engineering planning and design, including space and installation management. Conduct classes to teach procedures to staff. Dispose of, or oversee the disposal of, surplus or unclaimed property.

Personality Type: Enterprising. These occupations frequently involve starting up and carrying out projects and can involve leading people and making many decisions. They sometimes require risk taking and often deal with business.

GOE—Interest Area/Cluster: 04. Business and Administration. **Work Group:** 04.02. Managerial Work in Business Detail. **Other Jobs in This Work Group:** First-Line Supervisors/Managers of Housekeeping and Janitorial Workers; First-Line Supervisors/Managers of Office and Administrative Support Workers; Meeting and Convention Planners.

Skills—Management of Financial Resources: Determining how money will be spent to get the work done and accounting for these expenditures. **Management of Personnel Resources:** Motivating, developing, and directing people as they work; identifying the best people for the job. **Programming:** Writing computer programs for various purposes. **Service Orientation:** Actively looking for ways to help people. **Coordination:** Adjusting actions in relation to others' actions. **Monitoring:** Assessing how well one is doing when learning or doing something. **Writing:** Communicating effectively with others in writing as indicated by the needs of the audience. **Speaking:** Talking to others to effectively convey information.

Education and Training Programs: Business Administration and Management, General; Business/Commerce, General; Medical/Health Management and Clinical Assistant/Specialist Training; Public Administration; Purchasing, Procurement/Acquisitions, and Contracts Management; Transportation/Transportation Management. **Related Knowledge/Courses—Personnel and Human Resources:** Principles and procedures for personnel recruitment; selection; training; compensation and benefits; labor relations and negotiation; and personnel information systems. **Clerical Practices:** Administrative and clerical procedures and systems such as word-processing systems, filing and records management systems, stenography and transcription, forms, design principles, and other office procedures and terminology. **Economics and Accounting:** Economic and accounting principles and practices, the financial markets, banking, and the analysis and reporting of financial data. **Administration and Management:** Principles and processes involved in business and organizational planning, coordination, and execution. This includes strategic planning, resource allocation, manpower modeling, leadership techniques, and production methods. **Customer and Personal Service:** Principles and processes for providing customer and personal services, including needs assessment techniques, quality service standards, alternative delivery systems, and customer satisfaction evaluation techniques. **Law and Government:** Laws, legal codes, court procedures, precedents, government regulations, executive orders, agency rules, and the democratic political process.

Work Environment: Indoors; more often standing than sitting.

Adult Literacy, Remedial Education, and GED Teachers and Instructors

- ✸ Education/Training Required: Bachelor's degree
- ✸ Annual Earnings: $44,710
- ✸ Beginning Wage: $25,310
- ✸ Earnings Growth Potential: High
- ✸ Growth: 14.2%
- ✸ Annual Job Openings: 17,340
- ✸ Self-Employed: 0.0%
- ✸ Part-Time: 41.3%

Teach or instruct out-of-school youths and adults in remedial education classes, preparatory classes for the General Educational Development test, literacy, or English as a Second Language. Teaching may or may not take place in a traditional educational institution. Adapt teaching methods and instructional materials to meet students' varying needs, abilities, and interests. Observe and evaluate students' work to determine progress and make suggestions for improvement. Instruct students individually and in groups, using various teaching methods such as lectures, discussions, and demonstrations. Plan and conduct activities for a balanced program of instruction, demonstration, and work time that provides students with opportunities to observe, question, and investigate. Maintain accurate and complete student records as required by laws or administrative policies. Prepare materials and classrooms for class activities. Establish clear objectives for all lessons, units, and projects and communicate those objectives to students. Conduct classes, workshops, and demonstrations to teach principles, techniques, or methods in subjects such as basic English language skills, life skills, and workforce entry skills. Prepare students for further education by encouraging them to explore learning opportunities and to persevere with challenging tasks. Establish and enforce rules for behavior and procedures for maintaining order among the students for whom they are responsible. Provide information, guidance, and preparation for the General Equivalency Diploma (GED) examination. Assign and grade classwork and homework. Observe students to determine qualifications, limitations, abilities, interests, and other individual characteristics. Register, orient, and assess new students according to standards and procedures. Prepare and implement remedial programs for students requiring extra help. Prepare and administer written, oral, and performance tests and issue grades in accordance with performance. Use computers, audiovisual aids, and other equipment and materials to supplement presentations. Prepare objectives and outlines for courses of study, following curriculum guidelines or requirements of states and schools. Guide and counsel students with adjustment or academic problems or special academic interests. Enforce administration policies and rules governing students.

Personality Type: Social. These occupations frequently involve working with, communicating with, and teaching people and often involve helping or providing service to others.

GOE—Interest Area/Cluster: 05. Education and Training. **Work Group:** 05.03. Postsecondary and Adult Teaching and Instructing. **Other Jobs in This Work Group:** Agricultural Sciences Teachers, Postsecondary; Anthropology and Archeology Teachers, Postsecondary; Architecture Teachers, Postsecondary; Area, Ethnic, and Cultural Studies Teachers, Postsecondary; Art, Drama, and Music Teachers, Postsecondary; Atmospheric, Earth, Marine, and Space Sciences Teachers, Postsecondary; Biological Science Teachers, Postsecondary; Business Teachers, Postsecondary; Chemistry Teachers, Postsecondary; Communications Teachers, Postsecondary; Computer Science Teachers, Postsecondary; Criminal Justice and Law Enforcement Teachers, Postsecondary; Economics Teachers, Postsecondary; Education Teachers, Postsecondary; Engineering Teachers, Postsecondary; English Language and Literature Teachers, Postsecondary; Environmental Science Teachers, Postsecondary; Farm and Home Management Advisors; Foreign Language and Literature Teachers, Postsecondary; Forestry and Conservation Science Teachers, Postsecondary; Geography Teachers, Postsecondary; Graduate Teaching Assistants; Health Specialties Teachers, Postsecondary; History Teachers, Postsecondary; Home Economics Teachers, Postsecondary; Law Teachers, Postsecondary; Library Science Teachers, Postsecondary; Mathematical Science Teachers, Postsecondary; Nursing Instructors and Teachers, Postsecondary; Philosophy and Religion Teachers, Postsecondary; Physics Teachers, Postsecondary; Political Science Teachers, Postsecondary; Psychology Teachers, Postsecondary; Recreation and Fitness Studies Teachers, Postsecondary; Self-Enrichment Education Teachers; Social Work Teachers, Postsecondary; Sociology Teachers, Postsecondary; Vocational Education Teachers, Postsecondary.

Skills—Instructing: Teaching others how to do something. **Learning Strategies:** Using multiple approaches when learning or teaching new things. **Social Perceptiveness:** Being aware of others' reactions and understanding why they react the way they do. **Service Orientation:** Actively looking for ways to help people. **Monitoring:** Assessing how well one is doing when learning or doing something. **Speaking:** Talking to others to effectively convey information. **Persuasion:** Persuading others to approach things differently. **Writing:** Communicating effectively with others in writing as indicated by the needs of the audience.

Education and Training Programs: Adult and Continuing Education and Teaching; Adult Literacy Tutor/Instructor Training; Bilingual and Multilingual Education; Linguistics of ASL and Other Sign Languages; Multicultural Education; Teaching English as a Second or Foreign Language/ESL Language Instructor Training; Teaching French as a Second or Foreign Language. **Related Knowledge/Courses—History and Archeology:** Historical events and their causes, indicators, and impact on particular civilizations and cultures. **Sociology and Anthropology:** Group behavior and dynamics; societal trends and influences; and cultures and their history, migrations, ethnicity, and origins. **Therapy and Counseling:** Information and techniques needed to rehabilitate physical and mental ailments and to provide career guidance, including alternative treatments, rehabilitation equipment and its proper use, and methods to evaluate treatment effects. **Geography:** Various methods for describing the location and distribution of land, sea, and air masses, including their physical locations, relationships, and characteristics. **Education and Training:** Instructional methods and training techniques, including curriculum design principles, learning theory, group and individual teaching techniques, design of individual development plans, and test design principles. **English Language:** The structure and content of the English language, including the meaning and spelling of words, rules of composition, and grammar.

Work Environment: Indoors; more often standing than sitting.

Advertising and Promotions Managers

- ❋ Education/Training Required: Work experience plus degree
- ❋ Annual Earnings: $78,250
- ❋ Beginning Wage: $38,400
- ❋ Earnings Growth Potential: Very high
- ❋ Growth: 6.2%
- ❋ Annual Job Openings: 2,955
- ❋ Self-Employed: 13.4%
- ❋ Part-Time: 4.8%

Plan and direct advertising policies and programs or produce collateral materials, such as posters, contests, coupons, or giveaways, to create extra interest in the purchase of a product or service for a department, for an entire organization, or on an account basis. Prepare budgets and submit estimates for program costs as part of campaign plan development. Plan and prepare advertising and promotional material to increase sales of products or services, working with customers, company officials, sales departments, and advertising agencies. Assist with annual budget development. Inspect layouts and advertising copy and edit scripts, audiotapes and videotapes, and other promotional material for adherence to specifications. Coordinate activities of departments, such as sales, graphic arts, media, finance, and research. Prepare and negotiate advertising and sales contracts. Identify and develop contacts for promotional campaigns and industry programs that meet identified buyer targets, such as dealers, distributors, or consumers. Gather and organize information to plan advertising campaigns. Confer with department heads or staff to discuss topics such as contracts, selection of advertising media, or product to be advertised. Confer with clients to provide marketing or technical advice. Monitor and analyze sales promotion results to determine cost-effectiveness of promotion campaigns. Read trade journals and professional literature to stay informed on trends, innovations, and changes that affect media planning. Formulate plans to extend business with established accounts and to transact business as agent for advertising accounts. Provide presentation and product demonstration support during the introduction of new products and services to field staff and customers. Direct, motivate, and monitor the mobilization of a campaign team to advance campaign goals. Plan and execute advertising policies and strategies for organizations. Track program budgets and expenses and campaign response rates to evaluate each campaign based on program objectives and industry norms. Assemble and communicate with a strong, diverse coalition of organizations or public figures, securing their cooperation, support, and action to further campaign goals. Train and direct workers engaged in developing and producing advertisements. Coordinate with the media to disseminate advertising.

Personality Type: Enterprising. These occupations frequently involve starting up and carrying out projects and can involve leading people and making many decisions. They sometimes require risk taking and often deal with business.

GOE—Interest Area/Cluster: 14. Retail and Wholesale Sales and Service. **Work Group:** 14.01. Managerial Work in Retail/Wholesale Sales and Service. **Other Jobs in This Work Group:** First-Line Supervisors/Managers of Non-Retail Sales Workers; First-Line Supervisors/Managers of Retail Sales Workers; Funeral Directors; Marketing Managers; Property, Real Estate, and Community Association Managers; Purchasing Managers; Sales Managers.

Skills—Management of Financial Resources: Determining how money will be spent to get the work done and accounting for these expenditures. **Service Orientation:** Actively looking for ways to help people. **Persuasion:** Persuading others to approach things differently. **Negotiation:** Bringing others together and trying to reconcile differences. **Time Management:** Managing one's own time and the time of others. **Coordination:** Adjusting actions in relation to others' actions. **Management of Personnel Resources:** Motivating, developing, and directing people as they work; identifying the best people for the job. **Judgment and Decision Making:** Weighing the relative costs and benefits of a potential action.

Education and Training Programs: Advertising; Marketing/Marketing Management, General; Public Relations/Image Management. **Related Knowledge/Courses—Sales and Marketing:** Principles and methods involved in showing, promoting, and selling products or services. This includes marketing strategies and tactics, product demonstration and sales techniques, and sales control systems. **Fine Arts:** Theory and techniques required to produce, compose, and perform works of music, dance, visual arts, drama, and sculpture. **Design:** Design techniques, principles, tools, and instruments involved in the production and use of precision technical plans, blueprints, drawings, and models. **Production and Processing:** Inputs, outputs, raw materials, waste, quality control, costs, and techniques for maximizing the manufacture and distribution of goods. **Communications and Media:** Media production, communication, and dissemination techniques and methods, including alternative ways to inform and entertain via written, oral, and visual media. **Clerical Practices:** Administrative and clerical procedures and systems such as word-processing systems, filing and records management systems, stenography and transcription, forms, design principles, and other office procedures and terminology.

Work Environment: Sitting; repetitive motions.

Advertising Sales Agents

- ❋ Education/Training Required: Moderate-term on-the-job training
- ❋ Annual Earnings: $42,820
- ❋ Beginning Wage: $22,390
- ❋ Earnings Growth Potential: High
- ❋ Growth: 20.3%
- ❋ Annual Job Openings: 29,233
- ❋ Self-Employed: 5.6%
- ❋ Part-Time: 10.2%

Sell or solicit advertising, including graphic art, advertising space in publications, custom-made signs, or TV and radio advertising time. May obtain leases for outdoor advertising sites or persuade retailer to use sales promotion display items. Prepare and deliver sales presentations to new and existing customers to sell new advertising programs and to protect and increase existing advertising. Explain to customers how specific types of advertising will help promote their products or services in the most effective way possible. Maintain assigned account bases while developing new accounts. Process all correspondence and paperwork related to accounts. Deliver advertising or illustration proofs to customers for approval. Draw up contracts for advertising work and collect payments due. Locate and contact potential clients to offer advertising services. Provide clients with estimates of the costs of advertising products or services. Recommend appropriate sizes and formats for advertising, depending on medium being used. Inform customers of available options for advertisement artwork and provide samples. Obtain and study information about clients' products, needs, problems, advertising history, and business practices to offer effective sales presentations and appropriate product assistance. Determine advertising medium to be used and prepare sample advertisements within the selected medium for presentation to customers. Consult with company officials, sales departments, and advertising agencies to develop promotional plans. Prepare promotional plans, sales literature, media kits, and sales contracts, using computer. Identify new advertising markets and propose products to serve them. Write copy as part of layout. Attend sales meetings, industry trade shows, and training seminars to gather information, promote products, expand network of contacts, and increase knowledge. Gather all relevant material for bid processes and coordinate bidding and contract approval. Arrange for commercial taping sessions and accompany clients to sessions. Write sales outlines for use by staff.

Personality Type: Enterprising. These occupations frequently involve starting up and carrying out projects and can involve leading people and making many decisions. They sometimes require risk taking and often deal with business.

GOE—Interest Area/Cluster: 14. Retail and Wholesale Sales and Service. **Work Group:** 14.03. General Sales. **Other Jobs in This Work Group:** Insurance Sales Agents; Personal Financial Advisors; Sales Agents, Financial Services; Sales Agents, Securities and Commodities.

Skills—Negotiation: Bringing others together and trying to reconcile differences. **Management of Financial Resources:** Determining how money will be spent to get the work done and accounting for these expenditures. **Persuasion:** Persuading others to approach things differently. **Speaking:** Talking to others to effectively convey information. **Social Perceptiveness:** Being aware of others' reactions and understanding why they react the way they do. **Complex Problem Solving:** Identifying complex problems, reviewing the options, and implementing solutions. **Writing:** Communicating effectively with others in writing as indicated by the needs of the audience. **Service Orientation:** Actively looking for ways to help people.

Education and Training Program: Advertising. **Related Knowledge/Courses—Sales and Marketing:** Principles and methods involved in showing, promoting, and selling products or services. This includes marketing strategies and tactics, product demonstration and sales techniques, and sales control systems. **Economics and Accounting:** Economic and accounting principles and practices, the financial markets, banking, and the analysis and reporting of financial data. **Communications and Media:** Media production, communication, and dissemination techniques and methods, including alternative ways to inform and entertain via written, oral, and visual media. **Customer and Personal Service:** Principles and processes for providing customer and personal services, including needs assessment techniques, quality service standards, alternative delivery systems, and customer satisfaction evaluation techniques. **English Language:** The structure and content of the English language, including the meaning and spelling of words, rules of composition, and grammar. **Transportation:** Principles and methods for moving people or goods by air, rail, sea, or road, including their relative costs, advantages, and limitations.

Work Environment: More often outdoors than indoors; standing.

Aerospace Engineering and Operations Technicians

- ❋ Education/Training Required: Associate degree
- ❋ Annual Earnings: $54,930
- ❋ Beginning Wage: $38,330
- ❋ Earnings Growth Potential: Low
- ❋ Growth: 10.4%
- ❋ Annual Job Openings: 707
- ❋ Self-Employed: 0.9%
- ❋ Part-Time: 5.9%

Operate, install, calibrate, and maintain integrated computer/communications systems consoles; simulators; and other data acquisition, test, and measurement instruments and equipment to launch, track, position, and evaluate air and space vehicles. May record and interpret test data. Inspect, diagnose, maintain, and operate test setups and equipment to detect malfunctions. Record and interpret test data on parts, assemblies, and mechanisms. Confer with engineering personnel regarding details and implications of test procedures and results. Adjust, repair, or replace faulty components of test setups and equipment. Identify required data, data acquisition plans, and test parameters, setting up equipment to conform to these specifications. Construct and maintain test facilities for aircraft parts and systems according to specifications. Operate and calibrate computer systems and devices to comply with test requirements and to perform data acquisition and analysis. Test aircraft systems under simulated operational conditions, performing systems readiness tests and pre- and post-operational checkouts, to establish design or fabrication parameters. Fabricate and install parts and systems to be tested in test equipment, using hand tools, power tools, and test instruments. Finish vehicle instrumentation and deinstrumentation. Exchange cooling system components in various vehicles.

Personality Type: Realistic. These occupations frequently involve work activities that include practical, hands-on problems and solutions. They often deal with plants; animals; and real-world materials such as wood, tools, and machinery. Many of the occupations require working outside and don't involve a lot of paperwork or working closely with others.

GOE—Interest Area/Cluster: 15. Scientific Research, Engineering, and Mathematics. **Work Group:** 15.09.

Engineering Technology. **Other Jobs in This Work Group:** Cartographers and Photogrammetrists; Civil Engineering Technicians; Electrical and Electronic Engineering Technicians; Electrical and Electronics Drafters; Electrical Drafters; Electrical Engineering Technicians; Electro-Mechanical Technicians; Electronic Drafters; Electronics Engineering Technicians; Environmental Engineering Technicians; Mapping Technicians; Mechanical Drafters; Mechanical Engineering Technicians; Surveying and Mapping Technicians; Surveying Technicians.

Skills—Installation: Installing equipment, machines, wiring, or programs to meet specifications. **Technology Design:** Generating or adapting equipment and technology to serve user needs. **Operation Monitoring:** Watching gauges, dials, or other indicators to make sure a machine is working properly. **Science:** Using scientific methods to solve problems. **Troubleshooting:** Determining what is causing an operating error and deciding what to do about it. **Repairing:** Repairing machines or systems, using the needed tools. **Operations Analysis:** Analyzing needs and product requirements to create a design. **Operation and Control:** Controlling operations of equipment or systems.

Education and Training Program: Aeronautical/Aerospace Engineering Technology/Technician Training. **Related Knowledge/Courses—Engineering and Technology:** Equipment, tools, and mechanical devices and their uses to produce motion, light, power, technology, and other applications. **Mechanical Devices:** Machines and tools, including their designs, uses, benefits, repair, and maintenance. **Computers and Electronics:** Electric circuit boards, processors, chips, and computer hardware and software, including applications and programming. **Production and Processing:** Inputs, outputs, raw materials, waste, quality control, costs, and techniques for maximizing the manufacture and distribution of goods. **Public Safety and Security:** Weaponry; public safety; security operations, rules, regulations, precautions, and prevention; and the protection of people, data, and property. **Design:** Design techniques, principles, tools, and instruments involved in the production and use of precision technical plans, blueprints, drawings, and models.

Work Environment: Indoors; noisy; sitting; using hands on objects, tools, or controls; repetitive motions.

Aerospace Engineers

- ❊ Education/Training Required: Bachelor's degree
- ❊ Annual Earnings: $90,930
- ❊ Beginning Wage: $60,760
- ❊ Earnings Growth Potential: Low
- ❊ Growth: 10.2%
- ❊ Annual Job Openings: 6,498
- ❊ Self-Employed: 1.4%
- ❊ Part-Time: 2.6%

Perform a variety of engineering work in designing, constructing, and testing aircraft, missiles, and spacecraft. May conduct basic and applied research to evaluate adaptability of materials and equipment to aircraft design and manufacture. May recommend improvements in testing equipment and techniques. Formulate conceptual design of aeronautical or aerospace products or systems to meet customer requirements. Direct and coordinate activities of engineering or technical personnel designing, fabricating, modifying, or testing aircraft or aerospace products. Develop design criteria for aeronautical or aerospace products or systems, including testing methods, production costs, quality standards, and completion dates. Plan and conduct experimental, environmental, operational, and stress tests on models and prototypes of aircraft and aerospace systems and equipment. Evaluate product data and design from inspections and reports for conformance to engineering principles, customer requirements, and quality standards. Formulate mathematical models or other methods of computer analysis to develop, evaluate, or modify design according to customer engineering requirements. Write technical reports and other documentation, such as handbooks and bulletins, for use by engineering staff, management, and customers. Analyze project requests and proposals and engineering data to determine feasibility, productibility, cost, and production time of aerospace or aeronautical product. Review performance reports and documentation from customers and field engineers and inspect malfunctioning or damaged products to determine problem. Direct research and development programs. Evaluate and approve selection of vendors by study of past performance and new advertisements. Plan and coordinate activities concerned with investigating and resolving customers' reports of technical problems with aircraft or aerospace vehicles. Maintain records of performance reports for future reference.

Personality Type: Investigative. These occupations frequently involve working with ideas and require an extensive amount of thinking. They can involve searching for facts and figuring out problems mentally.

GOE—Interest Area/Cluster: 15. Scientific Research, Engineering, and Mathematics. **Work Group:** 15.07. Research and Design Engineering. **Other Jobs in This Work Group:** Biomedical Engineers; Chemical Engineers; Civil Engineers; Computer Hardware Engineers; Electrical Engineers; Electronics Engineers, Except Computer; Marine Architects; Marine Engineers; Marine Engineers and Naval Architects; Materials Engineers; Mechanical Engineers; Nuclear Engineers.

Skills—Science: Using scientific methods to solve problems. **Systems Evaluation:** Looking at many indicators of system performance and taking into account their accuracy. **Systems Analysis:** Determining how a system should work and how changes will affect outcomes. **Judgment and Decision Making:** Weighing the relative costs and benefits of a potential action. **Technology Design:** Generating or adapting equipment and technology to serve user needs. **Persuasion:** Persuading others to approach things differently. **Operations Analysis:** Analyzing needs and product requirements to create a design. **Management of Personnel Resources:** Motivating, developing, and directing people as they work; identifying the best people for the job.

Education and Training Program: Aerospace, Aeronautical, and Astronautical Engineering. **Related Knowledge/ Courses—Engineering and Technology:** Equipment, tools, and mechanical devices and their uses to produce motion, light, power, technology, and other applications. **Physics:** Physical principles, laws, and applications, including air, water, material dynamics, light, atomic principles, heat, electric theory, earth formations, and meteorological and related natural phenomena. **Design:** Design techniques, principles, tools, and instruments involved in the production and use of precision technical plans, blueprints, drawings, and models. **Mechanical Devices:** Machines and tools, including their designs, uses, benefits, repair, and maintenance. **Production and Processing:** Inputs, outputs, raw materials, waste, quality control, costs, and techniques for maximizing the manufacture and distribution of goods. **Mathematics:** Numbers and their operations and interrelationships, including arithmetic, algebra, geometry, calculus, and statistics and their applications.

Work Environment: Indoors; sitting; repetitive motions.

Agents and Business Managers of Artists, Performers, and Athletes

❋ Education/Training Required: Work experience plus degree
❋ Annual Earnings: $66,440
❋ Beginning Wage: $30,780
❋ Earnings Growth Potential: Very high
❋ Growth: 9.6%
❋ Annual Job Openings: 3,940
❋ Self-Employed: 55.8%
❋ Part-Time: 18.6%

Represent and promote artists, performers, and athletes to prospective employers. May handle contract negotiation and other business matters for clients. Manage business and financial affairs for clients, such as arranging travel and lodging, selling tickets, and directing marketing and advertising activities. Obtain information about and/ or inspect performance facilities, equipment, and accommodations to ensure that they meet specifications. Negotiate with managers, promoters, union officials, and other persons regarding clients' contractual rights and obligations. Advise clients on financial and legal matters such as investments and taxes. Hire trainers or coaches to advise clients on performance matters such as training techniques or performance presentations. Prepare periodic accounting statements for clients. Keep informed of industry trends and deals. Develop contacts with individuals and organizations and apply effective strategies and techniques to ensure their clients' success. Confer with clients to develop strategies for their careers and to explain actions taken on their behalf. Conduct auditions or interviews in order to evaluate potential clients. Schedule promotional or performance engagements for clients. Arrange meetings concerning issues involving their clients. Collect fees, commissions, or other payments according to contract terms.

Personality Type: Enterprising. These occupations frequently involve starting up and carrying out projects and can involve leading people and making many decisions. They sometimes require risk taking and often deal with business.

GOE—Interest Area/Cluster: 03. Arts and Communication. **Work Group:** 03.01. Managerial Work in Arts and Communication. **Other Jobs in This Work Group:** Art Directors; Producers; Producers and Directors; Program Directors; Public Relations Managers; Technical Directors/ Managers.

Skills—Management of Financial Resources: Determining how money will be spent to get the work done and accounting for these expenditures. **Negotiation:** Bringing others together and trying to reconcile differences. **Persuasion:** Persuading others to approach things differently. **Social Perceptiveness:** Being aware of others' reactions and understanding why they react the way they do. **Speaking:** Talking to others to effectively convey information. **Coordination:** Adjusting actions in relation to others' actions. **Judgment and Decision Making:** Weighing the relative costs and benefits of a potential action. **Management of Personnel Resources:** Motivating, developing, and directing people as they work; identifying the best people for the job.

Education and Training Programs: Arts Management; Purchasing, Procurement/Acquisitions, and Contracts Management. **Related Knowledge/Courses—Fine Arts:** Theory and techniques required to produce, compose, and perform works of music, dance, visual arts, drama, and sculpture. **Sales and Marketing:** Principles and methods involved in showing, promoting, and selling products or services. This includes marketing strategies and tactics, product demonstration and sales techniques, and sales control systems. **Communications and Media:** Media production, communication, and dissemination techniques and methods, including alternative ways to inform and entertain via written, oral, and visual media. **Clerical Practices:** Administrative and clerical procedures and systems such as word-processing systems, filing and records management systems, stenography and transcription, forms, design principles, and other office procedures and terminology. **Customer and Personal Service:** Principles and processes for providing customer and personal services, including needs assessment techniques, quality service standards, alternative delivery systems, and customer satisfaction evaluation techniques. **Economics and Accounting:** Economic and accounting principles and practices, the financial markets, banking, and the analysis and reporting of financial data.

Work Environment: Indoors; sitting.

Agricultural Engineers

- ❋ Education/Training Required: Bachelor's degree
- ❋ Annual Earnings: $67,710
- ❋ Beginning Wage: $45,020
- ❋ Earnings Growth Potential: Low
- ❋ Growth: 8.6%
- ❋ Annual Job Openings: 225
- ❋ Self-Employed: 0.0%
- ❋ Part-Time: 7.3%

Apply knowledge of engineering technology and biological science to agricultural problems concerned with power and machinery, electrification, structures, soil and water conservation, and processing of agricultural products. Visit sites to observe environmental problems, to consult with contractors, or to monitor construction activities. Design agricultural machinery components and equipment, using computer-aided design (CAD) technology. Test agricultural machinery and equipment to ensure adequate performance. Design structures for crop storage, animal shelter and loading, and animal and crop processing and supervise their construction. Provide advice on water quality and issues related to pollution management, river control, and ground and surface water resources. Conduct educational programs that provide farmers or farm cooperative members with information that can help them improve agricultural productivity. Discuss plans with clients, contractors, consultants, and other engineers so that they can be evaluated and necessary changes made. Supervise food processing or manufacturing plant operations. Design and supervise environmental and land reclamation projects in agriculture and related industries. Design food processing plants and related mechanical systems. Plan and direct construction of rural electric-power distribution systems and irrigation, drainage, and flood control systems for soil and water conservation. Prepare reports, sketches, working drawings, specifications, proposals, and budgets for proposed sites or systems. Meet with clients, such as district or regional councils, farmers, and developers, to discuss their needs. Design sensing, measuring, and recording devices and other instrumentation used to study plant or animal life.

Personality Type: Investigative. These occupations frequently involve working with ideas and require an extensive amount of thinking. They can involve searching for facts and figuring out problems mentally.

GOE—Interest Area/Cluster: 01. Agriculture and Natural Resources. **Work Group:** 01.02. Resource Science/Engineering for Plants, Animals, and the Environment. **Other Jobs in This Work Group:** Animal Scientists; Conservation Scientists; Environmental Engineers; Foresters; Mining and Geological Engineers, Including Mining Safety Engineers; Petroleum Engineers; Range Managers; Soil and Plant Scientists; Soil and Water Conservationists; Zoologists and Wildlife Biologists.

Skills—Science: Using scientific methods to solve problems. **Programming:** Writing computer programs for various purposes. **Technology Design:** Generating or adapting equipment and technology to serve user needs. **Operations Analysis:** Analyzing needs and product requirements to create a design. **Management of Material Resources:** Obtaining and seeing to the appropriate use of equipment, facilities, and materials needed to do certain work. **Mathematics:** Using mathematics to solve problems. **Management of Financial Resources:** Determining how money will be spent to get the work done and accounting for these expenditures. **Systems Analysis:** Determining how a system should work and how changes will affect outcomes.

Education and Training Program: Agricultural/Biological Engineering and Bioengineering. **Related Knowledge/Courses—Food Production:** Techniques and equipment for planting, growing, and harvesting of food for consumption, including crop-rotation methods, animal husbandry, and food storage/handling techniques. **Physics:** Physical principles, laws, and applications, including air, water, material dynamics, light, atomic principles, heat, electric theory, earth formations, and meteorological and related natural phenomena. **Engineering and Technology:** Equipment, tools, and mechanical devices and their uses to produce motion, light, power, technology, and other applications. **Design:** Design techniques, principles, tools, and instruments involved in the production and use of precision technical plans, blueprints, drawings, and models. **Biology:** Plant and animal living tissue, cells, organisms, and entities, including their functions, interdependencies, and interactions with each other and the environment. **Building and Construction:** Materials, methods, and the appropriate tools to construct objects, structures, and buildings.

Work Environment: More often indoors than outdoors; noisy; sitting.

Agricultural Sciences Teachers, Postsecondary

- ✸ Education/Training Required: Doctoral degree
- ✸ Annual Earnings: $78,460
- ✸ Beginning Wage: $43,050
- ✸ Earnings Growth Potential: High
- ✸ Growth: 22.9%
- ✸ Annual Job Openings: 1,840
- ✸ Self-Employed: 0.4%
- ✸ Part-Time: 27.8%

Teach courses in the agricultural sciences, including agronomy, dairy sciences, fisheries management, horticultural sciences, poultry sciences, range management, and agricultural soil conservation. Prepare course materials such as syllabi, homework assignments, and handouts. Evaluate and grade students' classwork, laboratory work, assignments, and papers. Keep abreast of developments in agriculture by reading current literature, talking with colleagues, and participating in professional conferences. Prepare and deliver lectures to undergraduate and/or graduate students on topics such as crop production, plant genetics, and soil chemistry. Initiate, facilitate, and moderate classroom discussions. Conduct research in a particular field of knowledge and publish findings in professional journals, books, and/or electronic media. Supervise laboratory sessions and fieldwork and coordinate laboratory operations. Supervise undergraduate and/or graduate teaching, internship, and research work. Compile, administer, and grade examinations or assign this work to others. Advise students on academic and vocational curricula and on career issues. Plan, evaluate, and revise curricula, course content, and course materials and methods of instruction. Maintain student attendance records, grades, and other required records. Write grant proposals to procure external research funding. Collaborate with colleagues to address teaching and research issues. Maintain regularly scheduled office hours in order to advise and assist students. Participate in student recruitment, registration, and placement activities. Select and obtain materials and supplies such as textbooks and laboratory equipment. Act as advisers to student organizations. Participate in campus and community events. Serve on academic or administrative committees that deal with institutional policies, departmental matters, and academic issues. Provide professional consulting services to government and/or industry. Perform administrative duties such as serving as department head. Compile bibliographies of specialized materials for outside reading assignments.

Personality Type: Social. These occupations frequently involve working with, communicating with, and teaching people and often involve helping or providing service to others.

GOE—Interest Area/Cluster: 05. Education and Training. **Work Group:** 05.03. Postsecondary and Adult Teaching and Instructing. **Other Jobs in This Work Group:** Adult Literacy, Remedial Education, and GED Teachers and Instructors; Anthropology and Archeology Teachers, Postsecondary; Architecture Teachers, Postsecondary; Area, Ethnic, and Cultural Studies Teachers, Postsecondary; Art, Drama, and Music Teachers, Postsecondary; Atmospheric, Earth, Marine, and Space Sciences Teachers, Postsecondary; Biological Science Teachers, Postsecondary; Business Teachers, Postsecondary; Chemistry Teachers, Postsecondary; Communications Teachers, Postsecondary; Computer Science Teachers, Postsecondary; Criminal Justice and Law Enforcement Teachers, Postsecondary; Economics Teachers, Postsecondary; Education Teachers, Postsecondary; Engineering Teachers, Postsecondary; English Language and Literature Teachers, Postsecondary; Environmental Science Teachers, Postsecondary; Farm and Home Management Advisors; Foreign Language and Literature Teachers, Postsecondary; Forestry and Conservation Science Teachers, Postsecondary; Geography Teachers, Postsecondary; Graduate Teaching Assistants; Health Specialties Teachers, Postsecondary; History Teachers, Postsecondary; Home Economics Teachers, Postsecondary; Law Teachers, Postsecondary; Library Science Teachers, Postsecondary; Mathematical Science Teachers, Postsecondary; Nursing Instructors and Teachers, Postsecondary; Philosophy and Religion Teachers, Postsecondary; Physics Teachers, Postsecondary; Political Science Teachers, Postsecondary; Psychology Teachers, Postsecondary; Recreation and Fitness Studies Teachers, Postsecondary; Self-Enrichment Education Teachers; Social Work Teachers, Postsecondary; Sociology Teachers, Postsecondary; Vocational Education Teachers, Postsecondary.

Skills—Science: Using scientific methods to solve problems. **Management of Financial Resources:** Determining how money will be spent to get the work done and accounting for these expenditures. **Writing:** Communicating effectively with others in writing as indicated by the needs of the audience. **Reading Comprehension:** Understanding written sentences and paragraphs in work-related documents. **Instructing:** Teaching others how to do something. **Complex Problem Solving:** Identifying complex problems, reviewing the options, and implementing solutions. **Active Learning:** Working with new material or information to grasp its implications. **Mathematics:** Using mathematics to solve problems.

Education and Training Programs: Agricultural and Food Products Processing; Agricultural Business and Management, General; Agricultural Production Operations, General; Agriculture, General; Agronomy and Crop Science; Animal Husbandry and Production; Aquaculture; Farm/Farm and Ranch Management; Food Science; Horticultural Science; Landscaping and Groundskeeping; Ornamental Horticulture; Plant Protection and Integrated Pest Management; Poultry Science; Range Science and Management; Soil Science and Agronomy, General; others. **Related Knowledge/Courses—Biology:** Plant and animal living tissue, cells, organisms, and entities, including their functions, interdependencies, and interactions with each other and the environment. **Food Production:** Techniques and equipment for planting, growing, and harvesting of food for consumption, including crop-rotation methods, animal husbandry, and food storage/handling techniques. **Education and Training:** Instructional methods and training techniques, including curriculum design principles, learning theory, group and individual teaching techniques, design of individual development plans, and test design principles. **Geography:** Various methods for describing the location and distribution of land, sea, and air masses, including their physical locations, relationships, and characteristics. **Chemistry:** The composition, structure, and properties of substances and of the chemical processes and transformations that they undergo. This includes uses of chemicals and their interactions, danger signs, production techniques, and disposal methods. **Communications and Media:** Media production, communication, and dissemination techniques and methods, including alternative ways to inform and entertain via written, oral, and visual media.

Work Environment: Indoors; sitting.

Air Traffic Controllers

* Education/Training Required: Long-term on-the-job training
* Annual Earnings: $112,930
* Beginning Wage: $47,290
* Earnings Growth Potential: Very high
* Growth: 10.2%
* Annual Job Openings: 1,213
* Self-Employed: 0.0%
* Part-Time: 2.1%

Control air traffic on and within vicinity of airport and movement of air traffic between altitude sectors and control centers according to established procedures and policies. Authorize, regulate, and control commercial airline flights according to government or company regulations to expedite and ensure flight safety. Issue landing and take-off authorizations and instructions. Monitor and direct the movement of aircraft within an assigned airspace and on the ground at airports to minimize delays and maximize safety. Monitor aircraft within a specific airspace, using radar, computer equipment, and visual references. Inform pilots about nearby planes as well as potentially hazardous conditions such as weather, speed and direction of wind, and visibility problems. Provide flight path changes or directions to emergency landing fields for pilots traveling in bad weather or in emergency situations. Alert airport emergency services in cases of emergency and when aircraft experience difficulties. Direct pilots to runways when space is available, or direct them to maintain a traffic pattern until there is space for them to land. Transfer control of departing flights to traffic control centers and accept control of arriving flights. Direct ground traffic, including taxiing aircraft, maintenance and baggage vehicles, and airport workers. Determine the timing and procedures for flight vector changes. Maintain radio and telephone contact with adjacent control towers, terminal control units, and other area control centers in order to coordinate aircraft movement. Contact pilots by radio to provide meteorological, navigational, and other information. Initiate and coordinate searches for missing aircraft. Check conditions and traffic at different altitudes in response to pilots' requests for altitude changes. Relay to control centers air traffic information such as courses, altitudes, and expected arrival times. Compile information about flights from flight plans, pilot reports, radar, and observations. Inspect, adjust, and control radio equipment and airport lights. Conduct preflight briefings on weather conditions, suggested routes, altitudes, indications of turbulence, and other flight safety information. Analyze factors such as weather reports, fuel requirements, and maps in order to determine air routes. Organize flight plans and traffic management plans to prepare for planes about to enter assigned airspace.

Personality Type: Enterprising. These occupations frequently involve starting up and carrying out projects and can involve leading people and making many decisions. They sometimes require risk taking and often deal with business.

GOE—Interest Area/Cluster: 03. Arts and Communication. **Work Group:** 03.10. Communications Technology. **Other Jobs in This Work Group:** Airfield Operations Specialists; Dispatchers, Except Police, Fire, and Ambulance; Police, Fire, and Ambulance Dispatchers; Telephone Operators.

Skills—Operation and Control: Controlling operations of equipment or systems. **Operation Monitoring:** Watching gauges, dials, or other indicators to make sure a machine is working properly. **Coordination:** Adjusting actions in relation to others' actions. **Complex Problem Solving:** Identifying complex problems, reviewing the options, and implementing solutions. **Active Listening:** Listening to what other people are saying and asking questions as appropriate. **Instructing:** Teaching others how to do something. **Judgment and Decision Making:** Weighing the relative costs and benefits of a potential action. **Monitoring:** Assessing how well one is doing when learning or doing something.

Education and Training Program: Air Traffic Controller Training. **Related Knowledge/Courses—Transportation:** Principles and methods for moving people or goods by air, rail, sea, or road, including their relative costs, advantages, and limitations. **Geography:** Various methods for describing the location and distribution of land, sea, and air masses, including their physical locations, relationships, and characteristics. **Telecommunications:** Transmission, broadcasting, switching, control, and operation of telecommunications systems. **Public Safety and Security:** Weaponry; public safety; security operations, rules, regulations, precautions, and prevention; and the protection of people, data, and property. **Physics:** Physical principles, laws, and applications, including air, water, material dynamics, light, atomic principles, heat, electric theory, earth formations, and meteorological and related natural phenomena. **Education and Training:** Instructional methods and training techniques, including curriculum design principles, learning theory, group and individual teaching techniques, design of individual development plans, and test design principles.

Work Environment: Indoors; noisy; sitting; using hands on objects, tools, or controls; repetitive motions.

Aircraft Cargo Handling Supervisors

- ❋ Education/Training Required: Work experience in a related occupation
- ❋ Annual Earnings: $37,760
- ❋ Beginning Wage: $24,030
- ❋ Earnings Growth Potential: Medium
- ❋ Growth: 23.3%
- ❋ Annual Job Openings: 523
- ❋ Self-Employed: 2.0%
- ❋ Part-Time: 5.3%

Direct ground crew in the loading, unloading, securing, and staging of aircraft cargo or baggage. Determine the quantity and orientation of cargo and compute aircraft center of gravity. May accompany aircraft as member of flight crew, monitor and handle cargo in flight, and assist and brief passengers on safety and emergency procedures. Calculate load weights for different aircraft compartments, using charts and computers. Distribute cargo in such a manner that space use is maximized.

Personality Type: Enterprising. These occupations frequently involve starting up and carrying out projects and can involve leading people and making many decisions. They sometimes require risk taking and often deal with business.

GOE—Interest Area/Cluster: 16. Transportation, Distribution, and Logistics. **Work Group:** 16.01. Managerial Work in Transportation. **Other Jobs in This Work Group:** First-Line Supervisors/Managers of Transportation and Material-Moving Machine and Vehicle Operators; Postmasters and Mail Superintendents; Railroad Conductors and Yardmasters; Storage and Distribution Managers; Transportation Managers; Transportation, Storage, and Distribution Managers.

Skills—Equipment Maintenance: Performing routine maintenance and determining when and what kind of maintenance is needed. **Service Orientation:** Actively looking for ways to help people. **Operation and Control:** Controlling operations of equipment or systems. **Operation Monitoring:** Watching gauges, dials, or other indicators to make sure a machine is working properly. **Management of Personnel Resources:** Motivating, developing, and directing people as they work; identifying the best people for the job.

Operations Analysis: Analyzing needs and product requirements to create a design. **Systems Evaluation:** Looking at many indicators of system performance and taking into account their accuracy. **Social Perceptiveness:** Being aware of others' reactions and understanding why they react the way they do.

Education and Training Program: Aviation/Airway Management and Operations. **Related Knowledge/Courses—Transportation:** Principles and methods for moving people or goods by air, rail, sea, or road, including their relative costs, advantages, and limitations. **Public Safety and Security:** Weaponry; public safety; security operations, rules, regulations, precautions, and prevention; and the protection of people, data, and property. **Geography:** Various methods for describing the location and distribution of land, sea, and air masses, including their physical locations, relationships, and characteristics. **Personnel and Human Resources:** Principles and procedures for personnel recruitment; selection; training; compensation and benefits; labor relations and negotiation; and personnel information systems. **Psychology:** Human behavior and performance, mental processes, psychological research methods, and the assessment and treatment of behavioral and affective disorders. **Customer and Personal Service:** Principles and processes for providing customer and personal services, including needs assessment techniques, quality service standards, alternative delivery systems, and customer satisfaction evaluation techniques.

Work Environment: Outdoors; noisy; very hot or cold; contaminants; hazardous equipment; standing.

Aircraft Mechanics and Service Technicians

- ❋ Education/Training Required: Postsecondary vocational training
- ❋ Annual Earnings: $49,010
- ❋ Beginning Wage: $32,160
- ❋ Earnings Growth Potential: Low
- ❋ Growth: 10.6%
- ❋ Annual Job Openings: 9,708
- ❋ Self-Employed: 0.4%
- ❋ Part-Time: 2.1%

Diagnose, adjust, repair, or overhaul aircraft engines and assemblies, such as hydraulic and pneumatic systems. Read and interpret maintenance manuals, service bulletins, and other specifications to determine the feasibility and method of repairing or replacing malfunctioning or damaged components. Inspect completed work to certify that maintenance meets standards and that aircraft are ready for operation. Maintain repair logs, documenting all preventive and corrective aircraft maintenance. Conduct routine and special inspections as required by regulations. Examine and inspect aircraft components, including landing gear, hydraulic systems, and de-icers, to locate cracks, breaks, leaks, or other problem. Inspect airframes for wear or other defects. Maintain, repair, and rebuild aircraft structures; functional components; and parts such as wings and fuselage, rigging, hydraulic units, oxygen systems, fuel systems, electrical systems, gaskets, and seals. Measure the tension of control cables. Replace or repair worn, defective, or damaged components, using hand tools, gauges, and testing equipment. Measure parts for wear, using precision instruments. Assemble and install electrical, plumbing, mechanical, hydraulic, and structural components and accessories, using hand tools and power tools. Test operation of engines and other systems, using test equipment such as ignition analyzers, compression checkers, distributor timers, and ammeters. Obtain fuel and oil samples and check them for contamination. Reassemble engines following repair or inspection and re-install engines in aircraft. Read and interpret pilots' descriptions of problems to diagnose causes. Modify aircraft structures, space vehicles, systems, or components, following drawings, schematics, charts, engineering orders, and technical publications. Install and align repaired or replacement parts for subsequent riveting or welding, using clamps and wrenches. Locate and mark dimensions and reference lines on defective or replacement parts, using templates, scribes, compasses, and steel rules. Clean, strip, prime, and sand structural surfaces and materials to prepare them for bonding. Service and maintain aircraft and related apparatus by performing activities such as flushing crankcases, cleaning screens, and lubricating moving parts.

Personality Type: Realistic. These occupations frequently involve work activities that include practical, hands-on problems and solutions. They often deal with plants; animals; and real-world materials such as wood, tools, and machinery. Many of the occupations require working outside and don't involve a lot of paperwork or working closely with others.

GOE—Interest Area/Cluster: 13. Manufacturing. **Work Group:** 13.14. Vehicle and Facility Mechanical Work. **Other Jobs in This Work Group:** Aircraft Structure, Surfaces, Rigging, and Systems Assemblers; Automotive Body and Related Repairers; Automotive Glass Installers and Repairers; Automotive Master Mechanics; Automotive Service Technicians and Mechanics; Automotive Specialty Technicians; Bus and Truck Mechanics and Diesel Engine Specialists; Farm Equipment Mechanics; Fiberglass Laminators and Fabricators; Mobile Heavy Equipment Mechanics, Except Engines; Motorboat Mechanics; Motorcycle Mechanics; Outdoor Power Equipment and Other Small Engine Mechanics; Rail Car Repairers; Recreational Vehicle Service Technicians; Tire Repairers and Changers.

Skills—Repairing: Repairing machines or systems, using the needed tools. **Equipment Maintenance:** Performing routine maintenance and determining when and what kind of maintenance is needed. **Installation:** Installing equipment, machines, wiring, or programs to meet specifications. **Operation Monitoring:** Watching gauges, dials, or other indicators to make sure a machine is working properly. **Troubleshooting:** Determining what is causing an operating error and deciding what to do about it. **Operation and Control:** Controlling operations of equipment or systems. **Quality Control Analysis:** Evaluating the quality or performance of products, services, or processes. **Complex Problem Solving:** Identifying complex problems, reviewing the options, and implementing solutions.

Education and Training Programs: Agricultural Mechanics and Equipment/Machine Technology; Aircraft Powerplant Technology/Technician Training; Airframe Mechanics and Aircraft Maintenance Technology/Technician Training. **Related Knowledge/Courses—Mechanical Devices:** Machines and tools, including their designs, uses, benefits, repair, and maintenance. **Design:** Design techniques, principles, tools, and instruments involved in the production and use of precision technical plans, blueprints, drawings, and models. **Physics:** Physical principles, laws, and applications, including air, water, material dynamics, light, atomic principles, heat, electric theory, earth formations, and meteorological and related natural phenomena. **Chemistry:** The composition, structure, and properties of substances and of the chemical processes and transformations that they undergo. This includes uses of chemicals and their interactions, danger signs, production techniques, and disposal methods. **Engineering and Technology:** Equipment, tools, and mechanical devices and their uses to produce motion, light, power, technology, and other applications. **Transportation:** Principles and methods for moving people or goods by air, rail, sea, or road, including their relative costs, advantages, and limitations.

Work Environment: Noisy; contaminants; cramped work space, awkward positions; standing; using hands on objects, tools, or controls; bending or twisting the body.

Aircraft Structure, Surfaces, Rigging, and Systems Assemblers

- ❀ Education/Training Required: Moderate-term on-the-job training
- ❀ Annual Earnings: $45,420
- ❀ Beginning Wage: $25,050
- ❀ Earnings Growth Potential: High
- ❀ Growth: 12.8%
- ❀ Annual Job Openings: 6,550
- ❀ Self-Employed: 0.0%
- ❀ Part-Time: 1.9%

Assemble, fit, fasten, and install parts of airplanes, space vehicles, or missiles, such as tails, wings, fuselage, bulkheads, stabilizers, landing gear, rigging and control equipment, or heating and ventilating systems. Form loops or splices in cables, using clamps and fittings, or reweave cable strands. Align and fit structural assemblies manually or signal crane operators to position assemblies for joining. Align, fit, assemble, connect, and install system components, using jigs, fixtures, measuring instruments, hand tools, and power tools. Assemble and fit prefabricated parts to form subassemblies. Assemble, install, and connect parts, fittings, and assemblies on aircraft, using layout tools; hand tools; power tools; and fasteners such as bolts, screws, rivets, and clamps. Attach brackets, hinges, or clips to secure or support components and subassemblies, using bolts, screws, rivets, chemical bonding, or welding. Select and install accessories in swaging machines, using hand tools. Fit and fasten sheet metal coverings to surface areas and other sections of aircraft prior to welding or riveting. Lay out and mark reference points and locations for installation of parts and components, using jigs, templates, and measuring and marking instruments. Inspect and test installed units, parts, systems, and assemblies for fit, alignment, performance, defects, and compliance with standards, using measuring instruments and test equipment. Install mechanical linkages and actuators and verify tension of cables, using tensiometers. Join structural assemblies such as wings, tails, and fuselage. Measure and cut cables and tubing, using master templates, measuring instruments, and cable cutters or saws. Read and interpret blueprints, illustrations, and specifications to determine layouts, sequences of operations, or identities and relationships of parts. Prepare and load live ammunition, missiles, and bombs onto aircraft according to established procedures. Adjust, repair, rework, or replace parts and assemblies to eliminate malfunctions and to ensure proper operation. Cut, trim, file, bend, and smooth parts and verify sizes and fitting tolerances in order to ensure proper fit and clearance of parts. Install and connect control cables to electronically controlled units, using hand tools, ring locks, cotter keys, threaded connectors, turnbuckles, and related devices.

Personality Type: Realistic. These occupations frequently involve work activities that include practical, hands-on problems and solutions. They often deal with plants; animals; and real-world materials such as wood, tools, and machinery. Many of the occupations require working outside and don't involve a lot of paperwork or working closely with others.

GOE—Interest Area/Cluster: 13. Manufacturing. **Work Group:** 13.14. Vehicle and Facility Mechanical Work. **Other Jobs in This Work Group:** Aircraft Mechanics and Service Technicians; Automotive Body and Related Repairers; Automotive Glass Installers and Repairers; Automotive Master Mechanics; Automotive Service Technicians and Mechanics; Automotive Specialty Technicians; Bus and Truck Mechanics and Diesel Engine Specialists; Farm Equipment Mechanics; Fiberglass Laminators and Fabricators; Mobile Heavy Equipment Mechanics, Except Engines; Motorboat Mechanics; Motorcycle Mechanics; Outdoor Power Equipment and Other Small Engine Mechanics; Rail Car Repairers; Recreational Vehicle Service Technicians; Tire Repairers and Changers.

Skills—Installation: Installing equipment, machines, wiring, or programs to meet specifications. **Equipment Maintenance:** Performing routine maintenance and determining when and what kind of maintenance is needed. **Repairing:** Repairing machines or systems, using the needed tools. **Quality Control Analysis:** Evaluating the quality or performance of products, services, or processes. **Equipment Selection:** Determining the kind of tools and equipment needed to do a job. **Operation Monitoring:** Watching gauges, dials, or other indicators to make sure a machine is working properly. **Mathematics:** Using mathematics to solve problems. **Troubleshooting:** Determining what is causing an operating error and deciding what to do about it.

Education and Training Programs: Aircraft Powerplant Technology/Technician Training; Airframe Mechanics and Aircraft Maintenance Technology/Technician Training; Avionics Maintenance Technology/Technician Training. **Related Knowledge/Courses—Mechanical Devices:** Machines and tools, including their designs, uses, benefits, repair, and maintenance. **Design:** Design techniques, principles, tools, and instruments involved in the production and use of precision technical plans, blueprints, drawings, and models. **Chemistry:** The composition, structure, and properties of substances and of the chemical processes and transformations that they undergo. This includes uses of chemicals and their interactions, danger signs, production techniques, and disposal methods. **Public Safety and Security:** Weaponry; public safety; security operations, rules, regulations, precautions, and prevention; and the protection of people, data, and property. **Production and Processing:** Inputs, outputs, raw materials, waste, quality control, costs, and techniques for maximizing the manufacture and distribution of goods.

Work Environment: Noisy; contaminants; hazardous conditions; hazardous equipment; standing; using hands on objects, tools, or controls.

Airline Pilots, Copilots, and Flight Engineers

* Education/Training Required: Bachelor's degree
* Annual Earnings: More than $145,600
* Beginning Wage: $56,540
* Earnings Growth Potential: Cannot be calculated
* Growth: 12.9%
* Annual Job Openings: 4,073
* Self-Employed: 2.5%
* Part-Time: 14.2%

Pilot and navigate the flight of multi-engine aircraft in regularly scheduled service for the transport of passengers and cargo. Requires Federal Air Transport rating and certification in specific aircraft type used. Use instrumentation to guide flights when visibility is poor. Respond to and report in-flight emergencies and malfunctions. Work as part of a flight team with other crew members, especially during takeoffs and landings. Contact control towers for takeoff clearances, arrival instructions, and other information, using radio equipment. Steer aircraft along planned routes with the assistance of autopilot and flight management computers. Monitor gauges, warning devices, and control panels to verify aircraft performance and to regulate engine speed. Start engines, operate controls, and pilot airplanes to transport passengers, mail, or freight while adhering to flight plans, regulations, and procedures. Inspect aircraft for defects and malfunctions according to pre-flight checklists. Check passenger and cargo distributions and fuel amounts to ensure that weight and balance specifications are met. Monitor engine operation, fuel consumption, and functioning of aircraft systems during flights. Confer with flight dispatchers and weather forecasters to keep abreast of flight conditions. Coordinate flight activities with ground crews and air-traffic control and inform crew members of flight and test procedures. Order changes in fuel supplies, loads, routes, or schedules to ensure safety of flights. Choose routes, altitudes, and speeds that will provide the fastest, safest, and smoothest flights. Direct activities of aircraft crews during flights. Brief crews about flight details such as destinations, duties, and responsibilities. Record in logbooks information such as flight times, distances flown, and fuel consumption. Make announcements regarding flights, using public address systems. File instrument flight plans with air traffic control to ensure that flights are coordinated with other air traffic. Perform minor maintenance work or arrange for major maintenance. Instruct other pilots and student pilots in aircraft operations and the principles of flight. Conduct in-flight tests and evaluations at specified altitudes and in all types of weather to determine the receptivity and other characteristics of equipment and systems.

Personality Type: Realistic. These occupations frequently involve work activities that include practical, hands-on problems and solutions. They often deal with plants; animals; and real-world materials such as wood, tools, and machinery. Many of the occupations require working outside and don't involve a lot of paperwork or working closely with others.

GOE—Interest Area/Cluster: 16. Transportation, Distribution, and Logistics. **Work Group:** 16.02. Air Vehicle Operation. **Other Jobs in This Work Group:** Commercial Pilots.

Skills—Operation Monitoring: Watching gauges, dials, or other indicators to make sure a machine is working properly. **Operation and Control:** Controlling operations of equipment or systems. **Systems Analysis:** Determining how a system should work and how changes will affect outcomes. **Judgment and Decision Making:** Weighing the relative costs and benefits of a potential action. **Troubleshooting:** Determining what is causing an operating error and deciding what to do about it. **Science:** Using scientific methods to solve problems. **Systems Evaluation:** Looking at many indicators of system performance and taking into account their accuracy. **Monitoring:** Assessing how well one is doing when learning or doing something.

Education and Training Programs: Airline/Commercial/Professional Pilot and Flight Crew Training; Flight Instructor

Training. **Related Knowledge/Courses—Transportation:** Principles and methods for moving people or goods by air, rail, sea, or road, including their relative costs, advantages, and limitations. **Geography:** Various methods for describing the location and distribution of land, sea, and air masses, including their physical locations, relationships, and characteristics. **Physics:** Physical principles, laws, and applications, including air, water, material dynamics, light, atomic principles, heat, electric theory, earth formations, and meteorological and related natural phenomena. **Public Safety and Security:** Weaponry; public safety; security operations, rules, regulations, precautions, and prevention; and the protection of people, data, and property. **Psychology:** Human behavior and performance, mental processes, psychological research methods, and the assessment and treatment of behavioral and affective disorders. **Law and Government:** Laws, legal codes, court procedures, precedents, government regulations, executive orders, agency rules, and the democratic political process.

Work Environment: Indoors; noisy; contaminants; radiation; sitting; using hands on objects, tools, or controls.

Ambulance Drivers and Attendants, Except Emergency Medical Technicians

- ❋ Education/Training Required: Moderate-term on-the-job training
- ❋ Annual Earnings: $21,140
- ❋ Beginning Wage: $14,870
- ❋ Earnings Growth Potential: Low
- ❋ Growth: 21.7%
- ❋ Annual Job Openings: 3,703
- ❋ Self-Employed: 0.1%
- ❋ Part-Time: 16.9%

Drive ambulance or assist ambulance driver in transporting sick, injured, or convalescent persons. Assist in lifting patients. Drive ambulances or assist ambulance drivers in transporting sick, injured, or convalescent persons. Remove and replace soiled linens and equipment to maintain sanitary conditions. Accompany and assist emergency medical technicians on calls. Place patients on stretchers and load stretchers into ambulances, usually with assistance from other attendants. Earn and maintain appropriate certifications. Replace supplies and disposable items on ambulances. Report facts concerning accidents or emergencies to hospital personnel or law enforcement officials. Administer first aid such as bandaging, splinting, and administering oxygen. Restrain or shackle violent patients.

Personality Type: Realistic. These occupations frequently involve work activities that include practical, hands-on problems and solutions. They often deal with plants; animals; and real-world materials such as wood, tools, and machinery. Many of the occupations require working outside and don't involve a lot of paperwork or working closely with others.

GOE—Interest Area/Cluster: 16. Transportation, Distribution, and Logistics. **Work Group:** 16.06. Other Services Requiring Driving. **Other Jobs in This Work Group:** Bus Drivers, School; Bus Drivers, Transit and Intercity; Couriers and Messengers; Driver/Sales Workers; Parking Lot Attendants; Postal Service Mail Carriers; Taxi Drivers and Chauffeurs.

Skills—Equipment Maintenance: Performing routine maintenance and determining when and what kind of maintenance is needed. **Operation Monitoring:** Watching gauges, dials, or other indicators to make sure a machine is working properly. **Operation and Control:** Controlling operations of equipment or systems. **Repairing:** Repairing machines or systems, using the needed tools. **Technology Design:** Generating or adapting equipment and technology to serve user needs. **Equipment Selection:** Determining the kind of tools and equipment needed to do a job. **Troubleshooting:** Determining what is causing an operating error and deciding what to do about it. **Service Orientation:** Actively looking for ways to help people.

Education and Training Program: Emergency Medical Technology/Technician Training (EMT Paramedic). **Related Knowledge/Courses—Transportation:** Principles and methods for moving people or goods by air, rail, sea, or road, including their relative costs, advantages, and limitations. **Psychology:** Human behavior and performance, mental processes, psychological research methods, and the assessment and treatment of behavioral and affective disorders. **Medicine and Dentistry:** The information and techniques needed to diagnose and treat injuries, diseases, and deformities. This includes symptoms, treatment alternatives, drug properties and interactions, and preventive health-care measures. **Customer and Personal Service:** Principles and processes for providing customer and personal services, including needs assessment techniques, quality service standards, alternative delivery systems, and customer satisfaction evaluation techniques. **Telecommunications:** Transmission, broadcasting, switching, control, and operation of telecommunications systems. **Public Safety and Security:** Weaponry; public safety; security operations, rules, regulations, precautions, and prevention; and the protection of people, data, and property.

Work Environment: Outdoors; noisy; very hot or cold; disease or infections; sitting; using hands on objects, tools, or controls.

Anesthesiologists

* Education/Training Required: First professional degree
* Annual Earnings: More than $145,600
* Beginning Wage: $118,320
* Earnings Growth Potential: Cannot be calculated
* Growth: 14.2%
* Annual Job Openings: 38,027
* Self-Employed: 14.7%
* Part-Time: 8.1%

The job openings listed here are shared with Family and General Practitioners; Internists, General; Obstetricians and Gynecologists; Pediatricians, General; Psychiatrists; and Surgeons.

Administer anesthetics during surgery or other medical procedures. Administer anesthetic or sedation during medical procedures, using local, intravenous, spinal, or caudal methods. Monitor patient before, during, and after anesthesia and counteract adverse reactions or complications. Provide and maintain life support and airway management and help prepare patients for emergency surgery. Record type and amount of anesthesia and patient condition throughout procedure. Examine patient; obtain medical history; and use diagnostic tests to determine risk during surgical, obstetrical, and other medical procedures. Position patient on operating table to maximize patient comfort and surgical accessibility. Decide when patients have recovered or stabilized enough to be sent to another room or ward or to be sent home following outpatient surgery. Coordinate administration of anesthetics with surgeons during operation. Confer with other medical professionals to determine type and method of anesthetic or sedation to render patient insensible to pain. Coordinate and direct work of nurses, medical technicians, and other health-care providers. Order laboratory tests, X rays, and other diagnostic procedures. Diagnose illnesses, using examinations, tests, and reports. Manage anesthesiological services, coordinating them with other medical activities

and formulating plans and procedures. Provide medical care and consultation in many settings, prescribing medication and treatment and referring patients for surgery. Inform students and staff of types and methods of anesthesia administration, signs of complications, and emergency methods to counteract reactions. Schedule and maintain use of surgical suite, including operating, wash-up, and waiting rooms and anesthetic and sterilizing equipment. Instruct individuals and groups on ways to preserve health and prevent disease. Conduct medical research to aid in controlling and curing disease, to investigate new medications, and to develop and test new medical techniques.

Personality Type: Investigative. These occupations frequently involve working with ideas and require an extensive amount of thinking. They can involve searching for facts and figuring out problems mentally.

GOE—Interest Area/Cluster: 08. Health Science. **Work Group:** 08.02. Medicine and Surgery. **Other Jobs in This Work Group:** Family and General Practitioners; Internists, General; Medical Assistants; Medical Transcriptionists; Obstetricians and Gynecologists; Pediatricians, General; Pharmacists; Pharmacy Aides; Pharmacy Technicians; Physician Assistants; Psychiatrists; Registered Nurses; Surgeons; Surgical Technologists.

Skills—Operation Monitoring: Watching gauges, dials, or other indicators to make sure a machine is working properly. **Science:** Using scientific methods to solve problems. **Operation and Control:** Controlling operations of equipment or systems. **Judgment and Decision Making:** Weighing the relative costs and benefits of a potential action. **Equipment Selection:** Determining the kind of tools and equipment needed to do a job. **Monitoring:** Assessing how well one is doing when learning or doing something. **Equipment Maintenance:** Performing routine maintenance and determining when and what kind of maintenance is needed. **Complex Problem Solving:** Identifying complex problems, reviewing the options, and implementing solutions.

Education and Training Programs: Anesthesiology; Critical Care Anesthesiology. **Related Knowledge/Courses—Medicine and Dentistry:** The information and techniques needed to diagnose and treat injuries, diseases, and deformities. This includes symptoms, treatment alternatives, drug properties and interactions, and preventive healthcare measures. **Biology:** Plant and animal living tissue, cells, organisms, and entities, including their functions, interdependencies, and interactions with each other and the environment. **Chemistry:** The composition, structure, and properties of substances and of the chemical processes and transformations that they undergo. This includes uses of chemicals and their interactions, danger signs, production techniques, and disposal methods. **Psychology:** Human behavior and performance, mental processes, psychological research methods, and the assessment and treatment of behavioral and affective disorders. **Physics:** Physical principles, laws, and applications, including air, water, material dynamics, light, atomic principles, heat, electric theory, earth formations, and meteorological and related natural phenomena. **Therapy and Counseling:** Information and techniques needed to rehabilitate physical and mental ailments and to provide career guidance, including alternative treatments, rehabilitation equipment and its proper use, and methods to evaluate treatment effects.

Work Environment: Indoors; contaminants; radiation; disease or infections; standing; using hands on objects, tools, or controls.

Animal Trainers

- ❋ Education/Training Required: Moderate-term on-the-job training
- ❋ Annual Earnings: $26,190
- ❋ Beginning Wage: $16,510
- ❋ Earnings Growth Potential: Medium
- ❋ Growth: 22.7%
- ❋ Annual Job Openings: 6,713
- ❋ Self-Employed: 56.9%
- ❋ Part-Time: 21.3%

Train animals for riding, harness, security, performance, or obedience or assisting persons with disabilities. Accustom animals to human voice and contact and condition animals to respond to commands. Train animals according to prescribed standards for show or competition. May train animals to carry pack loads or work as part of pack team. Observe animals' physical conditions to detect illness or unhealthy conditions requiring medical care. Cue or signal animals during performances. Administer prescribed medications to animals. Evaluate animals to determine their temperaments, abilities, and aptitude for training. Feed and exercise animals and provide other general care such as cleaning and maintaining holding and performance areas. Talk to and interact with animals in order to familiarize them to human voices and contact. Conduct training programs to develop and maintain desired animal behaviors for competition, entertainment, obedience, security, riding, and related areas. Keep records documenting animal health, diet, and

behavior. Advise animal owners regarding the purchase of specific animals. Instruct jockeys in handling specific horses during races. Train horses or other equines for riding, harness, show, racing, or other work, using knowledge of breed characteristics, training methods, performance standards, and the peculiarities of each animal. Use oral, spur, rein, and hand commands to condition horses to carry riders or to pull horse-drawn equipment. Place tack or harnesses on horses to accustom horses to the feel of equipment. Train dogs in human-assistance or property protection duties. Retrain horses to break bad habits, such as kicking, bolting, and resisting bridling and grooming. Train and rehearse animals, according to scripts, for motion picture, television, film, stage, or circus performances. Organize and conduct animal shows. Arrange for mating of stallions and mares and assist mares during foaling.

Personality Type: Realistic. These occupations frequently involve work activities that include practical, hands-on problems and solutions. They often deal with plants; animals; and real-world materials such as wood, tools, and machinery. Many of the occupations require working outside and don't involve a lot of paperwork or working closely with others.

GOE—Interest Area/Cluster: 08. Health Science. **Work Group:** 08.05. Animal Care. **Other Jobs in This Work Group:** Animal Breeders; Nonfarm Animal Caretakers; Veterinarians; Veterinary Assistants and Laboratory Animal Caretakers; Veterinary Technologists and Technicians.

Skills—Management of Financial Resources: Determining how money will be spent to get the work done and accounting for these expenditures. **Persuasion:** Persuading others to approach things differently. **Service Orientation:** Actively looking for ways to help people. **Instructing:** Teaching others how to do something. **Learning Strategies:** Using multiple approaches when learning or teaching new things. **Monitoring:** Assessing how well one is doing when learning or doing something. **Management of Material Resources:** Obtaining and seeing to the appropriate use of equipment, facilities, and materials needed to do certain work. **Social Perceptiveness:** Being aware of others' reactions and understanding why they react the way they do.

Education and Training Programs: Animal Training; Equestrian/Equine Studies. **Related Knowledge/Courses—Sales and Marketing:** Principles and methods involved in showing, promoting, and selling products or services. This includes marketing strategies and tactics, product demonstration and sales techniques, and sales control systems.

Biology: Plant and animal living tissue, cells, organisms, and entities, including their functions, interdependencies, and interactions with each other and the environment. **Economics and Accounting:** Economic and accounting principles and practices, the financial markets, banking, and the analysis and reporting of financial data. **Communications and Media:** Media production, communication, and dissemination techniques and methods, including alternative ways to inform and entertain via written, oral, and visual media. **Customer and Personal Service:** Principles and processes for providing customer and personal services, including needs assessment techniques, quality service standards, alternative delivery systems, and customer satisfaction evaluation techniques. **Clerical Practices:** Administrative and clerical procedures and systems such as word-processing systems, filing and records management systems, stenography and transcription, forms, design principles, and other office procedures and terminology.

Work Environment: Outdoors; noisy; standing; walking and running; using hands on objects, tools, or controls; repetitive motions.

Anthropologists

- ❊ Education/Training Required: Master's degree
- ❊ Annual Earnings: $53,080
- ❊ Beginning Wage: $31,130
- ❊ Earnings Growth Potential: High
- ❊ Growth: 15.0%
- ❊ Annual Job Openings: 446
- ❊ Self-Employed: 6.1%
- ❊ Part-Time: 20.1%

The job openings listed here are shared with Archeologists.

Research, evaluate, and establish public policy concerning the origins of humans; their physical, social, linguistic, and cultural development; and their behavior, as well as the cultures, organizations, and institutions they have created. Collect information and make judgments through observation, interviews, and the review of documents. Plan and direct research to characterize and compare the economic, demographic, health-care, social, political, linguistic, and religious institutions of distinct cultural groups, communities, and organizations. Write about and present research findings for a variety of specialized and general audiences. Advise government agencies, private organizations, and communities regarding proposed programs, plans, and policies and their potential impacts on cultural institutions, organizations, and communities. Identify culturally-specific beliefs and practices affecting health status and access to services for distinct populations and communities in collaboration with medical and public health officials. Build and use text-based database management systems to support the analysis of detailed first-hand observational records, or "field notes." Develop intervention procedures, utilizing techniques such as individual and focus group interviews, consultations, and participant observation of social interaction. Construct and test data collection methods. Explain the origins and physical, social, or cultural development of humans, including physical attributes, cultural traditions, beliefs, languages, resource management practices, and settlement patterns. Conduct participatory action research in communities and organizations to assess how work is done and to design work systems, technologies, and environments. Train others in the application of ethnographic research methods to solve problems in organizational effectiveness, communications, technology development, policy-making, and program planning. Formulate general rules that describe and predict the development and behavior of cultures and social institutions. Collaborate with economic development planners to decide on the implementation of proposed development policies, plans, and programs based on culturally institutionalized barriers and facilitating circumstances. Create data records for use in describing and analyzing social patterns and processes, using photography, videography, and audio recordings.

Personality Type: Investigative. These occupations frequently involve working with ideas and require an extensive amount of thinking. They can involve searching for facts and figuring out problems mentally.

GOE—Interest Area/Cluster: 15. Scientific Research, Engineering, and Mathematics. **Work Group:** 15.04. Social Sciences. **Other Jobs in This Work Group:** Anthropologists and Archeologists; Archeologists; Economists; Historians; Industrial-Organizational Psychologists; Political Scientists; School Psychologists; Sociologists.

Skills—Writing: Communicating effectively with others in writing as indicated by the needs of the audience. **Science:** Using scientific methods to solve problems. **Social Perceptiveness:** Being aware of others' reactions and understanding why they react the way they do. **Complex Problem Solving:** Identifying complex problems, reviewing the options, and implementing solutions. **Systems Evaluation:** Looking at many indicators of system performance and taking into account their accuracy. **Reading Comprehension:** Understanding written sentences and paragraphs in work-related documents. **Systems Analysis:** Determining how a system should work and how changes will affect outcomes. **Active Listening:** Listening to what other people are saying and asking questions as appropriate.

Education and Training Programs: Anthropology; Physical Anthropology. **Related Knowledge/Courses—Sociology and Anthropology:** Group behavior and dynamics; societal trends and influences; and cultures and their history, migrations, ethnicity, and origins. **History and Archeology:** Historical events and their causes, indicators, and impact on particular civilizations and cultures. **Foreign Language:** The structure and content of a foreign (non-English) language, including the meaning and spelling of words, rules of composition and grammar, and pronunciation. **Philosophy and Theology:** Different philosophical systems and religions, including their basic principles, values, ethics, ways of thinking, customs, and practices and their impact on human culture. **Geography:** Various methods for describing the location and distribution of land, sea, and air masses, including their physical locations, relationships, and characteristics. **Biology:** Plant and animal living tissue, cells, organisms, and entities, including their functions, interdependencies, and interactions with each other and the environment.

Work Environment: Indoors; sitting.

Anthropology and Archeology Teachers, Postsecondary

- ❋ Education/Training Required: Doctoral degree
- ❋ Annual Earnings: $64,530
- ❋ Beginning Wage: $38,840
- ❋ Earnings Growth Potential: Medium
- ❋ Growth: 22.9%
- ❋ Annual Job Openings: 910
- ❋ Self-Employed: 0.4%
- ❋ Part-Time: 27.8%

Teach courses in anthropology or archeology. Conduct research in a particular field of knowledge and publish findings in professional journals, books, and electronic media. Keep abreast of developments in their field by reading current literature, talking with colleagues, and participating in professional conferences. Prepare and deliver lectures to undergraduate and graduate students on topics such as research methods, urban anthropology, and language and culture. Evaluate and grade students' classwork, assignments, and papers. Initiate, facilitate, and moderate classroom discussions. Write grant proposals to procure external research funding. Supervise undergraduate and/or graduate teaching, internship, and research work. Prepare course materials such as syllabi, homework assignments, and handouts. Compile, administer, and grade examinations or assign this work to others. Supervise students' laboratory work or fieldwork. Plan, evaluate, and revise curricula, course content, and course materials and methods of instruction. Advise students on academic and vocational curricula, career issues, and laboratory and field research. Maintain student attendance records, grades, and other required records. Maintain regularly scheduled office hours in order to advise and assist students. Collaborate with colleagues to address teaching and research issues. Compile bibliographies of specialized materials for outside reading assignments. Perform administrative duties such as serving as department head. Select and obtain materials and supplies such as textbooks and laboratory equipment. Serve on academic or administrative committees that deal with institutional policies, departmental matters, and academic issues. Participate in student recruitment, registration, and placement activities. Participate in campus and community events. Provide professional consulting services to government and industry. Act as advisers to student organizations.

Personality Type: Social. These occupations frequently involve working with, communicating with, and teaching people and often involve helping or providing service to others.

GOE—Interest Area/Cluster: 05. Education and Training. **Work Group:** 05.03. Postsecondary and Adult Teaching and Instructing. **Other Jobs in This Work Group:** Adult Literacy, Remedial Education, and GED Teachers and Instructors; Agricultural Sciences Teachers, Postsecondary; Architecture Teachers, Postsecondary; Area, Ethnic, and Cultural Studies Teachers, Postsecondary; Art, Drama, and Music Teachers, Postsecondary; Atmospheric, Earth, Marine, and Space Sciences Teachers, Postsecondary; Biological Science Teachers, Postsecondary; Business Teachers, Postsecondary; Chemistry Teachers, Postsecondary; Communications Teachers, Postsecondary; Computer Science Teachers, Postsecondary; Criminal Justice and Law Enforcement Teachers, Postsecondary; Economics Teachers, Postsecondary; Education Teachers, Postsecondary; Engineering Teachers, Postsecondary; English Language and Literature

Teachers, Postsecondary; Environmental Science Teachers, Postsecondary; Farm and Home Management Advisors; Foreign Language and Literature Teachers, Postsecondary; Forestry and Conservation Science Teachers, Postsecondary; Geography Teachers, Postsecondary; Graduate Teaching Assistants; Health Specialties Teachers, Postsecondary; History Teachers, Postsecondary; Home Economics Teachers, Postsecondary; Law Teachers, Postsecondary; Library Science Teachers, Postsecondary; Mathematical Science Teachers, Postsecondary; Nursing Instructors and Teachers, Postsecondary; Philosophy and Religion Teachers, Postsecondary; Physics Teachers, Postsecondary; Political Science Teachers, Postsecondary; Psychology Teachers, Postsecondary; Recreation and Fitness Studies Teachers, Postsecondary; Self-Enrichment Education Teachers; Social Work Teachers, Postsecondary; Sociology Teachers, Postsecondary; Vocational Education Teachers, Postsecondary.

Skills—Science: Using scientific methods to solve problems. **Writing:** Communicating effectively with others in writing as indicated by the needs of the audience. **Critical Thinking:** Using logic and analysis to identify the strengths and weaknesses of different approaches. **Reading Comprehension:** Understanding written sentences and paragraphs in work-related documents. **Active Learning:** Working with new material or information to grasp its implications. **Instructing:** Teaching others how to do something. **Management of Financial Resources:** Determining how money will be spent to get the work done and accounting for these expenditures. **Active Listening:** Listening to what other people are saying and asking questions as appropriate.

Education and Training Programs: Anthropology; Archeology; Physical Anthropology; Social Science Teacher Education. **Related Knowledge/Courses—Sociology and Anthropology:** Group behavior and dynamics; societal trends and influences; and cultures and their history, migrations, ethnicity, and origins. **History and Archeology:** Historical events and their causes, indicators, and impact on particular civilizations and cultures. **Geography:** Various methods for describing the location and distribution of land, sea, and air masses, including their physical locations, relationships, and characteristics. **Foreign Language:** The structure and content of a foreign (non-English) language, including the meaning and spelling of words, rules of composition and grammar, and pronunciation. **Philosophy and Theology:** Different philosophical systems and religions, including their basic principles, values, ethics, ways of thinking, customs, and practices and their impact on human culture. **English Language:** The structure and content of the English language, including the meaning and spelling of words, rules of composition, and grammar.

Work Environment: Indoors; sitting.

Appraisers, Real Estate

- ❀ Education/Training Required: Bachelor's degree
- ❀ Annual Earnings: $46,130
- ❀ Beginning Wage: $25,110
- ❀ Earnings Growth Potential: High
- ❀ Growth: 16.9%
- ❀ Annual Job Openings: 6,493
- ❀ Self-Employed: 32.7%
- ❀ Part-Time: 8.4%

The job openings listed here are shared with Assessors.

Appraise real property to determine its value for purchase, sales, investment, mortgage, or loan purposes. Prepare written reports that estimate property values, outline methods by which the estimations were made, and meet appraisal standards. Compute final estimation of property values, taking into account such factors as depreciation, replacement costs, value comparisons of similar properties, and income potential. Search public records for transactions such as sales, leases, and assessments. Inspect properties to evaluate construction, condition, special features, and functional design and to take property measurements. Photograph interiors and exteriors of properties in order to assist in estimating property value, substantiate findings, and complete appraisal reports. Evaluate land and neighborhoods where properties are situated, considering locations and trends or impending changes that could influence future values. Obtain county land values and sales information about nearby properties in order to aid in establishment of property values. Verify legal descriptions of properties by comparing them to county records. Check building codes and zoning bylaws in order to determine any effects on the properties being appraised. Estimate building replacement costs, using building valuation manuals and professional cost estimators. Examine income records and operating costs of income properties. Interview persons familiar with properties and immediate surroundings, such as contractors, homeowners, and realtors, in order to obtain pertinent information. Examine the type and location of nearby services such as shopping centers, schools, parks, and other neighborhood features in order to evaluate their impact on property values. Draw land diagrams that will be used in appraisal reports to support findings. Testify in court as to the value of a piece of real estate property.

Personality Type: Enterprising. These occupations frequently involve starting up and carrying out projects and can involve leading people and making many decisions. They sometimes require risk taking and often deal with business.

GOE—Interest Area/Cluster: 06. Finance and Insurance. **Work Group:** 06.02. Finance/Insurance Investigation and Analysis. **Other Jobs in This Work Group:** Appraisers and Assessors of Real Estate; Assessors; Claims Adjusters, Examiners, and Investigators; Claims Examiners, Property and Casualty Insurance; Cost Estimators; Credit Analysts; Financial Analysts; Insurance Adjusters, Examiners, and Investigators; Insurance Appraisers, Auto Damage; Insurance Underwriters; Loan Counselors; Loan Officers; Market Research Analysts; Survey Researchers.

Skills—Mathematics: Using mathematics to solve problems. **Writing:** Communicating effectively with others in writing as indicated by the needs of the audience. **Critical Thinking:** Using logic and analysis to identify the strengths and weaknesses of different approaches. **Management of Financial Resources:** Determining how money will be spent to get the work done and accounting for these expenditures. **Equipment Selection:** Determining the kind of tools and equipment needed to do a job. **Complex Problem Solving:** Identifying complex problems, reviewing the options, and implementing solutions. **Speaking:** Talking to others to effectively convey information. **Technology Design:** Generating or adapting equipment and technology to serve user needs.

Education and Training Program: Real Estate. **Related Knowledge/Courses—Building and Construction:** Materials, methods, and the appropriate tools to construct objects, structures, and buildings. **Economics and Accounting:** Economic and accounting principles and practices, the financial markets, banking, and the analysis and reporting of financial data. **Geography:** Various methods for describing the location and distribution of land, sea, and air masses, including their physical locations, relationships, and characteristics. **Clerical Practices:** Administrative and clerical procedures and systems such as word-processing systems, filing and records management systems, stenography and transcription, forms, design principles, and other office procedures and terminology. **Law and Government:** Laws, legal codes, court procedures, precedents, government

regulations, executive orders, agency rules, and the democratic political process. **Sales and Marketing:** Principles and methods involved in showing, promoting, and selling products or services. This includes marketing strategies and tactics, product demonstration and sales techniques, and sales control systems.

Work Environment: More often outdoors than indoors; sitting.

Aquacultural Managers

- ✸ Education/Training Required: Work experience plus degree
- ✸ Annual Earnings: $53,720
- ✸ Beginning Wage: $31,100
- ✸ Earnings Growth Potential: High
- ✸ Growth: 1.1%
- ✸ Annual Job Openings: 18,101
- ✸ Self-Employed: 0.0%
- ✸ Part-Time: 9.3%

The job openings listed here are shared with Crop and Livestock Managers and with Nursery and Greenhouse Managers.

Direct and coordinate, through subordinate supervisory personnel, activities of workers engaged in fish hatchery production for corporations, cooperatives, or other owners. Grow fish and shellfish as cash crops or for release into freshwater or saltwater. Supervise and train aquaculture and fish hatchery support workers. Collect and record growth, production, and environmental data. Conduct and supervise stock examinations in order to identify diseases or parasites. Account for and disburse funds. Devise and participate in activities to improve fish hatching and growth rates and to prevent disease in hatcheries. Monitor environments to ensure maintenance of optimum conditions for aquatic life. Coordinate the selection and maintenance of brood stock. Direct and monitor trapping and spawning of fish, egg incubation, and fry rearing, applying knowledge of management and fish culturing techniques. Direct and monitor the transfer of mature fish to lakes, ponds, streams, or commercial tanks. Determine, administer, and execute policies relating to operations administration and standards and facility maintenance. Collect information regarding techniques for fish collection and fertilization, spawn incubation, and treatment of spawn and fry. Determine how to allocate resources and how to respond to unanticipated problems such as insect infestation, drought, and fire. Operate and maintain cultivating and harvesting equipment. Confer with biologists, fish pathologists, and other fishery personnel to obtain data concerning fish habits, diseases, food, and environmental requirements. Prepare reports required by state and federal laws. Identify environmental requirements of a particular species and select and oversee the preparation of sites for species cultivation. Scuba dive in order to inspect sea farm operations. Design and construct pens, floating stations, and collector strings or fences for sea farms.

Personality Type: Enterprising. These occupations frequently involve starting up and carrying out projects and can involve leading people and making many decisions. They sometimes require risk taking and often deal with business.

GOE—Interest Area/Cluster: 01. Agriculture and Natural Resources. **Work Group:** 01.01. Managerial Work in Agriculture and Natural Resources. **Other Jobs in This Work Group:** Crop and Livestock Managers; Farm Labor Contractors; Farm, Ranch, and Other Agricultural Managers; Farmers and Ranchers; First-Line Supervisors/Managers of Agricultural Crop and Horticultural Workers; First-Line Supervisors/Managers of Animal Husbandry and Animal Care Workers; First-Line Supervisors/Managers of Aquacultural Workers; First-Line Supervisors/Managers of Construction Trades and Extraction Workers; First-Line Supervisors/Managers of Farming, Fishing, and Forestry Workers; First-Line Supervisors/Managers of Landscaping, Lawn Service, and Groundskeeping Workers; First-Line Supervisors/Managers of Logging Workers; Nursery and Greenhouse Managers; Park Naturalists; Purchasing Agents and Buyers, Farm Products.

Skills—Management of Financial Resources: Determining how money will be spent to get the work done and accounting for these expenditures. **Science:** Using scientific methods to solve problems. **Technology Design:** Generating or adapting equipment and technology to serve user needs. **Management of Material Resources:** Obtaining and seeing to the appropriate use of equipment, facilities, and materials needed to do certain work. **Operations Analysis:** Analyzing needs and product requirements to create a design. **Systems Evaluation:** Looking at many indicators of system performance and taking into account their accuracy. **Management of Personnel Resources:** Motivating, developing, and directing people as they work; identifying the best people for the job. **Equipment Selection:** Determining the kind of tools and equipment needed to do a job.

Education and Training Programs: Agribusiness/Agricultural Business Operations; Agricultural Business and Management, General; Agricultural Business and Management,

Other; Agricultural Production Operations, General; Agricultural Production Operations, Other; Animal/Livestock Husbandry and Production; Crop Production; Farm/Farm and Ranch Management. **Related Knowledge/Courses— Food Production:** Techniques and equipment for planting, growing, and harvesting of food for consumption, including crop-rotation methods, animal husbandry, and food storage/handling techniques. **Biology:** Plant and animal living tissue, cells, organisms, and entities, including their functions, interdependencies, and interactions with each other and the environment. **Engineering and Technology:** Equipment, tools, and mechanical devices and their uses to produce motion, light, power, technology, and other applications. **Building and Construction:** Materials, methods, and the appropriate tools to construct objects, structures, and buildings. **Chemistry:** The composition, structure, and properties of substances and of the chemical processes and transformations that they undergo. This includes uses of chemicals and their interactions, danger signs, production techniques, and disposal methods. **Mechanical Devices:** Machines and tools, including their designs, uses, benefits, repair, and maintenance.

Work Environment: More often outdoors than indoors; noisy; very hot or cold; standing; using hands on objects, tools, or controls.

Arbitrators, Mediators, and Conciliators

* Education/Training Required: Work experience plus degree
* Annual Earnings: $48,840
* Beginning Wage: $28,530
* Earnings Growth Potential: High
* Growth: 10.6%
* Annual Job Openings: 546
* Self-Employed: 0.0%
* Part-Time: 5.9%

Facilitate negotiation and conflict resolution through dialogue. Resolve conflicts outside of the court system by mutual consent of parties involved. Conduct studies of appeals procedures in order to ensure adherence to legal requirements and to facilitate disposition of cases. Rule on exceptions, motions, and admissibility of evidence. Review and evaluate information from documents such as claim applications, birth or death certificates, and physician or employer records. Organize and deliver public presentations about mediation to organizations such as community agencies and schools. Prepare written opinions and decisions regarding cases. Prepare settlement agreements for disputants to sign. Use mediation techniques to facilitate communication between disputants, to further parties' understanding of different perspectives, and to guide parties toward mutual agreement. Notify claimants of denied claims and appeal rights. Analyze evidence and apply relevant laws, regulations, policies, and precedents in order to reach conclusions. Conduct initial meetings with disputants to outline the arbitration process, settle procedural matters such as fees, and determine details such as witness numbers and time requirements. Confer with disputants to clarify issues, identify underlying concerns, and develop an understanding of their respective needs and interests. Participate in court proceedings. Arrange and conduct hearings to obtain information and evidence relative to disposition of claims. Recommend acceptance or rejection of compromise settlement offers. Research laws, regulations, policies, and precedent decisions to prepare for hearings. Set up appointments for parties to meet for mediation. Authorize payment of valid claims. Determine existence and amount of liability according to evidence, laws, and administrative and judicial precedents. Issue subpoenas and administer oaths to prepare for formal hearings. Interview claimants, agents, or witnesses to obtain information about disputed issues.

Personality Type: Social. These occupations frequently involve working with, communicating with, and teaching people and often involve helping or providing service to others.

GOE—Interest Area/Cluster: 12. Law and Public Safety. **Work Group:** 12.02. Legal Practice and Justice Administration. **Other Jobs in This Work Group:** Administrative Law Judges, Adjudicators, and Hearing Officers; Judges, Magistrate Judges, and Magistrates; Lawyers.

Skills—Negotiation: Bringing others together and trying to reconcile differences. **Active Listening:** Listening to what other people are saying and asking questions as appropriate. **Persuasion:** Persuading others to approach things differently. **Judgment and Decision Making:** Weighing the relative costs and benefits of a potential action. **Social Perceptiveness:** Being aware of others' reactions and understanding why they react the way they do. **Complex Problem Solving:** Identifying complex problems, reviewing the options, and implementing solutions. **Critical Thinking:** Using logic and analysis to identify the strengths and weaknesses of different approaches. **Writing:** Communicating

effectively with others in writing as indicated by the needs of the audience.

Education and Training Programs: Law (LL.B., J.D.); Legal Professions and Studies, Other. **Related Knowledge/ Courses—Sociology and Anthropology:** Group behavior and dynamics; societal trends and influences; and cultures and their history, migrations, ethnicity, and origins. **Therapy and Counseling:** Information and techniques needed to rehabilitate physical and mental ailments and to provide career guidance, including alternative treatments, rehabilitation equipment and its proper use, and methods to evaluate treatment effects. **Law and Government:** Laws, legal codes, court procedures, precedents, government regulations, executive orders, agency rules, and the democratic political process. **Personnel and Human Resources:** Principles and procedures for personnel recruitment; selection; training; compensation and benefits; labor relations and negotiation; and personnel information systems. **Psychology:** Human behavior and performance, mental processes, psychological research methods, and the assessment and treatment of behavioral and affective disorders. **Philosophy and Theology:** Different philosophical systems and religions, including their basic principles, values, ethics, ways of thinking, customs, and practices and their impact on human culture.

Work Environment: Indoors; sitting.

Archeologists

- ❋ Education/Training Required: Master's degree
- ❋ Annual Earnings: $53,080
- ❋ Beginning Wage: $31,130
- ❋ Earnings Growth Potential: High
- ❋ Growth: 15.0%
- ❋ Annual Job Openings: 446
- ❋ Self-Employed: 6.1%
- ❋ Part-Time: 20.1%

The job openings listed here are shared with Anthropologists.

Conduct research to reconstruct record of past human life and culture from human remains, artifacts, architectural features, and structures recovered through excavation, underwater recovery, or other means of discovery. Write, present, and publish reports that record site history, methodology, and artifact analysis results, along with recommendations for conserving and interpreting findings. Compare findings from one site with archeological data from other sites to find similarities or differences. Research, survey, or assess sites of past societies and cultures in search of answers to specific research questions. Study objects and structures recovered by excavation to identify, date, and authenticate them and to interpret their significance. Develop and test theories concerning the origin and development of past cultures. Consult site reports, existing artifacts, and topographic maps to identify archeological sites. Create a grid of each site and draw and update maps of unit profiles, stratum surfaces, features, and findings. Record the exact locations and conditions of artifacts uncovered in diggings or surveys, using drawings and photographs as necessary. Assess archeological sites for resource management, development, or conservation purposes and recommend methods for site protection. Describe artifacts' physical properties or attributes, such as the materials from which artifacts are made and their size, shape, function, and decoration. Teach archeology at colleges and universities. Collect artifacts made of stone, bone, metal, and other materials, placing them in bags and marking them to show where they were found. Create artifact typologies to organize and make sense of past material cultures. Lead field training sites and train field staff, students, and volunteers in excavation methods. Clean, restore, and preserve artifacts.

Personality Type: Investigative. These occupations frequently involve working with ideas and require an extensive amount of thinking. They can involve searching for facts and figuring out problems mentally.

GOE—Interest Area/Cluster: 15. Scientific Research, Engineering, and Mathematics. **Work Group:** 15.04. Social Sciences. **Other Jobs in This Work Group:** Anthropologists; Anthropologists and Archeologists; Economists; Historians; Industrial-Organizational Psychologists; Political Scientists; School Psychologists; Sociologists.

Skills—Science: Using scientific methods to solve problems. **Management of Financial Resources:** Determining how money will be spent to get the work done and accounting for these expenditures. **Writing:** Communicating effectively with others in writing as indicated by the needs of the audience. **Management of Personnel Resources:** Motivating, developing, and directing people as they work; identifying the best people for the job. **Reading Comprehension:** Understanding written sentences and paragraphs in work-related documents. **Active Learning:** Working with new material or information to grasp its implications. **Management of Material Resources:** Obtaining and seeing to the appropriate use of equipment, facilities, and materials needed to do certain work. **Critical Thinking:** Using logic

and analysis to identify the strengths and weaknesses of different approaches.

Education and Training Program: Archeology. **Related Knowledge/Courses—History and Archeology:** Historical events and their causes, indicators, and impact on particular civilizations and cultures. **Sociology and Anthropology:** Group behavior and dynamics; societal trends and influences; and cultures and their history, migrations, ethnicity, and origins. **Geography:** Various methods for describing the location and distribution of land, sea, and air masses, including their physical locations, relationships, and characteristics. **Philosophy and Theology:** Different philosophical systems and religions, including their basic principles, values, ethics, ways of thinking, customs, and practices and their impact on human culture. **Foreign Language:** The structure and content of a foreign (non-English) language, including the meaning and spelling of words, rules of composition and grammar, and pronunciation. **Biology:** Plant and animal living tissue, cells, organisms, and entities, including their functions, interdependencies, and interactions with each other and the environment.

Work Environment: More often indoors than outdoors; sitting; using hands on objects, tools, or controls.

Architects, Except Landscape and Naval

- ❀ Education/Training Required: Bachelor's degree
- ❀ Annual Earnings: $67,620
- ❀ Beginning Wage: $40,250
- ❀ Earnings Growth Potential: High
- ❀ Growth: 17.7%
- ❀ Annual Job Openings: 11,324
- ❀ Self-Employed: 20.3%
- ❀ Part-Time: 6.1%

Plan and design structures, such as private residences, office buildings, theaters, factories, and other structural property. Prepare information regarding design, structure specifications, materials, color, equipment, estimated costs, or construction time. Consult with client to determine functional and spatial requirements of structure. Direct activities of workers engaged in preparing drawings and specification documents. Plan layout of project. Prepare contract documents for building contractors. Prepare scale drawings. Integrate engineering element into unified design. Conduct periodic on-site observation of work during construction to monitor compliance with plans. Administer construction contracts. Represent client in obtaining bids and awarding construction contracts. Prepare operating and maintenance manuals, studies, and reports.

Personality Type: Artistic. These occupations frequently involve working with forms, designs, and patterns. They often require self-expression, and the work can be done without following a clear set of rules.

GOE—Interest Area/Cluster: 02. Architecture and Construction. **Work Group:** 02.02. Architectural Design. **Other Jobs in This Work Group:** Landscape Architects.

Skills—Operations Analysis: Analyzing needs and product requirements to create a design. **Management of Financial Resources:** Determining how money will be spent to get the work done and accounting for these expenditures. **Complex Problem Solving:** Identifying complex problems, reviewing the options, and implementing solutions. **Management of Personnel Resources:** Motivating, developing, and directing people as they work; identifying the best people for the job. **Coordination:** Adjusting actions in relation to others' actions. **Negotiation:** Bringing others together and trying to reconcile differences. **Persuasion:** Persuading others to approach things differently. **Science:** Using scientific methods to solve problems.

Education and Training Programs: Architectural History and Criticism, General; Architecture (BArch, BA/BS, MArch, MA/MS, PhD); Architecture and Related Services, Other; Environmental Design/Architecture. **Related Knowledge/Courses—Building and Construction:** Materials, methods, and the appropriate tools to construct objects, structures, and buildings. **Design:** Design techniques, principles, tools, and instruments involved in the production and use of precision technical plans, blueprints, drawings, and models. **Engineering and Technology:** Equipment, tools, and mechanical devices and their uses to produce motion, light, power, technology, and other applications. **Fine Arts:** Theory and techniques required to produce, compose, and perform works of music, dance, visual arts, drama, and sculpture. **Law and Government:** Laws, legal codes, court procedures, precedents, government regulations, executive orders, agency rules, and the democratic political process. **Physics:** Physical principles, laws, and applications, including air, water, material dynamics, light, atomic principles, heat, electric theory, earth formations, and meteorological and related natural phenomena.

Work Environment: Indoors; sitting.

Architectural Drafters

- ❋ Education/Training Required: Postsecondary vocational training
- ❋ Annual Earnings: $43,310
- ❋ Beginning Wage: $27,680
- ❋ Earnings Growth Potential: Medium
- ❋ Growth: 6.1%
- ❋ Annual Job Openings: 16,238
- ❋ Self-Employed: 5.0%
- ❋ Part-Time: 5.9%

The job openings listed here are shared with Civil Drafters.

Prepare detailed drawings of architectural designs and plans for buildings and structures according to specifications provided by architect. Analyze building codes, by-laws, space and site requirements, and other technical documents and reports to determine their effect on architectural designs. Operate computer-aided drafting (CAD) equipment or conventional drafting station to produce designs, working drawings, charts, forms, and records. Coordinate structural, electrical, and mechanical designs and determine a method of presentation to graphically represent building plans. Obtain and assemble data to complete architectural designs, visiting job sites to compile measurements as necessary. Lay out and plan interior room arrangements for commercial buildings, using computer-assisted drafting (CAD) equipment and software. Draw rough and detailed scale plans for foundations, buildings, and structures based on preliminary concepts, sketches, engineering calculations, specification sheets, and other data. Supervise, coordinate, and inspect the work of draftspersons, technicians, and technologists on construction projects. Represent architect on construction site, ensuring builder compliance with design specifications and advising on design corrections under architect's supervision. Check dimensions of materials to be used and assign numbers to lists of materials. Determine procedures and instructions to be followed according to design specifications and quantity of required materials. Analyze technical implications of architect's design concept, calculating weights, volumes, and stress factors. Create freehand drawings and lettering to accompany drawings. Prepare colored drawings of landscape and interior designs for presentation to client. Reproduce drawings on copy machines or trace copies of plans and drawings, using transparent paper or cloth, ink, pencil, and standard drafting instruments. Prepare cost estimates, contracts, bidding documents, and technical reports for specific projects under an architect's supervision. Calculate heat loss and gain of buildings and structures to determine required equipment specifications, following standard procedures. Build landscape, architectural, and display models.

Personality Type: Artistic. These occupations frequently involve working with forms, designs, and patterns. They often require self-expression, and the work can be done without following a clear set of rules.

GOE—Interest Area/Cluster: 02. Architecture and Construction. **Work Group:** 02.03. Architecture/Construction Engineering Technologies. **Other Jobs in This Work Group:** Architectural and Civil Drafters; Civil Drafters; Surveyors.

Skills—Operations Analysis: Analyzing needs and product requirements to create a design. **Coordination:** Adjusting actions in relation to others' actions. **Active Learning:** Working with new material or information to grasp its implications. **Technology Design:** Generating or adapting equipment and technology to serve user needs. **Mathematics:** Using mathematics to solve problems. **Complex Problem Solving:** Identifying complex problems, reviewing the options, and implementing solutions. **Science:** Using scientific methods to solve problems. **Monitoring:** Assessing how well one is doing when learning or doing something.

Education and Training Programs: Architectural Drafting and Architectural CAD/CADD; Architectural Technology/Technician Training; CAD/CADD Drafting and/or Design Technology/Technician Training; Civil Drafting and Civil Engineering CAD/CADD; Drafting and Design Technology/Technician Training, General. **Related Knowledge/Courses—Design:** Design techniques, principles, tools, and instruments involved in the production and use of precision technical plans, blueprints, drawings, and models. **Building and Construction:** Materials, methods, and the appropriate tools to construct objects, structures, and buildings. **Engineering and Technology:** Equipment, tools, and mechanical devices and their uses to produce motion, light, power, technology, and other applications. **Computers and Electronics:** Electric circuit boards, processors, chips, and computer hardware and software, including applications and programming. **Mathematics:** Numbers and their operations and interrelationships, including arithmetic, algebra, geometry, calculus, and statistics and their applications. **Physics:** Physical principles, laws, and applications, including air, water, material dynamics, light, atomic principles, heat, electric theory, earth formations, and meteorological and related natural phenomena.

Work Environment: Indoors; noisy; sitting; using hands on objects, tools, or controls; repetitive motions.

Architecture Teachers, Postsecondary

* Education/Training Required: Doctoral degree
* Annual Earnings: $68,540
* Beginning Wage: $41,080
* Earnings Growth Potential: High
* Growth: 22.9%
* Annual Job Openings: 1,044
* Self-Employed: 0.4%
* Part-Time: 27.8%

Teach courses in architecture and architectural design, such as architectural environmental design, interior architecture/design, and landscape architecture. Evaluate and grade students' work, including work performed in design studios. Prepare and deliver lectures to undergraduate and/or graduate students on topics such as architectural design methods, aesthetics and design, and structures and materials. Prepare course materials such as syllabi, homework assignments, and handouts. Initiate, facilitate, and moderate classroom discussions. Plan, evaluate, and revise curricula, course content, and course materials and methods of instruction. Keep abreast of developments in their field by reading current literature, talking with colleagues, and participating in professional conferences. Maintain student attendance records, grades, and other required records. Maintain regularly scheduled office hours to advise and assist students. Compile, administer, and grade examinations or assign this work to others. Conduct research in a particular field of knowledge and publish findings in professional journals, books, and/or electronic media. Supervise undergraduate and/or graduate teaching, internship, and research work. Advise students on academic and vocational curricula and on career issues. Collaborate with colleagues to address teaching and research issues. Compile bibliographies of specialized materials for outside reading assignments. Serve on academic or administrative committees that deal with institutional policies, departmental matters, and academic issues. Participate in student recruitment, registration, and placement activities. Select and obtain materials and supplies such as textbooks and laboratory equipment. Write grant proposals to procure external research funding. Provide professional consulting services to government and/

or industry. Perform administrative duties such as serving as department head. Act as advisers to student organizations. Participate in campus and community events.

Personality Type: Social. These occupations frequently involve working with, communicating with, and teaching people and often involve helping or providing service to others.

GOE—Interest Area/Cluster: 05. Education and Training. **Work Group:** 05.03. Postsecondary and Adult Teaching and Instructing. **Other Jobs in This Work Group:** Adult Literacy, Remedial Education, and GED Teachers and Instructors; Agricultural Sciences Teachers, Postsecondary; Anthropology and Archeology Teachers, Postsecondary; Area, Ethnic, and Cultural Studies Teachers, Postsecondary; Art, Drama, and Music Teachers, Postsecondary; Atmospheric, Earth, Marine, and Space Sciences Teachers, Postsecondary; Biological Science Teachers, Postsecondary; Business Teachers, Postsecondary; Chemistry Teachers, Postsecondary; Communications Teachers, Postsecondary; Computer Science Teachers, Postsecondary; Criminal Justice and Law Enforcement Teachers, Postsecondary; Economics Teachers, Postsecondary; Education Teachers, Postsecondary; Engineering Teachers, Postsecondary; English Language and Literature Teachers, Postsecondary; Environmental Science Teachers, Postsecondary; Farm and Home Management Advisors; Foreign Language and Literature Teachers, Postsecondary; Forestry and Conservation Science Teachers, Postsecondary; Geography Teachers, Postsecondary; Graduate Teaching Assistants; Health Specialties Teachers, Postsecondary; History Teachers, Postsecondary; Home Economics Teachers, Postsecondary; Law Teachers, Postsecondary; Library Science Teachers, Postsecondary; Mathematical Science Teachers, Postsecondary; Nursing Instructors and Teachers, Postsecondary; Philosophy and Religion Teachers, Postsecondary; Physics Teachers, Postsecondary; Political Science Teachers, Postsecondary; Psychology Teachers, Postsecondary; Recreation and Fitness Studies Teachers, Postsecondary; Self-Enrichment Education Teachers; Social Work Teachers, Postsecondary; Sociology Teachers, Postsecondary; Vocational Education Teachers, Postsecondary.

Skills—Technology Design: Generating or adapting equipment and technology to serve user needs. **Operations Analysis:** Analyzing needs and product requirements to create a design. **Instructing:** Teaching others how to do something. **Writing:** Communicating effectively with others in writing as indicated by the needs of the audience. **Science:** Using scientific methods to solve problems. **Complex Problem Solving:** Identifying complex problems, reviewing the options, and implementing solutions. **Speaking:** Talking to others to effectively convey information. **Critical Thinking:** Using logic and analysis to identify the strengths and weaknesses of different approaches.

Education and Training Programs: Architectural Engineering; Architecture (BArch, BA/BS, MArch, MA/MS, PhD); City/Urban, Community, and Regional Planning; Environmental Design/Architecture; Interior Architecture; Landscape Architecture (BS, BSLA, BLA, MSLA, MLA, PhD); Teacher Education and Professional Development, Specific Subject Areas, Other. **Related Knowledge/Courses—Fine Arts:** Theory and techniques required to produce, compose, and perform works of music, dance, visual arts, drama, and sculpture. **Design:** Design techniques, principles, tools, and instruments involved in the production and use of precision technical plans, blueprints, drawings, and models. **Building and Construction:** Materials, methods, and the appropriate tools to construct objects, structures, and buildings. **History and Archeology:** Historical events and their causes, indicators, and impact on particular civilizations and cultures. **Philosophy and Theology:** Different philosophical systems and religions, including their basic principles, values, ethics, ways of thinking, customs, and practices and their impact on human culture. **Geography:** Various methods for describing the location and distribution of land, sea, and air masses, including their physical locations, relationships, and characteristics.

Work Environment: Indoors; sitting.

Archivists

* **Education/Training Required: Master's degree**
* **Annual Earnings: $43,110**
* **Beginning Wage: $26,330**
* **Earnings Growth Potential: Medium**
* **Growth: 14.4%**
* **Annual Job Openings: 795**
* **Self-Employed: 1.3%**
* **Part-Time: 18.4%**

Appraise, edit, and direct safekeeping of permanent records and historically valuable documents. Participate in research activities based on archival materials. Create and maintain accessible, retrievable computer archives and databases, incorporating current advances in electric information storage technology. Organize archival records and develop classification systems to facilitate access to archival materials. Authenticate and appraise historical documents and archival materials. Provide reference services and assistance for users needing archival materials. Direct activities of workers who assist in arranging, cataloguing, exhibiting, and maintaining collections of valuable materials. Prepare archival records, such as document descriptions, to allow easy access to information. Preserve records, documents, and objects, copying records to film, videotape, audiotape, disk, or computer formats as necessary. Establish and administer policy guidelines concerning public access and use of materials. Locate new materials and direct their acquisition and display. Research and record the origins and historical significance of archival materials. Specialize in an area of history or technology, researching topics or items relevant to collections to determine what should be retained or acquired. Coordinate educational and public outreach programs such as tours, workshops, lectures, and classes. Select and edit documents for publication and display, applying knowledge of subject, literary expression, and presentation techniques.

Personality Type: Conventional. These occupations frequently involve following set procedures and routines and can include working with data and details more than with ideas. Usually there is a clear line of authority to follow.

GOE—Interest Area/Cluster: 05. Education and Training. **Work Group:** 05.05. Archival and Museum Services. **Other Jobs in This Work Group:** Audio-Visual Collections Specialists; Curators; Museum Technicians and Conservators.

Skills—Programming: Writing computer programs for various purposes. **Writing:** Communicating effectively with others in writing as indicated by the needs of the audience. **Operations Analysis:** Analyzing needs and product requirements to create a design. **Reading Comprehension:** Understanding written sentences and paragraphs in work-related documents. **Quality Control Analysis:** Evaluating the quality or performance of products, services, or processes. **Persuasion:** Persuading others to approach things differently. **Judgment and Decision Making:** Weighing the relative costs and benefits of a potential action. **Active Listening:** Listening to what other people are saying and asking questions as appropriate.

Education and Training Programs: Art History, Criticism, and Conservation; Cultural Resource Management and Policy Analysis; Historic Preservation and Conservation; Historic Preservation and Conservation, Other; Museology/Museum Studies; Public/Applied History and Archival Administration. **Related Knowledge/Courses—Clerical**

Practices: Administrative and clerical procedures and systems such as word-processing systems, filing and records management systems, stenography and transcription, forms, design principles, and other office procedures and terminology. **History and Archeology:** Historical events and their causes, indicators, and impact on particular civilizations and cultures. **Computers and Electronics:** Electric circuit boards, processors, chips, and computer hardware and software, including applications and programming. **English Language:** The structure and content of the English language, including the meaning and spelling of words, rules of composition, and grammar. **Administration and Management:** Principles and processes involved in business and organizational planning, coordination, and execution. This includes strategic planning, resource allocation, manpower modeling, leadership techniques, and production methods. **Customer and Personal Service:** Principles and processes for providing customer and personal services, including needs assessment techniques, quality service standards, alternative delivery systems, and customer satisfaction evaluation techniques.

Work Environment: Indoors; sitting.

Area, Ethnic, and Cultural Studies Teachers, Postsecondary

* Education/Training Required: Doctoral degree
* Annual Earnings: $59,150
* Beginning Wage: $32,940
* Earnings Growth Potential: High
* Growth: 22.9%
* Annual Job Openings: 1,252
* Self-Employed: 0.4%
* Part-Time: 27.8%

Teach courses pertaining to the culture and development of an area (e.g., Latin America), an ethnic group, or any other group (e.g., women's studies, urban affairs). Keep abreast of developments in their field by reading current literature, talking with colleagues, and participating in professional conferences. Conduct research in a particular field of knowledge and publish findings in professional journals, books, and/or electronic media. Evaluate and grade students' classwork, assignments, and papers. Prepare course materials such as syllabi, homework assignments, and handouts. Prepare and deliver lectures to undergraduate and/or graduate students on topics such as race and ethnic relations, gender studies, and cross-cultural perspectives. Initiate, facilitate, and moderate classroom discussions. Compile, administer, and grade examinations or assign this work to others. Maintain regularly scheduled office hours in order to advise and assist students. Plan, evaluate, and revise curricula, course content, and course materials and methods of instruction. Maintain student attendance records, grades, and other required records. Advise students on academic and vocational curricula and on career issues. Supervise undergraduate and/or graduate teaching, internship, and research work. Select and obtain materials and supplies such as textbooks. Collaborate with colleagues to address teaching and research issues. Serve on academic or administrative committees that deal with institutional policies, departmental matters, and academic issues. Compile bibliographies of specialized materials for outside reading assignments. Write grant proposals to procure external research funding. Participate in campus and community events. Participate in student recruitment, registration, and placement activities. Act as advisers to student organizations. Incorporate experiential/site visit components into courses. Perform administrative duties such as serving as department head. Provide professional consulting services to government and/or industry.

Personality Type: Social. These occupations frequently involve working with, communicating with, and teaching people and often involve helping or providing service to others.

GOE—Interest Area/Cluster: 05. Education and Training. **Work Group:** 05.03. Postsecondary and Adult Teaching and Instructing. **Other Jobs in This Work Group:** Adult Literacy, Remedial Education, and GED Teachers and Instructors; Agricultural Sciences Teachers, Postsecondary; Anthropology and Archeology Teachers, Postsecondary; Architecture Teachers, Postsecondary; Art, Drama, and Music Teachers, Postsecondary; Atmospheric, Earth, Marine, and Space Sciences Teachers, Postsecondary; Biological Science Teachers, Postsecondary; Business Teachers, Postsecondary; Chemistry Teachers, Postsecondary; Communications Teachers, Postsecondary; Computer Science Teachers, Postsecondary; Criminal Justice and Law Enforcement Teachers, Postsecondary; Economics Teachers, Postsecondary; Education Teachers, Postsecondary; Engineering Teachers, Postsecondary; English Language and Literature Teachers, Postsecondary; Environmental Science Teachers, Postsecondary; Farm and Home Management Advisors; Foreign Language and Literature Teachers, Postsecondary; Forestry and Conservation Science Teachers, Postsecondary;

Geography Teachers, Postsecondary; Graduate Teaching Assistants; Health Specialties Teachers, Postsecondary; History Teachers, Postsecondary; Home Economics Teachers, Postsecondary; Law Teachers, Postsecondary; Library Science Teachers, Postsecondary; Mathematical Science Teachers, Postsecondary; Nursing Instructors and Teachers, Postsecondary; Philosophy and Religion Teachers, Postsecondary; Physics Teachers, Postsecondary; Political Science Teachers, Postsecondary; Psychology Teachers, Postsecondary; Recreation and Fitness Studies Teachers, Postsecondary; Self-Enrichment Education Teachers; Social Work Teachers, Postsecondary; Sociology Teachers, Postsecondary; Vocational Education Teachers, Postsecondary.

Skills—Writing: Communicating effectively with others in writing as indicated by the needs of the audience. **Critical Thinking:** Using logic and analysis to identify the strengths and weaknesses of different approaches. **Instructing:** Teaching others how to do something. **Persuasion:** Persuading others to approach things differently. **Active Learning:** Working with new material or information to grasp its implications. **Learning Strategies:** Using multiple approaches when learning or teaching new things. **Speaking:** Talking to others to effectively convey information. **Management of Financial Resources:** Determining how money will be spent to get the work done and accounting for these expenditures.

Education and Training Programs: African Studies; African-American/Black Studies; American Indian/Native American Studies; American/United States Studies/Civilization; Asian Studies/Civilization; Asian-American Studies; European Studies/Civilization; Gay/Lesbian Studies; Hispanic-American, Puerto Rican, and Mexican-American/Chicano Studies; Islamic Studies; Jewish/Judaic Studies; Near and Middle Eastern Studies; Regional Studies (U.S., Canadian, Foreign); Women's Studies; others. **Related Knowledge/Courses—History and Archeology:** Historical events and their causes, indicators, and impact on particular civilizations and cultures. **Sociology and Anthropology:** Group behavior and dynamics; societal trends and influences; and cultures and their history, migrations, ethnicity, and origins. **Foreign Language:** The structure and content of a foreign (non-English) language, including the meaning and spelling of words, rules of composition and grammar, and pronunciation. **Philosophy and Theology:** Different philosophical systems and religions, including their basic principles, values, ethics, ways of thinking, customs, and practices and their impact on human culture. **Geography:** Various methods for describing the location and distribution of land, sea, and air masses, including their physical locations, relationships, and characteristics. **Education and Training:** Instructional methods and training techniques, including curriculum design principles, learning theory, group and individual teaching techniques, design of individual development plans, and test design principles.

Work Environment: Indoors; sitting.

Art Directors

- ❋ Education/Training Required: Work experience plus degree
- ❋ Annual Earnings: $72,320
- ❋ Beginning Wage: $39,600
- ❋ Earnings Growth Potential: High
- ❋ Growth: 9.0%
- ❋ Annual Job Openings: 9,719
- ❋ Self-Employed: 59.0%
- ❋ Part-Time: 22.5%

Formulate design concepts and presentation approaches and direct workers engaged in art work, layout design, and copy writing for visual communications media, such as magazines, books, newspapers, and packaging. Formulate basic layout design or presentation approach and specify material details, such as style and size of type, photographs, graphics, animation, video, and sound. Review and approve proofs of printed copy and art and copy materials developed by staff members. Manage own accounts and projects, working within budget and scheduling requirements. Confer with creative, art, copy-writing, or production department heads to discuss client requirements and presentation concepts and to coordinate creative activities. Present final layouts to clients for approval. Confer with clients to determine objectives; budget; background information; and presentation approaches, styles, and techniques. Hire, train, and direct staff members who develop design concepts into art layouts or who prepare layouts for printing. Work with creative directors to develop design solutions. Review illustrative material to determine if it conforms to standards and specifications. Attend photo shoots and printing sessions to ensure that the products needed are obtained. Create custom illustrations or other graphic elements. Mark up, paste, and complete layouts and write typography instructions to prepare materials for typesetting or printing. Negotiate with printers and estimators to determine what services will be performed. Conceptualize and help design interfaces for multimedia games, products, and devices. Prepare detailed storyboards showing sequence and timing of story development for television production.

Personality Type: Artistic. These occupations frequently involve working with forms, designs, and patterns. They often require self-expression, and the work can be done without following a clear set of rules.

GOE—Interest Area/Cluster: 03. Arts and Communication. **Work Group:** 03.01. Managerial Work in Arts and Communication. **Other Jobs in This Work Group:** Agents and Business Managers of Artists, Performers, and Athletes; Producers; Producers and Directors; Program Directors; Public Relations Managers; Technical Directors/Managers.

Skills—Operations Analysis: Analyzing needs and product requirements to create a design. **Management of Financial Resources:** Determining how money will be spent to get the work done and accounting for these expenditures. **Coordination:** Adjusting actions in relation to others' actions. **Negotiation:** Bringing others together and trying to reconcile differences. **Persuasion:** Persuading others to approach things differently. **Service Orientation:** Actively looking for ways to help people. **Systems Evaluation:** Looking at many indicators of system performance and taking into account their accuracy. **Management of Personnel Resources:** Motivating, developing, and directing people as they work; identifying the best people for the job.

Education and Training Programs: Graphic Design; Intermedia/Multimedia. **Related Knowledge/Courses—Fine Arts:** Theory and techniques required to produce, compose, and perform works of music, dance, visual arts, drama, and sculpture. **Design:** Design techniques, principles, tools, and instruments involved in the production and use of precision technical plans, blueprints, drawings, and models. **Communications and Media:** Media production, communication, and dissemination techniques and methods, including alternative ways to inform and entertain via written, oral, and visual media. **Production and Processing:** Inputs, outputs, raw materials, waste, quality control, costs, and techniques for maximizing the manufacture and distribution of goods. **Computers and Electronics:** Electric circuit boards, processors, chips, and computer hardware and software, including applications and programming. **Administration and Management:** Principles and processes involved in business and organizational planning, coordination, and execution. This includes strategic planning, resource allocation, manpower modeling, leadership techniques, and production methods.

Work Environment: Indoors; sitting; using hands on objects, tools, or controls; repetitive motions.

Art, Drama, and Music Teachers, Postsecondary

- ❋ Education/Training Required: Doctoral degree
- ❋ Annual Earnings: $55,190
- ❋ Beginning Wage: $30,340
- ❋ Earnings Growth Potential: High
- ❋ Growth: 22.9%
- ❋ Annual Job Openings: 12,707
- ❋ Self-Employed: 0.4%
- ❋ Part-Time: 27.8%

Teach courses in drama; music; and the arts, including fine and applied art, such as painting and sculpture, or design and crafts. Evaluate and grade students' classwork, performances, projects, assignments, and papers. Explain and demonstrate artistic techniques. Prepare students for performances, exams, or assessments. Prepare and deliver lectures to undergraduate or graduate students on topics such as acting techniques, fundamentals of music, and art history. Organize performance groups and direct their rehearsals. Prepare course materials such as syllabi, homework assignments, and handouts. Initiate, facilitate, and moderate classroom discussions. Keep abreast of developments in their field by reading current literature, talking with colleagues, and participating in professional conferences. Advise students on academic and vocational curricula and on career issues. Maintain student attendance records, grades, and other required records. Conduct research in a particular field of knowledge and publish findings in professional journals, books, or electronic media. Supervise undergraduate and/or graduate teaching, internship, and research work. Plan, evaluate, and revise curricula, course content, and course materials and methods of instruction. Maintain regularly scheduled office hours to advise and assist students. Compile, administer, and grade examinations or assign this work to others. Participate in student recruitment, registration, and placement activities. Select and obtain materials and supplies such as textbooks and performance pieces. Collaborate with colleagues to address teaching and research issues. Serve on academic or administrative committees that deal with institutional policies, departmental matters, and academic issues. Participate in campus and community events. Keep students informed of community events such as plays and concerts. Compile bibliographies of specialized materials for outside reading assignments. Display students' work in schools, galleries, and exhibitions. Perform administrative duties such as serving as department head. Act as advisers to student organizations. Write grant proposals to procure external research funding. Provide professional consulting services to government or industry.

Personality Type: Social. These occupations frequently involve working with, communicating with, and teaching people and often involve helping or providing service to others.

GOE—Interest Area/Cluster: 05. Education and Training. **Work Group:** 05.03. Postsecondary and Adult Teaching and Instructing. **Other Jobs in This Work Group:** Adult Literacy, Remedial Education, and GED Teachers and Instructors; Agricultural Sciences Teachers, Postsecondary; Anthropology and Archeology Teachers, Postsecondary; Architecture Teachers, Postsecondary; Area, Ethnic, and Cultural Studies Teachers, Postsecondary; Atmospheric, Earth, Marine, and Space Sciences Teachers, Postsecondary; Biological Science Teachers, Postsecondary; Business Teachers, Postsecondary; Chemistry Teachers, Postsecondary; Communications Teachers, Postsecondary; Computer Science Teachers, Postsecondary; Criminal Justice and Law Enforcement Teachers, Postsecondary; Economics Teachers, Postsecondary; Education Teachers, Postsecondary; Engineering Teachers, Postsecondary; English Language and Literature Teachers, Postsecondary; Environmental Science Teachers, Postsecondary; Farm and Home Management Advisors; Foreign Language and Literature Teachers, Postsecondary; Forestry and Conservation Science Teachers, Postsecondary; Geography Teachers, Postsecondary; Graduate Teaching Assistants; Health Specialties Teachers, Postsecondary; History Teachers, Postsecondary; Home Economics Teachers, Postsecondary; Law Teachers, Postsecondary; Library Science Teachers, Postsecondary; Mathematical Science Teachers, Postsecondary; Nursing Instructors and Teachers, Postsecondary; Philosophy and Religion Teachers, Postsecondary; Physics Teachers, Postsecondary; Political Science Teachers, Postsecondary; Psychology Teachers, Postsecondary; Recreation and Fitness Studies Teachers, Postsecondary; Self-Enrichment Education Teachers; Social Work Teachers, Postsecondary; Sociology Teachers, Postsecondary; Vocational Education Teachers, Postsecondary.

Skills—Instructing: Teaching others how to do something. **Social Perceptiveness:** Being aware of others' reactions and understanding why they react the way they do. **Speaking:** Talking to others to effectively convey information. **Active Listening:** Listening to what other people are saying and asking questions as appropriate. **Persuasion:** Persuading others to approach things differently. **Learning Strategies:**

Using multiple approaches when learning or teaching new things. **Critical Thinking:** Using logic and analysis to identify the strengths and weaknesses of different approaches. **Monitoring:** Assessing how well one is doing when learning or doing something.

Education and Training Programs: Art History, Criticism, and Conservation; Art/Art Studies, General; Arts Management; Cinema Studies; Cinematography and Film/Video Production; Crafts/Craft Design; Dance, General; Fashion Design; Graphic Design; Industrial Design; Interior Design; Metal and Jewelry Arts; Music Performance, General; Painting; Photography; Playwriting and Screenwriting; Printmaking; Sculpture; Studio Arts, General; Technical Theatre/Theatre Design and Technology; Theatre Arts; Voice and Opera; others. **Related Knowledge/Courses—Fine Arts:** Theory and techniques required to produce, compose, and perform works of music, dance, visual arts, drama, and sculpture. **History and Archeology:** Historical events and their causes, indicators, and impact on particular civilizations and cultures. **Philosophy and Theology:** Different philosophical systems and religions, including their basic principles, values, ethics, ways of thinking, customs, and practices and their impact on human culture. **Education and Training:** Instructional methods and training techniques, including curriculum design principles, learning theory, group and individual teaching techniques, design of individual development plans, and test design principles. **Communications and Media:** Media production, communication, and dissemination techniques and methods, including alternative ways to inform and entertain via written, oral, and visual media. **Sociology and Anthropology:** Group behavior and dynamics; societal trends and influences; and cultures and their history, migrations, ethnicity, and origins.

Work Environment: Indoors; noisy; sitting.

Assessors

- ❋ Education/Training Required: Bachelor's degree
- ❋ Annual Earnings: $46,130
- ❋ Beginning Wage: $25,110
- ❋ Earnings Growth Potential: High
- ❋ Growth: 16.9%
- ❋ Annual Job Openings: 6,493
- ❋ Self-Employed: 32.7%
- ❋ Part-Time: 8.4%

The job openings listed here are shared with Appraisers, Real Estate.

Appraise real and personal property to determine its fair value. May assess taxes in accordance with prescribed schedules. Determine taxability and value of properties, using methods such as field inspection, structural measurement, calculation, sales analysis, market trend studies, and income and expense analysis. Inspect new construction and major improvements to existing structures to determine values. Explain assessed values to property owners and defend appealed assessments at public hearings. Inspect properties, considering factors such as market value, location, and building or replacement costs to determine appraisal value. Prepare and maintain current data on each parcel assessed, including maps of boundaries, inventories of land and structures, property characteristics, and any applicable exemptions. Identify the ownership of each piece of taxable property. Conduct regular reviews of property within jurisdictions to determine changes in property due to construction or demolition. Complete and maintain assessment rolls that show the assessed values and status of all property in a municipality. Issue notices of assessments and taxes. Review information about transfers of property to ensure its accuracy, checking basic information on buyers, sellers, and sales prices and making corrections as necessary. Maintain familiarity with aspects of local real estate markets. Analyze trends in sales prices, construction costs, and rents to assess property values or determine the accuracy of assessments. Approve applications for property tax exemptions or deductions. Establish uniform and equitable systems for assessing all classes and kinds of property. Write and submit appraisal and tax reports for public record. Serve on assessment review boards. Hire staff members. Provide sales analyses to be used for equalization of school aid. Calculate tax bills for properties by multiplying assessed values by jurisdiction tax rates.

Personality Type: Conventional. These occupations frequently involve following set procedures and routines and can include working with data and details more than with ideas. Usually there is a clear line of authority to follow.

GOE—Interest Area/Cluster: 06. Finance and Insurance. **Work Group:** 06.02. Finance/Insurance Investigation and Analysis. **Other Jobs in This Work Group:** Appraisers and Assessors of Real Estate; Appraisers, Real Estate; Claims Adjusters, Examiners, and Investigators; Claims Examiners, Property and Casualty Insurance; Cost Estimators; Credit Analysts; Financial Analysts; Insurance Adjusters, Examiners, and Investigators; Insurance Appraisers, Auto Damage; Insurance Underwriters; Loan Counselors; Loan Officers; Market Research Analysts; Survey Researchers.

Skills—Mathematics: Using mathematics to solve problems. **Systems Analysis:** Determining how a system should work and how changes will affect outcomes. **Speaking:** Talking to others to effectively convey information. **Negotiation:** Bringing others together and trying to reconcile differences. **Systems Evaluation:** Looking at many indicators of system performance and taking into account their accuracy. **Active Listening:** Listening to what other people are saying and asking questions as appropriate. **Management of Financial Resources:** Determining how money will be spent to get the work done and accounting for these expenditures. **Persuasion:** Persuading others to approach things differently.

Education and Training Program: Real Estate. **Related Knowledge/Courses—Building and Construction:** Materials, methods, and the appropriate tools to construct objects, structures, and buildings. **Clerical Practices:** Administrative and clerical procedures and systems such as word-processing systems, filing and records management systems, stenography and transcription, forms, design principles, and other office procedures and terminology. **Law and Government:** Laws, legal codes, court procedures, precedents, government regulations, executive orders, agency rules, and the democratic political process. **Mathematics:** Numbers and their operations and interrelationships, including arithmetic, algebra, geometry, calculus, and statistics and their applications. **Geography:** Various methods for describing the location and distribution of land, sea, and air masses, including their physical locations, relationships, and characteristics. **Economics and Accounting:** Economic and accounting principles and practices, the financial markets, banking, and the analysis and reporting of financial data.

Work Environment: More often indoors than outdoors; sitting; using hands on objects, tools, or controls; repetitive motions.

Astronomers

- ❋ Education/Training Required: Doctoral degree
- ❋ Annual Earnings: $99,020
- ❋ Beginning Wage: $44,490
- ❋ Earnings Growth Potential: Very high
- ❋ Growth: 5.6%
- ❋ Annual Job Openings: 128
- ❋ Self-Employed: 0.4%
- ❋ Part-Time: 5.2%

Observe, research, and interpret celestial and astronomical phenomena to increase basic knowledge and apply such information to practical problems. Study celestial phenomena, using a variety of ground-based and space-borne telescopes and scientific instruments. Analyze research data to determine its significance, using computers. Present research findings at scientific conferences and in papers written for scientific journals. Measure radio, infrared, gamma, and X-ray emissions from extraterrestrial sources. Develop theories based on personal observations or on observations and theories of other astronomers. Raise funds for scientific research. Collaborate with other astronomers to carry out research projects. Develop instrumentation and software for astronomical observation and analysis. Teach astronomy or astrophysics. Develop and modify astronomy-related programs for public presentation. Calculate orbits and determine sizes, shapes, brightness, and motions of different celestial bodies. Direct the operations of a planetarium.

Personality Type: Investigative. These occupations frequently involve working with ideas and require an extensive amount of thinking. They can involve searching for facts and figuring out problems mentally.

GOE—Interest Area/Cluster: 15. Scientific Research, Engineering, and Mathematics. **Work Group:** 15.02. Physical Sciences. **Other Jobs in This Work Group:** Atmospheric and Space Scientists; Chemists; Geographers; Geoscientists, Except Hydrologists and Geographers; Hydrologists; Materials Scientists; Physicists.

Skills—Science: Using scientific methods to solve problems. **Programming:** Writing computer programs for various purposes. **Mathematics:** Using mathematics to solve problems. **Complex Problem Solving:** Identifying complex problems, reviewing the options, and implementing solutions. **Technology Design:** Generating or adapting equipment and technology to serve user needs. **Active Learning:** Working with new material or information to grasp its implications. **Critical Thinking:** Using logic and analysis to identify the strengths and weaknesses of different approaches. **Reading Comprehension:** Understanding written sentences and paragraphs in work-related documents.

Education and Training Programs: Astronomy; Astronomy and Astrophysics, Other; Astrophysics; Planetary Astronomy and Science. **Related Knowledge/Courses—Physics:** Physical principles, laws, and applications, including air, water, material dynamics, light, atomic principles, heat, electric theory, earth formations, and meteorological and related natural phenomena. **Mathematics:** Numbers and their operations and interrelationships, including arithmetic, algebra, geometry, calculus, and statistics and their applications. **Engineering and Technology:** Equipment, tools, and mechanical devices and their uses to produce motion, light, power, technology, and other applications. **Chemistry:** The composition, structure, and properties of substances and of the chemical processes and transformations that they undergo. This includes uses of chemicals and their interactions, danger signs, production techniques, and disposal methods. **Computers and Electronics:** Electric circuit boards, processors, chips, and computer hardware and software, including applications and programming. **Education and Training:** Instructional methods and training techniques, including curriculum design principles, learning theory, group and individual teaching techniques, design of individual development plans, and test design principles.

Work Environment: Indoors; sitting.

Athletes and Sports Competitors

- ❋ Education/Training Required: Long-term on-the-job training
- ❋ Annual Earnings: $38,440
- ❋ Beginning Wage: $15,210
- ❋ Earnings Growth Potential: Very high
- ❋ Growth: 19.2%
- ❋ Annual Job Openings: 4,293
- ❋ Self-Employed: 27.0%
- ❋ Part-Time: 39.1%

Compete in athletic events. Assess performance following athletic competition, identifying strengths and weaknesses and making adjustments to improve future performance. Receive instructions from coaches and other sports staff prior to events and discuss performance afterwards. Lead teams by serving as captains. Maintain equipment used in a particular sport. Represent teams or professional sports clubs, performing such activities as meeting with members of the media, making speeches, or participating in charity events. Participate in athletic events and competitive sports according to established rules and regulations. Attend scheduled practice and training sessions. Exercise and practice under the direction of athletic trainers or professional coaches in order to develop skills, improve physical condition, and prepare for competitions. Maintain optimum physical fitness levels by training regularly, following nutrition plans, and consulting with health professionals.

Personality Type: Realistic. These occupations frequently involve work activities that include practical, hands-on

problems and solutions. They often deal with plants; animals; and real-world materials such as wood, tools, and machinery. Many of the occupations require working outside and don't involve a lot of paperwork or working closely with others.

GOE—Interest Area/Cluster: 09. Hospitality, Tourism, and Recreation. **Work Group:** 09.06. Sports. **Other Jobs in This Work Group:** Coaches and Scouts; Umpires, Referees, and Other Sports Officials.

Skills—Equipment Maintenance: Performing routine maintenance and determining when and what kind of maintenance is needed. **Equipment Selection:** Determining the kind of tools and equipment needed to do a job. **Troubleshooting:** Determining what is causing an operating error and deciding what to do about it. **Time Management:** Managing one's own time and the time of others. **Learning Strategies:** Using multiple approaches when learning or teaching new things. **Active Learning:** Working with new material or information to grasp its implications. **Judgment and Decision Making:** Weighing the relative costs and benefits of a potential action. **Repairing:** Repairing machines or systems, using the needed tools.

Education and Training Program: Health and Physical Education, General. **Related Knowledge/Courses—Therapy and Counseling:** Information and techniques needed to rehabilitate physical and mental ailments and to provide career guidance, including alternative treatments, rehabilitation equipment and its proper use, and methods to evaluate treatment effects. **Communications and Media:** Media production, communication, and dissemination techniques and methods, including alternative ways to inform and entertain via written, oral, and visual media. **Psychology:** Human behavior and performance, mental processes, psychological research methods, and the assessment and treatment of behavioral and affective disorders. **Sales and Marketing:** Principles and methods involved in showing, promoting, and selling products or services. This includes marketing strategies and tactics, product demonstration and sales techniques, and sales control systems. **Personnel and Human Resources:** Principles and procedures for personnel recruitment; selection; training; compensation and benefits; labor relations and negotiation; and personnel information systems.

Work Environment: Indoors; very hot or cold; keeping or regaining balance; using hands on objects, tools, or controls; bending or twisting the body; repetitive motions.

Athletic Trainers

- ❋ Education/Training Required: Bachelor's degree
- ❋ Annual Earnings: $38,360
- ❋ Beginning Wage: $23,430
- ❋ Earnings Growth Potential: Medium
- ❋ Growth: 24.3%
- ❋ Annual Job Openings: 1,669
- ❋ Self-Employed: 2.4%
- ❋ Part-Time: 8.0%

Evaluate, advise, and treat athletes to assist recovery from injury, avoid injury, or maintain peak physical fitness. Conduct an initial assessment of an athlete's injury or illness to provide emergency or continued care and to determine whether he or she should be referred to physicians for definitive diagnosis and treatment. Care for athletic injuries, using physical therapy equipment, techniques, and medication. Evaluate athletes' readiness to play and provide participation clearances when necessary and warranted. Apply protective or injury-preventive devices such as tape, bandages, or braces to body parts such as ankles, fingers, or wrists. Assess and report the progress of recovering athletes to coaches and physicians. Collaborate with physicians to develop and implement comprehensive rehabilitation programs for athletic injuries. Advise athletes on the proper use of equipment. Plan and implement comprehensive athletic injury and illness prevention programs. Develop training programs and routines designed to improve athletic performance. Travel with athletic teams to be available at sporting events. Instruct coaches, athletes, parents, medical personnel, and community members in the care and prevention of athletic injuries. Inspect playing fields to locate any items that could injure players. Conduct research and provide instruction on subject matter related to athletic training or sports medicine. Recommend special diets to improve athletes' health, increase their stamina, or alter their weight. Massage body parts to relieve soreness, strains, and bruises. Confer with coaches to select protective equipment. Accompany injured athletes to hospitals. Perform team-support duties such as running errands, maintaining equipment, and stocking supplies. Lead stretching exercises for team members before games and practices.

Personality Type: Social. These occupations frequently involve working with, communicating with, and teaching people and often involve helping or providing service to others.

GOE—Interest Area/Cluster: 08. Health Science. **Work Group:** 08.09. Health Protection and Promotion. **Other Jobs in This Work Group:** Dietetic Technicians; Dietitians and Nutritionists; Embalmers.

Skills—Science: Using scientific methods to solve problems. **Social Perceptiveness:** Being aware of others' reactions and understanding why they react the way they do. **Management of Material Resources:** Obtaining and seeing to the appropriate use of equipment, facilities, and materials needed to do certain work. **Management of Financial Resources:** Determining how money will be spent to get the work done and accounting for these expenditures. **Time Management:** Managing one's own time and the time of others. **Writing:** Communicating effectively with others in writing as indicated by the needs of the audience. **Management of Personnel Resources:** Motivating, developing, and directing people as they work; identifying the best people for the job. **Equipment Selection:** Determining the kind of tools and equipment needed to do a job.

Education and Training Program: Athletic Training/Trainer Training. **Related Knowledge/Courses—Therapy and Counseling:** Information and techniques needed to rehabilitate physical and mental ailments and to provide career guidance, including alternative treatments, rehabilitation equipment and its proper use, and methods to evaluate treatment effects. **Medicine and Dentistry:** The information and techniques needed to diagnose and treat injuries, diseases, and deformities. This includes symptoms, treatment alternatives, drug properties and interactions, and preventive health-care measures. **Biology:** Plant and animal living tissue, cells, organisms, and entities, including their functions, interdependencies, and interactions with each other and the environment. **Psychology:** Human behavior and performance, mental processes, psychological research methods, and the assessment and treatment of behavioral and affective disorders. **Sociology and Anthropology:** Group behavior and dynamics; societal trends and influences; and cultures and their history, migrations, ethnicity, and origins. **Physics:** Physical principles, laws, and applications, including air, water, material dynamics, light, atomic principles, heat, electric theory, earth formations, and meteorological and related natural phenomena.

Work Environment: More often indoors than outdoors; very hot or cold; contaminants; disease or infections; standing.

Atmospheric and Space Scientists

- ❋ Education/Training Required: Bachelor's degree
- ❋ Annual Earnings: $78,390
- ❋ Beginning Wage: $37,030
- ❋ Earnings Growth Potential: Very high
- ❋ Growth: 10.6%
- ❋ Annual Job Openings: 735
- ❋ Self-Employed: 0.0%
- ❋ Part-Time: 5.2%

Investigate atmospheric phenomena and interpret meteorological data gathered by surface and air stations, satellites, and radar to prepare reports and forecasts for public and other uses. Study and interpret data, reports, maps, photographs, and charts to predict long- and short-range weather conditions, using computer models and knowledge of climate theory, physics, and mathematics. Broadcast weather conditions, forecasts, and severe weather warnings to the public via television, radio, and the Internet or provide this information to the news media. Gather data from sources such as surface and upper air stations, satellites, weather bureaus, and radar for use in meteorological reports and forecasts. Prepare forecasts and briefings to meet the needs of industry, business, government, and other groups. Apply meteorological knowledge to problems in areas including agriculture, pollution control, and water management and to issues such as global warming or ozone depletion. Conduct basic or applied meteorological research into the processes and determinants of atmospheric phenomena, weather, and climate. Operate computer graphic equipment to produce weather reports and maps for analysis, distribution, or use in weather broadcasts. Measure wind, temperature, and humidity in the upper atmosphere, using weather balloons. Develop and use weather forecasting tools such as mathematical and computer models. Direct forecasting services at weather stations or at radio or television broadcasting facilities. Research and analyze the impact of industrial projects and pollution on climate, air quality, and weather phenomena. Collect air samples from planes and ships over land and sea to study atmospheric composition. Conduct numerical simulations of climate conditions to understand and predict global and regional weather patterns. Collect and analyze historical climate information such as precipitation and temperature records help predict future weather and climate trends. Consult with agencies, professionals, or researchers regarding the use and interpretation of climatological information. Design and develop new equipment and methods for meteorological data collection, remote sensing, or related applications. Make scientific presentations and publish reports, articles, or texts.

Personality Type: Investigative. These occupations frequently involve working with ideas and require an extensive amount of thinking. They can involve searching for facts and figuring out problems mentally.

GOE—Interest Area/Cluster: 15. Scientific Research, Engineering, and Mathematics. **Work Group:** 15.02. Physical Sciences. **Other Jobs in This Work Group:** Astronomers; Chemists; Geographers; Geoscientists, Except Hydrologists and Geographers; Hydrologists; Materials Scientists; Physicists.

Skills—Science: Using scientific methods to solve problems. **Programming:** Writing computer programs for various purposes. **Judgment and Decision Making:** Weighing the relative costs and benefits of a potential action. **Operation Monitoring:** Watching gauges, dials, or other indicators to make sure a machine is working properly. **Operations Analysis:** Analyzing needs and product requirements to create a design. **Technology Design:** Generating or adapting equipment and technology to serve user needs. **Quality Control Analysis:** Evaluating the quality or performance of products, services, or processes. **Operation and Control:** Controlling operations of equipment or systems.

Education and Training Programs: Atmospheric Chemistry and Climatology; Atmospheric Physics and Dynamics; Atmospheric Sciences and Meteorology, General; Atmospheric Sciences and Meteorology, Other; Meteorology. **Related Knowledge/Courses—Geography:** Various methods for describing the location and distribution of land, sea, and air masses, including their physical locations, relationships, and characteristics. **Physics:** Physical principles, laws, and applications, including air, water, material dynamics, light, atomic principles, heat, electric theory, earth formations, and meteorological and related natural phenomena. **Mathematics:** Numbers and their operations and interrelationships, including arithmetic, algebra, geometry, calculus, and statistics and their applications. **Computers and Electronics:** Electric circuit boards, processors, chips, and computer hardware and software, including applications and programming. **Communications and Media:** Media production, communication, and dissemination techniques and methods, including alternative ways to inform and entertain via written, oral, and visual media. **Customer and Personal Service:** Principles and processes for providing customer and personal services, including needs assessment techniques, quality service standards, alternative delivery systems, and customer satisfaction evaluation techniques.

Work Environment: Indoors; noisy; sitting; repetitive motions.

Atmospheric, Earth, Marine, and Space Sciences Teachers, Postsecondary

- ❋ Education/Training Required: Doctoral degree
- ❋ Annual Earnings: $73,280
- ❋ Beginning Wage: $39,840
- ❋ Earnings Growth Potential: High
- ❋ Growth: 22.9%
- ❋ Annual Job Openings: 1,553
- ❋ Self-Employed: 0.4%
- ❋ Part-Time: 27.8%

Teach courses in the physical sciences, except chemistry and physics. Conduct research in a particular field of knowledge and publish findings in professional journals, books, and/or electronic media. Write grant proposals to procure external research funding. Keep abreast of developments in their field by reading current literature, talking with colleagues, and participating in professional conferences. Supervise undergraduate and/or graduate teaching, internships, and research work. Prepare and deliver lectures to undergraduate and/or graduate students on topics such as structural geology, micrometeorology, and atmospheric thermodynamics. Supervise laboratory work and fieldwork. Evaluate and grade students' classwork, assignments, and papers. Prepare course materials such as syllabi, homework assignments, and handouts. Collaborate with colleagues to address teaching and research issues. Compile, administer, and grade examinations or assign this work to others. Plan, evaluate, and revise curricula, course content, course materials, and methods of instruction. Initiate, facilitate, and moderate classroom discussions. Maintain regularly scheduled office hours to advise and assist students. Advise students on academic and vocational curricula and on career issues. Maintain student attendance records, grades, and other required records. Participate in student recruitment, registration, and placement activities. Perform administrative duties such as serving as department head. Select and obtain materials and supplies such as textbooks and laboratory equipment. Serve on academic or administrative committees that deal with institutional policies, departmental matters, and academic issues. Compile bibliographies of specialized materials for outside reading assignments. Provide professional consulting services to government and/or industry. Act as adviser to student organizations. Participate in campus and community events.

Personality Type: Social. These occupations frequently involve working with, communicating with, and teaching people and often involve helping or providing service to others.

GOE—Interest Area/Cluster: 05. Education and Training. **Work Group:** 05.03. Postsecondary and Adult Teaching and Instructing. **Other Jobs in This Work Group:** Adult Literacy, Remedial Education, and GED Teachers and Instructors; Agricultural Sciences Teachers, Postsecondary; Anthropology and Archeology Teachers, Postsecondary; Architecture Teachers, Postsecondary; Area, Ethnic, and Cultural Studies Teachers, Postsecondary; Art, Drama, and Music Teachers, Postsecondary; Biological Science Teachers, Postsecondary; Business Teachers, Postsecondary; Chemistry Teachers, Postsecondary; Communications Teachers, Postsecondary; Computer Science Teachers, Postsecondary; Criminal Justice and Law Enforcement Teachers, Postsecondary; Economics Teachers, Postsecondary; Education Teachers, Postsecondary; Engineering Teachers, Postsecondary; English Language and Literature Teachers, Postsecondary; Environmental Science Teachers, Postsecondary; Farm and Home Management Advisors; Foreign Language and Literature Teachers, Postsecondary; Forestry and Conservation Science Teachers, Postsecondary; Geography Teachers, Postsecondary; Graduate Teaching Assistants; Health Specialties Teachers, Postsecondary; History Teachers, Postsecondary; Home Economics Teachers, Postsecondary; Law Teachers, Postsecondary; Library Science Teachers, Postsecondary; Mathematical Science Teachers, Postsecondary; Nursing Instructors and Teachers, Postsecondary; Philosophy and Religion Teachers, Postsecondary; Physics Teachers, Postsecondary; Political Science Teachers, Postsecondary; Psychology Teachers, Postsecondary; Recreation and Fitness Studies Teachers, Postsecondary; Self-Enrichment Education Teachers; Social Work Teachers, Postsecondary; Sociology Teachers, Postsecondary; Vocational Education Teachers, Postsecondary.

Skills—Science: Using scientific methods to solve problems. **Programming:** Writing computer programs for various purposes. **Mathematics:** Using mathematics to solve problems. **Management of Financial Resources:** Determining how money will be spent to get the work done and accounting for these expenditures. **Complex Problem Solving:** Identifying complex problems, reviewing the options, and implementing solutions. **Writing:** Communicating effectively with others in writing as indicated by the needs of the audience. **Active Learning:** Working with new material or information to grasp its implications. **Reading Comprehension:** Understanding written sentences and paragraphs in work-related documents.

Education and Training Programs: Acoustics; Astronomy; Astrophysics; Atmospheric Sciences and Meteorology, General; Atomic Physics; Geochemistry; Geochemistry and Petrology; Geology/Earth Science, General; Geophysics and Seismology; Hydrology and Water Resources Science; Meteorology; Nuclear Physics; Paleontology; Planetary Astronomy and Science; Plasma and High-Temperature Physics; Science Teacher Education/General Science Teacher Education; Solid State and Low-Temperature Physics; Theoretical and Mathematical Physics; others. **Related Knowledge/Courses—Physics:** Physical principles, laws, and applications, including air, water, material dynamics, light, atomic principles, heat, electric theory, earth formations, and meteorological and related natural phenomena. **Geography:** Various methods for describing the location and distribution of land, sea, and air masses, including their physical locations, relationships, and characteristics. **Chemistry:** The composition, structure, and properties of substances and of the chemical processes and transformations that they undergo. This includes uses of chemicals and their interactions, danger signs, production techniques, and disposal methods. **Biology:** Plant and animal living tissue, cells, organisms, and entities, including their functions, interdependencies, and interactions with each other and the environment. **Mathematics:** Numbers and their operations and interrelationships, including arithmetic, algebra, geometry, calculus, and statistics and their applications. **Education and Training:** Instructional methods and training techniques, including curriculum design principles, learning theory, group and individual teaching techniques, design of individual development plans, and test design principles.

Work Environment: Indoors; sitting.

Audio and Video Equipment Technicians

- ❋ Education/Training Required: Long-term on-the-job training
- ❋ Annual Earnings: $36,050
- ❋ Beginning Wage: $20,450
- ❋ Earnings Growth Potential: High
- ❋ Growth: 24.2%
- ❋ Annual Job Openings: 4,681
- ❋ Self-Employed: 12.8%
- ❋ Part-Time: 12.9%

Set up or set up and operate audio and video equipment, including microphones, sound speakers, video screens, projectors, video monitors, recording equipment, connecting wires and cables, sound and mixing boards, and related electronic equipment for concerts, sports events, meetings and conventions, presentations, and news conferences. May also set up and operate associated spotlights and other custom lighting systems. Notify supervisors when major equipment repairs are needed. Monitor incoming and outgoing pictures and sound feeds to ensure quality; notify directors of any possible problems. Mix and regulate sound inputs and feeds or coordinate audio feeds with television pictures. Install, adjust, and operate electronic equipment used to record, edit, and transmit radio and television programs, cable programs, and motion pictures. Design layouts of audio and video equipment and perform upgrades and maintenance. Perform minor repairs and routine cleaning of audio and video equipment. Diagnose and resolve media system problems in classrooms. Switch sources of video input from one camera or studio to another, from film to live programming, or from network to local programming. Meet with directors and senior members of camera crews to discuss assignments and determine filming sequences, camera movements, and picture composition. Construct and position properties, sets, lighting equipment, and other equipment. Compress, digitize, duplicate, and store audio and video data. Obtain, set up, and load videotapes for scheduled productions or broadcasts. Edit videotapes by erasing and removing portions of programs and adding video or sound as required. Direct and coordinate activities of assistants and other personnel during production. Plan and develop pre-production ideas into outlines, scripts, storyboards, and graphics, using own ideas or specifications of assignments. Maintain inventories of audiotapes and videotapes and related supplies.

Determine formats, approaches, content, levels, and media to effectively meet objectives within budgetary constraints, utilizing research, knowledge, and training. Record and edit audio material such as movie soundtracks, using audio recording and editing equipment. Inform users of audiotaping and videotaping service policies and procedures. Obtain and preview musical performance programs prior to events to become familiar with the order and approximate times of pieces. Produce rough and finished graphics and graphic designs. Locate and secure settings, properties, effects, and other production necessities.

Personality Type: Realistic. These occupations frequently involve work activities that include practical, hands-on problems and solutions. They often deal with plants; animals; and real-world materials such as wood, tools, and machinery. Many of the occupations require working outside and don't involve a lot of paperwork or working closely with others.

GOE—Interest Area/Cluster: 03. Arts and Communication. **Work Group:** 03.09. Media Technology. **Other Jobs in This Work Group:** Broadcast Technicians; Camera Operators, Television, Video, and Motion Picture; Film and Video Editors; Multi-Media Artists and Animators; Photographers; Radio Operators; Sound Engineering Technicians.

Skills—Installation: Installing equipment, machines, wiring, or programs to meet specifications. **Operation and Control:** Controlling operations of equipment or systems. **Equipment Maintenance:** Performing routine maintenance and determining when and what kind of maintenance is needed. **Troubleshooting:** Determining what is causing an operating error and deciding what to do about it. **Operation Monitoring:** Watching gauges, dials, or other indicators to make sure a machine is working properly. **Repairing:** Repairing machines or systems, using the needed tools. **Equipment Selection:** Determining the kind of tools and equipment needed to do a job. **Technology Design:** Generating or adapting equipment and technology to serve user needs.

Education and Training Programs: Agricultural Communication/Journalism; Photographic and Film/Video Technology/Technician and Assistant Training; Recording Arts Technology/Technician Training. **Related Knowledge/Courses—Computers and Electronics:** Electric circuit boards, processors, chips, and computer hardware and software, including applications and programming. **Telecommunications:** Transmission, broadcasting, switching, control, and operation of telecommunications

systems. **Engineering and Technology:** Equipment, tools, and mechanical devices and their uses to produce motion, light, power, technology, and other applications. **Communications and Media:** Media production, communication, and dissemination techniques and methods, including alternative ways to inform and entertain via written, oral, and visual media. **Mechanical Devices:** Machines and tools, including their designs, uses, benefits, repair, and maintenance. **Physics:** Physical principles, laws, and applications, including air, water, material dynamics, light, atomic principles, heat, electric theory, earth formations, and meteorological and related natural phenomena.

Work Environment: Indoors; standing; using hands on objects, tools, or controls.

Audiologists

* Education/Training Required: First professional degree
* Annual Earnings: $59,440
* Beginning Wage: $38,390
* Earnings Growth Potential: Medium
* Growth: 9.8%
* Annual Job Openings: 980
* Self-Employed: 10.2%
* Part-Time: 28.3%

Assess and treat persons with hearing and related disorders. May fit hearing aids and provide auditory training. May perform research related to hearing problems. Evaluate hearing and speech/language disorders to determine diagnoses and courses of treatment. Administer hearing or speech/language evaluations, tests, or examinations to patients to collect information on type and degree of impairment, using specialized instruments and electronic equipment. Fit and dispense assistive devices, such as hearing aids. Maintain client records at all stages, including initial evaluation and discharge. Refer clients to additional medical or educational services if needed. Counsel and instruct clients in techniques to improve hearing or speech impairment, including sign language or lipreading. Monitor clients' progress and discharge them from treatment when goals are attained. Plan and conduct treatment programs for clients' hearing or speech problems, consulting with physicians, nurses, psychologists, and other health-care personnel as necessary. Recommend assistive devices according to clients' needs or nature of impairments. Participate in conferences or training to update or share knowledge of new hearing or speech disorder treatment methods or technologies. Instruct clients, parents, teachers, or employers in how to avoid behavior patterns that lead to miscommunication. Examine and clean patients' ear canals. Advise educators or other medical staff on speech or hearing topics. Educate and supervise audiology students and health-care personnel. Fit and tune cochlear implants, providing rehabilitation for adjustment to listening with implant amplification systems. Work with multidisciplinary teams to assess and rehabilitate recipients of implanted hearing devices. Develop and supervise hearing screening programs. Conduct or direct research on hearing or speech topics and report findings to help in the development of procedures, technology, or treatments. Measure noise levels in workplaces and conduct hearing protection programs in industry, schools, and communities.

Personality Type: Investigative. These occupations frequently involve working with ideas and require an extensive amount of thinking. They can involve searching for facts and figuring out problems mentally.

GOE—Interest Area/Cluster: 08. Health Science. **Work Group:** 08.07. Medical Therapy. **Other Jobs in This Work Group:** Massage Therapists; Occupational Therapist Aides; Occupational Therapist Assistants; Occupational Therapists; Physical Therapist Aides; Physical Therapist Assistants; Physical Therapists; Radiation Therapists; Recreational Therapists; Respiratory Therapists; Respiratory Therapy Technicians; Speech-Language Pathologists.

Skills—Science: Using scientific methods to solve problems. **Social Perceptiveness:** Being aware of others' reactions and understanding why they react the way they do. **Service Orientation:** Actively looking for ways to help people. **Equipment Selection:** Determining the kind of tools and equipment needed to do a job. **Persuasion:** Persuading others to approach things differently. **Reading Comprehension:** Understanding written sentences and paragraphs in work-related documents. **Technology Design:** Generating or adapting equipment and technology to serve user needs. **Equipment Maintenance:** Performing routine maintenance and determining when and what kind of maintenance is needed.

Education and Training Programs: Audiology/Audiologist and Hearing Sciences; Audiology/Audiologist and Speech-Language Pathology/Pathologist Training; Communication Disorders Sciences and Services, Other; Communication Disorders, General. **Related Knowledge/Courses—Therapy and Counseling:** Information and techniques needed to rehabilitate physical and mental ailments and to provide career guidance, including alternative treatments, rehabilitation equipment and its proper use, and methods to evaluate treatment effects. **Medicine and Dentistry:** The information and techniques needed to diagnose and treat injuries, diseases, and deformities. This includes symptoms, treatment alternatives, drug properties and interactions, and preventive health-care measures. **Psychology:** Human behavior and performance, mental processes, psychological research methods, and the assessment and treatment of behavioral and affective disorders. **Sales and Marketing:** Principles and methods involved in showing, promoting, and selling products or services. This includes marketing strategies and tactics, product demonstration and sales techniques, and sales control systems. **Customer and Personal Service:** Principles and processes for providing customer and personal services, including needs assessment techniques, quality service standards, alternative delivery systems, and customer satisfaction evaluation techniques. **Sociology and Anthropology:** Group behavior and dynamics; societal trends and influences; and cultures and their history, migrations, ethnicity, and origins.

Work Environment: Indoors; disease or infections; sitting; using hands on objects, tools, or controls.

Auditors

- ❋ Education/Training Required: Bachelor's degree
- ❋ Annual Earnings: $57,060
- ❋ Beginning Wage: $35,570
- ❋ Earnings Growth Potential: Medium
- ❋ Growth: 17.7%
- ❋ Annual Job Openings: 134,463
- ❋ Self-Employed: 9.5%
- ❋ Part-Time: 9.3%

The job openings listed here are shared with Accountants.

Examine and analyze accounting records to determine financial status of establishment and prepare financial reports concerning operating procedures. Collect and analyze data to detect deficient controls; duplicated effort; extravagance; fraud; or non-compliance with laws, regulations, and management policies. Prepare detailed reports on audit findings. Supervise auditing of establishments and determine scope of investigation required. Report to management about asset utilization and audit results and recommend changes in operations and financial activities. Inspect account books and accounting systems for efficiency, effectiveness, and use of accepted accounting procedures to record transactions. Examine records and interview workers to ensure recording of transactions and compliance with laws and regulations. Examine and evaluate financial and information systems, recommending controls to ensure system reliability and data integrity. Review data about material assets, net worth, liabilities, capital stock, surplus, income, and expenditures. Confer with company officials about financial and regulatory matters. Examine whether the organization's objectives are reflected in its management activities and whether employees understand the objectives. Prepare, analyze, and verify annual reports, financial statements, and other records, using accepted accounting and statistical procedures to assess financial condition and facilitate financial planning. Inspect cash on hand, notes receivable and payable, negotiable securities, and canceled checks to confirm records are accurate. Examine inventory to verify journal and ledger entries. Direct activities of personnel engaged in filing, recording, compiling, and transmitting financial records. Conduct pre-implementation audits to determine whether systems and programs under development will work as planned. Audit payroll and personnel records to determine unemployment insurance premiums, workers' compensation coverage, liabilities, and compliance with tax laws. Evaluate taxpayer finances to determine tax liability, using knowledge of interest and discount rates, annuities, valuation of stocks and bonds, and amortization valuation of depletable assets. Review taxpayer accounts and conduct audits on-site, by correspondence, or by summoning taxpayers to office.

Personality Type: Conventional. These occupations frequently involve following set procedures and routines and can include working with data and details more than with ideas. Usually there is a clear line of authority to follow.

GOE—Interest Area/Cluster: 04. Business and Administration. **Work Group:** 04.05. Accounting, Auditing, and Analytical Support. **Other Jobs in This Work Group:** Accountants; Accountants and Auditors; Budget Analysts; Industrial Engineering Technicians; Logisticians; Management Analysts; Operations Research Analysts.

Skills—Systems Analysis: Determining how a system should work and how changes will affect outcomes. **Systems Evaluation:** Looking at many indicators of system performance and taking into account their accuracy.

Education and Training Programs: Accounting; Accounting and Business/Management; Accounting and Computer Science; Accounting and Finance; Auditing. **Related Knowledge/Courses—Economics and Accounting:** Economic and accounting principles and practices, the financial markets, banking, and the analysis and reporting of financial data. **Administration and Management:** Principles and processes involved in business and organizational planning, coordination, and execution. This includes strategic planning, resource allocation, manpower modeling, leadership techniques, and production methods. **Personnel and Human Resources:** Principles and procedures for personnel recruitment; selection; training; compensation and benefits; labor relations and negotiation; and personnel information systems. **Computers and Electronics:** Electric circuit boards, processors, chips, and computer hardware and software, including applications and programming. **Law and Government:** Laws, legal codes, court procedures, precedents, government regulations, executive orders, agency rules, and the democratic political process. **English Language:** The structure and content of the English language, including the meaning and spelling of words, rules of composition, and grammar.

Work Environment: Indoors; sitting.

Automotive Body and Related Repairers

- ❋ Education/Training Required: Long-term on-the-job training
- ❋ Annual Earnings: $35,690
- ❋ Beginning Wage: $21,480
- ❋ Earnings Growth Potential: Medium
- ❋ Growth: 11.6%
- ❋ Annual Job Openings: 37,469
- ❋ Self-Employed: 14.1%
- ❋ Part-Time: 5.6%

Repair and refinish automotive vehicle bodies and straighten vehicle frames. File, grind, sand, and smooth filled or repaired surfaces, using power tools and hand tools. Sand body areas to be painted and cover bumpers, windows, and trim with masking tape or paper to protect them from the paint. Follow supervisors' instructions as to which parts to restore or replace and how much time a job should take. Remove damaged sections of vehicles, using metal-cutting guns, air grinders, and wrenches, and install replacement parts, using wrenches or welding equipment. Cut and tape plastic separating film to outside repair areas to avoid damaging surrounding surfaces during repair procedure and remove tape and wash surfaces after repairs are complete. Prime and paint repaired surfaces, using paint spray guns and motorized sanders. Inspect repaired vehicles for dimensional accuracy and test-drive them to ensure proper alignment and handling. Mix polyester resins and hardeners to be used in restoring damaged areas. Chain or clamp frames and sections to alignment machines that use hydraulic pressure to align damaged components. Fill small dents that cannot be worked out with plastic or solder. Fit and weld replacement parts into place, using wrenches and welding equipment, and grind down welds to smooth them, using power grinders and other tools. Position dolly blocks against surfaces of dented areas and beat opposite surfaces to remove dents, using hammers. Remove damaged panels and identify the family and properties of the plastic used on a vehicle. Review damage reports, prepare or review repair cost estimates, and plan work to be performed. Remove small pits and dimples in body metal, using pick hammers and punches. Remove upholstery, accessories, electrical window- and seat-operating equipment, and trim to gain access to vehicle bodies and fenders. Clean work areas, using air hoses, to remove damaged material and discarded fiberglass strips used in repair procedures. Adjust or align headlights, wheels, and brake systems. Apply heat to plastic panels, using hot-air welding guns or immersion in hot water, and press the softened panels back into shape by hand. Soak fiberglass matting in resin mixtures and apply layers of matting over repair areas to specified thicknesses.

Personality Type: Realistic. These occupations frequently involve work activities that include practical, hands-on problems and solutions. They often deal with plants; animals; and real-world materials such as wood, tools, and machinery. Many of the occupations require working outside and don't involve a lot of paperwork or working closely with others.

GOE—Interest Area/Cluster: 13. Manufacturing. **Work Group:** 13.14. Vehicle and Facility Mechanical Work. **Other Jobs in This Work Group:** Aircraft Mechanics and Service Technicians; Aircraft Structure, Surfaces, Rigging, and Systems Assemblers; Automotive Glass Installers and Repairers; Automotive Master Mechanics; Automotive Service Technicians and Mechanics; Automotive Specialty Technicians; Bus and Truck Mechanics and Diesel Engine Specialists; Farm Equipment Mechanics; Fiberglass Laminators and Fabricators; Mobile Heavy Equipment Mechanics, Except Engines; Motorboat Mechanics; Motorcycle Mechanics; Outdoor Power Equipment and Other Small

Engine Mechanics; Rail Car Repairers; Recreational Vehicle Service Technicians; Tire Repairers and Changers.

Skills—Repairing: Repairing machines or systems, using the needed tools. **Installation:** Installing equipment, machines, wiring, or programs to meet specifications. **Equipment Maintenance:** Performing routine maintenance and determining when and what kind of maintenance is needed. **Troubleshooting:** Determining what is causing an operating error and deciding what to do about it. **Equipment Selection:** Determining the kind of tools and equipment needed to do a job. **Management of Financial Resources:** Determining how money will be spent to get the work done and accounting for these expenditures.

Education and Training Program: Autobody/Collision and Repair Technology/Technician Training. **Related Knowledge/Courses—Mechanical Devices:** Machines and tools, including their designs, uses, benefits, repair, and maintenance. **Building and Construction:** Materials, methods, and the appropriate tools to construct objects, structures, and buildings. **Chemistry:** The composition, structure, and properties of substances and of the chemical processes and transformations that they undergo. This includes uses of chemicals and their interactions, danger signs, production techniques, and disposal methods. **Production and Processing:** Inputs, outputs, raw materials, waste, quality control, costs, and techniques for maximizing the manufacture and distribution of goods. **Administration and Management:** Principles and processes involved in business and organizational planning, coordination, and execution. This includes strategic planning, resource allocation, manpower modeling, leadership techniques, and production methods. **Transportation:** Principles and methods for moving people or goods by air, rail, sea, or road, including their relative costs, advantages, and limitations.

Work Environment: Noisy; contaminants; hazardous equipment; standing; using hands on objects, tools, or controls; repetitive motions.

Automotive Glass Installers and Repairers

* Education/Training Required: Long-term on-the-job training
* Annual Earnings: $31,470
* Beginning Wage: $19,730
* Earnings Growth Potential: Medium
* Growth: 18.7%
* Annual Job Openings: 3,457
* Self-Employed: 20.7%
* Part-Time: 4.5%

Replace or repair broken windshields and window glass in motor vehicles. Remove all dirt, foreign matter, and loose glass from damaged areas; then apply primer along windshield or window edges and allow it to dry. Install replacement glass in vehicles after old glass has been removed and all necessary preparations have been made. Allow all glass parts installed with urethane ample time to cure, taking temperature and humidity into account. Prime all scratches on pinch welds with primer and allow primed scratches to dry. Obtain windshields or windows for specific automobile makes and models from stock and examine them for defects before installation. Apply a bead of urethane around the perimeter of each pinch weld and dress the remaining urethane on the pinch welds so that it is of uniform level and thickness all the way around. Check for moisture or contamination in damaged areas, dry out any moisture before making repairs, and keep damaged areas dry until repairs are complete. Select appropriate tools, safety equipment, and parts according to job requirements. Remove broken or damaged glass windshields or window glass from motor vehicles, using hand tools to remove screws from frames holding glass. Remove all moldings, clips, windshield wipers, screws, bolts, and inside A-pillar moldings; then lower headliners before beginning installation or repair work. Install, repair, and replace safety glass and related materials, such as back glass heating elements, on vehicles and equipment. Install rubber channeling strips around edges of glass or frames to weatherproof windows or to prevent rattling. Hold cut or uneven edges of glass against automated abrasive belts to shape or smooth edges. Cut flat safety glass according to specified patterns or perform precision pattern-making and glass-cutting to custom-fit replacement windows. Replace or adjust motorized or manual window-raising mechanisms. Install new foam dams on pinch welds if required. Cool or warm glass in the event of temperature extremes. Replace all moldings, clips, windshield wipers, and other parts that were removed before glass replacement or repair.

Personality Type: Realistic. These occupations frequently involve work activities that include practical, hands-on problems and solutions. They often deal with plants; animals; and real-world materials such as wood, tools, and machinery. Many of the occupations require working outside and don't involve a lot of paperwork or working closely with others.

GOE—Interest Area/Cluster: 13. Manufacturing. **Work Group:** 13.14. Vehicle and Facility Mechanical Work. **Other Jobs in This Work Group:** Aircraft Mechanics and Service Technicians; Aircraft Structure, Surfaces, Rigging, and Systems Assemblers; Automotive Body and Related Repairers; Automotive Master Mechanics; Automotive Service Technicians and Mechanics; Automotive Specialty Technicians; Bus and Truck Mechanics and Diesel Engine Specialists; Farm Equipment Mechanics; Fiberglass Laminators and Fabricators; Mobile Heavy Equipment Mechanics, Except Engines; Motorboat Mechanics; Motorcycle Mechanics; Outdoor Power Equipment and Other Small Engine Mechanics; Rail Car Repairers; Recreational Vehicle Service Technicians; Tire Repairers and Changers.

Skills—Installation: Installing equipment, machines, wiring, or programs to meet specifications. **Equipment Maintenance:** Performing routine maintenance and determining when and what kind of maintenance is needed. **Repairing:** Repairing machines or systems, using the needed tools. **Equipment Selection:** Determining the kind of tools and equipment needed to do a job. **Management of Material Resources:** Obtaining and seeing to the appropriate use of equipment, facilities, and materials needed to do certain work. **Quality Control Analysis:** Evaluating the quality or performance of products, services, or processes. **Operation and Control:** Controlling operations of equipment or systems.

Education and Training Program: Autobody/Collision and Repair Technology/Technician Training. **Related Knowledge/Courses—Mechanical Devices:** Machines and tools, including their designs, uses, benefits, repair, and maintenance. **Production and Processing:** Inputs, outputs, raw materials, waste, quality control, costs, and techniques for maximizing the manufacture and distribution of goods. **Customer and Personal Service:** Principles and processes for providing customer and personal services, including needs assessment techniques, quality service standards, alternative delivery systems, and customer satisfaction evaluation techniques. **Administration and Management:** Principles and processes involved in business and organizational planning, coordination, and execution. This includes strategic planning, resource allocation, manpower modeling, leadership techniques, and production methods. **Sales and Marketing:** Principles and methods involved in showing, promoting, and selling products or services. This includes marketing strategies and tactics, product demonstration and sales techniques, and sales control systems. **Transportation:** Principles and methods for moving people or goods by air, rail, sea, or road, including their relative costs, advantages, and limitations.

Work Environment: Outdoors; very hot or cold; contaminants; cramped work space, awkward positions; standing; using hands on objects, tools, or controls.

Automotive Master Mechanics

- ❋ Education/Training Required: Postsecondary vocational training
- ❋ Annual Earnings: $34,170
- ❋ Beginning Wage: $19,240
- ❋ Earnings Growth Potential: High
- ❋ Growth: 14.3%
- ❋ Annual Job Openings: 97,350
- ❋ Self-Employed: 16.8%
- ❋ Part-Time: 5.6%

The job openings listed here are shared with Automotive Specialty Technicians.

Repair automobiles, trucks, buses, and other vehicles. Master mechanics repair virtually any part on the vehicle or specialize in the transmission system. Examine vehicles to determine extent of damage or malfunctions. Test-drive vehicles and test components and systems, using equipment such as infrared engine analyzers, compression gauges, and computerized diagnostic devices. Repair, reline, replace, and adjust brakes. Review work orders and discuss work with supervisors. Follow checklists to ensure all important parts are examined, including belts, hoses, steering systems, spark plugs, brake and fuel systems, wheel bearings, and other potentially troublesome areas. Plan work procedures, using charts, technical manuals, and experience. Test and adjust repaired systems to meet manufacturers' performance specifications. Confer with customers to obtain descriptions of vehicle problems and to discuss work to be performed and future repair requirements. Perform routine and scheduled maintenance services such as oil changes, lubrications,

and tune-ups. Disassemble units and inspect parts for wear, using micrometers, calipers, and gauges. Overhaul or replace carburetors, blowers, generators, distributors, starters, and pumps. Repair and service air conditioning, heating, engine-cooling, and electrical systems. Repair or replace parts such as pistons, rods, gears, valves, and bearings. Tear down, repair, and rebuild faulty assemblies such as power systems, steering systems, and linkages. Rewire ignition systems, lights, and instrument panels. Repair radiator leaks. Install and repair accessories such as radios, heaters, mirrors, and windshield wipers. Repair manual and automatic transmissions. Repair or replace shock absorbers. Align vehicles' front ends. Rebuild parts such as crankshafts and cylinder blocks. Repair damaged automobile bodies. Replace and adjust headlights.

Personality Type: Realistic. These occupations frequently involve work activities that include practical, hands-on problems and solutions. They often deal with plants; animals; and real-world materials such as wood, tools, and machinery. Many of the occupations require working outside and don't involve a lot of paperwork or working closely with others.

GOE—Interest Area/Cluster: 13. Manufacturing. **Work Group:** 13.14. Vehicle and Facility Mechanical Work. **Other Jobs in This Work Group:** Aircraft Mechanics and Service Technicians; Aircraft Structure, Surfaces, Rigging, and Systems Assemblers; Automotive Body and Related Repairers; Automotive Glass Installers and Repairers; Automotive Service Technicians and Mechanics; Automotive Specialty Technicians; Bus and Truck Mechanics and Diesel Engine Specialists; Farm Equipment Mechanics; Fiberglass Laminators and Fabricators; Mobile Heavy Equipment Mechanics, Except Engines; Motorboat Mechanics; Motorcycle Mechanics; Outdoor Power Equipment and Other Small Engine Mechanics; Rail Car Repairers; Recreational Vehicle Service Technicians; Tire Repairers and Changers.

Skills—Repairing: Repairing machines or systems, using the needed tools. **Troubleshooting:** Determining what is causing an operating error and deciding what to do about it. **Installation:** Installing equipment, machines, wiring, or programs to meet specifications. **Equipment Maintenance:** Performing routine maintenance and determining when and what kind of maintenance is needed. **Equipment Selection:** Determining the kind of tools and equipment needed to do a job. **Operation Monitoring:** Watching gauges, dials, or other indicators to make sure a machine is working properly. **Complex Problem Solving:** Identifying complex problems, reviewing the options, and implementing solutions.

Technology Design: Generating or adapting equipment and technology to serve user needs.

Education and Training Programs: Automobile/Automotive Mechanics Technology/Technician Training; Automotive Engineering Technology/Technician Training; Medium/Heavy Vehicle and Truck Technology/Technician Training. **Related Knowledge/Courses—Mechanical Devices:** Machines and tools, including their designs, uses, benefits, repair, and maintenance. **Physics:** Physical principles, laws, and applications, including air, water, material dynamics, light, atomic principles, heat, electric theory, earth formations, and meteorological and related natural phenomena. **Computers and Electronics:** Electric circuit boards, processors, chips, and computer hardware and software, including applications and programming. **Engineering and Technology:** Equipment, tools, and mechanical devices and their uses to produce motion, light, power, technology, and other applications. **Chemistry:** The composition, structure, and properties of substances and of the chemical processes and transformations that they undergo. This includes uses of chemicals and their interactions, danger signs, production techniques, and disposal methods. **Public Safety and Security:** Weaponry; public safety; security operations, rules, regulations, precautions, and prevention; and the protection of people, data, and property.

Work Environment: Noisy; contaminants; hazardous equipment; minor burns, cuts, bites, or stings; standing; using hands on objects, tools, or controls.

Automotive Specialty Technicians

- ❈ Education/Training Required: Postsecondary vocational training
- ❈ Annual Earnings: $34,170
- ❈ Beginning Wage: $19,240
- ❈ Earnings Growth Potential: High
- ❈ Growth: 14.3%
- ❈ Annual Job Openings: 97,350
- ❈ Self-Employed: 16.8%
- ❈ Part-Time: 5.6%

The job openings listed here are shared with Automotive Master Mechanics.

Repair only one system or component on a vehicle, such as brakes, suspension, or radiator. Examine vehicles, compile estimates of repair costs, and secure customers' approval to perform repairs. Repair, overhaul, and adjust automobile brake systems. Use electronic test equipment to locate and correct malfunctions in fuel, ignition, and emissions control systems. Repair and replace defective ball joint suspensions, brake shoes, and wheel bearings. Inspect and test new vehicles for damage; then record findings so that necessary repairs can be made. Test electronic computer components in automobiles to ensure that they are working properly. Tune automobile engines to ensure proper and efficient functioning. Install and repair air conditioners and service components such as compressors, condensers, and controls. Repair, replace, and adjust defective carburetor parts and gasoline filters. Remove and replace defective mufflers and tailpipes. Repair and replace automobile leaf springs. Rebuild, repair, and test automotive fuel injection units. Align and repair wheels, axles, frames, torsion bars, and steering mechanisms of automobiles, using special alignment equipment and wheel-balancing machines. Repair, install, and adjust hydraulic and electromagnetic automatic lift mechanisms used to raise and lower automobile windows, seats, and tops. Repair and rebuild clutch systems. Convert vehicle fuel systems from gasoline to butane gas operations and repair and service operating butane fuel units.

Personality Type: Realistic. These occupations frequently involve work activities that include practical, hands-on problems and solutions. They often deal with plants; animals; and real-world materials such as wood, tools, and machinery. Many of the occupations require working outside and don't involve a lot of paperwork or working closely with others.

GOE—Interest Area/Cluster: 13. Manufacturing. **Work Group:** 13.14. Vehicle and Facility Mechanical Work. **Other Jobs in This Work Group:** Aircraft Mechanics and Service Technicians; Aircraft Structure, Surfaces, Rigging, and Systems Assemblers; Automotive Body and Related Repairers; Automotive Glass Installers and Repairers; Automotive Master Mechanics; Automotive Service Technicians and Mechanics; Bus and Truck Mechanics and Diesel Engine Specialists; Farm Equipment Mechanics; Fiberglass Laminators and Fabricators; Mobile Heavy Equipment Mechanics, Except Engines; Motorboat Mechanics; Motorcycle Mechanics; Outdoor Power Equipment and Other Small Engine Mechanics; Rail Car Repairers; Recreational Vehicle Service Technicians; Tire Repairers and Changers.

Skills—Repairing: Repairing machines or systems, using the needed tools. **Troubleshooting:** Determining what is causing an operating error and deciding what to do about it. **Operation Monitoring:** Watching gauges, dials, or other indicators to make sure a machine is working properly.

Equipment Maintenance: Performing routine maintenance and determining when and what kind of maintenance is needed. **Installation:** Installing equipment, machines, wiring, or programs to meet specifications. **Equipment Selection:** Determining the kind of tools and equipment needed to do a job. **Active Learning:** Working with new material or information to grasp its implications. **Operation and Control:** Controlling operations of equipment or systems.

Education and Training Programs: Alternative Fuel Vehicle Technology/Technician Training; Automotive Engineering Technology/Technician Training; Vehicle Emissions Inspection and Maintenance Technology/Technician Training. **Related Knowledge/Courses—Mechanical Devices:** Machines and tools, including their designs, uses, benefits, repair, and maintenance. **Physics:** Physical principles, laws, and applications, including air, water, material dynamics, light, atomic principles, heat, electric theory, earth formations, and meteorological and related natural phenomena. **Engineering and Technology:** Equipment, tools, and mechanical devices and their uses to produce motion, light, power, technology, and other applications. **Customer and Personal Service:** Principles and processes for providing customer and personal services, including needs assessment techniques, quality service standards, alternative delivery systems, and customer satisfaction evaluation techniques. **Sales and Marketing:** Principles and methods involved in showing, promoting, and selling products or services. This includes marketing strategies and tactics, product demonstration and sales techniques, and sales control systems. **Administration and Management:** Principles and processes involved in business and organizational planning, coordination, and execution. This includes strategic planning, resource allocation, manpower modeling, leadership techniques, and production methods.

Work Environment: Contaminants; cramped work space, awkward positions; minor burns, cuts, bites, or stings; standing; using hands on objects, tools, or controls; bending or twisting the body.

Aviation Inspectors

- ❋ Education/Training Required: Work experience in a related occupation
- ❋ Annual Earnings: $51,440
- ❋ Beginning Wage: $27,340
- ❋ Earnings Growth Potential: High
- ❋ Growth: 16.4%
- ❋ Annual Job Openings: 2,122
- ❋ Self-Employed: 5.9%
- ❋ Part-Time: 3.7%

The job openings listed here are shared with Freight and Cargo Inspectors and with Transportation Vehicle, Equipment, and Systems Inspectors, Except Aviation.

Inspect aircraft, maintenance procedures, air navigational aids, air traffic controls, and communications equipment to ensure conformance with federal safety regulations. Inspect work of aircraft mechanics performing maintenance, modification, or repair and overhaul of aircraft and aircraft mechanical systems to ensure adherence to standards and procedures. Start aircraft and observe gauges, meters, and other instruments to detect evidence of malfunctions. Examine aircraft access plates and doors for security. Examine landing gear, tires, and exteriors of fuselage, wings, and engines for evidence of damage or corrosion and to determine whether repairs are needed. Prepare and maintain detailed repair, inspection, investigation, and certification records and reports. Inspect new, repaired, or modified aircraft to identify damage or defects and to assess airworthiness and conformance to standards, using checklists, hand tools, and test instruments. Examine maintenance records and flight logs to determine if service and maintenance checks and overhauls were performed at prescribed intervals. Recommend replacement, repair, or modification of aircraft equipment. Recommend changes in rules, policies, standards, and regulations based on knowledge of operating conditions, aircraft improvements, and other factors. Issue pilots' licenses to individuals meeting standards. Investigate air accidents and complaints to determine causes. Observe flight activities of pilots to assess flying skills and to ensure conformance to flight and safety regulations. Conduct flight test programs to test equipment, instruments, and systems under a variety of conditions, using both manual and automatic controls. Approve or deny issuance of certificates of airworthiness. Analyze training programs and conduct oral and written examinations to ensure the competency of persons operating, installing, and repairing aircraft equipment.

Schedule and coordinate in-flight testing programs with ground crews and air traffic control to ensure availability of ground tracking, equipment monitoring, and related services.

Personality Type: Realistic. These occupations frequently involve work activities that include practical, hands-on problems and solutions. They often deal with plants; animals; and real-world materials such as wood, tools, and machinery. Many of the occupations require working outside and don't involve a lot of paperwork or working closely with others.

GOE—Interest Area/Cluster: 07. Government and Public Administration. **Work Group:** 07.03. Regulations Enforcement. **Other Jobs in This Work Group:** Agricultural Inspectors; Compliance Officers, Except Agriculture, Construction, Health and Safety, and Transportation; Construction and Building Inspectors; Environmental Compliance Inspectors; Equal Opportunity Representatives and Officers; Financial Examiners; Fire Inspectors; Fish and Game Wardens; Forest Fire Inspectors and Prevention Specialists; Freight and Cargo Inspectors; Government Property Inspectors and Investigators; Immigration and Customs Inspectors; Licensing Examiners and Inspectors; Nuclear Monitoring Technicians; Occupational Health and Safety Specialists; Occupational Health and Safety Technicians; Tax Examiners, Collectors, and Revenue Agents; Transportation Vehicle, Equipment, and Systems Inspectors, Except Aviation.

Skills—Systems Analysis: Determining how a system should work and how changes will affect outcomes. **Systems Evaluation:** Looking at many indicators of system performance and taking into account their accuracy. **Quality Control Analysis:** Evaluating the quality or performance of products, services, or processes. **Operation Monitoring:** Watching gauges, dials, or other indicators to make sure a machine is working properly. **Troubleshooting:** Determining what is causing an operating error and deciding what to do about it. **Operation and Control:** Controlling operations of equipment or systems. **Reading Comprehension:** Understanding written sentences and paragraphs in work-related documents. **Judgment and Decision Making:** Weighing the relative costs and benefits of a potential action.

Education and Training Program: Avionics Maintenance Technology/Technician Training. **Related Knowledge/Courses—Physics:** Physical principles, laws, and applications, including air, water, material dynamics, light, atomic principles, heat, electric theory, earth formations, and meteorological and related natural phenomena. **Mechanical Devices:** Machines and tools, including their designs, uses, benefits, repair, and maintenance. **Transportation:** Principles and methods for moving people or goods by air, rail, sea, or road, including their relative costs, advantages, and limitations. **Chemistry:** The composition, structure, and properties of substances and of the chemical processes and transformations that they undergo. This includes uses of chemicals and their interactions, danger signs, production techniques, and disposal methods. **Design:** Design techniques, principles, tools, and instruments involved in the production and use of precision technical plans, blueprints, drawings, and models. **Law and Government:** Laws, legal codes, court procedures, precedents, government regulations, executive orders, agency rules, and the democratic political process.

Work Environment: More often indoors than outdoors; noisy; sitting.

Bailiffs

* Education/Training Required: Moderate-term on-the-job training
* Annual Earnings: $36,900
* Beginning Wage: $19,130
* Earnings Growth Potential: High
* Growth: 11.2%
* Annual Job Openings: 2,223
* Self-Employed: 0.0%
* Part-Time: 1.8%

Maintain order in courts of law. Collect and retain unauthorized firearms from persons entering courtroom. Maintain order in courtroom during trial and guard jury from outside contact. Guard lodging of sequestered jury. Provide jury escort to restaurant and other areas outside of courtroom to prevent jury contact with public. Enforce courtroom rules of behavior and warn persons not to smoke or disturb court procedure. Report need for police or medical assistance to sheriff's office. Check courtroom for security and cleanliness and assure availability of sundry supplies for use of judge. Announce entrance of judge. Stop people from entering courtroom while judge charges jury.

Personality Type: Realistic. These occupations frequently involve work activities that include practical, hands-on problems and solutions. They often deal with plants; animals; and real-world materials such as wood, tools, and machinery. Many of the occupations require working outside and don't involve a lot of paperwork or working closely with others.

GOE—Interest Area/Cluster: 12. Law and Public Safety. **Work Group:** 12.04. Law Enforcement and Public Safety. **Other Jobs in This Work Group:** Correctional Officers and Jailers; Criminal Investigators and Special Agents; Detectives and Criminal Investigators; Fire Investigators; Forensic Science Technicians; Parking Enforcement Workers; Police and Sheriff's Patrol Officers; Police Detectives; Police Identification and Records Officers; Police Patrol Officers; Sheriffs and Deputy Sheriffs; Transit and Railroad Police.

Skills—Persuasion: Persuading others to approach things differently. **Social Perceptiveness:** Being aware of others' reactions and understanding why they react the way they do.

Education and Training Program: Criminal Justice/Police Science. **Related Knowledge/Courses—Public Safety and Security:** Weaponry; public safety; security operations, rules, regulations, precautions, and prevention; and the protection of people, data, and property. **Law and Government:** Laws, legal codes, court procedures, precedents, government regulations, executive orders, agency rules, and the democratic political process. **Philosophy and Theology:** Different philosophical systems and religions, including their basic principles, values, ethics, ways of thinking, customs, and practices and their impact on human culture. **Customer and Personal Service:** Principles and processes for providing customer and personal services, including needs assessment techniques, quality service standards, alternative delivery systems, and customer satisfaction evaluation techniques. **Psychology:** Human behavior and performance, mental processes, psychological research methods, and the assessment and treatment of behavioral and affective disorders. **Sociology and Anthropology:** Group behavior and dynamics; societal trends and influences; and cultures and their history, migrations, ethnicity, and origins.

Work Environment: Indoors; contaminants; disease or infections; sitting.

Bakers

- ❋ Education/Training Required: Long-term on-the-job training
- ❋ Annual Earnings: $22,590
- ❋ Beginning Wage: $15,760
- ❋ Earnings Growth Potential: Low
- ❋ Growth: 10.0%
- ❋ Annual Job Openings: 31,442
- ❋ Self-Employed: 4.3%
- ❋ Part-Time: 22.1%

Mix and bake ingredients according to recipes to produce breads, rolls, cookies, cakes, pies, pastries, or other baked goods. Observe color of products being baked and adjust oven temperatures, humidity, and conveyor speeds accordingly. Set oven temperatures and place items into hot ovens for baking. Combine measured ingredients in bowls of mixing, blending, or cooking machinery. Measure and weigh flour and other ingredients to prepare batters, doughs, fillings, and icings, using scales and graduated containers. Roll, knead, cut, and shape dough to form sweet rolls, pie crusts, tarts, cookies, and other products. Place dough in pans, in molds, or on sheets and bake in production ovens or on grills. Adapt the quantity of ingredients to match the amount of items to be baked. Check the quality of raw materials to ensure that standards and specifications are met. Apply glazes, icings, or other toppings to baked goods, using spatulas or brushes. Check equipment to ensure that it meets health and safety regulations and perform maintenance or cleaning as necessary. Decorate baked goods such as cakes and pastries. Set time and speed controls for mixing machines, blending machines, or steam kettles so that ingredients will be mixed or cooked according to instructions. Prepare and maintain inventory and production records. Direct and coordinate bakery deliveries. Order and receive supplies and equipment. Operate slicing and wrapping machines. Develop new recipes for baked goods.

Personality Type: Realistic. These occupations frequently involve work activities that include practical, hands-on problems and solutions. They often deal with plants; animals; and real-world materials such as wood, tools, and machinery. Many of the occupations require working outside and don't involve a lot of paperwork or working closely with others.

GOE—Interest Area/Cluster: 13. Manufacturing. **Work Group:** 13.03. Production Work, Assorted Materials

Processing. **Other Jobs in This Work Group:** Cementing and Gluing Machine Operators and Tenders; Chemical Equipment Operators and Tenders; Cleaning, Washing, and Metal Pickling Equipment Operators and Tenders; Coating, Painting, and Spraying Machine Setters, Operators, and Tenders; Cooling and Freezing Equipment Operators and Tenders; Cutting and Slicing Machine Setters, Operators, and Tenders; Extruding and Forming Machine Setters, Operators, and Tenders, Synthetic and Glass Fibers; Extruding, Forming, Pressing, and Compacting Machine Setters, Operators, and Tenders; Food and Tobacco Roasting, Baking, and Drying Machine Operators and Tenders; Food Batchmakers; Food Cooking Machine Operators and Tenders; Furnace, Kiln, Oven, Drier, and Kettle Operators and Tenders; Heat Treating Equipment Setters, Operators, and Tenders, Metal and Plastic; Helpers—Production Workers; Meat, Poultry, and Fish Cutters and Trimmers; Metal-Refining Furnace Operators and Tenders; Mixing and Blending Machine Setters, Operators, and Tenders; Packaging and Filling Machine Operators and Tenders; Plating and Coating Machine Setters, Operators, and Tenders, Metal and Plastic; Pourers and Casters, Metal; Sawing Machine Setters, Operators, and Tenders, Wood; Separating, Filtering, Clarifying, Precipitating, and Still Machine Setters, Operators, and Tenders; Sewing Machine Operators; Shoe Machine Operators and Tenders; Slaughterers and Meat Packers; Team Assemblers; Textile Bleaching and Dyeing Machine Operators and Tenders; Tire Builders; Woodworking Machine Setters, Operators, and Tenders, Except Sawing.

Skills—Quality Control Analysis: Evaluating the quality or performance of products, services, or processes. **Systems Evaluation:** Looking at many indicators of system performance and taking into account their accuracy. **Equipment Maintenance:** Performing routine maintenance and determining when and what kind of maintenance is needed. **Operation and Control:** Controlling operations of equipment or systems. **Troubleshooting:** Determining what is causing an operating error and deciding what to do about it. **Systems Analysis:** Determining how a system should work and how changes will affect outcomes. **Management of Personnel Resources:** Motivating, developing, and directing people as they work; identifying the best people for the job. **Operation Monitoring:** Watching gauges, dials, or other indicators to make sure a machine is working properly.

Education and Training Program: Baking and Pastry Arts/Baker/Pastry Chef Training. **Related Knowledge/Courses—Food Production:** Techniques and equipment for planting, growing, and harvesting of food for consumption, including crop-rotation methods, animal husbandry, and food storage/handling techniques. **Production and Processing:** Inputs, outputs, raw materials, waste, quality control, costs, and techniques for maximizing the manufacture and distribution of goods. **Personnel and Human Resources:** Principles and procedures for personnel recruitment; selection; training; compensation and benefits; labor relations and negotiation; and personnel information systems. **Mathematics:** Numbers and their operations and interrelationships, including arithmetic, algebra, geometry, calculus, and statistics and their applications. **Sales and Marketing:** Principles and methods involved in showing, promoting, and selling products or services. This includes marketing strategies and tactics, product demonstration and sales techniques, and sales control systems. **Administration and Management:** Principles and processes involved in business and organizational planning, coordination, and execution. This includes strategic planning, resource allocation, manpower modeling, leadership techniques, and production methods.

Work Environment: Indoors; very hot or cold; minor burns, cuts, bites, or stings; standing; walking and running; using hands on objects, tools, or controls.

Bill and Account Collectors

- Education/Training Required: Short-term on-the-job training
- Annual Earnings: $29,990
- Beginning Wage: $20,630
- Earnings Growth Potential: Low
- Growth: 22.9%
- Annual Job Openings: 118,709
- Self-Employed: 1.0%
- Part-Time: 10.7%

Locate and notify customers of delinquent accounts by mail, telephone, or personal visit to solicit payment. Duties include receiving payment and posting amount to customer's account, preparing statements to credit department if customer fails to respond, initiating repossession proceedings or service disconnection, and keeping records of collection and status of accounts. Receive payments and post amounts paid to customer accounts. Locate and monitor overdue accounts, using computers and a variety of automated systems. Record information about financial status of customers and status of collection efforts. Locate and notify customers of delinquent accounts by mail, telephone, or personal visits to solicit payment. Confer with customers by telephone or in person to determine reasons for overdue payments and to review the terms of sales, service, or credit contracts. Advise customers of necessary actions and strategies for debt repayment. Persuade customers to pay amounts due on credit accounts, damage claims, or nonpayable checks or to return merchandise. Sort and file correspondence and perform miscellaneous clerical duties such as answering correspondence and writing reports. Perform various administrative functions for assigned accounts, such as recording address changes and purging the records of deceased customers. Arrange for debt repayment or establish repayment schedules based on customers' financial situations. Negotiate credit extensions when necessary. Trace delinquent customers to new addresses by inquiring at post offices, telephone companies, or credit bureaus or through the questioning of neighbors. Notify credit departments, order merchandise repossession or service disconnection, and turn over account records to attorneys when customers fail to respond to collection attempts. Drive vehicles to visit customers, return merchandise to creditors, or deliver bills.

Personality Type: Conventional. These occupations frequently involve following set procedures and routines and can include working with data and details more than with ideas. Usually there is a clear line of authority to follow.

GOE—Interest Area/Cluster: 06. Finance and Insurance. **Work Group:** 06.04. Finance/Insurance Customer Service. **Other Jobs in This Work Group:** Loan Interviewers and Clerks; New Accounts Clerks; Tellers.

Skills—Management of Financial Resources: Determining how money will be spent to get the work done and accounting for these expenditures. **Speaking:** Talking to others to effectively convey information. **Management of Personnel Resources:** Motivating, developing, and directing people as they work; identifying the best people for the job. **Social Perceptiveness:** Being aware of others' reactions and understanding why they react the way they do. **Operations Analysis:** Analyzing needs and product requirements to create a design. **Time Management:** Managing one's own time and the time of others. **Service Orientation:** Actively looking for ways to help people. **Judgment and Decision Making:** Weighing the relative costs and benefits of a potential action.

Education and Training Program: Banking and Financial Support Services. **Related Knowledge/Courses—Clerical Practices:** Administrative and clerical procedures and systems such as word-processing systems, filing and records management systems, stenography and transcription, forms, design principles, and other office procedures and terminology. **Economics and Accounting:** Economic and accounting principles and practices, the financial markets, banking, and the analysis and reporting of financial data. **Law and Government:** Laws, legal codes, court procedures, precedents, government regulations, executive orders, agency rules, and the democratic political process. **Customer and Personal Service:** Principles and processes for providing customer and personal services, including needs assessment techniques, quality service standards, alternative delivery systems, and customer satisfaction evaluation techniques. **Computers and Electronics:** Electric circuit boards, processors, chips, and computer hardware and software, including applications and programming. **Personnel and Human Resources:** Principles and procedures for personnel recruitment; selection; training; compensation and benefits; labor relations and negotiation; and personnel information systems.

Work Environment: Indoors; sitting; using hands on objects, tools, or controls; repetitive motions.

Billing, Cost, and Rate Clerks

- ❋ Education/Training Required: Moderate-term on-the-job training
- ❋ Annual Earnings: $29,970
- ❋ Beginning Wage: $20,930
- ❋ Earnings Growth Potential: Low
- ❋ Growth: 4.4%
- ❋ Annual Job Openings: 81,885
- ❋ Self-Employed: 1.6%
- ❋ Part-Time: 14.3%

The job openings listed here are shared with Billing, Posting, and Calculating Machine Operators; and with Statement Clerks.

Compile data, compute fees and charges, and prepare invoices for billing purposes. Duties include computing costs and calculating rates for goods, services, and shipment of goods; posting data; and keeping other relevant records. May involve use of computer or typewriter, calculator, and adding and bookkeeping machines. Verify accuracy of billing data and revise any errors. Operate typing, adding, calculating, and billing machines. Prepare itemized statements, bills, or invoices and record amounts due for items purchased or services rendered. Review documents such as purchase orders, sales tickets, charge slips, or hospital records to compute fees and charges due. Perform bookkeeping work, including posting data and keeping other records concerning costs of goods and services and the shipment of goods. Keep records of invoices and support documents. Resolve discrepancies in accounting records. Type billing documents, shipping labels, credit memorandums, and credit forms, using typewriters or computers. Contact customers to obtain or relay account information. Compute credit terms, discounts, shipment charges, and rates for goods and services to complete billing documents. Answer mail and telephone inquiries regarding rates, routing, and procedures. Track accumulated hours and dollar amounts charged to each client job to calculate client fees for professional services such as legal and accounting services. Review compiled data on operating costs and revenues to set rates. Compile reports of cost factors, such as labor, production, storage, and equipment. Consult sources such as rate books, manuals, and insurance company representatives to determine specific charges and information such as rules, regulations, and government tax and tariff information. Update manuals when rates, rules, or regulations are amended. Estimate market value of products or services.

Personality Type: Conventional. These occupations frequently involve following set procedures and routines and can include working with data and details more than with ideas. Usually there is a clear line of authority to follow.

GOE—Interest Area/Cluster: 04. Business and Administration. **Work Group:** 04.06. Mathematical Clerical Support. **Other Jobs in This Work Group:** Billing and Posting Clerks and Machine Operators; Bookkeeping, Accounting, and Auditing Clerks; Brokerage Clerks; Payroll and Timekeeping Clerks; Statement Clerks; Tax Preparers.

Skills—Writing: Communicating effectively with others in writing as indicated by the needs of the audience. **Active Listening:** Listening to what other people are saying and asking questions as appropriate. **Service Orientation:** Actively looking for ways to help people. **Reading Comprehension:** Understanding written sentences and paragraphs in work-related documents. **Instructing:** Teaching others how to do something. **Speaking:** Talking to others to effectively convey information. **Social Perceptiveness:** Being aware of others' reactions and understanding why they react the way they do.

Education and Training Program: Accounting Technology/Technician Training and Bookkeeping. **Related Knowledge/Courses—Clerical Practices:** Administrative and clerical procedures and systems such as word-processing systems, filing and records management systems, stenography

and transcription, forms, design principles, and other office procedures and terminology. **Economics and Accounting:** Economic and accounting principles and practices, the financial markets, banking, and the analysis and reporting of financial data. **Computers and Electronics:** Electric circuit boards, processors, chips, and computer hardware and software, including applications and programming. **Mathematics:** Numbers and their operations and interrelationships, including arithmetic, algebra, geometry, calculus, and statistics and their applications.

Work Environment: Indoors; sitting.

Billing, Posting, and Calculating Machine Operators

* Education/Training Required: Moderate-term on-the-job training
* Annual Earnings: $29,970
* Beginning Wage: $20,930
* Earnings Growth Potential: Low
* Growth: 4.4%
* Annual Job Openings: 81,885
* Self-Employed: 1.6%
* Part-Time: 14.3%

The job openings listed here are shared with Billing, Cost, and Rate Clerks; and with Statement Clerks.

Operate machines that automatically perform mathematical processes, such as addition, subtraction, multiplication, and division, to calculate and record billing, accounting, statistical, and other numerical data. Duties include operating special billing machines to prepare statements, bills, and invoices and operating bookkeeping machines to copy and post data, make computations, and compile records of transactions. Enter into machines all information needed for bill generation. Train other calculating machine operators and review their work. Operate special billing machines to prepare statements, bills, and invoices. Operate bookkeeping machines to copy and post data, make computations, and compile records of transactions. Reconcile and post receipts for cash received by various departments. Prepare transmittal reports for changes to assessment and tax rolls; redemption file changes; and warrants, deposits, and invoices. Encode and add amounts of transaction documents, such as checks or money orders, using encoding machines. Balance and reconcile batch control totals with source documents or computer listings to locate errors, encode correct amounts, or prepare correction records. Compute payroll and retirement amounts, applying knowledge of payroll deductions, actuarial tables, disability factors, and survivor allowances. Maintain ledgers and registers, posting charges and refunds to individual funds and computing and verifying balances. Compute monies due on personal and real property, inventories, redemption payments, and other amounts, applying specialized knowledge of tax rates, formulas, interest rates, and other relevant information. Verify and post to ledgers purchase orders, reports of goods received, invoices, paid vouchers, and other information. Assign purchase order numbers to invoices, requisitions, and formal and informal bids. Verify completeness and accuracy of original documents such as business property statements, tax rolls, invoices, bonds and coupons, and redemption certificates. Bundle sorted documents to prepare those drawn on other banks for collection. Transcribe data from office records, using specified forms, billing machines, and transcribing machines. Sort and list items for proof or collection. Send completed bills to billing clerks for information verification. Transfer data from machines, such as encoding machines, to computers. Sort and microfilm transaction documents, such as checks, using sorting machines. Observe operation of sorters to locate documents that machines cannot read and manually record amounts of these documents.

Personality Type: Conventional. These occupations frequently involve following set procedures and routines and can include working with data and details more than with ideas. Usually there is a clear line of authority to follow.

GOE—Interest Area/Cluster: 04. Business and Administration. **Work Group:** 04.08. Clerical Machine Operation. **Other Jobs in This Work Group:** Data Entry Keyers; Mail Clerks and Mail Machine Operators, Except Postal Service; Office Machine Operators, Except Computer; Switchboard Operators, Including Answering Service; Word Processors and Typists.

Skills—Speaking: Talking to others to effectively convey information. **Active Listening:** Listening to what other people are saying and asking questions as appropriate. **Writing:** Communicating effectively with others in writing as indicated by the needs of the audience.

Education and Training Program: Accounting Technology/Technician Training and Bookkeeping. **Related Knowledge/Courses—Economics and Accounting:** Economic and accounting principles and practices, the financial markets, banking, and the analysis and reporting of financial

data. **Clerical Practices:** Administrative and clerical procedures and systems such as word-processing systems, filing and records management systems, stenography and transcription, forms, design principles, and other office procedures and terminology. **Personnel and Human Resources:** Principles and procedures for personnel recruitment; selection; training; compensation and benefits; labor relations and negotiation; and personnel information systems.

Work Environment: Indoors; noisy; contaminants; sitting; using hands on objects, tools, or controls; repetitive motions.

Biochemists and Biophysicists

* Education/Training Required: Doctoral degree
* Annual Earnings: $79,270
* Beginning Wage: $42,670
* Earnings Growth Potential: High
* Growth: 15.9%
* Annual Job Openings: 1,637
* Self-Employed: 2.5%
* Part-Time: 7.3%

Study the chemical composition and physical principles of living cells and organisms and their electrical and mechanical energy and related phenomena. May conduct research in order to further understanding of the complex chemical combinations and reactions involved in metabolism, reproduction, growth, and heredity. May determine the effects of foods, drugs, serums, hormones, and other substances on tissues and vital processes of living organisms. Design and perform experiments with equipment such as lasers, accelerators, and mass spectrometers. Analyze brain functions, such as learning, thinking, and memory, and analyze the dynamics of seeing and hearing. Share research findings by writing scientific articles and by making presentations at scientific conferences. Develop and test new drugs and medications intended for commercial distribution. Develop methods to process, store, and use foods, drugs, and chemical compounds. Develop new methods to study the mechanisms of biological processes. Examine the molecular and chemical aspects of immune system functioning. Investigate the nature, composition, and expression of genes and research how genetic engineering can impact these processes. Determine the three-dimensional structure of biological macromolecules. Prepare reports and recommendations based upon research outcomes. Design and build laboratory equipment needed for special research projects. Isolate, analyze, and synthesize vitamins, hormones, allergens, minerals, and enzymes and determine their effects on body functions. Research cancer treatment, using radiation and nuclear particles. Research transformations of substances in cells, using atomic isotopes. Study how light is absorbed in processes such as photosynthesis or vision. Analyze foods to determine their nutritional values and the effects of cooking, canning, and processing on these values. Study spatial configurations of submicroscopic molecules such as proteins, using X rays and electron microscopes. Teach and advise undergraduate and graduate students and supervise their research. Investigate the transmission of electrical impulses along nerves and muscles. Research how characteristics of plants and animals are carried through successive generations. Investigate damage to cells and tissues caused by X rays and nuclear particles. Research the chemical effects of substances such as drugs, serums, hormones, and food on tissues and vital processes. Develop and execute tests to detect diseases, genetic disorders, or other abnormalities. Produce pharmaceutically and industrially useful proteins, using recombinant DNA technology.

Personality Type: Investigative. These occupations frequently involve working with ideas and require an extensive amount of thinking. They can involve searching for facts and figuring out problems mentally.

GOE—Interest Area/Cluster: 15. Scientific Research, Engineering, and Mathematics. **Work Group:** 15.03. Life Sciences. **Other Jobs in This Work Group:** Biologists; Environmental Scientists and Specialists, Including Health; Epidemiologists; Medical Scientists, Except Epidemiologists; Microbiologists.

Skills—Science: Using scientific methods to solve problems. **Technology Design:** Generating or adapting equipment and technology to serve user needs. **Writing:** Communicating effectively with others in writing as indicated by the needs of the audience. **Equipment Selection:** Determining the kind of tools and equipment needed to do a job. **Operations Analysis:** Analyzing needs and product requirements to create a design. **Reading Comprehension:** Understanding written sentences and paragraphs in work-related documents. **Troubleshooting:** Determining what is causing an operating error and deciding what to do about it. **Quality Control Analysis:** Evaluating the quality or performance of products, services, or processes.

Education and Training Programs: Biochemistry/Biophysics and Molecular Biology; Biophysics; Cell/Cellular

Biology and Anatomical Sciences, Other; Molecular Biophysics; Soil Chemistry and Physics; Soil Microbiology. **Related Knowledge/Courses—Biology:** Plant and animal living tissue, cells, organisms, and entities, including their functions, interdependencies, and interactions with each other and the environment. **Chemistry:** The composition, structure, and properties of substances and of the chemical processes and transformations that they undergo. This includes uses of chemicals and their interactions, danger signs, production techniques, and disposal methods. **Physics:** Physical principles, laws, and applications, including air, water, material dynamics, light, atomic principles, heat, electric theory, earth formations, and meteorological and related natural phenomena. **Engineering and Technology:** Equipment, tools, and mechanical devices and their uses to produce motion, light, power, technology, and other applications. **Medicine and Dentistry:** The information and techniques needed to diagnose and treat injuries, diseases, and deformities. This includes symptoms, treatment alternatives, drug properties and interactions, and preventive health-care measures. **Design:** Design techniques, principles, tools, and instruments involved in the production and use of precision technical plans, blueprints, drawings, and models.

Work Environment: Indoors; disease or infections; sitting; using hands on objects, tools, or controls.

Biological Science Teachers, Postsecondary

- ✳ Education/Training Required: Doctoral degree
- ✳ Annual Earnings: $71,780
- ✳ Beginning Wage: $39,100
- ✳ Earnings Growth Potential: High
- ✳ Growth: 22.9%
- ✳ Annual Job Openings: 9,039
- ✳ Self-Employed: 0.4%
- ✳ Part-Time: 27.8%

Teach courses in biological sciences. Prepare and deliver lectures to undergraduate and/or graduate students on topics such as molecular biology, marine biology, and botany. Evaluate and grade students' classwork, laboratory work, assignments, and papers. Prepare course materials such as syllabi, homework assignments, and handouts. Compile, administer, and grade examinations or assign this work to others. Supervise students' laboratory work. Keep abreast of developments in their field by reading current literature, talking with colleagues, and participating in professional conferences. Maintain student attendance records, grades, and other required records. Initiate, facilitate, and moderate classroom discussions. Plan, evaluate, and revise curricula, course content, course materials, and methods of instruction. Advise students on academic and vocational curricula and on career issues. Maintain regularly scheduled office hours to advise and assist students. Supervise undergraduate and/or graduate teaching, internships, and research work. Select and obtain materials and supplies such as textbooks and laboratory equipment. Collaborate with colleagues to address teaching and research issues. Conduct research in a particular field of knowledge and publish findings in professional journals, books, and/or electronic media. Serve on academic or administrative committees that deal with institutional policies, departmental matters, and academic issues. Participate in student recruitment, registration, and placement activities. Write grant proposals to procure external research funding. Perform administrative duties such as serving as department head. Act as advisers to student organizations. Compile bibliographies of specialized materials for outside reading assignments. Participate in campus and community events. Provide professional consulting services to government and/or industry.

Personality Type: Social. These occupations frequently involve working with, communicating with, and teaching people and often involve helping or providing service to others.

GOE—Interest Area/Cluster: 05. Education and Training. **Work Group:** 05.03. Postsecondary and Adult Teaching and Instructing. **Other Jobs in This Work Group:** Adult Literacy, Remedial Education, and GED Teachers and Instructors; Agricultural Sciences Teachers, Postsecondary; Anthropology and Archeology Teachers, Postsecondary; Architecture Teachers, Postsecondary; Area, Ethnic, and Cultural Studies Teachers, Postsecondary; Art, Drama, and Music Teachers, Postsecondary; Atmospheric, Earth, Marine, and Space Sciences Teachers, Postsecondary; Business Teachers, Postsecondary; Chemistry Teachers, Postsecondary; Communications Teachers, Postsecondary; Computer Science Teachers, Postsecondary; Criminal Justice and Law Enforcement Teachers, Postsecondary; Economics Teachers, Postsecondary; Education Teachers, Postsecondary; Engineering Teachers, Postsecondary; English Language and Literature Teachers, Postsecondary; Environmental Science Teachers, Postsecondary; Farm and Home Management Advisors; Foreign Language and Literature Teachers, Postsecondary;

Forestry and Conservation Science Teachers, Postsecondary; Geography Teachers, Postsecondary; Graduate Teaching Assistants; Health Specialties Teachers, Postsecondary; History Teachers, Postsecondary; Home Economics Teachers, Postsecondary; Law Teachers, Postsecondary; Library Science Teachers, Postsecondary; Mathematical Science Teachers, Postsecondary; Nursing Instructors and Teachers, Postsecondary; Philosophy and Religion Teachers, Postsecondary; Physics Teachers, Postsecondary; Political Science Teachers, Postsecondary; Psychology Teachers, Postsecondary; Recreation and Fitness Studies Teachers, Postsecondary; Self-Enrichment Education Teachers; Social Work Teachers, Postsecondary; Sociology Teachers, Postsecondary; Vocational Education Teachers, Postsecondary.

Skills—Science: Using scientific methods to solve problems. **Instructing:** Teaching others how to do something. **Writing:** Communicating effectively with others in writing as indicated by the needs of the audience. **Reading Comprehension:** Understanding written sentences and paragraphs in work-related documents. **Learning Strategies:** Using multiple approaches when learning or teaching new things. **Speaking:** Talking to others to effectively convey information. **Active Learning:** Working with new material or information to grasp its implications. **Critical Thinking:** Using logic and analysis to identify the strengths and weaknesses of different approaches.

Education and Training Programs: Anatomy; Animal Physiology; Biochemistry; Biology/Biological Sciences, General; Biometry/Biometrics; Biophysics; Biotechnology; Botany/Plant Biology; Cell/Cellular Biology and Histology; Ecology; Entomology; Evolutionary Biology; Immunology; Marine Biology and Biological Oceanography; Microbiology, General; Molecular Biology; Neuroscience; Nutrition Sciences; Parasitology; Pharmacology; Plant Genetics; Plant Pathology/Phytopathology; Toxicology; Virology; Zoology/Animal Biology; others. **Related Knowledge/Courses—Biology:** Plant and animal living tissue, cells, organisms, and entities, including their functions, interdependencies, and interactions with each other and the environment. **Chemistry:** The composition, structure, and properties of substances and of the chemical processes and transformations that they undergo. This includes uses of chemicals and their interactions, danger signs, production techniques, and disposal methods. **Education and Training:** Instructional methods and training techniques, including curriculum design principles, learning theory, group and individual teaching techniques, design of individual development plans, and test design principles. **Medicine**

and Dentistry: The information and techniques needed to diagnose and treat injuries, diseases, and deformities. This includes symptoms, treatment alternatives, drug properties and interactions, and preventive health-care measures. **Physics:** Physical principles, laws, and applications, including air, water, material dynamics, light, atomic principles, heat, electric theory, earth formations, and meteorological and related natural phenomena. **Geography:** Various methods for describing the location and distribution of land, sea, and air masses, including their physical locations, relationships, and characteristics.

Work Environment: Indoors; more often sitting than standing.

Biological Technicians

- ❋ Education/Training Required: Bachelor's degree
- ❋ Annual Earnings: $37,810
- ❋ Beginning Wage: $24,360
- ❋ Earnings Growth Potential: Medium
- ❋ Growth: 16.0%
- ❋ Annual Job Openings: 15,374
- ❋ Self-Employed: 0.0%
- ❋ Part-Time: 6.2%

Assist biological and medical scientists in laboratories. Set up, operate, and maintain laboratory instruments and equipment; monitor experiments; make observations; and calculate and record results. May analyze organic substances, such as blood, food, and drugs. Keep detailed logs of all work-related activities. Monitor laboratory work to ensure compliance with set standards. Isolate, identify, and prepare specimens for examination. Use computers, computer-interfaced equipment, robotics, or high-technology industrial applications to perform work duties. Conduct research or assist in the conduct of research, including the collection of information and samples such as blood, water, soil, plants, and animals. Set up, adjust, calibrate, clean, maintain, and troubleshoot laboratory and field equipment. Provide technical support and services for scientists and engineers working in fields such as agriculture, environmental science, resource management, biology, and health sciences. Clean, maintain, and prepare supplies and work areas. Participate in the research, development, or manufacturing of medicinal and pharmaceutical preparations. Conduct standardized biological, microbiological, or biochemical tests and laboratory analyses to evaluate the

quantity or quality of physical or chemical substances in food or other products. Analyze experimental data and interpret results to write reports and summaries of findings. Measure or weigh compounds and solutions for use in testing or animal feed. Monitor and observe experiments, recording production and test data for evaluation by research personnel. Examine animals and specimens to detect the presence of disease or other problems. Conduct or supervise operational programs such as fish hatcheries, greenhouses, and livestock production programs. Feed livestock or laboratory animals.

Personality Type: Realistic. These occupations frequently involve work activities that include practical, hands-on problems and solutions. They often deal with plants; animals; and real-world materials such as wood, tools, and machinery. Many of the occupations require working outside and don't involve a lot of paperwork or working closely with others.

GOE—Interest Area/Cluster: 08. Health Science. **Work Group:** 08.06. Medical Technology. **Other Jobs in This Work Group:** Cardiovascular Technologists and Technicians; Diagnostic Medical Sonographers; Medical and Clinical Laboratory Technicians; Medical and Clinical Laboratory Technologists; Medical Equipment Preparers; Medical Records and Health Information Technicians; Nuclear Medicine Technologists; Opticians, Dispensing; Orthotists and Prosthetists; Radiologic Technicians; Radiologic Technologists; Radiologic Technologists and Technicians.

Skills—Science: Using scientific methods to solve problems. **Equipment Maintenance:** Performing routine maintenance and determining when and what kind of maintenance is needed. **Quality Control Analysis:** Evaluating the quality or performance of products, services, or processes. **Troubleshooting:** Determining what is causing an operating error and deciding what to do about it. **Mathematics:** Using mathematics to solve problems. **Active Learning:** Working with new material or information to grasp its implications. **Technology Design:** Generating or adapting equipment and technology to serve user needs. **Learning Strategies:** Using multiple approaches when learning or teaching new things.

Education and Training Program: Biology Technician Training/Biotechnology Laboratory Technician Training. **Related Knowledge/Courses—Chemistry:** The composition, structure, and properties of substances and of the chemical processes and transformations that they undergo. This includes uses of chemicals and their interactions, danger signs, production techniques, and disposal methods.

Biology: Plant and animal living tissue, cells, organisms, and entities, including their functions, interdependencies, and interactions with each other and the environment.

Work Environment: Indoors; standing; using hands on objects, tools, or controls; repetitive motions.

Biomedical Engineers

❋ Education/Training Required: Bachelor's degree
❋ Annual Earnings: $75,440
❋ Beginning Wage: $45,910
❋ Earnings Growth Potential: Medium
❋ Growth: 21.1%
❋ Annual Job Openings: 1,804
❋ Self-Employed: 0.0%
❋ Part-Time: 3.4%

Apply knowledge of engineering, biology, and biomechanical principles to the design, development, and evaluation of biological and health systems and products, such as artificial organs, prostheses, instrumentation, medical information systems, and health management and care delivery systems. Evaluate the safety, efficiency, and effectiveness of biomedical equipment. Install, adjust, maintain, and/or repair biomedical equipment. Advise hospital administrators on the planning, acquisition, and use of medical equipment. Advise and assist in the application of instrumentation in clinical environments. Develop models or computer simulations of human bio-behavioral systems in order to obtain data for measuring or controlling life processes. Research new materials to be used for products such as implanted artificial organs. Design and develop medical diagnostic and clinical instrumentation, equipment, and procedures, utilizing the principles of engineering and biobehavioral sciences. Conduct research, along with life scientists, chemists, and medical scientists, on the engineering aspects of the biological systems of humans and animals. Teach biomedical engineering or disseminate knowledge about field through writing or consulting. Design and deliver technology to assist people with disabilities. Diagnose and interpret bioelectric data, using signal-processing techniques. Adapt or design computer hardware or software for medical science uses. Analyze new medical procedures in order to forecast likely outcomes. Develop new applications for energy sources, such as using nuclear power for biomedical implants.

Personality Type: Investigative. These occupations frequently involve working with ideas and require an extensive amount of thinking. They can involve searching for facts and figuring out problems mentally.

GOE—Interest Area/Cluster: 15. Scientific Research, Engineering, and Mathematics. **Work Group:** 15.07. Research and Design Engineering. **Other Jobs in This Work Group:** Aerospace Engineers; Chemical Engineers; Civil Engineers; Computer Hardware Engineers; Electrical Engineers; Electronics Engineers, Except Computer; Marine Architects; Marine Engineers; Marine Engineers and Naval Architects; Materials Engineers; Mechanical Engineers; Nuclear Engineers.

Skills—Technology Design: Generating or adapting equipment and technology to serve user needs. **Science:** Using scientific methods to solve problems. **Installation:** Installing equipment, machines, wiring, or programs to meet specifications. **Operations Analysis:** Analyzing needs and product requirements to create a design. **Quality Control Analysis:** Evaluating the quality or performance of products, services, or processes. **Systems Evaluation:** Looking at many indicators of system performance and taking into account their accuracy. **Troubleshooting:** Determining what is causing an operating error and deciding what to do about it. **Management of Material Resources:** Obtaining and seeing to the appropriate use of equipment, facilities, and materials needed to do certain work.

Education and Training Program: Biomedical/Medical Engineering. **Related Knowledge/Courses—Engineering and Technology:** Equipment, tools, and mechanical devices and their uses to produce motion, light, power, technology, and other applications. **Computers and Electronics:** Electric circuit boards, processors, chips, and computer hardware and software, including applications and programming. **Physics:** Physical principles, laws, and applications, including air, water, material dynamics, light, atomic principles, heat, electric theory, earth formations, and meteorological and related natural phenomena. **Design:** Design techniques, principles, tools, and instruments involved in the production and use of precision technical plans, blueprints, drawings, and models. **Mechanical Devices:** Machines and tools, including their designs, uses, benefits, repair, and maintenance. **Chemistry:** The composition, structure, and properties of substances and of the chemical processes and transformations that they undergo. This includes uses of chemicals and their interactions, danger signs, production techniques, and disposal methods.

Work Environment: Indoors; contaminants; disease or infections; hazardous conditions; sitting; using hands on objects, tools, or controls.

Boilermakers

❋ Education/Training Required: Long-term on-the-job training
❋ Annual Earnings: $50,700
❋ Beginning Wage: $32,910
❋ Earnings Growth Potential: Medium
❋ Growth: 14.0%
❋ Annual Job Openings: 2,333
❋ Self-Employed: 0.2%
❋ Part-Time: 2.6%

Construct, assemble, maintain, and repair stationary steam boilers and boiler house auxiliaries. Align structures or plate sections to assemble boiler frame tanks or vats, following blueprints. Work involves use of hand and power tools, plumb bobs, levels, wedges, dogs, or turnbuckles. Assist in testing assembled vessels. Direct cleaning of boilers and boiler furnaces. Inspect and repair boiler fittings, such as safety valves, regulators, automatic-control mechanisms, water columns, and auxiliary machines. Examine boilers, pressure vessels, tanks, and vats to locate defects such as leaks, weak spots, and defective sections so that they can be repaired. Bolt or arc-weld pressure vessel structures and parts together, using wrenches and welding equipment. Inspect assembled vessels and individual components, such as tubes, fittings, valves, controls, and auxiliary mechanisms, to locate any defects. Repair or replace defective pressure vessel parts, such as safety valves and regulators, using torches, jacks, caulking hammers, power saws, threading dies, welding equipment, and metalworking machinery. Attach rigging and signal crane or hoist operators to lift heavy frame and plate sections and other parts into place. Bell, bead with power hammers, or weld pressure vessel tube ends in order to ensure leakproof joints. Lay out plate, sheet steel, or other heavy metal and locate and mark bending and cutting lines, using protractors, compasses, and drawing instruments or templates. Install manholes, handholes, taps, tubes, valves, gauges, and feedwater connections in drums of water tube boilers, using hand tools. Study blueprints to determine locations, relationships, and dimensions of parts. Straighten or reshape bent pressure vessel plates and structure parts, using hammers, jacks, and torches. Shape seams, joints, and irregular edges of pressure vessel sections and structural parts in order to attain specified fit of parts, using cutting torches, hammers, files, and metalworking machines. Position, align, and secure structural parts and related assemblies to boiler frames, tanks, or vats of pressure vessels, following blueprints. Locate and mark reference points for columns or plates on boiler foundations, following blueprints and using straightedges, squares, transits, and measuring instruments. Shape and fabricate parts, such as stacks, uptakes, and chutes, in order to adapt pressure vessels, heat exchangers, and piping to premises, using heavy-metalworking machines such as brakes, rolls, and drill presses. Clean pressure vessel equipment, using scrapers, wire brushes, and cleaning solvents.

Personality Type: Realistic. These occupations frequently involve work activities that include practical, hands-on problems and solutions. They often deal with plants; animals; and real-world materials such as wood, tools, and machinery. Many of the occupations require working outside and don't involve a lot of paperwork or working closely with others.

GOE—Interest Area/Cluster: 02. Architecture and Construction. **Work Group:** 02.04. Construction Crafts. **Other Jobs in This Work Group:** Brickmasons and Blockmasons; Carpet Installers; Cement Masons and Concrete Finishers; Commercial Divers; Construction Carpenters; Crane and Tower Operators; Drywall and Ceiling Tile Installers; Electricians; Fence Erectors; Floor Layers, Except Carpet, Wood, and Hard Tiles; Floor Sanders and Finishers; Glaziers; Hazardous Materials Removal Workers; Insulation Workers, Floor, Ceiling, and Wall; Insulation Workers, Mechanical; Manufactured Building and Mobile Home Installers; Operating Engineers and Other Construction Equipment Operators; Painters, Construction and Maintenance; Paperhangers; Paving, Surfacing, and Tamping Equipment Operators; Pile-Driver Operators; Pipe Fitters and Steamfitters; Pipelayers; Plasterers and Stucco Masons; Plumbers; Plumbers, Pipefitters, and Steamfitters; Rail-Track Laying and Maintenance Equipment Operators; Refractory Materials Repairers, Except Brickmasons; Reinforcing Iron and Rebar Workers; Riggers; Roofers; Rough Carpenters; Security and Fire Alarm Systems Installers; Segmental Pavers; Sheet Metal Workers; Stone Cutters and Carvers, Manufacturing; Stonemasons; Structural Iron and Steel Workers; Tapers; Terrazzo Workers and Finishers; Tile and Marble Setters.

Skills—Repairing: Repairing machines or systems, using the needed tools. **Installation:** Installing equipment, machines, wiring, or programs to meet specifications. **Equipment Maintenance:** Performing routine maintenance and determining when and what kind of maintenance is needed. **Operation Monitoring:** Watching gauges, dials, or other indicators to make sure a machine is working properly. **Mathematics:** Using mathematics to solve problems. **Troubleshooting:** Determining what is causing an operating error and deciding what to do about it. **Operation and Control:** Controlling operations of equipment or systems. **Equipment Selection:** Determining the kind of tools and equipment needed to do a job.

Education and Training Program: Boilermaking/Boilermaker Training. **Related Knowledge/Courses—Building and Construction:** Materials, methods, and the appropriate tools to construct objects, structures, and buildings. **Mechanical Devices:** Machines and tools, including their designs, uses, benefits, repair, and maintenance. **Engineering and Technology:** Equipment, tools, and mechanical devices and their uses to produce motion, light, power, technology, and other applications. **Design:** Design techniques, principles, tools, and instruments involved in the production and use of precision technical plans, blueprints, drawings, and models. **Physics:** Physical principles, laws, and applications, including air, water, material dynamics, light, atomic principles, heat, electric theory, earth formations, and meteorological and related natural phenomena. **Transportation:** Principles and methods for moving people or goods by air, rail, sea, or road, including their relative costs, advantages, and limitations.

Work Environment: Noisy; very hot or cold; contaminants; minor burns, cuts, bites, or stings; standing; using hands on objects, tools, or controls.

Bookkeeping, Accounting, and Auditing Clerks

- ✳ Education/Training Required: Moderate-term on-the-job training
- ✳ Annual Earnings: $31,560
- ✳ Beginning Wage: $20,310
- ✳ Earnings Growth Potential: Medium
- ✳ Growth: 12.5%
- ✳ Annual Job Openings: 286,854
- ✳ Self-Employed: 6.6%
- ✳ Part-Time: 24.8%

Compute, classify, and record numerical data to keep financial records complete. Perform any combination of routine calculating, posting, and verifying duties to obtain primary financial data for use in maintaining accounting records. May also check the accuracy of figures, calculations, and postings pertaining to business transactions recorded by other workers. Operate computers programmed with accounting software to record, store, and analyze information. Check figures, postings, and documents for correct entry, mathematical accuracy, and proper codes. Comply with federal, state, and company policies, procedures, and regulations. Debit, credit, and total accounts on computer spreadsheets and databases, using specialized accounting software. Classify, record, and summarize numerical and financial data to compile and keep financial records, using journals and ledgers or computers. Calculate, prepare, and issue bills, invoices, account statements, and other financial statements according to established procedures. Code documents according to company procedures. Compile statistical, financial, accounting, or auditing reports and tables pertaining to such matters as cash receipts, expenditures, accounts payable and receivable, and profits and losses. Operate 10-key calculators, typewriters, and copy machines to perform calculations and produce documents. Access computerized financial information to answer general questions as well as those related to specific accounts. Reconcile or note and report discrepancies found in records. Perform financial calculations such as amounts due, interest charges, balances, discounts, equity, and principal. Perform general office duties such as filing, answering telephones, and handling routine correspondence. Prepare bank deposits by compiling data from cashiers; verifying and balancing receipts; and sending cash, checks, or other forms of payment to banks. Receive, record, and bank cash, checks, and vouchers. Calculate and prepare checks for utilities, taxes, and other payments. Compare computer printouts to manually maintained journals to determine if they match. Reconcile records of bank transactions. Prepare trial balances of books. Monitor status of loans and accounts to ensure that payments are up to date. Transfer details from separate journals to general ledgers or data-processing sheets. Compile budget data and documents based on estimated revenues and expenses and previous budgets. Calculate costs of materials, overhead, and other expenses, based on estimates, quotations, and price lists.

Personality Type: Conventional. These occupations frequently involve following set procedures and routines and can include working with data and details more than with ideas. Usually there is a clear line of authority to follow.

GOE—Interest Area/Cluster: 04. Business and Administration. **Work Group:** 04.06. Mathematical Clerical

Support. **Other Jobs in This Work Group:** Billing and Posting Clerks and Machine Operators; Billing, Cost, and Rate Clerks; Brokerage Clerks; Payroll and Timekeeping Clerks; Statement Clerks; Tax Preparers.

Skills—Management of Financial Resources: Determining how money will be spent to get the work done and accounting for these expenditures. **Mathematics:** Using mathematics to solve problems. **Time Management:** Managing one's own time and the time of others.

Education and Training Programs: Accounting and Related Services, Other; Accounting Technology/Technician Training and Bookkeeping. **Related Knowledge/Courses—Clerical Practices:** Administrative and clerical procedures and systems such as word-processing systems, filing and records management systems, stenography and transcription, forms, design principles, and other office procedures and terminology. **Economics and Accounting:** Economic and accounting principles and practices, the financial markets, banking, and the analysis and reporting of financial data. **Mathematics:** Numbers and their operations and interrelationships, including arithmetic, algebra, geometry, calculus, and statistics and their applications. **Computers and Electronics:** Electric circuit boards, processors, chips, and computer hardware and software, including applications and programming.

Work Environment: Indoors; sitting; repetitive motions.

Brickmasons and Blockmasons

- ❈ Education/Training Required: Long-term on-the-job training
- ❈ Annual Earnings: $44,070
- ❈ Beginning Wage: $26,370
- ❈ Earnings Growth Potential: High
- ❈ Growth: 9.7%
- ❈ Annual Job Openings: 17,569
- ❈ Self-Employed: 24.5%
- ❈ Part-Time: 7.9%

Lay and bind building materials, such as brick, structural tile, concrete block, cinderblock, glass block, and terra-cotta block, with mortar and other substances to construct or repair walls, partitions, arches, sewers, and other structures. Construct corners by fastening in plumb position a corner pole or building a corner pyramid of bricks and filling in between the corners, using a line from corner to corner to guide each course, or layer, of brick. Measure

distance from reference points and mark guidelines to lay out work, using plumb bobs and levels. Fasten or fuse brick or other building material to structure with wire clamps, anchor holes, torch, or cement. Calculate angles and courses and determine vertical and horizontal alignment of courses. Break or cut bricks, tiles, or blocks to size, using trowel edge, hammer, or power saw. Remove excess mortar with trowels and hand tools and finish mortar joints with jointing tools for a sealed, uniform appearance. Interpret blueprints and drawings to determine specifications and to calculate the materials required. Apply and smooth mortar or other mixture over work surface. Mix specified amounts of sand, clay, dirt, or mortar powder with water to form refractory mixtures. Examine brickwork or structure to determine need for repair. Clean working surface to remove scale, dust, soot, or chips of brick and mortar, using broom, wire brush, or scraper. Lay and align bricks, blocks, or tiles to build or repair structures or high-temperature equipment, such as cupola, kilns, ovens, or furnaces. Remove burned or damaged brick or mortar, using sledgehammer, crowbar, chipping gun, or chisel. Spray or spread refractory material over brickwork to protect against deterioration.

Personality Type: Realistic. These occupations frequently involve work activities that include practical, hands-on problems and solutions. They often deal with plants; animals; and real-world materials such as wood, tools, and machinery. Many of the occupations require working outside and don't involve a lot of paperwork or working closely with others.

GOE—Interest Area/Cluster: 02. Architecture and Construction. **Work Group:** 02.04. Construction Crafts. **Other Jobs in This Work Group:** Boilermakers; Carpet Installers; Cement Masons and Concrete Finishers; Commercial Divers; Construction Carpenters; Crane and Tower Operators; Drywall and Ceiling Tile Installers; Electricians; Fence Erectors; Floor Layers, Except Carpet, Wood, and Hard Tiles; Floor Sanders and Finishers; Glaziers; Hazardous Materials Removal Workers; Insulation Workers, Floor, Ceiling, and Wall; Insulation Workers, Mechanical; Manufactured Building and Mobile Home Installers; Operating Engineers and Other Construction Equipment Operators; Painters, Construction and Maintenance; Paperhangers; Paving, Surfacing, and Tamping Equipment Operators; Pile-Driver Operators; Pipe Fitters and Steamfitters; Pipelayers; Plasterers and Stucco Masons; Plumbers; Plumbers, Pipefitters, and Steamfitters; Rail-Track Laying and Maintenance Equipment Operators; Refractory Materials Repairers, Except Brickmasons; Reinforcing Iron and Rebar Workers; Riggers; Roofers; Rough Carpenters; Security and Fire Alarm

Systems Installers; Segmental Pavers; Sheet Metal Workers; Stone Cutters and Carvers, Manufacturing; Stonemasons; Structural Iron and Steel Workers; Tapers; Terrazzo Workers and Finishers; Tile and Marble Setters.

Skills—Equipment Maintenance: Performing routine maintenance and determining when and what kind of maintenance is needed. **Mathematics:** Using mathematics to solve problems. **Installation:** Installing equipment, machines, wiring, or programs to meet specifications. **Repairing:** Repairing machines or systems, using the needed tools. **Technology Design:** Generating or adapting equipment and technology to serve user needs.

Education and Training Program: Mason Training/Masonry. **Related Knowledge/Courses—Building and Construction:** Materials, methods, and the appropriate tools to construct objects, structures, and buildings. **Design:** Design techniques, principles, tools, and instruments involved in the production and use of precision technical plans, blueprints, drawings, and models. **Mechanical Devices:** Machines and tools, including their designs, uses, benefits, repair, and maintenance. **Production and Processing:** Inputs, outputs, raw materials, waste, quality control, costs, and techniques for maximizing the manufacture and distribution of goods. **Public Safety and Security:** Weaponry; public safety; security operations, rules, regulations, precautions, and prevention; and the protection of people, data, and property. **Mathematics:** Numbers and their operations and interrelationships, including arithmetic, algebra, geometry, calculus, and statistics and their applications.

Work Environment: Outdoors; very hot or cold; hazardous equipment; standing; using hands on objects, tools, or controls; bending or twisting the body.

Broadcast Technicians

- ❇ Education/Training Required: Associate degree
- ❇ Annual Earnings: $32,230
- ❇ Beginning Wage: $17,060
- ❇ Earnings Growth Potential: High
- ❇ Growth: 12.1%
- ❇ Annual Job Openings: 2,955
- ❇ Self-Employed: 12.4%
- ❇ Part-Time: 12.9%

Set up, operate, and maintain the electronic equipment used to transmit radio and television programs. Control **audio equipment to regulate volume level and quality of sound during radio and television broadcasts. Operate radio transmitter to broadcast radio and television programs.** Maintain programming logs as required by station management and the Federal Communications Commission. Control audio equipment to regulate the volume and sound quality during radio and television broadcasts. Monitor strength, clarity, and reliability of incoming and outgoing signals and adjust equipment as necessary to maintain quality broadcasts. Regulate the fidelity, brightness, and contrast of video transmissions, using video console control panels. Observe monitors and converse with station personnel to determine audio and video levels and to ascertain that programs are airing. Preview scheduled programs to ensure that signals are functioning and programs are ready for transmission. Select sources from which programming will be received or through which programming will be transmitted. Report equipment problems, ensure that repairs are made; make emergency repairs to equipment when necessary and possible. Record sound onto tape or film for radio or television, checking its quality and making adjustments where necessary. Align antennae with receiving dishes to obtain the clearest signal for transmission of broadcasts from field locations. Substitute programs in cases where signals fail. Organize recording sessions and prepare areas such as radio booths and television stations for recording. Perform preventive and minor equipment maintenance, using hand tools. Instruct trainees in how to use television production equipment, how to film events, and how to copy and edit graphics or sound onto videotape. Schedule programming or read television programming logs to determine which programs are to be recorded or aired. Edit broadcast material electronically, using computers. Give technical directions to other personnel during filming. Set up and operate portable field transmission equipment outside the studio. Determine the number, type, and approximate location of microphones needed for best sound recording or transmission quality and position them appropriately. Design and modify equipment to employer specifications. Prepare reports outlining past and future programs, including content.

Personality Type: Realistic. These occupations frequently involve work activities that include practical, hands-on problems and solutions. They often deal with plants; animals; and real-world materials such as wood, tools, and machinery. Many of the occupations require working outside and don't involve a lot of paperwork or working closely with others.

GOE—Interest Area/Cluster: 03. Arts and Communication. **Work Group:** 03.09. Media Technology. **Other Jobs**

in This Work Group: Audio and Video Equipment Technicians; Camera Operators, Television, Video, and Motion Picture; Film and Video Editors; Multi-Media Artists and Animators; Photographers; Radio Operators; Sound Engineering Technicians.

Skills—Operation Monitoring: Watching gauges, dials, or other indicators to make sure a machine is working properly. **Operation and Control:** Controlling operations of equipment or systems. **Installation:** Installing equipment, machines, wiring, or programs to meet specifications. **Troubleshooting:** Determining what is causing an operating error and deciding what to do about it. **Equipment Maintenance:** Performing routine maintenance and determining when and what kind of maintenance is needed. **Repairing:** Repairing machines or systems, using the needed tools. **Operations Analysis:** Analyzing needs and product requirements to create a design. **Technology Design:** Generating or adapting equipment and technology to serve user needs.

Education and Training Programs: Audiovisual Communications Technologies/Technician Training, Other; Communications Technology/Technician Training; Radio and Television Broadcasting Technology/Technician Training. **Related Knowledge/Courses—Telecommunications:** Transmission, broadcasting, switching, control, and operation of telecommunications systems. **Communications and Media:** Media production, communication, and dissemination techniques and methods, including alternative ways to inform and entertain via written, oral, and visual media. **Engineering and Technology:** Equipment, tools, and mechanical devices and their uses to produce motion, light, power, technology, and other applications. **Computers and Electronics:** Electric circuit boards, processors, chips, and computer hardware and software, including applications and programming. **Mechanical Devices:** Machines and tools, including their designs, uses, benefits, repair, and maintenance. **Production and Processing:** Inputs, outputs, raw materials, waste, quality control, costs, and techniques for maximizing the manufacture and distribution of goods.

Work Environment: Indoors; noisy; sitting; using hands on objects, tools, or controls.

Brokerage Clerks

- ❋ Education/Training Required: Moderate-term on-the-job training
- ❋ Annual Earnings: $37,360
- ❋ Beginning Wage: $25,710
- ❋ Earnings Growth Potential: Low
- ❋ Growth: 20.0%
- ❋ Annual Job Openings: 10,826
- ❋ Self-Employed: 0.0%
- ❋ Part-Time: 19.4%

Perform clerical duties involving the purchase or sale of securities. Duties include writing orders for stock purchases and sales, computing transfer taxes, verifying stock transactions, accepting and delivering securities, tracking stock price fluctuations, computing equity, distributing dividends, and keeping records of daily transactions and holdings. Correspond with customers and confer with co-workers to answer inquiries, discuss market fluctuations, and resolve account problems. Record and document security transactions, such as purchases, sales, conversions, redemptions, and payments, using computers, accounting ledgers, and certificate records. Schedule and coordinate transfer and delivery of security certificates between companies, departments, and customers. Prepare forms, such as receipts, withdrawal orders, transmittal papers, and transfer confirmations, based on transaction requests from stockholders. File, type, and operate standard office machines. Monitor daily stock prices and compute fluctuations to determine the need for additional collateral to secure loans. Prepare reports summarizing daily transactions and earnings for individual customer accounts. Compute total holdings, dividends, interest, transfer taxes, brokerage fees, and commissions and allocate appropriate payments to customers. Verify ownership and transaction information and dividend distribution instructions to ensure conformance with governmental regulations, using stock records and reports.

Personality Type: Conventional. These occupations frequently involve following set procedures and routines and can include working with data and details more than with ideas. Usually there is a clear line of authority to follow.

GOE—Interest Area/Cluster: 04. Business and Administration. **Work Group:** 04.06. Mathematical Clerical Support. **Other Jobs in This Work Group:** Billing and Posting Clerks and Machine Operators; Billing, Cost, and Rate Clerks; Bookkeeping, Accounting, and Auditing Clerks;

Payroll and Timekeeping Clerks; Statement Clerks; Tax Preparers.

Skills—Service Orientation: Actively looking for ways to help people. **Mathematics:** Using mathematics to solve problems. **Speaking:** Talking to others to effectively convey information. **Active Listening:** Listening to what other people are saying and asking questions as appropriate. **Systems Evaluation:** Looking at many indicators of system performance and taking into account their accuracy.

Education and Training Program: Accounting Technology/Technician Training and Bookkeeping. **Related Knowledge/Courses—Economics and Accounting:** Economic and accounting principles and practices, the financial markets, banking, and the analysis and reporting of financial data. **Clerical Practices:** Administrative and clerical procedures and systems such as word-processing systems, filing and records management systems, stenography and transcription, forms, design principles, and other office procedures and terminology. **Customer and Personal Service:** Principles and processes for providing customer and personal services, including needs assessment techniques, quality service standards, alternative delivery systems, and customer satisfaction evaluation techniques. **Sales and Marketing:** Principles and methods involved in showing, promoting, and selling products or services. This includes marketing strategies and tactics, product demonstration and sales techniques, and sales control systems. **Computers and Electronics:** Electric circuit boards, processors, chips, and computer hardware and software, including applications and programming. **Mathematics:** Numbers and their operations and interrelationships, including arithmetic, algebra, geometry, calculus, and statistics and their applications.

Work Environment: Indoors; sitting; repetitive motions.

Budget Analysts

- ❋ Education/Training Required: Bachelor's degree
- ❋ Annual Earnings: $63,440
- ❋ Beginning Wage: $41,440
- ❋ Earnings Growth Potential: Low
- ❋ Growth: 7.1%
- ❋ Annual Job Openings: 6,423
- ❋ Self-Employed: 0.0%
- ❋ Part-Time: 3.2%

Examine budget estimates for completeness, accuracy, and conformance with procedures and regulations. Analyze budgeting and accounting reports for the purpose of maintaining expenditure controls. Direct the preparation of regular and special budget reports. Analyze monthly department budgeting and accounting reports to maintain expenditure controls. Provide advice and technical assistance with cost analysis, fiscal allocation, and budget preparation. Examine budget estimates for completeness, accuracy, and conformance with procedures and regulations. Summarize budgets and submit recommendations for the approval or disapproval of funds requests. Review operating budgets to analyze trends affecting budget needs. Consult with managers to ensure that budget adjustments are made in accordance with program changes. Compile and analyze accounting records and other data to determine the financial resources required to implement a program. Perform cost-benefit analyses to compare operating programs, review financial requests, or explore alternative financing methods. Interpret budget directives and establish policies for carrying out directives. Seek new ways to improve efficiency and increase profits. Testify before examining and fund-granting authorities, clarifying and promoting the proposed budgets. Match appropriations for specific programs with appropriations for broader programs, including items for emergency funds.

Personality Type: Conventional. These occupations frequently involve following set procedures and routines and can include working with data and details more than with ideas. Usually there is a clear line of authority to follow.

GOE—Interest Area/Cluster: 04. Business and Administration. **Work Group:** 04.05. Accounting, Auditing, and Analytical Support. **Other Jobs in This Work Group:** Accountants; Accountants and Auditors; Auditors; Industrial Engineering Technicians; Logisticians; Management Analysts; Operations Research Analysts.

Skills—Management of Financial Resources: Determining how money will be spent to get the work done and accounting for these expenditures. **Systems Analysis:** Determining how a system should work and how changes will affect outcomes. **Systems Evaluation:** Looking at many indicators of system performance and taking into account their accuracy. **Mathematics:** Using mathematics to solve problems. **Judgment and Decision Making:** Weighing the relative costs and benefits of a potential action. **Persuasion:** Persuading others to approach things differently.

Education and Training Programs: Accounting; Finance, General. **Related Knowledge/Courses—Economics and Accounting:** Economic and accounting principles and practices, the financial markets, banking, and the analysis and reporting of financial data. **Clerical Practices:** Administrative and clerical procedures and systems such as word-processing systems, filing and records management systems, stenography and transcription, forms, design principles, and other office procedures and terminology. **Administration and Management:** Principles and processes involved in business and organizational planning, coordination, and execution. This includes strategic planning, resource allocation, manpower modeling, leadership techniques, and production methods. **Mathematics:** Numbers and their operations and interrelationships, including arithmetic, algebra, geometry, calculus, and statistics and their applications. **Personnel and Human Resources:** Principles and procedures for personnel recruitment; selection; training; compensation and benefits; labor relations and negotiation; and personnel information systems. **Computers and Electronics:** Electric circuit boards, processors, chips, and computer hardware and software, including applications and programming.

Work Environment: Indoors; sitting; repetitive motions.

Bus and Truck Mechanics and Diesel Engine Specialists

- ❋ Education/Training Required: Postsecondary vocational training
- ❋ Annual Earnings: $38,640
- ❋ Beginning Wage: $25,210
- ❋ Earnings Growth Potential: Low
- ❋ Growth: 11.5%
- ❋ Annual Job Openings: 25,428
- ❋ Self-Employed: 5.8%
- ❋ Part-Time: 2.8%

Diagnose, adjust, repair, or overhaul trucks, buses, and all types of diesel engines. Includes mechanics working primarily with automobile diesel engines. Use hand tools such as screwdrivers, pliers, wrenches, pressure gauges, and precision instruments, as well as power tools such as pneumatic wrenches, lathes, welding equipment, and jacks and hoists. Inspect brake systems, steering mechanisms, wheel bearings, and other important parts to ensure that they are in proper operating condition. Perform routine maintenance such as changing oil, checking batteries, and lubricating equipment and machinery. Adjust and reline brakes, align wheels, tighten bolts and screws, and reassemble equipment. Raise trucks, buses, and heavy parts or equipment, using hydraulic jacks or hoists. Test drive trucks and buses to diagnose malfunctions or to ensure that they are working properly. Inspect, test, and listen to defective equipment to diagnose malfunctions, using test instruments such as handheld computers, motor analyzers, chassis charts, and pressure gauges. Examine and adjust protective guards, loose bolts, and specified safety devices. Inspect and verify dimensions and clearances of parts to ensure conformance to factory specifications. Specialize in repairing and maintaining parts of the engine, such as fuel injection systems. Attach test instruments to equipment and read dials and gauges to diagnose malfunctions. Rewire ignition systems, lights, and instrument panels. Recondition and replace parts, pistons, bearings, gears, and valves. Repair and adjust seats, doors, and windows and install and repair accessories. Inspect, repair, and maintain automotive and mechanical equipment and machinery such as pumps and compressors. Disassemble and overhaul internal combustion engines, pumps, generators, transmissions, clutches, and differential units. Rebuild gas or diesel engines. Align front ends and suspension systems. Operate valve-grinding machines to grind and reset valves.

Personality Type: Realistic. These occupations frequently involve work activities that include practical, hands-on problems and solutions. They often deal with plants; animals; and real-world materials such as wood, tools, and machinery. Many of the occupations require working outside and don't involve a lot of paperwork or working closely with others.

GOE—Interest Area/Cluster: 13. Manufacturing. **Work Group:** 13.14. Vehicle and Facility Mechanical Work. **Other Jobs in This Work Group:** Aircraft Mechanics and Service Technicians; Aircraft Structure, Surfaces, Rigging, and Systems Assemblers; Automotive Body and Related Repairers; Automotive Glass Installers and Repairers; Automotive Master Mechanics; Automotive Service Technicians and Mechanics; Automotive Specialty Technicians; Farm Equipment Mechanics; Fiberglass Laminators and Fabricators; Mobile Heavy Equipment Mechanics, Except Engines; Motorboat Mechanics; Motorcycle Mechanics; Outdoor Power Equipment and Other Small Engine Mechanics; Rail Car Repairers; Recreational Vehicle Service Technicians; Tire Repairers and Changers.

Skills—Repairing: Repairing machines or systems, using the needed tools. **Equipment Maintenance:** Performing routine maintenance and determining when and what kind of maintenance is needed. **Troubleshooting:** Determining what is causing an operating error and deciding what to do about it. **Installation:** Installing equipment, machines, wiring, or programs to meet specifications. **Science:** Using scientific methods to solve problems. **Technology Design:** Generating or adapting equipment and technology to serve user needs. **Equipment Selection:** Determining the kind of tools and equipment needed to do a job.

Education and Training Programs: Diesel Mechanics Technology/Technician Training; Medium/Heavy Vehicle and Truck Technology/Technician Training. **Related Knowledge/Courses—Mechanical Devices:** Machines and tools, including their designs, uses, benefits, repair, and maintenance. **Transportation:** Principles and methods for moving people or goods by air, rail, sea, or road, including their relative costs, advantages, and limitations. **Public Safety and Security:** Weaponry; public safety; security operations, rules, regulations, precautions, and prevention; and the protection of people, data, and property. **Physics:** Physical principles, laws, and applications, including air, water, material dynamics, light, atomic principles, heat, electric theory, earth formations, and meteorological and related natural phenomena. **Engineering and Technology:** Equipment, tools, and mechanical devices and their uses to produce motion, light, power, technology, and other applications. **Law and Government:** Laws, legal codes, court procedures, precedents, government regulations, executive orders, agency rules, and the democratic political process.

Work Environment: Noisy; very bright or dim lighting; contaminants; hazardous equipment; standing; using hands on objects, tools, or controls.

Bus Drivers, School

- ❋ Education/Training Required: Moderate-term on-the-job training
- ❋ Annual Earnings: $25,860
- ❋ Beginning Wage: $14,480
- ❋ Earnings Growth Potential: High
- ❋ Growth: 9.3%
- ❋ Annual Job Openings: 59,809
- ❋ Self-Employed: 1.4%
- ❋ Part-Time: 34.1%

Transport students or special clients, such as the elderly or persons with disabilities. Ensure adherence to safety rules. May assist passengers in boarding or exiting. Follow safety rules as students board and exit buses and as they cross streets near bus stops. Comply with traffic regulations to operate vehicles safely and courteously. Check the condition of a vehicle's tires, brakes, windshield wipers, lights, oil, fuel, water, and safety equipment to ensure that everything is in working order. Maintain order among pupils during trips to ensure safety. Pick up and drop off students at regularly scheduled neighborhood locations, following strict time schedules. Report any bus malfunctions or needed repairs. Drive gasoline, diesel, or electrically powered multi-passenger vehicles to transport students between neighborhoods, schools, and school activities. Prepare and submit reports that may include the number of passengers or trips, hours worked, mileage, fuel consumption, and fares received. Maintain knowledge of first-aid procedures. Keep bus interiors clean for passengers. Read maps and follow written and verbal geographic directions. Report delays, accidents, or other traffic and transportation situations, using telephones or mobile two-way radios. Regulate heating, lighting, and ventilation systems for passenger comfort. Escort small children across roads and highways. Make minor repairs to vehicles.

Personality Type: Realistic. These occupations frequently involve work activities that include practical, hands-on problems and solutions. They often deal with plants; animals; and real-world materials such as wood, tools, and machinery. Many of the occupations require working outside and don't involve a lot of paperwork or working closely with others.

GOE—Interest Area/Cluster: 16. Transportation, Distribution, and Logistics. **Work Group:** 16.06. Other Services Requiring Driving. **Other Jobs in This Work Group:** Ambulance Drivers and Attendants, Except Emergency Medical Technicians; Bus Drivers, Transit and Intercity; Couriers and Messengers; Driver/Sales Workers; Parking Lot Attendants; Postal Service Mail Carriers; Taxi Drivers and Chauffeurs.

Skills—Operation Monitoring: Watching gauges, dials, or other indicators to make sure a machine is working properly. **Equipment Maintenance:** Performing routine maintenance and determining when and what kind of maintenance is needed. **Operation and Control:** Controlling operations of equipment or systems. **Social Perceptiveness:** Being aware of others' reactions and understanding why they react the way they do. **Persuasion:** Persuading others to approach things differently. **Negotiation:** Bringing others together and trying to reconcile differences.

Education and Training Program: Truck and Bus Driver Training/Commercial Vehicle Operation. **Related Knowledge/Courses—Transportation:** Principles and methods for moving people or goods by air, rail, sea, or road, including their relative costs, advantages, and limitations. **Psychology:** Human behavior and performance, mental processes, psychological research methods, and the assessment and treatment of behavioral and affective disorders. **Public Safety and Security:** Weaponry; public safety; security operations, rules, regulations, precautions, and prevention; and the protection of people, data, and property.

Work Environment: Noisy; contaminants; disease or infections; sitting; using hands on objects, tools, or controls; repetitive motions.

Bus Drivers, Transit and Intercity

- ❋ Education/Training Required: Moderate-term on-the-job training
- ❋ Annual Earnings: $33,160
- ❋ Beginning Wage: $19,660
- ❋ Earnings Growth Potential: High
- ❋ Growth: 12.5%
- ❋ Annual Job Openings: 27,100
- ❋ Self-Employed: 1.3%
- ❋ Part-Time: 34.1%

Drive bus or motor coach, including regular route operations, charters, and private carriage. May assist passengers with baggage. May collect fares or tickets. Inspect vehicles and check gas, oil, and water levels prior to departure. Drive vehicles over specified routes or to specified destinations according to time schedules to transport passengers, complying with traffic regulations. Park vehicles at loading areas so that passengers can board. Assist passengers with baggage and collect tickets or cash fares. Report delays or accidents. Advise passengers to be seated and orderly while on vehicles. Regulate heating, lighting, and ventilating systems for passenger comfort. Load and unload baggage in baggage compartments. Record cash receipts and ticket fares. Make minor repairs to vehicle and change tires.

Personality Type: Realistic. These occupations frequently involve work activities that include practical, hands-on problems and solutions. They often deal with plants; animals; and real-world materials such as wood, tools, and machinery. Many of the occupations require working outside and don't involve a lot of paperwork or working closely with others.

GOE—Interest Area/Cluster: 16. Transportation, Distribution, and Logistics. **Work Group:** 16.06. Other Services Requiring Driving. **Other Jobs in This Work Group:** Ambulance Drivers and Attendants, Except Emergency Medical Technicians; Bus Drivers, School; Couriers and Messengers; Driver/Sales Workers; Parking Lot Attendants; Postal Service Mail Carriers; Taxi Drivers and Chauffeurs.

Skills—Equipment Maintenance: Performing routine maintenance and determining when and what kind of maintenance is needed. **Operation and Control:** Controlling operations of equipment or systems. **Social Perceptiveness:** Being aware of others' reactions and understanding why they react the way they do. **Operation Monitoring:** Watching gauges, dials, or other indicators to make sure a machine is working properly. **Troubleshooting:** Determining what is causing an operating error and deciding what to do about it. **Repairing:** Repairing machines or systems, using the needed tools.

Education and Training Program: Truck and Bus Driver Training/Commercial Vehicle Operation. **Related Knowledge/Courses—Transportation:** Principles and methods for moving people or goods by air, rail, sea, or road, including their relative costs, advantages, and limitations. **Geography:** Various methods for describing the location and distribution of land, sea, and air masses, including their physical locations, relationships, and characteristics. **Public Safety and Security:** Weaponry; public safety; security operations, rules, regulations, precautions, and prevention; and the protection of people, data, and property. **Psychology:** Human behavior and performance, mental processes, psychological research methods, and the assessment and treatment of behavioral and affective disorders. **Law and Government:** Laws, legal codes, court procedures, precedents, government regulations, executive orders, agency rules, and the democratic political process. **Customer and Personal Service:** Principles and processes for providing customer and personal services, including needs assessment techniques, quality service standards, alternative delivery systems, and customer satisfaction evaluation techniques.

Work Environment: Outdoors; noisy; contaminants; sitting; using hands on objects, tools, or controls; repetitive motions.

Business Teachers, Postsecondary

⊛ Education/Training Required: Doctoral degree
⊛ Annual Earnings: $64,900
⊛ Beginning Wage: $32,770
⊛ Earnings Growth Potential: High
⊛ Growth: 22.9%
⊛ Annual Job Openings: 11,643
⊛ Self-Employed: 0.4%
⊛ Part-Time: 27.8%

Teach courses in business administration and management, such as accounting, finance, human resources, labor relations, marketing, and operations research. Prepare and deliver lectures to undergraduate and/or graduate students on topics such as financial accounting, principles of marketing, and operations management. Evaluate and grade students' classwork, assignments, and papers. Compile, administer, and grade examinations or assign this work to others. Prepare course materials such as syllabi, homework assignments, and handouts. Maintain student attendance records, grades, and other required records. Initiate, facilitate, and moderate classroom discussions. Plan, evaluate, and revise curricula, course content, and course materials and methods of instruction. Keep abreast of developments in their field by reading current literature, talking with colleagues, and participating in professional organizations and conferences. Maintain regularly scheduled office hours to advise and assist students. Advise students on academic and vocational curricula and on career issues. Select and obtain materials and supplies such as textbooks. Collaborate with colleagues to address teaching and research issues. Collaborate with members of the business community to improve programs, to develop new programs, and to provide student access to learning opportunities such as internships. Participate in student recruitment, registration, and placement activities. Serve on academic or administrative committees that deal with institutional policies, departmental matters, and academic issues. Participate in campus and community events. Compile bibliographies of specialized materials for outside reading assignments. Perform administrative duties such as serving as department head. Supervise undergraduate and/or graduate teaching, internship, and research work. Conduct research in a particular field of knowledge and publish findings in professional journals, books, and/or electronic media. Act as advisers to student organizations. Provide professional consulting services to government and/or

industry. Write grant proposals to procure external research funding.

Personality Type: Social. These occupations frequently involve working with, communicating with, and teaching people and often involve helping or providing service to others.

GOE—Interest Area/Cluster: 05. Education and Training. **Work Group:** 05.03. Postsecondary and Adult Teaching and Instructing. **Other Jobs in This Work Group:** Adult Literacy, Remedial Education, and GED Teachers and Instructors; Agricultural Sciences Teachers, Postsecondary; Anthropology and Archeology Teachers, Postsecondary; Architecture Teachers, Postsecondary; Area, Ethnic, and Cultural Studies Teachers, Postsecondary; Art, Drama, and Music Teachers, Postsecondary; Atmospheric, Earth, Marine, and Space Sciences Teachers, Postsecondary; Biological Science Teachers, Postsecondary; Chemistry Teachers, Postsecondary; Communications Teachers, Postsecondary; Computer Science Teachers, Postsecondary; Criminal Justice and Law Enforcement Teachers, Postsecondary; Economics Teachers, Postsecondary; Education Teachers, Postsecondary; Engineering Teachers, Postsecondary; English Language and Literature Teachers, Postsecondary; Environmental Science Teachers, Postsecondary; Farm and Home Management Advisors; Foreign Language and Literature Teachers, Postsecondary; Forestry and Conservation Science Teachers, Postsecondary; Geography Teachers, Postsecondary; Graduate Teaching Assistants; Health Specialties Teachers, Postsecondary; History Teachers, Postsecondary; Home Economics Teachers, Postsecondary; Law Teachers, Postsecondary; Library Science Teachers, Postsecondary; Mathematical Science Teachers, Postsecondary; Nursing Instructors and Teachers, Postsecondary; Philosophy and Religion Teachers, Postsecondary; Physics Teachers, Postsecondary; Political Science Teachers, Postsecondary; Psychology Teachers, Postsecondary; Recreation and Fitness Studies Teachers, Postsecondary; Self-Enrichment Education Teachers; Social Work Teachers, Postsecondary; Sociology Teachers, Postsecondary; Vocational Education Teachers, Postsecondary.

Skills—Instructing: Teaching others how to do something. **Learning Strategies:** Using multiple approaches when learning or teaching new things. **Writing:** Communicating effectively with others in writing as indicated by the needs of the audience. **Monitoring:** Assessing how well one is doing when learning or doing something. **Speaking:** Talking to others to effectively convey information. **Active Learning:** Working with new material or information to grasp its implications. **Reading Comprehension:** Understanding

B

written sentences and paragraphs in work-related documents. **Critical Thinking:** Using logic and analysis to identify the strengths and weaknesses of different approaches.

Education and Training Programs: Accounting; Actuarial Science; Business Administration and Management, General; Business Statistics; Entrepreneurial Studies; Finance, General; Financial Planning and Services; Franchising and Franchise Operations; Human Resources Management; Insurance; International Business; Investments and Securities; Labor and Industrial Relations; Management Science, General; Marketing Management, General; Marketing Research; Public Finance; Purchasing, Procurement, and Contracts Management; others. **Related Knowledge/ Courses—Economics and Accounting:** Economic and accounting principles and practices, the financial markets, banking, and the analysis and reporting of financial data. **Education and Training:** Instructional methods and training techniques, including curriculum design principles, learning theory, group and individual teaching techniques, design of individual development plans, and test design principles. **Sociology and Anthropology:** Group behavior and dynamics; societal trends and influences; and cultures and their history, migrations, ethnicity, and origins. **Sales and Marketing:** Principles and methods involved in showing, promoting, and selling products or services. This includes marketing strategies and tactics, product demonstration and sales techniques, and sales control systems. **Philosophy and Theology:** Different philosophical systems and religions, including their basic principles, values, ethics, ways of thinking, customs, and practices and their impact on human culture. **English Language:** The structure and content of the English language, including the meaning and spelling of words, rules of composition, and grammar.

Work Environment: Indoors; sitting.

Camera Operators, Television, Video, and Motion Picture

- ❋ Education/Training Required: Postsecondary vocational training
- ❋ Annual Earnings: $41,850
- ❋ Beginning Wage: $21,050
- ❋ Earnings Growth Potential: High
- ❋ Growth: 11.5%
- ❋ Annual Job Openings: 3,496
- ❋ Self-Employed: 16.9%
- ❋ Part-Time: 18.9%

Operate television, video, or motion picture camera to photograph images or scenes for various purposes, such as TV broadcasts, advertising, video production, or motion pictures. Operate television or motion picture cameras to record scenes for television broadcasts, advertising, or motion pictures. Compose and frame each shot, applying the technical aspects of light, lenses, film, filters, and camera settings to achieve the effects sought by directors. Operate zoom lenses, changing images according to specifications and rehearsal instructions. Use cameras in any of several different camera mounts, such as stationary, track-mounted, or crane-mounted. Test, clean, and maintain equipment to ensure proper working condition. Adjust positions and controls of cameras, printers, and related equipment to change focus, exposure, and lighting. Gather and edit raw footage on location to send to television affiliates for broadcast, using electronic news-gathering or film-production equipment. Confer with directors, sound and lighting technicians, electricians, and other crew members to discuss assignments and determine filming sequences, desired effects, camera movements, and lighting requirements. Observe sets or locations for potential problems and to determine filming and lighting requirements. Instruct camera operators regarding camera setups, angles, distances, movement, and variables and cues for starting and stopping filming. Select and assemble cameras, accessories, equipment, and film stock to be used during filming, using knowledge of filming techniques, requirements, and computations. Label and record contents of exposed film and note details on report forms. Read charts and compute ratios to determine variables such as lighting, shutter angles, filter factors, and camera distances. Set up cameras, optical printers, and related equipment to produce photographs and special effects. View films to resolve problems of exposure control, subject and camera movement, changes in subject distance, and related variables. Reload camera magazines with fresh raw film stock. Read and analyze work orders and specifications to determine locations of subject material, work procedures, sequences of operations, and machine setups. Receive raw film stock and maintain film inventories.

Personality Type: Realistic. These occupations frequently involve work activities that include practical, hands-on problems and solutions. They often deal with plants; animals; and real-world materials such as wood, tools, and machinery. Many of the occupations require working outside and don't involve a lot of paperwork or working closely with others.

GOE—Interest Area/Cluster: 03. Arts and Communication. **Work Group:** 03.09. Media Technology. **Other Jobs**

in **This Work Group:** Audio and Video Equipment Technicians; Broadcast Technicians; Film and Video Editors; Multi-Media Artists and Animators; Photographers; Radio Operators; Sound Engineering Technicians.

Skills—Operation Monitoring: Watching gauges, dials, or other indicators to make sure a machine is working properly. **Operation and Control:** Controlling operations of equipment or systems. **Equipment Maintenance:** Performing routine maintenance and determining when and what kind of maintenance is needed. **Troubleshooting:** Determining what is causing an operating error and deciding what to do about it. **Equipment Selection:** Determining the kind of tools and equipment needed to do a job. **Operations Analysis:** Analyzing needs and product requirements to create a design. **Active Listening:** Listening to what other people are saying and asking questions as appropriate. **Installation:** Installing equipment, machines, wiring, or programs to meet specifications.

Education and Training Programs: Audiovisual Communications Technologies/Technician Training, Other; Cinematography and Film/Video Production; Radio and Television Broadcasting Technology/Technician Training. **Related Knowledge/Courses—Communications and Media:** Media production, communication, and dissemination techniques and methods, including alternative ways to inform and entertain via written, oral, and visual media. **Telecommunications:** Transmission, broadcasting, switching, control, and operation of telecommunications systems. **Computers and Electronics:** Electric circuit boards, processors, chips, and computer hardware and software, including applications and programming. **Engineering and Technology:** Equipment, tools, and mechanical devices and their uses to produce motion, light, power, technology, and other applications.

Work Environment: More often indoors than outdoors; very bright or dim lighting; standing; using hands on objects, tools, or controls.

Cardiovascular Technologists and Technicians

* Education/Training Required: Associate degree
* Annual Earnings: $44,940
* Beginning Wage: $24,650
* Earnings Growth Potential: High
* Growth: 25.5%
* Annual Job Openings: 3,550
* Self-Employed: 1.1%
* Part-Time: 17.3%

Conduct tests on pulmonary or cardiovascular systems of patients for diagnostic purposes. May conduct or assist in electrocardiograms, cardiac catheterizations, pulmonary-functions, lung capacity, and similar tests. Monitor patients' blood pressures and heart rates, using electrocardiogram (EKG) equipment during diagnostic and therapeutic procedures to notify physicians if something appears wrong. Explain testing procedures to patients to obtain cooperation and reduce anxiety. Observe gauges, recorders, and video screens of data analysis systems during imaging of cardiovascular systems. Monitor patients' comfort and safety during tests, alerting physicians to abnormalities or changes in patient responses. Obtain and record patients' identities, medical histories, or test results. Attach electrodes to patients' chests, arms, and legs; connect electrodes to leads from electrocardiogram (EKG) machines; and operate EKG machines to obtain readings. Adjust equipment and controls according to physicians' orders or established protocol. Prepare and position patients for testing. Check, test, and maintain cardiology equipment, making minor repairs when necessary, to ensure proper operation. Supervise and train other cardiology technologists and students. Perform general administrative tasks, such as scheduling appointments or ordering supplies and equipment. Maintain a proper sterile field during surgical procedures. Assist physicians in the diagnosis and treatment of cardiac and peripheral vascular treatments, such as implanting pacemakers or assisting with balloon angioplasties to treat blood vessel blockages. Inject contrast medium into patients' blood vessels. Assess cardiac physiology and calculate valve areas from blood flow velocity measurements. Operate diagnostic imaging equipment to produce contrast-enhanced radiographs of hearts and cardiovascular systems. Observe ultrasound display screens and listen to signals to record vascular information such as blood pressure, limb volume changes, oxygen saturation, and cerebral circulation. Transcribe, type, and distribute reports of diagnostic procedures for interpretation by physician. Conduct electrocardiogram (EKG), phonocardiogram, echocardiogram, stress testing, or other cardiovascular tests to record patients' cardiac activities, using specialized electronic test equipment, recording devices, and laboratory instruments.

Personality Type: Realistic. These occupations frequently involve work activities that include practical, hands-on problems and solutions. They often deal with plants; animals; and real-world materials such as wood, tools, and machinery. Many of the occupations require working outside and don't involve a lot of paperwork or working closely with others.

GOE—Interest Area/Cluster: 08. Health Science. **Work Group:** 08.06. Medical Technology. **Other Jobs in This Work Group:** Biological Technicians; Diagnostic Medical Sonographers; Medical and Clinical Laboratory Technicians; Medical and Clinical Laboratory Technologists; Medical Equipment Preparers; Medical Records and Health Information Technicians; Nuclear Medicine Technologists; Opticians, Dispensing; Orthotists and Prosthetists; Radiologic Technicians; Radiologic Technologists; Radiologic Technologists and Technicians.

Skills—Operation Monitoring: Watching gauges, dials, or other indicators to make sure a machine is working properly. **Management of Personnel Resources:** Motivating, developing, and directing people as they work; identifying the best people for the job. **Systems Analysis:** Determining how a system should work and how changes will affect outcomes. **Quality Control Analysis:** Evaluating the quality or performance of products, services, or processes. **Management of Material Resources:** Obtaining and seeing to the appropriate use of equipment, facilities, and materials needed to do certain work.

Education and Training Programs: Cardiopulmonary Technology/Technologist Training; Cardiovascular Technology/Technologist Training; Electrocardiograph Technology/Technician Training; Perfusion Technology/Perfusionist Training. **Related Knowledge/Courses—Medicine and Dentistry:** The information and techniques needed to diagnose and treat injuries, diseases, and deformities. This includes symptoms, treatment alternatives, drug properties and interactions, and preventive health-care measures. **Biology:** Plant and animal living tissue, cells, organisms, and entities, including their functions, interdependencies, and interactions with each other and the environment.

Psychology: Human behavior and performance, mental processes, psychological research methods, and the assessment and treatment of behavioral and affective disorders. **Customer and Personal Service:** Principles and processes for providing customer and personal services, including needs assessment techniques, quality service standards, alternative delivery systems, and customer satisfaction evaluation techniques. **Sociology and Anthropology:** Group behavior and dynamics; societal trends and influences; and cultures and their history, migrations, ethnicity, and origins. **Chemistry:** The composition, structure, and properties of substances and of the chemical processes and transformations that they undergo. This includes uses of chemicals and their interactions, danger signs, production techniques, and disposal methods.

Work Environment: Indoors; radiation; disease or infections; standing; using hands on objects, tools, or controls; repetitive motions.

Cargo and Freight Agents

* ❋ Education/Training Required: Moderate-term on-the-job training
* ❋ Annual Earnings: $37,060
* ❋ Beginning Wage: $22,720
* ❋ Earnings Growth Potential: Medium
* ❋ Growth: 16.5%
* ❋ Annual Job Openings: 9,967
* ❋ Self-Employed: 1.1%
* ❋ Part-Time: 6.1%

Expedite and route movement of incoming and outgoing cargo and freight shipments in airline, train, and trucking terminals and shipping docks. Take orders from customers and arrange pickup of freight and cargo for delivery to loading platform. Prepare and examine bills of lading to determine shipping charges and tariffs. Negotiate and arrange transport of goods with shipping or freight companies. Notify consignees, passengers, or customers of the arrival of freight or baggage and arrange for delivery. Advise clients on transportation and payment methods. Prepare manifests showing baggage, mail, and freight weights and number of passengers on airplanes and transmit data to destinations. Determine method of shipment and prepare bills of lading, invoices, and other shipping documents. Check import/export documentation to determine cargo contents and classify goods into different fee or tariff groups, using a tariff coding system. Estimate freight or postal rates and record shipment costs and weights. Enter shipping information into a computer by hand or by using a hand-held scanner that reads bar codes on goods. Retrieve stored items and trace lost shipments as necessary. Pack goods for shipping, using tools such as staplers, strapping machines, and hammers. Direct delivery trucks to shipping doors or designated marshalling areas and help load and unload goods safely. Inspect and count items received and check them against invoices or other documents, recording shortages and rejecting damaged goods. Install straps, braces, and padding to loads to prevent shifting or damage during shipment. Keep records of all goods shipped, received, and stored. Coordinate and supervise activities of workers engaged in packing and shipping merchandise. Arrange insurance coverage for goods. Direct or participate in cargo loading to ensure completeness of load and even distribution of weight. Open cargo containers and unwrap contents, using steel cutters, crowbars, or other hand tools. Attach address labels, identification codes, and shipping instructions to containers. Contact vendors or claims adjustment departments to resolve problems with shipments or contact service depots to arrange for repairs. Route received goods to first available flight or to appropriate storage areas or departments, using forklifts, handtrucks, or other equipment. Maintain a supply of packing materials.

Personality Type: Conventional. These occupations frequently involve following set procedures and routines and can include working with data and details more than with ideas. Usually there is a clear line of authority to follow.

GOE—Interest Area/Cluster: 16. Transportation, Distribution, and Logistics. **Work Group:** 16.07. Transportation Support Work. **Other Jobs in This Work Group:** Bridge and Lock Tenders; Cleaners of Vehicles and Equipment; Laborers and Freight, Stock, and Material Movers, Hand; Railroad Brake, Signal, and Switch Operators; Traffic Technicians.

Skills—Negotiation: Bringing others together and trying to reconcile differences. **Instructing:** Teaching others how to do something. **Writing:** Communicating effectively with others in writing as indicated by the needs of the audience. **Service Orientation:** Actively looking for ways to help people. **Monitoring:** Assessing how well one is doing when learning or doing something. **Speaking:** Talking to others to effectively convey information. **Learning Strategies:** Using multiple approaches when learning or teaching new things.

Education and Training Program: General Office Occupations and Clerical Services. **Related Knowledge/**

Courses—Transportation: Principles and methods for moving people or goods by air, rail, sea, or road, including their relative costs, advantages, and limitations. **Geography:** Various methods for describing the location and distribution of land, sea, and air masses, including their physical locations, relationships, and characteristics. **Customer and Personal Service:** Principles and processes for providing customer and personal services, including needs assessment techniques, quality service standards, alternative delivery systems, and customer satisfaction evaluation techniques. **Clerical Practices:** Administrative and clerical procedures and systems such as word-processing systems, filing and records management systems, stenography and transcription, forms, design principles, and other office procedures and terminology. **Computers and Electronics:** Electric circuit boards, processors, chips, and computer hardware and software, including applications and programming. **Administration and Management:** Principles and processes involved in business and organizational planning, coordination, and execution. This includes strategic planning, resource allocation, manpower modeling, leadership techniques, and production methods.

Work Environment: Indoors; sitting; repetitive motions.

Cartographers and Photogrammetrists

- ❋ Education/Training Required: Bachelor's degree
- ❋ Annual Earnings: $49,970
- ❋ Beginning Wage: $32,380
- ❋ Earnings Growth Potential: Medium
- ❋ Growth: 20.3%
- ❋ Annual Job Openings: 2,823
- ❋ Self-Employed: 3.4%
- ❋ Part-Time: 4.6%

Collect, analyze, and interpret geographic information provided by geodetic surveys, aerial photographs, and satellite data. Research, study, and prepare maps and other spatial data in digital or graphic form for legal, social, political, educational, and design purposes. May work with Geographic Information Systems (GIS). May design and evaluate algorithms, data structures, and user interfaces for GIS and mapping systems. Identify, scale, and orient geodetic points, elevations, and other planimetric or topographic features, applying standard mathematical formulas. Collect information about specific features of the Earth, using aerial photography and other digital remote sensing techniques. Revise existing maps and charts, making all necessary corrections and adjustments. Compile data required for map preparation, including aerial photographs, survey notes, records, reports, and original maps. Inspect final compositions to ensure completeness and accuracy. Determine map content and layout, as well as production specifications such as scale, size, projection, and colors, and direct production to ensure that specifications are followed. Examine and analyze data from ground surveys, reports, aerial photographs, and satellite images to prepare topographic maps, aerial-photograph mosaics, and related charts. Select aerial photographic and remote sensing techniques and plotting equipment needed to meet required standards of accuracy. Delineate aerial photographic detail such as control points, hydrography, topography, and cultural features, using precision stereoplotting apparatus or drafting instruments. Build and update digital databases. Prepare and alter trace maps, charts, tables, detailed drawings, and three-dimensional optical models of terrain, using stereoscopic plotting and computer graphics equipment. Determine guidelines that specify which source material is acceptable for use. Study legal records to establish boundaries of local, national, and international properties. Travel over photographed areas to observe, identify, record, and verify all relevant features.

Personality Type: Realistic. These occupations frequently involve work activities that include practical, hands-on problems and solutions. They often deal with plants; animals; and real-world materials such as wood, tools, and machinery. Many of the occupations require working outside and don't involve a lot of paperwork or working closely with others.

GOE—Interest Area/Cluster: 15. Scientific Research, Engineering, and Mathematics. **Work Group:** 15.09. Engineering Technology. **Other Jobs in This Work Group:** Aerospace Engineering and Operations Technicians; Civil Engineering Technicians; Electrical and Electronic Engineering Technicians; Electrical and Electronics Drafters; Electrical Drafters; Electrical Engineering Technicians; Electro-Mechanical Technicians; Electronic Drafters; Electronics Engineering Technicians; Environmental Engineering Technicians; Mapping Technicians; Mechanical Drafters; Mechanical Engineering Technicians; Surveying and Mapping Technicians; Surveying Technicians.

Skills—Science: Using scientific methods to solve problems. **Technology Design:** Generating or adapting equipment and technology to serve user needs. **Mathematics:** Using mathematics to solve problems. **Active Learning:** Working with new material or information to grasp its implications. **Troubleshooting:** Determining what is causing an operating error and deciding what to do about it. **Reading Comprehension:** Understanding written sentences and paragraphs in work-related documents. **Operation and Control:** Controlling operations of equipment or systems. **Writing:** Communicating effectively with others in writing as indicated by the needs of the audience.

Education and Training Programs: Cartography; Surveying Technology/Surveying. **Related Knowledge/Courses— Geography:** Various methods for describing the location and distribution of land, sea, and air masses, including their physical locations, relationships, and characteristics. **Design:** Design techniques, principles, tools, and instruments involved in the production and use of precision technical plans, blueprints, drawings, and models. **Engineering and Technology:** Equipment, tools, and mechanical devices and their uses to produce motion, light, power, technology, and other applications. **Computers and Electronics:** Electric circuit boards, processors, chips, and computer hardware and software, including applications and programming. **Production and Processing:** Inputs, outputs, raw materials, waste, quality control, costs, and techniques for maximizing the manufacture and distribution of goods. **Mathematics:** Numbers and their operations and interrelationships, including arithmetic, algebra, geometry, calculus, and statistics and their applications.

Work Environment: Indoors; sitting; using hands on objects, tools, or controls; repetitive motions.

Cement Masons and Concrete Finishers

- ❋ Education/Training Required: Moderate-term on-the-job training
- ❋ Annual Earnings: $33,840
- ❋ Beginning Wage: $21,980
- ❋ Earnings Growth Potential: Medium
- ❋ Growth: 11.4%
- ❋ Annual Job Openings: 34,625
- ❋ Self-Employed: 2.0%
- ❋ Part-Time: 6.0%

Smooth and finish surfaces of poured concrete, such as floors, walks, sidewalks, roads, or curbs, using a variety of hand and power tools. **Align forms for sidewalks, curbs, or gutters; patch voids; and use saws to cut expansion joints.** Check the forms that hold the concrete to see that they are properly constructed. Set the forms that hold concrete to the desired pitch and depth and align them. Spread, level, and smooth concrete, using rake, shovel, hand or power trowel, hand or power screed, and float. Mold expansion joints and edges, using edging tools, jointers, and straightedge. Monitor how the wind, heat, or cold affect the curing of the concrete throughout the entire process. Signal truck driver to position truck to facilitate pouring concrete and move chute to direct concrete on forms. Produce rough concrete surface, using broom. Operate power vibrator to compact concrete. Direct the casting of the concrete and supervise laborers who use shovels or special tools to spread it. Mix cement, sand, and water to produce concrete, grout, or slurry, using hoe, trowel, tamper, scraper, or concrete-mixing machine. Cut out damaged areas, drill holes for reinforcing rods, and position reinforcing rods to repair concrete, using power saw and drill. Wet surface to prepare for bonding, fill holes and cracks with grout or slurry, and smooth, using trowel. Wet concrete surface and rub with stone to smooth surface and obtain specified finish. Clean chipped area, using wire brush, and feel and observe surface to determine if it is rough or uneven. Apply hardening and sealing compounds to cure surface of concrete and waterproof or restore surface. Chip, scrape, and grind high spots, ridges, and rough projections to finish concrete, using pneumatic chisels, power grinders, or hand tools. Spread roofing paper on surface of foundation and spread concrete onto roofing paper with trowel to form terrazzo base. Build wooden molds and clamp molds around area to be repaired, using hand tools. Sprinkle colored marble or stone chips, powdered steel, or coloring powder over surface to produce prescribed finish. Cut metal division strips and press them into terrazzo base so that top edges form desired design or pattern. Fabricate concrete beams, columns, and panels. Waterproof or restore concrete surfaces, using appropriate compounds.

Personality Type: Realistic. These occupations frequently involve work activities that include practical, hands-on problems and solutions. They often deal with plants; animals; and real-world materials such as wood, tools, and machinery. Many of the occupations require working outside and don't involve a lot of paperwork or working closely with others.

GOE—Interest Area/Cluster: 02. Architecture and Construction. **Work Group:** 02.04. Construction Crafts.

Other Jobs in This Work Group: Boilermakers; Brickmasons and Blockmasons; Carpet Installers; Commercial Divers; Construction Carpenters; Crane and Tower Operators; Drywall and Ceiling Tile Installers; Electricians; Fence Erectors; Floor Layers, Except Carpet, Wood, and Hard Tiles; Floor Sanders and Finishers; Glaziers; Hazardous Materials Removal Workers; Insulation Workers, Floor, Ceiling, and Wall; Insulation Workers, Mechanical; Manufactured Building and Mobile Home Installers; Operating Engineers and Other Construction Equipment Operators; Painters, Construction and Maintenance; Paperhangers; Paving, Surfacing, and Tamping Equipment Operators; Pile-Driver Operators; Pipe Fitters and Steamfitters; Pipelayers; Plasterers and Stucco Masons; Plumbers; Plumbers, Pipefitters, and Steamfitters; Rail-Track Laying and Maintenance Equipment Operators; Refractory Materials Repairers, Except Brickmasons; Reinforcing Iron and Rebar Workers; Riggers; Roofers; Rough Carpenters; Security and Fire Alarm Systems Installers; Segmental Pavers; Sheet Metal Workers; Stone Cutters and Carvers, Manufacturing; Stonemasons; Structural Iron and Steel Workers; Tapers; Terrazzo Workers and Finishers; Tile and Marble Setters.

Skills—Mathematics: Using mathematics to solve problems. **Installation:** Installing equipment, machines, wiring, or programs to meet specifications. **Repairing:** Repairing machines or systems, using the needed tools. **Equipment Maintenance:** Performing routine maintenance and determining when and what kind of maintenance is needed. **Equipment Selection:** Determining the kind of tools and equipment needed to do a job. **Coordination:** Adjusting actions in relation to others' actions.

Education and Training Program: Concrete Finishing/Concrete Finisher Training. **Related Knowledge/Courses—Building and Construction:** Materials, methods, and the appropriate tools to construct objects, structures, and buildings. **Public Safety and Security:** Weaponry; public safety; security operations, rules, regulations, precautions, and prevention; and the protection of people, data, and property. **Mechanical Devices:** Machines and tools, including their designs, uses, benefits, repair, and maintenance. **Design:** Design techniques, principles, tools, and instruments involved in the production and use of precision technical plans, blueprints, drawings, and models. **Engineering and Technology:** Equipment, tools, and mechanical devices and their uses to produce motion, light, power, technology, and other applications.

Work Environment: Outdoors; noisy; hazardous equipment; standing; using hands on objects, tools, or controls; bending or twisting the body.

Chefs and Head Cooks

- ❇ Education/Training Required: Work experience in a related occupation
- ❇ Annual Earnings: $37,160
- ❇ Beginning Wage: $21,560
- ❇ Earnings Growth Potential: High
- ❇ Growth: 7.6%
- ❇ Annual Job Openings: 9,401
- ❇ Self-Employed: 7.2%
- ❇ Part-Time: 7.8%

Direct the preparation, seasoning, and cooking of salads, soups, fish, meats, vegetables, desserts, or other foods. May plan and price menu items, order supplies, and keep records and accounts. May participate in cooking. Check the quality of raw and cooked food products to ensure that standards are met. Monitor sanitation practices to ensure that employees follow standards and regulations. Check the quantity and quality of received products. Order or requisition food and other supplies needed to ensure efficient operation. Inspect supplies, equipment, and work areas to ensure conformance to established standards. Supervise and coordinate activities of cooks and workers engaged in food preparation. Determine how food should be presented and create decorative food displays. Instruct cooks and other workers in the preparation, cooking, garnishing, and presentation of food. Estimate amounts and costs of required supplies, such as food and ingredients. Collaborate with other personnel to plan and develop recipes and menus, taking into account such factors as seasonal availability of ingredients and the likely number of customers. Analyze recipes to assign prices to menu items, based on food, labor, and overhead costs. Prepare and cook foods of all types, either on a regular basis or for special guests or functions. Determine production schedules and staff requirements necessary to ensure timely delivery of services. Recruit and hire staff, including cooks and other kitchen workers. Meet with customers to discuss menus for special occasions such as weddings, parties, and banquets. Demonstrate new cooking techniques and equipment to staff. Meet with sales representatives in order to negotiate prices and order supplies. Arrange for equipment purchases and repairs. Record production and operational data on specified forms. Plan, direct, and supervise the food preparation and cooking activities of multiple kitchens or restaurants in an establishment such as a restaurant chain, hospital, or hotel. Coordinate planning, budgeting, and purchasing for all the food operations within establishments such as clubs, hotels, or restaurant chains.

Personality Type: Enterprising. These occupations frequently involve starting up and carrying out projects and can involve leading people and making many decisions. They sometimes require risk taking and often deal with business.

GOE—Interest Area/Cluster: 09. Hospitality, Tourism, and Recreation. **Work Group:** 09.04. Food and Beverage Preparation. **Other Jobs in This Work Group:** Butchers and Meat Cutters; Cooks, Fast Food; Cooks, Institution and Cafeteria; Cooks, Private Household; Cooks, Restaurant; Cooks, Short Order; Dishwashers; Food Preparation Workers.

Skills—Equipment Maintenance: Performing routine maintenance and determining when and what kind of maintenance is needed. **Management of Financial Resources:** Determining how money will be spent to get the work done and accounting for these expenditures. **Repairing:** Repairing machines or systems, using the needed tools. **Management of Personnel Resources:** Motivating, developing, and directing people as they work; identifying the best people for the job. **Service Orientation:** Actively looking for ways to help people. **Negotiation:** Bringing others together and trying to reconcile differences. **Quality Control Analysis:** Evaluating the quality or performance of products, services, or processes. **Systems Analysis:** Determining how a system should work and how changes will affect outcomes.

Education and Training Programs: Cooking and Related Culinary Arts, General; Culinary Arts/Chef Training. **Related Knowledge/Courses—Food Production:** Techniques and equipment for planting, growing, and harvesting of food for consumption, including crop-rotation methods, animal husbandry, and food storage/handling techniques. **Production and Processing:** Inputs, outputs, raw materials, waste, quality control, costs, and techniques for maximizing the manufacture and distribution of goods. **Administration and Management:** Principles and processes involved in business and organizational planning, coordination, and execution. This includes strategic planning, resource allocation, manpower modeling, leadership techniques, and production methods. **Chemistry:** The composition, structure, and properties of substances and of the chemical processes and transformations that they undergo. This includes uses of chemicals and their interactions, danger signs, production techniques, and disposal methods. **Education and Training:** Instructional methods and training techniques, including curriculum design principles, learning theory, group and individual teaching techniques, design of individual development plans, and test design principles. **Personnel and Human Resources:** Principles and procedures for personnel recruitment; selection; training; compensation and benefits; labor relations and negotiation; and personnel information systems.

Work Environment: Minor burns, cuts, bites, or stings; standing; walking and running; using hands on objects, tools, or controls; bending or twisting the body; repetitive motions.

Chemical Engineers

- ❈ Education/Training Required: Bachelor's degree
- ❈ Annual Earnings: $81,500
- ❈ Beginning Wage: $52,060
- ❈ Earnings Growth Potential: Medium
- ❈ Growth: 7.9%
- ❈ Annual Job Openings: 2,111
- ❈ Self-Employed: 1.9%
- ❈ Part-Time: 3.4%

Design chemical plant equipment and devise processes for manufacturing chemicals and products, such as gasoline, synthetic rubber, plastics, detergents, cement, paper, and pulp, by applying principles and technology of chemistry, physics, and engineering. Perform tests throughout stages of production to determine degree of control over variables, including temperature, density, specific gravity, and pressure. Develop safety procedures to be employed by workers operating equipment or working in close proximity to ongoing chemical reactions. Determine most effective arrangement of operations such as mixing, crushing, heat transfer, distillation, and drying. Prepare estimate of production costs and production progress reports for management. Direct activities of workers who operate or who are engaged in constructing and improving absorption, evaporation, or electromagnetic equipment. Perform laboratory studies of steps in manufacture of new product and test proposed process in small-scale operation such as a pilot plant. Develop processes to separate components of liquids or gases or generate electrical currents by using controlled chemical processes. Conduct research to develop new and improved chemical manufacturing processes. Design measurement and control systems for chemical plants based on data collected in laboratory experiments and in pilot plant operations. Design and plan layout of equipment.

Personality Type: Investigative. These occupations frequently involve working with ideas and require an extensive amount of thinking. They can involve searching for facts and figuring out problems mentally.

GOE—Interest Area/Cluster: 15. Scientific Research, Engineering, and Mathematics. **Work Group:** 15.07. Research and Design Engineering. **Other Jobs in This Work Group:** Aerospace Engineers; Biomedical Engineers; Civil Engineers; Computer Hardware Engineers; Electrical Engineers; Electronics Engineers, Except Computer; Marine Architects; Marine Engineers; Marine Engineers and Naval Architects; Materials Engineers; Mechanical Engineers; Nuclear Engineers.

Skills—Science: Using scientific methods to solve problems. **Technology Design:** Generating or adapting equipment and technology to serve user needs. **Troubleshooting:** Determining what is causing an operating error and deciding what to do about it. **Programming:** Writing computer programs for various purposes. **Operations Analysis:** Analyzing needs and product requirements to create a design. **Installation:** Installing equipment, machines, wiring, or programs to meet specifications. **Mathematics:** Using mathematics to solve problems. **Systems Analysis:** Determining how a system should work and how changes will affect outcomes.

Education and Training Program: Chemical Engineering. **Related Knowledge/Courses—Engineering and Technology:** Equipment, tools, and mechanical devices and their uses to produce motion, light, power, technology, and other applications. **Chemistry:** The composition, structure, and properties of substances and of the chemical processes and transformations that they undergo. This includes uses of chemicals and their interactions, danger signs, production techniques, and disposal methods. **Physics:** Physical principles, laws, and applications, including air, water, material dynamics, light, atomic principles, heat, electric theory, earth formations, and meteorological and related natural phenomena. **Design:** Design techniques, principles, tools, and instruments involved in the production and use of precision technical plans, blueprints, drawings, and models. **Production and Processing:** Inputs, outputs, raw materials, waste, quality control, costs, and techniques for maximizing the manufacture and distribution of goods.

Mathematics: Numbers and their operations and interrelationships, including arithmetic, algebra, geometry, calculus, and statistics and their applications.

Work Environment: Indoors; noisy; hazardous conditions; sitting.

Chemical Technicians

* ❋ Education/Training Required: Associate degree
* ❋ Annual Earnings: $40,740
* ❋ Beginning Wage: $25,380
* ❋ Earnings Growth Potential: Medium
* ❋ Growth: 5.8%
* ❋ Annual Job Openings: 4,010
* ❋ Self-Employed: 0.4%
* ❋ Part-Time: 3.9%

Conduct chemical and physical laboratory tests to assist scientists in making qualitative and quantitative analyses of solids, liquids, and gaseous materials for purposes such as research and development of new products or processes; quality control; maintenance of environmental standards; and other work involving experimental, theoretical, or practical application of chemistry and related sciences. Monitor product quality to ensure compliance to standards and specifications. Set up and conduct chemical experiments, tests, and analyses using techniques such as chromatography, spectroscopy, physical and chemical separation techniques, and microscopy. Conduct chemical and physical laboratory tests to assist scientists in making qualitative and quantitative analyses of solids, liquids, and gaseous materials. Compile and interpret results of tests and analyses. Provide technical support and assistance to chemists and engineers. Prepare chemical solutions for products and processes following standardized formulas or create experimental formulas. Maintain, clean, and sterilize laboratory instruments and equipment. Write technical reports or prepare graphs and charts to document experimental results. Order and inventory materials to maintain supplies. Develop and conduct programs of sampling and analysis to maintain quality standards of raw materials, chemical intermediates, and products. Direct or monitor other workers producing chemical products. Operate experimental pilot plants, assisting with experimental design. Develop new chemical engineering processes or production techniques. Design and fabricate experimental apparatus to develop new products and processes.

Personality Type: Investigative. These occupations frequently involve working with ideas and require an extensive amount of thinking. They can involve searching for facts and figuring out problems mentally.

GOE—Interest Area/Cluster: 15. Scientific Research, Engineering, and Mathematics. **Work Group:** 15.05. Physical Science Laboratory Technology. **Other Jobs in This Work Group:** Nuclear Equipment Operation Technicians; Nuclear Technicians.

Skills—Science: Using scientific methods to solve problems. **Operation Monitoring:** Watching gauges, dials, or other indicators to make sure a machine is working properly. **Quality Control Analysis:** Evaluating the quality or performance of products, services, or processes. **Equipment Maintenance:** Performing routine maintenance and determining when and what kind of maintenance is needed. **Operation and Control:** Controlling operations of equipment or systems. **Repairing:** Repairing machines or systems, using the needed tools. **Mathematics:** Using mathematics to solve problems. **Troubleshooting:** Determining what is causing an operating error and deciding what to do about it.

Education and Training Programs: Chemical Technology/Technician Training; Food Science. **Related Knowledge/Courses—Chemistry:** The composition, structure, and properties of substances and of the chemical processes and transformations that they undergo. This includes uses of chemicals and their interactions, danger signs, production techniques, and disposal methods. **Mechanical Devices:** Machines and tools, including their designs, uses, benefits, repair, and maintenance. **Computers and Electronics:** Electric circuit boards, processors, chips, and computer hardware and software, including applications and programming. **Mathematics:** Numbers and their operations and interrelationships, including arithmetic, algebra, geometry, calculus, and statistics and their applications.

Work Environment: Indoors; noisy; contaminants; hazardous conditions; standing.

Chemistry Teachers, Postsecondary

- ❋ Education/Training Required: Doctoral degree
- ❋ Annual Earnings: $63,870
- ❋ Beginning Wage: $37,810
- ❋ Earnings Growth Potential: High
- ❋ Growth: 22.9%
- ❋ Annual Job Openings: 3,405
- ❋ Self-Employed: 0.4%
- ❋ Part-Time: 27.8%

Teach courses pertaining to the chemical and physical properties and compositional changes of substances. Work may include instruction in the methods of qualitative and quantitative chemical analysis. Includes both teachers primarily engaged in teaching and those who do a combination of both teaching and research. Prepare and deliver lectures to undergraduate and/or graduate students on topics such as organic chemistry, analytical chemistry, and chemical separation. Supervise students' laboratory work. Evaluate and grade students' classwork, laboratory performance, assignments, and papers. Compile, administer, and grade examinations or assign this work to others. Maintain student attendance records, grades, and other required records. Prepare course materials such as syllabi, homework assignments, and handouts. Maintain regularly scheduled office hours to advise and assist students. Plan, evaluate, and revise curricula, course content, course materials, and methods of instruction. Supervise undergraduate and/or graduate teaching, internships, and research work. Keep abreast of developments in the field by reading current literature, talking with colleagues, and participating in professional conferences. Initiate, facilitate, and moderate classroom discussions. Select and obtain materials and supplies such as textbooks and laboratory equipment. Conduct research in a particular field of knowledge and publish findings in professional journals, books, and/or electronic media. Advise students on academic and vocational curricula and on career issues. Collaborate with colleagues to address teaching and research issues. Serve on academic or administrative committees that deal with institutional policies, departmental matters, and academic issues. Write grant proposals to procure external research funding. Participate in student recruitment, registration, and placement activities. Prepare and submit required reports related to instruction. Perform administrative duties such as serving as a department head. Act as advisers to student organizations. Compile bibliographies of specialized materials for outside reading assignments. Participate in campus and community events. Provide professional consulting services to government and/or industry.

Personality Type: Social. These occupations frequently involve working with, communicating with, and teaching people and often involve helping or providing service to others.

GOE—Interest Area/Cluster: 05. Education and Training. **Work Group:** 05.03. Postsecondary and Adult Teaching and Instructing. **Other Jobs in This Work Group:** Adult Literacy, Remedial Education, and GED Teachers and Instructors; Agricultural Sciences Teachers, Postsecondary; Anthropology and Archeology Teachers, Postsecondary; Architecture Teachers, Postsecondary; Area, Ethnic, and Cultural Studies Teachers, Postsecondary; Art, Drama, and Music Teachers, Postsecondary; Atmospheric, Earth, Marine, and Space Sciences Teachers, Postsecondary; Biological Science Teachers, Postsecondary; Business Teachers, Postsecondary; Communications Teachers, Postsecondary; Computer Science Teachers, Postsecondary; Criminal Justice and Law Enforcement Teachers, Postsecondary; Economics Teachers, Postsecondary; Education Teachers, Postsecondary; Engineering Teachers, Postsecondary; English Language and Literature Teachers, Postsecondary; Environmental Science Teachers, Postsecondary; Farm and Home Management Advisors; Foreign Language and Literature Teachers, Postsecondary; Forestry and Conservation Science Teachers, Postsecondary; Geography Teachers, Postsecondary; Graduate Teaching Assistants; Health Specialties Teachers, Postsecondary; History Teachers, Postsecondary; Home Economics Teachers, Postsecondary; Law Teachers, Postsecondary; Library Science Teachers, Postsecondary; Mathematical Science Teachers, Postsecondary; Nursing Instructors and Teachers, Postsecondary; Philosophy and Religion Teachers, Postsecondary; Physics Teachers, Postsecondary; Political Science Teachers, Postsecondary; Psychology Teachers, Postsecondary; Recreation and Fitness Studies Teachers, Postsecondary; Self-Enrichment Education Teachers; Social Work Teachers, Postsecondary; Sociology Teachers, Postsecondary; Vocational Education Teachers, Postsecondary.

Skills—Science: Using scientific methods to solve problems. **Mathematics:** Using mathematics to solve problems. **Instructing:** Teaching others how to do something. **Writing:** Communicating effectively with others in writing as indicated by the needs of the audience. **Reading Comprehension:** Understanding written sentences and paragraphs in work-related documents. **Active Learning:** Working with new material or information to grasp its implications.

Technology Design: Generating or adapting equipment and technology to serve user needs. **Complex Problem Solving:** Identifying complex problems, reviewing the options, and implementing solutions.

Education and Training Programs: Analytical Chemistry; Chemical Physics; Chemistry, General; Chemistry, Other; Geochemistry; Inorganic Chemistry; Organic Chemistry; Physical and Theoretical Chemistry; Polymer Chemistry. **Related Knowledge/Courses—Chemistry:** The composition, structure, and properties of substances and of the chemical processes and transformations that they undergo. This includes uses of chemicals and their interactions, danger signs, production techniques, and disposal methods. **Biology:** Plant and animal living tissue, cells, organisms, and entities, including their functions, interdependencies, and interactions with each other and the environment. **Physics:** Physical principles, laws, and applications, including air, water, material dynamics, light, atomic principles, heat, electric theory, earth formations, and meteorological and related natural phenomena. **Education and Training:** Instructional methods and training techniques, including curriculum design principles, learning theory, group and individual teaching techniques, design of individual development plans, and test design principles. **Mathematics:** Numbers and their operations and interrelationships, including arithmetic, algebra, geometry, calculus, and statistics and their applications. **English Language:** The structure and content of the English language, including the meaning and spelling of words, rules of composition, and grammar.

Work Environment: Indoors; contaminants; hazardous conditions; sitting.

Chemists

- ❋ Education/Training Required: Bachelor's degree
- ❋ Annual Earnings: $63,490
- ❋ Beginning Wage: $36,810
- ❋ Earnings Growth Potential: High
- ❋ Growth: 9.1%
- ❋ Annual Job Openings: 9,024
- ❋ Self-Employed: 1.2%
- ❋ Part-Time: 3.9%

Conduct qualitative and quantitative chemical analyses or chemical experiments in laboratories for quality or process control or to develop new products or

knowledge. Analyze organic and inorganic compounds to determine chemical and physical properties, composition, structure, relationships, and reactions, utilizing chromatography, spectroscopy, and spectrophotometry techniques. Develop, improve, and customize products, equipment, formulas, processes, and analytical methods. Compile and analyze test information to determine process or equipment operating efficiency and to diagnose malfunctions. Confer with scientists and engineers to conduct analyses of research projects, interpret test results, or develop nonstandard tests. Direct, coordinate, and advise personnel in test procedures for analyzing components and physical properties of materials. Induce changes in composition of substances by introducing heat, light, energy, and chemical catalysts for quantitative and qualitative analysis. Write technical papers and reports and prepare standards and specifications for processes, facilities, products, or tests. Study effects of various methods of processing, preserving, and packaging on composition and properties of foods. Prepare test solutions, compounds, and reagents for laboratory personnel to conduct test.

Personality Type: Investigative. These occupations frequently involve working with ideas and require an extensive amount of thinking. They can involve searching for facts and figuring out problems mentally.

GOE—Interest Area/Cluster: 15. Scientific Research, Engineering, and Mathematics. **Work Group:** 15.02. Physical Sciences. **Other Jobs in This Work Group:** Astronomers; Atmospheric and Space Scientists; Geographers; Geoscientists, Except Hydrologists and Geographers; Hydrologists; Materials Scientists; Physicists.

Skills—Science: Using scientific methods to solve problems. **Quality Control Analysis:** Evaluating the quality or performance of products, services, or processes. **Technology Design:** Generating or adapting equipment and technology to serve user needs. **Operation Monitoring:** Watching gauges, dials, or other indicators to make sure a machine is working properly. **Equipment Selection:** Determining the kind of tools and equipment needed to do a job. **Management of Material Resources:** Obtaining and seeing to the appropriate use of equipment, facilities, and materials needed to do certain work. **Management of Financial Resources:** Determining how money will be spent to get the work done and accounting for these expenditures. **Operations Analysis:** Analyzing needs and product requirements to create a design.

Education and Training Programs: Analytical Chemistry; Chemical Physics; Chemistry, General; Chemistry, Other; Inorganic Chemistry; Organic Chemistry; Physical and Theoretical Chemistry; Polymer Chemistry. **Related Knowledge/Courses—Chemistry:** The composition, structure, and properties of substances and of the chemical processes and transformations that they undergo. This includes uses of chemicals and their interactions, danger signs, production techniques, and disposal methods. **Mathematics:** Numbers and their operations and interrelationships, including arithmetic, algebra, geometry, calculus, and statistics and their applications. **Engineering and Technology:** Equipment, tools, and mechanical devices and their uses to produce motion, light, power, technology, and other applications. **Production and Processing:** Inputs, outputs, raw materials, waste, quality control, costs, and techniques for maximizing the manufacture and distribution of goods. **Computers and Electronics:** Electric circuit boards, processors, chips, and computer hardware and software, including applications and programming. **Law and Government:** Laws, legal codes, court procedures, precedents, government regulations, executive orders, agency rules, and the democratic political process.

Work Environment: Indoors; contaminants; hazardous conditions; standing.

Chief Executives

- ✴ Education/Training Required: Work experience plus degree
- ✴ Annual Earnings: More than $145,600
- ✴ Beginning Wage: $64,530
- ✴ Earnings Growth Potential: Cannot be calculated
- ✴ Growth: 2.0%
- ✴ Annual Job Openings: 21,209
- ✴ Self-Employed: 22.0%
- ✴ Part-Time: 5.5%

Determine and formulate policies and provide the overall direction of companies or private and public sector organizations within the guidelines set up by a board of directors or similar governing body. Plan, direct, or coordinate operational activities at the highest level of management with the help of subordinate executives and staff managers. Direct and coordinate an organization's financial and budget activities in order to fund operations, maximize investments, and increase efficiency. Confer with board members, organization officials, and staff members to discuss issues, coordinate activities, and resolve problems. Analyze operations to evaluate performance of a company and its staff in meeting objectives and to determine areas of potential cost reduction, program improvement, or policy change. Direct, plan, and implement policies, objectives, and activities of organizations or businesses in order to ensure continuing operations, to maximize returns on investments, and to increase productivity. Prepare budgets for approval, including those for funding and implementation of programs. Direct and coordinate activities of businesses or departments concerned with production, pricing, sales, and/or distribution of products. Negotiate or approve contracts and agreements with suppliers, distributors, federal and state agencies, and other organizational entities. Review reports submitted by staff members in order to recommend approval or to suggest changes. Appoint department heads or managers and assign or delegate responsibilities to them. Direct human resources activities, including the approval of human resource plans and activities, the selection of directors and other high-level staff, and establishment and organization of major departments. Preside over or serve on boards of directors, management committees, or other governing boards. Prepare and present reports concerning activities, expenses, budgets, government statutes and rulings, and other items affecting businesses or program services. Establish departmental responsibilities and coordinate functions among departments and sites. Implement corrective action plans to solve organizational or departmental problems. Coordinate the development and implementation of budgetary control systems, recordkeeping systems, and other administrative control processes. Direct non-merchandising departments such as advertising, purchasing, credit, and accounting. Deliver speeches, write articles, and present information at meetings or conventions in order to promote services, exchange ideas, and accomplish objectives.

Personality Type: Enterprising. These occupations frequently involve starting up and carrying out projects and can involve leading people and making many decisions. They sometimes require risk taking and often deal with business.

GOE—Interest Area/Cluster: 04. Business and Administration. **Work Group:** 04.01. Managerial Work in General Business. **Other Jobs in This Work Group:** Compensation and Benefits Managers; General and Operations Managers; Human Resources Managers; Training and Development Managers.

Skills—Management of Financial Resources: Determining how money will be spent to get the work done and accounting for these expenditures. **Management of Material Resources:** Obtaining and seeing to the appropriate use of equipment, facilities, and materials needed to do certain work. **Judgment and Decision Making:** Weighing the relative costs and benefits of a potential action. **Negotiation:** Bringing others together and trying to reconcile differences. **Management of Personnel Resources:** Motivating, developing, and directing people as they work; identifying the best people for the job. **Systems Evaluation:** Looking at many indicators of system performance and taking into account their accuracy. **Coordination:** Adjusting actions in relation to others' actions. **Operations Analysis:** Analyzing needs and product requirements to create a design.

Education and Training Programs: Business Administration/Management; Business/Commerce, General; Entrepreneurship/Entrepreneurial Studies; International Business/Trade/Commerce; International Relations and Affairs; Public Administration; Public Administration and Services, Other; Public Policy Analysis; Transportation/Transportation Management. **Related Knowledge/Courses—Economics and Accounting:** Economic and accounting principles and practices, the financial markets, banking, and the analysis and reporting of financial data. **Administration and Management:** Principles and processes involved in business and organizational planning, coordination, and execution. This includes strategic planning, resource allocation, manpower modeling, leadership techniques, and production methods. **Sales and Marketing:** Principles and methods involved in showing, promoting, and selling products or services. This includes marketing strategies and tactics, product demonstration and sales techniques, and sales control systems. **Personnel and Human Resources:** Principles and procedures for personnel recruitment; selection; training; compensation and benefits; labor relations and negotiation; and personnel information systems. **Law and Government:** Laws, legal codes, court procedures, precedents, government regulations, executive orders, agency rules, and the democratic political process. **Medicine and Dentistry:** The information and techniques needed to diagnose and treat injuries, diseases, and deformities. This includes symptoms, treatment alternatives, drug properties and interactions, and preventive health-care measures.

Work Environment: Indoors; sitting.

Child, Family, and School Social Workers

- ❋ Education/Training Required: Bachelor's degree
- ❋ Annual Earnings: $38,620
- ❋ Beginning Wage: $25,160
- ❋ Earnings Growth Potential: Low
- ❋ Growth: 19.1%
- ❋ Annual Job Openings: 35,402
- ❋ Self-Employed: 2.8%
- ❋ Part-Time: 9.4%

Provide social services and assistance to improve the social and psychological functioning of children and their families and to maximize the family well-being and the academic functioning of children. May assist single parents, arrange adoptions, and find foster homes for abandoned or abused children. In schools, they address such problems as teenage pregnancy, misbehavior, and truancy. May also advise teachers on how to deal with problem children. Interview clients individually, in families, or in groups, assessing their situations, capabilities, and problems, to determine what services are required to meet their needs. Counsel individuals, groups, families, or communities regarding issues including mental health, poverty, unemployment, substance abuse, physical abuse, rehabilitation, social adjustment, child care, or medical care. Maintain case history records and prepare reports. Counsel students whose behavior, school progress, or mental or physical impairment indicate a need for assistance, diagnosing students' problems and arranging for needed services. Consult with parents, teachers, and other school personnel to determine causes of problems such as truancy and misbehavior and to implement solutions. Counsel parents with child rearing problems, interviewing the child and family to determine whether further action is required. Develop and review service plans in consultation with clients and perform follow-ups assessing the quantity and quality of services provided. Collect supplementary information needed to assist clients, such as employment records, medical records, or school reports. Address legal issues, such as child abuse and discipline, assisting with hearings and providing testimony to inform custody arrangements. Provide, find, or arrange for support services, such as child care, homemaker service, prenatal care, substance abuse treatment, job training, counseling, or parenting classes, to prevent more serious problems from developing. Refer clients to community resources for services such as job placement, debt counseling, legal aid, housing, medical treatment, or financial assistance and provide concrete information, such as where to go and how to apply. Arrange for medical, psychiatric, and other tests that may disclose causes of difficulties and indicate remedial measures. Work in child and adolescent residential institutions. Administer welfare programs. Evaluate personal characteristics and home conditions of foster home or adoption applicants. Serve as liaisons between students, homes, schools, family services, child guidance clinics, courts, protective services, doctors, and other contacts to help children who face problems such as disabilities, abuse, or poverty.

Personality Type: Social. These occupations frequently involve working with, communicating with, and teaching people and often involve helping or providing service to others.

GOE—Interest Area/Cluster: 10. Human Service. **Work Group:** 10.01. Counseling and Social Work. **Other Jobs in This Work Group:** Clinical Psychologists; Clinical, Counseling, and School Psychologists; Counseling Psychologists; Marriage and Family Therapists; Medical and Public Health Social Workers; Mental Health and Substance Abuse Social Workers; Mental Health Counselors; Probation Officers and Correctional Treatment Specialists; Rehabilitation Counselors; Residential Advisors; Social and Human Service Assistants; Substance Abuse and Behavioral Disorder Counselors.

Skills—Social Perceptiveness: Being aware of others' reactions and understanding why they react the way they do. **Service Orientation:** Actively looking for ways to help people. **Speaking:** Talking to others to effectively convey information. **Monitoring:** Assessing how well one is doing when learning or doing something. **Writing:** Communicating effectively with others in writing as indicated by the needs of the audience. **Learning Strategies:** Using multiple approaches when learning or teaching new things. **Negotiation:** Bringing others together and trying to reconcile differences. **Active Listening:** Listening to what other people are saying and asking questions as appropriate.

Education and Training Programs: Juvenile Corrections; Social Work; Youth Services/Administration. **Related Knowledge/Courses—Therapy and Counseling:** Information and techniques needed to rehabilitate physical and mental ailments and to provide career guidance, including alternative treatments, rehabilitation equipment and its proper use, and methods to evaluate treatment effects. **Psychology:** Human behavior and performance, mental processes, psychological research methods, and the assessment and treatment of behavioral and affective disorders. **Sociology and Anthropology:** Group behavior and dynamics; societal trends and influences; and cultures and their history, migrations, ethnicity, and origins. **Philosophy and Theology:** Different philosophical systems and religions, including their basic principles, values, ethics, ways of thinking, customs, and practices and their impact on human culture. **Customer and Personal Service:** Principles and processes for providing customer and personal services, including needs assessment techniques, quality service standards, alternative delivery systems, and customer satisfaction evaluation techniques. **Law and Government:** Laws, legal codes, court procedures, precedents, government regulations, executive orders, agency rules, and the democratic political process.

Work Environment: Indoors; sitting.

Chiropractors

* Education/Training Required: First professional degree
* Annual Earnings: $65,890
* Beginning Wage: $32,530
* Earnings Growth Potential: Very high
* Growth: 14.4%
* Annual Job Openings: 3,179
* Self-Employed: 51.7%
* Part-Time: 23.6%

Adjust spinal column and other articulations of the body to correct abnormalities of the human body believed to be caused by interference with the nervous system. Examine patients to determine nature and extent of disorders. Manipulate spines or other involved areas. May utilize supplementary measures such as exercise, rest, water, light, heat, and nutritional therapy. Diagnose health problems by reviewing patients' health and medical histories; questioning, observing, and examining patients; and interpreting X rays. Maintain accurate case histories of patients. Evaluate the functioning of the neuromuscular-skeletal system and the spine, using systems of chiropractic diagnosis. Perform a series of manual adjustments to spines, or other articulations of the body, to correct musculoskeletal systems. Obtain and record patients' medical histories. Advise patients about recommended courses of treatment. Consult with and refer patients to appropriate health practitioners when necessary. Analyze X rays to locate the sources of patients' difficulties and to rule out fractures or diseases as sources of problems. Counsel patients about nutrition, exercise, sleeping habits, stress management, and other matters. Arrange for diagnostic X rays to be taken. Suggest and apply the use of supports such as straps, tapes, bandages, and braces if necessary.

Personality Type: Social. These occupations frequently involve working with, communicating with, and teaching people and often involve helping or providing service to others.

GOE—Interest Area/Cluster: 08. Health Science. **Work Group:** 08.04. Health Specialties. **Other Jobs in This Work Group:** Optometrists; Podiatrists.

Skills—Service Orientation: Actively looking for ways to help people. **Systems Analysis:** Determining how a system should work and how changes will affect outcomes. **Systems Evaluation:** Looking at many indicators of system performance and taking into account their accuracy. **Management of Personnel Resources:** Motivating, developing, and directing people as they work; identifying the best people for the job. **Writing:** Communicating effectively with others in writing as indicated by the needs of the audience.

Education and Training Program: Chiropractic (DC). **Related Knowledge/Courses—Medicine and Dentistry:** The information and techniques needed to diagnose and treat injuries, diseases, and deformities. This includes symptoms, treatment alternatives, drug properties and interactions, and preventive health-care measures. **Therapy and Counseling:** Information and techniques needed to rehabilitate physical and mental ailments and to provide career guidance, including alternative treatments, rehabilitation equipment and its proper use, and methods to evaluate treatment effects. **Biology:** Plant and animal living tissue, cells, organisms, and entities, including their functions, interdependencies, and interactions with each other and the environment. **Psychology:** Human behavior and performance, mental processes, psychological research methods, and the assessment and treatment of behavioral and affective disorders. **Personnel and Human Resources:** Principles and procedures for personnel recruitment; selection; training; compensation and benefits; labor relations and negotiation; and personnel information systems. **Sales and Marketing:** Principles and methods involved in showing, promoting, and selling products or services. This includes marketing strategies and tactics, product demonstration and sales techniques, and sales control systems.

Work Environment: Indoors; disease or infections; standing; using hands on objects, tools, or controls; bending or twisting the body; repetitive motions.

City and Regional Planning Aides

* Education/Training Required: Associate degree
* Annual Earnings: $35,870
* Beginning Wage: $21,940
* Earnings Growth Potential: Medium
* Growth: 12.4%
* Annual Job Openings: 3,571
* Self-Employed: 1.7%
* Part-Time: 19.4%

The job openings listed here are shared with Social Science Research Assistants.

Compile data from various sources, such as maps, reports, and field and file investigations, for use by city planner in making planning studies. Participate in and support team planning efforts. Prepare reports, using statistics, charts, and graphs, to illustrate planning studies in areas such as population, land use, or zoning. Research, compile, analyze, and organize information from maps, reports, investigations, and books for use in reports and special projects. Provide and process zoning and project permits and applications. Respond to public inquiries and complaints. Serve as liaison between planning department and other departments and agencies. Inspect sites and review plans for minor development permit applications. Conduct interviews, surveys, and site inspections concerning factors that affect land usage, such as zoning, traffic flow, and housing. Prepare, maintain, and update files and records, including land use data and statistics. Prepare, develop, and maintain maps and databases. Perform clerical duties such as composing, typing, and proofreading documents; scheduling appointments and meetings; handling mail; and posting public notices. Perform code enforcement tasks.

Personality Type: Conventional. These occupations frequently involve following set procedures and routines and can include working with data and details more than with ideas. Usually there is a clear line of authority to follow.

GOE—Interest Area/Cluster: 07. Government and Public Administration. **Work Group:** 07.02. Public Planning. **Other Jobs in This Work Group:** Urban and Regional Planners.

Skill—Systems Analysis: Determining how a system should work and how changes will affect outcomes.

Education and Training Program: Social Sciences, General. **Related Knowledge/Courses—Geography:** Various methods for describing the location and distribution of land, sea, and air masses, including their physical locations, relationships, and characteristics. **History and Archeology:** Historical events and their causes, indicators, and impact on particular civilizations and cultures. **Design:** Design techniques, principles, tools, and instruments involved in the production and use of precision technical plans, blueprints, drawings, and models. **Law and Government:** Laws, legal codes, court procedures, precedents, government regulations, executive orders, agency rules, and the democratic political process. **Building and Construction:** Materials, methods, and the appropriate tools to construct objects, structures, and buildings. **Sociology and Anthropology:** Group behavior and dynamics; societal trends and influences; and cultures and their history, migrations, ethnicity, and origins.

Work Environment: Indoors; sitting.

Civil Drafters

- ❋ Education/Training Required: Postsecondary vocational training
- ❋ Annual Earnings: $43,310
- ❋ Beginning Wage: $27,680
- ❋ Earnings Growth Potential: Medium
- ❋ Growth: 6.1%
- ❋ Annual Job Openings: 16,238
- ❋ Self-Employed: 5.0%
- ❋ Part-Time: 5.9%

The job openings listed here are shared with Architectural Drafters.

Prepare drawings and topographical and relief maps used in civil engineering projects such as highways, bridges, pipelines, flood control projects, and water and sewerage control systems. Produce drawings by using computer-assisted drafting systems (CAD) or drafting machines or by hand, using compasses, dividers, protractors, triangles, and other drafting devices. Draw maps, diagrams, and profiles, using cross-sections and surveys, to represent elevations, topographical contours, subsurface formations, and structures. Draft plans and detailed drawings for structures, installations, and construction projects such as highways, sewage disposal systems, and dikes, working from sketches or notes. Determine the order of work and method of presentation such as orthographic or isometric drawing. Finish and duplicate drawings and documentation packages according to required mediums and specifications for reproduction, using blueprinting, photography, or other duplication methods. Review rough sketches, drawings, specifications, and other engineering data received from civil engineers to ensure that they conform to design concepts. Calculate excavation tonnage and prepare graphs and fill-hauling diagrams for use in earth-moving operations. Supervise and train other technologists, technicians, and drafters. Correlate, interpret, and modify data obtained from topographical surveys, well logs, and geophysical prospecting reports. Determine quality, cost, strength, and quantity of required materials and enter figures on materials lists. Locate and identify symbols located on topographical surveys to denote geological and geophysical formations or oil field installations. Calculate weights, volumes, and stress factors and their implications for technical aspects of designs. Supervise or conduct field surveys, inspections, or technical investigations to obtain data required to revise construction drawings. Explain drawings to production or construction teams and provide adjustments as necessary. Plot characteristics of boreholes for oil and gas wells from photographic subsurface survey recordings and other data, representing depth, degree, and direction of inclination.

Personality Type: Realistic. These occupations frequently involve work activities that include practical, hands-on problems and solutions. They often deal with plants; animals; and real-world materials such as wood, tools, and machinery. Many of the occupations require working outside and don't involve a lot of paperwork or working closely with others.

GOE—Interest Area/Cluster: 02. Architecture and Construction. **Work Group:** 02.03. Architecture/Construction Engineering Technologies. **Other Jobs in This Work Group:** Architectural and Civil Drafters; Architectural Drafters; Surveyors.

Skills—Programming: Writing computer programs for various purposes. **Systems Analysis:** Determining how a system should work and how changes will affect outcomes. **Mathematics:** Using mathematics to solve problems. **Quality Control Analysis:** Evaluating the quality or performance of products, services, or processes. **Systems Evaluation:** Looking at many indicators of system performance and taking into account their accuracy.

Education and Training Programs: Architectural Drafting and Architectural CAD/CADD; Architectural Technology/Technician Training; CAD/CADD Drafting and/or Design Technology/Technician Training; Civil Drafting and Civil Engineering CAD/CADD; Drafting and Design Technology/Technician Training, General. **Related Knowledge/Courses—Design:** Design techniques, principles, tools, and instruments involved in the production and use of precision technical plans, blueprints, drawings, and models. **Engineering and Technology:** Equipment, tools, and mechanical devices and their uses to produce motion, light, power, technology, and other applications. **Building and Construction:** Materials, methods, and the appropriate tools to construct objects, structures, and buildings. **Geography:** Various methods for describing the location and distribution of land, sea, and air masses, including their physical locations, relationships, and characteristics. **Mathematics:** Numbers and their operations and interrelationships, including arithmetic, algebra, geometry, calculus, and statistics and their applications. **Physics:** Physical principles, laws, and applications, including air, water, material dynamics, light, atomic principles, heat, electric theory, earth formations, and meteorological and related natural phenomena.

Work Environment: Indoors; sitting; using hands on objects, tools, or controls; repetitive motions.

Civil Engineering Technicians

- ❀ Education/Training Required: Associate degree
- ❀ Annual Earnings: $42,580
- ❀ Beginning Wage: $25,390
- ❀ Earnings Growth Potential: High
- ❀ Growth: 10.2%
- ❀ Annual Job Openings: 7,499
- ❀ Self-Employed: 0.9%
- ❀ Part-Time: 5.9%

Apply theory and principles of civil engineering in planning, designing, and overseeing construction and maintenance of structures and facilities under the direction of engineering staff or physical scientists. Calculate dimensions, square footage, profile and component specifications, and material quantities, using calculator or computer. Draft detailed dimensional drawings and design layouts for projects and to ensure conformance to specifications. Analyze proposed site factors and design maps, graphs, tracings, and diagrams to illustrate findings. Read and review project blueprints and structural specifications to determine dimensions of structure or system and material requirements. Prepare reports and document project activities and data. Confer with supervisor to determine project details such as plan preparation, acceptance testing, and evaluation of field conditions. Inspect project site and evaluate contractor work to detect design malfunctions and ensure conformance to design specifications and applicable codes. Plan and conduct field surveys to locate new sites and analyze details of project sites. Develop plans and estimate costs for installation of systems, utilization of facilities, or construction of structures. Report maintenance problems occurring at project site to supervisor and negotiate changes to resolve system conflicts. Conduct materials test and analysis, using tools and equipment and applying engineering knowledge. Respond to public suggestions and complaints. Evaluate facility to determine suitability for occupancy and square footage availability.

Personality Type: Realistic. These occupations frequently involve work activities that include practical, hands-on problems and solutions. They often deal with plants; animals; and real-world materials such as wood, tools, and machinery. Many of the occupations require working outside and don't involve a lot of paperwork or working closely with others.

GOE—Interest Area/Cluster: 15. Scientific Research, Engineering, and Mathematics. **Work Group:** 15.09. Engineering Technology. **Other Jobs in This Work Group:** Aerospace Engineering and Operations Technicians; Cartographers and Photogrammetrists; Electrical and Electronic Engineering Technicians; Electrical and Electronics Drafters; Electrical Drafters; Electrical Engineering Technicians; Electro-Mechanical Technicians; Electronic Drafters; Electronics Engineering Technicians; Environmental Engineering Technicians; Mapping Technicians; Mechanical Drafters; Mechanical Engineering Technicians; Surveying and Mapping Technicians; Surveying Technicians.

Skills—Mathematics: Using mathematics to solve problems. **Science:** Using scientific methods to solve problems. **Operations Analysis:** Analyzing needs and product requirements to create a design. **Writing:** Communicating effectively with others in writing as indicated by the needs of the audience. **Complex Problem Solving:** Identifying complex problems, reviewing the options, and implementing solutions. **Reading Comprehension:** Understanding written sentences and paragraphs in work-related documents. **Technology Design:** Generating or adapting equipment and technology to serve user needs. **Active Learning:** Working with new material or information to grasp its implications.

Education and Training Programs: Civil Engineering Technology/Technician Training; Construction Engineering Technology/Technician Training. **Related Knowledge/ Courses—Building and Construction:** Materials, methods, and the appropriate tools to construct objects, structures, and buildings. **Design:** Design techniques, principles, tools, and instruments involved in the production and use of precision technical plans, blueprints, drawings, and models. **Engineering and Technology:** Equipment, tools, and mechanical devices and their uses to produce motion, light, power, technology, and other applications. **Mathematics:** Numbers and their operations and interrelationships, including arithmetic, algebra, geometry, calculus, and statistics and their applications. **Computers and Electronics:** Electric circuit boards, processors, chips, and computer hardware and software, including applications and programming. **Transportation:** Principles and methods for moving people or goods by air, rail, sea, or road, including their relative costs, advantages, and limitations.

Work Environment: More often indoors than outdoors; sitting.

Civil Engineers

- ❋ Education/Training Required: Bachelor's degree
- ❋ Annual Earnings: $71,710
- ❋ Beginning Wage: $46,420
- ❋ Earnings Growth Potential: Medium
- ❋ Growth: 18.0%
- ❋ Annual Job Openings: 15,979
- ❋ Self-Employed: 4.9%
- ❋ Part-Time: 3.2%

Perform engineering duties in planning, designing, and overseeing construction and maintenance of building structures and facilities such as roads, railroads, airports, bridges, harbors, channels, dams, irrigation projects, pipelines, power plants, water and sewage systems, and waste disposal units. Includes architectural, structural, traffic, ocean, and geo-technical engineers. Manage and direct staff members and the construction, operations, or maintenance activities at project site. Provide technical advice regarding design, construction, or program modifications and structural repairs to industrial and managerial personnel. Inspect project sites to monitor progress and ensure conformance to design specifications and safety or sanitation standards. Estimate quantities and cost of materials, equipment, or labor to determine project feasibility. Test soils and materials to determine the adequacy and strength of foundations, concrete, asphalt, or steel. Compute load and grade requirements, water flow rates, and material stress factors to determine design specifications. Plan and design transportation or hydraulic systems and structures, following construction and government standards and using design software and drawing tools. Analyze survey reports, maps, drawings, blueprints, aerial photography, and other topographical or geologic data to plan projects. Prepare or present public reports on topics such as bid proposals, deeds, environmental impact statements, or property and right-of-way descriptions. Direct or participate in surveying to lay out installations and establish reference points, grades, and elevations to guide construction. Conduct studies of traffic patterns or environmental conditions to identify engineering problems and assess the potential impact of projects.

Personality Type: Realistic. These occupations frequently involve work activities that include practical, hands-on problems and solutions. They often deal with plants; animals; and real-world materials such as wood, tools, and machinery. Many of the occupations require working outside and don't involve a lot of paperwork or working closely with others.

GOE—Interest Area/Cluster: 15. Scientific Research, Engineering, and Mathematics. **Work Group:** 15.07. Research and Design Engineering. **Other Jobs in This Work Group:** Aerospace Engineers; Biomedical Engineers; Chemical Engineers; Computer Hardware Engineers; Electrical Engineers; Electronics Engineers, Except Computer; Marine Architects; Marine Engineers; Marine Engineers and Naval Architects; Materials Engineers; Mechanical Engineers; Nuclear Engineers.

Skills—Management of Personnel Resources: Motivating, developing, and directing people as they work; identifying the best people for the job. **Systems Analysis:** Determining how a system should work and how changes will affect outcomes. **Systems Evaluation:** Looking at many indicators of system performance and taking into account their accuracy. **Management of Material Resources:** Obtaining and seeing to the appropriate use of equipment, facilities, and materials needed to do certain work. **Management of Financial Resources:** Determining how money will be spent to get the work done and accounting for these expenditures. **Operation Monitoring:** Watching gauges, dials, or other indicators to make sure a machine is working properly. **Negotiation:** Bringing others together and trying to reconcile differences. **Complex Problem Solving:** Identifying complex problems, reviewing the options, and implementing solutions.

Education and Training Programs: Civil Engineering, General; Civil Engineering, Other; Transportation and Highway Engineering; Water Resources Engineering. **Related Knowledge/Courses—Engineering and Technology:** Equipment, tools, and mechanical devices and their uses to produce motion, light, power, technology, and other applications. **Design:** Design techniques, principles, tools, and instruments involved in the production and use of precision technical plans, blueprints, drawings, and models. **Building and Construction:** Materials, methods, and the appropriate tools to construct objects, structures, and buildings. **Physics:** Physical principles, laws, and applications, including air, water, material dynamics, light, atomic principles, heat, electric theory, earth formations, and meteorological and related natural phenomena. **Transportation:** Principles and methods for moving people or goods by air, rail, sea, or road, including their relative costs, advantages, and limitations. **Geography:** Various methods for describing the location and distribution of land, sea, and air masses, including their physical locations, relationships, and characteristics.

Work Environment: Indoors; sitting.

Claims Examiners, Property and Casualty Insurance

* ❀ Education/Training Required: Long-term on-the-job training
* ❀ Annual Earnings: $53,560
* ❀ Beginning Wage: $33,010
* ❀ Earnings Growth Potential: Medium
* ❀ Growth: 8.9%
* ❀ Annual Job Openings: 22,024
* ❀ Self-Employed: 3.5%
* ❀ Part-Time: 4.0%

The job openings listed here are shared with Insurance Adjusters, Examiners, and Investigators.

Review settled insurance claims to determine that payments and settlements have been made in accordance with company practices and procedures. Report overpayments, underpayments, and other irregularities. Confer with legal counsel on claims requiring litigation.

Investigate, evaluate, and settle claims, applying technical knowledge and human relations skills to effect fair and prompt disposal of cases and to contribute to a reduced loss ratio. Pay and process claims within designated authority level. Adjust reserves or provide reserve recommendations to ensure that reserve activities are consistent with corporate policies. Enter claim payments, reserves, and new claims on computer system, inputting concise yet sufficient file documentation. Resolve complex severe exposure claims, using high-service-oriented file handling. Maintain claim files such as records of settled claims and an inventory of claims requiring detailed analysis. Verify and analyze data used in settling claims to ensure that claims are valid and that settlements are made according to company practices and procedures. Examine claims investigated by insurance adjusters, further investigating questionable claims to determine whether to authorize payments. Present cases and participate in their discussion at claim committee meetings. Contact or interview claimants, doctors, medical specialists, or employers to get additional information. Confer with legal counsel on claims requiring litigation. Report overpayments, underpayments, and other irregularities. Communicate with reinsurance brokers to obtain information necessary for processing claims. Supervise claims adjusters to ensure that adjusters have followed proper methods. Conduct detailed bill reviews to implement sound litigation management and expense control. Prepare reports to be submitted to company's data-processing department.

Personality Type: Conventional. These occupations frequently involve following set procedures and routines and can include working with data and details more than with ideas. Usually there is a clear line of authority to follow.

GOE—Interest Area/Cluster: 06. Finance and Insurance. **Work Group:** 06.02. Finance/Insurance Investigation and Analysis. **Other Jobs in This Work Group:** Appraisers and Assessors of Real Estate; Appraisers, Real Estate; Assessors; Claims Adjusters, Examiners, and Investigators; Cost Estimators; Credit Analysts; Financial Analysts; Insurance Adjusters, Examiners, and Investigators; Insurance Appraisers, Auto Damage; Insurance Underwriters; Loan Counselors; Loan Officers; Market Research Analysts; Survey Researchers.

Skills—Judgment and Decision Making: Weighing the relative costs and benefits of a potential action. **Writing:** Communicating effectively with others in writing as indicated by the needs of the audience. **Persuasion:** Persuading others to approach things differently. **Negotiation:** Bringing others together and trying to reconcile differences.

Reading Comprehension: Understanding written sentences and paragraphs in work-related documents. **Critical Thinking:** Using logic and analysis to identify the strengths and weaknesses of different approaches. **Instructing:** Teaching others how to do something. **Active Listening:** Listening to what other people are saying and asking questions as appropriate.

Education and Training Program: Health/Medical Claims Examiner Training. **Related Knowledge/Courses—Customer and Personal Service:** Principles and processes for providing customer and personal services, including needs assessment techniques, quality service standards, alternative delivery systems, and customer satisfaction evaluation techniques. **Medicine and Dentistry:** The information and techniques needed to diagnose and treat injuries, diseases, and deformities. This includes symptoms, treatment alternatives, drug properties and interactions, and preventive health-care measures. **Clerical Practices:** Administrative and clerical procedures and systems such as word-processing systems, filing and records management systems, stenography and transcription, forms, design principles, and other office procedures and terminology. **Law and Government:** Laws, legal codes, court procedures, precedents, government regulations, executive orders, agency rules, and the democratic political process. **Computers and Electronics:** Electric circuit boards, processors, chips, and computer hardware and software, including applications and programming. **English Language:** The structure and content of the English language, including the meaning and spelling of words, rules of composition, and grammar.

Work Environment: Indoors; sitting; using hands on objects, tools, or controls; repetitive motions.

Clergy

- ❀ Education/Training Required: Master's degree
- ❀ Annual Earnings: $40,460
- ❀ Beginning Wage: $20,240
- ❀ Earnings Growth Potential: High
- ❀ Growth: 18.9%
- ❀ Annual Job Openings: 35,092
- ❀ Self-Employed: 0.1%
- ❀ Part-Time: 10.0%

Conduct religious worship and perform other spiritual functions associated with beliefs and practices of religious faith or denomination. Provide spiritual and moral guidance and assistance to members. Pray and promote spirituality. Read from sacred texts such as the Bible, Torah, or Koran. Prepare and deliver sermons and other talks. Organize and lead regular religious services. Share information about religious issues by writing articles, giving speeches, or teaching. Instruct people who seek conversion to a particular faith. Counsel individuals and groups concerning their spiritual, emotional, and personal needs. Visit people in homes, hospitals, and prisons to provide them with comfort and support. Train leaders of church, community, and youth groups. Administer religious rites or ordinances. Study and interpret religious laws, doctrines, and/or traditions. Conduct special ceremonies such as weddings, funerals, and confirmations. Plan and lead religious education programs for their congregations. Respond to requests for assistance during emergencies or crises. Devise ways in which congregation membership can be expanded. Collaborate with committees and individuals to address financial and administrative issues pertaining to congregations. Prepare people for participation in religious ceremonies. Perform administrative duties such as overseeing building management, ordering supplies, contracting for services and repairs, and supervising the work of staff members and volunteers. Refer people to community support services, psychologists, and/or doctors as necessary. Participate in fundraising activities to support congregation activities and facilities. Organize and engage in interfaith, community, civic, educational, and recreational activities sponsored by or related to their religion.

Personality Type: Social. These occupations frequently involve working with, communicating with, and teaching people and often involve helping or providing service to others.

GOE—Interest Area/Cluster: 10. Human Service. **Work Group:** 10.02. Religious Work. **Other Jobs in This Work Group:** Directors, Religious Activities and Education.

Skills—Management of Personnel Resources: Motivating, developing, and directing people as they work; identifying the best people for the job. **Management of Financial Resources:** Determining how money will be spent to get the work done and accounting for these expenditures. **Service Orientation:** Actively looking for ways to help people. **Negotiation:** Bringing others together and trying to reconcile differences. **Judgment and Decision Making:** Weighing the relative costs and benefits of a potential action. **Persuasion:** Persuading others to approach things differently. **Social Perceptiveness:** Being aware of others' reactions and understanding why they react the way they do. **Coordination:** Adjusting actions in relation to others' actions.

Education and Training Programs: Clinical Pastoral Counseling/Patient Counseling; Divinity/Ministry (BD, MDiv.); Pastoral Counseling and Specialized Ministries, Other; Pastoral Studies/Counseling; Pre-Theology/Pre-Ministerial Studies; Rabbinical Studies; Theological and Ministerial Studies, Other; Theology and Religious Vocations, Other; Theology/Theological Studies; Youth Ministry. **Related Knowledge/Courses—Philosophy and Theology:** Different philosophical systems and religions, including their basic principles, values, ethics, ways of thinking, customs, and practices and their impact on human culture. **Therapy and Counseling:** Information and techniques needed to rehabilitate physical and mental ailments and to provide career guidance, including alternative treatments, rehabilitation equipment and its proper use, and methods to evaluate treatment effects. **Sociology and Anthropology:** Group behavior and dynamics; societal trends and influences; and cultures and their history, migrations, ethnicity, and origins. **Psychology:** Human behavior and performance, mental processes, psychological research methods, and the assessment and treatment of behavioral and affective disorders. **Public Safety and Security:** Weaponry; public safety; security operations, rules, regulations, precautions, and prevention; and the protection of people, data, and property. **Customer and Personal Service:** Principles and processes for providing customer and personal services, including needs assessment techniques, quality service standards, alternative delivery systems, and customer satisfaction evaluation techniques.

Work Environment: Indoors; sitting.

Clinical Psychologists

- ❇ Education/Training Required: Doctoral degree
- ❇ Annual Earnings: $62,210
- ❇ Beginning Wage: $37,300
- ❇ Earnings Growth Potential: High
- ❇ Growth: 15.8%
- ❇ Annual Job Openings: 8,309
- ❇ Self-Employed: 34.2%
- ❇ Part-Time: 24.0%

The job openings listed here are shared with Counseling Psychologists and with School Psychologists.

Diagnose or evaluate mental and emotional disorders of individuals through observation, interview, and psychological tests and formulate and administer programs of treatment. Identify psychological, emotional, or behavioral issues and diagnose disorders, using information obtained from interviews, tests, records, and reference materials. Develop and implement individual treatment plans, specifying type, frequency, intensity, and duration of therapy. Interact with clients to assist them in gaining insight, defining goals, and planning action to achieve effective personal, social, educational, and vocational development and adjustment. Discuss the treatment of problems with clients. Utilize a variety of treatment methods such as psychotherapy, hypnosis, behavior modification, stress reduction therapy, psychodrama, and play therapy. Counsel individuals and groups regarding problems such as stress, substance abuse, and family situations to modify behavior or to improve personal, social, and vocational adjustment. Write reports on clients and maintain required paperwork. Evaluate the effectiveness of counseling or treatments and the accuracy and completeness of diagnoses; then modify plans and diagnoses as necessary. Obtain and study medical, psychological, social, and family histories by interviewing individuals, couples, or families and by reviewing records. Consult reference material such as textbooks, manuals, and journals to identify symptoms, make diagnoses, and develop approaches to treatment. Maintain current knowledge of relevant research. Observe individuals at play, in group interactions, or in other contexts to detect indications of mental deficiency, abnormal behavior, or maladjustment. Select, administer, score, and interpret psychological tests to obtain information on individuals' intelligence, achievements, interests, and personalities. Refer clients to other specialists, institutions, or support services as necessary. Develop, direct, and participate in training programs for staff and students. Provide psychological or administrative services and advice to private firms and community agencies regarding mental health programs or individual cases. Provide occupational, educational, and other information to individuals so that they can make educational and vocational plans.

Personality Type: Investigative. These occupations frequently involve working with ideas and require an extensive amount of thinking. They can involve searching for facts and figuring out problems mentally.

GOE—Interest Area/Cluster: 10. Human Service. **Work Group:** 10.01. Counseling and Social Work. **Other Jobs in This Work Group:** Child, Family, and School Social Workers; Clinical, Counseling, and School Psychologists; Counseling Psychologists; Marriage and Family Therapists; Medical and Public Health Social Workers; Mental Health and Substance Abuse Social Workers; Mental Health

Counselors; Probation Officers and Correctional Treatment Specialists; Rehabilitation Counselors; Residential Advisors; Social and Human Service Assistants; Substance Abuse and Behavioral Disorder Counselors.

Skills—Social Perceptiveness: Being aware of others' reactions and understanding why they react the way they do. **Service Orientation:** Actively looking for ways to help people. **Complex Problem Solving:** Identifying complex problems, reviewing the options, and implementing solutions. **Learning Strategies:** Using multiple approaches when learning or teaching new things. **Active Listening:** Listening to what other people are saying and asking questions as appropriate. **Negotiation:** Bringing others together and trying to reconcile differences. **Active Learning:** Working with new material or information to grasp its implications. **Critical Thinking:** Using logic and analysis to identify the strengths and weaknesses of different approaches.

Education and Training Programs: Clinical Child Psychology; Clinical Psychology; Counseling Psychology; Developmental and Child Psychology; Psychoanalysis and Psychotherapy; Psychology, General; School Psychology. **Related Knowledge/Courses—Therapy and Counseling:** Information and techniques needed to rehabilitate physical and mental ailments and to provide career guidance, including alternative treatments, rehabilitation equipment and its proper use, and methods to evaluate treatment effects. **Psychology:** Human behavior and performance, mental processes, psychological research methods, and the assessment and treatment of behavioral and affective disorders. **Sociology and Anthropology:** Group behavior and dynamics; societal trends and influences; and cultures and their history, migrations, ethnicity, and origins. **Philosophy and Theology:** Different philosophical systems and religions, including their basic principles, values, ethics, ways of thinking, customs, and practices and their impact on human culture. **Customer and Personal Service:** Principles and processes for providing customer and personal services, including needs assessment techniques, quality service standards, alternative delivery systems, and customer satisfaction evaluation techniques. **Medicine and Dentistry:** The information and techniques needed to diagnose and treat injuries, diseases, and deformities. This includes symptoms, treatment alternatives, drug properties and interactions, and preventive health-care measures.

Work Environment: Indoors; sitting.

Coaches and Scouts

- ❋ Education/Training Required: Long-term on-the-job training
- ❋ Annual Earnings: $27,840
- ❋ Beginning Wage: $14,860
- ❋ Earnings Growth Potential: High
- ❋ Growth: 14.6%
- ❋ Annual Job Openings: 51,100
- ❋ Self-Employed: 22.7%
- ❋ Part-Time: 39.1%

Instruct or coach groups or individuals in the fundamentals of sports. Demonstrate techniques and methods of participation. May evaluate athletes' strengths and weaknesses as possible recruits or to improve the athletes' technique to prepare them for competition. Plan, organize, and conduct practice sessions. Provide training direction, encouragement, and motivation to prepare athletes for games, competitive events, or tours. Identify and recruit potential athletes, arranging and offering incentives such as athletic scholarships. Plan strategies and choose team members for individual games or sports seasons. Plan and direct physical conditioning programs that will enable athletes to achieve maximum performance. Adjust coaching techniques based on the strengths and weaknesses of athletes. File scouting reports that detail player assessments, provide recommendations on athlete recruitment, and identify locations and individuals to be targeted for future recruitment efforts. Keep records of athlete, team, and opposing team performance. Instruct individuals or groups in sports rules, game strategies, and performance principles such as specific ways of moving the body, hands, and feet in order to achieve desired results. Analyze the strengths and weaknesses of opposing teams to develop game strategies. Evaluate athletes' skills and review performance records to determine their fitness and potential in a particular area of athletics. Keep abreast of changing rules, techniques, technologies, and philosophies relevant to their sport. Monitor athletes' use of equipment to ensure safe and proper use. Explain and enforce safety rules and regulations. Develop and arrange competition schedules and programs. Serve as organizer, leader, instructor, or referee for outdoor and indoor games such as volleyball, football, and soccer. Explain and demonstrate the use of sports and training equipment, such as trampolines or weights. Perform activities that support a team or a specific sport, such as meeting with media representatives and appearing at fundraising events. Arrange and conduct sports-related activities such as training camps, skill-improvement courses, clinics, or pre-season try-outs. Select, acquire, store, and issue equipment and other materials as necessary. Negotiate with professional athletes or their representatives to obtain services and arrange contracts.

Personality Type: Social. These occupations frequently involve working with, communicating with, and teaching people and often involve helping or providing service to others.

GOE—Interest Area/Cluster: 09. Hospitality, Tourism, and Recreation. **Work Group:** 09.06. Sports. **Other Jobs in This Work Group:** Athletes and Sports Competitors; Umpires, Referees, and Other Sports Officials.

Skills—Social Perceptiveness: Being aware of others' reactions and understanding why they react the way they do. **Management of Personnel Resources:** Motivating, developing, and directing people as they work; identifying the best people for the job. **Management of Financial Resources:** Determining how money will be spent to get the work done and accounting for these expenditures. **Persuasion:** Persuading others to approach things differently. **Negotiation:** Bringing others together and trying to reconcile differences. **Instructing:** Teaching others how to do something. **Monitoring:** Assessing how well one is doing when learning or doing something. **Time Management:** Managing one's own time and the time of others.

Education and Training Programs: Health and Physical Education, General; Physical Education Teaching and Coaching; Sport and Fitness Administration/Management. **Related Knowledge/Courses—Psychology:** Human behavior and performance, mental processes, psychological research methods, and the assessment and treatment of behavioral and affective disorders. **Therapy and Counseling:** Information and techniques needed to rehabilitate physical and mental ailments and to provide career guidance, including alternative treatments, rehabilitation equipment and its proper use, and methods to evaluate treatment effects. **Education and Training:** Instructional methods and training techniques, including curriculum design principles, learning theory, group and individual teaching techniques, design of individual development plans, and test design principles. **Sales and Marketing:** Principles and methods involved in showing, promoting, and selling products or services. This includes marketing strategies and tactics, product demonstration and sales techniques, and sales control systems. **Personnel and Human Resources:** Principles and procedures for personnel recruitment; selection; training;

compensation and benefits; labor relations and negotiation; and personnel information systems. **Sociology and Anthropology:** Group behavior and dynamics; societal trends and influences; and cultures and their history, migrations, ethnicity, and origins.

Work Environment: More often indoors than outdoors; noisy; standing; walking and running.

Commercial and Industrial Designers

- ✸ Education/Training Required: Bachelor's degree
- ✸ Annual Earnings: $56,550
- ✸ Beginning Wage: $31,400
- ✸ Earnings Growth Potential: High
- ✸ Growth: 7.2%
- ✸ Annual Job Openings: 4,777
- ✸ Self-Employed: 29.8%
- ✸ Part-Time: 16.7%

Develop and design manufactured products, such as cars, home appliances, and children's toys. Combine artistic talent with research on product use, marketing, and materials to create the most functional and appealing product design. Prepare sketches of ideas, detailed drawings, illustrations, artwork, or blueprints, using drafting instruments, paints and brushes, or computer-aided design equipment. Direct and coordinate the fabrication of models or samples and the drafting of working drawings and specification sheets from sketches. Modify and refine designs, using working models, to conform with customer specifications, production limitations, or changes in design trends. Coordinate the look and function of product lines. Confer with engineering, marketing, production, or sales departments, or with customers, to establish and evaluate design concepts for manufactured products. Present designs and reports to customers or design committees for approval and discuss need for modification. Evaluate feasibility of design ideas based on factors such as appearance, safety, function, serviceability, budget, production costs/methods, and market characteristics. Read publications, attend showings, and study competing products and design styles and motifs to obtain perspective and generate design concepts. Research production specifications, costs, production materials, and manufacturing methods and provide cost estimates and itemized production requirements. Design graphic material for use as ornamentation, illustration, or advertising on manufactured materials and packaging or containers. Develop manufacturing procedures and monitor the manufacture of their designs in a factory to improve operations and product quality. Supervise assistants' work throughout the design process. Fabricate models or samples in paper, wood, glass, fabric, plastic, metal, or other materials, using hand or power tools. Investigate product characteristics such as the product's safety and handling qualities; its market appeal; how efficiently it can be produced; and ways of distributing, using, and maintaining it. Develop industrial standards and regulatory guidelines. Participate in new product planning or market research, including studying the potential need for new products. Advise corporations on issues involving corporate image projects or problems.

Personality Type: Artistic. These occupations frequently involve working with forms, designs, and patterns. They often require self-expression, and the work can be done without following a clear set of rules.

GOE—Interest Area/Cluster: 03. Arts and Communication. **Work Group:** 03.05. Design. **Other Jobs in This Work Group:** Fashion Designers; Floral Designers; Graphic Designers; Interior Designers; Merchandise Displayers and Window Trimmers; Set and Exhibit Designers.

Skills—Technology Design: Generating or adapting equipment and technology to serve user needs. **Operations Analysis:** Analyzing needs and product requirements to create a design. **Quality Control Analysis:** Evaluating the quality or performance of products, services, or processes. **Troubleshooting:** Determining what is causing an operating error and deciding what to do about it. **Equipment Selection:** Determining the kind of tools and equipment needed to do a job. **Installation:** Installing equipment, machines, wiring, or programs to meet specifications. **Mathematics:** Using mathematics to solve problems. **Systems Evaluation:** Looking at many indicators of system performance and taking into account their accuracy.

Education and Training Programs: Commercial and Advertising Art; Design and Applied Arts, Other; Design and Visual Communications, General; Industrial Design. **Related Knowledge/Courses—Design:** Design techniques, principles, tools, and instruments involved in the production and use of precision technical plans, blueprints, drawings, and models. **Engineering and Technology:** Equipment, tools, and mechanical devices and their uses to produce motion, light, power, technology, and other applications. **Mathematics:** Numbers and their operations and interrelationships, including arithmetic, algebra, geometry, calculus, and statistics and their applications. **Physics:** Physical principles, laws, and applications, including air, water, material dynamics, light, atomic principles, heat, electric theory, earth formations, and meteorological and related natural phenomena. **Mechanical Devices:** Machines and tools, including their designs, uses, benefits, repair, and maintenance. **Production and Processing:** Inputs, outputs, raw materials, waste, quality control, costs, and techniques for maximizing the manufacture and distribution of goods.

Work Environment: Indoors; sitting; using hands on objects, tools, or controls; repetitive motions.

Commercial Divers

- Education/Training Required: Postsecondary vocational training
- Annual Earnings: $41,610
- Beginning Wage: $28,640
- Earnings Growth Potential: Low
- Growth: 17.7%
- Annual Job Openings: 248
- Self-Employed: 12.7%
- Part-Time: 9.8%

Work below surface of water, using scuba gear to inspect, repair, remove, or install equipment and structures. May use a variety of power and hand tools such as drills, sledgehammers, torches, and welding equipment. May conduct tests or experiments, rig explosives, or photograph structures or marine life. Perform activities related to underwater search and rescue, salvage, recovery, and cleanup operations. Take appropriate safety precautions, such as monitoring dive lengths and depths and registering with authorities before diving expeditions begin. Set or guide placement of pilings and sandbags to provide support for structures such as docks, bridges, cofferdams, and platforms. Salvage wrecked ships and/or their cargoes, using pneumatic power velocity and hydraulic tools and explosive charges when necessary. Repair ships, bridge foundations, and other structures below the water line, using caulk, bolts, and hand tools. Remove obstructions from strainers and marine railway or launching ways, using pneumatic and power hand tools. Inspect and test docks; ships; buoyage systems; plant intakes and outflows; and underwater pipelines, cables, and sewers, using closed-circuit television, still photography, and testing equipment. Perform offshore oil and gas exploration and extraction duties such as conducting underwater surveys and repairing and maintaining drilling rigs and platforms. Install, inspect, clean, and repair piping and valves. Carry out non-destructive testing such as tests for cracks on the legs of oil rigs at sea. Check and maintain diving equipment such as helmets, masks, air tanks, harnesses, and gauges. Communicate with workers on the surface while underwater, using signal lines or telephones. Cut and weld steel, using underwater welding equipment, jigs, and supports. Descend into water with the aid of diver helpers, using scuba gear or diving suits. Recover objects by placing rigging around sunken objects; hooking rigging to crane lines; and operating winches, derricks, or cranes to raise objects. Install pilings or footings for piers and bridges. Supervise and train other divers, including hobby divers. Obtain information about diving tasks and environmental conditions. Remove rubbish and pollution from the sea. Cultivate and harvest marine species and perform routine work on fish farms. Set up dive sites for recreational instruction. Drill holes in rock and rig explosives for underwater demolitions.

Personality Type: Realistic. These occupations frequently involve work activities that include practical, hands-on problems and solutions. They often deal with plants; animals; and real-world materials such as wood, tools, and machinery. Many of the occupations require working outside and don't involve a lot of paperwork or working closely with others.

GOE—Interest Area/Cluster: 02. Architecture and Construction. **Work Group:** 02.04. Construction Crafts. **Other Jobs in This Work Group:** Boilermakers; Brickmasons and Blockmasons; Carpet Installers; Cement Masons and Concrete Finishers; Construction Carpenters; Crane and Tower Operators; Drywall and Ceiling Tile Installers; Electricians; Fence Erectors; Floor Layers, Except Carpet, Wood, and Hard Tiles; Floor Sanders and Finishers; Glaziers; Hazardous Materials Removal Workers; Insulation Workers, Floor, Ceiling, and Wall; Insulation Workers, Mechanical; Manufactured Building and Mobile Home Installers; Operating Engineers and Other Construction Equipment Operators; Painters, Construction and Maintenance; Paperhangers; Paving, Surfacing, and Tamping Equipment Operators; Pile-Driver Operators; Pipe Fitters and Steamfitters; Pipelayers; Plasterers and Stucco Masons; Plumbers; Plumbers, Pipefitters, and Steamfitters; Rail-Track Laying and Maintenance Equipment Operators; Refractory Materials Repairers, Except Brickmasons; Reinforcing Iron and Rebar Workers; Riggers; Roofers; Rough Carpenters; Security and Fire Alarm Systems Installers; Segmental Pavers; Sheet Metal Workers; Stone Cutters and Carvers, Manufacturing; Stonemasons; Structural Iron and Steel Workers; Tapers; Terrazzo Workers and Finishers; Tile and Marble Setters.

Skills—Repairing: Repairing machines or systems, using the needed tools. **Equipment Maintenance:** Performing routine maintenance and determining when and what kind of maintenance is needed. **Installation:** Installing equipment, machines, wiring, or programs to meet specifications. **Operation Monitoring:** Watching gauges, dials, or other indicators to make sure a machine is working properly. **Operation and Control:** Controlling operations of equipment or systems. **Equipment Selection:** Determining the kind of tools and equipment needed to do a job. **Troubleshooting:** Determining what is causing an operating error and deciding what to do about it. **Technology Design:** Generating or adapting equipment and technology to serve user needs.

Education and Training Program: Diver, Professional and Instructor Training. **Related Knowledge/Courses—Building and Construction:** Materials, methods, and the appropriate tools to construct objects, structures, and buildings. **Mechanical Devices:** Machines and tools, including their designs, uses, benefits, repair, and maintenance. **Physics:** Physical principles, laws, and applications, including air, water, material dynamics, light, atomic principles, heat, electric theory, earth formations, and meteorological and related natural phenomena. **Engineering and Technology:** Equipment, tools, and mechanical devices and their uses to produce motion, light, power, technology, and other applications. **Design:** Design techniques, principles, tools, and instruments involved in the production and use of precision technical plans, blueprints, drawings, and models. **Biology:** Plant and animal living tissue, cells, organisms, and entities, including their functions, interdependencies, and interactions with each other and the environment.

Work Environment: Outdoors; noisy; very hot or cold; hazardous equipment; standing; using hands on objects, tools, or controls.

Commercial Pilots

- ❋ Education/Training Required: Postsecondary vocational training
- ❋ Annual Earnings: $61,640
- ❋ Beginning Wage: $30,460
- ❋ Earnings Growth Potential: Very high
- ❋ Growth: 13.2%
- ❋ Annual Job Openings: 1,425
- ❋ Self-Employed: 1.9%
- ❋ Part-Time: 14.2%

Pilot and navigate the flight of small fixed or rotary winged aircraft primarily for the transport of cargo and passengers. Requires Commercial Rating. Check aircraft prior to flights to ensure that the engines, controls, instruments, and other systems are functioning properly. Start engines, operate controls, and pilot airplanes to transport passengers, mail, or freight while adhering to flight plans, regulations, and procedures. Contact control towers for takeoff clearances, arrival instructions, and other information, using radio equipment. Monitor engine operation, fuel consumption, and functioning of aircraft systems during flights. Consider airport altitudes, outside temperatures, plane weights, and wind speeds and directions to calculate the speed needed to become airborne. Order changes in fuel supplies, loads, routes, or schedules to ensure safety of flights. Obtain and review data such as load weights, fuel supplies, weather conditions, and flight schedules to determine flight plans and to see if changes might be necessary. Plan flights, following government and company regulations, using aeronautical charts and navigation instruments. Use instrumentation to pilot aircraft when visibility is poor. Check baggage or cargo to ensure that it has been loaded correctly. Request changes in altitudes or routes as circumstances dictate. Choose routes, altitudes, and speeds that will provide the fastest, safest, and smoothest flights. Coordinate flight activities with ground crews and air-traffic control and inform crew members of flight and test procedures. Write specified information in flight records, such as flight times, altitudes flown, and fuel consumption. Teach company regulations and procedures to other pilots. Instruct other pilots and student pilots in aircraft operations. Co-pilot aircraft or perform captain's duties if required. File instrument flight plans with air traffic control so that flights can be coordinated with other air traffic. Conduct in-flight tests and evaluations at specified altitudes and in all types of weather to determine the receptivity and other characteristics of equipment and systems. Rescue and evacuate injured persons. Supervise other crew members. Perform minor aircraft maintenance and repair work or arrange for major maintenance.

Personality Type: Realistic. These occupations frequently involve work activities that include practical, hands-on problems and solutions. They often deal with plants; animals; and real-world materials such as wood, tools, and machinery. Many of the occupations require working outside and don't involve a lot of paperwork or working closely with others.

GOE—Interest Area/Cluster: 16. Transportation, Distribution, and Logistics. **Work Group:** 16.02. Air Vehicle Operation. **Other Jobs in This Work Group:** Airline Pilots, Copilots, and Flight Engineers.

Skills—Operation Monitoring: Watching gauges, dials, or other indicators to make sure a machine is working properly. **Operation and Control:** Controlling operations of equipment or systems. **Troubleshooting:** Determining what is causing an operating error and deciding what to do about it. **Judgment and Decision Making:** Weighing the relative costs and benefits of a potential action. **Systems Evaluation:** Looking at many indicators of system performance and taking into account their accuracy. **Critical Thinking:** Using logic and analysis to identify the strengths and weaknesses of different approaches. **Systems Analysis:** Determining how a system should work and how changes will affect outcomes. **Mathematics:** Using mathematics to solve problems.

Education and Training Programs: Airline/Commercial/Professional Pilot and Flight Crew Training; Flight Instructor Training. **Related Knowledge/Courses—Transportation:** Principles and methods for moving people or goods by air, rail, sea, or road, including their relative costs, advantages, and limitations. **Geography:** Various methods for describing the location and distribution of land, sea, and air masses, including their physical locations, relationships, and characteristics. **Mechanical Devices:** Machines and tools, including their designs, uses, benefits, repair, and maintenance. **Physics:** Physical principles, laws, and applications, including air, water, material dynamics, light, atomic principles, heat, electric theory, earth formations, and meteorological and related natural phenomena. **Telecommunications:** Transmission, broadcasting, switching, control, and operation of telecommunications systems. **Psychology:** Human behavior and performance, mental processes, psychological research methods, and the assessment and treatment of behavioral and affective disorders.

Work Environment: Outdoors; noisy; very hot or cold; contaminants; sitting; using hands on objects, tools, or controls.

Communications Teachers, Postsecondary

- ❋ Education/Training Required: Doctoral degree
- ❋ Annual Earnings: $54,720
- ❋ Beginning Wage: $29,700
- ❋ Earnings Growth Potential: High
- ❋ Growth: 22.9%
- ❋ Annual Job Openings: 4,074
- ❋ Self-Employed: 0.4%
- ❋ Part-Time: 27.8%

Teach courses in communications, such as organizational communications, public relations, radio/television broadcasting, and journalism. Evaluate and grade students' classwork, assignments, and papers. Prepare course materials such as syllabi, homework assignments, and handouts. Initiate, facilitate, and moderate classroom discussions. Prepare and deliver lectures to undergraduate or graduate students on topics such as public speaking, media criticism, and oral traditions. Compile, administer, and grade examinations or assign this work to others. Maintain student attendance records, grades, and other required records. Plan, evaluate, and revise curricula, course content, and course materials and methods of instruction. Maintain regularly scheduled office hours to advise and assist students. Keep abreast of developments in their field by reading current literature, talking with colleagues, and participating in professional conferences. Advise students on academic and vocational curricula and on career issues. Supervise undergraduate or graduate teaching, internship, and research work. Select and obtain materials and supplies such as textbooks. Collaborate with colleagues to address teaching and research issues. Conduct research in a particular field of knowledge and publish findings in professional journals, books, or electronic media. Participate in student recruitment, registration, and placement activities. Serve on academic or administrative committees that deal with institutional policies, departmental matters, and academic issues. Compile bibliographies of specialized materials for outside reading assignments. Act as advisers to student organizations. Participate in campus and community events. Perform administrative duties such as serving as department head. Write grant proposals to procure external research funding. Provide professional consulting services to government or industry.

Personality Type: Social. These occupations frequently involve working with, communicating with, and teaching people and often involve helping or providing service to others.

GOE—Interest Area/Cluster: 05. Education and Training. **Work Group:** 05.03. Postsecondary and Adult Teaching and Instructing. **Other Jobs in This Work Group:** Adult Literacy, Remedial Education, and GED Teachers and Instructors; Agricultural Sciences Teachers, Postsecondary; Anthropology and Archeology Teachers, Postsecondary; Architecture Teachers, Postsecondary; Area, Ethnic, and Cultural Studies Teachers, Postsecondary; Art, Drama, and Music Teachers, Postsecondary; Atmospheric, Earth, Marine, and Space Sciences Teachers, Postsecondary; Biological Science Teachers, Postsecondary; Business Teachers, Postsecondary; Chemistry Teachers, Postsecondary; Computer Science Teachers, Postsecondary; Criminal Justice and Law Enforcement Teachers, Postsecondary; Economics Teachers, Postsecondary; Education Teachers, Postsecondary; Engineering Teachers, Postsecondary; English Language and Literature Teachers, Postsecondary; Environmental Science Teachers, Postsecondary; Farm and Home Management Advisors; Foreign Language and Literature Teachers, Postsecondary; Forestry and Conservation Science Teachers, Postsecondary; Geography Teachers, Postsecondary; Graduate Teaching Assistants; Health Specialties Teachers, Postsecondary; History Teachers, Postsecondary; Home Economics Teachers, Postsecondary; Law Teachers, Postsecondary; Library Science Teachers, Postsecondary; Mathematical Science Teachers, Postsecondary; Nursing Instructors and Teachers, Postsecondary; Philosophy and Religion Teachers, Postsecondary; Physics Teachers, Postsecondary; Political Science Teachers, Postsecondary; Psychology Teachers, Postsecondary; Recreation and Fitness Studies Teachers, Postsecondary; Self-Enrichment Education Teachers; Social Work Teachers, Postsecondary; Sociology Teachers, Postsecondary; Vocational Education Teachers, Postsecondary.

Skills—Instructing: Teaching others how to do something. **Writing:** Communicating effectively with others in writing as indicated by the needs of the audience. **Persuasion:** Persuading others to approach things differently. **Learning Strategies:** Using multiple approaches when learning or teaching new things. **Monitoring:** Assessing how well one is doing when learning or doing something. **Speaking:** Talking to others to effectively convey information. **Social Perceptiveness:** Being aware of others' reactions and understanding why they react the way they do. **Critical Thinking:** Using logic and analysis to identify the strengths and weaknesses of different approaches.

Education and Training Programs: Advertising; Broadcast Journalism; Communication Studies/Speech Communication and Rhetoric; Communication, Journalism, and Related Programs, Other; Digital Communication and Media/Multimedia; Health Communication; Journalism; Journalism, Other; Mass Communication/Media Studies; Political Communication; Public Relations/Image Management; Radio and Television. **Related Knowledge/Courses—Communications and Media:** Media production, communication, and dissemination techniques and methods, including alternative ways to inform and entertain via written, oral, and visual media. **Education and Training:** Instructional methods and training techniques, including curriculum design principles, learning theory, group and individual teaching techniques, design of individual development plans, and test design principles. **Philosophy and Theology:** Different philosophical systems and religions, including their basic principles, values, ethics, ways of thinking, customs, and practices and their impact on human culture. **Sociology and Anthropology:** Group behavior and dynamics; societal trends and influences; and cultures and their history, migrations, ethnicity, and origins. **English Language:** The structure and content of the English language, including the meaning and spelling of words, rules of composition, and grammar. **History and Archeology:** Historical events and their causes, indicators, and impact on particular civilizations and cultures.

Work Environment: Indoors; sitting.

Compensation and Benefits Managers

- ❀ Education/Training Required: Work experience plus degree
- ❀ Annual Earnings: $81,410
- ❀ Beginning Wage: $46,050
- ❀ Earnings Growth Potential: High
- ❀ Growth: 12.0%
- ❀ Annual Job Openings: 6,121
- ❀ Self-Employed: 1.4%
- ❀ Part-Time: 2.7%

Plan, direct, or coordinate compensation and benefits activities and staff of an organization. Design, evaluate, and modify benefits policies to ensure that programs are current, competitive, and in compliance with legal requirements. Analyze compensation policies, government regulations, and prevailing wage rates to develop competitive compensation plans. Fulfill all reporting requirements of all relevant government rules and regulations, including the Employee Retirement Income Security Act (ERISA). Direct preparation and distribution of written and verbal information to inform employees of benefits, compensation, and personnel policies. Administer, direct, and review employee benefit programs, including the integration of benefit programs following mergers and acquisitions. Plan, direct, supervise, and coordinate work activities of subordinates and staff relating to employment, compensation, labor relations, and employee relations. Identify and implement benefits to increase the quality of life for employees by working with brokers and researching benefits issues. Manage the design and development of tools to assist employees in benefits selection and to guide managers through compensation decisions. Prepare detailed job descriptions and classification systems and define job levels and families in partnership with other managers. Prepare budgets for personnel operations. Formulate policies, procedures, and programs for recruitment, testing, placement, classification, orientation, benefits and compensation, and labor and industrial relations. Mediate between benefits providers and employees, such as by assisting in handling employees' benefits-related questions or taking suggestions. Develop methods to improve employment policies, processes, and practices and recommend changes to management. Study legislation, arbitration decisions, and collective bargaining contracts to assess industry trends. Maintain records and compile statistical reports concerning personnel-related data such as hires, transfers, performance appraisals, and absenteeism rates. Negotiate bargaining agreements. Conduct exit interviews to identify reasons for employee termination. Plan and conduct new employee orientations to foster positive attitude toward organizational objectives.

Personality Type: Enterprising. These occupations frequently involve starting up and carrying out projects and can involve leading people and making many decisions. They sometimes require risk taking and often deal with business.

GOE—Interest Area/Cluster: 04. Business and Administration. **Work Group:** 04.01. Managerial Work in General Business. **Other Jobs in This Work Group:** Chief Executives; General and Operations Managers; Human Resources Managers; Training and Development Managers.

Skills—Management of Financial Resources: Determining how money will be spent to get the work done and accounting for these expenditures. **Management of Personnel Resources:** Motivating, developing, and directing people as they work; identifying the best people for the job. **Systems Analysis:** Determining how a system should work and how changes will affect outcomes. **Systems Evaluation:** Looking at many indicators of system performance and taking into account their accuracy. **Negotiation:** Bringing others together and trying to reconcile differences. **Writing:** Communicating effectively with others in writing as indicated by the needs of the audience. **Persuasion:** Persuading others to approach things differently. **Judgment and Decision Making:** Weighing the relative costs and benefits of a potential action.

Education and Training Programs: Human Resources Management/Personnel Administration, General; Labor and Industrial Relations. **Related Knowledge/Courses—Personnel and Human Resources:** Principles and procedures for personnel recruitment; selection; training; compensation and benefits; labor relations and negotiation; and personnel information systems. **Economics and Accounting:** Economic and accounting principles and practices, the financial markets, banking, and the analysis and reporting of financial data. **Administration and Management:** Principles and processes involved in business and organizational planning, coordination, and execution. This includes strategic planning, resource allocation, manpower modeling, leadership techniques, and production methods. **Mathematics:** Numbers and their operations and interrelationships, including arithmetic, algebra, geometry, calculus, and statistics and their applications. **Law and Government:** Laws, legal codes, court procedures, precedents, government regulations, executive orders, agency rules, and the democratic political process. **Communications and Media:** Media production, communication, and dissemination techniques and methods, including alternative ways to inform and entertain via written, oral, and visual media.

Work Environment: Indoors; sitting.

Compensation, Benefits, and Job Analysis Specialists

- ❋ Education/Training Required: Bachelor's degree
- ❋ Annual Earnings: $52,180
- ❋ Beginning Wage: $33,450
- ❋ Earnings Growth Potential: Medium
- ❋ Growth: 18.4%
- ❋ Annual Job Openings: 18,761
- ❋ Self-Employed: 2.1%
- ❋ Part-Time: 7.6%

Conduct programs of compensation and benefits and job analysis for employer. May specialize in specific areas, such as position classification and pension programs. Evaluate job positions, determining classification, exempt or non-exempt status, and salary. Ensure company compliance with federal and state laws, including reporting requirements. Advise managers and employees on state and federal employment regulations, collective agreements, benefit and compensation policies, personnel procedures, and classification programs. Plan, develop, evaluate, improve, and communicate methods and techniques for selecting, promoting, compensating, evaluating, and training workers. Provide advice on the resolution of classification and salary complaints. Prepare occupational classifications, job descriptions, and salary scales. Assist in preparing and maintaining personnel records and handbooks. Prepare reports such as organization and flow charts and career path reports to summarize job analysis and evaluation and compensation analysis information. Administer employee insurance, pension, and savings plans, working with insurance brokers and plan carriers. Negotiate collective agreements on behalf of employers or workers and mediate labor disputes and grievances. Develop, implement, administer, and evaluate personnel and labor relations programs, including performance appraisal, affirmative action, and employment equity programs. Perform multifactor data and cost analyses that may be used in areas such as support of collective bargaining agreements. Research employee benefit and health and safety practices and recommend changes or modifications to existing policies. Analyze organizational, occupational, and industrial data to facilitate organizational functions and provide technical information to business, industry, and government. Advise staff of individuals' qualifications. Assess need for and develop job analysis instruments and materials. Review occupational data on

Alien Employment Certification Applications to determine the appropriate occupational title and code; provide local offices with information about immigration and occupations. Research job and worker requirements, structural and functional relationships among jobs and occupations, and occupational trends.

Personality Type: Conventional. These occupations frequently involve following set procedures and routines and can include working with data and details more than with ideas. Usually there is a clear line of authority to follow.

GOE—Interest Area/Cluster: 04. Business and Administration. **Work Group:** 04.03. Human Resources Support. **Other Jobs in This Work Group:** Employment Interviewers; Employment, Recruitment, and Placement Specialists; Personnel Recruiters; Training and Development Specialists.

Skills—Service Orientation: Actively looking for ways to help people. **Judgment and Decision Making:** Weighing the relative costs and benefits of a potential action. **Management of Financial Resources:** Determining how money will be spent to get the work done and accounting for these expenditures. **Persuasion:** Persuading others to approach things differently. **Active Listening:** Listening to what other people are saying and asking questions as appropriate. **Negotiation:** Bringing others together and trying to reconcile differences. **Monitoring:** Assessing how well one is doing when learning or doing something. **Coordination:** Adjusting actions in relation to others' actions.

Education and Training Programs: Human Resources Management/Personnel Administration, General; Labor and Industrial Relations. **Related Knowledge/Courses—Personnel and Human Resources:** Principles and procedures for personnel recruitment; selection; training; compensation and benefits; labor relations and negotiation; and personnel information systems. **Clerical Practices:** Administrative and clerical procedures and systems such as word-processing systems, filing and records management systems, stenography and transcription, forms, design principles, and other office procedures and terminology. **Customer and Personal Service:** Principles and processes for providing customer and personal services, including needs assessment techniques, quality service standards, alternative delivery systems, and customer satisfaction evaluation techniques. **English Language:** The structure and content of the English language, including the meaning and spelling of words, rules of composition, and grammar. **Administration and Management:** Principles and processes involved in business

and organizational planning, coordination, and execution. This includes strategic planning, resource allocation, manpower modeling, leadership techniques, and production methods. **Law and Government:** Laws, legal codes, court procedures, precedents, government regulations, executive orders, agency rules, and the democratic political process.

Work Environment: Indoors; noisy; sitting; using hands on objects, tools, or controls; repetitive motions.

Computer and Information Scientists, Research

- ❈ Education/Training Required: Doctoral degree
- ❈ Annual Earnings: $97,970
- ❈ Beginning Wage: $55,930
- ❈ Earnings Growth Potential: High
- ❈ Growth: 21.5%
- ❈ Annual Job Openings: 2,901
- ❈ Self-Employed: 5.3%
- ❈ Part-Time: 5.6%

Conduct research into fundamental computer and information science as theorists, designers, or inventors. Solve or develop solutions to problems in the field of computer hardware and software. Analyze problems to develop solutions involving computer hardware and software. Assign or schedule tasks in order to meet work priorities and goals. Evaluate project plans and proposals to assess feasibility issues. Apply theoretical expertise and innovation to create or apply new technology, such as adapting principles for applying computers to new uses. Consult with users, management, vendors, and technicians to determine computing needs and system requirements. Meet with managers, vendors, and others to solicit cooperation and resolve problems. Conduct logical analyses of business, scientific, engineering, and other technical problems, formulating mathematical models of problems for solution by computers. Develop and interpret organizational goals, policies, and procedures. Participate in staffing decisions and direct training of subordinates. Develop performance standards and evaluate work in light of established standards. Design computers and the software that runs them. Maintain network hardware and software, direct network security measures, and monitor networks to ensure availability to system users. Participate in multidisciplinary projects in areas such as virtual reality, human-computer interaction, or robotics. Approve, prepare, monitor, and adjust operational budgets. Direct daily operations of departments, coordinating project activities with other departments.

Personality Type: Investigative. These occupations frequently involve working with ideas and require an extensive amount of thinking. They can involve searching for facts and figuring out problems mentally.

GOE—Interest Area/Cluster: 11. Information Technology. **Work Group:** 11.02. Information Technology Specialties. **Other Jobs in This Work Group:** Computer Operators; Computer Programmers; Computer Security Specialists; Computer Software Engineers, Applications; Computer Software Engineers, Systems Software; Computer Support Specialists; Computer Systems Analysts; Computer Systems Engineers/Architects; Database Administrators; Network Designers; Network Systems and Data Communications Analysts; Software Quality Assurance Engineers and Testers; Web Administrators; Web Developers.

Skills—Programming: Writing computer programs for various purposes. **Science:** Using scientific methods to solve problems. **Systems Analysis:** Determining how a system should work and how changes will affect outcomes. **Operations Analysis:** Analyzing needs and product requirements to create a design. **Technology Design:** Generating or adapting equipment and technology to serve user needs. **Active Learning:** Working with new material or information to grasp its implications. **Complex Problem Solving:** Identifying complex problems, reviewing the options, and implementing solutions. **Mathematics:** Using mathematics to solve problems.

Education and Training Programs: Artificial Intelligence and Robotics; Computer and Information Sciences and Support Services, Other; Computer and Information Sciences, General; Computer Science; Computer Systems Analysis/Analyst Training; Information Science/Studies; Medical Informatics. **Related Knowledge/Courses—Computers and Electronics:** Electric circuit boards, processors, chips, and computer hardware and software, including applications and programming. **Telecommunications:** Transmission, broadcasting, switching, control, and operation of telecommunications systems. **Engineering and Technology:** Equipment, tools, and mechanical devices and their uses to produce motion, light, power, technology, and other applications. **Mathematics:** Numbers and their operations and interrelationships, including arithmetic, algebra, geometry, calculus, and statistics and their applications. **Design:** Design techniques, principles, tools, and instruments

involved in the production and use of precision technical plans, blueprints, drawings, and models. **Education and Training:** Instructional methods and training techniques, including curriculum design principles, learning theory, group and individual teaching techniques, design of individual development plans, and test design principles.

Work Environment: Indoors; sitting; using hands on objects, tools, or controls; repetitive motions.

Computer and Information Systems Managers

❋ Education/Training Required: Work experience plus degree
❋ Annual Earnings: $108,070
❋ Beginning Wage: $65,760
❋ Earnings Growth Potential: Medium
❋ Growth: 16.4%
❋ Annual Job Openings: 30,887
❋ Self-Employed: 1.4%
❋ Part-Time: 2.1%

Plan, direct, or coordinate activities in such fields as electronic data processing, information systems, systems analysis, and computer programming. Review project plans to plan and coordinate project activity. Manage backup, security, and user help systems. Develop and interpret organizational goals, policies, and procedures. Develop computer information resources, providing for data security and control, strategic computing, and disaster recovery. Consult with users, management, vendors, and technicians to assess computing needs and system requirements. Stay abreast of advances in technology. Meet with department heads, managers, supervisors, vendors, and others to solicit cooperation and resolve problems. Provide users with technical support for computer problems. Recruit, hire, train, and supervise staff or participate in staffing decisions. Evaluate data processing proposals to assess project feasibility and requirements. Review and approve all systems charts and programs prior to their implementation. Control operational budget and expenditures. Direct daily operations of department, analyzing workflow, establishing priorities, developing standards, and setting deadlines. Assign and review the work of systems analysts, programmers, and other computer-related workers. Evaluate the organization's technology use and needs and recommend improvements such as hardware and software upgrades. Prepare and review operational reports or project progress reports. Purchase necessary equipment.

Personality Type: Enterprising. These occupations frequently involve starting up and carrying out projects and can involve leading people and making many decisions. They sometimes require risk taking and often deal with business.

GOE—Interest Area/Cluster: 11. Information Technology. **Work Group:** 11.01. Managerial Work in Information Technology. **Other Jobs in This Work Group:** Network and Computer Systems Administrators.

Skills—Programming: Writing computer programs for various purposes. **Systems Analysis:** Determining how a system should work and how changes will affect outcomes. **Management of Financial Resources:** Determining how money will be spent to get the work done and accounting for these expenditures. **Systems Evaluation:** Looking at many indicators of system performance and taking into account their accuracy. **Management of Material Resources:** Obtaining and seeing to the appropriate use of equipment, facilities, and materials needed to do certain work. **Management of Personnel Resources:** Motivating, developing, and directing people as they work; identifying the best people for the job. **Operation Monitoring:** Watching gauges, dials, or other indicators to make sure a machine is working properly. **Quality Control Analysis:** Evaluating the quality or performance of products, services, or processes.

Education and Training Programs: Computer and Information Sciences, General; Computer Science; Information Resources Management/CIO Training; Information Science/Studies; Knowledge Management; Management Information Systems, General; Operations Management and Supervision; System Administration/Administrator Training. **Related Knowledge/Courses—Telecommunications:** Transmission, broadcasting, switching, control, and operation of telecommunications systems. **Computers and Electronics:** Electric circuit boards, processors, chips, and computer hardware and software, including applications and programming. **Economics and Accounting:** Economic and accounting principles and practices, the financial markets, banking, and the analysis and reporting of financial data. **Personnel and Human Resources:** Principles and procedures for personnel recruitment; selection; training; compensation and benefits; labor relations and negotiation; and personnel information systems. **Production and Processing:** Inputs, outputs, raw materials, waste, quality control, costs, and techniques for maximizing the manufacture and distribution of goods. **Administration and Management:** Principles and processes involved in business and organizational planning, coordination, and execution. This includes strategic planning, resource allocation, manpower modeling, leadership techniques, and production methods.

Work Environment: Indoors; sitting; using hands on objects, tools, or controls.

Computer Hardware Engineers

* Education/Training Required: Bachelor's degree
* Annual Earnings: $91,860
* Beginning Wage: $55,880
* Earnings Growth Potential: Medium
* Growth: 4.6%
* Annual Job Openings: 3,572
* Self-Employed: 3.6%
* Part-Time: 2.7%

Research, design, develop, and test computer or computer-related equipment for commercial, industrial, military, or scientific use. May supervise the manufacturing and installation of computer or computer-related equipment and components. Update knowledge and skills to keep up with rapid advancements in computer technology. Provide technical support to designers, marketing and sales departments, suppliers, engineers, and other team members throughout the product development and implementation process. Test and verify hardware and support peripherals to ensure that they meet specifications and requirements, analyzing and recording test data. Monitor functioning of equipment and make necessary modifications to ensure system operates in conformance with specifications. Analyze information to determine, recommend, and plan layout, including type of computers and peripheral equipment modifications. Build, test, and modify product prototypes, using working models or theoretical models constructed using computer simulation. Analyze user needs and recommend appropriate hardware. Direct technicians, engineering designers, or other technical support personnel as needed. Confer with engineering staff and consult specifications to evaluate interface between hardware and software and operational and performance requirements of overall system. Select hardware and material, assuring compliance with specifications and product requirements. Store, retrieve, and manipulate data for analysis of system capabilities and requirements. Write detailed functional specifications that document the hardware development process and support hardware introduction. Specify power supply requirements and configuration, drawing on system performance expectations and design specifications. Provide training and support to system designers and users. Assemble and modify existing pieces of equipment to meet special needs. Evaluate factors such as reporting formats required, cost constraints, and need for security restrictions to determine hardware configuration. Design and develop computer hardware and support peripherals, including central processing units (CPUs), support logic, microprocessors, custom integrated circuits, and printers and disk drives. Recommend purchase of equipment to control dust, temperature, and humidity in area of system installation.

Personality Type: Investigative. These occupations frequently involve working with ideas and require an extensive amount of thinking. They can involve searching for facts and figuring out problems mentally.

GOE—Interest Area/Cluster: 15. Scientific Research, Engineering, and Mathematics. **Work Group:** 15.07. Research and Design Engineering. **Other Jobs in This Work Group:** Aerospace Engineers; Biomedical Engineers; Chemical Engineers; Civil Engineers; Electrical Engineers; Electronics Engineers, Except Computer; Marine Architects; Marine Engineers; Marine Engineers and Naval Architects; Materials Engineers; Mechanical Engineers; Nuclear Engineers.

Skills—Programming: Writing computer programs for various purposes. **Operations Analysis:** Analyzing needs and product requirements to create a design. **Systems Analysis:** Determining how a system should work and how changes will affect outcomes. **Systems Evaluation:** Looking at many indicators of system performance and taking into account their accuracy. **Troubleshooting:** Determining what is causing an operating error and deciding what to do about it. **Technology Design:** Generating or adapting equipment and technology to serve user needs. **Science:** Using scientific methods to solve problems. **Quality Control Analysis:** Evaluating the quality or performance of products, services, or processes.

Education and Training Programs: Computer Engineering, General; Computer Hardware Engineering. **Related Knowledge/Courses—Computers and Electronics:** Electric circuit boards, processors, chips, and computer hardware and software, including applications and programming. **Engineering and Technology:** Equipment, tools, and mechanical devices and their uses to produce motion, light, power, technology, and other applications. **Telecommunications:**

Transmission, broadcasting, switching, control, and operation of telecommunications systems. **Design:** Design techniques, principles, tools, and instruments involved in the production and use of precision technical plans, blueprints, drawings, and models. **Physics:** Physical principles, laws, and applications, including air, water, material dynamics, light, atomic principles, heat, electric theory, earth formations, and meteorological and related natural phenomena. **Communications and Media:** Media production, communication, and dissemination techniques and methods, including alternative ways to inform and entertain via written, oral, and visual media.

Work Environment: Indoors; sitting.

Computer Programmers

- ❋ Education/Training Required: Bachelor's degree
- ❋ Annual Earnings: $68,080
- ❋ Beginning Wage: $39,500
- ❋ Earnings Growth Potential: High
- ❋ Growth: –4.1%
- ❋ Annual Job Openings: 27,937
- ❋ Self-Employed: 3.9%
- ❋ Part-Time: 4.7%

Convert project specifications and statements of problems and procedures to detailed logical flow charts for coding into computer language. Develop and write computer programs to store, locate, and retrieve specific documents, data, and information. May program Web sites. Correct errors by making appropriate changes and rechecking the program to ensure that the desired results are produced. Conduct trial runs of programs and software applications to be sure that they will produce the desired information and that the instructions are correct. Compile and write documentation of program development and subsequent revisions, inserting comments in the coded instructions so others can understand the program. Write, update, and maintain computer programs or software packages to handle specific jobs such as tracking inventory, storing or retrieving data, or controlling other equipment. Consult with managerial, engineering, and technical personnel to clarify program intent, identify problems, and suggest changes. Perform or direct revision, repair, or expansion of existing programs to increase operating efficiency or adapt to new requirements. Write, analyze, review, and rewrite programs, using workflow chart and diagram and applying knowledge of computer capabilities, subject matter, and symbolic logic. Write or contribute to instructions or manuals to guide end users. Investigate whether networks, workstations, the central processing unit of the system, or peripheral equipment are responding to a program's instructions. Prepare detailed workflow charts and diagrams that describe input, output, and logical operation and convert them into a series of instructions coded in a computer language. Perform systems analysis and programming tasks to maintain and control the use of computer systems software as a systems programmer. Consult with and assist computer operators or system analysts to define and resolve problems in running computer programs. Assign, coordinate, and review work and activities of programming personnel. Collaborate with computer manufacturers and other users to develop new programming methods. Train subordinates in programming and program coding.

Personality Type: Investigative. These occupations frequently involve working with ideas and require an extensive amount of thinking. They can involve searching for facts and figuring out problems mentally.

GOE—Interest Area/Cluster: 11. Information Technology. **Work Group:** 11.02. Information Technology Specialties. **Other Jobs in This Work Group:** Computer and Information Scientists, Research; Computer Operators; Computer Security Specialists; Computer Software Engineers, Applications; Computer Software Engineers, Systems Software; Computer Support Specialists; Computer Systems Analysts; Computer Systems Engineers/Architects; Database Administrators; Network Designers; Network Systems and Data Communications Analysts; Software Quality Assurance Engineers and Testers; Web Administrators; Web Developers.

Skills—Programming: Writing computer programs for various purposes. **Operations Analysis:** Analyzing needs and product requirements to create a design. **Technology Design:** Generating or adapting equipment and technology to serve user needs. **Systems Analysis:** Determining how a system should work and how changes will affect outcomes. **Troubleshooting:** Determining what is causing an operating error and deciding what to do about it. **Installation:** Installing equipment, machines, wiring, or programs to meet specifications. **Complex Problem Solving:** Identifying complex problems, reviewing the options, and implementing solutions. **Systems Evaluation:** Looking at many indicators of system performance and taking into account their accuracy.

Education and Training Programs: Artificial Intelligence and Robotics; Bioinformatics; Computer Graphics; Computer Programming, Specific Applications; Computer Programming, Vendor/Product Certification; Computer Programming/Programmer, General; E-Commerce/Electronic Commerce; Management Information Systems, General; Medical Informatics; Medical Office Computer Specialist/Assistant Training; Web Page, Digital/Multimedia and Information Resources Design; Web/Multimedia Management and Webmaster Training. **Related Knowledge/Courses—Computers and Electronics:** Electric circuit boards, processors, chips, and computer hardware and software, including applications and programming. **Design:** Design techniques, principles, tools, and instruments involved in the production and use of precision technical plans, blueprints, drawings, and models. **Telecommunications:** Transmission, broadcasting, switching, control, and operation of telecommunications systems. **Mathematics:** Numbers and their operations and interrelationships, including arithmetic, algebra, geometry, calculus, and statistics and their applications. **Economics and Accounting:** Economic and accounting principles and practices, the financial markets, banking, and the analysis and reporting of financial data. **Engineering and Technology:** Equipment, tools, and mechanical devices and their uses to produce motion, light, power, technology, and other applications.

Work Environment: Indoors; sitting; using hands on objects, tools, or controls; repetitive motions.

Computer Science Teachers, Postsecondary

- ❊ Education/Training Required: Doctoral degree
- ❊ Annual Earnings: $62,020
- ❊ Beginning Wage: $33,720
- ❊ Earnings Growth Potential: High
- ❊ Growth: 22.9%
- ❊ Annual Job Openings: 5,820
- ❊ Self-Employed: 0.4%
- ❊ Part-Time: 27.8%

Teach courses in computer science. May specialize in a field of computer science, such as the design and function of computers or operations and research analysis. Evaluate and grade students' classwork, laboratory work, assignments, and papers. Maintain student attendance records, grades, and other required records. Prepare and deliver lectures to undergraduate and/or graduate students on topics such as programming, data structures, and software design. Prepare course materials such as syllabi, homework assignments, and handouts. Compile, administer, and grade examinations or assign this work to others. Keep abreast of developments in their field by reading current literature, talking with colleagues, and participating in professional conferences. Initiate, facilitate, and moderate classroom discussions. Plan, evaluate, and revise curricula, course content, and course materials and methods of instruction. Supervise students' laboratory work. Maintain regularly scheduled office hours to advise and assist students. Select and obtain materials and supplies such as textbooks and laboratory equipment. Advise students on academic and vocational curricula and on career issues. Participate in student recruitment, registration, and placement activities. Collaborate with colleagues to address teaching and research issues. Serve on academic or administrative committees that deal with institutional policies, departmental matters, and academic issues. Act as advisers to student organizations. Supervise undergraduate and/or graduate teaching, internship, and research work. Perform administrative duties such as serving as department head. Conduct research in a particular field of knowledge and publish findings in professional journals, books, and/or electronic media. Direct research of other teachers or of graduate students working for advanced academic degrees. Provide professional consulting services to government and/or industry. Participate in campus and community events. Compile bibliographies of specialized materials for outside reading assignments. Write grant proposals to procure external research funding.

Personality Type: Social. These occupations frequently involve working with, communicating with, and teaching people and often involve helping or providing service to others.

GOE—Interest Area/Cluster: 05. Education and Training. **Work Group:** 05.03. Postsecondary and Adult Teaching and Instructing. **Other Jobs in This Work Group:** Adult Literacy, Remedial Education, and GED Teachers and Instructors; Agricultural Sciences Teachers, Postsecondary; Anthropology and Archeology Teachers, Postsecondary; Architecture Teachers, Postsecondary; Area, Ethnic, and Cultural Studies Teachers, Postsecondary; Art, Drama, and Music Teachers, Postsecondary; Atmospheric, Earth, Marine, and Space Sciences Teachers, Postsecondary; Biological Science Teachers, Postsecondary; Business Teachers, Postsecondary; Chemistry Teachers, Postsecondary;

Communications Teachers, Postsecondary; Criminal Justice and Law Enforcement Teachers, Postsecondary; Economics Teachers, Postsecondary; Education Teachers, Postsecondary; Engineering Teachers, Postsecondary; English Language and Literature Teachers, Postsecondary; Environmental Science Teachers, Postsecondary; Farm and Home Management Advisors; Foreign Language and Literature Teachers, Postsecondary; Forestry and Conservation Science Teachers, Postsecondary; Geography Teachers, Postsecondary; Graduate Teaching Assistants; Health Specialties Teachers, Postsecondary; History Teachers, Postsecondary; Home Economics Teachers, Postsecondary; Law Teachers, Postsecondary; Library Science Teachers, Postsecondary; Mathematical Science Teachers, Postsecondary; Nursing Instructors and Teachers, Postsecondary; Philosophy and Religion Teachers, Postsecondary; Physics Teachers, Postsecondary; Political Science Teachers, Postsecondary; Psychology Teachers, Postsecondary; Recreation and Fitness Studies Teachers, Postsecondary; Self-Enrichment Education Teachers; Social Work Teachers, Postsecondary; Sociology Teachers, Postsecondary; Vocational Education Teachers, Postsecondary.

Skills—Programming: Writing computer programs for various purposes. **Instructing:** Teaching others how to do something. **Operations Analysis:** Analyzing needs and product requirements to create a design. **Technology Design:** Generating or adapting equipment and technology to serve user needs. **Science:** Using scientific methods to solve problems. **Mathematics:** Using mathematics to solve problems. **Learning Strategies:** Using multiple approaches when learning or teaching new things. **Complex Problem Solving:** Identifying complex problems, reviewing the options, and implementing solutions.

Education and Training Programs: Computer and Information Sciences, General; Computer Programming/Programmer, General; Computer Science; Computer Systems Analysis/Analyst Training; Information Science/Studies. **Related Knowledge/Courses—Computers and Electronics:** Electric circuit boards, processors, chips, and computer hardware and software, including applications and programming. **Education and Training:** Instructional methods and training techniques, including curriculum design principles, learning theory, group and individual teaching techniques, design of individual development plans, and test design principles. **Telecommunications:** Transmission, broadcasting, switching, control, and operation of telecommunications systems. **Mathematics:** Numbers and their operations and interrelationships, including arithmetic, algebra, geometry, calculus, and statistics and their applications. **Engineering and Technology:** Equipment, tools, and mechanical devices and their uses to produce motion, light, power, technology, and other applications. **English Language:** The structure and content of the English language, including the meaning and spelling of words, rules of composition, and grammar.

Work Environment: Indoors; sitting.

Computer Security Specialists

- ❋ Education/Training Required: Bachelor's degree
- ❋ Annual Earnings: $64,690
- ❋ Beginning Wage: $39,970
- ❋ Earnings Growth Potential: Medium
- ❋ Growth: 27.0%
- ❋ Annual Job Openings: 37,010
- ❋ Self-Employed: 0.4%
- ❋ Part-Time: 3.1%

The job openings listed here are shared with Network and Computer Systems Administrators.

Plan, coordinate, and implement security measures for information systems to regulate access to computer data files and prevent unauthorized modification, destruction, or disclosure of information. Train users and promote security awareness to ensure system security and to improve server and network efficiency. Develop plans to safeguard computer files against accidental or unauthorized modification, destruction, or disclosure and to meet emergency data processing needs. Confer with users to discuss issues such as computer data access needs, security violations, and programming changes. Monitor current reports of computer viruses to determine when to update virus protection systems. Modify computer security files to incorporate new software, correct errors, or change individual access status. Coordinate implementation of computer system plan with establishment personnel and outside vendors. Monitor use of data files and regulate access to safeguard information in computer files. Perform risk assessments and execute tests of data-processing system to ensure functioning of data-processing activities and security measures. Encrypt data transmissions and erect firewalls to conceal confidential information as it is being transmitted and to keep out tainted digital transfers. Document computer security and emergency measures policies, procedures, and tests. Review violations of computer security procedures and discuss procedures with violators to ensure violations are not repeated.

Maintain permanent fleet cryptologic and carry-on direct support systems required in special land, sea surface, and subsurface operations.

Personality Type: Conventional. These occupations frequently involve following set procedures and routines and can include working with data and details more than with ideas. Usually there is a clear line of authority to follow.

GOE—Interest Area/Cluster: 11. Information Technology. **Work Group:** 11.02. Information Technology Specialties. **Other Jobs in This Work Group:** Computer and Information Scientists, Research; Computer Operators; Computer Programmers; Computer Software Engineers, Applications; Computer Software Engineers, Systems Software; Computer Support Specialists; Computer Systems Analysts; Computer Systems Engineers/Architects; Database Administrators; Network Designers; Network Systems and Data Communications Analysts; Software Quality Assurance Engineers and Testers; Web Administrators; Web Developers.

Skills—Systems Evaluation: Looking at many indicators of system performance and taking into account their accuracy. **Systems Analysis:** Determining how a system should work and how changes will affect outcomes. **Operations Analysis:** Analyzing needs and product requirements to create a design. **Programming:** Writing computer programs for various purposes. **Installation:** Installing equipment, machines, wiring, or programs to meet specifications. **Management of Material Resources:** Obtaining and seeing to the appropriate use of equipment, facilities, and materials needed to do certain work. **Troubleshooting:** Determining what is causing an operating error and deciding what to do about it. **Management of Financial Resources:** Determining how money will be spent to get the work done and accounting for these expenditures.

Education and Training Programs: Computer and Information Sciences and Support Services, Other; Computer and Information Sciences, General; Computer and Information Systems Security; Computer Systems Analysis/Analyst Training; Computer Systems Networking and Telecommunications; Information Science/Studies; System Administration/Administrator Training; System, Networking, and LAN/WAN Management/Manager Training. **Related Knowledge/Courses—Computers and Electronics:** Electric circuit boards, processors, chips, and computer hardware and software, including applications and programming. **Telecommunications:** Transmission, broadcasting, switching, control, and operation of telecommunications systems. **Engineering and Technology:** Equipment, tools, and mechanical devices and their uses to produce motion, light, power, technology, and other applications. **Design:** Design techniques, principles, tools, and instruments involved in the production and use of precision technical plans, blueprints, drawings, and models. **Education and Training:** Instructional methods and training techniques, including curriculum design principles, learning theory, group and individual teaching techniques, design of individual development plans, and test design principles. **Therapy and Counseling:** Information and techniques needed to rehabilitate physical and mental ailments and to provide career guidance, including alternative treatments, rehabilitation equipment and its proper use, and methods to evaluate treatment effects.

Work Environment: Indoors; sitting.

Computer Software Engineers, Applications

- ❋ Education/Training Required: Bachelor's degree
- ❋ Annual Earnings: $83,130
- ❋ Beginning Wage: $52,090
- ❋ Earnings Growth Potential: Medium
- ❋ Growth: 44.6%
- ❋ Annual Job Openings: 58,690
- ❋ Self-Employed: 2.0%
- ❋ Part-Time: 2.6%

Develop, create, and modify general computer applications software or specialized utility programs. Analyze user needs and develop software solutions. Design software or customize software for client use with the aim of optimizing operational efficiency. May analyze and design databases within an application area, working individually or coordinating database development as part of a team. Confer with systems analysts, engineers, programmers, and others to design system and to obtain information on project limitations and capabilities, performance requirements, and interfaces. Modify existing software to correct errors, allow it to adapt to new hardware, or improve its performance. Analyze user needs and software requirements to determine feasibility of design within time and cost constraints. Consult with customers about software system design and maintenance. Coordinate software system installation and monitor equipment functioning to ensure specifications are met. Design, develop, and modify software systems, using scientific analysis and mathematical models to predict and measure outcome and consequences

of design. Develop and direct software system testing and validation procedures, programming, and documentation. Analyze information to determine, recommend, and plan computer specifications and layouts and peripheral equipment modifications. Supervise the work of programmers, technologists, and technicians and other engineering and scientific personnel. Obtain and evaluate information on factors such as reporting formats required, costs, and security needs to determine hardware configuration. Determine system performance standards. Train users to use new or modified equipment. Store, retrieve, and manipulate data for analysis of system capabilities and requirements. Specify power supply requirements and configuration. Recommend purchase of equipment to control dust, temperature, and humidity in area of system installation.

Personality Type: Investigative. These occupations frequently involve working with ideas and require an extensive amount of thinking. They can involve searching for facts and figuring out problems mentally.

GOE—Interest Area/Cluster: 11. Information Technology. **Work Group:** 11.02. Information Technology Specialties. **Other Jobs in This Work Group:** Computer and Information Scientists, Research; Computer Operators; Computer Programmers; Computer Security Specialists; Computer Software Engineers, Systems Software; Computer Support Specialists; Computer Systems Analysts; Computer Systems Engineers/Architects; Database Administrators; Network Designers; Network Systems and Data Communications Analysts; Software Quality Assurance Engineers and Testers; Web Administrators; Web Developers.

Skills—Programming: Writing computer programs for various purposes. **Troubleshooting:** Determining what is causing an operating error and deciding what to do about it. **Technology Design:** Generating or adapting equipment and technology to serve user needs. **Systems Analysis:** Determining how a system should work and how changes will affect outcomes. **Quality Control Analysis:** Evaluating the quality or performance of products, services, or processes. **Operations Analysis:** Analyzing needs and product requirements to create a design. **Installation:** Installing equipment, machines, wiring, or programs to meet specifications. **Complex Problem Solving:** Identifying complex problems, reviewing the options, and implementing solutions.

Education and Training Programs: Artificial Intelligence and Robotics; Bioinformatics; Computer Engineering Technologies/Technician Training, Other; Computer Engineering, General; Computer Science; Computer Software

Engineering; Information Technology; Medical Illustration and Informatics, Other; Medical Informatics. **Related Knowledge/Courses—Computers and Electronics:** Electric circuit boards, processors, chips, and computer hardware and software, including applications and programming. **Telecommunications:** Transmission, broadcasting, switching, control, and operation of telecommunications systems. **Engineering and Technology:** Equipment, tools, and mechanical devices and their uses to produce motion, light, power, technology, and other applications. **Design:** Design techniques, principles, tools, and instruments involved in the production and use of precision technical plans, blueprints, drawings, and models. **Mathematics:** Numbers and their operations and interrelationships, including arithmetic, algebra, geometry, calculus, and statistics and their applications. **Physics:** Physical principles, laws, and applications, including air, water, material dynamics, light, atomic principles, heat, electric theory, earth formations, and meteorological and related natural phenomena.

Work Environment: Indoors; sitting; using hands on objects, tools, or controls; repetitive motions.

Computer Software Engineers, Systems Software

- ❋ Education/Training Required: Bachelor's degree
- ❋ Annual Earnings: $89,070
- ❋ Beginning Wage: $55,870
- ❋ Earnings Growth Potential: Medium
- ❋ Growth: 28.2%
- ❋ Annual Job Openings: 33,139
- ❋ Self-Employed: 2.1%
- ❋ Part-Time: 2.6%

Research, design, develop, and test operating systems-level software, compilers, and network distribution software for medical, industrial, military, communications, aerospace, business, scientific, and general computing applications. Set operational specifications and formulate and analyze software requirements. Apply principles and techniques of computer science, engineering, and mathematical analysis. Modify existing software to correct errors, to adapt it to new hardware, or to upgrade interfaces and improve performance. Design and develop software systems, using scientific analysis and mathematical models to predict and measure outcome and consequences

of design. Consult with engineering staff to evaluate interface between hardware and software, develop specifications and performance requirements, and resolve customer problems. Analyze information to determine, recommend, and plan installation of a new system or modification of an existing system. Develop and direct software system testing and validation procedures. Direct software programming and development of documentation. Consult with customers or other departments on project status, proposals, and technical issues such as software system design and maintenance. Advise customer about, or perform, maintenance of software system. Coordinate installation of software system. Monitor functioning of equipment to ensure system operates in conformance with specifications. Store, retrieve, and manipulate data for analysis of system capabilities and requirements. Confer with data processing and project managers to obtain information on limitations and capabilities for data-processing projects. Prepare reports and correspondence concerning project specifications, activities, and status. Evaluate factors such as reporting formats required, cost constraints, and need for security restrictions to determine hardware configuration. Supervise and assign work to programmers, designers, technologists and technicians, and other engineering and scientific personnel. Train users to use new or modified equipment. Utilize microcontrollers to develop control signals; implement control algorithms; and measure process variables such as temperatures, pressures, and positions. Recommend purchase of equipment to control dust, temperature, and humidity in area of system installation. Specify power supply requirements and configuration.

Personality Type: Investigative. These occupations frequently involve working with ideas and require an extensive amount of thinking. They can involve searching for facts and figuring out problems mentally.

GOE—Interest Area/Cluster: 11. Information Technology. **Work Group:** 11.02. Information Technology Specialties. **Other Jobs in This Work Group:** Computer and Information Scientists, Research; Computer Operators; Computer Programmers; Computer Security Specialists; Computer Software Engineers, Applications; Computer Support Specialists; Computer Systems Analysts; Computer Systems Engineers/Architects; Database Administrators; Network Designers; Network Systems and Data Communications Analysts; Software Quality Assurance Engineers and Testers; Web Administrators; Web Developers.

Skills—Programming: Writing computer programs for various purposes. **Technology Design:** Generating or adapting equipment and technology to serve user needs. **Systems Analysis:** Determining how a system should work and how changes will affect outcomes. **Troubleshooting:** Determining what is causing an operating error and deciding what to do about it. **Operations Analysis:** Analyzing needs and product requirements to create a design. **Complex Problem Solving:** Identifying complex problems, reviewing the options, and implementing solutions. **Science:** Using scientific methods to solve problems. **Mathematics:** Using mathematics to solve problems.

Education and Training Programs: Artificial Intelligence and Robotics; Computer Engineering Technologies/Technician Training, Other; Computer Engineering, General; Computer Science; Information Science/Studies; Information Technology; System, Networking, and LAN/WAN Management/Manager Training. **Related Knowledge/Courses—Computers and Electronics:** Electric circuit boards, processors, chips, and computer hardware and software, including applications and programming. **Design:** Design techniques, principles, tools, and instruments involved in the production and use of precision technical plans, blueprints, drawings, and models. **Engineering and Technology:** Equipment, tools, and mechanical devices and their uses to produce motion, light, power, technology, and other applications. **Telecommunications:** Transmission, broadcasting, switching, control, and operation of telecommunications systems. **Mathematics:** Numbers and their operations and interrelationships, including arithmetic, algebra, geometry, calculus, and statistics and their applications. **Communications and Media:** Media production, communication, and dissemination techniques and methods, including alternative ways to inform and entertain via written, oral, and visual media.

Work Environment: Indoors; sitting; using hands on objects, tools, or controls; repetitive motions.

Computer Support Specialists

- ❈ Education/Training Required: Associate degree
- ❈ Annual Earnings: $42,400
- ❈ Beginning Wage: $25,950
- ❈ Earnings Growth Potential: Medium
- ❈ Growth: 12.9%
- ❈ Annual Job Openings: 97,334
- ❈ Self-Employed: 1.3%
- ❈ Part-Time: 6.9%

Provide technical assistance to computer system users. Answer questions or resolve computer problems for clients in person, via telephone, or from remote locations. May provide assistance concerning the use of computer hardware and software, including printing, installation, word processing, e-mail, and operating systems. Oversee the daily performance of computer systems. Answer user inquiries regarding computer software or hardware operation to resolve problems. Enter commands and observe system functioning to verify correct operations and detect errors. Set up equipment for employee use, performing or ensuring proper installation of cables, operating systems, or appropriate software. Install and perform minor repairs to hardware, software, or peripheral equipment, following design or installation specifications. Maintain records of daily data communication transactions, problems and remedial actions taken, or installation activities. Read technical manuals, confer with users, or conduct computer diagnostics to investigate and resolve problems or to provide technical assistance and support. Refer major hardware or software problems or defective products to vendors or technicians for service. Develop training materials and procedures or train users in the proper use of hardware or software. Confer with staff, users, and management to establish requirements for new systems or modifications. Prepare evaluations of software or hardware and recommend improvements or upgrades. Read trade magazines and technical manuals or attend conferences and seminars to maintain knowledge of hardware and software. Hire, supervise, and direct workers engaged in special project work, problem solving, monitoring, and installing data communication equipment and software. Inspect equipment and read order sheets to prepare for delivery to users. Modify and customize commercial programs for internal needs. Conduct office automation feasibility studies, including workflow analysis, space design, or cost comparison analysis.

Personality Type: Realistic. These occupations frequently involve work activities that include practical, hands-on problems and solutions. They often deal with plants; animals; and real-world materials such as wood, tools, and machinery. Many of the occupations require working outside and don't involve a lot of paperwork or working closely with others.

GOE—Interest Area/Cluster: 11. Information Technology. **Work Group:** 11.02. Information Technology Specialties. **Other Jobs in This Work Group:** Computer and Information Scientists, Research; Computer Operators; Computer Programmers; Computer Security Specialists;

Computer Software Engineers, Applications; Computer Software Engineers, Systems Software; Computer Systems Analysts; Computer Systems Engineers/Architects; Database Administrators; Network Designers; Network Systems and Data Communications Analysts; Software Quality Assurance Engineers and Testers; Web Administrators; Web Developers.

Skills—Programming: Writing computer programs for various purposes. **Installation:** Installing equipment, machines, wiring, or programs to meet specifications. **Systems Analysis:** Determining how a system should work and how changes will affect outcomes. **Operation Monitoring:** Watching gauges, dials, or other indicators to make sure a machine is working properly. **Repairing:** Repairing machines or systems, using the needed tools. **Systems Evaluation:** Looking at many indicators of system performance and taking into account their accuracy. **Troubleshooting:** Determining what is causing an operating error and deciding what to do about it. **Operation and Control:** Controlling operations of equipment or systems.

Education and Training Programs: Accounting and Computer Science; Agricultural Business Technology; Computer Hardware Technology/Technician Training; Computer Software Technology/Technician Training; Data Processing and Data Processing Technology/Technician Training; Medical Office Computer Specialist/Assistant Training. **Related Knowledge/Courses—Computers and Electronics:** Electric circuit boards, processors, chips, and computer hardware and software, including applications and programming. **Telecommunications:** Transmission, broadcasting, switching, control, and operation of telecommunications systems. **Engineering and Technology:** Equipment, tools, and mechanical devices and their uses to produce motion, light, power, technology, and other applications. **Clerical Practices:** Administrative and clerical procedures and systems such as word-processing systems, filing and records management systems, stenography and transcription, forms, design principles, and other office procedures and terminology. **Customer and Personal Service:** Principles and processes for providing customer and personal services, including needs assessment techniques, quality service standards, alternative delivery systems, and customer satisfaction evaluation techniques. **Communications and Media:** Media production, communication, and dissemination techniques and methods, including alternative ways to inform and entertain via written, oral, and visual media.

Work Environment: Indoors; sitting; using hands on objects, tools, or controls.

Computer Systems Analysts

- Education/Training Required: Bachelor's degree
- Annual Earnings: $73,090
- Beginning Wage: $43,930
- Earnings Growth Potential: Medium
- Growth: 29.0%
- Annual Job Openings: 63,166
- Self-Employed: 5.8%
- Part-Time: 5.6%

Analyze science, engineering, business, and all other data-processing problems for application to electronic data processing systems. Analyze user requirements, procedures, and problems to automate or improve existing systems and review computer system capabilities, workflow, and scheduling limitations. May analyze or recommend commercially available software. May supervise computer programmers. Provide staff and users with assistance solving computer-related problems, such as malfunctions and program problems. Test, maintain, and monitor computer programs and systems, including coordinating the installation of computer programs and systems. Use object-oriented programming languages as well as client and server applications development processes and multimedia and Internet technology. Confer with clients regarding the nature of the information processing or computation needs a computer program is to address. Coordinate and link the computer systems within an organization to increase compatibility and so information can be shared. Consult with management to ensure agreement on system principles. Expand or modify system to serve new purposes or improve workflow. Interview or survey workers, observe job performance, or perform the job to determine what information is processed and how it is processed. Determine computer software or hardware needed to set up or alter system. Train staff and users to work with computer systems and programs. Analyze information processing or computation needs and plan and design computer systems, using techniques such as structured analysis, data modeling, and information engineering. Assess the usefulness of pre-developed application packages and adapt them to a user environment. Define the goals of the system and devise flow charts and diagrams describing logical operational steps of programs. Develop, document, and revise system design procedures, test procedures, and quality standards. Review and analyze computer printouts and performance indicators to locate code problems; correct errors by correcting codes. Recommend new equipment or software packages. Read manuals, periodicals, and technical reports to learn how to develop programs that meet staff and user requirements. Supervise computer programmers or other systems analysts or serve as project leaders for particular systems projects. Utilize the computer in the analysis and solution of business problems such as development of integrated production and inventory control and cost analysis systems.

Personality Type: Investigative. These occupations frequently involve working with ideas and require an extensive amount of thinking. They can involve searching for facts and figuring out problems mentally.

GOE—Interest Area/Cluster: 11. Information Technology. **Work Group:** 11.02. Information Technology Specialties. **Other Jobs in This Work Group:** Computer and Information Scientists, Research; Computer Operators; Computer Programmers; Computer Security Specialists; Computer Software Engineers, Applications; Computer Software Engineers, Systems Software; Computer Support Specialists; Computer Systems Engineers/Architects; Database Administrators; Network Designers; Network Systems and Data Communications Analysts; Software Quality Assurance Engineers and Testers; Web Administrators; Web Developers.

Skills—Installation: Installing equipment, machines, wiring, or programs to meet specifications. **Quality Control Analysis:** Evaluating the quality or performance of products, services, or processes. **Technology Design:** Generating or adapting equipment and technology to serve user needs. **Programming:** Writing computer programs for various purposes. **Systems Analysis:** Determining how a system should work and how changes will affect outcomes. **Troubleshooting:** Determining what is causing an operating error and deciding what to do about it. **Operations Analysis:** Analyzing needs and product requirements to create a design. **Systems Evaluation:** Looking at many indicators of system performance and taking into account their accuracy.

Education and Training Programs: Computer and Information Sciences, General; Computer Systems Analysis/Analyst Training; Information Technology; Web/Multimedia Management and Webmaster Training. **Related Knowledge/Courses—Computers and Electronics:** Electric circuit boards, processors, chips, and computer hardware and software, including applications and programming. **Telecommunications:** Transmission, broadcasting, switching, control, and operation of telecommunications systems. **Design:** Design techniques, principles, tools, and instruments involved in the production and use of precision technical plans, blueprints, drawings, and models. **Customer and Personal Service:** Principles and processes for providing customer and personal services, including needs assessment techniques, quality service standards, alternative delivery systems, and customer satisfaction evaluation techniques. **Law and Government:** Laws, legal codes, court procedures, precedents, government regulations, executive orders, agency rules, and the democratic political process. **Communications and Media:** Media production, communication, and dissemination techniques and methods, including alternative ways to inform and entertain via written, oral, and visual media.

Work Environment: Indoors; sitting.

Computer Systems Engineers/ Architects

- ❋ **Education/Training Required: Bachelor's degree**
- ❋ **Annual Earnings: $71,510**
- ❋ **Beginning Wage: $37,600**
- ❋ **Earnings Growth Potential: High**
- ❋ **Growth: 15.1%**
- ❋ **Annual Job Openings: 14,374**
- ❋ **Self-Employed: 6.6%**
- ❋ **Part-Time: 5.6%**

The job openings listed here are shared with Network Designers; Software Quality Assurance Engineers and Testers; Web Administrators; and Web Developers.

Design and develop solutions to complex applications problems, system administration issues, or network concerns. Perform systems management and integration functions. Communicate with staff or clients to understand specific system requirements. Provide advice on project costs, design concepts, or design changes. Document design specifications, installation instructions, and other system-related information. Verify stability, interoperability, portability, security, or scalability of system architecture. Collaborate with engineers or software developers to select appropriate design solutions or ensure the compatibility of system components. Provide technical guidance or support for the development or troubleshooting of systems. Evaluate current or emerging technologies to consider factors such as cost, portability, compatibility, or usability. Identify system data, hardware, or software components required to meet user needs. Provide guidelines for implementing secure systems to customers or installation teams. Monitor system operation to detect potential problems. Direct the analysis, development, and operation of complete computer systems. Investigate system component suitability for specified purposes and make recommendations regarding component use. Perform ongoing hardware and software maintenance operations, including installing or upgrading hardware or software. Develop or approve project plans, schedules, or budgets. Configure servers to meet functional specifications. Design and conduct hardware or software tests. Define and analyze objectives, scope, issues, or organizational impact of information systems. Develop system engineering, software engineering, system integration, or distributed system architectures. Establish functional or system standards to ensure operational requirements, quality requirements, and design constraints are addressed. Evaluate existing systems to determine effectiveness and suggest changes to meet organizational requirements. Research, test, or verify proper functioning of software patches and fixes. Communicate project information through presentations, technical reports, or white papers. Complete models and simulations, using manual or automated tools, to analyze or predict system performance under different operating conditions.

Personality Type: Investigative. These occupations frequently involve working with ideas and require an extensive amount of thinking. They can involve searching for facts and figuring out problems mentally.

GOE—Interest Area/Cluster: 11. Information Technology. **Work Group:** 11.02. Information Technology Specialties. **Other Jobs in This Work Group:** Computer and Information Scientists, Research; Computer Operators; Computer Programmers; Computer Security Specialists; Computer Software Engineers, Applications; Computer Software Engineers, Systems Software; Computer Support Specialists; Computer Systems Analysts; Database Administrators; Network Designers; Network Systems and Data Communications Analysts; Software Quality Assurance Engineers and Testers; Web Administrators; Web Developers.

Skills—Programming: Writing computer programs for various purposes. **Systems Evaluation:** Looking at many indicators of system performance and taking into account their accuracy. **Technology Design:** Generating or adapting equipment and technology to serve user needs. **Systems Analysis:** Determining how a system should work and how changes will affect outcomes. **Troubleshooting:** Determining what is causing an operating error and deciding what to do about it. **Operations Analysis:** Analyzing

needs and product requirements to create a design. **Installation:** Installing equipment, machines, wiring, or programs to meet specifications. **Science:** Using scientific methods to solve problems.

Education and Training Programs: Computer Engineering, General; Computer Software Engineering. **Related Knowledge/Courses—Computers and Electronics:** Electric circuit boards, processors, chips, and computer hardware and software, including applications and programming. **Engineering and Technology:** Equipment, tools, and mechanical devices and their uses to produce motion, light, power, technology, and other applications. **Telecommunications:** Transmission, broadcasting, switching, control, and operation of telecommunications systems. **Design:** Design techniques, principles, tools, and instruments involved in the production and use of precision technical plans, blueprints, drawings, and models. **Mathematics:** Numbers and their operations and interrelationships, including arithmetic, algebra, geometry, calculus, and statistics and their applications. **Sales and Marketing:** Principles and methods involved in showing, promoting, and selling products or services. This includes marketing strategies and tactics, product demonstration and sales techniques, and sales control systems.

Work Environment: Indoors; sitting; repetitive motions.

Computer, Automated Teller, and Office Machine Repairers

- ✱ Education/Training Required: Postsecondary vocational training
- ✱ Annual Earnings: $37,100
- ✱ Beginning Wage: $22,640
- ✱ Earnings Growth Potential: Medium
- ✱ Growth: 3.0%
- ✱ Annual Job Openings: 22,330
- ✱ Self-Employed: 19.7%
- ✱ Part-Time: 9.0%

Repair, maintain, or install computers, word-processing systems, automated teller machines, and electronic office machines such as duplicating and fax machines. Converse with customers in order to determine details of equipment problems. Reassemble machines after making repairs or replacing parts. Travel to customers' stores or offices to service machines or to provide emergency repair service. Reinstall software programs or adjust settings on existing software in order to fix machine malfunctions. Advise customers concerning equipment operation, maintenance, and programming. Assemble machines according to specifications, using hand tools, power tools, and measuring devices. Test new systems in order to ensure that they are in working order. Operate machines in order to test functioning of parts and mechanisms. Maintain records of equipment maintenance work and repairs. Install and configure new equipment, including operating software and peripheral equipment. Maintain parts inventories and order any additional parts needed for repairs. Update existing equipment, performing tasks such as installing updated circuit boards or additional memory. Test components and circuits of faulty equipment in order to locate defects, using oscilloscopes, signal generators, ammeters, voltmeters, or special diagnostic software programs. Align, adjust, and calibrate equipment according to specifications. Repair, adjust, or replace electrical and mechanical components and parts, using hand tools, power tools, and soldering or welding equipment. Complete repair bills, shop records, time cards, and expense reports. Disassemble machine to examine parts such as wires, gears, and bearings for wear and defects, using hand tools, power tools, and measuring devices. Clean, oil, and adjust mechanical parts to maintain machines' operating efficiency and to prevent breakdowns. Read specifications such as blueprints, charts, and schematics in order to determine machine settings and adjustments. Enter information into computers to copy programs from one electronic component to another or to draw, modify, or store schematics. Lay cable and hook up electrical connections between machines, power sources, and phone lines. Analyze equipment performance records in order to assess equipment functioning.

Personality Type: Realistic. These occupations frequently involve work activities that include practical, hands-on problems and solutions. They often deal with plants; animals; and real-world materials such as wood, tools, and machinery. Many of the occupations require working outside and don't involve a lot of paperwork or working closely with others.

GOE—Interest Area/Cluster: 11. Information Technology. **Work Group:** 11.03. Digital Equipment Repair. **Other Jobs in This Work Group:** Coin, Vending, and Amusement Machine Servicers and Repairers.

Skills—Installation: Installing equipment, machines, wiring, or programs to meet specifications. **Repairing:** Repairing machines or systems, using the needed tools. **Troubleshooting:** Determining what is causing an operating error and deciding what to do about it. **Equipment Maintenance:** Performing routine maintenance and determining when

and what kind of maintenance is needed. **Management of Material Resources:** Obtaining and seeing to the appropriate use of equipment, facilities, and materials needed to do certain work. **Programming:** Writing computer programs for various purposes. **Technology Design:** Generating or adapting equipment and technology to serve user needs. **Systems Evaluation:** Looking at many indicators of system performance and taking into account their accuracy.

Education and Training Programs: Business Machine Repair; Computer Installation and Repair Technology/Technician Training. **Related Knowledge/Courses—Computers and Electronics:** Electric circuit boards, processors, chips, and computer hardware and software, including applications and programming. **Telecommunications:** Transmission, broadcasting, switching, control, and operation of telecommunications systems. **Mechanical Devices:** Machines and tools, including their designs, uses, benefits, repair, and maintenance. **Customer and Personal Service:** Principles and processes for providing customer and personal services, including needs assessment techniques, quality service standards, alternative delivery systems, and customer satisfaction evaluation techniques. **Engineering and Technology:** Equipment, tools, and mechanical devices and their uses to produce motion, light, power, technology, and other applications. **Sales and Marketing:** Principles and methods involved in showing, promoting, and selling products or services. This includes marketing strategies and tactics, product demonstration and sales techniques, and sales control systems.

Work Environment: Indoors; sitting; using hands on objects, tools, or controls; repetitive motions.

Concierges

- ❋ Education/Training Required: Moderate-term on-the-job training
- ❋ Annual Earnings: $25,540
- ❋ Beginning Wage: $16,910
- ❋ Earnings Growth Potential: Low
- ❋ Growth: 14.1%
- ❋ Annual Job Openings: 4,893
- ❋ Self-Employed: 0.3%
- ❋ Part-Time: 16.9%

Assist patrons at hotel, apartment, or office building with personal services. May take messages; arrange or give advice on transportation, business services, or

entertainment; or monitor guest requests for housekeeping and maintenance. Make dining and other reservations for patrons and obtain tickets for events. Provide information about local features such as shopping, dining, nightlife, and recreational destinations. Make travel arrangements for sightseeing and other tours. Receive, store, and deliver luggage and mail. Perform office duties on a temporary basis when needed. Pick up and deliver items or run errands for guests. Carry out unusual requests such as searching for hard-to-find items and arranging for exotic services such as hot-air balloon rides. Arrange for the replacement of items lost by travelers. Arrange for interpreters or translators when patrons require such services. Plan special events, parties, and meetings, which may include booking musicians or celebrities to appear.

Personality Type: Social. These occupations frequently involve working with, communicating with, and teaching people and often involve helping or providing service to others.

GOE—Interest Area/Cluster: 09. Hospitality, Tourism, and Recreation. **Work Group:** 09.03. Hospitality and Travel Services. **Other Jobs in This Work Group:** Baggage Porters and Bellhops; Flight Attendants; Hotel, Motel, and Resort Desk Clerks; Janitors and Cleaners, Except Maids and Housekeeping Cleaners; Maids and Housekeeping Cleaners; Reservation and Transportation Ticket Agents and Travel Clerks; Tour Guides and Escorts; Transportation Attendants, Except Flight Attendants and Baggage Porters; Travel Agents; Travel Guides.

Skills—Service Orientation: Actively looking for ways to help people. **Social Perceptiveness:** Being aware of others' reactions and understanding why they react the way they do. **Management of Personnel Resources:** Motivating, developing, and directing people as they work; identifying the best people for the job. **Critical Thinking:** Using logic and analysis to identify the strengths and weaknesses of different approaches.

Education and Training Programs: No related CIP programs; this job is learned through informal moderate-term on-the-job training. **Related Knowledge/Courses—Customer and Personal Service:** Principles and processes for providing customer and personal services, including needs assessment techniques, quality service standards, alternative delivery systems, and customer satisfaction evaluation techniques. **Philosophy and Theology:** Different philosophical systems and religions, including their basic principles, values, ethics, ways of thinking, customs, and practices and

their impact on human culture. **Clerical Practices:** Administrative and clerical procedures and systems such as word-processing systems, filing and records management systems, stenography and transcription, forms, design principles, and other office procedures and terminology. **Communications and Media:** Media production, communication, and dissemination techniques and methods, including alternative ways to inform and entertain via written, oral, and visual media. **Psychology:** Human behavior and performance, mental processes, psychological research methods, and the assessment and treatment of behavioral and affective disorders. **Public Safety and Security:** Weaponry; public safety; security operations, rules, regulations, precautions, and prevention; and the protection of people, data, and property.

Work Environment: Indoors; noisy; standing; repetitive motions.

Construction and Building Inspectors

- ❋ Education/Training Required: Work experience in a related occupation
- ❋ Annual Earnings: $48,330
- ❋ Beginning Wage: $30,450
- ❋ Earnings Growth Potential: Medium
- ❋ Growth: 18.2%
- ❋ Annual Job Openings: 12,606
- ❋ Self-Employed: 9.4%
- ❋ Part-Time: 4.6%

Inspect structures, using engineering skills to determine structural soundness and compliance with specifications, building codes, and other regulations. Inspections may be general in nature or may be limited to a specific area, such as electrical systems or plumbing. Issue violation notices and stop-work orders, conferring with owners, violators, and authorities to explain regulations and recommend rectifications. Inspect bridges, dams, highways, buildings, wiring, plumbing, electrical circuits, sewers, heating systems, and foundations during and after construction for structural quality, general safety, and conformance to specifications and codes. Approve and sign plans that meet required specifications. Review and interpret plans, blueprints, site layouts, specifications, and construction methods to ensure compliance to legal requirements and safety regulations. Monitor installation of plumbing, wiring, equipment, and appliances to ensure that installation is performed properly and is in compliance with applicable regulations. Inspect and monitor construction sites to ensure adherence to safety standards, building codes, and specifications. Measure dimensions and verify level, alignment, and elevation of structures and fixtures to ensure compliance to building plans and codes. Maintain daily logs and supplement inspection records with photographs. Use survey instruments, metering devices, tape measures, and test equipment such as concrete strength measurers to perform inspections. Train, direct, and supervise other construction inspectors. Issue permits for construction, relocation, demolition, and occupancy. Examine lifting and conveying devices such as elevators, escalators, moving sidewalks, lifts and hoists, inclined railways, ski lifts, and amusement rides to ensure safety and proper functioning. Compute estimates of work completed or of needed renovations or upgrades and approve payment for contractors. Evaluate premises for cleanliness, including proper garbage disposal and lack of vermin infestation.

Personality Type: Realistic. These occupations frequently involve work activities that include practical, hands-on problems and solutions. They often deal with plants; animals; and real-world materials such as wood, tools, and machinery. Many of the occupations require working outside and don't involve a lot of paperwork or working closely with others.

GOE—Interest Area/Cluster: 07. Government and Public Administration. **Work Group:** 07.03. Regulations Enforcement. **Other Jobs in This Work Group:** Agricultural Inspectors; Aviation Inspectors; Compliance Officers, Except Agriculture, Construction, Health and Safety, and Transportation; Environmental Compliance Inspectors; Equal Opportunity Representatives and Officers; Financial Examiners; Fire Inspectors; Fish and Game Wardens; Forest Fire Inspectors and Prevention Specialists; Freight and Cargo Inspectors; Government Property Inspectors and Investigators; Immigration and Customs Inspectors; Licensing Examiners and Inspectors; Nuclear Monitoring Technicians; Occupational Health and Safety Specialists; Occupational Health and Safety Technicians; Tax Examiners, Collectors, and Revenue Agents; Transportation Vehicle, Equipment, and Systems Inspectors, Except Aviation.

Skills—Quality Control Analysis: Evaluating the quality or performance of products, services, or processes. **Systems Analysis:** Determining how a system should work and how changes will affect outcomes. **Systems Evaluation:** Looking at many indicators of system performance and taking into account their accuracy. **Management of Personnel Resources:** Motivating, developing, and directing people as they work; identifying the best people for the job.

Operation Monitoring: Watching gauges, dials, or other indicators to make sure a machine is working properly.

Education and Training Program: Building/Home/Construction Inspection/Inspector Training. **Related Knowledge/Courses—Building and Construction:** Materials, methods, and the appropriate tools to construct objects, structures, and buildings. **Engineering and Technology:** Equipment, tools, and mechanical devices and their uses to produce motion, light, power, technology, and other applications. **Design:** Design techniques, principles, tools, and instruments involved in the production and use of precision technical plans, blueprints, drawings, and models. **Physics:** Physical principles, laws, and applications, including air, water, material dynamics, light, atomic principles, heat, electric theory, earth formations, and meteorological and related natural phenomena. **Public Safety and Security:** Weaponry; public safety; security operations, rules, regulations, precautions, and prevention; and the protection of people, data, and property. **Mechanical Devices:** Machines and tools, including their designs, uses, benefits, repair, and maintenance.

Work Environment: More often outdoors than indoors; very hot or cold; very bright or dim lighting; contaminants; cramped work space, awkward positions.

Construction Carpenters

- ❀ Education/Training Required: Long-term on-the-job training
- ❀ Annual Earnings: $37,660
- ❀ Beginning Wage: $23,370
- ❀ Earnings Growth Potential: Medium
- ❀ Growth: 10.3%
- ❀ Annual Job Openings: 223,225
- ❀ Self-Employed: 31.8%
- ❀ Part-Time: 6.1%

The job openings listed here are shared with Rough Carpenters.

Construct, erect, install, and repair structures and fixtures of wood, plywood, and wallboard, using carpenter's hand tools and power tools. Measure and mark cutting lines on materials, using ruler, pencil, chalk, and marking gauge. Follow established safety rules and regulations and maintain a safe and clean environment. Verify trueness of structure, using plumb bob and level. Shape or cut materials to specified measurements, using hand tools, machines, or power saw. Study specifications in blueprints, sketches, or building plans to prepare project layout and determine dimensions and materials required. Assemble and fasten materials to make framework or props, using hand tools and wood screws, nails, dowel pins, or glue. Build or repair cabinets, doors, frameworks, floors, and other wooden fixtures used in buildings, using woodworking machines, carpenter's hand tools, and power tools. Erect scaffolding and ladders for assembling structures above ground level. Remove damaged or defective parts or sections of structures and repair or replace, using hand tools. Install structures and fixtures, such as windows, frames, floorings, and trim, or hardware, using carpenter's hand and power tools. Select and order lumber and other required materials. Maintain records, document actions, and present written progress reports. Finish surfaces of woodwork or wallboard in houses and buildings, using paint, hand tools, and paneling. Prepare cost estimates for clients or employers. Arrange for subcontractors to deal with special areas such as heating and electrical wiring work. Inspect ceiling or floor tile, wall coverings, siding, glass, or woodwork to detect broken or damaged structures. Work with or remove hazardous material. Construct forms and chutes for pouring concrete. Cover subfloors with building paper to keep out moisture and lay hardwood, parquet, and wood-strip-block floors by nailing floors to subfloor or cementing them to mastic or asphalt base. Fill cracks and other defects in plaster or plasterboard and sand patch, using patching plaster, trowel, and sanding tool. Perform minor plumbing, welding, or concrete mixing work. Apply shock-absorbing, sound-deadening, and decorative paneling to ceilings and walls.

Personality Type: Realistic. These occupations frequently involve work activities that include practical, hands-on problems and solutions. They often deal with plants; animals; and real-world materials such as wood, tools, and machinery. Many of the occupations require working outside and don't involve a lot of paperwork or working closely with others.

GOE—Interest Area/Cluster: 02. Architecture and Construction. **Work Group:** 02.04. Construction Crafts. **Other Jobs in This Work Group:** Boilermakers; Brickmasons and Blockmasons; Carpet Installers; Cement Masons and Concrete Finishers; Commercial Divers; Crane and Tower Operators; Drywall and Ceiling Tile Installers; Electricians; Fence Erectors; Floor Layers, Except Carpet, Wood, and Hard Tiles; Floor Sanders and Finishers; Glaziers; Hazardous Materials Removal Workers; Insulation Workers, Floor, Ceiling, and Wall; Insulation Workers, Mechanical; Manufactured Building and Mobile Home Installers; Operating

Engineers and Other Construction Equipment Operators; Painters, Construction and Maintenance; Paperhangers; Paving, Surfacing, and Tamping Equipment Operators; Pile-Driver Operators; Pipe Fitters and Steamfitters; Pipelayers; Plasterers and Stucco Masons; Plumbers; Plumbers, Pipefitters, and Steamfitters; Rail-Track Laying and Maintenance Equipment Operators; Refractory Materials Repairers, Except Brickmasons; Reinforcing Iron and Rebar Workers; Riggers; Roofers; Rough Carpenters; Security and Fire Alarm Systems Installers; Segmental Pavers; Sheet Metal Workers; Stone Cutters and Carvers, Manufacturing; Stonemasons; Structural Iron and Steel Workers; Tapers; Terrazzo Workers and Finishers; Tile and Marble Setters.

Skills—Management of Personnel Resources: Motivating, developing, and directing people as they work; identifying the best people for the job. **Management of Material Resources:** Obtaining and seeing to the appropriate use of equipment, facilities, and materials needed to do certain work. **Management of Financial Resources:** Determining how money will be spent to get the work done and accounting for these expenditures. **Repairing:** Repairing machines or systems, using the needed tools. **Equipment Maintenance:** Performing routine maintenance and determining when and what kind of maintenance is needed. **Quality Control Analysis:** Evaluating the quality or performance of products, services, or processes. **Installation:** Installing equipment, machines, wiring, or programs to meet specifications. **Mathematics:** Using mathematics to solve problems.

Education and Training Program: Carpentry/Carpenter Training. **Related Knowledge/Courses—Building and Construction:** Materials, methods, and the appropriate tools to construct objects, structures, and buildings. **Mechanical Devices:** Machines and tools, including their designs, uses, benefits, repair, and maintenance. **Design:** Design techniques, principles, tools, and instruments involved in the production and use of precision technical plans, blueprints, drawings, and models. **Engineering and Technology:** Equipment, tools, and mechanical devices and their uses to produce motion, light, power, technology, and other applications. **Production and Processing:** Inputs, outputs, raw materials, waste, quality control, costs, and techniques for maximizing the manufacture and distribution of goods. **Public Safety and Security:** Weaponry; public safety; security operations, rules, regulations, precautions, and prevention; and the protection of people, data, and property.

Work Environment: Outdoors; noisy; hazardous equipment; standing; walking and running; using hands on objects, tools, or controls.

Construction Laborers

- ❋ Education/Training Required: Moderate-term on-the-job training
- ❋ Annual Earnings: $27,310
- ❋ Beginning Wage: $17,410
- ❋ Earnings Growth Potential: Medium
- ❋ Growth: 10.9%
- ❋ Annual Job Openings: 257,407
- ❋ Self-Employed: 16.4%
- ❋ Part-Time: 8.7%

Perform tasks involving physical labor at building, highway, and heavy construction projects; tunnel and shaft excavations; and demolition sites. May operate hand and power tools of all types: air hammers, earth tampers, cement mixers, small mechanical hoists, surveying and measuring equipment, and a variety of other equipment and instruments. May clean and prepare sites; dig trenches; set braces to support the sides of excavations; erect scaffolding; clean up rubble and debris; and remove asbestos, lead, and other hazardous waste materials. May assist other craft workers. Clean and prepare construction sites to eliminate possible hazards. Read and interpret plans, instructions, and specifications to determine work activities. Control traffic passing near, in, and around work zones. Signal equipment operators to facilitate alignment, movement, and adjustment of machinery, equipment, and materials. Dig ditches or trenches, backfill excavations, and compact and level earth to grade specifications, using picks, shovels, pneumatic tampers, and rakes. Measure, mark, and record openings and distances to lay out areas where construction work will be performed. Position, join, align, and seal structural components such as concrete wall sections and pipes. Load, unload, and identify building materials, machinery, and tools and distribute them to the appropriate locations according to project plans and specifications. Erect and disassemble scaffolding, shoring, braces, traffic barricades, ramps, and other temporary structures. Build and position forms for pouring concrete and dismantle forms after use, using saws, hammers, nails, or bolts. Lubricate, clean, and repair machinery, equipment, and tools. Operate jackhammers and drills to break up concrete or pavement. Smooth and finish freshly poured cement or concrete, using floats, trowels, screeds, or powered cement-finishing tools. Operate, read, and maintain air monitoring and other sampling devices in confined and/or hazardous environments. Install sewer, water, and storm drain pipes, using pipe-laying machinery and laser guidance equipment. Transport and set

explosives for tunnel, shaft, and road construction. Provide assistance to craft workers such as carpenters, plasterers, and masons. Tend pumps, compressors, and generators to provide power for tools, machinery, and equipment or to heat and move materials such as asphalt. Mop, brush, or spread paints, cleaning solutions, or other compounds over surfaces to clean them or to provide protection. Place, consolidate, and protect case-in-place concrete or masonry structures. Identify, pack, and transport hazardous and/or radioactive materials. Use computers and other input devices to control robotic pipe cutters and cleaners.

Personality Type: Realistic. These occupations frequently involve work activities that include practical, hands-on problems and solutions. They often deal with plants; animals; and real-world materials such as wood, tools, and machinery. Many of the occupations require working outside and don't involve a lot of paperwork or working closely with others.

GOE—Interest Area/Cluster: 02. Architecture and Construction. **Work Group:** 02.06. Construction Support/Labor. **Other Jobs in This Work Group:** Helpers—Brickmasons, Blockmasons, Stonemasons, and Tile and Marble Setters; Helpers—Carpenters; Helpers—Electricians; Helpers—Installation, Maintenance, and Repair Workers; Helpers—Painters, Paperhangers, Plasterers, and Stucco Masons; Helpers—Pipelayers, Plumbers, Pipefitters, and Steamfitters; Helpers—Roofers; Highway Maintenance Workers; Septic Tank Servicers and Sewer Pipe Cleaners.

Skills—Equipment Maintenance: Performing routine maintenance and determining when and what kind of maintenance is needed. **Repairing:** Repairing machines or systems, using the needed tools. **Equipment Selection:** Determining the kind of tools and equipment needed to do a job. **Installation:** Installing equipment, machines, wiring, or programs to meet specifications.

Education and Training Program: Construction Trades, Other. **Related Knowledge/Courses—Building and Construction:** Materials, methods, and the appropriate tools to construct objects, structures, and buildings. **Design:** Design techniques, principles, tools, and instruments involved in the production and use of precision technical plans, blueprints, drawings, and models. **Mechanical Devices:** Machines and tools, including their designs, uses, benefits, repair, and maintenance. **Transportation:** Principles and methods for moving people or goods by air, rail, sea, or road, including their relative costs, advantages, and limitations. **Engineering and Technology:** Equipment, tools, and mechanical devices and their uses to produce motion, light, power, technology, and other applications. **Public Safety and Security:** Weaponry; public safety; security operations, rules, regulations, precautions, and prevention; and the protection of people, data, and property.

Work Environment: Outdoors; noisy; very hot or cold; contaminants; standing; using hands on objects, tools, or controls.

Construction Managers

- ❀ Education/Training Required: Bachelor's degree
- ❀ Annual Earnings: $76,230
- ❀ Beginning Wage: $44,630
- ❀ Earnings Growth Potential: High
- ❀ Growth: 15.7%
- ❀ Annual Job Openings: 44,158
- ❀ Self-Employed: 56.3%
- ❀ Part-Time: 4.9%

Plan, direct, coordinate, or budget, usually through subordinate supervisory personnel, activities concerned with the construction and maintenance of structures, facilities, and systems. Participate in the conceptual development of a construction project and oversee its organization, scheduling, and implementation. Schedule the project in logical steps and budget time required to meet deadlines. Confer with supervisory personnel, owners, contractors, and design professionals to discuss and resolve matters such as work procedures, complaints, and construction problems. Prepare contracts and negotiate revisions, changes, and additions to contractual agreements with architects, consultants, clients, suppliers, and subcontractors. Prepare and submit budget estimates and progress and cost tracking reports. Interpret and explain plans and contract terms to administrative staff, workers, and clients, representing the owner or developer. Plan, organize, and direct activities concerned with the construction and maintenance of structures, facilities, and systems. Take actions to deal with the results of delays, bad weather, or emergencies at construction sites. Inspect and review projects to monitor compliance with building and safety codes and other regulations. Study job specifications to determine appropriate construction methods. Select, contract, and oversee workers who complete specific pieces of the project such as painting or plumbing. Obtain all necessary permits and licenses. Direct and supervise workers. Develop and implement quality

control programs. Investigate damage, accidents, or delays at construction sites to ensure that proper procedures are being carried out. Determine labor requirements and dispatch workers to construction sites. Evaluate construction methods and determine cost-effectiveness of plans, using computers. Requisition supplies and materials to complete construction projects. Direct acquisition of land for construction projects.

Personality Type: Enterprising. These occupations frequently involve starting up and carrying out projects and can involve leading people and making many decisions. They sometimes require risk taking and often deal with business.

GOE—Interest Area/Cluster: 02. Architecture and Construction. **Work Group:** 02.01. Managerial Work in Architecture and Construction. **Other Jobs in This Work Group:** No other jobs in this group.

Skills—Management of Financial Resources: Determining how money will be spent to get the work done and accounting for these expenditures. **Management of Material Resources:** Obtaining and seeing to the appropriate use of equipment, facilities, and materials needed to do certain work. **Management of Personnel Resources:** Motivating, developing, and directing people as they work; identifying the best people for the job. **Systems Analysis:** Determining how a system should work and how changes will affect outcomes. **Systems Evaluation:** Looking at many indicators of system performance and taking into account their accuracy. **Negotiation:** Bringing others together and trying to reconcile differences. **Persuasion:** Persuading others to approach things differently. **Monitoring:** Assessing how well one is doing when learning or doing something.

Education and Training Programs: Business Administration and Management, General; Business/Commerce, General; Construction Engineering Technology/Technician Training; Construction Management; Operations Management and Supervision. **Related Knowledge/Courses—Building and Construction:** Materials, methods, and the appropriate tools to construct objects, structures, and buildings. **Design:** Design techniques, principles, tools, and instruments involved in the production and use of precision technical plans, blueprints, drawings, and models. **Engineering and Technology:** Equipment, tools, and mechanical devices and their uses to produce motion, light, power, technology, and other applications. **Mechanical Devices:** Machines and tools, including their designs, uses, benefits, repair, and maintenance. **Administration and**

C

Management: Principles and processes involved in business and organizational planning, coordination, and execution. This includes strategic planning, resource allocation, manpower modeling, leadership techniques, and production methods. **Personnel and Human Resources:** Principles and procedures for personnel recruitment; selection; training; compensation and benefits; labor relations and negotiation; and personnel information systems.

Work Environment: More often outdoors than indoors; noisy; contaminants; hazardous equipment; sitting.

Cooks, Institution and Cafeteria

- ❈ Education/Training Required: Moderate-term on-the-job training
- ❈ Annual Earnings: $21,340
- ❈ Beginning Wage: $14,300
- ❈ Earnings Growth Potential: Low
- ❈ Growth: 10.8%
- ❈ Annual Job Openings: 111,898
- ❈ Self-Employed: 1.4%
- ❈ Part-Time: 29.9%

Prepare and cook large quantities of food for institutions, such as schools, hospitals, or cafeterias. Clean and inspect galley equipment, kitchen appliances, and work areas to ensure cleanliness and functional operation. Apportion and serve food to facility residents, employees, or patrons. Cook foodstuffs according to menus, special dietary or nutritional restrictions, and numbers of portions to be served. Clean, cut, and cook meat, fish, and poultry. Monitor use of government food commodities to ensure that proper procedures are followed. Wash pots, pans, dishes, utensils, and other cooking equipment. Compile and maintain records of food use and expenditures. Direct activities of one or more workers who assist in preparing and serving meals. Bake breads, rolls, and other pastries. Train new employees. Take inventory of supplies and equipment. Monitor menus and spending to ensure that meals are prepared economically. Plan menus that are varied, nutritionally balanced, and appetizing, taking advantage of foods in season and local availability. Requisition food supplies, kitchen equipment, and appliances based on estimates of future needs. Determine meal prices based on calculations of ingredient prices.

Personality Type: Realistic. These occupations frequently involve work activities that include practical, hands-on problems and solutions. They often deal with plants;

animals; and real-world materials such as wood, tools, and machinery. Many of the occupations require working outside and don't involve a lot of paperwork or working closely with others.

GOE—Interest Area/Cluster: 09. Hospitality, Tourism, and Recreation. **Work Group:** 09.04. Food and Beverage Preparation. **Other Jobs in This Work Group:** Butchers and Meat Cutters; Chefs and Head Cooks; Cooks, Fast Food; Cooks, Private Household; Cooks, Restaurant; Cooks, Short Order; Dishwashers; Food Preparation Workers.

Skills—Equipment Selection: Determining the kind of tools and equipment needed to do a job. **Instructing:** Teaching others how to do something. **Service Orientation:** Actively looking for ways to help people.

Education and Training Programs: Cooking and Related Culinary Arts, General; Culinary Arts and Related Services, Other; Food Preparation/Professional Cooking/Kitchen Assistant Training; Foodservice Systems Administration/Management; Institutional Food Worker Training. **Related Knowledge/Courses—Food Production:** Techniques and equipment for planting, growing, and harvesting of food for consumption, including crop-rotation methods, animal husbandry, and food storage/handling techniques. **Public Safety and Security:** Weaponry; public safety; security operations, rules, regulations, precautions, and prevention; and the protection of people, data, and property.

Work Environment: Indoors; very hot or cold; minor burns, cuts, bites, or stings; standing; walking and running; repetitive motions.

Cooks, Restaurant

- ❈ Education/Training Required: Long-term on-the-job training
- ❈ Annual Earnings: $21,220
- ❈ Beginning Wage: $15,120
- ❈ Earnings Growth Potential: Low
- ❈ Growth: 11.5%
- ❈ Annual Job Openings: 238,542
- ❈ Self-Employed: 1.2%
- ❈ Part-Time: 29.9%

Prepare, season, and cook soups, meats, vegetables, desserts, or other foodstuffs in restaurants. May order supplies, keep records and accounts, price items on menu, or plan menu. Inspect food preparation and serving areas to ensure observance of safe, sanitary food-handling practices. Turn or stir foods to ensure even cooking. Season and cook food according to recipes or personal judgment and experience. Observe and test foods to determine if they have been cooked sufficiently, using methods such as tasting them, smelling them, or piercing them with utensils. Weigh, measure, and mix ingredients according to recipes or personal judgment, using various kitchen utensils and equipment. Portion, arrange, and garnish food and serve food to waiters or patrons. Regulate temperature of ovens, broilers, grills, and roasters. Substitute for or assist other cooks during emergencies or rush periods. Bake, roast, broil, and steam meats, fish, vegetables, and other foods. Wash, peel, cut, and seed fruits and vegetables to prepare them for consumption. Estimate expected food consumption, requisition or purchase supplies, or procure food from storage. Carve and trim meats such as beef, veal, ham, pork, and lamb for hot or cold service or for sandwiches. Coordinate and supervise work of kitchen staff. Consult with supervisory staff to plan menus, taking into consideration factors such as costs and special event needs. Butcher and dress animals, fowl, or shellfish or cut and bone meat prior to cooking. Prepare relishes and hors d'oeuvres. Bake breads, rolls, cakes, and pastries. Keep records and accounts. Plan and price menu items.

Personality Type: Realistic. These occupations frequently involve work activities that include practical, hands-on problems and solutions. They often deal with plants; animals; and real-world materials such as wood, tools, and machinery. Many of the occupations require working outside and don't involve a lot of paperwork or working closely with others.

GOE—Interest Area/Cluster: 09. Hospitality, Tourism, and Recreation. **Work Group:** 09.04. Food and Beverage Preparation. **Other Jobs in This Work Group:** Butchers and Meat Cutters; Chefs and Head Cooks; Cooks, Fast Food; Cooks, Institution and Cafeteria; Cooks, Private Household; Cooks, Short Order; Dishwashers; Food Preparation Workers.

Skill—Equipment Maintenance: Performing routine maintenance and determining when and what kind of maintenance is needed.

Education and Training Programs: Cooking and Related Culinary Arts, General; Culinary Arts/Chef Training. **Related Knowledge/Courses—Food Production:** Techniques and equipment for planting, growing, and harvesting of food for consumption, including crop-rotation methods,

animal husbandry, and food storage/handling techniques. **Production and Processing:** Inputs, outputs, raw materials, waste, quality control, costs, and techniques for maximizing the manufacture and distribution of goods.

Work Environment: Indoors; very hot or cold; minor burns, cuts, bites, or stings; standing; using hands on objects, tools, or controls; repetitive motions.

Copy Writers

- ❋ Education/Training Required: Bachelor's degree
- ❋ Annual Earnings: $50,660
- ❋ Beginning Wage: $26,530
- ❋ Earnings Growth Potential: High
- ❋ Growth: 12.8%
- ❋ Annual Job Openings: 24,023
- ❋ Self-Employed: 65.9%
- ❋ Part-Time: 21.8%

The job openings listed here are shared with Poets, Lyricists, and Creative Writers.

Write advertising copy for use by publication or broadcast media to promote sale of goods and services. Write advertising copy for use by publication, broadcast, or Internet media to promote the sale of goods and services. Present drafts and ideas to clients. Discuss with the client the product, advertising themes and methods, and any changes that should be made in advertising copy. Consult with sales, media, and marketing representatives to obtain information on product or service and discuss style and length of advertising copy. Vary language and tone of messages based on product and medium. Edit or rewrite existing copy as necessary and submit copy for approval by supervisor. Write to customers in their terms and on their level so that the advertiser's sales message is more readily received. Write articles; bulletins; sales letters; speeches; and other related informative, marketing, and promotional material. Invent names for products and write the slogans that appear on packaging, brochures, and other promotional material. Review advertising trends, consumer surveys, and other data regarding marketing of goods and services to determine the best way to promote products. Develop advertising campaigns for a wide range of clients, working with an advertising agency's creative director and art director to determine the best way to present advertising information. Conduct research and interviews to determine which of a product's selling features should be promoted.

Personality Type: Enterprising. These occupations frequently involve starting up and carrying out projects and can involve leading people and making many decisions. They sometimes require risk taking and often deal with business.

GOE—Interest Area/Cluster: 03. Arts and Communication. **Work Group:** 03.02. Writing and Editing. **Other Jobs in This Work Group:** Editors; Poets, Lyricists, and Creative Writers; Technical Writers; Writers and Authors.

Skills—Persuasion: Persuading others to approach things differently. **Technology Design:** Generating or adapting equipment and technology to serve user needs. **Equipment Selection:** Determining the kind of tools and equipment needed to do a job. **Quality Control Analysis:** Evaluating the quality or performance of products, services, or processes. **Time Management:** Managing one's own time and the time of others. **Writing:** Communicating effectively with others in writing as indicated by the needs of the audience. **Active Listening:** Listening to what other people are saying and asking questions as appropriate. **Negotiation:** Bringing others together and trying to reconcile differences.

Education and Training Programs: Broadcast Journalism; Communication Studies/Speech Communication and Rhetoric; Communication, Journalism, and Related Programs, Other; English Composition; Journalism; Mass Communication/Media Studies. **Related Knowledge/Courses—Communications and Media:** Media production, communication, and dissemination techniques and methods, including alternative ways to inform and entertain via written, oral, and visual media. **Sales and Marketing:** Principles and methods involved in showing, promoting, and selling products or services. This includes marketing strategies and tactics, product demonstration and sales techniques, and sales control systems. **Sociology and Anthropology:** Group behavior and dynamics; societal trends and influences; and cultures and their history, migrations, ethnicity, and origins. **English Language:** The structure and content of the English language, including the meaning and spelling of words, rules of composition, and grammar. **Computers and Electronics:** Electric circuit boards, processors, chips, and computer hardware and software, including applications and programming. **Psychology:** Human behavior and performance, mental processes, psychological research methods, and the assessment and treatment of behavioral and affective disorders.

Work Environment: Indoors; sitting; using hands on objects, tools, or controls; repetitive motions.

Coroners

- ❋ Education/Training Required: Work experience in a related occupation
- ❋ Annual Earnings: $48,400
- ❋ Beginning Wage: $28,980
- ❋ Earnings Growth Potential: High
- ❋ Growth: 4.9%
- ❋ Annual Job Openings: 15,841
- ❋ Self-Employed: 0.4%
- ❋ Part-Time: 5.0%

The job openings listed here are shared with Environmental Compliance Inspectors; Equal Opportunity Representatives and Officers; Government Property Inspectors and Investigators; and Licensing Examiners and Inspectors.

Direct activities such as autopsies, pathological and toxicological analyses, and inquests relating to the investigation of deaths occurring within a legal jurisdiction to determine cause of death or to fix responsibility for accidental, violent, or unexplained deaths. Perform medicolegal examinations and autopsies, conducting preliminary examinations of the body in order to identify victims, to locate signs of trauma, and to identify factors that would indicate time of death. Inquire into the cause, manner, and circumstances of human deaths and establish the identities of deceased persons. Direct activities of workers who conduct autopsies, perform pathological and toxicological analyses, and prepare documents for permanent records. Complete death certificates, including the assignment of a cause and manner of death. Observe and record the positions and conditions of bodies and of related evidence. Collect and document any pertinent medical history information. Observe, record, and preserve any objects or personal property related to deaths, including objects such as medication containers and suicide notes. Complete reports and forms required to finalize cases. Remove or supervise removal of bodies from death scenes, using the proper equipment and supplies, and arrange for transportation to morgues. Testify at inquests, hearings, and court trials. Interview persons present at death scenes to obtain information useful in determining the manner of death. Provide information concerning the circumstances of death to relatives of the deceased. Locate and document information regarding the next of kin, including their relationship to the deceased and the status of notification attempts. Confer with officials of public health and law enforcement agencies in order to coordinate interdepartmental activities. Inventory personal effects, such as jewelry or wallets, that are recovered from bodies. Coordinate the release of personal effects to authorized persons and facilitate the disposition of unclaimed corpses and personal effects. Arrange for the next of kin to be notified of deaths. Record the disposition of minor children, as well as details of arrangements made for their care. Collect wills, burial instructions, and other documentation needed for investigations and for handling of the remains. Witness and certify deaths that are the result of a judicial order.

Personality Type: Investigative. These occupations frequently involve working with ideas and require an extensive amount of thinking. They can involve searching for facts and figuring out problems mentally.

GOE—Interest Area/Cluster: 08. Health Science. **Work Group:** 08.01. Managerial Work in Medical and Health Services. **Other Jobs in This Work Group:** Medical and Health Services Managers.

Skills—Science: Using scientific methods to solve problems. **Management of Financial Resources:** Determining how money will be spent to get the work done and accounting for these expenditures. **Reading Comprehension:** Understanding written sentences and paragraphs in work-related documents. **Critical Thinking:** Using logic and analysis to identify the strengths and weaknesses of different approaches. **Management of Personnel Resources:** Motivating, developing, and directing people as they work; identifying the best people for the job. **Speaking:** Talking to others to effectively convey information. **Management of Material Resources:** Obtaining and seeing to the appropriate use of equipment, facilities, and materials needed to do certain work. **Writing:** Communicating effectively with others in writing as indicated by the needs of the audience.

Education and Training Program: Public Administration. **Related Knowledge/Courses—Medicine and Dentistry:** The information and techniques needed to diagnose and treat injuries, diseases, and deformities. This includes symptoms, treatment alternatives, drug properties and interactions, and preventive health-care measures. **Biology:** Plant and animal living tissue, cells, organisms, and entities, including their functions, interdependencies, and interactions with each other and the environment. **Psychology:** Human behavior and performance, mental processes, psychological research methods, and the assessment and treatment of behavioral and affective disorders. **Therapy and Counseling:** Information and techniques needed to rehabilitate physical and mental ailments and to provide career guidance, including alternative treatments, rehabilitation equipment and its proper use, and methods to evaluate

treatment effects. **Chemistry:** The composition, structure, and properties of substances and of the chemical processes and transformations that they undergo. This includes uses of chemicals and their interactions, danger signs, production techniques, and disposal methods. **Law and Government:** Laws, legal codes, court procedures, precedents, government regulations, executive orders, agency rules, and the democratic political process.

Work Environment: More often indoors than outdoors; contaminants; disease or infections; hazardous equipment; using hands on objects, tools, or controls.

Correctional Officers and Jailers

- ❋ Education/Training Required: Moderate-term on-the-job training
- ❋ Annual Earnings: $36,970
- ❋ Beginning Wage: $24,820
- ❋ Earnings Growth Potential: Low
- ❋ Growth: 16.9%
- ❋ Annual Job Openings: 56,579
- ❋ Self-Employed: 0.0%
- ❋ Part-Time: 1.8%

Guard inmates in penal or rehabilitative institution in accordance with established regulations and procedures. May guard prisoners in transit between jail, courtroom, prison, or other point. Includes deputy sheriffs and police who spend the majority of their time guarding prisoners in correctional institutions. Conduct head counts to ensure that each prisoner is present. Monitor conduct of prisoners in housing unit or during work or recreational activities according to established policies, regulations, and procedures to prevent escape or violence. Inspect conditions of locks, window bars, grills, doors, and gates at correctional facilities to ensure security and help prevent escapes. Record information such as prisoner identification, charges, and incidences of inmate disturbance and keep daily logs of prisoner activities. Search prisoners and vehicles and conduct shakedowns of cells for valuables and contraband such as weapons or drugs. Use weapons, handcuffs, and physical force to maintain discipline and order among prisoners. Guard facility entrances to screen visitors. Inspect mail for the presence of contraband. Maintain records of prisoners' identification and charges. Process or book convicted individuals into prison. Settle disputes between inmates. Conduct fire, safety, and sanitation inspections. Provide to supervisors oral and written reports of the quality and quantity of work performed by inmates, inmate disturbances and rule violations, and unusual occurrences. Participate in required job training. Take prisoners into custody and escort to locations within and outside of facility such as visiting room, courtroom, or airport. Serve meals, distribute commissary items, and dispense prescribed medication to prisoners. Counsel inmates and respond to legitimate questions, concerns, and requests. Drive passenger vehicles and trucks used to transport inmates to other institutions, courtrooms, hospitals, and work sites. Use nondisciplinary tools and equipment such as a computer. Assign duties to inmates, providing instructions as needed. Investigate crimes that have occurred within an institution or assist police in their investigations of crimes and inmates. Issue clothing, tools, and other authorized items to inmates. Arrange daily schedules for prisoners, including library visits, work assignments, family visits, and counseling appointments. Search for and recapture escapees.

Personality Type: Realistic. These occupations frequently involve work activities that include practical, hands-on problems and solutions. They often deal with plants; animals; and real-world materials such as wood, tools, and machinery. Many of the occupations require working outside and don't involve a lot of paperwork or working closely with others.

GOE—Interest Area/Cluster: 12. Law and Public Safety. **Work Group:** 12.04. Law Enforcement and Public Safety. **Other Jobs in This Work Group:** Bailiffs; Criminal Investigators and Special Agents; Detectives and Criminal Investigators; Fire Investigators; Forensic Science Technicians; Parking Enforcement Workers; Police and Sheriff's Patrol Officers; Police Detectives; Police Identification and Records Officers; Police Patrol Officers; Sheriffs and Deputy Sheriffs; Transit and Railroad Police.

Skill—None met the criteria.

Education and Training Programs: Corrections; Corrections and Criminal Justice, Other; Juvenile Corrections. **Related Knowledge/Courses—Public Safety and Security:** Weaponry; public safety; security operations, rules, regulations, precautions, and prevention; and the protection of people, data, and property. **Psychology:** Human behavior and performance, mental processes, psychological research methods, and the assessment and treatment of behavioral and affective disorders. **Therapy and Counseling:** Information and techniques needed to rehabilitate physical and mental ailments and to provide career guidance, including alternative treatments, rehabilitation equipment and

its proper use, and methods to evaluate treatment effects. **Law and Government:** Laws, legal codes, court procedures, precedents, government regulations, executive orders, agency rules, and the democratic political process. **Medicine and Dentistry:** The information and techniques needed to diagnose and treat injuries, diseases, and deformities. This includes symptoms, treatment alternatives, drug properties and interactions, and preventive health-care measures. **Sociology and Anthropology:** Group behavior and dynamics; societal trends and influences; and cultures and their history, migrations, ethnicity, and origins.

Work Environment: Indoors; noisy; disease or infections; standing; walking and running; using hands on objects, tools, or controls.

Correspondence Clerks

- ❋ Education/Training Required: Short-term on-the-job training
- ❋ Annual Earnings: $29,500
- ❋ Beginning Wage: $20,350
- ❋ Earnings Growth Potential: Low
- ❋ Growth: 12.0%
- ❋ Annual Job Openings: 4,334
- ❋ Self-Employed: 0.0%
- ❋ Part-Time: 12.4%

Compose letters in reply to requests for merchandise, damage claims, credit and other information, delinquent accounts, incorrect billings, or unsatisfactory services. Duties may include gathering data to formulate reply and typing correspondence. Prepare documents and correspondence such as damage claims, credit and billing inquiries, invoices, and service complaints. Compile data from records to prepare periodic reports. Present clear and concise explanations of governing rules and regulations. Read incoming correspondence to ascertain nature of writers' concerns and to determine disposition of correspondence. Type acknowledgment letters to persons sending correspondence. Review correspondence for format and typographical accuracy, assemble the information into a prescribed form with the correct number of copies, and submit it to an authorized official for signature. Maintain files and control records to show correspondence activities. Gather records pertinent to specific problems, review them for completeness and accuracy, and attach records to correspondence as necessary. Complete form letters in response to requests or problems identified by correspondence. Route correspondence to other departments for reply. Compose letters in reply to correspondence concerning such items as requests for merchandise, damage claims, credit information requests, delinquent accounts, incorrect billing, or unsatisfactory service. Ensure that money collected is properly recorded and secured. Respond to internal and external requests for the release of information contained in medical records, copying medical records, and selective extracts in accordance with laws and regulations. Compute costs of records furnished to requesters and write letters to obtain payment. Compose correspondence requesting medical information and records. Prepare records for shipment by certified mail. Obtain written authorization to access required medical information. Confer with company personnel regarding feasibility of complying with writers' requests. Submit completed documents to typists for typing in final form and instruct typists in matters such as format, addresses, addressees, and the necessary number of copies. Process orders for goods requested in correspondence. Compile data pertinent to manufacture of special products for customers.

Personality Type: Conventional. These occupations frequently involve following set procedures and routines and can include working with data and details more than with ideas. Usually there is a clear line of authority to follow.

GOE—Interest Area/Cluster: 04. Business and Administration. **Work Group:** 04.07. Records and Materials Processing. **Other Jobs in This Work Group:** File Clerks; Human Resources Assistants, Except Payroll and Timekeeping; Marking Clerks; Meter Readers, Utilities; Office Clerks, General; Order Fillers, Wholesale and Retail Sales; Postal Service Clerks; Postal Service Mail Sorters, Processors, and Processing Machine Operators; Procurement Clerks; Production, Planning, and Expediting Clerks; Shipping, Receiving, and Traffic Clerks; Stock Clerks and Order Fillers; Stock Clerks, Sales Floor; Stock Clerks—Stockroom, Warehouse, or Storage Yard; Weighers, Measurers, Checkers, and Samplers, Recordkeeping.

Skills—Writing: Communicating effectively with others in writing as indicated by the needs of the audience. **Reading Comprehension:** Understanding written sentences and paragraphs in work-related documents. **Instructing:** Teaching others how to do something. **Active Listening:** Listening to what other people are saying and asking questions as appropriate.

Education and Training Program: General Office Occupations and Clerical Services. **Related Knowledge/Courses— Clerical Practices:** Administrative and clerical procedures

and systems such as word-processing systems, filing and records management systems, stenography and transcription, forms, design principles, and other office procedures and terminology. **Economics and Accounting:** Economic and accounting principles and practices, the financial markets, banking, and the analysis and reporting of financial data. **Therapy and Counseling:** Information and techniques needed to rehabilitate physical and mental ailments and to provide career guidance, including alternative treatments, rehabilitation equipment and its proper use, and methods to evaluate treatment effects. **Medicine and Dentistry:** The information and techniques needed to diagnose and treat injuries, diseases, and deformities. This includes symptoms, treatment alternatives, drug properties and interactions, and preventive health-care measures. **Personnel and Human Resources:** Principles and procedures for personnel recruitment; selection; training; compensation and benefits; labor relations and negotiation; and personnel information systems. **Customer and Personal Service:** Principles and processes for providing customer and personal services, including needs assessment techniques, quality service standards, alternative delivery systems, and customer satisfaction evaluation techniques.

Work Environment: Indoors; sitting; repetitive motions.

Cost Estimators

- ❋ Education/Training Required: Bachelor's degree
- ❋ Annual Earnings: $54,920
- ❋ Beginning Wage: $32,470
- ❋ Earnings Growth Potential: High
- ❋ Growth: 18.5%
- ❋ Annual Job Openings: 38,379
- ❋ Self-Employed: 1.1%
- ❋ Part-Time: 5.8%

Prepare cost estimates for product manufacturing, construction projects, or services to aid management in bidding on or determining prices of products or services. May specialize according to particular service performed or type of product manufactured. Consult with clients, vendors, personnel in other departments, or construction foremen to discuss and formulate estimates and resolve issues. Analyze blueprints and other documentation to prepare time, cost, materials, and labor estimates. Prepare estimates for use in selecting vendors or subcontractors. Confer with engineers, architects, owners, contractors, and subcontractors on changes and adjustments to cost estimates. Prepare estimates used by management for purposes such as planning, organizing, and scheduling work. Prepare cost and expenditure statements and other necessary documentation at regular intervals for the duration of the project. Assess cost-effectiveness of products, projects, or services, tracking actual costs relative to bids as projects develop. Set up cost-monitoring and cost-reporting systems and procedures. Conduct special studies to develop and establish standard hour and related cost data or to effect cost reductions. Review material and labor requirements to decide whether it is more cost-effective to produce or purchase components. Prepare and maintain a directory of suppliers, contractors, and subcontractors. Establish and maintain tendering processes and conduct negotiations. Visit sites and record information about access, drainage and topography, and availability of services such as water and electricity.

Personality Type: Conventional. These occupations frequently involve following set procedures and routines and can include working with data and details more than with ideas. Usually there is a clear line of authority to follow.

GOE—Interest Area/Cluster: 06. Finance and Insurance. **Work Group:** 06.02. Finance/Insurance Investigation and Analysis. **Other Jobs in This Work Group:** Appraisers and Assessors of Real Estate; Appraisers, Real Estate; Assessors; Claims Adjusters, Examiners, and Investigators; Claims Examiners, Property and Casualty Insurance; Credit Analysts; Financial Analysts; Insurance Adjusters, Examiners, and Investigators; Insurance Appraisers, Auto Damage; Insurance Underwriters; Loan Counselors; Loan Officers; Market Research Analysts; Survey Researchers.

Skills—Systems Analysis: Determining how a system should work and how changes will affect outcomes. **Management of Financial Resources:** Determining how money will be spent to get the work done and accounting for these expenditures. **Mathematics:** Using mathematics to solve problems. **Systems Evaluation:** Looking at many indicators of system performance and taking into account their accuracy. **Writing:** Communicating effectively with others in writing as indicated by the needs of the audience. **Negotiation:** Bringing others together and trying to reconcile differences.

Education and Training Programs: Business Administration and Management, General; Business/Commerce, General; Construction Engineering; Construction Engineering Technology/Technician Training; Manufacturing Engineering; Materials Engineering; Mechanical Engineering.

Related Knowledge/Courses—Engineering and Technology: Equipment, tools, and mechanical devices and their uses to produce motion, light, power, technology, and other applications. **Mathematics:** Numbers and their operations and interrelationships, including arithmetic, algebra, geometry, calculus, and statistics and their applications. **Economics and Accounting:** Economic and accounting principles and practices, the financial markets, banking, and the analysis and reporting of financial data. **Building and Construction:** Materials, methods, and the appropriate tools to construct objects, structures, and buildings. **Design:** Design techniques, principles, tools, and instruments involved in the production and use of precision technical plans, blueprints, drawings, and models. **Computers and Electronics:** Electric circuit boards, processors, chips, and computer hardware and software, including applications and programming.

Work Environment: Indoors; sitting.

Counseling Psychologists

* Education/Training Required: Doctoral degree
* Annual Earnings: $62,210
* Beginning Wage: $37,300
* Earnings Growth Potential: High
* Growth: 15.8%
* Annual Job Openings: 8,309
* Self-Employed: 34.2%
* Part-Time: 24.0%

The job openings listed here are shared with Clinical Psychologists and with School Psychologists.

Assess and evaluate individuals' problems through the use of case history, interview, and observation and provide individual or group counseling services to assist individuals in achieving more effective personal, social, educational, and vocational development and adjustment. Collect information about individuals or clients, using interviews, case histories, observational techniques, and other assessment methods. Counsel individuals, groups, or families to help them understand problems, define goals, and develop realistic action plans. Develop therapeutic and treatment plans based on clients' interests, abilities, and needs. Consult with other professionals to discuss therapies, treatments, counseling resources, or techniques and to share occupational information. Analyze data such as interview notes, test results, and reference manuals in order to identify symptoms and to diagnose the nature of clients' problems. Advise clients on how they could be helped by counseling. Evaluate the results of counseling methods to determine the reliability and validity of treatments. Provide consulting services to schools, social service agencies, and businesses. Refer clients to specialists or to other institutions for non-counseling treatment of problems. Select, administer, and interpret psychological tests to assess intelligence, aptitudes, abilities, or interests. Conduct research to develop or improve diagnostic or therapeutic counseling techniques.

Personality Type: Social. These occupations frequently involve working with, communicating with, and teaching people and often involve helping or providing service to others.

GOE—Interest Area/Cluster: 10. Human Service. **Work Group:** 10.01. Counseling and Social Work. **Other Jobs in This Work Group:** Child, Family, and School Social Workers; Clinical Psychologists; Clinical, Counseling, and School Psychologists; Marriage and Family Therapists; Medical and Public Health Social Workers; Mental Health and Substance Abuse Social Workers; Mental Health Counselors; Probation Officers and Correctional Treatment Specialists; Rehabilitation Counselors; Residential Advisors; Social and Human Service Assistants; Substance Abuse and Behavioral Disorder Counselors.

Skills—Social Perceptiveness: Being aware of others' reactions and understanding why they react the way they do. **Active Listening:** Listening to what other people are saying and asking questions as appropriate. **Persuasion:** Persuading others to approach things differently. **Service Orientation:** Actively looking for ways to help people. **Coordination:** Adjusting actions in relation to others' actions. **Monitoring:** Assessing how well one is doing when learning or doing something. **Negotiation:** Bringing others together and trying to reconcile differences. **Learning Strategies:** Using multiple approaches when learning or teaching new things.

Education and Training Programs: Clinical Child Psychology; Clinical Psychology; Counseling Psychology; Developmental and Child Psychology; Psychoanalysis and Psychotherapy; Psychology, General; School Psychology. **Related Knowledge/Courses—Therapy and Counseling:** Information and techniques needed to rehabilitate physical and mental ailments and to provide career guidance, including alternative treatments, rehabilitation equipment and its proper use, and methods to evaluate treatment effects. **Philosophy and Theology:** Different philosophical systems and religions, including their basic principles, values, ethics, ways of thinking, customs, and practices and their impact on human culture. **Sociology and Anthropology:** Group behavior and dynamics; societal trends and influences; and cultures and their history, migrations, ethnicity, and origins. **Psychology:** Human behavior and performance, mental processes, psychological research methods, and the assessment and treatment of behavioral and affective disorders. **English Language:** The structure and content of the English language, including the meaning and spelling of words, rules of composition, and grammar. **Customer and Personal Service:** Principles and processes for providing customer and personal services, including needs assessment techniques, quality service standards, alternative delivery systems, and customer satisfaction evaluation techniques.

Work Environment: Indoors; sitting.

Court Clerks

- ✽ Education/Training Required: Short-term on-the-job training
- ✽ Annual Earnings: $32,330
- ✽ Beginning Wage: $21,050
- ✽ Earnings Growth Potential: Low
- ✽ Growth: 8.8%
- ✽ Annual Job Openings: 16,163
- ✽ Self-Employed: 2.7%
- ✽ Part-Time: 9.6%

The job openings listed here are shared with License Clerks and with Municipal Clerks.

Perform clerical duties in court of law; prepare docket of cases to be called; secure information for judges; and contact witnesses, attorneys, and litigants to obtain information for court. Prepare dockets or calendars of cases to be called, using typewriters or computers. Record case dispositions, court orders, and arrangements made for payment of court fees. Answer inquiries from the general public regarding judicial procedures, court appearances, trial dates, adjournments, outstanding warrants, summonses, subpoenas, witness fees, and payment of fines. Prepare and issue orders of the court, including probation orders, release documentation, sentencing information, and summonses. Prepare documents recording the outcomes of court proceedings. Instruct parties about timing of court appearances. Explain procedures or forms to parties in cases or to the general public. Search files and contact witnesses, attorneys, and litigants to obtain information for the court. Follow procedures to secure courtrooms and exhibits such as money, drugs, and weapons. Amend indictments when necessary and endorse indictments with pertinent information. Read charges and related information to the court and, if necessary, record defendants' pleas. Swear in jury members, interpreters, witnesses, and defendants. Collect court fees or fines and record amounts collected. Direct support staff in handling of paperwork processed by clerks' offices. Examine legal documents submitted to courts for adherence to laws or court procedures. Prepare and mark all applicable court exhibits and evidence. Record court proceedings, using recording equipment, or record minutes of court proceedings, using stenotype machines or shorthand. Prepare courtrooms with paper, pens, water, easels, and electronic equipment and ensure that recording equipment is working. Conduct roll calls and poll jurors. Meet with judges, lawyers, parole officers, police, and social agency officials to coordinate the functions of the court. Open courts, calling them to order and announcing judges.

Personality Type: Conventional. These occupations frequently involve following set procedures and routines and can include working with data and details more than with ideas. Usually there is a clear line of authority to follow.

GOE—Interest Area/Cluster: 07. Government and Public Administration. **Work Group:** 07.04. Public Administration Clerical Support. **Other Jobs in This Work Group:** Court Reporters; Court, Municipal, and License Clerks; License Clerks; Municipal Clerks.

Skills—Active Listening: Listening to what other people are saying and asking questions as appropriate. **Writing:** Communicating effectively with others in writing as indicated by the needs of the audience. **Instructing:** Teaching others how to do something. **Service Orientation:** Actively looking for ways to help people. **Coordination:** Adjusting actions in relation to others' actions.

Education and Training Program: General Office Occupations and Clerical Services. **Related Knowledge/Courses—Clerical Practices:** Administrative and clerical procedures and systems such as word-processing systems, filing and records management systems, stenography and transcription, forms, design principles, and other office procedures and terminology. **Law and Government:** Laws, legal codes, court procedures, precedents, government regulations, executive orders, agency rules, and the democratic political process. **Computers and Electronics:** Electric circuit boards, processors, chips, and computer hardware and software, including applications and programming.

Work Environment: Indoors; noisy; sitting; using hands on objects, tools, or controls; repetitive motions.

Court Reporters

* Education/Training Required: Postsecondary vocational training
* Annual Earnings: $45,330
* Beginning Wage: $23,810
* Earnings Growth Potential: High
* Growth: 24.5%
* Annual Job Openings: 2,620
* Self-Employed: 7.9%
* Part-Time: 13.6%

Use verbatim methods and equipment to capture, store, retrieve, and transcribe pretrial and trial proceedings or other information. Includes stenocaptioners who operate computerized stenographic captioning equipment to provide captions of live or prerecorded broadcasts for hearing-impaired viewers. Take notes in shorthand or use a stenotype or shorthand machine that prints letters on a paper tape. Provide transcripts of proceedings upon request of judges, lawyers, or the public. Record verbatim proceedings of courts, legislative assemblies, committee meetings, and other proceedings, using computerized recording equipment, electronic stenograph machines, or stenomasks. Transcribe recorded proceedings in accordance with established formats. Ask speakers to clarify inaudible statements. File a legible transcript of records of a court case with the court clerk's office. File and store shorthand notes of court session. Respond to requests during court sessions to read portions of the proceedings already recorded. Record depositions and other proceedings for attorneys. Verify accuracy of transcripts by checking copies against original records of proceedings and accuracy of rulings by checking with judges. Record symbols on computer discs or CD-ROM; then translate and display them as text in computer-aided transcription process.

Personality Type: Conventional. These occupations frequently involve following set procedures and routines and can include working with data and details more than with ideas. Usually there is a clear line of authority to follow.

GOE—Interest Area/Cluster: 07. Government and Public Administration. **Work Group:** 07.04. Public Administration Clerical Support. **Other Jobs in This Work Group:** Court Clerks; Court, Municipal, and License Clerks; License Clerks; Municipal Clerks.

Skills—Reading Comprehension: Understanding written sentences and paragraphs in work-related documents.

Active Listening: Listening to what other people are saying and asking questions as appropriate. **Equipment Selection:** Determining the kind of tools and equipment needed to do a job. **Operation and Control:** Controlling operations of equipment or systems. **Equipment Maintenance:** Performing routine maintenance and determining when and what kind of maintenance is needed. **Operation Monitoring:** Watching gauges, dials, or other indicators to make sure a machine is working properly. **Operations Analysis:** Analyzing needs and product requirements to create a design. **Installation:** Installing equipment, machines, wiring, or programs to meet specifications.

Education and Training Program: Court Reporting/Court Reporter Training. **Related Knowledge/Courses—Clerical Practices:** Administrative and clerical procedures and systems such as word-processing systems, filing and records management systems, stenography and transcription, forms, design principles, and other office procedures and terminology. **English Language:** The structure and content of the English language, including the meaning and spelling of words, rules of composition, and grammar. **Law and Government:** Laws, legal codes, court procedures, precedents, government regulations, executive orders, agency rules, and the democratic political process. **Computers and Electronics:** Electric circuit boards, processors, chips, and computer hardware and software, including applications and programming. **Production and Processing:** Inputs, outputs, raw materials, waste, quality control, costs, and techniques for maximizing the manufacture and distribution of goods. **Customer and Personal Service:** Principles and processes for providing customer and personal services, including needs assessment techniques, quality service standards, alternative delivery systems, and customer satisfaction evaluation techniques.

Work Environment: Indoors; noisy; sitting; using hands on objects, tools, or controls; repetitive motions.

Credit Analysts

- ❋ Education/Training Required: Bachelor's degree
- ❋ Annual Earnings: $54,580
- ❋ Beginning Wage: $30,820
- ❋ Earnings Growth Potential: High
- ❋ Growth: 1.9%
- ❋ Annual Job Openings: 3,180
- ❋ Self-Employed: 0.0%
- ❋ Part-Time: 5.3%

Analyze current credit data and financial statements of individuals or firms to determine the degree of risk involved in extending credit or lending money. Prepare reports with this credit information for use in decision-making. Evaluate customer records and recommend payment plans based on earnings, savings data, payment history, and purchase activity. Confer with credit association and other business representatives to exchange credit information. Complete loan applications, including credit analyses and summaries of loan requests, and submit to loan committees for approval. Generate financial ratios, using computer programs, to evaluate customers' financial status. Review individual or commercial customer files to identify and select delinquent accounts for collection. Compare liquidity, profitability, and credit histories of establishments being evaluated with those of similar establishments in the same industries and geographic locations. Consult with customers to resolve complaints and verify financial and credit transactions. Analyze financial data such as income growth, quality of management, and market share to determine expected profitability of loans.

Personality Type: Conventional. These occupations frequently involve following set procedures and routines and can include working with data and details more than with ideas. Usually there is a clear line of authority to follow.

GOE—Interest Area/Cluster: 06. Finance and Insurance. **Work Group:** 06.02. Finance/Insurance Investigation and Analysis. **Other Jobs in This Work Group:** Appraisers and Assessors of Real Estate; Appraisers, Real Estate; Assessors; Claims Adjusters, Examiners, and Investigators; Claims Examiners, Property and Casualty Insurance; Cost Estimators; Financial Analysts; Insurance Adjusters, Examiners, and Investigators; Insurance Appraisers, Auto Damage; Insurance Underwriters; Loan Counselors; Loan Officers; Market Research Analysts; Survey Researchers.

Skills—Speaking: Talking to others to effectively convey information. **Writing:** Communicating effectively with others in writing as indicated by the needs of the audience. **Operations Analysis:** Analyzing needs and product requirements to create a design. **Active Listening:** Listening to what other people are saying and asking questions as appropriate. **Negotiation:** Bringing others together and trying to reconcile differences. **Systems Evaluation:** Looking at many indicators of system performance and taking into account their accuracy. **Judgment and Decision Making:** Weighing the relative costs and benefits of a potential action. **Monitoring:** Assessing how well one is doing when learning or doing something.

Education and Training Programs: Accounting; Credit Management; Finance, General. **Related Knowledge/ Courses—Economics and Accounting:** Economic and accounting principles and practices, the financial markets, banking, and the analysis and reporting of financial data. **Clerical Practices:** Administrative and clerical procedures and systems such as word-processing systems, filing and records management systems, stenography and transcription, forms, design principles, and other office procedures and terminology. **Mathematics:** Numbers and their operations and interrelationships, including arithmetic, algebra, geometry, calculus, and statistics and their applications. **Law and Government:** Laws, legal codes, court procedures, precedents, government regulations, executive orders, agency rules, and the democratic political process. **Administration and Management:** Principles and processes involved in business and organizational planning, coordination, and execution. This includes strategic planning, resource allocation, manpower modeling, leadership techniques, and production methods. **English Language:** The structure and content of the English language, including the meaning and spelling of words, rules of composition, and grammar.

Work Environment: Indoors; sitting; repetitive motions.

Criminal Investigators and Special Agents

- ❀ Education/Training Required: Work experience in a related occupation
- ❀ Annual Earnings: $59,930
- ❀ Beginning Wage: $35,600
- ❀ Earnings Growth Potential: High
- ❀ Growth: 17.3%
- ❀ Annual Job Openings: 14,746
- ❀ Self-Employed: 0.3%
- ❀ Part-Time: 2.2%

The job openings listed here are shared with Immigration and Customs Inspectors; Police Detectives; and Police Identification and Records Officers.

Investigate alleged or suspected criminal violations of federal, state, or local laws to determine if evidence is sufficient to recommend prosecution. Record evidence and documents, using equipment such as cameras and photocopy machines. Obtain and verify evidence by interviewing and observing suspects and witnesses or by analyzing records. Examine records to locate links in chains of evidence or information. Prepare reports that detail investigation findings. Determine scope, timing, and direction of investigations. Collaborate with other offices and agencies to exchange information and coordinate activities. Testify before grand juries concerning criminal activity investigations. Analyze evidence in laboratories or in the field. Investigate organized crime, public corruption, financial crime, copyright infringement, civil rights violations, bank robbery, extortion, kidnapping, and other violations of federal or state statutes. Identify case issues and evidence needed, based on analysis of charges, complaints, or allegations of law violations. Obtain and use search and arrest warrants. Serve subpoenas or other official papers. Collaborate with other authorities on activities such as surveillance, transcription, and research. Develop relationships with informants to obtain information related to cases. Search for and collect evidence such as fingerprints, using investigative equipment. Collect and record physical information about arrested suspects, including fingerprints, height and weight measurements, and photographs. Compare crime scene fingerprints with those from suspects or fingerprint files to identify perpetrators, using computers. Administer counter-terrorism and counter-narcotics reward programs. Provide protection for individuals such as government leaders, political candidates, and visiting foreign dignitaries. Perform undercover assignments and maintain surveillance, including monitoring authorized wiretaps. Manage security programs designed to protect personnel, facilities, and information. Issue security clearances.

Personality Type: Enterprising. These occupations frequently involve starting up and carrying out projects and can involve leading people and making many decisions. They sometimes require risk taking and often deal with business.

GOE—Interest Area/Cluster: 12. Law and Public Safety. **Work Group:** 12.04. Law Enforcement and Public Safety. **Other Jobs in This Work Group:** Bailiffs; Correctional Officers and Jailers; Detectives and Criminal Investigators; Fire Investigators; Forensic Science Technicians; Parking Enforcement Workers; Police and Sheriff's Patrol Officers; Police Detectives; Police Identification and Records Officers; Police Patrol Officers; Sheriffs and Deputy Sheriffs; Transit and Railroad Police.

Skills—Negotiation: Bringing others together and trying to reconcile differences. **Operations Analysis:** Analyzing needs and product requirements to create a design. **Programming:** Writing computer programs for various purposes. **Judgment and Decision Making:** Weighing the relative costs and benefits of a potential action. **Service Orientation:** Actively looking for ways to help people. **Complex Problem Solving:** Identifying complex problems, reviewing the options, and implementing solutions. **Equipment Selection:** Determining the kind of tools and equipment needed to do a job. **Persuasion:** Persuading others to approach things differently.

Education and Training Programs: Criminal Justice/ Police Science; Criminalistics and Criminal Science. **Related Knowledge/Courses—Law and Government:** Laws, legal codes, court procedures, precedents, government regulations, executive orders, agency rules, and the democratic political process. **Psychology:** Human behavior and performance, mental processes, psychological research methods, and the assessment and treatment of behavioral and affective disorders. **Geography:** Various methods for describing the location and distribution of land, sea, and air masses, including their physical locations, relationships, and characteristics. **Public Safety and Security:** Weaponry; public safety; security operations, rules, regulations, precautions, and prevention; and the protection of people, data, and property. **Clerical Practices:** Administrative and clerical procedures and systems such as word-processing systems, filing and records management systems, stenography

and transcription, forms, design principles, and other office procedures and terminology. **Telecommunications:** Transmission, broadcasting, switching, control, and operation of telecommunications systems.

Work Environment: More often outdoors than indoors; noisy; very hot or cold; standing.

Criminal Justice and Law Enforcement Teachers, Postsecondary

- ❋ Education/Training Required: Doctoral degree
- ❋ Annual Earnings: $51,060
- ❋ Beginning Wage: $30,420
- ❋ Earnings Growth Potential: High
- ❋ Growth: 22.9%
- ❋ Annual Job Openings: 1,911
- ❋ Self-Employed: 0.4%
- ❋ Part-Time: 27.8%

Teach courses in criminal justice, corrections, and law enforcement administration. Initiate, facilitate, and moderate classroom discussions. Keep abreast of developments in their field by reading current literature, talking with colleagues, and participating in professional conferences. Evaluate and grade students' classwork, assignments, and papers. Compile, administer, and grade examinations or assign this work to others. Prepare and deliver lectures to undergraduate or graduate students on topics such as criminal law, defensive policing, and investigation techniques. Prepare course materials such as syllabi, homework assignments, and handouts. Conduct research in a particular field of knowledge and publish findings in professional journals, books, and/or electronic media. Plan, evaluate, and revise curricula, course content, and course materials and methods of instruction. Supervise undergraduate and/or graduate teaching, internship, and research work. Maintain student attendance records, grades, and other required records. Select and obtain materials and supplies such as textbooks. Advise students on academic and vocational curricula and on career issues. Maintain regularly scheduled office hours to advise and assist students. Collaborate with colleagues to address teaching and research issues. Write grant proposals to procure external research funding. Serve on academic or administrative committees that deal with institutional policies, departmental matters, and academic issues. Compile bibliographies of specialized materials for outside reading assignments. Participate in student recruitment, registration, and placement activities. Provide professional consulting services to government and/or industry. Perform administrative duties such as serving as department head. Participate in campus and community events. Act as advisers to student organizations.

Personality Type: Social. These occupations frequently involve working with, communicating with, and teaching people and often involve helping or providing service to others.

GOE—Interest Area/Cluster: 05. Education and Training. **Work Group:** 05.03. Postsecondary and Adult Teaching and Instructing. **Other Jobs in This Work Group:** Adult Literacy, Remedial Education, and GED Teachers and Instructors; Agricultural Sciences Teachers, Postsecondary; Anthropology and Archeology Teachers, Postsecondary; Architecture Teachers, Postsecondary; Area, Ethnic, and Cultural Studies Teachers, Postsecondary; Art, Drama, and Music Teachers, Postsecondary; Atmospheric, Earth, Marine, and Space Sciences Teachers, Postsecondary; Biological Science Teachers, Postsecondary; Business Teachers, Postsecondary; Chemistry Teachers, Postsecondary; Communications Teachers, Postsecondary; Computer Science Teachers, Postsecondary; Economics Teachers, Postsecondary; Education Teachers, Postsecondary; Engineering Teachers, Postsecondary; English Language and Literature Teachers, Postsecondary; Environmental Science Teachers, Postsecondary; Farm and Home Management Advisors; Foreign Language and Literature Teachers, Postsecondary; Forestry and Conservation Science Teachers, Postsecondary; Geography Teachers, Postsecondary; Graduate Teaching Assistants; Health Specialties Teachers, Postsecondary; History Teachers, Postsecondary; Home Economics Teachers, Postsecondary; Law Teachers, Postsecondary; Library Science Teachers, Postsecondary; Mathematical Science Teachers, Postsecondary; Nursing Instructors and Teachers, Postsecondary; Philosophy and Religion Teachers, Postsecondary; Physics Teachers, Postsecondary; Political Science Teachers, Postsecondary; Psychology Teachers, Postsecondary; Recreation and Fitness Studies Teachers, Postsecondary; Self-Enrichment Education Teachers; Social Work Teachers, Postsecondary; Sociology Teachers, Postsecondary; Vocational Education Teachers, Postsecondary.

Skills—Writing: Communicating effectively with others in writing as indicated by the needs of the audience. **Critical Thinking:** Using logic and analysis to identify the strengths and weaknesses of different approaches. **Instructing:** Teaching others how to do something. **Active Learning:** Working with new material or information to grasp its implications. **Reading Comprehension:** Understanding written sentences and paragraphs in work-related documents. **Persuasion:** Persuading others to approach things differently. **Science:** Using scientific methods to solve problems. **Speaking:** Talking to others to effectively convey information.

Education and Training Programs: Corrections; Corrections Administration; Corrections and Criminal Justice, Other; Criminal Justice/Law Enforcement Administration; Criminal Justice/Police Science; Criminal Justice/Safety Studies; Criminalistics and Criminal Science; Forensic Science and Technology; Juvenile Corrections; Security and Loss Prevention Services; Teacher Education and Professional Development, Specific Subject Areas, Other. **Related Knowledge/Courses—Sociology and Anthropology:** Group behavior and dynamics; societal trends and influences; and cultures and their history, migrations, ethnicity, and origins. **Philosophy and Theology:** Different philosophical systems and religions, including their basic principles, values, ethics, ways of thinking, customs, and practices and their impact on human culture. **History and Archeology:** Historical events and their causes, indicators, and impact on particular civilizations and cultures. **Law and Government:** Laws, legal codes, court procedures, precedents, government regulations, executive orders, agency rules, and the democratic political process. **English Language:** The structure and content of the English language, including the meaning and spelling of words, rules of composition, and grammar. **Education and Training:** Instructional methods and training techniques, including curriculum design principles, learning theory, group and individual teaching techniques, design of individual development plans, and test design principles.

Work Environment: Indoors; sitting.

Crop and Livestock Managers

- ❋ Education/Training Required: Work experience plus degree
- ❋ Annual Earnings: $53,720
- ❋ Beginning Wage: $31,100
- ❋ Earnings Growth Potential: High
- ❋ Growth: 1.1%
- ❋ Annual Job Openings: 18,101
- ❋ Self-Employed: 0.0%
- ❋ Part-Time: 9.3%

The job openings listed here are shared with Aquacultural Managers and with Nursery and Greenhouse Managers.

Direct and coordinate, through subordinate supervisory personnel, activities of workers engaged in agricultural crop production for corporations, cooperatives, or other owners. Record information such as production figures, farm management practices, and parent stock data and prepare financial and operational reports. Confer with buyers to arrange for the sale of crops. Contract with farmers or independent owners for raising of crops or for management of crop production. Evaluate financial statements and make budget proposals. Analyze soil to determine types and quantities of fertilizer required for maximum production. Purchase machinery, equipment, and supplies, such as tractors, seed, fertilizer, and chemicals. Analyze market conditions to determine acreage allocations. Direct and coordinate worker activities such as planting, irrigation, chemical application, harvesting, and grading. Inspect orchards and fields to determine maturity dates of crops or to estimate potential crop damage from weather. Hire, discharge, transfer, and promote workers. Enforce applicable safety regulations. Negotiate with bank officials to obtain credit. Plan and direct development and production of hybrid plant varieties with high yields or with disease or insect resistance. Inspect equipment to ensure proper functioning. Determine procedural changes in drying, grading, storage, and shipment processes in order to provide greater efficiency and accuracy. Coordinate growing activities with activities of related departments such as engineering, equipment maintenance, and packing.

Personality Type: Enterprising. These occupations frequently involve starting up and carrying out projects and can involve leading people and making many decisions. They sometimes require risk taking and often deal with business.

GOE—Interest Area/Cluster: 01. Agriculture and Natural Resources. **Work Group:** 01.01. Managerial Work in Agriculture and Natural Resources. **Other Jobs in This Work Group:** Aquacultural Managers; Farm Labor Contractors; Farm, Ranch, and Other Agricultural Managers; Farmers and Ranchers; First-Line Supervisors/Managers of Agricultural Crop and Horticultural Workers; First-Line Supervisors/Managers of Animal Husbandry and Animal Care Workers; First-Line Supervisors/Managers of Aquacultural Workers; First-Line Supervisors/Managers of Construction Trades and Extraction Workers; First-Line Supervisors/Managers of Farming, Fishing, and Forestry Workers; First-Line Supervisors/Managers of Landscaping, Lawn Service, and Groundskeeping Workers; First-Line Supervisors/Managers of Logging Workers; Nursery and Greenhouse Managers; Park Naturalists; Purchasing Agents and Buyers, Farm Products.

Skills—Management of Financial Resources: Determining how money will be spent to get the work done and accounting for these expenditures. **Negotiation:** Bringing others together and trying to reconcile differences. **Management of Material Resources:** Obtaining and seeing to the appropriate use of equipment, facilities, and materials needed to do certain work. **Science:** Using scientific methods to solve problems. **Persuasion:** Persuading others to approach things differently. **Mathematics:** Using mathematics to solve problems. **Judgment and Decision Making:** Weighing the relative costs and benefits of a potential action. **Management of Personnel Resources:** Motivating, developing, and directing people as they work; identifying the best people for the job.

Education and Training Programs: Agribusiness/Agricultural Business Operations; Agricultural Animal Breeding; Agricultural Production Operations, General; Agronomy and Crop Science; Animal Nutrition; Animal Sciences, General; Crop Production; Dairy Husbandry and Production; Dairy Science; Equine Science and Management; Farm and Ranch Management; Horticultural Science; Livestock Management; Plant Protection and Integrated Pest Management; Plant Sciences, General; Poultry Science; Range Science and Management; others. **Related Knowledge/Courses—Food Production:** Techniques and equipment for planting, growing, and harvesting of food for consumption, including crop-rotation methods, animal husbandry, and food storage/handling techniques. **Biology:** Plant and animal living tissue, cells, organisms, and entities, including their functions, interdependencies, and interactions with each other and the environment. **Economics and Accounting:** Economic and accounting principles and practices, the financial markets, banking, and the analysis and reporting of financial data. **Geography:** Various methods for describing the location and distribution of land, sea, and air masses, including their physical locations, relationships, and characteristics. **Sales and Marketing:** Principles and methods involved in showing, promoting, and selling products or services. This includes marketing strategies and tactics, product demonstration and sales techniques, and sales control systems. **Chemistry:** The composition, structure, and properties of substances and of the chemical processes and transformations that they undergo. This includes uses of chemicals and their interactions, danger signs, production techniques, and disposal methods.

Work Environment: More often indoors than outdoors; sitting.

Curators

- ❀ Education/Training Required: Master's degree
- ❀ Annual Earnings: $46,000
- ❀ Beginning Wage: $26,100
- ❀ Earnings Growth Potential: High
- ❀ Growth: 23.3%
- ❀ Annual Job Openings: 1,416
- ❀ Self-Employed: 1.3%
- ❀ Part-Time: 18.4%

Administer affairs of museum and conduct research programs. Direct instructional, research, and public service activities of institution. Plan and organize the acquisition, storage, and exhibition of collections and related materials, including the selection of exhibition themes and designs. Develop and maintain an institution's registration, cataloging, and basic recordkeeping systems, using computer databases. Provide information from the institution's holdings to other curators and to the public. Inspect premises to assess the need for repairs and to ensure that climate and pest-control issues are addressed. Train and supervise curatorial, fiscal, technical, research, and clerical staff, as well as volunteers or interns. Negotiate and authorize purchase, sale, exchange, or loan of collections. Plan and conduct special research projects in area of interest or expertise. Conduct or organize tours, workshops, and instructional sessions to acquaint individuals with an institution's facilities and materials. Confer with the board of directors to formulate and interpret policies, to determine budget requirements, and to plan overall operations. Attend meetings, conventions, and civic events to promote use of institution's services, to seek financing, and to maintain community alliances. Schedule events and organize details, including refreshment, entertainment, decorations, and the collection of any fees. Write and review grant proposals, journal articles, institutional reports, and publicity materials. Study, examine, and test acquisitions to authenticate their origin, composition, and history and to assess their current value. Arrange insurance coverage for objects on loan or for special exhibits and recommend changes in coverage for the entire collection. Establish specifications for reproductions and oversee their manufacture or select items from commercially available replica sources.

Personality Type: Enterprising. These occupations frequently involve starting up and carrying out projects and can involve leading people and making many decisions. They sometimes require risk taking and often deal with business.

GOE—Interest Area/Cluster: 05. Education and Training. **Work Group:** 05.05. Archival and Museum Services. **Other Jobs in This Work Group:** Archivists; Audio-Visual Collections Specialists; Museum Technicians and Conservators.

Skills—Management of Financial Resources: Determining how money will be spent to get the work done and accounting for these expenditures. **Management of Personnel Resources:** Motivating, developing, and directing people as they work; identifying the best people for the job. **Writing:** Communicating effectively with others in writing as indicated by the needs of the audience. **Time Management:** Managing one's own time and the time of others. **Speaking:** Talking to others to effectively convey information. **Persuasion:** Persuading others to approach things differently. **Monitoring:** Assessing how well one is doing when learning or doing something. **Negotiation:** Bringing others together and trying to reconcile differences.

Education and Training Programs: Art History, Criticism and Conservation; Museology/Museum Studies; Public/Applied History and Archival Administration. **Related Knowledge/Courses—Fine Arts:** Theory and techniques required to produce, compose, and perform works of music, dance, visual arts, drama, and sculpture. **History and Archeology:** Historical events and their causes, indicators, and impact on particular civilizations and cultures. **Clerical Practices:** Administrative and clerical procedures and systems such as word-processing systems, filing and records management systems, stenography and transcription, forms, design principles, and other office procedures and terminology. **Philosophy and Theology:** Different philosophical systems and religions, including their basic principles, values, ethics, ways of thinking, customs, and practices and their impact on human culture. **Sociology and Anthropology:** Group behavior and dynamics; societal trends and influences; and cultures and their history, migrations, ethnicity, and origins. **Geography:** Various methods for describing the location and distribution of land, sea, and air masses, including their physical locations, relationships, and characteristics.

Work Environment: Indoors; sitting.

Customer Service Representatives

- ❋ Education/Training Required: Moderate-term on-the-job training
- ❋ Annual Earnings: $29,040
- ❋ Beginning Wage: $18,490
- ❋ Earnings Growth Potential: Medium
- ❋ Growth: 24.8%
- ❋ Annual Job Openings: 600,937
- ❋ Self-Employed: 0.4%
- ❋ Part-Time: 16.5%

Interact with customers to provide information in response to inquiries about products and services and to handle and resolve complaints. Confer with customers by telephone or in person to provide information about products and services, to take orders or cancel accounts, or to obtain details of complaints. Keep records of customer interactions and transactions, recording details of inquiries, complaints, and comments, as well as actions taken. Resolve customers' service or billing complaints by performing activities such as exchanging merchandise, refunding money, and adjusting bills. Check to ensure that appropriate changes were made to resolve customers' problems. Contact customers to respond to inquiries or to notify them of claim investigation results and any planned adjustments. Refer unresolved customer grievances to designated departments for further investigation. Determine charges for services requested, collect deposits or payments, or arrange for billing. Complete contract forms, prepare change of address records, and issue service discontinuance orders, using computers. Obtain and examine all relevant information to assess validity of complaints and to determine possible causes, such as extreme weather conditions, that could increase utility bills. Solicit sale of new or additional services or products. Review insurance policy terms to determine whether a particular loss is covered by insurance. Review claims adjustments with dealers, examining parts claimed to be defective and approving or disapproving dealers' claims. Compare disputed merchandise with original requisitions and information from invoices and prepare invoices for returned goods. Order tests that could determine the causes of product malfunctions. Recommend improvements in products, packaging, shipping, service, or billing methods and procedures to prevent future problems.

Personality Type: Enterprising. These occupations frequently involve starting up and carrying out projects and can involve leading people and making many decisions.

They sometimes require risk taking and often deal with business.

GOE—Interest Area/Cluster: 14. Retail and Wholesale Sales and Service. **Work Group:** 14.06. Customer Service. **Other Jobs in This Work Group:** Cashiers; Counter and Rental Clerks; Gaming Cage Workers; Gaming Change Persons and Booth Cashiers; Order Clerks; Receptionists and Information Clerks.

Skills—Service Orientation: Actively looking for ways to help people. **Monitoring:** Assessing how well one is doing when learning or doing something. **Reading Comprehension:** Understanding written sentences and paragraphs in work-related documents. **Active Listening:** Listening to what other people are saying and asking questions as appropriate. **Social Perceptiveness:** Being aware of others' reactions and understanding why they react the way they do.

Education and Training Programs: Customer Service Support/Call Center/Teleservice Operation; Receptionist Training. **Related Knowledge/Courses—Customer and Personal Service:** Principles and processes for providing customer and personal services, including needs assessment techniques, quality service standards, alternative delivery systems, and customer satisfaction evaluation techniques. **Clerical Practices:** Administrative and clerical procedures and systems such as word-processing systems, filing and records management systems, stenography and transcription, forms, design principles, and other office procedures and terminology. **Sales and Marketing:** Principles and methods involved in showing, promoting, and selling products or services. This includes marketing strategies and tactics, product demonstration and sales techniques, and sales control systems.

Work Environment: Indoors; sitting; using hands on objects, tools, or controls; repetitive motions.

Database Administrators

- ❋ Education/Training Required: Bachelor's degree
- ❋ Annual Earnings: $67,250
- ❋ Beginning Wage: $38,890
- ❋ Earnings Growth Potential: High
- ❋ Growth: 28.6%
- ❋ Annual Job Openings: 8,258
- ❋ Self-Employed: 1.3%
- ❋ Part-Time: 5.3%

Coordinate changes to computer databases. Test and implement the databases, applying knowledge of database management systems. May plan, coordinate, and implement security measures to safeguard computer databases. Test programs or databases, correct errors, and make necessary modifications. Modify existing databases and database management systems or direct programmers and analysts to make changes. Plan, coordinate, and implement security measures to safeguard information in computer files against accidental or unauthorized damage, modification, or disclosure. Work as part of project teams to coordinate database development and determine project scope and limitations. Write and code logical and physical database descriptions and specify identifiers of database to management system or direct others in coding descriptions. Train users and answer questions. Specify users and user access levels for each segment of databases. Approve, schedule, plan, and supervise the installation and testing of new products and improvements to computer systems such as the installation of new databases. Review project requests describing database user needs to estimate time and cost required to accomplish project. Develop standards and guidelines to guide the use and acquisition of software and to protect vulnerable information. Review procedures in database management system manuals for making changes to database. Develop methods for integrating different products so they work properly together such as customizing commercial databases to fit specific needs. Develop data models describing data elements and how they are used, following procedures and using pen, template, or computer software. Select and enter codes to monitor database performances and to create production databases. Establish and calculate optimum values for database parameters, using manuals and calculators. Revise company definition of data as defined in data dictionary. Review workflow charts developed by programmer analysts to understand tasks computer will perform, such as updating records. Identify and evaluate industry trends in database systems to serve as a source of information and advice for upper management.

Personality Type: Conventional. These occupations frequently involve following set procedures and routines and can include working with data and details more than with ideas. Usually there is a clear line of authority to follow.

GOE—Interest Area/Cluster: 11. Information Technology. **Work Group:** 11.02. Information Technology Specialties. **Other Jobs in This Work Group:** Computer and Information Scientists, Research; Computer Operators; Computer Programmers; Computer Security Specialists; Computer Software Engineers, Applications; Computer Software Engineers, Systems Software; Computer Support Specialists; Computer Systems Analysts; Computer Systems Engineers/Architects; Network Designers; Network Systems and Data Communications Analysts; Software Quality Assurance Engineers and Testers; Web Administrators; Web Developers.

Skills—Programming: Writing computer programs for various purposes. **Systems Analysis:** Determining how a system should work and how changes will affect outcomes. **Systems Evaluation:** Looking at many indicators of system performance and taking into account their accuracy.

Education and Training Programs: Computer and Information Sciences, General; Computer and Information Systems Security; Computer Systems Analysis/Analyst Training; Data Modeling/Warehousing and Database Administration; Management Information Systems, General. **Related Knowledge/Courses—Computers and Electronics:** Electric circuit boards, processors, chips, and computer hardware and software, including applications and programming. **Telecommunications:** Transmission, broadcasting, switching, control, and operation of telecommunications systems. **Clerical Practices:** Administrative and clerical procedures and systems such as word-processing systems, filing and records management systems, stenography and transcription, forms, design principles, and other office procedures and terminology. **Communications and Media:** Media production, communication, and dissemination techniques and methods, including alternative ways to inform and entertain via written, oral, and visual media. **Engineering and Technology:** Equipment, tools, and mechanical devices and their uses to produce motion, light, power, technology, and other applications. **Mathematics:** Numbers and their operations and interrelationships, including arithmetic, algebra, geometry, calculus, and statistics and their applications.

Work Environment: Indoors; noisy; sitting; using hands on objects, tools, or controls; repetitive motions.

Demonstrators and Product Promoters

- ❋ Education/Training Required: Moderate-term on-the-job training
- ❋ Annual Earnings: $22,570
- ❋ Beginning Wage: $16,440
- ❋ Earnings Growth Potential: Low
- ❋ Growth: 18.0%
- ❋ Annual Job Openings: 32,779
- ❋ Self-Employed: 20.8%
- ❋ Part-Time: 56.1%

Demonstrate merchandise and answer questions for the purpose of creating public interest in buying the product. May sell demonstrated merchandise. Demonstrate and explain products, methods, or services in order to persuade customers to purchase products or utilize services. Learn about competitors' products and consumers' interests and concerns in order to answer questions and provide more complete information. Recommend product or service improvements to employers. Train demonstrators to present a company's products or services. Give tours of plants where specific products are made. Develop lists of prospective clients from sources such as newspaper items, company records, local merchants, and customers. Contact businesses and civic establishments to arrange to exhibit and sell merchandise. Visit trade shows, stores, community organizations, and other venues to demonstrate products or services and to answer questions from potential customers. Write articles and pamphlets about products. Transport, assemble, and disassemble materials used in presentations. Instruct customers in alteration of products. Collect fees or accept donations. Identify interested and qualified customers in order to provide them with additional information. Work as part of a team of demonstrators to accommodate large crowds. Wear costumes or sign boards and walk in public to promote merchandise, services, or events. Provide product information, using lectures, films, charts, and/or slide shows. Prepare and alter presentation contents to target specific audiences. Keep areas neat while working and return items to correct locations following demonstrations. Record and report demonstration-related information such as the number of questions asked by the audience and the number of coupons distributed. Research and investigate products to be presented to prepare for demonstrations. Sell products being promoted and keep records of sales. Set up and arrange displays and demonstration areas to attract the attention of prospective customers. Stock shelves with products. Suggest specific product purchases to meet customers' needs. Provide product samples, coupons, informational brochures, and other incentives to persuade people to buy products. Practice demonstrations to ensure that they will run smoothly.

Personality Type: Enterprising. These occupations frequently involve starting up and carrying out projects and can involve leading people and making many decisions. They sometimes require risk taking and often deal with business.

GOE—Interest Area/Cluster: 14. Retail and Wholesale Sales and Service. **Work Group:** 14.04. Personal Soliciting. **Other Jobs in This Work Group:** Door-To-Door Sales Workers, News and Street Vendors, and Related Workers; Models; Telemarketers.

Skill—Persuasion: Persuading others to approach things differently.

Education and Training Program: Retailing and Retail Operations. **Related Knowledge/Courses—Sales and Marketing:** Principles and methods involved in showing, promoting, and selling products or services. This includes marketing strategies and tactics, product demonstration and sales techniques, and sales control systems. **Customer and Personal Service:** Principles and processes for providing customer and personal services, including needs assessment techniques, quality service standards, alternative delivery systems, and customer satisfaction evaluation techniques.

Work Environment: Standing.

Dental Assistants

- ❋ Education/Training Required: Moderate-term on-the-job training
- ❋ Annual Earnings: $31,550
- ❋ Beginning Wage: $21,550
- ❋ Earnings Growth Potential: Low
- ❋ Growth: 29.2%
- ❋ Annual Job Openings: 29,482
- ❋ Self-Employed: 0.0%
- ❋ Part-Time: 35.7%

Assist dentist, set up patient and equipment, and keep records. Prepare patient, sterilize and disinfect instruments, set up instrument trays, prepare materials, and assist dentist during dental procedures. Expose dental diagnostic X rays. Record treatment information in patient records. Take and record medical and dental histories and vital signs of patients. Provide postoperative instructions prescribed by dentist. Assist dentist in management of medical and dental emergencies. Pour, trim, and polish study casts. Instruct patients in oral hygiene and plaque control programs. Make preliminary impressions for study casts and occlusal registrations for mounting study casts. Clean and polish removable appliances. Clean teeth, using dental instruments. Apply protective coating of fluoride to teeth. Fabricate temporary restorations and custom impressions from preliminary impressions. Schedule appointments, prepare bills, and receive payment for dental services; complete insurance forms; and maintain records, manually or using computer.

Personality Type: Conventional. These occupations frequently involve following set procedures and routines and can include working with data and details more than with ideas. Usually there is a clear line of authority to follow.

GOE—Interest Area/Cluster: 08. Health Science. **Work Group:** 08.03. Dentistry. **Other Jobs in This Work Group:** Dental Hygienists; Dentists, General; Oral and Maxillofacial Surgeons; Orthodontists; Prosthodontists.

Skills—Equipment Maintenance: Performing routine maintenance and determining when and what kind of maintenance is needed. **Operation and Control:** Controlling operations of equipment or systems. **Social Perceptiveness:** Being aware of others' reactions and understanding why they react the way they do. **Management of Material Resources:** Obtaining and seeing to the appropriate use of equipment, facilities, and materials needed to do certain work. **Operation Monitoring:** Watching gauges, dials, or other indicators to make sure a machine is working properly. **Equipment Selection:** Determining the kind of tools and equipment needed to do a job. **Installation:** Installing equipment, machines, wiring, or programs to meet specifications. **Repairing:** Repairing machines or systems, using the needed tools.

Education and Training Program: Dental Assisting/Assistant Training. **Related Knowledge/Courses—Medicine and Dentistry:** The information and techniques needed to diagnose and treat injuries, diseases, and deformities. This includes symptoms, treatment alternatives, drug properties and interactions, and preventive health-care measures. **Chemistry:** The composition, structure, and properties of substances and of the chemical processes and transformations that they undergo. This includes uses of chemicals and their interactions, danger signs, production techniques, and disposal methods. **Clerical Practices:** Administrative and clerical procedures and systems such as word-processing systems, filing and records management systems, stenography and transcription, forms, design principles, and other office procedures and terminology. **Customer and Personal Service:** Principles and processes for providing customer and personal services, including needs assessment techniques, quality service standards, alternative delivery systems, and customer satisfaction evaluation techniques. **Psychology:** Human behavior and performance, mental processes, psychological research methods, and the assessment and treatment of behavioral and affective disorders.

Work Environment: Indoors; contaminants; disease or infections; using hands on objects, tools, or controls; bending or twisting the body; repetitive motions.

Dental Hygienists

- Education/Training Required: Associate degree
- Annual Earnings: $64,740
- Beginning Wage: $42,480
- Earnings Growth Potential: Low
- Growth: 30.1%
- Annual Job Openings: 10,433
- Self-Employed: 0.1%
- Part-Time: 58.7%

Clean teeth and examine oral areas, head, and neck for signs of oral disease. May educate patients on oral hygiene, take and develop X rays, or apply fluoride or sealants. Clean calcareous deposits, accretions, and stains from teeth and beneath margins of gums, using dental instruments. Feel and visually examine gums for sores and signs of disease. Chart conditions of decay and disease for diagnosis and treatment by dentist. Feel lymph nodes under patient's chin to detect swelling or tenderness that could indicate presence of oral cancer. Apply fluorides and other cavity-preventing agents to arrest dental decay. Examine gums, using probes, to locate periodontal recessed gums and signs of gum disease. Expose and develop X-ray film. Provide clinical services and health education to improve and maintain oral health of schoolchildren. Remove excess cement from coronal surfaces of teeth. Make impressions for study casts. Place, carve, and finish amalgam restorations. Administer local anesthetic agents. Conduct dental health clinics for community groups to augment services of dentist. Remove sutures and dressings. Place and remove rubber dams, matrices, and temporary restorations.

Personality Type: Social. These occupations frequently involve working with, communicating with, and teaching people and often involve helping or providing service to others.

GOE—Interest Area/Cluster: 08. Health Science. **Work Group:** 08.03. Dentistry. **Other Jobs in This Work Group:** Dental Assistants; Dentists, General; Oral and Maxillofacial Surgeons; Orthodontists; Prosthodontists.

Skills—Science: Using scientific methods to solve problems. **Active Learning:** Working with new material or information to grasp its implications. **Reading Comprehension:** Understanding written sentences and paragraphs in work-related documents. **Time Management:** Managing one's own time and the time of others. **Equipment Selection:** Determining the kind of tools and equipment needed to do a job. **Persuasion:** Persuading others to approach things differently. **Social Perceptiveness:** Being aware of others' reactions and understanding why they react the way they do. **Writing:** Communicating effectively with others in writing as indicated by the needs of the audience.

Education and Training Program: Dental Hygiene/Hygienist Training. **Related Knowledge/Courses—Biology:** Plant and animal living tissue, cells, organisms, and entities, including their functions, interdependencies, and interactions with each other and the environment. **Medicine and Dentistry:** The information and techniques needed to diagnose and treat injuries, diseases, and deformities. This includes symptoms, treatment alternatives, drug properties and interactions, and preventive health-care measures. **Chemistry:** The composition, structure, and properties of substances and of the chemical processes and transformations that they undergo. This includes uses of chemicals and their interactions, danger signs, production techniques, and disposal methods. **Psychology:** Human behavior and performance, mental processes, psychological research methods, and the assessment and treatment of behavioral and affective disorders. **Therapy and Counseling:** Information and techniques needed to rehabilitate physical and mental ailments and to provide career guidance, including alternative treatments, rehabilitation equipment and its proper use, and methods to evaluate treatment effects. **Sales and Marketing:** Principles and methods involved in showing, promoting, and selling products or services. This includes marketing strategies and tactics, product demonstration and sales techniques, and sales control systems.

Work Environment: Indoors; radiation; disease or infections; sitting; using hands on objects, tools, or controls; repetitive motions.

Dentists, General

- ❋ Education/Training Required: First professional degree
- ❋ Annual Earnings: $137,630
- ❋ Beginning Wage: $71,520
- ❋ Earnings Growth Potential: High
- ❋ Growth: 9.2%
- ❋ Annual Job Openings: 7,106
- ❋ Self-Employed: 36.6%
- ❋ Part-Time: 25.9%

Diagnose and treat diseases, injuries, and malformations of teeth and gums and related oral structures. May treat diseases of nerve, pulp, and other dental tissues affecting vitality of teeth. Use masks, gloves, and safety glasses to protect themselves and their patients from infectious diseases. Administer anesthetics to limit the amount of pain experienced by patients during procedures. Examine teeth, gums, and related tissues, using dental instruments, X rays, and other diagnostic equipment, to evaluate dental health, diagnose diseases or abnormalities, and plan appropriate treatments. Formulate plan of treatment for patient's teeth and mouth tissue. Use air turbine and hand instruments, dental appliances, and surgical implements. Advise and instruct patients regarding preventive dental care, the causes and treatment of dental problems, and oral health-care services. Design, make, and fit prosthodontic appliances such as space maintainers, bridges, and dentures or write fabrication instructions or prescriptions for denturists and dental technicians. Diagnose and treat diseases, injuries, and malformations of teeth, gums, and related oral structures and provide preventive and corrective services. Fill pulp chamber and canal with endodontic materials. Write prescriptions for antibiotics and other medications. Analyze and evaluate dental needs to determine changes and trends in patterns of dental disease. Treat exposure of pulp by pulp capping, removal of pulp from pulp chamber, or root canal, using dental instruments. Eliminate irritating margins of fillings and correct occlusions, using dental instruments. Perform oral and periodontal surgery on the jaw or mouth. Remove diseased tissue, using surgical instruments. Apply fluoride and sealants to teeth. Manage business, employing and supervising staff and handling paperwork and insurance claims. Bleach, clean, or polish teeth to restore natural color. Plan, organize, and maintain dental health programs. Produce and evaluate dental health educational materials.

Personality Type: Investigative. These occupations frequently involve working with ideas and require an extensive amount of thinking. They can involve searching for facts and figuring out problems mentally.

GOE—Interest Area/Cluster: 08. Health Science. **Work Group:** 08.03. Dentistry. **Other Jobs in This Work Group:** Dental Assistants; Dental Hygienists; Oral and Maxillofacial Surgeons; Orthodontists; Prosthodontists.

Skills—Science: Using scientific methods to solve problems. **Management of Financial Resources:** Determining how money will be spent to get the work done and accounting for these expenditures. **Management of Material Resources:** Obtaining and seeing to the appropriate use of equipment, facilities, and materials needed to do certain work. **Equipment Selection:** Determining the kind of tools and equipment needed to do a job. **Complex Problem Solving:** Identifying complex problems, reviewing the options, and implementing solutions. **Reading Comprehension:** Understanding written sentences and paragraphs in work-related documents. **Service Orientation:** Actively looking for ways to help people. **Management of Personnel Resources:** Motivating, developing, and directing people as they work; identifying the best people for the job.

Education and Training Programs: Advanced General Dentistry (Cert, MS, PhD); Dental Clinical Sciences, General (MS, PhD); Dental Materials (MS, PhD); Dental Public Health and Education (Cert, MS/MPH, PhD/DPH); Dental Public Health Specialty; Dentistry (DDS, DMD); Oral Biology and Oral Pathology (MS, PhD); Pediatric Dentistry/Pedodontics (Cert, MS, PhD); Pedodontics Specialty. **Related Knowledge/Courses—Medicine and Dentistry:** The information and techniques needed to diagnose and treat injuries, diseases, and deformities. This includes symptoms, treatment alternatives, drug properties and interactions, and preventive health-care measures. **Biology:** Plant and animal living tissue, cells, organisms, and entities, including their functions, interdependencies, and interactions with each other and the environment. **Psychology:** Human behavior and performance, mental processes, psychological research methods, and the assessment and treatment of behavioral and affective disorders. **Chemistry:** The composition, structure, and properties of substances and of the chemical processes and transformations that they undergo. This includes uses of chemicals and their interactions, danger signs, production techniques, and disposal methods. **Personnel and Human Resources:** Principles and procedures for personnel recruitment; selection; training; compensation and benefits; labor relations and negotiation; and personnel information systems. **Economics and Accounting:** Economic and accounting principles and practices, the financial markets, banking, and the analysis and reporting of financial data.

Work Environment: Indoors; contaminants; radiation; disease or infections; sitting; using hands on objects, tools, or controls.

Diagnostic Medical Sonographers

- ❋ Education/Training Required: Associate degree
- ❋ Annual Earnings: $59,860
- ❋ Beginning Wage: $42,250
- ❋ Earnings Growth Potential: Low
- ❋ Growth: 19.1%
- ❋ Annual Job Openings: 3,211
- ❋ Self-Employed: 1.1%
- ❋ Part-Time: 17.3%

Produce ultrasonic recordings of internal organs for use by physicians. Provide sonograms and oral or written summaries of technical findings to physicians for use in medical diagnosis. Decide which images to include, looking for differences between healthy and pathological areas. Operate ultrasound equipment to produce and record images of the motion, shape, and composition of blood, organs, tissues, and bodily masses such as fluid accumulations. Select appropriate equipment settings and adjust patient positions to obtain the best sites and angles. Observe screens during scans to ensure that images produced are satisfactory for diagnostic purposes, making adjustments to equipment as required. Prepare patients for exams by explaining procedures, transferring them to ultrasound tables, scrubbing skin and applying gel, and positioning them properly. Observe and care for patients throughout examinations to ensure their safety and comfort. Obtain and record accurate patient histories, including prior test results and information from physical examinations. Determine whether scope of exams should be extended, based on findings. Maintain records that include patient information; sonographs and interpretations; files of correspondence; publications and regulations; or quality assurance records such as pathology, biopsy, or post-operative reports. Record and store suitable images, using camera unit connected to the ultrasound equipment. Coordinate work with physicians and other health-care team members, including providing assistance during invasive procedures. Perform clerical duties such as scheduling exams and special procedures, keeping records, and archiving computerized images. Perform legal and ethical duties, including preparing safety and accident reports, obtaining written consent from patients to perform invasive procedures, and reporting symptoms of abuse and neglect. Clean, check, and maintain sonographic equipment, submitting maintenance requests or performing minor repairs as necessary. Supervise and train students and other medical sonographers. Maintain stock and supplies, preparing supplies for special examinations and ordering supplies when necessary. Process and code film from procedures and complete appropriate documentation.

Personality Type: Investigative. These occupations frequently involve working with ideas and require an extensive amount of thinking. They can involve searching for facts and figuring out problems mentally.

GOE—Interest Area/Cluster: 08. Health Science. **Work Group:** 08.06. Medical Technology. **Other Jobs in This Work Group:** Biological Technicians; Cardiovascular Technologists and Technicians; Medical and Clinical Laboratory Technicians; Medical and Clinical Laboratory Technologists; Medical Equipment Preparers; Medical Records and Health Information Technicians; Nuclear Medicine Technologists; Opticians, Dispensing; Orthotists and Prosthetists; Radiologic Technicians; Radiologic Technologists; Radiologic Technologists and Technicians.

Skills—Operation Monitoring: Watching gauges, dials, or other indicators to make sure a machine is working properly. **Service Orientation:** Actively looking for ways to help people. **Systems Analysis:** Determining how a system should work and how changes will affect outcomes. **Systems Evaluation:** Looking at many indicators of system performance and taking into account their accuracy.

Education and Training Programs: Allied Health Diagnostic, Intervention, and Treatment Professions, Other; Diagnostic Medical Sonography/Sonographer and Ultrasound Technician Training. **Related Knowledge/Courses—Medicine and Dentistry:** The information and techniques needed to diagnose and treat injuries, diseases, and deformities. This includes symptoms, treatment alternatives, drug properties and interactions, and preventive health-care measures. **Physics:** Physical principles, laws, and applications, including air, water, material dynamics, light, atomic principles, heat, electric theory, earth formations, and meteorological and related natural phenomena. **Biology:** Plant and animal living tissue, cells, organisms, and entities, including their functions, interdependencies, and interactions

with each other and the environment. **Psychology:** Human behavior and performance, mental processes, psychological research methods, and the assessment and treatment of behavioral and affective disorders. **Customer and Personal Service:** Principles and processes for providing customer and personal services, including needs assessment techniques, quality service standards, alternative delivery systems, and customer satisfaction evaluation techniques. **Clerical Practices:** Administrative and clerical procedures and systems such as word-processing systems, filing and records management systems, stenography and transcription, forms, design principles, and other office procedures and terminology.

Work Environment: Indoors; disease or infections; standing; using hands on objects, tools, or controls; bending or twisting the body; repetitive motions.

Dietitians and Nutritionists

- ❋ Education/Training Required: Bachelor's degree
- ❋ Annual Earnings: $49,010
- ❋ Beginning Wage: $31,830
- ❋ Earnings Growth Potential: Medium
- ❋ Growth: 8.6%
- ❋ Annual Job Openings: 4,996
- ❋ Self-Employed: 7.9%
- ❋ Part-Time: 27.0%

Plan and conduct food service or nutritional programs to assist in the promotion of health and control of disease. May supervise activities of a department providing quantity food services, counsel individuals, or conduct nutritional research. Assess nutritional needs, diet restrictions, and current health plans to develop and implement dietary-care plans and provide nutritional counseling. Consult with physicians and health-care personnel to determine nutritional needs and diet restrictions of patient or client. Advise patients and their families on nutritional principles, dietary plans and diet modifications, and food selection and preparation. Counsel individuals and groups on basic rules of good nutrition, healthy eating habits, and nutrition monitoring to improve their quality of life. Monitor food service operations to ensure conformance to nutritional, safety, sanitation, and quality standards. Coordinate recipe development and standardization and develop new menus for independent food service operations. Develop policies for food service or nutritional programs to assist in health promotion and disease control. Inspect meals served for conformance to prescribed diets and standards of palatability and appearance. Develop curriculum and prepare manuals, visual aids, course outlines, and other materials used in teaching. Prepare and administer budgets for food, equipment, and supplies. Purchase food in accordance with health and safety codes. Select, train, and supervise workers who plan, prepare, and serve meals. Manage quantity food service departments or clinical and community nutrition services. Coordinate diet counseling services. Advise food service managers and organizations on sanitation, safety procedures, menu development, budgeting, and planning to assist with the establishment, operation, and evaluation of food service facilities and nutrition programs. Organize, develop, analyze, test, and prepare special meals such as low-fat, low-cholesterol, and chemical-free meals. Plan, conduct, and evaluate dietary, nutritional, and epidemiological research. Plan and conduct training programs in dietetics, nutrition, and institutional management and administration for medical students, health-care personnel, and the general public. Make recommendations regarding public policy, such as nutrition labeling, food fortification, and nutrition standards for school programs.

Personality Type: Investigative. These occupations frequently involve working with ideas and require an extensive amount of thinking. They can involve searching for facts and figuring out problems mentally.

GOE—Interest Area/Cluster: 08. Health Science. **Work Group:** 08.09. Health Protection and Promotion. **Other Jobs in This Work Group:** Athletic Trainers; Dietetic Technicians; Embalmers.

Skills—Science: Using scientific methods to solve problems. **Writing:** Communicating effectively with others in writing as indicated by the needs of the audience. **Social Perceptiveness:** Being aware of others' reactions and understanding why they react the way they do. **Instructing:** Teaching others how to do something. **Reading Comprehension:** Understanding written sentences and paragraphs in work-related documents. **Speaking:** Talking to others to effectively convey information. **Learning Strategies:** Using multiple approaches when learning or teaching new things. **Persuasion:** Persuading others to approach things differently.

Education and Training Programs: Clinical Nutrition/Nutritionist Training; Dietetics and Clinical Nutrition Services, Other; Dietetics/Dietitian (RD); Foods, Nutrition, and Related Services, Other; Foods, Nutrition, and Wellness Studies, General; Foodservice Systems Administration/

Management; Human Nutrition; Nutrition Sciences. **Related Knowledge/Courses—Food Production:** Techniques and equipment for planting, growing, and harvesting of food for consumption, including crop-rotation methods, animal husbandry, and food storage/handling techniques. **Therapy and Counseling:** Information and techniques needed to rehabilitate physical and mental ailments and to provide career guidance, including alternative treatments, rehabilitation equipment and its proper use, and methods to evaluate treatment effects. **Sociology and Anthropology:** Group behavior and dynamics; societal trends and influences; and cultures and their history, migrations, ethnicity, and origins. **Medicine and Dentistry:** The information and techniques needed to diagnose and treat injuries, diseases, and deformities. This includes symptoms, treatment alternatives, drug properties and interactions, and preventive health-care measures. **Philosophy and Theology:** Different philosophical systems and religions, including their basic principles, values, ethics, ways of thinking, customs, and practices and their impact on human culture. **Psychology:** Human behavior and performance, mental processes, psychological research methods, and the assessment and treatment of behavioral and affective disorders.

Work Environment: Indoors; more often sitting than standing.

Directors, Religious Activities and Education

- ❋ Education/Training Required: Bachelor's degree
- ❋ Annual Earnings: $35,370
- ❋ Beginning Wage: $19,850
- ❋ Earnings Growth Potential: High
- ❋ Growth: 19.7%
- ❋ Annual Job Openings: 11,463
- ❋ Self-Employed: 0.0%
- ❋ Part-Time: 25.2%

Direct and coordinate activities of their chosen denominational groups to meet religious needs of students. Plan, direct, or coordinate church school programs designed to promote religious education among church membership. May provide counseling and guidance relative to marital, health, financial, and religious problems. Analyze member participation and changes in congregation emphasis to determine needs for religious education. Collaborate with other ministry members to establish goals and objectives for religious education programs and to develop ways to encourage program participation. Interpret religious education activities to the public through speaking, leading discussions, and writing articles for local and national publications. Implement program plans by ordering needed materials, scheduling speakers, reserving spaces, and handling other administrative details. Confer with clergy members, congregation officials, and congregation organizations to encourage support of and participation in religious education activities. Develop and direct study courses and religious education programs within congregations. Locate and distribute resources such as periodicals and curricula in order to enhance the effectiveness of educational programs. Visit congregation members' homes, or arrange for pastoral visits, in order to provide information and resources regarding religious education programs. Identify and recruit potential volunteer workers. Participate in denominational activities aimed at goals such as promoting interfaith understanding or providing aid to new or small congregations. Publicize programs through sources such as newsletters, bulletins, and mailings. Counsel individuals regarding interpersonal, health, financial, and religious problems. Attend workshops, seminars, and conferences to obtain program ideas, information, and resources. Analyze revenue and program cost data to determine budget priorities. Train and supervise religious education instructional staffs. Select appropriate curricula and class structures for educational programs. Schedule special events such as camps, conferences, meetings, seminars, and retreats. Plan and conduct conferences dealing with the interpretation of religious ideas and convictions.

Personality Type: Enterprising. These occupations frequently involve starting up and carrying out projects and can involve leading people and making many decisions. They sometimes require risk taking and often deal with business.

GOE—Interest Area/Cluster: 10. Human Service. **Work Group:** 10.02. Religious Work. **Other Jobs in This Work Group:** Clergy.

Skills—Management of Personnel Resources: Motivating, developing, and directing people as they work; identifying the best people for the job. **Social Perceptiveness:** Being aware of others' reactions and understanding why they react the way they do. **Negotiation:** Bringing others together and trying to reconcile differences. **Speaking:** Talking to others to effectively convey information. **Management of Financial Resources:** Determining how money will be spent to get the work done and accounting for these expenditures.

Service Orientation: Actively looking for ways to help people. **Coordination:** Adjusting actions in relation to others' actions. **Management of Material Resources:** Obtaining and seeing to the appropriate use of equipment, facilities, and materials needed to do certain work.

Education and Training Programs: Bible/Biblical Studies; Missions/Missionary Studies and Missiology; Religious Education; Youth Ministry. **Related Knowledge/Courses—Philosophy and Theology:** Different philosophical systems and religions, including their basic principles, values, ethics, ways of thinking, customs, and practices and their impact on human culture. **Education and Training:** Instructional methods and training techniques, including curriculum design principles, learning theory, group and individual teaching techniques, design of individual development plans, and test design principles. **Therapy and Counseling:** Information and techniques needed to rehabilitate physical and mental ailments and to provide career guidance, including alternative treatments, rehabilitation equipment and its proper use, and methods to evaluate treatment effects. **Sales and Marketing:** Principles and methods involved in showing, promoting, and selling products or services. This includes marketing strategies and tactics, product demonstration and sales techniques, and sales control systems. **History and Archeology:** Historical events and their causes, indicators, and impact on particular civilizations and cultures. **Economics and Accounting:** Economic and accounting principles and practices, the financial markets, banking, and the analysis and reporting of financial data.

Work Environment: Indoors; standing.

Directors—Stage, Motion Pictures, Television, and Radio

* Education/Training Required: Work experience plus degree
* Annual Earnings: $61,090
* Beginning Wage: $28,980
* Earnings Growth Potential: Very high
* Growth: 11.1%
* Annual Job Openings: 8,992
* Self-Employed: 29.5%
* Part-Time: 9.0%

The job openings listed here are shared with Producers, Program Directors, Talent Directors, and Technical Directors/Managers.

Interpret script, conduct rehearsals, and direct activities of cast and technical crew for stage, motion pictures, television, or radio programs. Direct live broadcasts, films and recordings, or non-broadcast programming for public entertainment or education. Supervise and coordinate the work of camera, lighting, design, and sound crew members. Study and research scripts to determine how they should be directed. Cut and edit film or tape to integrate component parts into desired sequences. Collaborate with film and sound editors during the post-production process as films are edited and soundtracks are added. Confer with technical directors, managers, crew members, and writers to discuss details of production, such as photography, script, music, sets, and costumes. Plan details such as framing, composition, camera movement, sound, and actor movement for each shot or scene. Communicate to actors the approach, characterization, and movement needed for each scene in such a way that rehearsals and takes are minimized. Establish pace of programs and sequences of scenes according to time requirements and cast and set accessibility. Choose settings and locations for films and determine how scenes will be shot in these settings. Identify and approve equipment and elements required for productions, such as scenery, lights, props, costumes, choreography, and music. Compile scripts, program notes, and other material related to productions. Perform producers' duties such as securing financial backing, establishing and administering budgets, and recruiting cast and crew. Select plays or scripts for production and determine how material should be interpreted and performed. Compile cue words and phrases; cue announcers, cast members, and technicians during performances. Consult with writers, producers, or actors about script changes or "workshop" scripts, through rehearsal with writers and actors, to create final drafts. Collaborate with producers to hire crew members such as art directors, cinematographers, and costumer designers. Review film daily to check on work in progress and to plan for future filming. Interpret stage-set diagrams to determine stage layouts and supervise placement of equipment and scenery. Hold auditions for parts or negotiate contracts with actors determined suitable for specific roles, working in conjunction with producers.

Personality Type: Enterprising. These occupations frequently involve starting up and carrying out projects and can involve leading people and making many decisions. They sometimes require risk taking and often deal with business.

GOE—Interest Area/Cluster: 03. Arts and Communication. **Work Group:** 03.06. Drama. **Other Jobs in This**

Work Group: Actors; Costume Attendants; Makeup Artists, Theatrical and Performance; Public Address System and Other Announcers; Radio and Television Announcers.

Skills—Management of Personnel Resources: Motivating, developing, and directing people as they work; identifying the best people for the job. **Time Management:** Managing one's own time and the time of others. **Judgment and Decision Making:** Weighing the relative costs and benefits of a potential action. **Operations Analysis:** Analyzing needs and product requirements to create a design. **Equipment Selection:** Determining the kind of tools and equipment needed to do a job. **Active Listening:** Listening to what other people are saying and asking questions as appropriate. **Speaking:** Talking to others to effectively convey information. **Critical Thinking:** Using logic and analysis to identify the strengths and weaknesses of different approaches.

Education and Training Programs: Cinematography and Film/Video Production; Directing and Theatrical Production; Drama and Dramatics/Theatre Arts, General; Dramatic/Theatre Arts and Stagecraft, Other; Film/Cinema Studies; Radio and Television; Theatre/Theatre Arts Management. **Related Knowledge/Courses—Communications and Media:** Media production, communication, and dissemination techniques and methods, including alternative ways to inform and entertain via written, oral, and visual media. **Telecommunications:** Transmission, broadcasting, switching, control, and operation of telecommunications systems. **Fine Arts:** Theory and techniques required to produce, compose, and perform works of music, dance, visual arts, drama, and sculpture. **Geography:** Various methods for describing the location and distribution of land, sea, and air masses, including their physical locations, relationships, and characteristics. **Computers and Electronics:** Electric circuit boards, processors, chips, and computer hardware and software, including applications and programming. **Education and Training:** Instructional methods and training techniques, including curriculum design principles, learning theory, group and individual teaching techniques, design of individual development plans, and test design principles.

Work Environment: More often indoors than outdoors; noisy; sitting; using hands on objects, tools, or controls.

Dispatchers, Except Police, Fire, and Ambulance

- ❋ Education/Training Required: Moderate-term on-the-job training
- ❋ Annual Earnings: $33,140
- ❋ Beginning Wage: $20,410
- ❋ Earnings Growth Potential: Medium
- ❋ Growth: 1.5%
- ❋ Annual Job Openings: 29,793
- ❋ Self-Employed: 1.1%
- ❋ Part-Time: 6.3%

Schedule and dispatch workers, work crews, equipment, or service vehicles for conveyance of materials, freight, or passengers or for normal installation, service, or emergency repairs rendered outside the place of business. Duties may include using radio, telephone, or computer to transmit assignments and compiling statistics and reports on work progress. Schedule and dispatch workers, work crews, equipment, or service vehicles to appropriate locations according to customer requests, specifications, or needs, using radios or telephones. Arrange for necessary repairs to restore service and schedules. Relay work orders, messages, and information to or from work crews, supervisors, and field inspectors, using telephones or two-way radios. Confer with customers or supervising personnel to address questions, problems, and requests for service or equipment. Prepare daily work and run schedules. Receive or prepare work orders. Oversee all communications within specifically assigned territories. Monitor personnel or equipment locations and utilization to coordinate service and schedules. Record and maintain files and records of customer requests, work or services performed, charges, expenses, inventory, and other dispatch information. Determine types or amounts of equipment, vehicles, materials, or personnel required according to work orders or specifications. Advise personnel about traffic problems such as construction areas, accidents, congestion, weather conditions, and other hazards. Ensure timely and efficient movement of trains according to train orders and schedules. Order supplies and equipment and issue them to personnel.

Personality Type: Conventional. These occupations frequently involve following set procedures and routines and can include working with data and details more than with ideas. Usually there is a clear line of authority to follow.

GOE—Interest Area/Cluster: 03. Arts and Communication. **Work Group:** 03.10. Communications Technology. **Other Jobs in This Work Group:** Air Traffic Controllers; Airfield Operations Specialists; Police, Fire, and Ambulance Dispatchers; Telephone Operators.

Skills—Operations Analysis: Analyzing needs and product requirements to create a design. **Service Orientation:** Actively looking for ways to help people. **Systems Evaluation:** Looking at many indicators of system performance and taking into account their accuracy. **Management of Personnel Resources:** Motivating, developing, and directing people as they work; identifying the best people for the job. **Troubleshooting:** Determining what is causing an operating error and deciding what to do about it. **Systems Analysis:** Determining how a system should work and how changes will affect outcomes. **Judgment and Decision Making:** Weighing the relative costs and benefits of a potential action. **Critical Thinking:** Using logic and analysis to identify the strengths and weaknesses of different approaches.

Education and Training Program: Logistics and Materials Management. **Related Knowledge/Courses—Transportation:** Principles and methods for moving people or goods by air, rail, sea, or road, including their relative costs, advantages, and limitations. **Clerical Practices:** Administrative and clerical procedures and systems such as word-processing systems, filing and records management systems, stenography and transcription, forms, design principles, and other office procedures and terminology. **Public Safety and Security:** Weaponry; public safety; security operations, rules, regulations, precautions, and prevention; and the protection of people, data, and property. **Communications and Media:** Media production, communication, and dissemination techniques and methods, including alternative ways to inform and entertain via written, oral, and visual media.

Work Environment: Indoors; noisy; sitting; using hands on objects, tools, or controls; repetitive motions.

Drywall and Ceiling Tile Installers

- ❋ Education/Training Required: Moderate-term on-the-job training
- ❋ Annual Earnings: $36,520
- ❋ Beginning Wage: $23,480
- ❋ Earnings Growth Potential: Medium
- ❋ Growth: 7.3%
- ❋ Annual Job Openings: 30,945
- ❋ Self-Employed: 23.0%
- ❋ Part-Time: 6.1%

Apply plasterboard or other wallboard to ceilings or interior walls of buildings. Apply or mount acoustical tiles or blocks, strips, or sheets of shock-absorbing materials to ceilings and walls of buildings to reduce or reflect sound. Materials may be of decorative quality. Includes lathers who fasten wooden, metal, or rockboard lath to walls, ceilings, or partitions of buildings to provide support base for plaster, fireproofing, or acoustical material. Inspect furrings, mechanical mountings, and masonry surface for plumbness and level, using spirit or water levels. Install metal lath where plaster applications will be exposed to weather or water or for curved or irregular surfaces. Install blanket insulation between studs and tack plastic moisture barriers over insulation. Coordinate work with drywall finishers who cover the seams between drywall panels. Trim rough edges from wallboard to maintain even joints, using knives. Seal joints between ceiling tiles and walls. Scribe and cut edges of tile to fit walls where wall molding is not specified. Read blueprints and other specifications to determine methods of installation, work procedures, and material and tool requirements. Nail channels or wood furring strips to surfaces to provide mounting for tile. Mount tile, using adhesives, or by nailing, screwing, stapling, or wire-tying lath directly to structural frameworks. Measure and mark surfaces to lay out work according to blueprints and drawings, using tape measures, straightedges or squares, and marking devices. Hang drywall panels on metal frameworks of walls and ceilings in offices, schools, and other large buildings, using lifts or hoists to adjust panel heights when necessary. Install horizontal and vertical metal or wooden studs to frames so that wallboard can be attached to interior walls. Fasten metal or rockboard lath to the structural framework of walls, ceilings, and partitions of buildings, using nails, screws, staples, or wire-ties. Apply or mount acoustical tile or blocks, strips, or sheets of shock-absorbing materials to ceilings and walls of buildings to reduce reflection of sound or to decorate rooms. Apply cement to backs of tiles and press tiles into place, aligning them with layout marks or joints of previously laid tile. Hang dry lines (stretched string) to wall moldings in order to guide positioning of main runners. Assemble and install metal framing and decorative trim for windows, doorways, and vents. Fit and fasten wallboard or drywall into position on wood or metal frameworks, using glue, nails, or screws.

Personality Type: Realistic. These occupations frequently involve work activities that include practical, hands-on problems and solutions. They often deal with plants; animals; and real-world materials such as wood, tools, and machinery. Many of the occupations require working outside and don't involve a lot of paperwork or working closely with others.

GOE—Interest Area/Cluster: 02. Architecture and Construction. **Work Group:** 02.04. Construction Crafts. **Other Jobs in This Work Group:** Boilermakers; Brickmasons and Blockmasons; Carpet Installers; Cement Masons and Concrete Finishers; Commercial Divers; Construction Carpenters; Crane and Tower Operators; Electricians; Fence Erectors; Floor Layers, Except Carpet, Wood, and Hard Tiles; Floor Sanders and Finishers; Glaziers; Hazardous Materials Removal Workers; Insulation Workers, Floor, Ceiling, and Wall; Insulation Workers, Mechanical; Manufactured Building and Mobile Home Installers; Operating Engineers and Other Construction Equipment Operators; Painters, Construction and Maintenance; Paperhangers; Paving, Surfacing, and Tamping Equipment Operators; Pile-Driver Operators; Pipe Fitters and Steamfitters; Pipelayers; Plasterers and Stucco Masons; Plumbers; Plumbers, Pipefitters, and Steamfitters; Rail-Track Laying and Maintenance Equipment Operators; Refractory Materials Repairers, Except Brickmasons; Reinforcing Iron and Rebar Workers; Riggers; Roofers; Rough Carpenters; Security and Fire Alarm Systems Installers; Segmental Pavers; Sheet Metal Workers; Stone Cutters and Carvers, Manufacturing; Stonemasons; Structural Iron and Steel Workers; Tapers; Terrazzo Workers and Finishers; Tile and Marble Setters.

Skills—Installation: Installing equipment, machines, wiring, or programs to meet specifications. **Management of Personnel Resources:** Motivating, developing, and directing people as they work; identifying the best people for the job. **Management of Material Resources:** Obtaining and seeing to the appropriate use of equipment, facilities, and materials needed to do certain work. **Management of Financial Resources:** Determining how money will be spent to get the work done and accounting for these expenditures. **Mathematics:** Using mathematics to solve problems. **Repairing:** Repairing machines or systems, using the needed tools. **Science:** Using scientific methods to solve problems. **Equipment Selection:** Determining the kind of tools and equipment needed to do a job.

Education and Training Program: Drywall Installation/ Drywaller Training. **Related Knowledge/Courses—Building and Construction:** Materials, methods, and the appropriate tools to construct objects, structures, and buildings. **Design:** Design techniques, principles, tools, and instruments involved in the production and use of precision technical plans, blueprints, drawings, and models. **Mechanical Devices:** Machines and tools, including their designs, uses, benefits, repair, and maintenance. **Mathematics:** Numbers and their operations and interrelationships, including arithmetic, algebra, geometry, calculus, and statistics and their applications. **Production and Processing:** Inputs, outputs, raw materials, waste, quality control, costs, and techniques for maximizing the manufacture and distribution of goods. **Public Safety and Security:** Weaponry; public safety; security operations, rules, regulations, precautions, and prevention; and the protection of people, data, and property.

Work Environment: High places; standing; walking and running; using hands on objects, tools, or controls; bending or twisting the body; repetitive motions.

Economics Teachers, Postsecondary

* Education/Training Required: Doctoral degree
* Annual Earnings: $75,300
* Beginning Wage: $41,650
* Earnings Growth Potential: High
* Growth: 22.9%
* Annual Job Openings: 2,208
* Self-Employed: 0.4%
* Part-Time: 27.8%

Teach courses in economics. Prepare and deliver lectures to undergraduate and/or graduate students on topics such as econometrics, price theory, and macroeconomics. Prepare course materials such as syllabi, homework assignments, and handouts. Evaluate and grade students' classwork, assignments, and papers. Compile, administer, and grade examinations or assign this work to others. Keep abreast of developments in their field by reading current literature, talking with colleagues, and participating in professional conferences. Maintain student attendance records, grades, and other required records. Initiate, facilitate, and moderate classroom discussions. Maintain regularly scheduled office hours in order to advise and assist students. Select and obtain materials and supplies such as textbooks. Plan, evaluate, and revise curricula, course content, and course materials and methods of instruction. Conduct research in a particular field of knowledge and publish findings in professional journals, books, and/or electronic media. Supervise undergraduate and/or graduate teaching, internship, and research work. Advise students on academic and vocational curricula and on career issues. Serve on academic or administrative committees that deal with institutional policies, departmental matters, and academic issues. Collaborate with colleagues to address teaching and research issues. Compile bibliographies of specialized materials for outside reading assignments. Participate in student recruitment, registration, and placement activities. Perform administrative duties such as serving as department head. Write grant proposals to procure external research funding. Participate in campus and community events. Provide professional consulting services to government and/or industry. Act as advisers to student organizations.

Personality Type: Social. These occupations frequently involve working with, communicating with, and teaching people and often involve helping or providing service to others.

GOE—Interest Area/Cluster: 05. Education and Training. **Work Group:** 05.03. Postsecondary and Adult Teaching and Instructing. **Other Jobs in This Work Group:** Adult Literacy, Remedial Education, and GED Teachers and Instructors; Agricultural Sciences Teachers, Postsecondary; Anthropology and Archeology Teachers, Postsecondary; Architecture Teachers, Postsecondary; Area, Ethnic, and Cultural Studies Teachers, Postsecondary; Art, Drama, and Music Teachers, Postsecondary; Atmospheric, Earth, Marine, and Space Sciences Teachers, Postsecondary; Biological Science Teachers, Postsecondary; Business Teachers, Postsecondary; Chemistry Teachers, Postsecondary; Communications Teachers, Postsecondary; Computer Science Teachers, Postsecondary; Criminal Justice and Law Enforcement Teachers, Postsecondary; Education Teachers, Postsecondary; Engineering Teachers, Postsecondary; English Language and Literature Teachers, Postsecondary; Environmental Science Teachers, Postsecondary; Farm and Home Management Advisors; Foreign Language and Literature Teachers, Postsecondary; Forestry and Conservation Science Teachers, Postsecondary; Geography Teachers, Postsecondary; Graduate Teaching

Assistants; Health Specialties Teachers, Postsecondary; History Teachers, Postsecondary; Home Economics Teachers, Postsecondary; Law Teachers, Postsecondary; Library Science Teachers, Postsecondary; Mathematical Science Teachers, Postsecondary; Nursing Instructors and Teachers, Postsecondary; Philosophy and Religion Teachers, Postsecondary; Physics Teachers, Postsecondary; Political Science Teachers, Postsecondary; Psychology Teachers, Postsecondary; Recreation and Fitness Studies Teachers, Postsecondary; Self-Enrichment Education Teachers; Social Work Teachers, Postsecondary; Sociology Teachers, Postsecondary; Vocational Education Teachers, Postsecondary.

Skills—Mathematics: Using mathematics to solve problems. **Writing:** Communicating effectively with others in writing as indicated by the needs of the audience. **Instructing:** Teaching others how to do something. **Speaking:** Talking to others to effectively convey information. **Reading Comprehension:** Understanding written sentences and paragraphs in work-related documents. **Critical Thinking:** Using logic and analysis to identify the strengths and weaknesses of different approaches. **Learning Strategies:** Using multiple approaches when learning or teaching new things. **Active Learning:** Working with new material or information to grasp its implications.

Education and Training Programs: Applied Economics; Business/Managerial Economics; Development Economics and International Development; Econometrics and Quantitative Economics; Economics, General; Economics, Other; International Economics; Social Science Teacher Education. **Related Knowledge/Courses—Economics and Accounting:** Economic and accounting principles and practices, the financial markets, banking, and the analysis and reporting of financial data. **History and Archeology:** Historical events and their causes, indicators, and impact on particular civilizations and cultures. **Mathematics:** Numbers and their operations and interrelationships, including arithmetic, algebra, geometry, calculus, and statistics and their applications. **Philosophy and Theology:** Different philosophical systems and religions, including their basic principles, values, ethics, ways of thinking, customs, and practices and their impact on human culture. **Education and Training:** Instructional methods and training techniques, including curriculum design principles, learning theory, group and individual teaching techniques, design of individual development plans, and test design principles. **English Language:** The structure and content of the English language, including the meaning and spelling of words, rules of composition, and grammar.

Work Environment: Indoors; sitting.

Economists

❋ Education/Training Required: Master's degree
❋ Annual Earnings: $80,220
❋ Beginning Wage: $43,540
❋ Earnings Growth Potential: High
❋ Growth: 7.5%
❋ Annual Job Openings: 1,555
❋ Self-Employed: 6.5%
❋ Part-Time: 3.3%

Conduct research, prepare reports, or formulate plans to aid in solution of economic problems arising from production and distribution of goods and services. May collect and process economic and statistical data, using econometric and sampling techniques. Study economic and statistical data in area of specialization, such as finance, labor, or agriculture. Provide advice and consultation on economic relationships to businesses, public and private agencies, and other employers. Compile, analyze, and report data to explain economic phenomena and forecast market trends, applying mathematical models and statistical techniques. Formulate recommendations, policies, or plans to solve economic problems or to interpret markets. Develop economic guidelines and standards and prepare points of view used in forecasting trends and formulating economic policy. Testify at regulatory or legislative hearings concerning the estimated effects of changes in legislation or public policy and present recommendations based on cost-benefit analyses. Supervise research projects and students' study projects. Forecast production and consumption of renewable resources and supply, consumption, and depletion of non-renewable resources. Teach theories, principles, and methods of economics.

Personality Type: Investigative. These occupations frequently involve working with ideas and require an extensive amount of thinking. They can involve searching for facts and figuring out problems mentally.

GOE—Interest Area/Cluster: 15. Scientific Research, Engineering, and Mathematics. **Work Group:** 15.04. Social Sciences. **Other Jobs in This Work Group:** Anthropologists; Anthropologists and Archeologists; Archeologists; Historians; Industrial-Organizational Psychologists; Political Scientists; School Psychologists; Sociologists.

Skills—Mathematics: Using mathematics to solve problems. **Programming:** Writing computer programs for various purposes. **Persuasion:** Persuading others to approach things differently. **Judgment and Decision Making:** Weighing the relative costs and benefits of a potential action. **Complex Problem Solving:** Identifying complex problems, reviewing the options, and implementing solutions. **Writing:** Communicating effectively with others in writing as indicated by the needs of the audience. **Critical Thinking:** Using logic and analysis to identify the strengths and weaknesses of different approaches. **Systems Analysis:** Determining how a system should work and how changes will affect outcomes.

Education and Training Programs: Agricultural Economics; Applied Economics; Business/Managerial Economics; Development Economics and International Development; Econometrics and Quantitative Economics; Economics, General; Economics, Other; International Economics. **Related Knowledge/Courses—Economics and Accounting:** Economic and accounting principles and practices, the financial markets, banking, and the analysis and reporting of financial data. **Mathematics:** Numbers and their operations and interrelationships, including arithmetic, algebra, geometry, calculus, and statistics and their applications. **Geography:** Various methods for describing the location and distribution of land, sea, and air masses, including their physical locations, relationships, and characteristics. **Sales and Marketing:** Principles and methods involved in showing, promoting, and selling products or services. This includes marketing strategies and tactics, product demonstration and sales techniques, and sales control systems. **Computers and Electronics:** Electric circuit boards, processors, chips, and computer hardware and software, including applications and programming. **English Language:** The structure and content of the English language, including the meaning and spelling of words, rules of composition, and grammar.

Work Environment: Indoors; sitting.

Editors

- ❋ Education/Training Required: Bachelor's degree
- ❋ Annual Earnings: $48,320
- ❋ Beginning Wage: $27,360
- ❋ Earnings Growth Potential: High
- ❋ Growth: 2.3%
- ❋ Annual Job Openings: 20,193
- ❋ Self-Employed: 13.4%
- ❋ Part-Time: 14.6%

Perform variety of editorial duties, such as laying out, indexing, and revising content of written materials, in preparation for final publication. Prepare, rewrite, and edit copy to improve readability or supervise others who do this work. Read copy or proof to detect and correct errors in spelling, punctuation, and syntax. Allocate print space for story text, photos, and illustrations according to space parameters and copy significance, using knowledge of layout principles. Plan the contents of publications according to the publication's style, editorial policy, and publishing requirements. Verify facts, dates, and statistics, using standard reference sources. Review and approve proofs submitted by composing room prior to publication production. Develop story or content ideas, considering reader or audience appeal. Oversee publication production, including artwork, layout, computer typesetting, and printing, ensuring adherence to deadlines and budget requirements. Confer with management and editorial staff members regarding placement and emphasis of developing news stories. Assign topics, events, and stories to individual writers or reporters for coverage. Read, evaluate, and edit manuscripts or other materials submitted for publication and confer with authors regarding changes in content, style or organization, or publication. Monitor news-gathering operations to ensure utilization of all news sources, such as press releases, telephone contacts, radio, television, wire services, and other reporters. Meet frequently with artists, typesetters, layout personnel, marketing directors, and production managers to discuss projects and resolve problems. Supervise and coordinate work of reporters and other editors. Make manuscript acceptance or revision recommendations to the publisher. Select local, state, national, and international news items received from wire services based on assessment of items' significance and interest value. Interview and hire writers and reporters or negotiate contracts, royalties, and payments for authors or freelancers. Direct the policies and departments of newspapers, magazines, and other publishing establishments. Arrange for copyright permissions. Read material to determine index items and arrange them alphabetically or topically, indicating page or chapter location.

Personality Type: Artistic. These occupations frequently involve working with forms, designs, and patterns. They often require self-expression, and the work can be done without following a clear set of rules.

GOE—Interest Area/Cluster: 03. Arts and Communication. **Work Group:** 03.02. Writing and Editing. **Other Jobs in This Work Group:** Copy Writers; Poets, Lyricists, and Creative Writers; Technical Writers; Writers and Authors.

Skills—Writing: Communicating effectively with others in writing as indicated by the needs of the audience. **Reading Comprehension:** Understanding written sentences and paragraphs in work-related documents. **Active Listening:** Listening to what other people are saying and asking questions as appropriate. **Judgment and Decision Making:** Weighing the relative costs and benefits of a potential action. **Time Management:** Managing one's own time and the time of others. **Critical Thinking:** Using logic and analysis to identify the strengths and weaknesses of different approaches. **Persuasion:** Persuading others to approach things differently. **Active Learning:** Working with new material or information to grasp its implications.

Education and Training Programs: Broadcast Journalism; Business/Corporate Communications; Communication, Journalism, and Related Programs, Other; Creative Writing; Family and Consumer Sciences/Human Sciences Communication; Journalism; Mass Communication/Media Studies; Publishing; Technical and Business Writing. **Related Knowledge/Courses—Communications and Media:** Media production, communication, and dissemination techniques and methods, including alternative ways to inform and entertain via written, oral, and visual media. **History and Archeology:** Historical events and their causes, indicators, and impact on particular civilizations and cultures. **Geography:** Various methods for describing the location and distribution of land, sea, and air masses, including their physical locations, relationships, and characteristics. **English Language:** The structure and content of the English language, including the meaning and spelling of words, rules of composition, and grammar. **Sales and Marketing:** Principles and methods involved in showing, promoting, and selling products or services. This includes marketing strategies and tactics, product demonstration and sales techniques, and sales control systems. **Clerical Practices:** Administrative and clerical procedures and systems such as word-processing systems, filing and records management systems, stenography and transcription, forms, design principles, and other office procedures and terminology.

Work Environment: Indoors; sitting; using hands on objects, tools, or controls; repetitive motions.

Education Administrators, Elementary and Secondary School

- ❋ Education/Training Required: Work experience plus degree
- ❋ Annual Earnings: $80,580
- ❋ Beginning Wage: $52,940
- ❋ Earnings Growth Potential: Low
- ❋ Growth: 7.6%
- ❋ Annual Job Openings: 27,143
- ❋ Self-Employed: 3.3%
- ❋ Part-Time: 8.3%

Plan, direct, or coordinate the academic, clerical, or auxiliary activities of public or private elementary or secondary-level schools. Review and approve new programs or recommend modifications to existing programs, submitting program proposals for school board approval as necessary. Prepare, maintain, or oversee the preparation and maintenance of attendance, activity, planning, or personnel reports and records. Confer with parents and staff to discuss educational activities, policies, and student behavioral or learning problems. Prepare and submit budget requests and recommendations or grant proposals to solicit program funding. Direct and coordinate school maintenance services and the use of school facilities. Counsel and provide guidance to students regarding personal, academic, vocational, or behavioral issues. Organize and direct committees of specialists, volunteers, and staff to provide technical and advisory assistance for programs. Teach classes or courses to students. Advocate for new schools to be built or for existing facilities to be repaired or remodeled. Plan and develop instructional methods and content for educational, vocational, or student activity programs. Develop partnerships with businesses, communities, and other organizations to help meet identified educational needs and to provide school-to-work programs. Direct and coordinate activities of teachers, administrators, and support staff at schools, public agencies, and institutions. Evaluate curricula, teaching methods, and programs to determine their effectiveness, efficiency, and utilization and to ensure that school activities comply with federal, state, and local regulations. Set educational standards and goals and help establish policies and procedures to carry them out. Recruit, hire, train, and evaluate primary and supplemental staff. Enforce discipline and attendance rules. Observe teaching methods and examine learning materials to evaluate and standardize curricula and teaching techniques and to determine areas where improvement is needed. Establish, coordinate, and oversee particular programs across school districts, such as programs to evaluate student academic achievement. Review and interpret government codes and develop programs to ensure adherence to codes and facility safety, security, and maintenance.

Personality Type: Enterprising. These occupations frequently involve starting up and carrying out projects and can involve leading people and making many decisions. They sometimes require risk taking and often deal with business.

GOE—Interest Area/Cluster: 05. Education and Training. **Work Group:** 05.01. Managerial Work in Education. **Other Jobs in This Work Group:** Education Administrators, Postsecondary; Education Administrators, Preschool and Child Care Center/Program; Instructional Coordinators.

Skills—Management of Personnel Resources: Motivating, developing, and directing people as they work; identifying the best people for the job. **Management of Financial Resources:** Determining how money will be spent to get the work done and accounting for these expenditures. **Negotiation:** Bringing others together and trying to reconcile differences. **Learning Strategies:** Using multiple approaches when learning or teaching new things. **Monitoring:** Assessing how well one is doing when learning or doing something. **Management of Material Resources:** Obtaining and seeing to the appropriate use of equipment, facilities, and materials needed to do certain work. **Systems Evaluation:** Looking at many indicators of system performance and taking into account their accuracy. **Social Perceptiveness:** Being aware of others' reactions and understanding why they react the way they do.

Education and Training Programs: Educational Administration and Supervision, Other; Educational Leadership and Administration, General; Educational, Instructional, and Curriculum Supervision; Elementary and Middle School Administration/Principalship; Secondary School Administration/Principalship. **Related Knowledge/Courses—Therapy and Counseling:** Information and techniques needed to rehabilitate physical and mental ailments and to provide career guidance, including alternative treatments, rehabilitation equipment and its proper use, and methods to evaluate treatment effects. **Education and Training:** Instructional methods and training techniques, including curriculum design principles, learning theory, group and individual teaching techniques, design of individual development plans, and test design principles. **Personnel and Human Resources:** Principles and procedures for personnel recruitment; selection; training; compensation and benefits; labor relations and negotiation; and personnel information systems. **Psychology:** Human behavior and performance, mental processes, psychological research methods, and the assessment and treatment of behavioral and affective disorders. **Sociology and Anthropology:** Group behavior and dynamics; societal trends and influences; and cultures and their history, migrations, ethnicity, and origins. **History and Archeology:** Historical events and their causes, indicators, and impact on particular civilizations and cultures.

Work Environment: Indoors; standing.

Education Administrators, Postsecondary

- ❋ Education/Training Required: Work experience plus degree
- ❋ Annual Earnings: $75,780
- ❋ Beginning Wage: $41,910
- ❋ Earnings Growth Potential: High
- ❋ Growth: 14.2%
- ❋ Annual Job Openings: 17,121
- ❋ Self-Employed: 3.3%
- ❋ Part-Time: 8.3%

Plan, direct, or coordinate research, instructional, student administration and services, and other educational activities at postsecondary institutions, including universities, colleges, and junior and community colleges. Recruit, hire, train, and terminate departmental personnel. Plan, administer, and control budgets; maintain financial records; and produce financial reports. Represent institutions at community and campus events, in meetings with other institution personnel, and during accreditation processes. Participate in faculty and college committee activities. Provide assistance to faculty and staff in duties such as teaching classes, conducting orientation programs, issuing transcripts, and scheduling events. Establish operational policies and procedures and make any necessary modifications, based on analysis of operations, demographics, and other research information. Confer with other academic staff to explain and formulate admission requirements and course credit policies. Appoint individuals to faculty positions and evaluate their performance. Direct activities of administrative departments such as admissions, registration, and career services. Develop curricula and recommend curricula revisions and additions. Determine course schedules and coordinate teaching assignments and room assignments to ensure optimum use of buildings and equipment. Consult with government regulatory and licensing agencies to ensure the institution's conformance with applicable standards. Direct, coordinate, and evaluate the activities of personnel engaged in administering academic institutions, departments, and/or alumni organizations. Teach courses within their department. Participate in student recruitment, selection, and admission, making admissions recommendations when required to do so. Review student misconduct reports requiring disciplinary action and counsel students regarding such reports. Supervise coaches. Assess and collect tuition and fees. Direct scholarship, fellowship, and loan programs, performing activities such as selecting recipients and distributing aid. Coordinate the production and dissemination of university publications such as course catalogs and class schedules. Review registration statistics and consult with faculty officials to develop registration policies. Audit the financial status of student organizations and facility accounts.

Personality Type: Enterprising. These occupations frequently involve starting up and carrying out projects and can involve leading people and making many decisions. They sometimes require risk taking and often deal with business.

GOE—Interest Area/Cluster: 05. Education and Training. **Work Group:** 05.01. Managerial Work in Education. **Other Jobs in This Work Group:** Education Administrators, Elementary and Secondary School; Education Administrators, Preschool and Child Care Center/Program; Instructional Coordinators.

Skills—Management of Financial Resources: Determining how money will be spent to get the work done and accounting for these expenditures. **Management of Personnel Resources:** Motivating, developing, and directing people as they work; identifying the best people for the job. **Systems Evaluation:** Looking at many indicators of system performance and taking into account their accuracy. **Persuasion:** Persuading others to approach things differently. **Monitoring:** Assessing how well one is doing when learning or doing something. **Judgment and Decision Making:** Weighing the relative costs and benefits of a potential action. **Management of Material Resources:** Obtaining and seeing to the appropriate use of equipment, facilities, and materials needed to do certain work. **Operations Analysis:** Analyzing needs and product requirements to create a design.

Education and Training Programs: Community College Education; Educational Administration and Supervision, Other; Educational Leadership and Administration, General; Educational, Instructional, and Curriculum Supervision; Higher Education/Higher Education Administration. **Related Knowledge/Courses—Personnel and Human Resources:** Principles and procedures for personnel recruitment; selection; training; compensation and benefits; labor relations and negotiation; and personnel information systems. **Education and Training:** Instructional methods and training techniques, including curriculum design principles, learning theory, group and individual teaching techniques, design of individual development plans, and test design principles. **Sociology and Anthropology:** Group behavior and dynamics; societal trends and influences; and cultures and their history, migrations, ethnicity, and origins. **Administration and Management:** Principles and processes involved in business and organizational planning, coordination, and execution. This includes strategic planning, resource allocation, manpower modeling, leadership techniques, and production methods. **Philosophy and Theology:** Different philosophical systems and religions, including their basic principles, values, ethics, ways of thinking, customs, and practices and their impact on human culture. **English Language:** The structure and content of the English language, including the meaning and spelling of words, rules of composition, and grammar.

Work Environment: Indoors; sitting.

Education Administrators, Preschool and Child Care Center/ Program

- ❋ Education/Training Required: Work experience plus degree
- ❋ Annual Earnings: $38,580
- ❋ Beginning Wage: $25,340
- ❋ Earnings Growth Potential: Low
- ❋ Growth: 23.5%
- ❋ Annual Job Openings: 8,113
- ❋ Self-Employed: 3.4%
- ❋ Part-Time: 8.3%

Plan, direct, or coordinate the academic and nonacademic activities of preschool and child care centers or programs. Confer with parents and staff to discuss educational activities and policies and students' behavioral or learning problems. Prepare and maintain attendance, activity, planning, accounting, or personnel reports and records for officials and agencies or direct preparation and maintenance activities. Set educational standards and goals and help establish policies, procedures, and programs to carry them out. Monitor students' progress and provide students and teachers with assistance in resolving any problems. Determine allocations of funds for staff, supplies, materials, and equipment and authorize purchases. Recruit, hire, train, and evaluate primary and supplemental staff and recommend personnel actions for programs and services. Direct and coordinate activities of teachers or administrators at daycare centers, schools, public agencies, or institutions. Plan, direct, and monitor instructional methods and content of educational, vocational, or student activity programs. Review and interpret government codes and develop procedures to meet codes and to ensure facility safety, security, and maintenance. Determine the scope of educational program offerings and prepare drafts of program schedules and descriptions to estimate staffing and facility requirements. Review and evaluate new and current programs to determine their efficiency; effectiveness; and compliance with state, local, and federal regulations, and recommend any necessary modifications. Teach classes or courses or provide direct care to children. Prepare and submit budget requests or grant proposals to solicit program funding. Write articles, manuals, and other publications and assist in the distribution of promotional literature about programs and facilities. Collect and analyze survey data, regulatory information, and demographic and employment trends to forecast enrollment patterns and the need for curriculum changes. Inform businesses, community groups, and governmental agencies about educational needs, available programs, and program policies. Organize and direct committees of specialists, volunteers, and staff to provide technical and advisory assistance for programs.

Personality Type: Social. These occupations frequently involve working with, communicating with, and teaching people and often involve helping or providing service to others.

GOE—Interest Area/Cluster: 05. Education and Training. **Work Group:** 05.01. Managerial Work in Education. **Other Jobs in This Work Group:** Education Administrators, Elementary and Secondary School; Education Administrators, Postsecondary; Instructional Coordinators.

Skills—Management of Financial Resources: Determining how money will be spent to get the work done and accounting for these expenditures. **Management of Personnel Resources:** Motivating, developing, and directing people as they work; identifying the best people for the job. **Management of Material Resources:** Obtaining and seeing to the appropriate use of equipment, facilities, and materials needed to do certain work. **Learning Strategies:** Using multiple approaches when learning or teaching new things. **Monitoring:** Assessing how well one is doing when learning or doing something. **Social Perceptiveness:** Being aware of others' reactions and understanding why they react the way they do. **Negotiation:** Bringing others together and trying to reconcile differences. **Persuasion:** Persuading others to approach things differently.

Education and Training Programs: Educational Administration and Supervision, Other; Educational Leadership and Administration, General; Educational, Instructional, and Curriculum Supervision; Elementary and Middle School Administration/Principalship. **Related Knowledge/Courses—Personnel and Human Resources:** Principles and procedures for personnel recruitment; selection; training; compensation and benefits; labor relations and negotiation; and personnel information systems. **Education and Training:** Instructional methods and training techniques, including curriculum design principles, learning theory, group and individual teaching techniques, design of individual development plans, and test design principles. **Clerical Practices:** Administrative and clerical procedures and systems such as word-processing systems, filing and records management systems, stenography and transcription, forms, design principles, and other office procedures and terminology. **Philosophy and Theology:** Different philosophical systems and religions, including their basic principles, values, ethics, ways of thinking, customs, and practices and their impact on human culture. **Therapy and Counseling:** Information and techniques needed to rehabilitate physical and mental ailments and to provide career guidance, including alternative treatments, rehabilitation equipment and its proper use, and methods to evaluate treatment effects. **Sociology and Anthropology:** Group behavior and dynamics; societal trends and influences; and cultures and their history, migrations, ethnicity, and origins.

Work Environment: Indoors; standing.

Education Teachers, Postsecondary

* Education/Training Required: Doctoral degree
* Annual Earnings: $54,220
* Beginning Wage: $29,060
* Earnings Growth Potential: High
* Growth: 22.9%
* Annual Job Openings: 9,359
* Self-Employed: 0.4%
* Part-Time: 27.8%

Teach courses pertaining to education, such as counseling, curriculum, guidance, instruction, teacher education, and teaching English as a second language. Prepare course materials such as syllabi, homework assignments, and handouts. Prepare and deliver lectures to undergraduate and/or graduate students on topics such as children's literature, learning and development, and reading instruction. Initiate, facilitate, and moderate classroom discussions. Evaluate and grade students' classwork, assignments, and papers. Plan, evaluate, and revise curricula, course content, and course materials and methods of instruction. Supervise students' fieldwork, internship, and research work. Keep abreast of developments in their field by reading current literature, talking with colleagues, and participating in professional conferences. Advise students on academic and vocational curricula and on career issues. Maintain regularly scheduled office hours to advise and assist students. Maintain student attendance records, grades, and other required records. Collaborate with colleagues to address teaching and research issues. Compile, administer, and grade examinations or assign this work to others. Conduct research in a particular field of knowledge and publish findings in professional journals, books, or electronic media. Select and obtain materials and supplies such as textbooks. Participate in student recruitment, registration, and placement activities. Advise and instruct teachers employed in school systems by providing activities such as in-service seminars. Serve on academic or administrative committees that deal with institutional policies, departmental matters, and academic issues. Compile bibliographies of specialized materials for outside reading assignments. Write grant proposals to procure external research funding. Participate in campus and community events. Perform administrative duties such as serving as department head. Act as advisers to student organizations. Provide professional consulting services to government and/or industry.

Personality Type: Social. These occupations frequently involve working with, communicating with, and teaching people and often involve helping or providing service to others.

GOE—Interest Area/Cluster: 05. Education and Training. **Work Group:** 05.03. Postsecondary and Adult Teaching and Instructing. **Other Jobs in This Work Group:** Adult Literacy, Remedial Education, and GED Teachers and Instructors; Agricultural Sciences Teachers, Postsecondary; Anthropology and Archeology Teachers, Postsecondary; Architecture Teachers, Postsecondary; Area, Ethnic, and Cultural Studies Teachers, Postsecondary; Art, Drama, and Music Teachers, Postsecondary; Atmospheric, Earth, Marine, and Space Sciences Teachers, Postsecondary; Biological Science Teachers, Postsecondary; Business Teachers, Postsecondary; Chemistry Teachers, Postsecondary; Communications Teachers, Postsecondary; Computer Science Teachers, Postsecondary; Criminal Justice and Law Enforcement Teachers, Postsecondary; Economics Teachers, Postsecondary; Engineering Teachers, Postsecondary; English Language and Literature Teachers, Postsecondary; Environmental Science Teachers, Postsecondary; Farm and Home Management Advisors; Foreign Language and Literature Teachers, Postsecondary; Forestry and Conservation Science Teachers, Postsecondary; Geography Teachers, Postsecondary; Graduate Teaching Assistants; Health Specialties Teachers, Postsecondary; History Teachers, Postsecondary; Home Economics Teachers, Postsecondary; Law Teachers, Postsecondary; Library Science Teachers, Postsecondary; Mathematical Science Teachers, Postsecondary; Nursing Instructors and Teachers, Postsecondary; Philosophy and Religion Teachers, Postsecondary; Physics Teachers, Postsecondary; Political Science Teachers, Postsecondary; Psychology Teachers, Postsecondary; Recreation and Fitness Studies Teachers, Postsecondary; Self-Enrichment Education Teachers; Social Work Teachers, Postsecondary; Sociology Teachers, Postsecondary; Vocational Education Teachers, Postsecondary.

Skills—Learning Strategies: Using multiple approaches when learning or teaching new things. **Instructing:** Teaching others how to do something. **Writing:** Communicating effectively with others in writing as indicated by the needs of the audience. **Social Perceptiveness:** Being aware of others' reactions and understanding why they react the way they do. **Speaking:** Talking to others to effectively convey information. **Persuasion:** Persuading others to approach things differently. **Science:** Using scientific methods to solve problems. **Monitoring:** Assessing how well one is doing when learning or doing something.

Education and Training Programs: Art Teacher Education; Biology Teacher Education; Business Teacher Education; Foreign Language Teacher Education; Geography Teacher Education; History Teacher Education; Mathematics Teacher Education; Physical Education Teaching and Coaching; Sales and Marketing Operations; Science Teacher Education; Social and Philosophical Foundations of Education; Social Studies Teacher Education; Speech Teacher Education; Technology Teacher Education/Industrial Arts Teacher Education; others. **Related Knowledge/Courses—Therapy and Counseling:** Information and techniques needed to rehabilitate physical and mental ailments and to provide career guidance, including alternative treatments, rehabilitation equipment and its proper use, and methods to evaluate treatment effects. **Education and Training:** Instructional methods and training techniques, including curriculum design principles, learning theory, group and individual teaching techniques, design of individual development plans, and test design principles. **Sociology and Anthropology:** Group behavior and dynamics; societal trends and influences; and cultures and their history, migrations, ethnicity, and origins. **Philosophy and Theology:** Different philosophical systems and religions, including their basic principles, values, ethics, ways of thinking, customs, and practices and their impact on human culture. **Psychology:** Human behavior and performance, mental processes, psychological research methods, and the assessment and treatment of behavioral and affective disorders. **English Language:** The structure and content of the English language, including the meaning and spelling of words, rules of composition, and grammar.

Work Environment: Indoors; sitting.

Educational, Vocational, and School Counselors

* Education/Training Required: Master's degree
* Annual Earnings: $49,450
* Beginning Wage: $28,430
* Earnings Growth Potential: High
* Growth: 12.6%
* Annual Job Openings: 54,025
* Self-Employed: 6.1%
* Part-Time: 15.4%

Counsel individuals and provide group educational and vocational guidance services. Counsel students regarding educational issues such as course and program selection, class scheduling, school adjustment, truancy, study habits, and career planning. Counsel individuals to help them understand and overcome personal, social, or behavioral problems affecting their educational or vocational situations. Maintain accurate and complete student records as required by laws, district policies, and administrative regulations. Confer with parents or guardians, teachers, other counselors, and administrators to resolve students' behavioral, academic, and other problems. Provide crisis intervention to students when difficult situations occur at schools. Identify cases involving domestic abuse or other family problems affecting students' development. Meet with parents and guardians to discuss their children's progress and to determine their priorities for their children and their resource needs. Prepare students for later educational experiences by encouraging them to explore learning opportunities and to persevere with challenging tasks. Encourage students and/or parents to seek additional assistance from mental health professionals when necessary. Observe and evaluate students' performance, behavior, social development, and physical health. Enforce all administration policies and rules governing students. Meet with other professionals to discuss individual students' needs and progress. Provide students with information on such topics as college degree programs and admission requirements, financial aid opportunities, trade and technical schools, and apprenticeship programs. Evaluate individuals' abilities, interests, and personality characteristics, using tests, records, interviews, and professional sources. Collaborate with teachers and administrators in the development, evaluation, and revision of school programs. Establish and enforce behavioral rules and procedures to maintain order among students. Teach classes and present self-help or information sessions on subjects related to education and career planning. Attend professional meetings, educational conferences, and teacher training workshops to maintain and improve professional competence.

Personality Type: Social. These occupations frequently involve working with, communicating with, and teaching people and often involve helping or providing service to others.

GOE—Interest Area/Cluster: 05. Education and Training. **Work Group:** 05.06. Counseling, Health, and Fitness Education. **Other Jobs in This Work Group:** Fitness Trainers and Aerobics Instructors; Health Educators.

Skills—Social Perceptiveness: Being aware of others' reactions and understanding why they react the way they do. **Service Orientation:** Actively looking for ways to help people. **Negotiation:** Bringing others together and trying to reconcile differences. **Active Listening:** Listening to what other people are saying and asking questions as appropriate. **Persuasion:** Persuading others to approach things differently. **Learning Strategies:** Using multiple approaches when learning or teaching new things. **Writing:** Communicating effectively with others in writing as indicated by the needs of the audience. **Monitoring:** Assessing how well one is doing when learning or doing something.

Education and Training Programs: College Student Counseling and Personnel Services; Counselor Education/School Counseling and Guidance Services. **Related Knowledge/Courses—Therapy and Counseling:** Information and techniques needed to rehabilitate physical and mental ailments and to provide career guidance, including alternative treatments, rehabilitation equipment and its proper use, and methods to evaluate treatment effects. **Psychology:** Human behavior and performance, mental processes, psychological research methods, and the assessment and treatment of behavioral and affective disorders. **Sociology and Anthropology:** Group behavior and dynamics; societal trends and influences; and cultures and their history, migrations, ethnicity, and origins. **Education and Training:** Instructional methods and training techniques, including curriculum design principles, learning theory, group and individual teaching techniques, design of individual development plans, and test design principles. **Philosophy and Theology:** Different philosophical systems and religions, including their basic principles, values, ethics, ways of thinking, customs, and practices and their impact on human culture. **Clerical Practices:** Administrative and clerical procedures and systems such as word-processing systems, filing and records management systems, stenography and transcription, forms, design principles, and other office procedures and terminology.

Work Environment: Indoors; sitting.

Electrical and Electronics Repairers, Commercial and Industrial Equipment

- ✱ Education/Training Required: Postsecondary vocational training
- ✱ Annual Earnings: $47,110
- ✱ Beginning Wage: $28,830
- ✱ Earnings Growth Potential: Medium
- ✱ Growth: 6.8%
- ✱ Annual Job Openings: 6,607
- ✱ Self-Employed: 0.0%
- ✱ Part-Time: 0.6%

Repair, test, adjust, or install electronic equipment, such as industrial controls, transmitters, and antennas. Perform scheduled preventive maintenance tasks, such as checking, cleaning, and repairing equipment, to detect and prevent problems. Examine work orders and converse with equipment operators to detect equipment problems and to ascertain whether mechanical or human errors contributed to the problems. Operate equipment to demonstrate proper use and to analyze malfunctions. Set up and test industrial equipment to ensure that it functions properly. Test faulty equipment to diagnose malfunctions, using test equipment and software and applying knowledge of the functional operation of electronic units and systems. Repair and adjust equipment, machines, and defective components, replacing worn parts such as gaskets and seals in watertight electrical equipment. Calibrate testing instruments and installed or repaired equipment to prescribed specifications. Advise management regarding customer satisfaction, product performance, and suggestions for product improvements. Study blueprints, schematics, manuals, and other specifications to determine installation procedures. Inspect components of industrial equipment for accurate assembly and installation and for defects such as loose connections and frayed wires. Maintain equipment logs that record performance problems, repairs, calibrations, and tests. Coordinate efforts with other workers involved in installing and maintaining equipment or components. Maintain inventory of spare parts. Consult with customers, supervisors, and engineers to plan layout of equipment and to resolve problems in system operation and maintenance. Install repaired equipment in various settings, such as industrial or military establishments. Send defective units to the manufacturer or to a specialized repair shop for repair. Determine feasibility of using standardized equipment and develop specifications for equipment required to perform additional functions. Enter information into computer to copy program or to draw, modify, or store schematics, applying knowledge of software package used. Sign overhaul documents for equipment replaced or repaired. Develop or modify industrial electronic devices, circuits, and equipment according to available specifications.

Personality Type: Realistic. These occupations frequently involve work activities that include practical, hands-on problems and solutions. They often deal with plants; animals; and real-world materials such as wood, tools, and machinery. Many of the occupations require working outside and don't involve a lot of paperwork or working closely with others.

GOE—Interest Area/Cluster: 13. Manufacturing. **Work Group:** 13.12. Electrical and Electronic Repair. **Other Jobs in This Work Group:** Avionics Technicians; Electric Motor, Power Tool, and Related Repairers; Electrical and Electronics Installers and Repairers, Transportation Equipment; Electronic Equipment Installers and Repairers, Motor Vehicles; Electronic Home Entertainment Equipment Installers and Repairers; Radio Mechanics.

Skills—Installation: Installing equipment, machines, wiring, or programs to meet specifications. **Repairing:** Repairing machines or systems, using the needed tools. **Operation Monitoring:** Watching gauges, dials, or other indicators to make sure a machine is working properly. **Troubleshooting:** Determining what is causing an operating error and deciding what to do about it. **Equipment Maintenance:** Performing routine maintenance and determining when and what kind of maintenance is needed. **Operation and Control:** Controlling operations of equipment or systems. **Systems Analysis:** Determining how a system should work and how changes will affect outcomes. **Science:** Using scientific methods to solve problems.

Education and Training Programs: Computer Installation and Repair Technology/Technician Training; Industrial Electronics Technology/Technician Training. **Related Knowledge/Courses—Mechanical Devices:** Machines and tools, including their designs, uses, benefits, repair, and maintenance. **Computers and Electronics:** Electric circuit boards, processors, chips, and computer hardware and software, including applications and programming. **Telecommunications:** Transmission, broadcasting, switching, control, and operation of telecommunications systems. **Engineering and Technology:** Equipment, tools, and mechanical devices and their uses to produce motion, light, power, technology, and other applications.

Work Environment: Indoors; noisy; cramped work space, awkward positions; hazardous conditions; standing; using hands on objects, tools, or controls.

Electrical Drafters

- ❋ Education/Training Required: Postsecondary vocational training
- ❋ Annual Earnings: $49,250
- ❋ Beginning Wage: $30,490
- ❋ Earnings Growth Potential: Medium
- ❋ Growth: 4.1%
- ❋ Annual Job Openings: 4,786
- ❋ Self-Employed: 5.7%
- ❋ Part-Time: 5.9%

The job openings listed here are shared with Electronic Drafters.

Develop specifications and instructions for installation of voltage transformers, overhead or underground cables, and related electrical equipment used to conduct electrical energy from transmission lines or high-voltage distribution lines to consumers. Use computer-aided drafting equipment and/or conventional drafting stations; technical handbooks; tables; calculators; and traditional drafting tools such as boards, pencils, protractors, and T-squares. Draft working drawings, wiring diagrams, wiring connection specifications, or cross-sections of underground cables as required for instructions to installation crew. Confer with engineering staff and other personnel to resolve problems. Draw master sketches to scale, showing relation of proposed installations to existing facilities and exact specifications and dimensions. Measure factors that affect installation and arrangement of equipment, such as distances to be spanned by wire and cable. Assemble documentation packages and produce drawing sets, which are then checked by an engineer or an architect. Review completed construction drawings and cost estimates for accuracy and conformity to standards and regulations. Prepare and interpret specifications, calculating weights, volumes, and stress factors. Explain drawings to production or construction teams and provide adjustments as necessary. Supervise and train other technologists, technicians, and drafters. Study work order requests to determine type of service, such as lighting or power, demanded by installation. Visit proposed installation sites and draw rough sketches of location. Determine the order of work and the method of presentation, such as orthographic or isometric drawing. Reproduce working drawings on copy machines or trace drawings in ink. Write technical reports and draw charts that display statistics and data.

Personality Type: Realistic. These occupations frequently involve work activities that include practical, hands-on problems and solutions. They often deal with plants; animals; and real-world materials such as wood, tools, and machinery. Many of the occupations require working outside and don't involve a lot of paperwork or working closely with others.

GOE—Interest Area/Cluster: 15. Scientific Research, Engineering, and Mathematics. **Work Group:** 15.09. Engineering Technology. **Other Jobs in This Work Group:** Aerospace Engineering and Operations Technicians; Cartographers and Photogrammetrists; Civil Engineering Technicians; Electrical and Electronic Engineering Technicians; Electrical and Electronics Drafters; Electrical Engineering Technicians; Electro-Mechanical Technicians; Electronic Drafters; Electronics Engineering Technicians; Environmental Engineering Technicians; Mapping Technicians; Mechanical Drafters; Mechanical Engineering Technicians; Surveying and Mapping Technicians; Surveying Technicians.

Skills—Mathematics: Using mathematics to solve problems. **Installation:** Installing equipment, machines, wiring, or programs to meet specifications. **Active Learning:** Working with new material or information to grasp its implications. **Critical Thinking:** Using logic and analysis to identify the strengths and weaknesses of different approaches. **Quality Control Analysis:** Evaluating the quality or performance of products, services, or processes. **Technology Design:** Generating or adapting equipment and technology to serve user needs. **Equipment Selection:** Determining the kind of tools and equipment needed to do a job. **Operations Analysis:** Analyzing needs and product requirements to create a design.

Education and Training Program: Electrical/Electronics Drafting and Electrical/Electronics CAD/CADD. **Related Knowledge/Courses—Design:** Design techniques, principles, tools, and instruments involved in the production and use of precision technical plans, blueprints, drawings, and models. **Engineering and Technology:** Equipment, tools, and mechanical devices and their uses to produce motion, light, power, technology, and other applications. **Building and Construction:** Materials, methods, and the appropriate tools to construct objects, structures, and buildings. **Computers and Electronics:** Electric circuit boards, processors, chips, and computer hardware and software, including applications and programming. **Telecommunications:** Transmission, broadcasting, switching, control, and operation of telecommunications systems. **Clerical Practices:** Administrative and clerical procedures and systems such as word-processing systems, filing and records management systems, stenography and transcription, forms, design principles, and other office procedures and terminology.

Work Environment: Indoors; sitting.

Electrical Engineering Technicians

- ❋ Education/Training Required: Associate degree
- ❋ Annual Earnings: $52,140
- ❋ Beginning Wage: $31,310
- ❋ Earnings Growth Potential: High
- ❋ Growth: 3.6%
- ❋ Annual Job Openings: 12,583
- ❋ Self-Employed: 0.9%
- ❋ Part-Time: 5.9%

The job openings listed here are shared with Electronics Engineering Technicians.

Apply electrical theory and related knowledge to test and modify developmental or operational electrical machinery and electrical control equipment and circuitry in industrial or commercial plants and laboratories. Usually work under direction of engineering staff. Assemble electrical and electronic systems and prototypes according to engineering data and knowledge of electrical principles, using hand tools and measuring instruments. Provide technical assistance and resolution when electrical or engineering problems are encountered before, during, and after construction. Install and maintain electrical control systems and solid state equipment. Modify electrical prototypes, parts, assemblies, and systems to correct functional deviations. Set up and operate test equipment to evaluate performance of developmental parts, assemblies, or systems under simulated operating conditions and record results. Collaborate with electrical engineers and other personnel to identify, define, and solve developmental problems. Build, calibrate, maintain, troubleshoot, and repair electrical instruments or testing equipment. Analyze and interpret test information to resolve design-related problems. Write commissioning procedures for electrical installations. Prepare project cost and work-time estimates. Evaluate engineering proposals, shop drawings, and design comments for sound electrical engineering practice and conformance with established safety and design criteria and recommend approval or disapproval. Draw or modify diagrams and write engineering specifications to clarify design details and functional criteria of experimental electronics units. Conduct inspections for quality control and assurance programs, reporting findings and recommendations. Prepare contracts and initiate, review, and coordinate modifications to contract specifications and plans throughout the construction process. Plan, schedule, and monitor work of support personnel to assist supervisor. Review existing electrical engineering criteria to identify necessary revisions, deletions, or amendments to outdated material. Perform supervisory duties such as recommending work assignments, approving leaves, and completing performance evaluations. Plan method and sequence of operations for developing and testing experimental electronic and electrical equipment. Visit construction sites to observe conditions impacting design and to identify solutions to technical design problems involving electrical systems equipment that arise during construction.

Personality Type: Realistic. These occupations frequently involve work activities that include practical, hands-on problems and solutions. They often deal with plants; animals; and real-world materials such as wood, tools, and machinery. Many of the occupations require working outside and don't involve a lot of paperwork or working closely with others.

GOE—Interest Area/Cluster: 15. Scientific Research, Engineering, and Mathematics. **Work Group:** 15.09. Engineering Technology. **Other Jobs in This Work Group:** Aerospace Engineering and Operations Technicians; Cartographers and Photogrammetrists; Civil Engineering Technicians; Electrical and Electronic Engineering Technicians; Electrical and Electronics Drafters; Electrical Drafters; Electro-Mechanical Technicians; Electronic Drafters; Electronics Engineering Technicians; Environmental Engineering Technicians; Mapping Technicians; Mechanical Drafters; Mechanical Engineering Technicians; Surveying and Mapping Technicians; Surveying Technicians.

Skills—Repairing: Repairing machines or systems, using the needed tools. **Installation:** Installing equipment, machines, wiring, or programs to meet specifications. **Troubleshooting:** Determining what is causing an operating error and deciding what to do about it. **Science:** Using scientific methods to solve problems. **Operations Analysis:** Analyzing needs and product requirements to create a design. **Technology Design:** Generating or adapting equipment and technology to serve user needs. **Mathematics:**

Using mathematics to solve problems. **Equipment Maintenance:** Performing routine maintenance and determining when and what kind of maintenance is needed.

Education and Training Programs: Computer Engineering Technology/Technician Training; Computer Technology/Computer Systems Technology; Electrical and Electronic Engineering Technologies/Technician Training, Other; Electrical, Electronic and Communications Engineering Technology/Technician Training; Telecommunications Technology/Technician Training. **Related Knowledge/Courses—Engineering and Technology:** Equipment, tools, and mechanical devices and their uses to produce motion, light, power, technology, and other applications. **Design:** Design techniques, principles, tools, and instruments involved in the production and use of precision technical plans, blueprints, drawings, and models. **Computers and Electronics:** Electric circuit boards, processors, chips, and computer hardware and software, including applications and programming. **Physics:** Physical principles, laws, and applications, including air, water, material dynamics, light, atomic principles, heat, electric theory, earth formations, and meteorological and related natural phenomena. **Mechanical Devices:** Machines and tools, including their designs, uses, benefits, repair, and maintenance. **Telecommunications:** Transmission, broadcasting, switching, control, and operation of telecommunications systems.

Work Environment: Indoors; noisy; sitting; using hands on objects, tools, or controls.

Electrical Engineers

- ❋ Education/Training Required: Bachelor's degree
- ❋ Annual Earnings: $79,240
- ❋ Beginning Wage: $51,220
- ❋ Earnings Growth Potential: Medium
- ❋ Growth: 6.3%
- ❋ Annual Job Openings: 6,806
- ❋ Self-Employed: 2.1%
- ❋ Part-Time: 2.0%

Design, develop, test, or supervise the manufacturing and installation of electrical equipment, components, or systems for commercial, industrial, military, or scientific use. Confer with engineers, customers, and others to discuss existing or potential engineering projects and products. Design, implement, maintain, and improve electrical instruments, equipment, facilities, components, products, and systems for commercial, industrial, and domestic purposes. Operate computer-assisted engineering and design software and equipment to perform engineering tasks. Direct and coordinate manufacturing, construction, installation, maintenance, support, documentation, and testing activities to ensure compliance with specifications, codes, and customer requirements. Perform detailed calculations to compute and establish manufacturing, construction, and installation standards and specifications. Inspect completed installations and observe operations to ensure conformance to design and equipment specifications and compliance with operational and safety standards. Plan and implement research methodology and procedures to apply principles of electrical theory to engineering projects. Prepare specifications for purchase of materials and equipment. Supervise and train project team members as necessary. Investigate and test vendors' and competitors' products. Oversee project production efforts to assure projects are completed satisfactorily, on time, and within budget. Prepare and study technical drawings, specifications of electrical systems, and topographical maps to ensure that installation and operations conform to standards and customer requirements. Investigate customer or public complaints, determine nature and extent of problem, and recommend remedial measures. Plan layout of electric-power-generating plants and distribution lines and stations. Assist in developing capital project programs for new equipment and major repairs. Develop budgets, estimating labor, material, and construction costs. Compile data and write reports regarding existing and potential engineering studies and projects. Collect data relating to commercial and residential development, population, and power system interconnection to determine operating efficiency of electrical systems. Conduct field surveys and study maps, graphs, diagrams, and other data to identify and correct power system problems.

Personality Type: Investigative. These occupations frequently involve working with ideas and require an extensive amount of thinking. They can involve searching for facts and figuring out problems mentally.

GOE—Interest Area/Cluster: 15. Scientific Research, Engineering, and Mathematics. **Work Group:** 15.07. Research and Design Engineering. **Other Jobs in This Work Group:** Aerospace Engineers; Biomedical Engineers; Chemical Engineers; Civil Engineers; Computer Hardware Engineers; Electronics Engineers, Except Computer; Marine Architects; Marine Engineers; Marine Engineers and Naval Architects; Materials Engineers; Mechanical Engineers; Nuclear Engineers.

Skills—Technology Design: Generating or adapting equipment and technology to serve user needs. **Science:** Using scientific methods to solve problems. **Systems Analysis:** Determining how a system should work and how changes will affect outcomes. **Troubleshooting:** Determining what is causing an operating error and deciding what to do about it. **Systems Evaluation:** Looking at many indicators of system performance and taking into account their accuracy. **Equipment Selection:** Determining the kind of tools and equipment needed to do a job. **Management of Material Resources:** Obtaining and seeing to the appropriate use of equipment, facilities, and materials needed to do certain work. **Programming:** Writing computer programs for various purposes.

Education and Training Program: Electrical, Electronics and Communications Engineering. **Related Knowledge/Courses—Engineering and Technology:** Equipment, tools, and mechanical devices and their uses to produce motion, light, power, technology, and other applications. **Design:** Design techniques, principles, tools, and instruments involved in the production and use of precision technical plans, blueprints, drawings, and models. **Physics:** Physical principles, laws, and applications, including air, water, material dynamics, light, atomic principles, heat, electric theory, earth formations, and meteorological and related natural phenomena. **Telecommunications:** Transmission, broadcasting, switching, control, and operation of telecommunications systems. **Computers and Electronics:** Electric circuit boards, processors, chips, and computer hardware and software, including applications and programming. **Mathematics:** Numbers and their operations and interrelationships, including arithmetic, algebra, geometry, calculus, and statistics and their applications.

Work Environment: Indoors; sitting.

Electrical Power-Line Installers and Repairers

- ❋ Education/Training Required: Long-term on-the-job training
- ❋ Annual Earnings: $52,570
- ❋ Beginning Wage: $29,780
- ❋ Earnings Growth Potential: High
- ❋ Growth: 7.2%
- ❋ Annual Job Openings: 6,401
- ❋ Self-Employed: 0.6%
- ❋ Part-Time: 1.3%

Install or repair cables or wires used in electrical power or distribution systems. May erect poles and light- or heavy-duty transmission towers. Adhere to safety practices and procedures, such as checking equipment regularly and erecting barriers around work areas. Open switches or attach grounding devices to remove electrical hazards from disturbed or fallen lines or to facilitate repairs. Climb poles or use truck-mounted buckets to access equipment. Place insulating or fireproofing materials over conductors and joints. Install, maintain, and repair electrical distribution and transmission systems, including conduits; cables; wires; and related equipment such as transformers, circuit breakers, and switches. Identify defective sectionalizing devices, circuit breakers, fuses, voltage regulators, transformers, switches, relays, or wiring, using wiring diagrams and electrical-testing instruments. Drive vehicles equipped with tools and materials to job sites. Coordinate work assignment preparation and completion with other workers. String wire conductors and cables between poles, towers, trenches, pylons, and buildings, setting lines in place and using winches to adjust tension. Inspect and test power lines and auxiliary equipment to locate and identify problems, using reading and testing instruments. Test conductors according to electrical diagrams and specifications to identify corresponding conductors and to prevent incorrect connections. Replace damaged poles with new poles and straighten the poles. Install watt-hour meters and connect service drops between power lines and consumers' facilities. Attach crossarms, insulators, and auxiliary equipment to poles prior to installing them. Travel in trucks, helicopters, and airplanes to inspect lines for freedom from obstruction and adequacy of insulation. Dig holes, using augers, and set poles, using cranes and power equipment. Trim trees that could be hazardous to the functioning of cables or wires. Splice or solder cables together or to overhead transmission lines, customer service lines, or street light lines, using hand tools, epoxies, or specialized equipment. Cut and peel lead sheathing and insulation from defective or newly installed cables and conduits prior to splicing.

Personality Type: Realistic. These occupations frequently involve work activities that include practical, hands-on problems and solutions. They often deal with plants; animals; and real-world materials such as wood, tools, and machinery. Many of the occupations require working outside and don't involve a lot of paperwork or working closely with others.

GOE—Interest Area/Cluster: 02. Architecture and Construction. **Work Group:** 02.05. Systems and Equipment

Installation, Maintenance, and Repair. **Other Jobs in This Work Group:** Electrical and Electronics Repairers, Powerhouse, Substation, and Relay; Elevator Installers and Repairers; Heating and Air Conditioning Mechanics and Installers; Maintenance and Repair Workers, General; Refrigeration Mechanics and Installers; Telecommunications Equipment Installers and Repairers, Except Line Installers; Telecommunications Line Installers and Repairers.

Skills—Repairing: Repairing machines or systems, using the needed tools. **Installation:** Installing equipment, machines, wiring, or programs to meet specifications. **Equipment Maintenance:** Performing routine maintenance and determining when and what kind of maintenance is needed. **Operation Monitoring:** Watching gauges, dials, or other indicators to make sure a machine is working properly. **Troubleshooting:** Determining what is causing an operating error and deciding what to do about it. **Operation and Control:** Controlling operations of equipment or systems. **Equipment Selection:** Determining the kind of tools and equipment needed to do a job. **Technology Design:** Generating or adapting equipment and technology to serve user needs.

Education and Training Programs: Electrical and Power Transmission Installation/Installer Training, General; Electrical and Power Transmission Installer Training, Other; Lineworker Training. **Related Knowledge/Courses— Building and Construction:** Materials, methods, and the appropriate tools to construct objects, structures, and buildings. **Mechanical Devices:** Machines and tools, including their designs, uses, benefits, repair, and maintenance. **Customer and Personal Service:** Principles and processes for providing customer and personal services, including needs assessment techniques, quality service standards, alternative delivery systems, and customer satisfaction evaluation techniques. **Engineering and Technology:** Equipment, tools, and mechanical devices and their uses to produce motion, light, power, technology, and other applications. **Transportation:** Principles and methods for moving people or goods by air, rail, sea, or road, including their relative costs, advantages, and limitations. **Design:** Design techniques, principles, tools, and instruments involved in the production and use of precision technical plans, blueprints, drawings, and models.

Work Environment: Outdoors; very hot or cold; high places; hazardous conditions; hazardous equipment; using hands on objects, tools, or controls.

Electricians

- ❈ Education/Training Required: Long-term on-the-job training
- ❈ Annual Earnings: $44,780
- ❈ Beginning Wage: $27,330
- ❈ Earnings Growth Potential: Medium
- ❈ Growth: 7.4%
- ❈ Annual Job Openings: 79,083
- ❈ Self-Employed: 10.7%
- ❈ Part-Time: 2.3%

Install, maintain, and repair electrical wiring, equipment, and fixtures. Ensure that work is in accordance with relevant codes. May install or service street lights, intercom systems, or electrical control systems. Maintain current electrician's license or identification card to meet governmental regulations. Connect wires to circuit breakers, transformers, or other components. Repair or replace wiring, equipment, and fixtures, using hand tools and power tools. Assemble, install, test, and maintain electrical or electronic wiring, equipment, appliances, apparatus, and fixtures, using hand tools and power tools. Test electrical systems and continuity of circuits in electrical wiring, equipment, and fixtures, using testing devices such as ohmmeters, voltmeters, and oscilloscopes, to ensure compatibility and safety of system. Use a variety of tools and equipment such as power construction equipment, measuring devices, power tools, and testing equipment, including oscilloscopes, ammeters, and test lamps. Plan layout and installation of electrical wiring, equipment, and fixtures based on job specifications and local codes. Inspect electrical systems, equipment, and components to identify hazards, defects, and the need for adjustment or repair and to ensure compliance with codes. Direct and train workers to install, maintain, or repair electrical wiring, equipment, and fixtures. Diagnose malfunctioning systems, apparatus, and components, using test equipment and hand tools, to locate the cause of a breakdown and correct the problem. Prepare sketches or follow blueprints to determine the location of wiring and equipment and to ensure conformance to building and safety codes. Install ground leads and connect power cables to equipment such as motors. Work from ladders, scaffolds, and roofs to install, maintain, or repair electrical wiring, equipment, and fixtures. Perform business management duties such as maintaining records and files, preparing reports, and ordering supplies and equipment. Fasten small metal or plastic boxes to walls to house electrical switches or outlets. Place conduit, pipes, or tubing inside designated partitions, walls, or other concealed areas and pull insulated wires or cables through the conduit to complete circuits between boxes. Advise management on whether continued operation of equipment could be hazardous.

Personality Type: Realistic. These occupations frequently involve work activities that include practical, hands-on problems and solutions. They often deal with plants; animals; and real-world materials such as wood, tools, and machinery. Many of the occupations require working outside and don't involve a lot of paperwork or working closely with others.

GOE—Interest Area/Cluster: 02. Architecture and Construction. **Work Group:** 02.04. Construction Crafts. **Other Jobs in This Work Group:** Boilermakers; Brickmasons and Blockmasons; Carpet Installers; Cement Masons and Concrete Finishers; Commercial Divers; Construction Carpenters; Crane and Tower Operators; Drywall and Ceiling Tile Installers; Fence Erectors; Floor Layers, Except Carpet, Wood, and Hard Tiles; Floor Sanders and Finishers; Glaziers; Hazardous Materials Removal Workers; Insulation Workers, Floor, Ceiling, and Wall; Insulation Workers, Mechanical; Manufactured Building and Mobile Home Installers; Operating Engineers and Other Construction Equipment Operators; Painters, Construction and Maintenance; Paperhangers; Paving, Surfacing, and Tamping Equipment Operators; Pile-Driver Operators; Pipe Fitters and Steamfitters; Pipelayers; Plasterers and Stucco Masons; Plumbers; Plumbers, Pipefitters, and Steamfitters; Rail-Track Laying and Maintenance Equipment Operators; Refractory Materials Repairers, Except Brickmasons; Reinforcing Iron and Rebar Workers; Riggers; Roofers; Rough Carpenters; Security and Fire Alarm Systems Installers; Segmental Pavers; Sheet Metal Workers; Stone Cutters and Carvers, Manufacturing; Stonemasons; Structural Iron and Steel Workers; Tapers; Terrazzo Workers and Finishers; Tile and Marble Setters.

Skills—Repairing: Repairing machines or systems, using the needed tools. **Operation Monitoring:** Watching gauges, dials, or other indicators to make sure a machine is working properly. **Installation:** Installing equipment, machines, wiring, or programs to meet specifications. **Equipment Maintenance:** Performing routine maintenance and determining when and what kind of maintenance is needed. **Troubleshooting:** Determining what is causing an operating error and deciding what to do about it. **Operation and Control:** Controlling operations of equipment or systems. **Quality Control Analysis:** Evaluating the quality or performance of products, services, or processes.

Education and Training Program: Electrician Training. **Related Knowledge/Courses—Building and Construction:** Materials, methods, and the appropriate tools to construct objects, structures, and buildings. **Mechanical Devices:** Machines and tools, including their designs, uses, benefits, repair, and maintenance. **Design:** Design techniques, principles, tools, and instruments involved in the production and use of precision technical plans, blueprints, drawings, and models. **Physics:** Physical principles, laws, and applications, including air, water, material dynamics, light, atomic principles, heat, electric theory, earth formations, and meteorological and related natural phenomena. **Telecommunications:** Transmission, broadcasting, switching, control, and operation of telecommunications systems. **Engineering and Technology:** Equipment, tools, and mechanical devices and their uses to produce motion, light, power, technology, and other applications.

Work Environment: Noisy; cramped work space, awkward positions; hazardous conditions; hazardous equipment; standing; using hands on objects, tools, or controls.

Electronic Drafters

❀ Education/Training Required: Postsecondary vocational training
❀ Annual Earnings: $49,250
❀ Beginning Wage: $30,490
❀ Earnings Growth Potential: Medium
❀ Growth: 4.1%
❀ Annual Job Openings: 4,786
❀ Self-Employed: 5.7%
❀ Part-Time: 5.9%

The job openings listed here are shared with Electrical Drafters.

Draw wiring diagrams, circuit board assembly diagrams, schematics, and layout drawings used for manufacture, installation, and repair of electronic equipment. Draft detail and assembly drawings of design components, circuitry, and printed circuit boards, using computer-assisted equipment or standard drafting techniques and devices. Consult with engineers to discuss and interpret design concepts and determine requirements of detailed working drawings. Locate files relating to specified design project in database library, load program into computer, and record completed job data. Examine electronic schematics and supporting documents to develop, compute, and verify specifications for drafting data, such as configuration of parts, dimensions, and tolerances. Supervise and coordinate work activities of workers engaged in drafting, designing layouts, assembling, and testing printed circuit boards. Compare logic element configuration on display screen with engineering schematics and calculate figures to convert, redesign, and modify element. Review work orders and procedural manuals and confer with vendors and design staff to resolve problems and modify design. Review blueprints to determine customer requirements and consult with assembler regarding schematics, wiring procedures, and conductor paths. Train students to use drafting machines and to prepare schematic diagrams, block diagrams, control drawings, logic diagrams, integrated circuit drawings, and interconnection diagrams. Generate computer tapes of final layout design to produce layered photo masks and photo plotting design onto film. Select drill size to drill test head, according to test design and specifications, and submit guide layout to designated department. Key and program specified commands and engineering specifications into computer system to change functions and test final layout. Copy drawings of printed circuit board fabrication, using print machine or blueprinting procedure. Plot electrical test points on layout sheets and draw schematics for wiring test fixture heads to frames.

Personality Type: Conventional. These occupations frequently involve following set procedures and routines and can include working with data and details more than with ideas. Usually there is a clear line of authority to follow.

GOE—Interest Area/Cluster: 15. Scientific Research, Engineering, and Mathematics. **Work Group:** 15.09. Engineering Technology. **Other Jobs in This Work Group:** Aerospace Engineering and Operations Technicians; Cartographers and Photogrammetrists; Civil Engineering Technicians; Electrical and Electronic Engineering Technicians; Electrical and Electronics Drafters; Electrical Drafters; Electrical Engineering Technicians; Electro-Mechanical Technicians; Electronics Engineering Technicians; Environmental Engineering Technicians; Mapping Technicians; Mechanical Drafters; Mechanical Engineering Technicians; Surveying and Mapping Technicians; Surveying Technicians.

Skills—Technology Design: Generating or adapting equipment and technology to serve user needs. **Operations Analysis:** Analyzing needs and product requirements to create a design. **Installation:** Installing equipment, machines, wiring, or programs to meet specifications. **Equipment Selection:** Determining the kind of tools and equipment needed to do a job. **Mathematics:** Using mathematics to solve problems. **Coordination:** Adjusting actions in relation to others' actions. **Negotiation:** Bringing others together and trying to reconcile differences. **Complex Problem Solving:** Identifying complex problems, reviewing the options, and implementing solutions.

Education and Training Program: Electrical/Electronics Drafting and Electrical/Electronics CAD/CADD. **Related Knowledge/Courses—Design:** Design techniques, principles, tools, and instruments involved in the production and use of precision technical plans, blueprints, drawings, and models. **Engineering and Technology:** Equipment, tools, and mechanical devices and their uses to produce motion, light, power, technology, and other applications. **Mechanical Devices:** Machines and tools, including their designs, uses, benefits, repair, and maintenance. **Physics:** Physical principles, laws, and applications, including air, water, material dynamics, light, atomic principles, heat, electric theory, earth formations, and meteorological and related natural phenomena. **Telecommunications:** Transmission, broadcasting, switching, control, and operation of telecommunications systems. **Mathematics:** Numbers and their operations and interrelationships, including arithmetic, algebra, geometry, calculus, and statistics and their applications.

Work Environment: Indoors; noisy; sitting; using hands on objects, tools, or controls; repetitive motions.

Electronics Engineering Technicians

- ❋ Education/Training Required: Associate degree
- ❋ Annual Earnings: $52,140
- ❋ Beginning Wage: $31,310
- ❋ Earnings Growth Potential: High
- ❋ Growth: 3.6%
- ❋ Annual Job Openings: 12,583
- ❋ Self-Employed: 0.9%
- ❋ Part-Time: 5.9%

The job openings listed here are shared with Electrical Engineering Technicians.

Lay out, build, test, troubleshoot, repair, and modify developmental and production electronic components, parts, equipment, and systems, such as computer equipment, missile control instrumentation, electron tubes, test equipment, and machine tool numerical controls, applying principles and theories of electronics, electrical circuitry, engineering mathematics, electronic and electrical testing, and physics. Usually work under direction of engineering staff. Read blueprints, wiring diagrams, schematic drawings, and engineering instructions for assembling electronics units, applying knowledge of electronic theory and components. Test electronics units, using standard test equipment, and analyze results to evaluate performance and determine need for adjustment. Perform preventative maintenance and calibration of equipment and systems. Assemble, test, and maintain circuitry or electronic components according to engineering instructions, technical manuals, and knowledge of electronics, using hand and power tools. Adjust and replace defective or improperly functioning circuitry and electronics components, using hand tools and soldering iron. Write reports and record data on testing techniques, laboratory equipment, and specifications to assist engineers. Identify and resolve equipment malfunctions, working with manufacturers and field representatives as necessary to procure replacement parts. Provide user applications and engineering support and recommendations for new and existing equipment with regard to installation, upgrades, and enhancement. Maintain system logs and manuals to document testing and operation of equipment. Provide customer support and education, working with users to identify needs, determine sources of problems, and to provide information on product use. Maintain working knowledge of state-of-the-art tools or software by reading or attending conferences, workshops, or other training. Build prototypes from rough sketches or plans. Design basic circuitry and draft sketches for clarification of details and design documentation under engineers' direction, using drafting instruments and computer aided design (CAD) equipment. Procure parts and maintain inventory and related documentation. Research equipment and component needs, sources, competitive prices, delivery times, and ongoing operational costs. Write computer or microprocessor software programs. Fabricate parts such as coils, terminal boards, and chassis, using bench lathes, drills, or other machine tools. Develop and upgrade preventative maintenance procedures for components, equipment, parts, and systems.

Personality Type: Realistic. These occupations frequently involve work activities that include practical, hands-on problems and solutions. They often deal with plants; animals; and real-world materials such as wood, tools, and machinery. Many of the occupations require working outside and don't involve a lot of paperwork or working closely with others.

GOE—Interest Area/Cluster: 15. Scientific Research, Engineering, and Mathematics. **Work Group:** 15.09.

Engineering Technology. **Other Jobs in This Work Group:** Aerospace Engineering and Operations Technicians; Cartographers and Photogrammetrists; Civil Engineering Technicians; Electrical and Electronic Engineering Technicians; Electrical and Electronics Drafters; Electrical Drafters; Electrical Engineering Technicians; Electro-Mechanical Technicians; Electronic Drafters; Environmental Engineering Technicians; Mapping Technicians; Mechanical Drafters; Mechanical Engineering Technicians; Surveying and Mapping Technicians; Surveying Technicians.

Skills—Repairing: Repairing machines or systems, using the needed tools. **Troubleshooting:** Determining what is causing an operating error and deciding what to do about it. **Operation Monitoring:** Watching gauges, dials, or other indicators to make sure a machine is working properly. **Equipment Maintenance:** Performing routine maintenance and determining when and what kind of maintenance is needed. **Systems Analysis:** Determining how a system should work and how changes will affect outcomes. **Quality Control Analysis:** Evaluating the quality or performance of products, services, or processes. **Systems Evaluation:** Looking at many indicators of system performance and taking into account their accuracy. **Operation and Control:** Controlling operations of equipment or systems.

Education and Training Programs: Computer Engineering Technology/Technician Training; Electrical and Electronic Engineering Technologies/Technician Training, Other; Electrical, Electronic and Communications Engineering Technology/Technician Training; Telecommunications Technology/Technician Training. **Related Knowledge/Courses—Telecommunications:** Transmission, broadcasting, switching, control, and operation of telecommunications systems. **Engineering and Technology:** Equipment, tools, and mechanical devices and their uses to produce motion, light, power, technology, and other applications. **Design:** Design techniques, principles, tools, and instruments involved in the production and use of precision technical plans, blueprints, drawings, and models. **Mechanical Devices:** Machines and tools, including their designs, uses, benefits, repair, and maintenance. **Computers and Electronics:** Electric circuit boards, processors, chips, and computer hardware and software, including applications and programming. **Physics:** Physical principles, laws, and applications, including air, water, material dynamics, light, atomic principles, heat, electric theory, earth formations, and meteorological and related natural phenomena.

Work Environment: Indoors; noisy; sitting; using hands on objects, tools, or controls.

Electronics Engineers, Except Computer

* Education/Training Required: Bachelor's degree
* Annual Earnings: $83,340
* Beginning Wage: $53,710
* Earnings Growth Potential: Medium
* Growth: 3.7%
* Annual Job Openings: 5,699
* Self-Employed: 2.2%
* Part-Time: 2.0%

Research, design, develop, and test electronic components and systems for commercial, industrial, military, or scientific use, utilizing knowledge of electronic theory and materials properties. Design electronic circuits and components for use in fields such as telecommunications, aerospace guidance and propulsion control, acoustics, or instruments and controls. Design electronic components, software, products, or systems for commercial, industrial, medical, military, or scientific applications. Provide technical support and instruction to staff or customers regarding equipment standards, assisting with specific, difficult in-service engineering. Operate computer-assisted engineering and design software and equipment to perform engineering tasks. Analyze system requirements, capacity, cost, and customer needs to determine feasibility of project and develop system plan. Confer with engineers, customers, vendors, or others to discuss existing and potential engineering projects or products. Review and evaluate work of others inside and outside the organization to ensure effectiveness, technical adequacy, and compatibility in the resolution of complex engineering problems. Determine material and equipment needs and order supplies. Inspect electronic equipment, instruments, products, and systems to ensure conformance to specifications, safety standards, and applicable codes and regulations. Evaluate operational systems, prototypes, and proposals and recommend repair or design modifications based on factors such as environment, service, cost, and system capabilities. Prepare documentation containing information such as confidential descriptions and specifications of proprietary hardware and software, product development and introduction schedules, product costs, and information about product performance weaknesses. Direct and coordinate activities concerned with manufacture, construction, installation, maintenance, operation, and modification of electronic equipment, products, and systems. Develop and perform operational, maintenance, and testing procedures for electronic products, components, equipment, and systems. Plan and develop applications and modifications for electronic properties used in components, products, and systems to improve technical performance. Plan and implement research, methodology, and procedures to apply principles of electronic theory to engineering projects. Prepare engineering sketches and specifications for construction, relocation, and installation of equipment, facilities, products, and systems.

Personality Type: Investigative. These occupations frequently involve working with ideas and require an extensive amount of thinking. They can involve searching for facts and figuring out problems mentally.

GOE—Interest Area/Cluster: 15. Scientific Research, Engineering, and Mathematics. **Work Group:** 15.07. Research and Design Engineering. **Other Jobs in This Work Group:** Aerospace Engineers; Biomedical Engineers; Chemical Engineers; Civil Engineers; Computer Hardware Engineers; Electrical Engineers; Marine Architects; Marine Engineers; Marine Engineers and Naval Architects; Materials Engineers; Mechanical Engineers; Nuclear Engineers.

Skills—Troubleshooting: Determining what is causing an operating error and deciding what to do about it. **Installation:** Installing equipment, machines, wiring, or programs to meet specifications. **Science:** Using scientific methods to solve problems. **Operations Analysis:** Analyzing needs and product requirements to create a design. **Technology Design:** Generating or adapting equipment and technology to serve user needs. **Equipment Selection:** Determining the kind of tools and equipment needed to do a job. **Systems Evaluation:** Looking at many indicators of system performance and taking into account their accuracy. **Quality Control Analysis:** Evaluating the quality or performance of products, services, or processes.

Education and Training Program: Electrical, Electronics and Communications Engineering. **Related Knowledge/Courses—Engineering and Technology:** Equipment, tools, and mechanical devices and their uses to produce motion, light, power, technology, and other applications. **Design:** Design techniques, principles, tools, and instruments involved in the production and use of precision technical plans, blueprints, drawings, and models. **Physics:** Physical principles, laws, and applications, including air, water, material dynamics, light, atomic principles, heat, electric theory, earth formations, and meteorological and related natural phenomena. **Computers and Electronics:** Electric circuit boards, processors, chips, and computer hardware and software, including applications and programming. **Telecommunications:** Transmission, broadcasting, switching, control, and operation of telecommunications systems. **Production and Processing:** Inputs, outputs, raw materials, waste, quality control, costs, and techniques for maximizing the manufacture and distribution of goods.

Work Environment: Indoors; noisy; sitting.

Elementary School Teachers, Except Special Education

* Education/Training Required: Bachelor's degree
* Annual Earnings: $47,330
* Beginning Wage: $31,480
* Earnings Growth Potential: Low
* Growth: 13.6%
* Annual Job Openings: 181,612
* Self-Employed: 0.0%
* Part-Time: 9.5%

Teach pupils in public or private schools at the elementary level basic academic, social, and other formative skills. Establish and enforce rules for behavior and procedures for maintaining order among the students for whom they are responsible. Observe and evaluate students' performance, behavior, social development, and physical health. Prepare materials and classrooms for class activities. Adapt teaching methods and instructional materials to meet students' varying needs and interests. Plan and conduct activities for a balanced program of instruction, demonstration, and work time that provides students with opportunities to observe, question, and investigate. Instruct students individually and in groups, using various teaching methods such as lectures, discussions, and demonstrations. Establish clear objectives for all lessons, units, and projects and communicate those objectives to students. Assign and grade classwork and homework. Read books to entire classes or small groups. Prepare, administer, and grade tests and assignments in order to evaluate students' progress. Confer with parents or guardians, teachers, counselors, and administrators to resolve students' behavioral and academic problems. Meet with parents and guardians to discuss their children's progress and to determine their priorities for their children and their resource needs. Prepare students for later grades by encouraging them to explore learning opportunities and to persevere with challenging tasks. Maintain accurate and complete student records as required by laws, district policies, and administrative regulations. Guide and counsel students with adjustment or academic problems or special academic interests. Prepare and implement remedial programs for students requiring extra help. Prepare objectives and outlines for courses of study, following curriculum guidelines or requirements of states and schools. Provide a variety of materials and resources for children to explore, manipulate, and use, both in learning activities and in imaginative play. Enforce administration policies and rules governing students. Confer with other staff members to plan and schedule lessons promoting learning, following approved curricula.

Personality Type: Social. These occupations frequently involve working with, communicating with, and teaching people and often involve helping or providing service to others.

GOE—Interest Area/Cluster: 05. Education and Training. **Work Group:** 05.02. Preschool, Elementary, and Secondary Teaching and Instructing. **Other Jobs in This Work Group:** Kindergarten Teachers, Except Special Education; Middle School Teachers, Except Special and Vocational Education; Preschool Teachers, Except Special Education; Secondary School Teachers, Except Special and Vocational Education; Special Education Teachers, Middle School; Special Education Teachers, Preschool, Kindergarten, and Elementary School; Special Education Teachers, Secondary School; Teacher Assistants; Vocational Education Teachers, Middle School; Vocational Education Teachers, Secondary School.

Skills—Instructing: Teaching others how to do something. **Learning Strategies:** Using multiple approaches when learning or teaching new things. **Monitoring:** Assessing how well one is doing when learning or doing something. **Social Perceptiveness:** Being aware of others' reactions and understanding why they react the way they do. **Speaking:** Talking to others to effectively convey information. **Persuasion:** Persuading others to approach things differently. **Writing:** Communicating effectively with others in writing as indicated by the needs of the audience. **Service Orientation:** Actively looking for ways to help people.

Education and Training Programs: Elementary Education and Teaching; Montessori Teacher Education; Teacher Education, Multiple Levels. **Related Knowledge/Courses—Geography:** Various methods for describing the location and distribution of land, sea, and air masses, including their

physical locations, relationships, and characteristics. **History and Archeology:** Historical events and their causes, indicators, and impact on particular civilizations and cultures. **Sociology and Anthropology:** Group behavior and dynamics; societal trends and influences; and cultures and their history, migrations, ethnicity, and origins. **Therapy and Counseling:** Information and techniques needed to rehabilitate physical and mental ailments and to provide career guidance, including alternative treatments, rehabilitation equipment and its proper use, and methods to evaluate treatment effects. **Philosophy and Theology:** Different philosophical systems and religions, including their basic principles, values, ethics, ways of thinking, customs, and practices and their impact on human culture. **Education and Training:** Instructional methods and training techniques, including curriculum design principles, learning theory, group and individual teaching techniques, design of individual development plans, and test design principles.

Work Environment: Indoors; noisy; disease or infections; standing.

Elevator Installers and Repairers

- ❀ Education/Training Required: Long-term on-the-job training
- ❀ Annual Earnings: $68,000
- ❀ Beginning Wage: $39,120
- ❀ Earnings Growth Potential: High
- ❀ Growth: 8.8%
- ❀ Annual Job Openings: 2,850
- ❀ Self-Employed: 0.0%
- ❀ Part-Time: 0.4%

Assemble, install, repair, or maintain electric or hydraulic freight or passenger elevators, escalators, or dumbwaiters. Assemble, install, repair, and maintain elevators, escalators, moving sidewalks, and dumbwaiters, using hand and power tools and testing devices such as test lamps, ammeters, and voltmeters. Test newly installed equipment to ensure that it meets specifications such as stopping at floors for set amounts of time. Check that safety regulations and building codes are met, and complete service reports verifying conformance to standards. Locate malfunctions in brakes, motors, switches, and signal and control systems, using test equipment. Connect electrical wiring to control panels and electric motors. Read and interpret blueprints to determine the layout of system components, frameworks, and foundations, and to select installation equipment. Adjust safety controls,

E

counterweights, door mechanisms, and components such as valves, ratchets, seals, and brake linings. Inspect wiring connections, control panel hookups, door installations, and alignments and clearances of cars and hoistways to ensure that equipment will operate properly. Disassemble defective units, and repair or replace parts such as locks, gears, cables, and electric wiring. Maintain log books that detail all repairs and checks performed. Participate in additional training to keep skills up-to-date. Attach guide shoes and rollers to minimize the lateral motion of cars as they travel through shafts. Connect car frames to counterweights, using steel cables. Bolt or weld steel rails to the walls of shafts to guide elevators, working from scaffolding or platforms. Assemble elevator cars, installing each car's platform, walls, and doors. Install outer doors and door frames at elevator entrances on each floor of a structure. Install electrical wires and controls by attaching conduit along shaft walls from floor to floor, then pulling plastic-covered wires through the conduit. Cut prefabricated sections of framework, rails, and other components to specified dimensions. Operate elevators to determine power demands, and test power consumption to detect overload factors. Assemble electrically powered stairs, steel frameworks, and tracks, and install associated motors and electrical wiring.

Personality Type: Realistic. These occupations frequently involve work activities that include practical, hands-on problems and solutions. They often deal with plants; animals; and real-world materials such as wood, tools, and machinery. Many of the occupations require working outside and don't involve a lot of paperwork or working closely with others.

GOE—Interest Area/Cluster: 02. Architecture and Construction. **Work Group:** 02.05. Systems and Equipment Installation, Maintenance, and Repair. **Other Jobs in This Work Group:** Electrical and Electronics Repairers, Powerhouse, Substation, and Relay; Electrical Power-Line Installers and Repairers; Heating and Air Conditioning Mechanics and Installers; Maintenance and Repair Workers, General; Refrigeration Mechanics and Installers; Telecommunications Equipment Installers and Repairers, Except Line Installers; Telecommunications Line Installers and Repairers.

Skills—Installation: Installing equipment, machines, wiring, or programs to meet specifications. **Repairing:** Repairing machines or systems, using the needed tools. **Equipment Maintenance:** Performing routine maintenance and determining when and what kind of maintenance is needed. **Troubleshooting:** Determining what is causing an operating error and deciding what to do about it. **Quality Control**

Analysis: Evaluating the quality or performance of products, services, or processes. **Technology Design:** Generating or adapting equipment and technology to serve user needs. **Equipment Selection:** Determining the kind of tools and equipment needed to do a job. **Science:** Using scientific methods to solve problems.

Education and Training Program: Industrial Mechanics and Maintenance Technology. **Related Knowledge/Courses—Building and Construction:** Materials, methods, and the appropriate tools to construct objects, structures, and buildings. **Mechanical Devices:** Machines and tools, including their designs, uses, benefits, repair, and maintenance. **Physics:** Physical principles, laws, and applications, including air, water, material dynamics, light, atomic principles, heat, electric theory, earth formations, and meteorological and related natural phenomena. **Design:** Design techniques, principles, tools, and instruments involved in the production and use of precision technical plans, blueprints, drawings, and models. **Engineering and Technology:** Equipment, tools, and mechanical devices and their uses to produce motion, light, power, technology, and other applications. **Public Safety and Security:** Weaponry; public safety; security operations, rules, regulations, precautions, and prevention; and the protection of people, data, and property.

Work Environment: Very bright or dim lighting; contaminants; high places; hazardous conditions; hazardous equipment; using hands on objects, tools, or controls.

Eligibility Interviewers, Government Programs

- ❋ Education/Training Required: Moderate-term on-the-job training
- ❋ Annual Earnings: $39,110
- ❋ Beginning Wage: $26,410
- ❋ Earnings Growth Potential: Low
- ❋ Growth: 3.1%
- ❋ Annual Job Openings: 11,337
- ❋ Self-Employed: 0.0%
- ❋ Part-Time: 4.7%

Determine eligibility of persons applying to receive assistance from government programs and agency resources, such as welfare, unemployment benefits, social security, and public housing. Answer applicants' questions about benefits and claim procedures. Interview benefits recipients at specified intervals to certify their eligibility for continuing benefits. Interpret and explain information such as eligibility requirements, application details, payment methods, and applicants' legal rights. Initiate procedures to grant, modify, deny, or terminate assistance or refer applicants to other agencies for assistance. Compile, record, and evaluate personal and financial data to verify completeness and accuracy and to determine eligibility status. Interview and investigate applicants for public assistance to gather information pertinent to their applications. Check with employers or other references to verify answers and obtain further information. Keep records of assigned cases and prepare required reports. Schedule benefits claimants for adjudication interviews to address questions of eligibility. Prepare applications and forms for applicants for such purposes as school enrollment, employment, and medical services. Refer applicants to job openings or to interviews with other staff in accordance with administrative guidelines or office procedures. Provide social workers with pertinent information gathered during applicant interviews. Compute and authorize amounts of assistance for programs such as grants, monetary payments, and food stamps. Monitor the payments of benefits throughout the duration of a claim. Provide applicants with assistance in completing application forms such as those for job referrals or unemployment compensation claims. Investigate claimants for the possibility of fraud or abuse. Conduct annual, interim, and special housing reviews and home visits to ensure conformance to regulations.

Personality Type: Social. These occupations frequently involve working with, communicating with, and teaching people and often involve helping or providing service to others.

GOE—Interest Area/Cluster: 10. Human Service. **Work Group:** 10.04. Client Interviewing. **Other Jobs in This Work Group:** Interviewers, Except Eligibility and Loan.

Skills—Service Orientation: Actively looking for ways to help people. **Speaking:** Talking to others to effectively convey information. **Active Listening:** Listening to what other people are saying and asking questions as appropriate. **Social Perceptiveness:** Being aware of others' reactions and understanding why they react the way they do. **Writing:** Communicating effectively with others in writing as indicated by the needs of the audience. **Active Learning:** Working with new material or information to grasp its implications. **Time Management:** Managing one's own time and the time of others. **Reading Comprehension:** Understanding written sentences and paragraphs in work-related documents.

Education and Training Program: Community Organization and Advocacy. **Related Knowledge/Courses—Clerical Practices:** Administrative and clerical procedures and systems such as word-processing systems, filing and records management systems, stenography and transcription, forms, design principles, and other office procedures and terminology. **Customer and Personal Service:** Principles and processes for providing customer and personal services, including needs assessment techniques, quality service standards, alternative delivery systems, and customer satisfaction evaluation techniques. **Law and Government:** Laws, legal codes, court procedures, precedents, government regulations, executive orders, agency rules, and the democratic political process. **Psychology:** Human behavior and performance, mental processes, psychological research methods, and the assessment and treatment of behavioral and affective disorders. **Sociology and Anthropology:** Group behavior and dynamics; societal trends and influences; and cultures and their history, migrations, ethnicity, and origins. **Computers and Electronics:** Electric circuit boards, processors, chips, and computer hardware and software, including applications and programming.

Work Environment: Indoors; contaminants; sitting; using hands on objects, tools, or controls; repetitive motions.

Embalmers

- ❋ Education/Training Required: Postsecondary vocational training
- ❋ Annual Earnings: $36,800
- ❋ Beginning Wage: $20,470
- ❋ Earnings Growth Potential: High
- ❋ Growth: 14.3%
- ❋ Annual Job Openings: 1,660
- ❋ Self-Employed: 0.7%
- ❋ Part-Time: 21.6%

Prepare bodies for interment in conformity with legal requirements. Conform to laws of health and sanitation and ensure that legal requirements concerning embalming are met. Apply cosmetics to impart lifelike appearance to the deceased. Incise stomach and abdominal walls and probe internal organs, using trocar, to withdraw blood and waste matter from organs. Close incisions, using needles and sutures. Reshape or reconstruct disfigured or maimed bodies when necessary, using derma-surgery techniques and materials such as clay, cotton, plaster of paris, and wax. Make incisions in arms or thighs and drain blood from circulatory system and replace it with embalming fluid, using pump. Dress bodies and place them in caskets. Join lips, using needles and thread or wire. Conduct interviews to arrange for the preparation of obituary notices, to assist with the selection of caskets or urns, and to determine the location and time of burials or cremations. Perform the duties of funeral directors, including coordinating funeral activities. Attach trocar to pump-tube, start pump, and repeat probing to force embalming fluid into organs. Perform special procedures necessary for remains that are to be transported to other states or overseas or where death was caused by infectious disease. Maintain records such as itemized lists of clothing or valuables delivered with body and names of persons embalmed. Insert convex celluloid or cotton between eyeballs and eyelids to prevent slipping and sinking of eyelids. Wash and dry bodies, using germicidal soap and towels or hot air dryers. Arrange for transporting the deceased to another state for interment. Supervise funeral attendants and other funeral home staff. Pack body orifices with cotton saturated with embalming fluid to prevent escape of gases or waste matter. Assist with placing caskets in hearses and organize cemetery processions. Serve as pallbearers, attend visiting rooms, and provide other assistance to the bereaved. Direct casket and floral display placement and arrange guest seating. Arrange funeral home equipment and perform general maintenance. Assist coroners at death scenes or at autopsies, file police reports, and testify at inquests or in court if employed by a coroner.

Personality Type: Realistic. These occupations frequently involve work activities that include practical, hands-on problems and solutions. They often deal with plants; animals; and real-world materials such as wood, tools, and machinery. Many of the occupations require working outside and don't involve a lot of paperwork or working closely with others.

GOE—Interest Area/Cluster: 08. Health Science. **Work Group:** 08.09. Health Protection and Promotion. **Other Jobs in This Work Group:** Athletic Trainers; Dietetic Technicians; Dietitians and Nutritionists.

Skills—Science: Using scientific methods to solve problems. **Service Orientation:** Actively looking for ways to help people. **Management of Financial Resources:** Determining how money will be spent to get the work done and accounting for these expenditures. **Management of Material Resources:** Obtaining and seeing to the appropriate use of equipment, facilities, and materials needed to do certain work. **Social Perceptiveness:** Being aware of others' reactions and understanding why they react the way they do.

Equipment Maintenance: Performing routine maintenance and determining when and what kind of maintenance is needed. **Operation Monitoring:** Watching gauges, dials, or other indicators to make sure a machine is working properly. **Equipment Selection:** Determining the kind of tools and equipment needed to do a job.

Education and Training Programs: Funeral Service and Mortuary Science, General; Mortuary Science and Embalming/Embalmer Training. **Related Knowledge/Courses—Chemistry:** The composition, structure, and properties of substances and of the chemical processes and transformations that they undergo. This includes uses of chemicals and their interactions, danger signs, production techniques, and disposal methods. **Biology:** Plant and animal living tissue, cells, organisms, and entities, including their functions, interdependencies, and interactions with each other and the environment. **Philosophy and Theology:** Different philosophical systems and religions, including their basic principles, values, ethics, ways of thinking, customs, and practices and their impact on human culture. **Customer and Personal Service:** Principles and processes for providing customer and personal services, including needs assessment techniques, quality service standards, alternative delivery systems, and customer satisfaction evaluation techniques. **Therapy and Counseling:** Information and techniques needed to rehabilitate physical and mental ailments and to provide career guidance, including alternative treatments, rehabilitation equipment and its proper use, and methods to evaluate treatment effects. **Medicine and Dentistry:** The information and techniques needed to diagnose and treat injuries, diseases, and deformities. This includes symptoms, treatment alternatives, drug properties and interactions, and preventive health-care measures.

Work Environment: Indoors; contaminants; disease or infections; hazardous conditions; standing; using hands on objects, tools, or controls.

Emergency Management Specialists

❀ Education/Training Required: Work experience in a related occupation

❀ Annual Earnings: $48,380

❀ Beginning Wage: $26,340

❀ Earnings Growth Potential: High

❀ Growth: 12.3%

❀ Annual Job Openings: 1,538

❀ Self-Employed: 0.1%

❀ Part-Time: 9.6%

Coordinate disaster response or crisis management activities, provide disaster-preparedness training, and prepare emergency plans and procedures for natural (e.g., hurricanes, floods, earthquakes), wartime, or technological (e.g., nuclear power plant emergencies, hazardous materials spills) disasters or hostage situations. Keep informed of activities or changes that could affect the likelihood of an emergency, as well as those that could affect response efforts and details of plan implementation. Prepare plans that outline operating procedures to be used in response to disasters or emergencies such as hurricanes, nuclear accidents, and terrorist attacks and in recovery from these events. Propose alteration of emergency response procedures based on regulatory changes, technological changes, or knowledge gained from outcomes of previous emergency situations. Maintain and update all resource materials associated with emergency-preparedness plans. Coordinate disaster response or crisis management activities such as ordering evacuations, opening public shelters, and implementing special needs plans and programs. Develop and maintain liaisons with municipalities, county departments, and similar entities in order to facilitate plan development, response effort coordination, and exchanges of personnel and equipment. Keep informed of federal, state, and local regulations affecting emergency plans and ensure that plans adhere to these regulations. Design and administer emergency and disaster-preparedness training courses that teach people how to effectively respond to major emergencies and disasters. Prepare emergency situation status reports that describe response and recovery efforts, needs, and preliminary damage assessments. Inspect facilities and equipment such as emergency management centers and communications equipment to determine their operational and functional capabilities in emergency situations. Consult with officials of local and area governments, schools, hospitals, and other institutions in order to determine their needs and capabilities in the event of a natural disaster or other emergency. Develop and perform tests and evaluations of emergency management plans in accordance with state and federal regulations. Attend meetings, conferences, and workshops related to emergency management to learn new information and to develop working relationships with other emergency management specialists.

Personality Type: Social. These occupations frequently involve working with, communicating with, and teaching people and often involve helping or providing service to others.

GOE—Interest Area/Cluster: 12. Law and Public Safety. **Work Group:** 12.01. Managerial Work in Law and Public Safety. **Other Jobs in This Work Group:** First-Line Supervisors/Managers of Correctional Officers; First-Line Supervisors/Managers of Fire Fighting and Prevention Workers; First-Line Supervisors/Managers of Police and Detectives; Forest Fire Fighting and Prevention Supervisors; Municipal Fire Fighting and Prevention Supervisors.

Skills—Management of Material Resources: Obtaining and seeing to the appropriate use of equipment, facilities, and materials needed to do certain work. **Service Orientation:** Actively looking for ways to help people. **Judgment and Decision Making:** Weighing the relative costs and benefits of a potential action. **Complex Problem Solving:** Identifying complex problems, reviewing the options, and implementing solutions. **Coordination:** Adjusting actions in relation to others' actions. **Operations Analysis:** Analyzing needs and product requirements to create a design. **Management of Financial Resources:** Determining how money will be spent to get the work done and accounting for these expenditures. **Writing:** Communicating effectively with others in writing as indicated by the needs of the audience.

Education and Training Programs: Community Organization and Advocacy; Public Administration. **Related Knowledge/Courses—Public Safety and Security:** Weaponry; public safety; security operations, rules, regulations, precautions, and prevention; and the protection of people, data, and property. **Customer and Personal Service:** Principles and processes for providing customer and personal services, including needs assessment techniques, quality service standards, alternative delivery systems, and customer satisfaction evaluation techniques. **Education and Training:** Instructional methods and training techniques, including curriculum design principles, learning theory, group and individual teaching techniques, design of individual development plans, and test design principles. **Law and Government:** Laws, legal codes, court procedures, precedents, government regulations, executive orders, agency rules, and the democratic political process. **Physics:** Physical principles, laws, and applications, including air, water, material dynamics, light, atomic principles, heat, electric theory, earth formations, and meteorological and related natural phenomena. **Telecommunications:** Transmission, broadcasting, switching, control, and operation of telecommunications systems.

Work Environment: Indoors; sitting.

Emergency Medical Technicians and Paramedics

- ❀ Education/Training Required: Postsecondary vocational training
- ❀ Annual Earnings: $28,400
- ❀ Beginning Wage: $18,150
- ❀ Earnings Growth Potential: Medium
- ❀ Growth: 19.2%
- ❀ Annual Job Openings: 19,513
- ❀ Self-Employed: 0.2%
- ❀ Part-Time: 10.5%

Assess injuries, administer emergency medical care, and extricate trapped individuals. Transport injured or sick persons to medical facilities. Administer first-aid treatment and life-support care to sick or injured persons in prehospital setting. Perform emergency diagnostic and treatment procedures, such as stomach suction, airway management, or heart monitoring, during ambulance ride. Observe, record, and report to physician the patient's condition or injury, the treatment provided, and reactions to drugs and treatment. Immobilize patient for placement on stretcher and ambulance transport, using backboard or other spinal immobilization device. Maintain vehicles and medical and communication equipment, and replenish first-aid equipment and supplies. Assess nature and extent of illness or injury to establish and prioritize medical procedures. Communicate with dispatchers and treatment center personnel to provide information about situation, to arrange reception of victims, and to receive instructions for further treatment. Comfort and reassure patients. Decontaminate ambulance interior following treatment of patient with infectious disease and report case to proper authorities. Operate equipment such as electrocardiograms (EKGs), external

defibrillators, and bag-valve mask resuscitators in advanced life-support environments. Drive mobile intensive care unit to specified location, following instructions from emergency medical dispatcher. Coordinate with treatment center personnel to obtain patients' vital statistics and medical history, to determine the circumstances of the emergency, and to administer emergency treatment. Coordinate work with other emergency medical team members and police and fire department personnel. Attend training classes to maintain certification licensure, keep abreast of new developments in the field, or maintain existing knowledge. Administer drugs, orally or by injection, and perform intravenous procedures under a physician's direction.

Personality Type: Social. These occupations frequently involve working with, communicating with, and teaching people and often involve helping or providing service to others.

GOE—Interest Area/Cluster: 12. Law and Public Safety. **Work Group:** 12.06. Emergency Responding. **Other Jobs in This Work Group:** Fire Fighters; Forest Fire Fighters; Municipal Fire Fighters.

Skills—Operation Monitoring: Watching gauges, dials, or other indicators to make sure a machine is working properly. **Operation and Control:** Controlling operations of equipment or systems. **Management of Personnel Resources:** Motivating, developing, and directing people as they work; identifying the best people for the job. **Systems Analysis:** Determining how a system should work and how changes will affect outcomes. **Systems Evaluation:** Looking at many indicators of system performance and taking into account their accuracy. **Service Orientation:** Actively looking for ways to help people.

Education and Training Programs: Emergency Care Attendant Training (EMT Ambulance); Emergency Medical Technology/Technician Training (EMT Paramedic). **Related Knowledge/Courses—Medicine and Dentistry:** The information and techniques needed to diagnose and treat injuries, diseases, and deformities. This includes symptoms, treatment alternatives, drug properties and interactions, and preventive health-care measures. **Customer and Personal Service:** Principles and processes for providing customer and personal services, including needs assessment techniques, quality service standards, alternative delivery systems, and customer satisfaction evaluation techniques. **Therapy and Counseling:** Information and techniques needed to rehabilitate physical and mental ailments and to provide career guidance, including alternative treatments, rehabilitation equipment and its proper use, and methods to evaluate treatment effects. **Psychology:** Human behavior and performance, mental processes, psychological research methods, and the assessment and treatment of behavioral and affective disorders. **Transportation:** Principles and methods for moving people or goods by air, rail, sea, or road, including their relative costs, advantages, and limitations. **Education and Training:** Instructional methods and training techniques, including curriculum design principles, learning theory, group and individual teaching techniques, design of individual development plans, and test design principles.

Work Environment: More often outdoors than indoors; noisy; very hot or cold; very bright or dim lighting; disease or infections.

Employment Interviewers

* Education/Training Required: Bachelor's degree
* Annual Earnings: $44,380
* Beginning Wage: $27,340
* Earnings Growth Potential: Medium
* Growth: 18.4%
* Annual Job Openings: 33,588
* Self-Employed: 2.1%
* Part-Time: 7.6%

The job openings listed here are shared with Personnel Recruiters.

Interview job applicants in employment office and refer them to prospective employers for consideration. Search application files, notify selected applicants of job openings, and refer qualified applicants to prospective employers. Contact employers to verify referral results. Record and evaluate various pertinent data. Inform applicants of job openings and details such as duties and responsibilities, compensation, benefits, schedules, working conditions, and promotion opportunities. Interview job applicants to match their qualifications with employers' needs, recording and evaluating applicant experience, education, training, and skills. Review employment applications and job orders to match applicants with job requirements, using manual or computerized file searches. Select qualified applicants or refer them to employers according to organization policy. Perform reference and background checks on applicants. Maintain records of applicants not selected for employment. Instruct job applicants in presenting a positive image

by providing help with resume writing, personal appearance, and interview techniques. Refer applicants to services such as vocational counseling, literacy or language instruction, transportation assistance, vocational training, and child care. Contact employers to solicit orders for job vacancies, determining their requirements and recording relevant data such as job descriptions. Conduct workshops and demonstrate the use of job listings to assist applicants with skill building. Search for and recruit applicants for open positions through campus job fairs and advertisements. Provide background information on organizations with which interviews are scheduled. Administer assessment tests to identify skill-building needs. Conduct or arrange for skill, intelligence, or psychological testing of applicants and current employees. Hire workers and place them with employers needing temporary help. Evaluate selection and testing techniques by conducting research or follow-up activities and conferring with management and supervisory personnel.

Personality Type: Enterprising. These occupations frequently involve starting up and carrying out projects and can involve leading people and making many decisions. They sometimes require risk taking and often deal with business.

GOE—Interest Area/Cluster: 04. Business and Administration. **Work Group:** 04.03. Human Resources Support. **Other Jobs in This Work Group:** Compensation, Benefits, and Job Analysis Specialists; Employment, Recruitment, and Placement Specialists; Personnel Recruiters; Training and Development Specialists.

Skills—Management of Personnel Resources: Motivating, developing, and directing people as they work; identifying the best people for the job. **Service Orientation:** Actively looking for ways to help people. **Social Perceptiveness:** Being aware of others' reactions and understanding why they react the way they do. **Persuasion:** Persuading others to approach things differently. **Negotiation:** Bringing others together and trying to reconcile differences. **Writing:** Communicating effectively with others in writing as indicated by the needs of the audience. **Speaking:** Talking to others to effectively convey information. **Instructing:** Teaching others how to do something.

Education and Training Programs: Human Resources Management/Personnel Administration, General; Labor and Industrial Relations. **Related Knowledge/Courses— Foreign Language:** The structure and content of a foreign (non-English) language, including the meaning and spelling of words, rules of composition and grammar, and pronunciation. **Clerical Practices:** Administrative and clerical procedures and systems such as word-processing systems, filing and records management systems, stenography and transcription, forms, design principles, and other office procedures and terminology. **Personnel and Human Resources:** Principles and procedures for personnel recruitment; selection; training; compensation and benefits; labor relations and negotiation; and personnel information systems. **Sales and Marketing:** Principles and methods involved in showing, promoting, and selling products or services. This includes marketing strategies and tactics, product demonstration and sales techniques, and sales control systems. **Customer and Personal Service:** Principles and processes for providing customer and personal services, including needs assessment techniques, quality service standards, alternative delivery systems, and customer satisfaction evaluation techniques. **English Language:** The structure and content of the English language, including the meaning and spelling of words, rules of composition, and grammar.

Work Environment: Indoors; sitting; repetitive motions.

Engineering Managers

* Education/Training Required: Work experience plus degree
* Annual Earnings: $111,020
* Beginning Wage: $70,640
* Earnings Growth Potential: Medium
* Growth: 7.3%
* Annual Job Openings: 7,404
* Self-Employed: 0.0%
* Part-Time: 2.0%

Plan, direct, or coordinate activities or research and development in such fields as architecture and engineering. Coordinate and direct projects, making detailed plans to accomplish goals and directing the integration of technical activities. Consult or negotiate with clients to prepare project specifications. Present and explain proposals, reports, and findings to clients. Direct, review, and approve product design and changes. Recruit employees, assign, direct, and evaluate their work, and oversee the development and maintenance of staff competence. Perform administrative functions such as reviewing and writing reports, approving expenditures, enforcing rules, and making decisions about the purchase of materials or services. Prepare budgets, bids, and contracts, and direct the negotiation of research contracts. Analyze technology, resource

needs, and market demand, to plan and assess the feasibility of projects. Confer with management, production, and marketing staff to discuss project specifications and procedures. Review and recommend or approve contracts and cost estimates. Develop and implement policies, standards, and procedures for the engineering and technical work performed in the department, service, laboratory, or firm. Plan and direct the installation, testing, operation, maintenance, and repair of facilities and equipment. Administer highway planning, construction, and maintenance. Confer with and report to officials and the public to provide information and solicit support for projects. Set scientific and technical goals within broad outlines provided by top management. Direct the engineering of water control, treatment, and distribution projects. Plan, direct, and coordinate survey work with other staff activities, certifying survey work, and writing land legal descriptions.

Personality Type: Enterprising. These occupations frequently involve starting up and carrying out projects and can involve leading people and making many decisions. They sometimes require risk taking and often deal with business.

GOE—Interest Area/Cluster: 15. Scientific Research, Engineering, and Mathematics. **Work Group:** 15.01. Managerial Work in Scientific Research, Engineering, and Mathematics. **Other Jobs in This Work Group:** Natural Sciences Managers.

Skills—Management of Financial Resources: Determining how money will be spent to get the work done and accounting for these expenditures. **Management of Personnel Resources:** Motivating, developing, and directing people as they work; identifying the best people for the job. **Systems Analysis:** Determining how a system should work and how changes will affect outcomes. **Management of Material Resources:** Obtaining and seeing to the appropriate use of equipment, facilities, and materials needed to do certain work. **Systems Evaluation:** Looking at many indicators of system performance and taking into account their accuracy. **Negotiation:** Bringing others together and trying to reconcile differences. **Mathematics:** Using mathematics to solve problems. **Writing:** Communicating effectively with others in writing as indicated by the needs of the audience.

Education and Training Programs: Aerospace Engineering; Agricultural/Biological Engineering; Architectural Engineering; Biomedical Engineering; Ceramic Sciences and Engineering; City/Urban, Community and Regional Planning; Civil Engineering, General; Computer

Engineering, General; Electrical, Electronics and Communications Engineering; Engineering, General; Industrial Engineering; Materials Engineering; Mechanical Engineering; Metallurgical Engineering; Nuclear Engineering; Ocean Engineering; Petroleum Engineering; others. **Related Knowledge/Courses—Engineering and Technology:** Equipment, tools, and mechanical devices and their uses to produce motion, light, power, technology, and other applications. **Design:** Design techniques, principles, tools, and instruments involved in the production and use of precision technical plans, blueprints, drawings, and models. **Physics:** Physical principles, laws, and applications, including air, water, material dynamics, light, atomic principles, heat, electric theory, earth formations, and meteorological and related natural phenomena. **Building and Construction:** Materials, methods, and the appropriate tools to construct objects, structures, and buildings. **Computers and Electronics:** Electric circuit boards, processors, chips, and computer hardware and software, including applications and programming. **Mathematics:** Numbers and their operations and interrelationships, including arithmetic, algebra, geometry, calculus, and statistics and their applications.

Work Environment: Indoors; noisy; sitting.

Engineering Teachers, Postsecondary

- ❋ Education/Training Required: Doctoral degree
- ❋ Annual Earnings: $79,510
- ❋ Beginning Wage: $43,090
- ❋ Earnings Growth Potential: High
- ❋ Growth: 22.9%
- ❋ Annual Job Openings: 5,565
- ❋ Self-Employed: 0.4%
- ❋ Part-Time: 27.8%

Teach courses pertaining to the application of physical laws and principles of engineering for the development of machines, materials, instruments, processes, and services. Includes teachers of subjects such as chemical, civil, electrical, industrial, mechanical, mineral, and petroleum engineering. Includes both teachers primarily engaged in teaching and those who do a combination of both teaching and research. Prepare and deliver lectures to undergraduate and/or graduate students on topics such as mechanics, hydraulics, and robotics. Keep abreast of developments in their field by reading current literature, talking with colleagues, and participating in professional conferences. Supervise undergraduate and/or graduate teaching, internship, and research work. Evaluate and grade students' classwork, laboratory work, assignments, and papers. Conduct research in a particular field of knowledge and publish findings in professional journals, books, and/or electronic media. Prepare course materials such as syllabi, homework assignments, and handouts. Compile, administer, and grade examinations or assign this work to others. Write grant proposals to procure external research funding. Supervise students' laboratory work. Initiate, facilitate, and moderate class discussions. Maintain regularly scheduled office hours to advise and assist students. Plan, evaluate, and revise curricula, course content, and course materials and methods of instruction. Advise students on academic and vocational curricula and on career issues. Maintain student attendance records, grades, and other required records. Collaborate with colleagues to address teaching and research issues. Select and obtain materials and supplies such as textbooks and laboratory equipment. Participate in student recruitment, registration, and placement activities. Serve on academic or administrative committees that deal with institutional policies, departmental matters, and academic issues. Perform administrative duties such as serving as department head. Provide professional consulting services to government and/or industry. Compile bibliographies of specialized materials for outside reading assignments. Act as advisers to student organizations. Participate in campus and community events.

Personality Type: Investigative. These occupations frequently involve working with ideas and require an extensive amount of thinking. They can involve searching for facts and figuring out problems mentally.

GOE—Interest Area/Cluster: 05. Education and Training. **Work Group:** 05.03. Postsecondary and Adult Teaching and Instructing. **Other Jobs in This Work Group:** Adult Literacy, Remedial Education, and GED Teachers and Instructors; Agricultural Sciences Teachers, Postsecondary; Anthropology and Archeology Teachers, Postsecondary; Architecture Teachers, Postsecondary; Area, Ethnic, and Cultural Studies Teachers, Postsecondary; Art, Drama, and Music Teachers, Postsecondary; Atmospheric, Earth, Marine, and Space Sciences Teachers, Postsecondary; Biological Science Teachers, Postsecondary; Business Teachers, Postsecondary; Chemistry Teachers, Postsecondary; Communications Teachers, Postsecondary; Computer Science Teachers, Postsecondary; Criminal Justice and Law

Enforcement Teachers, Postsecondary; Economics Teachers, Postsecondary; Education Teachers, Postsecondary; English Language and Literature Teachers, Postsecondary; Environmental Science Teachers, Postsecondary; Farm and Home Management Advisors; Foreign Language and Literature Teachers, Postsecondary; Forestry and Conservation Science Teachers, Postsecondary; Geography Teachers, Postsecondary; Graduate Teaching Assistants; Health Specialties Teachers, Postsecondary; History Teachers, Postsecondary; Home Economics Teachers, Postsecondary; Law Teachers, Postsecondary; Library Science Teachers, Postsecondary; Mathematical Science Teachers, Postsecondary; Nursing Instructors and Teachers, Postsecondary; Philosophy and Religion Teachers, Postsecondary; Physics Teachers, Postsecondary; Political Science Teachers, Postsecondary; Psychology Teachers, Postsecondary; Recreation and Fitness Studies Teachers, Postsecondary; Self-Enrichment Education Teachers; Social Work Teachers, Postsecondary; Sociology Teachers, Postsecondary; Vocational Education Teachers, Postsecondary.

Skills—Science: Using scientific methods to solve problems. **Programming:** Writing computer programs for various purposes. **Mathematics:** Using mathematics to solve problems. **Technology Design:** Generating or adapting equipment and technology to serve user needs. **Complex Problem Solving:** Identifying complex problems, reviewing the options, and implementing solutions. **Management of Financial Resources:** Determining how money will be spent to get the work done and accounting for these expenditures. **Critical Thinking:** Using logic and analysis to identify the strengths and weaknesses of different approaches. **Operations Analysis:** Analyzing needs and product requirements to create a design.

Education and Training Programs: Aerospace Engineering; Agricultural Engineering; Chemical Engineering; Computer Engineering; Construction Engineering; Electrical, Electronics and Communications Engineering; Environmental Engineering; Forest Engineering; Industrial Engineering; Manufacturing Engineering; Materials Engineering; Mechanical Engineering; Metallurgical Engineering; Mining and Mineral Engineering; Nuclear Engineering; Petroleum Engineering; Transportation and Highway Engineering; Water Resources Engineering; others. **Related Knowledge/Courses—Engineering and Technology:** Equipment, tools, and mechanical devices and their uses to produce motion, light, power, technology, and other applications. **Physics:** Physical principles, laws, and applications, including air, water, material dynamics, light, atomic principles, heat, electric theory, earth formations, and meteorological and related natural phenomena. **Design:** Design techniques, principles, tools, and instruments involved in the production and use of precision technical plans, blueprints, drawings, and models. **Mathematics:** Numbers and their operations and interrelationships, including arithmetic, algebra, geometry, calculus, and statistics and their applications. **Education and Training:** Instructional methods and training techniques, including curriculum design principles, learning theory, group and individual teaching techniques, design of individual development plans, and test design principles. **Telecommunications:** Transmission, broadcasting, switching, control, and operation of telecommunications systems.

Work Environment: Indoors; sitting.

English Language and Literature Teachers, Postsecondary

- ✾ Education/Training Required: Doctoral degree
- ✾ Annual Earnings: $54,000
- ✾ Beginning Wage: $30,680
- ✾ Earnings Growth Potential: High
- ✾ Growth: 22.9%
- ✾ Annual Job Openings: 10,475
- ✾ Self-Employed: 0.4%
- ✾ Part-Time: 27.8%

Teach courses in English language and literature, including linguistics and comparative literature. Initiate, facilitate, and moderate classroom discussions. Evaluate and grade students' classwork, assignments, and papers. Prepare course materials such as syllabi, homework assignments, and handouts. Prepare and deliver lectures to undergraduate and graduate students on topics such as poetry, novel structure, and translation and adaptation. Maintain student attendance records, grades, and other required records. Plan, evaluate, and revise curricula, course content, and course materials and methods of instruction. Compile, administer, and grade examinations or assign this work to others. Maintain regularly scheduled office hours in order to advise and assist students. Keep abreast of developments in their field by reading current literature, talking with colleagues, and participating in professional conferences. Select and obtain materials and supplies such as textbooks. Advise students on academic and vocational curricula and on career issues. Conduct research in a particular field of knowledge and publish findings in professional journals, books, or electronic media. Collaborate with colleagues to address teaching and research issues. Serve on academic or administrative committees that deal with institutional policies, departmental matters, and academic issues. Participate in campus and community events. Participate in student recruitment, registration, and placement activities. Compile bibliographies of specialized materials for outside reading assignments. Supervise undergraduate and/or graduate teaching, internship, and research work. Provide assistance to students in college writing centers. Perform administrative duties such as serving as department head. Recruit, train, and supervise student writing instructors. Act as advisers to student organizations. Write grant proposals to procure external research funding. Provide professional consulting services to government or industry.

Personality Type: Social. These occupations frequently involve working with, communicating with, and teaching people and often involve helping or providing service to others.

GOE—Interest Area/Cluster: 05. Education and Training. **Work Group:** 05.03. Postsecondary and Adult Teaching and Instructing. **Other Jobs in This Work Group:** Adult Literacy, Remedial Education, and GED Teachers and Instructors; Agricultural Sciences Teachers, Postsecondary; Anthropology and Archeology Teachers, Postsecondary; Architecture Teachers, Postsecondary; Area, Ethnic, and Cultural Studies Teachers, Postsecondary; Art, Drama, and Music Teachers, Postsecondary; Atmospheric, Earth, Marine, and Space Sciences Teachers, Postsecondary; Biological Science Teachers, Postsecondary; Business Teachers, Postsecondary; Chemistry Teachers, Postsecondary; Communications Teachers, Postsecondary; Computer Science Teachers, Postsecondary; Criminal Justice and Law Enforcement Teachers, Postsecondary; Economics Teachers, Postsecondary; Education Teachers, Postsecondary; Engineering Teachers, Postsecondary; Environmental Science Teachers, Postsecondary; Farm and Home Management Advisors; Foreign Language and Literature Teachers, Postsecondary; Forestry and Conservation Science Teachers, Postsecondary; Geography Teachers, Postsecondary; Graduate Teaching Assistants; Health Specialties Teachers, Postsecondary; History Teachers, Postsecondary; Home Economics Teachers, Postsecondary; Law Teachers, Postsecondary; Library Science Teachers, Postsecondary; Mathematical Science Teachers, Postsecondary; Nursing Instructors and Teachers, Postsecondary; Philosophy and Religion Teachers, Postsecondary; Physics Teachers, Postsecondary; Political Science Teachers, Postsecondary; Psychology Teachers, Postsecondary; Recreation and Fitness Studies Teachers, Postsecondary; Self-Enrichment Education Teachers; Social Work Teachers, Postsecondary; Sociology Teachers, Postsecondary; Vocational Education Teachers, Postsecondary.

Skills—Instructing: Teaching others how to do something. **Writing:** Communicating effectively with others in writing as indicated by the needs of the audience. **Learning Strategies:** Using multiple approaches when learning or teaching new things. **Social Perceptiveness:** Being aware of others' reactions and understanding why they react the way they do. **Reading Comprehension:** Understanding written sentences and paragraphs in work-related documents. **Persuasion:** Persuading others to approach things differently. **Critical Thinking:** Using logic and analysis to identify the strengths and weaknesses of different approaches. **Active Learning:** Working with new material or information to grasp its implications.

Education and Training Programs: American Literature (Canadian); American Literature (United States); Comparative Literature; Creative Writing; English Composition; English Language and Literature, General; English Language and Literature/Letters, Other; English Literature (British and Commonwealth); Technical and Business Writing. **Related Knowledge/Courses—Philosophy and Theology:** Different philosophical systems and religions, including their basic principles, values, ethics, ways of thinking, customs, and practices and their impact on human culture. **English Language:** The structure and content of the English language, including the meaning and spelling of words, rules of composition, and grammar. **History and Archeology:** Historical events and their causes, indicators, and impact on particular civilizations and cultures. **Education and Training:** Instructional methods and training techniques, including curriculum design principles, learning theory, group and individual teaching techniques, design of individual development plans, and test design principles. **Fine Arts:** Theory and techniques required to produce, compose, and perform works of music, dance, visual arts, drama, and sculpture. **Sociology and Anthropology:** Group behavior and dynamics; societal trends and influences; and cultures and their history, migrations, ethnicity, and origins.

Work Environment: Indoors; sitting.

Environmental Compliance Inspectors

- ❋ Education/Training Required: Long-term on-the-job training
- ❋ Annual Earnings: $48,400
- ❋ Beginning Wage: $28,980
- ❋ Earnings Growth Potential: High
- ❋ Growth: 4.9%
- ❋ Annual Job Openings: 15,841
- ❋ Self-Employed: 0.4%
- ❋ Part-Time: 5.0%

The job openings listed here are shared with Coroners; Equal Opportunity Representatives and Officers; Government Property Inspectors and Investigators; and Licensing Examiners and Inspectors.

Inspect and investigate sources of pollution to protect the public and environment and ensure conformance with federal, state, and local regulations and ordinances. Determine the nature of code violations and actions to be taken, and issue written notices of violation; participate in enforcement hearings as necessary. Examine permits, licenses, applications, and records to ensure compliance with licensing requirements. Prepare, organize, and maintain inspection records. Interview individuals to determine the nature of suspected violations and to obtain evidence of violations. Prepare written, oral, tabular, and graphic reports summarizing requirements and regulations, including enforcement and chain of custody documentation. Monitor follow-up actions in cases where violations were found, and review compliance monitoring reports. Investigate complaints and suspected violations regarding illegal dumping, pollution, pesticides, product quality, or labeling laws. Inspect waste pretreatment, treatment, and disposal facilities and systems for conformance to federal, state, or local regulations. Inform individuals and groups of pollution control regulations and inspection findings, and explain how problems can be corrected. Determine sampling locations and methods, and collect water or wastewater samples for analysis, preserving samples with appropriate containers and preservation methods. Verify that hazardous chemicals are handled, stored, and disposed of in accordance with regulations. Research and keep informed of pertinent information and developments in areas such as EPA laws and regulations. Determine which sites and violation reports to investigate, and coordinate compliance and enforcement activities with other government agencies. Observe and record field conditions, gathering, interpreting, and reporting data such as flow meter readings and chemical levels. Learn and observe proper safety precautions, rules, regulations, and practices so that unsafe conditions can be recognized and proper safety protocols implemented. Evaluate label information for accuracy and conformance to regulatory requirements. Inform health professionals, property owners, and the public about harmful properties and related problems of water pollution and contaminated wastewater.

Personality Type: Conventional. These occupations frequently involve following set procedures and routines and can include working with data and details more than with ideas. Usually there is a clear line of authority to follow.

GOE—Interest Area/Cluster: 07. Government and Public Administration. **Work Group:** 07.03. Regulations Enforcement. **Other Jobs in This Work Group:** Agricultural Inspectors; Aviation Inspectors; Compliance Officers, Except Agriculture, Construction, Health and Safety, and Transportation; Construction and Building Inspectors; Equal Opportunity Representatives and Officers; Financial Examiners; Fire Inspectors; Fish and Game Wardens; Forest Fire Inspectors and Prevention Specialists; Freight and Cargo Inspectors; Government Property Inspectors and Investigators; Immigration and Customs Inspectors; Licensing Examiners and Inspectors; Nuclear Monitoring Technicians; Occupational Health and Safety Specialists; Occupational Health and Safety Technicians; Tax Examiners, Collectors, and Revenue Agents; Transportation Vehicle, Equipment, and Systems Inspectors, Except Aviation.

Skills—Science: Using scientific methods to solve problems. **Negotiation:** Bringing others together and trying to reconcile differences. **Writing:** Communicating effectively with others in writing as indicated by the needs of the audience. **Reading Comprehension:** Understanding written sentences and paragraphs in work-related documents. **Mathematics:** Using mathematics to solve problems. **Active Listening:** Listening to what other people are saying and asking questions as appropriate. **Persuasion:** Persuading others to approach things differently. **Operation Monitoring:** Watching gauges, dials, or other indicators to make sure a machine is working properly.

Education and Training Program: Natural Resources Management and Policy, Other. **Related Knowledge/Courses—Biology:** Plant and animal living tissue, cells, organisms, and entities, including their functions, interdependencies, and interactions with each other and the environment. **Chemistry:** The composition, structure, and properties of substances and of the chemical processes and transformations that they undergo. This includes uses of chemicals and their interactions, danger signs, production techniques, and disposal methods. **Law and Government:** Laws, legal codes, court procedures, precedents, government regulations, executive orders, agency rules, and the democratic political process. **Geography:** Various methods for describing the location and distribution of land, sea, and air masses, including their physical locations, relationships, and characteristics. **Physics:** Physical principles, laws, and applications, including air, water, material dynamics, light, atomic principles, heat, electric theory, earth formations, and meteorological and related natural phenomena. **Engineering and Technology:** Equipment, tools, and mechanical devices and their uses to produce motion, light, power, technology, and other applications.

Work Environment: More often indoors than outdoors; contaminants; sitting.

Environmental Engineering Technicians

- ❋ Education/Training Required: Associate degree
- ❋ Annual Earnings: $40,690
- ❋ Beginning Wage: $25,360
- ❋ Earnings Growth Potential: Medium
- ❋ Growth: 24.8%
- ❋ Annual Job Openings: 2,162
- ❋ Self-Employed: 0.8%
- ❋ Part-Time: 5.9%

Apply theory and principles of environmental engineering to modify, test, and operate equipment and devices used in the prevention, control, and remediation of environmental pollution, including waste treatment and site remediation. May assist in the development of environmental pollution remediation devices under direction of engineer. Receive, set up, test, and decontaminate equipment. Maintain project logbook records and computer program files. Perform environmental quality work in field and office settings. Conduct pollution surveys, collecting and analyzing samples such as air and groundwater. Review technical documents to ensure completeness and conformance to requirements. Perform laboratory work such as logging numerical and visual observations, preparing and packaging samples, recording test results, and performing photo documentation. Review work plans to schedule activities.

Obtain product information, identify vendors and suppliers, and order materials and equipment to maintain inventory. Arrange for the disposal of lead, asbestos, and other hazardous materials. Inspect facilities to monitor compliance with regulations governing substances such as asbestos, lead, and wastewater. Provide technical engineering support in the planning of projects such as wastewater treatment plants to ensure compliance with environmental regulations and policies. Improve chemical processes to reduce toxic emissions. Oversee support staff. Assist in the cleanup of hazardous material spills. Produce environmental assessment reports, tabulating data and preparing charts, graphs, and sketches. Maintain process parameters and evaluate process anomalies. Work with customers to assess the environmental impact of proposed construction and to develop pollution prevention programs. Perform statistical analysis and correction of air or water pollution data submitted by industry and other agencies. Develop work plans, including writing specifications and establishing material, manpower, and facilities needs.

Personality Type: Realistic. These occupations frequently involve work activities that include practical, hands-on problems and solutions. They often deal with plants; animals; and real-world materials such as wood, tools, and machinery. Many of the occupations require working outside and don't involve a lot of paperwork or working closely with others.

GOE—Interest Area/Cluster: 15. Scientific Research, Engineering, and Mathematics. **Work Group:** 15.09. Engineering Technology. **Other Jobs in This Work Group:** Aerospace Engineering and Operations Technicians; Cartographers and Photogrammetrists; Civil Engineering Technicians; Electrical and Electronic Engineering Technicians; Electrical and Electronics Drafters; Electrical Drafters; Electrical Engineering Technicians; Electro-Mechanical Technicians; Electronic Drafters; Electronics Engineering Technicians; Mapping Technicians; Mechanical Drafters; Mechanical Engineering Technicians; Surveying and Mapping Technicians; Surveying Technicians.

Skills—Science: Using scientific methods to solve problems. **Repairing:** Repairing machines or systems, using the needed tools. **Troubleshooting:** Determining what is causing an operating error and deciding what to do about it. **Equipment Maintenance:** Performing routine maintenance and determining when and what kind of maintenance is needed. **Operation Monitoring:** Watching gauges, dials, or other indicators to make sure a machine is working properly. **Mathematics:** Using mathematics to solve problems.

Quality Control Analysis: Evaluating the quality or performance of products, services, or processes. **Installation:** Installing equipment, machines, wiring, or programs to meet specifications.

Education and Training Programs: Environmental Engineering Technology/Environmental Technology; Hazardous Materials Information Systems Technology/Technician Training. **Related Knowledge/Courses—Engineering and Technology:** Equipment, tools, and mechanical devices and their uses to produce motion, light, power, technology, and other applications. **Building and Construction:** Materials, methods, and the appropriate tools to construct objects, structures, and buildings. **Physics:** Physical principles, laws, and applications, including air, water, material dynamics, light, atomic principles, heat, electric theory, earth formations, and meteorological and related natural phenomena. **Design:** Design techniques, principles, tools, and instruments involved in the production and use of precision technical plans, blueprints, drawings, and models. **Biology:** Plant and animal living tissue, cells, organisms, and entities, including their functions, interdependencies, and interactions with each other and the environment. **Chemistry:** The composition, structure, and properties of substances and of the chemical processes and transformations that they undergo. This includes uses of chemicals and their interactions, danger signs, production techniques, and disposal methods.

Work Environment: More often indoors than outdoors; contaminants; hazardous conditions; hazardous equipment; standing.

Environmental Engineers

- ❈ Education/Training Required: Bachelor's degree
- ❈ Annual Earnings: $72,350
- ❈ Beginning Wage: $44,090
- ❈ Earnings Growth Potential: Medium
- ❈ Growth: 25.4%
- ❈ Annual Job Openings: 5,003
- ❈ Self-Employed: 2.7%
- ❈ Part-Time: 3.0%

Design, plan, or perform engineering duties in the prevention, control, and remediation of environmental health hazards, using various engineering disciplines. Work may include waste treatment, site remediation, or pollution control technology. Collaborate with environmental scientists, planners, hazardous waste technicians, engineers, and other specialists, and experts in law and business to address environmental problems. Inspect industrial and municipal facilities and programs to evaluate operational effectiveness and ensure compliance with environmental regulations. Prepare, review, and update environmental investigation and recommendation reports. Design and supervise the development of systems processes or equipment for control, management, or remediation of water, air, or soil quality. Provide environmental engineering assistance in network analysis, regulatory analysis, and planning or reviewing database development. Obtain, update, and maintain plans, permits, and standard operating procedures. Provide technical-level support for environmental remediation and litigation projects, including remediation system design and determination of regulatory applicability. Monitor progress of environmental improvement programs. Inform company employees and other interested parties of environmental issues. Advise corporations and government agencies of procedures to follow in cleaning up contaminated sites to protect people and the environment. Develop proposed project objectives and targets, and report to management on progress in attaining them. Request bids from suppliers or consultants. Advise industries and government agencies about environmental policies and standards. Assess the existing or potential environmental impact of land use projects on air, water, and land. Assist in budget implementation, forecasts, and administration. Serve on teams conducting multimedia inspections at complex facilities, providing assistance with planning, quality assurance, safety inspection protocols, and sampling. Coordinate and manage environmental protection programs and projects, assigning and evaluating work. Maintain, write, and revise quality assurance documentation and procedures. Provide administrative support for projects by collecting data, providing project documentation, training staff, and performing other general administrative duties.

Personality Type: Investigative. These occupations frequently involve working with ideas and require an extensive amount of thinking. They can involve searching for facts and figuring out problems mentally.

GOE—Interest Area/Cluster: 01. Agriculture and Natural Resources. **Work Group:** 01.02. Resource Science/Engineering for Plants, Animals, and the Environment. **Other Jobs in This Work Group:** Agricultural Engineers; Animal Scientists; Conservation Scientists; Foresters; Mining and Geological Engineers, Including Mining Safety Engineers;

Petroleum Engineers; Range Managers; Soil and Plant Scientists; Soil and Water Conservationists; Zoologists and Wildlife Biologists.

Skills—Management of Financial Resources: Determining how money will be spent to get the work done and accounting for these expenditures. **Systems Analysis:** Determining how a system should work and how changes will affect outcomes. **Mathematics:** Using mathematics to solve problems. **Systems Evaluation:** Looking at many indicators of system performance and taking into account their accuracy. **Management of Personnel Resources:** Motivating, developing, and directing people as they work; identifying the best people for the job. **Writing:** Communicating effectively with others in writing as indicated by the needs of the audience. **Operation Monitoring:** Watching gauges, dials, or other indicators to make sure a machine is working properly. **Complex Problem Solving:** Identifying complex problems, reviewing the options, and implementing solutions.

Education and Training Program: Environmental/Environmental Health Engineering. **Related Knowledge/Courses—Engineering and Technology:** Equipment, tools, and mechanical devices and their uses to produce motion, light, power, technology, and other applications. **Physics:** Physical principles, laws, and applications, including air, water, material dynamics, light, atomic principles, heat, electric theory, earth formations, and meteorological and related natural phenomena. **Design:** Design techniques, principles, tools, and instruments involved in the production and use of precision technical plans, blueprints, drawings, and models. **Chemistry:** The composition, structure, and properties of substances and of the chemical processes and transformations that they undergo. This includes uses of chemicals and their interactions, danger signs, production techniques, and disposal methods. **Building and Construction:** Materials, methods, and the appropriate tools to construct objects, structures, and buildings. **Biology:** Plant and animal living tissue, cells, organisms, and entities, including their functions, interdependencies, and interactions with each other and the environment.

Work Environment: More often indoors than outdoors; noisy; contaminants; sitting; using hands on objects, tools, or controls.

Environmental Science and Protection Technicians, Including Health

❋ Education/Training Required: Associate degree
❋ Annual Earnings: $39,370
❋ Beginning Wage: $25,090
❋ Earnings Growth Potential: Medium
❋ Growth: 28.0%
❋ Annual Job Openings: 8,404
❋ Self-Employed: 1.5%
❋ Part-Time: 19.4%

Perform laboratory and field tests to monitor the environment and investigate sources of pollution, including those that affect health. Under direction of environmental scientists or specialists, may collect samples of gases, soil, water, and other materials for testing and take corrective actions as assigned. Collect samples of gases, soils, water, industrial wastewater, and asbestos products to conduct tests on pollutant levels and identify sources of pollution. Record test data and prepare reports, summaries, and charts that interpret test results. Develop and implement programs for monitoring of environmental pollution and radiation. Discuss test results and analyses with customers. Set up equipment or stations to monitor and collect pollutants from sites such as smoke stacks, manufacturing plants, or mechanical equipment. Maintain files such as hazardous waste databases, chemical usage data, personnel exposure information, and diagrams showing equipment locations. Develop testing procedures or direct activities of workers in laboratory. Prepare samples or photomicrographs for testing and analysis. Calibrate microscopes and test instruments. Examine and analyze material for presence and concentration of contaminants such as asbestos, using variety of microscopes. Calculate amount of pollutant in samples or compute air pollution or gas flow in industrial processes, using chemical and mathematical formulas. Make recommendations to control or eliminate unsafe conditions at workplaces or public facilities. Weigh, analyze, and measure collected sample particles such as lead, coal dust, or rock, to determine concentration of pollutants. Provide information and technical and program assistance to government representatives, employers, and the general public on the issues of public health, environmental protection, or workplace safety. Conduct standardized tests to ensure materials and supplies used throughout power supply systems meet processing and safety specifications. Perform statistical analysis of environmental data. Respond to and investigate hazardous conditions or spills or outbreaks of disease or food poisoning, collecting samples for analysis. Determine amounts and kinds of chemicals to use in destroying harmful organisms and removing impurities from purification systems. Inspect sanitary conditions at public facilities. Inspect workplaces to ensure the absence of health and safety hazards such as high noise levels, radiation, or potential lighting hazards.

Personality Type: Investigative. These occupations frequently involve working with ideas and require an extensive amount of thinking. They can involve searching for facts and figuring out problems mentally.

GOE—Interest Area/Cluster: 01. Agriculture and Natural Resources. **Work Group:** 01.03. Resource Technologies for Plants, Animals, and the Environment. **Other Jobs in This Work Group:** Agricultural and Food Science Technicians; Agricultural Technicians; Food Science Technicians; Food Scientists and Technologists; Geological and Petroleum Technicians; Geological Sample Test Technicians; Geophysical Data Technicians.

Skills—Quality Control Analysis: Evaluating the quality or performance of products, services, or processes. **Systems Analysis:** Determining how a system should work and how changes will affect outcomes. **Systems Evaluation:** Looking at many indicators of system performance and taking into account their accuracy. **Operation Monitoring:** Watching gauges, dials, or other indicators to make sure a machine is working properly. **Operation and Control:** Controlling operations of equipment or systems. **Science:** Using scientific methods to solve problems.

Education and Training Programs: Environmental Science; Environmental Studies; Physical Science Technologies/Technician Training, Other; Science Technologies/Technician Training, Other. **Related Knowledge/Courses—Biology:** Plant and animal living tissue, cells, organisms, and entities, including their functions, interdependencies, and interactions with each other and the environment. **Chemistry:** The composition, structure, and properties of substances and of the chemical processes and transformations that they undergo. This includes uses of chemicals and their interactions, danger signs, production techniques, and disposal methods. **Geography:** Various methods for describing the location and distribution of land, sea, and air masses, including their physical locations, relationships, and characteristics. **Physics:** Physical principles, laws, and applications, including air, water, material dynamics, light, atomic principles, heat, electric theory, earth formations, and meteorological and related natural phenomena. **Computers and Electronics:** Electric circuit boards, processors, chips, and computer hardware and software, including applications and programming. **Building and Construction:** Materials, methods, and the appropriate tools to construct objects, structures, and buildings.

Work Environment: More often outdoors than indoors; very hot or cold; contaminants; hazardous equipment; standing.

Environmental Science Teachers, Postsecondary

- ❈ Education/Training Required: Doctoral degree
- ❈ Annual Earnings: $64,850
- ❈ Beginning Wage: $35,120
- ❈ Earnings Growth Potential: High
- ❈ Growth: 22.9%
- ❈ Annual Job Openings: 769
- ❈ Self-Employed: 0.4%
- ❈ Part-Time: 27.8%

Teach courses in environmental science. Supervise undergraduate and/or graduate teaching, internship, and research work. Conduct research in a particular field of knowledge and publish findings in professional journals, books, and/or electronic media. Keep abreast of developments in their field by reading current literature, talking with colleagues, and participating in professional conferences. Evaluate and grade students' classwork, laboratory work, assignments, and papers. Write grant proposals to procure external research funding. Supervise students' laboratory work and fieldwork. Prepare course materials such as syllabi, homework assignments, and handouts. Plan, evaluate, and revise curricula, course content, and course materials and methods of instruction. Compile, administer, and grade examinations or assign this work to others. Initiate, facilitate, and moderate classroom discussions. Advise students on academic and vocational curricula and on career issues. Prepare and deliver lectures to undergraduate and/or graduate students on topics such as hazardous waste management, industrial safety, and environmental toxicology. Maintain student attendance records, grades, and other required records. Select and obtain materials and supplies such as textbooks and laboratory equipment. Maintain regularly scheduled office hours in order to advise and assist students. Collaborate with colleagues to address teaching and research issues. Perform administrative duties such as serving as department head. Participate in student recruitment, registration, and placement activities. Provide professional consulting services to government and/or industry. Serve on academic or administrative committees that deal with institutional policies, departmental matters, and academic issues. Compile bibliographies of specialized materials for outside reading assignments. Participate in campus and community events. Act as advisers to student organizations.

Personality Type: Social. These occupations frequently involve working with, communicating with, and teaching people and often involve helping or providing service to others.

GOE—Interest Area/Cluster: 05. Education and Training. **Work Group:** 05.03. Postsecondary and Adult Teaching and Instructing. **Other Jobs in This Work Group:** Adult Literacy, Remedial Education, and GED Teachers and Instructors; Agricultural Sciences Teachers, Postsecondary; Anthropology and Archeology Teachers, Postsecondary; Architecture Teachers, Postsecondary; Area, Ethnic, and Cultural Studies Teachers, Postsecondary; Art, Drama, and Music Teachers, Postsecondary; Atmospheric, Earth, Marine, and Space Sciences Teachers, Postsecondary; Biological Science Teachers, Postsecondary; Business Teachers, Postsecondary; Chemistry Teachers, Postsecondary; Communications Teachers, Postsecondary; Computer Science Teachers, Postsecondary; Criminal Justice and Law Enforcement Teachers, Postsecondary; Economics Teachers, Postsecondary; Education Teachers, Postsecondary; Engineering Teachers, Postsecondary; English Language and Literature Teachers, Postsecondary; Farm and Home Management Advisors; Foreign Language and Literature Teachers, Postsecondary; Forestry and Conservation Science Teachers, Postsecondary; Geography Teachers, Postsecondary; Graduate Teaching Assistants; Health Specialties Teachers, Postsecondary; History Teachers, Postsecondary; Home Economics Teachers, Postsecondary; Law Teachers, Postsecondary; Library Science Teachers, Postsecondary; Mathematical Science Teachers, Postsecondary; Nursing Instructors and Teachers, Postsecondary; Philosophy and Religion Teachers, Postsecondary; Physics Teachers, Postsecondary; Political Science Teachers, Postsecondary; Psychology Teachers, Postsecondary; Recreation and Fitness Studies Teachers, Postsecondary; Self-Enrichment Education Teachers; Social Work Teachers, Postsecondary; Sociology Teachers, Postsecondary; Vocational Education Teachers, Postsecondary.

Skills—Science: Using scientific methods to solve problems. **Writing:** Communicating effectively with others in writing as indicated by the needs of the audience. **Reading Comprehension:** Understanding written sentences and paragraphs in work-related documents. **Instructing:** Teaching others how to do something. **Mathematics:** Using mathematics to solve problems. **Management of Financial Resources:** Determining how money will be spent to get the work done and accounting for these expenditures. **Programming:** Writing computer programs for various purposes. **Critical Thinking:** Using logic and analysis to identify the strengths and weaknesses of different approaches.

Education and Training Programs: Environmental Science; Environmental Studies; Science Teacher Education/General Science Teacher Education. **Related Knowledge/Courses—Biology:** Plant and animal living tissue, cells, organisms, and entities, including their functions, interdependencies, and interactions with each other and the environment. **Geography:** Various methods for describing the location and distribution of land, sea, and air masses, including their physical locations, relationships, and characteristics. **Chemistry:** The composition, structure, and properties of substances and of the chemical processes and transformations that they undergo. This includes uses of chemicals and their interactions, danger signs, production techniques, and disposal methods. **Education and Training:** Instructional methods and training techniques, including curriculum design principles, learning theory, group and individual teaching techniques, design of individual development plans, and test design principles. **Physics:** Physical principles, laws, and applications, including air, water, material dynamics, light, atomic principles, heat, electric theory, earth formations, and meteorological and related natural phenomena. **History and Archeology:** Historical events and their causes, indicators, and impact on particular civilizations and cultures.

Work Environment: Indoors; sitting.

Environmental Scientists and Specialists, Including Health

* Education/Training Required: Master's degree
* Annual Earnings: $58,380
* Beginning Wage: $35,630
* Earnings Growth Potential: Medium
* Growth: 25.1%
* Annual Job Openings: 6,961
* Self-Employed: 2.2%
* Part-Time: 5.3%

Conduct research or perform investigation for the purpose of identifying, abating, or eliminating sources of pollutants or hazards that affect either the environment or the health of the population. Using knowledge of various scientific disciplines, may collect, synthesize, study, report, and take action based on data derived from measurements or observations of air, food, soil, water, and other sources. Collect, synthesize, analyze, manage, and report environmental data such as pollution emission measurements, atmospheric monitoring measurements, meteorological and mineralogical information, and soil or water samples. Analyze data to determine validity, quality, and scientific significance, and to interpret correlations between human activities and environmental effects. Communicate scientific and technical information to the public, organizations, or internal audiences through oral briefings, written documents, workshops, conferences, training sessions, or public hearings. Provide scientific and technical guidance, support, coordination, and oversight to governmental agencies, environmental programs, industry, or the public. Process and review environmental permits, licenses, and related materials. Review and implement environmental technical standards, guidelines, policies, and formal regulations that meet all appropriate requirements. Prepare charts or graphs from data samples, providing summary information on the environmental relevance of the data. Determine data collection methods to be employed in research projects and surveys. Investigate and report on accidents affecting the environment. Research sources of pollution to determine their effects on the environment and to develop theories or methods of pollution abatement or control. Provide advice on proper standards and regulations or the development of policies, strategies, and codes of practice for environmental management. Monitor effects of pollution and land degradation, and recommend means of prevention or control. Supervise or train students, environmental technologists, technicians, or other related staff. Evaluate violations or problems discovered during inspections to determine appropriate regulatory actions or to provide advice on the development and prosecution of regulatory cases. Conduct environmental audits and inspections, and investigations of violations. Plan and develop research models, using knowledge of mathematical and statistical concepts. Conduct applied research on environmental topics such as waste control and treatment and pollution abatement methods.

Personality Type: Investigative. These occupations frequently involve working with ideas and require an extensive amount of thinking. They can involve searching for facts and figuring out problems mentally.

GOE—Interest Area/Cluster: 15. Scientific Research, Engineering, and Mathematics. **Work Group:** 15.03. Life Sciences. **Other Jobs in This Work Group:** Biochemists and Biophysicists; Biologists; Epidemiologists; Medical Scientists, Except Epidemiologists; Microbiologists.

Skills—Science: Using scientific methods to solve problems. **Systems Analysis:** Determining how a system should work and how changes will affect outcomes. **Systems Evaluation:** Looking at many indicators of system performance and taking into account their accuracy. **Writing:** Communicating effectively with others in writing as indicated by the needs of the audience. **Reading Comprehension:** Understanding written sentences and paragraphs in work-related documents. **Management of Personnel Resources:** Motivating, developing, and directing people as they work; identifying the best people for the job. **Management of Material Resources:** Obtaining and seeing to the appropriate use of equipment, facilities, and materials needed to do certain work. **Operation Monitoring:** Watching gauges, dials, or other indicators to make sure a machine is working properly.

Education and Training Programs: Environmental Science; Environmental Studies. **Related Knowledge/Courses—Biology:** Plant and animal living tissue, cells, organisms, and entities, including their functions, interdependencies, and interactions with each other and the environment. **Geography:** Various methods for describing the location and distribution of land, sea, and air masses, including their physical locations, relationships, and characteristics. **Chemistry:** The composition, structure, and properties of substances and of the chemical processes and transformations that they undergo. This includes uses of chemicals and their interactions, danger signs, production techniques, and disposal methods. **Physics:** Physical principles, laws, and applications, including air, water, material dynamics, light, atomic principles, heat, electric theory, earth formations, and meteorological and related natural phenomena. **Law and Government:** Laws, legal codes, court procedures, precedents, government regulations, executive orders, agency rules, and the democratic political process. **Engineering and Technology:** Equipment, tools, and mechanical devices and their uses to produce motion, light, power, technology, and other applications.

Work Environment: More often indoors than outdoors; noisy; sitting.

Epidemiologists

- ❋ Education/Training Required: Master's degree
- ❋ Annual Earnings: $60,010
- ❋ Beginning Wage: $40,140
- ❋ Earnings Growth Potential: Low
- ❋ Growth: 13.6%
- ❋ Annual Job Openings: 503
- ❋ Self-Employed: 2.6%
- ❋ Part-Time: 5.9%

Investigate and describe the determinants and distribution of disease, disability, and other health outcomes and develop the means for prevention and control. Monitor and report incidents of infectious diseases to local and state health agencies. Plan and direct studies to investigate human or animal disease, preventive methods, and treatments for disease. Communicate research findings on various types of diseases to health practitioners, policy makers, and the public. Provide expertise in the design, management, and evaluation of study protocols and health status questionnaires, sample selection, and analysis. Oversee public health programs, including statistical analysis, health care planning, surveillance systems, and public health improvement. Investigate diseases or parasites to determine cause and risk factors, progress, life cycle, or mode of transmission. Educate healthcare workers, patients, and the public about infectious and communicable diseases, including disease transmission and prevention. Conduct research to develop methodologies, instrumentation, and procedures for medical application, analyzing data and presenting findings. Identify and analyze public health issues related to foodborne parasitic diseases and their impact on public policies or scientific studies or surveys. Supervise professional,

technical, and clerical personnel. Plan, administer, and evaluate health safety standards and programs to improve public health, conferring with health department, industry personnel, physicians, and others. Prepare and analyze samples to study effects of drugs, gases, pesticides, or microorganisms on cell structure and tissue. Consult with and advise physicians, educators, researchers, government health officials, and others regarding medical applications of sciences such as physics, biology, and chemistry. Teach principles of medicine and medical and laboratory procedures to physicians, residents, students, and technicians. Standardize drug dosages, methods of immunization, and procedures for manufacture of drugs and medicinal compounds.

Personality Type: Investigative. These occupations frequently involve working with ideas and require an extensive amount of thinking. They can involve searching for facts and figuring out problems mentally.

GOE—Interest Area/Cluster: 15. Scientific Research, Engineering, and Mathematics. **Work Group:** 15.03. Life Sciences. **Other Jobs in This Work Group:** Biochemists and Biophysicists; Biologists; Environmental Scientists and Specialists, Including Health; Medical Scientists, Except Epidemiologists; Microbiologists.

Skills—Science: Using scientific methods to solve problems. **Systems Analysis:** Determining how a system should work and how changes will affect outcomes. **Systems Evaluation:** Looking at many indicators of system performance and taking into account their accuracy. **Programming:** Writing computer programs for various purposes. **Complex Problem Solving:** Identifying complex problems, reviewing the options, and implementing solutions. **Reading Comprehension:** Understanding written sentences and paragraphs in work-related documents. **Management of Personnel Resources:** Motivating, developing, and directing people as they work; identifying the best people for the job. **Judgment and Decision Making:** Weighing the relative costs and benefits of a potential action.

Education and Training Programs: Biophysics; Cell/Cellular Biology and Histology; Epidemiology; Medical Scientist (MS, PhD). **Related Knowledge/Courses—Biology:** Plant and animal living tissue, cells, organisms, and entities, including their functions, interdependencies, and interactions with each other and the environment. **Medicine and Dentistry:** The information and techniques needed to diagnose and treat injuries, diseases, and deformities. This includes symptoms, treatment alternatives, drug properties and interactions, and preventive health-care measures.

Sociology and Anthropology: Group behavior and dynamics; societal trends and influences; and cultures and their history, migrations, ethnicity, and origins. **Geography:** Various methods for describing the location and distribution of land, sea, and air masses, including their physical locations, relationships, and characteristics. **Mathematics:** Numbers and their operations and interrelationships, including arithmetic, algebra, geometry, calculus, and statistics and their applications. **Education and Training:** Instructional methods and training techniques, including curriculum design principles, learning theory, group and individual teaching techniques, design of individual development plans, and test design principles.

Work Environment: Indoors; sitting.

Equal Opportunity Representatives and Officers

- ❋ Education/Training Required: Long-term on-the-job training
- ❋ Annual Earnings: $48,400
- ❋ Beginning Wage: $28,980
- ❋ Earnings Growth Potential: High
- ❋ Growth: 4.9%
- ❋ Annual Job Openings: 15,841
- ❋ Self-Employed: 0.4%
- ❋ Part-Time: 5.0%

The job openings listed here are shared with Coroners; Environmental Compliance Inspectors; Government Property Inspectors and Investigators; and Licensing Examiners and Inspectors.

Monitor and evaluate compliance with equal opportunity laws, guidelines, and policies to ensure that employment practices and contracting arrangements give equal opportunity without regard to race, religion, color, national origin, sex, age, or disability. Investigate employment practices and alleged violations of laws, in order to document and correct discriminatory factors. Interpret civil rights laws and equal opportunity regulations for individuals and employers. Study equal opportunity complaints in order to clarify issues. Meet with persons involved in equal opportunity complaints in order to verify case information, and to arbitrate and settle disputes. Coordinate, monitor, and revise complaint procedures to ensure timely processing and review of complaints. Prepare reports of selection, survey, and other statistics, and recommendations for corrective action. Conduct surveys and evaluate findings in order to determine if systematic discrimination exists. Develop guidelines for non-discriminatory employment practices, and monitor their implementation and impact. Review company contracts to determine actions required to meet governmental equal opportunity provisions. Counsel newly hired members of minority and disadvantaged groups, informing them about details of civil rights laws. Provide information, technical assistance, and training to supervisors, managers, and employees on topics such as employee supervision, hiring, grievance procedures, and staff development. Verify that all job descriptions are submitted for review and approval, and that descriptions meet regulatory standards. Act as liaisons between minority placement agencies and employers, or between job search committees and other equal opportunity administrators. Consult with community representatives to develop technical assistance agreements in accordance with governmental regulations. Meet with job search committees or coordinators to explain the role of the equal opportunity coordinator, to provide resources for advertising, and to explain expectations for future contacts. Participate in the recruitment of employees through job fairs, career days, and advertising plans.

Personality Type: Social. These occupations frequently involve working with, communicating with, and teaching people and often involve helping or providing service to others.

GOE—Interest Area/Cluster: 07. Government and Public Administration. **Work Group:** 07.03. Regulations Enforcement. **Other Jobs in This Work Group:** Agricultural Inspectors; Aviation Inspectors; Compliance Officers, Except Agriculture, Construction, Health and Safety, and Transportation; Construction and Building Inspectors; Environmental Compliance Inspectors; Financial Examiners; Fire Inspectors; Fish and Game Wardens; Forest Fire Inspectors and Prevention Specialists; Freight and Cargo Inspectors; Government Property Inspectors and Investigators; Immigration and Customs Inspectors; Licensing Examiners and Inspectors; Nuclear Monitoring Technicians; Occupational Health and Safety Specialists; Occupational Health and Safety Technicians; Tax Examiners, Collectors, and Revenue Agents; Transportation Vehicle, Equipment, and Systems Inspectors, Except Aviation.

Skills—Negotiation: Bringing others together and trying to reconcile differences. **Persuasion:** Persuading others to approach things differently. **Social Perceptiveness:** Being aware of others' reactions and understanding why they react the way they do. **Service Orientation:** Actively looking for ways to help people. **Complex Problem Solving:**

Identifying complex problems, reviewing the options, and implementing solutions. **Judgment and Decision Making:** Weighing the relative costs and benefits of a potential action. **Active Listening:** Listening to what other people are saying and asking questions as appropriate. **Writing:** Communicating effectively with others in writing as indicated by the needs of the audience.

Education and Training Program: Public Administration and Social Service Professions, Other. **Related Knowledge/ Courses—Law and Government:** Laws, legal codes, court procedures, precedents, government regulations, executive orders, agency rules, and the democratic political process. **Personnel and Human Resources:** Principles and procedures for personnel recruitment; selection; training; compensation and benefits; labor relations and negotiation; and personnel information systems. **Clerical Practices:** Administrative and clerical procedures and systems such as word-processing systems, filing and records management systems, stenography and transcription, forms, design principles, and other office procedures and terminology. **English Language:** The structure and content of the English language, including the meaning and spelling of words, rules of composition, and grammar. **Customer and Personal Service:** Principles and processes for providing customer and personal services, including needs assessment techniques, quality service standards, alternative delivery systems, and customer satisfaction evaluation techniques. **Administration and Management:** Principles and processes involved in business and organizational planning, coordination, and execution. This includes strategic planning, resource allocation, manpower modeling, leadership techniques, and production methods.

Work Environment: Indoors; sitting; repetitive motions.

Excavating and Loading Machine and Dragline Operators

- ❋ Education/Training Required: Moderate-term on-the-job training
- ❋ Annual Earnings: $34,050
- ❋ Beginning Wage: $23,140
- ❋ Earnings Growth Potential: Low
- ❋ Growth: 8.3%
- ❋ Annual Job Openings: 6,562
- ❋ Self-Employed: 14.9%
- ❋ Part-Time: 3.2%

Operate or tend machinery equipped with scoops, shovels, or buckets to excavate and load loose materials. Move levers, depress foot pedals, and turn dials to operate power machinery such as power shovels, stripping-shovels, scraper loaders, or backhoes. Set up and inspect equipment prior to operation. Observe hand signals, grade stakes, and other markings when operating machines so that work can be performed to specifications. Become familiar with digging plans, machine capabilities and limitations, and with efficient and safe digging procedures in a given application. Operate machinery to perform activities such as backfilling excavations, vibrating or breaking rock or concrete, and making winter roads. Lubricate, adjust, and repair machinery, and replace parts such as gears, bearings, and bucket teeth. Create and maintain inclines and ramps, and handle slides, mud, and pit cleanings and maintenance. Move materials over short distances such as around a construction site, factory, or warehouse. Measure and verify levels of rock or gravel, bases, and other excavated material. Receive written or oral instructions regarding material movement or excavation. Adjust dig face angles for varying overburden depths and set lengths. Drive machines to work sites. Perform manual labor to prepare or finish sites, such as shoveling materials by hand. Direct ground workers engaged in activities such as moving stakes or markers or changing positions of towers. Direct workers engaged in placing blocks and outriggers in order to prevent capsizing of machines when lifting heavy loads.

Personality Type: Realistic. These occupations frequently involve work activities that include practical, hands-on problems and solutions. They often deal with plants; animals; and real-world materials such as wood, tools, and machinery. Many of the occupations require working outside and don't involve a lot of paperwork or working closely with others.

GOE—Interest Area/Cluster: 01. Agriculture and Natural Resources. **Work Group:** 01.08. Mining and Drilling. **Other Jobs in This Work Group:** Continuous Mining Machine Operators; Derrick Operators, Oil and Gas; Earth Drillers, Except Oil and Gas; Explosives Workers, Ordnance Handling Experts, and Blasters; Helpers—Extraction Workers; Loading Machine Operators, Underground Mining; Mine Cutting and Channeling Machine Operators; Rock Splitters, Quarry; Roof Bolters, Mining; Rotary Drill Operators, Oil and Gas; Roustabouts, Oil and Gas; Service Unit Operators, Oil, Gas, and Mining; Shuttle Car Operators; Wellhead Pumpers.

Skills—Repairing: Repairing machines or systems, using the needed tools. **Equipment Maintenance:** Performing routine maintenance and determining when and what kind of maintenance is needed. **Operation and Control:** Controlling operations of equipment or systems. **Operation Monitoring:** Watching gauges, dials, or other indicators to make sure a machine is working properly. **Installation:** Installing equipment, machines, wiring, or programs to meet specifications. **Equipment Selection:** Determining the kind of tools and equipment needed to do a job. **Systems Analysis:** Determining how a system should work and how changes will affect outcomes. **Technology Design:** Generating or adapting equipment and technology to serve user needs.

Education and Training Program: Construction/Heavy Equipment/Earthmoving Equipment Operation. **Related Knowledge/Courses—Building and Construction:** Materials, methods, and the appropriate tools to construct objects, structures, and buildings. **Mechanical Devices:** Machines and tools, including their designs, uses, benefits, repair, and maintenance. **Transportation:** Principles and methods for moving people or goods by air, rail, sea, or road, including their relative costs, advantages, and limitations. **Production and Processing:** Inputs, outputs, raw materials, waste, quality control, costs, and techniques for maximizing the manufacture and distribution of goods. **Public Safety and Security:** Weaponry; public safety; security operations, rules, regulations, precautions, and prevention; and the protection of people, data, and property. **Engineering and Technology:** Equipment, tools, and mechanical devices and their uses to produce motion, light, power, technology, and other applications.

Work Environment: Outdoors; noisy; contaminants; whole-body vibration; sitting; using hands on objects, tools, or controls.

Executive Secretaries and Administrative Assistants

- ❋ Education/Training Required: Work experience in a related occupation
- ❋ Annual Earnings: $38,640
- ❋ Beginning Wage: $26,060
- ❋ Earnings Growth Potential: Low
- ❋ Growth: 14.8%
- ❋ Annual Job Openings: 235,314
- ❋ Self-Employed: 1.4%
- ❋ Part-Time: 18.9%

Provide high-level administrative support by conducting research; preparing statistical reports; handling information requests; and performing clerical functions such as preparing correspondence, receiving visitors, arranging conference calls, and scheduling meetings. May also train and supervise lower-level clerical staff. Manage and maintain executives' schedules. Prepare invoices, reports, memos, letters, financial statements, and other documents, using word-processing, spreadsheet, database, or presentation software. Open, sort, and distribute incoming correspondence, including faxes and e-mail. Read and analyze incoming memos, submissions, and reports to determine their significance and plan their distribution. File and retrieve corporate documents, records, and reports. Greet visitors and determine whether they should be given access to specific individuals. Prepare responses to correspondence containing routine inquiries. Perform general office duties such as ordering supplies, maintaining records management systems, and performing basic bookkeeping work. Prepare agendas and make arrangements for committee, board, and other meetings. Make travel arrangements for executives. Conduct research, compile data, and prepare papers for consideration and presentation by executives, committees, and boards of directors. Compile, transcribe, and distribute minutes of meetings. Attend meetings to record minutes. Coordinate and direct office services, such as records and budget preparation, personnel, and housekeeping, to aid executives. Meet with individuals, special-interest groups, and others on behalf of executives, committees, and boards of directors. Set up and oversee administrative policies and procedures for offices or organizations. Supervise and train other clerical staff. Review operating practices and procedures to determine whether improvements can be made in areas such as workflow, reporting procedures, or expenditures. Interpret administrative and operating policies and procedures for employees.

Personality Type: Conventional. These occupations frequently involve following set procedures and routines and can include working with data and details more than with ideas. Usually there is a clear line of authority to follow.

GOE—Interest Area/Cluster: 04. Business and Administration. **Work Group:** 04.04. Secretarial Support. **Other Jobs in This Work Group:** Legal Secretaries; Medical Secretaries; Secretaries, Except Legal, Medical, and Executive.

Skills—Writing: Communicating effectively with others in writing as indicated by the needs of the audience. **Active Listening:** Listening to what other people are saying and asking questions as appropriate. **Speaking:** Talking to others to effectively convey information. **Management of Financial Resources:** Determining how money will be spent to get the work done and accounting for these expenditures.

Education and Training Programs: Administrative Assistant and Secretarial Science, General; Executive Assistant/Executive Secretary Training; Medical Administrative/Executive Assistant and Medical Secretary Training. **Related Knowledge/Courses—Clerical Practices:** Administrative and clerical procedures and systems such as word-processing systems, filing and records management systems, stenography and transcription, forms, design principles, and other office procedures and terminology. **Customer and Personal Service:** Principles and processes for providing customer and personal services, including needs assessment techniques, quality service standards, alternative delivery systems, and customer satisfaction evaluation techniques. **English Language:** The structure and content of the English language, including the meaning and spelling of words, rules of composition, and grammar. **Computers and Electronics:** Electric circuit boards, processors, chips, and computer hardware and software, including applications and programming. **Communications and Media:** Media production, communication, and dissemination techniques and methods, including alternative ways to inform and entertain via written, oral, and visual media. **Personnel and Human Resources:** Principles and procedures for personnel recruitment; selection; training; compensation and benefits; labor relations and negotiation; and personnel information systems.

Work Environment: Indoors; sitting; repetitive motions.

Family and General Practitioners

- ✳ Education/Training Required: First professional degree
- ✳ Annual Earnings: More than $145,600
- ✳ Beginning Wage: $67,400
- ✳ Earnings Growth Potential: Cannot be calculated
- ✳ Growth: 14.2%
- ✳ Annual Job Openings: 38,027
- ✳ Self-Employed: 14.7%
- ✳ Part-Time: 8.1%

The job openings listed here are shared with Anesthesiologists; Internists, General; Obstetricians and Gynecologists; Pediatricians, General; Psychiatrists; and Surgeons.

Diagnose, treat, and help prevent diseases and injuries that commonly occur in the general population. Prescribe or administer treatment, therapy, medication, vaccination, and other specialized medical care to treat or prevent illness, disease, or injury. Order, perform, and interpret tests and analyze records, reports, and examination information to diagnose patients' condition. Monitor the patients' conditions and progress and re-evaluate treatments as necessary. Explain procedures and discuss test results or prescribed treatments with patients. Collect, record, and maintain patient information, such as medical history, reports, and examination results. Advise patients and community members concerning diet, activity, hygiene, and disease prevention. Refer patients to medical specialists or other practitioners when necessary. Direct and coordinate activities of nurses, students, assistants, specialists, therapists, and other medical staff. Coordinate work with nurses, social workers, rehabilitation therapists, pharmacists, psychologists, and other health-care providers. Deliver babies. Operate on patients to remove, repair, or improve functioning of diseased or injured body parts and systems. Plan, implement, or administer health programs or standards in hospital, business, or community for information, prevention, or treatment of injury or illness. Prepare reports for government or management of birth, death, and disease statistics; workforce evaluations; or medical status of individuals. Conduct research to study anatomy and develop or test medications, treatments, or procedures to prevent or control disease or injury.

Personality Type: Investigative. These occupations frequently involve working with ideas and require an extensive amount of thinking. They can involve searching for facts and figuring out problems mentally.

GOE—Interest Area/Cluster: 08. Health Science. **Work Group:** 08.02. Medicine and Surgery. **Other Jobs in This Work Group:** Anesthesiologists; Internists, General; Medical Assistants; Medical Transcriptionists; Obstetricians and Gynecologists; Pediatricians, General; Pharmacists; Pharmacy Aides; Pharmacy Technicians; Physician Assistants; Psychiatrists; Registered Nurses; Surgeons; Surgical Technologists.

Skills—Science: Using scientific methods to solve problems. **Social Perceptiveness:** Being aware of others' reactions and understanding why they react the way they do. **Reading Comprehension:** Understanding written sentences and paragraphs in work-related documents. **Complex Problem Solving:** Identifying complex problems, reviewing the options, and implementing solutions. **Persuasion:** Persuading others to approach things differently.

Service Orientation: Actively looking for ways to help people. **Management of Financial Resources:** Determining how money will be spent to get the work done and accounting for these expenditures. **Active Learning:** Working with new material or information to grasp its implications.

Education and Training Programs: Family Medicine; Medicine (MD); Osteopathic Medicine/Osteopathy (DO). **Related Knowledge/Courses—Medicine and Dentistry:** The information and techniques needed to diagnose and treat injuries, diseases, and deformities. This includes symptoms, treatment alternatives, drug properties and interactions, and preventive health-care measures. **Biology:** Plant and animal living tissue, cells, organisms, and entities, including their functions, interdependencies, and interactions with each other and the environment. **Therapy and Counseling:** Information and techniques needed to rehabilitate physical and mental ailments and to provide career guidance, including alternative treatments, rehabilitation equipment and its proper use, and methods to evaluate treatment effects. **Psychology:** Human behavior and performance, mental processes, psychological research methods, and the assessment and treatment of behavioral and affective disorders. **Sociology and Anthropology:** Group behavior and dynamics; societal trends and influences; and cultures and their history, migrations, ethnicity, and origins. **Chemistry:** The composition, structure, and properties of substances and of the chemical processes and transformations that they undergo. This includes uses of chemicals and their interactions, danger signs, production techniques, and disposal methods.

Work Environment: Indoors; disease or infections; standing; using hands on objects, tools, or controls.

Farmers and Ranchers

- ❋ Education/Training Required: Long-term on-the-job training
- ❋ Annual Earnings: $33,360
- ❋ Beginning Wage: $21,230
- ❋ Earnings Growth Potential: Medium
- ❋ Growth: –8.5%
- ❋ Annual Job Openings: 129,552
- ❋ Self-Employed: 100.0%
- ❋ Part-Time: 18.8%

On an ownership or rental basis, operate farms, ranches, greenhouses, nurseries, timber tracts, or other agricultural production establishments that produce crops, horticultural specialties, livestock, poultry, finfish, shellfish, or animal specialties. May plant, cultivate, harvest, perform post-harvest activities on, and market crops and livestock; may hire, train, and supervise farm workers or supervise a farm labor contractor; may prepare cost, production, and other records. May maintain and operate machinery and perform physical work. Breed and raise stock such as cattle, poultry, and honeybees, using recognized breeding practices to ensure continued improvement in stock. Lubricate, adjust, and make minor repairs to farm equipment, using oilcans, grease guns, and hand tools. Assist in animal births, and care for newborn livestock. Assemble, position, and secure structures such as trellises, beehives, or fences, using hand tools. Operate dairy farms that produce bulk milk. Manage and oversee the day-to-day running of farms raising poultry or pigs for the production of meat and breeding stock. Maintain colonies of bees to produce honey and hive byproducts, pollinate crops, and/or produce queens and bees for sale. Keep hens in order to produce table eggs for eating or fertile eggs for breeding. Maintain financial, tax, production, and employee records. Maintain facilities such as fencing, water supplies, and outdoor housing and wind shelters. Hire, train, and direct workers engaged in planting, cultivating, irrigating, harvesting, and marketing crops, and in raising livestock. Grow out-of-season or early crops in greenhouses or cold-frame beds, or bud and graft plant stock. Herd cattle, using horses or all-terrain vehicles. Buy or sell futures contracts, or price products in advance of future sales so that risk is limited and/or profit is increased. Clean and disinfect buildings and yards, and remove manure. Transport grain to silos for storage, and burn or bale any straw that is left behind. Set up and operate farm machinery to cultivate, harvest, and haul crops. Select animals for market, and provide transportation of livestock to market. Select and purchase supplies and equipment such as seed, fertilizers, and farm machinery. Remove lower quality or older animals from herds and purchase other livestock to replace culled animals. Purchase and store livestock feed. Control the spread of disease and parasites in herds by using vaccination and medication and by separating sick animals. Clean, grade, and package crops for marketing. Clean and sanitize milking equipment, storage tanks, collection cups, and cows' udders, or ensure that procedures are followed to maintain sanitary conditions for handling of milk.

Personality Type: Realistic. These occupations frequently involve work activities that include practical, hands-on problems and solutions. They often deal with plants; animals; and real-world materials such as wood, tools, and machinery. Many of the occupations require working outside and don't involve a lot of paperwork or working closely with others.

GOE—Interest Area/Cluster: 01. Agriculture and Natural Resources. **Work Group:** 01.01. Managerial Work in Agriculture and Natural Resources. **Other Jobs in This Work Group:** Aquacultural Managers; Crop and Livestock Managers; Farm Labor Contractors; Farm, Ranch, and Other Agricultural Managers; First-Line Supervisors/Managers of Agricultural Crop and Horticultural Workers; First-Line Supervisors/Managers of Animal Husbandry and Animal Care Workers; First-Line Supervisors/Managers of Aquacultural Workers; First-Line Supervisors/Managers of Construction Trades and Extraction Workers; First-Line Supervisors/Managers of Farming, Fishing, and Forestry Workers; First-Line Supervisors/Managers of Landscaping, Lawn Service, and Groundskeeping Workers; First-Line Supervisors/Managers of Logging Workers; Nursery and Greenhouse Managers; Park Naturalists; Purchasing Agents and Buyers, Farm Products.

Skills—Repairing: Repairing machines or systems, using the needed tools. **Equipment Maintenance:** Performing routine maintenance and determining when and what kind of maintenance is needed. **Management of Financial Resources:** Determining how money will be spent to get the work done and accounting for these expenditures. **Installation:** Installing equipment, machines, wiring, or programs to meet specifications. **Operation Monitoring:** Watching gauges, dials, or other indicators to make sure a machine is working properly. **Operation and Control:** Controlling operations of equipment or systems. **Management of Material Resources:** Obtaining and seeing to the appropriate use of equipment, facilities, and materials needed to do certain work. **Troubleshooting:** Determining what is causing an operating error and deciding what to do about it.

Education and Training Programs: Agribusiness/Agricultural Business Operations; Agricultural Animal Breeding; Agricultural Business and Management, General; Agronomy and Crop Science; Animal Nutrition; Animal Sciences, General; Aquaculture; Crop Production; Dairy Science; Farm/Farm and Ranch Management; Greenhouse Operations and Management; Horticultural Science; Livestock Management; Ornamental Horticulture; Plant Nursery Operations and Management; Poultry Science; Range Science and Management; others. **Related Knowledge/Courses—Food Production:** Techniques and equipment for planting, growing, and harvesting of food for consumption, including crop-rotation methods, animal husbandry,

and food storage/handling techniques. **Building and Construction:** Materials, methods, and the appropriate tools to construct objects, structures, and buildings. **Biology:** Plant and animal living tissue, cells, organisms, and entities, including their functions, interdependencies, and interactions with each other and the environment. **Mechanical Devices:** Machines and tools, including their designs, uses, benefits, repair, and maintenance. **Sales and Marketing:** Principles and methods involved in showing, promoting, and selling products or services. This includes marketing strategies and tactics, product demonstration and sales techniques, and sales control systems. **Economics and Accounting:** Economic and accounting principles and practices, the financial markets, banking, and the analysis and reporting of financial data.

Work Environment: Outdoors; noisy; very hot or cold; contaminants; hazardous equipment; using hands on objects, tools, or controls.

Fashion Designers

- ✽ Education/Training Required: Associate degree
- ✽ Annual Earnings: $62,810
- ✽ Beginning Wage: $31,340
- ✽ Earnings Growth Potential: Very high
- ✽ Growth: 5.0%
- ✽ Annual Job Openings: 1,968
- ✽ Self-Employed: 23.6%
- ✽ Part-Time: 16.7%

Design clothing and accessories. Create original garments or design garments that follow well-established fashion trends. May develop the line of color and kinds of materials. Examine sample garments on and off models; then modify designs to achieve desired effects. Determine prices for styles. Select materials and production techniques to be used for products. Draw patterns for articles designed; then cut patterns, and cut material according to patterns, using measuring instruments and scissors. Design custom clothing and accessories for individuals, retailers, or theatrical, television, or film productions. Attend fashion shows and review garment magazines and manuals in order to gather information about fashion trends and consumer preferences. Develop a group of products and/or accessories, and market them through venues such as boutiques or mail-order catalogs. Test fabrics or oversee testing so that garment care labels can be created. Visit textile showrooms to keep up-to-date on the latest fabrics. Sew together sections of material to form mockups or samples of garments or articles, using sewing equipment. Research the styles and periods of clothing needed for film or theatrical productions. Direct and coordinate workers involved in drawing and cutting patterns and constructing samples or finished garments. Purchase new or used clothing and accessory items as needed to complete designs. Provide sample garments to agents and sales representatives, and arrange for showings of sample garments at sales meetings or fashion shows. Identify target markets for designs, looking at factors such as age, gender, and socioeconomic status. Read scripts and consult directors and other production staff in order to develop design concepts and plan productions. Confer with sales and management executives or with clients in order to discuss design ideas. Collaborate with other designers to coordinate special products and designs. Sketch rough and detailed drawings of apparel or accessories, and write specifications such as color schemes, construction, material types, and accessory requirements. Adapt other designers' ideas for the mass market.

Personality Type: Artistic. These occupations frequently involve working with forms, designs, and patterns. They often require self-expression, and the work can be done without following a clear set of rules.

GOE—Interest Area/Cluster: 03. Arts and Communication. **Work Group:** 03.05. Design. **Other Jobs in This Work Group:** Commercial and Industrial Designers; Floral Designers; Graphic Designers; Interior Designers; Merchandise Displayers and Window Trimmers; Set and Exhibit Designers.

Skills—Technology Design: Generating or adapting equipment and technology to serve user needs. **Operations Analysis:** Analyzing needs and product requirements to create a design. **Quality Control Analysis:** Evaluating the quality or performance of products, services, or processes. **Negotiation:** Bringing others together and trying to reconcile differences. **Time Management:** Managing one's own time and the time of others. **Systems Evaluation:** Looking at many indicators of system performance and taking into account their accuracy. **Mathematics:** Using mathematics to solve problems. **Active Learning:** Working with new material or information to grasp its implications.

Education and Training Programs: Apparel and Textile Manufacture; Fashion and Fabric Consultant; Fashion/Apparel Design; Textile Science. **Related Knowledge/Courses—Fine Arts:** Theory and techniques required to produce, compose, and perform works of music, dance, visual arts, drama, and sculpture. **Design:** Design techniques, principles, tools, and instruments involved in the production and use of precision technical plans, blueprints, drawings, and models. **Sales and Marketing:** Principles and methods involved in showing, promoting, and selling products or services. This includes marketing strategies and tactics, product demonstration and sales techniques, and sales control systems. **Production and Processing:** Inputs, outputs, raw materials, waste, quality control, costs, and techniques for maximizing the manufacture and distribution of goods. **Communications and Media:** Media production, communication, and dissemination techniques and methods, including alternative ways to inform and entertain via written, oral, and visual media. **Administration and Management:** Principles and processes involved in business and organizational planning, coordination, and execution. This includes strategic planning, resource allocation, manpower modeling, leadership techniques, and production methods.

Work Environment: Indoors; noisy; cramped work space, awkward positions; sitting; using hands on objects, tools, or controls; repetitive motions.

Film and Video Editors

* Education/Training Required: Bachelor's degree
* Annual Earnings: $47,870
* Beginning Wage: $24,270
* Earnings Growth Potential: High
* Growth: 12.7%
* Annual Job Openings: 2,707
* Self-Employed: 15.9%
* Part-Time: 18.9%

Edit motion picture soundtracks, film, and video. Cut shot sequences to different angles at specific points in scenes, making each individual cut as fluid and seamless as possible. Study scripts to become familiar with production concepts and requirements. Edit films and videotapes to insert music, dialogue, and sound effects; to arrange films into sequences; and to correct errors, using editing equipment. Select and combine the most effective shots of each scene to form a logical and smoothly running story. Mark frames where a particular shot or piece of sound is to begin or end. Determine the specific audio and visual effects and music necessary to complete films. Verify key numbers and time codes on materials. Organize and string together raw footage into a continuous whole according to scripts or the instructions of directors and producers. Review assembled films or edited videotapes on screens or monitors to determine if corrections are necessary. Program computerized graphic effects. Review footage sequence by sequence to become familiar with it before assembling it into a final product. Set up and operate computer editing systems, electronic titling systems, video switching equipment, and digital video effects units to produce a final product. Record needed sounds or obtain them from sound effects libraries. Confer with producers and directors concerning layout or editing approaches needed to increase dramatic or entertainment value of productions. Manipulate plot, score, sound, and graphics to make the parts into a continuous whole, working closely with people in audio, visual, music, optical, or special effects departments. Supervise and coordinate activities of workers engaged in film editing, assembling, and recording activities. Trim film segments to specified lengths and reassemble segments in sequences that present stories with maximum effect. Develop post-production models for films. Piece sounds together to develop film soundtracks. Conduct film screenings for directors and members of production staffs. Collaborate with music editors to select appropriate passages of music and develop production scores. Discuss the sound requirements of pictures with sound effects editors.

Personality Type: Artistic. These occupations frequently involve working with forms, designs, and patterns. They often require self-expression, and the work can be done without following a clear set of rules.

GOE—Interest Area/Cluster: 03. Arts and Communication. **Work Group:** 03.09. Media Technology. **Other Jobs in This Work Group:** Audio and Video Equipment Technicians; Broadcast Technicians; Camera Operators, Television, Video, and Motion Picture; Multi-Media Artists and Animators; Photographers; Radio Operators; Sound Engineering Technicians.

Skills—Equipment Selection: Determining the kind of tools and equipment needed to do a job. **Operation and Control:** Controlling operations of equipment or systems. **Operations Analysis:** Analyzing needs and product requirements to create a design. **Equipment Maintenance:** Performing routine maintenance and determining when and what kind of maintenance is needed. **Installation:** Installing equipment, machines, wiring, or programs to meet specifications. **Troubleshooting:** Determining what is causing an operating error and deciding what to do about it. **Operation Monitoring:** Watching gauges, dials, or other indicators to make sure a machine is working properly. **Active**

Learning: Working with new material or information to grasp its implications.

Education and Training Programs: Audiovisual Communications Technologies/Technician Training, Other; Cinematography and Film/Video Production; Communications Technology/Technician Training; Photojournalism; Radio and Television; Radio and Television Broadcasting Technology/Technician Training. **Related Knowledge/Courses— Fine Arts:** Theory and techniques required to produce, compose, and perform works of music, dance, visual arts, drama, and sculpture. **Communications and Media:** Media production, communication, and dissemination techniques and methods, including alternative ways to inform and entertain via written, oral, and visual media. **Design:** Design techniques, principles, tools, and instruments involved in the production and use of precision technical plans, blueprints, drawings, and models. **Computers and Electronics:** Electric circuit boards, processors, chips, and computer hardware and software, including applications and programming. **Telecommunications:** Transmission, broadcasting, switching, control, and operation of telecommunications systems. **English Language:** The structure and content of the English language, including the meaning and spelling of words, rules of composition, and grammar.

Work Environment: Indoors; sitting; using hands on objects, tools, or controls; repetitive motions.

Financial Analysts

- ❈ Education/Training Required: Bachelor's degree
- ❈ Annual Earnings: $70,400
- ❈ Beginning Wage: $42,280
- ❈ Earnings Growth Potential: Medium
- ❈ Growth: 33.8%
- ❈ Annual Job Openings: 29,317
- ❈ Self-Employed: 8.3%
- ❈ Part-Time: 7.1%

Conduct quantitative analyses of information affecting investment programs of public or private institutions. Assemble spreadsheets and draw charts and graphs used to illustrate technical reports, using computer. Analyze financial information to produce forecasts of business, industry, and economic conditions for use in making investment decisions. Maintain knowledge and stay abreast of developments in the fields of industrial technology, business, finance, and economic theory. Interpret data affecting investment programs, such as price, yield, stability, future trends in investment risks, and economic influences. Monitor fundamental economic, industrial, and corporate developments through the analysis of information obtained from financial publications and services, investment banking firms, government agencies, trade publications, company sources, and personal interviews. Recommend investments and investment timing to companies, investment firm staff, or the investing public. Determine the prices at which securities should be syndicated and offered to the public. Prepare plans of action for investment based on financial analyses. Evaluate and compare the relative quality of various securities in a given industry. Present oral and written reports on general economic trends, individual corporations, and entire industries. Contact brokers and purchase investments for companies according to company policy. Collaborate with investment bankers to attract new corporate clients to securities firms.

Personality Type: Conventional. These occupations frequently involve following set procedures and routines and can include working with data and details more than with ideas. Usually there is a clear line of authority to follow.

GOE—Interest Area/Cluster: 06. Finance and Insurance. **Work Group:** 06.02. Finance/Insurance Investigation and Analysis. **Other Jobs in This Work Group:** Appraisers and Assessors of Real Estate; Appraisers, Real Estate; Assessors; Claims Adjusters, Examiners, and Investigators; Claims Examiners, Property and Casualty Insurance; Cost Estimators; Credit Analysts; Insurance Adjusters, Examiners, and Investigators; Insurance Appraisers, Auto Damage; Insurance Underwriters; Loan Counselors; Loan Officers; Market Research Analysts; Survey Researchers.

Skills—Management of Financial Resources: Determining how money will be spent to get the work done and accounting for these expenditures. **Judgment and Decision Making:** Weighing the relative costs and benefits of a potential action. **Mathematics:** Using mathematics to solve problems. **Systems Evaluation:** Looking at many indicators of system performance and taking into account their accuracy. **Programming:** Writing computer programs for various purposes. **Complex Problem Solving:** Identifying complex problems, reviewing the options, and implementing solutions. **Operations Analysis:** Analyzing needs and product requirements to create a design. **Systems Analysis:** Determining how a system should work and how changes will affect outcomes.

Education and Training Programs: Accounting and Business/Management; Accounting and Finance; Finance, General. **Related Knowledge/Courses—Economics and Accounting:** Economic and accounting principles and practices, the financial markets, banking, and the analysis and reporting of financial data. **Mathematics:** Numbers and their operations and interrelationships, including arithmetic, algebra, geometry, calculus, and statistics and their applications. **Law and Government:** Laws, legal codes, court procedures, precedents, government regulations, executive orders, agency rules, and the democratic political process. **Clerical Practices:** Administrative and clerical procedures and systems such as word-processing systems, filing and records management systems, stenography and transcription, forms, design principles, and other office procedures and terminology. **English Language:** The structure and content of the English language, including the meaning and spelling of words, rules of composition, and grammar. **Administration and Management:** Principles and processes involved in business and organizational planning, coordination, and execution. This includes strategic planning, resource allocation, manpower modeling, leadership techniques, and production methods.

Work Environment: Indoors; sitting.

Financial Examiners

- ✱ Education/Training Required: Bachelor's degree
- ✱ Annual Earnings: $66,670
- ✱ Beginning Wage: $36,400
- ✱ Earnings Growth Potential: High
- ✱ Growth: 10.7%
- ✱ Annual Job Openings: 2,449
- ✱ Self-Employed: 0.0%
- ✱ Part-Time: 9.3%

Enforce or ensure compliance with laws and regulations governing financial and securities institutions and financial and real estate transactions. May examine, verify correctness of, or establish authenticity of records. Investigate activities of institutions in order to enforce laws and regulations and to ensure legality of transactions and operations or financial solvency. Review and analyze new, proposed, or revised laws, regulations, policies, and procedures in order to interpret their meaning and determine their impact. Plan, supervise, and review work of assigned subordinates. Recommend actions to ensure compliance with laws and regulations or to protect solvency of institutions. Examine the minutes of meetings of directors, stockholders, and committees in order to investigate the specific authority extended at various levels of management. Prepare reports, exhibits, and other supporting schedules that detail an institution's safety and soundness, compliance with laws and regulations, and recommended solutions to questionable financial conditions. Review balance sheets, operating income and expense accounts, and loan documentation in order to confirm institution assets and liabilities. Review audit reports of internal and external auditors in order to monitor adequacy of scope of reports or to discover specific weaknesses in internal routines. Train other examiners in the financial examination process. Establish guidelines for procedures and policies that comply with new and revised regulations and direct their implementation. Direct and participate in formal and informal meetings with bank directors, trustees, senior management, counsels, outside accountants, and consultants in order to gather information and discuss findings. Verify and inspect cash reserves, assigned collateral, and bank-owned securities in order to check internal control procedures. Review applications for mergers, acquisitions, establishment of new institutions, acceptance in Federal Reserve System, or registration of securities sales in order to determine their public interest value and conformance to regulations and recommend acceptance or rejection. Resolve problems concerning the overall financial integrity of banking institutions, including loan investment portfolios, capital, earnings, and specific or large troubled accounts.

Personality Type: Enterprising. These occupations frequently involve starting up and carrying out projects and can involve leading people and making many decisions. They sometimes require risk taking and often deal with business.

GOE—Interest Area/Cluster: 07. Government and Public Administration. **Work Group:** 07.03. Regulations Enforcement. **Other Jobs in This Work Group:** Agricultural Inspectors; Aviation Inspectors; Compliance Officers, Except Agriculture, Construction, Health and Safety, and Transportation; Construction and Building Inspectors; Environmental Compliance Inspectors; Equal Opportunity Representatives and Officers; Fire Inspectors; Fish and Game Wardens; Forest Fire Inspectors and Prevention Specialists; Freight and Cargo Inspectors; Government Property Inspectors and Investigators; Immigration and Customs Inspectors; Licensing Examiners and Inspectors; Nuclear Monitoring Technicians; Occupational Health and Safety Specialists; Occupational Health and Safety Technicians;

Tax Examiners, Collectors, and Revenue Agents; Transportation Vehicle, Equipment, and Systems Inspectors, Except Aviation.

Skills—Quality Control Analysis: Evaluating the quality or performance of products, services, or processes. **Monitoring:** Assessing how well one is doing when learning or doing something. **Management of Financial Resources:** Determining how money will be spent to get the work done and accounting for these expenditures. **Systems Analysis:** Determining how a system should work and how changes will affect outcomes. **Systems Evaluation:** Looking at many indicators of system performance and taking into account their accuracy. **Operations Analysis:** Analyzing needs and product requirements to create a design. **Writing:** Communicating effectively with others in writing as indicated by the needs of the audience. **Reading Comprehension:** Understanding written sentences and paragraphs in work-related documents.

Education and Training Programs: Accounting; Taxation. **Related Knowledge/Courses—Economics and Accounting:** Economic and accounting principles and practices, the financial markets, banking, and the analysis and reporting of financial data. **Law and Government:** Laws, legal codes, court procedures, precedents, government regulations, executive orders, agency rules, and the democratic political process. **Clerical Practices:** Administrative and clerical procedures and systems such as word-processing systems, filing and records management systems, stenography and transcription, forms, design principles, and other office procedures and terminology. **Mathematics:** Numbers and their operations and interrelationships, including arithmetic, algebra, geometry, calculus, and statistics and their applications. **English Language:** The structure and content of the English language, including the meaning and spelling of words, rules of composition, and grammar. **Administration and Management:** Principles and processes involved in business and organizational planning, coordination, and execution. This includes strategic planning, resource allocation, manpower modeling, leadership techniques, and production methods.

Work Environment: Indoors; sitting.

Financial Managers, Branch or Department

❋ Education/Training Required: Work experience plus degree

❋ Annual Earnings: $95,310

❋ Beginning Wage: $51,910

❋ Earnings Growth Potential: High

❋ Growth: 12.6%

❋ Annual Job Openings: 57,589

❋ Self-Employed: 4.6%

❋ Part-Time: 4.2%

The job openings listed here are shared with Treasurers and Controllers.

Direct and coordinate financial activities of workers in a branch, office, or department of an establishment, such as branch bank, brokerage firm, risk and insurance department, or credit department. Establish and maintain relationships with individual and business customers and provide assistance with problems these customers may encounter. Examine, evaluate, and process loan applications. Plan, direct, and coordinate the activities of workers in branches, offices, or departments of such establishments as branch banks, brokerage firms, risk and insurance departments, or credit departments. Oversee the flow of cash and financial instruments. Recruit staff members and oversee training programs. Network within communities to find and attract new business. Approve or reject, or coordinate the approval and rejection of, lines of credit and commercial, real estate, and personal loans. Prepare financial and regulatory reports required by laws, regulations, and boards of directors. Establish procedures for custody and control of assets, records, loan collateral, and securities in order to ensure safekeeping. Review collection reports to determine the status of collections and the amounts of outstanding balances. Prepare operational and risk reports for management analysis. Evaluate financial reporting systems, accounting and collection procedures, and investment activities and make recommendations for changes to procedures, operating systems, budgets, and other financial control functions. Plan, direct, and coordinate risk and insurance programs of establishments to control risks and losses. Submit delinquent accounts to attorneys or outside agencies for collection. Communicate with stockholders and other investors to provide information and to raise capital. Evaluate data pertaining to costs in order to plan budgets. Analyze and classify risks and investments to determine their potential impacts on companies.

Review reports of securities transactions and price lists in order to analyze market conditions. Develop and analyze information to assess the current and future financial status of firms. Direct insurance negotiations, select insurance brokers and carriers, and place insurance.

Personality Type: Enterprising. These occupations frequently involve starting up and carrying out projects and can involve leading people and making many decisions. They sometimes require risk taking and often deal with business.

GOE—Interest Area/Cluster: 06. Finance and Insurance. **Work Group:** 06.01. Managerial Work in Finance and Insurance. **Other Jobs in This Work Group:** Financial Managers; Treasurers and Controllers.

Skills—Management of Personnel Resources: Motivating, developing, and directing people as they work; identifying the best people for the job. **Management of Financial Resources:** Determining how money will be spent to get the work done and accounting for these expenditures. **Service Orientation:** Actively looking for ways to help people. **Time Management:** Managing one's own time and the time of others. **Persuasion:** Persuading others to approach things differently. **Negotiation:** Bringing others together and trying to reconcile differences. **Instructing:** Teaching others how to do something. **Systems Evaluation:** Looking at many indicators of system performance and taking into account their accuracy.

Education and Training Programs: Accounting and Finance; Credit Management; Finance and Financial Management Services, Other; Finance, General; International Finance; Public Finance. **Related Knowledge/Courses— Economics and Accounting:** Economic and accounting principles and practices, the financial markets, banking, and the analysis and reporting of financial data. **Sales and Marketing:** Principles and methods involved in showing, promoting, and selling products or services. This includes marketing strategies and tactics, product demonstration and sales techniques, and sales control systems. **Personnel and Human Resources:** Principles and procedures for personnel recruitment; selection; training; compensation and benefits; labor relations and negotiation; and personnel information systems. **Clerical Practices:** Administrative and clerical procedures and systems such as word-processing systems, filing and records management systems, stenography and transcription, forms, design principles, and other office procedures and terminology. **Customer and Personal Service:** Principles and processes for providing customer and personal services, including needs assessment techniques, quality service standards, alternative delivery systems, and customer satisfaction evaluation techniques. **Mathematics:** Numbers and their operations and interrelationships, including arithmetic, algebra, geometry, calculus, and statistics and their applications.

Work Environment: Indoors; sitting.

Fine Artists, Including Painters, Sculptors, and Illustrators

- ❀ Education/Training Required: Long-term on-the-job training
- ❀ Annual Earnings: $42,070
- ❀ Beginning Wage: $18,650
- ❀ Earnings Growth Potential: Very high
- ❀ Growth: 9.9%
- ❀ Annual Job Openings: 3,830
- ❀ Self-Employed: 62.6%
- ❀ Part-Time: 22.5%

Create original artwork, using any of a wide variety of mediums and techniques such as painting and sculpture. Use materials such as pens and ink, watercolors, charcoal, oil, or computer software to create artwork. Integrate and develop visual elements such as line, space, mass, color, and perspective, in order to produce desired effects such as the illustration of ideas, emotions, or moods. Confer with clients, editors, writers, art directors, and other interested parties regarding the nature and content of artwork to be produced. Submit preliminary or finished artwork or project plans to clients for approval, incorporating changes as necessary. Maintain portfolios of artistic work to demonstrate styles, interests, and abilities. Create finished art work as decoration or to elucidate or substitute for spoken or written messages. Cut, bend, laminate, arrange, and fasten individual or mixed raw and manufactured materials and products to form works of art. Monitor events, trends, and other circumstances, research specific subject areas, attend art exhibitions, and read art publications in order to develop ideas and keep current on art world activities. Study different techniques to learn how to apply them to artistic endeavors. Render drawings, illustrations, and sketches of buildings, manufactured products, or models, working from sketches, blueprints, memory, models, or reference materials. Create sculptures, statues, and other three-dimensional artwork by using abrasives and tools to shape, carve, and fabricate materials such as clay, stone, wood, or metal. Create sketches, profiles, or likenesses of posed subjects or photographs, using any combination of freehand drawing, mechanical assembly kits, and computer imaging. Develop project budgets for approval, estimating time lines and material costs. Study styles, techniques, colors, textures, and materials used in works undergoing restoration to ensure consistency during the restoration process. Shade and fill in sketch outlines and backgrounds, using a variety of media such as water colors, markers, and transparent washes, labeling designated colors when necessary. Collaborate with engineers, mechanics, and other technical experts as necessary to build and install creations.

Personality Type: Artistic. These occupations frequently involve working with forms, designs, and patterns. They often require self-expression, and the work can be done without following a clear set of rules.

GOE—Interest Area/Cluster: 03. Arts and Communication. **Work Group:** 03.04. Studio Art. **Other Jobs in This Work Group:** Craft Artists; Potters, Manufacturing.

Skills—Management of Financial Resources: Determining how money will be spent to get the work done and accounting for these expenditures. **Equipment Selection:** Determining the kind of tools and equipment needed to do a job. **Operations Analysis:** Analyzing needs and product requirements to create a design. **Repairing:** Repairing machines or systems, using the needed tools. **Equipment Maintenance:** Performing routine maintenance and determining when and what kind of maintenance is needed. **Installation:** Installing equipment, machines, wiring, or programs to meet specifications. **Complex Problem Solving:** Identifying complex problems, reviewing the options, and implementing solutions. **Mathematics:** Using mathematics to solve problems.

Education and Training Programs: Art/Art Studies, General; Drawing; Fine Arts and Art Studies, Other; Fine/Studio Arts, General; Painting; Visual and Performing Arts, General. **Related Knowledge/Courses—Fine Arts:** Theory and techniques required to produce, compose, and perform works of music, dance, visual arts, drama, and sculpture. **Design:** Design techniques, principles, tools, and instruments involved in the production and use of precision technical plans, blueprints, drawings, and models. **Sales and Marketing:** Principles and methods involved in showing, promoting, and selling products or services. This includes marketing strategies and tactics, product demonstration and sales techniques, and sales control systems. **Production and**

Processing: Inputs, outputs, raw materials, waste, quality control, costs, and techniques for maximizing the manufacture and distribution of goods. **Economics and Accounting:** Economic and accounting principles and practices, the financial markets, banking, and the analysis and reporting of financial data. **Communications and Media:** Media production, communication, and dissemination techniques and methods, including alternative ways to inform and entertain via written, oral, and visual media.

Work Environment: Indoors; contaminants; standing; using hands on objects, tools, or controls; repetitive motions.

Fire Inspectors

- ❋ Education/Training Required: Work experience in a related occupation
- ❋ Annual Earnings: $50,830
- ❋ Beginning Wage: $31,170
- ❋ Earnings Growth Potential: Medium
- ❋ Growth: 11.0%
- ❋ Annual Job Openings: 644
- ❋ Self-Employed: 0.0%
- ❋ Part-Time: 2.2%

The job openings listed here are shared with Fire Investigators.

Inspect buildings and equipment to detect fire hazards and enforce state and local regulations. Inspect buildings to locate hazardous conditions and fire code violations such as accumulations of combustible material, electrical wiring problems, and inadequate or non-functional fire exits. Identify corrective actions necessary to bring properties into compliance with applicable fire codes, laws, regulations, and standards and explain these measures to property owners or their representatives. Conduct inspections and acceptance testing of newly installed fire protection systems. Inspect and test fire protection or fire detection systems to verify that such systems are installed in accordance with appropriate laws, codes, ordinances, regulations, and standards. Conduct fire code compliance follow-ups to ensure that corrective actions have been taken in cases where violations were found. Inspect properties that store, handle, and use hazardous materials to ensure compliance with laws, codes, and regulations; issue hazardous materials permits to facilities found in compliance. Write detailed reports of fire inspections performed, fire code violations observed, and corrective recommendations offered. Review blueprints and plans for new or remodeled buildings to ensure the structures meet fire safety codes. Develop or review fire exit plans.

Attend training classes to maintain current knowledge of fire prevention, safety, and firefighting procedures. Present and explain fire code requirements and fire prevention information to architects, contractors, attorneys, engineers, developers, fire service personnel, and the general public. Conduct fire exit drills to monitor and evaluate evacuation procedures. Inspect liquefied petroleum installations, storage containers, and transportation and delivery systems for compliance with fire laws. Search for clues as to the cause of a fire after the fire is completely extinguished. Develop and coordinate fire prevention programs such as false alarm billing, fire inspection reporting, and hazardous materials management. Testify in court regarding fire code and fire safety issues. Recommend changes to fire prevention, inspection, and fire code endorsement procedures.

Personality Type: Conventional. These occupations frequently involve following set procedures and routines and can include working with data and details more than with ideas. Usually there is a clear line of authority to follow.

GOE—Interest Area/Cluster: 07. Government and Public Administration. **Work Group:** 07.03. Regulations Enforcement. **Other Jobs in This Work Group:** Agricultural Inspectors; Aviation Inspectors; Compliance Officers, Except Agriculture, Construction, Health and Safety, and Transportation; Construction and Building Inspectors; Environmental Compliance Inspectors; Equal Opportunity Representatives and Officers; Financial Examiners; Fish and Game Wardens; Forest Fire Inspectors and Prevention Specialists; Freight and Cargo Inspectors; Government Property Inspectors and Investigators; Immigration and Customs Inspectors; Licensing Examiners and Inspectors; Nuclear Monitoring Technicians; Occupational Health and Safety Specialists; Occupational Health and Safety Technicians; Tax Examiners, Collectors, and Revenue Agents; Transportation Vehicle, Equipment, and Systems Inspectors, Except Aviation.

Skills—Science: Using scientific methods to solve problems. **Persuasion:** Persuading others to approach things differently. **Operations Analysis:** Analyzing needs and product requirements to create a design. **Service Orientation:** Actively looking for ways to help people. **Negotiation:** Bringing others together and trying to reconcile differences. **Operation Monitoring:** Watching gauges, dials, or other indicators to make sure a machine is working properly. **Writing:** Communicating effectively with others in writing as indicated by the needs of the audience. **Complex Problem Solving:** Identifying complex problems, reviewing the options, and implementing solutions.

Education and Training Programs: Fire Protection and Safety Technology/Technician Training; Fire Science/Firefighting. **Related Knowledge/Courses—Building and Construction:** Materials, methods, and the appropriate tools to construct objects, structures, and buildings. **Public Safety and Security:** Weaponry; public safety; security operations, rules, regulations, precautions, and prevention; and the protection of people, data, and property. **Physics:** Physical principles, laws, and applications, including air, water, material dynamics, light, atomic principles, heat, electric theory, earth formations, and meteorological and related natural phenomena. **Customer and Personal Service:** Principles and processes for providing customer and personal services, including needs assessment techniques, quality service standards, alternative delivery systems, and customer satisfaction evaluation techniques. **Law and Government:** Laws, legal codes, court procedures, precedents, government regulations, executive orders, agency rules, and the democratic political process. **Design:** Design techniques, principles, tools, and instruments involved in the production and use of precision technical plans, blueprints, drawings, and models.

Work Environment: More often outdoors than indoors; noisy; very hot or cold; very bright or dim lighting; hazardous equipment.

Fire Investigators

- ❀ Education/Training Required: Work experience in a related occupation
- ❀ Annual Earnings: $50,830
- ❀ Beginning Wage: $31,170
- ❀ Earnings Growth Potential: Medium
- ❀ Growth: 11.0%
- ❀ Annual Job Openings: 644
- ❀ Self-Employed: 0.0%
- ❀ Part-Time: 2.2%

The job openings listed here are shared with Fire Inspectors.

Conduct investigations to determine causes of fires and explosions. Package collected pieces of evidence in securely closed containers such as bags, crates, or boxes to protect them. Examine fire sites and collect evidence such as glass, metal fragments, charred wood, and accelerant residue for use in determining the cause of a fire. Instruct children about the dangers of fire. Analyze evidence and other information to determine probable cause of fire or explosion. Photograph

damage and evidence related to causes of fires or explosions to document investigation findings. Subpoena and interview witnesses, property owners, and building occupants to obtain information and sworn testimony. Swear out warrants and arrest and process suspected arsonists. Testify in court cases involving fires, suspected arson, and false alarms. Prepare and maintain reports of investigation results and records of convicted arsonists and arson suspects. Test sites and materials to establish facts such as burn patterns and flash points of materials, using test equipment. Conduct internal investigation to determine negligence and violation of laws and regulations by fire department employees. Dust evidence or portions of fire scenes for latent fingerprints.

Personality Type: Investigative. These occupations frequently involve working with ideas and require an extensive amount of thinking. They can involve searching for facts and figuring out problems mentally.

GOE—Interest Area/Cluster: 12. Law and Public Safety. **Work Group:** 12.04. Law Enforcement and Public Safety. **Other Jobs in This Work Group:** Bailiffs; Correctional Officers and Jailers; Criminal Investigators and Special Agents; Detectives and Criminal Investigators; Forensic Science Technicians; Parking Enforcement Workers; Police and Sheriff's Patrol Officers; Police Detectives; Police Identification and Records Officers; Police Patrol Officers; Sheriffs and Deputy Sheriffs; Transit and Railroad Police.

Skills—Science: Using scientific methods to solve problems. **Equipment Maintenance:** Performing routine maintenance and determining when and what kind of maintenance is needed. **Management of Personnel Resources:** Motivating, developing, and directing people as they work; identifying the best people for the job. **Operation and Control:** Controlling operations of equipment or systems. **Equipment Selection:** Determining the kind of tools and equipment needed to do a job. **Repairing:** Repairing machines or systems, using the needed tools. **Judgment and Decision Making:** Weighing the relative costs and benefits of a potential action. **Operations Analysis:** Analyzing needs and product requirements to create a design.

Education and Training Programs: Fire Protection and Safety Technology/Technician Training; Fire Science/Firefighting. **Related Knowledge/Courses—Building and Construction:** Materials, methods, and the appropriate tools to construct objects, structures, and buildings. **Public Safety and Security:** Weaponry; public safety; security operations, rules, regulations, precautions, and prevention; and the protection of people, data, and property. **Physics:**

Physical principles, laws, and applications, including air, water, material dynamics, light, atomic principles, heat, electric theory, earth formations, and meteorological and related natural phenomena. **Chemistry:** The composition, structure, and properties of substances and of the chemical processes and transformations that they undergo. This includes uses of chemicals and their interactions, danger signs, production techniques, and disposal methods. **Mechanical Devices:** Machines and tools, including their designs, uses, benefits, repair, and maintenance. **Law and Government:** Laws, legal codes, court procedures, precedents, government regulations, executive orders, agency rules, and the democratic political process.

Work Environment: Indoors; noisy; contaminants; hazardous conditions; hazardous equipment; using hands on objects, tools, or controls.

Fire-Prevention and Protection Engineers

- ❋ Education/Training Required: Bachelor's degree
- ❋ Annual Earnings: $69,580
- ❋ Beginning Wage: $42,200
- ❋ Earnings Growth Potential: Medium
- ❋ Growth: 9.6%
- ❋ Annual Job Openings: 1,105
- ❋ Self-Employed: 1.1%
- ❋ Part-Time: 2.0%

The job openings listed here are shared with Industrial Safety and Health Engineers and with Product Safety Engineers.

Research causes of fires, determine fire protection methods, and design or recommend materials or equipment such as structural components or fire-detection equipment to assist organizations in safeguarding life and property against fire, explosion, and related hazards. Design fire detection equipment, alarm systems, and fire extinguishing devices and systems. Inspect buildings or building designs to determine fire protection system requirements and potential problems in areas such as water supplies, exit locations, and construction materials. Advise architects, builders, and other construction personnel on fire prevention equipment and techniques and on fire code and standard interpretation and compliance. Prepare and write reports detailing specific fire prevention and protection issues, such as work performed and proposed review

schedules. Determine causes of fires and ways in which they could have been prevented. Direct the purchase, modification, installation, maintenance, and operation of fire protection systems. Consult with authorities to discuss safety regulations and to recommend changes as necessary. Develop plans for the prevention of destruction by fire, wind, and water. Study the relationships between ignition sources and materials to determine how fires start. Attend workshops, seminars, or conferences to present or obtain information regarding fire prevention and protection. Develop training materials and conduct training sessions on fire protection. Evaluate fire department performance and the laws and regulations affecting fire prevention or fire safety. Conduct research on fire retardants and the fire safety of materials and devices.

Personality Type: Investigative. These occupations frequently involve working with ideas and require an extensive amount of thinking. They can involve searching for facts and figuring out problems mentally.

GOE—Interest Area/Cluster: 15. Scientific Research, Engineering, and Mathematics. **Work Group:** 15.08. Industrial and Safety Engineering. **Other Jobs in This Work Group:** Health and Safety Engineers, Except Mining Safety Engineers and Inspectors; Industrial Engineers; Industrial Safety and Health Engineers; Product Safety Engineers.

Skills—Science: Using scientific methods to solve problems. **Management of Financial Resources:** Determining how money will be spent to get the work done and accounting for these expenditures. **Operations Analysis:** Analyzing needs and product requirements to create a design. **Mathematics:** Using mathematics to solve problems. **Systems Analysis:** Determining how a system should work and how changes will affect outcomes. **Negotiation:** Bringing others together and trying to reconcile differences. **Complex Problem Solving:** Identifying complex problems, reviewing the options, and implementing solutions. **Management of Personnel Resources:** Motivating, developing, and directing people as they work; identifying the best people for the job.

Education and Training Program: Environmental/Environmental Health Engineering. **Related Knowledge/Courses—Design:** Design techniques, principles, tools, and instruments involved in the production and use of precision technical plans, blueprints, drawings, and models. **Engineering and Technology:** Equipment, tools, and mechanical devices and their uses to produce motion, light, power, technology, and other applications. **Building and Construction:** Materials, methods, and the appropriate tools to construct objects, structures, and buildings. **Physics:** Physical principles, laws, and applications, including air, water, material dynamics, light, atomic principles, heat, electric theory, earth formations, and meteorological and related natural phenomena. **Chemistry:** The composition, structure, and properties of substances and of the chemical processes and transformations that they undergo. This includes uses of chemicals and their interactions, danger signs, production techniques, and disposal methods. **Public Safety and Security:** Weaponry; public safety; security operations, rules, regulations, precautions, and prevention; and the protection of people, data, and property.

Work Environment: Indoors; sitting.

First-Line Supervisors/Managers of Construction Trades and Extraction Workers

* Education/Training Required: Work experience in a related occupation
* Annual Earnings: $55,950
* Beginning Wage: $34,870
* Earnings Growth Potential: Medium
* Growth: 9.1%
* Annual Job Openings: 82,923
* Self-Employed: 24.4%
* Part-Time: 3.0%

Directly supervise and coordinate activities of construction or extraction workers. Examine and inspect work progress, equipment, and construction sites to verify safety and to ensure that specifications are met. Read specifications such as blueprints to determine construction requirements and to plan procedures. Estimate material and worker requirements to complete jobs. Supervise, coordinate, and schedule the activities of construction or extractive workers. Confer with managerial and technical personnel, other departments, and contractors in order to resolve problems and to coordinate activities. Coordinate work activities with other construction project activities. Locate, measure, and mark site locations and placement of structures and equipment, using measuring and marking equipment. Order or requisition materials and supplies. Record information such as personnel, production, and operational data on specified forms and reports. Assign work to employees, based on material and worker requirements of specific jobs. Provide assistance to workers engaged in construction or extraction

activities, using hand tools and equipment. Train workers in construction methods, operation of equipment, safety procedures, and company policies. Analyze worker and production problems and recommend solutions such as improving production methods or implementing motivational plans. Arrange for repairs of equipment and machinery. Suggest or initiate personnel actions such as promotions, transfers, and hires.

Personality Type: Enterprising. These occupations frequently involve starting up and carrying out projects and can involve leading people and making many decisions. They sometimes require risk taking and often deal with business.

GOE—Interest Area/Cluster: 01. Agriculture and Natural Resources. **Work Group:** 01.01. Managerial Work in Agriculture and Natural Resources. **Other Jobs in This Work Group:** Aquacultural Managers; Crop and Livestock Managers; Farm Labor Contractors; Farm, Ranch, and Other Agricultural Managers; Farmers and Ranchers; First-Line Supervisors/Managers of Agricultural Crop and Horticultural Workers; First-Line Supervisors/Managers of Animal Husbandry and Animal Care Workers; First-Line Supervisors/Managers of Aquacultural Workers; First-Line Supervisors/Managers of Farming, Fishing, and Forestry Workers; First-Line Supervisors/Managers of Landscaping, Lawn Service, and Groundskeeping Workers; First-Line Supervisors/Managers of Logging Workers; Nursery and Greenhouse Managers; Park Naturalists; Purchasing Agents and Buyers, Farm Products.

Skills—Management of Material Resources: Obtaining and seeing to the appropriate use of equipment, facilities, and materials needed to do certain work. **Installation:** Installing equipment, machines, wiring, or programs to meet specifications. **Equipment Maintenance:** Performing routine maintenance and determining when and what kind of maintenance is needed. **Repairing:** Repairing machines or systems, using the needed tools. **Coordination:** Adjusting actions in relation to others' actions. **Equipment Selection:** Determining the kind of tools and equipment needed to do a job. **Management of Personnel Resources:** Motivating, developing, and directing people as they work; identifying the best people for the job. **Mathematics:** Using mathematics to solve problems.

Education and Training Programs: Blasting/Blaster Training; Building/Construction Site Management/Manager Training; Building/Home/Construction Inspection/Inspector Training; Building/Property Maintenance and

Management; Carpentry; Concrete Finishing; Drywall Installation; Electrical and Power Transmission Installation, General; Electrician Training; Glazier Training; Lineworker Training; Masonry; Painting; Plumbing Technology; Roofer Training; Well Drilling. **Related Knowledge/Courses— Building and Construction:** Materials, methods, and the appropriate tools to construct objects, structures, and buildings. **Mechanical Devices:** Machines and tools, including their designs, uses, benefits, repair, and maintenance. **Design:** Design techniques, principles, tools, and instruments involved in the production and use of precision technical plans, blueprints, drawings, and models. **Engineering and Technology:** Equipment, tools, and mechanical devices and their uses to produce motion, light, power, technology, and other applications. **Production and Processing:** Inputs, outputs, raw materials, waste, quality control, costs, and techniques for maximizing the manufacture and distribution of goods. **Administration and Management:** Principles and processes involved in business and organizational planning, coordination, and execution. This includes strategic planning, resource allocation, manpower modeling, leadership techniques, and production methods.

Work Environment: Outdoors; noisy; very hot or cold; contaminants; hazardous equipment; standing.

First-Line Supervisors/Managers of Correctional Officers

- ❈ Education/Training Required: Work experience in a related occupation
- ❈ Annual Earnings: $55,720
- ❈ Beginning Wage: $31,780
- ❈ Earnings Growth Potential: High
- ❈ Growth: 12.5%
- ❈ Annual Job Openings: 4,180
- ❈ Self-Employed: 0.0%
- ❈ Part-Time: 0.0%

Supervise and coordinate activities of correctional officers and jailers. Take, receive, and check periodic inmate counts. Maintain order, discipline, and security within assigned areas in accordance with relevant rules, regulations, policies, and laws. Respond to emergencies such as escapes. Maintain knowledge of, comply with, and enforce all institutional policies, rules, procedures, and regulations. Supervise and direct the work of correctional officers to ensure the safe custody, discipline, and welfare of inmates. Restrain,

secure, and control offenders, using chemical agents, firearms, and other weapons of force as necessary. Supervise and perform searches of inmates and their quarters to locate contraband items. Monitor behavior of subordinates to ensure alert, courteous, and professional behavior toward inmates, parolees, fellow employees, visitors, and the public. Complete administrative paperwork and supervise the preparation and maintenance of records, forms, and reports. Instruct employees and provide on-the-job training. Conduct roll calls of correctional officers. Supervise activities such as searches, shakedowns, riot control, and institutional tours. Carry injured offenders or employees to safety and provide emergency first aid when necessary. Supervise and provide security for offenders performing tasks such as construction, maintenance, laundry, food service, and other industrial or agricultural operations. Develop work and security procedures. Set up employee work schedules. Resolve problems between inmates. Read and review offender information to identify issues that require special attention. Rate behavior of inmates, promoting acceptable attitudes and behaviors to those with low ratings. Transfer and transport offenders on foot or by driving vehicles such as trailers, vans, and buses. Examine incoming and outgoing mail to ensure conformance with regulations. Convey correctional officers' and inmates' complaints to superiors.

Personality Type: Enterprising. These occupations frequently involve starting up and carrying out projects and can involve leading people and making many decisions. They sometimes require risk taking and often deal with business.

GOE—Interest Area/Cluster: 12. Law and Public Safety. **Work Group:** 12.01. Managerial Work in Law and Public Safety. **Other Jobs in This Work Group:** Emergency Management Specialists; First-Line Supervisors/Managers of Fire Fighting and Prevention Workers; First-Line Supervisors/ Managers of Police and Detectives; Forest Fire Fighting and Prevention Supervisors; Municipal Fire Fighting and Prevention Supervisors.

Skills—Social Perceptiveness: Being aware of others' reactions and understanding why they react the way they do. **Negotiation:** Bringing others together and trying to reconcile differences. **Management of Personnel Resources:** Motivating, developing, and directing people as they work; identifying the best people for the job. **Persuasion:** Persuading others to approach things differently. **Monitoring:** Assessing how well one is doing when learning or doing something. **Writing:** Communicating effectively with others in writing as indicated by the needs of the audience.

Service Orientation: Actively looking for ways to help people. **Complex Problem Solving:** Identifying complex problems, reviewing the options, and implementing solutions.

Education and Training Programs: Corrections; Corrections Administration. **Related Knowledge/Courses—Public Safety and Security:** Weaponry; public safety; security operations, rules, regulations, precautions, and prevention; and the protection of people, data, and property. **Psychology:** Human behavior and performance, mental processes, psychological research methods, and the assessment and treatment of behavioral and affective disorders. **Therapy and Counseling:** Information and techniques needed to rehabilitate physical and mental ailments and to provide career guidance, including alternative treatments, rehabilitation equipment and its proper use, and methods to evaluate treatment effects. **Personnel and Human Resources:** Principles and procedures for personnel recruitment; selection; training; compensation and benefits; labor relations and negotiation; and personnel information systems. **Clerical Practices:** Administrative and clerical procedures and systems such as word-processing systems, filing and records management systems, stenography and transcription, forms, design principles, and other office procedures and terminology. **Law and Government:** Laws, legal codes, court procedures, precedents, government regulations, executive orders, agency rules, and the democratic political process.

Work Environment: More often indoors than outdoors; noisy; very bright or dim lighting; contaminants; disease or infections.

First-Line Supervisors/Managers of Food Preparation and Serving Workers

- ❋ Education/Training Required: Work experience in a related occupation
- ❋ Annual Earnings: $28,040
- ❋ Beginning Wage: $17,920
- ❋ Earnings Growth Potential: Medium
- ❋ Growth: 11.3%
- ❋ Annual Job Openings: 154,175
- ❋ Self-Employed: 4.1%
- ❋ Part-Time: 14.5%

Supervise workers engaged in preparing and serving food. Compile and balance cash receipts at the end of the day or shift. Resolve customer complaints regarding food service. Inspect supplies, equipment, and work areas to ensure efficient service and conformance to standards. Train workers in food preparation and in service, sanitation, and safety procedures. Control inventories of food, equipment, smallware, and liquor and report shortages to designated personnel. Observe and evaluate workers and work procedures to ensure quality standards and service. Assign duties, responsibilities, and workstations to employees in accordance with work requirements. Estimate ingredients and supplies required to prepare a recipe. Perform personnel actions such as hiring and firing staff, consulting with other managers as necessary. Analyze operational problems, such as theft and wastage, and establish procedures to alleviate these problems. Specify food portions and courses, production and time sequences, and workstation and equipment arrangements. Recommend measures for improving work procedures and worker performance to increase service quality and enhance job safety. Greet and seat guests and present menus and wine lists. Present bills and accept payments. Forecast staff, equipment, and supply requirements based on a master menu. Record production and operational data on specified forms. Perform serving duties such as carving meat, preparing flambé dishes, or serving wine and liquor. Purchase or requisition supplies and equipment needed to ensure quality and timely delivery of services. Collaborate with other personnel to plan menus, serving arrangements, and related details. Supervise and check the assembly of regular and special diet trays and the delivery of food trolleys to hospital patients. Schedule parties and take reservations. Develop departmental objectives, budgets, policies, procedures, and strategies. Develop equipment maintenance schedules and arrange for repairs. Evaluate new products for usefulness and suitability.

Personality Type: Enterprising. These occupations frequently involve starting up and carrying out projects and can involve leading people and making many decisions. They sometimes require risk taking and often deal with business.

GOE—Interest Area/Cluster: 09. Hospitality, Tourism, and Recreation. **Work Group:** 09.01. Managerial Work in Hospitality and Tourism. **Other Jobs in This Work Group:** First-Line Supervisors/Managers of Personal Service Workers; Food Service Managers; Gaming Managers; Gaming Supervisors; Lodging Managers.

Skills—Equipment Maintenance: Performing routine maintenance and determining when and what kind of maintenance is needed. **Management of Financial Resources:**

Determining how money will be spent to get the work done and accounting for these expenditures. **Management of Personnel Resources:** Motivating, developing, and directing people as they work; identifying the best people for the job. **Operation Monitoring:** Watching gauges, dials, or other indicators to make sure a machine is working properly. **Management of Material Resources:** Obtaining and seeing to the appropriate use of equipment, facilities, and materials needed to do certain work. **Monitoring:** Assessing how well one is doing when learning or doing something.

Education and Training Programs: Cooking and Related Culinary Arts, General; Foodservice Systems Administration/Management; Restaurant, Culinary, and Catering Management/Manager Training. **Related Knowledge/Courses—Food Production:** Techniques and equipment for planting, growing, and harvesting of food for consumption, including crop-rotation methods, animal husbandry, and food storage/handling techniques. **Administration and Management:** Principles and processes involved in business and organizational planning, coordination, and execution. This includes strategic planning, resource allocation, manpower modeling, leadership techniques, and production methods. **Customer and Personal Service:** Principles and processes for providing customer and personal services, including needs assessment techniques, quality service standards, alternative delivery systems, and customer satisfaction evaluation techniques. **Economics and Accounting:** Economic and accounting principles and practices, the financial markets, banking, and the analysis and reporting of financial data. **Sales and Marketing:** Principles and methods involved in showing, promoting, and selling products or services. This includes marketing strategies and tactics, product demonstration and sales techniques, and sales control systems. **Production and Processing:** Inputs, outputs, raw materials, waste, quality control, costs, and techniques for maximizing the manufacture and distribution of goods.

Work Environment: Indoors; minor burns, cuts, bites, or stings; standing; walking and running; using hands on objects, tools, or controls; repetitive motions.

First-Line Supervisors/Managers of Helpers, Laborers, and Material Movers, Hand

- ❋ Education/Training Required: Work experience in a related occupation
- ❋ Annual Earnings: $40,640
- ❋ Beginning Wage: $25,430
- ❋ Earnings Growth Potential: Medium
- ❋ Growth: 12.5%
- ❋ Annual Job Openings: 13,877
- ❋ Self-Employed: 1.4%
- ❋ Part-Time: 5.3%

Supervise and coordinate the activities of helpers, laborers, or material movers. Plan work schedules and assign duties to maintain adequate staffing levels, to ensure that activities are performed effectively, and to respond to fluctuating workloads. Collaborate with workers and managers to solve work-related problems. Review work throughout the work process and at completion to ensure that it has been performed properly. Transmit and explain work orders to laborers. Check specifications of materials loaded or unloaded against information contained in work orders. Inform designated employees or departments of items loaded and problems encountered. Examine freight to determine loading sequences. Evaluate employee performance and prepare performance appraisals. Perform the same work duties as those whom they supervise or perform more difficult or skilled tasks or assist in their performance. Prepare and maintain work records and reports that include information such as employee time and wages, daily receipts, and inspection results. Counsel employees in work-related activities, personal growth, and career development. Conduct staff meetings to relay general information or to address specific topics such as safety. Inspect equipment for wear and for conformance to specifications. Resolve personnel problems, complaints, and formal grievances when possible or refer them to higher-level supervisors for resolution. Recommend or initiate personnel actions such as promotions, transfers, and disciplinary measures. Assess training needs of staff; then arrange for or provide appropriate instruction. Schedule times of shipment and modes of transportation for materials. Quote prices to customers. Estimate material, time, and staffing requirements for a given project based on work orders, job specifications, and experience. Provide assistance in balancing books; tracking, monitoring, and projecting a unit's budget needs; and developing unit policies and procedures. Inspect job sites to determine the extent of maintenance or repairs needed. Participate in the hiring process by reviewing credentials, conducting interviews, and making hiring decisions or recommendations.

Personality Type: Enterprising. These occupations frequently involve starting up and carrying out projects and can involve leading people and making many decisions. They sometimes require risk taking and often deal with business.

GOE—Interest Area/Cluster: 13. Manufacturing. **Work Group:** 13.01. Managerial Work in Manufacturing. **Other Jobs in This Work Group:** First-Line Supervisors/Managers of Mechanics, Installers, and Repairers; First-Line Supervisors/Managers of Production and Operating Workers; Industrial Production Managers.

Skills—Management of Personnel Resources: Motivating, developing, and directing people as they work; identifying the best people for the job. **Monitoring:** Assessing how well one is doing when learning or doing something. **Persuasion:** Persuading others to approach things differently. **Time Management:** Managing one's own time and the time of others. **Social Perceptiveness:** Being aware of others' reactions and understanding why they react the way they do. **Quality Control Analysis:** Evaluating the quality or performance of products, services, or processes. **Systems Evaluation:** Looking at many indicators of system performance and taking into account their accuracy. **Judgment and Decision Making:** Weighing the relative costs and benefits of a potential action.

Education and Training Programs: No related CIP programs; this job is learned through work experience in a related occupation; this job is learned through work experience in a related occupation. **Related Knowledge/Courses—Production and Processing:** Inputs, outputs, raw materials, waste, quality control, costs, and techniques for maximizing the manufacture and distribution of goods. **Transportation:** Principles and methods for moving people or goods by air, rail, sea, or road, including their relative costs, advantages, and limitations. **Personnel and Human Resources:** Principles and procedures for personnel recruitment; selection; training; compensation and benefits; labor relations and negotiation; and personnel information systems. **Administration and Management:** Principles and processes involved in business and organizational planning, coordination, and execution. This includes strategic planning, resource allocation, manpower modeling, leadership techniques, and production methods. **Public Safety and Security:** Weaponry; public safety; security operations, rules, regulations, precautions, and prevention; and the protection of people, data, and property. **Psychology:** Human behavior and performance, mental processes, psychological research methods, and the assessment and treatment of behavioral and affective disorders.

Work Environment: Indoors; noisy; very hot or cold; contaminants; standing; walking and running.

First-Line Supervisors/Managers of Housekeeping and Janitorial Workers

- ✽ Education/Training Required: Work experience in a related occupation
- ✽ Annual Earnings: $32,850
- ✽ Beginning Wage: $20,650
- ✽ Earnings Growth Potential: Medium
- ✽ Growth: 12.7%
- ✽ Annual Job Openings: 30,613
- ✽ Self-Employed: 30.7%
- ✽ Part-Time: 10.8%

Supervise work activities of cleaning personnel in hotels, hospitals, offices, and other establishments. Direct activities for stopping the spread of infections in facilities such as hospitals. Inspect work performed to ensure that it meets specifications and established standards. Plan and prepare employee work schedules. Perform or assist with cleaning duties as necessary. Investigate complaints about service and equipment and take corrective action. Coordinate activities with other departments to ensure that services are provided in an efficient and timely manner. Check equipment to ensure that it is in working order. Inspect and evaluate the physical condition of facilities to determine the type of work required. Select the most suitable cleaning materials for different types of linens, furniture, flooring, and surfaces. Instruct staff in work policies and procedures and the use and maintenance of equipment. Issue supplies and equipment to workers. Forecast necessary levels of staffing and stock at different times to facilitate effective scheduling and ordering. Inventory stock to ensure that supplies and equipment are available in adequate amounts. Evaluate employee performance and recommend personnel actions such as promotions, transfers, and dismissals. Confer with staff to resolve performance and personnel problems and to discuss company policies. Establish and implement operational standards and procedures for the departments they supervise. Recommend or arrange for additional services such as painting, repair work, renovations, and the replacement of furnishings and equipment. Select and order or purchase new equipment, supplies, and furnishings. Recommend changes that could improve service and increase operational efficiency. Maintain required records of work hours, budgets, payrolls, and other information. Screen job applicants and hire new employees. Supervise in-house services such as laundries, maintenance and repair, dry cleaning, and valet services. Advise managers, desk clerks, or admitting personnel of rooms ready for occupancy. Perform financial tasks such as estimating costs and preparing and managing budgets. Prepare activity and personnel reports and reports containing information such as occupancy, hours worked, facility usage, work performed, and departmental expenses.

Personality Type: Enterprising. These occupations frequently involve starting up and carrying out projects and can involve leading people and making many decisions. They sometimes require risk taking and often deal with business.

GOE—Interest Area/Cluster: 04. Business and Administration. **Work Group:** 04.02. Managerial Work in Business Detail. **Other Jobs in This Work Group:** Administrative Services Managers; First-Line Supervisors/Managers of Office and Administrative Support Workers; Meeting and Convention Planners.

Skills—Management of Personnel Resources: Motivating, developing, and directing people as they work; identifying the best people for the job. **Monitoring:** Assessing how well one is doing when learning or doing something. **Equipment Maintenance:** Performing routine maintenance and determining when and what kind of maintenance is needed. **Equipment Selection:** Determining the kind of tools and equipment needed to do a job. **Service Orientation:** Actively looking for ways to help people. **Writing:** Communicating effectively with others in writing as indicated by the needs of the audience. **Systems Evaluation:** Looking at many indicators of system performance and taking into account their accuracy. **Science:** Using scientific methods to solve problems.

Education and Training Programs: No related CIP programs; this job is learned through work experience in a related occupation; this job is learned through work experience in a related occupation. **Related Knowledge/Courses—Chemistry:** The composition, structure, and properties of substances and of the chemical processes

and transformations that they undergo. This includes uses of chemicals and their interactions, danger signs, production techniques, and disposal methods. **Building and Construction:** Materials, methods, and the appropriate tools to construct objects, structures, and buildings. **Public Safety and Security:** Weaponry; public safety; security operations, rules, regulations, precautions, and prevention; and the protection of people, data, and property. **Physics:** Physical principles, laws, and applications, including air, water, material dynamics, light, atomic principles, heat, electric theory, earth formations, and meteorological and related natural phenomena. **Mechanical Devices:** Machines and tools, including their designs, uses, benefits, repair, and maintenance. **Administration and Management:** Principles and processes involved in business and organizational planning, coordination, and execution. This includes strategic planning, resource allocation, manpower modeling, leadership techniques, and production methods.

Work Environment: Indoors; contaminants; disease or infections; standing; walking and running.

First-Line Supervisors/Managers of Landscaping, Lawn Service, and Groundskeeping Workers

- ✱ Education/Training Required: Work experience in a related occupation
- ✱ Annual Earnings: $38,720
- ✱ Beginning Wage: $25,270
- ✱ Earnings Growth Potential: Low
- ✱ Growth: 17.6%
- ✱ Annual Job Openings: 18,956
- ✱ Self-Employed: 44.1%
- ✱ Part-Time: 6.1%

Plan, organize, direct, or coordinate activities of workers engaged in landscaping or groundskeeping activities such as planting and maintaining ornamental trees, shrubs, flowers, and lawns and applying fertilizers, pesticides, and other chemicals, according to contract specifications. May also coordinate activities of workers engaged in terracing hillsides, building retaining walls, constructing pathways, installing patios, and similar activities in following a landscape design plan. Work may involve reviewing contracts to ascertain service, machine, and work force requirements; answering inquiries from potential customers regarding methods,

material, and price ranges; and preparing estimates according to labor, material, and machine costs. Establish and enforce operating procedures and work standards that will ensure adequate performance and personnel safety. Inspect completed work to ensure conformance to specifications, standards, and contract requirements. Direct activities of workers who perform duties such as landscaping, cultivating lawns, or pruning trees and shrubs. Schedule work for crews depending on work priorities, crew and equipment availability, and weather conditions. Plant and maintain vegetation through activities such as mulching, fertilizing, watering, mowing, and pruning. Monitor project activities to ensure that instructions are followed, deadlines are met, and schedules are maintained. Train workers in tasks such as transplanting and pruning trees and shrubs, finishing cement, using equipment, and caring for turf. Provide workers with assistance in performing duties as necessary to meet deadlines. Inventory supplies of tools, equipment, and materials to ensure that sufficient supplies are available and items are in usable condition. Confer with other supervisors to coordinate work activities with those of other departments or units. Perform personnel-related activities such as hiring workers, evaluating staff performance, and taking disciplinary actions when performance problems occur. Direct or perform mixing and application of fertilizers, insecticides, herbicides, and fungicides. Review contracts or work assignments to determine service, machine, and workforce requirements for jobs. Maintain required records such as personnel information and project records. Prepare and maintain required records such as work activity and personnel reports. Order the performance of corrective work when problems occur, and recommend procedural changes to avoid such problems. Identify diseases and pests affecting landscaping, and order appropriate treatments. Investigate work-related complaints in order to verify problems, and to determine responses. Direct and assist workers engaged in the maintenance and repair of equipment such as power tools and motorized equipment. Install and maintain landscaped areas, performing tasks such as removing snow, pouring cement curbs, and repairing sidewalks.

Personality Type: Enterprising. These occupations frequently involve starting up and carrying out projects and can involve leading people and making many decisions. They sometimes require risk taking and often deal with business.

GOE—Interest Area/Cluster: 01. Agriculture and Natural Resources. **Work Group:** 01.01. Managerial Work in Agriculture and Natural Resources. **Other Jobs in This**

Work Group: Aquacultural Managers; Crop and Livestock Managers; Farm Labor Contractors; Farm, Ranch, and Other Agricultural Managers; Farmers and Ranchers; First-Line Supervisors/Managers of Agricultural Crop and Horticultural Workers; First-Line Supervisors/Managers of Animal Husbandry and Animal Care Workers; First-Line Supervisors/Managers of Aquacultural Workers; First-Line Supervisors/Managers of Construction Trades and Extraction Workers; First-Line Supervisors/Managers of Farming, Fishing, and Forestry Workers; First-Line Supervisors/Managers of Logging Workers; Nursery and Greenhouse Managers; Park Naturalists; Purchasing Agents and Buyers, Farm Products.

Skills—Repairing: Repairing machines or systems, using the needed tools. **Equipment Maintenance:** Performing routine maintenance and determining when and what kind of maintenance is needed. **Systems Analysis:** Determining how a system should work and how changes will affect outcomes. **Operations Analysis:** Analyzing needs and product requirements to create a design. **Management of Personnel Resources:** Motivating, developing, and directing people as they work; identifying the best people for the job. **Equipment Selection:** Determining the kind of tools and equipment needed to do a job. **Monitoring:** Assessing how well one is doing when learning or doing something. **Operation and Control:** Controlling operations of equipment or systems.

Education and Training Programs: Landscaping and Groundskeeping; Ornamental Horticulture; Turf and Turfgrass Management. **Related Knowledge/Courses—Mechanical Devices:** Machines and tools, including their designs, uses, benefits, repair, and maintenance. **Building and Construction:** Materials, methods, and the appropriate tools to construct objects, structures, and buildings. **Biology:** Plant and animal living tissue, cells, organisms, and entities, including their functions, interdependencies, and interactions with each other and the environment. **Design:** Design techniques, principles, tools, and instruments involved in the production and use of precision technical plans, blueprints, drawings, and models. **Chemistry:** The composition, structure, and properties of substances and of the chemical processes and transformations that they undergo. This includes uses of chemicals and their interactions, danger signs, production techniques, and disposal methods. **Education and Training:** Instructional methods and training techniques, including curriculum design principles, learning theory, group and individual teaching techniques, design of individual development plans, and test design principles.

Work Environment: Outdoors; noisy; very hot or cold; contaminants; minor burns, cuts, bites, or stings; standing.

First-Line Supervisors/Managers of Mechanics, Installers, and Repairers

- ✱ Education/Training Required: Work experience in a related occupation
- ✱ Annual Earnings: $55,380
- ✱ Beginning Wage: $33,620
- ✱ Earnings Growth Potential: Medium
- ✱ Growth: 7.3%
- ✱ Annual Job Openings: 24,361
- ✱ Self-Employed: 1.5%
- ✱ Part-Time: 0.9%

Supervise and coordinate the activities of mechanics, installers, and repairers. Determine schedules, sequences, and assignments for work activities, based on work priority, quantity of equipment, and skill of personnel. Monitor employees' work levels and review work performance. Monitor tool and part inventories and the condition and maintenance of shops to ensure adequate working conditions. Recommend or initiate personnel actions such as hires, promotions, transfers, discharges, and disciplinary measures. Investigate accidents and injuries, and prepare reports of findings. Compile operational and personnel records such as time and production records, inventory data, repair and maintenance statistics, and test results. Develop, implement, and evaluate maintenance policies and procedures. Counsel employees about work-related issues and assist employees to correct job-skill deficiencies. Examine objects, systems, or facilities, and analyze information to determine needed installations, services, or repairs. Conduct or arrange for worker training in safety, repair, and maintenance techniques, operational procedures, or equipment use. Inspect and monitor work areas, examine tools and equipment, and provide employee safety training to prevent, detect, and correct unsafe conditions or violations of procedures and safety rules. Inspect, test, and measure completed work, using devices such as hand tools and gauges to verify conformance to standards and repair requirements. Requisition materials and supplies such as tools, equipment, and replacement parts. Participate in budget preparation and administration, coordinating purchasing and documentation, and monitoring departmental expenditures. Perform skilled repair and maintenance operations, using equipment such as hand and power tools, hydraulic presses and shears, and welding equipment. Meet with vendors and suppliers to discuss products used in repair work. Compute estimates and actual costs of factors such as materials, labor, and outside contractors. Review, evaluate, accept, and coordinate completion of work bid from contractors. Confer with personnel, such as management, engineering, quality control, customer, and union workers' representatives, to coordinate work activities, resolve employee grievances, and identify and review resource needs.

Personality Type: Enterprising. These occupations frequently involve starting up and carrying out projects and can involve leading people and making many decisions. They sometimes require risk taking and often deal with business.

GOE—Interest Area/Cluster: 13. Manufacturing. **Work Group:** 13.01. Managerial Work in Manufacturing. **Other Jobs in This Work Group:** First-Line Supervisors/Managers of Helpers, Laborers, and Material Movers, Hand; First-Line Supervisors/Managers of Production and Operating Workers; Industrial Production Managers.

Skills—Repairing: Repairing machines or systems, using the needed tools. **Operation Monitoring:** Watching gauges, dials, or other indicators to make sure a machine is working properly. **Management of Personnel Resources:** Motivating, developing, and directing people as they work; identifying the best people for the job. **Equipment Maintenance:** Performing routine maintenance and determining when and what kind of maintenance is needed. **Management of Financial Resources:** Determining how money will be spent to get the work done and accounting for these expenditures. **Systems Analysis:** Determining how a system should work and how changes will affect outcomes. **Operation and Control:** Controlling operations of equipment or systems. **Quality Control Analysis:** Evaluating the quality or performance of products, services, or processes.

Education and Training Program: Operations Management and Supervision. **Related Knowledge/Courses— Mechanical Devices:** Machines and tools, including their designs, uses, benefits, repair, and maintenance. **Personnel and Human Resources:** Principles and procedures for personnel recruitment; selection; training; compensation and benefits; labor relations and negotiation; and personnel information systems. **Production and Processing:** Inputs, outputs, raw materials, waste, quality control, costs, and techniques for maximizing the manufacture and distribution of goods. **Engineering and Technology:** Equipment, tools, and mechanical devices and their uses to produce motion, light, power, technology, and other applications. **Building and Construction:** Materials, methods, and the appropriate tools to construct objects, structures, and buildings. **Economics and Accounting:** Economic and accounting principles and practices, the financial markets, banking, and the analysis and reporting of financial data.

Work Environment: More often indoors than outdoors; noisy; contaminants; hazardous conditions; standing.

First-Line Supervisors/Managers of Non-Retail Sales Workers

- ❊ Education/Training Required: Work experience in a related occupation
- ❊ Annual Earnings: $67,020
- ❊ Beginning Wage: $36,120
- ❊ Earnings Growth Potential: High
- ❊ Growth: 3.7%
- ❊ Annual Job Openings: 48,883
- ❊ Self-Employed: 45.4%
- ❊ Part-Time: 5.3%

Directly supervise and coordinate activities of sales workers other than retail sales workers. May perform duties such as budgeting, accounting, and personnel work in addition to supervisory duties. Listen to and resolve customer complaints regarding services, products, or personnel. Monitor sales staff performance to ensure that goals are met. Hire, train, and evaluate personnel. Confer with company officials to develop methods and procedures to increase sales, expand markets, and promote business. Direct and supervise employees engaged in sales, inventory-taking, reconciling cash receipts, or performing specific services such as pumping gasoline for customers. Provide staff with assistance in performing difficult or complicated duties. Plan and prepare work schedules and assign employees to specific duties. Attend company meetings to exchange product information and coordinate work activities with other departments. Prepare sales and inventory reports for management and budget departments. Formulate pricing policies on merchandise according to profitability requirements. Examine merchandise to ensure correct pricing and display and ensure that it functions as advertised. Analyze details of sales territories to assess their growth potential and to set quotas. Visit retailers and sales representatives to promote products and gather information. Keep records pertaining to purchases, sales, and requisitions. Coordinate sales promotion activities and prepare merchandise displays and advertising copy. Prepare rental or lease agreements, specifying charges and payment procedures for use of machinery, tools, or other items. Inventory stock and reorder when inventories drop to specified levels. Examine products purchased for resale or received for storage to determine product condition.

Personality Type: Enterprising. These occupations frequently involve starting up and carrying out projects and can involve leading people and making many decisions. They sometimes require risk taking and often deal with business.

GOE—Interest Area/Cluster: 14. Retail and Wholesale Sales and Service. **Work Group:** 14.01. Managerial Work in Retail/Wholesale Sales and Service. **Other Jobs in This Work Group:** Advertising and Promotions Managers; First-Line Supervisors/Managers of Retail Sales Workers; Funeral Directors; Marketing Managers; Property, Real Estate, and Community Association Managers; Purchasing Managers; Sales Managers.

Skills—Management of Personnel Resources: Motivating, developing, and directing people as they work; identifying the best people for the job. **Negotiation:** Bringing others together and trying to reconcile differences. **Persuasion:** Persuading others to approach things differently. **Time Management:** Managing one's own time and the time of others. **Social Perceptiveness:** Being aware of others' reactions and understanding why they react the way they do. **Operations Analysis:** Analyzing needs and product requirements to create a design. **Monitoring:** Assessing how well one is doing when learning or doing something. **Judgment and Decision Making:** Weighing the relative costs and benefits of a potential action.

Education and Training Programs: Business, Management, Marketing, and Related Support Services, Other; General Merchandising, Sales, and Related Marketing Operations, Other; Special Products Marketing Operations; Specialized Merchandising, Sales, and Related Marketing Operations, Other. **Related Knowledge/Courses—Sales and Marketing:** Principles and methods involved in showing, promoting, and selling products or services. This includes marketing strategies and tactics, product demonstration and sales techniques, and sales control systems. **Economics and Accounting:** Economic and accounting principles and practices, the financial markets, banking, and the analysis and reporting of financial data. **Personnel and Human Resources:** Principles and procedures for personnel recruitment; selection; training; compensation and benefits; labor relations and negotiation; and personnel information systems. **Administration and Management:** Principles and processes involved in business and organizational planning, coordination, and execution. This includes strategic planning, resource allocation, manpower modeling, leadership techniques, and production methods. **Mathematics:** Numbers and their operations and interrelationships, including arithmetic, algebra, geometry, calculus, and statistics and their applications. **Education and Training:** Instructional methods and training techniques, including curriculum design principles, learning theory, group and individual teaching techniques, design of individual development plans, and test design principles.

Work Environment: Indoors; noisy.

First-Line Supervisors/Managers of Office and Administrative Support Workers

* ❋ Education/Training Required: Work experience in a related occupation
* ❋ Annual Earnings: $44,650
* ❋ Beginning Wage: $27,190
* ❋ Earnings Growth Potential: Medium
* ❋ Growth: 5.8%
* ❋ Annual Job Openings: 138,420
* ❋ Self-Employed: 1.6%
* ❋ Part-Time: 7.9%

Supervise and coordinate the activities of clerical and administrative support workers. Resolve customer complaints and answer customers' questions regarding policies and procedures. Supervise the work of office, administrative, or customer service employees to ensure adherence to quality standards, deadlines, and proper procedures, correcting errors or problems. Provide employees with guidance in handling difficult or complex problems and in resolving escalated complaints or disputes. Implement corporate and departmental policies, procedures, and service standards in conjunction with management. Discuss job performance problems with employees to identify causes and issues and to work on resolving problems. Train and instruct employees in job duties and company policies or arrange for training to be provided. Evaluate employees' job performance and conformance to regulations and recommend

appropriate personnel action. Recruit, interview, and select employees. Review records and reports pertaining to activities such as production, payroll, and shipping to verify details, monitor work activities, and evaluate performance. Interpret and communicate work procedures and company policies to staff. Prepare and issue work schedules, deadlines, and duty assignments of office or administrative staff. Maintain records pertaining to inventory, personnel, orders, supplies, and machine maintenance. Compute figures such as balances, totals, and commissions. Research, compile, and prepare reports, manuals, correspondence, and other information required by management or governmental agencies. Coordinate activities with other supervisory personnel and with other work units or departments. Analyze financial activities of establishments or departments and provide input into budget planning and preparation processes. Develop or update procedures, policies, and standards. Make recommendations to management concerning such issues as staffing decisions and procedural changes. Consult with managers and other personnel to resolve problems in areas such as equipment performance, output quality, and work schedules. Participate in the work of subordinates to facilitate productivity or to overcome difficult aspects of work.

Personality Type: Enterprising. These occupations frequently involve starting up and carrying out projects and can involve leading people and making many decisions. They sometimes require risk taking and often deal with business.

GOE—Interest Area/Cluster: 04. Business and Administration. **Work Group:** 04.02. Managerial Work in Business Detail. **Other Jobs in This Work Group:** Administrative Services Managers; First-Line Supervisors/Managers of Housekeeping and Janitorial Workers; Meeting and Convention Planners.

Skills—Management of Personnel Resources: Motivating, developing, and directing people as they work; identifying the best people for the job. **Management of Financial Resources:** Determining how money will be spent to get the work done and accounting for these expenditures. **Negotiation:** Bringing others together and trying to reconcile differences. **Management of Material Resources:** Obtaining and seeing to the appropriate use of equipment, facilities, and materials needed to do certain work. **Monitoring:** Assessing how well one is doing when learning or doing something. **Service Orientation:** Actively looking for ways to help people. **Persuasion:** Persuading others to approach things differently. **Judgment and Decision Making:** Weighing the relative costs and benefits of a potential action.

Education and Training Programs: No related CIP programs; this job is learned through work experience in a related occupation; this job is learned through work experience in a related occupation. **Related Knowledge/Courses—Clerical Practices:** Administrative and clerical procedures and systems such as word-processing systems, filing and records management systems, stenography and transcription, forms, design principles, and other office procedures and terminology. **Economics and Accounting:** Economic and accounting principles and practices, the financial markets, banking, and the analysis and reporting of financial data. **Administration and Management:** Principles and processes involved in business and organizational planning, coordination, and execution. This includes strategic planning, resource allocation, manpower modeling, leadership techniques, and production methods. **Personnel and Human Resources:** Principles and procedures for personnel recruitment; selection; training; compensation and benefits; labor relations and negotiation; and personnel information systems. **Customer and Personal Service:** Principles and processes for providing customer and personal services, including needs assessment techniques, quality service standards, alternative delivery systems, and customer satisfaction evaluation techniques. **Education and Training:** Instructional methods and training techniques, including curriculum design principles, learning theory, group and individual teaching techniques, design of individual development plans, and test design principles.

Work Environment: Indoors; noisy; sitting.

First-Line Supervisors/Managers of Personal Service Workers

- ❀ Education/Training Required: Work experience in a related occupation
- ❀ Annual Earnings: $33,900
- ❀ Beginning Wage: $20,820
- ❀ Earnings Growth Potential: Medium
- ❀ Growth: 15.5%
- ❀ Annual Job Openings: 37,555
- ❀ Self-Employed: 38.6%
- ❀ Part-Time: 15.8%

Supervise and coordinate activities of personal service workers such as flight attendants, hairdressers, or caddies. Requisition necessary supplies, equipment, and services. Inform workers about interests and special needs of specific groups. Participate in continuing education to stay abreast of industry trends and developments. Meet with managers and other supervisors to stay informed of changes affecting operations. Collaborate with staff members to plan and develop programs of events, schedules of activities, or menus. Train workers in proper operational procedures and functions, and explain company policies. Furnish customers with information on events and activities. Resolve customer complaints regarding worker performance and services rendered. Analyze and record personnel and operational data, and write related activity reports. Observe and evaluate workers' appearance and performance to ensure quality service and compliance with specifications. Inspect work areas and operating equipment to ensure conformance to established standards in areas such as cleanliness and maintenance. Direct and coordinate the activities of workers such as flight attendants, hotel staff, or hair stylists. Assign work schedules, following work requirements, to ensure quality and timely delivery of service. Apply customer/guest feedback to service improvement efforts. Direct marketing, advertising, and other customer recruitment efforts. Take disciplinary action to address performance problems. Recruit and hire staff members.

Personality Type: Enterprising. These occupations frequently involve starting up and carrying out projects and can involve leading people and making many decisions. They sometimes require risk taking and often deal with business.

GOE—Interest Area/Cluster: 09. Hospitality, Tourism, and Recreation. **Work Group:** 09.01. Managerial Work in Hospitality and Tourism. **Other Jobs in This Work Group:** First-Line Supervisors/Managers of Food Preparation and Serving Workers; Food Service Managers; Gaming Managers; Gaming Supervisors; Lodging Managers.

Skills—Management of Personnel Resources: Motivating, developing, and directing people as they work; identifying the best people for the job. **Social Perceptiveness:** Being aware of others' reactions and understanding why they react the way they do. **Service Orientation:** Actively looking for ways to help people. **Learning Strategies:** Using multiple approaches when learning or teaching new things. **Coordination:** Adjusting actions in relation to others' actions. **Judgment and Decision Making:** Weighing the relative costs and benefits of a potential action. **Writing:** Communicating effectively with others in writing as indicated by the needs of the audience. **Time Management:** Managing one's own time and the time of others.

Education and Training Program: Personal and Culinary Services, Other. **Related Knowledge/Courses—Psychology:** Human behavior and performance, mental processes, psychological research methods, and the assessment and treatment of behavioral and affective disorders. **Therapy and Counseling:** Information and techniques needed to rehabilitate physical and mental ailments and to provide career guidance, including alternative treatments, rehabilitation equipment and its proper use, and methods to evaluate treatment effects. **Education and Training:** Instructional methods and training techniques, including curriculum design principles, learning theory, group and individual teaching techniques, design of individual development plans, and test design principles. **Philosophy and Theology:** Different philosophical systems and religions, including their basic principles, values, ethics, ways of thinking, customs, and practices and their impact on human culture. **Medicine and Dentistry:** The information and techniques needed to diagnose and treat injuries, diseases, and deformities. This includes symptoms, treatment alternatives, drug properties and interactions, and preventive health-care measures. **Public Safety and Security:** Weaponry; public safety; security operations, rules, regulations, precautions, and prevention; and the protection of people, data, and property.

Work Environment: Indoors; noisy; contaminants; standing; walking and running; using hands on objects, tools, or controls.

First-Line Supervisors/Managers of Police and Detectives

- ✱ Education/Training Required: Work experience in a related occupation
- ✱ Annual Earnings: $72,620
- ✱ Beginning Wage: $43,720
- ✱ Earnings Growth Potential: Medium
- ✱ Growth: 9.2%
- ✱ Annual Job Openings: 9,373
- ✱ Self-Employed: 0.0%
- ✱ Part-Time: 0.8%

Supervise and coordinate activities of members of police force. Supervise and coordinate the investigation of criminal cases, offering guidance and expertise to investigators, and ensuring that procedures are conducted in accordance with laws and regulations. Maintain logs, prepare reports, and direct the preparation, handling, and maintenance of departmental records. Explain police operations to subordinates to assist them in performing their job duties. Cooperate with court personnel and officials from other law enforcement agencies and testify in court as necessary. Review contents of written orders to ensure adherence to legal requirements. Investigate and resolve personnel problems within organization and charges of misconduct against staff. Direct collection, preparation, and handling of evidence and personal property of prisoners. Inform personnel of changes in regulations and policies, implications of new or amended laws, and new techniques of police work. Train staff in proper police work procedures. Monitor and evaluate the job performance of subordinates, and authorize promotions and transfers. Prepare work schedules and assign duties to subordinates. Conduct raids and order detention of witnesses and suspects for questioning. Discipline staff for violation of departmental rules and regulations. Develop, implement, and revise departmental policies and procedures. Inspect facilities, supplies, vehicles, and equipment to ensure conformance to standards. Requisition and issue equipment and supplies. Meet with civic, educational, and community groups to develop community programs and events, and to discuss law enforcement subjects. Prepare news releases and respond to police correspondence. Prepare budgets and manage expenditures of department funds. Direct release or transfer of prisoners.

Personality Type: Enterprising. These occupations frequently involve starting up and carrying out projects and can involve leading people and making many decisions. They sometimes require risk taking and often deal with business.

GOE—Interest Area/Cluster: 12. Law and Public Safety. **Work Group:** 12.01. Managerial Work in Law and Public Safety. **Other Jobs in This Work Group:** Emergency Management Specialists; First-Line Supervisors/Managers of Correctional Officers; First-Line Supervisors/Managers of Fire Fighting and Prevention Workers; Forest Fire Fighting and Prevention Supervisors; Municipal Fire Fighting and Prevention Supervisors.

Skills—Management of Personnel Resources: Motivating, developing, and directing people as they work; identifying the best people for the job. **Systems Analysis:** Determining how a system should work and how changes will affect outcomes. **Negotiation:** Bringing others together and trying to reconcile differences. **Systems Evaluation:** Looking at many indicators of system performance and taking into account their accuracy. **Operation Monitoring:** Watching gauges, dials, or other indicators to make sure a machine is working properly. **Writing:** Communicating effectively with others in writing as indicated by the needs of the audience. **Social Perceptiveness:** Being aware of others' reactions and understanding why they react the way they do. **Persuasion:** Persuading others to approach things differently.

Education and Training Programs: Corrections; Criminal Justice/Law Enforcement Administration; Criminal Justice/Safety Studies. **Related Knowledge/Courses—Public Safety and Security:** Weaponry; public safety; security operations, rules, regulations, precautions, and prevention; and the protection of people, data, and property. **Law and Government:** Laws, legal codes, court procedures, precedents, government regulations, executive orders, agency rules, and the democratic political process. **Psychology:** Human behavior and performance, mental processes, psychological research methods, and the assessment and treatment of behavioral and affective disorders. **Sociology and Anthropology:** Group behavior and dynamics; societal trends and influences; and cultures and their history, migrations, ethnicity, and origins. **Therapy and Counseling:** Information and techniques needed to rehabilitate physical and mental ailments and to provide career guidance, including alternative treatments, rehabilitation equipment and its proper use, and methods to evaluate treatment effects. **Personnel and Human Resources:** Principles and procedures for personnel recruitment; selection; training; compensation and benefits; labor relations and negotiation; and personnel information systems.

Work Environment: More often indoors than outdoors; noisy; very hot or cold; contaminants; sitting.

First-Line Supervisors/Managers of Production and Operating Workers

* Education/Training Required: Work experience in a related occupation
* Annual Earnings: $48,670
* Beginning Wage: $29,830
* Earnings Growth Potential: Medium
* Growth: –4.8%
* Annual Job Openings: 46,144
* Self-Employed: 2.4%
* Part-Time: 1.9%

Supervise and coordinate the activities of production and operating workers, such as inspectors, precision workers, machine setters and operators, assemblers, fabricators, and plant and system operators. Enforce safety and sanitation regulations. Direct and coordinate the activities of employees engaged in the production or processing of goods, such as inspectors, machine setters, and fabricators. Read and analyze charts, work orders, production schedules, and other records and reports to determine production requirements and to evaluate current production estimates and outputs. Confer with other supervisors to coordinate operations and activities within or between departments. Plan and establish work schedules, assignments, and production sequences to meet production goals. Inspect materials, products, or equipment to detect defects or malfunctions. Demonstrate equipment operations and work and safety procedures to new employees or assign employees to experienced workers for training. Observe work and monitor gauges, dials, and other indicators to ensure that operators conform to production or processing standards. Interpret specifications, blueprints, job orders, and company policies and procedures for workers. Confer with management or subordinates to resolve worker problems, complaints, or grievances. Maintain operations data such as time, production, and cost records and prepare management reports of production results. Recommend or implement measures to motivate employees and to improve production methods, equipment performance, product quality, or efficiency. Determine standards, budgets, production goals, and rates based on company policies, equipment and labor availability, and workloads. Requisition materials, supplies, equipment parts, or repair services. Recommend personnel actions such as hirings and promotions. Set up and adjust machines and equipment. Calculate labor and equipment requirements and production specifications, using standard formulas. Plan and develop new products and production processes.

Personality Type: Enterprising. These occupations frequently involve starting up and carrying out projects and can involve leading people and making many decisions. They sometimes require risk taking and often deal with business.

GOE—Interest Area/Cluster: 13. Manufacturing. **Work Group:** 13.01. Managerial Work in Manufacturing. **Other Jobs in This Work Group:** First-Line Supervisors/Managers of Helpers, Laborers, and Material Movers, Hand; First-Line Supervisors/Managers of Mechanics, Installers, and Repairers; Industrial Production Managers.

Skills—Management of Personnel Resources: Motivating, developing, and directing people as they work; identifying the best people for the job. **Operation Monitoring:**

Watching gauges, dials, or other indicators to make sure a machine is working properly. **Operation and Control:** Controlling operations of equipment or systems. **Quality Control Analysis:** Evaluating the quality or performance of products, services, or processes. **Operations Analysis:** Analyzing needs and product requirements to create a design. **Systems Analysis:** Determining how a system should work and how changes will affect outcomes. **Monitoring:** Assessing how well one is doing when learning or doing something. **Systems Evaluation:** Looking at many indicators of system performance and taking into account their accuracy.

Education and Training Program: Operations Management and Supervision. **Related Knowledge/Courses— Production and Processing:** Inputs, outputs, raw materials, waste, quality control, costs, and techniques for maximizing the manufacture and distribution of goods. **Mechanical Devices:** Machines and tools, including their designs, uses, benefits, repair, and maintenance. **Personnel and Human Resources:** Principles and procedures for personnel recruitment; selection; training; compensation and benefits; labor relations and negotiation; and personnel information systems. **Engineering and Technology:** Equipment, tools, and mechanical devices and their uses to produce motion, light, power, technology, and other applications. **Administration and Management:** Principles and processes involved in business and organizational planning, coordination, and execution. This includes strategic planning, resource allocation, manpower modeling, leadership techniques, and production methods. **Psychology:** Human behavior and performance, mental processes, psychological research methods, and the assessment and treatment of behavioral and affective disorders.

Work Environment: Indoors; noisy; contaminants; hazardous equipment; standing; walking and running.

First-Line Supervisors/Managers of Retail Sales Workers

- ❋ Education/Training Required: Work experience in a related occupation
- ❋ Annual Earnings: $34,470
- ❋ Beginning Wage: $21,760
- ❋ Earnings Growth Potential: Medium
- ❋ Growth: 4.2%
- ❋ Annual Job Openings: 221,241
- ❋ Self-Employed: 34.2%
- ❋ Part-Time: 7.8%

Directly supervise sales workers in a retail establishment or department. Duties may include management functions, such as purchasing, budgeting, accounting, and personnel work, in addition to supervisory duties. Provide customer service by greeting and assisting customers and responding to customer inquiries and complaints. Assign employees to specific duties. Monitor sales activities to ensure that customers receive satisfactory service and quality goods. Direct and supervise employees engaged in sales, inventory-taking, reconciling cash receipts, or performing services for customers. Inventory stock and reorder when inventory drops to a specified level. Keep records of purchases, sales, and requisitions. Enforce safety, health, and security rules. Examine products purchased for resale or received for storage to assess the condition of each product or item. Hire, train, and evaluate personnel in sales or marketing establishments, promoting or firing workers when appropriate. Perform work activities of subordinates, such as cleaning and organizing shelves and displays and selling merchandise. Establish and implement policies, goals, objectives, and procedures for their department. Instruct staff on how to handle difficult and complicated sales. Formulate pricing policies for merchandise according to profitability requirements. Estimate consumer demand and determine the types and amounts of goods to be sold. Examine merchandise to ensure that it is correctly priced and displayed and that it functions as advertised. Plan and prepare work schedules and keep records of employees' work schedules and time cards. Review inventory and sales records to prepare reports for management and budget departments. Plan and coordinate advertising campaigns and sales promotions and prepare merchandise displays and advertising copy. Confer with company officials to develop methods and procedures to increase sales, expand markets, and promote business. Establish credit policies and operating procedures. Plan budgets and authorize payments and merchandise returns.

Personality Type: Enterprising. These occupations frequently involve starting up and carrying out projects and can involve leading people and making many decisions. They sometimes require risk taking and often deal with business.

GOE—Interest Area/Cluster: 14. Retail and Wholesale Sales and Service. **Work Group:** 14.01. Managerial Work in Retail/Wholesale Sales and Service. **Other Jobs in This Work Group:** Advertising and Promotions Managers; First-Line Supervisors/Managers of Non-Retail Sales Workers; Funeral Directors; Marketing Managers; Property, Real Estate, and Community Association Managers; Purchasing Managers; Sales Managers.

Skills—Management of Personnel Resources: Motivating, developing, and directing people as they work; identifying the best people for the job. **Management of Financial Resources:** Determining how money will be spent to get the work done and accounting for these expenditures. **Persuasion:** Persuading others to approach things differently. **Repairing:** Repairing machines or systems, using the needed tools. **Equipment Maintenance:** Performing routine maintenance and determining when and what kind of maintenance is needed. **Monitoring:** Assessing how well one is doing when learning or doing something. **Troubleshooting:** Determining what is causing an operating error and deciding what to do about it. **Social Perceptiveness:** Being aware of others' reactions and understanding why they react the way they do.

Education and Training Programs: Business, Management, Marketing, and Related Support Services, Other; Consumer Merchandising/Retailing Management; E-Commerce/Electronic Commerce; Floriculture/Floristry Operations and Management; Retailing and Retail Operations; Selling Skills and Sales Operations; Special Products Marketing Operations; Specialized Merchandising, Sales, and Related Marketing Operations, Other. **Related Knowledge/Courses—Sales and Marketing:** Principles and methods involved in showing, promoting, and selling products or services. This includes marketing strategies and tactics, product demonstration and sales techniques, and sales control systems. **Personnel and Human Resources:** Principles and procedures for personnel recruitment; selection; training; compensation and benefits; labor relations and negotiation; and personnel information systems. **Administration and Management:** Principles and processes involved in business and organizational planning, coordination, and execution. This includes strategic planning, resource allocation, manpower modeling, leadership techniques, and production methods. **Economics and Accounting:** Economic and accounting principles and practices, the financial markets, banking, and the analysis and reporting of financial data. **Customer and Personal Service:** Principles and processes for providing customer and personal services, including needs assessment techniques, quality service standards, alternative delivery systems, and customer satisfaction evaluation techniques.

Work Environment: Indoors; hazardous equipment; standing; walking and running; using hands on objects, tools, or controls.

First-Line Supervisors/Managers of Transportation and Material-Moving Machine and Vehicle Operators

* Education/Training Required: Work experience in a related occupation
* Annual Earnings: $49,850
* Beginning Wage: $29,760
* Earnings Growth Potential: High
* Growth: 10.2%
* Annual Job Openings: 16,580
* Self-Employed: 1.5%
* Part-Time: 5.3%

Directly supervise and coordinate activities of transportation and material-moving machine and vehicle operators and helpers. Enforce safety rules and regulations. Plan work assignments and equipment allocations to meet transportation, operations, or production goals. Confer with customers, supervisors, contractors, and other personnel to exchange information and to resolve problems. Direct workers in transportation or related services, such as pumping, moving, storing, and loading and unloading of materials or people. Resolve worker problems or collaborate with employees to assist in problem resolution. Review orders, production schedules, blueprints, and shipping and receiving notices to determine work sequences and material shipping dates, types, volumes, and destinations. Monitor fieldwork to ensure that it is being performed properly and that materials are being used as they should be. Recommend and implement measures to improve worker motivation, equipment performance, work methods, and customer services. Maintain or verify records of time, materials, expenditures, and crew activities. Interpret transportation and tariff regulations, shipping orders, safety regulations, and company policies and procedures for workers. Explain and demonstrate work tasks to new workers or assign workers to more experienced workers for further training. Prepare, compile, and submit reports on work activities, operations, production, and work-related accidents. Recommend or implement personnel actions such as employee selection, evaluation, and rewards or disciplinary actions. Requisition needed personnel, supplies, equipment, parts, or repair services. Inspect or test materials, stock, vehicles, equipment, and facilities to ensure that they are safe, are free of defects, and meet specifications. Plan and establish transportation routes. Compute and estimate cash, payroll, transportation, personnel, and storage requirements. Dispatch personnel and vehicles in response to telephone or radio reports of emergencies. Perform or schedule repairs and preventive maintenance of vehicles and other equipment. Examine, measure, and weigh cargo or materials to determine specific handling requirements. Provide workers with assistance in performing tasks such as coupling railroad cars or loading vehicles.

Personality Type: Enterprising. These occupations frequently involve starting up and carrying out projects and can involve leading people and making many decisions. They sometimes require risk taking and often deal with business.

GOE—Interest Area/Cluster: 16. Transportation, Distribution, and Logistics. **Work Group:** 16.01. Managerial Work in Transportation. **Other Jobs in This Work Group:** Aircraft Cargo Handling Supervisors; Postmasters and Mail Superintendents; Railroad Conductors and Yardmasters; Storage and Distribution Managers; Transportation Managers; Transportation, Storage, and Distribution Managers.

Skills—Management of Personnel Resources: Motivating, developing, and directing people as they work; identifying the best people for the job. **Management of Financial Resources:** Determining how money will be spent to get the work done and accounting for these expenditures. **Management of Material Resources:** Obtaining and seeing to the appropriate use of equipment, facilities, and materials needed to do certain work. **Social Perceptiveness:** Being aware of others' reactions and understanding why they react the way they do. **Operations Analysis:** Analyzing needs and product requirements to create a design. **Equipment Selection:** Determining the kind of tools and equipment needed to do a job. **Systems Evaluation:** Looking at many indicators of system performance and taking into account their accuracy. **Monitoring:** Assessing how well one is doing when learning or doing something.

Education and Training Programs: No related CIP programs; this job is learned through work experience in a related occupation; this job is learned through work experience in a related occupation. **Related Knowledge/ Courses—Transportation:** Principles and methods for moving people or goods by air, rail, sea, or road, including their relative costs, advantages, and limitations. **Production and Processing:** Inputs, outputs, raw materials, waste, quality control, costs, and techniques for maximizing the manufacture and distribution of goods. **Personnel and Human Resources:** Principles and procedures for personnel recruitment; selection; training; compensation and benefits; labor relations and negotiation; and personnel information systems. **Customer and Personal Service:** Principles and processes for providing customer and personal services, including needs assessment techniques, quality service standards, alternative delivery systems, and customer satisfaction evaluation techniques. **Public Safety and Security:** Weaponry; public safety; security operations, rules, regulations, precautions, and prevention; and the protection of people, data, and property. **Administration and Management:** Principles and processes involved in business and organizational planning, coordination, and execution. This includes strategic planning, resource allocation, manpower modeling, leadership techniques, and production methods.

Work Environment: Indoors; noisy; contaminants; sitting.

Fitness Trainers and Aerobics Instructors

- ❋ Education/Training Required: Postsecondary vocational training
- ❋ Annual Earnings: $27,680
- ❋ Beginning Wage: $15,550
- ❋ Earnings Growth Potential: High
- ❋ Growth: 26.8%
- ❋ Annual Job Openings: 51,235
- ❋ Self-Employed: 7.6%
- ❋ Part-Time: 38.2%

Instruct or coach groups or individuals in exercise activities and the fundamentals of sports. Demonstrate techniques and methods of participation. Observe participants and inform them of corrective measures necessary to improve their skills. Explain and enforce safety rules and regulations governing sports, recreational activities, and the use of exercise equipment. Offer alternatives during classes to accommodate different levels of fitness. Plan routines, choose appropriate music, and choose different movements for each set of muscles, depending on participants' capabilities and limitations. Observe participants and inform them of corrective measures necessary for skill improvement. Teach proper breathing techniques used during physical exertion. Teach and demonstrate use of gymnastic and training equipment such as trampolines and weights. Instruct participants in maintaining exertion levels to maximize benefits from exercise routines. Maintain fitness equipment. Conduct therapeutic, recreational, or athletic activities. Monitor participants' progress and adapt programs as needed. Evaluate individuals' abilities, needs, and physical conditions and develop suitable training programs to meet any special requirements. Plan physical education programs to promote development of participants' physical attributes and social skills. Provide students with information and resources regarding nutrition, weight control, and lifestyle issues. Administer emergency first aid, wrap injuries, treat minor chronic disabilities, or refer injured persons to physicians. Advise clients about proper clothing and shoes. Wrap ankles, fingers, wrists, or other body parts with synthetic skin, gauze, or adhesive tape to support muscles and ligaments. Teach individual and team sports to participants through instruction and demonstration, utilizing knowledge of sports techniques and of participants' physical capabilities. Promote health clubs through membership sales and record member information. Organize, lead, and referee indoor and outdoor games such as volleyball, baseball, and basketball. Maintain equipment inventories and select, store, or issue equipment as needed. Organize and conduct competitions and tournaments. Advise participants in use of heat or ultraviolet treatments and hot baths. Massage body parts to relieve soreness, strains, and bruises.

Personality Type: Social. These occupations frequently involve working with, communicating with, and teaching people and often involve helping or providing service to others.

GOE—Interest Area/Cluster: 05. Education and Training. **Work Group:** 05.06. Counseling, Health, and Fitness Education. **Other Jobs in This Work Group:** Educational, Vocational, and School Counselors; Health Educators.

Skills—Instructing: Teaching others how to do something. **Equipment Selection:** Determining the kind of tools and equipment needed to do a job. **Monitoring:** Assessing how well one is doing when learning or doing something. **Service Orientation:** Actively looking for ways to help people. **Coordination:** Adjusting actions in relation to others' actions. **Science:** Using scientific methods to solve problems. **Social Perceptiveness:** Being aware of others' reactions and understanding why they react the way they do. **Time Management:** Managing one's own time and the time of others.

Education and Training Programs: Health and Physical Education, General; Physical Education Teaching and Coaching; Sport and Fitness Administration/Management. **Related Knowledge/Courses—Customer and Personal Service:** Principles and processes for providing customer

and personal services, including needs assessment techniques, quality service standards, alternative delivery systems, and customer satisfaction evaluation techniques. **Psychology:** Human behavior and performance, mental processes, psychological research methods, and the assessment and treatment of behavioral and affective disorders. **Sociology and Anthropology:** Group behavior and dynamics; societal trends and influences; and cultures and their history, migrations, ethnicity, and origins. **Education and Training:** Instructional methods and training techniques, including curriculum design principles, learning theory, group and individual teaching techniques, design of individual development plans, and test design principles. **Sales and Marketing:** Principles and methods involved in showing, promoting, and selling products or services. This includes marketing strategies and tactics, product demonstration and sales techniques, and sales control systems. **Personnel and Human Resources:** Principles and procedures for personnel recruitment; selection; training; compensation and benefits; labor relations and negotiation; and personnel information systems.

Work Environment: Indoors; standing; walking and running; repetitive motions.

Flight Attendants

- ❋ Education/Training Required: Long-term on-the-job training
- ❋ Annual Earnings: $61,120
- ❋ Beginning Wage: $28,880
- ❋ Earnings Growth Potential: Very high
- ❋ Growth: 10.6%
- ❋ Annual Job Openings: 10,773
- ❋ Self-Employed: 0.0%
- ❋ Part-Time: 24.9%

Provide personal services to ensure the safety and comfort of airline passengers during flight. Greet passengers, verify tickets, explain use of safety equipment, and serve food or beverages. Direct and assist passengers in the event of an emergency, such as directing passengers to evacuate a plane following an emergency landing. Announce and demonstrate safety and emergency procedures such as the use of oxygen masks, seat belts, and life jackets. Walk aisles of planes to verify that passengers have complied with federal regulations prior to takeoffs and landings. Verify that first aid kits and other emergency equipment, including fire extinguishers and oxygen bottles, are in working order. Administer first aid to passengers in distress. Attend preflight briefings concerning weather, altitudes, routes, emergency procedures, crew coordination, lengths of flights, food and beverage services offered, and numbers of passengers. Prepare passengers and aircraft for landing, following procedures. Determine special assistance needs of passengers such as small children, the elderly, or disabled persons. Check to ensure that food, beverages, blankets, reading material, emergency equipment, and other supplies are aboard and are in adequate supply. Reassure passengers when situations such as turbulence are encountered. Announce flight delays and descent preparations. Inspect passenger tickets to verify information and to obtain destination information. Answer passengers' questions about flights, aircraft, weather, travel routes and services, arrival times, and schedules. Assist passengers while entering or disembarking the aircraft. Inspect and clean cabins, checking for any problems and making sure that cabins are in order. Greet passengers boarding aircraft and direct them to assigned seats. Conduct periodic trips through the cabin to ensure passenger comfort and to distribute reading material, headphones, pillows, playing cards, and blankets. Take inventory of headsets, alcoholic beverages, and money collected. Operate audio and video systems. Assist passengers in placing carry-on luggage in overhead, garment, or under-seat storage. Prepare reports showing places of departure and destination, passenger ticket numbers, meal and beverage inventories, the conditions of cabin equipment, and any problems encountered by passengers.

Personality Type: Enterprising. These occupations frequently involve starting up and carrying out projects and can involve leading people and making many decisions. They sometimes require risk taking and often deal with business.

GOE—Interest Area/Cluster: 09. Hospitality, Tourism, and Recreation. **Work Group:** 09.03. Hospitality and Travel Services. **Other Jobs in This Work Group:** Baggage Porters and Bellhops; Concierges; Hotel, Motel, and Resort Desk Clerks; Janitors and Cleaners, Except Maids and Housekeeping Cleaners; Maids and Housekeeping Cleaners; Reservation and Transportation Ticket Agents and Travel Clerks; Tour Guides and Escorts; Transportation Attendants, Except Flight Attendants and Baggage Porters; Travel Agents; Travel Guides.

Skills—Service Orientation: Actively looking for ways to help people. **Social Perceptiveness:** Being aware of others' reactions and understanding why they react the way they do. **Reading Comprehension:** Understanding written sentences and paragraphs in work-related documents. **Critical**

Thinking: Using logic and analysis to identify the strengths and weaknesses of different approaches.

Education and Training Program: Airline Flight Attendant Training. **Related Knowledge/Courses—Customer and Personal Service:** Principles and processes for providing customer and personal services, including needs assessment techniques, quality service standards, alternative delivery systems, and customer satisfaction evaluation techniques. **Psychology:** Human behavior and performance, mental processes, psychological research methods, and the assessment and treatment of behavioral and affective disorders. **Geography:** Various methods for describing the location and distribution of land, sea, and air masses, including their physical locations, relationships, and characteristics. **Transportation:** Principles and methods for moving people or goods by air, rail, sea, or road, including their relative costs, advantages, and limitations. **Philosophy and Theology:** Different philosophical systems and religions, including their basic principles, values, ethics, ways of thinking, customs, and practices and their impact on human culture. **Public Safety and Security:** Weaponry; public safety; security operations, rules, regulations, precautions, and prevention; and the protection of people, data, and property.

Work Environment: Indoors; noisy; contaminants; disease or infections; high places; standing.

Food Batchmakers

* Education/Training Required: Short-term on-the-job training
* Annual Earnings: $23,730
* Beginning Wage: $15,670
* Earnings Growth Potential: Low
* Growth: 10.9%
* Annual Job Openings: 15,704
* Self-Employed: 1.7%
* Part-Time: 15.7%

Set up and operate equipment that mixes or blends ingredients used in the manufacturing of food products. Includes candy makers and cheese makers. Record production and test data for each food product batch, such as the ingredients used, temperature, test results, and time cycle. Observe gauges and thermometers to determine if the mixing chamber temperature is within specified limits and turn valves to control the temperature. Clean and sterilize vats and factory processing areas. Press switches and turn knobs to start, adjust, and regulate equipment such as beaters, extruders, discharge pipes, and salt pumps. Observe and listen to equipment to detect possible malfunctions, such as leaks or plugging, and report malfunctions or undesirable tastes to supervisors. Set up, operate, and tend equipment that cooks, mixes, blends, or processes ingredients in the manufacturing of food products according to formulas or recipes. Mix or blend ingredients according to recipes by using a paddle or an agitator or by controlling vats that heat and mix ingredients. Select and measure or weigh ingredients, using English or metric measures and balance scales. Follow recipes to produce food products of specified flavor, texture, clarity, bouquet, or color. Turn valve controls to start equipment and to adjust operation to maintain product quality. Determine mixing sequences, based on knowledge of temperature effects and of the solubility of specific ingredients. Fill processing or cooking containers, such as kettles, rotating cookers, pressure cookers, or vats, with ingredients by opening valves, by starting pumps or injectors, or by hand. Give directions to other workers who are assisting in the batchmaking process. Homogenize or pasteurize material to prevent separation or to obtain prescribed butterfat content, using a homogenizing device. Inspect vats after cleaning to ensure that fermentable residue has been removed. Examine, feel, and taste product samples during production to evaluate quality, color, texture, flavor, and bouquet and document the results. Test food product samples for moisture content, acidity level, specific gravity, or butterfat content and continue processing until desired levels are reached. Formulate or modify recipes for specific kinds of food products.

Personality Type: Realistic. These occupations frequently involve work activities that include practical, hands-on problems and solutions. They often deal with plants; animals; and real-world materials such as wood, tools, and machinery. Many of the occupations require working outside and don't involve a lot of paperwork or working closely with others.

GOE—Interest Area/Cluster: 13. Manufacturing. **Work Group:** 13.03. Production Work, Assorted Materials Processing. **Other Jobs in This Work Group:** Bakers; Cementing and Gluing Machine Operators and Tenders; Chemical Equipment Operators and Tenders; Cleaning, Washing, and Metal Pickling Equipment Operators and Tenders; Coating, Painting, and Spraying Machine Setters, Operators, and Tenders; Cooling and Freezing Equipment Operators and Tenders; Cutting and Slicing Machine Setters, Operators, and Tenders; Extruding and Forming Machine Setters, Operators, and Tenders, Synthetic and Glass Fibers; Extruding, Forming, Pressing, and Compacting Machine Setters, Operators, and Tenders; Food and Tobacco Roasting, Baking, and Drying Machine Operators and Tenders; Food Cooking Machine Operators and Tenders; Furnace, Kiln, Oven, Drier, and Kettle Operators and Tenders; Heat Treating Equipment Setters, Operators, and Tenders, Metal and Plastic; Helpers—Production Workers; Meat, Poultry, and Fish Cutters and Trimmers; Metal-Refining Furnace Operators and Tenders; Mixing and Blending Machine Setters, Operators, and Tenders; Packaging and Filling Machine Operators and Tenders; Plating and Coating Machine Setters, Operators, and Tenders, Metal and Plastic; Pourers and Casters, Metal; Sawing Machine Setters, Operators, and Tenders, Wood; Separating, Filtering, Clarifying, Precipitating, and Still Machine Setters, Operators, and Tenders; Sewing Machine Operators; Shoe Machine Operators and Tenders; Slaughterers and Meat Packers; Team Assemblers; Textile Bleaching and Dyeing Machine Operators and Tenders; Tire Builders; Woodworking Machine Setters, Operators, and Tenders, Except Sawing.

Skills—Operation Monitoring: Watching gauges, dials, or other indicators to make sure a machine is working properly. **Operation and Control:** Controlling operations of equipment or systems. **Equipment Maintenance:** Performing routine maintenance and determining when and what kind of maintenance is needed. **Repairing:** Repairing machines or systems, using the needed tools. **Quality Control Analysis:** Evaluating the quality or performance of products, services, or processes. **Troubleshooting:** Determining what is causing an operating error and deciding what to do about it.

Education and Training Programs: Agricultural and Food Products Processing; Foodservice Systems Administration/Management. **Related Knowledge/Courses—Production and Processing:** Inputs, outputs, raw materials, waste, quality control, costs, and techniques for maximizing the manufacture and distribution of goods. **Public Safety and Security:** Weaponry; public safety; security operations, rules, regulations, precautions, and prevention; and the protection of people, data, and property. **Chemistry:** The composition, structure, and properties of substances and of the chemical processes and transformations that they undergo. This includes uses of chemicals and their interactions, danger signs, production techniques, and disposal methods.

Work Environment: Noisy; contaminants; standing; using hands on objects, tools, or controls; bending or twisting the body; repetitive motions.

Food Scientists and Technologists

* Education/Training Required: Bachelor's degree
* Annual Earnings: $57,870
* Beginning Wage: $32,090
* Earnings Growth Potential: High
* Growth: 10.3%
* Annual Job Openings: 663
* Self-Employed: 16.3%
* Part-Time: 11.4%

Use chemistry, microbiology, engineering, and other sciences to study the principles underlying the processing and deterioration of foods; analyze food content to determine levels of vitamins, fat, sugar, and protein; discover new food sources; research ways to make processed foods safe, palatable, and healthful; and apply food science knowledge to determine the best ways to process, package, preserve, store, and distribute food. Test new products for flavor, texture, color, nutritional content, and adherence to government and industry standards. Check raw ingredients for maturity or stability for processing and finished products for safety, quality, and nutritional value. Confer with process engineers, plant operators, flavor experts, and packaging and marketing specialists in order to resolve problems in product development. Evaluate food processing and storage operations and assist in the development of quality assurance programs for such operations. Study methods to improve aspects of foods such as chemical composition, flavor, color, texture, nutritional value, and convenience. Study the structure and composition of food or the changes foods undergo in storage and processing. Develop new or improved ways of preserving, processing, packaging, storing, and delivering foods, using knowledge of chemistry, microbiology, and other sciences. Develop food standards and production specifications, safety and sanitary regulations, and waste management and water supply specifications. Demonstrate products to clients. Inspect food processing areas in order to ensure compliance with government regulations and standards for sanitation, safety, quality, and waste management standards. Search for substitutes for harmful or undesirable additives, such as nitrites.

Personality Type: Investigative. These occupations frequently involve working with ideas and require an extensive amount of thinking. They can involve searching for facts and figuring out problems mentally.

GOE—Interest Area/Cluster: 01. Agriculture and Natural Resources. **Work Group:** 01.03. Resource Technologies for Plants, Animals, and the Environment. **Other Jobs in This Work Group:** Agricultural and Food Science Technicians; Agricultural Technicians; Environmental Science and Protection Technicians, Including Health; Food Science Technicians; Geological and Petroleum Technicians; Geological Sample Test Technicians; Geophysical Data Technicians.

Skills—Quality Control Analysis: Evaluating the quality or performance of products, services, or processes. **Science:** Using scientific methods to solve problems. **Troubleshooting:** Determining what is causing an operating error and deciding what to do about it. **Operations Analysis:** Analyzing needs and product requirements to create a design. **Mathematics:** Using mathematics to solve problems. **Reading Comprehension:** Understanding written sentences and paragraphs in work-related documents. **Operation Monitoring:** Watching gauges, dials, or other indicators to make sure a machine is working properly. **Monitoring:** Assessing how well one is doing when learning or doing something.

Education and Training Programs: Agriculture, General; Food Science; Food Technology and Processing; International Agriculture. **Related Knowledge/Courses—Food Production:** Techniques and equipment for planting, growing, and harvesting of food for consumption, including crop-rotation methods, animal husbandry, and food storage/handling techniques. **Chemistry:** The composition, structure, and properties of substances and of the chemical processes and transformations that they undergo. This includes uses of chemicals and their interactions, danger signs, production techniques, and disposal methods. **Production and Processing:** Inputs, outputs, raw materials, waste, quality control, costs, and techniques for maximizing the manufacture and distribution of goods. **Biology:** Plant and animal living tissue, cells, organisms, and entities, including their functions, interdependencies, and interactions with each other and the environment. **Physics:** Physical principles, laws, and applications, including air, water, material dynamics, light, atomic principles, heat, electric theory, earth formations, and meteorological and related natural phenomena. **Engineering and Technology:** Equipment, tools, and mechanical devices and their uses to produce motion, light, power, technology, and other applications.

Work Environment: Indoors; noisy; hazardous conditions; sitting.

Food Service Managers

❋ Education/Training Required: Work experience in a related occupation

❋ Annual Earnings: $44,570

❋ Beginning Wage: $28,240

❋ Earnings Growth Potential: Medium

❋ Growth: 5.0%

❋ Annual Job Openings: 59,302

❋ Self-Employed: 44.8%

❋ Part-Time: 8.0%

Plan, direct, or coordinate activities of an organization or department that serves food and beverages. Monitor compliance with health and fire regulations regarding food preparation and serving, and building maintenance in lodging and dining facilities. Monitor food preparation methods, portion sizes, and garnishing and presentation of food to ensure that food is prepared and presented in an acceptable manner. Count money and make bank deposits. Investigate and resolve complaints regarding food quality, service, or accommodations. Coordinate assignments of cooking personnel to ensure economical use of food and timely preparation. Schedule and receive food and beverage deliveries, checking delivery contents to verify product quality and quantity. Monitor budgets and payroll records, and review financial transactions to ensure that expenditures are authorized and budgeted. Schedule staff hours and assign duties. Maintain food and equipment inventories, and keep inventory records. Establish standards for personnel performance and customer service. Perform some food preparation or service tasks such as cooking, clearing tables, and serving food and drinks when necessary. Plan menus and food utilization based on anticipated number of guests, nutritional value, palatability, popularity, and costs. Keep records required by government agencies regarding sanitation, and food subsidies when appropriate. Test cooked food by tasting and smelling it to ensure palatability and flavor conformity. Organize and direct worker training programs, resolve personnel problems, hire new staff, and evaluate employee performance in dining and lodging facilities. Order and purchase equipment and supplies. Review work procedures and operational problems to determine ways to improve service, performance, or safety. Assess staffing needs, and recruit staff using methods such as newspaper advertisements or attendance at job fairs. Arrange for equipment maintenance and repairs, and coordinate a variety of services such as waste removal and pest control. Record the number, type, and cost of items sold to determine which items may be unpopular or less profitable. Review menus and analyze recipes to determine labor and overhead costs, and assign prices to menu items.

Personality Type: Enterprising. These occupations frequently involve starting up and carrying out projects and can involve leading people and making many decisions. They sometimes require risk taking and often deal with business.

GOE—Interest Area/Cluster: 09. Hospitality, Tourism, and Recreation. **Work Group:** 09.01. Managerial Work in Hospitality and Tourism. **Other Jobs in This Work Group:** First-Line Supervisors/Managers of Food Preparation and Serving Workers; First-Line Supervisors/Managers of Personal Service Workers; Gaming Managers; Gaming Supervisors; Lodging Managers.

Skills—Management of Financial Resources: Determining how money will be spent to get the work done and accounting for these expenditures. **Management of Personnel Resources:** Motivating, developing, and directing people as they work; identifying the best people for the job. **Systems Evaluation:** Looking at many indicators of system performance and taking into account their accuracy. **Management of Material Resources:** Obtaining and seeing to the appropriate use of equipment, facilities, and materials needed to do certain work. **Systems Analysis:** Determining how a system should work and how changes will affect outcomes. **Negotiation:** Bringing others together and trying to reconcile differences. **Service Orientation:** Actively looking for ways to help people. **Persuasion:** Persuading others to approach things differently.

Education and Training Programs: Hospitality Administration/Management, General; Hotel/Motel Administration/Management; Restaurant, Culinary, and Catering Management/Manager Training; Restaurant/Food Services Management. **Related Knowledge/Courses—Food Production:** Techniques and equipment for planting, growing, and harvesting of food for consumption, including crop-rotation methods, animal husbandry, and food storage/handling techniques. **Sales and Marketing:** Principles and methods involved in showing, promoting, and selling products or services. This includes marketing strategies and tactics, product demonstration and sales techniques, and sales control systems. **Personnel and Human Resources:** Principles and procedures for personnel recruitment; selection; training; compensation and benefits; labor relations and negotiation; and personnel information systems. **Production and Processing:** Inputs, outputs, raw materials, waste, quality control, costs, and techniques for maximizing the manufacture and distribution of goods. **Education and Training:** Instructional methods and training techniques, including curriculum design principles, learning theory, group and individual teaching techniques, design of individual development plans, and test design principles. **Administration and Management:** Principles and processes involved in business and organizational planning, coordination, and execution. This includes strategic planning, resource allocation, manpower modeling, leadership techniques, and production methods.

Work Environment: Indoors; noisy; standing; walking and running; using hands on objects, tools, or controls; repetitive motions.

Foreign Language and Literature Teachers, Postsecondary

- ❋ Education/Training Required: Doctoral degree
- ❋ Annual Earnings: $53,610
- ❋ Beginning Wage: $30,590
- ❋ Earnings Growth Potential: High
- ❋ Growth: 22.9%
- ❋ Annual Job Openings: 4,317
- ❋ Self-Employed: 0.4%
- ❋ Part-Time: 27.8%

Teach courses in foreign (i.e., other than English) languages and literature. Evaluate and grade students' classwork, assignments, and papers. Prepare course materials such as syllabi, homework assignments, and handouts. Initiate, facilitate, and moderate classroom discussions. Maintain student attendance records, grades, and other required records. Compile, administer, and grade examinations or assign this work to others. Plan, evaluate, and revise curricula, course content, and course materials and methods of instruction. Prepare and deliver lectures to undergraduate and graduate students on topics such as how to speak and write a foreign language and the cultural aspects of areas where a particular language is used. Maintain regularly scheduled office hours to advise and assist students. Select and obtain materials and supplies such as textbooks. Keep abreast of developments in their field by reading current literature, talking with colleagues, and participating in professional organizations and activities. Advise students on academic and vocational curricula and on career issues.

Conduct research in a particular field of knowledge and publish findings in scholarly journals, books, and/or electronic media. Collaborate with colleagues to address teaching and research issues. Serve on academic or administrative committees that deal with institutional policies, departmental matters, and academic issues. Participate in student recruitment, registration, and placement activities. Compile bibliographies of specialized materials for outside reading assignments. Participate in campus and community events. Act as advisers to student organizations. Perform administrative duties such as serving as department head. Supervise undergraduate and graduate teaching, internship, and research work. Write grant proposals to procure external research funding. Provide professional consulting services to government or industry.

Personality Type: Social. These occupations frequently involve working with, communicating with, and teaching people and often involve helping or providing service to others.

GOE—Interest Area/Cluster: 05. Education and Training. **Work Group:** 05.03. Postsecondary and Adult Teaching and Instructing. **Other Jobs in This Work Group:** Adult Literacy, Remedial Education, and GED Teachers and Instructors; Agricultural Sciences Teachers, Postsecondary; Anthropology and Archeology Teachers, Postsecondary; Architecture Teachers, Postsecondary; Area, Ethnic, and Cultural Studies Teachers, Postsecondary; Art, Drama, and Music Teachers, Postsecondary; Atmospheric, Earth, Marine, and Space Sciences Teachers, Postsecondary; Biological Science Teachers, Postsecondary; Business Teachers, Postsecondary; Chemistry Teachers, Postsecondary; Communications Teachers, Postsecondary; Computer Science Teachers, Postsecondary; Criminal Justice and Law Enforcement Teachers, Postsecondary; Economics Teachers, Postsecondary; Education Teachers, Postsecondary; Engineering Teachers, Postsecondary; English Language and Literature Teachers, Postsecondary; Environmental Science Teachers, Postsecondary; Farm and Home Management Advisors; Forestry and Conservation Science Teachers, Postsecondary; Geography Teachers, Postsecondary; Graduate Teaching Assistants; Health Specialties Teachers, Postsecondary; History Teachers, Postsecondary; Home Economics Teachers, Postsecondary; Law Teachers, Postsecondary; Library Science Teachers, Postsecondary; Mathematical Science Teachers, Postsecondary; Nursing Instructors and Teachers, Postsecondary; Philosophy and Religion Teachers, Postsecondary; Physics Teachers, Postsecondary; Political Science Teachers, Postsecondary; Psychology Teachers, Postsecondary; Recreation and Fitness

Studies Teachers, Postsecondary; Self-Enrichment Education Teachers; Social Work Teachers, Postsecondary; Sociology Teachers, Postsecondary; Vocational Education Teachers, Postsecondary.

Skills—Learning Strategies: Using multiple approaches when learning or teaching new things. **Instructing:** Teaching others how to do something. **Writing:** Communicating effectively with others in writing as indicated by the needs of the audience. **Reading Comprehension:** Understanding written sentences and paragraphs in work-related documents. **Speaking:** Talking to others to effectively convey information. **Persuasion:** Persuading others to approach things differently. **Social Perceptiveness:** Being aware of others' reactions and understanding why they react the way they do. **Critical Thinking:** Using logic and analysis to identify the strengths and weaknesses of different approaches.

Education and Training Programs: Arabic Language and Literature; Chinese Language and Literature; Classics and Classical Languages, Literatures, and Linguistics, General; Foreign Languages, Literatures, and Linguistics, others; French Language and Literature; German Language and Literature; Italian Language and Literature; Japanese Language and Literature; Russian Language and Literature; Spanish Language and Literature. **Related Knowledge/Courses— Foreign Language:** The structure and content of a foreign (non-English) language, including the meaning and spelling of words, rules of composition and grammar, and pronunciation. **Philosophy and Theology:** Different philosophical systems and religions, including their basic principles, values, ethics, ways of thinking, customs, and practices and their impact on human culture. **History and Archeology:** Historical events and their causes, indicators, and impact on particular civilizations and cultures. **Sociology and Anthropology:** Group behavior and dynamics; societal trends and influences; and cultures and their history, migrations, ethnicity, and origins. **Geography:** Various methods for describing the location and distribution of land, sea, and air masses, including their physical locations, relationships, and characteristics. **English Language:** The structure and content of the English language, including the meaning and spelling of words, rules of composition, and grammar.

Work Environment: Indoors; sitting.

Forensic Science Technicians

✳ Education/Training Required: Bachelor's degree
✳ Annual Earnings: $47,680
✳ Beginning Wage: $29,170
✳ Earnings Growth Potential: Medium
✳ Growth: 30.7%
✳ Annual Job Openings: 3,074
✳ Self-Employed: 1.3%
✳ Part-Time: 19.4%

Collect, identify, classify, and analyze physical evidence related to criminal investigations. Perform tests on weapons or substances such as fiber, hair, and tissue to determine significance to investigation. May testify as expert witnesses on evidence or crime laboratory techniques. May serve as specialists in area of expertise, such as ballistics, fingerprinting, handwriting, or biochemistry. Testify in court about investigative and analytical methods and findings. Keep records and prepare reports detailing findings, investigative methods, and laboratory techniques. Interpret laboratory findings and test results to identify and classify substances, materials, and other evidence collected at crime scenes. Operate and maintain laboratory equipment and apparatus. Prepare solutions, reagents, and sample formulations needed for laboratory work. Analyze and classify biological fluids, using DNA typing or serological techniques. Collect evidence from crime scenes, storing it in conditions that preserve its integrity. Identify and quantify drugs and poisons found in biological fluids and tissues, in foods, and at crime scenes. Analyze handwritten and machine-produced textual evidence to decipher altered or obliterated text or to determine authorship, age, or source. Reconstruct crime scenes to determine relationships among pieces of evidence. Examine DNA samples to determine if they match other samples. Collect impressions of dust from surfaces to obtain and identify fingerprints. Analyze gunshot residue and bullet paths to determine how shootings occurred. Visit morgues, examine scenes of crimes, or contact other sources to obtain evidence or information to be used in investigations. Examine physical evidence such as hair, fiber, wood, or soil residues to obtain information about its source and composition. Determine types of bullets used in shooting and whether they were fired from a specific weapon. Examine firearms to determine mechanical condition and legal status, performing restoration work on damaged firearms to obtain information such as serial numbers. Confer with ballistics, fingerprinting, handwriting, document, electronics, medical, chemical, or metallurgical experts concerning evidence and its interpretation. Interpret the pharmacological effects of a drug or a combination of drugs on an individual. Compare objects such as tools with impression marks to determine whether a specific object is responsible for a specific mark.

Personality Type: Investigative. These occupations frequently involve working with ideas and require an extensive amount of thinking. They can involve searching for facts and figuring out problems mentally.

GOE—Interest Area/Cluster: 12. Law and Public Safety. **Work Group:** 12.04. Law Enforcement and Public Safety. **Other Jobs in This Work Group:** Bailiffs; Correctional Officers and Jailers; Criminal Investigators and Special Agents; Detectives and Criminal Investigators; Fire Investigators; Parking Enforcement Workers; Police and Sheriff's Patrol Officers; Police Detectives; Police Identification and Records Officers; Police Patrol Officers; Sheriffs and Deputy Sheriffs; Transit and Railroad Police.

Skills—Science: Using scientific methods to solve problems. **Quality Control Analysis:** Evaluating the quality or performance of products, services, or processes. **Troubleshooting:** Determining what is causing an operating error and deciding what to do about it. **Speaking:** Talking to others to effectively convey information. **Equipment Selection:** Determining the kind of tools and equipment needed to do a job. **Active Learning:** Working with new material or information to grasp its implications. **Reading Comprehension:** Understanding written sentences and paragraphs in work-related documents. **Monitoring:** Assessing how well one is doing when learning or doing something.

Education and Training Program: Forensic Science and Technology. **Related Knowledge/Courses—Chemistry:** The composition, structure, and properties of substances and of the chemical processes and transformations that they undergo. This includes uses of chemicals and their interactions, danger signs, production techniques, and disposal methods. **Law and Government:** Laws, legal codes, court procedures, precedents, government regulations, executive orders, agency rules, and the democratic political process. **Biology:** Plant and animal living tissue, cells, organisms, and entities, including their functions, interdependencies, and interactions with each other and the environment. **Public Safety and Security:** Weaponry; public safety; security operations, rules, regulations, precautions, and prevention; and the protection of people, data, and property. **English Language:** The structure and content of the English language, including the meaning and spelling of words, rules of composition, and grammar. **Clerical Practices:** Administrative and clerical procedures and systems such as word-processing systems, filing and records management systems, stenography and transcription, forms, design principles, and other office procedures and terminology.

Work Environment: Indoors; contaminants; disease or infections; hazardous conditions; sitting.

Forest Fire Fighters

- ❊ Education/Training Required: Long-term on-the-job training
- ❊ Annual Earnings: $43,170
- ❊ Beginning Wage: $21,530
- ❊ Earnings Growth Potential: Very high
- ❊ Growth: 12.1%
- ❊ Annual Job Openings: 18,887
- ❊ Self-Employed: 0.0%
- ❊ Part-Time: 1.3%

The job openings listed here are shared with Municipal Fire Fighters.

Control and suppress fires in forests or vacant public land. Maintain contact with fire dispatchers at all times to notify them of the need for additional firefighters and supplies or to detail any difficulties encountered. Rescue fire victims and administer emergency medical aid. Collaborate with other firefighters as a member of a firefighting crew. Patrol burned areas after fires to locate and eliminate hot spots that may restart fires. Extinguish flames and embers to suppress fires, using shovels or engine- or hand-driven water or chemical pumps. Fell trees, cut and clear brush, and dig trenches to create firelines, using axes, chain saws, or shovels. Maintain knowledge of current firefighting practices by participating in drills and by attending seminars, conventions, and conferences. Operate pumps connected to high-pressure hoses. Participate in physical training to maintain high levels of physical fitness. Establish water supplies, connect hoses, and direct water onto fires. Maintain fire equipment and firehouse living quarters. Inform and educate the public about fire prevention. Take action to contain any hazardous chemicals that could catch fire, leak, or spill. Organize fire caches, positioning equipment for the most effective response. Transport personnel and cargo to and from fire areas. Participate in fire prevention and inspection programs. Perform forest maintenance and improvement tasks such as cutting brush, planting trees, building trails, and marking timber. Test and maintain tools, equipment, jump gear, and parachutes to ensure readiness for fire-suppression activities. Observe forest areas from fire lookout towers to spot potential problems. Orient self in relation to fire, using compass and map, and collect supplies and equipment dropped by parachute. Serve as fully trained lead helicopter crewmember and as helispot manager. Drop weighted paper streamers from aircraft to determine the speed and direction of the wind at fire sites.

Personality Type: Realistic. These occupations frequently involve work activities that include practical, hands-on problems and solutions. They often deal with plants; animals; and real-world materials such as wood, tools, and machinery. Many of the occupations require working outside and don't involve a lot of paperwork or working closely with others.

GOE—Interest Area/Cluster: 12. Law and Public Safety. **Work Group:** 12.06. Emergency Responding. **Other Jobs in This Work Group:** Emergency Medical Technicians and Paramedics; Fire Fighters; Municipal Fire Fighters.

Skills—Repairing: Repairing machines or systems, using the needed tools. **Equipment Maintenance:** Performing routine maintenance and determining when and what kind of maintenance is needed. **Management of Personnel Resources:** Motivating, developing, and directing people as they work; identifying the best people for the job. **Operation Monitoring:** Watching gauges, dials, or other indicators to make sure a machine is working properly. **Equipment Selection:** Determining the kind of tools and equipment needed to do a job. **Operation and Control:** Controlling operations of equipment or systems. **Systems Analysis:** Determining how a system should work and how changes will affect outcomes. **Operations Analysis:** Analyzing needs and product requirements to create a design.

Education and Training Programs: Fire Protection, Other; Fire Science/Firefighting. **Related Knowledge/Courses—Geography:** Various methods for describing the location and distribution of land, sea, and air masses, including their physical locations, relationships, and characteristics. **Customer and Personal Service:** Principles and processes for providing customer and personal services, including needs assessment techniques, quality service standards, alternative delivery systems, and customer satisfaction evaluation techniques. **Mechanical Devices:** Machines and tools, including their designs, uses, benefits, repair, and maintenance. **Public Safety and Security:** Weaponry; public safety; security operations, rules, regulations, precautions, and prevention;

and the protection of people, data, and property. **Education and Training:** Instructional methods and training techniques, including curriculum design principles, learning theory, group and individual teaching techniques, design of individual development plans, and test design principles. **Psychology:** Human behavior and performance, mental processes, psychological research methods, and the assessment and treatment of behavioral and affective disorders.

Work Environment: Outdoors; very hot or cold; contaminants; hazardous conditions; minor burns, cuts, bites, or stings; using hands on objects, tools, or controls.

Forest Fire Fighting and Prevention Supervisors

- ❋ Education/Training Required: Work experience in a related occupation
- ❋ Annual Earnings: $65,040
- ❋ Beginning Wage: $37,930
- ❋ Earnings Growth Potential: High
- ❋ Growth: 11.5%
- ❋ Annual Job Openings: 3,771
- ❋ Self-Employed: 0.0%
- ❋ Part-Time: 0.4%

The job openings listed here are shared with Municipal Fire Fighting and Prevention Supervisors.

Supervise fire fighters who control and suppress fires in forests or vacant public land. Communicate fire details to superiors, subordinates, and interagency dispatch centers, using two-way radios. Serve as working leader of an engine, hand, helicopter, or prescribed fire crew of three or more firefighters. Maintain fire suppression equipment in good condition, checking equipment periodically to ensure that it is ready for use. Evaluate size, location, and condition of forest fires in order to request and dispatch crews and position equipment so fires can be contained safely and effectively. Operate wildland fire engines and hoselays. Direct and supervise prescribed burn projects and prepare post-burn reports analyzing burn conditions and results. Monitor prescribed burns to ensure that they are conducted safely and effectively. Identify staff training and development needs to ensure that appropriate training can be arranged. Maintain knowledge of forest fire laws and fire prevention techniques and tactics. Recommend equipment modifications or new equipment purchases. Perform administrative duties such as compiling and maintaining records, completing forms, preparing reports, and composing correspondence. Recruit and hire forest fire-fighting personnel. Train workers in such skills as parachute jumping, fire suppression, aerial observation, and radio communication, both in the classroom and on the job. Review and evaluate employee performance. Observe fires and crews from air to determine fire-fighting force requirements and to note changing conditions that will affect fire-fighting efforts. Inspect all stations, uniforms, equipment, and recreation areas to ensure compliance with safety standards, taking corrective action as necessary. Schedule employee work assignments and set work priorities. Regulate open burning by issuing burning permits, inspecting problem sites, issuing citations for violations of laws and ordinances, and educating the public in proper burning practices. Direct investigations of suspected arsons in wildfires, working closely with other investigating agencies. Monitor fire suppression expenditures to ensure that they are necessary and reasonable.

Personality Type: Enterprising. These occupations frequently involve starting up and carrying out projects and can involve leading people and making many decisions. They sometimes require risk taking and often deal with business.

GOE—Interest Area/Cluster: 12. Law and Public Safety. **Work Group:** 12.01. Managerial Work in Law and Public Safety. **Other Jobs in This Work Group:** Emergency Management Specialists; First-Line Supervisors/Managers of Correctional Officers; First-Line Supervisors/Managers of Fire Fighting and Prevention Workers; First-Line Supervisors/Managers of Police and Detectives; Municipal Fire Fighting and Prevention Supervisors.

Skills—Equipment Maintenance: Performing routine maintenance and determining when and what kind of maintenance is needed. **Repairing:** Repairing machines or systems, using the needed tools. **Operation Monitoring:** Watching gauges, dials, or other indicators to make sure a machine is working properly. **Management of Personnel Resources:** Motivating, developing, and directing people as they work; identifying the best people for the job. **Operation and Control:** Controlling operations of equipment or systems. **Science:** Using scientific methods to solve problems. **Management of Material Resources:** Obtaining and seeing to the appropriate use of equipment, facilities, and materials needed to do certain work. **Equipment Selection:** Determining the kind of tools and equipment needed to do a job.

Education and Training Programs: Fire Protection and Safety Technology/Technician Training; Fire Services Administration. **Related Knowledge/Courses—Public Safety and Security:** Weaponry; public safety; security operations, rules, regulations, precautions, and prevention; and the protection of people, data, and property. **Building and Construction:** Materials, methods, and the appropriate tools to construct objects, structures, and buildings. **Mechanical Devices:** Machines and tools, including their designs, uses, benefits, repair, and maintenance. **Customer and Personal Service:** Principles and processes for providing customer and personal services, including needs assessment techniques, quality service standards, alternative delivery systems, and customer satisfaction evaluation techniques. **Personnel and Human Resources:** Principles and procedures for personnel recruitment; selection; training; compensation and benefits; labor relations and negotiation; and personnel information systems. **Transportation:** Principles and methods for moving people or goods by air, rail, sea, or road, including their relative costs, advantages, and limitations.

Work Environment: Outdoors; noisy; very hot or cold; hazardous equipment; minor burns, cuts, bites, or stings; standing.

Forestry and Conservation Science Teachers, Postsecondary

- ❀ Education/Training Required: Doctoral degree
- ❀ Annual Earnings: $63,790
- ❀ Beginning Wage: $36,270
- ❀ Earnings Growth Potential: High
- ❀ Growth: 22.9%
- ❀ Annual Job Openings: 454
- ❀ Self-Employed: 0.4%
- ❀ Part-Time: 27.8%

Teach courses in environmental and conservation science. Conduct research in a particular field of knowledge and publish findings in books, professional journals, and/or electronic media. Keep abreast of developments in their field by reading current literature, talking with colleagues, and participating in professional conferences. Prepare and deliver lectures to undergraduate and/or graduate students on topics such as forest resource policy, forest pathology, and mapping. Evaluate and grade students' classwork, assignments, and papers. Write grant proposals to procure external research funding. Supervise undergraduate and/or graduate teaching, internship, and research work. Plan, evaluate, and revise curricula, course content, and course materials and methods of instruction. Prepare course materials such as syllabi, homework assignments, and handouts. Compile, administer, and grade examinations or assign this work to others. Advise students on academic and vocational curricula and on career issues. Initiate, facilitate, and moderate classroom discussions. Supervise students' laboratory work and fieldwork. Maintain student attendance records, grades, and other required records. Collaborate with colleagues to address teaching and research issues. Maintain regularly scheduled office hours in order to advise and assist students. Select and obtain materials and supplies such as textbooks and laboratory equipment. Participate in student recruitment, registration, and placement activities. Serve on academic or administrative committees that deal with institutional policies, departmental matters, and academic issues. Provide professional consulting services to government and/or industry. Perform administrative duties such as serving as department head. Compile bibliographies of specialized materials for outside reading assignments. Act as advisers to student organizations. Participate in campus and community events.

Personality Type: Social. These occupations frequently involve working with, communicating with, and teaching people and often involve helping or providing service to others.

GOE—Interest Area/Cluster: 05. Education and Training. **Work Group:** 05.03. Postsecondary and Adult Teaching and Instructing. **Other Jobs in This Work Group:** Adult Literacy, Remedial Education, and GED Teachers and Instructors; Agricultural Sciences Teachers, Postsecondary; Anthropology and Archeology Teachers, Postsecondary; Architecture Teachers, Postsecondary; Area, Ethnic, and Cultural Studies Teachers, Postsecondary; Art, Drama, and Music Teachers, Postsecondary; Atmospheric, Earth, Marine, and Space Sciences Teachers, Postsecondary; Biological Science Teachers, Postsecondary; Business Teachers, Postsecondary; Chemistry Teachers, Postsecondary; Communications Teachers, Postsecondary; Computer Science Teachers, Postsecondary; Criminal Justice and Law Enforcement Teachers, Postsecondary; Economics Teachers, Postsecondary; Education Teachers, Postsecondary; Engineering Teachers, Postsecondary; English Language and Literature Teachers, Postsecondary; Environmental Science Teachers, Postsecondary; Farm and Home Management Advisors; Foreign Language and Literature Teachers, Postsecondary; Geography Teachers, Postsecondary; Graduate Teaching Assistants; Health Specialties Teachers, Postsecondary; History Teachers, Postsecondary; Home Economics Teachers, Postsecondary; Law Teachers, Postsecondary; Library Science Teachers, Postsecondary; Mathematical Science Teachers, Postsecondary; Nursing Instructors and Teachers, Postsecondary; Philosophy and Religion Teachers, Postsecondary; Physics Teachers, Postsecondary; Political Science Teachers, Postsecondary; Psychology Teachers, Postsecondary; Recreation and Fitness Studies Teachers, Postsecondary; Self-Enrichment Education Teachers; Social Work Teachers, Postsecondary; Sociology Teachers, Postsecondary; Vocational Education Teachers, Postsecondary.

Skills—Science: Using scientific methods to solve problems. **Management of Financial Resources:** Determining how money will be spent to get the work done and accounting for these expenditures. **Writing:** Communicating effectively with others in writing as indicated by the needs of the audience. **Instructing:** Teaching others how to do something. **Mathematics:** Using mathematics to solve problems. **Management of Personnel Resources:** Motivating, developing, and directing people as they work; identifying the best people for the job. **Complex Problem Solving:** Identifying complex problems, reviewing the options, and implementing solutions. **Active Learning:** Working with new material or information to grasp its implications.

Education and Training Program: Science Teacher Education/General Science Teacher Education. **Related Knowledge/Courses—Biology:** Plant and animal living tissue, cells, organisms, and entities, including their functions, interdependencies, and interactions with each other and the environment. **Geography:** Various methods for describing the location and distribution of land, sea, and air masses, including their physical locations, relationships, and characteristics. **Education and Training:** Instructional methods and training techniques, including curriculum design principles, learning theory, group and individual teaching techniques, design of individual development plans, and test design principles. **Mathematics:** Numbers and their operations and interrelationships, including arithmetic, algebra, geometry, calculus, and statistics and their applications. **Chemistry:** The composition, structure, and properties of substances and of the chemical processes and transformations that they undergo. This includes uses of chemicals and their interactions, danger signs, production techniques, and disposal methods. **History and Archeology:** Historical events and their causes, indicators, and impact on particular civilizations and cultures.

Work Environment: Indoors; sitting.

Freight and Cargo Inspectors

- ❋ Education/Training Required: Work experience in a related occupation
- ❋ Annual Earnings: $51,440
- ❋ Beginning Wage: $27,340
- ❋ Earnings Growth Potential: High
- ❋ Growth: 16.4%
- ❋ Annual Job Openings: 2,122
- ❋ Self-Employed: 5.9%
- ❋ Part-Time: 3.7%

The job openings listed here are shared with Aviation Inspectors; and with Transportation Vehicle, Equipment, and Systems Inspectors, Except Aviation.

Inspect the handling, storage, and stowing of freight and cargoes. Prepare and submit reports after completion of freight shipments. Inspect shipments to ensure that freight is securely braced and blocked. Record details about freight conditions, handling of freight, and any problems encountered. Advise crews in techniques of stowing dangerous and heavy cargo. Observe loading of freight to ensure that crews comply with procedures. Recommend remedial procedures to correct any violations found during inspections. Inspect loaded cargo, cargo lashed to decks or in storage facilities, and cargo handling devices to determine compliance with health and safety regulations and need for maintenance. Measure ships' holds and depths of fuel and water in tanks, using sounding lines and tape measures. Notify workers of any special treatment required for shipments. Direct crews to reload freight or to insert additional bracing or packing as necessary. Check temperatures and humidities of shipping and storage areas to ensure that they are at appropriate levels to protect cargo. Determine cargo transportation capabilities by reading documents that set forth cargo loading and securing procedures, capacities, and stability factors. Read draft markings to determine depths of vessels in water. Issue certificates of compliance for vessels without violations. Write certificates of admeasurement that list details such as designs, lengths, depths, and breadths of vessels, and methods of propulsion. Calculate gross and net tonnage, hold capacities, volumes of stored fuel and water, cargo weights, and ship stability factors, using mathematical formulas. Post warning signs on vehicles containing explosives or flammable or radioactive materials. Measure heights and widths of loads to ensure they will pass over bridges or through tunnels on scheduled routes. Time rolls of ships, using stopwatches. Determine types of licenses and safety equipment required, and compute applicable fees such as tolls and wharfage fees.

Personality Type: Realistic. These occupations frequently involve work activities that include practical, hands-on problems and solutions. They often deal with plants; animals; and real-world materials such as wood, tools, and machinery. Many of the occupations require working outside and don't involve a lot of paperwork or working closely with others.

GOE—Interest Area/Cluster: 07. Government and Public Administration. **Work Group:** 07.03. Regulations Enforcement. **Other Jobs in This Work Group:** Agricultural Inspectors; Aviation Inspectors; Compliance Officers, Except Agriculture, Construction, Health and Safety, and Transportation; Construction and Building Inspectors; Environmental Compliance Inspectors; Equal Opportunity Representatives and Officers; Financial Examiners; Fire Inspectors; Fish and Game Wardens; Forest Fire Inspectors and Prevention Specialists; Government Property Inspectors and Investigators; Immigration and Customs Inspectors; Licensing Examiners and Inspectors; Nuclear Monitoring Technicians; Occupational Health and Safety Specialists; Occupational Health and Safety Technicians; Tax Examiners, Collectors, and Revenue Agents; Transportation Vehicle, Equipment, and Systems Inspectors, Except Aviation.

Skills—Operation Monitoring: Watching gauges, dials, or other indicators to make sure a machine is working properly. **Quality Control Analysis:** Evaluating the quality or performance of products, services, or processes. **Science:** Using scientific methods to solve problems. **Mathematics:** Using mathematics to solve problems. **Writing:** Communicating effectively with others in writing as indicated by the needs of the audience. **Service Orientation:** Actively looking for ways to help people. **Equipment Selection:** Determining the kind of tools and equipment needed to do a job. **Troubleshooting:** Determining what is causing an operating error and deciding what to do about it.

Education and Training Programs: No related CIP programs; this job is learned through work experience in a related occupation; this job is learned through work experience in a related occupation. **Related Knowledge/Courses—Transportation:** Principles and methods for moving people or goods by air, rail, sea, or road, including their relative costs, advantages, and limitations. **Engineering and Technology:** Equipment, tools, and mechanical devices and their uses to produce motion, light, power, technology, and other applications. **Public Safety and Security:** Weaponry; public safety;

security operations, rules, regulations, precautions, and prevention; and the protection of people, data, and property. **Physics:** Physical principles, laws, and applications, including air, water, material dynamics, light, atomic principles, heat, electric theory, earth formations, and meteorological and related natural phenomena. **Geography:** Various methods for describing the location and distribution of land, sea, and air masses, including their physical locations, relationships, and characteristics. **Mechanical Devices:** Machines and tools, including their designs, uses, benefits, repair, and maintenance.

Work Environment: More often outdoors than indoors; noisy; very hot or cold; very bright or dim lighting; contaminants.

Funeral Directors

- ❈ Education/Training Required: Associate degree
- ❈ Annual Earnings: $50,370
- ❈ Beginning Wage: $28,890
- ❈ Earnings Growth Potential: High
- ❈ Growth: 12.5%
- ❈ Annual Job Openings: 3,939
- ❈ Self-Employed: 19.7%
- ❈ Part-Time: 8.5%

Perform various tasks to arrange and direct funeral services, such as coordinating transportation of bodies to mortuaries for embalming, interviewing families or other authorized people to arrange details, selecting pallbearers, procuring officials for religious rites, and providing transportation for mourners. Obtain information needed to complete legal documents such as death certificates and burial permits. Oversee the preparation and care of the remains of people who have died. Consult with families or friends of the deceased to arrange funeral details such as obituary notice wording, casket selection, and plans for services. Plan, schedule, and coordinate funerals, burials, and cremations, arranging details such as floral delivery and the time and place of services. Perform embalming duties as necessary. Arrange for clergy members to perform needed services. Contact cemeteries to schedule the opening and closing of graves. Provide information on funeral service options, products, and merchandise, and maintain a casket display area. Close caskets and lead funeral corteges to churches or burial sites. Offer counsel and comfort to bereaved families and friends. Inform survivors of benefits for which they may be eligible. Discuss and negotiate prearranged funerals with clients. Maintain financial records, order merchandise, and prepare accounts. Provide or arrange transportation between sites for the remains, mourners, pallbearers, clergy, and flowers. Plan placement of caskets at funeral sites, and place and adjust lights, fixtures, and floral displays. Direct preparations and shipment of bodies for out-of-state burials. Manage funeral home operations, including the hiring, training, and supervision of embalmers, funeral attendants, or other staff. Clean funeral home facilities and grounds. Arrange for pallbearers, and inform pallbearers and honorary groups of their duties. Receive and usher people to their seats for services. Participate in community activities for funeral home promotion or other purposes.

Personality Type: Enterprising. These occupations frequently involve starting up and carrying out projects and can involve leading people and making many decisions. They sometimes require risk taking and often deal with business.

GOE—Interest Area/Cluster: 14. Retail and Wholesale Sales and Service. **Work Group:** 14.01. Managerial Work in Retail/Wholesale Sales and Service. **Other Jobs in This Work Group:** Advertising and Promotions Managers; First-Line Supervisors/Managers of Non-Retail Sales Workers; First-Line Supervisors/Managers of Retail Sales Workers; Marketing Managers; Property, Real Estate, and Community Association Managers; Purchasing Managers; Sales Managers.

Skills—Management of Personnel Resources: Motivating, developing, and directing people as they work; identifying the best people for the job. **Social Perceptiveness:** Being aware of others' reactions and understanding why they react the way they do. **Negotiation:** Bringing others together and trying to reconcile differences. **Management of Financial Resources:** Determining how money will be spent to get the work done and accounting for these expenditures. **Service Orientation:** Actively looking for ways to help people.

Education and Training Programs: Funeral Direction/Service; Funeral Service and Mortuary Science, General. **Related Knowledge/Courses—Chemistry:** The composition, structure, and properties of substances and of the chemical processes and transformations that they undergo. This includes uses of chemicals and their interactions, danger signs, production techniques, and disposal methods. **Philosophy and Theology:** Different philosophical systems and religions, including their basic principles, values, ethics, ways of thinking, customs, and practices and their impact on human culture. **Therapy and Counseling:** Information and techniques needed to rehabilitate physical and mental ailments and to provide career guidance, including alternative treatments, rehabilitation equipment and its proper use, and methods to evaluate treatment effects. **Customer and Personal Service:** Principles and processes for providing customer and personal services, including needs assessment techniques, quality service standards, alternative delivery systems, and customer satisfaction evaluation techniques. **Biology:** Plant and animal living tissue, cells, organisms, and entities, including their functions, interdependencies, and interactions with each other and the environment. **Sales and Marketing:** Principles and methods involved in showing, promoting, and selling products or services. This includes marketing strategies and tactics, product demonstration and sales techniques, and sales control systems.

Work Environment: More often indoors than outdoors; contaminants; disease or infections; standing; using hands on objects, tools, or controls.

Gaming Managers

- ❋ Education/Training Required: Work experience in a related occupation
- ❋ Annual Earnings: $64,410
- ❋ Beginning Wage: $36,740
- ❋ Earnings Growth Potential: High
- ❋ Growth: 24.4%
- ❋ Annual Job Openings: 549
- ❋ Self-Employed: 16.3%
- ❋ Part-Time: 4.5%

Plan, organize, direct, control, or coordinate gaming operations in a casino. Formulate gaming policies for their area of responsibility. Resolve customer complaints regarding problems such as payout errors. Remove suspected cheaters, such as card counters and other players who may have systems that shift the odds of winning to their favor. Maintain familiarity with all games used at a facility, as well as strategies and tricks employed in those games. Train new workers and evaluate their performance. Circulate among gaming tables to ensure that operations are conducted properly, that dealers follow house rules, and that players are not cheating. Explain and interpret house rules, such as game rules and betting limits. Monitor staffing levels to ensure that games and tables are adequately staffed for each shift, arranging for staff rotations and breaks and locating substitute employees as necessary. Interview and hire workers.

Prepare work schedules and station assignments and keep attendance records. Direct the distribution of complimentary hotel rooms, meals, and other discounts or free items given to players based on their length of play and betting totals. Establish policies on issues such as the type of gambling offered and the odds, the extension of credit, and the serving of food and beverages. Track supplies of money to tables and perform any required paperwork. Set and maintain a bank and table limit for each game. Monitor credit extended to players. Review operational expenses, budget estimates, betting accounts, and collection reports for accuracy. Record, collect, and pay off bets, issuing receipts as necessary. Direct workers compiling summary sheets that show wager amounts and payoffs for races and events. Notify board attendants of table vacancies so that waiting patrons can play.

Personality Type: Enterprising. These occupations frequently involve starting up and carrying out projects and can involve leading people and making many decisions. They sometimes require risk taking and often deal with business.

GOE—Interest Area/Cluster: 09. Hospitality, Tourism, and Recreation. **Work Group:** 09.01. Managerial Work in Hospitality and Tourism. **Other Jobs in This Work Group:** First-Line Supervisors/Managers of Food Preparation and Serving Workers; First-Line Supervisors/Managers of Personal Service Workers; Food Service Managers; Gaming Supervisors; Lodging Managers.

Skills—Management of Personnel Resources: Motivating, developing, and directing people as they work; identifying the best people for the job. **Management of Financial Resources:** Determining how money will be spent to get the work done and accounting for these expenditures. **Systems Evaluation:** Looking at many indicators of system performance and taking into account their accuracy. **Service Orientation:** Actively looking for ways to help people. **Negotiation:** Bringing others together and trying to reconcile differences. **Operations Analysis:** Analyzing needs and product requirements to create a design. **Social Perceptiveness:** Being aware of others' reactions and understanding why they react the way they do. **Mathematics:** Using mathematics to solve problems.

Education and Training Program: Personal and Culinary Services, Other. **Related Knowledge/Courses—Sales and Marketing:** Principles and methods involved in showing, promoting, and selling products or services. This includes marketing strategies and tactics, product demonstration and sales techniques, and sales control systems. **Personnel and Human Resources:** Principles and procedures for personnel recruitment; selection; training; compensation and benefits; labor relations and negotiation; and personnel information systems. **Customer and Personal Service:** Principles and processes for providing customer and personal services, including needs assessment techniques, quality service standards, alternative delivery systems, and customer satisfaction evaluation techniques. **Administration and Management:** Principles and processes involved in business and organizational planning, coordination, and execution. This includes strategic planning, resource allocation, manpower modeling, leadership techniques, and production methods. **Economics and Accounting:** Economic and accounting principles and practices, the financial markets, banking, and the analysis and reporting of financial data. **Mathematics:** Numbers and their operations and interrelationships, including arithmetic, algebra, geometry, calculus, and statistics and their applications.

Work Environment: Indoors; noisy; contaminants; standing; walking and running.

Gaming Supervisors

- ❋ Education/Training Required: Work experience in a related occupation
- ❋ Annual Earnings: $42,980
- ❋ Beginning Wage: $26,310
- ❋ Earnings Growth Potential: Medium
- ❋ Growth: 23.4%
- ❋ Annual Job Openings: 4,602
- ❋ Self-Employed: 29.2%
- ❋ Part-Time: 12.8%

Supervise gaming operations and personnel in an assigned area. Circulate among tables and observe operations. Ensure that stations and games are covered for each shift. May explain and interpret operating rules of house to patrons. May plan and organize activities and create friendly atmosphere for guests in hotels/casinos. May adjust service complaints. Monitor game operations to ensure that house rules are followed, that tribal, state, and federal regulations are adhered to, and that employees provide prompt and courteous service. Observe gamblers' behavior for signs of cheating such as marking, switching, or counting cards; notify security staff of suspected cheating. Maintain familiarity with the games at a facility and with strategies and tricks used by cheaters at such games.

Perform paperwork required for monetary transactions. Resolve customer and employee complaints. Greet customers and ask about the quality of service they are receiving. Establish and maintain banks and table limits for each game. Report customer-related incidents occurring in gaming areas to supervisors. Monitor stations and games and move dealers from game to game to ensure adequate staffing. Explain and interpret house rules, such as game rules and betting limits, for patrons. Supervise the distribution of complimentary meals, hotel rooms, discounts, and other items given to players based on length of play and amount bet. Evaluate workers' performance and prepare written performance evaluations. Monitor patrons for signs of compulsive gambling, offering assistance if necessary. Record, issue receipts for, and pay off bets. Monitor and verify the counting, wrapping, weighing, and distribution of currency and coins. Direct workers compiling summary sheets for each race or event to record amounts wagered and amounts to be paid to winners. Determine how many gaming tables to open each day and schedule staff accordingly. Establish policies on types of gambling offered, odds, and extension of credit. Interview, hire, and train workers. Provide fire protection and first-aid assistance when necessary. Review operational expenses, budget estimates, betting accounts, and collection reports for accuracy.

Personality Type: Enterprising. These occupations frequently involve starting up and carrying out projects and can involve leading people and making many decisions. They sometimes require risk taking and often deal with business.

GOE—Interest Area/Cluster: 09. Hospitality, Tourism, and Recreation. **Work Group:** 09.01. Managerial Work in Hospitality and Tourism. **Other Jobs in This Work Group:** First-Line Supervisors/Managers of Food Preparation and Serving Workers; First-Line Supervisors/Managers of Personal Service Workers; Food Service Managers; Gaming Managers; Lodging Managers.

Skills—Management of Personnel Resources: Motivating, developing, and directing people as they work; identifying the best people for the job. **Instructing:** Teaching others how to do something. **Service Orientation:** Actively looking for ways to help people. **Monitoring:** Assessing how well one is doing when learning or doing something. **Social Perceptiveness:** Being aware of others' reactions and understanding why they react the way they do. **Mathematics:** Using mathematics to solve problems. **Critical Thinking:** Using logic and analysis to identify the strengths and weaknesses of different approaches. **Judgment and Decision**

Making: Weighing the relative costs and benefits of a potential action.

Education and Training Program: Personal and Culinary Services, Other. **Related Knowledge/Courses—Customer and Personal Service:** Principles and processes for providing customer and personal services, including needs assessment techniques, quality service standards, alternative delivery systems, and customer satisfaction evaluation techniques. **Psychology:** Human behavior and performance, mental processes, psychological research methods, and the assessment and treatment of behavioral and affective disorders. **Mathematics:** Numbers and their operations and interrelationships, including arithmetic, algebra, geometry, calculus, and statistics and their applications. **Law and Government:** Laws, legal codes, court procedures, precedents, government regulations, executive orders, agency rules, and the democratic political process. **Sales and Marketing:** Principles and methods involved in showing, promoting, and selling products or services. This includes marketing strategies and tactics, product demonstration and sales techniques, and sales control systems. **Personnel and Human Resources:** Principles and procedures for personnel recruitment; selection; training; compensation and benefits; labor relations and negotiation; and personnel information systems.

Work Environment: Indoors; noisy; contaminants; standing; walking and running.

Gaming Surveillance Officers and Gaming Investigators

- ❋ Education/Training Required: Moderate-term on-the-job training
- ❋ Annual Earnings: $27,440
- ❋ Beginning Wage: $19,170
- ❋ Earnings Growth Potential: Low
- ❋ Growth: 33.6%
- ❋ Annual Job Openings: 2,124
- ❋ Self-Employed: 0.7%
- ❋ Part-Time: 15.5%

Act as oversight and security agent for management and customers. Observe casino or casino hotel operation for irregular activities such as cheating or theft by either employees or patrons. May utilize one-way mirrors above the casino floor and cashier's cage and from desk. Use of audio/video equipment is also common to observe operation of the business. Usually required to **provide verbal and written reports of all violations and suspicious behavior to supervisor.** Report all violations and suspicious behaviors to supervisors, verbally or in writing. Monitor establishment activities to ensure adherence to all state gaming regulations and company policies and procedures. Act as oversight or security agents for management or customers. Supervise or train surveillance observers.

Personality Type: Realistic. These occupations frequently involve work activities that include practical, hands-on problems and solutions. They often deal with plants; animals; and real-world materials such as wood, tools, and machinery. Many of the occupations require working outside and don't involve a lot of paperwork or working closely with others.

GOE—Interest Area/Cluster: 12. Law and Public Safety. **Work Group:** 12.05. Safety and Security. **Other Jobs in This Work Group:** Animal Control Workers; Crossing Guards; Lifeguards, Ski Patrol, and Other Recreational Protective Service Workers; Private Detectives and Investigators; Security Guards; Transportation Security Screeners.

Skills—Management of Personnel Resources: Motivating, developing, and directing people as they work; identifying the best people for the job. **Active Listening:** Listening to what other people are saying and asking questions as appropriate. **Writing:** Communicating effectively with others in writing as indicated by the needs of the audience. **Negotiation:** Bringing others together and trying to reconcile differences. **Learning Strategies:** Using multiple approaches when learning or teaching new things. **Social Perceptiveness:** Being aware of others' reactions and understanding why they react the way they do. **Installation:** Installing equipment, machines, wiring, or programs to meet specifications. **Critical Thinking:** Using logic and analysis to identify the strengths and weaknesses of different approaches.

Education and Training Program: Personal and Culinary Services, Other. **Related Knowledge/Courses—Public Safety and Security:** Weaponry; public safety; security operations, rules, regulations, precautions, and prevention; and the protection of people, data, and property. **Computers and Electronics:** Electric circuit boards, processors, chips, and computer hardware and software, including applications and programming. **Telecommunications:** Transmission, broadcasting, switching, control, and operation of telecommunications systems. **Law and Government:** Laws, legal codes, court procedures, precedents, government regulations, executive orders, agency rules, and the democratic political process. **Clerical Practices:** Administrative and clerical procedures and systems such as word-processing systems, filing and records management systems, stenography and transcription, forms, design principles, and other office procedures and terminology. **Education and Training:** Instructional methods and training techniques, including curriculum design principles, learning theory, group and individual teaching techniques, design of individual development plans, and test design principles.

Work Environment: Indoors; contaminants; sitting; using hands on objects, tools, or controls; repetitive motions.

General and Operations Managers

- ❋ Education/Training Required: Work experience plus degree
- ❋ Annual Earnings: $88,700
- ❋ Beginning Wage: $43,990
- ❋ Earnings Growth Potential: Very high
- ❋ Growth: 1.5%
- ❋ Annual Job Openings: 112,072
- ❋ Self-Employed: 0.9%
- ❋ Part-Time: 3.2%

Plan, direct, or coordinate the operations of companies or public and private sector organizations. Duties and responsibilities include formulating policies, managing daily operations, and planning the use of materials and human resources, but are too diverse and general in nature to be classified in any one functional area of management or administration, such as personnel, purchasing, or administrative services. Includes owners and managers who head small business establishments whose duties are primarily managerial. Oversee activities directly related to making products or providing services. Direct and coordinate activities of businesses or departments concerned with the production, pricing, sales, or distribution of products. Review financial statements, sales and activity reports, and other performance data to measure productivity and goal achievement and to determine areas needing cost reduction and program improvement. Manage staff, preparing work schedules and assigning specific duties. Direct and coordinate organization's financial and budget activities to fund operations, maximize investments, and increase efficiency. Establish and implement departmental policies, goals, objectives, and procedures, conferring with board members, organization officials, and staff members as necessary. Determine staffing requirements, and interview, hire, and train new employees, or oversee those personnel processes.

Plan and direct activities such as sales promotions, coordinating with other department heads as required. Determine goods and services to be sold, and set prices and credit terms based on forecasts of customer demand. Monitor businesses and agencies to ensure that they efficiently and effectively provide needed services while staying within budgetary limits. Locate, select, and procure merchandise for resale, representing management in purchase negotiations. Perform sales floor work such as greeting and assisting customers, stocking shelves, and taking inventory. Manage the movement of goods into and out of production facilities. Develop and implement product marketing strategies including advertising campaigns and sales promotions. Recommend locations for new facilities or oversee the remodeling of current facilities. Direct non-merchandising departments of businesses such as advertising and purchasing. Plan store layouts, and design displays.

Personality Type: Enterprising. These occupations frequently involve starting up and carrying out projects and can involve leading people and making many decisions. They sometimes require risk taking and often deal with business.

GOE—Interest Area/Cluster: 04. Business and Administration. **Work Group:** 04.01. Managerial Work in General Business. **Other Jobs in This Work Group:** Chief Executives; Compensation and Benefits Managers; Human Resources Managers; Training and Development Managers.

Skills—Management of Financial Resources: Determining how money will be spent to get the work done and accounting for these expenditures. **Management of Material Resources:** Obtaining and seeing to the appropriate use of equipment, facilities, and materials needed to do certain work. **Systems Analysis:** Determining how a system should work and how changes will affect outcomes. **Management of Personnel Resources:** Motivating, developing, and directing people as they work; identifying the best people for the job. **Systems Evaluation:** Looking at many indicators of system performance and taking into account their accuracy. **Negotiation:** Bringing others together and trying to reconcile differences. **Persuasion:** Persuading others to approach things differently. **Operation Monitoring:** Watching gauges, dials, or other indicators to make sure a machine is working properly.

Education and Training Programs: Business Administration and Management, General; Business/Commerce, General; Entrepreneurship/Entrepreneurial Studies; International Business/Trade/Commerce; Public Administration.

Related Knowledge/Courses—Economics and Accounting: Economic and accounting principles and practices, the financial markets, banking, and the analysis and reporting of financial data. **Personnel and Human Resources:** Principles and procedures for personnel recruitment; selection; training; compensation and benefits; labor relations and negotiation; and personnel information systems. **Administration and Management:** Principles and processes involved in business and organizational planning, coordination, and execution. This includes strategic planning, resource allocation, manpower modeling, leadership techniques, and production methods. **Sales and Marketing:** Principles and methods involved in showing, promoting, and selling products or services. This includes marketing strategies and tactics, product demonstration and sales techniques, and sales control systems. **Clerical Practices:** Administrative and clerical procedures and systems such as word-processing systems, filing and records management systems, stenography and transcription, forms, design principles, and other office procedures and terminology. **Building and Construction:** Materials, methods, and the appropriate tools to construct objects, structures, and buildings.

Work Environment: Indoors; noisy; more often sitting than standing.

Geography Teachers, Postsecondary

- ❈ Education/Training Required: Doctoral degree
- ❈ Annual Earnings: $61,310
- ❈ Beginning Wage: $36,070
- ❈ Earnings Growth Potential: High
- ❈ Growth: 22.9%
- ❈ Annual Job Openings: 697
- ❈ Self-Employed: 0.4%
- ❈ Part-Time: 27.8%

Teach courses in geography. Prepare and deliver lectures to undergraduate and/or graduate students on topics such as urbanization, environmental systems, and cultural geography. Evaluate and grade students' classwork, assignments, and papers. Compile, administer, and grade examinations or assign this work to others. Initiate, facilitate, and moderate classroom discussions. Maintain student attendance records, grades, and other required records. Prepare course materials such as syllabi, homework assignments, and handouts. Keep abreast of developments in their field by reading current

literature, talking with colleagues, and participating in professional conferences. Supervise undergraduate and/or graduate teaching, internship, and research work. Plan, evaluate, and revise curricula, course content, and course materials and methods of instruction. Maintain regularly scheduled office hours to advise and assist students. Supervise students' laboratory work and fieldwork. Conduct research in a particular field of knowledge and publish findings in professional journals, books, and electronic media. Collaborate with colleagues to address teaching and research issues. Select and obtain materials and supplies such as textbooks. Advise students on academic and vocational curricula and on career issues. Serve on academic or administrative committees that deal with institutional policies, departmental matters, and academic issues. Participate in student recruitment, registration, and placement activities. Participate in campus and community events. Compile bibliographies of specialized materials for outside reading assignments. Perform administrative duties such as serving as department head. Write grant proposals to procure external research funding. Maintain geographic information systems laboratories, performing duties such as updating software. Perform spatial analysis and modeling, using geographic information system techniques. Act as advisers to student organizations. Provide professional consulting services to government and industry.

Personality Type: Social. These occupations frequently involve working with, communicating with, and teaching people and often involve helping or providing service to others.

GOE—Interest Area/Cluster: 05. Education and Training. **Work Group:** 05.03. Postsecondary and Adult Teaching and Instructing. **Other Jobs in This Work Group:** Adult Literacy, Remedial Education, and GED Teachers and Instructors; Agricultural Sciences Teachers, Postsecondary; Anthropology and Archeology Teachers, Postsecondary; Architecture Teachers, Postsecondary; Area, Ethnic, and Cultural Studies Teachers, Postsecondary; Art, Drama, and Music Teachers, Postsecondary; Atmospheric, Earth, Marine, and Space Sciences Teachers, Postsecondary; Biological Science Teachers, Postsecondary; Business Teachers, Postsecondary; Chemistry Teachers, Postsecondary; Communications Teachers, Postsecondary; Computer Science Teachers, Postsecondary; Criminal Justice and Law Enforcement Teachers, Postsecondary; Economics Teachers, Postsecondary; Education Teachers, Postsecondary; Engineering Teachers, Postsecondary; English Language and Literature Teachers, Postsecondary; Environmental Science Teachers, Postsecondary; Farm and Home Management Advisors;

Foreign Language and Literature Teachers, Postsecondary; Forestry and Conservation Science Teachers, Postsecondary; Graduate Teaching Assistants; Health Specialties Teachers, Postsecondary; History Teachers, Postsecondary; Home Economics Teachers, Postsecondary; Law Teachers, Postsecondary; Library Science Teachers, Postsecondary; Mathematical Science Teachers, Postsecondary; Nursing Instructors and Teachers, Postsecondary; Philosophy and Religion Teachers, Postsecondary; Physics Teachers, Postsecondary; Political Science Teachers, Postsecondary; Psychology Teachers, Postsecondary; Recreation and Fitness Studies Teachers, Postsecondary; Self-Enrichment Education Teachers; Social Work Teachers, Postsecondary; Sociology Teachers, Postsecondary; Vocational Education Teachers, Postsecondary.

Skills—Science: Using scientific methods to solve problems. **Writing:** Communicating effectively with others in writing as indicated by the needs of the audience. **Instructing:** Teaching others how to do something. **Learning Strategies:** Using multiple approaches when learning or teaching new things. **Reading Comprehension:** Understanding written sentences and paragraphs in work-related documents. **Speaking:** Talking to others to effectively convey information. **Critical Thinking:** Using logic and analysis to identify the strengths and weaknesses of different approaches. **Active Learning:** Working with new material or information to grasp its implications.

Education and Training Programs: Geography; Geography Teacher Education. **Related Knowledge/Courses— Geography:** Various methods for describing the location and distribution of land, sea, and air masses, including their physical locations, relationships, and characteristics. **Sociology and Anthropology:** Group behavior and dynamics; societal trends and influences; and cultures and their history, migrations, ethnicity, and origins. **History and Archeology:** Historical events and their causes, indicators, and impact on particular civilizations and cultures. **Philosophy and Theology:** Different philosophical systems and religions, including their basic principles, values, ethics, ways of thinking, customs, and practices and their impact on human culture. **Education and Training:** Instructional methods and training techniques, including curriculum design principles, learning theory, group and individual teaching techniques, design of individual development plans, and test design principles. **Communications and Media:** Media production, communication, and dissemination techniques and methods, including alternative ways to inform and entertain via written, oral, and visual media.

Work Environment: Indoors; sitting.

Geological Sample Test Technicians

- ❋ Education/Training Required: Associate degree
- ❋ Annual Earnings: $50,950
- ❋ Beginning Wage: $25,160
- ❋ Earnings Growth Potential: Very high
- ❋ Growth: 8.6%
- ❋ Annual Job Openings: 1,895
- ❋ Self-Employed: 0.0%
- ❋ Part-Time: 1.0%

The job openings listed here are shared with Geophysical Data Technicians.

Test and analyze geological samples, crude oil, or petroleum products to detect presence of petroleum, gas, or mineral deposits indicating potential for exploration and production or to determine physical and chemical properties to ensure that products meet quality standards. Test and analyze samples in order to determine their content and characteristics, using laboratory apparatus and testing equipment. Collect and prepare solid and fluid samples for analysis. Assemble, operate, and maintain field and laboratory testing, measuring, and mechanical equipment, working as part of a crew when required. Compile and record testing and operational data for review and further analysis. Adjust and repair testing, electrical, and mechanical equipment and devices. Supervise well exploration and drilling activities and well completions. Inspect engines for wear and defective parts, using equipment and measuring devices. Prepare notes, sketches, geological maps, and cross sections. Participate in geological, geophysical, geochemical, hydrographic, or oceanographic surveys; prospecting field trips; exploratory drilling; well logging; or underground mine survey programs. Plot information from aerial photographs, well logs, section descriptions, and other databases. Assess the environmental impacts of development projects on subsurface materials. Collaborate with hydrogeologists to evaluate groundwater and well circulation. Prepare, transcribe, and/or analyze seismic, gravimetric, well log, or other geophysical and survey data. Participate in the evaluation of possible mining locations.

Personality Type: Realistic. These occupations frequently involve work activities that include practical, hands-on problems and solutions. They often deal with plants; animals; and real-world materials such as wood, tools, and machinery. Many of the occupations require working outside and don't involve a lot of paperwork or working closely with others.

GOE—**Interest Area/Cluster:** 01. Agriculture and Natural Resources. **Work Group:** 01.03. Resource Technologies for Plants, Animals, and the Environment. **Other Jobs in This Work Group:** Agricultural and Food Science Technicians; Agricultural Technicians; Environmental Science and Protection Technicians, Including Health; Food Science Technicians; Food Scientists and Technologists; Geological and Petroleum Technicians; Geophysical Data Technicians.

Skills—Science: Using scientific methods to solve problems. **Equipment Maintenance:** Performing routine maintenance and determining when and what kind of maintenance is needed. **Operation Monitoring:** Watching gauges, dials, or other indicators to make sure a machine is working properly. **Quality Control Analysis:** Evaluating the quality or performance of products, services, or processes. **Mathematics:** Using mathematics to solve problems. **Operations Analysis:** Analyzing needs and product requirements to create a design. **Installation:** Installing equipment, machines, wiring, or programs to meet specifications. **Operation and Control:** Controlling operations of equipment or systems.

Education and Training Program: Petroleum Technology/Technician Training. **Related Knowledge/Courses— Chemistry:** The composition, structure, and properties of substances and of the chemical processes and transformations that they undergo. This includes uses of chemicals and their interactions, danger signs, production techniques, and disposal methods. **Geography:** Various methods for describing the location and distribution of land, sea, and air masses, including their physical locations, relationships, and characteristics. **Physics:** Physical principles, laws, and applications, including air, water, material dynamics, light, atomic principles, heat, electric theory, earth formations, and meteorological and related natural phenomena. **Mechanical Devices:** Machines and tools, including their designs, uses, benefits, repair, and maintenance. **Mathematics:** Numbers and their operations and interrelationships, including arithmetic, algebra, geometry, calculus, and statistics and their applications. **Computers and Electronics:** Electric circuit boards, processors, chips, and computer hardware and software, including applications and programming.

Work Environment: Indoors; noisy; contaminants; more often standing than sitting; using hands on objects, tools, or controls.

Geophysical Data Technicians

- ❋ Education/Training Required: Associate degree
- ❋ Annual Earnings: $50,950
- ❋ Beginning Wage: $25,160
- ❋ Earnings Growth Potential: Very high
- ❋ Growth: 8.6%
- ❋ Annual Job Openings: 1,895
- ❋ Self-Employed: 0.0%
- ❋ Part-Time: 1.0%

The job openings listed here are shared with Geological Sample Test Technicians.

Measure, record, and evaluate geological data by using sonic, electronic, electrical, seismic, or gravity-measuring instruments to prospect for oil or gas. May collect and evaluate core samples and cuttings. Prepare notes, sketches, geological maps, and cross-sections. Read and study reports in order to compile information and data for geological and geophysical prospecting. Interview individuals, and research public databases in order to obtain information. Assemble, maintain, and distribute information for library or record systems. Operate and adjust equipment and apparatus used to obtain geological data. Plan and direct activities of workers who operate equipment to collect data. Set up, or direct set-up of instruments used to collect geological data. Record readings in order to compile data used in prospecting for oil or gas. Supervise oil, water, and gas well drilling activities. Collect samples and cuttings, using equipment and hand tools. Develop and print photographic recordings of information, using equipment. Measure geological characteristics used in prospecting for oil or gas, using measuring instruments. Evaluate and interpret core samples and cuttings, and other geological data used in prospecting for oil or gas. Diagnose and repair malfunctioning instruments and equipment, using manufacturers' manuals and hand tools. Prepare and attach packing instructions to shipping containers. Develop and design packing materials and handling procedures for shipping of objects.

Personality Type: Conventional. These occupations frequently involve following set procedures and routines and can include working with data and details more than with ideas. Usually there is a clear line of authority to follow.

GOE—**Interest Area/Cluster:** 01. Agriculture and Natural Resources. **Work Group:** 01.03. Resource Technologies for Plants, Animals, and the Environment. **Other Jobs in**

This Work Group: Agricultural and Food Science Technicians; Agricultural Technicians; Environmental Science and Protection Technicians, Including Health; Food Science Technicians; Food Scientists and Technologists; Geological and Petroleum Technicians; Geological Sample Test Technicians.

Skills—Science: Using scientific methods to solve problems. **Technology Design:** Generating or adapting equipment and technology to serve user needs. **Mathematics:** Using mathematics to solve problems. **Operations Analysis:** Analyzing needs and product requirements to create a design. **Operation Monitoring:** Watching gauges, dials, or other indicators to make sure a machine is working properly. **Persuasion:** Persuading others to approach things differently. **Equipment Selection:** Determining the kind of tools and equipment needed to do a job. **Management of Financial Resources:** Determining how money will be spent to get the work done and accounting for these expenditures.

Education and Training Program: Petroleum Technology/Technician Training. **Related Knowledge/Courses— Geography:** Various methods for describing the location and distribution of land, sea, and air masses, including their physical locations, relationships, and characteristics. **Engineering and Technology:** Equipment, tools, and mechanical devices and their uses to produce motion, light, power, technology, and other applications. **Physics:** Physical principles, laws, and applications, including air, water, material dynamics, light, atomic principles, heat, electric theory, earth formations, and meteorological and related natural phenomena. **Computers and Electronics:** Electric circuit boards, processors, chips, and computer hardware and software, including applications and programming. **Mathematics:** Numbers and their operations and interrelationships, including arithmetic, algebra, geometry, calculus, and statistics and their applications. **Chemistry:** The composition, structure, and properties of substances and of the chemical processes and transformations that they undergo. This includes uses of chemicals and their interactions, danger signs, production techniques, and disposal methods.

Work Environment: Indoors; sitting.

Geoscientists, Except Hydrologists and Geographers

* Education/Training Required: Master's degree
* Annual Earnings: $75,800
* Beginning Wage: $41,020
* Earnings Growth Potential: High
* Growth: 21.9%
* Annual Job Openings: 2,471
* Self-Employed: 2.2%
* Part-Time: 5.3%

Study the composition, structure, and other physical aspects of the Earth. May use knowledge of geology, physics, and mathematics in exploration for oil, gas, minerals, or underground water or in waste disposal, land reclamation, or other environmental problems. May study the Earth's internal composition, atmospheres, and oceans and its magnetic, electrical, and gravitational forces. Includes mineralogists, crystallographers, paleontologists, stratigraphers, geodesists, and seismologists. Analyze and interpret geological, geochemical, and geophysical information from sources such as survey data, well logs, bore holes, and aerial photos. Locate and estimate probable natural gas, oil, and mineral ore deposits and underground water resources, using aerial photographs, charts, or research and survey results. Plan and conduct geological, geochemical, and geophysical field studies and surveys, sample collection, or drilling and testing programs used to collect data for research or application. Analyze and interpret geological data, using computer software. Search for and review research articles or environmental, historical, and technical reports. Assess ground and surface water movement to provide advice regarding issues such as waste management, route and site selection, and the restoration of contaminated sites. Prepare geological maps, cross-sectional diagrams, charts, and reports concerning mineral extraction, land use, and resource management, using results of field work and laboratory research. Investigate the composition, structure, and history of the Earth's crust through the collection, examination, measurement, and classification of soils, minerals, rocks, or fossil remains. Conduct geological and geophysical studies to provide information for use in regional development, site selection, and development of public works projects. Measure characteristics of the Earth, such as gravity and magnetic fields, using equipment such as seismographs, gravimeters, torsion balances, and magnetometers.

Inspect construction projects to analyze engineering problems, applying geological knowledge and using test equipment and drilling machinery. Design geological mine maps, monitor mine structural integrity, or advise and monitor mining crews. Identify risks for natural disasters such as mud slides, earthquakes, and volcanic eruptions, providing advice on mitigation of potential damage. Advise construction firms and government agencies on dam and road construction, foundation design, or land use and resource management. Test industrial diamonds and abrasives, soil, or rocks to determine their geological characteristics, using optical, x-ray, heat, acid, and precision instruments.

Personality Type: Investigative. These occupations frequently involve working with ideas and require an extensive amount of thinking. They can involve searching for facts and figuring out problems mentally.

GOE—Interest Area/Cluster: 15. Scientific Research, Engineering, and Mathematics. **Work Group:** 15.02. Physical Sciences. **Other Jobs in This Work Group:** Astronomers; Atmospheric and Space Scientists; Chemists; Geographers; Hydrologists; Materials Scientists; Physicists.

Skills—Systems Analysis: Determining how a system should work and how changes will affect outcomes. **Science:** Using scientific methods to solve problems. **Systems Evaluation:** Looking at many indicators of system performance and taking into account their accuracy. **Mathematics:** Using mathematics to solve problems. **Writing:** Communicating effectively with others in writing as indicated by the needs of the audience. **Operation Monitoring:** Watching gauges, dials, or other indicators to make sure a machine is working properly. **Speaking:** Talking to others to effectively convey information.

Education and Training Programs: Geochemistry; Geochemistry and Petrology; Geological and Earth Sciences/Geosciences, Other; Geology/Earth Science, General; Geophysics and Seismology; Oceanography, Chemical and Physical; Paleontology. **Related Knowledge/Courses—Geography:** Various methods for describing the location and distribution of land, sea, and air masses, including their physical locations, relationships, and characteristics. **Engineering and Technology:** Equipment, tools, and mechanical devices and their uses to produce motion, light, power, technology, and other applications. **Physics:** Physical principles, laws, and applications, including air, water, material dynamics, light, atomic principles, heat, electric theory, earth formations, and meteorological and related natural phenomena. **Chemistry:** The composition, structure, and

properties of substances and of the chemical processes and transformations that they undergo. This includes uses of chemicals and their interactions, danger signs, production techniques, and disposal methods. **Mathematics:** Numbers and their operations and interrelationships, including arithmetic, algebra, geometry, calculus, and statistics and their applications. **Design:** Design techniques, principles, tools, and instruments involved in the production and use of precision technical plans, blueprints, drawings, and models.

Work Environment: Indoors; sitting.

Glaziers

- ❋ Education/Training Required: Long-term on-the-job training
- ❋ Annual Earnings: $35,230
- ❋ Beginning Wage: $21,670
- ❋ Earnings Growth Potential: Medium
- ❋ Growth: 11.9%
- ❋ Annual Job Openings: 6,416
- ❋ Self-Employed: 5.3%
- ❋ Part-Time: 2.7%

Install glass in windows, skylights, storefronts, and display cases or on surfaces such as building fronts, interior walls, ceilings, and tabletops. Read and interpret blueprints and specifications to determine size, shape, color, type, and thickness of glass; location of framing; installation procedures; and staging and scaffolding materials required. Determine plumb of walls or ceilings, using plumb-lines and levels. Fabricate and install metal sashes and moldings for glass installation, using aluminum or steel framing. Measure mirrors and dimensions of areas to be covered in order to determine work procedures. Fasten glass panes into wood sashes or frames with clips, points, or moldings, adding weather seals or putty around pane edges to seal joints. Secure mirrors in position, using mastic cement, putty, bolts, or screws. Cut, fit, install, repair, and replace glass and glass substitutes, such as plastic and aluminum, in building interiors or exteriors and in furniture or other products. Cut and remove broken glass prior to installing replacement glass. Set glass doors into frames, and bolt metal hinges, handles, locks, and other hardware to attach doors to frames and walls. Score glass with cutters' wheels, breaking off excess glass by hand or with notched tools. Cut, assemble, fit, and attach metal-framed glass enclosures for showers, bathtubs, display cases, skylights, solariums, and other structures. Drive trucks to installation sites, and unload mirrors, glass equipment, and tools. Install pre-assembled metal or wood frameworks for windows or doors to be fitted with glass panels, using hand tools. Cut and attach mounting strips, metal or wood moldings, rubber gaskets, or metal clips to surfaces in preparation for mirror installation. Assemble, erect, and dismantle scaffolds, rigging, and hoisting equipment. Load and arrange glass and mirrors onto delivery trucks, using suction cups or cranes to lift glass. Measure and mark outlines or patterns on glass to indicate cutting lines. Grind and polish glass and smooth edges when necessary. Prepare glass for cutting by resting it on rack edges or against cutting tables, and brushing a thin layer of oil along cutting lines or dipping cutting tools in oil. Pack spaces between moldings and glass with glazing compounds, and trim excess material with glazing knives.

Personality Type: Realistic. These occupations frequently involve work activities that include practical, hands-on problems and solutions. They often deal with plants; animals; and real-world materials such as wood, tools, and machinery. Many of the occupations require working outside and don't involve a lot of paperwork or working closely with others.

GOE—Interest Area/Cluster: 02. Architecture and Construction. **Work Group:** 02.04. Construction Crafts. **Other Jobs in This Work Group:** Boilermakers; Brickmasons and Blockmasons; Carpet Installers; Cement Masons and Concrete Finishers; Commercial Divers; Construction Carpenters; Crane and Tower Operators; Drywall and Ceiling Tile Installers; Electricians; Fence Erectors; Floor Layers, Except Carpet, Wood, and Hard Tiles; Floor Sanders and Finishers; Hazardous Materials Removal Workers; Insulation Workers, Floor, Ceiling, and Wall; Insulation Workers, Mechanical; Manufactured Building and Mobile Home Installers; Operating Engineers and Other Construction Equipment Operators; Painters, Construction and Maintenance; Paperhangers; Paving, Surfacing, and Tamping Equipment Operators; Pile-Driver Operators; Pipe Fitters and Steamfitters; Pipelayers; Plasterers and Stucco Masons; Plumbers; Plumbers, Pipefitters, and Steamfitters; Rail-Track Laying and Maintenance Equipment Operators; Refractory Materials Repairers, Except Brickmasons; Reinforcing Iron and Rebar Workers; Riggers; Roofers; Rough Carpenters; Security and Fire Alarm Systems Installers; Segmental Pavers; Sheet Metal Workers; Stone Cutters and Carvers, Manufacturing; Stonemasons; Structural Iron and Steel Workers; Tapers; Terrazzo Workers and Finishers; Tile and Marble Setters.

Skills—Installation: Installing equipment, machines, wiring, or programs to meet specifications. **Mathematics:**

Using mathematics to solve problems. **Repairing:** Repairing machines or systems, using the needed tools.

Education and Training Program: Glazier Training. **Related Knowledge/Courses—Building and Construction:** Materials, methods, and the appropriate tools to construct objects, structures, and buildings. **Mechanical Devices:** Machines and tools, including their designs, uses, benefits, repair, and maintenance. **Design:** Design techniques, principles, tools, and instruments involved in the production and use of precision technical plans, blueprints, drawings, and models. **Engineering and Technology:** Equipment, tools, and mechanical devices and their uses to produce motion, light, power, technology, and other applications. **Mathematics:** Numbers and their operations and interrelationships, including arithmetic, algebra, geometry, calculus, and statistics and their applications. **Public Safety and Security:** Weaponry; public safety; security operations, rules, regulations, precautions, and prevention; and the protection of people, data, and property.

Work Environment: Outdoors; noisy; very hot or cold; contaminants; standing; using hands on objects, tools, or controls.

Government Property Inspectors and Investigators

- ❀ Education/Training Required: Long-term on-the-job training
- ❀ Annual Earnings: $48,400
- ❀ Beginning Wage: $28,980
- ❀ Earnings Growth Potential: High
- ❀ Growth: 4.9%
- ❀ Annual Job Openings: 15,841
- ❀ Self-Employed: 0.4%
- ❀ Part-Time: 5.0%

The job openings listed here are shared with Coroners; Environmental Compliance Inspectors; Equal Opportunity Representatives and Officers; and Licensing Examiners and Inspectors.

Investigate or inspect government property to ensure compliance with contract agreements and government regulations. Prepare correspondence, reports of inspections or investigations, and recommendations for action. Inspect government-owned equipment and materials in the possession of private contractors in order to ensure compliance with contracts and regulations and to prevent misuse. Examine records, reports, and documents in order to establish facts and detect discrepancies. Inspect manufactured or processed products to ensure compliance with contract specifications and legal requirements. Locate and interview plaintiffs, witnesses, or representatives of business or government in order to gather facts relevant to inspections or alleged violations. Recommend legal or administrative action to protect government property. Submit samples of products to government laboratories for testing as required. Coordinate with and assist law enforcement agencies in matters of mutual concern. Testify in court or at administrative proceedings concerning investigation findings. Collect, identify, evaluate, and preserve case evidence. Monitor investigations of suspected offenders to ensure that they are conducted in accordance with constitutional requirements. Investigate applications for special licenses or permits, as well as alleged license or permit violations.

Personality Type: Conventional. These occupations frequently involve following set procedures and routines and can include working with data and details more than with ideas. Usually there is a clear line of authority to follow.

GOE—Interest Area/Cluster: 07. Government and Public Administration. **Work Group:** 07.03. Regulations Enforcement. **Other Jobs in This Work Group:** Agricultural Inspectors; Aviation Inspectors; Compliance Officers, Except Agriculture, Construction, Health and Safety, and Transportation; Construction and Building Inspectors; Environmental Compliance Inspectors; Equal Opportunity Representatives and Officers; Financial Examiners; Fire Inspectors; Fish and Game Wardens; Forest Fire Inspectors and Prevention Specialists; Freight and Cargo Inspectors; Immigration and Customs Inspectors; Licensing Examiners and Inspectors; Nuclear Monitoring Technicians; Occupational Health and Safety Specialists; Occupational Health and Safety Technicians; Tax Examiners, Collectors, and Revenue Agents; Transportation Vehicle, Equipment, and Systems Inspectors, Except Aviation.

Skills—Quality Control Analysis: Evaluating the quality or performance of products, services, or processes. **Technology Design:** Generating or adapting equipment and technology to serve user needs. **Science:** Using scientific methods to solve problems. **Troubleshooting:** Determining what is causing an operating error and deciding what to do about it. **Equipment Selection:** Determining the kind of tools and equipment needed to do a job. **Coordination:** Adjusting actions in relation to others' actions. **Operation and Control:** Controlling operations of equipment or systems. **Service Orientation:** Actively looking for ways to help people.

Education and Training Program: Building/Home/Construction Inspection/Inspector Training. **Related Knowledge/Courses—Building and Construction:** Materials, methods, and the appropriate tools to construct objects, structures, and buildings. **Engineering and Technology:** Equipment, tools, and mechanical devices and their uses to produce motion, light, power, technology, and other applications. **Public Safety and Security:** Weaponry; public safety; security operations, rules, regulations, precautions, and prevention; and the protection of people, data, and property. **Mechanical Devices:** Machines and tools, including their designs, uses, benefits, repair, and maintenance. **Computers and Electronics:** Electric circuit boards, processors, chips, and computer hardware and software, including applications and programming. **Transportation:** Principles and methods for moving people or goods by air, rail, sea, or road, including their relative costs, advantages, and limitations.

Work Environment: More often outdoors than indoors; noisy; very hot or cold; contaminants; sitting.

Graduate Teaching Assistants

* Education/Training Required: Bachelor's degree
* Annual Earnings: $28,060
* Beginning Wage: $15,660
* Earnings Growth Potential: High
* Growth: 22.9%
* Annual Job Openings: 20,601
* Self-Employed: 0.4%
* Part-Time: 27.8%

Assist department chairperson, faculty members, or other professional staff members in colleges or universities by performing teaching or teaching-related duties such as teaching lower-level courses, developing teaching materials, preparing and giving examinations, and grading examinations or papers. Graduate assistants must be enrolled in graduate school programs. Graduate assistants who primarily perform non-teaching duties such as laboratory research, should be reported in the occupational category related to the work performed. Lead discussion sections, tutorials, and laboratory sections. Evaluate and grade examinations, assignments, and papers and record grades. Return assignments to students in accordance with established deadlines. Schedule and maintain regular office hours to meet with students. Inform students of the procedures for completing and submitting class work such as lab reports. Prepare and proctor examinations. Notify instructors of errors or problems with assignments. Meet with supervisors to discuss students' grades and to complete required grade-related paperwork. Copy and distribute classroom materials. Demonstrate use of laboratory equipment and enforce laboratory rules. Teach undergraduate-level courses. Complete laboratory projects prior to assigning them to students so that any needed modifications can be made. Develop teaching materials such as syllabi, visual aids, answer keys, supplementary notes, and course websites. Provide assistance to faculty members or staff with laboratory or field research. Arrange for supervisors to conduct teaching observations; meet with supervisors to receive feedback about teaching performance. Attend lectures given by the instructors whom they are assisting. Order or obtain materials needed for classes. Provide instructors with assistance in the use of audiovisual equipment. Assist faculty members or staff with student conferences.

Personality Type: Social. These occupations frequently involve working with, communicating with, and teaching people and often involve helping or providing service to others.

GOE—Interest Area/Cluster: 05. Education and Training. **Work Group:** 05.03. Postsecondary and Adult Teaching and Instructing. **Other Jobs in This Work Group:** Adult Literacy, Remedial Education, and GED Teachers and Instructors; Agricultural Sciences Teachers, Postsecondary; Anthropology and Archeology Teachers, Postsecondary; Architecture Teachers, Postsecondary; Area, Ethnic, and Cultural Studies Teachers, Postsecondary; Art, Drama, and Music Teachers, Postsecondary; Atmospheric, Earth, Marine, and Space Sciences Teachers, Postsecondary; Biological Science Teachers, Postsecondary; Business Teachers, Postsecondary; Chemistry Teachers, Postsecondary; Communications Teachers, Postsecondary; Computer Science Teachers, Postsecondary; Criminal Justice and Law Enforcement Teachers, Postsecondary; Economics Teachers, Postsecondary; Education Teachers, Postsecondary; Engineering Teachers, Postsecondary; English Language and Literature Teachers, Postsecondary; Environmental Science Teachers, Postsecondary; Farm and Home Management Advisors; Foreign Language and Literature Teachers, Postsecondary; Forestry and Conservation Science Teachers, Postsecondary; Geography Teachers, Postsecondary; Health Specialties Teachers, Postsecondary; History Teachers, Postsecondary; Home Economics Teachers, Postsecondary; Law Teachers, Postsecondary; Library Science Teachers, Postsecondary; Mathematical Science Teachers, Postsecondary; Nursing Instructors and Teachers,

Postsecondary; Philosophy and Religion Teachers, Postsecondary; Physics Teachers, Postsecondary; Political Science Teachers, Postsecondary; Psychology Teachers, Postsecondary; Recreation and Fitness Studies Teachers, Postsecondary; Self-Enrichment Education Teachers; Social Work Teachers, Postsecondary; Sociology Teachers, Postsecondary; Vocational Education Teachers, Postsecondary.

Skills—Learning Strategies: Using multiple approaches when learning or teaching new things. **Instructing:** Teaching others how to do something. **Social Perceptiveness:** Being aware of others' reactions and understanding why they react the way they do. **Reading Comprehension:** Understanding written sentences and paragraphs in work-related documents. **Writing:** Communicating effectively with others in writing as indicated by the needs of the audience. **Speaking:** Talking to others to effectively convey information. **Time Management:** Managing one's own time and the time of others. **Active Learning:** Working with new material or information to grasp its implications.

Education and Training Program: Education, General. **Related Knowledge/Courses—Sociology and Anthropology:** Group behavior and dynamics; societal trends and influences; and cultures and their history, migrations, ethnicity, and origins. **Education and Training:** Instructional methods and training techniques, including curriculum design principles, learning theory, group and individual teaching techniques, design of individual development plans, and test design principles. **English Language:** The structure and content of the English language, including the meaning and spelling of words, rules of composition, and grammar. **Philosophy and Theology:** Different philosophical systems and religions, including their basic principles, values, ethics, ways of thinking, customs, and practices and their impact on human culture. **Communications and Media:** Media production, communication, and dissemination techniques and methods, including alternative ways to inform and entertain via written, oral, and visual media. **Psychology:** Human behavior and performance, mental processes, psychological research methods, and the assessment and treatment of behavioral and affective disorders.

Work Environment: Indoors; sitting.

Graphic Designers

- ❋ Education/Training Required: Bachelor's degree
- ❋ Annual Earnings: $41,280
- ❋ Beginning Wage: $25,090
- ❋ Earnings Growth Potential: Medium
- ❋ Growth: 9.8%
- ❋ Annual Job Openings: 26,968
- ❋ Self-Employed: 25.3%
- ❋ Part-Time: 16.7%

Design or create graphics to meet specific commercial or promotional needs such as packaging, displays, or logos. May use a variety of media to achieve artistic or decorative effects. Create designs, concepts, and sample layouts based on knowledge of layout principles and esthetic design concepts. Determine size and arrangement of illustrative material and copy, and select style and size of type. Confer with clients to discuss and determine layout designs. Develop graphics and layouts for product illustrations, company logos, and Internet Web sites. Review final layouts and suggest improvements as needed. Prepare illustrations or rough sketches of material, discussing them with clients or supervisors and making necessary changes. Use computer software to generate new images. Key information into computer equipment to create layouts for client or supervisor. Maintain archive of images, photos, or previous work products. Prepare notes and instructions for workers who assemble and prepare final layouts for printing. Draw and print charts, graphs, illustrations, and other artwork, using computer. Study illustrations and photographs to plan presentations of materials, products, or services. Research new software or design concepts. Mark up, paste, and assemble final layouts to prepare layouts for printer. Produce still and animated graphics for on-air and taped portions of television news broadcasts, using electronic video equipment. Photograph layouts, using cameras, to make layout prints for supervisors or clients. Develop negatives and prints to produce layout photographs, using negative and print developing equipment and tools.

Personality Type: Artistic. These occupations frequently involve working with forms, designs, and patterns. They often require self-expression, and the work can be done without following a clear set of rules.

GOE—Interest Area/Cluster: 03. Arts and Communication. **Work Group:** 03.05. Design. **Other Jobs in This**

Work Group: Commercial and Industrial Designers; Fashion Designers; Floral Designers; Interior Designers; Merchandise Displayers and Window Trimmers; Set and Exhibit Designers.

Skills—Programming: Writing computer programs for various purposes. **Systems Analysis:** Determining how a system should work and how changes will affect outcomes.

Education and Training Programs: Agricultural Communication/Journalism; Commercial and Advertising Art; Computer Graphics; Design and Visual Communications, General; Graphic Design; Industrial Design; Web Page, Digital/Multimedia and Information Resources Design. **Related Knowledge/Courses—Fine Arts:** Theory and techniques required to produce, compose, and perform works of music, dance, visual arts, drama, and sculpture. **Design:** Design techniques, principles, tools, and instruments involved in the production and use of precision technical plans, blueprints, drawings, and models. **Communications and Media:** Media production, communication, and dissemination techniques and methods, including alternative ways to inform and entertain via written, oral, and visual media. **Sales and Marketing:** Principles and methods involved in showing, promoting, and selling products or services. This includes marketing strategies and tactics, product demonstration and sales techniques, and sales control systems. **Sociology and Anthropology:** Group behavior and dynamics; societal trends and influences; and cultures and their history, migrations, ethnicity, and origins. **Computers and Electronics:** Electric circuit boards, processors, chips, and computer hardware and software, including applications and programming.

Work Environment: Indoors; sitting; using hands on objects, tools, or controls; repetitive motions.

Hairdressers, Hairstylists, and Cosmetologists

- ❋ Education/Training Required: Postsecondary vocational training
- ❋ Annual Earnings: $22,210
- ❋ Beginning Wage: $14,790
- ❋ Earnings Growth Potential: Low
- ❋ Growth: 12.4%
- ❋ Annual Job Openings: 73,030
- ❋ Self-Employed: 44.5%
- ❋ Part-Time: 31.1%

Provide beauty services, such as shampooing, cutting, coloring, and styling hair and massaging and treating scalp. May also apply makeup, dress wigs, perform hair removal, and provide nail and skin care services. Keep work stations clean and sanitize tools such as scissors and combs. Cut, trim, and shape hair or hairpieces based on customers' instructions, hair type, and facial features, using clippers, scissors, trimmers, and razors. Analyze patrons' hair and other physical features to determine and recommend beauty treatment or suggest hairstyles. Schedule client appointments. Bleach, dye, or tint hair, using applicator or brush. Update and maintain customer information records, such as beauty services provided. Shampoo, rinse, condition, and dry hair and scalp or hairpieces with water, liquid soap, or other solutions. Operate cash registers to receive payments from patrons. Demonstrate and sell hair care products and cosmetics. Apply water, setting, straightening, or waving solutions to hair and use curlers, rollers, hot combs, and curling irons to press and curl hair. Develop new styles and techniques. Comb, brush, and spray hair or wigs to set style. Shape eyebrows and remove facial hair, using depilatory cream, tweezers, electrolysis, or wax. Administer therapeutic medication and advise patron to seek medical treatment for chronic or contagious scalp conditions. Massage and treat scalp for hygienic and remedial purposes, using hands, fingers, or vibrating equipment. Shave, trim, and shape beards and moustaches. Train or supervise other hairstylists, hairdressers, and assistants. Recommend and explain the use of cosmetics, lotions, and creams to soften and lubricate skin and enhance and restore natural appearance. Give facials to patrons, using special compounds such as lotions and creams. Clean, shape, and polish fingernails and toenails, using files and nail polish. Apply artificial fingernails. Attach wigs or hairpieces to model heads and dress wigs and hairpieces according to instructions, samples, sketches, or photographs.

Personality Type: Artistic. These occupations frequently involve working with forms, designs, and patterns. They often require self-expression, and the work can be done without following a clear set of rules.

GOE—Interest Area/Cluster: 09. Hospitality, Tourism, and Recreation. **Work Group:** 09.07. Barber and Beauty Services. **Other Jobs in This Work Group:** Barbers; Manicurists and Pedicurists; Shampooers; Skin Care Specialists.

Skills—Science: Using scientific methods to solve problems. **Operations Analysis:** Analyzing needs and product requirements to create a design. **Equipment Selection:** Determining the kind of tools and equipment needed to do a job. **Management of Financial Resources:** Determining how money will be spent to get the work done and accounting for these expenditures. **Equipment Maintenance:** Performing routine maintenance and determining when and what kind of maintenance is needed. **Learning Strategies:** Using multiple approaches when learning or teaching new things. **Social Perceptiveness:** Being aware of others' reactions and understanding why they react the way they do. **Management of Material Resources:** Obtaining and seeing to the appropriate use of equipment, facilities, and materials needed to do certain work.

Education and Training Programs: Cosmetology and Related Personal Grooming Arts, Other; Cosmetology, Barber/Styling, and Nail Instructor Training; Cosmetology/Cosmetologist Training, General; Electrolysis/Electrology and Electrolysis Technician Training; Hair Styling/Stylist and Hair Design; Make-Up Artist/Specialist Training; Permanent Cosmetics/Makeup and Tattooing; Salon/Beauty Salon Management/Manager Training. **Related Knowledge/Courses—Chemistry:** The composition, structure, and properties of substances and of the chemical processes and transformations that they undergo. This includes uses of chemicals and their interactions, danger signs, production techniques, and disposal methods. **Sales and Marketing:** Principles and methods involved in showing, promoting, and selling products or services. This includes marketing strategies and tactics, product demonstration and sales techniques, and sales control systems. **Customer and Personal Service:** Principles and processes for providing customer and personal services, including needs assessment techniques, quality service standards, alternative delivery systems, and customer satisfaction evaluation techniques.

Work Environment: Indoors; contaminants; minor burns, cuts, bites, or stings; standing; using hands on objects, tools, or controls; repetitive motions.

Hazardous Materials Removal Workers

❋ Education/Training Required: Moderate-term on-the-job training
❋ Annual Earnings: $36,330
❋ Beginning Wage: $23,200
❋ Earnings Growth Potential: Medium
❋ Growth: 11.2%
❋ Annual Job Openings: 1,933
❋ Self-Employed: 1.6%
❋ Part-Time: 5.7%

Identify, remove, pack, transport, or dispose of hazardous materials, including asbestos, lead-based paint, waste oil, fuel, transmission fluid, radioactive materials, contaminated soil, and so on. Specialized training and certification in hazardous materials handling or a confined entry permit are generally required. May operate earth-moving equipment or trucks. Follow prescribed safety procedures, and comply with federal laws regulating waste disposal methods. Record numbers of containers stored at disposal sites, and specify amounts and types of equipment and waste disposed. Drive trucks or other heavy equipment to convey contaminated waste to designated sea or ground locations. Operate machines and equipment to remove, package, store, or transport loads of waste materials. Load and unload materials into containers and onto trucks, using hoists or forklifts. Clean contaminated equipment or areas for reuse, using detergents and solvents, sandblasters, filter pumps, and steam cleaners. Construct scaffolding or build containment areas prior to beginning abatement or decontamination work. Remove asbestos and/or lead from surfaces, using hand and power tools such as scrapers, vacuums, and high-pressure sprayers. Unload baskets of irradiated elements onto packaging machines that automatically insert fuel elements into canisters and secure lids. Apply chemical compounds to lead-based paint, allow compounds to dry, then scrape the hazardous material into containers for removal and/or storage. Identify asbestos, lead, or other hazardous materials that need to be removed, using monitoring devices. Pull tram cars along underwater tracks, and position cars to receive irradiated fuel elements; then pull loaded cars to mechanisms that automatically unload elements onto underwater tables. Package, store, and move irradiated fuel elements in the underwater storage basin of a nuclear reactor plant, using machines and equipment. Organize and track the locations of hazardous items in landfills.

Operate cranes to move and load baskets, casks, and canisters. Manipulate handgrips of mechanical arms to place irradiated fuel elements into baskets. Mix and pour concrete into forms to encase waste material for disposal.

Personality Type: Realistic. These occupations frequently involve work activities that include practical, hands-on problems and solutions. They often deal with plants; animals; and real-world materials such as wood, tools, and machinery. Many of the occupations require working outside and don't involve a lot of paperwork or working closely with others.

GOE—Interest Area/Cluster: 02. Architecture and Construction. **Work Group:** 02.04. Construction Crafts. **Other Jobs in This Work Group:** Boilermakers; Brickmasons and Blockmasons; Carpet Installers; Cement Masons and Concrete Finishers; Commercial Divers; Construction Carpenters; Crane and Tower Operators; Drywall and Ceiling Tile Installers; Electricians; Fence Erectors; Floor Layers, Except Carpet, Wood, and Hard Tiles; Floor Sanders and Finishers; Glaziers; Insulation Workers, Floor, Ceiling, and Wall; Insulation Workers, Mechanical; Manufactured Building and Mobile Home Installers; Operating Engineers and Other Construction Equipment Operators; Painters, Construction and Maintenance; Paperhangers; Paving, Surfacing, and Tamping Equipment Operators; Pile-Driver Operators; Pipe Fitters and Steamfitters; Pipelayers; Plasterers and Stucco Masons; Plumbers; Plumbers, Pipefitters, and Steamfitters; Rail-Track Laying and Maintenance Equipment Operators; Refractory Materials Repairers, Except Brickmasons; Reinforcing Iron and Rebar Workers; Riggers; Roofers; Rough Carpenters; Security and Fire Alarm Systems Installers; Segmental Pavers; Sheet Metal Workers; Stone Cutters and Carvers, Manufacturing; Stonemasons; Structural Iron and Steel Workers; Tapers; Terrazzo Workers and Finishers; Tile and Marble Setters.

Skills—Equipment Maintenance: Performing routine maintenance and determining when and what kind of maintenance is needed. **Operation Monitoring:** Watching gauges, dials, or other indicators to make sure a machine is working properly. **Repairing:** Repairing machines or systems, using the needed tools. **Operation and Control:** Controlling operations of equipment or systems. **Science:** Using scientific methods to solve problems. **Troubleshooting:** Determining what is causing an operating error and deciding what to do about it. **Quality Control Analysis:** Evaluating the quality or performance of products, services, or processes. **Systems Analysis:** Determining how a system should work and how changes will affect outcomes.

Education and Training Programs: Construction Trades, Other; Hazardous Materials Management and Waste Technology/Technician Training; Mechanic and Repair Technologies/Technician Training, Other. **Related Knowledge/Courses—Chemistry:** The composition, structure, and properties of substances and of the chemical processes and transformations that they undergo. This includes uses of chemicals and their interactions, danger signs, production techniques, and disposal methods. **Mechanical Devices:** Machines and tools, including their designs, uses, benefits, repair, and maintenance. **Building and Construction:** Materials, methods, and the appropriate tools to construct objects, structures, and buildings. **Transportation:** Principles and methods for moving people or goods by air, rail, sea, or road, including their relative costs, advantages, and limitations. **Physics:** Physical principles, laws, and applications, including air, water, material dynamics, light, atomic principles, heat, electric theory, earth formations, and meteorological and related natural phenomena. **Public Safety and Security:** Weaponry; public safety; security operations, rules, regulations, precautions, and prevention; and the protection of people, data, and property.

Work Environment: Outdoors; very hot or cold; contaminants; hazardous conditions; using hands on objects, tools, or controls; repetitive motions.

Health Educators

- ❋ Education/Training Required: Bachelor's degree
- ❋ Annual Earnings: $42,920
- ❋ Beginning Wage: $25,340
- ❋ Earnings Growth Potential: High
- ❋ Growth: 26.2%
- ❋ Annual Job Openings: 13,707
- ❋ Self-Employed: 0.1%
- ❋ Part-Time: 12.0%

Promote, maintain, and improve individual and community health by assisting individuals and communities to adopt healthy behaviors. Collect and analyze data to identify community needs prior to planning, implementing, monitoring, and evaluating programs designed to encourage healthy lifestyles, policies, and environments. May also serve as a resource to assist individuals, other professionals, or the community and may administer fiscal resources for health education programs. Document activities, recording information such as the numbers of applications completed, presentations conducted, and persons assisted. Develop and present health education and promotion programs such as training workshops, conferences, and school or community presentations. Develop and maintain cooperative working relationships with agencies and organizations interested in public health care. Prepare and distribute health education materials, including reports; bulletins; and visual aids such as films, videotapes, photographs, and posters. Develop operational plans and policies necessary to achieve health education objectives and services. Collaborate with health specialists and civic groups to determine community health needs and the availability of services and to develop goals for meeting needs. Maintain databases, mailing lists, telephone networks, and other information to facilitate the functioning of health education programs. Supervise professional and technical staff in implementing health programs, objectives, and goals. Design and conduct evaluations and diagnostic studies to assess the quality and performance of health education programs. Provide program information to the public by preparing and presenting press releases, conducting media campaigns, and/or maintaining program-related Web sites. Develop, prepare, and coordinate grant applications and grant-related activities to obtain funding for health education programs and related work. Provide guidance to agencies and organizations in the assessment of health education needs and in the development and delivery of health education programs. Develop and maintain health education libraries to provide resources for staff and community agencies. Develop, conduct, or coordinate health needs assessments and other public health surveys.

Personality Type: Social. These occupations frequently involve working with, communicating with, and teaching people and often involve helping or providing service to others.

GOE—Interest Area/Cluster: 05. Education and Training. **Work Group:** 05.06. Counseling, Health, and Fitness Education. **Other Jobs in This Work Group:** Educational, Vocational, and School Counselors; Fitness Trainers and Aerobics Instructors.

Skills—Service Orientation: Actively looking for ways to help people. **Social Perceptiveness:** Being aware of others' reactions and understanding why they react the way they do. **Monitoring:** Assessing how well one is doing when learning or doing something. **Learning Strategies:** Using multiple approaches when learning or teaching new things. **Instructing:** Teaching others how to do something. **Speaking:** Talking to others to effectively convey information.

Coordination: Adjusting actions in relation to others' actions. **Active Learning:** Working with new material or information to grasp its implications.

Education and Training Programs: Bioethics/Medical Ethics; Community Health Services/Liaison/Counseling; Health Communication; International Public Health/International Health; Maternal and Child Health; Public Health Education and Promotion. **Related Knowledge/Courses—Sociology and Anthropology:** Group behavior and dynamics; societal trends and influences; and cultures and their history, migrations, ethnicity, and origins. **Customer and Personal Service:** Principles and processes for providing customer and personal services, including needs assessment techniques, quality service standards, alternative delivery systems, and customer satisfaction evaluation techniques. **Education and Training:** Instructional methods and training techniques, including curriculum design principles, learning theory, group and individual teaching techniques, design of individual development plans, and test design principles. **Personnel and Human Resources:** Principles and procedures for personnel recruitment; selection; training; compensation and benefits; labor relations and negotiation; and personnel information systems. **Psychology:** Human behavior and performance, mental processes, psychological research methods, and the assessment and treatment of behavioral and affective disorders. **Therapy and Counseling:** Information and techniques needed to rehabilitate physical and mental ailments and to provide career guidance, including alternative treatments, rehabilitation equipment and its proper use, and methods to evaluate treatment effects.

Work Environment: Indoors; disease or infections; sitting; using hands on objects, tools, or controls.

Health Specialties Teachers, Postsecondary

- ✸ Education/Training Required: Doctoral degree
- ✸ Annual Earnings: $80,700
- ✸ Beginning Wage: $37,890
- ✸ Earnings Growth Potential: Very high
- ✸ Growth: 22.9%
- ✸ Annual Job Openings: 19,617
- ✸ Self-Employed: 0.4%
- ✸ Part-Time: 27.8%

Teach courses in health specialties, such as veterinary medicine, dentistry, pharmacy, therapy, laboratory technology, and public health. Initiate, facilitate, and moderate classroom discussions. Keep abreast of developments in their field by reading current literature, talking with colleagues, and participating in professional conferences. Compile, administer, and grade examinations or assign this work to others. Evaluate and grade students' classwork, assignments, and papers. Prepare course materials such as syllabi, homework assignments, and handouts. Prepare and deliver lectures to undergraduate or graduate students on topics such as public health, stress management, and worksite health promotion. Plan, evaluate, and revise curricula, course content, and course materials and methods of instruction. Supervise undergraduate or graduate teaching, internship, and research work. Conduct research in a particular field of knowledge and publish findings in professional journals, books, or electronic media. Collaborate with colleagues to address teaching and research issues. Supervise laboratory sessions. Maintain student attendance records, grades, and other required records. Maintain regularly scheduled office hours in order to advise and assist students. Advise students on academic and vocational curricula and on career issues. Participate in student recruitment, registration, and placement activities. Write grant proposals to procure external research funding. Serve on academic or administrative committees that deal with institutional policies, departmental matters, and academic issues. Select and obtain materials and supplies such as textbooks and laboratory equipment. Act as advisers to student organizations. Perform administrative duties such as serving as department head. Compile bibliographies of specialized materials for outside reading assignments. Provide professional consulting services to government and industry. Participate in campus and community events.

Personality Type: Social. These occupations frequently involve working with, communicating with, and teaching people and often involve helping or providing service to others.

GOE—Interest Area/Cluster: 05. Education and Training. **Work Group:** 05.03. Postsecondary and Adult Teaching and Instructing. **Other Jobs in This Work Group:** Adult Literacy, Remedial Education, and GED Teachers and Instructors; Agricultural Sciences Teachers, Postsecondary; Anthropology and Archeology Teachers, Postsecondary; Architecture Teachers, Postsecondary; Area, Ethnic, and Cultural Studies Teachers, Postsecondary; Art, Drama, and Music Teachers, Postsecondary; Atmospheric, Earth,

Marine, and Space Sciences Teachers, Postsecondary; Biological Science Teachers, Postsecondary; Business Teachers, Postsecondary; Chemistry Teachers, Postsecondary; Communications Teachers, Postsecondary; Computer Science Teachers, Postsecondary; Criminal Justice and Law Enforcement Teachers, Postsecondary; Economics Teachers, Postsecondary; Education Teachers, Postsecondary; Engineering Teachers, Postsecondary; English Language and Literature Teachers, Postsecondary; Environmental Science Teachers, Postsecondary; Farm and Home Management Advisors; Foreign Language and Literature Teachers, Postsecondary; Forestry and Conservation Science Teachers, Postsecondary; Geography Teachers, Postsecondary; Graduate Teaching Assistants; History Teachers, Postsecondary; Home Economics Teachers, Postsecondary; Law Teachers, Postsecondary; Library Science Teachers, Postsecondary; Mathematical Science Teachers, Postsecondary; Nursing Instructors and Teachers, Postsecondary; Philosophy and Religion Teachers, Postsecondary; Physics Teachers, Postsecondary; Political Science Teachers, Postsecondary; Psychology Teachers, Postsecondary; Recreation and Fitness Studies Teachers, Postsecondary; Self-Enrichment Education Teachers; Social Work Teachers, Postsecondary; Sociology Teachers, Postsecondary; Vocational Education Teachers, Postsecondary.

Skills—Science: Using scientific methods to solve problems. **Instructing:** Teaching others how to do something. **Writing:** Communicating effectively with others in writing as indicated by the needs of the audience. **Reading Comprehension:** Understanding written sentences and paragraphs in work-related documents. **Learning Strategies:** Using multiple approaches when learning or teaching new things. **Complex Problem Solving:** Identifying complex problems, reviewing the options, and implementing solutions. **Critical Thinking:** Using logic and analysis to identify the strengths and weaknesses of different approaches. **Speaking:** Talking to others to effectively convey information.

Education and Training Programs: Allied Health and Medical Assisting Services, others; Art Therapy; Audiology and Speech-Language Pathology; Biostatistics; Cardiovascular Technology; Chiropractic; Clinical Laboratory Sciencet; Dental Hygiene; Dentistry; Electrocardiograph Technology; Massage Therapy; Medical Radiologic Technology; Nuclear Medical Technology; Occupational Health and Industrial Hygiene; Perfusion Technology; Pharmacy; Physical Therapy; Respiratory Care Therapy; Surgical Technology; Veterinary Medicine. **Related Knowledge/Courses—Biology:** Plant and animal living tissue, cells, organisms, and entities, including their functions, interdependencies, and

interactions with each other and the environment. **Medicine and Dentistry:** The information and techniques needed to diagnose and treat injuries, diseases, and deformities. This includes symptoms, treatment alternatives, drug properties and interactions, and preventive health-care measures. **Education and Training:** Instructional methods and training techniques, including curriculum design principles, learning theory, group and individual teaching techniques, design of individual development plans, and test design principles. **Therapy and Counseling:** Information and techniques needed to rehabilitate physical and mental ailments and to provide career guidance, including alternative treatments, rehabilitation equipment and its proper use, and methods to evaluate treatment effects. **Sociology and Anthropology:** Group behavior and dynamics; societal trends and influences; and cultures and their history, migrations, ethnicity, and origins. **Psychology:** Human behavior and performance, mental processes, psychological research methods, and the assessment and treatment of behavioral and affective disorders.

Work Environment: Indoors; sitting.

Heating and Air Conditioning Mechanics and Installers

- ❋ Education/Training Required: Long-term on-the-job training
- ❋ Annual Earnings: $38,360
- ❋ Beginning Wage: $24,240
- ❋ Earnings Growth Potential: Medium
- ❋ Growth: 8.7%
- ❋ Annual Job Openings: 29,719
- ❋ Self-Employed: 12.7%
- ❋ Part-Time: 3.6%

The job openings listed here are shared with Refrigeration Mechanics and Installers.

Install, service, and repair heating and air conditioning systems in residences and commercial establishments. Obtain and maintain required certifications. Comply with all applicable standards, policies, and procedures, including safety procedures and the maintenance of a clean work area. Repair or replace defective equipment, components, or wiring. Test electrical circuits and components for continuity, using electrical test equipment. Reassemble and test equipment following repairs. Inspect and test system to verify system compliance with plans and specifications and to detect and locate malfunctions. Discuss heating-cooling system malfunctions with users to isolate problems or to verify that malfunctions have been corrected. Test pipe or tubing joints and connections for leaks, using pressure gauge or soap-and-water solution. Record and report all faults, deficiencies, and other unusual occurrences, as well as the time and materials expended on work orders. Adjust system controls to setting recommended by manufacturer to balance system, using hand tools. Recommend, develop, and perform preventive and general maintenance procedures such as cleaning, power-washing, and vacuuming equipment; oiling parts; and changing filters. Lay out and connect electrical wiring between controls and equipment according to wiring diagram, using electrician's hand tools. Install auxiliary components to heating-cooling equipment, such as expansion and discharge valves, air ducts, pipes, blowers, dampers, flues, and stokers, following blueprints. Assist with other work in coordination with repair and maintenance teams. Install, connect, and adjust thermostats, humidistats, and timers, using hand tools. Generate work orders that address deficiencies in need of correction. Join pipes or tubing to equipment and to fuel, water, or refrigerant source to form complete circuit. Assemble, position, and mount heating or cooling equipment, following blueprints. Study blueprints, design specifications, and manufacturers' recommendations to ascertain the configuration of heating or cooling equipment components and to ensure the proper installation of components. Cut and drill holes in floors, walls, and roof to install equipment, using power saws and drills.

Personality Type: Realistic. These occupations frequently involve work activities that include practical, hands-on problems and solutions. They often deal with plants; animals; and real-world materials such as wood, tools, and machinery. Many of the occupations require working outside and don't involve a lot of paperwork or working closely with others.

GOE—Interest Area/Cluster: 02. Architecture and Construction. **Work Group:** 02.05. Systems and Equipment Installation, Maintenance, and Repair. **Other Jobs in This Work Group:** Electrical and Electronics Repairers, Powerhouse, Substation, and Relay; Electrical Power-Line Installers and Repairers; Elevator Installers and Repairers; Maintenance and Repair Workers, General; Refrigeration Mechanics and Installers; Telecommunications Equipment Installers and Repairers, Except Line Installers; Telecommunications Line Installers and Repairers.

Skills—Repairing: Repairing machines or systems, using the needed tools. **Installation:** Installing equipment, machines, wiring, or programs to meet specifications. **Equipment Maintenance:** Performing routine maintenance and determining when and what kind of maintenance is needed. **Troubleshooting:** Determining what is causing an operating error and deciding what to do about it. **Systems Evaluation:** Looking at many indicators of system performance and taking into account their accuracy. **Science:** Using scientific methods to solve problems. **Systems Analysis:** Determining how a system should work and how changes will affect outcomes. **Coordination:** Adjusting actions in relation to others' actions.

Education and Training Programs: Heating, Air Conditioning and Refrigeration Technology/Technician Training (ACH/ACR/ACHR/HRAC/HVAC/; Heating, Air Conditioning, Ventilation and Refrigeration Maintenance Technology/Technician Training; Solar Energy Technology/Technician Training. **Related Knowledge/Courses—Mechanical Devices:** Machines and tools, including their designs, uses, benefits, repair, and maintenance. **Building and Construction:** Materials, methods, and the appropriate tools to construct objects, structures, and buildings. **Design:** Design techniques, principles, tools, and instruments involved in the production and use of precision technical plans, blueprints, drawings, and models. **Physics:** Physical principles, laws, and applications, including air, water, material dynamics, light, atomic principles, heat, electric theory, earth formations, and meteorological and related natural phenomena. **Engineering and Technology:** Equipment, tools, and mechanical devices and their uses to produce motion, light, power, technology, and other applications. **Sales and Marketing:** Principles and methods involved in showing, promoting, and selling products or services. This includes marketing strategies and tactics, product demonstration and sales techniques, and sales control systems.

Work Environment: Outdoors; contaminants; hazardous conditions; minor burns, cuts, bites, or stings; standing; using hands on objects, tools, or controls.

Helpers—Brickmasons, Blockmasons, Stonemasons, and Tile and Marble Setters

- ❀ Education/Training Required: Short-term on-the-job training
- ❀ Annual Earnings: $26,260
- ❀ Beginning Wage: $18,340
- ❀ Earnings Growth Potential: Low
- ❀ Growth: 11.0%
- ❀ Annual Job Openings: 22,500
- ❀ Self-Employed: 3.0%
- ❀ Part-Time: 10.4%

Help brickmasons, blockmasons, stonemasons, or tile and marble setters by performing duties of lesser skill. Duties include using, supplying, or holding materials or tools and cleaning work area and equipment. Transport materials, tools, and machines to installation sites, manually or using conveyance equipment. Move or position materials such as marble slabs, using cranes, hoists, or dollies. Modify material moving, mixing, grouting, grinding, polishing, or cleaning procedures according to installation or material requirements. Correct surface imperfections or fill chipped, cracked, or broken bricks or tiles, using fillers, adhesives, and grouting materials. Arrange and store materials, machines, tools, and equipment. Apply caulk, sealants, or other agents to installed surfaces. Select or locate and supply materials to masons for installation, following drawings or numbered sequences. Remove excess grout and residue from tile or brick joints, using sponges or trowels. Remove damaged tile, brick, or mortar, and clean and prepare surfaces, using pliers, hammers, chisels, drills, wire brushes, and metal wire anchors. Provide assistance in the preparation, installation, repair, and/or rebuilding of tile, brick, or stone surfaces. Mix mortar, plaster, and grout, manually or using machines, according to standard formulas. Erect scaffolding or other installation structures. Cut materials to specified sizes for installation, using power saws or tile cutters. Clean installation surfaces, equipment, tools, work sites, and storage areas, using water, chemical solutions, oxygen lances, or polishing machines. Apply grout between joints of bricks or tiles, using grouting trowels.

Personality Type: Realistic. These occupations frequently involve work activities that include practical, hands-on problems and solutions. They often deal with plants; animals; and real-world materials such as wood, tools, and machinery. Many of the occupations require working outside and don't involve a lot of paperwork or working closely with others.

GOE—Interest Area/Cluster: 02. Architecture and Construction. **Work Group:** 02.06. Construction Support/Labor. **Other Jobs in This Work Group:** Construction Laborers; Helpers—Carpenters; Helpers—Electricians; Helpers—Installation, Maintenance, and Repair Workers; Helpers—Painters, Paperhangers, Plasterers, and Stucco Masons; Helpers—Pipelayers, Plumbers, Pipefitters, and Steamfitters; Helpers—Roofers; Highway Maintenance Workers; Septic Tank Servicers and Sewer Pipe Cleaners.

Skills—Repairing: Repairing machines or systems, using the needed tools. **Equipment Maintenance:** Performing routine maintenance and determining when and what kind of maintenance is needed. **Installation:** Installing equipment, machines, wiring, or programs to meet specifications. **Management of Material Resources:** Obtaining and seeing to the appropriate use of equipment, facilities, and materials needed to do certain work. **Operation and Control:** Controlling operations of equipment or systems. **Mathematics:** Using mathematics to solve problems. **Operations Analysis:** Analyzing needs and product requirements to create a design.

Education and Training Program: Mason Training/Masonry. **Related Knowledge/Courses—Building and Construction:** Materials, methods, and the appropriate tools to construct objects, structures, and buildings. **Chemistry:** The composition, structure, and properties of substances and of the chemical processes and transformations that they undergo. This includes uses of chemicals and their interactions, danger signs, production techniques, and disposal methods. **Transportation:** Principles and methods for moving people or goods by air, rail, sea, or road, including their relative costs, advantages, and limitations. **Production and Processing:** Inputs, outputs, raw materials, waste, quality control, costs, and techniques for maximizing the manufacture and distribution of goods. **Mechanical Devices:** Machines and tools, including their designs, uses, benefits, repair, and maintenance. **Design:** Design techniques, principles, tools, and instruments involved in the production and use of precision technical plans, blueprints, drawings, and models.

Work Environment: Outdoors; noisy; very hot or cold; high places; using hands on objects, tools, or controls; repetitive motions.

Helpers—Carpenters

- ❋ Education/Training Required: Short-term on-the-job training
- ❋ Annual Earnings: $24,340
- ❋ Beginning Wage: $16,790
- ❋ Earnings Growth Potential: Low
- ❋ Growth: 11.7%
- ❋ Annual Job Openings: 37,731
- ❋ Self-Employed: 3.2%
- ❋ Part-Time: 10.4%

Help carpenters by performing duties of lesser skill. Duties include using, supplying, or holding materials or tools and cleaning work area and equipment. Position and hold timbers, lumber, and paneling in place for fastening or cutting. Erect scaffolding, shoring, and braces. Select tools, equipment, and materials from storage and transport items to worksite. Fasten timbers or lumber with glue, screws, pegs, or nails and install hardware. Clean work areas, machines, and equipment to maintain a clean and safe jobsite. Align, straighten, plumb, and square forms for installation. Hold plumb bobs, sighting rods, and other equipment to aid in establishing reference points and lines. Cut timbers, lumber, or paneling to specified dimensions and drill holes in timbers or lumber. Smooth and sand surfaces to remove ridges, tool marks, glue, or caulking. Perform tie spacing layout; then measure, mark, drill, and cut. Secure stakes to grids for constructions of footings, nail scabs to footing forms, and vibrate and float concrete. Construct forms; then assist in raising them to the required elevation. Install handrails under the direction of a carpenter. Glue and clamp edges or joints of assembled parts. Cut and install insulating or sound-absorbing material. Cut tile or linoleum to fit and spread adhesives on flooring to install tile or linoleum. Cover surfaces with laminated-plastic covering material.

Personality Type: Realistic. These occupations frequently involve work activities that include practical, hands-on problems and solutions. They often deal with plants; animals; and real-world materials such as wood, tools, and machinery. Many of the occupations require working outside and don't involve a lot of paperwork or working closely with others.

GOE—Interest Area/Cluster: 02. Architecture and Construction. **Work Group:** 02.06. Construction Support/Labor. **Other Jobs in This Work Group:** Construction Laborers; Helpers—Brickmasons, Blockmasons, Stonemasons, and Tile and Marble Setters; Helpers—Electricians; Helpers—Installation, Maintenance, and Repair Workers; Helpers—Painters, Paperhangers, Plasterers, and Stucco Masons; Helpers—Pipelayers, Plumbers, Pipefitters, and Steamfitters; Helpers—Roofers; Highway Maintenance Workers; Septic Tank Servicers and Sewer Pipe Cleaners.

Skills—Installation: Installing equipment, machines, wiring, or programs to meet specifications. **Repairing:** Repairing machines or systems, using the needed tools. **Equipment Maintenance:** Performing routine maintenance and determining when and what kind of maintenance is needed. **Management of Material Resources:** Obtaining and seeing to the appropriate use of equipment, facilities, and materials needed to do certain work. **Troubleshooting:** Determining what is causing an operating error and deciding what to do about it. **Equipment Selection:** Determining the kind of tools and equipment needed to do a job. **Mathematics:** Using mathematics to solve problems. **Operation and Control:** Controlling operations of equipment or systems.

Education and Training Program: Carpentry/Carpenter Training. **Related Knowledge/Courses—Building and Construction:** Materials, methods, and the appropriate tools to construct objects, structures, and buildings. **Design:** Design techniques, principles, tools, and instruments involved in the production and use of precision technical plans, blueprints, drawings, and models. **Engineering and Technology:** Equipment, tools, and mechanical devices and their uses to produce motion, light, power, technology, and other applications.

Work Environment: Noisy; very hot or cold; hazardous equipment; standing; walking and running; using hands on objects, tools, or controls.

Helpers—Electricians

- ❋ Education/Training Required: Short-term on-the-job training
- ❋ Annual Earnings: $24,880
- ❋ Beginning Wage: $17,580
- ❋ Earnings Growth Potential: Low
- ❋ Growth: 6.8%
- ❋ Annual Job Openings: 35,109
- ❋ Self-Employed: 2.9%
- ❋ Part-Time: 10.4%

Help electricians by performing duties of lesser skill. Duties include using, supplying, or holding materials

or tools and cleaning work area and equipment. Trace out short circuits in wiring, using test meter. Measure, cut, and bend wire and conduit, using measuring instruments and hand tools. Maintain tools, vehicles, and equipment and keep parts and supplies in order. Drill holes and pull or push wiring through openings, using hand and power tools. Perform semi-skilled and unskilled laboring duties related to the installation, maintenance, and repair of a wide variety of electrical systems and equipment. Disassemble defective electrical equipment, replace defective or worn parts, and reassemble equipment, using hand tools. Transport tools, materials, equipment, and supplies to worksite by hand; handtruck; or heavy, motorized truck. Examine electrical units for loose connections and broken insulation and tighten connections, using hand tools. Strip insulation from wire ends, using wire-stripping pliers, and attach wires to terminals for subsequent soldering. Construct controllers and panels, using power drills, drill presses, taps, saws, and punches. Thread conduit ends, connect couplings, and fabricate and secure conduit support brackets, using hand tools. String transmission lines or cables through ducts or conduits, under the ground, through equipment, or to towers. Clean work area and wash parts. Erect electrical system components and barricades and rig scaffolds, hoists, and shoring. Install copper-clad ground rods, using a manual post driver. Raise, lower, or position equipment, tools, and materials, using hoist, hand line, or block and tackle. Dig trenches or holes for installation of conduit or supports. Requisition materials, using warehouse requisition or release forms. Bolt component parts together to form tower assemblies, using hand tools. Paint a variety of objects related to electrical functions. Operate cutting torches and welding equipment while working with conduit and metal components to construct devices associated with electrical functions. Break up concrete, using air hammer, to facilitate installation, construction, or repair of equipment. Solder electrical connections, using soldering iron. Trim trees and clear undergrowth along right-of-way.

Personality Type: Realistic. These occupations frequently involve work activities that include practical, hands-on problems and solutions. They often deal with plants; animals; and real-world materials such as wood, tools, and machinery. Many of the occupations require working outside and don't involve a lot of paperwork or working closely with others.

GOE—Interest Area/Cluster: 02. Architecture and Construction. **Work Group:** 02.06. Construction Support/ Labor. **Other Jobs in This Work Group:** Construction Laborers; Helpers—Brickmasons, Blockmasons, Stonemasons, and Tile and Marble Setters; Helpers—Carpenters; Helpers—Installation, Maintenance, and Repair Workers; Helpers—Painters, Paperhangers, Plasterers, and Stucco Masons; Helpers—Pipelayers, Plumbers, Pipefitters, and Steamfitters; Helpers—Roofers; Highway Maintenance Workers; Septic Tank Servicers and Sewer Pipe Cleaners.

Skills—Installation: Installing equipment, machines, wiring, or programs to meet specifications. **Troubleshooting:** Determining what is causing an operating error and deciding what to do about it. **Repairing:** Repairing machines or systems, using the needed tools. **Mathematics:** Using mathematics to solve problems. **Equipment Selection:** Determining the kind of tools and equipment needed to do a job. **Complex Problem Solving:** Identifying complex problems, reviewing the options, and implementing solutions. **Operation and Control:** Controlling operations of equipment or systems. **Science:** Using scientific methods to solve problems.

Education and Training Program: Electrician Training. **Related Knowledge/Courses—Building and Construction:** Materials, methods, and the appropriate tools to construct objects, structures, and buildings. **Mechanical Devices:** Machines and tools, including their designs, uses, benefits, repair, and maintenance. **Design:** Design techniques, principles, tools, and instruments involved in the production and use of precision technical plans, blueprints, drawings, and models. **Engineering and Technology:** Equipment, tools, and mechanical devices and their uses to produce motion, light, power, technology, and other applications. **Mathematics:** Numbers and their operations and interrelationships, including arithmetic, algebra, geometry, calculus, and statistics and their applications. **Public Safety and Security:** Weaponry; public safety; security operations, rules, regulations, precautions, and prevention; and the protection of people, data, and property.

Work Environment: Outdoors; very hot or cold; contaminants; high places; standing; using hands on objects, tools, or controls.

Helpers—Installation, Maintenance, and Repair Workers

* Education/Training Required: Short-term on-the-job training
* Annual Earnings: $22,920
* Beginning Wage: $15,530
* Earnings Growth Potential: Low
* Growth: 11.8%
* Annual Job Openings: 52,058
* Self-Employed: 0.1%
* Part-Time: 22.7%

Help installation, maintenance, and repair workers in maintenance, parts replacement, and repair of vehicles, industrial machinery, and electrical and electronic equipment. Perform duties such as furnishing tools, materials, and supplies to other workers; cleaning work area, machines, and tools; and holding materials or tools for other workers. Tend and observe equipment and machinery to verify efficient and safe operation. Examine and test machinery, equipment, components, and parts for defects and to ensure proper functioning. Adjust, connect, or disconnect wiring, piping, tubing, and other parts, using hand tools or power tools. Install or replace machinery, equipment, and new or replacement parts and instruments, using hand tools or power tools. Clean or lubricate vehicles, machinery, equipment, instruments, tools, work areas, and other objects, using hand tools, power tools, and cleaning equipment. Apply protective materials to equipment, components, and parts to prevent defects and corrosion. Transfer tools, parts, equipment, and supplies to and from workstations and other areas. Disassemble broken or defective equipment in order to facilitate repair; reassemble equipment when repairs are complete. Assemble and maintain physical structures, using hand tools or power tools. Provide assistance to more skilled workers involved in the adjustment, maintenance, part replacement, and repair of tools, equipment, and machines. Position vehicles, machinery, equipment, physical structures, and other objects for assembly or installation, using hand tools, power tools, and moving equipment. Hold or supply tools, parts, equipment, and supplies for other workers. Prepare work stations so mechanics and repairers can conduct work.

Personality Type: Realistic. These occupations frequently involve work activities that include practical, hands-on problems and solutions. They often deal with plants; animals; and real-world materials such as wood, tools, and machinery. Many of the occupations require working outside and don't involve a lot of paperwork or working closely with others.

GOE—Interest Area/Cluster: 02. Architecture and Construction. **Work Group:** 02.06. Construction Support/Labor. **Other Jobs in This Work Group:** Construction Laborers; Helpers—Brickmasons, Blockmasons, Stonemasons, and Tile and Marble Setters; Helpers—Carpenters; Helpers—Electricians; Helpers—Painters, Paperhangers, Plasterers, and Stucco Masons; Helpers—Pipelayers, Plumbers, Pipefitters, and Steamfitters; Helpers—Roofers; Highway Maintenance Workers; Septic Tank Servicers and Sewer Pipe Cleaners.

Skills—Installation: Installing equipment, machines, wiring, or programs to meet specifications. **Operation Monitoring:** Watching gauges, dials, or other indicators to make sure a machine is working properly. **Repairing:** Repairing machines or systems, using the needed tools. **Equipment Maintenance:** Performing routine maintenance and determining when and what kind of maintenance is needed. **Troubleshooting:** Determining what is causing an operating error and deciding what to do about it. **Operations Analysis:** Analyzing needs and product requirements to create a design. **Operation and Control:** Controlling operations of equipment or systems. **Science:** Using scientific methods to solve problems.

Education and Training Program: Industrial Mechanics and Maintenance Technology. **Related Knowledge/Courses—Mechanical Devices:** Machines and tools, including their designs, uses, benefits, repair, and maintenance. **Engineering and Technology:** Equipment, tools, and mechanical devices and their uses to produce motion, light, power, technology, and other applications. **Building and Construction:** Materials, methods, and the appropriate tools to construct objects, structures, and buildings. **Chemistry:** The composition, structure, and properties of substances and of the chemical processes and transformations that they undergo. This includes uses of chemicals and their interactions, danger signs, production techniques, and disposal methods. **Design:** Design techniques, principles, tools, and instruments involved in the production and use of precision technical plans, blueprints, drawings, and models. **Public Safety and Security:** Weaponry; public safety; security operations, rules, regulations, precautions, and prevention; and the protection of people, data, and property.

Work Environment: Noisy; hazardous conditions; hazardous equipment; standing; using hands on objects, tools, or controls; bending or twisting the body.

Helpers—Pipelayers, Plumbers, Pipefitters, and Steamfitters

- ❋ Education/Training Required: Short-term on-the-job training
- ❋ Annual Earnings: $25,350
- ❋ Beginning Wage: $17,700
- ❋ Earnings Growth Potential: Low
- ❋ Growth: 11.9%
- ❋ Annual Job Openings: 29,332
- ❋ Self-Employed: 2.9%
- ❋ Part-Time: 10.4%

Help plumbers, pipefitters, steamfitters, or pipelayers by performing duties of lesser skill. Duties include using, supplying, or holding materials or tools and cleaning work area and equipment. Assist plumbers by performing rough-ins, repairing and replacing fixtures, and locating and repairing leaking or broken pipes. Cut or drill holes in walls or floors to accommodate the passage of pipes. Measure, cut, thread, and assemble new pipe, placing the assembled pipe in hangers or other supports. Mount brackets and hangers on walls and ceilings to hold pipes and set sleeves or inserts to provide support for pipes. Requisition tools and equipment, select type and size of pipe, and collect and transport materials and equipment to worksite. Fit or assist in fitting valves, couplings, or assemblies to tanks, pumps, or systems, using hand tools. Assist pipe fitters in the layout, assembly, and installation of piping for air, ammonia, gas, and water systems. Excavate and grade ditches and lay and join pipe for water and sewer service. Cut pipe and lift up to fitters. Disassemble and remove damaged or worn pipe. Clean shop, work area, and machines, using solvent and rags. Install gas burners to convert furnaces from wood, coal, or oil. Immerse pipe in chemical solution to remove dirt, oil, and scale. Clean and renew steam traps. Fill pipes with sand or resin to prevent distortion and hold pipes during bending and installation.

Personality Type: Realistic. These occupations frequently involve work activities that include practical, hands-on problems and solutions. They often deal with plants; animals; and real-world materials such as wood, tools, and machinery. Many of the occupations require working outside and don't involve a lot of paperwork or working closely with others.

GOE—Interest Area/Cluster: 02. Architecture and Construction. **Work Group:** 02.06. Construction Support/ Labor. **Other Jobs in This Work Group:** Construction Laborers; Helpers—Brickmasons, Blockmasons, Stonemasons, and Tile and Marble Setters; Helpers—Carpenters; Helpers—Electricians; Helpers—Installation, Maintenance, and Repair Workers; Helpers—Painters, Paperhangers, Plasterers, and Stucco Masons; Helpers—Roofers; Highway Maintenance Workers; Septic Tank Servicers and Sewer Pipe Cleaners.

Skills—Installation: Installing equipment, machines, wiring, or programs to meet specifications. **Repairing:** Repairing machines or systems, using the needed tools. **Equipment Maintenance:** Performing routine maintenance and determining when and what kind of maintenance is needed. **Troubleshooting:** Determining what is causing an operating error and deciding what to do about it. **Mathematics:** Using mathematics to solve problems. **Quality Control Analysis:** Evaluating the quality or performance of products, services, or processes. **Equipment Selection:** Determining the kind of tools and equipment needed to do a job. **Negotiation:** Bringing others together and trying to reconcile differences.

Education and Training Program: Plumbing Technology/Plumber Training. **Related Knowledge/Courses— Building and Construction:** Materials, methods, and the appropriate tools to construct objects, structures, and buildings. **Mechanical Devices:** Machines and tools, including their designs, uses, benefits, repair, and maintenance. **Design:** Design techniques, principles, tools, and instruments involved in the production and use of precision technical plans, blueprints, drawings, and models. **Public Safety and Security:** Weaponry; public safety; security operations, rules, regulations, precautions, and prevention; and the protection of people, data, and property. **Engineering and Technology:** Equipment, tools, and mechanical devices and their uses to produce motion, light, power, technology, and other applications. **Law and Government:** Laws, legal codes, court procedures, precedents, government regulations, executive orders, agency rules, and the democratic political process.

Work Environment: Outdoors; noisy; contaminants; hazardous equipment; standing; using hands on objects, tools, or controls.

Highway Maintenance Workers

- ❊ Education/Training Required: Moderate-term on-the-job training
- ❊ Annual Earnings: $32,600
- ❊ Beginning Wage: $20,960
- ❊ Earnings Growth Potential: Medium
- ❊ Growth: 8.9%
- ❊ Annual Job Openings: 24,774
- ❊ Self-Employed: 0.9%
- ❊ Part-Time: 1.9%

Maintain highways, municipal and rural roads, airport runways, and rights-of-way. Duties include patching broken or eroded pavement and repairing guardrails, highway markers, and snow fences. May also mow or clear brush from along road or plow snow from roadway. Flag motorists to warn them of obstacles or repair work ahead. Set out signs and cones around work areas to divert traffic. Drive trucks or tractors with adjustable attachments to sweep debris from paved surfaces, mow grass and weeds, and remove snow and ice. Dump, spread, and tamp asphalt, using pneumatic tampers, to repair joints and patch broken pavement. Drive trucks to transport crews and equipment to worksites. Inspect, clean, and repair drainage systems, bridges, tunnels, and other structures. Haul and spread sand, gravel, and clay to fill washouts and repair road shoulders. Erect, install, or repair guardrails, road shoulders, berms, highway markers, warning signals, and highway lighting, using hand tools and power tools. Remove litter and debris from roadways, including debris from rock slides and mudslides. Clean and clear debris from culverts, catch basins, drop inlets, ditches, and other drain structures. Perform roadside landscaping work, such as clearing weeds and brush and planting and trimming trees. Paint traffic control lines and place pavement traffic messages by hand or using machines. Inspect markers to verify accurate installation. Apply poisons along roadsides and in animal burrows to eliminate unwanted roadside vegetation and rodents. Measure and mark locations for installation of markers, using tape, string, or chalk. Apply oil to road surfaces, using sprayers. Blend compounds to form adhesive mixtures used for marker installation. Place and remove snow fences used to prevent the accumulation of drifting snow on highways.

Personality Type: Realistic. These occupations frequently involve work activities that include practical, hands-on problems and solutions. They often deal with plants; animals; and real-world materials such as wood, tools, and machinery. Many of the occupations require working outside and don't involve a lot of paperwork or working closely with others.

GOE—Interest Area/Cluster: 02. Architecture and Construction. **Work Group:** 02.06. Construction Support/Labor. **Other Jobs in This Work Group:** Construction Laborers; Helpers—Brickmasons, Blockmasons, Stonemasons, and Tile and Marble Setters; Helpers—Carpenters; Helpers—Electricians; Helpers—Installation, Maintenance, and Repair Workers; Helpers—Painters, Paperhangers, Plasterers, and Stucco Masons; Helpers—Pipelayers, Plumbers, Pipefitters, and Steamfitters; Helpers—Roofers; Septic Tank Servicers and Sewer Pipe Cleaners.

Skills—Equipment Maintenance: Performing routine maintenance and determining when and what kind of maintenance is needed. **Repairing:** Repairing machines or systems, using the needed tools. **Installation:** Installing equipment, machines, wiring, or programs to meet specifications. **Operation and Control:** Controlling operations of equipment or systems. **Management of Material Resources:** Obtaining and seeing to the appropriate use of equipment, facilities, and materials needed to do certain work. **Equipment Selection:** Determining the kind of tools and equipment needed to do a job. **Troubleshooting:** Determining what is causing an operating error and deciding what to do about it. **Technology Design:** Generating or adapting equipment and technology to serve user needs.

Education and Training Program: Construction/Heavy Equipment/Earthmoving Equipment Operation. **Related Knowledge/Courses—Building and Construction:** Materials, methods, and the appropriate tools to construct objects, structures, and buildings. **Transportation:** Principles and methods for moving people or goods by air, rail, sea, or road, including their relative costs, advantages, and limitations. **Mechanical Devices:** Machines and tools, including their designs, uses, benefits, repair, and maintenance. **Public Safety and Security:** Weaponry; public safety; security operations, rules, regulations, precautions, and prevention; and the protection of people, data, and property. **Customer and Personal Service:** Principles and processes for providing customer and personal services, including needs assessment techniques, quality service standards, alternative delivery systems, and customer satisfaction evaluation techniques. **Geography:** Various methods for describing the location and distribution of land, sea, and air masses, including their physical locations, relationships, and characteristics.

Work Environment: Outdoors; noisy; very hot or cold; contaminants; hazardous equipment; using hands on objects, tools, or controls.

History Teachers, Postsecondary

* Education/Training Required: Doctoral degree
* Annual Earnings: $59,160
* Beginning Wage: $33,540
* Earnings Growth Potential: High
* Growth: 22.9%
* Annual Job Openings: 3,570
* Self-Employed: 0.4%
* Part-Time: 27.8%

Teach courses in human history and historiography. Prepare and deliver lectures to undergraduate and/or graduate students on topics such as ancient history, postwar civilizations, and the history of third-world countries. Evaluate and grade students' classwork, assignments, and papers. Prepare course materials such as syllabi, homework assignments, and handouts. Compile, administer, and grade examinations or assign this work to others. Initiate, facilitate, and moderate classroom discussions. Keep abreast of developments in their field by reading current literature, talking with colleagues, and participating in professional conferences. Plan, evaluate, and revise curricula, course content, and course materials and methods of instruction. Maintain student attendance records, grades, and other required records. Maintain regularly scheduled office hours to advise and assist students. Conduct research in a particular field of knowledge and publish findings in professional journals, books, or electronic media. Select and obtain materials and supplies such as textbooks. Advise students on academic and vocational curricula and on career issues. Collaborate with colleagues to address teaching and research issues. Serve on academic or administrative committees that deal with institutional policies, departmental matters, and academic issues. Participate in campus and community events. Act as advisers to student organizations. Participate in student recruitment, registration, and placement activities. Compile bibliographies of specialized materials for outside reading assignments. Supervise undergraduate and graduate teaching, internship, and research work. Perform administrative duties such as serving as department head. Write grant proposals to procure external research funding. Provide professional consulting services to government, educational institutions, and industry.

Personality Type: Social. These occupations frequently involve working with, communicating with, and teaching people and often involve helping or providing service to others.

GOE—Interest Area/Cluster: 05. Education and Training. **Work Group:** 05.03. Postsecondary and Adult Teaching and Instructing. **Other Jobs in This Work Group:** Adult Literacy, Remedial Education, and GED Teachers and Instructors; Agricultural Sciences Teachers, Postsecondary; Anthropology and Archeology Teachers, Postsecondary; Architecture Teachers, Postsecondary; Area, Ethnic, and Cultural Studies Teachers, Postsecondary; Art, Drama, and Music Teachers, Postsecondary; Atmospheric, Earth, Marine, and Space Sciences Teachers, Postsecondary; Biological Science Teachers, Postsecondary; Business Teachers, Postsecondary; Chemistry Teachers, Postsecondary; Communications Teachers, Postsecondary; Computer Science Teachers, Postsecondary; Criminal Justice and Law Enforcement Teachers, Postsecondary; Economics Teachers, Postsecondary; Education Teachers, Postsecondary; Engineering Teachers, Postsecondary; English Language and Literature Teachers, Postsecondary; Environmental Science Teachers, Postsecondary; Farm and Home Management Advisors; Foreign Language and Literature Teachers, Postsecondary; Forestry and Conservation Science Teachers, Postsecondary; Geography Teachers, Postsecondary; Graduate Teaching Assistants; Health Specialties Teachers, Postsecondary; Home Economics Teachers, Postsecondary; Law Teachers, Postsecondary; Library Science Teachers, Postsecondary; Mathematical Science Teachers, Postsecondary; Nursing Instructors and Teachers, Postsecondary; Philosophy and Religion Teachers, Postsecondary; Physics Teachers, Postsecondary; Political Science Teachers, Postsecondary; Psychology Teachers, Postsecondary; Recreation and Fitness Studies Teachers, Postsecondary; Self-Enrichment Education Teachers; Social Work Teachers, Postsecondary; Sociology Teachers, Postsecondary; Vocational Education Teachers, Postsecondary.

Skills—Writing: Communicating effectively with others in writing as indicated by the needs of the audience. **Instructing:** Teaching others how to do something. **Learning Strategies:** Using multiple approaches when learning or teaching new things. **Reading Comprehension:** Understanding written sentences and paragraphs in work-related documents. **Speaking:** Talking to others to effectively convey information. **Persuasion:** Persuading others to approach things differently. **Critical Thinking:** Using logic and analysis to identify the strengths and weaknesses of different approaches. **Active Learning:** Working with new material or information to grasp its implications.

Education and Training Programs: American History (United States); Asian History; Canadian History; European History; History and Philosophy of Science and Technology; History, General; History, Other; Public/Applied History and Archival Administration. **Related Knowledge/ Courses—History and Archeology:** Historical events and their causes, indicators, and impact on particular civilizations and cultures. **Philosophy and Theology:** Different philosophical systems and religions, including their basic principles, values, ethics, ways of thinking, customs, and practices and their impact on human culture. **Geography:** Various methods for describing the location and distribution of land, sea, and air masses, including their physical locations, relationships, and characteristics. **Sociology and Anthropology:** Group behavior and dynamics; societal trends and influences; and cultures and their history, migrations, ethnicity, and origins. **Education and Training:** Instructional methods and training techniques, including curriculum design principles, learning theory, group and individual teaching techniques, design of individual development plans, and test design principles. **English Language:** The structure and content of the English language, including the meaning and spelling of words, rules of composition, and grammar.

Work Environment: Indoors; sitting.

Home Economics Teachers, Postsecondary

- ❋ Education/Training Required: Doctoral degree
- ❋ Annual Earnings: $58,170
- ❋ Beginning Wage: $29,510
- ❋ Earnings Growth Potential: High
- ❋ Growth: 22.9%
- ❋ Annual Job Openings: 820
- ❋ Self-Employed: 0.4%
- ❋ Part-Time: 27.8%

Teach courses in child care, family relations, finance, nutrition, and related subjects as pertaining to home management. Evaluate and grade students' classwork, laboratory work, projects, assignments, and papers. Initiate, facilitate, and moderate classroom discussions. Prepare and deliver lectures to undergraduate or graduate students on topics such as food science, nutrition, and child care. Prepare course materials such as syllabi, homework assignments, and handouts. Keep abreast of developments in their field by reading current literature, talking with colleagues, and participating in professional conferences. Maintain student attendance records, grades, and other required records. Plan, evaluate, and revise curricula, course content, and course materials and methods of instruction. Compile, administer, and grade examinations or assign this work to others. Advise students on academic and vocational curricula and on career issues. Maintain regularly scheduled office hours to advise and assist students. Supervise undergraduate or graduate teaching, internship, and research work. Select and obtain materials and supplies such as textbooks. Conduct research in a particular field of knowledge and publish findings in professional journals, books, and/or electronic media. Collaborate with colleagues to address teaching and research issues. Act as advisers to student organizations. Participate in student recruitment, registration, and placement activities. Serve on academic or administrative committees that deal with institutional policies, departmental matters, and academic issues. Participate in campus and community events. Compile bibliographies of specialized materials for outside reading assignments. Perform administrative duties such as serving as department head. Write grant proposals to procure external research funding. Provide professional consulting services to government and industry.

Personality Type: Social. These occupations frequently involve working with, communicating with, and teaching people and often involve helping or providing service to others.

GOE—Interest Area/Cluster: 05. Education and Training. **Work Group:** 05.03. Postsecondary and Adult Teaching and Instructing. **Other Jobs in This Work Group:** Adult Literacy, Remedial Education, and GED Teachers and Instructors; Agricultural Sciences Teachers, Postsecondary; Anthropology and Archeology Teachers, Postsecondary; Architecture Teachers, Postsecondary; Area, Ethnic, and Cultural Studies Teachers, Postsecondary; Art, Drama, and Music Teachers, Postsecondary; Atmospheric, Earth, Marine, and Space Sciences Teachers, Postsecondary; Biological Science Teachers, Postsecondary; Business Teachers, Postsecondary; Chemistry Teachers, Postsecondary; Communications Teachers, Postsecondary; Computer Science Teachers, Postsecondary; Criminal Justice and Law Enforcement Teachers, Postsecondary; Economics Teachers, Postsecondary; Education Teachers, Postsecondary; Engineering Teachers, Postsecondary; English Language and Literature Teachers, Postsecondary; Environmental Science Teachers, Postsecondary; Farm and Home Management Advisors;

Foreign Language and Literature Teachers, Postsecondary; Forestry and Conservation Science Teachers, Postsecondary; Geography Teachers, Postsecondary; Graduate Teaching Assistants; Health Specialties Teachers, Postsecondary; History Teachers, Postsecondary; Law Teachers, Postsecondary; Library Science Teachers, Postsecondary; Mathematical Science Teachers, Postsecondary; Nursing Instructors and Teachers, Postsecondary; Philosophy and Religion Teachers, Postsecondary; Physics Teachers, Postsecondary; Political Science Teachers, Postsecondary; Psychology Teachers, Postsecondary; Recreation and Fitness Studies Teachers, Postsecondary; Self-Enrichment Education Teachers; Social Work Teachers, Postsecondary; Sociology Teachers, Postsecondary; Vocational Education Teachers, Postsecondary.

Skills—Writing: Communicating effectively with others in writing as indicated by the needs of the audience. **Instructing:** Teaching others how to do something. **Learning Strategies:** Using multiple approaches when learning or teaching new things. **Service Orientation:** Actively looking for ways to help people. **Active Learning:** Working with new material or information to grasp its implications. **Operations Analysis:** Analyzing needs and product requirements to create a design. **Social Perceptiveness:** Being aware of others' reactions and understanding why they react the way they do. **Speaking:** Talking to others to effectively convey information.

Education and Training Programs: Business Family and Consumer Sciences/Human Sciences; Child Care and Support Services Management; Family and Consumer Sciences/Human Sciences, General; Foodservice Systems Administration/Management; Human Development and Family Studies, General. **Related Knowledge/Courses—Sociology and Anthropology:** Group behavior and dynamics; societal trends and influences; and cultures and their history, migrations, ethnicity, and origins. **Philosophy and Theology:** Different philosophical systems and religions, including their basic principles, values, ethics, ways of thinking, customs, and practices and their impact on human culture. **Education and Training:** Instructional methods and training techniques, including curriculum design principles, learning theory, group and individual teaching techniques, design of individual development plans, and test design principles. **Therapy and Counseling:** Information and techniques needed to rehabilitate physical and mental ailments and to provide career guidance, including alternative treatments, rehabilitation equipment and its proper use, and methods to evaluate treatment effects. **Psychology:** Human behavior and performance, mental processes, psychological research methods, and the assessment and treatment of behavioral and affective disorders. **English Language:** The structure and content of the English language, including the meaning and spelling of words, rules of composition, and grammar.

Work Environment: Indoors; sitting.

Human Resources Assistants, Except Payroll and Timekeeping

- ✱ Education/Training Required: Short-term on-the-job training
- ✱ Annual Earnings: $34,970
- ✱ Beginning Wage: $23,750
- ✱ Earnings Growth Potential: Low
- ✱ Growth: 11.3%
- ✱ Annual Job Openings: 18,647
- ✱ Self-Employed: 0.0%
- ✱ Part-Time: 9.3%

Compile and keep personnel records. Record data for each employee, such as address, weekly earnings, absences, amount of sales or production, supervisory reports on ability, and date of and reason for termination. Compile and type reports from employment records. File employment records. Search employee files and furnish information to authorized persons. Explain company personnel policies, benefits, and procedures to employees or job applicants. Process, verify, and maintain documentation relating to personnel activities such as staffing, recruitment, training, grievances, performance evaluations, and classifications. Record data for each employee, including such information as addresses, weekly earnings, absences, amount of sales or production, supervisory reports on performance, and dates of and reasons for terminations. Process and review employment applications to evaluate qualifications or eligibility of applicants. Answer questions regarding examinations, eligibility, salaries, benefits, and other pertinent information. Examine employee files to answer inquiries and provide information for personnel actions. Gather personnel records from other departments or employees. Search employee files to obtain information for authorized persons and organizations such as credit bureaus and finance companies. Interview job applicants to obtain and verify information used to screen and evaluate them. Request information from law enforcement officials, previous employers, and other references to determine applicants' employment acceptability.

Compile and prepare reports and documents pertaining to personnel activities. Inform job applicants of their acceptance or rejection of employment. Select applicants meeting specified job requirements and refer them to hiring personnel. Arrange for in-house and external training activities. Arrange for advertising or posting of job vacancies and notify eligible workers of position availability. Provide assistance in administering employee benefit programs and worker's compensation plans. Prepare badges, passes, and identification cards and perform other security-related duties. Administer and score applicant and employee aptitude, personality, and interest assessment instruments.

Personality Type: Conventional. These occupations frequently involve following set procedures and routines and can include working with data and details more than with ideas. Usually there is a clear line of authority to follow.

GOE—Interest Area/Cluster: 04. Business and Administration. **Work Group:** 04.07. Records and Materials Processing. **Other Jobs in This Work Group:** Correspondence Clerks; File Clerks; Marking Clerks; Meter Readers, Utilities; Office Clerks, General; Order Fillers, Wholesale and Retail Sales; Postal Service Clerks; Postal Service Mail Sorters, Processors, and Processing Machine Operators; Procurement Clerks; Production, Planning, and Expediting Clerks; Shipping, Receiving, and Traffic Clerks; Stock Clerks and Order Fillers; Stock Clerks, Sales Floor; Stock Clerks—Stockroom, Warehouse, or Storage Yard; Weighers, Measurers, Checkers, and Samplers, Recordkeeping.

Skills—Writing: Communicating effectively with others in writing as indicated by the needs of the audience. **Active Listening:** Listening to what other people are saying and asking questions as appropriate. **Management of Personnel Resources:** Motivating, developing, and directing people as they work; identifying the best people for the job.

Education and Training Program: General Office Occupations and Clerical Services. **Related Knowledge/Courses—Clerical Practices:** Administrative and clerical procedures and systems such as word-processing systems, filing and records management systems, stenography and transcription, forms, design principles, and other office procedures and terminology. **Personnel and Human Resources:** Principles and procedures for personnel recruitment; selection; training; compensation and benefits; labor relations and negotiation; and personnel information systems. **Customer and Personal Service:** Principles and processes for providing customer and personal services, including needs assessment techniques, quality service standards, alternative delivery systems, and customer satisfaction evaluation techniques. **Computers and Electronics:** Electric circuit boards, processors, chips, and computer hardware and software, including applications and programming. **Economics and Accounting:** Economic and accounting principles and practices, the financial markets, banking, and the analysis and reporting of financial data. **Sociology and Anthropology:** Group behavior and dynamics; societal trends and influences; and cultures and their history, migrations, ethnicity, and origins.

Work Environment: Indoors; noisy; sitting.

Hydrologists

- ❋ Education/Training Required: Master's degree
- ❋ Annual Earnings: $68,140
- ❋ Beginning Wage: $42,450
- ❋ Earnings Growth Potential: Medium
- ❋ Growth: 24.3%
- ❋ Annual Job Openings: 687
- ❋ Self-Employed: 2.4%
- ❋ Part-Time: 5.3%

Research the distribution, circulation, and physical properties of underground and surface waters; study the form and intensity of precipitation, its rate of infiltration into the soil, its movement through the earth, and its return to the ocean and atmosphere. Study and document quantities, distribution, disposition, and development of underground and surface waters. Draft final reports describing research results, including illustrations, appendices, maps, and other attachments. Coordinate and supervise the work of professional and technical staff, including research assistants, technologists, and technicians. Prepare hydrogeologic evaluations of known or suspected hazardous waste sites and land treatment and feedlot facilities. Design and conduct scientific hydrogeological investigations to ensure that accurate and appropriate information is available for use in water resource management decisions. Study public water supply issues, including flood and drought risks, water quality, wastewater, and impacts on wetland habitats. Collect and analyze water samples as part of field investigations and/or to validate data from automatic monitors. Apply research findings to help minimize the environmental impacts of pollution, water-borne diseases, erosion, and sedimentation. Measure and graph phenomena such as lake levels, stream flows, and changes in water volumes. Investigate complaints or conflicts related to the alteration of public waters, gathering information, recommending alternatives, informing participants of progress, and preparing draft orders. Develop or modify methods of conducting hydrologic studies. Answer questions and provide technical assistance and information to contractors and/or the public regarding issues such as well drilling, code requirements, hydrology, and geology. Install, maintain, and calibrate instruments such as those that monitor water levels, rainfall, and sediments. Evaluate data and provide recommendations regarding the feasibility of municipal projects such as hydroelectric power plants, irrigation systems, flood warning systems, and waste treatment facilities. Conduct short-term and long-term climate assessments and study storm occurrences. Study and analyze the physical aspects of the Earth in terms of the hydrological components, including atmosphere, hydrosphere, and interior structure. Conduct research and communicate information to promote the conservation and preservation of water resources.

Personality Type: Investigative. These occupations frequently involve working with ideas and require an extensive amount of thinking. They can involve searching for facts and figuring out problems mentally.

GOE—Interest Area/Cluster: 15. Scientific Research, Engineering, and Mathematics. **Work Group:** 15.02. Physical Sciences. **Other Jobs in This Work Group:** Astronomers; Atmospheric and Space Scientists; Chemists; Geographers; Geoscientists, Except Hydrologists and Geographers; Materials Scientists; Physicists.

Skills—Science: Using scientific methods to solve problems. **Programming:** Writing computer programs for various purposes. **Management of Financial Resources:** Determining how money will be spent to get the work done and accounting for these expenditures. **Mathematics:** Using mathematics to solve problems. **Management of Personnel Resources:** Motivating, developing, and directing people as they work; identifying the best people for the job. **Complex Problem Solving:** Identifying complex problems, reviewing the options, and implementing solutions. **Systems Analysis:** Determining how a system should work and how changes will affect outcomes. **Management of Material Resources:** Obtaining and seeing to the appropriate use of equipment, facilities, and materials needed to do certain work.

Education and Training Programs: Geology/Earth Science, General; Hydrology and Water Resources Science; Oceanography, Chemical and Physical. **Related Knowledge/ Courses—Geography:** Various methods for describing

the location and distribution of land, sea, and air masses, including their physical locations, relationships, and characteristics. **Physics:** Physical principles, laws, and applications, including air, water, material dynamics, light, atomic principles, heat, electric theory, earth formations, and meteorological and related natural phenomena. **Engineering and Technology:** Equipment, tools, and mechanical devices and their uses to produce motion, light, power, technology, and other applications. **Biology:** Plant and animal living tissue, cells, organisms, and entities, including their functions, interdependencies, and interactions with each other and the environment. **Chemistry:** The composition, structure, and properties of substances and of the chemical processes and transformations that they undergo. This includes uses of chemicals and their interactions, danger signs, production techniques, and disposal methods. **Mathematics:** Numbers and their operations and interrelationships, including arithmetic, algebra, geometry, calculus, and statistics and their applications.

Work Environment: More often indoors than outdoors; sitting.

Immigration and Customs Inspectors

- ❋ Education/Training Required: Work experience in a related occupation
- ❋ Annual Earnings: $59,930
- ❋ Beginning Wage: $35,600
- ❋ Earnings Growth Potential: High
- ❋ Growth: 17.3%
- ❋ Annual Job Openings: 14,746
- ❋ Self-Employed: 0.3%
- ❋ Part-Time: 2.2%

The job openings listed here are shared with Criminal Investigators and Special Agents; Police Detectives; and Police Identification and Records Officers.

Investigate and inspect persons, common carriers, goods, and merchandise arriving in or departing from the United States or moving between states to detect violations of immigration and customs laws and regulations. Examine immigration applications, visas, and passports and interview persons to determine eligibility for admission, residence, and travel in U.S. Detain persons found to be in violation of customs or immigration laws and arrange for legal action such as deportation. Locate and seize contraband or undeclared merchandise and vehicles, aircraft, or boats that contain such merchandise. Interpret and explain laws and regulations to travelers, prospective immigrants, shippers, and manufacturers. Inspect cargo, baggage, and personal articles entering or leaving U.S. for compliance with revenue laws and U.S. Customs Service regulations. Record and report job-related activities, findings, transactions, violations, discrepancies, and decisions. Institute civil and criminal prosecutions and cooperate with other law enforcement agencies in the investigation and prosecution of those in violation of immigration or customs laws. Testify regarding decisions at immigration appeals or in federal court. Determine duty and taxes to be paid on goods. Collect samples of merchandise for examination, appraisal, or testing. Investigate applications for duty refunds and petition for remission or mitigation of penalties when warranted.

Personality Type: Conventional. These occupations frequently involve following set procedures and routines and can include working with data and details more than with ideas. Usually there is a clear line of authority to follow.

GOE—Interest Area/Cluster: 07. Government and Public Administration. **Work Group:** 07.03. Regulations Enforcement. **Other Jobs in This Work Group:** Agricultural Inspectors; Aviation Inspectors; Compliance Officers, Except Agriculture, Construction, Health and Safety, and Transportation; Construction and Building Inspectors; Environmental Compliance Inspectors; Equal Opportunity Representatives and Officers; Financial Examiners; Fire Inspectors; Fish and Game Wardens; Forest Fire Inspectors and Prevention Specialists; Freight and Cargo Inspectors; Government Property Inspectors and Investigators; Licensing Examiners and Inspectors; Nuclear Monitoring Technicians; Occupational Health and Safety Specialists; Occupational Health and Safety Technicians; Tax Examiners, Collectors, and Revenue Agents; Transportation Vehicle, Equipment, and Systems Inspectors, Except Aviation.

Skills—Persuasion: Persuading others to approach things differently. **Operations Analysis:** Analyzing needs and product requirements to create a design. **Equipment Selection:** Determining the kind of tools and equipment needed to do a job. **Negotiation:** Bringing others together and trying to reconcile differences. **Speaking:** Talking to others to effectively convey information. **Social Perceptiveness:** Being aware of others' reactions and understanding why they react the way they do. **Active Listening:** Listening to what other people are saying and asking questions as appropriate. **Judgment and Decision Making:** Weighing the relative costs and benefits of a potential action.

Education and Training Programs: Criminal Justice/Police Science; Criminalistics and Criminal Science. **Related Knowledge/Courses—Public Safety and Security:** Weaponry; public safety; security operations, rules, regulations, precautions, and prevention; and the protection of people, data, and property. **Law and Government:** Laws, legal codes, court procedures, precedents, government regulations, executive orders, agency rules, and the democratic political process. **Foreign Language:** The structure and content of a foreign (non-English) language, including the meaning and spelling of words, rules of composition and grammar, and pronunciation. **Geography:** Various methods for describing the location and distribution of land, sea, and air masses, including their physical locations, relationships, and characteristics. **Customer and Personal Service:** Principles and processes for providing customer and personal services, including needs assessment techniques, quality service standards, alternative delivery systems, and customer satisfaction evaluation techniques. **Philosophy and Theology:** Different philosophical systems and religions, including their basic principles, values, ethics, ways of thinking, customs, and practices and their impact on human culture.

Work Environment: More often outdoors than indoors; noisy; contaminants; radiation; hazardous equipment.

Industrial Engineering Technicians

- ❀ Education/Training Required: Associate degree
- ❀ Annual Earnings: $47,490
- ❀ Beginning Wage: $31,130
- ❀ Earnings Growth Potential: Low
- ❀ Growth: 9.9%
- ❀ Annual Job Openings: 6,172
- ❀ Self-Employed: 0.8%
- ❀ Part-Time: 5.9%

Apply engineering theory and principles to problems of industrial layout or manufacturing production, usually under the direction of engineering staff. May study and record time, motion, method, and speed involved in performance of production, maintenance, clerical, and other worker operations for such purposes as establishing standard production rates or improving efficiency. Recommend revision to methods of operation, material handling, equipment layout, or other changes to increase production or improve standards. Study time, motion, methods, and speed involved in maintenance, production, and other operations to establish standard production rate and improve efficiency. Interpret engineering drawings, schematic diagrams, or formulas and confer with management or engineering staff to determine quality and reliability standards. Recommend modifications to existing quality or production standards to achieve optimum quality within limits of equipment capability. Aid in planning work assignments in accordance with worker performance, machine capacity, production schedules, and anticipated delays. Observe workers using equipment to verify that equipment is being operated and maintained according to quality assurance standards. Observe workers operating equipment or performing tasks to determine time involved and fatigue rate, using timing devices. Prepare charts, graphs, and diagrams to illustrate workflow, routing, floor layouts, material handling, and machine utilization. Evaluate data and write reports to validate or indicate deviations from existing standards. Read worker logs, product processing sheets, and specification sheets to verify that records adhere to quality assurance specifications. Prepare graphs or charts of data or enter data into computer for analysis. Record test data, applying statistical quality control procedures. Select products for tests at specified stages in production process and test products for performance characteristics and adherence to specifications. Compile and evaluate statistical data to determine and maintain quality and reliability of products.

Personality Type: Investigative. These occupations frequently involve working with ideas and require an extensive amount of thinking. They can involve searching for facts and figuring out problems mentally.

GOE—Interest Area/Cluster: 04. Business and Administration. **Work Group:** 04.05. Accounting, Auditing, and Analytical Support. **Other Jobs in This Work Group:** Accountants; Accountants and Auditors; Auditors; Budget Analysts; Logisticians; Management Analysts; Operations Research Analysts.

Skills—Operations Analysis: Analyzing needs and product requirements to create a design. **Technology Design:** Generating or adapting equipment and technology to serve user needs. **Repairing:** Repairing machines or systems, using the needed tools. **Troubleshooting:** Determining what is causing an operating error and deciding what to do about it. **Systems Evaluation:** Looking at many indicators of system performance and taking into account their accuracy. **Systems Analysis:** Determining how a system should work and how changes will affect outcomes. **Quality Control Analysis:** Evaluating the quality or performance of products, services, or processes. **Mathematics:** Using mathematics to solve problems.

Education and Training Programs: Engineering/Industrial Management; Industrial Production Technologies/Technician Training, Other; Industrial Technology/Technician Training; Manufacturing Technology/Technician Training. **Related Knowledge/Courses—Production and Processing:** Inputs, outputs, raw materials, waste, quality control, costs, and techniques for maximizing the manufacture and distribution of goods. **Engineering and Technology:** Equipment, tools, and mechanical devices and their uses to produce motion, light, power, technology, and other applications. **Design:** Design techniques, principles, tools, and instruments involved in the production and use of precision technical plans, blueprints, drawings, and models. **Clerical Practices:** Administrative and clerical procedures and systems such as word-processing systems, filing and records management systems, stenography and transcription, forms, design principles, and other office procedures and terminology. **Mathematics:** Numbers and their operations and interrelationships, including arithmetic, algebra, geometry, calculus, and statistics and their applications. **Mechanical Devices:** Machines and tools, including their designs, uses, benefits, repair, and maintenance.

Work Environment: Indoors; noisy; contaminants; hazardous equipment; standing; walking and running.

Industrial Engineers

* Education/Training Required: Bachelor's degree
* Annual Earnings: $71,430
* Beginning Wage: $46,340
* Earnings Growth Potential: Medium
* Growth: 20.3%
* Annual Job Openings: 11,272
* Self-Employed: 0.9%
* Part-Time: 2.0%

Design, develop, test, and evaluate integrated systems for managing industrial production processes, including human work factors, quality control, inventory control, logistics and material flow, cost analysis, and production coordination. Analyze statistical data and product specifications to determine standards and establish quality and reliability objectives of finished product. Develop manufacturing methods, labor utilization standards, and cost analysis systems to promote efficient staff and facility utilization. Recommend methods for improving utilization of personnel, material, and utilities. Plan and establish sequence of operations to fabricate and assemble parts or products and to promote efficient utilization. Apply statistical methods and perform mathematical calculations to determine manufacturing processes, staff requirements, and production standards. Coordinate quality control objectives and activities to resolve production problems, maximize product reliability, and minimize cost. Confer with vendors, staff, and management personnel regarding purchases, procedures, product specifications, manufacturing capabilities, and project status. Draft and design layout of equipment, materials, and workspace to illustrate maximum efficiency, using drafting tools and computer. Review production schedules, engineering specifications, orders, and related information to obtain knowledge of manufacturing methods, procedures, and activities. Communicate with management and user personnel to develop production and design standards. Estimate production cost and effect of product design changes for management review, action, and control. Formulate sampling procedures and designs and develop forms and instructions for recording, evaluating, and reporting quality and reliability data. Record or oversee recording of information to ensure currency of engineering drawings and documentation of production problems. Study operations sequence, material flow, functional statements, organization charts, and project information to determine worker functions and responsibilities. Direct workers engaged in product measurement, inspection, and testing activities to ensure quality control and reliability. Implement methods and procedures for disposition of discrepant material and defective or damaged parts and assess cost and responsibility.

Personality Type: Investigative. These occupations frequently involve working with ideas and require an extensive amount of thinking. They can involve searching for facts and figuring out problems mentally.

GOE—Interest Area/Cluster: 15. Scientific Research, Engineering, and Mathematics. **Work Group:** 15.08. Industrial and Safety Engineering. **Other Jobs in This Work Group:** Fire-Prevention and Protection Engineers; Health and Safety Engineers, Except Mining Safety Engineers and Inspectors; Industrial Safety and Health Engineers; Product Safety Engineers.

Skills—Equipment Selection: Determining the kind of tools and equipment needed to do a job. **Technology Design:** Generating or adapting equipment and technology to serve user needs. **Troubleshooting:** Determining what is causing an operating error and deciding what to do about it. **Installation:** Installing equipment, machines, wiring, or programs to meet specifications. **Systems Analysis:** Determining how a system should work and how changes will affect outcomes. **Mathematics:** Using mathematics to solve problems. **Judgment and Decision Making:** Weighing the relative costs and benefits of a potential action. **Negotiation:** Bringing others together and trying to reconcile differences.

Education and Training Program: Industrial Engineering. **Related Knowledge/Courses—Engineering and Technology:** Equipment, tools, and mechanical devices and their uses to produce motion, light, power, technology, and other applications. **Design:** Design techniques, principles, tools, and instruments involved in the production and use of precision technical plans, blueprints, drawings, and models. **Production and Processing:** Inputs, outputs, raw materials, waste, quality control, costs, and techniques for maximizing the manufacture and distribution of goods. **Mechanical Devices:** Machines and tools, including their designs, uses, benefits, repair, and maintenance. **Physics:** Physical principles, laws, and applications, including air, water, material dynamics, light, atomic principles, heat, electric theory, earth formations, and meteorological and related natural phenomena. **Mathematics:** Numbers and their operations and interrelationships, including arithmetic, algebra, geometry, calculus, and statistics and their applications.

Work Environment: Indoors; noisy; contaminants; hazardous equipment; more often sitting than standing.

Industrial Machinery Mechanics

- ❋ Education/Training Required: Long-term on-the-job training
- ❋ Annual Earnings: $42,350
- ❋ Beginning Wage: $27,650
- ❋ Earnings Growth Potential: Low
- ❋ Growth: 9.0%
- ❋ Annual Job Openings: 23,361
- ❋ Self-Employed: 2.5%
- ❋ Part-Time: 1.7%

Repair, install, adjust, or maintain industrial production and processing machinery or refinery and pipeline distribution systems. Disassemble machinery and equipment to remove parts and make repairs. Repair and replace broken or malfunctioning components of machinery and equipment. Repair and maintain the operating condition of industrial production and processing machinery and equipment. Examine parts for defects such as breakage and excessive wear. Reassemble equipment after completion of inspections, testing, or repairs. Observe and test the operation of machinery and equipment in order to diagnose malfunctions, using voltmeters and other testing devices. Operate newly repaired machinery and equipment to verify the adequacy of repairs. Clean, lubricate, and adjust parts, equipment, and machinery. Analyze test results, machine error messages, and information obtained from operators in order to diagnose equipment problems. Record repairs and maintenance performed. Study blueprints and manufacturers' manuals to determine correct installation and operation of machinery. Record parts and materials used, and order or requisition new parts and materials as necessary. Cut and weld metal to repair broken metal parts, fabricate new parts, and assemble new equipment. Demonstrate equipment functions and features to machine operators. Enter codes and instructions to program computer-controlled machinery.

Personality Type: Realistic. These occupations frequently involve work activities that include practical, hands-on problems and solutions. They often deal with plants; animals; and real-world materials such as wood, tools, and machinery. Many of the occupations require working outside and don't involve a lot of paperwork or working closely with others.

GOE—Interest Area/Cluster: 13. Manufacturing. **Work Group:** 13.13. Machinery Repair. **Other Jobs in This Work Group:** Bicycle Repairers; Control and Valve Installers and Repairers, Except Mechanical Door; Home Appliance Repairers; Locksmiths and Safe Repairers; Maintenance Workers, Machinery; Mechanical Door Repairers; Millwrights; Signal and Track Switch Repairers.

Skills—Installation: Installing equipment, machines, wiring, or programs to meet specifications. **Repairing:** Repairing machines or systems, using the needed tools. **Equipment Maintenance:** Performing routine maintenance and determining when and what kind of maintenance is needed. **Operation Monitoring:** Watching gauges, dials, or other indicators to make sure a machine is working properly. **Troubleshooting:** Determining what is causing an operating error and deciding what to do about it. **Technology Design:** Generating or adapting equipment and technology to serve user needs. **Equipment Selection:** Determining the kind of tools and equipment needed to do a job. **Operation and Control:** Controlling operations of equipment or systems.

Education and Training Programs: Heavy/Industrial Equipment Maintenance Technologies, Other; Industrial Mechanics and Maintenance Technology. **Related Knowledge/Courses—Mechanical Devices:** Machines and tools, including their designs, uses, benefits, repair, and maintenance. **Engineering and Technology:** Equipment, tools, and mechanical devices and their uses to produce motion, light, power, technology, and other applications. **Building and Construction:** Materials, methods, and the appropriate tools to construct objects, structures, and buildings. **Design:** Design techniques, principles, tools, and instruments involved in the production and use of precision technical plans, blueprints, drawings, and models. **Chemistry:** The composition, structure, and properties of substances and of the chemical processes and transformations that they undergo. This includes uses of chemicals and their interactions, danger signs, production techniques, and disposal methods. **Physics:** Physical principles, laws, and applications, including air, water, material dynamics, light, atomic principles, heat, electric theory, earth formations, and meteorological and related natural phenomena.

Work Environment: Noisy; contaminants; hazardous conditions; hazardous equipment; standing; using hands on objects, tools, or controls.

Industrial Production Managers

- ❋ Education/Training Required: Work experience in a related occupation
- ❋ Annual Earnings: $80,560
- ❋ Beginning Wage: $48,670
- ❋ Earnings Growth Potential: Medium
- ❋ Growth: –5.9%
- ❋ Annual Job Openings: 14,889
- ❋ Self-Employed: 2.0%
- ❋ Part-Time: 1.6%

Plan, direct, or coordinate the work activities and resources necessary for manufacturing products in accordance with cost, quality, and quantity specifications. Direct and coordinate production, processing, distribution, and marketing activities of industrial organization. Review processing schedules and production orders to make decisions concerning inventory requirements, staffing requirements, work procedures, and duty assignments, considering budgetary limitations and time constraints. Review operations and confer with technical or administrative staff to resolve production or processing problems. Develop and implement production tracking and quality control systems, analyzing production, quality control, maintenance, and other operational reports, to detect production problems. Hire, train, evaluate, and discharge staff, and resolve personnel grievances. Set and monitor product standards, examining samples of raw products or directing testing during processing, to ensure finished products are of prescribed quality. Prepare and maintain production reports and personnel records. Coordinate and recommend procedures for facility and equipment maintenance or modification, including the replacement of machines. Initiate and coordinate inventory and cost control programs. Institute employee suggestion or involvement programs. Maintain current knowledge of the quality control field, relying on current literature pertaining to materials use, technological advances, and statistical studies. Review plans and confer with research and support staff to develop new products and processes. Develop budgets and approve expenditures for supplies, materials, and human resources, ensuring that materials, labor, and equipment are used efficiently to meet production targets. Negotiate prices of materials with suppliers.

Personality Type: Enterprising. These occupations frequently involve starting up and carrying out projects and can involve leading people and making many decisions. They sometimes require risk taking and often deal with business.

GOE—Interest Area/Cluster: 13. Manufacturing. **Work Group:** 13.01. Managerial Work in Manufacturing. **Other Jobs in This Work Group:** First-Line Supervisors/Managers of Helpers, Laborers, and Material Movers, Hand; First-Line Supervisors/Managers of Mechanics, Installers, and Repairers; First-Line Supervisors/Managers of Production and Operating Workers.

Skills—Management of Personnel Resources: Motivating, developing, and directing people as they work; identifying the best people for the job. **Systems Analysis:** Determining how a system should work and how changes will affect outcomes. **Systems Evaluation:** Looking at many indicators of system performance and taking into account their accuracy. **Management of Financial Resources:** Determining how money will be spent to get the work done and accounting for these expenditures. **Management of Material Resources:** Obtaining and seeing to the appropriate use of equipment, facilities, and materials needed to do certain work. **Negotiation:** Bringing others together and trying to reconcile differences. **Operation Monitoring:** Watching gauges, dials, or other indicators to make sure a machine is working properly. **Monitoring:** Assessing how well one is doing when learning or doing something.

Education and Training Programs: Business Administration and Management, General; Business/Commerce, General; Operations Management and Supervision. **Related Knowledge/Courses—Production and Processing:** Inputs, outputs, raw materials, waste, quality control, costs, and techniques for maximizing the manufacture and distribution of goods. **Mechanical Devices:** Machines and tools, including their designs, uses, benefits, repair, and maintenance. **Administration and Management:** Principles and processes involved in business and organizational planning, coordination, and execution. This includes strategic planning, resource allocation, manpower modeling, leadership techniques, and production methods. **Design:** Design techniques, principles, tools, and instruments involved in the production and use of precision technical plans, blueprints, drawings, and models. **Personnel and Human Resources:** Principles and procedures for personnel recruitment; selection; training; compensation and benefits; labor relations and negotiation; and personnel information systems. **Engineering and Technology:** Equipment, tools, and mechanical devices and their uses to produce motion, light, power, technology, and other applications.

Work Environment: Indoors; noisy; contaminants; hazardous equipment; minor burns, cuts, bites, or stings; standing.

Industrial Safety and Health Engineers

- ❋ Education/Training Required: Bachelor's degree
- ❋ Annual Earnings: $69,580
- ❋ Beginning Wage: $42,200
- ❋ Earnings Growth Potential: Medium
- ❋ Growth: 9.6%
- ❋ Annual Job Openings: 1,105
- ❋ Self-Employed: 1.1%
- ❋ Part-Time: 2.0%

The job openings listed here are shared with Fire-Prevention and Protection Engineers and with Product Safety Engineers.

Plan, implement, and coordinate safety programs requiring application of engineering principles and technology to prevent or correct unsafe environmental working conditions. Investigate industrial accidents, injuries, or occupational diseases to determine causes and preventive measures. Report or review findings from accident investigations, facilities inspections, or environmental testing. Maintain and apply knowledge of current policies, regulations, and industrial processes. Inspect facilities, machinery, and safety equipment to identify and correct potential hazards and to ensure safety regulation compliance. Conduct or coordinate worker training in areas such as safety laws and regulations, hazardous condition monitoring, and use of safety equipment. Review employee safety programs to determine their adequacy. Interview employers and employees to obtain information about work environments and workplace incidents. Review plans and specifications for construction of new machinery or equipment to determine whether all safety requirements have been met. Compile, analyze, and interpret statistical data related to occupational illnesses and accidents. Interpret safety regulations for others interested in industrial safety, such as safety engineers, labor representatives, and safety inspectors. Recommend process and product safety features that will reduce employees' exposure to chemical, physical, and biological work hazards. Conduct or direct testing of air quality, noise, temperature, or radiation levels to verify compliance with health and safety regulations. Provide technical advice and guidance to organizations on how to handle health-related problems and make needed changes. Confer with medical professionals to assess health risks and to develop ways to manage health issues and concerns. Install safety devices on machinery or direct device installation. Maintain liaisons with outside organizations such as fire departments, mutual aid societies, and rescue teams so that emergency responses can be facilitated. Evaluate adequacy of actions taken to correct health inspection violations. Write and revise safety regulations and codes. Check floors of plants to ensure that they are strong enough to support heavy machinery. Plan and conduct industrial hygiene research.

Personality Type: Investigative. These occupations frequently involve working with ideas and require an extensive amount of thinking. They can involve searching for facts and figuring out problems mentally.

GOE—Interest Area/Cluster: 15. Scientific Research, Engineering, and Mathematics. **Work Group:** 15.08. Industrial and Safety Engineering. **Other Jobs in This Work Group:** Fire-Prevention and Protection Engineers; Health and Safety Engineers, Except Mining Safety Engineers and Inspectors; Industrial Engineers; Product Safety Engineers.

Skills—Management of Financial Resources: Determining how money will be spent to get the work done and accounting for these expenditures. **Science:** Using scientific methods to solve problems. **Systems Analysis:** Determining how a system should work and how changes will affect outcomes. **Persuasion:** Persuading others to approach things differently. **Operations Analysis:** Analyzing needs and product requirements to create a design. **Systems Evaluation:** Looking at many indicators of system performance and taking into account their accuracy. **Management of Material Resources:** Obtaining and seeing to the appropriate use of equipment, facilities, and materials needed to do certain work. **Management of Personnel Resources:** Motivating, developing, and directing people as they work; identifying the best people for the job.

Education and Training Program: Environmental/Environmental Health Engineering. **Related Knowledge/Courses—Building and Construction:** Materials, methods, and the appropriate tools to construct objects, structures, and buildings. **Physics:** Physical principles, laws, and applications, including air, water, material dynamics, light, atomic principles, heat, electric theory, earth formations, and meteorological and related natural phenomena. **Chemistry:** The composition, structure, and properties of substances and of the chemical processes and transformations that they undergo. This includes uses of chemicals and their interactions, danger signs, production techniques, and disposal methods. **Biology:** Plant and animal living tissue, cells, organisms, and entities, including their functions, interdependencies, and interactions with each other and the environment. **Engineering and Technology:** Equipment, tools, and mechanical devices and their uses to produce motion, light, power, technology, and other applications. **Education and Training:** Instructional methods and training techniques, including curriculum design principles, learning theory, group and individual teaching techniques, design of individual development plans, and test design principles.

Work Environment: More often indoors than outdoors; noisy; sitting.

Industrial Truck and Tractor Operators

- ❋ Education/Training Required: Short-term on-the-job training
- ❋ Annual Earnings: $28,010
- ❋ Beginning Wage: $19,510
- ❋ Earnings Growth Potential: Low
- ❋ Growth: –2.0%
- ❋ Annual Job Openings: 89,547
- ❋ Self-Employed: 0.3%
- ❋ Part-Time: 2.7%

Operate industrial trucks or tractors equipped to move materials around a warehouse, storage yard, factory, construction site, or similar location. Inspect product load for accuracy, and safely move it around the warehouse or facility to ensure timely and complete delivery. Move controls to drive gasoline- or electric-powered trucks, cars, or tractors and transport materials between loading, processing, and storage areas. Move levers and controls that operate lifting devices, such as forklifts, lift beams and swivel-hooks, hoists, and elevating platforms, to load, unload, transport, and stack material. Position lifting devices under, over, or around loaded pallets, skids, and boxes, and secure material or products for transport to designated areas. Manually or mechanically load and unload materials from pallets, skids, platforms, cars, lifting devices, or other transport vehicles. Perform routine maintenance on vehicles and auxiliary equipment, such as cleaning, lubricating, recharging batteries, fueling, or replacing liquefied-gas tank. Weigh materials or products, and record weight and other production data on tags or labels. Operate or tend automatic stacking, loading, packaging, or cutting machines. Turn valves and open chutes to dump, spray, or release materials from dump cars or storage bins into hoppers. Signal workers to discharge, dump, or level materials. Hook tow trucks to trailer hitches and fasten attachments such as graders, plows, rollers, and winch cables to tractors, using hitchpins.

Personality Type: Realistic. These occupations frequently involve work activities that include practical, hands-on problems and solutions. They often deal with plants; animals; and real-world materials such as wood, tools, and machinery. Many of the occupations require working outside and don't involve a lot of paperwork or working closely with others.

GOE—Interest Area/Cluster: 13. Manufacturing. **Work Group:** 13.17. Loading, Moving, Hoisting, and Conveying. **Other Jobs in This Work Group:** Conveyor Operators and Tenders; Hoist and Winch Operators; Machine Feeders and Offbearers; Packers and Packagers, Hand; Pump Operators, Except Wellhead Pumpers; Refuse and Recyclable Material Collectors; Tank Car, Truck, and Ship Loaders.

Skills—Operation Monitoring: Watching gauges, dials, or other indicators to make sure a machine is working properly. **Operation and Control:** Controlling operations of equipment or systems.

Education and Training Program: Ground Transportation, Other. **Related Knowledge/Course—Production and Processing:** Inputs, outputs, raw materials, waste, quality control, costs, and techniques for maximizing the manufacture and distribution of goods.

Work Environment: Very hot or cold; contaminants; sitting; using hands on objects, tools, or controls; bending or twisting the body; repetitive motions.

Industrial-Organizational Psychologists

- ❋ Education/Training Required: Master's degree
- ❋ Annual Earnings: $80,820
- ❋ Beginning Wage: $38,910
- ❋ Earnings Growth Potential: Very high
- ❋ Growth: 21.3%
- ❋ Annual Job Openings: 118
- ❋ Self-Employed: 39.3%
- ❋ Part-Time: 24.0%

Apply principles of psychology to personnel, administration, management, sales, and marketing problems. Activities may include policy planning; employee screening, training, and development; and organizational development and analysis. May work with management to reorganize the work setting to improve worker productivity. Develop and implement employee selection and placement programs. Analyze job requirements and content to establish criteria for classification, selection, training, and other related personnel functions. Develop interview techniques, rating scales, and psychological tests used to assess skills, abilities, and interests for the purpose of employee selection, placement, and promotion. Advise management concerning personnel, managerial, and marketing policies and practices and their potential effects on organizational effectiveness and efficiency. Analyze data, using statistical methods and applications, to evaluate the outcomes and effectiveness of workplace programs. Assess employee performance. Observe and interview workers to obtain information about the physical, mental, and educational requirements of jobs as well as information about aspects such as job satisfaction. Write reports on research findings and implications to contribute to general knowledge and to suggest potential changes in organizational functioning. Facilitate organizational development and change. Identify training and development needs. Formulate and implement training programs, applying principles of learning and individual differences. Study organizational effectiveness, productivity, and efficiency, including the nature of workplace supervision and leadership. Conduct research studies of physical work environments, organizational structures, communication systems, group interactions, morale, and motivation to assess organizational functioning. Counsel workers about job and career-related issues. Study consumers' reactions to new products and package designs, and to advertising efforts, using surveys and tests. Participate in mediation and dispute resolution.

Personality Type: Investigative. These occupations frequently involve working with ideas and require an extensive amount of thinking. They can involve searching for facts and figuring out problems mentally.

GOE—Interest Area/Cluster: 15. Scientific Research, Engineering, and Mathematics. **Work Group:** 15.04. Social Sciences. **Other Jobs in This Work Group:** Anthropologists; Anthropologists and Archeologists; Archeologists; Economists; Historians; Political Scientists; School Psychologists; Sociologists.

Skills—Science: Using scientific methods to solve problems. **Systems Evaluation:** Looking at many indicators of system performance and taking into account their accuracy. **Judgment and Decision Making:** Weighing the relative costs and benefits of a potential action. **Writing:** Communicating effectively with others in writing as indicated by the needs of the audience. **Monitoring:** Assessing how well one is doing when learning or doing something. **Time Management:** Managing one's own time and the time of others. **Coordination:** Adjusting actions in relation to others' actions. **Critical Thinking:** Using logic and analysis to identify the strengths and weaknesses of different approaches.

Education and Training Programs: Industrial and Organizational Psychology; Psychology, General. **Related**

Knowledge/Courses—Personnel and Human Resources: Principles and procedures for personnel recruitment; selection; training; compensation and benefits; labor relations and negotiation; and personnel information systems. **Psychology:** Human behavior and performance, mental processes, psychological research methods, and the assessment and treatment of behavioral and affective disorders. **Sociology and Anthropology:** Group behavior and dynamics; societal trends and influences; and cultures and their history, migrations, ethnicity, and origins. **Education and Training:** Instructional methods and training techniques, including curriculum design principles, learning theory, group and individual teaching techniques, design of individual development plans, and test design principles. **Therapy and Counseling:** Information and techniques needed to rehabilitate physical and mental ailments and to provide career guidance, including alternative treatments, rehabilitation equipment and its proper use, and methods to evaluate treatment effects. **Mathematics:** Numbers and their operations and interrelationships, including arithmetic, algebra, geometry, calculus, and statistics and their applications.

Work Environment: Indoors; sitting.

Inspectors, Testers, Sorters, Samplers, and Weighers

* Education/Training Required: Moderate-term on-the-job training
* Annual Earnings: $30,310
* Beginning Wage: $18,630
* Earnings Growth Potential: Medium
* Growth: –7.0%
* Annual Job Openings: 75,361
* Self-Employed: 1.5%
* Part-Time: 4.9%

Inspect, test, sort, sample, or weigh nonagricultural raw materials or processed, machined, fabricated, or assembled parts or products for defects, wear, and deviations from specifications. May use precision measuring instruments and complex test equipment. Discard or reject products, materials, and equipment not meeting specifications. Analyze and interpret blueprints, data, manuals, and other materials to determine specifications, inspection and testing procedures, adjustment and certification methods, formulas, and measuring instruments required. Inspect, test, or measure materials, products, installations, and work for conformance to specifications. Notify supervisors and other personnel of production problems, and assist in identifying and correcting these problems. Discuss inspection results with those responsible for products, and recommend necessary corrective actions. Record inspection or test data such as weights, temperatures, grades, or moisture content, and quantities inspected or graded. Mark items with details such as grade and acceptance or rejection status. Observe and monitor production operations and equipment to ensure conformance to specifications and make or order necessary process or assembly adjustments. Measure dimensions of products to verify conformance to specifications, using measuring instruments such as rulers, calipers, gauges, or micrometers. Analyze test data and make computations as necessary to determine test results. Collect or select samples for testing or for use as models. Check arriving materials to ensure that they match purchase orders and submit discrepancy reports when problems are found. Compare colors, shapes, textures, or grades of products or materials with color charts, templates, or samples to verify conformance to standards. Write test and inspection reports describing results, recommendations, and needed repairs. Read dials and meters to verify that equipment is functioning at specified levels. Remove defects such as chips and burrs and lap corroded or pitted surfaces. Clean, maintain, repair, and calibrate measuring instruments and test equipment such as dial indicators, fixed gauges, and height gauges. Adjust, clean, or repair products or processing equipment to correct defects found during inspections. Stack and arrange tested products for further processing, shipping, or packaging and transport products to other work stations as necessary.

Personality Type: Conventional. These occupations frequently involve following set procedures and routines and can include working with data and details more than with ideas. Usually there is a clear line of authority to follow.

GOE—Interest Area/Cluster: 13. Manufacturing. **Work Group:** 13.07. Production Quality Control. **Other Jobs in This Work Group:** Graders and Sorters, Agricultural Products.

Skills—Quality Control Analysis: Evaluating the quality or performance of products, services, or processes. **Operation Monitoring:** Watching gauges, dials, or other indicators to make sure a machine is working properly. **Operation and Control:** Controlling operations of equipment or systems. **Repairing:** Repairing machines or systems, using the needed tools. **Systems Evaluation:** Looking at many indicators of system performance and taking into account their

accuracy. **Troubleshooting:** Determining what is causing an operating error and deciding what to do about it.

Education and Training Program: Quality Control Technology/Technician. **Related Knowledge/Course—Production and Processing:** Inputs, outputs, raw materials, waste, quality control, costs, and techniques for maximizing the manufacture and distribution of goods.

Work Environment: Noisy; standing; using hands on objects, tools, or controls; repetitive motions.

Instructional Coordinators

- ❋ Education/Training Required: Master's degree
- ❋ Annual Earnings: $55,270
- ❋ Beginning Wage: $30,580
- ❋ Earnings Growth Potential: High
- ❋ Growth: 22.5%
- ❋ Annual Job Openings: 21,294
- ❋ Self-Employed: 3.1%
- ❋ Part-Time: 19.7%

Develop instructional material, coordinate educational content, and incorporate current technology in specialized fields that provide guidelines to educators and instructors for developing curricula and conducting courses. Conduct or participate in workshops, committees, and conferences designed to promote the intellectual, social, and physical welfare of students. Plan and conduct teacher training programs and conferences dealing with new classroom procedures, instructional materials and equipment, and teaching aids. Advise teaching and administrative staff in curriculum development, use of materials and equipment, and implementation of state and federal programs and procedures. Recommend, order, or authorize purchase of instructional materials, supplies, equipment, and visual aids designed to meet student educational needs and district standards. Interpret and enforce provisions of state education codes and rules and regulations of state education boards. Confer with members of educational committees and advisory groups to obtain knowledge of subject areas and to relate curriculum materials to specific subjects, individual student needs, and occupational areas. Organize production and design of curriculum materials. Research, evaluate, and prepare recommendations on curricula, instructional methods, and materials for school systems. Observe work of teaching staff to evaluate performance and to recommend changes that could strengthen teaching skills. Develop instructional materials to be used by educators and instructors. Prepare grant proposals, budgets, and program policies and goals or assist in their preparation. Develop tests, questionnaires, and procedures that measure the effectiveness of curricula and use these tools to determine whether program objectives are being met. Update the content of educational programs to ensure that students are being trained with equipment and processes that are technologically current. Address public audiences to explain program objectives and to elicit support. Advise and teach students. Prepare or approve manuals, guidelines, and reports on state educational policies and practices for distribution to school districts. Develop classroom-based and distance-learning training courses, using needs assessments and skill level analyses. Inspect instructional equipment to determine if repairs are needed and authorize necessary repairs.

Personality Type: Social. These occupations frequently involve working with, communicating with, and teaching people and often involve helping or providing service to others.

GOE—Interest Area/Cluster: 05. Education and Training. **Work Group:** 05.01. Managerial Work in Education. **Other Jobs in This Work Group:** Education Administrators, Elementary and Secondary School; Education Administrators, Postsecondary; Education Administrators, Preschool and Child Care Center/Program.

Skills—Management of Financial Resources: Determining how money will be spent to get the work done and accounting for these expenditures. **Learning Strategies:** Using multiple approaches when learning or teaching new things. **Monitoring:** Assessing how well one is doing when learning or doing something. **Social Perceptiveness:** Being aware of others' reactions and understanding why they react the way they do. **Coordination:** Adjusting actions in relation to others' actions. **Time Management:** Managing one's own time and the time of others. **Management of Personnel Resources:** Motivating, developing, and directing people as they work; identifying the best people for the job. **Persuasion:** Persuading others to approach things differently.

Education and Training Programs: Curriculum and Instruction; Educational/Instructional Media Design; International and Comparative Education. **Related Knowledge/Courses—Education and Training:** Instructional methods and training techniques, including curriculum design principles, learning theory, group and individual teaching techniques, design of individual development plans, and test design principles. **Sociology and Anthropology:** Group

behavior and dynamics; societal trends and influences; and cultures and their history, migrations, ethnicity, and origins. **English Language:** The structure and content of the English language, including the meaning and spelling of words, rules of composition, and grammar. **Personnel and Human Resources:** Principles and procedures for personnel recruitment; selection; training; compensation and benefits; labor relations and negotiation; and personnel information systems. **Communications and Media:** Media production, communication, and dissemination techniques and methods, including alternative ways to inform and entertain via written, oral, and visual media. **Psychology:** Human behavior and performance, mental processes, psychological research methods, and the assessment and treatment of behavioral and affective disorders.

Work Environment: Indoors; sitting.

Insulation Workers, Mechanical

* Education/Training Required: Moderate-term on-the-job training
* Annual Earnings: $36,570
* Beginning Wage: $22,840
* Earnings Growth Potential: Medium
* Growth: 8.6%
* Annual Job Openings: 5,787
* Self-Employed: 0.7%
* Part-Time: 3.1%

Apply insulating materials to pipes or ductwork or other mechanical systems to help control and maintain temperature. Cover, seal, or finish insulated surfaces or access holes with plastic covers, canvas strips, sealants, tape, cement, or asphalt mastic. Measure and cut insulation for covering surfaces, using tape measures, handsaws, knives, and scissors. Prepare surfaces for insulation application by brushing or spreading on adhesives, cement, or asphalt, or by attaching metal pins to surfaces. Select appropriate insulation such as fiberglass, Styrofoam, or cork, based on the heat retaining or excluding characteristics of the material. Read blueprints and specifications to determine job requirements. Install sheet metal around insulated pipes with screws in order to protect the insulation from weather conditions or physical damage. Determine the amounts and types of insulation needed, and methods of installation, based on factors such as location, surface shape, and equipment use. Apply, remove, and repair insulation on industrial equipment, pipes, ductwork, or other mechanical systems such as heat exchangers, tanks, and vessels, to help control noise and maintain temperatures. Remove or seal off old asbestos insulation, following safety procedures. Move controls, buttons, or levers to start blowers and to regulate flow of materials through nozzles. Fill blower hoppers with insulating materials. Distribute insulating materials evenly into small spaces within floors, ceilings, or walls, using blowers and hose attachments or cement mortar. Fit insulation around obstructions, and shape insulating materials and protective coverings as required.

Personality Type: Realistic. These occupations frequently involve work activities that include practical, hands-on problems and solutions. They often deal with plants; animals; and real-world materials such as wood, tools, and machinery. Many of the occupations require working outside and don't involve a lot of paperwork or working closely with others.

GOE—Interest Area/Cluster: 02. Architecture and Construction. **Work Group:** 02.04. Construction Crafts. **Other Jobs in This Work Group:** Boilermakers; Brickmasons and Blockmasons; Carpet Installers; Cement Masons and Concrete Finishers; Commercial Divers; Construction Carpenters; Crane and Tower Operators; Drywall and Ceiling Tile Installers; Electricians; Fence Erectors; Floor Layers, Except Carpet, Wood, and Hard Tiles; Floor Sanders and Finishers; Glaziers; Hazardous Materials Removal Workers; Insulation Workers, Floor, Ceiling, and Wall; Manufactured Building and Mobile Home Installers; Operating Engineers and Other Construction Equipment Operators; Painters, Construction and Maintenance; Paperhangers; Paving, Surfacing, and Tamping Equipment Operators; Pile-Driver Operators; Pipe Fitters and Steamfitters; Pipelayers; Plasterers and Stucco Masons; Plumbers; Plumbers, Pipefitters, and Steamfitters; Rail-Track Laying and Maintenance Equipment Operators; Refractory Materials Repairers, Except Brickmasons; Reinforcing Iron and Rebar Workers; Riggers; Roofers; Rough Carpenters; Security and Fire Alarm Systems Installers; Segmental Pavers; Sheet Metal Workers; Stone Cutters and Carvers, Manufacturing; Stonemasons; Structural Iron and Steel Workers; Tapers; Terrazzo Workers and Finishers; Tile and Marble Setters.

Skills—Installation: Installing equipment, machines, wiring, or programs to meet specifications. **Repairing:** Repairing machines or systems, using the needed tools. **Mathematics:** Using mathematics to solve problems. **Coordination:** Adjusting actions in relation to others' actions. **Management of Personnel Resources:** Motivating, developing, and directing people as they work; identifying the best people for the job. **Equipment Selection:** Determining the kind of tools and equipment needed to do a job. **Management of Material Resources:** Obtaining and seeing to the appropriate use of equipment, facilities, and materials needed to do certain work. **Equipment Maintenance:** Performing routine maintenance and determining when and what kind of maintenance is needed.

Education and Training Program: Construction Trades, Other. **Related Knowledge/Courses—Building and Construction:** Materials, methods, and the appropriate tools to construct objects, structures, and buildings. **Design:** Design techniques, principles, tools, and instruments involved in the production and use of precision technical plans, blueprints, drawings, and models. **Mechanical Devices:** Machines and tools, including their designs, uses, benefits, repair, and maintenance. **Transportation:** Principles and methods for moving people or goods by air, rail, sea, or road, including their relative costs, advantages, and limitations. **Education and Training:** Instructional methods and training techniques, including curriculum design principles, learning theory, group and individual teaching techniques, design of individual development plans, and test design principles. **Public Safety and Security:** Weaponry; public safety; security operations, rules, regulations, precautions, and prevention; and the protection of people, data, and property.

Work Environment: Noisy; contaminants; cramped work space, awkward positions; high places; standing; using hands on objects, tools, or controls.

Insurance Adjusters, Examiners, and Investigators

- ❋ Education/Training Required: Long-term on-the-job training
- ❋ Annual Earnings: $53,560
- ❋ Beginning Wage: $33,010
- ❋ Earnings Growth Potential: Medium
- ❋ Growth: 8.9%
- ❋ Annual Job Openings: 22,024
- ❋ Self-Employed: 3.5%
- ❋ Part-Time: 4.0%

The job openings listed here are shared with Claims Examiners, Property and Casualty Insurance.

Investigate, analyze, and determine the extent of insurance company's liability concerning personal, casualty, or property loss or damages and attempt to effect

settlement with claimants. **Correspond with or interview medical specialists, agents, witnesses, or claimants to compile information. Calculate benefit payments and approve payment of claims within a certain monetary limit.** Interview or correspond with claimant and witnesses, consult police and hospital records, and inspect property damage to determine extent of liability. Investigate and assess damage to property. Examine claims forms and other records to determine insurance coverage. Analyze information gathered by investigation and report findings and recommendations. Negotiate claim settlements and recommend litigation when settlement cannot be negotiated. Collect evidence to support contested claims in court. Prepare report of findings of investigation. Interview or correspond with agents and claimants to correct errors or omissions and to investigate questionable claims. Refer questionable claims to investigator or claims adjuster for investigation or settlement. Examine titles to property to determine validity and act as company agent in transactions with property owners. Obtain credit information from banks and other credit services. Communicate with former associates to verify employment record and to obtain background information regarding persons or businesses applying for credit.

Personality Type: Conventional. These occupations frequently involve following set procedures and routines and can include working with data and details more than with ideas. Usually there is a clear line of authority to follow.

GOE—Interest Area/Cluster: 06. Finance and Insurance. **Work Group:** 06.02. Finance/Insurance Investigation and Analysis. **Other Jobs in This Work Group:** Appraisers and Assessors of Real Estate; Appraisers, Real Estate; Assessors; Claims Adjusters, Examiners, and Investigators; Claims Examiners, Property and Casualty Insurance; Cost Estimators; Credit Analysts; Financial Analysts; Insurance Appraisers, Auto Damage; Insurance Underwriters; Loan Counselors; Loan Officers; Market Research Analysts; Survey Researchers.

Skills—Negotiation: Bringing others together and trying to reconcile differences. **Persuasion:** Persuading others to approach things differently. **Judgment and Decision Making:** Weighing the relative costs and benefits of a potential action. **Time Management:** Managing one's own time and the time of others. **Management of Financial Resources:** Determining how money will be spent to get the work done and accounting for these expenditures. **Reading Comprehension:** Understanding written sentences and paragraphs in work-related documents. **Writing:** Communicating effectively with others in writing as indicated by the needs of the audience. **Critical Thinking:** Using logic and analysis to identify the strengths and weaknesses of different approaches.

Education and Training Program: Insurance. **Related Knowledge/Courses—Customer and Personal Service:** Principles and processes for providing customer and personal services, including needs assessment techniques, quality service standards, alternative delivery systems, and customer satisfaction evaluation techniques. **Clerical Practices:** Administrative and clerical procedures and systems such as word-processing systems, filing and records management systems, stenography and transcription, forms, design principles, and other office procedures and terminology. **Computers and Electronics:** Electric circuit boards, processors, chips, and computer hardware and software, including applications and programming. **Law and Government:** Laws, legal codes, court procedures, precedents, government regulations, executive orders, agency rules, and the democratic political process. **Medicine and Dentistry:** The information and techniques needed to diagnose and treat injuries, diseases, and deformities. This includes symptoms, treatment alternatives, drug properties and interactions, and preventive health-care measures. **Therapy and Counseling:** Information and techniques needed to rehabilitate physical and mental ailments and to provide career guidance, including alternative treatments, rehabilitation equipment and its proper use, and methods to evaluate treatment effects.

Work Environment: Indoors; noisy; sitting; using hands on objects, tools, or controls; repetitive motions.

Insurance Appraisers, Auto Damage

* ❋ Education/Training Required: Postsecondary vocational training
* ❋ Annual Earnings: $51,500
* ❋ Beginning Wage: $35,750
* ❋ Earnings Growth Potential: Low
* ❋ Growth: 12.5%
* ❋ Annual Job Openings: 1,030
* ❋ Self-Employed: 4.1%
* ❋ Part-Time: 4.0%

Appraise automobile or other vehicle damage to determine cost of repair for insurance claim settlement and seek agreement with automotive repair shop on cost of repair. Prepare insurance forms to indicate repair cost or cost estimates and recommendations. Estimate parts and labor to repair damage, using standard automotive labor and parts-cost manuals and knowledge of automotive repair. Review repair-cost estimates with automobile-repair shop to secure agreement on cost of repairs. Examine damaged vehicle to determine extent of structural, body, mechanical, electrical, or interior damage. Evaluate practicality of repair as opposed to payment of market value of vehicle before accident. Determine salvage value on total-loss vehicle. Prepare insurance forms to indicate repair-cost estimates and recommendations. Arrange to have damage appraised by another appraiser to resolve disagreement with shop on repair cost.

Personality Type: Conventional. These occupations frequently involve following set procedures and routines and can include working with data and details more than with ideas. Usually there is a clear line of authority to follow.

GOE—Interest Area/Cluster: 06. Finance and Insurance. **Work Group:** 06.02. Finance/Insurance Investigation and Analysis. **Other Jobs in This Work Group:** Appraisers and Assessors of Real Estate; Appraisers, Real Estate; Assessors; Claims Adjusters, Examiners, and Investigators; Claims Examiners, Property and Casualty Insurance; Cost Estimators; Credit Analysts; Financial Analysts; Insurance Adjusters, Examiners, and Investigators; Insurance Underwriters; Loan Counselors; Loan Officers; Market Research Analysts; Survey Researchers.

Skills—Negotiation: Bringing others together and trying to reconcile differences. **Service Orientation:** Actively looking for ways to help people. **Persuasion:** Persuading others to approach things differently. **Judgment and Decision Making:** Weighing the relative costs and benefits of a potential action. **Active Listening:** Listening to what other people are saying and asking questions as appropriate. **Time Management:** Managing one's own time and the time of others. **Equipment Selection:** Determining the kind of tools and equipment needed to do a job. **Speaking:** Talking to others to effectively convey information.

Education and Training Program: Insurance. **Related Knowledge/Courses—Customer and Personal Service:** Principles and processes for providing customer and personal services, including needs assessment techniques, quality service standards, alternative delivery systems, and customer satisfaction evaluation techniques. **Law and Government:** Laws, legal codes, court procedures, precedents, government regulations, executive orders, agency rules, and the democratic political process. **Medicine and Dentistry:** The information and techniques needed to diagnose and treat injuries, diseases, and deformities. This includes symptoms,

treatment alternatives, drug properties and interactions, and preventive health-care measures. **Computers and Electronics:** Electric circuit boards, processors, chips, and computer hardware and software, including applications and programming. **Transportation:** Principles and methods for moving people or goods by air, rail, sea, or road, including their relative costs, advantages, and limitations. **Telecommunications:** Transmission, broadcasting, switching, control, and operation of telecommunications systems.

Work Environment: More often indoors than outdoors; noisy; very hot or cold; contaminants; sitting.

Insurance Claims Clerks

- ❋ Education/Training Required: Moderate-term on-the-job training
- ❋ Annual Earnings: $32,040
- ❋ Beginning Wage: $21,950
- ❋ Earnings Growth Potential: Low
- ❋ Growth: −1.3%
- ❋ Annual Job Openings: 42,246
- ❋ Self-Employed: 0.4%
- ❋ Part-Time: 9.7%

The job openings listed here are shared with Insurance Policy Processing Clerks.

Obtain information from insured or designated persons for purpose of settling claim with insurance carrier. Review insurance policy to determine coverage. Prepare and review insurance-claim forms and related documents for completeness. Provide customer service, such as giving limited instructions on how to proceed with claims or providing referrals to auto repair facilities or local contractors. Organize and work with detailed office or warehouse records, using computers to enter, access, search, and retrieve data. Post or attach information to claim file. Pay small claims. Transmit claims for payment or further investigation. Contact insured or other involved persons to obtain missing information. Calculate amount of claim. Apply insurance rating systems.

Personality Type: Conventional. These occupations frequently involve following set procedures and routines and can include working with data and details more than with ideas. Usually there is a clear line of authority to follow.

GOE—Interest Area/Cluster: 06. Finance and Insurance. **Work Group:** 06.03. Finance/Insurance Records Processing.

Other Jobs in This Work Group: Credit Authorizers; Credit Authorizers, Checkers, and Clerks; Credit Checkers; Insurance Claims and Policy Processing Clerks; Insurance Policy Processing Clerks; Proofreaders and Copy Markers.

Skill—Service Orientation: Actively looking for ways to help people.

Education and Training Program: General Office Occupations and Clerical Services. **Related Knowledge/Courses—Clerical Practices:** Administrative and clerical procedures and systems such as word-processing systems, filing and records management systems, stenography and transcription, forms, design principles, and other office procedures and terminology. **Customer and Personal Service:** Principles and processes for providing customer and personal services, including needs assessment techniques, quality service standards, alternative delivery systems, and customer satisfaction evaluation techniques. **Computers and Electronics:** Electric circuit boards, processors, chips, and computer hardware and software, including applications and programming. **Economics and Accounting:** Economic and accounting principles and practices, the financial markets, banking, and the analysis and reporting of financial data.

Work Environment: Indoors; sitting; repetitive motions.

Insurance Policy Processing Clerks

- ❋ Education/Training Required: Moderate-term on-the-job training
- ❋ Annual Earnings: $32,040
- ❋ Beginning Wage: $21,950
- ❋ Earnings Growth Potential: Low
- ❋ Growth: –1.3%
- ❋ Annual Job Openings: 42,246
- ❋ Self-Employed: 0.4%
- ❋ Part-Time: 9.7%

The job openings listed here are shared with Insurance Claims Clerks.

Process applications for, changes to, reinstatement of, and cancellation of insurance policies. Duties include reviewing insurance applications to ensure that all questions have been answered, compiling data on insurance policy changes, changing policy records to conform to insured party's specifications, compiling data on lapsed insurance policies to determine automatic reinstatement according to company policies, canceling insurance policies as requested by agents, and verifying the accuracy of insurance company records. Modify, update, and process existing policies and claims to reflect any change in beneficiary, amount of coverage, or type of insurance. Process and record new insurance policies and claims. Review and verify data, such as age, name, address, and principal sum and value of property, on insurance applications and policies. Organize and work with detailed office or warehouse records, maintaining files for each policyholder, including policies that are to be reinstated or cancelled. Examine letters from policyholders or agents, original insurance applications, and other company documents to determine whether changes are needed and effects of changes. Correspond with insured or agent to obtain information or inform them of account status or changes. Transcribe data to worksheets and enter data into computer for use in preparing documents and adjusting accounts. Notify insurance agent and accounting department of policy cancellation. Interview clients and take their calls to provide customer service and obtain information on claims. Compare information from application to criteria for policy reinstatement and approve reinstatement when criteria are met. Process, prepare, and submit business or government forms, such as submitting applications for coverage to insurance carriers. Collect initial premiums and issue receipts. Calculate premiums, refunds, commissions, adjustments, and new reserve requirements, using insurance rate standards. Obtain computer printout of policy cancellations or retrieve cancellation cards from file. Compose business correspondence for supervisors, managers, and professionals. Check computations of interest accrued, premiums due, and settlement surrender on loan values.

Personality Type: Conventional. These occupations frequently involve following set procedures and routines and can include working with data and details more than with ideas. Usually there is a clear line of authority to follow.

GOE—Interest Area/Cluster: 06. Finance and Insurance. **Work Group:** 06.03. Finance/Insurance Records Processing. **Other Jobs in This Work Group:** Credit Authorizers; Credit Authorizers, Checkers, and Clerks; Credit Checkers; Insurance Claims and Policy Processing Clerks; Insurance Claims Clerks; Proofreaders and Copy Markers.

Skill—Critical Thinking: Using logic and analysis to identify the strengths and weaknesses of different approaches.

Education and Training Program: General Office Occupations and Clerical Services. **Related Knowledge/Courses—Clerical Practices:** Administrative and clerical procedures and systems such as word-processing systems, filing and records management systems, stenography and transcription, forms, design principles, and other office procedures and terminology. **Customer and Personal Service:** Principles and processes for providing customer and personal services, including needs assessment techniques, quality service standards, alternative delivery systems, and customer satisfaction evaluation techniques. **Computers and Electronics:** Electric circuit boards, processors, chips, and computer hardware and software, including applications and programming. **Economics and Accounting:** Economic and accounting principles and practices, the financial markets, banking, and the analysis and reporting of financial data. **Sales and Marketing:** Principles and methods involved in showing, promoting, and selling products or services. This includes marketing strategies and tactics, product demonstration and sales techniques, and sales control systems. **Production and Processing:** Inputs, outputs, raw materials, waste, quality control, costs, and techniques for maximizing the manufacture and distribution of goods.

Work Environment: Sitting; repetitive motions.

Insurance Sales Agents

- ❋ Education/Training Required: Bachelor's degree
- ❋ Annual Earnings: $44,110
- ❋ Beginning Wage: $25,230
- ❋ Earnings Growth Potential: High
- ❋ Growth: 12.9%
- ❋ Annual Job Openings: 64,162
- ❋ Self-Employed: 25.5%
- ❋ Part-Time: 9.8%

Sell life, property, casualty, health, automotive, or other types of insurance. May refer clients to independent brokers, work as independent broker, or be employed by an insurance company. Call on policyholders to deliver and explain policy, to analyze insurance program and suggest additions or changes, or to change beneficiaries. Calculate premiums and establish payment method. Customize insurance programs to suit individual customers, often covering a variety of risks. Sell various types of insurance policies to businesses and individuals on behalf of insurance companies, including automobile, fire, life, property, medical, and dental insurance or specialized policies such as marine, farm/crop, and medical malpractice. Interview prospective clients to obtain data about their financial resources and needs and the physical condition of the person or property

to be insured and to discuss any existing coverage. Seek out new clients and develop clientele by networking to find new customers and generate lists of prospective clients. Explain features, advantages, and disadvantages of various policies to promote sale of insurance plans. Contact underwriter and submit forms to obtain binder coverage. Ensure that policy requirements are fulfilled, including any necessary medical examinations and the completion of appropriate forms. Confer with clients to obtain and provide information when claims are made on a policy. Perform administrative tasks, such as maintaining records and handling policy renewals. Select company that offers type of coverage requested by client to underwrite policy. Monitor insurance claims to ensure that they are settled equitably for both the client and the insurer. Develop marketing strategies to compete with other individuals or companies who sell insurance. Attend meetings, seminars, and programs to learn about new products and services, learn new skills, and receive technical assistance in developing new accounts. Inspect property, examining its general condition, type of construction, age, and other characteristics, to decide if it is a good insurance risk. Install bookkeeping systems and resolve system problems. Plan and oversee incorporation of insurance program into bookkeeping system of company. Explain necessary bookkeeping requirements for customer to implement and provide group insurance program.

Personality Type: Enterprising. These occupations frequently involve starting up and carrying out projects and can involve leading people and making many decisions. They sometimes require risk taking and often deal with business.

GOE—Interest Area/Cluster: 06. Finance and Insurance. **Work Group:** 06.05. Finance/Insurance Sales and Support. **Other Jobs in This Work Group:** Advertising Sales Agents; Personal Financial Advisors; Sales Agents, Financial Services; Sales Agents, Securities and Commodities; Securities, Commodities, and Financial Services Sales Agents.

Skills—Persuasion: Persuading others to approach things differently. **Judgment and Decision Making:** Weighing the relative costs and benefits of a potential action. **Time Management:** Managing one's own time and the time of others. **Negotiation:** Bringing others together and trying to reconcile differences. **Service Orientation:** Actively looking for ways to help people. **Speaking:** Talking to others to effectively convey information. **Active Listening:** Listening to what other people are saying and asking questions as appropriate. **Social Perceptiveness:** Being aware of others' reactions and understanding why they react the way they do.

Education and Training Program: Insurance. **Related Knowledge/Courses—Sales and Marketing:** Principles and methods involved in showing, promoting, and selling products or services. This includes marketing strategies and tactics, product demonstration and sales techniques, and sales control systems. **Economics and Accounting:** Economic and accounting principles and practices, the financial markets, banking, and the analysis and reporting of financial data. **Customer and Personal Service:** Principles and processes for providing customer and personal services, including needs assessment techniques, quality service standards, alternative delivery systems, and customer satisfaction evaluation techniques. **Computers and Electronics:** Electric circuit boards, processors, chips, and computer hardware and software, including applications and programming. **Clerical Practices:** Administrative and clerical procedures and systems such as word-processing systems, filing and records management systems, stenography and transcription, forms, design principles, and other office procedures and terminology. **Law and Government:** Laws, legal codes, court procedures, precedents, government regulations, executive orders, agency rules, and the democratic political process.

Work Environment: Indoors; sitting.

Insurance Underwriters

- ❋ Education/Training Required: Bachelor's degree
- ❋ Annual Earnings: $54,530
- ❋ Beginning Wage: $33,550
- ❋ Earnings Growth Potential: Medium
- ❋ Growth: 6.3%
- ❋ Annual Job Openings: 6,880
- ❋ Self-Employed: 0.0%
- ❋ Part-Time: 3.6%

Review individual applications for insurance to evaluate degree of risk involved and determine acceptance of applications. Examine documents to determine degree of risk from such factors as applicant financial standing and value and condition of property. Decline excessive risks. Write to field representatives, medical personnel, and others to obtain further information, quote rates, or explain company underwriting policies. Evaluate possibility of losses due to catastrophe or excessive insurance. Decrease value of policy when risk is substandard and specify applicable endorsements or apply rating to ensure safe profitable distribution of risks, using reference materials. Review company records

to determine amount of insurance in force on single risk or group of closely related risks. Authorize reinsurance of policy when risk is high.

Personality Type: Conventional. These occupations frequently involve following set procedures and routines and can include working with data and details more than with ideas. Usually there is a clear line of authority to follow.

GOE—Interest Area/Cluster: 06. Finance and Insurance. **Work Group:** 06.02. Finance/Insurance Investigation and Analysis. **Other Jobs in This Work Group:** Appraisers and Assessors of Real Estate; Appraisers, Real Estate; Assessors; Claims Adjusters, Examiners, and Investigators; Claims Examiners, Property and Casualty Insurance; Cost Estimators; Credit Analysts; Financial Analysts; Insurance Adjusters, Examiners, and Investigators; Insurance Appraisers, Auto Damage; Loan Counselors; Loan Officers; Market Research Analysts; Survey Researchers.

Skills—Writing: Communicating effectively with others in writing as indicated by the needs of the audience. **Service Orientation:** Actively looking for ways to help people. **Speaking:** Talking to others to effectively convey information. **Active Listening:** Listening to what other people are saying and asking questions as appropriate. **Learning Strategies:** Using multiple approaches when learning or teaching new things. **Active Learning:** Working with new material or information to grasp its implications. **Monitoring:** Assessing how well one is doing when learning or doing something. **Persuasion:** Persuading others to approach things differently.

Education and Training Program: Insurance. **Related Knowledge/Courses—Clerical Practices:** Administrative and clerical procedures and systems such as word-processing systems, filing and records management systems, stenography and transcription, forms, design principles, and other office procedures and terminology. **Customer and Personal Service:** Principles and processes for providing customer and personal services, including needs assessment techniques, quality service standards, alternative delivery systems, and customer satisfaction evaluation techniques. **Sales and Marketing:** Principles and methods involved in showing, promoting, and selling products or services. This includes marketing strategies and tactics, product demonstration and sales techniques, and sales control systems. **Economics and Accounting:** Economic and accounting principles and practices, the financial markets, banking, and the analysis and reporting of financial data. **Law and Government:** Laws, legal codes, court procedures, precedents, government regulations, executive orders, agency rules, and the democratic political process. **Computers and Electronics:** Electric circuit boards, processors, chips, and computer hardware and software, including applications and programming.

Work Environment: Indoors; sitting; using hands on objects, tools, or controls; repetitive motions.

Interior Designers

* ❋ Education/Training Required: Associate degree
* ❋ Annual Earnings: $43,970
* ❋ Beginning Wage: $25,920
* ❋ Earnings Growth Potential: High
* ❋ Growth: 19.5%
* ❋ Annual Job Openings: 8,434
* ❋ Self-Employed: 26.3%
* ❋ Part-Time: 16.7%

Plan, design, and furnish interiors of residential, commercial, or industrial buildings. Formulate design that is practical, aesthetic, and conducive to intended purposes, such as raising productivity, selling merchandise, or improving lifestyle. May specialize in a particular field, style, or phase of interior design. Estimate material requirements and costs and present design to client for approval. Confer with client to determine factors affecting planning interior environments, such as budget, architectural preferences, and purpose and function. Advise client on interior design factors such as space planning, layout, and utilization of furnishings or equipment and color coordination. Select or design and purchase furnishings, artwork, and accessories. Formulate environmental plan to be practical, esthetic, and conducive to intended purposes such as raising productivity or selling merchandise. Subcontract fabrication, installation, and arrangement of carpeting, fixtures, accessories, draperies, paint and wall coverings, artwork, furniture, and related items. Render design ideas in form of paste-ups or drawings. Plan and design interior environments for boats, planes, buses, trains, and other enclosed spaces.

Personality Type: Artistic. These occupations frequently involve working with forms, designs, and patterns. They often require self-expression, and the work can be done without following a clear set of rules.

GOE—Interest Area/Cluster: 03. Arts and Communication. **Work Group:** 03.05. Design. **Other Jobs in This Work Group:** Commercial and Industrial Designers; Fashion Designers; Floral Designers; Graphic Designers; Merchandise Displayers and Window Trimmers; Set and Exhibit Designers.

Skills—Installation: Installing equipment, machines, wiring, or programs to meet specifications. **Management of Financial Resources:** Determining how money will be spent to get the work done and accounting for these expenditures. **Persuasion:** Persuading others to approach things differently. **Operations Analysis:** Analyzing needs and product requirements to create a design. **Negotiation:** Bringing others together and trying to reconcile differences. **Active Learning:** Working with new material or information to grasp its implications. **Mathematics:** Using mathematics to solve problems. **Speaking:** Talking to others to effectively convey information.

Education and Training Programs: Facilities Planning and Management; Interior Architecture; Interior Design; Textile Science. **Related Knowledge/Courses—Design:** Design techniques, principles, tools, and instruments involved in the production and use of precision technical plans, blueprints, drawings, and models. **Sales and Marketing:** Principles and methods involved in showing, promoting, and selling products or services. This includes marketing strategies and tactics, product demonstration and sales techniques, and sales control systems. **Building and Construction:** Materials, methods, and the appropriate tools to construct objects, structures, and buildings. **Clerical Practices:** Administrative and clerical procedures and systems such as word-processing systems, filing and records management systems, stenography and transcription, forms, design principles, and other office procedures and terminology. **Fine Arts:** Theory and techniques required to produce, compose, and perform works of music, dance, visual arts, drama, and sculpture. **Administration and Management:** Principles and processes involved in business and organizational planning, coordination, and execution. This includes strategic planning, resource allocation, manpower modeling, leadership techniques, and production methods.

Work Environment: Indoors; sitting.

Internists, General

- ❀ Education/Training Required: First professional degree
- ❀ Annual Earnings: More than $145,600
- ❀ Beginning Wage: $89,130
- ❀ Earnings Growth Potential: Cannot be calculated
- ❀ Growth: 14.2%
- ❀ Annual Job Openings: 38,027
- ❀ Self-Employed: 14.7%
- ❀ Part-Time: 8.1%

The job openings listed here are shared with Anesthesiologists; Family and General Practitioners; Obstetricians and Gynecologists; Pediatricians, General; Psychiatrists; and Surgeons.

Diagnose and provide non-surgical treatment of diseases and injuries of internal organ systems. Provide care mainly for adults who have a wide range of problems associated with the internal organs. Treat internal disorders, such as hypertension; heart disease; diabetes; and problems of the lung, brain, kidney, and gastrointestinal tract. Analyze records, reports, test results, or examination information to diagnose medical condition of patient. Prescribe or administer medication, therapy, and other specialized medical care to treat or prevent illness, disease, or injury. Provide and manage long-term, comprehensive medical care, including diagnosis and non-surgical treatment of diseases, for adult patients in an office or hospital. Manage and treat common health problems, such as infections, influenza and pneumonia, as well as serious, chronic, and complex illnesses, in adolescents, adults, and the elderly. Monitor patients' conditions and progress and re-evaluate treatments as necessary. Collect, record, and maintain patient information, such as medical history, reports, and examination results. Make diagnoses when different illnesses occur together or in situations where the diagnosis may be obscure. Explain procedures and discuss test results or prescribed treatments with patients. Advise patients and community members concerning diet, activity, hygiene, and disease prevention. Refer patient to medical specialist or other practitioner when necessary. Immunize patients to protect them from preventable diseases. Advise surgeon of a patient's risk status and recommend appropriate intervention to minimize risk. Direct and coordinate activities of nurses, students, assistants, specialists, therapists, and other medical staff. Provide consulting services to other doctors caring for patients with special or difficult problems. Operate on patients to remove, repair, or improve functioning of diseased or injured body parts and systems. Plan, implement, or administer health programs in hospitals, businesses, or communities for prevention and treatment of injuries or illnesses. Conduct research to develop or test medications, treatments, or procedures to prevent or control disease or injury. Prepare government or organizational reports on birth, death, and disease statistics; workforce evaluations; or the medical status of individuals.

Personality Type: Investigative. These occupations frequently involve working with ideas and require an extensive amount of thinking. They can involve searching for facts and figuring out problems mentally.

GOE—Interest Area/Cluster: 08. Health Science. **Work Group:** 08.02. Medicine and Surgery. **Other Jobs in This Work Group:** Anesthesiologists; Family and General Practitioners; Medical Assistants; Medical Transcriptionists; Obstetricians and Gynecologists; Pediatricians, General; Pharmacists; Pharmacy Aides; Pharmacy Technicians; Physician Assistants; Psychiatrists; Registered Nurses; Surgeons; Surgical Technologists.

Skills—Science: Using scientific methods to solve problems. **Judgment and Decision Making:** Weighing the relative costs and benefits of a potential action. **Complex Problem Solving:** Identifying complex problems, reviewing the options, and implementing solutions. **Reading Comprehension:** Understanding written sentences and paragraphs in work-related documents. **Social Perceptiveness:** Being aware of others' reactions and understanding why they react the way they do. **Service Orientation:** Actively looking for ways to help people. **Management of Financial Resources:** Determining how money will be spent to get the work done and accounting for these expenditures. **Persuasion:** Persuading others to approach things differently.

Education and Training Programs: Cardiology; Critical Care Medicine; Endocrinology and Metabolism; Gastroenterology; Geriatric Medicine; Hematology; Infectious Disease; Internal Medicine; Nephrology; Neurology; Nuclear Medicine; Oncology; Pulmonary Disease; Rheumatology. **Related Knowledge/Courses—Medicine and Dentistry:** The information and techniques needed to diagnose and treat injuries, diseases, and deformities. This includes symptoms, treatment alternatives, drug properties and interactions, and preventive health-care measures. **Biology:** Plant and animal living tissue, cells, organisms, and entities, including their functions, interdependencies, and interactions with each other and the environment. **Therapy and Counseling:** Information and techniques needed to rehabilitate physical and mental ailments and to provide career guidance, including alternative treatments, rehabilitation equipment and its proper use, and methods to evaluate treatment effects. **Psychology:** Human behavior and performance, mental processes, psychological research methods, and the assessment and treatment of behavioral and affective disorders. **Chemistry:** The composition, structure, and properties of substances and of the chemical processes and transformations that they undergo. This includes uses of chemicals and their interactions, danger signs, production techniques, and disposal methods. **Education and Training:** Instructional methods and training techniques, including curriculum design principles, learning theory, group and individual teaching techniques, design of individual development plans, and test design principles.

Work Environment: Indoors; disease or infections; standing.

Interpreters and Translators

- ❋ Education/Training Required: Long-term on-the-job training
- ❋ Annual Earnings: $37,490
- ❋ Beginning Wage: $21,500
- ❋ Earnings Growth Potential: High
- ❋ Growth: 23.6%
- ❋ Annual Job Openings: 6,630
- ❋ Self-Employed: 21.6%
- ❋ Part-Time: 28.5%

Translate or interpret written, oral, or sign language text into another language for others. Follow ethical codes that protect the confidentiality of information. Identify and resolve conflicts related to the meanings of words, concepts, practices, or behaviors. Proofread, edit, and revise translated materials. Translate messages simultaneously or consecutively into specified languages orally or by using hand signs, maintaining message content, context, and style as much as possible. Check translations of technical terms and terminology to ensure that they are accurate and remain consistent throughout translation revisions. Read written materials such as legal documents, scientific works, or news reports and rewrite material into specified languages. Refer to reference materials such as dictionaries, lexicons, encyclopedias, and computerized terminology banks as needed to ensure translation accuracy. Compile terminology and information to be used in translations, including technical terms such as those for legal or medical material. Adapt

translations to students' cognitive and grade levels, collaborating with educational team members as necessary. Listen to speakers' statements to determine meanings and to prepare translations, using electronic listening systems as necessary. Check original texts or confer with authors to ensure that translations retain the content, meaning, and feeling of the original material. Compile information about the content and context of information to be translated, as well as details of the groups for whom translation or interpretation is being performed. Discuss translation requirements with clients and determine any fees to be charged for services provided. Adapt software and accompanying technical documents to another language and culture. Educate students, parents, staff, and teachers about the roles and functions of educational interpreters. Train and supervise other translators/interpreters. Travel with or guide tourists who speak another language.

Personality Type: Artistic. These occupations frequently involve working with forms, designs, and patterns. They often require self-expression, and the work can be done without following a clear set of rules.

GOE—Interest Area/Cluster: 03. Arts and Communication. **Work Group:** 03.03. News, Broadcasting, and Public Relations. **Other Jobs in This Work Group:** Broadcast News Analysts; Public Relations Specialists; Reporters and Correspondents.

Skills—Social Perceptiveness: Being aware of others' reactions and understanding why they react the way they do. **Speaking:** Talking to others to effectively convey information. **Active Listening:** Listening to what other people are saying and asking questions as appropriate. **Writing:** Communicating effectively with others in writing as indicated by the needs of the audience. **Reading Comprehension:** Understanding written sentences and paragraphs in work-related documents.

Education and Training Programs: American Sign Language (ASL); Chinese Language and Literature; Classics; Education/Teaching of Individuals with Hearing Impairments; Foreign Languages, Literatures, and Linguistics, others; French Language and Literature; German Language and Literature; Italian Language and Literature; Japanese Language and Literature; Language Interpretation and Translation; Linguistics; Russian Language and Literature; Spanish Language and Literature. **Related Knowledge/Courses— Foreign Language:** The structure and content of a foreign (non-English) language, including the meaning and spelling of words, rules of composition and grammar, and pronunciation. **English Language:** The structure and content of the English language, including the meaning and spelling of words, rules of composition, and grammar. **Geography:** Various methods for describing the location and distribution of land, sea, and air masses, including their physical locations, relationships, and characteristics. **Sociology and Anthropology:** Group behavior and dynamics; societal trends and influences; and cultures and their history, migrations, ethnicity, and origins. **Computers and Electronics:** Electric circuit boards, processors, chips, and computer hardware and software, including applications and programming. **Communications and Media:** Media production, communication, and dissemination techniques and methods, including alternative ways to inform and entertain via written, oral, and visual media.

Work Environment: Indoors; sitting; repetitive motions.

Interviewers, Except Eligibility and Loan

- ❋ Education/Training Required: Short-term on-the-job training
- ❋ Annual Earnings: $27,320
- ❋ Beginning Wage: $17,960
- ❋ Earnings Growth Potential: Low
- ❋ Growth: 9.5%
- ❋ Annual Job Openings: 54,060
- ❋ Self-Employed: 0.8%
- ❋ Part-Time: 23.4%

Interview persons by telephone, by mail, in person, or by other means for the purpose of completing forms, applications, or questionnaires. Ask specific questions, record answers, and assist persons with completing form. May sort, classify, and file forms. Ask questions in accordance with instructions to obtain various specified information such as person's name, address, age, religious preference, and state of residency. Identify and resolve inconsistencies in interviewees' responses by means of appropriate questioning or explanation. Compile, record, and code results and data from interview or survey, using computer or specified form. Review data obtained from interview for completeness and accuracy. Contact individuals to be interviewed at home, place of business, or field location by telephone, by mail, or in person. Assist individuals in filling out applications or questionnaires. Ensure payment for services by verifying benefits with the person's insurance provider or working out

financing options. Identify and report problems in obtaining valid data. Explain survey objectives and procedures to interviewees and interpret survey questions to help interviewees' comprehension. Perform patient services, such as answering the telephone and assisting patients with financial and medical questions. Prepare reports to provide answers in response to specific problems. Locate and list addresses and households. Perform other office duties as needed, such as telemarketing and customer service inquiries, billing patients, and receiving payments. Meet with supervisor daily to submit completed assignments and discuss progress. Collect and analyze data, such as studying old records; tallying the number of outpatients entering each day or week; or participating in federal, state, or local population surveys as a census enumerator.

Personality Type: Conventional. These occupations frequently involve following set procedures and routines and can include working with data and details more than with ideas. Usually there is a clear line of authority to follow.

GOE—Interest Area/Cluster: 10. Human Service. **Work Group:** 10.04. Client Interviewing. **Other Jobs in This Work Group:** Eligibility Interviewers, Government Programs.

Skills—Service Orientation: Actively looking for ways to help people. **Speaking:** Talking to others to effectively convey information.

Education and Training Program: Receptionist Training. **Related Knowledge/Courses—Therapy and Counseling:** Information and techniques needed to rehabilitate physical and mental ailments and to provide career guidance, including alternative treatments, rehabilitation equipment and its proper use, and methods to evaluate treatment effects. **Sales and Marketing:** Principles and methods involved in showing, promoting, and selling products or services. This includes marketing strategies and tactics, product demonstration and sales techniques, and sales control systems. **Customer and Personal Service:** Principles and processes for providing customer and personal services, including needs assessment techniques, quality service standards, alternative delivery systems, and customer satisfaction evaluation techniques. **Psychology:** Human behavior and performance, mental processes, psychological research methods, and the assessment and treatment of behavioral and affective disorders. **Medicine and Dentistry:** The information and techniques needed to diagnose and treat injuries, diseases, and deformities. This includes symptoms, treatment alternatives, drug properties and interactions, and preventive health-care measures. **Education and Training:** Instructional methods and training techniques, including curriculum design principles, learning theory, group and individual teaching techniques, design of individual development plans, and test design principles.

Work Environment: Indoors; sitting; using hands on objects, tools, or controls; repetitive motions.

Judges, Magistrate Judges, and Magistrates

- ❋ Education/Training Required: Work experience plus degree
- ❋ Annual Earnings: $107,230
- ❋ Beginning Wage: $31,100
- ❋ Earnings Growth Potential: Very high
- ❋ Growth: 5.1%
- ❋ Annual Job Openings: 1,567
- ❋ Self-Employed: 0.0%
- ❋ Part-Time: 5.9%

Arbitrate, advise, adjudicate, or administer justice in a court of law. May sentence defendant in criminal cases according to government statutes. May determine liability of defendant in civil cases. May issue marriage licenses and perform wedding ceremonies. Instruct juries on applicable laws, direct juries to deduce the facts from the evidence presented, and hear their verdicts. Sentence defendants in criminal cases on conviction by jury according to applicable government statutes. Rule on admissibility of evidence and methods of conducting testimony. Preside over hearings and listen to allegations made by plaintiffs to determine whether the evidence supports the charges. Read documents on pleadings and motions to ascertain facts and issues. Interpret and enforce rules of procedure or establish new rules in situations where there are no procedures already established by law. Monitor proceedings to ensure that all applicable rules and procedures are followed. Advise attorneys, juries, litigants, and court personnel regarding conduct, issues, and proceedings. Research legal issues and write opinions on the issues. Conduct preliminary hearings to decide issues such as whether there is reasonable and probable cause to hold defendants in felony cases. Write decisions on cases. Award compensation for damages to litigants in civil cases in relation to findings by juries or by the court. Settle disputes between opposing attorneys. Supervise other judges, court officers, and the court's administrative staff.

Impose restrictions upon parties in civil cases until trials can be held. Rule on custody and access disputes and enforce court orders regarding custody and support of children. Grant divorces and divide assets between spouses. Participate in judicial tribunals to help resolve disputes. Perform wedding ceremonies.

Personality Type: Enterprising. These occupations frequently involve starting up and carrying out projects and can involve leading people and making many decisions. They sometimes require risk taking and often deal with business.

GOE—Interest Area/Cluster: 12. Law and Public Safety. **Work Group:** 12.02. Legal Practice and Justice Administration. **Other Jobs in This Work Group:** Administrative Law Judges, Adjudicators, and Hearing Officers; Arbitrators, Mediators, and Conciliators; Lawyers.

Skills—Judgment and Decision Making: Weighing the relative costs and benefits of a potential action. **Persuasion:** Persuading others to approach things differently. **Negotiation:** Bringing others together and trying to reconcile differences. **Critical Thinking:** Using logic and analysis to identify the strengths and weaknesses of different approaches. **Active Listening:** Listening to what other people are saying and asking questions as appropriate. **Reading Comprehension:** Understanding written sentences and paragraphs in work-related documents. **Social Perceptiveness:** Being aware of others' reactions and understanding why they react the way they do. **Management of Personnel Resources:** Motivating, developing, and directing people as they work; identifying the best people for the job.

Education and Training Programs: Law (LL.B., J.D.); Legal Professions and Studies, Other. **Related Knowledge/Courses—Law and Government:** Laws, legal codes, court procedures, precedents, government regulations, executive orders, agency rules, and the democratic political process. **Therapy and Counseling:** Information and techniques needed to rehabilitate physical and mental ailments and to provide career guidance, including alternative treatments, rehabilitation equipment and its proper use, and methods to evaluate treatment effects. **Philosophy and Theology:** Different philosophical systems and religions, including their basic principles, values, ethics, ways of thinking, customs, and practices and their impact on human culture. **English Language:** The structure and content of the English language, including the meaning and spelling of words, rules of composition, and grammar. **Psychology:** Human behavior and performance, mental processes, psychological research methods, and the assessment and treatment of behavioral and affective disorders. **Sociology and Anthropology:** Group behavior and dynamics; societal trends and influences; and cultures and their history, migrations, ethnicity, and origins.

Work Environment: Indoors; sitting.

Kindergarten Teachers, Except Special Education

- ❋ Education/Training Required: Bachelor's degree
- ❋ Annual Earnings: $45,120
- ❋ Beginning Wage: $29,300
- ❋ Earnings Growth Potential: Medium
- ❋ Growth: 16.3%
- ❋ Annual Job Openings: 27,603
- ❋ Self-Employed: 1.1%
- ❋ Part-Time: 25.1%

Teach elemental natural and social science, personal hygiene, music, art, and literature to children from 4 to 6 years old. Promote physical, mental, and social development. May be required to hold state certification. Teach basic skills such as color, shape, number, and letter recognition; personal hygiene; and social skills. Establish and enforce rules for behavior and policies and procedures to maintain order among students. Observe and evaluate children's performance, behavior, social development, and physical health. Instruct students individually and in groups, adapting teaching methods to meet students' varying needs and interests. Read books to entire classes or to small groups. Demonstrate activities to children. Provide a variety of materials and resources for children to explore, manipulate, and use, both in learning activities and in imaginative play. Plan and conduct activities for a balanced program of instruction, demonstration, and work time that provides students with opportunities to observe, question, and investigate. Confer with parents or guardians, other teachers, counselors, and administrators to resolve students' behavioral and academic problems. Prepare children for later grades by encouraging them to explore learning opportunities and to persevere with challenging tasks. Establish clear objectives for all lessons, units, and projects and communicate those objectives to children. Prepare and implement remedial programs for students requiring extra help. Meet with parents and guardians to discuss their children's progress and to determine

their priorities for their children and their resource needs. Prepare objectives and outlines for courses of study, following curriculum guidelines or requirements of states and schools. Organize and lead activities designed to promote physical, mental, and social development such as games, arts and crafts, music, and storytelling. Guide and counsel students with adjustment or academic problems or special academic interests. Identify children showing signs of emotional, developmental, or health-related problems and discuss them with supervisors, parents or guardians, and child development specialists. Instruct and monitor students in the use and care of equipment and materials to prevent injuries and damage. Assimilate arriving children to the school environment by greeting them, helping them remove outerwear, and selecting activities of interest to them.

Personality Type: Social. These occupations frequently involve working with, communicating with, and teaching people and often involve helping or providing service to others.

GOE—Interest Area/Cluster: 05. Education and Training. **Work Group:** 05.02. Preschool, Elementary, and Secondary Teaching and Instructing. **Other Jobs in This Work Group:** Elementary School Teachers, Except Special Education; Middle School Teachers, Except Special and Vocational Education; Preschool Teachers, Except Special Education; Secondary School Teachers, Except Special and Vocational Education; Special Education Teachers, Middle School; Special Education Teachers, Preschool, Kindergarten, and Elementary School; Special Education Teachers, Secondary School; Teacher Assistants; Vocational Education Teachers, Middle School; Vocational Education Teachers, Secondary School.

Skills—Learning Strategies: Using multiple approaches when learning or teaching new things. **Instructing:** Teaching others how to do something. **Monitoring:** Assessing how well one is doing when learning or doing something. **Social Perceptiveness:** Being aware of others' reactions and understanding why they react the way they do. **Writing:** Communicating effectively with others in writing as indicated by the needs of the audience. **Time Management:** Managing one's own time and the time of others. **Coordination:** Adjusting actions in relation to others' actions. **Speaking:** Talking to others to effectively convey information.

Education and Training Programs: Early Childhood Education and Teaching; Kindergarten/Preschool Education and Teaching; Montessori Teacher Education; Waldorf/Steiner Teacher Education. **Related Knowledge/**

Courses—History and Archeology: Historical events and their causes, indicators, and impact on particular civilizations and cultures. **Geography:** Various methods for describing the location and distribution of land, sea, and air masses, including their physical locations, relationships, and characteristics. **Sociology and Anthropology:** Group behavior and dynamics; societal trends and influences; and cultures and their history, migrations, ethnicity, and origins. **Philosophy and Theology:** Different philosophical systems and religions, including their basic principles, values, ethics, ways of thinking, customs, and practices and their impact on human culture. **Psychology:** Human behavior and performance, mental processes, psychological research methods, and the assessment and treatment of behavioral and affective disorders. **Education and Training:** Instructional methods and training techniques, including curriculum design principles, learning theory, group and individual teaching techniques, design of individual development plans, and test design principles.

Work Environment: Indoors; disease or infections; standing.

Laborers and Freight, Stock, and Material Movers, Hand

- ✸ Education/Training Required: Short-term on-the-job training
- ✸ Annual Earnings: $21,900
- ✸ Beginning Wage: $15,420
- ✸ Earnings Growth Potential: Low
- ✸ Growth: 2.1%
- ✸ Annual Job Openings: 630,487
- ✸ Self-Employed: 1.1%
- ✸ Part-Time: 20.8%

Manually move freight, stock, or other materials or perform other unskilled general labor. Includes all unskilled manual laborers not elsewhere classified. Attach identifying tags to containers or mark them with identifying information. Read work orders or receive oral instructions to determine work assignments and material and equipment needs. Record numbers of units handled and moved, using daily production sheets or work tickets. Move freight, stock, and other materials to and from storage and production areas, loading docks, delivery vehicles, ships, and containers by hand or using trucks, tractors, and other equipment. Sort cargo before loading and unloading. Assemble product containers and crates, using hand tools and precut lumber. Load and unload ship cargo, using winches and other hoisting devices. Connect hoses and operate equipment to move liquid materials into and out of storage tanks on vessels. Pack containers and re-pack damaged containers. Carry needed tools and supplies from storage or trucks and return them after use. Install protective devices, such as bracing, padding, or strapping, to prevent shifting or damage to items being transported. Maintain equipment storage areas to ensure that inventory is protected. Attach slings, hooks, and other devices to lift cargo and guide loads. Carry out general yard duties such as performing shunting on railway lines. Adjust controls to guide, position, and move equipment such as cranes, booms, and cameras. Guide loads being lifted to prevent swinging. Adjust or replace equipment parts such as rollers, belts, plugs, and caps, using hand tools. Stack cargo in locations such as transit sheds or in holds of ships as directed, using pallets or cargo boards. Connect electrical equipment to power sources so that it can be tested before use. Set up the equipment needed to produce special lighting and sound effects during performances. Bundle and band material such as fodder and tobacco leaves, using banding machines. Rig and dismantle props and equipment such as frames, scaffolding, platforms, or backdrops, using hand tools. Check out, rent, or requisition all equipment needed for productions or for set construction. Direct spouts and position receptacles such as bins, carts, and containers so they can be loaded.

Personality Type: Realistic. These occupations frequently involve work activities that include practical, hands-on problems and solutions. They often deal with plants; animals; and real-world materials such as wood, tools, and machinery. Many of the occupations require working outside and don't involve a lot of paperwork or working closely with others.

GOE—Interest Area/Cluster: 16. Transportation, Distribution, and Logistics. **Work Group:** 16.07. Transportation Support Work. **Other Jobs in This Work Group:** Bridge and Lock Tenders; Cargo and Freight Agents; Cleaners of Vehicles and Equipment; Railroad Brake, Signal, and Switch Operators; Traffic Technicians.

Skill—None met the criteria.

Education and Training Programs: No related CIP programs; this job is learned through informal short-term on-the-job training. **Related Knowledge/Courses—Transportation:** Principles and methods for moving people or goods by air, rail, sea, or road, including their relative costs, advantages, and limitations. **Public Safety and Security:** Weaponry; public safety; security operations, rules, regulations, precautions, and prevention; and the protection of people, data, and property. **Production and Processing:** Inputs, outputs, raw materials, waste, quality control, costs, and techniques for maximizing the manufacture and distribution of goods.

Work Environment: Outdoors; noisy; very hot or cold; contaminants; standing; using hands on objects, tools, or controls.

Landscape Architects

- ❋ Education/Training Required: Bachelor's degree
- ❋ Annual Earnings: $57,580
- ❋ Beginning Wage: $36,250
- ❋ Earnings Growth Potential: Medium
- ❋ Growth: 16.4%
- ❋ Annual Job Openings: 2,342
- ❋ Self-Employed: 18.5%
- ❋ Part-Time: 6.1%

Plan and design land areas for such projects as parks and other recreational facilities; airports; highways; hospitals; schools; land subdivisions; and commercial, industrial, and residential sites. Prepare site plans, specifications, and cost estimates for land development, coordinating arrangement of existing and proposed land features and structures. Confer with clients, engineering personnel, and architects on overall program. Compile and analyze data on conditions such as location, drainage, and location of structures for environmental reports and landscaping plans. Inspect landscape work to ensure compliance with specifications, approve quality of materials and work, and advise client and construction personnel.

Personality Type: Artistic. These occupations frequently involve working with forms, designs, and patterns. They often require self-expression, and the work can be done without following a clear set of rules.

GOE—Interest Area/Cluster: 02. Architecture and Construction. **Work Group:** 02.02. Architectural Design. **Other Jobs in This Work Group:** Architects, Except Landscape and Naval.

Skills—Operations Analysis: Analyzing needs and product requirements to create a design. **Management of Financial Resources:** Determining how money will be spent to get the work done and accounting for these expenditures. **Coordination:** Adjusting actions in relation to others' actions. **Mathematics:** Using mathematics to solve problems. **Complex Problem Solving:** Identifying complex problems, reviewing the options, and implementing solutions. **Social Perceptiveness:** Being aware of others' reactions and understanding why they react the way they do. **Persuasion:** Persuading others to approach things differently. **Writing:** Communicating effectively with others in writing as indicated by the needs of the audience.

Education and Training Programs: Environmental Design/Architecture; Landscape Architecture (BS, BSLA, BLA, MSLA, MLA, PhD). **Related Knowledge/Courses— Design:** Design techniques, principles, tools, and instruments involved in the production and use of precision technical plans, blueprints, drawings, and models. **Building and Construction:** Materials, methods, and the appropriate tools to construct objects, structures, and buildings. **Geography:** Various methods for describing the location and distribution of land, sea, and air masses, including their physical locations, relationships, and characteristics. **Biology:** Plant and animal living tissue, cells, organisms, and entities, including their functions, interdependencies, and interactions with each other and the environment. **Engineering and Technology:** Equipment, tools, and mechanical devices and their uses to produce motion, light, power, technology, and other applications. **Fine Arts:** Theory and techniques required to produce, compose, and perform works of music, dance, visual arts, drama, and sculpture.

Work Environment: More often indoors than outdoors; very hot or cold; hazardous equipment; minor burns, cuts, bites, or stings; sitting.

Landscaping and Groundskeeping Workers

- ❋ Education/Training Required: Short-term on-the-job training
- ❋ Annual Earnings: $22,240
- ❋ Beginning Wage: $15,970
- ❋ Earnings Growth Potential: Low
- ❋ Growth: 18.1%
- ❋ Annual Job Openings: 307,138
- ❋ Self-Employed: 20.5%
- ❋ Part-Time: 14.6%

Landscape or maintain grounds of property, using hand or power tools or equipment. Workers typically perform a variety of tasks, which may include any combination of the following: sod laying, mowing, trimming, planting, watering, fertilizing, digging, raking, sprinkler installation, and installation of mortarless segmental concrete masonry wall units. Operate powered equipment such as mowers, tractors, twin-axle vehicles, snowblowers, chain saws, electric clippers, sod cutters, and pruning saws. Mow and edge lawns, using power mowers and edgers. Shovel snow from walks, driveways, and parking lots and spread salt in those areas. Care for established lawns by mulching; aerating; weeding; grubbing and removing thatch; and trimming and edging around flower beds, walks, and walls. Use hand tools such as shovels, rakes, pruning saws, saws, hedge and brush trimmers, and axes. Prune and trim trees, shrubs, and hedges, using shears, pruners, or chain saws. Maintain and repair tools; equipment; and structures such as buildings, greenhouses, fences, and benches, using hand and power tools. Gather and remove litter. Mix and spray or spread fertilizers, herbicides, or insecticides onto grass, shrubs, and trees, using hand or automatic sprayers or spreaders. Provide proper upkeep of sidewalks, driveways, parking lots, fountains, planters, burial sites, and other grounds features. Water lawns, trees, and plants, using portable sprinkler systems, hoses, or watering cans. Trim and pick flowers and clean flowerbeds. Rake, mulch, and compost leaves. Plant seeds, bulbs, foliage, flowering plants, grass, ground covers, trees, and shrubs and apply mulch for protection, using gardening tools. Follow planned landscaping designs to determine where to lay sod, sow grass, or plant flowers and foliage. Decorate gardens with stones and plants. Maintain irrigation systems, including winterizing the systems and starting them up in spring. Care for natural turf fields, making sure the underlying soil has the required composition to allow proper drainage and to support the grasses used on the fields. Use irrigation methods to adjust the amount of water consumption and to prevent waste. Haul or spread topsoil and spread straw over seeded soil to hold soil in place. Advise customers on plant selection and care. Care for artificial turf fields, periodically removing the turf and replacing cushioning pads and vacuuming and disinfecting the turf after use to prevent the growth of harmful bacteria.

Personality Type: Realistic. These occupations frequently involve work activities that include practical, hands-on problems and solutions. They often deal with plants; animals; and real-world materials such as wood, tools, and machinery. Many of the occupations require working outside and don't involve a lot of paperwork or working closely with others.

GOE—Interest Area/Cluster: 01. Agriculture and Natural Resources. **Work Group:** 01.05. Nursery, Groundskeeping, and Pest Control. **Other Jobs in This Work Group:** Nursery Workers; Pest Control Workers; Pesticide Handlers, Sprayers, and Applicators, Vegetation; Tree Trimmers and Pruners.

Skills—Equipment Maintenance: Performing routine maintenance and determining when and what kind of maintenance is needed. **Repairing:** Repairing machines or systems, using the needed tools. **Operation Monitoring:** Watching gauges, dials, or other indicators to make sure a machine is working properly. **Installation:** Installing equipment, machines, wiring, or programs to meet specifications. **Equipment Selection:** Determining the kind of tools and equipment needed to do a job.

Education and Training Programs: Landscaping and Groundskeeping; Turf and Turfgrass Management. **Related Knowledge/Course—Mechanical Devices:** Machines and tools, including their designs, uses, benefits, repair, and maintenance.

Work Environment: Outdoors; noisy; very hot or cold; contaminants; standing; using hands on objects, tools, or controls.

Law Teachers, Postsecondary

- ❋ Education/Training Required: First professional degree
- ❋ Annual Earnings: $87,730
- ❋ Beginning Wage: $39,670
- ❋ Earnings Growth Potential: Very high
- ❋ Growth: 22.9%
- ❋ Annual Job Openings: 2,169
- ❋ Self-Employed: 0.4%
- ❋ Part-Time: 27.8%

Teach courses in law. Evaluate and grade students' classwork, assignments, papers, and oral presentations. Compile, administer, and grade examinations or assign this work to others. Prepare and deliver lectures to undergraduate or graduate students on topics such as civil procedure, contracts, and torts. Initiate, facilitate, and moderate classroom discussions. Prepare course materials such as syllabi, homework assignments, and handouts. Keep abreast of developments in their field by reading current literature, talking with colleagues, and participating in professional conferences. Plan, evaluate, and revise curricula, course content, and course materials and methods of instruction. Maintain regularly scheduled office hours to advise and assist students. Conduct research in a particular field of knowledge and publish findings in professional journals, books, or electronic media. Advise students on academic and vocational curricula and on career issues. Supervise undergraduate and/or graduate teaching, internship, and research work. Select and obtain materials and supplies such as textbooks. Maintain student attendance records, grades, and other required records. Serve on academic or administrative committees that deal with institutional policies, departmental matters, and academic issues. Perform administrative duties such as serving as department head. Collaborate with colleagues to address teaching and research issues. Participate in student recruitment, registration, and placement activities. Compile bibliographies of specialized materials for outside reading assignments. Participate in campus and community events. Act as advisers to student organizations. Assign cases for students to hear and try. Provide professional consulting services to government or industry. Write grant proposals to procure external research funding.

Personality Type: Social. These occupations frequently involve working with, communicating with, and teaching people and often involve helping or providing service to others.

GOE—Interest Area/Cluster: 05. Education and Training. **Work Group:** 05.03. Postsecondary and Adult Teaching and Instructing. **Other Jobs in This Work Group:** Adult Literacy, Remedial Education, and GED Teachers and Instructors; Agricultural Sciences Teachers, Postsecondary; Anthropology and Archeology Teachers, Postsecondary; Architecture Teachers, Postsecondary; Area, Ethnic, and Cultural Studies Teachers, Postsecondary; Art, Drama, and Music Teachers, Postsecondary; Atmospheric, Earth, Marine, and Space Sciences Teachers, Postsecondary; Biological Science Teachers, Postsecondary; Business Teachers, Postsecondary; Chemistry Teachers, Postsecondary; Communications Teachers, Postsecondary; Computer Science Teachers, Postsecondary; Criminal Justice and Law Enforcement Teachers, Postsecondary; Economics Teachers, Postsecondary; Education Teachers, Postsecondary; Engineering Teachers, Postsecondary; English Language and Literature Teachers, Postsecondary; Environmental Science Teachers, Postsecondary; Farm and Home Management Advisors; Foreign Language and Literature Teachers, Postsecondary; Forestry and Conservation Science Teachers, Postsecondary; Geography Teachers, Postsecondary; Graduate Teaching Assistants; Health Specialties Teachers, Postsecondary; History Teachers, Postsecondary; Home Economics Teachers, Postsecondary; Library Science Teachers, Postsecondary; Mathematical Science Teachers, Postsecondary; Nursing Instructors and Teachers, Postsecondary; Philosophy and Religion Teachers, Postsecondary; Physics Teachers, Postsecondary; Political Science Teachers, Postsecondary; Psychology Teachers, Postsecondary; Recreation and Fitness Studies Teachers, Postsecondary; Self-Enrichment Education Teachers; Social Work Teachers, Postsecondary; Sociology Teachers, Postsecondary; Vocational Education Teachers, Postsecondary.

Skills—Instructing: Teaching others how to do something. **Critical Thinking:** Using logic and analysis to identify the strengths and weaknesses of different approaches. **Writing:** Communicating effectively with others in writing as indicated by the needs of the audience. **Reading Comprehension:** Understanding written sentences and paragraphs in work-related documents. **Persuasion:** Persuading others to approach things differently. **Speaking:** Talking to others to effectively convey information. **Active Listening:** Listening to what other people are saying and asking questions as appropriate. **Learning Strategies:** Using multiple approaches when learning or teaching new things.

Education and Training Programs: Law (LL.B., J.D.); Legal Studies, General. **Related Knowledge/Courses— Law and Government:** Laws, legal codes, court procedures, precedents, government regulations, executive orders, agency rules, and the democratic political process. **English Language:** The structure and content of the English language, including the meaning and spelling of words, rules of composition, and grammar. **History and Archeology:** Historical events and their causes, indicators, and impact on particular civilizations and cultures. **Education and Training:** Instructional methods and training techniques, including curriculum design principles, learning theory, group and individual teaching techniques, design of individual development plans, and test design principles. **Philosophy and Theology:** Different philosophical systems and religions, including their basic principles, values, ethics, ways of thinking, customs, and practices and their impact on human culture. **Communications and Media:** Media production, communication, and dissemination techniques and methods, including alternative ways to inform and entertain via written, oral, and visual media.

Work Environment: Indoors; sitting.

Lawyers

- ❋ Education/Training Required: First professional degree
- ❋ Annual Earnings: $106,120
- ❋ Beginning Wage: $52,280
- ❋ Earnings Growth Potential: Very high
- ❋ Growth: 11.0%
- ❋ Annual Job Openings: 49,445
- ❋ Self-Employed: 26.7%
- ❋ Part-Time: 5.9%

Represent clients in criminal and civil litigation and other legal proceedings, draw up legal documents, and manage or advise clients on legal transactions. May specialize in a single area or may practice broadly in many areas of law. Advise clients concerning business transactions, claim liability, advisability of prosecuting or defending lawsuits, or legal rights and obligations. Interpret laws, rulings, and regulations for individuals and businesses. Analyze the probable outcomes of cases, using knowledge of legal precedents. Present and summarize cases to judges and juries. Gather evidence to formulate defense or to initiate legal actions by such means as interviewing clients and witnesses to ascertain the facts of a case. Evaluate findings and develop strategies and arguments in preparation for presentation of cases. Represent clients in court or before government agencies. Examine legal data to determine advisability of defending or prosecuting lawsuit. Select jurors, argue motions, meet with judges, and question witnesses during the course of a trial. Present evidence to defend clients or prosecute defendants in criminal or civil litigation. Study Constitution, statutes, decisions, regulations, and ordinances of quasi-judicial bodies to determine ramifications for cases. Prepare and draft legal documents, such as wills, deeds, patent applications, mortgages, leases, and contracts. Prepare legal briefs and opinions and file appeals in state and federal courts of appeal. Negotiate settlements of civil disputes. Confer with colleagues with specialties in appropriate areas of legal issue to establish and verify bases for legal proceedings. Search for and examine public and other legal records to write opinions or establish ownership. Supervise legal assistants. Perform administrative and management functions related to the practice of law. Act as agent, trustee, guardian, or executor for businesses or individuals. Probate wills and represent and advise executors and administrators of estates. Help develop federal and state programs, draft and interpret laws and legislation, and establish enforcement procedures. Work in environmental law, representing public interest groups, waste disposal companies, or construction firms in their dealings with state and federal agencies.

Personality Type: Enterprising. These occupations frequently involve starting up and carrying out projects and can involve leading people and making many decisions. They sometimes require risk taking and often deal with business.

GOE—Interest Area/Cluster: 12. Law and Public Safety. **Work Group:** 12.02. Legal Practice and Justice Administration. **Other Jobs in This Work Group:** Administrative Law Judges, Adjudicators, and Hearing Officers; Arbitrators, Mediators, and Conciliators; Judges, Magistrate Judges, and Magistrates.

Skills—Persuasion: Persuading others to approach things differently. **Negotiation:** Bringing others together and trying to reconcile differences. **Writing:** Communicating effectively with others in writing as indicated by the needs of the audience. **Judgment and Decision Making:** Weighing the relative costs and benefits of a potential action. **Critical Thinking:** Using logic and analysis to identify the strengths and weaknesses of different approaches. **Reading Comprehension:** Understanding written sentences and paragraphs in work-related documents. **Speaking:** Talking to others to effectively convey information. **Active Listening:** Listening to what other people are saying and asking questions as appropriate.

Education and Training Programs: American/U.S. Law/Legal Studies/Jurisprudence (LL.M., M.C.J., J.S.D./S.J.D.); Banking, Corporate, Finance, and Securities Law (LL.M., J.S.D./S.J.D.); Comparative Law (LL.M., M.C.L., J.S.D./S.J.D.); Energy, Environment, and Natural Resources Law (LL.M., M.S., J.S.D./S.J.D.); Health Law (LL.M., M.J., J.S.D./S.J.D.); International Law and Legal Studies (LL.M., J.S.D./S.J.D.); Law (LL.B., J.D.); Programs for Foreign Lawyers (LL.M., M.C.L.); Tax Law/Taxation (LL.M, J.S.D./S.J.D.); others. **Related Knowledge/Courses—Law and Government:** Laws, legal codes, court procedures, precedents, government regulations, executive orders, agency rules, and the democratic political process. **English Language:** The structure and content of the English language, including the meaning and spelling of words, rules of composition, and grammar. **Personnel and Human Resources:** Principles and procedures for personnel recruitment; selection; training; compensation and benefits; labor relations and negotiation; and personnel information systems. **Economics and Accounting:** Economic and accounting principles and practices, the financial markets, banking, and the analysis and reporting of financial data. **Psychology:** Human behavior and performance, mental processes, psychological research methods, and the assessment and treatment of behavioral and affective disorders. **Administration and Management:** Principles and processes involved in business and organizational planning, coordination, and execution. This includes strategic planning, resource allocation, manpower modeling, leadership techniques, and production methods.

Work Environment: Indoors; sitting.

Legal Secretaries

- ✳ Education/Training Required: Associate degree
- ✳ Annual Earnings: $38,810
- ✳ Beginning Wage: $24,380
- ✳ Earnings Growth Potential: Medium
- ✳ Growth: 11.7%
- ✳ Annual Job Openings: 38,682
- ✳ Self-Employed: 1.4%
- ✳ Part-Time: 18.9%

Perform secretarial duties, utilizing legal terminology, procedures, and documents. Prepare legal papers and correspondence, such as summonses, complaints, motions, and subpoenas. May also assist with legal research. Prepare and process legal documents and papers, such as summonses, subpoenas, complaints, appeals, motions, and pretrial agreements. Mail, fax, or arrange for delivery of legal correspondence to clients, witnesses, and court officials. Receive and place telephone calls. Schedule and make appointments. Make photocopies of correspondence, documents, and other printed matter. Organize and maintain law libraries, documents, and case files. Assist attorneys in collecting information such as employment, medical, and other records. Attend legal meetings, such as client interviews, hearings, or depositions, and take notes. Draft and type office memos. Review legal publications and perform database searches to identify laws and court decisions relevant to pending cases. Submit articles and information from searches to attorneys for review and approval for use. Complete various forms such as accident reports, trial and courtroom requests, and applications for clients.

Personality Type: Conventional. These occupations frequently involve following set procedures and routines and can include working with data and details more than with ideas. Usually there is a clear line of authority to follow.

GOE—Interest Area/Cluster: 04. Business and Administration. **Work Group:** 04.04. Secretarial Support. **Other Jobs in This Work Group:** Executive Secretaries and Administrative Assistants; Medical Secretaries; Secretaries, Except Legal, Medical, and Executive.

Skills—Writing: Communicating effectively with others in writing as indicated by the needs of the audience. **Reading Comprehension:** Understanding written sentences and paragraphs in work-related documents. **Time Management:** Managing one's own time and the time of others. **Social Perceptiveness:** Being aware of others' reactions and understanding why they react the way they do. **Judgment and Decision Making:** Weighing the relative costs and benefits of a potential action. **Operation and Control:** Controlling operations of equipment or systems. **Active Listening:** Listening to what other people are saying and asking questions as appropriate. **Speaking:** Talking to others to effectively convey information.

Education and Training Program: Legal Administrative Assistant/Secretary Training. **Related Knowledge/Courses—Clerical Practices:** Administrative and clerical procedures and systems such as word-processing systems, filing and records management systems, stenography and transcription, forms, design principles, and other office procedures and terminology. **Law and Government:** Laws, legal codes, court procedures, precedents, government regulations, executive orders, agency rules, and the democratic political process. **Economics and Accounting:** Economic and accounting principles and practices, the financial markets, banking, and the analysis and reporting of financial data. **Computers and Electronics:** Electric circuit boards, processors, chips, and computer hardware and software, including applications and programming. **Customer and Personal Service:** Principles and processes for providing customer and personal services, including needs assessment techniques, quality service standards, alternative delivery systems, and customer satisfaction evaluation techniques.

Work Environment: Indoors; sitting; repetitive motions.

Librarians

❋ Education/Training Required: Master's degree
❋ Annual Earnings: $50,970
❋ Beginning Wage: $31,960
❋ Earnings Growth Potential: Medium
❋ Growth: 3.6%
❋ Annual Job Openings: 18,945
❋ Self-Employed: 0.6%
❋ Part-Time: 21.2%

Administer libraries and perform related library services. Work in a variety of settings, including public libraries, schools, colleges and universities, museums, corporations, government agencies, law firms, non-profit organizations, and health-care providers. Tasks may include selecting, acquiring, cataloguing, classifying, circulating, and maintaining library materials and furnishing reference, bibliographical, and readers' advisory services. May perform in-depth, strategic research and synthesize, analyze, edit, and filter information. May set up or work with databases and information systems to catalogue and access information. Search standard reference materials, including online sources and the Internet, to answer patrons' reference questions. Analyze patrons' requests to determine needed information and assist in furnishing or locating that information. Teach library patrons to search for information by using databases. Keep records of circulation and materials. Supervise budgeting, planning, and personnel activities. Check books in and out of the library. Explain use of library facilities, resources, equipment, and services and provide information about library policies. Review and evaluate resource material, such as book reviews and catalogs, to select and order print, audiovisual, and electronic resources. Code, classify, and catalog books, publications, films, audiovisual aids, and other library materials based on subject matter or standard library classification systems. Locate unusual or unique information in response to specific requests. Direct and train library staff in duties such as receiving, shelving, researching, cataloging, and equipment use. Respond to customer complaints, taking action as necessary. Organize collections of books, publications, documents, audiovisual aids, and other reference materials for convenient access. Develop library policies and procedures. Evaluate materials to determine outdated or unused items to be discarded. Develop information access aids such as indexes and annotated bibliographies, Web pages, electronic pathfinders, and online tutorials. Plan and deliver client-centered programs and services such as special services for corporate clients, storytelling for children, newsletters, or programs for special groups. Compile lists of books, periodicals, articles, and audiovisual materials on particular subjects. Arrange for interlibrary loans of materials not available in a particular library. Assemble and arrange display materials. Confer with teachers, parents, and community organizations to develop, plan, and conduct programs in reading, viewing, and communication skills. Compile lists of overdue materials and notify borrowers that their materials are overdue.

Personality Type: Conventional. These occupations frequently involve following set procedures and routines and can include working with data and details more than with ideas. Usually there is a clear line of authority to follow.

GOE—Interest Area/Cluster: 05. Education and Training. **Work Group:** 05.04. Library Services. **Other Jobs in This Work Group:** Library Assistants, Clerical; Library Technicians.

Skills—Management of Financial Resources: Determining how money will be spent to get the work done and accounting for these expenditures. **Management of Material Resources:** Obtaining and seeing to the appropriate use of equipment, facilities, and materials needed to do certain work. **Learning Strategies:** Using multiple approaches when learning or teaching new things. **Equipment Selection:** Determining the kind of tools and equipment needed to do a job. **Service Orientation:** Actively looking for ways to help people. **Systems Evaluation:** Looking at many indicators of system performance and taking into account their accuracy. **Persuasion:** Persuading others to approach things differently. **Monitoring:** Assessing how well one is doing when learning or doing something.

Education and Training Programs: Library Science, Other; Library Science/Librarianship; School Librarian/School Library Media Specialist Training. **Related Knowledge/Courses—Communications and Media:** Media production, communication, and dissemination techniques and methods, including alternative ways to inform and entertain via written, oral, and visual media. **Clerical Practices:** Administrative and clerical procedures and systems such as word-processing systems, filing and records management systems, stenography and transcription, forms, design principles, and other office procedures and terminology. **Customer and Personal Service:** Principles and processes for providing customer and personal services, including needs assessment techniques, quality service standards, alternative delivery systems, and customer satisfaction evaluation techniques. **Personnel and Human Resources:** Principles and procedures for personnel recruitment; selection; training; compensation and benefits; labor relations and negotiation; and personnel information systems. **English Language:** The structure and content of the English language, including the meaning and spelling of words, rules of composition, and grammar. **Computers and Electronics:** Electric circuit boards, processors, chips, and computer hardware and software, including applications and programming.

Work Environment: Indoors; sitting; using hands on objects, tools, or controls; repetitive motions.

Library Science Teachers, Postsecondary

- ❋ Education/Training Required: Doctoral degree
- ❋ Annual Earnings: $56,810
- ❋ Beginning Wage: $34,850
- ❋ Earnings Growth Potential: Medium
- ❋ Growth: 22.9%
- ❋ Annual Job Openings: 702
- ❋ Self-Employed: 0.4%
- ❋ Part-Time: 27.8%

Teach courses in library science. Prepare course materials such as syllabi, homework assignments, and handouts. Prepare and deliver lectures to undergraduate or graduate students on topics such as collection development, archival methods, and indexing and abstracting. Evaluate and grade students' classwork, assignments, and papers. Keep abreast of developments in their field by reading current literature, talking with colleagues, and participating in professional conferences. Initiate, facilitate, and moderate classroom discussions. Plan, evaluate, and revise curricula, course content, and course materials and methods of instruction. Conduct research in a particular field of knowledge and publish findings in professional journals, books, and/or electronic media. Maintain student attendance records, grades, and other required records. Collaborate with colleagues to address teaching and research issues. Advise students on academic and vocational curricula and on career issues. Compile, administer, and grade examinations or assign this work to others. Supervise undergraduate or graduate teaching, internship, and research work. Maintain regularly scheduled office hours in order to advise and assist students.

Write grant proposals to procure external research funding. Select and obtain materials and supplies such as textbooks. Serve on academic or administrative committees that deal with institutional policies, departmental matters, and academic issues. Compile bibliographies of specialized materials for outside reading assignments. Participate in student recruitment, registration, and placement activities. Perform administrative duties such as serving as department head. Participate in campus and community events. Act as advisers to student organizations. Provide professional consulting services to government and/or industry.

Personality Type: Social. These occupations frequently involve working with, communicating with, and teaching people and often involve helping or providing service to others.

GOE—Interest Area/Cluster: 05. Education and Training. **Work Group:** 05.03. Postsecondary and Adult Teaching and Instructing. **Other Jobs in This Work Group:** Adult Literacy, Remedial Education, and GED Teachers and Instructors; Agricultural Sciences Teachers, Postsecondary; Anthropology and Archeology Teachers, Postsecondary; Architecture Teachers, Postsecondary; Area, Ethnic, and Cultural Studies Teachers, Postsecondary; Art, Drama, and Music Teachers, Postsecondary; Atmospheric, Earth, Marine, and Space Sciences Teachers, Postsecondary; Biological Science Teachers, Postsecondary; Business Teachers, Postsecondary; Chemistry Teachers, Postsecondary; Communications Teachers, Postsecondary; Computer Science Teachers, Postsecondary; Criminal Justice and Law Enforcement Teachers, Postsecondary; Economics Teachers, Postsecondary; Education Teachers, Postsecondary; Engineering Teachers, Postsecondary; English Language and Literature Teachers, Postsecondary; Environmental Science Teachers, Postsecondary; Farm and Home Management Advisors; Foreign Language and Literature Teachers, Postsecondary; Forestry and Conservation Science Teachers, Postsecondary; Geography Teachers, Postsecondary; Graduate Teaching Assistants; Health Specialties Teachers, Postsecondary; History Teachers, Postsecondary; Home Economics Teachers, Postsecondary; Law Teachers, Postsecondary; Mathematical Science Teachers, Postsecondary; Nursing Instructors and Teachers, Postsecondary; Philosophy and Religion Teachers, Postsecondary; Physics Teachers, Postsecondary; Political Science Teachers, Postsecondary; Psychology Teachers, Postsecondary; Recreation and Fitness Studies Teachers, Postsecondary; Self-Enrichment Education Teachers; Social Work Teachers, Postsecondary; Sociology Teachers, Postsecondary; Vocational Education Teachers, Postsecondary.

Skills—Writing: Communicating effectively with others in writing as indicated by the needs of the audience. **Learning Strategies:** Using multiple approaches when learning or teaching new things. **Instructing:** Teaching others how to do something. **Reading Comprehension:** Understanding written sentences and paragraphs in work-related documents. **Active Learning:** Working with new material or information to grasp its implications. **Monitoring:** Assessing how well one is doing when learning or doing something. **Operations Analysis:** Analyzing needs and product requirements to create a design. **Speaking:** Talking to others to effectively convey information.

Education and Training Programs: Library Science/Librarianship; Teacher Education and Professional Development, Specific Subject Areas, Other. **Related Knowledge/Courses—Education and Training:** Instructional methods and training techniques, including curriculum design principles, learning theory, group and individual teaching techniques, design of individual development plans, and test design principles. **Sociology and Anthropology:** Group behavior and dynamics; societal trends and influences; and cultures and their history, migrations, ethnicity, and origins. **English Language:** The structure and content of the English language, including the meaning and spelling of words, rules of composition, and grammar. **Communications and Media:** Media production, communication, and dissemination techniques and methods, including alternative ways to inform and entertain via written, oral, and visual media. **History and Archeology:** Historical events and their causes, indicators, and impact on particular civilizations and cultures. **Philosophy and Theology:** Different philosophical systems and religions, including their basic principles, values, ethics, ways of thinking, customs, and practices and their impact on human culture.

Work Environment: Indoors; sitting.

Library Technicians

- ❀ Education/Training Required: Postsecondary vocational training
- ❀ Annual Earnings: $27,680
- ❀ Beginning Wage: $16,430
- ❀ Earnings Growth Potential: High
- ❀ Growth: 8.5%
- ❀ Annual Job Openings: 29,075
- ❀ Self-Employed: 0.0%
- ❀ Part-Time: 65.0%

Assist librarians by helping readers in the use of library catalogs, databases, and indexes to locate books and other materials and by answering questions that require only brief consultation of standard reference. Compile records; sort and shelve books; remove or repair damaged books; register patrons; check materials in and out of the circulation process. Replace materials in shelving area (stacks) or files. Includes bookmobile drivers who operate bookmobiles or light trucks that pull trailers to specific locations on a predetermined schedule and assist with providing services in mobile libraries. Reserve, circulate, renew, and discharge books and other materials. Enter and update patrons' records on computers. Provide assistance to teachers and students by locating materials and helping to complete special projects. Guide patrons in finding and using library resources, including reference materials, audiovisual equipment, computers, and electronic resources. Answer routine reference inquiries and refer patrons needing further assistance to librarians. Train other staff, volunteers, or student assistants, and schedule and supervise their work. Sort books, publications, and other items according to procedure and return them to shelves, files, or other designated storage areas. Conduct reference searches, using printed materials and in-house and online databases. Deliver and retrieve items throughout the library by hand or using pushcart. Take actions to halt disruption of library activities by problem patrons. Process interlibrary loans for patrons. Process print and non-print library materials to prepare them for inclusion in library collections. Retrieve information from central databases for storage in a library's computer. Organize and maintain periodicals and reference materials. Compile and maintain records relating to circulation, materials, and equipment. Collect fines and respond to complaints about fines. Issue identification cards to borrowers. Verify bibliographical data for materials, including author, title, publisher, publication date, and edition. Review subject matter of materials to be classified and select classification numbers and headings according to classification systems. Send out notices about lost or overdue books. Prepare order slips for materials to be acquired, checking prices and figuring costs. Design, customize, and maintain databases, Web pages, and local area networks. Operate and maintain audiovisual equipment such as projectors, tape recorders, and videocassette recorders. File catalog cards according to system used. Prepare volumes for binding. Conduct children's programs and other specialized programs such as library tours. Compose explanatory summaries of contents of books and other reference materials.

Personality Type: Conventional. These occupations frequently involve following set procedures and routines and can include working with data and details more than with ideas. Usually there is a clear line of authority to follow.

GOE—Interest Area/Cluster: 05. Education and Training. **Work Group:** 05.04. Library Services. **Other Jobs in This Work Group:** Librarians; Library Assistants, Clerical.

Skills—Service Orientation: Actively looking for ways to help people. **Reading Comprehension:** Understanding written sentences and paragraphs in work-related documents. **Writing:** Communicating effectively with others in writing as indicated by the needs of the audience.

Education and Training Program: Library Assistant/Technician Training. **Related Knowledge/Courses—Clerical Practices:** Administrative and clerical procedures and systems such as word-processing systems, filing and records management systems, stenography and transcription, forms, design principles, and other office procedures and terminology. **Computers and Electronics:** Electric circuit boards, processors, chips, and computer hardware and software, including applications and programming. **Customer and Personal Service:** Principles and processes for providing customer and personal services, including needs assessment techniques, quality service standards, alternative delivery systems, and customer satisfaction evaluation techniques. **English Language:** The structure and content of the English language, including the meaning and spelling of words, rules of composition, and grammar. **Education and Training:** Instructional methods and training techniques, including curriculum design principles, learning theory, group and individual teaching techniques, design of individual development plans, and test design principles. **Administration and Management:** Principles and processes involved in business and organizational planning, coordination, and execution. This includes strategic planning, resource allocation, manpower modeling, leadership techniques, and production methods.

Work Environment: Indoors; sitting; using hands on objects, tools, or controls; repetitive motions.

License Clerks

❋ Education/Training Required: Short-term on-the-job training
❋ Annual Earnings: $32,330
❋ Beginning Wage: $21,050
❋ Earnings Growth Potential: Low
❋ Growth: 8.8%
❋ Annual Job Openings: 16,163
❋ Self-Employed: 2.7%
❋ Part-Time: 9.6%

The job openings listed here are shared with Court Clerks and with Municipal Clerks.

Issue licenses or permits to qualified applicants. Obtain necessary information, record data, advise applicants on requirements, collect fees, and issue licenses. May conduct oral, written, visual, or performance testing. Collect prescribed fees for licenses. Code information on license applications for entry into computers. Evaluate information on applications to verify completeness and accuracy and to determine whether applicants are qualified to obtain desired licenses. Answer questions and provide advice to the public regarding licensing policies, procedures, and regulations. Maintain records of applications made and licensing fees collected. Question applicants to obtain required information, such as name, address, and age, and record data on prescribed forms. Update operational records and licensing information, using computer terminals. Inform customers by mail or telephone of additional steps they need to take to obtain licenses. Perform routine data entry and other office support activities, including creating, sorting, photocopying, distributing, and filing documents. Stock counters with adequate supplies of forms, film, licenses, and other required materials. Enforce canine licensing regulations, contacting non-compliant owners in person or by mail to inform them of the required regulations and potential enforcement actions. Assemble photographs with printed license information to produce completed documents. Prepare bank deposits and take them to banks. Operate specialized photographic equipment to obtain photographs for drivers' licenses and photo identification cards. Instruct customers in the completion of drivers' license application forms and other forms such as voter registration cards and organ donor forms. Conduct and score oral, visual, written, or performance tests to determine applicant qualifications and notify applicants of their scores. Send by mail drivers' licenses to out-of-county or out-of-state applicants. Perform record checks on past and current licensees as required by investigations. Respond to correspondence from insurance companies regarding the licensure of agents, brokers, and adjusters. Prepare lists of overdue accounts and license suspensions and issuances. Train other workers and coordinate their work as necessary.

Personality Type: Conventional. These occupations frequently involve following set procedures and routines and can include working with data and details more than with ideas. Usually there is a clear line of authority to follow.

GOE—Interest Area/Cluster: 07. Government and Public Administration. **Work Group:** 07.04. Public Administration Clerical Support. **Other Jobs in This Work Group:** Court Clerks; Court Reporters; Court, Municipal, and License Clerks; Municipal Clerks.

Skills—Reading Comprehension: Understanding written sentences and paragraphs in work-related documents. **Service Orientation:** Actively looking for ways to help people. **Instructing:** Teaching others how to do something. **Active Listening:** Listening to what other people are saying and asking questions as appropriate.

Education and Training Program: General Office Occupations and Clerical Services. **Related Knowledge/Courses—Clerical Practices:** Administrative and clerical procedures and systems such as word-processing systems, filing and records management systems, stenography and transcription, forms, design principles, and other office procedures and terminology. **Customer and Personal Service:** Principles and processes for providing customer and personal services, including needs assessment techniques, quality service standards, alternative delivery systems, and customer satisfaction evaluation techniques. **Law and Government:** Laws, legal codes, court procedures, precedents, government regulations, executive orders, agency rules, and the democratic political process. **Computers and Electronics:** Electric circuit boards, processors, chips, and computer hardware and software, including applications and programming.

Work Environment: Indoors; noisy; sitting; using hands on objects, tools, or controls; repetitive motions.

Licensed Practical and Licensed Vocational Nurses

- ❋ Education/Training Required: Postsecondary vocational training
- ❋ Annual Earnings: $37,940
- ❋ Beginning Wage: $27,370
- ❋ Earnings Growth Potential: Low
- ❋ Growth: 14.0%
- ❋ Annual Job Openings: 70,610
- ❋ Self-Employed: 1.5%
- ❋ Part-Time: 18.3%

Care for ill, injured, convalescent, or disabled persons in hospitals, nursing homes, clinics, private homes, group homes, and similar institutions. May work under the supervision of a registered nurse. Licensing required. Administer prescribed medications or start intravenous fluids, and note times and amounts on patients' charts. Observe patients, charting and reporting changes in patients' conditions, such as adverse reactions to medication or treatment, and taking any necessary actions. Provide basic patient care and treatments such as taking temperatures or blood pressures, dressing wounds, treating bedsores, giving enemas or douches, rubbing with alcohol, massaging, or performing catheterizations. Sterilize equipment and supplies, using germicides, sterilizer, or autoclave. Answer patients' calls and determine how to assist them. Work as part of a health-care team to assess patient needs, plan and modify care, and implement interventions. Measure and record patients' vital signs such as height, weight, temperature, blood pressure, pulse, and respiration. Collect samples such as blood, urine, and sputum from patients and perform routine laboratory tests on samples. Prepare patients for examinations, tests, or treatments and explain procedures. Assemble and use equipment such as catheters, tracheotomy tubes, and oxygen suppliers. Evaluate nursing intervention outcomes, conferring with other health-care team members as necessary. Record food and fluid intake and output. Help patients with bathing, dressing, maintaining personal hygiene, moving in bed, or standing and walking. Apply compresses, ice bags, and hot water bottles. Inventory and requisition supplies and instruments. Clean rooms and make beds. Supervise nurses' aides and assistants. Make appointments, keep records, and perform other clerical duties in doctors' offices and clinics. Provide medical treatment and personal care to patients in private home settings such as cooking, keeping rooms orderly, seeing that patients are comfortable and in good spirits, and instructing family members in simple nursing tasks. Set up equipment and prepare medical treatment rooms. Prepare food trays and examine them for conformance to prescribed diet. Wash and dress bodies of deceased persons. Assist in delivery, care, and feeding of infants.

Personality Type: Social. These occupations frequently involve working with, communicating with, and teaching people and often involve helping or providing service to others.

GOE—Interest Area/Cluster: 08. Health Science. **Work Group:** 08.08. Patient Care and Assistance. **Other Jobs in This Work Group:** Home Health Aides; Nursing Aides, Orderlies, and Attendants; Psychiatric Aides; Psychiatric Technicians.

Skills—Service Orientation: Actively looking for ways to help people. **Systems Analysis:** Determining how a system should work and how changes will affect outcomes. **Management of Personnel Resources:** Motivating, developing, and directing people as they work; identifying the best people for the job. **Social Perceptiveness:** Being aware of others' reactions and understanding why they react the way they do. **Systems Evaluation:** Looking at many indicators of system performance and taking into account their accuracy.

Education and Training Program: Licensed Practical/Vocational Nurse Training (LPN, LVN, Cert, Dipl, AAS). **Related Knowledge/Courses—Psychology:** Human behavior and performance, mental processes, psychological research methods, and the assessment and treatment of behavioral and affective disorders. **Medicine and Dentistry:** The information and techniques needed to diagnose and treat injuries, diseases, and deformities. This includes symptoms, treatment alternatives, drug properties and interactions, and preventive health-care measures. **Therapy and Counseling:** Information and techniques needed to rehabilitate physical and mental ailments and to provide career guidance, including alternative treatments, rehabilitation equipment and its proper use, and methods to evaluate treatment effects. **Biology:** Plant and animal living tissue, cells, organisms, and entities, including their functions, interdependencies, and interactions with each other and the environment. **Philosophy and Theology:** Different philosophical systems and religions, including their basic principles, values, ethics, ways of thinking, customs, and practices and their impact on human culture. **Customer and Personal Service:** Principles and processes for providing customer and personal services, including needs assessment techniques, quality service standards, alternative delivery systems, and customer satisfaction evaluation techniques.

Work Environment: Indoors; contaminants; disease or infections; standing; walking and running; using hands on objects, tools, or controls.

Licensing Examiners and Inspectors

* Education/Training Required: Long-term on-the-job training
* Annual Earnings: $48,400
* Beginning Wage: $28,980
* Earnings Growth Potential: High
* Growth: 4.9%
* Annual Job Openings: 15,841
* Self-Employed: 0.4%
* Part-Time: 5.0%

The job openings listed here are shared with Coroners; Environmental Compliance Inspectors; Equal Opportunity Representatives and Officers; and Government Property Inspectors and Investigators.

Examine, evaluate, and investigate eligibility for, conformity with, or liability under licenses or permits. Issue licenses to individuals meeting standards. Evaluate applications, records, and documents in order to gather information about eligibility or liability issues. Administer oral, written, road, or flight tests to license applicants. Score tests and observe equipment operation and control in order to rate ability of applicants. Advise licensees and other individuals or groups concerning licensing, permit, or passport regulations. Warn violators of infractions or penalties. Prepare reports of activities, evaluations, recommendations, and decisions. Prepare correspondence to inform concerned parties of licensing decisions and of appeals processes. Confer with and interview officials, technical or professional specialists, and applicants in order to obtain information or to clarify facts relevant to licensing decisions. Report law or regulation violations to appropriate boards and agencies. Visit establishments to verify that valid licenses and permits are displayed, and that licensing standards are being upheld.

Personality Type: Conventional. These occupations frequently involve following set procedures and routines and can include working with data and details more than with ideas. Usually there is a clear line of authority to follow.

GOE—Interest Area/Cluster: 07. Government and Public Administration. **Work Group:** 07.03. Regulations Enforcement. **Other Jobs in This Work Group:** Agricultural Inspectors; Aviation Inspectors; Compliance Officers,

Except Agriculture, Construction, Health and Safety, and Transportation; Construction and Building Inspectors; Environmental Compliance Inspectors; Equal Opportunity Representatives and Officers; Financial Examiners; Fire Inspectors; Fish and Game Wardens; Forest Fire Inspectors and Prevention Specialists; Freight and Cargo Inspectors; Government Property Inspectors and Investigators; Immigration and Customs Inspectors; Nuclear Monitoring Technicians; Occupational Health and Safety Specialists; Occupational Health and Safety Technicians; Tax Examiners, Collectors, and Revenue Agents; Transportation Vehicle, Equipment, and Systems Inspectors, Except Aviation.

Skills—Speaking: Talking to others to effectively convey information. **Service Orientation:** Actively looking for ways to help people. **Judgment and Decision Making:** Weighing the relative costs and benefits of a potential action. **Active Listening:** Listening to what other people are saying and asking questions as appropriate. **Reading Comprehension:** Understanding written sentences and paragraphs in work-related documents.

Education and Training Program: Public Administration and Social Service Professions, Other. **Related Knowledge/ Courses—Clerical Practices:** Administrative and clerical procedures and systems such as word-processing systems, filing and records management systems, stenography and transcription, forms, design principles, and other office procedures and terminology. **Customer and Personal Service:** Principles and processes for providing customer and personal services, including needs assessment techniques, quality service standards, alternative delivery systems, and customer satisfaction evaluation techniques. **Law and Government:** Laws, legal codes, court procedures, precedents, government regulations, executive orders, agency rules, and the democratic political process. **Foreign Language:** The structure and content of a foreign (non-English) language, including the meaning and spelling of words, rules of composition and grammar, and pronunciation. **Psychology:** Human behavior and performance, mental processes, psychological research methods, and the assessment and treatment of behavioral and affective disorders. **Public Safety and Security:** Weaponry; public safety; security operations, rules, regulations, precautions, and prevention; and the protection of people, data, and property.

Work Environment: More often indoors than outdoors; contaminants; sitting; using hands on objects, tools, or controls; repetitive motions.

Loan Interviewers and Clerks

* Education/Training Required: Short-term on-the-job training
* Annual Earnings: $31,680
* Beginning Wage: $21,070
* Earnings Growth Potential: Low
* Growth: –0.9%
* Annual Job Openings: 40,217
* Self-Employed: 2.5%
* Part-Time: 6.3%

Interview loan applicants to elicit information; investigate applicants' backgrounds and verify references; prepare loan request papers; and forward findings, reports, and documents to appraisal department. Review loan papers to ensure completeness and complete transactions between loan establishment, borrowers, and sellers upon approval of loan. Verify and examine information and accuracy of loan application and closing documents. Interview loan applicants in order to obtain personal and financial data, and to assist in completing applications. Assemble and compile documents for loan closings, such as title abstracts, insurance forms, loan forms, and tax receipts. Answer questions and advise customers regarding loans and transactions. Contact customers by mail, telephone, or in person concerning acceptance or rejection of applications. Record applications for loan and credit, loan information, and disbursements of funds, using computers. Prepare and type loan applications, closing documents, legal documents, letters, forms, government notices, and checks, using computers. Present loan and repayment schedules to customers. Calculate, review, and correct errors on interest, principal, payment, and closing costs, using computers or calculators. Check value of customer collateral to be held as loan security. Contact credit bureaus, employers, and other sources in order to check applicants' credit and personal references. File and maintain loan records. Schedule and conduct closings of mortgage transactions. Accept payment on accounts. Submit loan applications with recommendation for underwriting approval. Order property insurance or mortgage insurance policies in order to ensure protection against loss on mortgaged property. Review customer accounts in order to determine whether payments are made on time and that other loan terms are being followed. Establish credit limits and grant extensions of credit on overdue accounts.

Personality Type: Conventional. These occupations frequently involve following set procedures and routines and can include working with data and details more than with ideas. Usually there is a clear line of authority to follow.

GOE—Interest Area/Cluster: 06. Finance and Insurance. **Work Group:** 06.04. Finance/Insurance Customer Service. **Other Jobs in This Work Group:** Bill and Account Collectors; New Accounts Clerks; Tellers.

Skills—Service Orientation: Actively looking for ways to help people. **Learning Strategies:** Using multiple approaches when learning or teaching new things. **Mathematics:** Using mathematics to solve problems. **Time Management:** Managing one's own time and the time of others. **Speaking:** Talking to others to effectively convey information. **Writing:** Communicating effectively with others in writing as indicated by the needs of the audience. **Persuasion:** Persuading others to approach things differently. **Operations Analysis:** Analyzing needs and product requirements to create a design.

Education and Training Program: Banking and Financial Support Services. **Related Knowledge/Courses—Economics and Accounting:** Economic and accounting principles and practices, the financial markets, banking, and the analysis and reporting of financial data. **Clerical Practices:** Administrative and clerical procedures and systems such as word-processing systems, filing and records management systems, stenography and transcription, forms, design principles, and other office procedures and terminology. **Mathematics:** Numbers and their operations and interrelationships, including arithmetic, algebra, geometry, calculus, and statistics and their applications. **Customer and Personal Service:** Principles and processes for providing customer and personal services, including needs assessment techniques, quality service standards, alternative delivery systems, and customer satisfaction evaluation techniques. **Law and Government:** Laws, legal codes, court procedures, precedents, government regulations, executive orders, agency rules, and the democratic political process.

Work Environment: Indoors; sitting.

Loan Officers

- ❋ Education/Training Required: Bachelor's degree
- ❋ Annual Earnings: $53,000
- ❋ Beginning Wage: $30,340
- ❋ Earnings Growth Potential: High
- ❋ Growth: 11.5%
- ❋ Annual Job Openings: 54,237
- ❋ Self-Employed: 2.9%
- ❋ Part-Time: 6.6%

Evaluate, authorize, or recommend approval of commercial, real estate, or credit loans. Advise borrowers on financial status and methods of payments. Includes mortgage loan officers and agents, collection analysts, loan servicing officers, and loan underwriters. Meet with applicants to obtain information for loan applications and to answer questions about the process. Approve loans within specified limits and refer loan applications outside those limits to management for approval. Analyze applicants' financial status, credit, and property evaluations to determine feasibility of granting loans. Explain to customers the different types of loans and credit options that are available, as well as the terms of those services. Obtain and compile copies of loan applicants' credit histories, corporate financial statements, and other financial information. Review and update credit and loan files. Review loan agreements to ensure that they are complete and accurate according to policy. Compute payment schedules. Stay abreast of new types of loans and other financial services and products to better meet customers' needs. Submit applications to credit analysts for verification and recommendation. Handle customer complaints and take appropriate action to resolve them. Work with clients to identify their financial goals and to find ways of reaching those goals. Confer with underwriters to aid in resolving mortgage application problems. Negotiate payment arrangements with customers who have delinquent loans. Market bank products to individuals and firms, promoting bank services that may meet customers' needs. Supervise loan personnel. Set credit policies, credit lines, procedures, and standards in conjunction with senior managers. Provide special services such as investment banking for clients with more specialized needs. Analyze potential loan markets and develop referral networks to locate prospects for loans. Prepare reports to send to customers whose accounts are delinquent and forward irreconcilable accounts for collector action. Arrange for maintenance and liquidation of delinquent properties. Interview, hire, and train new employees. Petition courts to transfer titles and deeds of collateral to banks.

Personality Type: Conventional. These occupations frequently involve following set procedures and routines and can include working with data and details more than with ideas. Usually there is a clear line of authority to follow.

GOE—Interest Area/Cluster: 06. Finance and Insurance. **Work Group:** 06.02. Finance/Insurance Investigation and Analysis. **Other Jobs in This Work Group:** Appraisers and Assessors of Real Estate; Appraisers, Real Estate; Assessors; Claims Adjusters, Examiners, and Investigators; Claims Examiners, Property and Casualty Insurance; Cost Estimators; Credit Analysts; Financial Analysts; Insurance Adjusters, Examiners, and Investigators; Insurance Appraisers, Auto Damage; Insurance Underwriters; Loan Counselors; Market Research Analysts; Survey Researchers.

Skills—Persuasion: Persuading others to approach things differently. **Social Perceptiveness:** Being aware of others' reactions and understanding why they react the way they do. **Service Orientation:** Actively looking for ways to help people. **Complex Problem Solving:** Identifying complex problems, reviewing the options, and implementing solutions. **Negotiation:** Bringing others together and trying to reconcile differences. **Instructing:** Teaching others how to do something. **Speaking:** Talking to others to effectively convey information. **Judgment and Decision Making:** Weighing the relative costs and benefits of a potential action.

Education and Training Programs: Credit Management; Finance, General. **Related Knowledge/Courses—Economics and Accounting:** Economic and accounting principles and practices, the financial markets, banking, and the analysis and reporting of financial data. **Sales and Marketing:** Principles and methods involved in showing, promoting, and selling products or services. This includes marketing strategies and tactics, product demonstration and sales techniques, and sales control systems. **Law and Government:** Laws, legal codes, court procedures, precedents, government regulations, executive orders, agency rules, and the democratic political process. **English Language:** The structure and content of the English language, including the meaning and spelling of words, rules of composition, and grammar. **Mathematics:** Numbers and their operations and interrelationships, including arithmetic, algebra, geometry, calculus, and statistics and their applications. **Customer and Personal Service:** Principles and processes for providing customer and personal services, including needs assessment techniques, quality service standards, alternative delivery systems, and customer satisfaction evaluation techniques.

Work Environment: Indoors; sitting; repetitive motions.

Locksmiths and Safe Repairers

* Education/Training Required: Moderate-term on-the-job training
* Annual Earnings: $33,230
* Beginning Wage: $18,580
* Earnings Growth Potential: High
* Growth: 22.1%
* Annual Job Openings: 3,545
* Self-Employed: 28.3%
* Part-Time: 10.6%

Repair and open locks, make keys, change locks and safe combinations, and install and repair safes. Cut new or duplicate keys, using keycutting machines. Keep records of company locks and keys. Insert new or repaired tumblers into locks to change combinations. Move picklocks in cylinders to open door locks without keys. Disassemble mechanical or electrical locking devices and repair or replace worn tumblers, springs, and other parts, using hand tools. Repair and adjust safes, vault doors, and vault components, using hand tools, lathes, drill presses, and welding and acetylene cutting apparatus. Install safes, vault doors, and deposit boxes according to blueprints, using equipment such as powered drills, taps, dies, truck cranes, and dollies. Open safe locks by drilling. Remove interior and exterior finishes on safes and vaults and spray on new finishes.

Personality Type: Realistic. These occupations frequently involve work activities that include practical, hands-on problems and solutions. They often deal with plants; animals; and real-world materials such as wood, tools, and machinery. Many of the occupations require working outside and don't involve a lot of paperwork or working closely with others.

GOE—Interest Area/Cluster: 13. Manufacturing. **Work Group:** 13.13. Machinery Repair. **Other Jobs in This Work Group:** Bicycle Repairers; Control and Valve Installers and Repairers, Except Mechanical Door; Home Appliance Repairers; Industrial Machinery Mechanics; Maintenance Workers, Machinery; Mechanical Door Repairers; Millwrights; Signal and Track Switch Repairers.

Skills—Installation: Installing equipment, machines, wiring, or programs to meet specifications. **Repairing:** Repairing machines or systems, using the needed tools. **Equipment Maintenance:** Performing routine maintenance and determining when and what kind of maintenance is needed. **Troubleshooting:** Determining what is causing an operating error and deciding what to do about it. **Equipment Selection:** Determining the kind of tools and equipment needed to do a job. **Service Orientation:** Actively looking for ways to help people. **Technology Design:** Generating or adapting equipment and technology to serve user needs. **Management of Material Resources:** Obtaining and seeing to the appropriate use of equipment, facilities, and materials needed to do certain work.

Education and Training Program: Locksmithing and Safe Repair. **Related Knowledge/Courses—Sales and Marketing:** Principles and methods involved in showing, promoting, and selling products or services. This includes marketing strategies and tactics, product demonstration and sales techniques, and sales control systems. **Clerical Practices:** Administrative and clerical procedures and systems such as word-processing systems, filing and records management systems, stenography and transcription, forms, design principles, and other office procedures and terminology. **Customer and Personal Service:** Principles and processes for providing customer and personal services, including needs assessment techniques, quality service standards, alternative delivery systems, and customer satisfaction evaluation techniques. **Administration and Management:** Principles and processes involved in business and organizational planning, coordination, and execution. This includes strategic planning, resource allocation, manpower modeling, leadership techniques, and production methods. **Mechanical Devices:** Machines and tools, including their designs, uses, benefits, repair, and maintenance. **Public Safety and Security:** Weaponry; public safety; security operations, rules, regulations, precautions, and prevention; and the protection of people, data, and property.

Work Environment: More often outdoors than indoors; noisy; very bright or dim lighting; standing; using hands on objects, tools, or controls.

Lodging Managers

- ❀ Education/Training Required: Work experience in a related occupation
- ❀ Annual Earnings: $44,240
- ❀ Beginning Wage: $26,880
- ❀ Earnings Growth Potential: Medium
- ❀ Growth: 12.2%
- ❀ Annual Job Openings: 5,529
- ❀ Self-Employed: 53.0%
- ❀ Part-Time: 8.5%

Plan, direct, or coordinate activities of an organization or department that provides lodging and other accommodations. Greet and register guests. Answer inquiries pertaining to hotel policies and services and resolve occupants' complaints. Assign duties to workers and schedule shifts. Coordinate front-office activities of hotels or motels and resolve problems. Participate in financial activities such as the setting of room rates, the establishment of budgets, and the allocation of funds to departments. Confer and cooperate with other managers to ensure coordination of hotel activities. Collect payments and record data pertaining to funds and expenditures. Manage and maintain temporary or permanent lodging facilities. Observe and monitor staff performance to ensure efficient operations and adherence to facility's policies and procedures. Train staff members. Show, rent, or assign accommodations. Develop and implement policies and procedures for the operation of a department or establishment. Inspect guest rooms, public areas, and grounds for cleanliness and appearance. Prepare required paperwork pertaining to departmental functions. Interview and hire applicants. Purchase supplies and arrange for outside services such as deliveries, laundry, maintenance and repair, and trash collection. Arrange telephone answering services, deliver mail and packages, or answer questions regarding locations for eating and entertainment. Organize and coordinate the work of staff and convention personnel for meetings to be held at a particular facility. Perform marketing and public relations activities. Receive and process advance registration payments, mail letters of confirmation, or return checks when registrations cannot be accepted. Meet with clients to schedule and plan details of conventions, banquets, receptions, and other functions. Provide assistance to staff members by inspecting rooms, setting tables, or doing laundry. Book tickets for guests for local tours and attractions.

Personality Type: Enterprising. These occupations frequently involve starting up and carrying out projects and can involve leading people and making many decisions. They sometimes require risk taking and often deal with business.

GOE—Interest Area/Cluster: 09. Hospitality, Tourism, and Recreation. **Work Group:** 09.01. Managerial Work in Hospitality and Tourism. **Other Jobs in This Work Group:** First-Line Supervisors/Managers of Food Preparation and Serving Workers; First-Line Supervisors/Managers of Personal Service Workers; Food Service Managers; Gaming Managers; Gaming Supervisors.

Skills—Management of Financial Resources: Determining how money will be spent to get the work done and accounting for these expenditures. **Management of Material Resources:** Obtaining and seeing to the appropriate use of equipment, facilities, and materials needed to do certain work. **Negotiation:** Bringing others together and trying to reconcile differences. **Social Perceptiveness:** Being aware of others' reactions and understanding why they react the way they do. **Monitoring:** Assessing how well one is doing when learning or doing something. **Management of Personnel Resources:** Motivating, developing, and directing people as they work; identifying the best people for the job. **Persuasion:** Persuading others to approach things differently. **Active Listening:** Listening to what other people are saying and asking questions as appropriate.

Education and Training Programs: Hospitality Administration/Management, General; Hospitality and Recreation Marketing Operations; Hotel/Motel Administration/Management; Resort Management; Selling Skills and Sales Operations. **Related Knowledge/Courses—Sales and Marketing:** Principles and methods involved in showing, promoting, and selling products or services. This includes marketing strategies and tactics, product demonstration and sales techniques, and sales control systems. **Clerical Practices:** Administrative and clerical procedures and systems such as word-processing systems, filing and records management systems, stenography and transcription, forms, design principles, and other office procedures and terminology. **Personnel and Human Resources:** Principles and procedures for personnel recruitment; selection; training; compensation and benefits; labor relations and negotiation; and personnel information systems. **Economics and Accounting:** Economic and accounting principles and practices, the financial markets, banking, and the analysis and reporting of financial data. **Psychology:** Human behavior and performance, mental processes, psychological research methods, and the assessment and treatment of behavioral and affective disorders. **Customer and Personal Service:** Principles and processes for providing customer and personal services, including needs assessment techniques, quality service standards, alternative delivery systems, and customer satisfaction evaluation techniques.

Work Environment: Indoors; sitting.

Logisticians

- ❀ Education/Training Required: Bachelor's degree
- ❀ Annual Earnings: $64,250
- ❀ Beginning Wage: $38,280
- ❀ Earnings Growth Potential: High
- ❀ Growth: 17.3%
- ❀ Annual Job Openings: 9,671
- ❀ Self-Employed: 1.5%
- ❀ Part-Time: 3.6%

Analyze and coordinate the logistical functions of a firm or organization. Responsible for the entire life cycle of a product, including acquisition, distribution, internal allocation, delivery, and final disposal of resources. Maintain and develop positive business relationships with a customer's key personnel involved in or directly relevant to a logistics activity. Develop an understanding of customers' needs and take actions to ensure that such needs are met. Direct availability and allocation of materials, supplies, and finished products. Collaborate with other departments as necessary to meet customer requirements, to take advantage of sales opportunities, or, in the case of shortages, to minimize negative impacts on a business. Protect and control proprietary materials. Review logistics performance with customers against targets, benchmarks, and service agreements. Develop and implement technical project management tools such as plans, schedules, and responsibility and compliance matrices. Direct team activities, establishing task priorities, scheduling and tracking work assignments, providing guidance, and ensuring the availability of resources. Report project plans, progress, and results. Direct and support the compilation and analysis of technical source data necessary for product development. Explain proposed solutions to customers, management, or other interested parties through written proposals and oral presentations. Provide project management services, including the provision and analysis of technical data. Develop proposals that include documentation for estimates. Plan, organize, and execute logistics support activities such as maintenance planning, repair analysis, and test equipment recommendations. Participate in the assessment and review of design alternatives and design change proposal impacts. Support the development of training materials and technical manuals. Stay informed of logistics technology advances and apply appropriate technology in order to improve logistics processes. Redesign the movement of goods in order to maximize value and minimize costs. Manage subcontractor activities, reviewing proposals, developing performance specifications, and serving as liaisons between subcontractors and organizations. Manage the logistical aspects of product life cycles, including coordination or provisioning of samples and the minimization of obsolescence.

Personality Type: Enterprising. These occupations frequently involve starting up and carrying out projects and can involve leading people and making many decisions. They sometimes require risk taking and often deal with business.

GOE—Interest Area/Cluster: 04. Business and Administration. **Work Group:** 04.05. Accounting, Auditing, and Analytical Support. **Other Jobs in This Work Group:** Accountants; Accountants and Auditors; Auditors; Budget Analysts; Industrial Engineering Technicians; Management Analysts; Operations Research Analysts.

Skills—Management of Financial Resources: Determining how money will be spent to get the work done and accounting for these expenditures. **Management of Material Resources:** Obtaining and seeing to the appropriate use of equipment, facilities, and materials needed to do certain work. **Systems Analysis:** Determining how a system should work and how changes will affect outcomes. **Operations Analysis:** Analyzing needs and product requirements to create a design. **Management of Personnel Resources:** Motivating, developing, and directing people as they work; identifying the best people for the job. **Service Orientation:** Actively looking for ways to help people. **Persuasion:** Persuading others to approach things differently. **Technology Design:** Generating or adapting equipment and technology to serve user needs.

Education and Training Programs: Logistics and Materials Management; Operations Management and Supervision; Transportation/Transportation Management. **Related Knowledge/Courses—Telecommunications:** Transmission, broadcasting, switching, control, and operation of telecommunications systems. **Geography:** Various methods for describing the location and distribution of land, sea, and air

masses, including their physical locations, relationships, and characteristics. **Computers and Electronics:** Electric circuit boards, processors, chips, and computer hardware and software, including applications and programming. **Administration and Management:** Principles and processes involved in business and organizational planning, coordination, and execution. This includes strategic planning, resource allocation, manpower modeling, leadership techniques, and production methods. **Economics and Accounting:** Economic and accounting principles and practices, the financial markets, banking, and the analysis and reporting of financial data. **Public Safety and Security:** Weaponry; public safety; security operations, rules, regulations, precautions, and prevention; and the protection of people, data, and property.

Work Environment: Indoors; sitting.

Machinists

- ❀ Education/Training Required: Long-term on-the-job training
- ❀ Annual Earnings: $35,230
- ❀ Beginning Wage: $21,670
- ❀ Earnings Growth Potential: Medium
- ❀ Growth: –3.1%
- ❀ Annual Job Openings: 39,505
- ❀ Self-Employed: 1.7%
- ❀ Part-Time: 1.7%

Set up and operate a variety of machine tools to produce precision parts and instruments. Includes precision instrument makers who fabricate, modify, or repair mechanical instruments. May also fabricate and modify parts to make or repair machine tools or maintain industrial machines, applying knowledge of mechanics, shop mathematics, metal properties, layout, and machining procedures. Calculate dimensions and tolerances using knowledge of mathematics and instruments such as micrometers and vernier calipers. Align and secure holding fixtures, cutting tools, attachments, accessories, and materials onto machines. Select the appropriate tools, machines, and materials to be used in preparation of machinery work. Monitor the feed and speed of machines during the machining process. Machine parts to specifications using machine tools such as lathes, milling machines, shapers, or grinders. Set up, adjust, and operate all of the basic machine tools and many specialized or advanced variation tools to perform precision machining operations. Measure, examine, and test completed units to detect defects and ensure conformance to specifications, using precision instruments such as micrometers. Set controls to regulate machining, or enter commands to retrieve, input, or edit computerized machine control media. Position and fasten work pieces. Maintain industrial machines, applying knowledge of mechanics, shop mathematics, metal properties, layout, and machining procedures. Observe and listen to operating machines or equipment to diagnose machine malfunctions and to determine need for adjustments or repairs. Check work pieces to ensure that they are properly lubricated and cooled. Lay out, measure, and mark metal stock to display placement of cuts. Study sample parts, blueprints, drawings, and engineering information to determine methods and sequences of operations needed to fabricate products, and determine product dimensions and tolerances. Confer with engineering, supervisory, and manufacturing personnel to exchange technical information. Program computers and electronic instruments such as numerically controlled machine tools. Operate equipment to verify operational efficiency. Clean and lubricate machines, tools, and equipment to remove grease, rust, stains, and foreign matter. Design fixtures, tooling, and experimental parts to meet special engineering needs. Evaluate experimental procedures, and recommend changes or modifications for improved efficiency and adaptability to setup and production.

Personality Type: Realistic. These occupations frequently involve work activities that include practical, hands-on problems and solutions. They often deal with plants; animals; and real-world materials such as wood, tools, and machinery. Many of the occupations require working outside and don't involve a lot of paperwork or working closely with others.

GOE—Interest Area/Cluster: 13. Manufacturing. **Work Group:** 13.05. Production Machining Technology. **Other Jobs in This Work Group:** Computer-Controlled Machine Tool Operators, Metal and Plastic; Foundry Mold and Coremakers; Lay-Out Workers, Metal and Plastic; Model Makers, Metal and Plastic; Numerical Tool and Process Control Programmers; Patternmakers, Metal and Plastic; Tool and Die Makers; Tool Grinders, Filers, and Sharpeners.

Skills—Operation Monitoring: Watching gauges, dials, or other indicators to make sure a machine is working properly. **Repairing:** Repairing machines or systems, using the needed tools. **Operation and Control:** Controlling operations of equipment or systems. **Quality Control Analysis:** Evaluating the quality or performance of products, services, or processes. **Equipment Maintenance:** Performing routine maintenance and determining when and what kind

of maintenance is needed. **Troubleshooting:** Determining what is causing an operating error and deciding what to do about it.

Education and Training Programs: Machine Shop Technology/Assistant Training; Machine Tool Technology/Machinist Training. **Related Knowledge/Courses—Mechanical Devices:** Machines and tools, including their designs, uses, benefits, repair, and maintenance. **Design:** Design techniques, principles, tools, and instruments involved in the production and use of precision technical plans, blueprints, drawings, and models. **Engineering and Technology:** Equipment, tools, and mechanical devices and their uses to produce motion, light, power, technology, and other applications. **Production and Processing:** Inputs, outputs, raw materials, waste, quality control, costs, and techniques for maximizing the manufacture and distribution of goods. **Mathematics:** Numbers and their operations and interrelationships, including arithmetic, algebra, geometry, calculus, and statistics and their applications.

Work Environment: Noisy; contaminants; hazardous equipment; minor burns, cuts, bites, or stings; standing; using hands on objects, tools, or controls.

Maintenance and Repair Workers, General

* Education/Training Required: Moderate-term on-the-job training
* Annual Earnings: $32,570
* Beginning Wage: $19,590
* Earnings Growth Potential: Medium
* Growth: 10.1%
* Annual Job Openings: 165,502
* Self-Employed: 1.5%
* Part-Time: 5.2%

Perform work involving the skills of two or more maintenance or craft occupations to keep machines, mechanical equipment, or the structure of an establishment in repair. Duties may involve pipe fitting; boiler making; insulating; welding; machining; carpentry; repairing electrical or mechanical equipment; installing, aligning, and balancing new equipment; and repairing buildings, floors, or stairs. Repair or replace defective equipment parts, using hand tools and power tools, and reassemble equipment. Perform routine preventive maintenance to ensure that machines continue to run smoothly, building systems operate efficiently, and the physical condition of buildings does not deteriorate. Inspect drives, motors, and belts; check fluid levels; replace filters; and perform other maintenance actions, following checklists. Use tools ranging from common hand and power tools, such as hammers, hoists, saws, drills, and wrenches, to precision measuring instruments and electrical and electronic testing devices. Assemble, install, or repair wiring, electrical and electronic components, pipe systems and plumbing, machinery, and equipment. Diagnose mechanical problems and determine how to correct them, checking blueprints, repair manuals, and parts catalogs as necessary. Inspect, operate, and test machinery and equipment to diagnose machine malfunctions. Record maintenance and repair work performed and the costs of the work. Clean and lubricate shafts, bearings, gears, and other parts of machinery. Dismantle devices to gain access to and remove defective parts, using hoists, cranes, hand tools, and power tools. Plan and lay out repair work, using diagrams, drawings, blueprints, maintenance manuals, and schematic diagrams. Adjust functional parts of devices and control instruments, using hand tools, levels, plumb bobs, and straightedges. Order parts, supplies, and equipment from catalogs and suppliers or obtain them from storerooms. Paint and repair roofs, windows, doors, floors, woodwork, plaster, drywall, and other parts of building structures. Operate cutting torches or welding equipment to cut or join metal parts. Align and balance new equipment after installation. Inspect used parts to determine changes in dimensional requirements, using rules, calipers, micrometers, and other measuring instruments. Set up and operate machine tools to repair or fabricate machine parts, jigs and fixtures, and tools. Maintain and repair specialized equipment and machinery found in cafeterias, laundries, hospitals, stores, offices, and factories.

Personality Type: Realistic. These occupations frequently involve work activities that include practical, hands-on problems and solutions. They often deal with plants; animals; and real-world materials such as wood, tools, and machinery. Many of the occupations require working outside and don't involve a lot of paperwork or working closely with others.

GOE—Interest Area/Cluster: 02. Architecture and Construction. **Work Group:** 02.05. Systems and Equipment Installation, Maintenance, and Repair. **Other Jobs in This Work Group:** Electrical and Electronics Repairers, Powerhouse, Substation, and Relay; Electrical Power-Line Installers and Repairers; Elevator Installers and Repairers; Heating and Air Conditioning Mechanics and Installers; Refrigeration Mechanics and Installers; Telecommunications Equipment Installers and Repairers, Except Line Installers; Telecommunications Line Installers and Repairers.

Skills—Equipment Maintenance: Performing routine maintenance and determining when and what kind of maintenance is needed. **Installation:** Installing equipment, machines, wiring, or programs to meet specifications. **Repairing:** Repairing machines or systems, using the needed tools. **Troubleshooting:** Determining what is causing an operating error and deciding what to do about it. **Operation Monitoring:** Watching gauges, dials, or other indicators to make sure a machine is working properly. **Operation and Control:** Controlling operations of equipment or systems. **Equipment Selection:** Determining the kind of tools and equipment needed to do a job. **Technology Design:** Generating or adapting equipment and technology to serve user needs.

Education and Training Program: Building/Construction Site Management/Manager Training. **Related Knowledge/Courses—Building and Construction:** Materials, methods, and the appropriate tools to construct objects, structures, and buildings. **Mechanical Devices:** Machines and tools, including their designs, uses, benefits, repair, and maintenance. **Design:** Design techniques, principles, tools, and instruments involved in the production and use of precision technical plans, blueprints, drawings, and models. **Physics:** Physical principles, laws, and applications, including air, water, material dynamics, light, atomic principles, heat, electric theory, earth formations, and meteorological and related natural phenomena. **Engineering and Technology:** Equipment, tools, and mechanical devices and their uses to produce motion, light, power, technology, and other applications. **Public Safety and Security:** Weaponry; public safety; security operations, rules, regulations, precautions, and prevention; and the protection of people, data, and property.

Work Environment: Indoors; noisy; minor burns, cuts, bites, or stings; standing; walking and running; using hands on objects, tools, or controls.

Maintenance Workers, Machinery

- ❋ Education/Training Required: Moderate-term on-the-job training
- ❋ Annual Earnings: $35,590
- ❋ Beginning Wage: $21,890
- ❋ Earnings Growth Potential: Medium
- ❋ Growth: –1.1%
- ❋ Annual Job Openings: 15,055
- ❋ Self-Employed: 0.0%
- ❋ Part-Time: 4.0%

Lubricate machinery, change parts, or perform other routine machinery maintenance. Reassemble machines after the completion of repair or maintenance work. Start machines and observe mechanical operation to determine efficiency and to detect problems. Inspect or test damaged machine parts, and mark defective areas or advise supervisors of repair needs. Lubricate or apply adhesives or other materials to machines, machine parts, or other equipment, according to specified procedures. Install, replace, or change machine parts and attachments, according to production specifications. Dismantle machines and remove parts for repair, using hand tools, chain falls, jacks, cranes, or hoists. Record production, repair, and machine maintenance information. Read work orders and specifications to determine machines and equipment requiring repair or maintenance. Set up and operate machines, and adjust controls to regulate operations. Collaborate with other workers to repair or move machines, machine parts, or equipment. Inventory and requisition machine parts, equipment, and other supplies so that stock can be maintained and replenished. Transport machine parts, tools, equipment, and other material between work areas and storage, using cranes, hoists, or dollies. Clean machines and machine parts, using cleaning solvents, cloths, air guns, hoses, vacuums, or other equipment. Collect and discard worn machine parts and other refuse in order to maintain machinery and work areas. Replace or repair metal, wood, leather, glass, or other lining in machines or in equipment compartments or containers. Remove hardened material from machines or machine parts, using abrasives, power and hand tools, jackhammers, sledgehammers, or other equipment. Measure, mix, prepare, and test chemical solutions used to clean or repair machinery and equipment. Replace, empty, or replenish machine and equipment containers such as gas tanks or boxes.

Personality Type: Realistic. These occupations frequently involve work activities that include practical, hands-on problems and solutions. They often deal with plants; animals; and real-world materials such as wood, tools, and machinery. Many of the occupations require working outside and don't involve a lot of paperwork or working closely with others.

GOE—Interest Area/Cluster: 13. Manufacturing. **Work Group:** 13.13. Machinery Repair. **Other Jobs in This Work Group:** Bicycle Repairers; Control and Valve Installers and Repairers, Except Mechanical Door; Home Appliance Repairers; Industrial Machinery Mechanics; Locksmiths and Safe Repairers; Mechanical Door Repairers; Millwrights; Signal and Track Switch Repairers.

Skills—Installation: Installing equipment, machines, wiring, or programs to meet specifications. **Repairing:** Repairing machines or systems, using the needed tools. **Equipment Maintenance:** Performing routine maintenance and determining when and what kind of maintenance is needed. **Troubleshooting:** Determining what is causing an operating error and deciding what to do about it. **Operation Monitoring:** Watching gauges, dials, or other indicators to make sure a machine is working properly. **Operation and Control:** Controlling operations of equipment or systems. **Technology Design:** Generating or adapting equipment and technology to serve user needs. **Equipment Selection:** Determining the kind of tools and equipment needed to do a job.

Education and Training Programs: Heavy/Industrial Equipment Maintenance Technologies, Other; Industrial Mechanics and Maintenance Technology. **Related Knowledge/Courses—Mechanical Devices:** Machines and tools, including their designs, uses, benefits, repair, and maintenance. **Building and Construction:** Materials, methods, and the appropriate tools to construct objects, structures, and buildings. **Engineering and Technology:** Equipment, tools, and mechanical devices and their uses to produce motion, light, power, technology, and other applications. **Physics:** Physical principles, laws, and applications, including air, water, material dynamics, light, atomic principles, heat, electric theory, earth formations, and meteorological and related natural phenomena. **Chemistry:** The composition, structure, and properties of substances and of the chemical processes and transformations that they undergo. This includes uses of chemicals and their interactions, danger signs, production techniques, and disposal methods. **Design:** Design techniques, principles, tools, and instruments involved in the production and use of precision technical plans, blueprints, drawings, and models.

Work Environment: Noisy; very hot or cold; contaminants; hazardous equipment; standing; using hands on objects, tools, or controls.

Makeup Artists, Theatrical and Performance

- ❋ Education/Training Required: Postsecondary vocational training
- ❋ Annual Earnings: $35,250
- ❋ Beginning Wage: $15,920
- ❋ Earnings Growth Potential: Very high
- ❋ Growth: 39.8%
- ❋ Annual Job Openings: 392
- ❋ Self-Employed: 39.7%
- ❋ Part-Time: 26.3%

Apply makeup to performers to reflect period, setting, and situation of their role. Confer with stage or motion picture officials and performers in order to determine desired effects. Duplicate work precisely in order to replicate characters' appearances on a daily basis. Establish budgets, and work within budgetary limits. Apply makeup to enhance and/or alter the appearance of people appearing in productions such as movies. Alter or maintain makeup during productions as necessary to compensate for lighting changes or to achieve continuity of effect. Select desired makeup shades from stock, or mix oil, grease, and coloring in order to achieve specific color effects. Cleanse and tone the skin in order to prepare it for makeup application. Assess performers' skin-type in order to ensure that make-up will not cause break-outs or skin irritations. Analyze a script, noting events that affect each character's appearance, so that plans can be made for each scene. Requisition or acquire needed materials for special effects, including wigs, beards, and special cosmetics. Write makeup sheets and take photos in order to document specific looks and the products that were used to achieve the looks. Examine sketches, photographs, and plaster models in order to obtain desired character image depiction. Attach prostheses to performers and apply makeup in order to create special features or effects such as scars, aging, or illness. Evaluate environmental characteristics such as venue size and lighting plans in order to determine makeup requirements. Design rubber or plastic prostheses that can be used to change performers' appearances. Create character drawings or models, based upon independent research, in order to augment period production files. Advise hairdressers on the hairstyles required for character parts. Study production information such as character descriptions, period settings, and situations in order to determine makeup requirements. Provide performers with makeup removal assistance after performances have been completed. Wash and reset wigs. Demonstrate products to clients, and provide instruction in makeup application.

Personality Type: Artistic. These occupations frequently involve working with forms, designs, and patterns. They often require self-expression, and the work can be done without following a clear set of rules.

GOE—Interest Area/Cluster: 03. Arts and Communication. **Work Group:** 03.06. Drama. **Other Jobs in This Work Group:** Actors; Costume Attendants; Directors—Stage, Motion Pictures, Television, and Radio; Public Address System and Other Announcers; Radio and Television Announcers.

Skills—Management of Financial Resources: Determining how money will be spent to get the work done and accounting for these expenditures. **Equipment Selection:** Determining the kind of tools and equipment needed to do a job. **Time Management:** Managing one's own time and the time of others. **Operations Analysis:** Analyzing needs and product requirements to create a design. **Management of Material Resources:** Obtaining and seeing to the appropriate use of equipment, facilities, and materials needed to do certain work. **Management of Personnel Resources:** Motivating, developing, and directing people as they work; identifying the best people for the job. **Negotiation:** Bringing others together and trying to reconcile differences. **Coordination:** Adjusting actions in relation to others' actions.

Education and Training Programs: Cosmetology/Cosmetologist Training, General; Make-Up Artist/Specialist Training; Permanent Cosmetics/Makeup and Tattooing. **Related Knowledge/Courses—Fine Arts:** Theory and techniques required to produce, compose, and perform works of music, dance, visual arts, drama, and sculpture. **Chemistry:** The composition, structure, and properties of substances and of the chemical processes and transformations that they undergo. This includes uses of chemicals and their interactions, danger signs, production techniques, and disposal methods. **Design:** Design techniques, principles, tools, and instruments involved in the production and use of precision technical plans, blueprints, drawings, and models. **Sales and Marketing:** Principles and methods involved in showing, promoting, and selling products or services. This includes marketing strategies and tactics, product demonstration and sales techniques, and sales control systems. **Personnel and**

Human Resources: Principles and procedures for personnel recruitment; selection; training; compensation and benefits; labor relations and negotiation; and personnel information systems. **Psychology:** Human behavior and performance, mental processes, psychological research methods, and the assessment and treatment of behavioral and affective disorders.

Work Environment: More often indoors than outdoors; very bright or dim lighting; standing; using hands on objects, tools, or controls; repetitive motions.

Management Analysts

- ❋ Education/Training Required: Work experience plus degree
- ❋ Annual Earnings: $71,150
- ❋ Beginning Wage: $40,860
- ❋ Earnings Growth Potential: High
- ❋ Growth: 21.9%
- ❋ Annual Job Openings: 125,669
- ❋ Self-Employed: 27.0%
- ❋ Part-Time: 13.2%

Conduct organizational studies and evaluations, design systems and procedures, conduct work simplifications and measurement studies, and prepare operations and procedures manuals to assist management in operating more efficiently and effectively. Includes program analysts and management consultants. Gather and organize information on problems or procedures. Analyze data gathered and develop solutions or alternative methods of proceeding. Confer with personnel concerned to ensure successful functioning of newly implemented systems or procedures. Develop and implement records management program for filing, protection, and retrieval of records and assure compliance with program. Review forms and reports and confer with management and users about format, distribution, and purpose and to identify problems and improvements. Document findings of study and prepare recommendations for implementation of new systems, procedures, or organizational changes. Interview personnel and conduct on-site observation to ascertain unit functions; work performed; and methods, equipment, and personnel used. Prepare manuals and train workers in use of new forms, reports, procedures, or equipment according to organizational policy. Design, evaluate, recommend, and approve changes of forms and reports. Plan study of work problems and procedures, such as organizational change, communications,

information flow, integrated production methods, inventory control, or cost analysis. Recommend purchase of storage equipment and design area layout to locate equipment in space available.

Personality Type: Investigative. These occupations frequently involve working with ideas and require an extensive amount of thinking. They can involve searching for facts and figuring out problems mentally.

GOE—Interest Area/Cluster: 04. Business and Administration. **Work Group:** 04.05. Accounting, Auditing, and Analytical Support. **Other Jobs in This Work Group:** Accountants; Accountants and Auditors; Auditors; Budget Analysts; Industrial Engineering Technicians; Logisticians; Operations Research Analysts.

Skills—Operations Analysis: Analyzing needs and product requirements to create a design. **Systems Evaluation:** Looking at many indicators of system performance and taking into account their accuracy. **Installation:** Installing equipment, machines, wiring, or programs to meet specifications. **Management of Financial Resources:** Determining how money will be spent to get the work done and accounting for these expenditures. **Quality Control Analysis:** Evaluating the quality or performance of products, services, or processes. **Operation and Control:** Controlling operations of equipment or systems. **Systems Analysis:** Determining how a system should work and how changes will affect outcomes. **Equipment Maintenance:** Performing routine maintenance and determining when and what kind of maintenance is needed.

Education and Training Programs: Business Administration and Management, General; Business/Commerce, General. **Related Knowledge/Courses—Personnel and Human Resources:** Principles and procedures for personnel recruitment; selection; training; compensation and benefits; labor relations and negotiation; and personnel information systems. **Clerical Practices:** Administrative and clerical procedures and systems such as word-processing systems, filing and records management systems, stenography and transcription, forms, design principles, and other office procedures and terminology. **Sales and Marketing:** Principles and methods involved in showing, promoting, and selling products or services. This includes marketing strategies and tactics, product demonstration and sales techniques, and sales control systems. **Economics and Accounting:** Economic and accounting principles and practices, the financial markets, banking, and the analysis and reporting of financial data. **Customer and Personal Service:** Principles and processes for providing customer and personal services, including needs assessment techniques, quality service standards, alternative delivery systems, and customer satisfaction evaluation techniques. **Administration and Management:** Principles and processes involved in business and organizational planning, coordination, and execution. This includes strategic planning, resource allocation, manpower modeling, leadership techniques, and production methods.

Work Environment: Indoors; sitting.

Mapping Technicians

- ❋ Education/Training Required: Moderate-term on-the-job training
- ❋ Annual Earnings: $33,640
- ❋ Beginning Wage: $20,670
- ❋ Earnings Growth Potential: Medium
- ❋ Growth: 19.4%
- ❋ Annual Job Openings: 8,299
- ❋ Self-Employed: 4.2%
- ❋ Part-Time: 4.5%

The job openings listed here are shared with Surveying Technicians.

Calculate mapmaking information from field notes and draw and verify accuracy of topographical maps. Check all layers of maps to ensure accuracy, identifying and marking errors and making corrections. Determine scales, line sizes, and colors to be used for hard copies of computerized maps, using plotters. Monitor mapping work and the updating of maps to ensure accuracy, the inclusion of new and/or changed information, and compliance with rules and regulations. Identify and compile database information to create maps in response to requests. Produce and update overlay maps to show information boundaries, water locations, and topographic features on various base maps and at different scales. Trace contours and topographic details to generate maps that denote specific land and property locations and geographic attributes. Lay out and match aerial photographs in sequences in which they were taken and identify any areas missing from photographs. Compare topographical features and contour lines with images from aerial photographs, old maps, and other reference materials to verify the accuracy of their identification. Compute and measure scaled distances between reference points to establish relative positions of adjoining prints and enable the creation of photographic mosaics. Research resources such as survey maps and legal descriptions to verify property lines

and to obtain information needed for mapping. Form three-dimensional images of aerial photographs taken from different locations, using mathematical techniques and plotting instruments. Enter GPS data, legal deeds, field notes, and land survey reports into GIS workstations so that information can be transformed into graphic land descriptions such as maps and drawings. Analyze aerial photographs to detect and interpret significant military, industrial, resource, or topographical data. Redraw and correct maps, such as revising parcel maps to reflect tax code area changes, using information from official records and surveys. Train staff members in duties such as tax mapping, the use of computerized mapping equipment, and the interpretation of source documents.

Personality Type: Conventional. These occupations frequently involve following set procedures and routines and can include working with data and details more than with ideas. Usually there is a clear line of authority to follow.

GOE—Interest Area/Cluster: 15. Scientific Research, Engineering, and Mathematics. **Work Group:** 15.09. Engineering Technology. **Other Jobs in This Work Group:** Aerospace Engineering and Operations Technicians; Cartographers and Photogrammetrists; Civil Engineering Technicians; Electrical and Electronic Engineering Technicians; Electrical and Electronics Drafters; Electrical Drafters; Electrical Engineering Technicians; Electro-Mechanical Technicians; Electronic Drafters; Electronics Engineering Technicians; Environmental Engineering Technicians; Mechanical Drafters; Mechanical Engineering Technicians; Surveying and Mapping Technicians; Surveying Technicians.

Skills—Technology Design: Generating or adapting equipment and technology to serve user needs. **Operations Analysis:** Analyzing needs and product requirements to create a design. **Programming:** Writing computer programs for various purposes. **Quality Control Analysis:** Evaluating the quality or performance of products, services, or processes. **Science:** Using scientific methods to solve problems. **Troubleshooting:** Determining what is causing an operating error and deciding what to do about it. **Mathematics:** Using mathematics to solve problems. **Complex Problem Solving:** Identifying complex problems, reviewing the options, and implementing solutions.

Education and Training Programs: Cartography; Surveying Technology/Surveying. **Related Knowledge/Courses—Geography:** Various methods for describing the location and distribution of land, sea, and air masses, including their physical locations, relationships, and characteristics.

Design: Design techniques, principles, tools, and instruments involved in the production and use of precision technical plans, blueprints, drawings, and models. **Computers and Electronics:** Electric circuit boards, processors, chips, and computer hardware and software, including applications and programming. **Engineering and Technology:** Equipment, tools, and mechanical devices and their uses to produce motion, light, power, technology, and other applications. **Mathematics:** Numbers and their operations and interrelationships, including arithmetic, algebra, geometry, calculus, and statistics and their applications. **Clerical Practices:** Administrative and clerical procedures and systems such as word-processing systems, filing and records management systems, stenography and transcription, forms, design principles, and other office procedures and terminology.

Work Environment: Indoors; sitting; using hands on objects, tools, or controls; repetitive motions.

Marine Architects

- ❋ Education/Training Required: Bachelor's degree
- ❋ Annual Earnings: $76,200
- ❋ Beginning Wage: $47,920
- ❋ Earnings Growth Potential: Medium
- ❋ Growth: 10.9%
- ❋ Annual Job Openings: 495
- ❋ Self-Employed: 12.4%
- ❋ Part-Time: 2.6%

The job openings listed here are shared with Marine Engineers.

Design and oversee construction and repair of marine craft and floating structures such as ships, barges, tugs, dredges, submarines, torpedoes, floats, and buoys. May confer with marine engineers. Design complete hull and superstructure according to specifications and test data and in conformity with standards of safety, efficiency, and economy. Design layout of craft interior, including cargo space, passenger compartments, ladder wells, and elevators. Study design proposals and specifications to establish basic characteristics of craft, such as size, weight, speed, propulsion, displacement, and draft. Confer with marine engineering personnel to establish arrangement of boiler room equipment and propulsion machinery, heating and ventilating systems, refrigeration equipment, piping, and other functional equipment. Evaluate performance of craft during dock and sea trials to determine design changes and conformance with national and international standards. Oversee construction and testing of prototype in model basin and develop sectional and waterline curves of hull to establish center of gravity, ideal hull form, and buoyancy and stability data.

Personality Type: Investigative. These occupations frequently involve working with ideas and require an extensive amount of thinking. They can involve searching for facts and figuring out problems mentally.

GOE—Interest Area/Cluster: 15. Scientific Research, Engineering, and Mathematics. **Work Group:** 15.07. Research and Design Engineering. **Other Jobs in This Work Group:** Aerospace Engineers; Biomedical Engineers; Chemical Engineers; Civil Engineers; Computer Hardware Engineers; Electrical Engineers; Electronics Engineers, Except Computer; Marine Engineers; Marine Engineers and Naval Architects; Materials Engineers; Mechanical Engineers; Nuclear Engineers.

Skills—Science: Using scientific methods to solve problems. **Mathematics:** Using mathematics to solve problems. **Operations Analysis:** Analyzing needs and product requirements to create a design. **Technology Design:** Generating or adapting equipment and technology to serve user needs. **Complex Problem Solving:** Identifying complex problems, reviewing the options, and implementing solutions. **Equipment Selection:** Determining the kind of tools and equipment needed to do a job. **Installation:** Installing equipment, machines, wiring, or programs to meet specifications. **Systems Analysis:** Determining how a system should work and how changes will affect outcomes.

Education and Training Program: Naval Architecture and Marine Engineering. **Related Knowledge/Courses—Engineering and Technology:** Equipment, tools, and mechanical devices and their uses to produce motion, light, power, technology, and other applications. **Design:** Design techniques, principles, tools, and instruments involved in the production and use of precision technical plans, blueprints, drawings, and models. **Physics:** Physical principles, laws, and applications, including air, water, material dynamics, light, atomic principles, heat, electric theory, earth formations, and meteorological and related natural phenomena. **Building and Construction:** Materials, methods, and the appropriate tools to construct objects, structures, and buildings. **Mechanical Devices:** Machines and tools, including their designs, uses, benefits, repair, and maintenance. **Production and Processing:** Inputs, outputs, raw materials, waste, quality control, costs, and techniques for maximizing the manufacture and distribution of goods.

Work Environment: Indoors; sitting.

Marine Engineers

- ❀ Education/Training Required: Bachelor's degree
- ❀ Annual Earnings: $76,200
- ❀ Beginning Wage: $47,920
- ❀ Earnings Growth Potential: Medium
- ❀ Growth: 10.9%
- ❀ Annual Job Openings: 495
- ❀ Self-Employed: 12.4%
- ❀ Part-Time: 2.6%

The job openings listed here are shared with Marine Architects.

Design, develop, and take responsibility for the installation of ship machinery and related equipment, including propulsion machines and power supply systems. Prepare, or direct the preparation of, product or system layouts and detailed drawings and schematics. Inspect marine equipment and machinery in order to draw up work requests and job specifications. Conduct analytical, environmental, operational, or performance studies in order to develop designs for products such as marine engines, equipment, and structures. Design and oversee testing, installation, and repair of marine apparatus and equipment. Prepare plans, estimates, design and construction schedules, and contract specifications, including any special provisions. Investigate and observe tests on machinery and equipment for compliance with standards. Coordinate activities with regulatory bodies in order to ensure repairs and alterations are at minimum cost consistent with safety. Prepare technical reports for use by engineering, management, or sales personnel. Conduct environmental, operational, or performance tests on marine machinery and equipment. Maintain contact with, and formulate reports for, contractors and clients to ensure completion of work at minimum cost. Evaluate operation of marine equipment during acceptance testing and shakedown cruises. Analyze data in order to determine feasibility of product proposals. Determine conditions under which tests are to be conducted, as well as sequences and phases of test operations. Procure materials needed to repair marine equipment and machinery. Confer with research personnel to clarify or resolve problems and to develop or modify designs. Review work requests and compare them with previous work completed on ships to ensure that costs are economically sound. Act as liaisons between ships' captains and shore personnel to ensure that schedules and budgets are maintained and that ships are operated safely and efficiently. Perform monitoring activities to ensure that ships comply with international regulations and standards for life-saving equipment and pollution preventatives. Check, test, and maintain automatic controls and alarm systems. Supervise other engineers and crewmembers and train them for routine and emergency duties.

Personality Type: Investigative. These occupations frequently involve working with ideas and require an extensive amount of thinking. They can involve searching for facts and figuring out problems mentally.

GOE—Interest Area/Cluster: 15. Scientific Research, Engineering, and Mathematics. **Work Group:** 15.07. Research and Design Engineering. **Other Jobs in This Work Group:** Aerospace Engineers; Biomedical Engineers; Chemical Engineers; Civil Engineers; Computer Hardware Engineers; Electrical Engineers; Electronics Engineers, Except Computer; Marine Architects; Marine Engineers and Naval Architects; Materials Engineers; Mechanical Engineers; Nuclear Engineers.

Skills—Science: Using scientific methods to solve problems. **Technology Design:** Generating or adapting equipment and technology to serve user needs. **Installation:** Installing equipment, machines, wiring, or programs to meet specifications. **Mathematics:** Using mathematics to solve problems. **Operations Analysis:** Analyzing needs and product requirements to create a design. **Equipment Selection:** Determining the kind of tools and equipment needed to do a job. **Systems Analysis:** Determining how a system should work and how changes will affect outcomes. **Troubleshooting:** Determining what is causing an operating error and deciding what to do about it.

Education and Training Program: Naval Architecture and Marine Engineering. **Related Knowledge/Courses—Engineering and Technology:** Equipment, tools, and mechanical devices and their uses to produce motion, light, power, technology, and other applications. **Design:** Design techniques, principles, tools, and instruments involved in the production and use of precision technical plans, blueprints, drawings, and models. **Physics:** Physical principles, laws, and applications, including air, water, material dynamics, light, atomic principles, heat, electric theory, earth formations, and meteorological and related natural phenomena. **Mechanical Devices:** Machines and tools, including their designs, uses, benefits, repair, and maintenance. **Building and Construction:** Materials, methods, and the appropriate tools to construct objects, structures, and buildings.

Computers and Electronics: Electric circuit boards, processors, chips, and computer hardware and software, including applications and programming.

Work Environment: Outdoors; noisy; sitting.

Market Research Analysts

- ❋ Education/Training Required: Bachelor's degree
- ❋ Annual Earnings: $60,300
- ❋ Beginning Wage: $33,310
- ❋ Earnings Growth Potential: High
- ❋ Growth: 20.1%
- ❋ Annual Job Openings: 45,015
- ❋ Self-Employed: 6.6%
- ❋ Part-Time: 12.5%

Research market conditions in local, regional, or national areas to determine potential sales of a product or service. May gather information on competitors, prices, sales, and methods of marketing and distribution. May use survey results to create a marketing campaign based on regional preferences and buying habits. Collect and analyze data on customer demographics, preferences, needs, and buying habits to identify potential markets and factors affecting product demand. Prepare reports of findings, illustrating data graphically and translating complex findings into written text. Measure and assess customer and employee satisfaction. Forecast and track marketing and sales trends, analyzing collected data. Seek and provide information to help companies determine their position in the marketplace. Measure the effectiveness of marketing, advertising, and communications programs and strategies. Conduct research on consumer opinions and marketing strategies, collaborating with marketing professionals, statisticians, pollsters, and other professionals. Attend staff conferences to provide management with information and proposals concerning the promotion, distribution, design, and pricing of company products or services. Gather data on competitors and analyze their prices, sales, and method of marketing and distribution. Monitor industry statistics and follow trends in trade literature. Devise and evaluate methods and procedures for collecting data, such as surveys, opinion polls, or questionnaires, or arrange to obtain existing data. Develop and implement procedures for identifying advertising needs. Direct trained survey interviewers.

Personality Type: Investigative. These occupations frequently involve working with ideas and require an extensive amount of thinking. They can involve searching for facts and figuring out problems mentally.

GOE—Interest Area/Cluster: 06. Finance and Insurance. **Work Group:** 06.02. Finance/Insurance Investigation and Analysis. **Other Jobs in This Work Group:** Appraisers and Assessors of Real Estate; Appraisers, Real Estate; Assessors; Claims Adjusters, Examiners, and Investigators; Claims Examiners, Property and Casualty Insurance; Cost Estimators; Credit Analysts; Financial Analysts; Insurance Adjusters, Examiners, and Investigators; Insurance Appraisers, Auto Damage; Insurance Underwriters; Loan Counselors; Loan Officers; Survey Researchers.

Skills—Writing: Communicating effectively with others in writing as indicated by the needs of the audience. **Negotiation:** Bringing others together and trying to reconcile differences. **Persuasion:** Persuading others to approach things differently. **Judgment and Decision Making:** Weighing the relative costs and benefits of a potential action. **Reading Comprehension:** Understanding written sentences and paragraphs in work-related documents. **Management of Financial Resources:** Determining how money will be spent to get the work done and accounting for these expenditures. **Coordination:** Adjusting actions in relation to others' actions. **Active Listening:** Listening to what other people are saying and asking questions as appropriate.

Education and Training Programs: Applied Economics; Business/Managerial Economics; Econometrics and Quantitative Economics; Economics, General; International Economics; Marketing Research. **Related Knowledge/Courses—Sales and Marketing:** Principles and methods involved in showing, promoting, and selling products or services. This includes marketing strategies and tactics, product demonstration and sales techniques, and sales control systems. **Communications and Media:** Media production, communication, and dissemination techniques and methods, including alternative ways to inform and entertain via written, oral, and visual media. **Administration and Management:** Principles and processes involved in business and organizational planning, coordination, and execution. This includes strategic planning, resource allocation, manpower modeling, leadership techniques, and production methods. **Economics and Accounting:** Economic and accounting principles and practices, the financial markets, banking, and the analysis and reporting of financial data. **Clerical Practices:** Administrative and clerical procedures and systems such as word-processing systems, filing and records management systems, stenography and transcription, forms, design principles, and other office procedures and terminology. **Computers and Electronics:** Electric circuit boards, processors, chips, and computer hardware and software, including applications and programming.

Work Environment: Indoors; sitting.

Marketing Managers

- ❋ Education/Training Required: Work experience plus degree
- ❋ Annual Earnings: $104,400
- ❋ Beginning Wage: $53,520
- ❋ Earnings Growth Potential: High
- ❋ Growth: 14.4%
- ❋ Annual Job Openings: 20,189
- ❋ Self-Employed: 2.3%
- ❋ Part-Time: 4.1%

Determine the demand for products and services offered by firms and their competitors and identify potential customers. Develop pricing strategies with the goal of maximizing firms' profits or shares of the market while ensuring that firms' customers are satisfied. Oversee product development or monitor trends that indicate the need for new products and services. Formulate, direct, and coordinate marketing activities and policies to promote products and services, working with advertising and promotion managers. Identify, develop, and evaluate marketing strategies based on knowledge of establishment objectives, market characteristics, and cost and markup factors. Direct the hiring, training, and performance evaluations of marketing and sales staff and oversee their daily activities. Evaluate the financial aspects of product development, such as budgets, expenditures, research and development appropriations, and return-on-investment and profit-loss projections. Develop pricing strategies, balancing firm objectives and customer satisfaction. Compile lists describing product or service offerings. Initiate market research studies and analyze their findings. Use sales forecasting and strategic planning to ensure the sale and profitability of products, lines, or services, analyzing business developments and monitoring market trends. Coordinate and participate in promotional activities and trade shows, working with developers, advertisers, and production managers, to market products and services. Consult with buying personnel to gain advice regarding the types of products or services expected to be in demand. Conduct economic and commercial surveys to identify potential markets for products and services. Select products and accessories to be displayed at trade or special production shows. Negotiate contracts with vendors and distributors to manage product distribution, establishing distribution networks and developing distribution strategies. Consult with product development personnel on product specifications such as design, color, and packaging. Advise businesses and other groups on local, national, and international factors affecting the buying and selling of products and services. Confer with legal staff to resolve problems such as copyright infringement and royalty sharing with outside producers and distributors.

Personality Type: Enterprising. These occupations frequently involve starting up and carrying out projects and can involve leading people and making many decisions. They sometimes require risk taking and often deal with business.

GOE—Interest Area/Cluster: 14. Retail and Wholesale Sales and Service. **Work Group:** 14.01. Managerial Work in Retail/Wholesale Sales and Service. **Other Jobs in This Work Group:** Advertising and Promotions Managers; First-Line Supervisors/Managers of Non-Retail Sales Workers; First-Line Supervisors/Managers of Retail Sales Workers; Funeral Directors; Property, Real Estate, and Community Association Managers; Purchasing Managers; Sales Managers.

Skills—Management of Personnel Resources: Motivating, developing, and directing people as they work; identifying the best people for the job. **Systems Analysis:** Determining how a system should work and how changes will affect outcomes. **Systems Evaluation:** Looking at many indicators of system performance and taking into account their accuracy. **Persuasion:** Persuading others to approach things differently. **Negotiation:** Bringing others together and trying to reconcile differences. **Management of Financial Resources:** Determining how money will be spent to get the work done and accounting for these expenditures. **Writing:** Communicating effectively with others in writing as indicated by the needs of the audience. **Social Perceptiveness:** Being aware of others' reactions and understanding why they react the way they do.

Education and Training Programs: Apparel and Textile Marketing Management; Consumer Merchandising/Retailing Management; International Marketing; Marketing Research; Marketing, Other; Marketing/Marketing Management, General. **Related Knowledge/Courses—Sales and Marketing:** Principles and methods involved in showing, promoting, and selling products or services. This includes marketing strategies and tactics, product demonstration and sales techniques, and sales control systems. **Personnel and Human Resources:** Principles and procedures for personnel recruitment; selection; training; compensation and benefits; labor relations and negotiation; and personnel information systems. **Customer and Personal Service:** Principles and processes for providing customer and personal services, including needs assessment techniques, quality service standards, alternative delivery systems, and customer satisfaction evaluation techniques. **Communications and Media:** Media production, communication, and dissemination techniques and methods, including alternative ways to inform and entertain via written, oral, and visual media. **Sociology and Anthropology:** Group behavior and dynamics; societal trends and influences; and cultures and their history, migrations, ethnicity, and origins. **Economics and Accounting:** Economic and accounting principles and practices, the financial markets, banking, and the analysis and reporting of financial data.

Work Environment: Indoors; sitting.

Marriage and Family Therapists

* Education/Training Required: Master's degree
* Annual Earnings: $43,600
* Beginning Wage: $26,080
* Earnings Growth Potential: High
* Growth: 29.8%
* Annual Job Openings: 5,953
* Self-Employed: 6.2%
* Part-Time: 15.4%

Diagnose and treat mental and emotional disorders, whether cognitive, affective, or behavioral, within the context of marriage and family systems. Apply psychotherapeutic and family systems theories and techniques in the delivery of professional services to individuals, couples, and families for the purpose of treating such diagnosed nervous and mental disorders. Ask questions that will help clients identify their feelings and behaviors. Counsel clients on concerns such as unsatisfactory relationships, divorce and separation, child rearing, home management, and financial difficulties. Encourage individuals and family members to develop and use skills and strategies for confronting their problems in a constructive manner. Maintain case files that include activities, progress notes,

evaluations, and recommendations. Collect information about clients, using techniques such as testing, interviewing, discussion, and observation. Develop and implement individualized treatment plans addressing family relationship problems. Determine whether clients should be counseled or referred to other specialists in such fields as medicine, psychiatry, and legal aid. Confer with clients in order to develop plans for post-treatment activities. Confer with other counselors to analyze individual cases and to coordinate counseling services. Follow up on results of counseling programs and clients' adjustments to determine effectiveness of programs. Provide instructions to clients on how to obtain help with legal, financial, and other personal issues. Contact doctors, schools, social workers, juvenile counselors, law enforcement personnel, and others to gather information in order to make recommendations to courts for the resolution of child custody or visitation disputes. Provide public education and consultation to other professionals or groups regarding counseling services, issues, and methods. Supervise other counselors, social service staff, and assistants. Provide family counseling and treatment services to inmates participating in substance abuse programs. Write evaluations of parents and children for use by courts deciding divorce and custody cases, testifying in court if necessary.

Personality Type: Social. These occupations frequently involve working with, communicating with, and teaching people and often involve helping or providing service to others.

GOE—Interest Area/Cluster: 10. Human Service. **Work Group:** 10.01. Counseling and Social Work. **Other Jobs in This Work Group:** Child, Family, and School Social Workers; Clinical Psychologists; Clinical, Counseling, and School Psychologists; Counseling Psychologists; Medical and Public Health Social Workers; Mental Health and Substance Abuse Social Workers; Mental Health Counselors; Probation Officers and Correctional Treatment Specialists; Rehabilitation Counselors; Residential Advisors; Social and Human Service Assistants; Substance Abuse and Behavioral Disorder Counselors.

Skills—Social Perceptiveness: Being aware of others' reactions and understanding why they react the way they do. **Negotiation:** Bringing others together and trying to reconcile differences. **Active Listening:** Listening to what other people are saying and asking questions as appropriate. **Persuasion:** Persuading others to approach things differently. **Service Orientation:** Actively looking for ways to help people. **Monitoring:** Assessing how well one is doing when learning or doing something. **Judgment and Decision**

Making: Weighing the relative costs and benefits of a potential action. **Writing:** Communicating effectively with others in writing as indicated by the needs of the audience.

Education and Training Programs: Clinical Pastoral Counseling/Patient Counseling; Marriage and Family Therapy/Counseling; Social Work. **Related Knowledge/ Courses—Therapy and Counseling:** Information and techniques needed to rehabilitate physical and mental ailments and to provide career guidance, including alternative treatments, rehabilitation equipment and its proper use, and methods to evaluate treatment effects. **Psychology:** Human behavior and performance, mental processes, psychological research methods, and the assessment and treatment of behavioral and affective disorders. **Philosophy and Theology:** Different philosophical systems and religions, including their basic principles, values, ethics, ways of thinking, customs, and practices and their impact on human culture. **Sociology and Anthropology:** Group behavior and dynamics; societal trends and influences; and cultures and their history, migrations, ethnicity, and origins. **Medicine and Dentistry:** The information and techniques needed to diagnose and treat injuries, diseases, and deformities. This includes symptoms, treatment alternatives, drug properties and interactions, and preventive health-care measures. **Customer and Personal Service:** Principles and processes for providing customer and personal services, including needs assessment techniques, quality service standards, alternative delivery systems, and customer satisfaction evaluation techniques.

Work Environment: Indoors; sitting.

Massage Therapists

- ❋ Education/Training Required: Postsecondary vocational training
- ❋ Annual Earnings: $34,870
- ❋ Beginning Wage: $16,000
- ❋ Earnings Growth Potential: Very high
- ❋ Growth: 20.3%
- ❋ Annual Job Openings: 9,193
- ❋ Self-Employed: 64.0%
- ❋ Part-Time: 42.9%

Massage customers for hygienic or remedial purposes. Confer with clients about their medical histories and any problems with stress or pain to determine whether massage would be helpful. Apply finger and hand pressure to specific points of the body. Massage and knead the muscles and soft tissues of the human body to provide courses of treatment for medical conditions and injuries or wellness maintenance. Maintain treatment records. Provide clients with guidance and information about techniques for postural improvement and stretching, strengthening, relaxation, and rehabilitative exercises. Assess clients' soft tissue condition, joint quality and function, muscle strength, and range of motion. Develop and propose client treatment plans that specify which types of massage are to be used. Refer clients to other types of therapists when necessary. Use complementary aids, such as infrared lamps, wet compresses, ice, and whirlpool baths, to promote clients' recovery, relaxation, and well-being. Treat clients in own offices or travel to clients' offices and homes. Consult with other health-care professionals such as physiotherapists, chiropractors, physicians, and psychologists to develop treatment plans for clients. Prepare and blend oils and apply the blends to clients' skin.

Personality Type: Social. These occupations frequently involve working with, communicating with, and teaching people and often involve helping or providing service to others.

GOE—Interest Area/Cluster: 08. Health Science. **Work Group:** 08.07. Medical Therapy. **Other Jobs in This Work Group:** Audiologists; Occupational Therapist Aides; Occupational Therapist Assistants; Occupational Therapists; Physical Therapist Aides; Physical Therapist Assistants; Physical Therapists; Radiation Therapists; Recreational Therapists; Respiratory Therapists; Respiratory Therapy Technicians; Speech-Language Pathologists.

Skills—Service Orientation: Actively looking for ways to help people. **Active Listening:** Listening to what other people are saying and asking questions as appropriate.

Education and Training Programs: Asian Bodywork Therapy; Massage Therapy/Therapeutic Massage; Somatic Bodywork; Somatic Bodywork and Related Therapeutic Services, Other. **Related Knowledge/Courses—Therapy and Counseling:** Information and techniques needed to rehabilitate physical and mental ailments and to provide career guidance, including alternative treatments, rehabilitation equipment and its proper use, and methods to evaluate treatment effects. **Psychology:** Human behavior and performance, mental processes, psychological research methods, and the assessment and treatment of behavioral and affective disorders. **Sales and Marketing:** Principles and methods involved in showing, promoting, and selling products or services. This includes marketing strategies and tactics, product demonstration and sales techniques, and sales control systems. **Medicine and Dentistry:** The information and techniques needed to diagnose and treat injuries, diseases, and deformities. This includes symptoms, treatment alternatives, drug properties and interactions, and preventive health-care measures. **Chemistry:** The composition, structure, and properties of substances and of the chemical processes and transformations that they undergo. This includes uses of chemicals and their interactions, danger signs, production techniques, and disposal methods. **English Language:** The structure and content of the English language, including the meaning and spelling of words, rules of composition, and grammar.

Work Environment: Indoors; standing; using hands on objects, tools, or controls; repetitive motions.

Materials Engineers

- ❋ Education/Training Required: Bachelor's degree
- ❋ Annual Earnings: $77,170
- ❋ Beginning Wage: $47,140
- ❋ Earnings Growth Potential: Medium
- ❋ Growth: 4.0%
- ❋ Annual Job Openings: 1,390
- ❋ Self-Employed: 0.0%
- ❋ Part-Time: 3.2%

Evaluate materials and develop machinery and processes to manufacture materials for use in products that must meet specialized design and performance specifications. Develop new uses for known materials. Includes those working with composite materials or specializing in one type of material, such as graphite, metal and metal alloys, ceramics and glass, plastics and polymers, and naturally occurring materials. Analyze product failure data and laboratory test results in order to determine causes of problems and develop solutions. Monitor material performance and evaluate material deterioration. Supervise the work of technologists, technicians, and other engineers and scientists. Design and direct the testing and/or control of processing procedures. Evaluate technical specifications and economic factors relating to process or product design objectives. Conduct or supervise tests on raw materials or finished products in order to ensure their quality. Perform managerial functions such as preparing proposals and budgets, analyzing labor costs, and writing reports. Solve problems in a

number of engineering fields, such as mechanical, chemical, electrical, civil, nuclear, and aerospace. Plan and evaluate new projects, consulting with other engineers and corporate executives as necessary. Review new product plans and make recommendations for material selection based on design objectives, such as strength, weight, heat resistance, electrical conductivity, and cost. Design processing plants and equipment. Modify properties of metal alloys, using thermal and mechanical treatments. Guide technical staff engaged in developing materials for specific uses in projected products or devices. Plan and implement laboratory operations for the purpose of developing material and fabrication procedures that meet cost, product specification, and performance standards. Determine appropriate methods for fabricating and joining materials. Conduct training sessions on new material products, applications, or manufacturing methods for customers and their employees. Supervise production and testing processes in industrial settings such as metal refining facilities, smelting or foundry operations, or non-metallic materials production operations. Write for technical magazines, journals, and trade association publications. Replicate the characteristics of materials and their components with computers. Teach in colleges and universities.

Personality Type: Investigative. These occupations frequently involve working with ideas and require an extensive amount of thinking. They can involve searching for facts and figuring out problems mentally.

GOE—Interest Area/Cluster: 15. Scientific Research, Engineering, and Mathematics. **Work Group:** 15.07. Research and Design Engineering. **Other Jobs in This Work Group:** Aerospace Engineers; Biomedical Engineers; Chemical Engineers; Civil Engineers; Computer Hardware Engineers; Electrical Engineers; Electronics Engineers, Except Computer; Marine Architects; Marine Engineers; Marine Engineers and Naval Architects; Mechanical Engineers; Nuclear Engineers.

Skills—Science: Using scientific methods to solve problems. **Mathematics:** Using mathematics to solve problems. **Quality Control Analysis:** Evaluating the quality or performance of products, services, or processes. **Equipment Selection:** Determining the kind of tools and equipment needed to do a job. **Reading Comprehension:** Understanding written sentences and paragraphs in work-related documents. **Technology Design:** Generating or adapting equipment and technology to serve user needs. **Troubleshooting:** Determining what is causing an operating error and deciding what to do about it. **Complex Problem Solving:**

Identifying complex problems, reviewing the options, and implementing solutions.

Education and Training Programs: Ceramic Sciences and Engineering; Materials Engineering; Metallurgical Engineering. **Related Knowledge/Courses—Engineering and Technology:** Equipment, tools, and mechanical devices and their uses to produce motion, light, power, technology, and other applications. **Chemistry:** The composition, structure, and properties of substances and of the chemical processes and transformations that they undergo. This includes uses of chemicals and their interactions, danger signs, production techniques, and disposal methods. **Physics:** Physical principles, laws, and applications, including air, water, material dynamics, light, atomic principles, heat, electric theory, earth formations, and meteorological and related natural phenomena. **Design:** Design techniques, principles, tools, and instruments involved in the production and use of precision technical plans, blueprints, drawings, and models. **Mathematics:** Numbers and their operations and interrelationships, including arithmetic, algebra, geometry, calculus, and statistics and their applications. **Mechanical Devices:** Machines and tools, including their designs, uses, benefits, repair, and maintenance.

Work Environment: Indoors; noisy; contaminants; sitting.

Materials Scientists

- ❋ Education/Training Required: Bachelor's degree
- ❋ Annual Earnings: $76,160
- ❋ Beginning Wage: $43,180
- ❋ Earnings Growth Potential: High
- ❋ Growth: 8.7%
- ❋ Annual Job Openings: 1,039
- ❋ Self-Employed: 1.0%
- ❋ Part-Time: 3.9%

Research and study the structures and chemical properties of various natural and manmade materials, including metals, alloys, rubber, ceramics, semiconductors, polymers, and glass. Determine ways to strengthen or combine materials or develop new materials with new or specific properties for use in a variety of products and applications. Plan laboratory experiments to confirm feasibility of processes and techniques used in the production of materials having special characteristics. Confer with customers in order to determine how materials can be tailored to suit their needs. Conduct research into the structures and properties of materials such as metals, alloys, polymers, and ceramics to obtain information that could be used to develop new products or enhance existing ones. Prepare reports of materials study findings for the use of other scientists and requestors. Devise testing methods to evaluate the effects of various conditions on particular materials. Determine ways to strengthen or combine materials or develop new materials with new or specific properties for use in a variety of products and applications. Recommend materials for reliable performance in various environments. Test individual parts and products to ensure that manufacturer and governmental quality and safety standards are met. Visit suppliers of materials or users of products to gather specific information. Research methods of processing, forming, and firing materials to develop such products as ceramic fillings for teeth, unbreakable dinner plates, and telescope lenses. Study the nature, structure, and physical properties of metals and their alloys and their responses to applied forces. Monitor production processes to ensure that equipment is used efficiently and that projects are completed within appropriate time frames and budgets. Test material samples for tolerance under tension, compression, and shear to determine the cause of metal failures. Test metals to determine whether they meet specifications of mechanical strength; strength-weight ratio; ductility; magnetic and electrical properties; and resistance to abrasion, corrosion, heat, and cold. Teach in colleges and universities.

Personality Type: Investigative. These occupations frequently involve working with ideas and require an extensive amount of thinking. They can involve searching for facts and figuring out problems mentally.

GOE—Interest Area/Cluster: 15. Scientific Research, Engineering, and Mathematics. **Work Group:** 15.02. Physical Sciences. **Other Jobs in This Work Group:** Astronomers; Atmospheric and Space Scientists; Chemists; Geographers; Geoscientists, Except Hydrologists and Geographers; Hydrologists; Physicists.

Skills—Science: Using scientific methods to solve problems. **Programming:** Writing computer programs for various purposes. **Technology Design:** Generating or adapting equipment and technology to serve user needs. **Quality Control Analysis:** Evaluating the quality or performance of products, services, or processes. **Mathematics:** Using mathematics to solve problems. **Equipment Selection:** Determining the kind of tools and equipment needed to do a job. **Installation:** Installing equipment, machines, wiring, or programs to meet specifications. **Troubleshooting:**

Determining what is causing an operating error and deciding what to do about it.

Education and Training Program: Materials Science. **Related Knowledge/Courses—Chemistry:** The composition, structure, and properties of substances and of the chemical processes and transformations that they undergo. This includes uses of chemicals and their interactions, danger signs, production techniques, and disposal methods. **Engineering and Technology:** Equipment, tools, and mechanical devices and their uses to produce motion, light, power, technology, and other applications. **Mathematics:** Numbers and their operations and interrelationships, including arithmetic, algebra, geometry, calculus, and statistics and their applications. **Physics:** Physical principles, laws, and applications, including air, water, material dynamics, light, atomic principles, heat, electric theory, earth formations, and meteorological and related natural phenomena. **Production and Processing:** Inputs, outputs, raw materials, waste, quality control, costs, and techniques for maximizing the manufacture and distribution of goods. **Administration and Management:** Principles and processes involved in business and organizational planning, coordination, and execution. This includes strategic planning, resource allocation, manpower modeling, leadership techniques, and production methods.

Work Environment: Indoors; noisy; hazardous conditions; sitting.

Mates—Ship, Boat, and Barge

* ❋ Education/Training Required: Work experience in a related occupation
* ❋ Annual Earnings: $57,210
* ❋ Beginning Wage: $29,530
* ❋ Earnings Growth Potential: High
* ❋ Growth: 17.9%
* ❋ Annual Job Openings: 2,665
* ❋ Self-Employed: 6.8%
* ❋ Part-Time: 4.8%

The job openings listed here are shared with Pilots, Ship; and with Ship and Boat Captains.

Supervise and coordinate activities of crew aboard ships, boats, barges, or dredges. Determine geographical positions of ships, using lorans, azimuths of celestial bodies, or computers and use this information to determine the course and speed of a ship. Supervise crews in cleaning and maintaining decks, superstructures, and bridges. Supervise crew

members in the repair or replacement of defective gear and equipment. Steer vessels, using navigational devices such as compasses and sextons and navigational aids such as lighthouses and buoys. Observe water from ships' mastheads in order to advise on navigational direction. Inspect equipment such as cargo-handling gear, lifesaving equipment, visual-signaling equipment, and fishing, towing, or dredging gear, in order to detect problems. Arrange for ships to be stocked, fueled, and repaired. Assume command of vessels in the event that ships' masters become incapacitated. Participate in activities related to maintenance of vessel security. Stand watches on vessels during specified periods while vessels are under way. Observe loading and unloading of cargo and equipment to ensure that handling and storage are performed according to specifications.

Personality Type: Enterprising. These occupations frequently involve starting up and carrying out projects and can involve leading people and making many decisions. They sometimes require risk taking and often deal with business.

GOE—Interest Area/Cluster: 16. Transportation, Distribution, and Logistics. **Work Group:** 16.05. Water Vehicle Operation. **Other Jobs in This Work Group:** Captains, Mates, and Pilots of Water Vessels; Dredge Operators; Motorboat Operators; Pilots, Ship; Sailors and Marine Oilers; Ship and Boat Captains.

Skills—Equipment Maintenance: Performing routine maintenance and determining when and what kind of maintenance is needed. **Repairing:** Repairing machines or systems, using the needed tools. **Operation and Control:** Controlling operations of equipment or systems. **Operation Monitoring:** Watching gauges, dials, or other indicators to make sure a machine is working properly. **Troubleshooting:** Determining what is causing an operating error and deciding what to do about it. **Installation:** Installing equipment, machines, wiring, or programs to meet specifications. **Equipment Selection:** Determining the kind of tools and equipment needed to do a job. **Judgment and Decision Making:** Weighing the relative costs and benefits of a potential action.

Education and Training Programs: Commercial Fishing; Marine Science/Merchant Marine Officer Training; Marine Transportation, Other. **Related Knowledge/Courses— Geography:** Various methods for describing the location and distribution of land, sea, and air masses, including their physical locations, relationships, and characteristics. **Transportation:** Principles and methods for moving people or goods by air, rail, sea, or road, including their relative costs, advantages, and limitations. **Public Safety and Security:** Weaponry; public safety; security operations, rules, regulations, precautions, and prevention; and the protection of people, data, and property. **Telecommunications:** Transmission, broadcasting, switching, control, and operation of telecommunications systems. **Personnel and Human Resources:** Principles and procedures for personnel recruitment; selection; training; compensation and benefits; labor relations and negotiation; and personnel information systems. **Mechanical Devices:** Machines and tools, including their designs, uses, benefits, repair, and maintenance.

Work Environment: Outdoors; noisy; very hot or cold; very bright or dim lighting; contaminants; hazardous equipment.

Mathematical Science Teachers, Postsecondary

- ❋ Education/Training Required: Doctoral degree
- ❋ Annual Earnings: $58,560
- ❋ Beginning Wage: $32,690
- ❋ Earnings Growth Potential: High
- ❋ Growth: 22.9%
- ❋ Annual Job Openings: 7,663
- ❋ Self-Employed: 0.4%
- ❋ Part-Time: 27.8%

Teach courses pertaining to mathematical concepts, statistics, and actuarial science and to the application of original and standardized mathematical techniques in solving specific problems and situations. Evaluate and grade students' classwork, assignments, and papers. Compile, administer, and grade examinations or assign this work to others. Prepare and deliver lectures to undergraduate and/or graduate students on topics such as linear algebra, differential equations, and discrete mathematics. Prepare course materials such as syllabi, homework assignments, and handouts. Maintain student attendance records, grades, and other required records. Maintain regularly scheduled office hours to advise and assist students. Plan, evaluate, and revise curricula, course content, and course materials and methods of instruction. Initiate, facilitate, and moderate classroom discussions. Select and obtain materials and supplies such as textbooks. Keep abreast of developments in their fields by reading current literature, talking with colleagues, and

participating in professional conferences. Advise students on academic and vocational curricula and on career issues. Collaborate with colleagues to address teaching and research issues. Serve on academic or administrative committees that deal with institutional policies, departmental matters, and academic issues. Participate in student recruitment, registration, and placement activities. Perform administrative duties such as serving as department head. Conduct research in a particular field of knowledge and publish findings in books, professional journals, and/or electronic media. Supervise undergraduate and/or graduate teaching, internship, and research work. Act as advisers to student organizations. Participate in campus and community events. Write grant proposals to procure external research funding. Compile bibliographies of specialized materials for outside reading assignments. Provide professional consulting services to government and/or industry.

Personality Type: Social. These occupations frequently involve working with, communicating with, and teaching people and often involve helping or providing service to others.

GOE—Interest Area/Cluster: 05. Education and Training. **Work Group:** 05.03. Postsecondary and Adult Teaching and Instructing. **Other Jobs in This Work Group:** Adult Literacy, Remedial Education, and GED Teachers and Instructors; Agricultural Sciences Teachers, Postsecondary; Anthropology and Archeology Teachers, Postsecondary; Architecture Teachers, Postsecondary; Area, Ethnic, and Cultural Studies Teachers, Postsecondary; Art, Drama, and Music Teachers, Postsecondary; Atmospheric, Earth, Marine, and Space Sciences Teachers, Postsecondary; Biological Science Teachers, Postsecondary; Business Teachers, Postsecondary; Chemistry Teachers, Postsecondary; Communications Teachers, Postsecondary; Computer Science Teachers, Postsecondary; Criminal Justice and Law Enforcement Teachers, Postsecondary; Economics Teachers, Postsecondary; Education Teachers, Postsecondary; Engineering Teachers, Postsecondary; English Language and Literature Teachers, Postsecondary; Environmental Science Teachers, Postsecondary; Farm and Home Management Advisors; Foreign Language and Literature Teachers, Postsecondary; Forestry and Conservation Science Teachers, Postsecondary; Geography Teachers, Postsecondary; Graduate Teaching Assistants; Health Specialties Teachers, Postsecondary; History Teachers, Postsecondary; Home Economics Teachers, Postsecondary; Law Teachers, Postsecondary; Library Science Teachers, Postsecondary; Nursing Instructors and Teachers, Postsecondary; Philosophy and Religion Teachers,

Postsecondary; Physics Teachers, Postsecondary; Political Science Teachers, Postsecondary; Psychology Teachers, Postsecondary; Recreation and Fitness Studies Teachers, Postsecondary; Self-Enrichment Education Teachers; Social Work Teachers, Postsecondary; Sociology Teachers, Postsecondary; Vocational Education Teachers, Postsecondary.

Skills—Mathematics: Using mathematics to solve problems. **Instructing:** Teaching others how to do something. **Science:** Using scientific methods to solve problems. **Learning Strategies:** Using multiple approaches when learning or teaching new things. **Critical Thinking:** Using logic and analysis to identify the strengths and weaknesses of different approaches. **Complex Problem Solving:** Identifying complex problems, reviewing the options, and implementing solutions. **Speaking:** Talking to others to effectively convey information. **Reading Comprehension:** Understanding written sentences and paragraphs in work-related documents.

Education and Training Programs: Algebra and Number Theory; Analysis and Functional Analysis; Applied Mathematics; Business Statistics; Geometry/Geometric Analysis; Logic; Mathematical Statistics and Probability; Mathematics and Statistics, Other; Mathematics, General; Mathematics, Other; Statistics, General; Topology and Foundations. **Related Knowledge/Courses—Mathematics:** Numbers and their operations and interrelationships, including arithmetic, algebra, geometry, calculus, and statistics and their applications. **Education and Training:** Instructional methods and training techniques, including curriculum design principles, learning theory, group and individual teaching techniques, design of individual development plans, and test design principles. **Physics:** Physical principles, laws, and applications, including air, water, material dynamics, light, atomic principles, heat, electric theory, earth formations, and meteorological and related natural phenomena. **Computers and Electronics:** Electric circuit boards, processors, chips, and computer hardware and software, including applications and programming. **English Language:** The structure and content of the English language, including the meaning and spelling of words, rules of composition, and grammar. **Communications and Media:** Media production, communication, and dissemination techniques and methods, including alternative ways to inform and entertain via written, oral, and visual media.

Work Environment: Indoors; more often standing than sitting.

Mathematicians

* Education/Training Required: Doctoral degree
* Annual Earnings: $90,870
* Beginning Wage: $51,240
* Earnings Growth Potential: High
* Growth: 10.2%
* Annual Job Openings: 473
* Self-Employed: 0.0%
* Part-Time: 5.6%

Conduct research in fundamental mathematics or in application of mathematical techniques to science, management, and other fields. Solve or direct solutions to problems in various fields by mathematical methods. Apply mathematical theories and techniques to the solution of practical problems in business, engineering, the sciences, or other fields. Develop computational methods for solving problems that occur in areas of science and engineering or that come from applications in business or industry. Maintain knowledge in the field by reading professional journals, talking with other mathematicians, and attending professional conferences. Perform computations and apply methods of numerical analysis to data. Develop mathematical or statistical models of phenomena to be used for analysis or for computational simulation. Assemble sets of assumptions and explore the consequences of each set. Address the relationships of quantities, magnitudes, and forms through the use of numbers and symbols. Develop new principles and new relationships between existing mathematical principles to advance mathematical science. Design, analyze, and decipher encryption systems designed to transmit military, political, financial, or law-enforcement-related information in code. Conduct research to extend mathematical knowledge in traditional areas, such as algebra, geometry, probability, and logic.

Personality Type: Investigative. These occupations frequently involve working with ideas and require an extensive amount of thinking. They can involve searching for facts and figuring out problems mentally.

GOE—Interest Area/Cluster: 15. Scientific Research, Engineering, and Mathematics. **Work Group:** 15.06. Mathematics and Data Analysis. **Other Jobs in This Work Group:** Actuaries; Mathematical Technicians; Social Science Research Assistants; Statistical Assistants; Statisticians.

Skills—**Programming:** Writing computer programs for various purposes. **Science:** Using scientific methods to solve problems. **Mathematics:** Using mathematics to solve problems. **Complex Problem Solving:** Identifying complex problems, reviewing the options, and implementing solutions. **Operations Analysis:** Analyzing needs and product requirements to create a design. **Reading Comprehension:** Understanding written sentences and paragraphs in work-related documents. **Critical Thinking:** Using logic and analysis to identify the strengths and weaknesses of different approaches. **Active Learning:** Working with new material or information to grasp its implications.

Education and Training Programs: Algebra and Number Theory; Analysis and Functional Analysis; Applied Mathematics; Applied Mathematics, Other; Computational Mathematics; Geometry/Geometric Analysis; Logic; Mathematical Statistics and Probability; Mathematics and Statistics, Other; Mathematics, General; Mathematics, Other; Topology and Foundations. **Related Knowledge/Courses— Mathematics:** Numbers and their operations and interrelationships, including arithmetic, algebra, geometry, calculus, and statistics and their applications. **Physics:** Physical principles, laws, and applications, including air, water, material dynamics, light, atomic principles, heat, electric theory, earth formations, and meteorological and related natural phenomena. **Computers and Electronics:** Electric circuit boards, processors, chips, and computer hardware and software, including applications and programming. **Engineering and Technology:** Equipment, tools, and mechanical devices and their uses to produce motion, light, power, technology, and other applications. **English Language:** The structure and content of the English language, including the meaning and spelling of words, rules of composition, and grammar.

Work Environment: Indoors; sitting.

Meat, Poultry, and Fish Cutters and Trimmers

- ❋ Education/Training Required: Short-term on-the-job training
- ❋ Annual Earnings: $21,050
- ❋ Beginning Wage: $15,780
- ❋ Earnings Growth Potential: Low
- ❋ Growth: 10.9%
- ❋ Annual Job Openings: 17,920
- ❋ Self-Employed: 1.1%
- ❋ Part-Time: 8.3%

Use hand tools to perform routine cutting and trimming of meat, poultry, and fish. Use knives, cleavers, meat saws, band saws, or other equipment to perform meat cutting and trimming. Clean, trim, slice, and section carcasses for future processing. Cut and trim meat to prepare for packing. Remove parts, such as skin, feathers, scales, or bones, from carcass. Inspect meat products for defects, bruises, or blemishes and remove them along with any excess fat. Produce hamburger meat and meat trimmings. Process primal parts into cuts that are ready for retail use. Obtain and distribute specified meat or carcass. Separate meats and byproducts into specified containers and seal containers. Weigh meats and tag containers for weight and contents. Clean and salt hides. Prepare sausages, luncheon meats, hot dogs, and other fabricated meat products, using meat trimmings and hamburger meat. Prepare ready-to-heat foods by filleting meat or fish or cutting it into bite-sized pieces, preparing and adding vegetables or applying sauces or breading.

Personality Type: Realistic. These occupations frequently involve work activities that include practical, hands-on problems and solutions. They often deal with plants; animals; and real-world materials such as wood, tools, and machinery. Many of the occupations require working outside and don't involve a lot of paperwork or working closely with others.

GOE—Interest Area/Cluster: 13. Manufacturing. **Work Group:** 13.03. Production Work, Assorted Materials Processing. **Other Jobs in This Work Group:** Bakers; Cementing and Gluing Machine Operators and Tenders; Chemical Equipment Operators and Tenders; Cleaning, Washing, and Metal Pickling Equipment Operators and Tenders; Coating, Painting, and Spraying Machine Setters, Operators, and Tenders; Cooling and Freezing Equipment Operators and Tenders; Cutting and Slicing Machine Setters,

Operators, and Tenders; Extruding and Forming Machine Setters, Operators, and Tenders, Synthetic and Glass Fibers; Extruding, Forming, Pressing, and Compacting Machine Setters, Operators, and Tenders; Food and Tobacco Roasting, Baking, and Drying Machine Operators and Tenders; Food Batchmakers; Food Cooking Machine Operators and Tenders; Furnace, Kiln, Oven, Drier, and Kettle Operators and Tenders; Heat Treating Equipment Setters, Operators, and Tenders, Metal and Plastic; Helpers—Production Workers; Metal-Refining Furnace Operators and Tenders; Mixing and Blending Machine Setters, Operators, and Tenders; Packaging and Filling Machine Operators and Tenders; Plating and Coating Machine Setters, Operators, and Tenders, Metal and Plastic; Pourers and Casters, Metal; Sawing Machine Setters, Operators, and Tenders, Wood; Separating, Filtering, Clarifying, Precipitating, and Still Machine Setters, Operators, and Tenders; Sewing Machine Operators; Shoe Machine Operators and Tenders; Slaughterers and Meat Packers; Team Assemblers; Textile Bleaching and Dyeing Machine Operators and Tenders; Tire Builders; Woodworking Machine Setters, Operators, and Tenders, Except Sawing.

Skill—None met the criteria.

Education and Training Program: Meat Cutting/Meat Cutter Training. **Related Knowledge/Courses—Food Production:** Techniques and equipment for planting, growing, and harvesting of food for consumption, including crop-rotation methods, animal husbandry, and food storage/handling techniques. **Production and Processing:** Inputs, outputs, raw materials, waste, quality control, costs, and techniques for maximizing the manufacture and distribution of goods. **Mechanical Devices:** Machines and tools, including their designs, uses, benefits, repair, and maintenance.

Work Environment: Indoors; very hot or cold; hazardous equipment; standing; using hands on objects, tools, or controls; repetitive motions.

Mechanical Drafters

- ❋ Education/Training Required: Postsecondary vocational training
- ❋ Annual Earnings: $44,740
- ❋ Beginning Wage: $28,540
- ❋ Earnings Growth Potential: Medium
- ❋ Growth: 5.2%
- ❋ Annual Job Openings: 10,902
- ❋ Self-Employed: 5.5%
- ❋ Part-Time: 5.9%

Prepare detailed working diagrams of machinery and mechanical devices, including dimensions, fastening methods, and other engineering information. Develop detailed design drawings and specifications for mechanical equipment, dies, tools, and controls, using computer-assisted drafting (CAD) equipment. Coordinate with and consult other workers to design, lay out, or detail components and systems and to resolve design or other problems. Review and analyze specifications, sketches, drawings, ideas, and related data to assess factors affecting component designs and the procedures and instructions to be followed. Position instructions and comments onto drawings. Compute mathematical formulas to develop and design detailed specifications for components or machinery, using computer-assisted equipment. Modify and revise designs to correct operating deficiencies or to reduce production problems. Design scale or full-size blueprints of specialty items such as furniture and automobile body or chassis components. Check dimensions of materials to be used and assign numbers to the materials. Lay out and draw schematic, orthographic, or angle views to depict functional relationships of components, assemblies, systems, and machines. Confer with customer representatives to review schematics and answer questions pertaining to installation of systems. Draw freehand sketches of designs, trace finished drawings onto designated paper for the reproduction of blueprints, and reproduce working drawings on copy machines. Supervise and train other drafters, technologists, and technicians. Lay out, draw, and reproduce illustrations for reference manuals and technical publications to describe operation and maintenance of mechanical systems. Shade or color drawings to clarify and emphasize details and dimensions or eliminate background, using ink, crayon, airbrush, and overlays.

Personality Type: Realistic. These occupations frequently involve work activities that include practical, hands-on problems and solutions. They often deal with plants;

animals; and real-world materials such as wood, tools, and machinery. Many of the occupations require working outside and don't involve a lot of paperwork or working closely with others.

GOE—Interest Area/Cluster: 15. Scientific Research, Engineering, and Mathematics. **Work Group:** 15.09. Engineering Technology. **Other Jobs in This Work Group:** Aerospace Engineering and Operations Technicians; Cartographers and Photogrammetrists; Civil Engineering Technicians; Electrical and Electronic Engineering Technicians; Electrical and Electronics Drafters; Electrical Drafters; Electrical Engineering Technicians; Electro-Mechanical Technicians; Electronic Drafters; Electronics Engineering Technicians; Environmental Engineering Technicians; Mapping Technicians; Mechanical Engineering Technicians; Surveying and Mapping Technicians; Surveying Technicians.

Skills—Technology Design: Generating or adapting equipment and technology to serve user needs. **Installation:** Installing equipment, machines, wiring, or programs to meet specifications. **Equipment Selection:** Determining the kind of tools and equipment needed to do a job. **Operations Analysis:** Analyzing needs and product requirements to create a design. **Quality Control Analysis:** Evaluating the quality or performance of products, services, or processes. **Mathematics:** Using mathematics to solve problems. **Repairing:** Repairing machines or systems, using the needed tools. **Science:** Using scientific methods to solve problems.

Education and Training Program: Mechanical Drafting and Mechanical Drafting CAD/CADD. **Related Knowledge/Courses—Design:** Design techniques, principles, tools, and instruments involved in the production and use of precision technical plans, blueprints, drawings, and models. **Engineering and Technology:** Equipment, tools, and mechanical devices and their uses to produce motion, light, power, technology, and other applications. **Building and Construction:** Materials, methods, and the appropriate tools to construct objects, structures, and buildings. **Physics:** Physical principles, laws, and applications, including air, water, material dynamics, light, atomic principles, heat, electric theory, earth formations, and meteorological and related natural phenomena. **Mathematics:** Numbers and their operations and interrelationships, including arithmetic, algebra, geometry, calculus, and statistics and their applications. **English Language:** The structure and content of the English language, including the meaning and spelling of words, rules of composition, and grammar.

Work Environment: Indoors; noisy; sitting; using hands on objects, tools, or controls; repetitive motions.

Mechanical Engineering Technicians

* Education/Training Required: Associate degree
* Annual Earnings: $47,280
* Beginning Wage: $30,960
* Earnings Growth Potential: Low
* Growth: 6.4%
* Annual Job Openings: 3,710
* Self-Employed: 0.8%
* Part-Time: 5.9%

Apply theory and principles of mechanical engineering to modify, develop, and test machinery and equipment under direction of engineering staff or physical scientists. Prepare parts sketches and write work orders and purchase requests to be furnished by outside contractors. Draft detail drawing or sketch for drafting room completion or to request parts fabrication by machine, sheet, or wood shops. Review project instructions and blueprints to ascertain test specifications, procedures, and objectives and test nature of technical problems such as redesign. Review project instructions and specifications to identify, modify, and plan requirements fabrication, assembly, and testing. Devise, fabricate, and assemble new or modified mechanical components for products such as industrial machinery or equipment and measuring instruments. Discuss changes in design, method of manufacture and assembly, and drafting techniques and procedures with staff and coordinate corrections. Set up and conduct tests of complete units and components under operational conditions to investigate proposals for improving equipment performance. Inspect lines and figures for clarity and return erroneous drawings to designer for correction. Analyze test results in relation to design or rated specifications and test objectives and modify or adjust equipment to meet specifications. Evaluate tool drawing designs by measuring drawing dimensions and comparing with original specifications for form and function, using engineering skills. Confer with technicians and submit reports of test results to engineering department and recommend design or material changes. Calculate required capacities for equipment of proposed system to obtain specified performance and submit data to engineering personnel for approval. Record test procedures and results, numerical and graphical data, and recommendations for changes in product or test methods. Read dials and meters to determine amperage, voltage, and electrical output and input at specific operating temperature to analyze parts performance. Estimate cost factors, including labor and material, for purchased and fabricated parts and costs for assembly, testing, or installing. Set up prototype and test apparatus and operate test-controlling equipment to observe and record prototype test results.

Personality Type: Realistic. These occupations frequently involve work activities that include practical, hands-on problems and solutions. They often deal with plants; animals; and real-world materials such as wood, tools, and machinery. Many of the occupations require working outside and don't involve a lot of paperwork or working closely with others.

GOE—Interest Area/Cluster: 15. Scientific Research, Engineering, and Mathematics. **Work Group:** 15.09. Engineering Technology. **Other Jobs in This Work Group:** Aerospace Engineering and Operations Technicians; Cartographers and Photogrammetrists; Civil Engineering Technicians; Electrical and Electronic Engineering Technicians; Electrical and Electronics Drafters; Electrical Drafters; Electrical Engineering Technicians; Electro-Mechanical Technicians; Electronic Drafters; Electronics Engineering Technicians; Environmental Engineering Technicians; Mapping Technicians; Mechanical Drafters; Surveying and Mapping Technicians; Surveying Technicians.

Skills—Installation: Installing equipment, machines, wiring, or programs to meet specifications. **Troubleshooting:** Determining what is causing an operating error and deciding what to do about it. **Technology Design:** Generating or adapting equipment and technology to serve user needs. **Operations Analysis:** Analyzing needs and product requirements to create a design. **Equipment Selection:** Determining the kind of tools and equipment needed to do a job. **Science:** Using scientific methods to solve problems. **Mathematics:** Using mathematics to solve problems. **Systems Evaluation:** Looking at many indicators of system performance and taking into account their accuracy.

Education and Training Programs: Mechanical Engineering Related Technologies/Technician Training, Other; Mechanical Engineering/Mechanical Technology/Technician Training. **Related Knowledge/Courses—Engineering and Technology:** Equipment, tools, and mechanical devices and their uses to produce motion, light, power, technology, and other applications. **Design:** Design techniques,

principles, tools, and instruments involved in the production and use of precision technical plans, blueprints, drawings, and models. **Mechanical Devices:** Machines and tools, including their designs, uses, benefits, repair, and maintenance. **Physics:** Physical principles, laws, and applications, including air, water, material dynamics, light, atomic principles, heat, electric theory, earth formations, and meteorological and related natural phenomena. **Chemistry:** The composition, structure, and properties of substances and of the chemical processes and transformations that they undergo. This includes uses of chemicals and their interactions, danger signs, production techniques, and disposal methods. **Production and Processing:** Inputs, outputs, raw materials, waste, quality control, costs, and techniques for maximizing the manufacture and distribution of goods.

Work Environment: Indoors; noisy; contaminants; hazardous equipment; sitting.

Mechanical Engineers

- ❀ Education/Training Required: Bachelor's degree
- ❀ Annual Earnings: $72,300
- ❀ Beginning Wage: $46,560
- ❀ Earnings Growth Potential: Medium
- ❀ Growth: 4.2%
- ❀ Annual Job Openings: 12,394
- ❀ Self-Employed: 2.2%
- ❀ Part-Time: 1.9%

Perform engineering duties in planning and designing tools, engines, machines, and other mechanically functioning equipment. Oversee installation, operation, maintenance, and repair of such equipment as centralized heat, gas, water, and steam systems. Read and interpret blueprints, technical drawings, schematics, and computer-generated reports. Confer with engineers and other personnel to implement operating procedures, resolve system malfunctions, and provide technical information. Research and analyze customer design proposals, specifications, manuals, and other data to evaluate the feasibility, cost, and maintenance requirements of designs or applications. Specify system components or direct modification of products to ensure conformance with engineering design and performance specifications. Research, design, evaluate, install, operate, and maintain mechanical products, equipment, systems, and processes to meet requirements, applying knowledge of engineering principles. Investigate equipment failures and difficulties to diagnose faulty operation and to make recommendations to maintenance crew. Assist drafters in developing the structural design of products, using drafting tools or computer-assisted design (CAD) or drafting equipment and software. Provide feedback to design engineers on customer problems and needs. Oversee installation, operation, maintenance, and repair to ensure that machines and equipment are installed and functioning according to specifications. Conduct research that tests and analyzes the feasibility, design, operation, and performance of equipment, components, and systems. Recommend design modifications to eliminate machine or system malfunctions. Develop and test models of alternate designs and processing methods to assess feasibility, operating condition effects, possible new applications, and necessity of modification. Develop, coordinate, and monitor all aspects of production, including selection of manufacturing methods, fabrication, and operation of product designs. Estimate costs and submit bids for engineering, construction, or extraction projects and prepare contract documents. Perform personnel functions such as supervision of production workers, technicians, technologists, and other engineers or design of evaluation programs. Solicit new business and provide technical customer service. Establish and coordinate the maintenance and safety procedures, service schedule, and supply of materials required to maintain machines and equipment in the prescribed condition.

Personality Type: Investigative. These occupations frequently involve working with ideas and require an extensive amount of thinking. They can involve searching for facts and figuring out problems mentally.

GOE—Interest Area/Cluster: 15. Scientific Research, Engineering, and Mathematics. **Work Group:** 15.07. Research and Design Engineering. **Other Jobs in This Work Group:** Aerospace Engineers; Biomedical Engineers; Chemical Engineers; Civil Engineers; Computer Hardware Engineers; Electrical Engineers; Electronics Engineers, Except Computer; Marine Architects; Marine Engineers; Marine Engineers and Naval Architects; Materials Engineers; Nuclear Engineers.

Skills—Science: Using scientific methods to solve problems. **Operations Analysis:** Analyzing needs and product requirements to create a design. **Installation:** Installing equipment, machines, wiring, or programs to meet specifications. **Complex Problem Solving:** Identifying complex problems, reviewing the options, and implementing solutions. **Mathematics:** Using mathematics to solve problems. **Systems Analysis:** Determining how a system should work

and how changes will affect outcomes. **Judgment and Decision Making:** Weighing the relative costs and benefits of a potential action. **Coordination:** Adjusting actions in relation to others' actions.

Education and Training Program: Mechanical Engineering. **Related Knowledge/Courses—Design:** Design techniques, principles, tools, and instruments involved in the production and use of precision technical plans, blueprints, drawings, and models. **Engineering and Technology:** Equipment, tools, and mechanical devices and their uses to produce motion, light, power, technology, and other applications. **Mechanical Devices:** Machines and tools, including their designs, uses, benefits, repair, and maintenance. **Production and Processing:** Inputs, outputs, raw materials, waste, quality control, costs, and techniques for maximizing the manufacture and distribution of goods. **Physics:** Physical principles, laws, and applications, including air, water, material dynamics, light, atomic principles, heat, electric theory, earth formations, and meteorological and related natural phenomena. **Administration and Management:** Principles and processes involved in business and organizational planning, coordination, and execution. This includes strategic planning, resource allocation, manpower modeling, leadership techniques, and production methods.

Work Environment: Indoors; sitting.

Medical and Clinical Laboratory Technicians

- ❋ Education/Training Required: Associate degree
- ❋ Annual Earnings: $34,270
- ❋ Beginning Wage: $22,670
- ❋ Earnings Growth Potential: Low
- ❋ Growth: 15.0%
- ❋ Annual Job Openings: 10,866
- ❋ Self-Employed: 0.7%
- ❋ Part-Time: 14.3%

Perform routine medical laboratory tests for the diagnosis, treatment, and prevention of disease. May work under the supervision of a medical technologist. Conduct chemical analyses of bodily fluids, such as blood and urine, using microscope or automatic analyzer to detect abnormalities or diseases, and enter findings into computer. Set up, adjust, maintain, and clean medical laboratory equipment. Analyze the results of tests and experiments to ensure conformity to specifications, using special mechanical and electrical devices. Analyze and record test data to issue reports that use charts, graphs and narratives. Conduct blood tests for transfusion purposes and perform blood counts. Perform medical research to further control and cure disease. Obtain specimens, cultivating, isolating, and identifying microorganisms for analysis. Examine cells stained with dye to locate abnormalities. Collect blood or tissue samples from patients, observing principles of asepsis to obtain blood sample. Consult with a pathologist to determine a final diagnosis when abnormal cells are found. Inoculate fertilized eggs, broths, or other bacteriological media with organisms. Cut, stain, and mount tissue samples for examination by pathologists. Supervise and instruct other technicians and laboratory assistants. Prepare standard volumetric solutions and reagents to be combined with samples, following standardized formulas or experimental procedures. Prepare vaccines and serums by standard laboratory methods, testing for virus inactivity and sterility. Test raw materials, processes, and finished products to determine quality and quantity of materials or characteristics of a substance.

Personality Type: Realistic. These occupations frequently involve work activities that include practical, hands-on problems and solutions. They often deal with plants; animals; and real-world materials such as wood, tools, and machinery. Many of the occupations require working outside and don't involve a lot of paperwork or working closely with others.

GOE—Interest Area/Cluster: 08. Health Science. **Work Group:** 08.06. Medical Technology. **Other Jobs in This Work Group:** Biological Technicians; Cardiovascular Technologists and Technicians; Diagnostic Medical Sonographers; Medical and Clinical Laboratory Technologists; Medical Equipment Preparers; Medical Records and Health Information Technicians; Nuclear Medicine Technologists; Opticians, Dispensing; Orthotists and Prosthetists; Radiologic Technicians; Radiologic Technologists; Radiologic Technologists and Technicians.

Skills—Science: Using scientific methods to solve problems. **Equipment Maintenance:** Performing routine maintenance and determining when and what kind of maintenance is needed. **Troubleshooting:** Determining what is causing an operating error and deciding what to do about it. **Quality Control Analysis:** Evaluating the quality or performance of products, services, or processes. **Operation Monitoring:** Watching gauges, dials, or other indicators to make sure a machine is working properly. **Operation and Control:** Controlling operations of equipment or systems. **Monitoring:** Assessing how well one is doing when learning or doing something. **Installation:** Installing equipment, machines, wiring, or programs to meet specifications.

Education and Training Programs: Blood Bank Technology Specialist Training; Clinical/Medical Laboratory Assistant Training; Clinical/Medical Laboratory Technician Training; Hematology Technology/Technician Training; Histologic Technician Training. **Related Knowledge/Courses—Medicine and Dentistry:** The information and techniques needed to diagnose and treat injuries, diseases, and deformities. This includes symptoms, treatment alternatives, drug properties and interactions, and preventive healthcare measures. **Therapy and Counseling:** Information and techniques needed to rehabilitate physical and mental ailments and to provide career guidance, including alternative treatments, rehabilitation equipment and its proper use, and methods to evaluate treatment effects. **Biology:** Plant and animal living tissue, cells, organisms, and entities, including their functions, interdependencies, and interactions with each other and the environment. **Clerical Practices:** Administrative and clerical procedures and systems such as word-processing systems, filing and records management systems, stenography and transcription, forms, design principles, and other office procedures and terminology.

Work Environment: Indoors; disease or infections; standing; walking and running; using hands on objects, tools, or controls.

Medical and Clinical Laboratory Technologists

* Education/Training Required: Bachelor's degree
* Annual Earnings: $51,720
* Beginning Wage: $35,460
* Earnings Growth Potential: Low
* Growth: 12.4%
* Annual Job Openings: 11,457
* Self-Employed: 0.7%
* Part-Time: 14.3%

Perform complex medical laboratory tests for diagnosis, treatment, and prevention of disease. May train or supervise staff. Conduct chemical analysis of bodily fluids, including blood, urine, and spinal fluid, to determine presence of normal and abnormal components. Analyze laboratory findings to check the accuracy of the results. Enter data from analysis of medical tests and clinical results into computer for storage. Operate, calibrate, and maintain equipment used in quantitative and qualitative analysis, such as spectrophotometers, calorimeters, flame photometers, and computer-controlled analyzers. Establish and monitor quality assurance programs and activities to ensure the accuracy of laboratory results. Set up, clean, and maintain laboratory equipment. Provide technical information about test results to physicians, family members, and researchers. Supervise, train, and direct lab assistants, medical and clinical laboratory technicians and technologists, and other medical laboratory workers engaged in laboratory testing. Collect and study blood samples to determine the number of cells, their morphology, or their blood group, blood type, and compatibility for transfusion purposes, using microscopic techniques. Analyze samples of biological material for chemical content or reaction. Cultivate, isolate, and assist in identifying microbial organisms, and perform various tests on these microorganisms. Obtain, cut, stain, and mount biological material on slides for microscopic study and diagnosis, following standard laboratory procedures. Select and prepare specimen and media for cell culture, using aseptic technique and knowledge of medium components and cell requirements. Develop, standardize, evaluate, and modify procedures, techniques, and tests used in the analysis of specimens and in medical laboratory experiments. Harvest cell cultures at optimum time based on knowledge of cell cycle differences and culture conditions. Conduct medical research under direction of microbiologist or biochemist.

Personality Type: Investigative. These occupations frequently involve working with ideas and require an extensive amount of thinking. They can involve searching for facts and figuring out problems mentally.

GOE—Interest Area/Cluster: 08. Health Science. **Work Group:** 08.06. Medical Technology. **Other Jobs in This Work Group:** Biological Technicians; Cardiovascular Technologists and Technicians; Diagnostic Medical Sonographers; Medical and Clinical Laboratory Technicians; Medical Equipment Preparers; Medical Records and Health Information Technicians; Nuclear Medicine Technologists; Opticians, Dispensing; Orthotists and Prosthetists; Radiologic Technicians; Radiologic Technologists; Radiologic Technologists and Technicians.

Skills—Operation Monitoring: Watching gauges, dials, or other indicators to make sure a machine is working properly. **Management of Personnel Resources:** Motivating, developing, and directing people as they work; identifying the best people for the job. **Quality Control Analysis:** Evaluating the quality or performance of products, services, or processes.

Education and Training Programs: Clinical Laboratory Science/Medical Technology/Technologist Training; Clinical/Medical Laboratory Science and Allied Professions, Other; Cytogenetics/Genetics/Clinical Genetics Technology/Technologist Training; Cytotechnology/Cytotechnologist Training; Histologic Technology/Histotechnologist Training; Renal/Dialysis Technologist/Technician Training. **Related Knowledge/Courses—Biology:** Plant and animal living tissue, cells, organisms, and entities, including their functions, interdependencies, and interactions with each other and the environment. **Chemistry:** The composition, structure, and properties of substances and of the chemical processes and transformations that they undergo. This includes uses of chemicals and their interactions, danger signs, production techniques, and disposal methods. **Medicine and Dentistry:** The information and techniques needed to diagnose and treat injuries, diseases, and deformities. This includes symptoms, treatment alternatives, drug properties and interactions, and preventive health-care measures. **Mechanical Devices:** Machines and tools, including their designs, uses, benefits, repair, and maintenance. **Clerical Practices:** Administrative and clerical procedures and systems such as word-processing systems, filing and records management systems, stenography and transcription, forms, design principles, and other office procedures and terminology. **Mathematics:** Numbers and their operations and interrelationships, including arithmetic, algebra, geometry, calculus, and statistics and their applications.

Work Environment: Indoors; noisy; contaminants; disease or infections; standing; using hands on objects, tools, or controls.

Medical and Health Services Managers

❋ Education/Training Required: Work experience plus degree
❋ Annual Earnings: $76,990
❋ Beginning Wage: $46,860
❋ Earnings Growth Potential: Medium
❋ Growth: 16.4%
❋ Annual Job Openings: 31,877
❋ Self-Employed: 8.2%
❋ Part-Time: 5.5%

Plan, direct, or coordinate medicine and health services in hospitals, clinics, managed care organizations, public health agencies, or similar organizations. Conduct and administer fiscal operations, including accounting, planning budgets, authorizing expenditures, establishing rates for services, and coordinating financial reporting. Direct, supervise, and evaluate work activities of medical, nursing, technical, clerical, service, maintenance, and other personnel. Maintain communication between governing boards, medical staff, and department heads by attending board meetings and coordinating interdepartmental functioning. Review and analyze facility activities and data to aid planning and cash and risk management and to improve service utilization. Plan, implement, and administer programs and services in a health-care or medical facility, including personnel administration, training, and coordination of medical, nursing, and physical plant staff. Direct or conduct recruitment, hiring, and training of personnel. Establish work schedules and assignments for staff, according to workload, space, and equipment availability. Maintain awareness of advances in medicine, computerized diagnostic and treatment equipment, data processing technology, government regulations, health insurance changes, and financing options. Monitor the use of diagnostic services, inpatient beds, facilities, and staff to ensure effective use of resources and assess the need

for additional staff, equipment, and services. Develop and maintain computerized record management systems to store and process data such as personnel activities and information and to produce reports. Establish objectives and evaluative or operational criteria for units they manage. Prepare activity reports to inform management of the status and implementation plans of programs, services, and quality initiatives. Inspect facilities and recommend building or equipment modifications to ensure emergency readiness and compliance to access, safety, and sanitation regulations. Develop and implement organizational policies and procedures for the facility or medical unit. Manage change in integrated health-care delivery systems such as work restructuring, technological innovations, and shifts in the focus of care.

Personality Type: Enterprising. These occupations frequently involve starting up and carrying out projects and can involve leading people and making many decisions. They sometimes require risk taking and often deal with business.

GOE—Interest Area/Cluster: 08. Health Science. **Work Group:** 08.01. Managerial Work in Medical and Health Services. **Other Jobs in This Work Group:** Coroners.

Skills—Management of Financial Resources: Determining how money will be spent to get the work done and accounting for these expenditures. **Management of Personnel Resources:** Motivating, developing, and directing people as they work; identifying the best people for the job. **Systems Analysis:** Determining how a system should work and how changes will affect outcomes. **Systems Evaluation:** Looking at many indicators of system performance and taking into account their accuracy. **Management of Material Resources:** Obtaining and seeing to the appropriate use of equipment, facilities, and materials needed to do certain work. **Negotiation:** Bringing others together and trying to reconcile differences. **Persuasion:** Persuading others to approach things differently. **Monitoring:** Assessing how well one is doing when learning or doing something.

Education and Training Programs: Community Health and Preventive Medicine; Health and Medical Administrative Services, Other; Health Information/Medical Records Administration/Administrator Training; Health Services Administration; Health Unit Manager/Ward Supervisor Training; Health/Health Care Administration/Management; Hospital and Health Care Facilities Administration/Management; Medical Staff Services Technology/Technician Training; Nursing Administration (MSN, MS, PhD);

Public Health, General (MPH, DPH). **Related Knowledge/Courses—Economics and Accounting:** Economic and accounting principles and practices, the financial markets, banking, and the analysis and reporting of financial data. **Personnel and Human Resources:** Principles and procedures for personnel recruitment; selection; training; compensation and benefits; labor relations and negotiation; and personnel information systems. **Administration and Management:** Principles and processes involved in business and organizational planning, coordination, and execution. This includes strategic planning, resource allocation, manpower modeling, leadership techniques, and production methods. **Sales and Marketing:** Principles and methods involved in showing, promoting, and selling products or services. This includes marketing strategies and tactics, product demonstration and sales techniques, and sales control systems. **Medicine and Dentistry:** The information and techniques needed to diagnose and treat injuries, diseases, and deformities. This includes symptoms, treatment alternatives, drug properties and interactions, and preventive health-care measures. **Law and Government:** Laws, legal codes, court procedures, precedents, government regulations, executive orders, agency rules, and the democratic political process.

Work Environment: Indoors; disease or infections; sitting.

Medical and Public Health Social Workers

- ❋ Education/Training Required: Bachelor's degree
- ❋ Annual Earnings: $44,670
- ❋ Beginning Wage: $28,160
- ❋ Earnings Growth Potential: Medium
- ❋ Growth: 24.2%
- ❋ Annual Job Openings: 16,429
- ❋ Self-Employed: 2.6%
- ❋ Part-Time: 9.4%

Provide persons, families, or vulnerable populations with the psychosocial support needed to cope with chronic, acute, or terminal illnesses such as Alzheimer's, cancer, or AIDS. Services include advising family caregivers, providing patient education and counseling, and making necessary referrals for other social services. Advocate for clients or patients to resolve crises. Collaborate with other professionals to evaluate patients' medical or physical condition and to assess client needs. Refer patients, clients, or families to community resources to assist in recovery from mental or physical illnesses and to provide access to services such as financial assistance, legal aid, housing, job placement, or education. Counsel clients and patients in individual and group sessions to help them overcome dependencies, recover from illnesses, and adjust to life. Use consultation data and social work experience to plan and coordinate client or patient care and rehabilitation, following through to ensure service efficacy. Plan discharge from care facility to home or other care facility. Organize support groups or counsel family members to assist them in understanding, dealing with, and supporting clients or patients. Modify treatment plans to comply with changes in clients' statuses. Monitor, evaluate, and record client progress according to measurable goals described in treatment and care plans. Identify environmental impediments to client or patient progress through interviews and review of patient records. Supervise and direct other workers providing services to clients or patients. Develop or advise on social policy and assist in community development. Investigate child abuse or neglect cases and take authorized protective action when necessary. Oversee Medicaid- and Medicare-related paperwork and recordkeeping in hospitals. Plan and conduct programs to combat social problems, prevent substance abuse, or improve community health and counseling services. Conduct social research to advance knowledge in the social work field.

Personality Type: Social. These occupations frequently involve working with, communicating with, and teaching people and often involve helping or providing service to others.

GOE—Interest Area/Cluster: 10. Human Service. **Work Group:** 10.01. Counseling and Social Work. **Other Jobs in This Work Group:** Child, Family, and School Social Workers; Clinical Psychologists; Clinical, Counseling, and School Psychologists; Counseling Psychologists; Marriage and Family Therapists; Mental Health and Substance Abuse Social Workers; Mental Health Counselors; Probation Officers and Correctional Treatment Specialists; Rehabilitation Counselors; Residential Advisors; Social and Human Service Assistants; Substance Abuse and Behavioral Disorder Counselors.

Skills—Social Perceptiveness: Being aware of others' reactions and understanding why they react the way they do. **Systems Evaluation:** Looking at many indicators of system performance and taking into account their accuracy. **Service Orientation:** Actively looking for ways to help people. **Systems Analysis:** Determining how a system should work and how changes will affect outcomes. **Negotiation:** Bringing others together and trying to reconcile differences. **Speaking:** Talking to others to effectively convey information. **Writing:** Communicating effectively with others in writing as indicated by the needs of the audience.

Education and Training Program: Clinical/Medical Social Work. **Related Knowledge/Courses—Therapy and Counseling:** Information and techniques needed to rehabilitate physical and mental ailments and to provide career guidance, including alternative treatments, rehabilitation equipment and its proper use, and methods to evaluate treatment effects. **Sociology and Anthropology:** Group behavior and dynamics; societal trends and influences; and cultures and their history, migrations, ethnicity, and origins. **Psychology:** Human behavior and performance, mental processes, psychological research methods, and the assessment and treatment of behavioral and affective disorders. **Philosophy and Theology:** Different philosophical systems and religions, including their basic principles, values, ethics, ways of thinking, customs, and practices and their impact on human culture. **Customer and Personal Service:** Principles and processes for providing customer and personal services, including needs assessment techniques, quality service standards, alternative delivery systems, and customer satisfaction evaluation techniques. **Medicine and Dentistry:** The information and techniques needed to diagnose and treat injuries, diseases, and deformities. This includes symptoms, treatment alternatives, drug properties and interactions, and preventive health-care measures.

Work Environment: Indoors; noisy; disease or infections; sitting.

Medical Assistants

- ❋ Education/Training Required: Moderate-term on-the-job training
- ❋ Annual Earnings: $27,430
- ❋ Beginning Wage: $19,850
- ❋ Earnings Growth Potential: Low
- ❋ Growth: 35.4%
- ❋ Annual Job Openings: 92,977
- ❋ Self-Employed: 0.0%
- ❋ Part-Time: 23.2%

Perform administrative and certain clinical duties under the direction of physicians. Administrative duties may include scheduling appointments, maintaining medical records, billing, and coding for insurance purposes. Clinical duties may include taking and recording vital signs and medical histories, preparing patients for examination, drawing blood, and administering medications as directed by physician. Record patients' medical history, vital statistics, and information such as test results in medical records. Prepare treatment rooms for patient examinations, keeping the rooms neat and clean. Interview patients to obtain medical information and measure their vital signs, weights, and heights. Authorize drug refills and provide prescription information to pharmacies. Clean and sterilize instruments and dispose of contaminated supplies. Prepare and administer medications as directed by a physician. Show patients to examination rooms and prepare them for the physician. Explain treatment procedures, medications, diets, and physicians' instructions to patients. Help physicians examine and treat patients, handing them instruments and materials or performing such tasks as giving injections or removing sutures. Collect blood, tissue, or other laboratory specimens; log the specimens; and prepare them for testing. Perform routine laboratory tests and sample analyses. Contact medical facilities or departments to schedule patients for tests or admission. Operate X-ray, electrocardiogram (EKG), and other equipment to administer routine diagnostic tests. Change dressings on wounds. Set up medical laboratory equipment. Perform general office duties such as answering telephones, taking dictation, or completing insurance forms. Greet and log in patients arriving at office or clinic. Schedule appointments for patients. Inventory and order medical, lab, or office supplies and equipment. Keep financial records and perform other bookkeeping duties such as handling credit and collections and mailing monthly statements to patients.

Personality Type: Social. These occupations frequently involve working with, communicating with, and teaching people and often involve helping or providing service to others.

GOE—Interest Area/Cluster: 08. Health Science. **Work Group:** 08.02. Medicine and Surgery. **Other Jobs in This Work Group:** Anesthesiologists; Family and General Practitioners; Internists, General; Medical Transcriptionists; Obstetricians and Gynecologists; Pediatricians, General; Pharmacists; Pharmacy Aides; Pharmacy Technicians; Physician Assistants; Psychiatrists; Registered Nurses; Surgeons; Surgical Technologists.

Skill—Systems Analysis: Determining how a system should work and how changes will affect outcomes.

Education and Training Programs: Allied Health and Medical Assisting Services, Other; Anesthesiologist Assistant Training; Chiropractic Assistant/Technician Training; Medical Administrative/Executive Assistant and Medical Secretary Training; Medical Insurance Coding Specialist/Coder Training; Medical Office Assistant/Specialist Training; Medical Office Management/Administration; Medical Reception/Receptionist Training; Medical/Clinical Assistant Training; Opthalmic Technician/Technologist Training; Optomeric Technician/Assistant Training; Orthoptics/Orthoptist Training. **Related Knowledge/Courses—Medicine and Dentistry:** The information and techniques needed to diagnose and treat injuries, diseases, and deformities. This includes symptoms, treatment alternatives, drug properties and interactions, and preventive health-care measures. **Clerical Practices:** Administrative and clerical procedures and systems such as word-processing systems, filing and records management systems, stenography and transcription, forms, design principles, and other office procedures and terminology. **Psychology:** Human behavior and performance, mental processes, psychological research methods, and the assessment and treatment of behavioral and affective disorders. **Therapy and Counseling:** Information and techniques needed to rehabilitate physical and mental ailments and to provide career guidance, including alternative treatments, rehabilitation equipment and its proper use, and methods to evaluate treatment effects. **Customer and Personal Service:** Principles and processes for providing customer and personal services, including needs assessment techniques, quality service standards, alternative delivery systems, and customer satisfaction evaluation techniques. **Public Safety and Security:** Weaponry; public safety; security operations, rules, regulations, precautions, and prevention; and the protection of people, data, and property.

Work Environment: Indoors; disease or infections; standing; walking and running; using hands on objects, tools, or controls; repetitive motions.

Medical Equipment Preparers

* Education/Training Required: Short-term on-the-job training
* Annual Earnings: $27,040
* Beginning Wage: $19,490
* Earnings Growth Potential: Low
* Growth: 14.2%
* Annual Job Openings: 8,363
* Self-Employed: 2.8%
* Part-Time: 23.2%

Prepare, sterilize, install, or clean laboratory or health-care equipment. May perform routine laboratory tasks and operate or inspect equipment. Organize and assemble routine and specialty surgical instrument trays and other sterilized supplies, filling special requests as needed. Clean instruments to prepare them for sterilization. Operate and maintain steam autoclaves, keeping records of loads completed, items in loads, and maintenance procedures performed. Record sterilizer test results. Disinfect and sterilize equipment such as respirators, hospital beds, and oxygen and dialysis equipment, using sterilizers, aerators, and washers. Start equipment and observe gauges and equipment operation to detect malfunctions and to ensure equipment is operating to prescribed standards. Examine equipment to detect leaks, worn or loose parts, or other indications of disrepair. Report defective equipment to appropriate supervisors or staff. Check sterile supplies to ensure that they are not outdated. Maintain records of inventory and equipment usage. Attend hospital in-service programs related to areas of work specialization. Purge wastes from equipment by connecting equipment to water sources and flushing water through systems. Deliver equipment to specified hospital locations or to patients' residences. Assist hospital staff with patient care duties such as providing transportation or setting up traction. Install and set up medical equipment, using hand tools.

Personality Type: Realistic. These occupations frequently involve work activities that include practical, hands-on problems and solutions. They often deal with plants; animals; and real-world materials such as wood, tools, and machinery. Many of the occupations require working outside and don't involve a lot of paperwork or working closely with others.

GOE—**Interest Area/Cluster:** 08. Health Science. **Work Group:** 08.06. Medical Technology. **Other Jobs in This Work Group:** Biological Technicians; Cardiovascular Technologists and Technicians; Diagnostic Medical Sonographers; Medical and Clinical Laboratory Technicians; Medical and Clinical Laboratory Technologists; Medical Records and Health Information Technicians; Nuclear Medicine Technologists; Opticians, Dispensing; Orthotists and Prosthetists; Radiologic Technicians; Radiologic Technologists; Radiologic Technologists and Technicians.

Skills—Operation Monitoring: Watching gauges, dials, or other indicators to make sure a machine is working properly. **Equipment Maintenance:** Performing routine maintenance and determining when and what kind of maintenance is needed. **Management of Material Resources:** Obtaining and seeing to the appropriate use of equipment, facilities, and materials needed to do certain work. **Quality Control Analysis:** Evaluating the quality or performance of products, services, or processes. **Operation and Control:** Controlling operations of equipment or systems. **Service Orientation:** Actively looking for ways to help people. **Monitoring:** Assessing how well one is doing when learning or doing something. **Science:** Using scientific methods to solve problems.

Education and Training Programs: Allied Health and Medical Assisting Services, Other; Medical/Clinical Assistant Training. **Related Knowledge/Courses—Chemistry:** The composition, structure, and properties of substances and of the chemical processes and transformations that they undergo. This includes uses of chemicals and their interactions, danger signs, production techniques, and disposal methods. **Biology:** Plant and animal living tissue, cells, organisms, and entities, including their functions, interdependencies, and interactions with each other and the environment. **Medicine and Dentistry:** The information and techniques needed to diagnose and treat injuries, diseases, and deformities. This includes symptoms, treatment alternatives, drug properties and interactions, and preventive health-care measures. **Production and Processing:** Inputs, outputs, raw materials, waste, quality control, costs, and techniques for maximizing the manufacture and distribution of goods. **Education and Training:** Instructional methods and training techniques, including curriculum design principles, learning theory, group and individual teaching techniques, design of individual development plans, and test design principles. **Customer and Personal Service:** Principles and processes for providing customer and personal services, including needs assessment techniques, quality service

standards, alternative delivery systems, and customer satisfaction evaluation techniques.

Work Environment: Indoors; contaminants; disease or infections; standing; using hands on objects, tools, or controls; repetitive motions.

Medical Equipment Repairers

* Education/Training Required: Associate degree
* Annual Earnings: $40,320
* Beginning Wage: $24,680
* Earnings Growth Potential: Medium
* Growth: 21.7%
* Annual Job Openings: 2,351
* Self-Employed: 14.0%
* Part-Time: 10.1%

Test, adjust, or repair biomedical or electromedical equipment. Inspect and test malfunctioning medical and related equipment following manufacturers' specifications, using test and analysis instruments. Examine medical equipment and facility's structural environment and check for proper use of equipment to protect patients and staff from electrical or mechanical hazards and to ensure compliance with safety regulations. Disassemble malfunctioning equipment and remove, repair, and replace defective parts such as motors, clutches, or transformers. Keep records of maintenance, repair, and required updates of equipment. Perform preventive maintenance or service such as cleaning, lubricating, and adjusting equipment. Test and calibrate components and equipment, following manufacturers' manuals and troubleshooting techniques and using hand tools, power tools, and measuring devices. Explain and demonstrate correct operation and preventive maintenance of medical equipment to personnel. Study technical manuals and attend training sessions provided by equipment manufacturers to maintain current knowledge. Plan and carry out work assignments, using blueprints, schematic drawings, technical manuals, wiring diagrams, and liquid and air flow sheets, following prescribed regulations, directives, and other instructions as required. Solder loose connections, using soldering iron. Test, evaluate, and classify excess or in-use medical equipment and determine serviceability, condition, and disposition in accordance with regulations. Research catalogs and repair part lists to locate sources for repair parts, requisitioning parts and recording their receipt. Evaluate technical specifications to identify equipment and systems best suited for intended use and possible purchase based on specifications, user needs, and technical requirements. Contribute expertise to develop medical maintenance standard operating procedures. Compute power and space requirements for installing medical, dental, or related equipment and install units to manufacturers' specifications. Supervise and advise subordinate personnel. Repair shop equipment, metal furniture, and hospital equipment, including welding broken parts and replacing missing parts, or bring item into local shop for major repairs.

Personality Type: Realistic. These occupations frequently involve work activities that include practical, hands-on problems and solutions. They often deal with plants; animals; and real-world materials such as wood, tools, and machinery. Many of the occupations require working outside and don't involve a lot of paperwork or working closely with others.

GOE—Interest Area/Cluster: 13. Manufacturing. **Work Group:** 13.15. Medical and Technical Equipment Repair. **Other Jobs in This Work Group:** Camera and Photographic Equipment Repairers; Watch Repairers.

Skills—Repairing: Repairing machines or systems, using the needed tools. **Installation:** Installing equipment, machines, wiring, or programs to meet specifications. **Equipment Maintenance:** Performing routine maintenance and determining when and what kind of maintenance is needed. **Troubleshooting:** Determining what is causing an operating error and deciding what to do about it. **Science:** Using scientific methods to solve problems. **Operation Monitoring:** Watching gauges, dials, or other indicators to make sure a machine is working properly. **Systems Analysis:** Determining how a system should work and how changes will affect outcomes. **Quality Control Analysis:** Evaluating the quality or performance of products, services, or processes.

Education and Training Program: Biomedical Technology/Technician Training. **Related Knowledge/Courses—Mechanical Devices:** Machines and tools, including their designs, uses, benefits, repair, and maintenance. **Computers and Electronics:** Electric circuit boards, processors, chips, and computer hardware and software, including applications and programming. **Engineering and Technology:** Equipment, tools, and mechanical devices and their uses to produce motion, light, power, technology, and other applications. **Physics:** Physical principles, laws, and applications, including air, water, material dynamics, light, atomic principles, heat, electric theory, earth formations, and meteorological and related natural phenomena. **Telecommunications:**

Transmission, broadcasting, switching, control, and operation of telecommunications systems. **Medicine and Dentistry:** The information and techniques needed to diagnose and treat injuries, diseases, and deformities. This includes symptoms, treatment alternatives, drug properties and interactions, and preventive health-care measures.

Work Environment: Indoors; contaminants; disease or infections; standing; using hands on objects, tools, or controls.

Medical Records and Health Information Technicians

- ❋ Education/Training Required: Associate degree
- ❋ Annual Earnings: $29,290
- ❋ Beginning Wage: $19,690
- ❋ Earnings Growth Potential: Low
- ❋ Growth: 17.8%
- ❋ Annual Job Openings: 39,048
- ❋ Self-Employed: 0.2%
- ❋ Part-Time: 12.5%

Compile, process, and maintain medical records of hospital and clinic patients in a manner consistent with medical, administrative, ethical, legal, and regulatory requirements of the health care system. Process, maintain, compile, and report patient information for health requirements and standards. Protect the security of medical records to ensure that confidentiality is maintained. Review records for completeness, accuracy, and compliance with regulations. Retrieve patient medical records for physicians, technicians, or other medical personnel. Release information to persons and agencies according to regulations. Plan, develop, maintain, and operate a variety of health record indexes and storage and retrieval systems to collect, classify, store, and analyze information. Enter data such as demographic characteristics, history and extent of disease, diagnostic procedures, and treatment into computer. Process and prepare business and government forms. Compile and maintain patients' medical records to document condition and treatment and to provide data for research or cost control and care improvement efforts. Process patient admission and discharge documents. Assign the patient to diagnosis-related groups (DRGs), using appropriate computer software. Transcribe medical reports. Identify, compile, abstract, and code patient data, using standard classification systems.

Resolve or clarify codes and diagnoses with conflicting, missing, or unclear information by consulting with doctors or others or by participating in the coding team's regular meetings. Compile medical care and census data for statistical reports on diseases treated, surgeries performed, or use of hospital beds. Post medical insurance billings. Train medical records staff. Prepare statistical reports, narrative reports, and graphic presentations of information such as tumor registry data for use by hospital staff, researchers, or other users. Manage the department and supervise clerical workers, directing and controlling activities of personnel in the medical records department. Develop in-service educational materials. Consult classification manuals to locate information about disease processes.

Personality Type: Conventional. These occupations frequently involve following set procedures and routines and can include working with data and details more than with ideas. Usually there is a clear line of authority to follow.

GOE—Interest Area/Cluster: 08. Health Science. **Work Group:** 08.06. Medical Technology. **Other Jobs in This Work Group:** Biological Technicians; Cardiovascular Technologists and Technicians; Diagnostic Medical Sonographers; Medical and Clinical Laboratory Technicians; Medical and Clinical Laboratory Technologists; Medical Equipment Preparers; Nuclear Medicine Technologists; Opticians, Dispensing; Orthotists and Prosthetists; Radiologic Technicians; Radiologic Technologists; Radiologic Technologists and Technicians.

Skill—Systems Analysis: Determining how a system should work and how changes will affect outcomes.

Education and Training Programs: Health Information/Medical Records Technology/Technician Training; Medical Insurance Coding Specialist/Coder Training. **Related Knowledge/Courses—Clerical Practices:** Administrative and clerical procedures and systems such as word-processing systems, filing and records management systems, stenography and transcription, forms, design principles, and other office procedures and terminology. **Law and Government:** Laws, legal codes, court procedures, precedents, government regulations, executive orders, agency rules, and the democratic political process. **Customer and Personal Service:** Principles and processes for providing customer and personal services, including needs assessment techniques, quality service standards, alternative delivery systems, and customer satisfaction evaluation techniques.

Work Environment: Indoors; disease or infections; sitting; using hands on objects, tools, or controls; repetitive motions.

Medical Scientists, Except Epidemiologists

* Education/Training Required: Doctoral degree
* Annual Earnings: $64,200
* Beginning Wage: $36,730
* Earnings Growth Potential: High
* Growth: 20.2%
* Annual Job Openings: 10,596
* Self-Employed: 2.0%
* Part-Time: 5.9%

Conduct research dealing with the understanding of human diseases and the improvement of human health. Engage in clinical investigation or other research, production, technical writing, or related activities. Conduct research to develop methodologies, instrumentation, and procedures for medical application, analyzing data and presenting findings. Plan and direct studies to investigate human or animal disease, preventive methods, and treatments for disease. Follow strict safety procedures when handling toxic materials to avoid contamination. Evaluate effects of drugs, gases, pesticides, parasites, and microorganisms at various levels. Teach principles of medicine and medical and laboratory procedures to physicians, residents, students, and technicians. Prepare and analyze organ, tissue, and cell samples to identify toxicity, bacteria, or microorganisms or to study cell structure. Standardize drug dosages, methods of immunization, and procedures for manufacture of drugs and medicinal compounds. Investigate cause, progress, life cycle, or mode of transmission of diseases or parasites. Confer with health department, industry personnel, physicians, and others to develop health safety standards and public health improvement programs. Study animal and human health and physiological processes. Consult with and advise physicians, educators, researchers, and others regarding medical applications of physics, biology, and chemistry. Use equipment such as atomic absorption spectrometers, electron microscopes, flow cytometers, and chromatography systems.

Personality Type: Investigative. These occupations frequently involve working with ideas and require an extensive amount of thinking. They can involve searching for facts and figuring out problems mentally.

GOE—Interest Area/Cluster: 15. Scientific Research, Engineering, and Mathematics. **Work Group:** 15.03. Life

Sciences. **Other Jobs in This Work Group:** Biochemists and Biophysicists; Biologists; Environmental Scientists and Specialists, Including Health; Epidemiologists; Microbiologists.

Skills—Science: Using scientific methods to solve problems. **Management of Financial Resources:** Determining how money will be spent to get the work done and accounting for these expenditures. **Judgment and Decision Making:** Weighing the relative costs and benefits of a potential action. **Reading Comprehension:** Understanding written sentences and paragraphs in work-related documents. **Writing:** Communicating effectively with others in writing as indicated by the needs of the audience. **Time Management:** Managing one's own time and the time of others. **Complex Problem Solving:** Identifying complex problems, reviewing the options, and implementing solutions. **Active Listening:** Listening to what other people are saying and asking questions as appropriate.

Education and Training Programs: Anatomy; Biochemistry; Biomedical Sciences, General; Biophysics; Biostatistics; Cardiovascular Science; Cell Physiology; Endocrinology; Epidemiology; Human/Medical Genetics; Immunology; Medical Microbiology and Bacteriology; Molecular Biology; Molecular Pharmacology; Neurobiology and Neurophysiology; Oncology and Cancer Biology; Pathology; Pharmacology; Pharmacology and Toxicology; Physiology, General; Reproductive Biology; Toxicology; Vision Science/Physiological Optics; others. **Related Knowledge/ Courses—Biology:** Plant and animal living tissue, cells, organisms, and entities, including their functions, interdependencies, and interactions with each other and the environment. **Medicine and Dentistry:** The information and techniques needed to diagnose and treat injuries, diseases, and deformities. This includes symptoms, treatment alternatives, drug properties and interactions, and preventive health-care measures. **Chemistry:** The composition, structure, and properties of substances and of the chemical processes and transformations that they undergo. This includes uses of chemicals and their interactions, danger signs, production techniques, and disposal methods. **Communications and Media:** Media production, communication, and dissemination techniques and methods, including alternative ways to inform and entertain via written, oral, and visual media. **Personnel and Human Resources:** Principles and procedures for personnel recruitment; selection; training; compensation and benefits; labor relations and negotiation; and personnel information systems. **Sociology and Anthropology:** Group behavior and dynamics; societal trends and influences; and cultures and their history, migrations, ethnicity, and origins.

Work Environment: Indoors; sitting; using hands on objects, tools, or controls.

Medical Secretaries

- ❋ Education/Training Required: Moderate-term on-the-job training
- ❋ Annual Earnings: $28,950
- ❋ Beginning Wage: $20,260
- ❋ Earnings Growth Potential: Low
- ❋ Growth: 16.7%
- ❋ Annual Job Openings: 60,659
- ❋ Self-Employed: 1.3%
- ❋ Part-Time: 18.9%

Perform secretarial duties, using specific knowledge of medical terminology and hospital, clinical, or laboratory procedures. Duties include scheduling appointments; billing patients; and compiling and recording medical charts, reports, and correspondence. Answer telephones, and direct calls to appropriate staff. Schedule and confirm patient diagnostic appointments, surgeries, and medical consultations. Greet visitors, ascertain purpose of visit, and direct them to appropriate staff. Operate office equipment such as voice mail messaging systems, and use word processing, spreadsheet, and other software applications to prepare reports, invoices, financial statements, letters, case histories, and medical records. Complete insurance and other claim forms. Interview patients to complete documents, case histories, and forms such as intake and insurance forms. Receive and route messages and documents such as laboratory results to appropriate staff. Compile and record medical charts, reports, and correspondence, using typewriter or personal computer. Transmit correspondence and medical records by mail, e-mail, or fax. Maintain medical records, technical library documents, and correspondence files. Perform various clerical and administrative functions such as ordering and maintaining an inventory of supplies. Perform bookkeeping duties such as credits and collections, preparing and sending financial statements and bills, and keeping financial records. Transcribe recorded messages and practitioners' diagnoses and recommendations into patients' medical records. Arrange hospital admissions for patients. Prepare correspondence and assist physicians or medical scientists with preparation of reports, speeches, articles, and conference proceedings.

Personality Type: Conventional. These occupations frequently involve following set procedures and routines and can include working with data and details more than with ideas. Usually there is a clear line of authority to follow.

GOE—Interest Area/Cluster: 04. Business and Administration. **Work Group:** 04.04. Secretarial Support. **Other Jobs in This Work Group:** Executive Secretaries and Administrative Assistants; Legal Secretaries; Secretaries, Except Legal, Medical, and Executive.

Skill—None met the criteria.

Education and Training Programs: Medical Administrative/Executive Assistant and Medical Secretary Training; Medical Insurance Specialist/Medical Biller Training; Medical Office Assistant/Specialist Training. **Related Knowledge/Courses—Clerical Practices:** Administrative and clerical procedures and systems such as word-processing systems, filing and records management systems, stenography and transcription, forms, design principles, and other office procedures and terminology. **Medicine and Dentistry:** The information and techniques needed to diagnose and treat injuries, diseases, and deformities. This includes symptoms, treatment alternatives, drug properties and interactions, and preventive health-care measures. **Customer and Personal Service:** Principles and processes for providing customer and personal services, including needs assessment techniques, quality service standards, alternative delivery systems, and customer satisfaction evaluation techniques. **Computers and Electronics:** Electric circuit boards, processors, chips, and computer hardware and software, including applications and programming. **Economics and Accounting:** Economic and accounting principles and practices, the financial markets, banking, and the analysis and reporting of financial data.

Work Environment: Indoors; disease or infections; sitting; repetitive motions.

Medical Transcriptionists

- ❋ Education/Training Required: Postsecondary vocational training
- ❋ Annual Earnings: $31,250
- ❋ Beginning Wage: $22,160
- ❋ Earnings Growth Potential: Low
- ❋ Growth: 13.5%
- ❋ Annual Job Openings: 18,080
- ❋ Self-Employed: 9.7%
- ❋ Part-Time: 23.2%

Use transcribing machines with headset and foot pedal to listen to recordings by physicians and other health-care professionals dictating a variety of medical reports, such as emergency room visits, diagnostic imaging studies, operations, chart reviews, and final summaries. Transcribe dictated reports and translate medical jargon and abbreviations into their expanded forms. Edit as necessary and return reports in either printed or electronic form to the dictator for review and signature or correction. Transcribe dictation for a variety of medical reports such as patient histories, physical examinations, emergency room visits, operations, chart reviews, consultation, or discharge summaries. Review and edit transcribed reports or dictated material for spelling, grammar, clarity, consistency, and proper medical terminology. Distinguish between homonyms and recognize inconsistencies and mistakes in medical terms, referring to dictionaries; drug references; and other sources on anatomy, physiology, and medicine. Return dictated reports in printed or electronic form for physicians' review, signature, and corrections and for inclusion in patients' medical records. Translate medical jargon and abbreviations into their expanded forms to ensure the accuracy of patient and health-care facility records. Take dictation, using either shorthand or a stenotype machine or using headsets and transcribing machines; then convert dictated materials or rough notes to written form. Identify mistakes in reports and check with doctors to obtain the correct information. Perform data entry and data retrieval services, providing data for inclusion in medical records and for transmission to physicians. Produce medical reports, correspondence, records, patient-care information, statistics, medical research, and administrative material. Answer inquiries concerning the progress of medical cases within the limits of confidentiality laws. Set up and maintain medical files and databases, including records such as X-ray, lab, and procedure reports; medical histories; diagnostic workups; admission and discharge summaries; and clinical resumes. Perform a variety of clerical and office tasks, such as handling incoming and outgoing mail, completing and submitting insurance claims, typing, filing, and operating office machines. Decide which information should be included or excluded in reports. Receive patients, schedule appointments, and maintain patient records. Receive and screen telephone calls and visitors.

Personality Type: Conventional. These occupations frequently involve following set procedures and routines and can include working with data and details more than with ideas. Usually there is a clear line of authority to follow.

GOE—Interest Area/Cluster: 08. Health Science. **Work Group:** 08.02. Medicine and Surgery. **Other Jobs in This Work Group:** Anesthesiologists; Family and General Practitioners; Internists, General; Medical Assistants; Obstetricians and Gynecologists; Pediatricians, General; Pharmacists; Pharmacy Aides; Pharmacy Technicians; Physician Assistants; Psychiatrists; Registered Nurses; Surgeons; Surgical Technologists.

Skills—Active Listening: Listening to what other people are saying and asking questions as appropriate. **Reading Comprehension:** Understanding written sentences and paragraphs in work-related documents. **Time Management:** Managing one's own time and the time of others.

Education and Training Program: Medical Transcription/Transcriptionist Training. **Related Knowledge/Courses—Clerical Practices:** Administrative and clerical procedures and systems such as word-processing systems, filing and records management systems, stenography and transcription, forms, design principles, and other office procedures and terminology. **English Language:** The structure and content of the English language, including the meaning and spelling of words, rules of composition, and grammar. **Medicine and Dentistry:** The information and techniques needed to diagnose and treat injuries, diseases, and deformities. This includes symptoms, treatment alternatives, drug properties and interactions, and preventive health-care measures. **Computers and Electronics:** Electric circuit boards, processors, chips, and computer hardware and software, including applications and programming.

Work Environment: Indoors; sitting; using hands on objects, tools, or controls; repetitive motions.

Meeting and Convention Planners

- ❋ Education/Training Required: Bachelor's degree
- ❋ Annual Earnings: $43,530
- ❋ Beginning Wage: $26,880
- ❋ Earnings Growth Potential: Medium
- ❋ Growth: 19.9%
- ❋ Annual Job Openings: 8,318
- ❋ Self-Employed: 5.6%
- ❋ Part-Time: 13.8%

Coordinate activities of staff and convention personnel to make arrangements for group meetings and conventions. Monitor event activities to ensure compliance with applicable regulations and laws, satisfaction of participants, and resolution of any problems that arise. Confer with staff at chosen event sites to coordinate details. Inspect event facilities to ensure that they conform to customer requirements. Coordinate services for events, such as accommodation and transportation for participants, facilities, catering, signage, displays, special needs requirements, printing, and event security. Consult with customers to determine objectives and requirements for events such as meetings, conferences, and conventions. Meet with sponsors and organizing committees to plan scope and format of events, to establish and monitor budgets, or to review administrative procedures and event progress. Review event bills for accuracy and approve payments. Evaluate and select providers of services according to customer requirements. Arrange the availability of audio-visual equipment, transportation, displays, and other event needs. Plan and develop programs, agendas, budgets, and services according to customer requirements. Negotiate contracts with such service providers and suppliers as hotels, convention centers, and speakers. Maintain records of event aspects, including financial details. Conduct post-event evaluations to determine how future events could be improved. Organize registration of event participants. Hire, train, and supervise volunteers and support staff required for events. Read trade publications, attend seminars, and consult with other meeting professionals to keep abreast of meeting management standards and trends. Direct administrative details such as financial operations, dissemination of promotional materials, and responses to inquiries. Promote conference, convention, and trade show services by performing tasks such as meeting with professional and trade associations and producing brochures and other publications. Develop event topics and choose featured speakers. Obtain permits from fire and health departments to erect displays and exhibits and serve food at events. Design and implement efforts to publicize events and promote sponsorships.

Personality Type: Enterprising. These occupations frequently involve starting up and carrying out projects and can involve leading people and making many decisions. They sometimes require risk taking and often deal with business.

GOE—Interest Area/Cluster: 04. Business and Administration. **Work Group:** 04.02. Managerial Work in Business Detail. **Other Jobs in This Work Group:** Administrative Services Managers; First-Line Supervisors/Managers of Housekeeping and Janitorial Workers; First-Line Supervisors/Managers of Office and Administrative Support Workers.

Skills—Management of Financial Resources: Determining how money will be spent to get the work done and accounting for these expenditures. **Systems Evaluation:** Looking at many indicators of system performance and taking into account their accuracy. **Management of Material Resources:** Obtaining and seeing to the appropriate use of equipment, facilities, and materials needed to do certain work. **Systems Analysis:** Determining how a system should work and how changes will affect outcomes. **Negotiation:** Bringing others together and trying to reconcile differences. **Management of Personnel Resources:** Motivating, developing, and directing people as they work; identifying the best people for the job. **Service Orientation:** Actively looking for ways to help people. **Coordination:** Adjusting actions in relation to others' actions.

Education and Training Program: Selling Skills and Sales Operations. **Related Knowledge/Courses—Sales and Marketing:** Principles and methods involved in showing, promoting, and selling products or services. This includes marketing strategies and tactics, product demonstration and sales techniques, and sales control systems. **Clerical Practices:** Administrative and clerical procedures and systems such as word-processing systems, filing and records management systems, stenography and transcription, forms, design principles, and other office procedures and terminology. **Customer and Personal Service:** Principles and processes for providing customer and personal services, including needs assessment techniques, quality service standards, alternative delivery systems, and customer satisfaction evaluation techniques. **English Language:** The structure and content of the English language, including the meaning and spelling of words, rules of composition, and grammar. **Economics and Accounting:** Economic and accounting principles and

practices, the financial markets, banking, and the analysis and reporting of financial data. **Administration and Management:** Principles and processes involved in business and organizational planning, coordination, and execution. This includes strategic planning, resource allocation, manpower modeling, leadership techniques, and production methods.

Work Environment: Indoors; noisy; sitting.

Mental Health and Substance Abuse Social Workers

* Education/Training Required: Master's degree
* Annual Earnings: $36,640
* Beginning Wage: $23,820
* Earnings Growth Potential: Medium
* Growth: 29.9%
* Annual Job Openings: 17,289
* Self-Employed: 2.8%
* Part-Time: 9.4%

Assess and treat individuals with mental, emotional, or substance abuse problems, including abuse of alcohol, tobacco, and/or other drugs. Activities may include individual and group therapy, crisis intervention, case management, client advocacy, prevention, and education. Counsel clients in individual and group sessions to assist them in dealing with substance abuse, mental and physical illness, poverty, unemployment, or physical abuse. Interview clients, review records, and confer with other professionals to evaluate mental or physical condition of client or patient. Collaborate with counselors, physicians, and nurses to plan and coordinate treatment, drawing on social work experience and patient needs. Monitor, evaluate, and record client progress with respect to treatment goals. Refer patient, client, or family to community resources for housing or treatment to assist in recovery from mental or physical illness, following through to ensure service efficacy. Counsel and aid family members to assist them in understanding, dealing with, and supporting the client or patient. Modify treatment plans according to changes in client status. Plan and conduct programs to prevent substance abuse, to combat social problems, or to improve health and counseling services in community. Supervise and direct other workers who provide services to clients or patients. Develop or advise on social policy and assist in community development. Conduct social research to advance knowledge in the social work field.

Personality Type: Social. These occupations frequently involve working with, communicating with, and teaching people and often involve helping or providing service to others.

GOE—Interest Area/Cluster: 10. Human Service. **Work Group:** 10.01. Counseling and Social Work. **Other Jobs in This Work Group:** Child, Family, and School Social Workers; Clinical Psychologists; Clinical, Counseling, and School Psychologists; Counseling Psychologists; Marriage and Family Therapists; Medical and Public Health Social Workers; Mental Health Counselors; Probation Officers and Correctional Treatment Specialists; Rehabilitation Counselors; Residential Advisors; Social and Human Service Assistants; Substance Abuse and Behavioral Disorder Counselors.

Skills—Social Perceptiveness: Being aware of others' reactions and understanding why they react the way they do. **Service Orientation:** Actively looking for ways to help people. **Negotiation:** Bringing others together and trying to reconcile differences. **Judgment and Decision Making:** Weighing the relative costs and benefits of a potential action. **Active Listening:** Listening to what other people are saying and asking questions as appropriate. **Persuasion:** Persuading others to approach things differently. **Complex Problem Solving:** Identifying complex problems, reviewing the options, and implementing solutions. **Writing:** Communicating effectively with others in writing as indicated by the needs of the audience.

Education and Training Program: Clinical/Medical Social Work. **Related Knowledge/Courses—Psychology:** Human behavior and performance, mental processes, psychological research methods, and the assessment and treatment of behavioral and affective disorders. **Therapy and Counseling:** Information and techniques needed to rehabilitate physical and mental ailments and to provide career guidance, including alternative treatments, rehabilitation equipment and its proper use, and methods to evaluate treatment effects. **Sociology and Anthropology:** Group behavior and dynamics; societal trends and influences; and cultures and their history, migrations, ethnicity, and origins. **Customer and Personal Service:** Principles and processes for providing customer and personal services, including needs assessment techniques, quality service standards, alternative delivery systems, and customer satisfaction evaluation techniques.

Work Environment: Indoors; noisy; sitting.

Mental Health Counselors

- ❋ Education/Training Required: Master's degree
- ❋ Annual Earnings: $36,000
- ❋ Beginning Wage: $22,900
- ❋ Earnings Growth Potential: Medium
- ❋ Growth: 30.0%
- ❋ Annual Job Openings: 24,103
- ❋ Self-Employed: 6.1%
- ❋ Part-Time: 15.4%

Counsel with emphasis on prevention. Work with individuals and groups to promote optimum mental health. May help individuals deal with addictions and substance abuse; family, parenting, and marital problems; suicide; stress management; problems with self-esteem; and issues associated with aging and mental and emotional health. Maintain confidentiality of records relating to clients' treatment. Guide clients in the development of skills and strategies for dealing with their problems. Encourage clients to express their feelings and discuss what is happening in their lives and help them to develop insight into themselves and their relationships. Prepare and maintain all required treatment records and reports. Counsel clients and patients, individually and in group sessions, to assist in overcoming dependencies, adjusting to life, and making changes. Collect information about clients through interviews, observation, and tests. Act as client advocates to coordinate required services or to resolve emergency problems in crisis situations. Develop and implement treatment plans based on clinical experience and knowledge. Collaborate with other staff members to perform clinical assessments and develop treatment plans. Evaluate clients' physical or mental condition based on review of client information. Meet with families, probation officers, police, and other interested parties to exchange necessary information during the treatment process. Refer patients, clients, or family members to community resources or to specialists as necessary. Evaluate the effectiveness of counseling programs and clients' progress in resolving identified problems and moving towards defined objectives. Counsel family members to assist them in understanding, dealing with, and supporting clients or patients. Plan, organize, and lead structured programs of counseling, work, study, recreation, and social activities for clients. Modify treatment activities and approaches as needed to comply with changes in clients' status. Learn about new developments in their field by reading professional literature, attending courses and seminars, and establishing and maintaining contact with other social service agencies. Discuss with individual patients their plans for life after leaving therapy. Gather information about community mental health needs and resources that could be used in conjunction with therapy. Monitor clients' use of medications. Supervise other counselors, social service staff, and assistants.

Personality Type: Social. These occupations frequently involve working with, communicating with, and teaching people and often involve helping or providing service to others.

GOE—Interest Area/Cluster: 10. Human Service. **Work Group:** 10.01. Counseling and Social Work. **Other Jobs in This Work Group:** Child, Family, and School Social Workers; Clinical Psychologists; Clinical, Counseling, and School Psychologists; Counseling Psychologists; Marriage and Family Therapists; Medical and Public Health Social Workers; Mental Health and Substance Abuse Social Workers; Probation Officers and Correctional Treatment Specialists; Rehabilitation Counselors; Residential Advisors; Social and Human Service Assistants; Substance Abuse and Behavioral Disorder Counselors.

Skills—Social Perceptiveness: Being aware of others' reactions and understanding why they react the way they do. **Service Orientation:** Actively looking for ways to help people. **Negotiation:** Bringing others together and trying to reconcile differences. **Active Listening:** Listening to what other people are saying and asking questions as appropriate. **Persuasion:** Persuading others to approach things differently. **Learning Strategies:** Using multiple approaches when learning or teaching new things. **Speaking:** Talking to others to effectively convey information. **Critical Thinking:** Using logic and analysis to identify the strengths and weaknesses of different approaches.

Education and Training Programs: Clinical/Medical Social Work; Mental and Social Health Services and Allied Professions, Other; Mental Health Counseling/Counselor Training; Substance Abuse/Addiction Counseling. **Related Knowledge/Courses—Therapy and Counseling:** Information and techniques needed to rehabilitate physical and mental ailments and to provide career guidance, including alternative treatments, rehabilitation equipment and its proper use, and methods to evaluate treatment effects. **Psychology:** Human behavior and performance, mental processes, psychological research methods, and the assessment and treatment of behavioral and affective disorders. **Sociology and Anthropology:** Group behavior and dynamics; societal trends and influences; and cultures and their history,

migrations, ethnicity, and origins. **Philosophy and Theology:** Different philosophical systems and religions, including their basic principles, values, ethics, ways of thinking, customs, and practices and their impact on human culture. **Medicine and Dentistry:** The information and techniques needed to diagnose and treat injuries, diseases, and deformities. This includes symptoms, treatment alternatives, drug properties and interactions, and preventive health-care measures. **Law and Government:** Laws, legal codes, court procedures, precedents, government regulations, executive orders, agency rules, and the democratic political process.

Work Environment: Indoors; noisy; sitting.

Merchandise Displayers and Window Trimmers

- ❋ Education/Training Required: Moderate-term on-the-job training
- ❋ Annual Earnings: $24,830
- ❋ Beginning Wage: $16,300
- ❋ Earnings Growth Potential: Low
- ❋ Growth: 10.7%
- ❋ Annual Job Openings: 9,103
- ❋ Self-Employed: 28.6%
- ❋ Part-Time: 16.7%

Plan and erect commercial displays, such as those in windows and interiors of retail stores and at trade exhibitions. Take photographs of displays and signage. Plan and erect commercial displays to entice and appeal to customers. Place prices and descriptive signs on backdrops, fixtures, merchandise, or floor. Change or rotate window displays, interior display areas, and signage to reflect changes in inventory or promotion. Obtain plans from display designers or display managers and discuss their implementation with clients or supervisors. Develop ideas or plans for merchandise displays or window decorations. Consult with advertising and sales staff to determine type of merchandise to be featured and time and place for each display. Arrange properties, furniture, merchandise, backdrops, and other accessories as shown in prepared sketches. Construct or assemble displays and display components from fabric, glass, paper, and plastic according to specifications, using hand tools and woodworking power tools. Collaborate with others to obtain products and other display items. Use computers to produce signage. Dress mannequins for displays. Maintain props and mannequins, inspecting them for imperfections and applying preservative coatings as necessary. Select themes, lighting, colors, and props to be used. Attend training sessions and corporate planning meetings to obtain new ideas for product launches. Instruct sales staff in color-coordination of clothing racks and counter displays. Store, pack, and maintain records of props and display items. Prepare sketches, floor plans, or models of proposed displays. Cut out designs on cardboard, hardboard, and plywood according to motif of event. Install booths, exhibits, displays, carpets, and drapes as guided by floor plan of building and specifications. Install decorations such as flags, banners, festive lights, and bunting on or in building, street, exhibit hall, or booth. Create and enhance mannequin faces by mixing and applying paint and attaching measured eyelash strips, using artist's brush, airbrush, pins, ruler, and scissors.

Personality Type: Artistic. These occupations frequently involve working with forms, designs, and patterns. They often require self-expression, and the work can be done without following a clear set of rules.

GOE—Interest Area/Cluster: 03. Arts and Communication. **Work Group:** 03.05. Design. **Other Jobs in This Work Group:** Commercial and Industrial Designers; Fashion Designers; Floral Designers; Graphic Designers; Interior Designers; Set and Exhibit Designers.

Skills—Persuasion: Persuading others to approach things differently. **Negotiation:** Bringing others together and trying to reconcile differences. **Management of Personnel Resources:** Motivating, developing, and directing people as they work; identifying the best people for the job.

Education and Training Program: Commercial and Advertising Art. **Related Knowledge/Courses—Sales and Marketing:** Principles and methods involved in showing, promoting, and selling products or services. This includes marketing strategies and tactics, product demonstration and sales techniques, and sales control systems. **Design:** Design techniques, principles, tools, and instruments involved in the production and use of precision technical plans, blueprints, drawings, and models. **Administration and Management:** Principles and processes involved in business and organizational planning, coordination, and execution. This includes strategic planning, resource allocation, manpower modeling, leadership techniques, and production methods. **Computers and Electronics:** Electric circuit boards, processors, chips, and computer hardware and software, including applications and programming.

Work Environment: Indoors; contaminants; walking and running; using hands on objects, tools, or controls; bending or twisting the body; repetitive motions.

Microbiologists

- ❋ Education/Training Required: Doctoral degree
- ❋ Annual Earnings: $60,680
- ❋ Beginning Wage: $37,180
- ❋ Earnings Growth Potential: Medium
- ❋ Growth: 11.2%
- ❋ Annual Job Openings: 1,306
- ❋ Self-Employed: 2.7%
- ❋ Part-Time: 7.3%

Investigate the growth, structure, development, and other characteristics of microscopic organisms such as bacteria, algae, or fungi. Includes medical microbiologists who study the relationship between organisms and disease or the effects of antibiotics on microorganisms. Investigate the relationship between organisms and disease including the control of epidemics and the effects of antibiotics on microorganisms. Prepare technical reports and recommendations based upon research outcomes. Supervise biological technologists and technicians and other scientists. Provide laboratory services for health departments, for community environmental health programs, and for physicians needing information for diagnosis and treatment. Use a variety of specialized equipment such as electron microscopes, gas chromatographs, and high pressure liquid chromatographs, electrophoresis units, thermocyclers, fluorescence activated cell sorters and phosphoimagers. Examine physiological, morphological, and cultural characteristics, using microscopes, to identify and classify microorganisms in human, water, and food specimens. Study growth, structure, development, and general characteristics of bacteria and other microorganisms to understand their relationships to human, plant, and animal health. Isolate and maintain cultures of bacteria or other microorganisms in prescribed or developed media, controlling moisture, aeration, temperature, and nutrition. Observe action of microorganisms upon living tissues of plants, higher animals, and other microorganisms, and on dead organic matter. Study the structure and function of human, animal, and plant tissues, cells, pathogens, and toxins. Conduct chemical analyses of substances such as acids, alcohols, and enzymes. Monitor and perform tests on water, food, and the environment to detect harmful microorganisms or to obtain information about sources of pollution, contamination, or infection. Develop new products and procedures for sterilization, food and pharmaceutical supply preservation, or microbial contamination detection. Research use of bacteria and microorganisms to develop vitamins, antibiotics, amino acids, grain alcohol, sugars, and polymers.

Personality Type: Investigative. These occupations frequently involve working with ideas and require an extensive amount of thinking. They can involve searching for facts and figuring out problems mentally.

GOE—Interest Area/Cluster: 15. Scientific Research, Engineering, and Mathematics. **Work Group:** 15.03. Life Sciences. **Other Jobs in This Work Group:** Biochemists and Biophysicists; Biologists; Environmental Scientists and Specialists, Including Health; Epidemiologists; Medical Scientists, Except Epidemiologists.

Skills—Science: Using scientific methods to solve problems. **Writing:** Communicating effectively with others in writing as indicated by the needs of the audience. **Reading Comprehension:** Understanding written sentences and paragraphs in work-related documents. **Systems Analysis:** Determining how a system should work and how changes will affect outcomes. **Operation Monitoring:** Watching gauges, dials, or other indicators to make sure a machine is working properly. **Complex Problem Solving:** Identifying complex problems, reviewing the options, and implementing solutions. **Systems Evaluation:** Looking at many indicators of system performance and taking into account their accuracy. **Management of Personnel Resources:** Motivating, developing, and directing people as they work; identifying the best people for the job.

Education and Training Programs: Biochemistry/Biophysics and Molecular Biology; Cell/Cellular Biology and Anatomical Sciences, Other; Microbiology, General; Neuroanatomy; Soil Microbiology; Structural Biology. **Related Knowledge/Courses—Biology:** Plant and animal living tissue, cells, organisms, and entities, including their functions, interdependencies, and interactions with each other and the environment. **Chemistry:** The composition, structure, and properties of substances and of the chemical processes and transformations that they undergo. This includes uses of chemicals and their interactions, danger signs, production techniques, and disposal methods. **Medicine and Dentistry:** The information and techniques needed to diagnose and treat injuries, diseases, and deformities. This includes symptoms, treatment alternatives, drug properties

and interactions, and preventive health-care measures. **English Language:** The structure and content of the English language, including the meaning and spelling of words, rules of composition, and grammar. **Education and Training:** Instructional methods and training techniques, including curriculum design principles, learning theory, group and individual teaching techniques, design of individual development plans, and test design principles. **Mathematics:** Numbers and their operations and interrelationships, including arithmetic, algebra, geometry, calculus, and statistics and their applications.

Work Environment: Indoors; disease or infections; hazardous conditions; sitting; using hands on objects, tools, or controls.

Middle School Teachers, Except Special and Vocational Education

* Education/Training Required: Bachelor's degree
* Annual Earnings: $47,900
* Beginning Wage: $32,630
* Earnings Growth Potential: Low
* Growth: 11.2%
* Annual Job Openings: 75,270
* Self-Employed: 0.0%
* Part-Time: 9.5%

Teach students in public or private schools in one or more subjects at the middle, intermediate, or junior high level, which falls between elementary and senior high school as defined by applicable state laws and regulations. Establish and enforce rules for behavior and procedures for maintaining order among the students for whom they are responsible. Adapt teaching methods and instructional materials to meet students' varying needs and interests. Instruct through lectures, discussions, and demonstrations in one or more subjects such as English, mathematics, or social studies. Prepare, administer, and grade tests and assignments to evaluate students' progress. Establish clear objectives for all lessons, units, and projects and communicate these objectives to students. Plan and conduct activities for a balanced program of instruction, demonstration, and work time that provides students with opportunities to observe, question, and investigate. Maintain accurate, complete, and correct student records as required by laws, district policies, and administrative regulations. Observe and evaluate students' performance, behavior, social development, and physical health. Assign lessons and correct homework. Prepare materials and classrooms for class activities. Enforce all administration policies and rules governing students. Confer with parents or guardians, other teachers, counselors, and administrators to resolve students' behavioral and academic problems. Prepare students for later grades by encouraging them to explore learning opportunities and to persevere with challenging tasks. Prepare objectives and outlines for courses of study, following curriculum guidelines or requirements of states and schools. Guide and counsel students with adjustment or academic problems or special academic interests. Meet with parents and guardians to discuss their children's progress and to determine their priorities for their children and their resource needs. Meet with other professionals to discuss individual students' needs and progress. Prepare and implement remedial programs for students requiring extra help. Prepare for assigned classes and show written evidence of preparation upon request of immediate supervisors. Instruct and monitor students in the use and care of equipment and materials to prevent injury and damage.

Personality Type: Social. These occupations frequently involve working with, communicating with, and teaching people and often involve helping or providing service to others.

GOE—Interest Area/Cluster: 05. Education and Training. **Work Group:** 05.02. Preschool, Elementary, and Secondary Teaching and Instructing. **Other Jobs in This Work Group:** Elementary School Teachers, Except Special Education; Kindergarten Teachers, Except Special Education; Preschool Teachers, Except Special Education; Secondary School Teachers, Except Special and Vocational Education; Special Education Teachers, Middle School; Special Education Teachers, Preschool, Kindergarten, and Elementary School; Special Education Teachers, Secondary School; Teacher Assistants; Vocational Education Teachers, Middle School; Vocational Education Teachers, Secondary School.

Skills—Learning Strategies: Using multiple approaches when learning or teaching new things. **Instructing:** Teaching others how to do something. **Monitoring:** Assessing how well one is doing when learning or doing something. **Social Perceptiveness:** Being aware of others' reactions and understanding why they react the way they do. **Time Management:** Managing one's own time and the time of others. **Persuasion:** Persuading others to approach things differently. **Negotiation:** Bringing others together and trying to reconcile differences. **Speaking:** Talking to others to effectively convey information.

Education and Training Programs: Art Teacher Education; Computer Teacher Education; Family and Consumer Sciences Teacher Education; Foreign Language Teacher Education; Health Teacher Education; History Teacher Education; Mathematics Teacher Education; Music Teacher Education; Physical Education Teaching and Coaching; Reading Teacher Education; Science Teacher Education; Social Science Teacher Education; Social Studies Teacher Education; Technology Teacher Education Teacher Education; others. **Related Knowledge/Courses—Sociology and Anthropology:** Group behavior and dynamics; societal trends and influences; and cultures and their history, migrations, ethnicity, and origins. **History and Archeology:** Historical events and their causes, indicators, and impact on particular civilizations and cultures. **Philosophy and Theology:** Different philosophical systems and religions, including their basic principles, values, ethics, ways of thinking, customs, and practices and their impact on human culture. **Education and Training:** Instructional methods and training techniques, including curriculum design principles, learning theory, group and individual teaching techniques, design of individual development plans, and test design principles. **Geography:** Various methods for describing the location and distribution of land, sea, and air masses, including their physical locations, relationships, and characteristics. **Therapy and Counseling:** Information and techniques needed to rehabilitate physical and mental ailments and to provide career guidance, including alternative treatments, rehabilitation equipment and its proper use, and methods to evaluate treatment effects.

Work Environment: Indoors; noisy; standing.

Millwrights

* Education/Training Required: Long-term on-the-job training
* Annual Earnings: $46,090
* Beginning Wage: $28,940
* Earnings Growth Potential: Medium
* Growth: 5.8%
* Annual Job Openings: 4,758
* Self-Employed: 3.2%
* Part-Time: 1.5%

Install, dismantle, or move machinery and heavy equipment according to layout plans, blueprints, or other drawings. Replace defective parts of machine or adjust clearances and alignment of moving parts. Align machines and equipment, using hoists, jacks, hand tools, squares, rules, micrometers, and plumb bobs. Connect power unit to machines or steam piping to equipment and test unit to evaluate its mechanical operation. Repair and lubricate machines and equipment. Assemble and install equipment, using hand tools and power tools. Position steel beams to support bedplates of machines and equipment, using blueprints and schematic drawings to determine work procedures. Signal crane operator to lower basic assembly units to bedplate and align unit to centerline. Insert shims, adjust tension on nuts and bolts, or position parts, using hand tools and measuring instruments to set specified clearances between moving and stationary parts. Move machinery and equipment, using hoists, dollies, rollers, and trucks. Attach moving parts and subassemblies to basic assembly unit, using hand tools and power tools. Assemble machines and bolt, weld, rivet, or otherwise fasten them to foundation or other structures, using hand tools and power tools. Lay out mounting holes, using measuring instruments, and drill holes with power drill. Bolt parts, such as side and deck plates, jaw plates, and journals, to basic assembly unit. Dismantle machines, using hammers, wrenches, crowbars, and other hand tools. Level bedplate and establish centerline, using straightedge, levels, and transit. Shrink-fit bushings, sleeves, rings, liners, gears, and wheels to specified items, using portable gas heating equipment. Dismantle machinery and equipment for shipment to installation site, usually performing installation and maintenance work as part of team. Construct foundation for machines, using hand tools and building materials such as wood, cement, and steel. Install robot and modify its program, using teach pendant. Operate engine lathe to grind, file, and turn machine parts to dimensional specifications.

Personality Type: Realistic. These occupations frequently involve work activities that include practical, hands-on problems and solutions. They often deal with plants; animals; and real-world materials such as wood, tools, and machinery. Many of the occupations require working outside and don't involve a lot of paperwork or working closely with others.

GOE—Interest Area/Cluster: 13. Manufacturing. **Work Group:** 13.13. Machinery Repair. **Other Jobs in This Work Group:** Bicycle Repairers; Control and Valve Installers and Repairers, Except Mechanical Door; Home Appliance Repairers; Industrial Machinery Mechanics; Locksmiths and Safe Repairers; Maintenance Workers, Machinery; Mechanical Door Repairers; Signal and Track Switch Repairers.

Skills—Installation: Installing equipment, machines, wiring, or programs to meet specifications. **Repairing:** Repairing machines or systems, using the needed tools. **Troubleshooting:** Determining what is causing an operating error and deciding what to do about it. **Equipment Maintenance:** Performing routine maintenance and determining when and what kind of maintenance is needed. **Equipment Selection:** Determining the kind of tools and equipment needed to do a job. **Mathematics:** Using mathematics to solve problems. **Technology Design:** Generating or adapting equipment and technology to serve user needs. **Operation Monitoring:** Watching gauges, dials, or other indicators to make sure a machine is working properly.

Education and Training Programs: Heavy/Industrial Equipment Maintenance Technologies, Other; Industrial Mechanics and Maintenance Technology. **Related Knowledge/Courses—Mechanical Devices:** Machines and tools, including their designs, uses, benefits, repair, and maintenance. **Building and Construction:** Materials, methods, and the appropriate tools to construct objects, structures, and buildings. **Physics:** Physical principles, laws, and applications, including air, water, material dynamics, light, atomic principles, heat, electric theory, earth formations, and meteorological and related natural phenomena. **Engineering and Technology:** Equipment, tools, and mechanical devices and their uses to produce motion, light, power, technology, and other applications. **Design:** Design techniques, principles, tools, and instruments involved in the production and use of precision technical plans, blueprints, drawings, and models. **Public Safety and Security:** Weaponry; public safety; security operations, rules, regulations, precautions, and prevention; and the protection of people, data, and property.

Work Environment: Noisy; very hot or cold; very bright or dim lighting; contaminants; hazardous equipment; using hands on objects, tools, or controls.

Mining and Geological Engineers, Including Mining Safety Engineers

- ✳ Education/Training Required: Bachelor's degree
- ✳ Annual Earnings: $74,330
- ✳ Beginning Wage: $44,690
- ✳ Earnings Growth Potential: Medium
- ✳ Growth: 10.0%
- ✳ Annual Job Openings: 456
- ✳ Self-Employed: 0.0%
- ✳ Part-Time: 5.3%

Determine the location and plan the extraction of coal, metallic ores, nonmetallic minerals, and building materials such as stone and gravel. Work involves conducting preliminary surveys of deposits or undeveloped mines and planning their development; examining deposits or mines to determine whether they can be worked at a profit; making geological and topographical surveys; evolving methods of mining best suited to character, type, and size of deposits; and supervising mining operations. Inspect mining areas for unsafe structures, equipment, and working conditions. Select locations and plan underground or surface mining operations, specifying processes, labor usage, and equipment that will result in safe, economical, and environmentally sound extraction of minerals and ores. Examine maps, deposits, drilling locations, or mines to determine the location, size, accessibility, contents, value, and potential profitability of mineral, oil, and gas deposits. Supervise and coordinate the work of technicians, technologists, survey personnel, engineers, scientists, and other mine personnel. Prepare schedules, reports, and estimates of the costs involved in developing and operating mines. Monitor mine production rates to assess operational effectiveness. Design, implement, and monitor the development of mines, facilities, systems, or equipment. Select or develop mineral location, extraction, and production methods based on factors such as safety, cost, and deposit characteristics. Prepare technical reports for use by mining, engineering, and management personnel. Implement and coordinate mine safety programs, including the design and maintenance of protective and rescue equipment and safety devices. Test air to detect toxic gases and recommend measures to remove them, such as installation of ventilation shafts. Design, develop, and implement computer applications for use in mining operations such as mine design, modeling, or mapping or for monitoring mine conditions. Select or devise materials-handling methods and equipment to transport ore, waste materials, and mineral products efficiently and economically. Devise solutions to problems of land reclamation and water and air pollution, such as methods of storing excavated soil and returning exhausted mine sites to natural states. Lay out, direct, and supervise mine construction operations, such as the construction of shafts and tunnels. Evaluate data to develop new mining products, equipment, or processes. Conduct or direct mining experiments to test or prove research findings. Design mining and mineral treatment equipment and machinery in collaboration with other engineering specialists.

Personality Type: Investigative. These occupations frequently involve working with ideas and require an extensive amount of thinking. They can involve searching for facts and figuring out problems mentally.

GOE—Interest Area/Cluster: 01. Agriculture and Natural Resources. **Work Group:** 01.02. Resource Science/Engineering for Plants, Animals, and the Environment. **Other Jobs in This Work Group:** Agricultural Engineers; Animal Scientists; Conservation Scientists; Environmental Engineers; Foresters; Petroleum Engineers; Range Managers; Soil and Plant Scientists; Soil and Water Conservationists; Zoologists and Wildlife Biologists.

Skills—Operations Analysis: Analyzing needs and product requirements to create a design. **Science:** Using scientific methods to solve problems. **Programming:** Writing computer programs for various purposes. **Management of Financial Resources:** Determining how money will be spent to get the work done and accounting for these expenditures. **Mathematics:** Using mathematics to solve problems. **Management of Material Resources:** Obtaining and seeing to the appropriate use of equipment, facilities, and materials needed to do certain work. **Systems Analysis:** Determining how a system should work and how changes will affect outcomes. **Technology Design:** Generating or adapting equipment and technology to serve user needs.

Education and Training Program: Mining and Mineral Engineering. **Related Knowledge/Courses—Engineering and Technology:** Equipment, tools, and mechanical devices and their uses to produce motion, light, power, technology, and other applications. **Design:** Design techniques, principles, tools, and instruments involved in the production and use of precision technical plans, blueprints, drawings, and models. **Chemistry:** The composition, structure, and properties of substances and of the chemical processes and transformations that they undergo. This includes uses of chemicals and their interactions, danger signs, production techniques, and disposal methods. **Physics:** Physical principles, laws, and applications, including air, water, material dynamics, light, atomic principles, heat, electric theory, earth formations, and meteorological and related natural phenomena. **Production and Processing:** Inputs, outputs, raw materials, waste, quality control, costs, and techniques for maximizing the manufacture and distribution of goods. **Geography:** Various methods for describing the location and distribution of land, sea, and air masses, including their physical locations, relationships, and characteristics.

Work Environment: More often indoors than outdoors; very hot or cold; contaminants; hazardous equipment; sitting.

Mobile Heavy Equipment Mechanics, Except Engines

- ❋ Education/Training Required: Long-term on-the-job training
- ❋ Annual Earnings: $41,450
- ❋ Beginning Wage: $27,200
- ❋ Earnings Growth Potential: Low
- ❋ Growth: 12.3%
- ❋ Annual Job Openings: 11,037
- ❋ Self-Employed: 5.0%
- ❋ Part-Time: 2.3%

Diagnose, adjust, repair, or overhaul mobile mechanical, hydraulic, and pneumatic equipment, such as cranes, bulldozers, graders, and conveyors, used in construction, logging, and surface mining. Test mechanical products and equipment after repair or assembly to ensure proper performance and compliance with manufacturers' specifications. Repair and replace damaged or worn parts. Diagnose faults or malfunctions to determine required repairs, using engine diagnostic equipment such as computerized test equipment and calibration devices. Operate and inspect machines or heavy equipment to diagnose defects. Dismantle and reassemble heavy equipment, using hoists and hand tools. Clean, lubricate, and perform other routine maintenance work on equipment and vehicles. Examine parts for damage or excessive wear, using micrometers and gauges. Read and understand operating manuals, blueprints, and technical drawings. Schedule maintenance for industrial machines and equipment and keep equipment service records. Overhaul and test machines or equipment to ensure operating efficiency. Assemble gear systems and align frames and gears. Fit bearings to adjust, repair, or overhaul mobile mechanical, hydraulic, and pneumatic equipment. Weld or solder broken parts and structural members, using electric or gas welders and soldering tools. Clean parts by spraying them with grease solvent or immersing them in tanks of solvent. Adjust, maintain, and repair or replace subassemblies, such as transmissions and crawler heads, using hand tools, jacks, and cranes. Adjust and maintain industrial machinery, using control and regulating devices. Fabricate needed parts or items from sheet metal. Direct workers who are assembling or disassembling equipment or cleaning parts.

Personality Type: Realistic. These occupations frequently involve work activities that include practical, hands-on problems and solutions. They often deal with plants; animals; and real-world materials such as wood, tools, and machinery. Many of the occupations require working outside and don't involve a lot of paperwork or working closely with others.

GOE—Interest Area/Cluster: 13. Manufacturing. **Work Group:** 13.14. Vehicle and Facility Mechanical Work. **Other Jobs in This Work Group:** Aircraft Mechanics and Service Technicians; Aircraft Structure, Surfaces, Rigging, and Systems Assemblers; Automotive Body and Related Repairers; Automotive Glass Installers and Repairers; Automotive Master Mechanics; Automotive Service Technicians and Mechanics; Automotive Specialty Technicians; Bus and Truck Mechanics and Diesel Engine Specialists; Farm Equipment Mechanics; Fiberglass Laminators and Fabricators; Motorboat Mechanics; Motorcycle Mechanics; Outdoor Power Equipment and Other Small Engine Mechanics; Rail Car Repairers; Recreational Vehicle Service Technicians; Tire Repairers and Changers.

Skills—Installation: Installing equipment, machines, wiring, or programs to meet specifications. **Repairing:** Repairing machines or systems, using the needed tools. **Equipment Maintenance:** Performing routine maintenance and determining when and what kind of maintenance is needed. **Operation Monitoring:** Watching gauges, dials, or other indicators to make sure a machine is working properly. **Troubleshooting:** Determining what is causing an operating error and deciding what to do about it. **Operation and Control:** Controlling operations of equipment or systems. **Equipment Selection:** Determining the kind of tools and equipment needed to do a job. **Technology Design:** Generating or adapting equipment and technology to serve user needs.

Education and Training Programs: Agricultural Mechanics and Equipment/Machine Technology; Heavy Equipment Maintenance Technology/Technician Training. **Related Knowledge/Courses—Mechanical Devices:** Machines and tools, including their designs, uses, benefits, repair, and maintenance. **Engineering and Technology:** Equipment, tools, and mechanical devices and their uses to produce motion, light, power, technology, and other applications. **Physics:** Physical principles, laws, and applications, including air, water, material dynamics, light, atomic principles, heat, electric theory, earth formations, and meteorological and related natural phenomena.

Work Environment: Noisy; contaminants; hazardous equipment; minor burns, cuts, bites, or stings; standing; using hands on objects, tools, or controls.

Motorboat Mechanics

* Education/Training Required: Long-term on-the-job training
* Annual Earnings: $34,210
* Beginning Wage: $21,430
* Earnings Growth Potential: Medium
* Growth: 19.0%
* Annual Job Openings: 4,326
* Self-Employed: 22.6%
* Part-Time: 11.4%

Repairs and adjusts electrical and mechanical equipment of gasoline or diesel-powered inboard or inboard-outboard boat engines. Disassemble and inspect motors to locate defective parts, using mechanic's hand tools and gauges. Adjust generators and replace faulty wiring, using hand tools and soldering irons. Start motors and monitor performance for signs of malfunctioning such as smoke, excessive vibration, and misfiring. Adjust carburetor mixtures, electrical point settings, and timing while motors are running in water-filled test tanks. Idle motors and observe thermometers to determine the effectiveness of cooling systems. Inspect and repair or adjust propellers and propeller shafts. Mount motors to boats and operate boats at various speeds on waterways to conduct operational tests. Replace parts such as gears, magneto points, piston rings, and spark plugs, and reassemble engines. Repair or rework parts, using machine tools such as lathes, mills, drills, and grinders. Repair engine mechanical equipment such as power-tilts, bilge pumps, or power take-offs. Set starter locks, and align and repair steering or throttle controls, using gauges, screwdrivers, and wrenches. Document inspection and test results, and work performed or to be performed.

Personality Type: Realistic. These occupations frequently involve work activities that include practical, hands-on problems and solutions. They often deal with plants; animals; and real-world materials such as wood, tools, and machinery. Many of the occupations require working outside and don't involve a lot of paperwork or working closely with others.

GOE—Interest Area/Cluster: 13. Manufacturing. **Work Group:** 13.14. Vehicle and Facility Mechanical Work. **Other Jobs in This Work Group:** Aircraft Mechanics and Service Technicians; Aircraft Structure, Surfaces, Rigging, and Systems Assemblers; Automotive Body and Related Repairers; Automotive Glass Installers and Repairers; Automotive Master Mechanics; Automotive Service Technicians and Mechanics; Automotive Specialty Technicians; Bus and Truck Mechanics and Diesel Engine Specialists; Farm Equipment Mechanics; Fiberglass Laminators and Fabricators; Mobile Heavy Equipment Mechanics, Except Engines; Motorcycle Mechanics; Outdoor Power Equipment and Other Small Engine Mechanics; Rail Car Repairers; Recreational Vehicle Service Technicians; Tire Repairers and Changers.

Skills—Repairing: Repairing machines or systems, using the needed tools. **Installation:** Installing equipment, machines, wiring, or programs to meet specifications. **Equipment Maintenance:** Performing routine maintenance and determining when and what kind of maintenance is needed. **Troubleshooting:** Determining what is causing an operating error and deciding what to do about it. **Technology Design:** Generating or adapting equipment and technology to serve user needs. **Operation Monitoring:** Watching gauges, dials, or other indicators to make sure a machine is working properly. **Operation and Control:** Controlling operations of equipment or systems. **Equipment Selection:** Determining the kind of tools and equipment needed to do a job.

Education and Training Programs: Marine Maintenance/Fitter and Ship Repair Technology/Technician Training; Small Engine Mechanics and Repair Technology/Technician Training. **Related Knowledge/Courses—Mechanical Devices:** Machines and tools, including their designs, uses, benefits, repair, and maintenance. **Engineering and Technology:** Equipment, tools, and mechanical devices and their uses to produce motion, light, power, technology, and other applications. **Design:** Design techniques, principles, tools, and instruments involved in the production and use of precision technical plans, blueprints, drawings, and models. **Physics:** Physical principles, laws, and applications, including air, water, material dynamics, light, atomic principles, heat, electric theory, earth formations, and meteorological and related natural phenomena. **Chemistry:** The composition, structure, and properties of substances and of the chemical processes and transformations that they undergo. This includes uses of chemicals and their interactions, danger signs, production techniques, and disposal methods. **Transportation:** Principles and methods for moving people or goods by air, rail, sea, or road, including their relative costs, advantages, and limitations.

Work Environment: Outdoors; noisy; contaminants; cramped work space, awkward positions; standing; using hands on objects, tools, or controls.

Motorcycle Mechanics

- ❋ Education/Training Required: Long-term on-the-job training
- ❋ Annual Earnings: $30,300
- ❋ Beginning Wage: $19,070
- ❋ Earnings Growth Potential: Medium
- ❋ Growth: 12.5%
- ❋ Annual Job Openings: 3,564
- ❋ Self-Employed: 21.9%
- ❋ Part-Time: 11.4%

Diagnose, adjust, repair, or overhaul motorcycles, scooters, mopeds, dirt bikes, or similar motorized vehicles. Repair and adjust motorcycle subassemblies such as forks, transmissions, brakes, and drive chains according to specifications. Replace defective parts, using hand tools, arbor presses, flexible power presses, or power tools. Connect test panels to engines and measure generator output, ignition timing, and other engine performance indicators. Listen to engines, examine vehicle frames, and confer with customers to determine nature and extent of malfunction or damage. Reassemble and test subassembly units. Dismantle engines and repair or replace defective parts, such as magnetos, carburetors, and generators. Remove cylinder heads; grind valves; scrape off carbon; and replace defective valves, pistons, cylinders, and rings, using hand tools and power tools. Repair or replace other parts, such as headlights, horns, handlebar controls, gasoline and oil tanks, starters, and mufflers. Disassemble subassembly units and examine condition, movement, or alignment of parts visually or by using gauges. Hammer out dents and bends in frames, weld tears and breaks, and reassemble frames and reinstall engines.

Personality Type: Realistic. These occupations frequently involve work activities that include practical, hands-on problems and solutions. They often deal with plants; animals; and real-world materials such as wood, tools, and machinery. Many of the occupations require working outside and don't involve a lot of paperwork or working closely with others.

GOE—Interest Area/Cluster: 13. Manufacturing. **Work Group:** 13.14. Vehicle and Facility Mechanical Work. **Other Jobs in This Work Group:** Aircraft Mechanics and Service Technicians; Aircraft Structure, Surfaces, Rigging, and Systems Assemblers; Automotive Body and Related Repairers; Automotive Glass Installers and Repairers; Automotive Master Mechanics; Automotive Service Technicians and Mechanics; Automotive Specialty Technicians; Bus and Truck Mechanics and Diesel Engine Specialists; Farm Equipment Mechanics; Fiberglass Laminators and Fabricators; Mobile Heavy Equipment Mechanics, Except Engines; Motorboat Mechanics; Outdoor Power Equipment and Other Small Engine Mechanics; Rail Car Repairers; Recreational Vehicle Service Technicians; Tire Repairers and Changers.

Skills—Repairing: Repairing machines or systems, using the needed tools. **Installation:** Installing equipment, machines, wiring, or programs to meet specifications. **Troubleshooting:** Determining what is causing an operating error and deciding what to do about it. **Equipment Maintenance:** Performing routine maintenance and determining when and what kind of maintenance is needed. **Science:** Using scientific methods to solve problems. **Technology Design:** Generating or adapting equipment and technology to serve user needs. **Mathematics:** Using mathematics to solve problems. **Equipment Selection:** Determining the kind of tools and equipment needed to do a job.

Education and Training Program: Motorcycle Maintenance and Repair Technology/Technician Training. **Related Knowledge/Courses—Mechanical Devices:** Machines and tools, including their designs, uses, benefits, repair, and maintenance. **Design:** Design techniques, principles, tools, and instruments involved in the production and use of precision technical plans, blueprints, drawings, and models. **Engineering and Technology:** Equipment, tools, and mechanical devices and their uses to produce motion, light, power, technology, and other applications. **Physics:** Physical principles, laws, and applications, including air, water, material dynamics, light, atomic principles, heat, electric theory, earth formations, and meteorological and related natural phenomena. **Transportation:** Principles and methods for moving people or goods by air, rail, sea, or road, including their relative costs, advantages, and limitations. **Chemistry:** The composition, structure, and properties of substances and of the chemical processes and transformations that they undergo. This includes uses of chemicals and their interactions, danger signs, production techniques, and disposal methods.

Work Environment: Indoors; noisy; contaminants; standing; using hands on objects, tools, or controls; bending or twisting the body.

Multi-Media Artists and Animators

* Education/Training Required: Bachelor's degree
* Annual Earnings: $54,550
* Beginning Wage: $30,620
* Earnings Growth Potential: High
* Growth: 25.8%
* Annual Job Openings: 13,182
* Self-Employed: 69.7%
* Part-Time: 22.5%

Create special effects, animation, or other visual images, using film, video, computers, or other electronic tools and media, for use in products or creations such as computer games, movies, music videos, and commercials. Design complex graphics and animation, using independent judgment, creativity, and computer equipment. Create two-dimensional and three-dimensional images depicting objects in motion or illustrating a process, using computer animation or modeling programs. Make objects or characters appear lifelike by manipulating light, color, texture, shadow, and transparency or manipulating static images to give the illusion of motion. Apply story development, directing, cinematography, and editing to animation to create storyboards that show the flow of the animation and map out key scenes and characters. Assemble, typeset, scan, and produce digital camera-ready art or film negatives and printer's proofs. Script, plan, and create animated narrative sequences under tight deadlines, using computer software and hand-drawing techniques. Create basic designs, drawings, and illustrations for product labels, cartons, direct mail, or television. Create pen-and-paper images to be scanned, edited, colored, textured, or animated by computer. Develop briefings, brochures, multimedia presentations, Web pages, promotional products, technical illustrations, and computer artwork for use in products, technical manuals, literature, newsletters, and slide shows. Use models to simulate the behavior of animated objects in the finished sequence. Create and install special effects as required by the script, mixing chemicals and fabricating needed parts from wood, metal, plaster, and clay. Participate in design and production of multimedia campaigns, handling budgeting and scheduling and assisting with such responsibilities as production coordination, background design, and progress tracking. Convert real objects to animated objects through modeling, using techniques such as optical scanning. Implement and maintain configuration control systems.

Personality Type: Artistic. These occupations frequently involve working with forms, designs, and patterns. They often require self-expression, and the work can be done without following a clear set of rules.

GOE—Interest Area/Cluster: 03. Arts and Communication. **Work Group:** 03.09. Media Technology. **Other Jobs in This Work Group:** Audio and Video Equipment Technicians; Broadcast Technicians; Camera Operators, Television, Video, and Motion Picture; Film and Video Editors; Photographers; Radio Operators; Sound Engineering Technicians.

Skills—Operations Analysis: Analyzing needs and product requirements to create a design. **Technology Design:** Generating or adapting equipment and technology to serve user needs. **Time Management:** Managing one's own time and the time of others. **Judgment and Decision Making:** Weighing the relative costs and benefits of a potential action. **Science:** Using scientific methods to solve problems. **Reading Comprehension:** Understanding written sentences and paragraphs in work-related documents. **Active Listening:** Listening to what other people are saying and asking questions as appropriate. **Programming:** Writing computer programs for various purposes.

Education and Training Programs: Animation, Interactive Technology, Video Graphics and Special Effects; Drawing; Graphic Design; Intermedia/Multimedia; Painting; Printmaking; Web Page, Digital/Multimedia and Information Resources Design. **Related Knowledge/Courses—Fine Arts:** Theory and techniques required to produce, compose, and perform works of music, dance, visual arts, drama, and sculpture. **Design:** Design techniques, principles, tools, and instruments involved in the production and use of precision technical plans, blueprints, drawings, and models. **Computers and Electronics:** Electric circuit boards, processors, chips, and computer hardware and software, including applications and programming. **Communications and Media:** Media production, communication, and dissemination techniques and methods, including alternative ways to inform and entertain via written, oral, and visual media. **English Language:** The structure and content of the English language, including the meaning and spelling of words, rules of composition, and grammar.

Work Environment: Indoors; sitting; using hands on objects, tools, or controls; repetitive motions.

M

Municipal Clerks

- ❀ Education/Training Required: Short-term on-the-job training
- ❀ Annual Earnings: $32,330
- ❀ Beginning Wage: $21,050
- ❀ Earnings Growth Potential: Low
- ❀ Growth: 8.8%
- ❀ Annual Job Openings: 16,163
- ❀ Self-Employed: 2.7%
- ❀ Part-Time: 9.6%

The job openings listed here are shared with Court Clerks and with License Clerks.

Draft agendas and bylaws for town or city council, record minutes of council meetings, answer official correspondence, keep fiscal records and accounts, and prepare reports on civic needs. Participate in the administration of municipal elections, including preparation and distribution of ballots, appointment and training of election officers, and tabulation and certification of results. Record and edit the minutes of meetings; then distribute them to appropriate officials and staff members. Plan and direct the maintenance, filing, safekeeping, and computerization of all municipal documents. Issue public notification of all official activities and meetings. Maintain and update documents such as municipal codes and city charters. Prepare meeting agendas and packets of related information. Prepare ordinances, resolutions, and proclamations so that they can be executed, recorded, archived, and distributed. Respond to requests for information from the public, other municipalities, state officials, and state and federal legislative offices. Maintain fiscal records and accounts. Perform budgeting duties, including assisting in budget preparation, expenditure review, and budget administration. Perform general office duties such as taking and transcribing dictation, typing and proofreading correspondence, distributing and filing official forms, and scheduling appointments. Coordinate and maintain office-tracking systems for correspondence and follow-up actions. Research information in the municipal archives upon request of public officials and private citizens. Perform contract administration duties, assisting with bid openings and the awarding of contracts. Collaborate with other staff to assist in the development and implementation of goals, objectives, policies, and priorities. Represent municipalities at community events and serve as liaisons on community committees. Serve as a notary of the public. Issue various permits and licenses, including marriage, fishing, hunting, and dog licenses, and collect appropriate fees. Provide assistance to persons with disabilities in reaching less-accessible areas of municipal facilities. Process claims against the municipality, maintaining files and log of claims, and coordinate claim response and handling with municipal claims administrators.

Personality Type: Conventional. These occupations frequently involve following set procedures and routines and can include working with data and details more than with ideas. Usually there is a clear line of authority to follow.

GOE—Interest Area/Cluster: 07. Government and Public Administration. **Work Group:** 07.04. Public Administration Clerical Support. **Other Jobs in This Work Group:** Court Clerks; Court Reporters; Court, Municipal, and License Clerks; License Clerks.

Skills—Service Orientation: Actively looking for ways to help people. **Management of Financial Resources:** Determining how money will be spent to get the work done and accounting for these expenditures. **Writing:** Communicating effectively with others in writing as indicated by the needs of the audience. **Social Perceptiveness:** Being aware of others' reactions and understanding why they react the way they do. **Active Listening:** Listening to what other people are saying and asking questions as appropriate. **Operations Analysis:** Analyzing needs and product requirements to create a design. **Persuasion:** Persuading others to approach things differently. **Management of Personnel Resources:** Motivating, developing, and directing people as they work; identifying the best people for the job.

Education and Training Program: General Office Occupations and Clerical Services. **Related Knowledge/ Courses—Clerical Practices:** Administrative and clerical procedures and systems such as word-processing systems, filing and records management systems, stenography and transcription, forms, design principles, and other office procedures and terminology. **Law and Government:** Laws, legal codes, court procedures, precedents, government regulations, executive orders, agency rules, and the democratic political process. **Economics and Accounting:** Economic and accounting principles and practices, the financial markets, banking, and the analysis and reporting of financial data. **English Language:** The structure and content of the English language, including the meaning and spelling of words, rules of composition, and grammar. **Personnel and Human Resources:** Principles and procedures for personnel recruitment; selection; training; compensation and benefits; labor relations and negotiation; and personnel information systems. **Administration and Management:** Principles and processes involved in business and organizational planning, coordination, and execution. This includes strategic planning, resource allocation, manpower modeling, leadership techniques, and production methods.

Work Environment: Indoors; sitting.

Municipal Fire Fighters

- ❋ Education/Training Required: Long-term on-the-job training
- ❋ Annual Earnings: $43,170
- ❋ Beginning Wage: $21,530
- ❋ Earnings Growth Potential: Very high
- ❋ Growth: 12.1%
- ❋ Annual Job Openings: 18,887
- ❋ Self-Employed: 0.0%
- ❋ Part-Time: 1.3%

The job openings listed here are shared with Forest Fire Fighters.

Control and extinguish municipal fires, protect life and property, and conduct rescue efforts. Administer first aid and cardiopulmonary resuscitation to injured persons. Rescue victims from burning buildings and accident sites. Search burning buildings to locate fire victims. Drive and operate fire fighting vehicles and equipment. Move toward the source of a fire, using knowledge of types of fires, construction design, building materials, and physical layout of properties. Dress with equipment such as fire-resistant clothing and breathing apparatus. Position and climb ladders to gain access to upper levels of buildings or to rescue individuals from burning structures. Take action to contain hazardous chemicals that might catch fire, leak, or spill. Assess fires and situations and report conditions to superiors to receive instructions, using two-way radios. Respond to fire alarms and other calls for assistance, such as automobile and industrial accidents. Operate pumps connected to high-pressure hoses. Select and attach hose nozzles, depending on fire type, and direct streams of water or chemicals onto fires. Create openings in buildings for ventilation or entrance, using axes, chisels, crowbars, electric saws, or core cutters. Inspect fire sites after flames have been extinguished to ensure that there is no further danger. Lay hose lines and connect them to water supplies. Protect property from water and smoke, using waterproof salvage covers, smoke ejectors, and deodorants. Participate in physical training activities to maintain a high level of physical fitness. Salvage property

by removing broken glass, pumping out water, and ventilating buildings to remove smoke. Participate in fire drills and demonstrations of fire fighting techniques. Clean and maintain fire stations and fire fighting equipment and apparatus. Collaborate with police to respond to accidents, disasters, and arson investigation calls. Establish firelines to prevent unauthorized persons from entering areas near fires. Inform and educate the public on fire prevention. Inspect buildings for fire hazards and compliance with fire prevention ordinances, testing and checking smoke alarms and fire suppression equipment as necessary.

Personality Type: Realistic. These occupations frequently involve work activities that include practical, hands-on problems and solutions. They often deal with plants; animals; and real-world materials such as wood, tools, and machinery. Many of the occupations require working outside and don't involve a lot of paperwork or working closely with others.

GOE—Interest Area/Cluster: 12. Law and Public Safety. **Work Group:** 12.06. Emergency Responding. **Other Jobs in This Work Group:** Emergency Medical Technicians and Paramedics; Fire Fighters; Forest Fire Fighters.

Skills—Equipment Maintenance: Performing routine maintenance and determining when and what kind of maintenance is needed. **Equipment Selection:** Determining the kind of tools and equipment needed to do a job. **Service Orientation:** Actively looking for ways to help people. **Operation Monitoring:** Watching gauges, dials, or other indicators to make sure a machine is working properly. **Science:** Using scientific methods to solve problems. **Social Perceptiveness:** Being aware of others' reactions and understanding why they react the way they do. **Coordination:** Adjusting actions in relation to others' actions. **Complex Problem Solving:** Identifying complex problems, reviewing the options, and implementing solutions.

Education and Training Programs: Fire Protection, Other; Fire Science/Firefighting. **Related Knowledge/Courses— Medicine and Dentistry:** The information and techniques needed to diagnose and treat injuries, diseases, and deformities. This includes symptoms, treatment alternatives, drug properties and interactions, and preventive health-care measures. **Physics:** Physical principles, laws, and applications, including air, water, material dynamics, light, atomic principles, heat, electric theory, earth formations, and meteorological and related natural phenomena. **Customer and Personal Service:** Principles and processes for providing customer and personal services, including needs assessment techniques, quality service standards, alternative delivery systems, and customer satisfaction evaluation techniques. **Building and Construction:** Materials, methods, and the appropriate tools to construct objects, structures, and buildings. **Chemistry:** The composition, structure, and properties of substances and of the chemical processes and transformations that they undergo. This includes uses of chemicals and their interactions, danger signs, production techniques, and disposal methods. **Public Safety and Security:** Weaponry; public safety; security operations, rules, regulations, precautions, and prevention; and the protection of people, data, and property.

Work Environment: More often outdoors than indoors; noisy; contaminants; disease or infections; hazardous equipment.

Municipal Fire Fighting and Prevention Supervisors

- ❈ Education/Training Required: Work experience in a related occupation
- ❈ Annual Earnings: $65,040
- ❈ Beginning Wage: $37,930
- ❈ Earnings Growth Potential: High
- ❈ Growth: 11.5%
- ❈ Annual Job Openings: 3,771
- ❈ Self-Employed: 0.0%
- ❈ Part-Time: 0.4%

The job openings listed here are shared with Forest Fire Fighting and Prevention Supervisors.

Supervise fire fighters who control and extinguish municipal fires, protect life and property, and conduct rescue efforts. Assign firefighters to jobs at strategic locations to facilitate rescue of persons and maximize application of extinguishing agents. Provide emergency medical services as required and perform light to heavy rescue functions at emergencies. Assess nature and extent of fire, condition of building, danger to adjacent buildings, and water supply status to determine crew or company requirements. Instruct and drill fire department personnel in assigned duties, including firefighting, medical care, hazardous materials response, fire prevention, and related subjects. Evaluate the performance of assigned firefighting personnel. Direct the training of firefighters, assigning of instructors to training classes, and providing of supervisors with reports on training progress and status. Prepare activity reports listing fire call locations, actions taken, fire types and probable causes, damage estimates, and situation dispositions. Maintain required maps and records. Attend in-service training classes to remain current in knowledge of codes, laws, ordinances, and regulations. Evaluate fire station procedures to ensure efficiency and enforcement of departmental regulations. Direct firefighters in station maintenance duties and participate in these duties. Compile and maintain equipment and personnel records, including accident reports. Direct investigation of cases of suspected arson, hazards, and false alarms and submit reports outlining findings. Recommend personnel actions related to disciplinary procedures, performance, leaves of absence, and grievances. Supervise and participate in the inspection of properties to ensure that they are in compliance with applicable fire codes, ordinances, laws, regulations, and standards. Write and submit proposals for repair, modification, or replacement of firefighting equipment. Coordinate the distribution of fire prevention promotional materials. Identify corrective actions needed to bring properties into compliance with applicable fire codes and ordinances and conduct follow-up inspections to see if corrective actions have been taken. Participate in creating fire safety guidelines and evacuation schemes for non-residential buildings.

Personality Type: Enterprising. These occupations frequently involve starting up and carrying out projects and can involve leading people and making many decisions. They sometimes require risk taking and often deal with business.

GOE—Interest Area/Cluster: 12. Law and Public Safety. **Work Group:** 12.01. Managerial Work in Law and Public Safety. **Other Jobs in This Work Group:** Emergency Management Specialists; First-Line Supervisors/Managers of Correctional Officers; First-Line Supervisors/Managers of Fire Fighting and Prevention Workers; First-Line Supervisors/Managers of Police and Detectives; Forest Fire Fighting and Prevention Supervisors.

Skills—Equipment Maintenance: Performing routine maintenance and determining when and what kind of maintenance is needed. **Management of Personnel Resources:** Motivating, developing, and directing people as they work; identifying the best people for the job. **Service Orientation:** Actively looking for ways to help people. **Operation Monitoring:** Watching gauges, dials, or other indicators to make sure a machine is working properly. **Management of Material Resources:** Obtaining and seeing to the appropriate use of equipment, facilities, and materials needed to do certain work. **Coordination:** Adjusting actions in relation to others' actions. **Operation and Control:** Controlling operations of equipment or systems. **Equipment Selection:** Determining the kind of tools and equipment needed to do a job.

Education and Training Programs: Fire Protection and Safety Technology/Technician Training; Fire Services Administration. **Related Knowledge/Courses—Public Safety and Security:** Weaponry; public safety; security operations, rules, regulations, precautions, and prevention; and the protection of people, data, and property. **Building and Construction:** Materials, methods, and the appropriate tools to construct objects, structures, and buildings. **Medicine and Dentistry:** The information and techniques needed to diagnose and treat injuries, diseases, and deformities. This includes symptoms, treatment alternatives, drug properties and interactions, and preventive health-care measures. **Education and Training:** Instructional methods and training techniques, including curriculum design principles, learning theory, group and individual teaching techniques, design of individual development plans, and test design principles. **Mechanical Devices:** Machines and tools, including their designs, uses, benefits, repair, and maintenance. **Therapy and Counseling:** Information and techniques needed to rehabilitate physical and mental ailments and to provide career guidance, including alternative treatments, rehabilitation equipment and its proper use, and methods to evaluate treatment effects.

Work Environment: More often outdoors than indoors; noisy; contaminants; hazardous equipment; using hands on objects, tools, or controls.

Museum Technicians and Conservators

- ❈ Education/Training Required: Bachelor's degree
- ❈ Annual Earnings: $35,350
- ❈ Beginning Wage: $21,630
- ❈ Earnings Growth Potential: Medium
- ❈ Growth: 15.9%
- ❈ Annual Job Openings: 1,341
- ❈ Self-Employed: 1.3%
- ❈ Part-Time: 18.4%

Prepare specimens, such as fossils, skeletal parts, lace, and textiles, for museum collection and exhibits. May restore documents or install, arrange, and exhibit materials.

Install, arrange, assemble, and prepare artifacts for exhibition, ensuring the artifacts' safety, reporting their status and condition, and identifying and correcting any problems with the setup. Coordinate exhibit installations, assisting with design; constructing displays, dioramas, display cases, and models; and ensuring the availability of necessary materials. Determine whether objects need repair and choose the safest and most effective method of repair. Clean objects, such as paper, textiles, wood, metal, glass, rock, pottery, and furniture, using cleansers, solvents, soap solutions, and polishes. Prepare artifacts for storage and shipping. Supervise and work with volunteers. Present public programs and tours. Specialize in particular materials or types of object, such as documents and books, paintings, decorative arts, textiles, metals, or architectural materials. Recommend preservation procedures, such as control of temperature and humidity, to curatorial and building staff. Classify and assign registration numbers to artifacts and supervise inventory control. Direct and supervise curatorial and technical staff in the handling, mounting, care, and storage of art objects. Perform on-site fieldwork, which may involve interviewing people, inspecting and identifying artifacts, note-taking, viewing sites and collections, and repainting exhibition spaces. Repair, restore, and reassemble artifacts, designing and fabricating missing or broken parts, to restore them to their original appearance and prevent deterioration. Prepare reports on the operation of conservation laboratories, documenting the condition of artifacts, treatment options, and the methods of preservation and repair used. Study object documentation or conduct standard chemical and physical tests to ascertain the object's age, composition, original appearance, need for treatment or restoration, and appropriate preservation method. Cut and weld metal sections in reconstruction or renovation of exterior structural sections and accessories of exhibits. Perform tests and examinations to establish storage and conservation requirements, policies, and procedures.

Personality Type: Realistic. These occupations frequently involve work activities that include practical, hands-on problems and solutions. They often deal with plants; animals; and real-world materials such as wood, tools, and machinery. Many of the occupations require working outside and don't involve a lot of paperwork or working closely with others.

GOE—Interest Area/Cluster: 05. Education and Training. **Work Group:** 05.05. Archival and Museum Services. **Other Jobs in This Work Group:** Archivists; Audio-Visual Collections Specialists; Curators.

Skills—Management of Material Resources: Obtaining and seeing to the appropriate use of equipment, facilities, and materials needed to do certain work. **Repairing:** Repairing machines or systems, using the needed tools. **Installation:** Installing equipment, machines, wiring, or programs to meet specifications. **Technology Design:** Generating or adapting equipment and technology to serve user needs. **Equipment Maintenance:** Performing routine maintenance and determining when and what kind of maintenance is needed. **Equipment Selection:** Determining the kind of tools and equipment needed to do a job. **Operations Analysis:** Analyzing needs and product requirements to create a design. **Science:** Using scientific methods to solve problems.

Education and Training Programs: Art History, Criticism and Conservation; Museology/Museum Studies; Public/Applied History and Archival Administration. **Related Knowledge/Courses—History and Archeology:** Historical events and their causes, indicators, and impact on particular civilizations and cultures. **Fine Arts:** Theory and techniques required to produce, compose, and perform works of music, dance, visual arts, drama, and sculpture. **Sociology and Anthropology:** Group behavior and dynamics; societal trends and influences; and cultures and their history, migrations, ethnicity, and origins. **Design:** Design techniques, principles, tools, and instruments involved in the production and use of precision technical plans, blueprints, drawings, and models. **Clerical Practices:** Administrative and clerical procedures and systems such as word-processing systems, filing and records management systems, stenography and transcription, forms, design principles, and other office procedures and terminology. **Building and Construction:** Materials, methods, and the appropriate tools to construct objects, structures, and buildings.

Work Environment: Indoors; standing; using hands on objects, tools, or controls.

Music Composers and Arrangers

* Education/Training Required: Work experience plus degree
* Annual Earnings: $40,150
* Beginning Wage: $16,110
* Earnings Growth Potential: Very high
* Growth: 12.9%
* Annual Job Openings: 8,597
* Self-Employed: 44.7%
* Part-Time: 37.0%

The job openings listed here are shared with Music Directors.

Write and transcribe musical scores. Copy parts from scores for individual performers. Transpose music from one voice or instrument to another to accommodate particular musicians. Use computers and synthesizers to compose, orchestrate, and arrange music. Write changes directly into compositions or use computer software to make changes. Confer with producers and directors to define the nature and placement of film or television music. Guide musicians during rehearsals, performances, or recording sessions. Study original pieces of music to become familiar with them prior to making any changes. Study films or scripts to determine how musical scores can be used to create desired effects or moods. Write music for commercial mediums, including advertising jingles or film soundtracks. Accept commissions to create music for special occasions. Arrange music composed by others, changing the music to achieve desired effects. Write musical scores for orchestras, bands, choral groups, or individual instrumentalists or vocalists, using knowledge of music theory and of instrumental and vocal capabilities. Score compositions so that they are consistent with instrumental and vocal capabilities such as ranges and keys, using knowledge of music theory. Apply elements of music theory to create musical and tonal structures, including harmonies and melodies. Collaborate with other colleagues such as copyists to complete final scores. Determine voices, instruments, harmonic structures, rhythms, tempos, and tone balances required to achieve the effects desired in musical compositions. Experiment with different sounds and types and pieces of music, using synthesizers and computers as necessary to test and evaluate ideas. Explore and develop musical ideas based on sources such as imagination or sounds in the environment. Rewrite original musical scores in different musical styles by changing rhythms, harmonies, or tempos. Transcribe ideas for musical compositions into musical notation, using instruments, pen and paper, or computers. Create original musical forms or write within circumscribed musical forms such as sonatas, symphonies, or operas.

Personality Type: Artistic. These occupations frequently involve working with forms, designs, and patterns. They often require self-expression, and the work can be done without following a clear set of rules.

GOE—Interest Area/Cluster: 03. Arts and Communication. **Work Group:** 03.07. Music. **Other Jobs in This Work Group:** Music Directors; Music Directors and Composers; Musicians and Singers; Musicians, Instrumental; Singers; Talent Directors.

Skills—Management of Financial Resources: Determining how money will be spent to get the work done and accounting for these expenditures. **Installation:** Installing equipment, machines, wiring, or programs to meet specifications. **Equipment Maintenance:** Performing routine maintenance and determining when and what kind of maintenance is needed. **Operation and Control:** Controlling operations of equipment or systems. **Management of Material Resources:** Obtaining and seeing to the appropriate use of equipment, facilities, and materials needed to do certain work. **Writing:** Communicating effectively with others in writing as indicated by the needs of the audience. **Technology Design:** Generating or adapting equipment and technology to serve user needs. **Operations Analysis:** Analyzing needs and product requirements to create a design.

Education and Training Programs: Conducting; Music Management and Merchandising; Music Performance, General; Music Theory and Composition; Music, Other; Musicology and Ethnomusicology; Religious/Sacred Music; Voice and Opera. **Related Knowledge/Courses—Fine Arts:** Theory and techniques required to produce, compose, and perform works of music, dance, visual arts, drama, and sculpture. **Communications and Media:** Media production, communication, and dissemination techniques and methods, including alternative ways to inform and entertain via written, oral, and visual media. **Computers and Electronics:** Electric circuit boards, processors, chips, and computer hardware and software, including applications and programming. **Sales and Marketing:** Principles and methods involved in showing, promoting, and selling products or services. This includes marketing strategies and tactics, product demonstration and sales techniques, and sales control systems. **Production and Processing:** Inputs, outputs, raw materials, waste, quality control, costs, and techniques for maximizing the manufacture and distribution of goods.

Design: Design techniques, principles, tools, and instruments involved in the production and use of precision technical plans, blueprints, drawings, and models.

Work Environment: Indoors; sitting; using hands on objects, tools, or controls; repetitive motions.

Music Directors

* Education/Training Required: Work experience plus degree
* Annual Earnings: $40,150
* Beginning Wage: $16,110
* Earnings Growth Potential: Very high
* Growth: 12.9%
* Annual Job Openings: 8,597
* Self-Employed: 44.7%
* Part-Time: 37.0%

The job openings listed here are shared with Music Composers and Arrangers.

Direct and conduct instrumental or vocal performances by musical groups such as orchestras or choirs. Study scores to learn the music in detail, and to develop interpretations. Consider such factors as ensemble size and abilities, availability of scores, and the need for musical variety in order to select music to be performed. Use gestures to shape the music being played, communicating desired tempo, phrasing, tone, color, pitch, volume, and other performance aspects. Engage services of composers to write scores. Plan and implement fund-raising and promotional activities. Coordinate and organize tours or hire touring companies to arrange concert dates, venues, accommodations, and transportation for longer tours. Confer with clergy to select music for church services. Transcribe musical compositions and melodic lines to adapt them to a particular group or to create a particular musical style. Audition and select performers for musical presentations. Meet with composers to discuss interpretations of their works. Conduct guest soloists in addition to ensemble members. Collaborate with music librarians to ensure availability of scores. Assign and review staff work in such areas as scoring, arranging, and copying music and vocal coaching. Position members within groups to obtain balance among instrumental or vocal sections. Plan and schedule rehearsals and performances, and arrange details such as locations, accompanists, and instrumentalists. Meet with soloists and concertmasters to discuss and prepare for performances. Direct groups at rehearsals and live or recorded performances in order to achieve desired effects such as tonal and harmonic balance, dynamics, rhythm, and tempo. Perform administrative tasks such as applying for grants, developing budgets, negotiating contracts, and designing and printing programs and other promotional materials.

Personality Type: Artistic. These occupations frequently involve working with forms, designs, and patterns. They often require self-expression, and the work can be done without following a clear set of rules.

GOE—Interest Area/Cluster: 03. Arts and Communication. **Work Group:** 03.07. Music. **Other Jobs in This Work Group:** Music Composers and Arrangers; Music Directors and Composers; Musicians and Singers; Musicians, Instrumental; Singers; Talent Directors.

Skills—Coordination: Adjusting actions in relation to others' actions. **Management of Personnel Resources:** Motivating, developing, and directing people as they work; identifying the best people for the job. **Social Perceptiveness:** Being aware of others' reactions and understanding why they react the way they do. **Negotiation:** Bringing others together and trying to reconcile differences. **Monitoring:** Assessing how well one is doing when learning or doing something. **Learning Strategies:** Using multiple approaches when learning or teaching new things. **Persuasion:** Persuading others to approach things differently. **Instructing:** Teaching others how to do something.

Education and Training Programs: Conducting; Music Management and Merchandising; Music Performance, General; Music Theory and Composition; Music, Other; Musicology and Ethnomusicology; Religious/Sacred Music; Voice and Opera. **Related Knowledge/Courses—Fine Arts:** Theory and techniques required to produce, compose, and perform works of music, dance, visual arts, drama, and sculpture. **Philosophy and Theology:** Different philosophical systems and religions, including their basic principles, values, ethics, ways of thinking, customs, and practices and their impact on human culture. **Education and Training:** Instructional methods and training techniques, including curriculum design principles, learning theory, group and individual teaching techniques, design of individual development plans, and test design principles. **History and Archeology:** Historical events and their causes, indicators, and impact on particular civilizations and cultures. **Communications and Media:** Media production, communication, and dissemination techniques and methods, including alternative ways to inform and entertain via written, oral, and visual media. **Personnel and Human Resources:** Principles

and procedures for personnel recruitment; selection; training; compensation and benefits; labor relations and negotiation; and personnel information systems.

Work Environment: More often sitting than standing.

Natural Sciences Managers

- ❋ Education/Training Required: Work experience plus degree
- ❋ Annual Earnings: $104,040
- ❋ Beginning Wage: $62,880
- ❋ Earnings Growth Potential: Medium
- ❋ Growth: 11.4%
- ❋ Annual Job Openings: 3,661
- ❋ Self-Employed: 0.6%
- ❋ Part-Time: 4.4%

Plan, direct, or coordinate activities in such fields as life sciences, physical sciences, mathematics, and statistics and research and development in these fields. Confer with scientists, engineers, regulators, and others to plan and review projects and to provide technical assistance. Develop client relationships and communicate with clients to explain proposals, present research findings, establish specifications, or discuss project status. Plan and direct research, development, and production activities. Prepare project proposals. Design and coordinate successive phases of problem analysis, solution proposals, and testing. Review project activities and prepare and review research, testing, and operational reports. Hire, supervise, and evaluate engineers, technicians, researchers, and other staff. Determine scientific and technical goals within broad outlines provided by top management and make detailed plans to accomplish these goals. Develop and implement policies, standards, and procedures for the architectural, scientific, and technical work performed to ensure regulatory compliance and operations enhancement. Develop innovative technology and train staff for its implementation. Provide for stewardship of plant and animal resources and habitats, studying land use; monitoring animal populations; and providing shelter, resources, and medical treatment for animals. Conduct own research in field of expertise. Recruit personnel and oversee the development and maintenance of staff competence. Advise and assist in obtaining patents or meeting other legal requirements. Prepare and administer budget, approve and review expenditures, and prepare financial reports. Make presentations at professional meetings to further knowledge in the field.

Personality Type: Enterprising. These occupations frequently involve starting up and carrying out projects and can involve leading people and making many decisions. They sometimes require risk taking and often deal with business.

GOE—Interest Area/Cluster: 15. Scientific Research, Engineering, and Mathematics. **Work Group:** 15.01. Managerial Work in Scientific Research, Engineering, and Mathematics. **Other Jobs in This Work Group:** Engineering Managers.

Skills—Science: Using scientific methods to solve problems. **Mathematics:** Using mathematics to solve problems. **Active Learning:** Working with new material or information to grasp its implications. **Reading Comprehension:** Understanding written sentences and paragraphs in work-related documents. **Writing:** Communicating effectively with others in writing as indicated by the needs of the audience. **Management of Personnel Resources:** Motivating, developing, and directing people as they work; identifying the best people for the job. **Complex Problem Solving:** Identifying complex problems, reviewing the options, and implementing solutions. **Critical Thinking:** Using logic and analysis to identify the strengths and weaknesses of different approaches.

Education and Training Programs: Analytical Chemistry; Astronomy; Biology/Biological Sciences; Botany/Plant Biology; Chemistry, General; Entomology; Geology/Earth Science; Inorganic Chemistry; Marine Biology and Biological Oceanography; Mathematics, General; Meteorology; Microbiology; Molecular Biology; Nutrition Sciences; Oceanography, Organic Chemistry; Paleontology; Physics, General; Plant Pathology/Phytopathology; Statistics, General; Theoretical and Mathematical Physics; Toxicology; Virology; Zoology; others. **Related Knowledge/Courses—Biology:** Plant and animal living tissue, cells, organisms, and entities, including their functions, interdependencies, and interactions with each other and the environment. **Chemistry:** The composition, structure, and properties of substances and of the chemical processes and transformations that they undergo. This includes uses of chemicals and their interactions, danger signs, production techniques, and disposal methods. **Engineering and Technology:** Equipment, tools, and mechanical devices and their uses to produce motion, light, power, technology, and other applications. **Law and Government:** Laws, legal codes, court procedures, precedents, government regulations, executive orders, agency rules, and the democratic political process. **Administration and Management:** Principles and processes involved

in business and organizational planning, coordination, and execution. This includes strategic planning, resource allocation, manpower modeling, leadership techniques, and production methods. **Physics:** Physical principles, laws, and applications, including air, water, material dynamics, light, atomic principles, heat, electric theory, earth formations, and meteorological and related natural phenomena.

Work Environment: Indoors; noisy; sitting.

Network and Computer Systems Administrators

- ❋ Education/Training Required: Bachelor's degree
- ❋ Annual Earnings: $64,690
- ❋ Beginning Wage: $39,970
- ❋ Earnings Growth Potential: Medium
- ❋ Growth: 27.0%
- ❋ Annual Job Openings: 37,010
- ❋ Self-Employed: 0.4%
- ❋ Part-Time: 3.1%

The job openings listed here are shared with Computer Security Specialists.

Install, configure, and support organizations' local area networks (LANs), wide area networks (WANs), and Internet systems or segments of network systems. Maintain network hardware and software. Monitor networks to ensure network availability to all system users and perform necessary maintenance to support network availability. May supervise other network support and client server specialists and plan, coordinate, and implement network security measures. Maintain and administer computer networks and related computing environments, including computer hardware, systems software, applications software, and all configurations. Perform data backups and disaster recovery operations. Diagnose, troubleshoot, and resolve hardware, software, or other network and system problems and replace defective components when necessary. Plan, coordinate, and implement network security measures to protect data, software, and hardware. Configure, monitor, and maintain e-mail applications or virus protection software. Operate master consoles to monitor the performance of computer systems and networks and to coordinate computer network access and use. Load computer tapes and disks and install software and printer paper or forms. Design, configure, and test computer hardware, networking software, and operating system software. Monitor network performance to determine whether adjustments need to be made and to determine where changes will need to be made in the future. Confer with network users about how to solve existing system problems. Research new technologies by attending seminars, reading trade articles, or taking classes and implement or recommend the implementation of new technologies. Analyze equipment performance records to determine the need for repair or replacement. Implement and provide technical support for voice services and equipment such as private branch exchanges, voice mail systems, and telecom systems. Maintain inventories of parts for emergency repairs. Recommend changes to improve systems and network configurations and determine hardware or software requirements related to such changes. Gather data pertaining to customer needs and use the information to identify, predict, interpret, and evaluate system and network requirements. Train people in computer system use. Coordinate with vendors and with company personnel to facilitate purchases. Perform routine network startup and shutdown procedures and maintain control records. Maintain logs related to network functions as well as maintenance and repair records.

Personality Type: Investigative. These occupations frequently involve working with ideas and require an extensive amount of thinking. They can involve searching for facts and figuring out problems mentally.

GOE—Interest Area/Cluster: 11. Information Technology. **Work Group:** 11.01. Managerial Work in Information Technology. **Other Jobs in This Work Group:** Computer and Information Systems Managers.

Skills—Programming: Writing computer programs for various purposes. **Systems Analysis:** Determining how a system should work and how changes will affect outcomes. **Systems Evaluation:** Looking at many indicators of system performance and taking into account their accuracy. **Operation Monitoring:** Watching gauges, dials, or other indicators to make sure a machine is working properly. **Quality Control Analysis:** Evaluating the quality or performance of products, services, or processes. **Troubleshooting:** Determining what is causing an operating error and deciding what to do about it. **Management of Personnel Resources:** Motivating, developing, and directing people as they work; identifying the best people for the job. **Operation and Control:** Controlling operations of equipment or systems.

Education and Training Programs: Computer and Information Sciences and Support Services, Other;

Computer and Information Sciences, General; Computer and Information Systems Security; Computer Systems Analysis/Analyst Training; Computer Systems Networking and Telecommunications; Information Science/Studies; System Administration/Administrator Training; System, Networking, and LAN/WAN Management/Manager Training. **Related Knowledge/Courses—Telecommunications:** Transmission, broadcasting, switching, control, and operation of telecommunications systems. **Computers and Electronics:** Electric circuit boards, processors, chips, and computer hardware and software, including applications and programming. **Clerical Practices:** Administrative and clerical procedures and systems such as word-processing systems, filing and records management systems, stenography and transcription, forms, design principles, and other office procedures and terminology. **Administration and Management:** Principles and processes involved in business and organizational planning, coordination, and execution. This includes strategic planning, resource allocation, manpower modeling, leadership techniques, and production methods. **Engineering and Technology:** Equipment, tools, and mechanical devices and their uses to produce motion, light, power, technology, and other applications.

Work Environment: Indoors; noisy; sitting; using hands on objects, tools, or controls; repetitive motions.

Network Designers

* Education/Training Required: Bachelor's degree
* Annual Earnings: $71,510
* Beginning Wage: $37,600
* Earnings Growth Potential: High
* Growth: 15.1%
* Annual Job Openings: 14,374
* Self-Employed: 6.6%
* Part-Time: 5.6%

The job openings listed here are shared with Computer Systems Engineers/Architects; Software Quality Assurance Engineers and Testers; Web Administrators; and Web Developers.

Determine user requirements and design specifications for computer networks. Plan and implement network upgrades. Develop network-related documentation. Design, build, or operate equipment configuration prototypes, including network hardware, software, servers, or server operation systems. Coordinate network operations, maintenance, repairs, or upgrades. Adjust network sizes to meet volume or capacity demands. Communicate with vendors to gather information about products, to alert them to future needs, to resolve problems, or to address system maintenance issues. Coordinate installation of new equipment. Coordinate network or design activities with designers of associated networks. Design, organize, and deliver product awareness, skills transfer, and product education sessions for staff and suppliers. Determine specific network hardware or software requirements, such as platforms, interfaces, bandwidths, or routine schemas. Develop disaster recovery plans. Communicate with customers, sales staff, or marketing staff to determine customer needs. Explain design specifications to integration or test engineers. Develop plans or budgets for network equipment replacement. Prepare design presentations and proposals for staff or customers. Supervise engineers and other staff in the design or implementation of network solutions. Use network computer-aided design (CAD) software packages to optimize network designs. Develop or maintain project reporting systems. Participate in network technology upgrade or expansion projects, including installation of hardware and software and integration testing. Research and test new or modified hardware or software products to determine performance and interoperability. Develop and implement solutions for network problems. Prepare or monitor project schedules, budgets, or cost control systems. Monitor and analyze network performance and data input/output reports to detect problems, identify inefficient use of computer resources, or perform capacity planning. Evaluate network designs to determine whether customer requirements are met efficiently and effectively. Estimate time and materials needed to complete projects. Develop or recommend network security measures, such as firewalls, network security audits, or automated security probes.

Personality Type: Conventional. These occupations frequently involve following set procedures and routines and can include working with data and details more than with ideas. Usually there is a clear line of authority to follow.

GOE—Interest Area/Cluster: 11. Information Technology. **Work Group:** 11.02. Information Technology Specialties. **Other Jobs in This Work Group:** Computer and Information Scientists, Research; Computer Operators; Computer Programmers; Computer Security Specialists; Computer Software Engineers, Applications; Computer Software Engineers, Systems Software; Computer Support Specialists; Computer Systems Analysts; Computer Systems Engineers/Architects; Database Administrators; Network Systems and Data Communications Analysts; Software

Quality Assurance Engineers and Testers; Web Administrators; Web Developers.

Skills—No data available.

Education and Training Programs: Computer and Information Sciences, General; Computer Engineering, General; Computer Science; Computer Software Engineering; Computer Systems Networking and Telecommunications. **Related Knowledge/Courses**—No data available.

Work Environment: No data available.

Network Systems and Data Communications Analysts

- ❋ Education/Training Required: Bachelor's degree
- ❋ Annual Earnings: $68,220
- ❋ Beginning Wage: $40,100
- ❋ Earnings Growth Potential: High
- ❋ Growth: 53.4%
- ❋ Annual Job Openings: 35,086
- ❋ Self-Employed: 17.5%
- ❋ Part-Time: 8.6%

Analyze, design, test, and evaluate network systems, such as local area networks (LAN); wide area networks (WAN); and Internet, intranet, and other data communications systems. Perform network modeling, analysis, and planning. Research and recommend network and data communications hardware and software. Includes telecommunications specialists who deal with the interfacing of computer and communications equipment. May supervise computer programmers. Maintain needed files by adding and deleting files on the network server and backing up files to guarantee their safety in the event of problems with the network. Monitor system performance and provide security measures, troubleshooting, and maintenance as needed. Assist users to diagnose and solve data communication problems. Set up user accounts, regulating and monitoring file access to ensure confidentiality and proper use. Design and implement systems, network configurations, and network architecture, including hardware and software technology, site locations, and integration of technologies. Maintain the peripherals, such as printers, that are connected to the network. Identify areas of operation that need upgraded equipment such as modems, fiber-optic cables, and telephone wires. Train users in use of equipment.

Develop and write procedures for installation, use, and troubleshooting of communications hardware and software. Adapt and modify existing software to meet specific needs. Work with other engineers, systems analysts, programmers, technicians, scientists, and top-level managers in the design, testing, and evaluation of systems. Test and evaluate hardware and software to determine efficiency, reliability, and compatibility with existing system and make purchase recommendations. Read technical manuals and brochures to determine which equipment meets establishment requirements. Consult customers, visit workplaces, or conduct surveys to determine present and future user needs. Visit vendors, attend conferences or training, and study technical journals to keep up with changes in technology.

Personality Type: Investigative. These occupations frequently involve working with ideas and require an extensive amount of thinking. They can involve searching for facts and figuring out problems mentally.

GOE—Interest Area/Cluster: 11. Information Technology. **Work Group:** 11.02. Information Technology Specialties. **Other Jobs in This Work Group:** Computer and Information Scientists, Research; Computer Operators; Computer Programmers; Computer Security Specialists; Computer Software Engineers, Applications; Computer Software Engineers, Systems Software; Computer Support Specialists; Computer Systems Analysts; Computer Systems Engineers/Architects; Database Administrators; Network Designers; Software Quality Assurance Engineers and Testers; Web Administrators; Web Developers.

Skills—Installation: Installing equipment, machines, wiring, or programs to meet specifications. **Technology Design:** Generating or adapting equipment and technology to serve user needs. **Troubleshooting:** Determining what is causing an operating error and deciding what to do about it. **Systems Analysis:** Determining how a system should work and how changes will affect outcomes. **Programming:** Writing computer programs for various purposes. **Systems Evaluation:** Looking at many indicators of system performance and taking into account their accuracy. **Management of Material Resources:** Obtaining and seeing to the appropriate use of equipment, facilities, and materials needed to do certain work. **Operations Analysis:** Analyzing needs and product requirements to create a design.

Education and Training Programs: Computer and Information Sciences, General; Computer and Information Systems Security; Computer Systems Analysis/Analyst Training; Computer Systems Networking and Telecommunications;

Information Technology; System, Networking, and LAN/WAN Management/Manager Training. **Related Knowledge/Courses—Telecommunications:** Transmission, broadcasting, switching, control, and operation of telecommunications systems. **Computers and Electronics:** Electric circuit boards, processors, chips, and computer hardware and software, including applications and programming. **Customer and Personal Service:** Principles and processes for providing customer and personal services, including needs assessment techniques, quality service standards, alternative delivery systems, and customer satisfaction evaluation techniques. **Engineering and Technology:** Equipment, tools, and mechanical devices and their uses to produce motion, light, power, technology, and other applications. **Education and Training:** Instructional methods and training techniques, including curriculum design principles, learning theory, group and individual teaching techniques, design of individual development plans, and test design principles. **Design:** Design techniques, principles, tools, and instruments involved in the production and use of precision technical plans, blueprints, drawings, and models.

Work Environment: Indoors; sitting.

Nuclear Engineers

- ❋ Education/Training Required: Bachelor's degree
- ❋ Annual Earnings: $94,420
- ❋ Beginning Wage: $66,460
- ❋ Earnings Growth Potential: Low
- ❋ Growth: 7.2%
- ❋ Annual Job Openings: 1,046
- ❋ Self-Employed: 0.0%
- ❋ Part-Time: 2.9%

Conduct research on nuclear engineering problems or apply principles and theory of nuclear science to problems concerned with release, control, and utilization of nuclear energy and nuclear waste disposal. Examine accidents to obtain data that can be used to design preventive measures. Monitor nuclear facility operations to identify any design, construction, or operation practices that violate safety regulations and laws or that could jeopardize the safety of operations. Keep abreast of developments and changes in the nuclear field by reading technical journals and by independent study and research. Perform experiments that will provide information about acceptable methods of nuclear material usage, nuclear fuel reclamation, and waste disposal. Design and oversee construction and operation of nuclear reactors and power plants and nuclear fuels reprocessing and reclamation systems. Design and develop nuclear equipment such as reactor cores, radiation shielding, and associated instrumentation and control mechanisms. Initiate corrective actions or order plant shutdowns in emergency situations. Recommend preventive measures to be taken in the handling of nuclear technology, based on data obtained from operations monitoring or from evaluation of test results. Write operational instructions to be used in nuclear plant operation and nuclear fuel and waste handling and disposal. Conduct tests of nuclear fuel behavior and cycles and performance of nuclear machinery and equipment to optimize performance of existing plants. Direct operating and maintenance activities of operational nuclear power plants to ensure efficiency and conformity to safety standards. Synthesize analyses of test results and use the results to prepare technical reports of findings and recommendations. Prepare construction project proposals that include cost estimates and discuss proposals with interested parties such as vendors, contractors, and nuclear facility review boards. Analyze available data and consult with other scientists to determine parameters of experimentation and suitability of analytical models. Design and direct nuclear research projects to discover facts, to test or modify theoretical models, or to develop new theoretical models or new uses for current models.

Personality Type: Investigative. These occupations frequently involve working with ideas and require an extensive amount of thinking. They can involve searching for facts and figuring out problems mentally.

GOE—Interest Area/Cluster: 15. Scientific Research, Engineering, and Mathematics. **Work Group:** 15.07. Research and Design Engineering. **Other Jobs in This Work Group:** Aerospace Engineers; Biomedical Engineers; Chemical Engineers; Civil Engineers; Computer Hardware Engineers; Electrical Engineers; Electronics Engineers, Except Computer; Marine Architects; Marine Engineers; Marine Engineers and Naval Architects; Materials Engineers; Mechanical Engineers.

Skills—Operation Monitoring: Watching gauges, dials, or other indicators to make sure a machine is working properly. **Technology Design:** Generating or adapting equipment and technology to serve user needs. **Systems Evaluation:** Looking at many indicators of system performance and taking into account their accuracy. **Systems Analysis:** Determining how a system should work and how changes will affect outcomes. **Operations Analysis:** Analyzing needs and

product requirements to create a design. **Quality Control Analysis:** Evaluating the quality or performance of products, services, or processes. **Science:** Using scientific methods to solve problems. **Mathematics:** Using mathematics to solve problems.

Education and Training Program: Nuclear Engineering. **Related Knowledge/Courses—Engineering and Technology:** Equipment, tools, and mechanical devices and their uses to produce motion, light, power, technology, and other applications. **Physics:** Physical principles, laws, and applications, including air, water, material dynamics, light, atomic principles, heat, electric theory, earth formations, and meteorological and related natural phenomena. **Design:** Design techniques, principles, tools, and instruments involved in the production and use of precision technical plans, blueprints, drawings, and models. **Chemistry:** The composition, structure, and properties of substances and of the chemical processes and transformations that they undergo. This includes uses of chemicals and their interactions, danger signs, production techniques, and disposal methods. **Mechanical Devices:** Machines and tools, including their designs, uses, benefits, repair, and maintenance. **Building and Construction:** Materials, methods, and the appropriate tools to construct objects, structures, and buildings.

Work Environment: Indoors; noisy; radiation; sitting.

Nuclear Equipment Operation Technicians

* Education/Training Required: Associate degree
* Annual Earnings: $66,140
* Beginning Wage: $40,520
* Earnings Growth Potential: Medium
* Growth: 6.7%
* Annual Job Openings: 1,021
* Self-Employed: 0.0%
* Part-Time: 3.9%

The job openings listed here are shared with Nuclear Monitoring Technicians.

Operate equipment used for the release, control, and utilization of nuclear energy to assist scientists in laboratory and production activities. Follow policies and procedures for radiation workers to ensure personnel safety. Modify, devise, and maintain equipment used in operations. Set control panel switches, according to standard procedures, to route electric power from sources and direct particle beams through injector units. Submit computations to supervisors for review. Calculate equipment operating factors, such as radiation times, dosages, temperatures, gamma intensities, and pressures, using standard formulas and conversion tables. Perform testing, maintenance, repair, and upgrading of accelerator systems. Warn maintenance workers of radiation hazards and direct workers to vacate hazardous areas. Monitor instruments, gauges, and recording devices in control rooms during operation of equipment under direction of nuclear experimenters. Write summaries of activities and record experimental data, such as accelerator performance, systems status, particle beam specification, and beam conditions obtained.

Personality Type: Realistic. These occupations frequently involve work activities that include practical, hands-on problems and solutions. They often deal with plants; animals; and real-world materials such as wood, tools, and machinery. Many of the occupations require working outside and don't involve a lot of paperwork or working closely with others.

GOE—Interest Area/Cluster: 15. Scientific Research, Engineering, and Mathematics. **Work Group:** 15.05. Physical Science Laboratory Technology. **Other Jobs in This Work Group:** Chemical Technicians; Nuclear Technicians.

Skills—Operation Monitoring: Watching gauges, dials, or other indicators to make sure a machine is working properly. **Operation and Control:** Controlling operations of equipment or systems. **Science:** Using scientific methods to solve problems. **Mathematics:** Using mathematics to solve problems. **Equipment Maintenance:** Performing routine maintenance and determining when and what kind of maintenance is needed. **Quality Control Analysis:** Evaluating the quality or performance of products, services, or processes. **Troubleshooting:** Determining what is causing an operating error and deciding what to do about it. **Reading Comprehension:** Understanding written sentences and paragraphs in work-related documents.

Education and Training Programs: Industrial Radiologic Technology/Technician Training; Nuclear and Industrial Radiologic Technologies/Technician Training, Other; Nuclear Engineering Technology/Technician Training; Nuclear/Nuclear Power Technology/Technician Training; Radiation Protection/Health Physics Technician Training. **Related Knowledge/Courses—Physics:** Physical principles, laws, and applications, including air, water, material dynamics, light, atomic principles, heat, electric theory,

earth formations, and meteorological and related natural phenomena. **Chemistry:** The composition, structure, and properties of substances and of the chemical processes and transformations that they undergo. This includes uses of chemicals and their interactions, danger signs, production techniques, and disposal methods. **Engineering and Technology:** Equipment, tools, and mechanical devices and their uses to produce motion, light, power, technology, and other applications. **Public Safety and Security:** Weaponry; public safety; security operations, rules, regulations, precautions, and prevention; and the protection of people, data, and property. **Mechanical Devices:** Machines and tools, including their designs, uses, benefits, repair, and maintenance. **Telecommunications:** Transmission, broadcasting, switching, control, and operation of telecommunications systems.

Work Environment: Indoors; noisy; very hot or cold; radiation; hazardous conditions; hazardous equipment.

Nuclear Medicine Technologists

- ❀ Education/Training Required: Associate degree
- ❀ Annual Earnings: $64,670
- ❀ Beginning Wage: $47,370
- ❀ Earnings Growth Potential: Low
- ❀ Growth: 14.8%
- ❀ Annual Job Openings: 1,290
- ❀ Self-Employed: 1.0%
- ❀ Part-Time: 17.3%

Prepare, administer, and measure radioactive isotopes in therapeutic, diagnostic, and tracer studies, using a variety of radioisotope equipment. Prepare stock solutions of radioactive materials and calculate doses to be administered by radiologists. Subject patients to radiation. Execute blood volume, red cell survival, and fat absorption studies, following standard laboratory techniques. Detect and map radiopharmaceuticals in patients' bodies, using a camera to produce photographic or computer images. Administer radiopharmaceuticals or radiation intravenously to detect or treat diseases, using radioisotope equipment, under direction of a physician. Produce computer-generated or film images for interpretation by physicians. Calculate, measure, and record radiation dosages or radiopharmaceuticals received, used, and disposed, using computers and following physicians' prescriptions. Perform quality control checks on laboratory equipment and cameras. Maintain and calibrate radioisotope and laboratory equipment. Dispose of radioactive materials and store radiopharmaceuticals, following radiation safety procedures. Process cardiac function studies, using computers. Prepare stock radiopharmaceuticals, adhering to safety standards that minimize radiation exposure to workers and patients. Record and process results of procedures. Explain test procedures and safety precautions to patients and provide them with assistance during test procedures. Gather information on patients' illnesses and medical histories to guide choices of diagnostic procedures for therapies. Measure glandular activity, blood volume, red cell survival, and radioactivity of patient, using scanners, Geiger counters, scintillation counters, and other laboratory equipment. Train and supervise student or subordinate nuclear medicine technologists. Position radiation fields, radiation beams, and patients to allow for most effective treatment of patients' diseases, using computers. Add radioactive substances to biological specimens such as blood, urine, and feces to determine therapeutic drug or hormone levels. Develop treatment procedures for nuclear medicine treatment programs.

Personality Type: Investigative. These occupations frequently involve working with ideas and require an extensive amount of thinking. They can involve searching for facts and figuring out problems mentally.

GOE—Interest Area/Cluster: 08. Health Science. **Work Group:** 08.06. Medical Technology. **Other Jobs in This Work Group:** Biological Technicians; Cardiovascular Technologists and Technicians; Diagnostic Medical Sonographers; Medical and Clinical Laboratory Technicians; Medical and Clinical Laboratory Technologists; Medical Equipment Preparers; Medical Records and Health Information Technicians; Opticians, Dispensing; Orthotists and Prosthetists; Radiologic Technicians; Radiologic Technologists; Radiologic Technologists and Technicians.

Skills—Operation Monitoring: Watching gauges, dials, or other indicators to make sure a machine is working properly. **Equipment Maintenance:** Performing routine maintenance and determining when and what kind of maintenance is needed. **Quality Control Analysis:** Evaluating the quality or performance of products, services, or processes. **Systems Analysis:** Determining how a system should work and how changes will affect outcomes. **Operation and Control:** Controlling operations of equipment or systems. **Systems Evaluation:** Looking at many indicators of system performance and taking into account their accuracy.

Education and Training Programs: Nuclear Medical Technology/Technologist Training; Radiation Protection/

Health Physics Technician Training. **Related Knowledge/Courses—Medicine and Dentistry:** The information and techniques needed to diagnose and treat injuries, diseases, and deformities. This includes symptoms, treatment alternatives, drug properties and interactions, and preventive health-care measures. **Biology:** Plant and animal living tissue, cells, organisms, and entities, including their functions, interdependencies, and interactions with each other and the environment. **Chemistry:** The composition, structure, and properties of substances and of the chemical processes and transformations that they undergo. This includes uses of chemicals and their interactions, danger signs, production techniques, and disposal methods. **Physics:** Physical principles, laws, and applications, including air, water, material dynamics, light, atomic principles, heat, electric theory, earth formations, and meteorological and related natural phenomena. **Customer and Personal Service:** Principles and processes for providing customer and personal services, including needs assessment techniques, quality service standards, alternative delivery systems, and customer satisfaction evaluation techniques. **Therapy and Counseling:** Information and techniques needed to rehabilitate physical and mental ailments and to provide career guidance, including alternative treatments, rehabilitation equipment and its proper use, and methods to evaluate treatment effects.

Work Environment: Indoors; contaminants; radiation; disease or infections; standing; using hands on objects, tools, or controls.

Nuclear Monitoring Technicians

- ❋ Education/Training Required: Associate degree
- ❋ Annual Earnings: $66,140
- ❋ Beginning Wage: $40,520
- ❋ Earnings Growth Potential: Medium
- ❋ Growth: 6.7%
- ❋ Annual Job Openings: 1,021
- ❋ Self-Employed: 0.0%
- ❋ Part-Time: 3.9%

The job openings listed here are shared with Nuclear Equipment Operation Technicians.

Collect and test samples to monitor results of nuclear experiments and contamination of humans, facilities, and environment. Calculate safe radiation exposure times for personnel, using plant contamination readings and prescribed safe levels of radiation. Provide initial response to abnormal events and to alarms from radiation monitoring equipment. Monitor personnel in order to determine the amounts and intensities of radiation exposure. Inform supervisors when individual exposures or area radiation levels approach maximum permissible limits. Instruct personnel in radiation safety procedures and demonstrate use of protective clothing and equipment. Determine intensities and types of radiation in work areas, equipment, and materials, using radiation detectors and other instruments. Collect samples of air, water, gases, and solids to determine radioactivity levels of contamination. Set up equipment that automatically detects area radiation deviations and test detection equipment to ensure its accuracy. Determine or recommend radioactive decontamination procedures according to the size and nature of equipment and the degree of contamination. Decontaminate objects by cleaning with soap or solvents or by abrading with wire brushes, buffing wheels, or sandblasting machines. Place radioactive waste, such as sweepings and broken sample bottles, into containers for disposal. Calibrate and maintain chemical instrumentation sensing elements and sampling system equipment, using calibration instruments and hand tools. Place irradiated nuclear fuel materials in environmental chambers for testing and observe reactions through cell windows. Enter data into computers in order to record characteristics of nuclear events and locating coordinates of particles. Operate manipulators from outside cells to move specimens into and out of shielded containers, to remove specimens from cells, or to place specimens on benches or equipment workstations. Prepare reports describing contamination tests, material and equipment decontaminated, and methods used in decontamination processes. Confer with scientists directing projects to determine significant events to monitor during tests. Immerse samples in chemical compounds to prepare them for testing.

Personality Type: Realistic. These occupations frequently involve work activities that include practical, hands-on problems and solutions. They often deal with plants; animals; and real-world materials such as wood, tools, and machinery. Many of the occupations require working outside and don't involve a lot of paperwork or working closely with others.

GOE—Interest Area/Cluster: 07. Government and Public Administration. **Work Group:** 07.03. Regulations Enforcement. **Other Jobs in This Work Group:** Agricultural Inspectors; Aviation Inspectors; Compliance Officers, Except Agriculture, Construction, Health and Safety, and Transportation; Construction and Building Inspectors;

Environmental Compliance Inspectors; Equal Opportunity Representatives and Officers; Financial Examiners; Fire Inspectors; Fish and Game Wardens; Forest Fire Inspectors and Prevention Specialists; Freight and Cargo Inspectors; Government Property Inspectors and Investigators; Immigration and Customs Inspectors; Licensing Examiners and Inspectors; Occupational Health and Safety Specialists; Occupational Health and Safety Technicians; Tax Examiners, Collectors, and Revenue Agents; Transportation Vehicle, Equipment, and Systems Inspectors, Except Aviation.

Skills—Science: Using scientific methods to solve problems. **Operation Monitoring:** Watching gauges, dials, or other indicators to make sure a machine is working properly. **Equipment Maintenance:** Performing routine maintenance and determining when and what kind of maintenance is needed. **Mathematics:** Using mathematics to solve problems. **Operation and Control:** Controlling operations of equipment or systems. **Equipment Selection:** Determining the kind of tools and equipment needed to do a job. **Technology Design:** Generating or adapting equipment and technology to serve user needs. **Systems Analysis:** Determining how a system should work and how changes will affect outcomes.

Education and Training Programs: Industrial Radiologic Technology/Technician Training; Nuclear and Industrial Radiologic Technologies/Technician Training, Other; Nuclear Engineering Technology/Technician Training; Nuclear/Nuclear Power Technology/Technician Training; Radiation Protection/Health Physics Technician Training. **Related Knowledge/Courses—Physics:** Physical principles, laws, and applications, including air, water, material dynamics, light, atomic principles, heat, electric theory, earth formations, and meteorological and related natural phenomena. **Chemistry:** The composition, structure, and properties of substances and of the chemical processes and transformations that they undergo. This includes uses of chemicals and their interactions, danger signs, production techniques, and disposal methods. **Public Safety and Security:** Weaponry; public safety; security operations, rules, regulations, precautions, and prevention; and the protection of people, data, and property. **Engineering and Technology:** Equipment, tools, and mechanical devices and their uses to produce motion, light, power, technology, and other applications. **Biology:** Plant and animal living tissue, cells, organisms, and entities, including their functions, interdependencies, and interactions with each other and the environment. **Design:** Design techniques, principles, tools, and instruments involved in the production and use of precision technical plans, blueprints, drawings, and models.

Work Environment: Indoors; noisy; very hot or cold; contaminants; radiation; hazardous conditions.

Nuclear Power Reactor Operators

- ❀ Education/Training Required: Long-term on-the-job training
- ❀ Annual Earnings: $70,410
- ❀ Beginning Wage: $53,730
- ❀ Earnings Growth Potential: Very low
- ❀ Growth: 10.6%
- ❀ Annual Job Openings: 233
- ❀ Self-Employed: 0.0%
- ❀ Part-Time: 0.6%

Control nuclear reactors. Adjust controls to position rod and to regulate flux level, reactor period, coolant temperature, and rate of power flow, following standard procedures. Respond to system or unit abnormalities, diagnosing the cause and recommending or taking corrective action. Monitor all systems for normal running conditions, performing activities such as checking gauges to assess output or assess the effects of generator loading on other equipment. Implement operational procedures such as those controlling startup and shutdown activities. Note malfunctions of equipment, instruments, or controls and report these conditions to supervisors. Monitor and operate boilers, turbines, wells, and auxiliary power plant equipment. Dispatch orders and instructions to personnel through radiotelephone or intercommunication systems to coordinate auxiliary equipment operation. Record operating data such as the results of surveillance tests. Participate in nuclear fuel element handling activities such as preparation, transfer, loading, and unloading. Conduct inspections and operations outside of control rooms as necessary. Direct reactor operators in emergency situations in accordance with emergency operating procedures. Authorize maintenance activities on units and changes in equipment and system operational status.

Personality Type: Realistic. These occupations frequently involve work activities that include practical, hands-on problems and solutions. They often deal with plants; animals; and real-world materials such as wood, tools, and machinery. Many of the occupations require working outside and don't involve a lot of paperwork or working closely with others.

GOE—Interest Area/Cluster: 13. Manufacturing. **Work Group:** 13.16. Utility Operation and Energy Distribution.

Other Jobs in This Work Group: Chemical Plant and System Operators; Gas Compressor and Gas Pumping Station Operators; Gas Plant Operators; Petroleum Pump System Operators, Refinery Operators, and Gaugers; Power Distributors and Dispatchers; Power Plant Operators; Ship Engineers; Stationary Engineers and Boiler Operators; Water and Liquid Waste Treatment Plant and System Operators.

Skills—Operation Monitoring: Watching gauges, dials, or other indicators to make sure a machine is working properly. **Operation and Control:** Controlling operations of equipment or systems. **Science:** Using scientific methods to solve problems. **Systems Analysis:** Determining how a system should work and how changes will affect outcomes. **Troubleshooting:** Determining what is causing an operating error and deciding what to do about it. **Equipment Maintenance:** Performing routine maintenance and determining when and what kind of maintenance is needed. **Quality Control Analysis:** Evaluating the quality or performance of products, services, or processes. **Reading Comprehension:** Understanding written sentences and paragraphs in work-related documents.

Education and Training Program: Nuclear/Nuclear Power Technology/Technician Training. **Related Knowledge/Courses—Physics:** Physical principles, laws, and applications, including air, water, material dynamics, light, atomic principles, heat, electric theory, earth formations, and meteorological and related natural phenomena. **Engineering and Technology:** Equipment, tools, and mechanical devices and their uses to produce motion, light, power, technology, and other applications. **Chemistry:** The composition, structure, and properties of substances and of the chemical processes and transformations that they undergo. This includes uses of chemicals and their interactions, danger signs, production techniques, and disposal methods. **Mechanical Devices:** Machines and tools, including their designs, uses, benefits, repair, and maintenance. **Public Safety and Security:** Weaponry; public safety; security operations, rules, regulations, precautions, and prevention; and the protection of people, data, and property. **Design:** Design techniques, principles, tools, and instruments involved in the production and use of precision technical plans, blueprints, drawings, and models.

Work Environment: Indoors; noisy; radiation; hazardous conditions; hazardous equipment; using hands on objects, tools, or controls.

Nursery and Greenhouse Managers

- ❋ Education/Training Required: Work experience plus degree
- ❋ Annual Earnings: $53,720
- ❋ Beginning Wage: $31,100
- ❋ Earnings Growth Potential: High
- ❋ Growth: 1.1%
- ❋ Annual Job Openings: 18,101
- ❋ Self-Employed: 0.0%
- ❋ Part-Time: 9.3%

The job openings listed here are shared with Aquacultural Managers and with Crop and Livestock Managers.

Plan, organize, direct, control, and coordinate activities of workers engaged in propagating, cultivating, and harvesting horticultural specialties such as trees, shrubs, flowers, mushrooms, and other plants. Construct structures and accessories such as greenhouses and benches. Coordinate clerical, recordkeeping, inventory, requisitioning, and marketing activities. Cut and prune trees, shrubs, flowers, and plants. Graft plants. Inspect facilities and equipment for signs of disrepair and perform necessary maintenance work. Position and regulate plant irrigation systems and program environmental and irrigation control computers. Provide information to customers on the care of trees, shrubs, flowers, plants, and lawns. Confer with horticultural personnel in order to plan facility renovations or additions. Determine plant growing conditions, such as in greenhouses, hydroponic environments, or natural settings, and set planting and care schedules. Prepare soil for planting and plant or transplant seeds, bulbs, and cuttings. Negotiate contracts such as those for land leases or tree purchases. Apply pesticides and fertilizers to plants. Tour work areas to observe work being done, to inspect crops, and to evaluate plant and soil conditions. Hire employees and train them in gardening techniques. Select and purchase seeds, plant nutrients, disease control chemicals, and garden and lawn care equipment. Manage nurseries that grow horticultural plants for sale to trade or retail customers, for display or exhibition, or for research. Assign work schedules and duties to nursery or greenhouse staff and supervise their work. Determine types and quantities of horticultural plants to be grown, based on budgets, projected sales volumes, and/or executive directives. Explain and enforce safety regulations and policies. Identify plants as well as problems such as diseases, weeds, and insect pests.

Personality Type: Enterprising. These occupations frequently involve starting up and carrying out projects and can involve leading people and making many decisions. They sometimes require risk taking and often deal with business.

GOE—Interest Area/Cluster: 01. Agriculture and Natural Resources. **Work Group:** 01.01. Managerial Work in Agriculture and Natural Resources. **Other Jobs in This Work Group:** Aquacultural Managers; Crop and Livestock Managers; Farm Labor Contractors; Farm, Ranch, and Other Agricultural Managers; Farmers and Ranchers; First-Line Supervisors/Managers of Agricultural Crop and Horticultural Workers; First-Line Supervisors/Managers of Animal Husbandry and Animal Care Workers; First-Line Supervisors/Managers of Aquacultural Workers; First-Line Supervisors/Managers of Construction Trades and Extraction Workers; First-Line Supervisors/Managers of Farming, Fishing, and Forestry Workers; First-Line Supervisors/Managers of Landscaping, Lawn Service, and Groundskeeping Workers; First-Line Supervisors/Managers of Logging Workers; Park Naturalists; Purchasing Agents and Buyers, Farm Products.

Skills—Management of Financial Resources: Determining how money will be spent to get the work done and accounting for these expenditures. **Management of Material Resources:** Obtaining and seeing to the appropriate use of equipment, facilities, and materials needed to do certain work. **Science:** Using scientific methods to solve problems. **Management of Personnel Resources:** Motivating, developing, and directing people as they work; identifying the best people for the job. **Systems Evaluation:** Looking at many indicators of system performance and taking into account their accuracy. **Installation:** Installing equipment, machines, wiring, or programs to meet specifications. **Operation Monitoring:** Watching gauges, dials, or other indicators to make sure a machine is working properly. **Equipment Maintenance:** Performing routine maintenance and determining when and what kind of maintenance is needed.

Education and Training Programs: Agribusiness/Agricultural Business Operations; Agricultural Business and Management, General; Greenhouse Operations and Management; Horticultural Science; Ornamental Horticulture; Plant Nursery Operations and Management; Plant Protection and Integrated Pest Management. **Related Knowledge/Courses—Biology:** Plant and animal living tissue, cells, organisms, and entities, including their functions, interdependencies, and interactions with each other and the environment. **Production and Processing:** Inputs, outputs, raw materials, waste, quality control, costs, and techniques for maximizing the manufacture and distribution of goods. **Sales and Marketing:** Principles and methods involved in showing, promoting, and selling products or services. This includes marketing strategies and tactics, product demonstration and sales techniques, and sales control systems. **Chemistry:** The composition, structure, and properties of substances and of the chemical processes and transformations that they undergo. This includes uses of chemicals and their interactions, danger signs, production techniques, and disposal methods. **Personnel and Human Resources:** Principles and procedures for personnel recruitment; selection; training; compensation and benefits; labor relations and negotiation; and personnel information systems. **Design:** Design techniques, principles, tools, and instruments involved in the production and use of precision technical plans, blueprints, drawings, and models.

Work Environment: More often outdoors than indoors; very hot or cold; contaminants; minor burns, cuts, bites, or stings; standing.

Nursing Aides, Orderlies, and Attendants

- ❋ Education/Training Required: Postsecondary vocational training
- ❋ Annual Earnings: $23,160
- ❋ Beginning Wage: $16,850
- ❋ Earnings Growth Potential: Low
- ❋ Growth: 18.2%
- ❋ Annual Job Openings: 321,036
- ❋ Self-Employed: 2.4%
- ❋ Part-Time: 24.0%

Provide basic patient care under direction of nursing staff. Perform duties such as feeding, bathing, dressing, grooming, or moving patients or changing linens. Answer patients' call signals. Turn and reposition bedridden patients, alone or with assistance, to prevent bedsores. Observe patients' conditions, measuring and recording food and liquid intake and output and vital signs, and report changes to professional staff. Feed patients who are unable to feed themselves. Provide patients with help walking, exercising, and moving in and out of bed. Provide patient care by supplying and emptying bed pans, applying dressings and supervising exercise routines. Bathe, groom, shave, dress, or drape patients to prepare them for surgery, treatment, or examination. Transport patients to treatment units, using

a wheelchair or stretcher. Clean rooms and change linens. Collect specimens such as urine, feces, or sputum. Prepare, serve, and collect food trays. Deliver messages, documents, and specimens. Answer phones and direct visitors. Restrain patients if necessary. Set up equipment such as oxygen tents, portable X-ray machines, and overhead irrigation bottles. Explain medical instructions to patients and family members. Work as part of a medical team that examines and treats clinic outpatients. Maintain inventories by storing, preparing, sterilizing, and issuing supplies such as dressing packs and treatment trays. Administer medications and treatments such as catheterizations, suppositories, irrigations, enemas, massages, and douches as directed by a physician or nurse. Perform clerical duties such as processing documents and scheduling appointments.

Personality Type: Social. These occupations frequently involve working with, communicating with, and teaching people and often involve helping or providing service to others.

GOE—Interest Area/Cluster: 08. Health Science. **Work Group:** 08.08. Patient Care and Assistance. **Other Jobs in This Work Group:** Home Health Aides; Licensed Practical and Licensed Vocational Nurses; Psychiatric Aides; Psychiatric Technicians.

Skill—None met the criteria.

Education and Training Programs: Health Aide Training; Nurse/Nursing Assistant/Aide and Patient Care Assistant Training. **Related Knowledge/Courses—Medicine and Dentistry:** The information and techniques needed to diagnose and treat injuries, diseases, and deformities. This includes symptoms, treatment alternatives, drug properties and interactions, and preventive health-care measures. **Psychology:** Human behavior and performance, mental processes, psychological research methods, and the assessment and treatment of behavioral and affective disorders. **Therapy and Counseling:** Information and techniques needed to rehabilitate physical and mental ailments and to provide career guidance, including alternative treatments, rehabilitation equipment and its proper use, and methods to evaluate treatment effects. **Customer and Personal Service:** Principles and processes for providing customer and personal services, including needs assessment techniques, quality service standards, alternative delivery systems, and customer satisfaction evaluation techniques.

Work Environment: Disease or infections; standing; walking and running; using hands on objects, tools, or controls; bending or twisting the body; repetitive motions.

Nursing Instructors and Teachers, Postsecondary

* Education/Training Required: Doctoral degree
* Annual Earnings: $57,500
* Beginning Wage: $36,020
* Earnings Growth Potential: Medium
* Growth: 22.9%
* Annual Job Openings: 7,337
* Self-Employed: 0.4%
* Part-Time: 27.8%

Demonstrate and teach patient care in classroom and clinical units to nursing students. Includes both teachers primarily engaged in teaching and those who do a combination of both teaching and research. Initiate, facilitate, and moderate classroom discussions. Prepare and deliver lectures to undergraduate or graduate students on topics such as pharmacology, mental health nursing, and community health-care practices. Keep abreast of developments in their field by reading current literature, talking with colleagues, and participating in professional conferences. Prepare course materials such as syllabi, homework assignments, and handouts. Supervise students' laboratory and clinical work. Evaluate and grade students' classwork, laboratory and clinic work, assignments, and papers. Collaborate with colleagues to address teaching and research issues. Plan, evaluate, and revise curricula, course content, and course materials and methods of instruction. Assess clinical education needs and patient and client teaching needs, utilizing a variety of methods. Compile, administer, and grade examinations or assign this work to others. Advise students on academic and vocational curricula and on career issues. Maintain student attendance records, grades, and other required records. Maintain regularly scheduled office hours to advise and assist students. Supervise undergraduate or graduate teaching, internship, and research work. Conduct research in a particular field of knowledge and publish findings in professional journals, books, and/or electronic media. Participate in student recruitment, registration, and placement activities. Serve on academic or administrative committees that deal with institutional policies, departmental matters, and academic issues. Coordinate training programs with area universities, clinics, hospitals, health agencies, and/or vocational schools. Compile bibliographies of specialized materials for outside reading assignments. Select and obtain materials and supplies such as textbooks and laboratory equipment. Participate in campus and community events. Write grant proposals to procure external research funding. Act as advisers to student organizations. Demonstrate patient care in clinical units of hospitals. Perform administrative duties such as serving as department head.

Personality Type: Social. These occupations frequently involve working with, communicating with, and teaching people and often involve helping or providing service to others.

GOE—Interest Area/Cluster: 05. Education and Training. **Work Group:** 05.03. Postsecondary and Adult Teaching and Instructing. **Other Jobs in This Work Group:** Adult Literacy, Remedial Education, and GED Teachers and Instructors; Agricultural Sciences Teachers, Postsecondary; Anthropology and Archeology Teachers, Postsecondary; Architecture Teachers, Postsecondary; Area, Ethnic, and Cultural Studies Teachers, Postsecondary; Art, Drama, and Music Teachers, Postsecondary; Atmospheric, Earth, Marine, and Space Sciences Teachers, Postsecondary; Biological Science Teachers, Postsecondary; Business Teachers, Postsecondary; Chemistry Teachers, Postsecondary; Communications Teachers, Postsecondary; Computer Science Teachers, Postsecondary; Criminal Justice and Law Enforcement Teachers, Postsecondary; Economics Teachers, Postsecondary; Education Teachers, Postsecondary; Engineering Teachers, Postsecondary; English Language and Literature Teachers, Postsecondary; Environmental Science Teachers, Postsecondary; Farm and Home Management Advisors; Foreign Language and Literature Teachers, Postsecondary; Forestry and Conservation Science Teachers, Postsecondary; Geography Teachers, Postsecondary; Graduate Teaching Assistants; Health Specialties Teachers, Postsecondary; History Teachers, Postsecondary; Home Economics Teachers, Postsecondary; Law Teachers, Postsecondary; Library Science Teachers, Postsecondary; Mathematical Science Teachers, Postsecondary; Philosophy and Religion Teachers, Postsecondary; Physics Teachers, Postsecondary; Political Science Teachers, Postsecondary; Psychology Teachers, Postsecondary; Recreation and Fitness Studies Teachers, Postsecondary; Self-Enrichment Education Teachers; Social Work Teachers, Postsecondary; Sociology Teachers, Postsecondary; Vocational Education Teachers, Postsecondary.

Skills—Science: Using scientific methods to solve problems. **Instructing:** Teaching others how to do something. **Writing:** Communicating effectively with others in writing as indicated by the needs of the audience. **Social Perceptiveness:** Being aware of others' reactions and understanding why they react the way they do. **Reading Comprehension:**

Understanding written sentences and paragraphs in work-related documents. **Learning Strategies:** Using multiple approaches when learning or teaching new things. **Service Orientation:** Actively looking for ways to help people. **Critical Thinking:** Using logic and analysis to identify the strengths and weaknesses of different approaches.

Education and Training Programs: Adult Health Nurse Training/Nursing; Clinical Nurse Specialist Training; Family Practice Nurse/Nurse Practitioner Training; Maternal/Child Health and Neonatal Nurse Training/Nursing; Nurse Anesthetist Training; Nurse Midwife Training/Nursing Midwifery; Nursing Science (MS, PhD); Nursing, Other; Nursing—Registered Nurse Training (RN, ASN, BSN, MSN); Pediatric Nurse Training/Nursing; Perioperative/Operating Room and Surgical Nurse Training/Nursing; Pre-Nursing Studies; Psychiatric/Mental Health Nurse Training/Nursing; Public Health/Community Nurse Training/Nursing. **Related Knowledge/Courses—Therapy and Counseling:** Information and techniques needed to rehabilitate physical and mental ailments and to provide career guidance, including alternative treatments, rehabilitation equipment and its proper use, and methods to evaluate treatment effects. **Biology:** Plant and animal living tissue, cells, organisms, and entities, including their functions, interdependencies, and interactions with each other and the environment. **Sociology and Anthropology:** Group behavior and dynamics; societal trends and influences; and cultures and their history, migrations, ethnicity, and origins. **Medicine and Dentistry:** The information and techniques needed to diagnose and treat injuries, diseases, and deformities. This includes symptoms, treatment alternatives, drug properties and interactions, and preventive health-care measures. **Philosophy and Theology:** Different philosophical systems and religions, including their basic principles, values, ethics, ways of thinking, customs, and practices and their impact on human culture. **Psychology:** Human behavior and performance, mental processes, psychological research methods, and the assessment and treatment of behavioral and affective disorders.

Work Environment: Indoors; disease or infections; sitting.

Obstetricians and Gynecologists

- ❋ Education/Training Required: First professional degree
- ❋ Annual Earnings: More than $145,600
- ❋ Beginning Wage: $100,770
- ❋ Earnings Growth Potential: Cannot be calculated
- ❋ Growth: 14.2%
- ❋ Annual Job Openings: 38,027
- ❋ Self-Employed: 14.7%
- ❋ Part-Time: 8.1%

The job openings listed here are shared with Anesthesiologists; Family and General Practitioners; Internists, General; Pediatricians, General; Psychiatrists; and Surgeons.

Diagnose, treat, and help prevent diseases of women, especially those affecting the reproductive system and the process of childbirth. Care for and treat women during prenatal, natal, and post-natal periods. Explain procedures and discuss test results or prescribed treatments with patients. Treat diseases of female organs. Monitor patients' condition and progress and re-evaluate treatments as necessary. Perform cesarean sections or other surgical procedures as needed to preserve patients' health and deliver babies safely. Prescribe or administer therapy, medication, and other specialized medical care to treat or prevent illness, disease, or injury. Analyze records, reports, test results, or examination information to diagnose medical condition of patient. Collect, record, and maintain patient information, such as medical histories, reports, and examination results. Advise patients and community members concerning diet, activity, hygiene, and disease prevention. Refer patient to medical specialist or other practitioner when necessary. Consult with, or provide consulting services to, other physicians. Direct and coordinate activities of nurses, students, assistants, specialists, therapists, and other medical staff. Plan, implement, or administer health programs in hospitals, businesses, or communities for prevention and treatment of injuries or illnesses. Prepare government and organizational reports on birth, death, and disease statistics; workforce evaluations; or the medical status of individuals. Conduct research to develop or test medications, treatments, or procedures to prevent or control disease or injury.

Personality Type: Investigative. These occupations frequently involve working with ideas and require an extensive amount of thinking. They can involve searching for facts and figuring out problems mentally.

GOE—**Interest Area/Cluster:** 08. Health Science. **Work Group:** 08.02. Medicine and Surgery. **Other Jobs in This Work Group:** Anesthesiologists; Family and General Practitioners; Internists, General; Medical Assistants; Medical Transcriptionists; Pediatricians, General; Pharmacists; Pharmacy Aides; Pharmacy Technicians; Physician Assistants; Psychiatrists; Registered Nurses; Surgeons; Surgical Technologists.

Skills—Science: Using scientific methods to solve problems. **Judgment and Decision Making:** Weighing the relative costs and benefits of a potential action. **Reading Comprehension:** Understanding written sentences and paragraphs in work-related documents. **Complex Problem Solving:** Identifying complex problems, reviewing the options, and implementing solutions. **Active Learning:** Working with new material or information to grasp its implications. **Social Perceptiveness:** Being aware of others' reactions and understanding why they react the way they do. **Critical Thinking:** Using logic and analysis to identify the strengths and weaknesses of different approaches. **Instructing:** Teaching others how to do something.

Education and Training Programs: Neonatal-Perinatal Medicine; Obstetrics and Gynecology. **Related Knowledge/Courses—Medicine and Dentistry:** The information and techniques needed to diagnose and treat injuries, diseases, and deformities. This includes symptoms, treatment alternatives, drug properties and interactions, and preventive health-care measures. **Therapy and Counseling:** Information and techniques needed to rehabilitate physical and mental ailments and to provide career guidance, including alternative treatments, rehabilitation equipment and its proper use, and methods to evaluate treatment effects. **Biology:** Plant and animal living tissue, cells, organisms, and entities, including their functions, interdependencies, and interactions with each other and the environment. **Psychology:** Human behavior and performance, mental processes, psychological research methods, and the assessment and treatment of behavioral and affective disorders. **Sociology and Anthropology:** Group behavior and dynamics; societal trends and influences; and cultures and their history, migrations, ethnicity, and origins. **Chemistry:** The composition, structure, and properties of substances and of the chemical processes and transformations that they undergo. This includes uses of chemicals and their interactions, danger signs, production techniques, and disposal methods.

Work Environment: Indoors; disease or infections; standing; using hands on objects, tools, or controls.

Occupational Health and Safety Specialists

* Education/Training Required: Bachelor's degree
* Annual Earnings: $60,140
* Beginning Wage: $35,990
* Earnings Growth Potential: High
* Growth: 8.1%
* Annual Job Openings: 3,440
* Self-Employed: 2.4%
* Part-Time: 8.0%

Review, evaluate, and analyze work environments and design programs and procedures to control, eliminate, and prevent diseases or injuries caused by chemical, physical, and biological agents or ergonomic factors. May conduct inspections and enforce adherence to laws and regulations governing health and safety of individuals. May be employed in public or private sector. Order suspension of activities that pose threats to workers' health and safety. Recommend measures to help protect workers from potentially hazardous work methods, processes, or materials. Investigate accidents to identify causes and to determine how such accidents might be prevented in the future. Investigate the adequacy of ventilation, exhaust equipment, lighting, and other conditions that could affect employee health, comfort, or performance. Develop and maintain hygiene programs such as noise surveys, continuous atmosphere monitoring, ventilation surveys, and asbestos management plans. Inspect and evaluate workplace environments, equipment, and practices in order to ensure compliance with safety standards and government regulations. Collaborate with engineers and physicians to institute control and remedial measures for hazardous and potentially hazardous conditions or equipment. Conduct safety training and education programs and demonstrate the use of safety equipment. Provide new-employee health and safety orientations and develop materials for these presentations. Collect samples of dust, gases, vapors, and other potentially toxic materials for analysis. Investigate health-related complaints and inspect facilities to ensure that they comply with public health legislation and regulations. Coordinate "right-to-know" programs regarding hazardous chemicals and other substances. Maintain and update emergency response plans and procedures. Develop and maintain medical monitoring programs for employees. Inspect specified areas to ensure the presence of fire prevention equipment, safety equipment, and first-aid supplies. Conduct audits at hazardous waste sites or industrial sites and participate in hazardous waste site investigations. Collect samples of hazardous materials or arrange for sample collection. Maintain inventories of hazardous materials and hazardous wastes, using waste tracking systems, to ensure that materials are handled properly. Prepare hazardous, radioactive, and mixed waste samples for transportation and storage by treating, compacting, packaging, and labeling them.

Personality Type: Investigative. These occupations frequently involve working with ideas and require an extensive amount of thinking. They can involve searching for facts and figuring out problems mentally.

GOE—Interest Area/Cluster: 07. Government and Public Administration. **Work Group:** 07.03. Regulations Enforcement. **Other Jobs in This Work Group:** Agricultural Inspectors; Aviation Inspectors; Compliance Officers, Except Agriculture, Construction, Health and Safety, and Transportation; Construction and Building Inspectors; Environmental Compliance Inspectors; Equal Opportunity Representatives and Officers; Financial Examiners; Fire Inspectors; Fish and Game Wardens; Forest Fire Inspectors and Prevention Specialists; Freight and Cargo Inspectors; Government Property Inspectors and Investigators; Immigration and Customs Inspectors; Licensing Examiners and Inspectors; Nuclear Monitoring Technicians; Occupational Health and Safety Technicians; Tax Examiners, Collectors, and Revenue Agents; Transportation Vehicle, Equipment, and Systems Inspectors, Except Aviation.

Skills—Science: Using scientific methods to solve problems. **Management of Financial Resources:** Determining how money will be spent to get the work done and accounting for these expenditures. **Technology Design:** Generating or adapting equipment and technology to serve user needs. **Persuasion:** Persuading others to approach things differently. **Systems Analysis:** Determining how a system should work and how changes will affect outcomes. **Management of Material Resources:** Obtaining and seeing to the appropriate use of equipment, facilities, and materials needed to do certain work. **Systems Evaluation:** Looking at many indicators of system performance and taking into account their accuracy. **Operations Analysis:** Analyzing needs and product requirements to create a design.

Education and Training Programs: Environmental Health; Industrial Safety Technology/Technician Training; Occupational Health and Industrial Hygiene; Occupational Safety and Health Technology/Technician Training; Quality Control and Safety Technologies/Technician Training, Other. **Related Knowledge/Courses—Chemistry:** The composition, structure, and properties of substances and of the chemical processes and transformations that they undergo. This includes uses of chemicals and their interactions, danger signs, production techniques, and disposal methods. **Biology:** Plant and animal living tissue, cells, organisms, and entities, including their functions, interdependencies, and interactions with each other and the environment. **Physics:** Physical principles, laws, and applications, including air, water, material dynamics, light, atomic principles, heat, electric theory, earth formations, and meteorological and related natural phenomena. **Engineering and Technology:** Equipment, tools, and mechanical devices and their uses to produce motion, light, power, technology, and other applications. **Public Safety and Security:** Weaponry; public safety; security operations, rules, regulations, precautions, and prevention; and the protection of people, data, and property. **Psychology:** Human behavior and performance, mental processes, psychological research methods, and the assessment and treatment of behavioral and affective disorders.

Work Environment: More often indoors than outdoors; noisy; contaminants; sitting.

Occupational Health and Safety Technicians

- ❋ Education/Training Required: Bachelor's degree
- ❋ Annual Earnings: $44,020
- ❋ Beginning Wage: $25,280
- ❋ Earnings Growth Potential: High
- ❋ Growth: 14.6%
- ❋ Annual Job Openings: 886
- ❋ Self-Employed: 0.0%
- ❋ Part-Time: 8.0%

Collect data on work environments for analysis by occupational health and safety specialists. Implement and conduct evaluation of programs designed to limit chemical, physical, biological, and ergonomic risks to workers. Maintain all required records and documentation. Supply, operate, and maintain personal protective equipment. Verify that safety equipment such as hearing protection and respirators is available to employees and monitor their use of such equipment to ensure proper fit and use. Evaluate situations where a worker has refused to work on the grounds that danger or potential harm exists and determine how such situations should be handled. Prepare and calibrate equipment used to collect and analyze samples. Test workplaces for environmental hazards such as exposure to radiation, chemical and biological hazards, and excessive noise. Prepare and review specifications and orders for the purchase of safety equipment, ensuring that proper features are present and that items conform to health and safety standards. Report the results of environmental contaminant analyses and recommend corrective measures to be applied. Review physicians' reports and conduct worker studies in order to determine whether specific instances of disease or illness are job-related. Examine credentials, licenses, or permits to ensure compliance with licensing requirements. Conduct fire drills and inspect fire suppression systems and portable fire systems to ensure that they are in working order. Educate the public about health issues and enforce health legislation in order to prevent diseases, to promote health, and to help people understand health protection procedures and regulations. Provide consultation to organizations or agencies on the application of safety principles, practices, and techniques in the workplace. Conduct interviews to obtain information and evidence regarding communicable diseases or violations of health and sanitation regulations. Review records and reports concerning laboratory results, staffing, floor plans, fire inspections, and sanitation in order to gather information for the development and enforcement of safety activities. Prepare documents to be used in legal proceedings, testifying in such proceedings when necessary. Plan emergency response drills. Maintain logbooks of daily activities, including areas visited and activities performed.

Personality Type: Conventional. These occupations frequently involve following set procedures and routines and can include working with data and details more than with ideas. Usually there is a clear line of authority to follow.

GOE—Interest Area/Cluster: 07. Government and Public Administration. **Work Group:** 07.03. Regulations Enforcement. **Other Jobs in This Work Group:** Agricultural Inspectors; Aviation Inspectors; Compliance Officers, Except Agriculture, Construction, Health and Safety, and Transportation; Construction and Building Inspectors; Environmental Compliance Inspectors; Equal Opportunity Representatives and Officers; Financial Examiners; Fire Inspectors; Fish and Game Wardens; Forest Fire Inspectors and Prevention Specialists; Freight and Cargo Inspectors; Government Property Inspectors and Investigators; Immigration and Customs Inspectors; Licensing Examiners and Inspectors; Nuclear Monitoring Technicians; Occupational Health and Safety Specialists; Tax Examiners, Collectors, and Revenue Agents; Transportation Vehicle, Equipment, and Systems Inspectors, Except Aviation.

Skills—Science: Using scientific methods to solve problems. **Persuasion:** Persuading others to approach things differently. **Operations Analysis:** Analyzing needs and product requirements to create a design. **Technology Design:** Generating or adapting equipment and technology to serve user needs. **Negotiation:** Bringing others together and trying to reconcile differences. **Mathematics:** Using mathematics to solve problems. **Equipment Selection:** Determining the kind of tools and equipment needed to do a job. **Operation Monitoring:** Watching gauges, dials, or other indicators to make sure a machine is working properly.

Education and Training Programs: Environmental Health; Occupational Health and Industrial Hygiene; Radiation Protection/Health Physics Technician Training. **Related Knowledge/Courses—Building and Construction:** Materials, methods, and the appropriate tools to construct objects, structures, and buildings. **Chemistry:** The composition, structure, and properties of substances and of the chemical processes and transformations that they undergo. This includes uses of chemicals and their interactions, danger signs, production techniques, and disposal methods. **Public Safety and Security:** Weaponry; public safety; security operations, rules, regulations, precautions, and prevention; and the protection of people, data, and property. **Engineering and Technology:** Equipment, tools, and mechanical devices and their uses to produce motion, light, power, technology, and other applications. **Physics:** Physical principles, laws, and applications, including air, water, material dynamics, light, atomic principles, heat, electric theory, earth formations, and meteorological and related natural phenomena. **Education and Training:** Instructional methods and training techniques, including curriculum design principles, learning theory, group and individual teaching techniques, design of individual development plans, and test design principles.

Work Environment: More often outdoors than indoors; noisy; hazardous conditions; hazardous equipment; standing.

Occupational Therapist Assistants

* ❀ Education/Training Required: Associate degree
* ❀ Annual Earnings: $45,050
* ❀ Beginning Wage: $27,870
* ❀ Earnings Growth Potential: Medium
* ❀ Growth: 25.4%
* ❀ Annual Job Openings: 2,634
* ❀ Self-Employed: 3.5%
* ❀ Part-Time: 17.8%

Assist occupational therapists in providing occupational therapy treatments and procedures. May, in accordance with state laws, assist in development of treatment plans, carry out routine functions, direct activity programs, and document the progress of treatments. Generally requires formal training. Observe and record patients' progress, attitudes, and behavior and maintain this information in client records. Maintain and promote a positive attitude toward clients and their treatment programs. Monitor patients' performance in therapy activities, providing encouragement. Select therapy activities to fit patients' needs and capabilities. Instruct, or assist in instructing, patients and families in home programs, basic living skills, and the care and use of adaptive equipment. Evaluate the daily living skills and capacities of physically, developmentally, or emotionally disabled clients. Aid patients in dressing and grooming themselves. Implement, or assist occupational therapists with implementing, treatment plans designed to help clients function independently. Report to supervisors, verbally or in writing, on patients' progress, attitudes, and behavior. Alter treatment programs to obtain better results if treatment is not having the intended effect. Work under the direction of occupational therapists to plan, implement, and administer educational, vocational, and recreational programs that restore and enhance performance in individuals with functional impairments. Design, fabricate, and repair assistive devices and make adaptive changes to equipment and environments. Assemble, clean, and maintain equipment and materials for patient use. Teach patients how to deal constructively with their emotions. Perform clerical duties such as scheduling appointments, collecting data, and documenting health insurance billings. Transport patients to and from the occupational therapy work area. Demonstrate therapy techniques such as manual and creative arts or games. Order any needed educational or treatment supplies. Assist educational specialists or clinical psychologists in administering situational or diagnostic tests to measure client's abilities or progress.

Personality Type: Social. These occupations frequently involve working with, communicating with, and teaching people and often involve helping or providing service to others.

GOE—Interest Area/Cluster: 08. Health Science. **Work Group:** 08.07. Medical Therapy. **Other Jobs in This Work Group:** Audiologists; Massage Therapists; Occupational Therapist Aides; Occupational Therapists; Physical Therapist Aides; Physical Therapist Assistants; Physical Therapists; Radiation Therapists; Recreational Therapists; Respiratory Therapists; Respiratory Therapy Technicians; Speech-Language Pathologists.

Skills—Social Perceptiveness: Being aware of others' reactions and understanding why they react the way they do. **Operations Analysis:** Analyzing needs and product requirements to create a design. **Equipment Selection:** Determining the kind of tools and equipment needed to do a job. **Service Orientation:** Actively looking for ways to help people. **Writing:** Communicating effectively with others in writing as indicated by the needs of the audience. **Persuasion:** Persuading others to approach things differently. **Monitoring:** Assessing how well one is doing when learning or doing something. **Time Management:** Managing one's own time and the time of others.

Education and Training Program: Occupational Therapist Assistant Training. **Related Knowledge/Courses—Therapy and Counseling:** Information and techniques needed to rehabilitate physical and mental ailments and to provide career guidance, including alternative treatments, rehabilitation equipment and its proper use, and methods to evaluate treatment effects. **Psychology:** Human behavior and performance, mental processes, psychological research methods, and the assessment and treatment of behavioral and affective disorders. **Sociology and Anthropology:** Group behavior and dynamics; societal trends and influences; and cultures and their history, migrations, ethnicity, and origins. **Philosophy and Theology:** Different philosophical systems and religions, including their basic principles, values, ethics, ways of thinking, customs, and practices and their impact on human culture. **Medicine and Dentistry:** The information and techniques needed to diagnose and treat injuries, diseases, and deformities. This includes symptoms, treatment alternatives, drug properties and interactions, and preventive health-care measures. **Biology:** Plant and animal living tissue, cells, organisms, and entities, including their functions, interdependencies, and interactions with each other and the environment.

Work Environment: Indoors; disease or infections; standing; walking and running; using hands on objects, tools, or controls; bending or twisting the body.

Occupational Therapists

- ❋ Education/Training Required: Master's degree
- ❋ Annual Earnings: $63,790
- ❋ Beginning Wage: $42,330
- ❋ Earnings Growth Potential: Low
- ❋ Growth: 23.1%
- ❋ Annual Job Openings: 8,338
- ❋ Self-Employed: 8.6%
- ❋ Part-Time: 29.8%

Assess, plan, organize, and participate in rehabilitative programs that help restore vocational, homemaking, and daily living skills, as well as general independence, to disabled persons. Plan, organize, and conduct occupational therapy programs in hospital, institutional, or community settings to help rehabilitate those impaired because of illness, injury, or psychological or developmental problems. Test and evaluate patients' physical and mental abilities and analyze medical data to determine realistic rehabilitation goals for patients. Select activities that will help individuals learn work and life-management skills within limits of their mental and physical capabilities. Evaluate patients' progress and prepare reports that detail progress. Complete and maintain necessary records. Train caregivers to provide for the needs of patients during and after therapies. Recommend changes in patients' work or living environments consistent with their needs and capabilities. Develop and participate in health promotion programs, group activities, or discussions to promote client health, facilitate social adjustment, alleviate stress, and prevent physical or mental disability. Consult with rehabilitation team to select activity programs and coordinate occupational therapy with other therapeutic activities. Plan and implement programs and social activities to help patients learn work and school skills and adjust to handicaps. Design and create, or requisition, special supplies and equipment such as splints, braces and computer-aided adaptive equipment. Conduct research in occupational therapy. Provide training and supervision in therapy techniques and objectives for students and nurses and other medical staff. Help clients improve decision making, abstract reasoning, memory, sequencing, coordination, and perceptual skills, using computer programs. Advise on health risks in the workplace and on health-related transition to retirement. Lay out materials such as puzzles, scissors, and eating utensils for use in therapy and clean and repair these tools after therapy sessions. Provide patients with assistance in locating and holding jobs.

Personality Type: Social. These occupations frequently involve working with, communicating with, and teaching people and often involve helping or providing service to others.

GOE—Interest Area/Cluster: 08. Health Science. **Work Group:** 08.07. Medical Therapy. **Other Jobs in This Work Group:** Audiologists; Massage Therapists; Occupational Therapist Aides; Occupational Therapist Assistants; Physical Therapist Aides; Physical Therapist Assistants; Physical Therapists; Radiation Therapists; Recreational Therapists; Respiratory Therapists; Respiratory Therapy Technicians; Speech-Language Pathologists.

Skills—Systems Evaluation: Looking at many indicators of system performance and taking into account their accuracy. **Systems Analysis:** Determining how a system should work and how changes will affect outcomes. **Social Perceptiveness:** Being aware of others' reactions and understanding why they react the way they do. **Judgment and Decision Making:** Weighing the relative costs and benefits of a potential action. **Service Orientation:** Actively looking for ways to help people. **Persuasion:** Persuading others to approach things differently. **Management of Personnel Resources:** Motivating, developing, and directing people as they work; identifying the best people for the job. **Complex Problem Solving:** Identifying complex problems, reviewing the options, and implementing solutions.

Education and Training Program: Occupational Therapy/Therapist Training. **Related Knowledge/Courses—Therapy and Counseling:** Information and techniques needed to rehabilitate physical and mental ailments and to provide career guidance, including alternative treatments, rehabilitation equipment and its proper use, and methods to evaluate treatment effects. **Psychology:** Human behavior and performance, mental processes, psychological research methods, and the assessment and treatment of behavioral and affective disorders. **Sociology and Anthropology:** Group behavior and dynamics; societal trends and influences; and cultures and their history, migrations, ethnicity, and origins.

Medicine and Dentistry: The information and techniques needed to diagnose and treat injuries, diseases, and deformities. This includes symptoms, treatment alternatives, drug properties and interactions, and preventive healthcare measures. **Biology:** Plant and animal living tissue, cells, organisms, and entities, including their functions, interdependencies, and interactions with each other and the environment. **Education and Training:** Instructional methods and training techniques, including curriculum design principles, learning theory, group and individual teaching techniques, design of individual development plans, and test design principles.

Work Environment: Indoors; disease or infections; standing; using hands on objects, tools, or controls; bending or twisting the body.

Office Clerks, General

- ✱ Education/Training Required: Short-term on-the-job training
- ✱ Annual Earnings: $24,460
- ✱ Beginning Wage: $15,490
- ✱ Earnings Growth Potential: Medium
- ✱ Growth: 12.6%
- ✱ Annual Job Openings: 765,803
- ✱ Self-Employed: 0.7%
- ✱ Part-Time: 26.0%

Perform duties too varied and diverse to be classified in any specific office clerical occupation requiring limited knowledge of office management systems and procedures. Clerical duties may be assigned in accordance with the office procedures of individual establishments and may include a combination of answering telephones, bookkeeping, typing or word processing, stenography, office machine operation, and filing. Collect, count, and disburse money; do basic bookkeeping; and complete banking transactions. Communicate with customers, employees, and other individuals to answer questions, disseminate or explain information, take orders, and address complaints. Answer telephones, direct calls, and take messages. Compile, copy, sort, and file records of office activities, business transactions, and other activities. Complete and mail bills, contracts, policies, invoices, or checks. Operate office machines such as photocopiers and scanners, facsimile machines, voice mail systems, and personal computers. Compute, record, and proofread data and other information, such as records or reports. Maintain and update filing, inventory, mailing, and database systems, either manually or using a computer. Open, sort, and route incoming mail; answer correspondence; and prepare outgoing mail. Review files, records, and other documents to obtain information to respond to requests. Deliver messages and run errands. Inventory and order materials, supplies, and services. Complete work schedules, manage calendars, and arrange appointments. Process and prepare documents such as business or government forms and expense reports. Monitor and direct the work of lower-level clerks. Type, format, proofread, and edit correspondence and other documents from notes or dictating machines, using computers or typewriters. Count, weigh, measure, or organize materials. Train other staff members to perform work activities, such as using computer applications. Prepare meeting agendas, attend meetings, and record and transcribe minutes. Troubleshoot problems involving office equipment, such as computer hardware and software. Make travel arrangements for office personnel.

Personality Type: Conventional. These occupations frequently involve following set procedures and routines and can include working with data and details more than with ideas. Usually there is a clear line of authority to follow.

GOE—Interest Area/Cluster: 04. Business and Administration. **Work Group:** 04.07. Records and Materials Processing. **Other Jobs in This Work Group:** Correspondence Clerks; File Clerks; Human Resources Assistants, Except Payroll and Timekeeping; Marking Clerks; Meter Readers, Utilities; Order Fillers, Wholesale and Retail Sales; Postal Service Clerks; Postal Service Mail Sorters, Processors, and Processing Machine Operators; Procurement Clerks; Production, Planning, and Expediting Clerks; Shipping, Receiving, and Traffic Clerks; Stock Clerks and Order Fillers; Stock Clerks, Sales Floor; Stock Clerks—Stockroom, Warehouse, or Storage Yard; Weighers, Measurers, Checkers, and Samplers, Recordkeeping.

Skill—None met the criteria.

Education and Training Program: General Office Occupations and Clerical Services. **Related Knowledge/Courses— Clerical Practices:** Administrative and clerical procedures and systems such as word-processing systems, filing and records management systems, stenography and transcription, forms, design principles, and other office procedures and terminology. **Economics and Accounting:** Economic and accounting principles and practices, the financial markets, banking, and the analysis and reporting of financial data. **Customer and Personal Service:** Principles and processes for providing customer and personal services, including needs assessment techniques, quality service standards, alternative delivery systems, and customer satisfaction evaluation techniques. **Personnel and Human Resources:** Principles and procedures for personnel recruitment; selection; training; compensation and benefits; labor relations and negotiation; and personnel information systems. **Mathematics:** Numbers and their operations and interrelationships, including arithmetic, algebra, geometry, calculus, and statistics and their applications. **Computers and Electronics:** Electric circuit boards, processors, chips, and computer hardware and software, including applications and programming.

Work Environment: Indoors; sitting; using hands on objects, tools, or controls.

Operating Engineers and Other Construction Equipment Operators

- ❀ Education/Training Required: Moderate-term on-the-job training
- ❀ Annual Earnings: $38,130
- ❀ Beginning Wage: $24,840
- ❀ Earnings Growth Potential: Low
- ❀ Growth: 8.4%
- ❀ Annual Job Openings: 55,468
- ❀ Self-Employed: 5.7%
- ❀ Part-Time: 2.1%

Operate one or several types of power construction equipment, such as motor graders, bulldozers, scrapers, compressors, pumps, derricks, shovels, tractors, or front-end loaders, to excavate, move, and grade earth; erect structures; or pour concrete or other hard-surface pavement. May repair and maintain equipment in addition to other duties. Learn and follow safety regulations. Take actions to avoid potential hazards and obstructions such as utility lines, other equipment, other workers, and falling objects. Adjust handwheels and depress pedals to control attachments such as blades, buckets, scrapers, and swing booms. Start engines; move throttles, switches, and levers; and depress pedals to operate machines such as bulldozers, trench excavators, road graders, and backhoes. Locate underground services, such as pipes and wires, prior to beginning work. Monitor operations to ensure that health and safety standards are met. Align machines, cutterheads, or depth gauge makers with reference stakes and guidelines or ground or position

equipment by following hand signals of other workers. Load and move dirt, rocks, equipment, and materials, using trucks, crawler tractors, power cranes, shovels, graders, and related equipment. Drive and maneuver equipment equipped with blades in successive passes over working areas to remove topsoil, vegetation, and rocks and to distribute and level earth or terrain. Coordinate machine actions with other activities, positioning or moving loads in response to hand or audio signals from crew members. Operate tractors and bulldozers to perform such tasks as clearing land, mixing sludge, trimming backfills, and building roadways and parking lots. Repair and maintain equipment, making emergency adjustments or assisting with major repairs as necessary. Check fuel supplies at sites to ensure adequate availability. Connect hydraulic hoses, belts, mechanical linkages, or power take-off shafts to tractors. Operate loaders to pull out stumps, rip asphalt or concrete, rough-grade properties, bury refuse, or perform general cleanup. Select and fasten bulldozer blades or other attachments to tractors, using hitches. Test atmosphere for adequate oxygen and explosive conditions when working in confined spaces. Operate compactors, scrapers, and rollers to level, compact, and cover refuse at disposal grounds. Talk to clients and study instructions, plans, and diagrams to establish work requirements.

Personality Type: Realistic. These occupations frequently involve work activities that include practical, hands-on problems and solutions. They often deal with plants; animals; and real-world materials such as wood, tools, and machinery. Many of the occupations require working outside and don't involve a lot of paperwork or working closely with others.

GOE—Interest Area/Cluster: 02. Architecture and Construction. **Work Group:** 02.04. Construction Crafts. **Other Jobs in This Work Group:** Boilermakers; Brickmasons and Blockmasons; Carpet Installers; Cement Masons and Concrete Finishers; Commercial Divers; Construction Carpenters; Crane and Tower Operators; Drywall and Ceiling Tile Installers; Electricians; Fence Erectors; Floor Layers, Except Carpet, Wood, and Hard Tiles; Floor Sanders and Finishers; Glaziers; Hazardous Materials Removal Workers; Insulation Workers, Floor, Ceiling, and Wall; Insulation Workers, Mechanical; Manufactured Building and Mobile Home Installers; Painters, Construction and Maintenance; Paperhangers; Paving, Surfacing, and Tamping Equipment Operators; Pile-Driver Operators; Pipe Fitters and Steamfitters; Pipelayers; Plasterers and Stucco Masons; Plumbers; Plumbers, Pipefitters, and Steamfitters; Rail-Track Laying and Maintenance Equipment Operators; Refractory Materials

Repairers, Except Brickmasons; Reinforcing Iron and Rebar Workers; Riggers; Roofers; Rough Carpenters; Security and Fire Alarm Systems Installers; Segmental Pavers; Sheet Metal Workers; Stone Cutters and Carvers, Manufacturing; Stonemasons; Structural Iron and Steel Workers; Tapers; Terrazzo Workers and Finishers; Tile and Marble Setters.

Skills—Equipment Maintenance: Performing routine maintenance and determining when and what kind of maintenance is needed. **Installation:** Installing equipment, machines, wiring, or programs to meet specifications. **Operation and Control:** Controlling operations of equipment or systems. **Operation Monitoring:** Watching gauges, dials, or other indicators to make sure a machine is working properly. **Repairing:** Repairing machines or systems, using the needed tools. **Equipment Selection:** Determining the kind of tools and equipment needed to do a job. **Management of Financial Resources:** Determining how money will be spent to get the work done and accounting for these expenditures. **Management of Material Resources:** Obtaining and seeing to the appropriate use of equipment, facilities, and materials needed to do certain work.

Education and Training Programs: Construction/Heavy Equipment/Earthmoving Equipment Operation; Mobile Crane Operation/Operator Training. **Related Knowledge/ Courses—Building and Construction:** Materials, methods, and the appropriate tools to construct objects, structures, and buildings. **Mechanical Devices:** Machines and tools, including their designs, uses, benefits, repair, and maintenance. **Engineering and Technology:** Equipment, tools, and mechanical devices and their uses to produce motion, light, power, technology, and other applications. **Design:** Design techniques, principles, tools, and instruments involved in the production and use of precision technical plans, blueprints, drawings, and models. **Production and Processing:** Inputs, outputs, raw materials, waste, quality control, costs, and techniques for maximizing the manufacture and distribution of goods. **Public Safety and Security:** Weaponry; public safety; security operations, rules, regulations, precautions, and prevention; and the protection of people, data, and property.

Work Environment: Outdoors; noisy; very hot or cold; contaminants; whole-body vibration; using hands on objects, tools, or controls.

Operations Research Analysts

❋ Education/Training Required: Master's degree
❋ Annual Earnings: $66,950
❋ Beginning Wage: $39,760
❋ Earnings Growth Potential: High
❋ Growth: 10.6%
❋ Annual Job Openings: 5,727
❋ Self-Employed: 0.2%
❋ Part-Time: 5.6%

Formulate and apply mathematical modeling and other optimizing methods, using a computer to develop and interpret information that assists management with decision making, policy formulation, or other managerial functions. May develop related software, service, or products. Frequently concentrates on collecting and analyzing data and developing decision support software. May develop and supply optimal time, cost, or logistics networks for program evaluation, review, or implementation. Formulate mathematical or simulation models of problems, relating constants and variables, restrictions, alternatives, and conflicting objectives and their numerical parameters. Collaborate with others in the organization to ensure successful implementation of chosen problem solutions. Analyze information obtained from management in order to conceptualize and define operational problems. Perform validation and testing of models to ensure adequacy; reformulate models as necessary. Collaborate with senior managers and decision-makers to identify and solve a variety of problems and to clarify management objectives. Define data requirements; then gather and validate information, applying judgment and statistical tests. Study and analyze information about alternative courses of action in order to determine which plan will offer the best outcomes. Prepare management reports defining and evaluating problems and recommending solutions. Break systems into their component parts, assign numerical values to each component, and examine the mathematical relationships between them. Specify manipulative or computational methods to be applied to models. Observe the current system in operation and gather and analyze information about each of the parts of component problems, using a variety of sources. Design, conduct, and evaluate experimental operational models in cases where models cannot be developed from existing data. Develop and apply time and cost networks in order to plan, control, and review large projects. Develop business methods and procedures, including accounting systems, file systems, office systems, logistics systems, and production schedules.

Personality Type: Investigative. These occupations frequently involve working with ideas and require an extensive amount of thinking. They can involve searching for facts and figuring out problems mentally.

GOE—Interest Area/Cluster: 04. Business and Administration. **Work Group:** 04.05. Accounting, Auditing, and Analytical Support. **Other Jobs in This Work Group:** Accountants; Accountants and Auditors; Auditors; Budget Analysts; Industrial Engineering Technicians; Logisticians; Management Analysts.

Skills—Programming: Writing computer programs for various purposes. **Systems Analysis:** Determining how a system should work and how changes will affect outcomes. **Operations Analysis:** Analyzing needs and product requirements to create a design. **Science:** Using scientific methods to solve problems. **Mathematics:** Using mathematics to solve problems. **Systems Evaluation:** Looking at many indicators of system performance and taking into account their accuracy. **Complex Problem Solving:** Identifying complex problems, reviewing the options, and implementing solutions. **Judgment and Decision Making:** Weighing the relative costs and benefits of a potential action.

Education and Training Programs: Educational Evaluation and Research; Educational Statistics and Research Methods; Management Science, General; Management Sciences and Quantitative Methods, Other; Operations Research. **Related Knowledge/Courses—Mathematics:** Numbers and their operations and interrelationships, including arithmetic, algebra, geometry, calculus, and statistics and their applications. **Engineering and Technology:** Equipment, tools, and mechanical devices and their uses to produce motion, light, power, technology, and other applications. **Computers and Electronics:** Electric circuit boards, processors, chips, and computer hardware and software, including applications and programming. **Production and Processing:** Inputs, outputs, raw materials, waste, quality control, costs, and techniques for maximizing the manufacture and distribution of goods. **Economics and Accounting:** Economic and accounting principles and practices, the financial markets, banking, and the analysis and reporting of financial data. **Administration and Management:** Principles and processes involved in business and organizational planning, coordination, and execution. This includes strategic planning, resource allocation, manpower modeling, leadership techniques, and production methods.

Work Environment: Indoors; sitting.

Optometrists

* **Education/Training Required: First professional degree**
* **Annual Earnings: $93,800**
* **Beginning Wage: $47,980**
* **Earnings Growth Potential: High**
* **Growth: 11.3%**
* **Annual Job Openings: 1,789**
* **Self-Employed: 25.5%**
* **Part-Time: 20.8%**

Diagnose, manage, and treat conditions and diseases of the human eye and visual system. Examine eyes and visual systems, diagnose problems or impairments, prescribe corrective lenses, and provide treatment. May prescribe therapeutic drugs to treat specific eye conditions. Examine eyes, using observation, instruments, and pharmaceutical agents, to determine visual acuity and perception, focus, and coordination and to diagnose diseases and other abnormalities such as glaucoma or color blindness. Prescribe medications to treat eye diseases if state laws permit. Analyze test results and develop treatment plans. Prescribe, supply, fit, and adjust eyeglasses, contact lenses, and other vision aids. Educate and counsel patients on contact lens care, visual hygiene, lighting arrangements, and safety factors. Remove foreign bodies from eyes. Consult with and refer patients to ophthalmologist or other health-care practitioners if additional medical treatment is determined necessary. Provide patients undergoing eye surgeries, such as cataract and laser vision correction, with pre- and postoperative care. Prescribe therapeutic procedures to correct or conserve vision. Provide vision therapy and low vision rehabilitation.

Personality Type: Investigative. These occupations frequently involve working with ideas and require an extensive amount of thinking. They can involve searching for facts and figuring out problems mentally.

GOE—Interest Area/Cluster: 08. Health Science. **Work Group:** 08.04. Health Specialties. **Other Jobs in This Work Group:** Chiropractors; Podiatrists.

Skills—Management of Personnel Resources: Motivating, developing, and directing people as they work; identifying the best people for the job. **Systems Evaluation:** Looking at many indicators of system performance and taking into account their accuracy. **Writing:** Communicating effectively with others in writing as indicated by the needs of the audience. **Systems Analysis:** Determining how a system should work and how changes will affect outcomes.

Education and Training Program: Optometry (OD). **Related Knowledge/Courses—Medicine and Dentistry:** The information and techniques needed to diagnose and treat injuries, diseases, and deformities. This includes symptoms, treatment alternatives, drug properties and interactions, and preventive health-care measures. **Biology:** Plant and animal living tissue, cells, organisms, and entities, including their functions, interdependencies, and interactions with each other and the environment. **Therapy and Counseling:** Information and techniques needed to rehabilitate physical and mental ailments and to provide career guidance, including alternative treatments, rehabilitation equipment and its proper use, and methods to evaluate treatment effects. **Physics:** Physical principles, laws, and applications, including air, water, material dynamics, light, atomic principles, heat, electric theory, earth formations, and meteorological and related natural phenomena. **Sales and Marketing:** Principles and methods involved in showing, promoting, and selling products or services. This includes marketing strategies and tactics, product demonstration and sales techniques, and sales control systems. **Economics and Accounting:** Economic and accounting principles and practices, the financial markets, banking, and the analysis and reporting of financial data.

Work Environment: Indoors; disease or infections; sitting; using hands on objects, tools, or controls.

Oral and Maxillofacial Surgeons

- ❀ Education/Training Required: First professional degree
- ❀ Annual Earnings: More than $145,600
- ❀ Beginning Wage: $63,850
- ❀ Earnings Growth Potential: Cannot be calculated
- ❀ Growth: 9.1%
- ❀ Annual Job Openings: 400
- ❀ Self-Employed: 30.6%
- ❀ Part-Time: 25.9%

Perform surgery on mouth, jaws, and related head and neck structure to execute difficult and multiple extractions of teeth, to remove tumors and other abnormal **growths, to correct abnormal jaw relations by mandibular or maxillary revision, to prepare mouth for insertion of dental prosthesis, or to treat fractured jaws.** Administer general and local anesthetics. Remove impacted, damaged, and non-restorable teeth. Evaluate the position of the wisdom teeth in order to determine whether problems exist currently or might occur in the future. Collaborate with other professionals such as restorative dentists and orthodontists in order to plan treatment. Perform surgery to prepare the mouth for dental implants and to aid in the regeneration of deficient bone and gum tissues. Remove tumors and other abnormal growths of the oral and facial regions, using surgical instruments. Treat infections of the oral cavity, salivary glands, jaws, and neck. Treat problems affecting the oral mucosa such as mouth ulcers and infections. Provide emergency treatment of facial injuries, including facial lacerations, intra-oral lacerations, and fractured facial bones. Perform surgery on the mouth and jaws in order to treat conditions such as cleft lip and palate and jaw growth problems. Restore form and function by moving skin, bone, nerves, and other tissues from other parts of the body in order to reconstruct the jaws and face. Perform minor cosmetic procedures such as chin and cheekbone enhancements and minor facial rejuvenation procedures including the use of Botox and laser technology. Treat snoring problems, using laser surgery.

Personality Type: Realistic. These occupations frequently involve work activities that include practical, hands-on problems and solutions. They often deal with plants; animals; and real-world materials such as wood, tools, and machinery. Many of the occupations require working outside and don't involve a lot of paperwork or working closely with others.

GOE—Interest Area/Cluster: 08. Health Science. **Work Group:** 08.03. Dentistry. **Other Jobs in This Work Group:** Dental Assistants; Dental Hygienists; Dentists, General; Orthodontists; Prosthodontists.

Skills—Science: Using scientific methods to solve problems. **Management of Financial Resources:** Determining how money will be spent to get the work done and accounting for these expenditures. **Equipment Selection:** Determining the kind of tools and equipment needed to do a job. **Service Orientation:** Actively looking for ways to help people. **Complex Problem Solving:** Identifying complex problems, reviewing the options, and implementing solutions. **Management of Personnel Resources:** Motivating, developing, and directing people as they work; identifying the best people for the job. **Active Learning:** Working with new material or information to grasp its implications. **Reading Comprehension:** Understanding written sentences and paragraphs in work-related documents.

Education and Training Programs: Dental/Oral Surgery Specialty; Oral/Maxillofacial Surgery (Cert, MS, PhD). **Related Knowledge/Courses—Medicine and Dentistry:** The information and techniques needed to diagnose and treat injuries, diseases, and deformities. This includes symptoms, treatment alternatives, drug properties and interactions, and preventive health-care measures. **Biology:** Plant and animal living tissue, cells, organisms, and entities, including their functions, interdependencies, and interactions with each other and the environment. **Therapy and Counseling:** Information and techniques needed to rehabilitate physical and mental ailments and to provide career guidance, including alternative treatments, rehabilitation equipment and its proper use, and methods to evaluate treatment effects. **Chemistry:** The composition, structure, and properties of substances and of the chemical processes and transformations that they undergo. This includes uses of chemicals and their interactions, danger signs, production techniques, and disposal methods. **Psychology:** Human behavior and performance, mental processes, psychological research methods, and the assessment and treatment of behavioral and affective disorders. **Personnel and Human Resources:** Principles and procedures for personnel recruitment; selection; training; compensation and benefits; labor relations and negotiation; and personnel information systems.

Work Environment: Indoors; disease or infections; standing; using hands on objects, tools, or controls; bending or twisting the body; repetitive motions.

Orthodontists

- ❇ Education/Training Required: First professional degree
- ❇ Annual Earnings: More than $145,600
- ❇ Beginning Wage: $95,740
- ❇ Earnings Growth Potential: Cannot be calculated
- ❇ Growth: 9.2%
- ❇ Annual Job Openings: 479
- ❇ Self-Employed: 43.3%
- ❇ Part-Time: 25.9%

Examine, diagnose, and treat dental malocclusions and oral cavity anomalies. Design and fabricate appliances to realign teeth and jaws to produce and maintain normal function and to improve appearance. Fit dental appliances in patients' mouths to alter the position and relationship of teeth and jaws and to realign teeth. Study diagnostic records such as medical/dental histories, plaster models of the teeth, photos of a patient's face and teeth, and X rays to develop patient treatment plans. Diagnose teeth and jaw or other dental-facial abnormalities. Examine patients to assess abnormalities of jaw development, tooth position, and other dental-facial structures. Prepare diagnostic and treatment records. Adjust dental appliances periodically to produce and maintain normal function. Provide patients with proposed treatment plans and cost estimates. Instruct dental officers and technical assistants in orthodontic procedures and techniques. Coordinate orthodontic services with other dental and medical services. Design and fabricate appliances, such as space maintainers, retainers, and labial and lingual arch wires.

Personality Type: Investigative. These occupations frequently involve working with ideas and require an extensive amount of thinking. They can involve searching for facts and figuring out problems mentally.

GOE—Interest Area/Cluster: 08. Health Science. **Work Group:** 08.03. Dentistry. **Other Jobs in This Work Group:** Dental Assistants; Dental Hygienists; Dentists, General; Oral and Maxillofacial Surgeons; Prosthodontists.

Skills—Management of Financial Resources: Determining how money will be spent to get the work done and accounting for these expenditures. **Equipment Selection:** Determining the kind of tools and equipment needed to do a job. **Management of Personnel Resources:** Motivating, developing, and directing people as they work; identifying the best people for the job. **Management of Material Resources:** Obtaining and seeing to the appropriate use of equipment, facilities, and materials needed to do certain work. **Technology Design:** Generating or adapting equipment and technology to serve user needs. **Judgment and Decision Making:** Weighing the relative costs and benefits of a potential action. **Operations Analysis:** Analyzing needs and product requirements to create a design. **Service Orientation:** Actively looking for ways to help people.

Education and Training Programs: Orthodontics Specialty; Orthodontics/Orthodontology (Cert, MS, PhD). **Related Knowledge/Courses—Medicine and Dentistry:** The information and techniques needed to diagnose and treat injuries, diseases, and deformities. This includes symptoms, treatment alternatives, drug properties and interactions, and preventive health-care measures. **Biology:** Plant and animal living tissue, cells, organisms, and entities, including their functions, interdependencies, and interactions with each other and the environment. **Sales and Marketing:** Principles and methods involved in showing, promoting, and selling products or services. This includes marketing strategies and tactics, product demonstration and sales techniques, and sales control systems. **Economics and Accounting:** Economic and accounting principles and practices, the financial markets, banking, and the analysis and reporting of financial data. **Personnel and Human Resources:** Principles and procedures for personnel recruitment; selection; training; compensation and benefits; labor relations and negotiation; and personnel information systems. **Customer and Personal Service:** Principles and processes for providing customer and personal services, including needs assessment techniques, quality service standards, alternative delivery systems, and customer satisfaction evaluation techniques.

Work Environment: Indoors; disease or infections; sitting; using hands on objects, tools, or controls; bending or twisting the body; repetitive motions.

Orthotists and Prosthetists

- ❋ Education/Training Required: Bachelor's degree
- ❋ Annual Earnings: $60,520
- ❋ Beginning Wage: $31,670
- ❋ Earnings Growth Potential: High
- ❋ Growth: 11.8%
- ❋ Annual Job Openings: 295
- ❋ Self-Employed: 6.5%
- ❋ Part-Time: 15.4%

Assist patients with disabling conditions of limbs and spine or with partial or total absence of limb by fitting and preparing orthopedic braces or prostheses. Examine, interview, and measure patients in order to determine their appliance needs and to identify factors that could affect appliance fit. Fit, test, and evaluate devices on patients and make adjustments for proper fit, function, and comfort. Instruct patients in the use and care of orthoses and prostheses. Design orthopedic and prosthetic devices based on physicians' prescriptions and examination and measurement of patients. Maintain patients' records. Make and

modify plaster casts of areas that will be fitted with prostheses or orthoses for use in the device construction process. Select materials and components to be used, based on device design. Confer with physicians to formulate specifications and prescriptions for orthopedic or prosthetic devices. Repair, rebuild, and modify prosthetic and orthopedic appliances. Construct and fabricate appliances or supervise others who are constructing the appliances. Train and supervise orthopedic and prosthetic assistants and technicians and other support staff. Update skills and knowledge by attending conferences and seminars. Show and explain orthopedic and prosthetic appliances to health-care workers. Research new ways to construct and use orthopedic and prosthetic devices. Publish research findings and present them at conferences and seminars.

Personality Type: Social. These occupations frequently involve working with, communicating with, and teaching people and often involve helping or providing service to others.

GOE—Interest Area/Cluster: 08. Health Science. **Work Group:** 08.06. Medical Technology. **Other Jobs in This Work Group:** Biological Technicians; Cardiovascular Technologists and Technicians; Diagnostic Medical Sonographers; Medical and Clinical Laboratory Technicians; Medical and Clinical Laboratory Technologists; Medical Equipment Preparers; Medical Records and Health Information Technicians; Nuclear Medicine Technologists; Opticians, Dispensing; Radiologic Technicians; Radiologic Technologists; Radiologic Technologists and Technicians.

Skills—Technology Design: Generating or adapting equipment and technology to serve user needs. **Management of Financial Resources:** Determining how money will be spent to get the work done and accounting for these expenditures. **Management of Material Resources:** Obtaining and seeing to the appropriate use of equipment, facilities, and materials needed to do certain work. **Operations Analysis:** Analyzing needs and product requirements to create a design. **Service Orientation:** Actively looking for ways to help people. **Science:** Using scientific methods to solve problems. **Equipment Selection:** Determining the kind of tools and equipment needed to do a job. **Management of Personnel Resources:** Motivating, developing, and directing people as they work; identifying the best people for the job.

Education and Training Programs: Assistive/Augmentative Technology and Rehabiliation Engineering; Orthotist/Prosthetist Training. **Related Knowledge/Courses—Engineering and Technology:** Equipment, tools, and mechanical devices and their uses to produce motion, light, power, technology, and other applications. **Medicine and Dentistry:** The information and techniques needed to diagnose and treat injuries, diseases, and deformities. This includes symptoms, treatment alternatives, drug properties and interactions, and preventive health-care measures. **Design:** Design techniques, principles, tools, and instruments involved in the production and use of precision technical plans, blueprints, drawings, and models. **Therapy and Counseling:** Information and techniques needed to rehabilitate physical and mental ailments and to provide career guidance, including alternative treatments, rehabilitation equipment and its proper use, and methods to evaluate treatment effects. **Psychology:** Human behavior and performance, mental processes, psychological research methods, and the assessment and treatment of behavioral and affective disorders. **Production and Processing:** Inputs, outputs, raw materials, waste, quality control, costs, and techniques for maximizing the manufacture and distribution of goods.

Work Environment: Indoors; noisy; contaminants; disease or infections; hazardous equipment; using hands on objects, tools, or controls.

Painters, Construction and Maintenance

- ❈ Education/Training Required: Moderate-term on-the-job training
- ❈ Annual Earnings: $32,080
- ❈ Beginning Wage: $21,720
- ❈ Earnings Growth Potential: Low
- ❈ Growth: 11.8%
- ❈ Annual Job Openings: 101,140
- ❈ Self-Employed: 42.2%
- ❈ Part-Time: 9.8%

Paint walls, equipment, buildings, bridges, and other structural surfaces with brushes, rollers, and spray guns. May remove old paint to prepare surfaces before painting. May mix colors or oils to obtain desired color or consistency. Cover surfaces with dropcloths or masking tape and paper to protect surfaces during painting. Fill cracks, holes, and joints with caulk, putty, plaster, or other fillers, using caulking guns or putty knives. Apply primers or sealers to prepare new surfaces such as bare wood or metal for finish coats. Apply paint, stain, varnish, enamel, and other finishes to equipment, buildings, bridges, and/or other structures,

using brushes, spray guns, or rollers. Calculate amounts of required materials and estimate costs, based on surface measurements and/or work orders. Read work orders or receive instructions from supervisors or homeowners in order to determine work requirements. Erect scaffolding and swing gates, or set up ladders, to work above ground level. Remove fixtures such as pictures, door knobs, lamps, and electric switch covers prior to painting. Wash and treat surfaces with oil, turpentine, mildew remover, or other preparations and sand rough spots to ensure that finishes will adhere properly. Mix and match colors of paint, stain, or varnish with oil and thinning and drying additives in order to obtain desired colors and consistencies. Remove old finishes by stripping, sanding, wire brushing, burning, or using water and/or abrasive blasting. Select and purchase tools and finishes for surfaces to be covered, considering durability, ease of handling, methods of application, and customers' wishes. Smooth surfaces, using sandpaper, scrapers, brushes, steel wool, and/or sanding machines. Polish final coats to specified finishes. Use special finishing techniques such as sponging, ragging, layering, or faux finishing. Waterproof buildings, using waterproofers and caulking. Cut stencils and brush and spray lettering and decorations on surfaces. Spray or brush hot plastics or pitch onto surfaces. Bake finishes on painted and enameled articles, using baking ovens.

Personality Type: Realistic. These occupations frequently involve work activities that include practical, hands-on problems and solutions. They often deal with plants; animals; and real-world materials such as wood, tools, and machinery. Many of the occupations require working outside and don't involve a lot of paperwork or working closely with others.

GOE—Interest Area/Cluster: 02. Architecture and Construction. **Work Group:** 02.04. Construction Crafts. **Other Jobs in This Work Group:** Boilermakers; Brickmasons and Blockmasons; Carpet Installers; Cement Masons and Concrete Finishers; Commercial Divers; Construction Carpenters; Crane and Tower Operators; Drywall and Ceiling Tile Installers; Electricians; Fence Erectors; Floor Layers, Except Carpet, Wood, and Hard Tiles; Floor Sanders and Finishers; Glaziers; Hazardous Materials Removal Workers; Insulation Workers, Floor, Ceiling, and Wall; Insulation Workers, Mechanical; Manufactured Building and Mobile Home Installers; Operating Engineers and Other Construction Equipment Operators; Paperhangers; Paving, Surfacing, and Tamping Equipment Operators; Pile-Driver Operators; Pipe Fitters and Steamfitters; Pipelayers; Plasterers and Stucco Masons; Plumbers; Plumbers, Pipefitters, and

Steamfitters; Rail-Track Laying and Maintenance Equipment Operators; Refractory Materials Repairers, Except Brickmasons; Reinforcing Iron and Rebar Workers; Riggers; Roofers; Rough Carpenters; Security and Fire Alarm Systems Installers; Segmental Pavers; Sheet Metal Workers; Stone Cutters and Carvers, Manufacturing; Stonemasons; Structural Iron and Steel Workers; Tapers; Terrazzo Workers and Finishers; Tile and Marble Setters.

Skills—Equipment Maintenance: Performing routine maintenance and determining when and what kind of maintenance is needed. **Management of Material Resources:** Obtaining and seeing to the appropriate use of equipment, facilities, and materials needed to do certain work. **Equipment Selection:** Determining the kind of tools and equipment needed to do a job. **Repairing:** Repairing machines or systems, using the needed tools. **Management of Personnel Resources:** Motivating, developing, and directing people as they work; identifying the best people for the job. **Monitoring:** Assessing how well one is doing when learning or doing something. **Coordination:** Adjusting actions in relation to others' actions.

Education and Training Program: Painting/Painter and Wall Coverer Training. **Related Knowledge/Courses—Building and Construction:** Materials, methods, and the appropriate tools to construct objects, structures, and buildings. **Design:** Design techniques, principles, tools, and instruments involved in the production and use of precision technical plans, blueprints, drawings, and models. **Transportation:** Principles and methods for moving people or goods by air, rail, sea, or road, including their relative costs, advantages, and limitations. **Customer and Personal Service:** Principles and processes for providing customer and personal services, including needs assessment techniques, quality service standards, alternative delivery systems, and customer satisfaction evaluation techniques. **Production and Processing:** Inputs, outputs, raw materials, waste, quality control, costs, and techniques for maximizing the manufacture and distribution of goods. **Administration and Management:** Principles and processes involved in business and organizational planning, coordination, and execution. This includes strategic planning, resource allocation, manpower modeling, leadership techniques, and production methods.

Work Environment: Contaminants; standing; climbing ladders, scaffolds, or poles; using hands on objects, tools, or controls; bending or twisting the body; repetitive motions.

Paralegals and Legal Assistants

* Education/Training Required: Associate degree
* Annual Earnings: $44,990
* Beginning Wage: $28,360
* Earnings Growth Potential: Medium
* Growth: 22.2%
* Annual Job Openings: 22,756
* Self-Employed: 2.2%
* Part-Time: 11.0%

Assist lawyers by researching legal precedent, investigating facts, or preparing legal documents. Conduct research to support a legal proceeding, to formulate a defense, or to initiate legal action. Prepare legal documents, including briefs, pleadings, appeals, wills, contracts, and real estate closing statements. Prepare affidavits or other documents, maintain document file, and file pleadings with court clerk. Gather and analyze research data, such as statutes; decisions; and legal articles, codes, and documents. Investigate facts and law of cases to determine causes of action and to prepare cases. Call upon witnesses to testify at hearing. Direct and coordinate law office activity, including delivery of subpoenas. Arbitrate disputes between parties and assist in real estate closing process. Keep and monitor legal volumes to ensure that law library is up to date. Appraise and inventory real and personal property for estate planning.

Personality Type: Conventional. These occupations frequently involve following set procedures and routines and can include working with data and details more than with ideas. Usually there is a clear line of authority to follow.

GOE—Interest Area/Cluster: 12. Law and Public Safety. **Work Group:** 12.03. Legal Support. **Other Jobs in This Work Group:** Law Clerks; Title Examiners, Abstractors, and Searchers.

Skills—Writing: Communicating effectively with others in writing as indicated by the needs of the audience. **Active Listening:** Listening to what other people are saying and asking questions as appropriate. **Speaking:** Talking to others to effectively convey information. **Time Management:** Managing one's own time and the time of others. **Reading Comprehension:** Understanding written sentences and paragraphs in work-related documents. **Monitoring:** Assessing how well one is doing when learning or doing something.

Education and Training Program: Legal Assistant/Paralegal. **Related Knowledge/Courses—Clerical Practices:** Administrative and clerical procedures and systems such as word-processing systems, filing and records management systems, stenography and transcription, forms, design principles, and other office procedures and terminology. **Law and Government:** Laws, legal codes, court procedures, precedents, government regulations, executive orders, agency rules, and the democratic political process. **Computers and Electronics:** Electric circuit boards, processors, chips, and computer hardware and software, including applications and programming. **Personnel and Human Resources:** Principles and procedures for personnel recruitment; selection; training; compensation and benefits; labor relations and negotiation; and personnel information systems. **English Language:** The structure and content of the English language, including the meaning and spelling of words, rules of composition, and grammar. **Customer and Personal Service:** Principles and processes for providing customer and personal services, including needs assessment techniques, quality service standards, alternative delivery systems, and customer satisfaction evaluation techniques.

Work Environment: Indoors; sitting; repetitive motions.

Parts Salespersons

* Education/Training Required: Moderate-term on-the-job training
* Annual Earnings: $28,130
* Beginning Wage: $17,310
* Earnings Growth Potential: Medium
* Growth: –2.2%
* Annual Job Openings: 52,414
* Self-Employed: 1.6%
* Part-Time: 8.3%

Sell spare and replacement parts and equipment in repair shop or parts store. Read catalogs, microfiche viewers, or computer displays to determine replacement part stock numbers and prices. Determine replacement parts required according to inspections of old parts, customer requests, or customers' descriptions of malfunctions. Receive and fill telephone orders for parts. Fill customer orders from stock. Prepare sales slips or sales contracts. Receive payment or obtain credit authorization. Take inventory of stock. Advise customers on substitution or modification of parts when identical replacements are not available. Examine returned parts for defects and exchange defective parts or refund money.

Mark and store parts in stockrooms according to prearranged systems. Discuss use and features of various parts, based on knowledge of machines or equipment. Demonstrate equipment to customers and explain functioning of equipment. Place new merchandise on display. Measure parts, using precision measuring instruments, to determine whether similar parts may be machined to required sizes. Repair parts or equipment.

Personality Type: Enterprising. These occupations frequently involve starting up and carrying out projects and can involve leading people and making many decisions. They sometimes require risk taking and often deal with business.

GOE—Interest Area/Cluster: 14. Retail and Wholesale Sales and Service. **Work Group:** 14.03. General Sales. **Other Jobs in This Work Group:** Real Estate Brokers; Real Estate Sales Agents; Retail Salespersons; Sales Representatives, Wholesale and Manufacturing, Except Technical and Scientific Products; Service Station Attendants.

Skills—Service Orientation: Actively looking for ways to help people. **Management of Personnel Resources:** Motivating, developing, and directing people as they work; identifying the best people for the job. **Negotiation:** Bringing others together and trying to reconcile differences. **Equipment Selection:** Determining the kind of tools and equipment needed to do a job. **Operations Analysis:** Analyzing needs and product requirements to create a design. **Management of Financial Resources:** Determining how money will be spent to get the work done and accounting for these expenditures. **Social Perceptiveness:** Being aware of others' reactions and understanding why they react the way they do. **Persuasion:** Persuading others to approach things differently.

Education and Training Programs: Selling Skills and Sales Operations; Vehicle and Vehicle Parts and Accessories Marketing Operations. **Related Knowledge/Courses—Sales and Marketing:** Principles and methods involved in showing, promoting, and selling products or services. This includes marketing strategies and tactics, product demonstration and sales techniques, and sales control systems. **Customer and Personal Service:** Principles and processes for providing customer and personal services, including needs assessment techniques, quality service standards, alternative delivery systems, and customer satisfaction evaluation techniques. **Mechanical Devices:** Machines and tools, including their designs, uses, benefits, repair, and maintenance. **Computers and Electronics:** Electric circuit boards, processors, chips, and computer hardware and software, including applications and programming. **Production and Processing:** Inputs, outputs, raw materials, waste, quality control, costs, and techniques for maximizing the manufacture and distribution of goods. **Mathematics:** Numbers and their operations and interrelationships, including arithmetic, algebra, geometry, calculus, and statistics and their applications.

Work Environment: Indoors; noisy; contaminants; standing; repetitive motions.

Payroll and Timekeeping Clerks

* Education/Training Required: Moderate-term on-the-job training
* Annual Earnings: $33,810
* Beginning Wage: $22,450
* Earnings Growth Potential: Low
* Growth: 3.1%
* Annual Job Openings: 18,544
* Self-Employed: 1.2%
* Part-Time: 15.9%

Compile and post employee time and payroll data. May compute employees' time worked, production, and commission. May compute and post wages and deductions. May prepare paychecks. Process and issue employee paychecks and statements of earnings and deductions. Compute wages and deductions and enter data into computers. Compile employee time, production, and payroll data from time sheets and other records. Review time sheets, work charts, wage computation, and other information to detect and reconcile payroll discrepancies. Verify attendance, hours worked, and pay adjustments and post information onto designated records. Record employee information, such as exemptions, transfers, and resignations, to maintain and update payroll records. Keep informed about changes in tax and deduction laws that apply to the payroll process. Issue and record adjustments to pay related to previous errors or retroactive increases. Provide information to employees and managers on payroll matters, tax issues, benefit plans, and collective agreement provisions. Complete time sheets showing employees' arrival and departure times. Post relevant work hours to client files to bill clients properly. Distribute and collect timecards each pay period. Complete, verify, and process forms and documentation for administration of benefits such as pension plans and unemployment and medical insurance. Prepare and balance period-end reports and reconcile issued payrolls to bank statements. Compile statistical reports, statements, and summaries related to pay and benefits accounts and submit them to appropriate departments. Coordinate special programs, such as United Way campaigns, that involve payroll deductions.

Personality Type: Conventional. These occupations frequently involve following set procedures and routines and can include working with data and details more than with ideas. Usually there is a clear line of authority to follow.

GOE—Interest Area/Cluster: 04. Business and Administration. **Work Group:** 04.06. Mathematical Clerical Support. **Other Jobs in This Work Group:** Billing and Posting Clerks and Machine Operators; Billing, Cost, and Rate Clerks; Bookkeeping, Accounting, and Auditing Clerks; Brokerage Clerks; Statement Clerks; Tax Preparers.

Skills—Mathematics: Using mathematics to solve problems. **Time Management:** Managing one's own time and the time of others. **Writing:** Communicating effectively with others in writing as indicated by the needs of the audience. **Active Listening:** Listening to what other people are saying and asking questions as appropriate. **Judgment and Decision Making:** Weighing the relative costs and benefits of a potential action. **Speaking:** Talking to others to effectively convey information. **Learning Strategies:** Using multiple approaches when learning or teaching new things. **Reading Comprehension:** Understanding written sentences and paragraphs in work-related documents.

Education and Training Program: Accounting Technology/Technician Training and Bookkeeping. **Related Knowledge/Courses—Clerical Practices:** Administrative and clerical procedures and systems such as word-processing systems, filing and records management systems, stenography and transcription, forms, design principles, and other office procedures and terminology. **Economics and Accounting:** Economic and accounting principles and practices, the financial markets, banking, and the analysis and reporting of financial data. **Mathematics:** Numbers and their operations and interrelationships, including arithmetic, algebra, geometry, calculus, and statistics and their applications. **Administration and Management:** Principles and processes involved in business and organizational planning, coordination, and execution. This includes strategic planning, resource allocation, manpower modeling, leadership techniques, and production methods. **Personnel and Human Resources:** Principles and procedures for personnel recruitment; selection; training; compensation and benefits; labor relations and negotiation; and personnel information systems. **Computers and Electronics:** Electric circuit boards, processors, chips, and computer hardware and software, including applications and programming.

Work Environment: Indoors; noisy; sitting; repetitive motions.

Pediatricians, General

- ❀ Education/Training Required: First professional degree
- ❀ Annual Earnings: $140,690
- ❀ Beginning Wage: $67,430
- ❀ Earnings Growth Potential: Very high
- ❀ Growth: 14.2%
- ❀ Annual Job Openings: 38,027
- ❀ Self-Employed: 14.7%
- ❀ Part-Time: 8.1%

The job openings listed here are shared with Anesthesiologists; Family and General Practitioners; Internists, General; Obstetricians and Gynecologists; Psychiatrists; and Surgeons.

Diagnose, treat, and help prevent children's diseases and injuries. Examine patients or order, perform, and interpret diagnostic tests to obtain information on medical condition and determine diagnosis. Examine children regularly to assess their growth and development. Prescribe or administer treatment, therapy, medication, vaccination, and other specialized medical care to treat or prevent illness, disease, or injury in infants and children. Collect, record, and maintain patient information, such as medical history, reports, and examination results. Advise patients, parents or guardians, and community members concerning diet, activity, hygiene, and disease prevention. Treat children who have minor illnesses, acute and chronic health problems, and growth and development concerns. Explain procedures and discuss test results or prescribed treatments with patients and parents or guardians. Monitor patients' condition and progress and re-evaluate treatments as necessary. Plan and execute medical care programs to aid in the mental and physical growth and development of children and adolescents. Refer patient to medical specialist or other practitioner when necessary. Direct and coordinate activities of nurses, students, assistants, specialists, therapists, and other medical staff. Provide consulting services to other physicians. Plan, implement, or administer health programs or standards in hospital, business, or community for information, prevention, or treatment of injury or illness. Operate on patients to remove, repair, or improve functioning of diseased or injured body parts and systems. Conduct research to study anatomy and develop or test medications, treatments, or procedures to prevent or control disease or injury. Prepare reports for government or management of birth, death, and disease statistics; workforce evaluations; or medical status of individuals.

Personality Type: Investigative. These occupations frequently involve working with ideas and require an extensive amount of thinking. They can involve searching for facts and figuring out problems mentally.

GOE—Interest Area/Cluster: 08. Health Science. **Work Group:** 08.02. Medicine and Surgery. **Other Jobs in This Work Group:** Anesthesiologists; Family and General Practitioners; Internists, General; Medical Assistants; Medical Transcriptionists; Obstetricians and Gynecologists; Pharmacists; Pharmacy Aides; Pharmacy Technicians; Physician Assistants; Psychiatrists; Registered Nurses; Surgeons; Surgical Technologists.

Skills—Science: Using scientific methods to solve problems. **Social Perceptiveness:** Being aware of others' reactions and understanding why they react the way they do. **Active Learning:** Working with new material or information to grasp its implications. **Reading Comprehension:** Understanding written sentences and paragraphs in work-related documents. **Persuasion:** Persuading others to approach things differently. **Critical Thinking:** Using logic and analysis to identify the strengths and weaknesses of different approaches. **Management of Financial Resources:** Determining how money will be spent to get the work done and accounting for these expenditures. **Monitoring:** Assessing how well one is doing when learning or doing something.

Education and Training Programs: Child/Pediatric Neurology; Family Medicine; Neonatal-Perinatal Medicine; Pediatric Cardiology; Pediatric Endocrinology; Pediatric Hemato-Oncology; Pediatric Nephrology; Pediatric Orthopedics; Pediatric Surgery; Pediatrics. **Related Knowledge/ Courses—Medicine and Dentistry:** The information and techniques needed to diagnose and treat injuries, diseases, and deformities. This includes symptoms, treatment alternatives, drug properties and interactions, and preventive health-care measures. **Therapy and Counseling:** Information and techniques needed to rehabilitate physical and mental ailments and to provide career guidance, including alternative treatments, rehabilitation equipment and its proper use, and methods to evaluate treatment effects. **Biology:** Plant and animal living tissue, cells, organisms, and entities, including their functions, interdependencies, and interactions with each other and the environment. **Psychology:**

Human behavior and performance, mental processes, psychological research methods, and the assessment and treatment of behavioral and affective disorders. **Chemistry:** The composition, structure, and properties of substances and of the chemical processes and transformations that they undergo. This includes uses of chemicals and their interactions, danger signs, production techniques, and disposal methods. **Sociology and Anthropology:** Group behavior and dynamics; societal trends and influences; and cultures and their history, migrations, ethnicity, and origins.

Work Environment: Indoors; disease or infections; standing; using hands on objects, tools, or controls.

Personal Financial Advisors

- ❀ Education/Training Required: Bachelor's degree
- ❀ Annual Earnings: $67,660
- ❀ Beginning Wage: $33,100
- ❀ Earnings Growth Potential: Very high
- ❀ Growth: 41.0%
- ❀ Annual Job Openings: 17,114
- ❀ Self-Employed: 30.9%
- ❀ Part-Time: 7.7%

Advise clients on financial plans, using knowledge of tax and investment strategies, securities, insurance, pension plans, and real estate. Duties include assessing clients' assets, liabilities, cash flow, insurance coverage, tax status, and financial objectives to establish investment strategies. Prepare and interpret for clients information such as investment performance reports, financial document summaries, and income projections. Recommend strategies clients can use to achieve their financial goals and objectives, including specific recommendations in such areas as cash management, insurance coverage, and investment planning. Build and maintain client bases, keeping current client plans up to date and recruiting new clients on an ongoing basis. Devise debt liquidation plans that include payoff priorities and timelines. Implement financial planning recommendations or refer clients to someone who can assist them with plan implementation. Interview clients to determine their current income, expenses, insurance coverage, tax status, financial objectives, risk tolerance, and other information needed to develop a financial plan. Monitor financial market trends to ensure that plans are effective and to identify any necessary updates. Explain and document for clients the types of services that are to be provided and the responsibilities to be taken by the personal financial advisor. Explain to individuals and groups the details of financial assistance available to college and university students, such as loans, grants, and scholarships. Guide clients in the gathering of information such as bank account records, income tax returns, life and disability insurance records, pension plan information, and wills. Analyze financial information obtained from clients to determine strategies for meeting clients' financial objectives. Meet with clients' other advisors, including attorneys, accountants, trust officers, and investment bankers, to fully understand clients' financial goals and circumstances. Answer clients' questions about the purposes and details of financial plans and strategies. Open accounts for clients and disburse funds from account to creditors as agents for clients. Authorize release of financial aid funds to students. Participate in the selection of candidates for specific financial aid awards. Research and investigate available investment opportunities to determine whether they fit into financial plans.

Personality Type: Enterprising. These occupations frequently involve starting up and carrying out projects and can involve leading people and making many decisions. They sometimes require risk taking and often deal with business.

GOE—Interest Area/Cluster: 06. Finance and Insurance. **Work Group:** 06.05. Finance/Insurance Sales and Support. **Other Jobs in This Work Group:** Advertising Sales Agents; Insurance Sales Agents; Sales Agents, Financial Services; Sales Agents, Securities and Commodities; Securities, Commodities, and Financial Services Sales Agents.

Skills—Management of Financial Resources: Determining how money will be spent to get the work done and accounting for these expenditures. **Persuasion:** Persuading others to approach things differently. **Mathematics:** Using mathematics to solve problems. **Speaking:** Talking to others to effectively convey information. **Complex Problem Solving:** Identifying complex problems, reviewing the options, and implementing solutions. **Active Listening:** Listening to what other people are saying and asking questions as appropriate. **Service Orientation:** Actively looking for ways to help people. **Judgment and Decision Making:** Weighing the relative costs and benefits of a potential action.

Education and Training Programs: Finance, General; Financial Planning and Services. **Related Knowledge/Courses—Economics and Accounting:** Economic and accounting principles and practices, the financial markets, banking, and the analysis and reporting of financial data.

Sales and Marketing: Principles and methods involved in showing, promoting, and selling products or services. This includes marketing strategies and tactics, product demonstration and sales techniques, and sales control systems. **Law and Government:** Laws, legal codes, court procedures, precedents, government regulations, executive orders, agency rules, and the democratic political process. **Customer and Personal Service:** Principles and processes for providing customer and personal services, including needs assessment techniques, quality service standards, alternative delivery systems, and customer satisfaction evaluation techniques. **Mathematics:** Numbers and their operations and interrelationships, including arithmetic, algebra, geometry, calculus, and statistics and their applications. **Computers and Electronics:** Electric circuit boards, processors, chips, and computer hardware and software, including applications and programming.

Work Environment: Indoors; sitting.

Personnel Recruiters

- ❋ Education/Training Required: Bachelor's degree
- ❋ Annual Earnings: $44,380
- ❋ Beginning Wage: $27,340
- ❋ Earnings Growth Potential: Medium
- ❋ Growth: 18.4%
- ❋ Annual Job Openings: 33,588
- ❋ Self-Employed: 2.1%
- ❋ Part-Time: 7.6%

The job openings listed here are shared with Employment Interviewers.

Seek out, interview, and screen applicants to fill existing and future job openings and promote career opportunities within an organization. Establish and maintain relationships with hiring managers to stay abreast of current and future hiring and business needs. Interview applicants to obtain information on work history, training, education, and job skills. Maintain current knowledge of Equal Employment Opportunity (EEO) and affirmative action guidelines and laws, such as the Americans with Disabilities Act (ADA). Perform searches for qualified candidates according to relevant job criteria, using computer databases, networking, Internet recruiting resources, cold calls, media, recruiting firms, and employee referrals. Prepare and maintain employment records. Contact applicants to inform them of employment possibilities, consideration,

and selection. Inform potential applicants about facilities, operations, benefits, and job or career opportunities in organizations. Screen and refer applicants to hiring personnel in the organization, making hiring recommendations when appropriate. Arrange for interviews and provide travel arrangements as necessary. Advise managers and employees on staffing policies and procedures. Review and evaluate applicant qualifications or eligibility for specified licensing according to established guidelines and designated licensing codes. Hire applicants and authorize paperwork assigning them to positions. Conduct reference and background checks on applicants. Evaluate recruitment and selection criteria to ensure conformance to professional, statistical, and testing standards, recommending revision as needed. Recruit applicants for open positions, arranging job fairs with college campus representatives. Advise management on organizing, preparing, and implementing recruiting and retention programs. Supervise personnel clerks performing filing, typing, and recordkeeping duties. Project yearly recruitment expenditures for budgetary consideration and control. Serve on selection and examination boards to evaluate applicants according to test scores, contacting promising candidates for interviews. Address civic and social groups and attend conferences to disseminate information concerning possible job openings and career opportunities.

Personality Type: Enterprising. These occupations frequently involve starting up and carrying out projects and can involve leading people and making many decisions. They sometimes require risk taking and often deal with business.

GOE—Interest Area/Cluster: 04. Business and Administration. **Work Group:** 04.03. Human Resources Support. **Other Jobs in This Work Group:** Compensation, Benefits, and Job Analysis Specialists; Employment Interviewers; Employment, Recruitment, and Placement Specialists; Training and Development Specialists.

Skills—Management of Personnel Resources: Motivating, developing, and directing people as they work; identifying the best people for the job. **Negotiation:** Bringing others together and trying to reconcile differences. **Persuasion:** Persuading others to approach things differently. **Management of Financial Resources:** Determining how money will be spent to get the work done and accounting for these expenditures. **Service Orientation:** Actively looking for ways to help people. **Judgment and Decision Making:** Weighing the relative costs and benefits of a potential action. **Monitoring:** Assessing how well one is doing when learning or doing something. **Active Listening:** Listening to what other people are saying and asking questions as appropriate.

Education and Training Programs: Human Resources Management/Personnel Administration, General; Labor and Industrial Relations. **Related Knowledge/Courses—Personnel and Human Resources:** Principles and procedures for personnel recruitment; selection; training; compensation and benefits; labor relations and negotiation; and personnel information systems. **Clerical Practices:** Administrative and clerical procedures and systems such as word-processing systems, filing and records management systems, stenography and transcription, forms, design principles, and other office procedures and terminology. **Sales and Marketing:** Principles and methods involved in showing, promoting, and selling products or services. This includes marketing strategies and tactics, product demonstration and sales techniques, and sales control systems. **Education and Training:** Instructional methods and training techniques, including curriculum design principles, learning theory, group and individual teaching techniques, design of individual development plans, and test design principles. **Administration and Management:** Principles and processes involved in business and organizational planning, coordination, and execution. This includes strategic planning, resource allocation, manpower modeling, leadership techniques, and production methods. **Communications and Media:** Media production, communication, and dissemination techniques and methods, including alternative ways to inform and entertain via written, oral, and visual media.

Work Environment: Indoors; sitting.

Pest Control Workers

- ❋ Education/Training Required: Moderate-term on-the-job training
- ❋ Annual Earnings: $29,030
- ❋ Beginning Wage: $18,970
- ❋ Earnings Growth Potential: Low
- ❋ Growth: 15.5%
- ❋ Annual Job Openings: 6,006
- ❋ Self-Employed: 8.7%
- ❋ Part-Time: 4.4%

Spray or release chemical solutions or toxic gases and set traps to kill pests and vermin, such as mice, termites, and roaches, that infest buildings and surrounding areas. Record work activities performed. Inspect premises to identify infestation source and extent of damage to property, wall and roof porosity, and access to infested locations. Spray or dust chemical solutions, powders, or gases into rooms; onto clothing, furnishings, or wood; and over marshlands, ditches, and catch-basins. Clean work site after completion of job. Direct or assist other workers in treatment and extermination processes to eliminate and control rodents, insects, and weeds. Drive truck equipped with power spraying equipment. Measure area dimensions requiring treatment, using rule; calculate fumigant requirements; and estimate cost for service. Post warning signs and lock building doors to secure area to be fumigated. Cut or bore openings in building or surrounding concrete, access infested areas, insert nozzle, and inject pesticide to impregnate ground. Study preliminary reports and diagrams of infested area and determine treatment type required to eliminate and prevent recurrence of infestation. Dig up and burn or spray weeds with herbicides. Set mechanical traps and place poisonous paste or bait in sewers, burrows, and ditches. Clean and remove blockages from infested areas to facilitate spraying procedure and provide drainage, using broom, mop, shovel, and rake. Position and fasten edges of tarpaulins over building and tape vents to ensure airtight environment and check for leaks.

Personality Type: Realistic. These occupations frequently involve work activities that include practical, hands-on problems and solutions. They often deal with plants; animals; and real-world materials such as wood, tools, and machinery. Many of the occupations require working outside and don't involve a lot of paperwork or working closely with others.

GOE—Interest Area/Cluster: 01. Agriculture and Natural Resources. **Work Group:** 01.05. Nursery, Groundskeeping, and Pest Control. **Other Jobs in This Work Group:** Landscaping and Groundskeeping Workers; Nursery Workers; Pesticide Handlers, Sprayers, and Applicators, Vegetation; Tree Trimmers and Pruners.

Skills—Equipment Selection: Determining the kind of tools and equipment needed to do a job. **Persuasion:** Persuading others to approach things differently. **Service Orientation:** Actively looking for ways to help people. **Social Perceptiveness:** Being aware of others' reactions and understanding why they react the way they do. **Management of Material Resources:** Obtaining and seeing to the appropriate use of equipment, facilities, and materials needed to do certain work. **Active Learning:** Working with new material or information to grasp its implications. **Equipment Maintenance:** Performing routine maintenance and determining when and what kind of maintenance is needed.

Coordination: Adjusting actions in relation to others' actions.

Education and Training Program: Agricultural/Farm Supplies Retailing and Wholesaling. **Related Knowledge/ Courses—Sales and Marketing:** Principles and methods involved in showing, promoting, and selling products or services. This includes marketing strategies and tactics, product demonstration and sales techniques, and sales control systems. **Biology:** Plant and animal living tissue, cells, organisms, and entities, including their functions, interdependencies, and interactions with each other and the environment. **Chemistry:** The composition, structure, and properties of substances and of the chemical processes and transformations that they undergo. This includes uses of chemicals and their interactions, danger signs, production techniques, and disposal methods. **Customer and Personal Service:** Principles and processes for providing customer and personal services, including needs assessment techniques, quality service standards, alternative delivery systems, and customer satisfaction evaluation techniques. **Building and Construction:** Materials, methods, and the appropriate tools to construct objects, structures, and buildings. **Law and Government:** Laws, legal codes, court procedures, precedents, government regulations, executive orders, agency rules, and the democratic political process.

Work Environment: More often outdoors than indoors; very hot or cold; contaminants; hazardous conditions; using hands on objects, tools, or controls.

Pesticide Handlers, Sprayers, and Applicators, Vegetation

- ❋ Education/Training Required: Moderate-term on-the-job training
- ❋ Annual Earnings: $28,560
- ❋ Beginning Wage: $18,780
- ❋ Earnings Growth Potential: Low
- ❋ Growth: 14.0%
- ❋ Annual Job Openings: 7,443
- ❋ Self-Employed: 20.5%
- ❋ Part-Time: 14.6%

Mix or apply pesticides, herbicides, fungicides, or insecticides through sprays, dusts, vapors, soil incorporation, or chemical application on trees, shrubs, lawns, or botanical crops. Usually requires specific training and state or federal certification. Fill sprayer tanks with water and chemicals according to formulas. Mix pesticides, herbicides, and fungicides for application to trees, shrubs, lawns, or botanical crops. Cover areas to specified depths with pesticides, applying knowledge of weather conditions, droplet sizes, elevation-to-distance ratios, and obstructions. Lift, push, and swing nozzles, hoses, and tubes in order to direct spray over designated areas. Start motors and engage machinery such as sprayer agitators and pumps or portable spray equipment. Connect hoses and nozzles selected according to terrain, distribution pattern requirements, types of infestations, and velocities. Clean and service machinery to ensure operating efficiency, using water, gasoline, lubricants, and/ or hand tools. Provide driving instructions to truck drivers to ensure complete coverage of designated areas, using hand and horn signals. Plant grass with seed spreaders and operate straw blowers to cover seeded areas with mixtures of asphalt and straw.

Personality Type: Realistic. These occupations frequently involve work activities that include practical, hands-on problems and solutions. They often deal with plants; animals; and real-world materials such as wood, tools, and machinery. Many of the occupations require working outside and don't involve a lot of paperwork or working closely with others.

GOE—Interest Area/Cluster: 01. Agriculture and Natural Resources. **Work Group:** 01.05. Nursery, Groundskeeping, and Pest Control. **Other Jobs in This Work Group:** Landscaping and Groundskeeping Workers; Nursery Workers; Pest Control Workers; Tree Trimmers and Pruners.

Skills—Repairing: Repairing machines or systems, using the needed tools. **Equipment Maintenance:** Performing routine maintenance and determining when and what kind of maintenance is needed. **Operation Monitoring:** Watching gauges, dials, or other indicators to make sure a machine is working properly. **Management of Material Resources:** Obtaining and seeing to the appropriate use of equipment, facilities, and materials needed to do certain work. **Installation:** Installing equipment, machines, wiring, or programs to meet specifications. **Operation and Control:** Controlling operations of equipment or systems. **Quality Control Analysis:** Evaluating the quality or performance of products, services, or processes. **Science:** Using scientific methods to solve problems.

Education and Training Programs: Landscaping and Groundskeeping; Plant Nursery Operations and Management; Turf and Turfgrass Management. **Related Knowledge/Courses—Biology:** Plant and animal living tissue, cells, organisms, and entities, including their functions, interdependencies, and interactions with each other and the environment. **Chemistry:** The composition, structure, and properties of substances and of the chemical processes and transformations that they undergo. This includes uses of chemicals and their interactions, danger signs, production techniques, and disposal methods. **Mechanical Devices:** Machines and tools, including their designs, uses, benefits, repair, and maintenance. **Transportation:** Principles and methods for moving people or goods by air, rail, sea, or road, including their relative costs, advantages, and limitations. **Customer and Personal Service:** Principles and processes for providing customer and personal services, including needs assessment techniques, quality service standards, alternative delivery systems, and customer satisfaction evaluation techniques. **Public Safety and Security:** Weaponry; public safety; security operations, rules, regulations, precautions, and prevention; and the protection of people, data, and property.

Work Environment: Outdoors; noisy; contaminants; hazardous conditions; using hands on objects, tools, or controls; repetitive motions.

Petroleum Engineers

- ❋ Education/Training Required: Bachelor's degree
- ❋ Annual Earnings: $103,960
- ❋ Beginning Wage: $58,840
- ❋ Earnings Growth Potential: High
- ❋ Growth: 5.2%
- ❋ Annual Job Openings: 1,016
- ❋ Self-Employed: 9.2%
- ❋ Part-Time: 2.9%

Devise methods to improve oil and gas well production and determine the need for new or modified tool designs. Oversee drilling and offer technical advice to achieve economical and satisfactory progress. Assess costs and estimate the production capabilities and economic value of oil and gas wells to evaluate the economic viability of potential drilling sites. Monitor production rates and plan rework processes to improve production. Analyze data to recommend placement of wells and supplementary processes to enhance production. Specify and supervise well modification and stimulation programs to maximize oil and gas recovery. Direct and monitor the completion and evaluation of wells, well testing, or well surveys. Assist engineering and other personnel to solve operating problems. Develop plans for oil and gas field drilling and for product recovery and treatment. Maintain records of drilling and production operations. Confer with scientific, engineering, and technical personnel to resolve design, research, and testing problems. Write technical reports for engineering and management personnel. Evaluate findings to develop, design, or test equipment or processes. Assign work to staff to obtain maximum utilization of personnel. Interpret drilling and testing information for personnel. Design and implement environmental controls on oil and gas operations. Coordinate the installation, maintenance, and operation of mining and oilfield equipment. Supervise the removal of drilling equipment, the removal of any waste, and the safe return of land to structural stability when wells or pockets are exhausted. Inspect oil and gas wells to determine that installations are completed. Simulate reservoir performance for different recovery techniques, using computer models. Take samples to assess the amount and quality of oil, the depth at which resources lie, and the equipment needed to properly extract them. Coordinate activities of workers engaged in research, planning, and development. Design or modify mining and oilfield machinery and tools, applying engineering principles. Test machinery and equipment to ensure that it is safe and conforms to performance specifications. Conduct engineering research experiments to improve or modify mining and oil machinery and operations.

Personality Type: Investigative. These occupations frequently involve working with ideas and require an extensive amount of thinking. They can involve searching for facts and figuring out problems mentally.

GOE—Interest Area/Cluster: 01. Agriculture and Natural Resources. **Work Group:** 01.02. Resource Science/Engineering for Plants, Animals, and the Environment. **Other Jobs in This Work Group:** Agricultural Engineers; Animal Scientists; Conservation Scientists; Environmental Engineers; Foresters; Mining and Geological Engineers, Including Mining Safety Engineers; Range Managers; Soil and Plant Scientists; Soil and Water Conservationists; Zoologists and Wildlife Biologists.

Skills—Management of Financial Resources: Determining how money will be spent to get the work done and accounting for these expenditures. **Science:** Using scientific methods to solve problems. **Operations Analysis:** Analyzing needs and product requirements to create a design. **Troubleshooting:** Determining what is causing an operating error and deciding what to do about it. **Mathematics:** Using mathematics to solve problems. **Technology Design:**

Generating or adapting equipment and technology to serve user needs. **Judgment and Decision Making:** Weighing the relative costs and benefits of a potential action. **Operation Monitoring:** Watching gauges, dials, or other indicators to make sure a machine is working properly.

Education and Training Program: Petroleum Engineering. **Related Knowledge/Courses—Engineering and Technology:** Equipment, tools, and mechanical devices and their uses to produce motion, light, power, technology, and other applications. **Physics:** Physical principles, laws, and applications, including air, water, material dynamics, light, atomic principles, heat, electric theory, earth formations, and meteorological and related natural phenomena. **Geography:** Various methods for describing the location and distribution of land, sea, and air masses, including their physical locations, relationships, and characteristics. **Chemistry:** The composition, structure, and properties of substances and of the chemical processes and transformations that they undergo. This includes uses of chemicals and their interactions, danger signs, production techniques, and disposal methods. **Design:** Design techniques, principles, tools, and instruments involved in the production and use of precision technical plans, blueprints, drawings, and models. **Economics and Accounting:** Economic and accounting principles and practices, the financial markets, banking, and the analysis and reporting of financial data.

Work Environment: Indoors; sitting.

Pharmacists

- ❋ Education/Training Required: First professional degree
- ❋ Annual Earnings: $100,480
- ❋ Beginning Wage: $73,010
- ❋ Earnings Growth Potential: Low
- ❋ Growth: 21.7%
- ❋ Annual Job Openings: 16,358
- ❋ Self-Employed: 0.5%
- ❋ Part-Time: 18.1%

Compound and dispense medications, following prescriptions issued by physicians, dentists, or other authorized medical practitioners. Review prescriptions to assure accuracy, to ascertain the needed ingredients, and to evaluate their suitability. Provide information and advice regarding drug interactions, side effects, dosage, and proper medication storage. Analyze prescribing trends to monitor patient compliance and to prevent excessive usage or harmful interactions. Order and purchase pharmaceutical supplies, medical supplies, and drugs, maintaining stock and storing and handling it properly. Maintain records, such as pharmacy files; patient profiles; charge system files; inventories; control records for radioactive nuclei; and registries of poisons, narcotics, and controlled drugs. Provide specialized services to help patients manage conditions such as diabetes, asthma, smoking cessation, or high blood pressure. Advise customers on the selection of medication brands, medical equipment, and health-care supplies. Collaborate with other health-care professionals to plan, monitor, review, and evaluate the quality and effectiveness of drugs and drug regimens, providing advice on drug applications and characteristics. Compound and dispense medications as prescribed by doctors and dentists by calculating, weighing, measuring, and mixing ingredients or oversee these activities. Offer health promotion and prevention activities—for example, training people to use devices such as blood-pressure or diabetes monitors. Refer patients to other health professionals and agencies when appropriate. Prepare sterile solutions and infusions for use in surgical procedures, emergency rooms, or patients' homes. Plan, implement, and maintain procedures for mixing, packaging, and labeling pharmaceuticals according to policy and legal requirements to ensure quality, security, and proper disposal. Assay radiopharmaceuticals, verify rates of disintegration, and calculate the volume required to produce the desired results to ensure proper dosages. Manage pharmacy operations, hiring and supervising staff, performing administrative duties, and buying and selling nonpharmaceutical merchandise. Work in hospitals, clinics, or for health maintenance organizations (HMOs), dispensing prescriptions, serving as a medical team consultant, or specializing in specific drug therapy areas such as oncology or nuclear pharmacotherapy.

Personality Type: Investigative. These occupations frequently involve working with ideas and require an extensive amount of thinking. They can involve searching for facts and figuring out problems mentally.

GOE—Interest Area/Cluster: 08. Health Science. **Work Group:** 08.02. Medicine and Surgery. **Other Jobs in This Work Group:** Anesthesiologists; Family and General Practitioners; Internists, General; Medical Assistants; Medical Transcriptionists; Obstetricians and Gynecologists; Pediatricians, General; Pharmacy Aides; Pharmacy Technicians; Physician Assistants; Psychiatrists; Registered Nurses; Surgeons; Surgical Technologists.

Skills—Science: Using scientific methods to solve problems. **Reading Comprehension:** Understanding written sentences and paragraphs in work-related documents. **Social Perceptiveness:** Being aware of others' reactions and understanding why they react the way they do. **Active Listening:** Listening to what other people are saying and asking questions as appropriate. **Instructing:** Teaching others how to do something. **Mathematics:** Using mathematics to solve problems. **Speaking:** Talking to others to effectively convey information. **Critical Thinking:** Using logic and analysis to identify the strengths and weaknesses of different approaches.

Education and Training Programs: Clinical and Industrial Drug Development (MS, PhD); Clinical, Hospital, and Managed Care Pharmacy (MS, PhD); Industrial and Physical Pharmacy and Cosmetic Sciences (MS, PhD); Medicinal and Pharmaceutical Chemistry (MS, PhD); Natural Products Chemistry and Pharmacognosy (MS, PhD); Pharmaceutical Economics (MS, PhD); Pharmaceutics and Drug Design (MS, PhD); Pharmacy (PharmD [USA] PharmD, BS/BPharm [Canada]); Pharmacy Administration and Pharmacy Policy and Regulatory Affairs (MS, PhD); others. **Related Knowledge/Courses—Medicine and Dentistry:** The information and techniques needed to diagnose and treat injuries, diseases, and deformities. This includes symptoms, treatment alternatives, drug properties and interactions, and preventive health-care measures. **Chemistry:** The composition, structure, and properties of substances and of the chemical processes and transformations that they undergo. This includes uses of chemicals and their interactions, danger signs, production techniques, and disposal methods. **Therapy and Counseling:** Information and techniques needed to rehabilitate physical and mental ailments and to provide career guidance, including alternative treatments, rehabilitation equipment and its proper use, and methods to evaluate treatment effects. **Biology:** Plant and animal living tissue, cells, organisms, and entities, including their functions, interdependencies, and interactions with each other and the environment. **Psychology:** Human behavior and performance, mental processes, psychological research methods, and the assessment and treatment of behavioral and affective disorders. **Mathematics:** Numbers and their operations and interrelationships, including arithmetic, algebra, geometry, calculus, and statistics and their applications.

Work Environment: Indoors; disease or infections; standing; repetitive motions.

Pharmacy Technicians

❋ Education/Training Required: Moderate-term on-the-job training
❋ Annual Earnings: $26,720
❋ Beginning Wage: $18,520
❋ Earnings Growth Potential: Low
❋ Growth: 32.0%
❋ Annual Job Openings: 54,453
❋ Self-Employed: 0.2%
❋ Part-Time: 20.8%

Prepare medications under the direction of a pharmacist. May measure, mix, count out, label, and record amounts and dosages of medications. Receive written prescription or refill requests and verify that information is complete and accurate. Maintain proper storage and security conditions for drugs. Answer telephones, responding to questions or requests. Fill bottles with prescribed medications and type and affix labels. Assist customers by answering simple questions, locating items, or referring them to the pharmacist for medication information. Price and file prescriptions that have been filled. Clean and help maintain equipment and work areas and sterilize glassware according to prescribed methods. Establish and maintain patient profiles, including lists of medications taken by individual patients. Order, label, and count stock of medications, chemicals, and supplies and enter inventory data into computer. Receive and store incoming supplies, verify quantities against invoices, and inform supervisors of stock needs and shortages. Transfer medication from vials to the appropriate number of sterile disposable syringes, using aseptic techniques. Under pharmacist supervision, add measured drugs or nutrients to intravenous solutions under sterile conditions to prepare intravenous (IV) packs. Supply and monitor robotic machines that dispense medicine into containers and label the containers. Prepare and process medical insurance claim forms and records. Mix pharmaceutical preparations according to written prescriptions. Operate cash registers to accept payment from customers. Compute charges for medication and equipment dispensed to hospital patients and enter data in computer. Deliver medications and pharmaceutical supplies to patients, nursing stations, or surgery. Price stock and mark items for sale. Maintain and merchandise home health-care products and services.

Personality Type: Conventional. These occupations frequently involve following set procedures and routines and can include working with data and details more than with ideas. Usually there is a clear line of authority to follow.

GOE—**Interest Area/Cluster:** 08. Health Science. **Work Group:** 08.02. Medicine and Surgery. **Other Jobs in This Work Group:** Anesthesiologists; Family and General Practitioners; Internists, General; Medical Assistants; Medical Transcriptionists; Obstetricians and Gynecologists; Pediatricians, General; Pharmacists; Pharmacy Aides; Physician Assistants; Psychiatrists; Registered Nurses; Surgeons; Surgical Technologists.

Skills—Service Orientation: Actively looking for ways to help people. **Active Listening:** Listening to what other people are saying and asking questions as appropriate. **Instructing:** Teaching others how to do something. **Mathematics:** Using mathematics to solve problems. **Speaking:** Talking to others to effectively convey information. **Active Learning:** Working with new material or information to grasp its implications. **Troubleshooting:** Determining what is causing an operating error and deciding what to do about it. **Writing:** Communicating effectively with others in writing as indicated by the needs of the audience.

Education and Training Program: Pharmacy Technician/Assistant Training. **Related Knowledge/Courses—Medicine and Dentistry:** The information and techniques needed to diagnose and treat injuries, diseases, and deformities. This includes symptoms, treatment alternatives, drug properties and interactions, and preventive health-care measures. **Chemistry:** The composition, structure, and properties of substances and of the chemical processes and transformations that they undergo. This includes uses of chemicals and their interactions, danger signs, production techniques, and disposal methods. **Customer and Personal Service:** Principles and processes for providing customer and personal services, including needs assessment techniques, quality service standards, alternative delivery systems, and customer satisfaction evaluation techniques. **Mathematics:** Numbers and their operations and interrelationships, including arithmetic, algebra, geometry, calculus, and statistics and their applications. **Clerical Practices:** Administrative and clerical procedures and systems such as word-processing systems, filing and records management systems, stenography and transcription, forms, design principles, and other office procedures and terminology.

Work Environment: Indoors; standing; using hands on objects, tools, or controls; repetitive motions.

Philosophy and Religion Teachers, Postsecondary

- ❁ Education/Training Required: Doctoral degree
- ❁ Annual Earnings: $56,380
- ❁ Beginning Wage: $32,640
- ❁ Earnings Growth Potential: High
- ❁ Growth: 22.9%
- ❁ Annual Job Openings: 3,120
- ❁ Self-Employed: 0.4%
- ❁ Part-Time: 27.8%

Teach courses in philosophy, religion, and theology. Evaluate and grade students' classwork, assignments, and papers. Initiate, facilitate, and moderate classroom discussions. Prepare and deliver lectures to undergraduate and graduate students on topics such as ethics, logic, and contemporary religious thought. Prepare course materials such as syllabi, homework assignments, and handouts. Compile, administer, and grade examinations or assign this work to others. Keep abreast of developments in their field by reading current literature, talking with colleagues, and participating in professional conferences. Maintain student attendance records, grades, and other required records. Plan, evaluate, and revise curricula, course content, and course materials and methods of instruction. Maintain regularly scheduled office hours to advise and assist students. Select and obtain materials and supplies such as textbooks. Advise students on academic and vocational curricula and on career issues. Conduct research in a particular field of knowledge and publish findings in professional journals, books, or electronic media. Perform administrative duties such as serving as department head. Serve on academic or administrative committees that deal with institutional policies, departmental matters, and academic issues. Collaborate with colleagues to address teaching and research issues. Participate in campus and community events. Participate in student recruitment, registration, and placement activities. Compile bibliographies of specialized materials for outside reading assignments. Supervise undergraduate and graduate teaching, internship, and research work. Act as advisers to student organizations. Write grant proposals to procure external research funding. Provide professional consulting services to government or industry.

Personality Type: Social. These occupations frequently involve working with, communicating with, and teaching people and often involve helping or providing service to others.

GOE—Interest Area/Cluster: 05. Education and Training. **Work Group:** 05.03. Postsecondary and Adult Teaching and Instructing. **Other Jobs in This Work Group:** Adult Literacy, Remedial Education, and GED Teachers and Instructors; Agricultural Sciences Teachers, Postsecondary; Anthropology and Archeology Teachers, Postsecondary; Architecture Teachers, Postsecondary; Area, Ethnic, and Cultural Studies Teachers, Postsecondary; Art, Drama, and Music Teachers, Postsecondary; Atmospheric, Earth, Marine, and Space Sciences Teachers, Postsecondary; Biological Science Teachers, Postsecondary; Business Teachers, Postsecondary; Chemistry Teachers, Postsecondary; Communications Teachers, Postsecondary; Computer Science Teachers, Postsecondary; Criminal Justice and Law Enforcement Teachers, Postsecondary; Economics Teachers, Postsecondary; Education Teachers, Postsecondary; Engineering Teachers, Postsecondary; English Language and Literature Teachers, Postsecondary; Environmental Science Teachers, Postsecondary; Farm and Home Management Advisors; Foreign Language and Literature Teachers, Postsecondary; Forestry and Conservation Science Teachers, Postsecondary; Geography Teachers, Postsecondary; Graduate Teaching Assistants; Health Specialties Teachers, Postsecondary; History Teachers, Postsecondary; Home Economics Teachers, Postsecondary; Law Teachers, Postsecondary; Library Science Teachers, Postsecondary; Mathematical Science Teachers, Postsecondary; Nursing Instructors and Teachers, Postsecondary; Physics Teachers, Postsecondary; Political Science Teachers, Postsecondary; Psychology Teachers, Postsecondary; Recreation and Fitness Studies Teachers, Postsecondary; Self-Enrichment Education Teachers; Social Work Teachers, Postsecondary; Sociology Teachers, Postsecondary; Vocational Education Teachers, Postsecondary.

Skills—Writing: Communicating effectively with others in writing as indicated by the needs of the audience. **Instructing:** Teaching others how to do something. **Reading Comprehension:** Understanding written sentences and paragraphs in work-related documents. **Critical Thinking:** Using logic and analysis to identify the strengths and weaknesses of different approaches. **Speaking:** Talking to others to effectively convey information. **Learning Strategies:** Using multiple approaches when learning or teaching new things. **Social Perceptiveness:** Being aware of others' reactions and understanding why they react the way they do. **Persuasion:** Persuading others to approach things differently.

Education and Training Programs: Bible/Biblical Studies; Buddhist Studies; Christian Studies; Divinity/Ministry (BD, MDiv.); Ethics; Hindu Studies; Missions/Missionary Studies and Missiology; Pastoral Studies/Counseling; Philosophy; Pre-Theology/Pre-Ministerial Studies; Rabbinical Studies; Religion/Religious Studies; Religious Education; Religious/Sacred Music; Talmudic Studies; Theological and Ministerial Studies, Other; Theology and Religious Vocations, Other; Theology/Theological Studies; others. **Related Knowledge/Courses—Philosophy and Theology:** Different philosophical systems and religions, including their basic principles, values, ethics, ways of thinking, customs, and practices and their impact on human culture. **History and Archeology:** Historical events and their causes, indicators, and impact on particular civilizations and cultures. **Sociology and Anthropology:** Group behavior and dynamics; societal trends and influences; and cultures and their history, migrations, ethnicity, and origins. **Foreign Language:** The structure and content of a foreign (non-English) language, including the meaning and spelling of words, rules of composition and grammar, and pronunciation. **English Language:** The structure and content of the English language, including the meaning and spelling of words, rules of composition, and grammar. **Education and Training:** Instructional methods and training techniques, including curriculum design principles, learning theory, group and individual teaching techniques, design of individual development plans, and test design principles.

Work Environment: Indoors; sitting.

Photographers

- ❋ Education/Training Required: Long-term on-the-job training
- ❋ Annual Earnings: $27,720
- ❋ Beginning Wage: $16,170
- ❋ Earnings Growth Potential: High
- ❋ Growth: 10.3%
- ❋ Annual Job Openings: 16,100
- ❋ Self-Employed: 54.3%
- ❋ Part-Time: 22.1%

Photograph persons, subjects, merchandise, or other commercial products. May develop negatives and produce finished prints. Take pictures of individuals, families, and small groups, either in studio or on location. Adjust apertures, shutter speeds, and camera focus based on a combination of factors such as lighting, field depth, subject motion, film type, and film speed. Use traditional or digital cameras, along with a variety of equipment such as tripods, filters, and flash attachments. Create artificial light, using flashes and reflectors. Determine desired images and picture composition; select and adjust subjects, equipment, and lighting to achieve desired effects. Scan photographs into computers for editing, storage, and electronic transmission. Test equipment prior to use to ensure that it is in good working order. Review sets of photographs to select the best work. Estimate or measure light levels, distances, and numbers of exposures needed, using measuring devices and formulas. Manipulate and enhance scanned or digital images to create desired effects, using computers and specialized software. Perform maintenance tasks necessary to keep equipment working properly. Perform general office duties such as scheduling appointments, keeping books, and ordering supplies. Consult with clients or advertising staff and study assignments to determine project goals, locations, and equipment needs. Select and assemble equipment and required background properties according to subjects, materials, and conditions. Enhance, retouch, and resize photographs and negatives, using airbrushing and other techniques. Set up, mount, or install photographic equipment and cameras. Produce computer-readable digital images from film, using flatbed scanners and photofinishing laboratories. Develop and print exposed film, using chemicals, touchup tools, and developing and printing equipment, or send film to photofinishing laboratories for processing. Direct activities of workers who are setting up photographic equipment. Employ a variety of specialized photographic materials and techniques, including infrared and ultraviolet films, macro-photography, photogrammetry, and sensitometry. Engage in research to develop new photographic procedures and materials.

Personality Type: Artistic. These occupations frequently involve working with forms, designs, and patterns. They often require self-expression, and the work can be done without following a clear set of rules.

GOE—Interest Area/Cluster: 03. Arts and Communication. **Work Group:** 03.09. Media Technology. **Other Jobs in This Work Group:** Audio and Video Equipment Technicians; Broadcast Technicians; Camera Operators, Television, Video, and Motion Picture; Film and Video Editors; Multi-Media Artists and Animators; Radio Operators; Sound Engineering Technicians.

Skills—Persuasion: Persuading others to approach things differently. **Equipment Maintenance:** Performing routine maintenance and determining when and what kind of maintenance is needed. **Management of Financial Resources:** Determining how money will be spent to get the work done and accounting for these expenditures. **Operation Monitoring:** Watching gauges, dials, or other indicators to make sure a machine is working properly. **Service Orientation:** Actively looking for ways to help people. **Equipment Selection:** Determining the kind of tools and equipment needed to do a job. **Technology Design:** Generating or adapting equipment and technology to serve user needs. **Operations Analysis:** Analyzing needs and product requirements to create a design.

Education and Training Programs: Art/Art Studies, General; Commercial Photography; Film/Video and Photographic Arts, Other; Photography; Photojournalism; Visual and Performing Arts, General. **Related Knowledge/Courses—Sales and Marketing:** Principles and methods involved in showing, promoting, and selling products or services. This includes marketing strategies and tactics, product demonstration and sales techniques, and sales control systems. **Fine Arts:** Theory and techniques required to produce, compose, and perform works of music, dance, visual arts, drama, and sculpture. **Clerical Practices:** Administrative and clerical procedures and systems such as word-processing systems, filing and records management systems, stenography and transcription, forms, design principles, and other office procedures and terminology. **Customer and Personal Service:** Principles and processes for providing customer and personal services, including needs assessment techniques, quality service standards, alternative delivery systems, and customer satisfaction evaluation techniques. **Communications and Media:** Media production, communication, and dissemination techniques and methods, including alternative ways to inform and entertain via written, oral, and visual media. **Production and Processing:** Inputs, outputs, raw materials, waste, quality control, costs, and techniques for maximizing the manufacture and distribution of goods.

Work Environment: More often indoors than outdoors; sitting; using hands on objects, tools, or controls.

Physical Therapist Aides

- ❋ Education/Training Required: Short-term on-the-job training
- ❋ Annual Earnings: $22,990
- ❋ Beginning Wage: $16,740
- ❋ Earnings Growth Potential: Low
- ❋ Growth: 24.4%
- ❋ Annual Job Openings: 4,092
- ❋ Self-Employed: 0.2%
- ❋ Part-Time: 27.1%

Under close supervision of a physical therapist or physical therapy assistant, perform delegated, selected, or routine tasks in specific situations. These duties include preparing patients and treatment areas. Clean and organize work areas and disinfect equipment after treatment. Administer active and passive manual therapeutic exercises; therapeutic massage; and heat, light, sound, water, or electrical modality treatments such as ultrasound. Instruct, motivate, safeguard, and assist patients practicing exercises and functional activities under direction of medical staff. Record treatment given and equipment used. Confer with physical therapy staff or others to discuss and evaluate patient information for planning, modifying, and coordinating treatment. Observe patients during treatment to compile and evaluate data on patients' responses and progress and report to physical therapist. Secure patients into or onto therapy equipment. Change linens such as bed sheets and pillow cases. Transport patients to and from treatment areas, using wheelchairs or providing standing support. Arrange treatment supplies to keep them in order. Maintain equipment and furniture to keep it in good working condition, including performing the assembly and disassembly of equipment and accessories. Assist patients to dress, undress, and put on and remove supportive devices such as braces, splints, and slings. Perform clerical duties such as taking inventory, ordering supplies, answering telephones, taking messages, and filling out forms. Administer traction to relieve neck and back pain, using intermittent and static traction equipment. Schedule patient appointments with physical therapists and coordinate therapists' schedules. Train patients to use orthopedic braces, prostheses, or supportive devices. Measure patient's range-of-joint motion, body parts, and vital signs to determine effects of treatments or for patient evaluations. Participate in patient care tasks such as assisting with passing food trays, feeding residents, or bathing residents on bed rest. Fit patients for orthopedic braces, prostheses, or supportive devices, adjusting fit as needed.

Personality Type: Social. These occupations frequently involve working with, communicating with, and teaching people and often involve helping or providing service to others.

GOE—Interest Area/Cluster: 08. Health Science. **Work Group:** 08.07. Medical Therapy. **Other Jobs in This Work Group:** Audiologists; Massage Therapists; Occupational Therapist Aides; Occupational Therapist Assistants; Occupational Therapists; Physical Therapist Assistants; Physical Therapists; Radiation Therapists; Recreational Therapists; Respiratory Therapists; Respiratory Therapy Technicians; Speech-Language Pathologists.

Skill—None met the criteria.

Education and Training Program: Physical Therapist Assistant Training. **Related Knowledge/Courses—Medicine and Dentistry:** The information and techniques needed to diagnose and treat injuries, diseases, and deformities. This includes symptoms, treatment alternatives, drug properties and interactions, and preventive health-care measures. **Therapy and Counseling:** Information and techniques needed to rehabilitate physical and mental ailments and to provide career guidance, including alternative treatments, rehabilitation equipment and its proper use, and methods to evaluate treatment effects. **Customer and Personal Service:** Principles and processes for providing customer and personal services, including needs assessment techniques, quality service standards, alternative delivery systems, and customer satisfaction evaluation techniques. **Psychology:** Human behavior and performance, mental processes, psychological research methods, and the assessment and treatment of behavioral and affective disorders. **Public Safety and Security:** Weaponry; public safety; security operations, rules, regulations, precautions, and prevention; and the protection of people, data, and property.

Work Environment: Indoors; disease or infections; standing; walking and running; using hands on objects, tools, or controls; bending or twisting the body.

Physical Therapist Assistants

- ❋ Education/Training Required: Associate degree
- ❋ Annual Earnings: $44,130
- ❋ Beginning Wage: $27,800
- ❋ Earnings Growth Potential: Medium
- ❋ Growth: 32.4%
- ❋ Annual Job Openings: 5,957
- ❋ Self-Employed: 0.2%
- ❋ Part-Time: 27.1%

Assist physical therapists in providing physical therapy treatments and procedures. May, in accordance with state laws, assist in the development of treatment plans, carry out routine functions, document the progress of treatment, and modify specific treatments in accordance with patient status and within the scope of treatment plans established by physical therapists. Generally requires formal training. Instruct, motivate, safeguard, and assist patients as they practice exercises and functional activities.

Observe patients during treatments to compile and evaluate data on their responses and progress and provide results to physical therapists in person or through progress notes. Confer with physical therapy staffs or others to discuss and evaluate patient information for planning, modifying, and coordinating treatment. Transport patients to and from treatment areas, lifting and transferring them according to positioning requirements. Secure patients into or onto therapy equipment. Administer active and passive manual therapeutic exercises; therapeutic massage; aquatic physical therapy; and heat, light, sound, and electrical modality treatments such as ultrasound. Communicate with or instruct caregivers and family members on patient therapeutic activities and treatment plans. Measure patients' range of joint motion, body parts, and vital signs to determine effects of treatments or for patient evaluations. Monitor operation of equipment and record use of equipment and administration of treatment. Fit patients for orthopedic braces, prostheses, and supportive devices such as crutches. Train patients in the use of orthopedic braces, prostheses, or supportive devices. Clean work areas and check and store equipment after treatments. Assist patients to dress, undress, or put on and remove supportive devices such as braces, splints, and slings. Attend or conduct continuing education courses, seminars, or in-service activities. Perform clerical duties such as taking inventory, ordering supplies, answering telephones, taking messages, and filling out forms. Prepare treatment areas and electrotherapy equipment for use by physiotherapists. Administer traction to relieve neck and back pain, using intermittent and static traction equipment. Perform postural drainage, percussions, and vibrations and teach deep breathing exercises to treat respiratory conditions.

Personality Type: Social. These occupations frequently involve working with, communicating with, and teaching people and often involve helping or providing service to others.

GOE—Interest Area/Cluster: 08. Health Science. **Work Group:** 08.07. Medical Therapy. **Other Jobs in This Work Group:** Audiologists; Massage Therapists; Occupational Therapist Aides; Occupational Therapist Assistants; Occupational Therapists; Physical Therapist Aides; Physical Therapists; Radiation Therapists; Recreational Therapists; Respiratory Therapists; Respiratory Therapy Technicians; Speech-Language Pathologists.

Skill—Service Orientation: Actively looking for ways to help people.

Education and Training Program: Physical Therapist Assistant Training. **Related Knowledge/Courses—Therapy and Counseling:** Information and techniques needed to rehabilitate physical and mental ailments and to provide career guidance, including alternative treatments, rehabilitation equipment and its proper use, and methods to evaluate treatment effects. **Medicine and Dentistry:** The information and techniques needed to diagnose and treat injuries, diseases, and deformities. This includes symptoms, treatment alternatives, drug properties and interactions, and preventive health-care measures. **Psychology:** Human behavior and performance, mental processes, psychological research methods, and the assessment and treatment of behavioral and affective disorders. **Biology:** Plant and animal living tissue, cells, organisms, and entities, including their functions, interdependencies, and interactions with each other and the environment. **Customer and Personal Service:** Principles and processes for providing customer and personal services, including needs assessment techniques, quality service standards, alternative delivery systems, and customer satisfaction evaluation techniques. **Education and Training:** Instructional methods and training techniques, including curriculum design principles, learning theory, group and individual teaching techniques, design of individual development plans, and test design principles.

Work Environment: Indoors; disease or infections; standing; walking and running.

Physical Therapists

- ✴ Education/Training Required: Master's degree
- ✴ Annual Earnings: $69,760
- ✴ Beginning Wage: $48,530
- ✴ Earnings Growth Potential: Low
- ✴ Growth: 27.1%
- ✴ Annual Job Openings: 12,072
- ✴ Self-Employed: 8.4%
- ✴ Part-Time: 22.7%

Assess, plan, organize, and participate in rehabilitative programs that improve mobility, relieve pain, increase strength, and decrease or prevent deformity of patients suffering from disease or injury. Perform and document initial exams, evaluating data to identify problems and determine diagnoses prior to interventions. Plan, prepare, and carry out individually designed programs of physical treatment to maintain, improve, or restore physical functioning; alleviate pain; and prevent physical dysfunction in patients. Record prognoses, treatments, responses, and progresses in patients' charts or enter information into computers. Identify and document goals, anticipated progresses, and plans for reevaluation. Evaluate effects of treatments at various stages and adjust treatments to achieve maximum benefits. Administer manual exercises, massage, or traction to help relieve pain; increase patient strength; or decrease or prevent deformity or crippling. Test and measure patients' strength, motor development and function, sensory perception, functional capacity, and respiratory and circulatory efficiency and record data. Instruct patients and families in treatment procedures to be continued at home. Confer with patients, medical practitioners, and appropriate others to plan, implement, and assess intervention programs. Review physicians' referrals and patients' medical records to help determine diagnoses and physical therapy treatments required. Obtain patients' informed consent to proposed interventions. Discharge patients from physical therapy when goals or projected outcomes have been attained and provide for appropriate follow-up care or referrals. Provide information to patients about proposed interventions, material risks, and expected benefits and any reasonable alternatives. Inform patients when diagnoses reveal findings outside the scope of physical therapy and refer to appropriate practitioners. Direct, supervise, assess, and communicate with supportive personnel. Provide educational information about physical therapy and physical therapists, injury prevention, ergonomics, and ways to promote health. Refer clients to community resources and services. Administer treatment involving application of physical agents, using equipment, moist packs, ultraviolet and infrared lamps, and ultrasound machines.

Personality Type: Social. These occupations frequently involve working with, communicating with, and teaching people and often involve helping or providing service to others.

GOE—Interest Area/Cluster: 08. Health Science. **Work Group:** 08.07. Medical Therapy. **Other Jobs in This Work Group:** Audiologists; Massage Therapists; Occupational Therapist Aides; Occupational Therapist Assistants; Occupational Therapists; Physical Therapist Aides; Physical Therapist Assistants; Radiation Therapists; Recreational Therapists; Respiratory Therapists; Respiratory Therapy Technicians; Speech-Language Pathologists.

Skills—Management of Personnel Resources: Motivating, developing, and directing people as they work; identifying the best people for the job. **Systems Analysis:** Determining how a system should work and how changes will affect outcomes. **Social Perceptiveness:** Being aware of others' reactions and understanding why they react the way they do. **Complex Problem Solving:** Identifying complex problems, reviewing the options, and implementing solutions. **Systems Evaluation:** Looking at many indicators of system performance and taking into account their accuracy. **Judgment and Decision Making:** Weighing the relative costs and benefits of a potential action. **Monitoring:** Assessing how well one is doing when learning or doing something. **Speaking:** Talking to others to effectively convey information.

Education and Training Programs: Kinesiotherapy/Kinesiotherapist Training; Physical Therapy/Therapist Training. **Related Knowledge/Courses—Therapy and Counseling:** Information and techniques needed to rehabilitate physical and mental ailments and to provide career guidance, including alternative treatments, rehabilitation equipment and its proper use, and methods to evaluate treatment effects. **Medicine and Dentistry:** The information and techniques needed to diagnose and treat injuries, diseases, and deformities. This includes symptoms, treatment alternatives, drug properties and interactions, and preventive health-care measures. **Psychology:** Human behavior and performance, mental processes, psychological research methods, and the assessment and treatment of behavioral and affective disorders. **Education and Training:** Instructional methods and training techniques, including curriculum design principles, learning theory, group and individual teaching techniques, design of individual development plans, and test design principles. **Biology:** Plant and animal living tissue, cells, organisms, and entities, including their functions, interdependencies, and interactions with each other and the environment. **Customer and Personal Service:** Principles and processes for providing customer and personal services, including needs assessment techniques, quality service standards, alternative delivery systems, and customer satisfaction evaluation techniques.

Work Environment: Indoors; disease or infections; standing.

P

Physician Assistants

- ❋ Education/Training Required: Master's degree
- ❋ Annual Earnings: $78,450
- ❋ Beginning Wage: $46,750
- ❋ Earnings Growth Potential: High
- ❋ Growth: 27.0%
- ❋ Annual Job Openings: 7,147
- ❋ Self-Employed: 1.8%
- ❋ Part-Time: 15.6%

Under the supervision of physicians, provide health-care services typically performed by a physician. Conduct complete physicals, provide treatment, and counsel patients. May, in some cases, prescribe medication. Must graduate from an accredited educational program for physician assistants. Examine patients to obtain information about their physical conditions. Obtain, compile, and record patient medical data, including health history, progress notes, and results of physical examinations. Interpret diagnostic test results for deviations from normal. Make tentative diagnoses and decisions about management and treatment of patients. Prescribe therapy or medication with physician approval. Administer or order diagnostic tests, such as X-ray, electrocardiogram, and laboratory tests. Instruct and counsel patients about prescribed therapeutic regimens, normal growth and development, family planning, emotional problems of daily living, and health maintenance. Perform therapeutic procedures such as injections, immunizations, suturing and wound care, and infection management. Provide physicians with assistance during surgery or complicated medical procedures. Visit and observe patients on hospital rounds or house calls, updating charts, ordering therapy, and reporting back to physicians. Supervise and coordinate activities of technicians and technical assistants. Order medical and laboratory supplies and equipment.

Personality Type: Social. These occupations frequently involve working with, communicating with, and teaching people and often involve helping or providing service to others.

GOE—Interest Area/Cluster: 08. Health Science. **Work Group:** 08.02. Medicine and Surgery. **Other Jobs in This Work Group:** Anesthesiologists; Family and General Practitioners; Internists, General; Medical Assistants; Medical Transcriptionists; Obstetricians and Gynecologists; Pediatricians, General; Pharmacists; Pharmacy Aides; Pharmacy Technicians; Psychiatrists; Registered Nurses; Surgeons; Surgical Technologists.

Skills—Social Perceptiveness: Being aware of others' reactions and understanding why they react the way they do. **Systems Analysis:** Determining how a system should work and how changes will affect outcomes. **Systems Evaluation:** Looking at many indicators of system performance and taking into account their accuracy. **Persuasion:** Persuading others to approach things differently. **Complex Problem Solving:** Identifying complex problems, reviewing the options, and implementing solutions. **Reading Comprehension:** Understanding written sentences and paragraphs in work-related documents. **Service Orientation:** Actively looking for ways to help people. **Speaking:** Talking to others to effectively convey information.

Education and Training Program: Physician Assistant Training. **Related Knowledge/Courses—Medicine and Dentistry:** The information and techniques needed to diagnose and treat injuries, diseases, and deformities. This includes symptoms, treatment alternatives, drug properties and interactions, and preventive health-care measures. **Biology:** Plant and animal living tissue, cells, organisms, and entities, including their functions, interdependencies, and interactions with each other and the environment. **Therapy and Counseling:** Information and techniques needed to rehabilitate physical and mental ailments and to provide career guidance, including alternative treatments, rehabilitation equipment and its proper use, and methods to evaluate treatment effects. **Psychology:** Human behavior and performance, mental processes, psychological research methods, and the assessment and treatment of behavioral and affective disorders. **Chemistry:** The composition, structure, and properties of substances and of the chemical processes and transformations that they undergo. This includes uses of chemicals and their interactions, danger signs, production techniques, and disposal methods. **Sociology and Anthropology:** Group behavior and dynamics; societal trends and influences; and cultures and their history, migrations, ethnicity, and origins.

Work Environment: Indoors; disease or infections; standing; using hands on objects, tools, or controls.

Physicists

- ❀ Education/Training Required: Doctoral degree
- ❀ Annual Earnings: $96,850
- ❀ Beginning Wage: $51,870
- ❀ Earnings Growth Potential: High
- ❀ Growth: 6.8%
- ❀ Annual Job Openings: 1,302
- ❀ Self-Employed: 0.8%
- ❀ Part-Time: 5.2%

Conduct research into phases of physical phenomena, develop theories and laws on basis of observation and experiments, and devise methods to apply laws and theories to industry and other fields. Perform complex calculations as part of the analysis and evaluation of data, using computers. Describe and express observations and conclusions in mathematical terms. Analyze data from research conducted to detect and measure physical phenomena. Report experimental results by writing papers for scientific journals or by presenting information at scientific conferences. Design computer simulations to model physical data so that it can be better understood. Collaborate with other scientists in the design, development, and testing of experimental, industrial, or medical equipment, instrumentation, and procedures. Direct testing and monitoring of contamination of radioactive equipment and recording of personnel and plant area radiation exposure data. Observe the structure and properties of matter and the transformation and propagation of energy, using equipment such as masers, lasers, and telescopes, in order to explore and identify the basic principles governing these phenomena. Develop theories and laws on the basis of observation and experiments and apply these theories and laws to problems in areas such as nuclear energy, optics, and aerospace technology. Teach physics to students. Develop manufacturing, assembly, and fabrication processes of laser, maser, infrared, and other light-emitting and light-sensitive devices. Conduct application evaluations and analyze results in order to determine commercial, industrial, scientific, medical, military, or other uses for electro-optical devices. Develop standards of permissible concentrations of radioisotopes in liquids and gases. Conduct research pertaining to potential environmental impacts of atomic energy-related industrial development in order to determine licensing qualifications. Advise authorities of procedures to be followed in radiation incidents or hazards and assist in civil defense planning.

Personality Type: Investigative. These occupations frequently involve working with ideas and require an extensive amount of thinking. They can involve searching for facts and figuring out problems mentally.

GOE—Interest Area/Cluster: 15. Scientific Research, Engineering, and Mathematics. **Work Group:** 15.02. Physical Sciences. **Other Jobs in This Work Group:** Astronomers; Atmospheric and Space Scientists; Chemists; Geographers; Geoscientists, Except Hydrologists and Geographers; Hydrologists; Materials Scientists.

Skills—Programming: Writing computer programs for various purposes. **Science:** Using scientific methods to solve problems. **Mathematics:** Using mathematics to solve problems. **Complex Problem Solving:** Identifying complex problems, reviewing the options, and implementing solutions. **Management of Financial Resources:** Determining how money will be spent to get the work done and accounting for these expenditures. **Systems Analysis:** Determining how a system should work and how changes will affect outcomes. **Writing:** Communicating effectively with others in writing as indicated by the needs of the audience. **Critical Thinking:** Using logic and analysis to identify the strengths and weaknesses of different approaches.

Education and Training Programs: Acoustics; Astrophysics; Atomic/Molecular Physics; Elementary Particle Physics; Health/Medical Physics; Nuclear Physics; Optics/Optical Sciences; Physics, General; Physics, Other; Plasma and High-Temperature Physics; Solid State and Low-Temperature Physics; Theoretical and Mathematical Physics. **Related Knowledge/Courses—Physics:** Physical principles, laws, and applications, including air, water, material dynamics, light, atomic principles, heat, electric theory, earth formations, and meteorological and related natural phenomena. **Mathematics:** Numbers and their operations and interrelationships, including arithmetic, algebra, geometry, calculus, and statistics and their applications. **Engineering and Technology:** Equipment, tools, and mechanical devices and their uses to produce motion, light, power, technology, and other applications. **Computers and Electronics:** Electric circuit boards, processors, chips, and computer hardware and software, including applications and programming. **English Language:** The structure and content of the English language, including the meaning and spelling of words, rules of composition, and grammar. **Telecommunications:** Transmission, broadcasting, switching, control, and operation of telecommunications systems.

Work Environment: Indoors; sitting.

Physics Teachers, Postsecondary

⬢ Education/Training Required: Doctoral degree
⬢ Annual Earnings: $70,090
⬢ Beginning Wage: $40,580
⬢ Earnings Growth Potential: High
⬢ Growth: 22.9%
⬢ Annual Job Openings: 2,155
⬢ Self-Employed: 0.4%
⬢ Part-Time: 27.8%

Teach courses pertaining to the laws of matter and energy. Includes both teachers primarily engaged in teaching and those who do a combination of both teaching and research. Evaluate and grade students' classwork, laboratory work, assignments, and papers. Prepare and deliver lectures to undergraduate and/or graduate students on topics such as quantum mechanics, particle physics, and optics. Compile, administer, and grade examinations or assign this work to others. Maintain student attendance records, grades, and other required records. Supervise students' laboratory work. Prepare course materials such as syllabi, homework assignments, and handouts. Maintain regularly scheduled office hours to advise and assist students. Supervise undergraduate and/or graduate teaching, internship, and research work. Keep abreast of developments in their field by reading current literature, talking with colleagues, and participating in professional conferences. Plan, evaluate, and revise curricula, course content, and course materials and methods of instruction. Initiate, facilitate, and moderate classroom discussions. Conduct research in a particular field of knowledge and publish findings in professional journals, books, and/or electronic media. Advise students on academic and vocational curricula and on career issues. Select and obtain materials and supplies such as textbooks and laboratory equipment. Collaborate with colleagues to address teaching and research issues. Participate in student recruitment, registration, and placement activities. Serve on academic or administrative committees that deal with institutional policies, departmental matters, and academic issues. Write grant proposals to procure external research funding. Perform administrative duties such as serving as department head. Act as advisers to student organizations. Provide professional consulting services to government and/or industry. Compile bibliographies of specialized materials for outside reading assignments. Participate in campus and community events.

Personality Type: Social. These occupations frequently involve working with, communicating with, and teaching people and often involve helping or providing service to others.

GOE—Interest Area/Cluster: 05. Education and Training. **Work Group:** 05.03. Postsecondary and Adult Teaching and Instructing. **Other Jobs in This Work Group:** Adult Literacy, Remedial Education, and GED Teachers and Instructors; Agricultural Sciences Teachers, Postsecondary; Anthropology and Archeology Teachers, Postsecondary; Architecture Teachers, Postsecondary; Area, Ethnic, and Cultural Studies Teachers, Postsecondary; Art, Drama, and Music Teachers, Postsecondary; Atmospheric, Earth, Marine, and Space Sciences Teachers, Postsecondary; Biological Science Teachers, Postsecondary; Business Teachers, Postsecondary; Chemistry Teachers, Postsecondary; Communications Teachers, Postsecondary; Computer Science Teachers, Postsecondary; Criminal Justice and Law Enforcement Teachers, Postsecondary; Economics Teachers, Postsecondary; Education Teachers, Postsecondary; Engineering Teachers, Postsecondary; English Language and Literature Teachers, Postsecondary; Environmental Science Teachers, Postsecondary; Farm and Home Management Advisors; Foreign Language and Literature Teachers, Postsecondary; Forestry and Conservation Science Teachers, Postsecondary; Geography Teachers, Postsecondary; Graduate Teaching Assistants; Health Specialties Teachers, Postsecondary; History Teachers, Postsecondary; Home Economics Teachers, Postsecondary; Law Teachers, Postsecondary; Library Science Teachers, Postsecondary; Mathematical Science Teachers, Postsecondary; Nursing Instructors and Teachers, Postsecondary; Philosophy and Religion Teachers, Postsecondary; Political Science Teachers, Postsecondary; Psychology Teachers, Postsecondary; Recreation and Fitness Studies Teachers, Postsecondary; Self-Enrichment Education Teachers; Social Work Teachers, Postsecondary; Sociology Teachers, Postsecondary; Vocational Education Teachers, Postsecondary.

Skills—Science: Using scientific methods to solve problems. **Programming:** Writing computer programs for various purposes. **Mathematics:** Using mathematics to solve problems. **Instructing:** Teaching others how to do something. **Writing:** Communicating effectively with others in writing as indicated by the needs of the audience. **Reading Comprehension:** Understanding written sentences and paragraphs in work-related documents. **Learning Strategies:** Using multiple approaches when learning or teaching new things. **Critical Thinking:** Using logic and analysis to identify the strengths and weaknesses of different approaches.

Education and Training Programs: Acoustics; Atomic/Molecular Physics; Elementary Particle Physics; Nuclear Physics; Optics/Optical Sciences; Physics, General; Physics, Other; Plasma and High-Temperature Physics; Solid State and Low-Temperature Physics; Theoretical and Mathematical Physics. **Related Knowledge/Courses—Physics:** Physical principles, laws, and applications, including air, water, material dynamics, light, atomic principles, heat, electric theory, earth formations, and meteorological and related natural phenomena. **Mathematics:** Numbers and their operations and interrelationships, including arithmetic, algebra, geometry, calculus, and statistics and their applications. **Chemistry:** The composition, structure, and properties of substances and of the chemical processes and transformations that they undergo. This includes uses of chemicals and their interactions, danger signs, production techniques, and disposal methods. **Engineering and Technology:** Equipment, tools, and mechanical devices and their uses to produce motion, light, power, technology, and other applications. **Education and Training:** Instructional methods and training techniques, including curriculum design principles, learning theory, group and individual teaching techniques, design of individual development plans, and test design principles. **Computers and Electronics:** Electric circuit boards, processors, chips, and computer hardware and software, including applications and programming.

Work Environment: Indoors; sitting.

Pilots, Ship

* ❋ Education/Training Required: Work experience in a related occupation
* ❋ Annual Earnings: $57,210
* ❋ Beginning Wage: $29,530
* ❋ Earnings Growth Potential: High
* ❋ Growth: 17.9%
* ❋ Annual Job Openings: 2,665
* ❋ Self-Employed: 6.8%
* ❋ Part-Time: 4.8%

The job openings listed here are shared with Mates—Ship, Boat, and Barge; and with Ship and Boat Captains.

Command ships to steer them into and out of harbors, estuaries, straits, and sounds and on rivers, lakes, and bays. Must be licensed by U.S. Coast Guard with limitations indicating class and tonnage of vessels for which licenses are valid and routes and waters that may be piloted. Maintain and repair boats and equipment. Give directions to crew members who are steering ships. Make nautical maps. Set ships' courses to avoid reefs, outlying shoals, and other hazards, using navigational aids such as lighthouses and buoys. Report to appropriate authorities any violations of federal or state pilotage laws. Relieve crew members on tugs and launches. Provide assistance to vessels approaching or leaving seacoasts, navigating harbors, and docking and undocking. Provide assistance in maritime rescue operations. Prevent ships under their navigational control from engaging in unsafe operations. Operate amphibious craft during troop landings. Maintain ships' logs. Learn to operate new technology systems and procedures through the use of instruction, simulators, and models. Advise ships' masters on harbor rules and customs procedures. Steer ships into and out of berths or signal tugboat captains to berth and unberth ships. Serve as vessels' docking masters upon arrival at a port and when at a berth. Operate ship-to-shore radios to exchange information needed for ship operations. Consult maps, charts, weather reports, and navigation equipment to determine and direct ship movements. Direct courses and speeds of ships based on specialized knowledge of local winds, weather, water depths, tides, currents, and hazards. Oversee cargo storage on or below decks.

Personality Type: Realistic. These occupations frequently involve work activities that include practical, hands-on problems and solutions. They often deal with plants; animals; and real-world materials such as wood, tools, and machinery. Many of the occupations require working outside and don't involve a lot of paperwork or working closely with others.

GOE—Interest Area/Cluster: 16. Transportation, Distribution, and Logistics. **Work Group:** 16.05. Water Vehicle Operation. **Other Jobs in This Work Group:** Captains, Mates, and Pilots of Water Vessels; Dredge Operators; Mates—Ship, Boat, and Barge; Motorboat Operators; Sailors and Marine Oilers; Ship and Boat Captains.

Skills—Operation and Control: Controlling operations of equipment or systems. **Operation Monitoring:** Watching gauges, dials, or other indicators to make sure a machine is working properly. **Judgment and Decision Making:** Weighing the relative costs and benefits of a potential action. **Management of Personnel Resources:** Motivating, developing, and directing people as they work; identifying the best people for the job. **Troubleshooting:** Determining what is causing an operating error and deciding what to do about it. **Equipment Maintenance:** Performing routine maintenance and determining when and what kind of maintenance is needed. **Negotiation:** Bringing others together and trying to reconcile differences. **Coordination:** Adjusting actions in relation to others' actions.

Education and Training Programs: Commercial Fishing; Marine Science/Merchant Marine Officer Training; Marine Transportation, Other. **Related Knowledge/Courses— Transportation:** Principles and methods for moving people or goods by air, rail, sea, or road, including their relative costs, advantages, and limitations. **Geography:** Various methods for describing the location and distribution of land, sea, and air masses, including their physical locations, relationships, and characteristics. **Public Safety and Security:** Weaponry; public safety; security operations, rules, regulations, precautions, and prevention; and the protection of people, data, and property. **Telecommunications:** Transmission, broadcasting, switching, control, and operation of telecommunications systems. **Mechanical Devices:** Machines and tools, including their designs, uses, benefits, repair, and maintenance. **Law and Government:** Laws, legal codes, court procedures, precedents, government regulations, executive orders, agency rules, and the democratic political process.

Work Environment: Outdoors; noisy; very hot or cold; very bright or dim lighting; contaminants; using hands on objects, tools, or controls.

Pipe Fitters and Steamfitters

* Education/Training Required: Long-term on-the-job training
* Annual Earnings: $44,090
* Beginning Wage: $26,550
* Earnings Growth Potential: Medium
* Growth: 10.6%
* Annual Job Openings: 68,643
* Self-Employed: 12.3%
* Part-Time: 3.4%

The job openings listed here are shared with Plumbers.

Lay out, assemble, install, and maintain pipe systems, pipe supports, and related hydraulic and pneumatic equipment for steam, hot water, heating, cooling, lubricating, sprinkling, and industrial production and processing systems. Cut, thread, and hammer pipe to specifications, using tools such as saws, cutting torches, and pipe threaders and benders. Assemble and secure pipes, tubes, fittings, and related equipment according to specifications by welding, brazing, cementing, soldering, and threading

joints. Attach pipes to walls, structures, and fixtures, such as radiators or tanks, using brackets, clamps, tools, or welding equipment. Inspect, examine, and test installed systems and pipelines, using pressure gauge, hydrostatic testing, observation, or other methods. Measure and mark pipes for cutting and threading. Lay out full scale drawings of pipe systems, supports, and related equipment, following blueprints. Plan pipe system layout, installation, or repair according to specifications. Select pipe sizes and types and related materials, such as supports, hangers, and hydraulic cylinders, according to specifications. Cut and bore holes in structures such as bulkheads, decks, walls, and mains prior to pipe installation, using hand and power tools. Modify, clean, and maintain pipe systems, units, fittings, and related machines and equipment, following specifications and using hand and power tools. Install automatic controls used to regulate pipe systems. Turn valves to shut off steam, water, or other gases or liquids from pipe sections, using valve keys or wrenches. Remove and replace worn components. Prepare cost estimates for clients. Inspect work sites for obstructions and to ensure that holes will not cause structural weakness. Operate motorized pumps to remove water from flooded manholes, basements, or facility floors. Dip nonferrous piping materials in a mixture of molten tin and lead to obtain a coating that prevents erosion or galvanic and electrolytic action.

Personality Type: Realistic. These occupations frequently involve work activities that include practical, hands-on problems and solutions. They often deal with plants; animals; and real-world materials such as wood, tools, and machinery. Many of the occupations require working outside and don't involve a lot of paperwork or working closely with others.

GOE—Interest Area/Cluster: 02. Architecture and Construction. **Work Group:** 02.04. Construction Crafts. **Other Jobs in This Work Group:** Boilermakers; Brickmasons and Blockmasons; Carpet Installers; Cement Masons and Concrete Finishers; Commercial Divers; Construction Carpenters; Crane and Tower Operators; Drywall and Ceiling Tile Installers; Electricians; Fence Erectors; Floor Layers, Except Carpet, Wood, and Hard Tiles; Floor Sanders and Finishers; Glaziers; Hazardous Materials Removal Workers; Insulation Workers, Floor, Ceiling, and Wall; Insulation Workers, Mechanical; Manufactured Building and Mobile Home Installers; Operating Engineers and Other Construction Equipment Operators; Painters, Construction and Maintenance; Paperhangers; Paving, Surfacing, and Tamping Equipment Operators; Pile-Driver Operators; Pipelayers; Plasterers and Stucco Masons; Plumbers; Plumbers,

Pipefitters, and Steamfitters; Rail-Track Laying and Maintenance Equipment Operators; Refractory Materials Repairers, Except Brickmasons; Reinforcing Iron and Rebar Workers; Riggers; Roofers; Rough Carpenters; Security and Fire Alarm Systems Installers; Segmental Pavers; Sheet Metal Workers; Stone Cutters and Carvers, Manufacturing; Stonemasons; Structural Iron and Steel Workers; Tapers; Terrazzo Workers and Finishers; Tile and Marble Setters.

Skills—Installation: Installing equipment, machines, wiring, or programs to meet specifications. **Repairing:** Repairing machines or systems, using the needed tools. **Systems Analysis:** Determining how a system should work and how changes will affect outcomes. **Management of Personnel Resources:** Motivating, developing, and directing people as they work; identifying the best people for the job. **Equipment Maintenance:** Performing routine maintenance and determining when and what kind of maintenance is needed. **Operation Monitoring:** Watching gauges, dials, or other indicators to make sure a machine is working properly. **Operation and Control:** Controlling operations of equipment or systems. **Technology Design:** Generating or adapting equipment and technology to serve user needs.

Education and Training Program: Pipefitting/Pipefitter and Sprinkler Fitter Training. **Related Knowledge/ Courses—Building and Construction:** Materials, methods, and the appropriate tools to construct objects, structures, and buildings. **Design:** Design techniques, principles, tools, and instruments involved in the production and use of precision technical plans, blueprints, drawings, and models. **Mechanical Devices:** Machines and tools, including their designs, uses, benefits, repair, and maintenance. **Engineering and Technology:** Equipment, tools, and mechanical devices and their uses to produce motion, light, power, technology, and other applications. **Economics and Accounting:** Economic and accounting principles and practices, the financial markets, banking, and the analysis and reporting of financial data. **Transportation:** Principles and methods for moving people or goods by air, rail, sea, or road, including their relative costs, advantages, and limitations.

Work Environment: Outdoors; hazardous equipment; minor burns, cuts, bites, or stings; standing; using hands on objects, tools, or controls; repetitive motions.

Pipelayers

- Education/Training Required: Moderate-term on-the-job training
- Annual Earnings: $31,280
- Beginning Wage: $21,270
- Earnings Growth Potential: Low
- Growth: 8.7%
- Annual Job Openings: 8,902
- Self-Employed: 11.6%
- Part-Time: 3.4%

Lay pipe for storm or sanitation sewers, drains, and water mains. Perform any combination of these tasks: grade trenches or culverts, position pipe, or seal joints. Check slopes for conformance to requirements, using levels or lasers. Cover pipes with earth or other materials. Cut pipes to required lengths. Connect pipe pieces and seal joints, using welding equipment, cement, or glue. Install and repair sanitary and stormwater sewer structures and pipe systems. Install and use instruments such as lasers, grade rods, and transit levels. Grade and level trench bases, using tamping machines and hand tools. Lay out pipe routes, following written instructions or blueprints and coordinating layouts with supervisors. Align and position pipes to prepare them for welding or sealing. Dig trenches to desired or required depths by hand or using trenching tools. Operate mechanized equipment such as pickup trucks, rollers, tandem dump trucks, front-end loaders, and backhoes. Train others in pipe-laying and provide supervision. Tap and drill holes into pipes to introduce auxiliary lines or devices. Locate existing pipes needing repair or replacement, using magnetic or radio indicators.

Personality Type: Realistic. These occupations frequently involve work activities that include practical, hands-on problems and solutions. They often deal with plants; animals; and real-world materials such as wood, tools, and machinery. Many of the occupations require working outside and don't involve a lot of paperwork or working closely with others.

GOE—Interest Area/Cluster: 02. Architecture and Construction. **Work Group:** 02.04. Construction Crafts. **Other Jobs in This Work Group:** Boilermakers; Brickmasons and Blockmasons; Carpet Installers; Cement Masons and Concrete Finishers; Commercial Divers; Construction Carpenters; Crane and Tower Operators; Drywall and Ceiling Tile Installers; Electricians; Fence Erectors; Floor Layers, Except

Carpet, Wood, and Hard Tiles; Floor Sanders and Finishers; Glaziers; Hazardous Materials Removal Workers; Insulation Workers, Floor, Ceiling, and Wall; Insulation Workers, Mechanical; Manufactured Building and Mobile Home Installers; Operating Engineers and Other Construction Equipment Operators; Painters, Construction and Maintenance; Paperhangers; Paving, Surfacing, and Tamping Equipment Operators; Pile-Driver Operators; Pipe Fitters and Steamfitters; Plasterers and Stucco Masons; Plumbers; Plumbers, Pipefitters, and Steamfitters; Rail-Track Laying and Maintenance Equipment Operators; Refractory Materials Repairers, Except Brickmasons; Reinforcing Iron and Rebar Workers; Riggers; Roofers; Rough Carpenters; Security and Fire Alarm Systems Installers; Segmental Pavers; Sheet Metal Workers; Stone Cutters and Carvers, Manufacturing; Stonemasons; Structural Iron and Steel Workers; Tapers; Terrazzo Workers and Finishers; Tile and Marble Setters.

Skills—Installation: Installing equipment, machines, wiring, or programs to meet specifications. **Quality Control Analysis:** Evaluating the quality or performance of products, services, or processes. **Operation and Control:** Controlling operations of equipment or systems. **Operation Monitoring:** Watching gauges, dials, or other indicators to make sure a machine is working properly. **Equipment Maintenance:** Performing routine maintenance and determining when and what kind of maintenance is needed. **Equipment Selection:** Determining the kind of tools and equipment needed to do a job. **Repairing:** Repairing machines or systems, using the needed tools. **Technology Design:** Generating or adapting equipment and technology to serve user needs.

Education and Training Program: Plumbing Technology/Plumber Training. **Related Knowledge/Courses—Building and Construction:** Materials, methods, and the appropriate tools to construct objects, structures, and buildings. **Mechanical Devices:** Machines and tools, including their designs, uses, benefits, repair, and maintenance.

Work Environment: Outdoors; noisy; hazardous equipment; standing; using hands on objects, tools, or controls; repetitive motions.

Plasterers and Stucco Masons

* Education/Training Required: Long-term on-the-job training
* Annual Earnings: $36,430
* Beginning Wage: $23,670
* Earnings Growth Potential: Medium
* Growth: 8.1%
* Annual Job Openings: 4,509
* Self-Employed: 15.7%
* Part-Time: 4.3%

Apply interior or exterior plaster, cement, stucco, or similar materials. May also set ornamental plaster. Apply coats of plaster or stucco to walls, ceilings, or partitions of buildings, using trowels, brushes, or spray guns. Mix mortar and plaster to desired consistency or direct workers who perform mixing. Create decorative textures in finish coat, using brushes or trowels, sand, pebbles, or stones. Apply insulation to building exteriors by installing prefabricated insulation systems over existing walls or by covering the outer wall with insulation board, reinforcing mesh, and a base coat. Cure freshly plastered surfaces. Clean and prepare surfaces for applications of plaster, cement, stucco, or similar materials, such as by drywall taping. Rough the undercoat surface with a scratcher so the finish coat will adhere. Apply weatherproof decorative coverings to exterior surfaces of buildings, such as troweling or spraying on coats of stucco. Install guide wires on exterior surfaces of buildings to indicate thickness of plaster or stucco and nail wire mesh, lath, or similar materials to the outside surface to hold stucco in place. Spray acoustic materials or texture finish over walls and ceilings. Mold and install ornamental plaster pieces, panels, and trim.

Personality Type: Realistic. These occupations frequently involve work activities that include practical, hands-on problems and solutions. They often deal with plants; animals; and real-world materials such as wood, tools, and machinery. Many of the occupations require working outside and don't involve a lot of paperwork or working closely with others.

GOE—Interest Area/Cluster: 02. Architecture and Construction. **Work Group:** 02.04. Construction Crafts. **Other Jobs in This Work Group:** Boilermakers; Brickmasons and Blockmasons; Carpet Installers; Cement Masons and Concrete Finishers; Commercial Divers; Construction Carpenters; Crane and Tower Operators; Drywall and Ceiling Tile

Installers; Electricians; Fence Erectors; Floor Layers, Except Carpet, Wood, and Hard Tiles; Floor Sanders and Finishers; Glaziers; Hazardous Materials Removal Workers; Insulation Workers, Floor, Ceiling, and Wall; Insulation Workers, Mechanical; Manufactured Building and Mobile Home Installers; Operating Engineers and Other Construction Equipment Operators; Painters, Construction and Maintenance; Paperhangers; Paving, Surfacing, and Tamping Equipment Operators; Pile-Driver Operators; Pipe Fitters and Steamfitters; Pipelayers; Plumbers; Plumbers, Pipefitters, and Steamfitters; Rail-Track Laying and Maintenance Equipment Operators; Refractory Materials Repairers, Except Brickmasons; Reinforcing Iron and Rebar Workers; Riggers; Roofers; Rough Carpenters; Security and Fire Alarm Systems Installers; Segmental Pavers; Sheet Metal Workers; Stone Cutters and Carvers, Manufacturing; Stonemasons; Structural Iron and Steel Workers; Tapers; Terrazzo Workers and Finishers; Tile and Marble Setters.

Skills—Management of Material Resources: Obtaining and seeing to the appropriate use of equipment, facilities, and materials needed to do certain work. **Repairing:** Repairing machines or systems, using the needed tools. **Installation:** Installing equipment, machines, wiring, or programs to meet specifications. **Technology Design:** Generating or adapting equipment and technology to serve user needs. **Equipment Maintenance:** Performing routine maintenance and determining when and what kind of maintenance is needed. **Management of Financial Resources:** Determining how money will be spent to get the work done and accounting for these expenditures. **Equipment Selection:** Determining the kind of tools and equipment needed to do a job. **Operations Analysis:** Analyzing needs and product requirements to create a design.

Education and Training Program: Construction Trades, Other. **Related Knowledge/Courses—Building and Construction:** Materials, methods, and the appropriate tools to construct objects, structures, and buildings. **Public Safety and Security:** Weaponry; public safety; security operations, rules, regulations, precautions, and prevention; and the protection of people, data, and property.

Work Environment: High places; standing; walking and running; using hands on objects, tools, or controls; bending or twisting the body; repetitive motions.

Plumbers

- ❋ Education/Training Required: Long-term on-the-job training
- ❋ Annual Earnings: $44,090
- ❋ Beginning Wage: $26,550
- ❋ Earnings Growth Potential: Medium
- ❋ Growth: 10.6%
- ❋ Annual Job Openings: 68,643
- ❋ Self-Employed: 12.3%
- ❋ Part-Time: 3.4%

The job openings listed here are shared with Pipe Fitters and Steamfitters.

Assemble, install, and repair pipes, fittings, and fixtures of heating, water, and drainage systems according to specifications and plumbing codes. Measure, cut, thread, and bend pipe to required angles, using hand and power tools or machines such as pipe cutters, pipe-threading machines, and pipe-bending machines. Study building plans and inspect structures to assess material and equipment needs, to establish the sequence of pipe installations, and to plan installation around obstructions such as electrical wiring. Locate and mark the position of pipe installations, connections, passage holes, and fixtures in structures, using measuring instruments such as rulers and levels. Assemble pipe sections, tubing, and fittings, using couplings; clamps; screws; bolts; cement; plastic solvent; caulking; or soldering, brazing, and welding equipment. Fill pipes or plumbing fixtures with water or air and observe pressure gauges to detect and locate leaks. Install pipe assemblies, fittings, valves, appliances such as dishwashers and water heaters, and fixtures such as sinks and toilets, using hand and power tools. Direct workers engaged in pipe cutting and preassembly and installation of plumbing systems and components. Cut openings in structures to accommodate pipes and pipe fittings, using hand and power tools. Review blueprints and building codes and specifications to determine work details and procedures. Install underground storm, sanitary, and water piping systems and extend piping to connect fixtures and plumbing to these systems. Repair and maintain plumbing, replacing defective washers, replacing or mending broken pipes, and opening clogged drains. Keep records of assignments and produce detailed work reports. Hang steel supports from ceiling joists to hold pipes in place. Perform complex calculations and planning for special or very large jobs. Clear away debris in renovations. Install oxygen and medical gas in hospitals. Prepare written work cost estimates and negotiate contracts. Use specialized techniques, equipment, or materials, such as performing computer-assisted welding of small pipes or working with the special piping used in microchip fabrication.

Personality Type: Realistic. These occupations frequently involve work activities that include practical, hands-on problems and solutions. They often deal with plants; animals; and real-world materials such as wood, tools, and machinery. Many of the occupations require working outside and don't involve a lot of paperwork or working closely with others.

GOE—Interest Area/Cluster: 02. Architecture and Construction. **Work Group:** 02.04. Construction Crafts. **Other Jobs in This Work Group:** Boilermakers; Brickmasons and Blockmasons; Carpet Installers; Cement Masons and Concrete Finishers; Commercial Divers; Construction Carpenters; Crane and Tower Operators; Drywall and Ceiling Tile Installers; Electricians; Fence Erectors; Floor Layers, Except Carpet, Wood, and Hard Tiles; Floor Sanders and Finishers; Glaziers; Hazardous Materials Removal Workers; Insulation Workers, Floor, Ceiling, and Wall; Insulation Workers, Mechanical; Manufactured Building and Mobile Home Installers; Operating Engineers and Other Construction Equipment Operators; Painters, Construction and Maintenance; Paperhangers; Paving, Surfacing, and Tamping Equipment Operators; Pile-Driver Operators; Pipe Fitters and Steamfitters; Pipelayers; Plasterers and Stucco Masons; Plumbers, Pipefitters, and Steamfitters; Rail-Track Laying and Maintenance Equipment Operators; Refractory Materials Repairers, Except Brickmasons; Reinforcing Iron and Rebar Workers; Riggers; Roofers; Rough Carpenters; Security and Fire Alarm Systems Installers; Segmental Pavers; Sheet Metal Workers; Stone Cutters and Carvers, Manufacturing; Stonemasons; Structural Iron and Steel Workers; Tapers; Terrazzo Workers and Finishers; Tile and Marble Setters.

Skills—Installation: Installing equipment, machines, wiring, or programs to meet specifications. **Quality Control Analysis:** Evaluating the quality or performance of products, services, or processes. **Repairing:** Repairing machines or systems, using the needed tools. **Operation and Control:** Controlling operations of equipment or systems. **Operation Monitoring:** Watching gauges, dials, or other indicators to make sure a machine is working properly. **Mathematics:** Using mathematics to solve problems. **Systems Analysis:** Determining how a system should work and how changes will affect outcomes.

Education and Training Programs: Pipefitting/Pipefitter and Sprinkler Fitter Training; Plumbing and Related Water Supply Services, Other; Plumbing Technology/Plumber Training. **Related Knowledge/Courses—Building and Construction:** Materials, methods, and the appropriate tools to construct objects, structures, and buildings. **Physics:** Physical principles, laws, and applications, including air, water, material dynamics, light, atomic principles, heat, electric theory, earth formations, and meteorological and related natural phenomena. **Mechanical Devices:** Machines and tools, including their designs, uses, benefits, repair, and maintenance. **Design:** Design techniques, principles, tools, and instruments involved in the production and use of precision technical plans, blueprints, drawings, and models. **Engineering and Technology:** Equipment, tools, and mechanical devices and their uses to produce motion, light, power, technology, and other applications. **Customer and Personal Service:** Principles and processes for providing customer and personal services, including needs assessment techniques, quality service standards, alternative delivery systems, and customer satisfaction evaluation techniques.

Work Environment: Outdoors; noisy; very hot or cold; hazardous equipment; standing; using hands on objects, tools, or controls.

Podiatrists

- ❋ Education/Training Required: First professional degree
- ❋ Annual Earnings: $110,510
- ❋ Beginning Wage: $45,260
- ❋ Earnings Growth Potential: Very high
- ❋ Growth: 9.5%
- ❋ Annual Job Openings: 648
- ❋ Self-Employed: 23.9%
- ❋ Part-Time: 23.6%

Diagnose and treat diseases and deformities of the human foot. Treat bone, muscle, and joint disorders affecting the feet. Diagnose diseases and deformities of the foot, using medical histories, physical examinations, X rays, and laboratory test results. Prescribe medications, corrective devices, physical therapy, or surgery. Treat conditions such as corns, calluses, ingrown nails, tumors, shortened tendons, bunions, cysts, and abscesses by surgical methods. Advise patients about treatments and foot care techniques necessary for prevention of future problems. Refer patients to physicians when symptoms indicative of systemic disorders, such as arthritis or diabetes, are observed in feet and legs. Correct deformities by means of plaster casts and strapping. Make and fit prosthetic appliances. Perform administrative duties such as hiring employees, ordering supplies, and keeping records. Educate the public about the benefits of foot care through techniques such as speaking engagements, advertising, and other forums. Treat deformities, using mechanical methods, such as whirlpool or paraffin baths, and electrical methods, such as shortwave and low-voltage currents.

Personality Type: Investigative. These occupations frequently involve working with ideas and require an extensive amount of thinking. They can involve searching for facts and figuring out problems mentally.

GOE—Interest Area/Cluster: 08. Health Science. **Work Group:** 08.04. Health Specialties. **Other Jobs in This Work Group:** Chiropractors; Optometrists.

Skills—Science: Using scientific methods to solve problems. **Active Listening:** Listening to what other people are saying and asking questions as appropriate. **Complex Problem Solving:** Identifying complex problems, reviewing the options, and implementing solutions. **Management of Financial Resources:** Determining how money will be spent to get the work done and accounting for these expenditures. **Reading Comprehension:** Understanding written sentences and paragraphs in work-related documents. **Equipment Selection:** Determining the kind of tools and equipment needed to do a job. **Active Learning:** Working with new material or information to grasp its implications. **Judgment and Decision Making:** Weighing the relative costs and benefits of a potential action.

Education and Training Program: Podiatric Medicine/Podiatry (DPM). **Related Knowledge/Courses—Medicine and Dentistry:** The information and techniques needed to diagnose and treat injuries, diseases, and deformities. This includes symptoms, treatment alternatives, drug properties and interactions, and preventive health-care measures. **Biology:** Plant and animal living tissue, cells, organisms, and entities, including their functions, interdependencies, and interactions with each other and the environment. **Therapy and Counseling:** Information and techniques needed to rehabilitate physical and mental ailments and to provide career guidance, including alternative treatments, rehabilitation equipment and its proper use, and methods to evaluate treatment effects. **Sales and Marketing:** Principles and methods involved in showing, promoting, and selling products or services. This includes marketing strategies and tactics, product demonstration and sales techniques, and sales

control systems. **Chemistry:** The composition, structure, and properties of substances and of the chemical processes and transformations that they undergo. This includes uses of chemicals and their interactions, danger signs, production techniques, and disposal methods. **Psychology:** Human behavior and performance, mental processes, psychological research methods, and the assessment and treatment of behavioral and affective disorders.

Work Environment: Indoors; contaminants; disease or infections; sitting; using hands on objects, tools, or controls; repetitive motions.

Poets, Lyricists, and Creative Writers

* Education/Training Required: Bachelor's degree
* Annual Earnings: $50,660
* Beginning Wage: $26,530
* Earnings Growth Potential: High
* Growth: 12.8%
* Annual Job Openings: 24,023
* Self-Employed: 65.9%
* Part-Time: 21.8%

The job openings listed here are shared with Copy Writers.

Create original written works, such as scripts, essays, prose, poetry, or song lyrics, for publication or performance. Revise written material to meet personal standards and to satisfy needs of clients, publishers, directors, or producers. Choose subject matter and suitable form to express personal feelings and experiences or ideas, or to narrate stories or events. Plan project arrangements or outlines, and organize material accordingly. Prepare works in appropriate format for publication, and send them to publishers or producers. Follow appropriate procedures to get copyrights for completed work. Write fiction or nonfiction prose such as short stories, novels, biographies, articles, descriptive or critical analyses, and essays. Develop factors such as themes, plots, characterizations, psychological analyses, historical environments, action, and dialogue, to create material. Confer with clients, editors, publishers, or producers to discuss changes or revisions to written material. Conduct research to obtain factual information and authentic detail, using sources such as newspaper accounts, diaries, and interviews. Write narrative, dramatic, lyric, or other types of poetry for publication. Attend book launches and publicity events, or conduct public readings. Write words to fit musical compositions, including lyrics for operas, musical plays, and choral works. Adapt text to accommodate musical requirements of composers and singers. Teach writing classes. Write humorous material for publication, or for performances such as comedy routines, gags, and comedy shows. Collaborate with other writers on specific projects.

Personality Type: Artistic. These occupations frequently involve working with forms, designs, and patterns. They often require self-expression, and the work can be done without following a clear set of rules.

GOE—Interest Area/Cluster: 03. Arts and Communication. **Work Group:** 03.02. Writing and Editing. **Other Jobs in This Work Group:** Copy Writers; Editors; Technical Writers; Writers and Authors.

Skills—Writing: Communicating effectively with others in writing as indicated by the needs of the audience. **Social Perceptiveness:** Being aware of others' reactions and understanding why they react the way they do. **Management of Financial Resources:** Determining how money will be spent to get the work done and accounting for these expenditures. **Persuasion:** Persuading others to approach things differently. **Active Listening:** Listening to what other people are saying and asking questions as appropriate. **Reading Comprehension:** Understanding written sentences and paragraphs in work-related documents. **Speaking:** Talking to others to effectively convey information. **Critical Thinking:** Using logic and analysis to identify the strengths and weaknesses of different approaches.

Education and Training Programs: Communication Studies/Speech Communication and Rhetoric; Creative Writing; English Composition; Family and Consumer Sciences/Human Sciences Communication; Mass Communication/Media Studies; Playwriting and Screenwriting. **Related Knowledge/Courses—Fine Arts:** Theory and techniques required to produce, compose, and perform works of music, dance, visual arts, drama, and sculpture. **Communications and Media:** Media production, communication, and dissemination techniques and methods, including alternative ways to inform and entertain via written, oral, and visual media. **Philosophy and Theology:** Different philosophical systems and religions, including their basic principles, values, ethics, ways of thinking, customs, and practices and their impact on human culture. **Sociology and Anthropology:** Group behavior and dynamics; societal trends and influences; and cultures and their history, migrations, ethnicity, and origins. **Sales and Marketing:** Principles and methods involved in showing, promoting, and selling products or services. This includes marketing strategies and tactics, product demonstration and sales techniques, and sales control systems. **English Language:** The structure and content of the English language, including the meaning and spelling of words, rules of composition, and grammar.

Work Environment: Indoors; sitting; using hands on objects, tools, or controls; repetitive motions.

Police Detectives

- ❋ Education/Training Required: Work experience in a related occupation
- ❋ Annual Earnings: $59,930
- ❋ Beginning Wage: $35,600
- ❋ Earnings Growth Potential: High
- ❋ Growth: 17.3%
- ❋ Annual Job Openings: 14,746
- ❋ Self-Employed: 0.3%
- ❋ Part-Time: 2.2%

The job openings listed here are shared with Criminal Investigators and Special Agents; Immigration and Customs Inspectors; and Police Identification and Records Officers.

Conduct investigations to prevent crimes or solve criminal cases. Provide testimony as a witness in court. Secure deceased bodies and obtain evidence from them, preventing bystanders from tampering with bodies prior to medical examiner's arrival. Examine crime scenes to obtain clues and evidence such as loose hairs, fibers, clothing, or weapons. Obtain evidence from suspects. Record progress of investigations, maintain informational files on suspects, and submit reports to commanding officers or magistrates to authorize warrants. Check victims for signs of life such as breathing and pulse. Prepare charges or responses to charges, or information for court cases, according to formalized procedures. Obtain facts or statements from complainants, witnesses, and accused persons and record interviews, using recording devices. Prepare and serve search and arrest warrants. Note, mark, and photograph locations of objects found, such as footprints, tire tracks, bullets, and bloodstains, and take measurements of each scene. Question individuals or observe persons and establishments to confirm information given to patrol officers. Preserve, process, and analyze items of evidence obtained from crime scenes and suspects, placing them in proper containers and destroying evidence no longer needed. Secure persons at scenes, keeping witnesses from conversing or leaving scenes before investigators arrive.

Take photographs from all angles of relevant parts of crime scenes, including entrance and exit routes and streets and intersections. Analyze completed police reports to determine what additional information and investigative work is needed. Obtain summary of incidents from officers in charge at crime scenes, taking care to avoid disturbing evidence. Provide information to lab personnel concerning the source of each item of evidence and tests to be performed. Examine records and governmental agency files to find identifying data about suspects. Block or rope off scenes and check perimeters to ensure that scenes are completely secured. Summon medical help for injured individuals and alert medical personnel to take statements from them. Observe and photograph narcotic purchase transactions to compile evidence and protect undercover investigators.

Personality Type: Enterprising. These occupations frequently involve starting up and carrying out projects and can involve leading people and making many decisions. They sometimes require risk taking and often deal with business.

GOE—Interest Area/Cluster: 12. Law and Public Safety. **Work Group:** 12.04. Law Enforcement and Public Safety. **Other Jobs in This Work Group:** Bailiffs; Correctional Officers and Jailers; Criminal Investigators and Special Agents; Detectives and Criminal Investigators; Fire Investigators; Forensic Science Technicians; Parking Enforcement Workers; Police and Sheriff's Patrol Officers; Police Identification and Records Officers; Police Patrol Officers; Sheriffs and Deputy Sheriffs; Transit and Railroad Police.

Skills—Persuasion: Persuading others to approach things differently. **Systems Analysis:** Determining how a system should work and how changes will affect outcomes. **Social Perceptiveness:** Being aware of others' reactions and understanding why they react the way they do. **Systems Evaluation:** Looking at many indicators of system performance and taking into account their accuracy. **Complex Problem Solving:** Identifying complex problems, reviewing the options, and implementing solutions. **Critical Thinking:** Using logic and analysis to identify the strengths and weaknesses of different approaches. **Negotiation:** Bringing others together and trying to reconcile differences. **Active Listening:** Listening to what other people are saying and asking questions as appropriate.

Education and Training Programs: Criminal Justice/Police Science; Criminalistics and Criminal Science. **Related Knowledge/Courses—Public Safety and Security:** Weaponry; public safety; security operations, rules, regulations,

precautions, and prevention; and the protection of people, data, and property. **Law and Government:** Laws, legal codes, court procedures, precedents, government regulations, executive orders, agency rules, and the democratic political process. **Psychology:** Human behavior and performance, mental processes, psychological research methods, and the assessment and treatment of behavioral and affective disorders. **Therapy and Counseling:** Information and techniques needed to rehabilitate physical and mental ailments and to provide career guidance, including alternative treatments, rehabilitation equipment and its proper use, and methods to evaluate treatment effects. **Customer and Personal Service:** Principles and processes for providing customer and personal services, including needs assessment techniques, quality service standards, alternative delivery systems, and customer satisfaction evaluation techniques. **Philosophy and Theology:** Different philosophical systems and religions, including their basic principles, values, ethics, ways of thinking, customs, and practices and their impact on human culture.

Work Environment: More often outdoors than indoors; noisy; very hot or cold; contaminants; sitting.

Police Identification and Records Officers

- ❋ Education/Training Required: Work experience in a related occupation
- ❋ Annual Earnings: $59,930
- ❋ Beginning Wage: $35,600
- ❋ Earnings Growth Potential: High
- ❋ Growth: 17.3%
- ❋ Annual Job Openings: 14,746
- ❋ Self-Employed: 0.3%
- ❋ Part-Time: 2.2%

The job openings listed here are shared with Criminal Investigators and Special Agents; Immigration and Customs Inspectors; and Police Detectives.

Collect evidence at crime scene, classify and identify fingerprints, and photograph evidence for use in criminal and civil cases. Photograph crime or accident scenes for evidence records. Analyze and process evidence at crime scenes and in the laboratory, wearing protective equipment and using powders and chemicals. Look for trace evidence, such as fingerprints, hairs, fibers, or shoe impressions, using alternative light sources when necessary. Dust selected areas of crime scene and lift latent fingerprints, adhering to proper preservation procedures. Testify in court and present evidence. Package, store, and retrieve evidence. Serve as technical advisor and coordinate with other law enforcement workers to exchange information on crime scene collection activities. Perform emergency work during off-hours. Submit evidence to supervisors. Process film and prints from crime or accident scenes. Identify, classify, and file fingerprints, using systems such as the Henry Classification system.

Personality Type: Conventional. These occupations frequently involve following set procedures and routines and can include working with data and details more than with ideas. Usually there is a clear line of authority to follow.

GOE—Interest Area/Cluster: 12. Law and Public Safety. **Work Group:** 12.04. Law Enforcement and Public Safety. **Other Jobs in This Work Group:** Bailiffs; Correctional Officers and Jailers; Criminal Investigators and Special Agents; Detectives and Criminal Investigators; Fire Investigators; Forensic Science Technicians; Parking Enforcement Workers; Police and Sheriff's Patrol Officers; Police Detectives; Police Patrol Officers; Sheriffs and Deputy Sheriffs; Transit and Railroad Police.

Skills—Persuasion: Persuading others to approach things differently. **Judgment and Decision Making:** Weighing the relative costs and benefits of a potential action. **Negotiation:** Bringing others together and trying to reconcile differences. **Service Orientation:** Actively looking for ways to help people. **Social Perceptiveness:** Being aware of others' reactions and understanding why they react the way they do. **Critical Thinking:** Using logic and analysis to identify the strengths and weaknesses of different approaches. **Speaking:** Talking to others to effectively convey information. **Science:** Using scientific methods to solve problems.

Education and Training Programs: Criminal Justice/Police Science; Criminalistics and Criminal Science. **Related Knowledge/Courses—Law and Government:** Laws, legal codes, court procedures, precedents, government regulations, executive orders, agency rules, and the democratic political process. **Public Safety and Security:** Weaponry; public safety; security operations, rules, regulations, precautions, and prevention; and the protection of people, data, and property. **Telecommunications:** Transmission, broadcasting, switching, control, and operation of telecommunications systems. **Customer and Personal Service:** Principles and processes for providing customer and personal services, including needs assessment techniques,

quality service standards, alternative delivery systems, and customer satisfaction evaluation techniques. **Psychology:** Human behavior and performance, mental processes, psychological research methods, and the assessment and treatment of behavioral and affective disorders. **Computers and Electronics:** Electric circuit boards, processors, chips, and computer hardware and software, including applications and programming.

Work Environment: More often outdoors than indoors; noisy; very hot or cold; contaminants; using hands on objects, tools, or controls.

Police Patrol Officers

* Education/Training Required: Long-term on-the-job training
* Annual Earnings: $49,630
* Beginning Wage: $28,820
* Earnings Growth Potential: High
* Growth: 10.8%
* Annual Job Openings: 37,842
* Self-Employed: 0.0%
* Part-Time: 1.1%

The job openings listed here are shared with Sheriffs and Deputy Sheriffs.

Patrol assigned areas to enforce laws and ordinances, regulate traffic, control crowds, prevent crime, and arrest violators. Provide for public safety by maintaining order, responding to emergencies, protecting people and property, enforcing motor vehicle and criminal laws, and promoting good community relations. Monitor, note, report, and investigate suspicious persons and situations, safety hazards, and unusual or illegal activity in patrol area. Record facts to prepare reports that document incidents and activities. Identify, pursue, and arrest suspects and perpetrators of criminal acts. Patrol specific areas on foot, horseback, or motorized conveyance, responding promptly to calls for assistance. Review facts of incidents to determine if criminal acts or statute violations were involved. Investigate traffic accidents and other accidents to determine causes and to determine if crimes have been committed. Render aid to accident victims and other persons requiring first aid for physical injuries. Testify in court to present evidence or act as witness in traffic and criminal cases. Photograph or draw diagrams of crime or accident scenes and interview principals and eyewitnesses. Relay complaint and emergency-request information to appropriate agency dispatchers. Evaluate complaint and emergency-request information to determine response requirements. Process prisoners, and prepare and maintain records of prisoner bookings and prisoner statuses during booking and pre-trial processes. Monitor traffic to ensure motorists observe traffic regulations and exhibit safe driving procedures. Issue citations or warnings to violators of motor vehicle ordinances. Direct traffic flow and reroute traffic in case of emergencies. Inform citizens of community services and recommend options to facilitate longer-term problem resolution. Provide road information to assist motorists. Inspect public establishments to ensure compliance with rules and regulations. Act as official escorts at times such as when leading funeral processions or firefighters.

Personality Type: Realistic. These occupations frequently involve work activities that include practical, hands-on problems and solutions. They often deal with plants; animals; and real-world materials such as wood, tools, and machinery. Many of the occupations require working outside and don't involve a lot of paperwork or working closely with others.

GOE—Interest Area/Cluster: 12. Law and Public Safety. **Work Group:** 12.04. Law Enforcement and Public Safety. **Other Jobs in This Work Group:** Bailiffs; Correctional Officers and Jailers; Criminal Investigators and Special Agents; Detectives and Criminal Investigators; Fire Investigators; Forensic Science Technicians; Parking Enforcement Workers; Police and Sheriff's Patrol Officers; Police Detectives; Police Identification and Records Officers; Sheriffs and Deputy Sheriffs; Transit and Railroad Police.

Skills—Negotiation: Bringing others together and trying to reconcile differences. **Service Orientation:** Actively looking for ways to help people. **Management of Personnel Resources:** Motivating, developing, and directing people as they work; identifying the best people for the job. **Systems Analysis:** Determining how a system should work and how changes will affect outcomes. **Systems Evaluation:** Looking at many indicators of system performance and taking into account their accuracy.

Education and Training Programs: Criminal Justice/Police Science; Criminalistics and Criminal Science. **Related Knowledge/Courses—Psychology:** Human behavior and performance, mental processes, psychological research methods, and the assessment and treatment of behavioral and affective disorders. **Public Safety and Security:** Weaponry; public safety; security operations, rules, regulations, precautions, and prevention; and the protection of people, data, and property. **Law and Government:** Laws, legal codes, court procedures, precedents, government regulations, executive orders, agency rules, and the democratic political process. **Customer and Personal Service:** Principles and processes for providing customer and personal services, including needs assessment techniques, quality service standards, alternative delivery systems, and customer satisfaction evaluation techniques. **Therapy and Counseling:** Information and techniques needed to rehabilitate physical and mental ailments and to provide career guidance, including alternative treatments, rehabilitation equipment and its proper use, and methods to evaluate treatment effects. **Sociology and Anthropology:** Group behavior and dynamics; societal trends and influences; and cultures and their history, migrations, ethnicity, and origins.

Work Environment: More often outdoors than indoors; noisy; very hot or cold; hazardous equipment; sitting.

Police, Fire, and Ambulance Dispatchers

- ❀ Education/Training Required: Moderate-term on-the-job training
- ❀ Annual Earnings: $32,660
- ❀ Beginning Wage: $20,910
- ❀ Earnings Growth Potential: Medium
- ❀ Growth: 13.6%
- ❀ Annual Job Openings: 17,628
- ❀ Self-Employed: 1.2%
- ❀ Part-Time: 6.3%

Receive complaints from public concerning crimes and police emergencies. Broadcast orders to police patrol units in vicinity of complaint to investigate. Operate radio, telephone, or computer equipment to receive reports of fires and medical emergencies and relay information or orders to proper officials. Question callers to determine their locations and the nature of their problems to determine types of response needed. Receive incoming telephone or alarm system calls regarding emergency and non-emergency police and fire service, emergency ambulance service, information, and after-hours calls for departments within a city. Determine response requirements and relative priorities of situations and dispatch units in accordance with established procedures. Record details of calls, dispatches, and messages. Enter, update, and retrieve information from teletype networks and computerized data systems regarding such things as wanted persons, stolen

P

property, vehicle registration, and stolen vehicles. Maintain access to, and security of, highly sensitive materials. Relay information and messages to and from emergency sites, to law enforcement agencies, and to all other individuals or groups requiring notification. Scan status charts and computer screens and contact emergency response field units to determine emergency units available for dispatch. Observe alarm registers and scan maps to determine whether a specific emergency is in the dispatch service area. Maintain files of information relating to emergency calls such as personnel rosters and emergency call-out and pager files. Monitor various radio frequencies such as those used by public works departments, school security, and civil defense to keep apprised of developing situations. Learn material and pass required tests for certification. Read and effectively interpret small-scale maps and information from a computer screen to determine locations and provide directions. Answer routine inquiries and refer calls not requiring dispatches to appropriate departments and agencies. Test and adjust communication and alarm systems and report malfunctions to maintenance units. Provide emergency medical instructions to callers. Monitor alarm systems to detect emergencies such as fires and illegal entry into establishments. Operate and maintain mobile dispatch vehicles and equipment.

Personality Type: Conventional. These occupations frequently involve following set procedures and routines and can include working with data and details more than with ideas. Usually there is a clear line of authority to follow.

GOE—Interest Area/Cluster: 03. Arts and Communication. **Work Group:** 03.10. Communications Technology. **Other Jobs in This Work Group:** Air Traffic Controllers; Airfield Operations Specialists; Dispatchers, Except Police, Fire, and Ambulance; Telephone Operators.

Skills—Negotiation: Bringing others together and trying to reconcile differences. **Operation Monitoring:** Watching gauges, dials, or other indicators to make sure a machine is working properly.

Education and Training Program: No related CIP programs; this job is learned through moderate-term on-the-job training. **Related Knowledge/Courses—Telecommunications:** Transmission, broadcasting, switching, control, and operation of telecommunications systems. **Customer and Personal Service:** Principles and processes for providing customer and personal services, including needs assessment techniques, quality service standards, alternative delivery systems, and customer satisfaction evaluation techniques. **Clerical Practices:** Administrative and clerical procedures

and systems such as word-processing systems, filing and records management systems, stenography and transcription, forms, design principles, and other office procedures and terminology. **Law and Government:** Laws, legal codes, court procedures, precedents, government regulations, executive orders, agency rules, and the democratic political process. **Psychology:** Human behavior and performance, mental processes, psychological research methods, and the assessment and treatment of behavioral and affective disorders. **Public Safety and Security:** Weaponry; public safety; security operations, rules, regulations, precautions, and prevention; and the protection of people, data, and property.

Work Environment: Indoors; noisy; contaminants; sitting; using hands on objects, tools, or controls; repetitive motions.

Political Science Teachers, Postsecondary

- ❋ Education/Training Required: Doctoral degree
- ❋ Annual Earnings: $63,100
- ❋ Beginning Wage: $35,600
- ❋ Earnings Growth Potential: High
- ❋ Growth: 22.9%
- ❋ Annual Job Openings: 2,435
- ❋ Self-Employed: 0.4%
- ❋ Part-Time: 27.8%

Teach courses in political science, international affairs, and international relations. Initiate, facilitate, and moderate classroom discussions. Prepare and deliver lectures to undergraduate or graduate students on topics such as classical political thought, international relations, and democracy and citizenship. Evaluate and grade students' classwork, assignments, and papers. Compile, administer, and grade examinations or assign this work to others. Prepare course materials such as syllabi, homework assignments, and handouts. Keep abreast of developments in their field by reading current literature, talking with colleagues, and participating in professional conferences. Plan, evaluate, and revise curricula, course content, and course materials and methods of instruction. Maintain student attendance records, grades, and other required records. Maintain regularly scheduled office hours in order to advise and assist students. Advise students on academic and vocational curricula and on career issues. Select and obtain materials and supplies such as textbooks. Conduct research in a particular field of knowledge and publish findings in professional journals, books, and electronic media. Supervise undergraduate and graduate teaching, internship, and research work. Collaborate with colleagues to address teaching and research issues. Serve on academic or administrative committees that deal with institutional policies, departmental matters, and academic issues. Participate in student recruitment, registration, and placement activities. Participate in campus and community events. Compile bibliographies of specialized materials for outside reading assignments. Act as advisers to student organizations. Perform administrative duties such as serving as department head. Write grant proposals to procure external research funding. Provide professional consulting services to government and industry.

Personality Type: Social. These occupations frequently involve working with, communicating with, and teaching people and often involve helping or providing service to others.

GOE—Interest Area/Cluster: 05. Education and Training. **Work Group:** 05.03. Postsecondary and Adult Teaching and Instructing. **Other Jobs in This Work Group:** Adult Literacy, Remedial Education, and GED Teachers and Instructors; Agricultural Sciences Teachers, Postsecondary; Anthropology and Archeology Teachers, Postsecondary; Architecture Teachers, Postsecondary; Area, Ethnic, and Cultural Studies Teachers, Postsecondary; Art, Drama, and Music Teachers, Postsecondary; Atmospheric, Earth, Marine, and Space Sciences Teachers, Postsecondary; Biological Science Teachers, Postsecondary; Business Teachers, Postsecondary; Chemistry Teachers, Postsecondary; Communications Teachers, Postsecondary; Computer Science Teachers, Postsecondary; Criminal Justice and Law Enforcement Teachers, Postsecondary; Economics Teachers, Postsecondary; Education Teachers, Postsecondary; Engineering Teachers, Postsecondary; English Language and Literature Teachers, Postsecondary; Environmental Science Teachers, Postsecondary; Farm and Home Management Advisors; Foreign Language and Literature Teachers, Postsecondary; Forestry and Conservation Science Teachers, Postsecondary; Geography Teachers, Postsecondary; Graduate Teaching Assistants; Health Specialties Teachers, Postsecondary; History Teachers, Postsecondary; Home Economics Teachers, Postsecondary; Law Teachers, Postsecondary; Library Science Teachers, Postsecondary; Mathematical Science Teachers, Postsecondary; Nursing Instructors and Teachers, Postsecondary; Philosophy and Religion Teachers, Postsecondary; Physics Teachers, Postsecondary; Psychology Teachers, Postsecondary;

Recreation and Fitness Studies Teachers, Postsecondary; Self-Enrichment Education Teachers; Social Work Teachers, Postsecondary; Sociology Teachers, Postsecondary; Vocational Education Teachers, Postsecondary.

Skills—Writing: Communicating effectively with others in writing as indicated by the needs of the audience. **Instructing:** Teaching others how to do something. **Reading Comprehension:** Understanding written sentences and paragraphs in work-related documents. **Learning Strategies:** Using multiple approaches when learning or teaching new things. **Persuasion:** Persuading others to approach things differently. **Critical Thinking:** Using logic and analysis to identify the strengths and weaknesses of different approaches. **Speaking:** Talking to others to effectively convey information. **Active Learning:** Working with new material or information to grasp its implications.

Education and Training Programs: American Government and Politics (United States); Political Science and Government, General; Political Science and Government, Other; Social Science Teacher Education. **Related Knowledge/Courses—History and Archeology:** Historical events and their causes, indicators, and impact on particular civilizations and cultures. **Philosophy and Theology:** Different philosophical systems and religions, including their basic principles, values, ethics, ways of thinking, customs, and practices and their impact on human culture. **Sociology and Anthropology:** Group behavior and dynamics; societal trends and influences; and cultures and their history, migrations, ethnicity, and origins. **Geography:** Various methods for describing the location and distribution of land, sea, and air masses, including their physical locations, relationships, and characteristics. **Law and Government:** Laws, legal codes, court procedures, precedents, government regulations, executive orders, agency rules, and the democratic political process. **English Language:** The structure and content of the English language, including the meaning and spelling of words, rules of composition, and grammar.

Work Environment: Indoors; sitting.

Political Scientists

❀ Education/Training Required: Master's degree
❀ Annual Earnings: $91,580
❀ Beginning Wage: $37,960
❀ Earnings Growth Potential: Very high
❀ Growth: 5.3%
❀ Annual Job Openings: 318
❀ Self-Employed: 7.5%
❀ Part-Time: 20.1%

Study the origin, development, and operation of political systems. Research a wide range of subjects, such as relations between the United States and foreign countries, the beliefs and institutions of foreign nations, or the politics of small towns or a major metropolis. May study topics such as public opinion, political decision making, and ideology. May analyze the structure and operation of governments, as well as various political entities. May conduct public opinion surveys, analyze election results, or analyze public documents. Teach political science. Disseminate research results through academic publications, written reports, or public presentations. Identify issues for research and analysis. Develop and test theories, using information from interviews, newspapers, periodicals, case law, historical papers, polls, and/or statistical sources. Maintain current knowledge of government policy decisions. Collect, analyze, and interpret data such as election results and public opinion surveys; report on findings, recommendations, and conclusions. Interpret and analyze policies; public issues; legislation; and the operations of governments, businesses, and organizations. Evaluate programs and policies and make related recommendations to institutions and organizations. Write drafts of legislative proposals and prepare speeches, correspondence, and policy papers for governmental use. Forecast political, economic, and social trends. Consult with and advise government officials, civic bodies, research agencies, the media, political parties, and others concerned with political issues. Provide media commentary and/or criticism related to public policy and political issues and events.

Personality Type: Investigative. These occupations frequently involve working with ideas and require an extensive amount of thinking. They can involve searching for facts and figuring out problems mentally.

GOE—Interest Area/Cluster: 15. Scientific Research, Engineering, and Mathematics. **Work Group:** 15.04. Social

Sciences. **Other Jobs in This Work Group:** Anthropologists; Anthropologists and Archeologists; Archeologists; Economists; Historians; Industrial-Organizational Psychologists; School Psychologists; Sociologists.

Skills—Writing: Communicating effectively with others in writing as indicated by the needs of the audience. **Reading Comprehension:** Understanding written sentences and paragraphs in work-related documents. **Critical Thinking:** Using logic and analysis to identify the strengths and weaknesses of different approaches. **Speaking:** Talking to others to effectively convey information. **Active Learning:** Working with new material or information to grasp its implications. **Instructing:** Teaching others how to do something. **Complex Problem Solving:** Identifying complex problems, reviewing the options, and implementing solutions. **Persuasion:** Persuading others to approach things differently.

Education and Training Programs: American Government and Politics (United States); Canadian Government and Politics; International/Global Studies; Political Science and Government, General; Political Science and Government, Other. **Related Knowledge/Courses—History and Archeology:** Historical events and their causes, indicators, and impact on particular civilizations and cultures. **Law and Government:** Laws, legal codes, court procedures, precedents, government regulations, executive orders, agency rules, and the democratic political process. **Philosophy and Theology:** Different philosophical systems and religions, including their basic principles, values, ethics, ways of thinking, customs, and practices and their impact on human culture. **Sociology and Anthropology:** Group behavior and dynamics; societal trends and influences; and cultures and their history, migrations, ethnicity, and origins. **Foreign Language:** The structure and content of a foreign (non-English) language, including the meaning and spelling of words, rules of composition and grammar, and pronunciation. **Geography:** Various methods for describing the location and distribution of land, sea, and air masses, including their physical locations, relationships, and characteristics.

Work Environment: Indoors; sitting.

Postal Service Mail Carriers

- ❈ Education/Training Required: Short-term on-the-job training
- ❈ Annual Earnings: $44,500
- ❈ Beginning Wage: $34,990
- ❈ Earnings Growth Potential: Very low
- ❈ Growth: 1.0%
- ❈ Annual Job Openings: 16,710
- ❈ Self-Employed: 0.0%
- ❈ Part-Time: 7.1%

Sort mail for delivery. Deliver mail on established routes by vehicle or on foot. Obtain signed receipts for registered, certified, and insured mail; collect associated charges; and complete any necessary paperwork. Sort mail for delivery, arranging it in delivery sequence. Deliver mail to residences and business establishments along specified routes by walking and/or driving, using a combination of satchels, carts, cars, and small trucks. Return to the post office with mail collected from homes, businesses, and public mailboxes. Turn in money and receipts collected along mail routes. Sign for cash-on-delivery and registered mail before leaving the post office. Record address changes and redirect mail for those addresses. Hold mail for customers who are away from delivery locations. Bundle mail in preparation for delivery or transportation to relay boxes. Leave notices telling patrons where to collect mail that could not be delivered. Meet schedules for the collection and return of mail. Return incorrectly addressed mail to senders. Maintain accurate records of deliveries. Answer customers' questions about postal services and regulations. Provide customers with change of address cards and other forms. Report any unusual circumstances concerning mail delivery, including the condition of street letter boxes. Register, certify, and insure parcels and letters. Travel to post offices to pick up the mail for routes and/or pick up mail from postal relay boxes. Enter change-of-address orders into computers that process forwarding address stickers. Complete forms that notify publishers of address changes. Sell stamps and money orders.

Personality Type: Conventional. These occupations frequently involve following set procedures and routines and can include working with data and details more than with ideas. Usually there is a clear line of authority to follow.

GOE—Interest Area/Cluster: 16. Transportation, Distribution, and Logistics. **Work Group:** 16.06. Other Services Requiring Driving. **Other Jobs in This Work Group:** Ambulance Drivers and Attendants, Except Emergency Medical Technicians; Bus Drivers, School; Bus Drivers, Transit and Intercity; Couriers and Messengers; Driver/Sales Workers; Parking Lot Attendants; Taxi Drivers and Chauffeurs.

Skill—None met the criteria.

Education and Training Program: General Office Occupations and Clerical Services. **Related Knowledge/Courses— Transportation:** Principles and methods for moving people or goods by air, rail, sea, or road, including their relative costs, advantages, and limitations. **Public Safety and Security:** Weaponry; public safety; security operations, rules, regulations, precautions, and prevention; and the protection of people, data, and property.

Work Environment: Outdoors; very hot or cold; contaminants; standing; using hands on objects, tools, or controls; repetitive motions.

Preschool Teachers, Except Special Education

- ❈ Education/Training Required: Postsecondary vocational training
- ❈ Annual Earnings: $23,130
- ❈ Beginning Wage: $15,380
- ❈ Earnings Growth Potential: Low
- ❈ Growth: 26.3%
- ❈ Annual Job Openings: 78,172
- ❈ Self-Employed: 1.1%
- ❈ Part-Time: 25.1%

Instruct children (normally up to 5 years of age) in activities designed to promote social, physical, and intellectual growth needed for primary school in preschool, day care center, or other child development facility. May be required to hold state certification. Provide a variety of materials and resources for children to explore, manipulate, and use, both in learning activities and in imaginative play. Attend to children's basic needs by feeding them, dressing them, and changing their diapers. Establish and enforce rules for behavior and procedures for maintaining order. Read books to entire classes or to small groups. Teach basic skills such as color, shape, number, and letter recognition; personal hygiene; and social skills. Organize and lead activities designed to promote physical, mental, and social development, such as games, arts and crafts, music, storytelling, and field trips. Observe and evaluate children's performance, behavior, social development, and physical health. Meet with parents and guardians to discuss their children's progress and needs, determine their priorities for their children, and suggest ways that they can promote learning and development. Identify children showing signs of emotional, developmental, or health-related problems and discuss them with supervisors, parents or guardians, and child development specialists. Enforce all administration policies and rules governing students. Prepare materials and classrooms for class activities. Serve meals and snacks in accordance with nutritional guidelines. Teach proper eating habits and personal hygiene. Assimilate arriving children to the school environment by greeting them, helping them remove outerwear, and selecting activities of interest to them. Adapt teaching methods and instructional materials to meet students' varying needs and interests. Establish clear objectives for all lessons, units, and projects and communicate those objectives to children. Demonstrate activities to children. Arrange indoor and outdoor space to facilitate creative play, motor-skill activities, and safety. Plan and conduct activities for a balanced program of instruction, demonstration, and work time that provides students with opportunities to observe, question, and investigate. Maintain accurate and complete student records as required by laws, district policies, and administrative regulations.

Personality Type: Social. These occupations frequently involve working with, communicating with, and teaching people and often involve helping or providing service to others.

GOE—Interest Area/Cluster: 05. Education and Training. **Work Group:** 05.02. Preschool, Elementary, and Secondary Teaching and Instructing. **Other Jobs in This Work Group:** Elementary School Teachers, Except Special Education; Kindergarten Teachers, Except Special Education; Middle School Teachers, Except Special and Vocational Education; Secondary School Teachers, Except Special and Vocational Education; Special Education Teachers, Middle School; Special Education Teachers, Preschool, Kindergarten, and Elementary School; Special Education Teachers, Secondary School; Teacher Assistants; Vocational Education Teachers, Middle School; Vocational Education Teachers, Secondary School.

Skills—Learning Strategies: Using multiple approaches when learning or teaching new things. **Social Perceptiveness:** Being aware of others' reactions and understanding why they react the way they do. **Writing:** Communicating effectively with others in writing as indicated by the needs of the audience. **Negotiation:** Bringing others together and trying to reconcile differences.

Education and Training Programs: Child Care and Support Services Management; Early Childhood Education and Teaching; Montessori Teacher Education. **Related Knowledge/Courses—Philosophy and Theology:** Different philosophical systems and religions, including their basic principles, values, ethics, ways of thinking, customs, and practices and their impact on human culture. **Sociology and Anthropology:** Group behavior and dynamics; societal trends and influences; and cultures and their history, migrations, ethnicity, and origins. **Psychology:** Human behavior and performance, mental processes, psychological research methods, and the assessment and treatment of behavioral and affective disorders. **Customer and Personal Service:** Principles and processes for providing customer and personal services, including needs assessment techniques, quality service standards, alternative delivery systems, and customer satisfaction evaluation techniques. **Education and Training:** Instructional methods and training techniques, including curriculum design principles, learning theory, group and individual teaching techniques, design of individual development plans, and test design principles.

Work Environment: Indoors; standing; walking and running; bending or twisting the body.

Private Detectives and Investigators

* Education/Training Required: Work experience in a related occupation
* Annual Earnings: $37,640
* Beginning Wage: $20,990
* Earnings Growth Potential: High
* Growth: 18.2%
* Annual Job Openings: 7,329
* Self-Employed: 29.7%
* Part-Time: 11.1%

Detect occurrences of unlawful acts or infractions of rules in private establishments or seek, examine, and compile information for clients. Question persons to obtain evidence for cases of divorce, child custody, or missing persons or information about an individual's character or financial status. Conduct private investigations on a paid basis. Confer with establishment officials, security departments, police, or postal officials to identify problems, provide information, and receive instructions. Observe and document activities of individuals to detect unlawful acts or to obtain evidence for cases, using binoculars and still or video cameras. Investigate companies' financial standings or locate funds stolen by embezzlers, using accounting skills. Monitor industrial or commercial properties to enforce conformance to establishment rules and to protect people or property. Search computer databases, credit reports, public records, tax and legal filings, and other resources to locate persons or to compile information for investigations. Write reports and case summaries to document investigations. Count cash and review transactions, sales checks, and register tapes to verify amounts and to identify shortages. Perform undercover operations such as evaluating employee performance and honesty by posing as customers or employees. Expose fraudulent insurance claims or stolen funds. Alert appropriate personnel to suspects' locations. Conduct background investigations of individuals, such as pre-employment checks, to obtain information about each individual's character, financial status, or personal history. Testify at hearings and court trials to present evidence. Warn troublemakers causing problems on establishment premises and eject them from premises when necessary. Obtain and analyze information on suspects, crimes, and disturbances to solve cases, identify criminal activity, and gather information for court cases. Apprehend suspects and release them to law-enforcement authorities or security personnel.

Personality Type: Enterprising. These occupations frequently involve starting up and carrying out projects and can involve leading people and making many decisions. They sometimes require risk taking and often deal with business.

GOE—Interest Area/Cluster: 12. Law and Public Safety. **Work Group:** 12.05. Safety and Security. **Other Jobs in This Work Group:** Animal Control Workers; Crossing Guards; Gaming Surveillance Officers and Gaming Investigators; Lifeguards, Ski Patrol, and Other Recreational Protective Service Workers; Security Guards; Transportation Security Screeners.

Skills—Management of Financial Resources: Determining how money will be spent to get the work done and accounting for these expenditures. **Persuasion:** Persuading others to approach things differently. **Time Management:** Managing one's own time and the time of others. **Writing:** Communicating effectively with others in writing as indicated by the needs of the audience. **Service Orientation:** Actively looking for ways to help people. **Technology Design:** Generating or adapting equipment and technology

to serve user needs. **Speaking:** Talking to others to effectively convey information. **Judgment and Decision Making:** Weighing the relative costs and benefits of a potential action.

Education and Training Program: Criminal Justice/Police Science. **Related Knowledge/Courses—Clerical Practices:** Administrative and clerical procedures and systems such as word-processing systems, filing and records management systems, stenography and transcription, forms, design principles, and other office procedures and terminology. **Law and Government:** Laws, legal codes, court procedures, precedents, government regulations, executive orders, agency rules, and the democratic political process. **Customer and Personal Service:** Principles and processes for providing customer and personal services, including needs assessment techniques, quality service standards, alternative delivery systems, and customer satisfaction evaluation techniques. **Computers and Electronics:** Electric circuit boards, processors, chips, and computer hardware and software, including applications and programming. **Sales and Marketing:** Principles and methods involved in showing, promoting, and selling products or services. This includes marketing strategies and tactics, product demonstration and sales techniques, and sales control systems. **Mathematics:** Numbers and their operations and interrelationships, including arithmetic, algebra, geometry, calculus, and statistics and their applications.

Work Environment: Outdoors; noisy; very hot or cold; very bright or dim lighting; sitting; using hands on objects, tools, or controls.

Probation Officers and Correctional Treatment Specialists

- ❋ Education/Training Required: Bachelor's degree
- ❋ Annual Earnings: $44,510
- ❋ Beginning Wage: $28,400
- ❋ Earnings Growth Potential: Medium
- ❋ Growth: 10.9%
- ❋ Annual Job Openings: 18,335
- ❋ Self-Employed: 0.1%
- ❋ Part-Time: 12.0%

Provide social services to assist in rehabilitation of law offenders in custody or on probation or parole. Make recommendations for actions involving formulation of

rehabilitation plan and treatment of offender, including conditional release and education and employment stipulations. Prepare and maintain case folder for each assigned inmate or offender. Write reports describing offenders' progress. Inform offenders or inmates of requirements of conditional release, such as office visits, restitution payments, or educational and employment stipulations. Discuss with offenders how such issues as drug and alcohol abuse and anger management problems might have played roles in their criminal behavior. Gather information about offenders' backgrounds by talking to offenders, their families and friends, and other people who have relevant information. Develop rehabilitation programs for assigned offenders or inmates, establishing rules of conduct, goals, and objectives. Develop liaisons and networks with other parole officers, community agencies, staff in correctional institutions, psychiatric facilities, and after-care agencies to make plans for helping offenders with life adjustments. Arrange for medical, mental health, or substance abuse treatment services according to individual needs and court orders. Provide offenders or inmates with assistance in matters concerning detainers, sentences in other jurisdictions, writs, and applications for social assistance. Arrange for post-release services such as employment, housing, counseling, education, and social activities. Recommend remedial action or initiate court action when terms of probation or parole are not complied with. Interview probationers and parolees regularly to evaluate their progress in accomplishing goals and maintaining the terms specified in their probation contracts and rehabilitation plans. Supervise people on community-based sentences, including people on electronically monitored home detention. Assess the suitability of penitentiary inmates for release under parole and statutory release programs and submit recommendations to parole boards. Investigate alleged parole violations, using interviews, surveillance, and search and seizure. Conduct prehearing and presentencing investigations and testify in court regarding offenders' backgrounds and recommended sentences and sentencing conditions.

Personality Type: Social. These occupations frequently involve working with, communicating with, and teaching people and often involve helping or providing service to others.

GOE—Interest Area/Cluster: 10. Human Service. **Work Group:** 10.01. Counseling and Social Work. **Other Jobs in This Work Group:** Child, Family, and School Social Workers; Clinical Psychologists; Clinical, Counseling, and School Psychologists; Counseling Psychologists; Marriage and Family Therapists; Medical and Public Health Social Workers; Mental Health and Substance Abuse Social Workers; Mental Health Counselors; Rehabilitation Counselors; Residential Advisors; Social and Human Service Assistants; Substance Abuse and Behavioral Disorder Counselors.

Skills—Social Perceptiveness: Being aware of others' reactions and understanding why they react the way they do. **Persuasion:** Persuading others to approach things differently. **Negotiation:** Bringing others together and trying to reconcile differences. **Management of Personnel Resources:** Motivating, developing, and directing people as they work; identifying the best people for the job. **Time Management:** Managing one's own time and the time of others. **Monitoring:** Assessing how well one is doing when learning or doing something. **Writing:** Communicating effectively with others in writing as indicated by the needs of the audience. **Learning Strategies:** Using multiple approaches when learning or teaching new things.

Education and Training Program: Social Work. **Related Knowledge/Courses—Therapy and Counseling:** Information and techniques needed to rehabilitate physical and mental ailments and to provide career guidance, including alternative treatments, rehabilitation equipment and its proper use, and methods to evaluate treatment effects. **Psychology:** Human behavior and performance, mental processes, psychological research methods, and the assessment and treatment of behavioral and affective disorders. **Sociology and Anthropology:** Group behavior and dynamics; societal trends and influences; and cultures and their history, migrations, ethnicity, and origins. **Philosophy and Theology:** Different philosophical systems and religions, including their basic principles, values, ethics, ways of thinking, customs, and practices and their impact on human culture. **Law and Government:** Laws, legal codes, court procedures, precedents, government regulations, executive orders, agency rules, and the democratic political process. **Public Safety and Security:** Weaponry; public safety; security operations, rules, regulations, precautions, and prevention; and the protection of people, data, and property.

Work Environment: More often indoors than outdoors; very hot or cold; disease or infections; sitting.

Producers

- ✳ Education/Training Required: Work experience plus degree
- ✳ Annual Earnings: $61,090
- ✳ Beginning Wage: $28,980
- ✳ Earnings Growth Potential: Very high
- ✳ Growth: 11.1%
- ✳ Annual Job Openings: 8,992
- ✳ Self-Employed: 29.5%
- ✳ Part-Time: 9.0%

The job openings listed here are shared with Directors—Stage, Motion Pictures, Television, and Radio; Program Directors; Talent Directors; and Technical Directors/Managers.

Plan and coordinate various aspects of radio, television, stage, or motion picture production, such as selecting script; coordinating writing, directing, and editing; and arranging financing. Coordinate the activities of writers, directors, managers, and other personnel throughout the production process. Monitor post-production processes to ensure accurate completion of all details. Perform management activities such as budgeting, scheduling, planning, and marketing. Determine production size, content, and budget, establishing details such as production schedules and management policies. Compose and edit scripts or provide screenwriters with story outlines from which scripts can be written. Conduct meetings with staff to discuss production progress and to ensure production objectives are attained. Resolve personnel problems that arise during the production process by acting as liaisons between dissenting parties when necessary. Produce shows for special occasions, such as holidays or testimonials. Edit and write news stories from information collected by reporters. Write and submit proposals to bid on contracts for projects. Hire directors, principal cast members, and key production staff members. Arrange financing for productions. Select plays, scripts, books, or ideas to be produced. Review film, recordings, or rehearsals to ensure conformance to production and broadcast standards. Perform administrative duties such as preparing operational reports, distributing rehearsal call sheets and script copies, and arranging for rehearsal quarters. Obtain and distribute costumes, props, music, and studio equipment needed to complete productions. Negotiate contracts with artistic personnel, often in accordance with collective bargaining agreements. Maintain knowledge of minimum wages and working conditions established by unions or associations of actors and technicians. Plan and coordinate the production of musical recordings, selecting music and directing performers. Negotiate with parties, including independent producers and the distributors and broadcasters who will be handling completed productions. Develop marketing plans for finished products, collaborating with sales associates to supervise product distribution. Determine and direct the content of radio programming.

Personality Type: Enterprising. These occupations frequently involve starting up and carrying out projects and can involve leading people and making many decisions. They sometimes require risk taking and often deal with business.

GOE—Interest Area/Cluster: 03. Arts and Communication. **Work Group:** 03.01. Managerial Work in Arts and Communication. **Other Jobs in This Work Group:** Agents and Business Managers of Artists, Performers, and Athletes; Art Directors; Producers and Directors; Program Directors; Public Relations Managers; Technical Directors/Managers.

Skills—Monitoring: Assessing how well one is doing when learning or doing something. **Writing:** Communicating effectively with others in writing as indicated by the needs of the audience. **Management of Financial Resources:** Determining how money will be spent to get the work done and accounting for these expenditures. **Management of Personnel Resources:** Motivating, developing, and directing people as they work; identifying the best people for the job. **Negotiation:** Bringing others together and trying to reconcile differences. **Coordination:** Adjusting actions in relation to others' actions. **Equipment Selection:** Determining the kind of tools and equipment needed to do a job. **Speaking:** Talking to others to effectively convey information.

Education and Training Programs: Cinematography and Film/Video Production; Directing and Theatrical Production; Drama and Dramatics/Theatre Arts, General; Dramatic/Theatre Arts and Stagecraft, Other; Film/Cinema Studies; Radio and Television; Theatre/Theatre Arts Management. **Related Knowledge/Courses—Communications and Media:** Media production, communication, and dissemination techniques and methods, including alternative ways to inform and entertain via written, oral, and visual media. **Fine Arts:** Theory and techniques required to produce, compose, and perform works of music, dance, visual arts, drama, and sculpture. **Clerical Practices:** Administrative and clerical procedures and systems such as word-processing systems, filing and records management systems, stenography and transcription, forms, design principles, and other office procedures and terminology. **Sales and**

Marketing: Principles and methods involved in showing, promoting, and selling products or services. This includes marketing strategies and tactics, product demonstration and sales techniques, and sales control systems. Telecommunications: Transmission, broadcasting, switching, control, and operation of telecommunications systems. English Language: The structure and content of the English language, including the meaning and spelling of words, rules of composition, and grammar.

Work Environment: Indoors; sitting.

Product Safety Engineers

- ❋ Education/Training Required: Bachelor's degree
- ❋ Annual Earnings: $69,580
- ❋ Beginning Wage: $42,200
- ❋ Earnings Growth Potential: Medium
- ❋ Growth: 9.6%
- ❋ Annual Job Openings: 1,105
- ❋ Self-Employed: 1.1%
- ❋ Part-Time: 2.0%

The job openings listed here are shared with Fire-Prevention and Protection Engineers and with Industrial Safety and Health Engineers.

Develop and conduct tests to evaluate product safety levels and recommend measures to reduce or eliminate hazards. Report accident investigation findings. Conduct research to evaluate safety levels for products. Evaluate potential health hazards or damage that could occur from product misuse. Investigate causes of accidents, injuries, or illnesses related to product usage in order to develop solutions to minimize or prevent recurrence. Recommend procedures for detection, prevention, and elimination of physical, chemical, or other product hazards. Participate in preparation of product usage and precautionary label instructions.

Personality Type: Investigative. These occupations frequently involve working with ideas and require an extensive amount of thinking. They can involve searching for facts and figuring out problems mentally.

GOE—Interest Area/Cluster: 15. Scientific Research, Engineering, and Mathematics. **Work Group:** 15.08. Industrial and Safety Engineering. **Other Jobs in This Work Group:** Fire-Prevention and Protection Engineers; Health and Safety Engineers, Except Mining Safety Engineers

and Inspectors; Industrial Engineers; Industrial Safety and Health Engineers.

Skills—Science: Using scientific methods to solve problems. **Systems Analysis:** Determining how a system should work and how changes will affect outcomes. **Technology Design:** Generating or adapting equipment and technology to serve user needs. **Operations Analysis:** Analyzing needs and product requirements to create a design. **Quality Control Analysis:** Evaluating the quality or performance of products, services, or processes. **Mathematics:** Using mathematics to solve problems. **Systems Evaluation:** Looking at many indicators of system performance and taking into account their accuracy. **Persuasion:** Persuading others to approach things differently.

Education and Training Program: Environmental/Environmental Health Engineering. **Related Knowledge/Courses—Engineering and Technology:** Equipment, tools, and mechanical devices and their uses to produce motion, light, power, technology, and other applications. **Design:** Design techniques, principles, tools, and instruments involved in the production and use of precision technical plans, blueprints, drawings, and models. **Physics:** Physical principles, laws, and applications, including air, water, material dynamics, light, atomic principles, heat, electric theory, earth formations, and meteorological and related natural phenomena. **Mechanical Devices:** Machines and tools, including their designs, uses, benefits, repair, and maintenance. **Chemistry:** The composition, structure, and properties of substances and of the chemical processes and transformations that they undergo. This includes uses of chemicals and their interactions, danger signs, production techniques, and disposal methods. **Public Safety and Security:** Weaponry; public safety; security operations, rules, regulations, precautions, and prevention; and the protection of people, data, and property.

Work Environment: Indoors; sitting.

Production, Planning, and Expediting Clerks

- ❋ Education/Training Required: Moderate-term on-the-job training
- ❋ Annual Earnings: $39,690
- ❋ Beginning Wage: $24,520
- ❋ Earnings Growth Potential: Medium
- ❋ Growth: 4.2%
- ❋ Annual Job Openings: 52,735
- ❋ Self-Employed: 1.4%
- ❋ Part-Time: 6.7%

Coordinate and expedite the flow of work and materials within or between departments of an establishment according to production schedules. Duties include reviewing and distributing production, work, and shipment schedules; conferring with department supervisors to determine progress of work and completion dates; and compiling reports on progress of work, inventory levels, costs, and production problems. Examine documents, materials, and products and monitor work processes in order to assess completeness, accuracy, and conformance to standards and specifications. Review documents such as production schedules, work orders, and staffing tables to determine personnel and materials requirements and material priorities. Revise production schedules when required due to design changes, labor or material shortages, backlogs, or other interruptions, collaborating with management, marketing, sales, production, and engineering. Confer with department supervisors and other personnel to assess progress and discuss needed changes. Confer with establishment personnel, vendors, and customers to coordinate production and shipping activities and to resolve complaints or eliminate delays. Record production data, including volume produced, consumption of raw materials, and quality control measures. Requisition and maintain inventories of materials and supplies necessary to meet production demands. Calculate figures such as required amounts of labor and materials, manufacturing costs, and wages, using pricing schedules, adding machines, calculators, or computers. Distribute production schedules and work orders to departments. Compile information such as production rates and progress, materials inventories, materials used, and customer information so that status reports can be completed. Arrange for delivery, assembly, and distribution of supplies and parts in order to expedite flow of materials and meet production schedules. Contact suppliers to verify shipment details. Maintain files such as maintenance records, bills of lading, and cost reports. Plan production commitments and timetables for business units, specific programs, and/or jobs, using sales forecasts. Establish and prepare product construction directions and locations; information on required tools, materials, and equipment; numbers of workers needed; and cost projections. Compile and prepare documentation related to production sequences; transportation; personnel schedules; and purchase, maintenance, and repair orders. Provide documentation and information to account for delays, difficulties, and changes to cost estimates.

Personality Type: Conventional. These occupations frequently involve following set procedures and routines and can include working with data and details more than with ideas. Usually there is a clear line of authority to follow.

GOE—Interest Area/Cluster: 04. Business and Administration. **Work Group:** 04.07. Records and Materials Processing. **Other Jobs in This Work Group:** Correspondence Clerks; File Clerks; Human Resources Assistants, Except Payroll and Timekeeping; Marking Clerks; Meter Readers, Utilities; Office Clerks, General; Order Fillers, Wholesale and Retail Sales; Postal Service Clerks; Postal Service Mail Sorters, Processors, and Processing Machine Operators; Procurement Clerks; Shipping, Receiving, and Traffic Clerks; Stock Clerks and Order Fillers; Stock Clerks, Sales Floor; Stock Clerks—Stockroom, Warehouse, or Storage Yard; Weighers, Measurers, Checkers, and Samplers, Recordkeeping.

Skills—Management of Material Resources: Obtaining and seeing to the appropriate use of equipment, facilities, and materials needed to do certain work. **Operations Analysis:** Analyzing needs and product requirements to create a design. **Management of Financial Resources:** Determining how money will be spent to get the work done and accounting for these expenditures. **Systems Evaluation:** Looking at many indicators of system performance and taking into account their accuracy. **Negotiation:** Bringing others together and trying to reconcile differences. **Mathematics:** Using mathematics to solve problems. **Coordination:** Adjusting actions in relation to others' actions. **Persuasion:** Persuading others to approach things differently.

Education and Training Program: Parts, Warehousing, and Inventory Management Operations. **Related Knowledge/Courses—Production and Processing:** Inputs, outputs, raw materials, waste, quality control, costs, and techniques for maximizing the manufacture and distribution of goods. **Clerical Practices:** Administrative and clerical procedures and systems such as word-processing systems, filing and records management systems, stenography and transcription, forms, design principles, and other office procedures and terminology. **Computers and Electronics:** Electric circuit boards, processors, chips, and computer hardware and software, including applications and programming. **Administration and Management:** Principles and processes involved in business and organizational planning, coordination, and execution. This includes strategic planning, resource allocation, manpower modeling, leadership techniques, and production methods. **Mathematics:** Numbers and their operations and interrelationships, including arithmetic, algebra, geometry, calculus, and statistics and their applications. **Customer and Personal Service:** Principles and processes for providing customer and personal services, including needs assessment techniques, quality service standards, alternative delivery systems, and customer satisfaction evaluation techniques.

Work Environment: Indoors; noisy; contaminants; sitting.

Program Directors

- ❈ Education/Training Required: Work experience plus degree
- ❈ Annual Earnings: $61,090
- ❈ Beginning Wage: $28,980
- ❈ Earnings Growth Potential: Very high
- ❈ Growth: 11.1%
- ❈ Annual Job Openings: 8,992
- ❈ Self-Employed: 29.5%
- ❈ Part-Time: 9.0%

The job openings listed here are shared with Directors—Stage, Motion Pictures, Television, and Radio; Producers; Talent Directors; Technical Directors/Managers.

Direct and coordinate activities of personnel engaged in preparation of radio or television station program schedules and programs such as sports or news. Plan and schedule programming and event coverage based on broadcast length; time availability; and other factors such as community needs, ratings data, and viewer demographics. Monitor and review programming to ensure that schedules are met, guidelines are adhered to, and performances are of adequate quality. Direct and coordinate activities of personnel engaged in broadcast news, sports, or programming. Check completed program logs for accuracy and conformance with FCC rules and regulations and resolve program log inaccuracies. Establish work schedules and assign work to staff members. Coordinate activities between departments such

as news and programming. Perform personnel duties such as hiring staff and evaluating work performance. Evaluate new and existing programming for suitability and to assess the need for changes, using information such as audience surveys and feedback. Develop budgets for programming and broadcasting activities and monitor expenditures to ensure that they remain within budgetary limits. Confer with directors and production staff to discuss issues such as production and casting problems, budgets, policies, and news coverage. Select, acquire, and maintain programs, music, films, and other needed materials and obtain legal clearances for their use as necessary. Monitor network transmissions for advisories concerning daily program schedules, program content, special feeds, or program changes. Develop promotions for current programs and specials. Prepare copy and edit tape so that material is ready for broadcasting. Develop ideas for programs and features that a station could produce. Participate in the planning and execution of fundraising activities. Review information about programs and schedules to ensure accuracy and provide such information to local media outlets as necessary. Read news, read or record public service and promotional announcements, and otherwise participate as a member of an on-air shift as required. Operate and maintain on-air and production audio equipment. Direct setup of remote facilities and install or cancel programs at remote stations.

Personality Type: Enterprising. These occupations frequently involve starting up and carrying out projects and can involve leading people and making many decisions. They sometimes require risk taking and often deal with business.

GOE—Interest Area/Cluster: 03. Arts and Communication. **Work Group:** 03.01. Managerial Work in Arts and Communication. **Other Jobs in This Work Group:** Agents and Business Managers of Artists, Performers, and Athletes; Art Directors; Producers; Producers and Directors; Public Relations Managers; Technical Directors/Managers.

Skills—Operations Analysis: Analyzing needs and product requirements to create a design. **Management of Financial Resources:** Determining how money will be spent to get the work done and accounting for these expenditures. **Management of Personnel Resources:** Motivating, developing, and directing people as they work; identifying the best people for the job. **Coordination:** Adjusting actions in relation to others' actions. **Writing:** Communicating effectively with others in writing as indicated by the needs of the audience. **Time Management:** Managing one's own time and the time of others. **Equipment Selection:** Determining the kind of tools and equipment needed to do a job. **Monitoring:** Assessing how well one is doing when learning or doing something.

Education and Training Programs: Cinematography and Film/Video Production; Directing and Theatrical Production; Drama and Dramatics/Theatre Arts, General; Dramatic/Theatre Arts and Stagecraft, Other; Film/Cinema Studies; Radio and Television; Theatre/Theatre Arts Management. **Related Knowledge/Courses—Telecommunications:** Transmission, broadcasting, switching, control, and operation of telecommunications systems. **Communications and Media:** Media production, communication, and dissemination techniques and methods, including alternative ways to inform and entertain via written, oral, and visual media. **Computers and Electronics:** Electric circuit boards, processors, chips, and computer hardware and software, including applications and programming. **Clerical Practices:** Administrative and clerical procedures and systems such as word-processing systems, filing and records management systems, stenography and transcription, forms, design principles, and other office procedures and terminology. **Personnel and Human Resources:** Principles and procedures for personnel recruitment; selection; training; compensation and benefits; labor relations and negotiation; and personnel information systems. **Engineering and Technology:** Equipment, tools, and mechanical devices and their uses to produce motion, light, power, technology, and other applications.

Work Environment: Indoors; noisy; sitting.

Property, Real Estate, and Community Association Managers

* Education/Training Required: Bachelor's degree
* Annual Earnings: $43,670
* Beginning Wage: $20,800
* Earnings Growth Potential: Very high
* Growth: 15.1%
* Annual Job Openings: 49,916
* Self-Employed: 50.9%
* Part-Time: 16.1%

Plan, direct, or coordinate selling, buying, leasing, or governance activities of commercial, industrial, or residential real estate properties. Meet with prospective tenants to show properties, explain terms of occupancy, and provide information about local areas. Direct collection of monthly assessments; rental fees; and deposits and payment of insurance premiums, mortgage, taxes, and incurred operating expenses. Inspect grounds, facilities, and equipment routinely to determine necessity of repairs or maintenance. Investigate complaints, disturbances, and violations and resolve problems, following management rules and regulations. Manage and oversee operations, maintenance, administration, and improvement of commercial, industrial, or residential properties. Plan, schedule, and coordinate general maintenance, major repairs, and remodeling or construction projects for commercial or residential properties. Negotiate the sale, lease, or development of property and complete or review appropriate documents and forms. Maintain records of sales, rental or usage activity, special permits issued, maintenance and operating costs, or property availability. Determine and certify the eligibility of prospective tenants, following government regulations. Prepare detailed budgets and financial reports for properties. Direct and coordinate the activities of staff and contract personnel and evaluate their performance. Maintain contact with insurance carriers, fire and police departments, and other agencies to ensure protection and compliance with codes and regulations. Market vacant space to prospective tenants through leasing agents, advertising, or other methods. Solicit and analyze bids from contractors for repairs, renovations, and maintenance. Review rents to ensure that they are in line with rental markets. Prepare and administer contracts for provision of property services such as cleaning, maintenance, and security services. Purchase building and maintenance supplies, equipment, or furniture. Act as liaisons between on-site managers or tenants and owners. Confer regularly with community association members to ensure their needs are being met. Meet with boards of directors and committees to discuss and resolve legal and environmental issues or disputes between neighbors.

Personality Type: Enterprising. These occupations frequently involve starting up and carrying out projects and can involve leading people and making many decisions. They sometimes require risk taking and often deal with business.

GOE—Interest Area/Cluster: 14. Retail and Wholesale Sales and Service. **Work Group:** 14.01. Managerial Work in Retail/Wholesale Sales and Service. **Other Jobs in This Work Group:** Advertising and Promotions Managers; First-Line Supervisors/Managers of Non-Retail Sales Workers; First-Line Supervisors/Managers of Retail Sales Workers; Funeral Directors; Marketing Managers; Purchasing Managers; Sales Managers.

Skills—Management of Financial Resources: Determining how money will be spent to get the work done and accounting for these expenditures. **Management of Personnel Resources:** Motivating, developing, and directing people as they work; identifying the best people for the job. **Management of Material Resources:** Obtaining and seeing to the appropriate use of equipment, facilities, and materials needed to do certain work. **Time Management:** Managing one's own time and the time of others. **Repairing:** Repairing machines or systems, using the needed tools. **Judgment and Decision Making:** Weighing the relative costs and benefits of a potential action. **Installation:** Installing equipment, machines, wiring, or programs to meet specifications. **Coordination:** Adjusting actions in relation to others' actions.

Education and Training Program: Real Estate. **Related Knowledge/Courses—Sales and Marketing:** Principles and methods involved in showing, promoting, and selling products or services. This includes marketing strategies and tactics, product demonstration and sales techniques, and sales control systems. **Clerical Practices:** Administrative and clerical procedures and systems such as word-processing systems, filing and records management systems, stenography and transcription, forms, design principles, and other office procedures and terminology. **Economics and Accounting:** Economic and accounting principles and practices, the financial markets, banking, and the analysis and reporting of financial data. **Administration and Management:** Principles and processes involved in business and organizational planning, coordination, and execution. This includes strategic planning, resource allocation, manpower modeling, leadership techniques, and production methods. **Customer and Personal Service:** Principles and processes for providing customer and personal services, including needs assessment techniques, quality service standards, alternative delivery systems, and customer satisfaction evaluation techniques. **Building and Construction:** Materials, methods, and the appropriate tools to construct objects, structures, and buildings.

Work Environment: More often indoors than outdoors; sitting.

Prosthodontists

- ❋ Education/Training Required: First professional degree
- ❋ Annual Earnings: More than $145,600
- ❋ Beginning Wage: $75,450
- ❋ Earnings Growth Potential: Cannot be calculated
- ❋ Growth: 10.7%
- ❋ Annual Job Openings: 54
- ❋ Self-Employed: 51.3%
- ❋ Part-Time: 25.9%

Construct oral prostheses to replace missing teeth and other oral structures to correct natural and acquired deformation of mouth and jaws; to restore and maintain oral function, such as chewing and speaking; and to improve appearance. Replace missing teeth and associated oral structures with permanent fixtures, such as crowns and bridges, or removable fixtures, such as dentures. Fit prostheses to patients, making any necessary adjustments and modifications. Design and fabricate dental prostheses or supervise dental technicians and laboratory bench workers who construct the devices. Measure and take impressions of patients' jaws and teeth to determine the shape and size of dental prostheses, using face bows, dental articulators, recording devices, and other materials. Collaborate with general dentists, specialists, and other health professionals to develop solutions to dental and oral health concerns. Repair, reline, and/or rebase dentures. Restore function and aesthetics to traumatic injury victims or to individuals with diseases or birth defects. Use bonding technology on the surface of the teeth to change tooth shape or to close gaps. Treat facial pain and jaw joint problems. Place veneers onto teeth to conceal defects. Bleach discolored teeth to brighten and whiten them.

Personality Type: Investigative. These occupations frequently involve working with ideas and require an extensive amount of thinking. They can involve searching for facts and figuring out problems mentally.

GOE—Interest Area/Cluster: 08. Health Science. **Work Group:** 08.03. Dentistry. **Other Jobs in This Work Group:** Dental Assistants; Dental Hygienists; Dentists, General; Oral and Maxillofacial Surgeons; Orthodontists.

Skills—Science: Using scientific methods to solve problems. Management of Financial Resources: Determining how money will be spent to get the work done and accounting for these expenditures. Social Perceptiveness: Being aware of others' reactions and understanding why they react the way they do. Equipment Selection: Determining the kind of tools and equipment needed to do a job. Reading Comprehension: Understanding written sentences and paragraphs in work-related documents. Active Learning: Working with new material or information to grasp its implications. Complex Problem Solving: Identifying complex problems, reviewing the options, and implementing solutions. Technology Design: Generating or adapting equipment and technology to serve user needs.

Education and Training Programs: Prosthodontics Specialty; Prosthodontics/Prosthodontology (Cert, MS, PhD). Related Knowledge/Courses—Medicine and Dentistry: The information and techniques needed to diagnose and treat injuries, diseases, and deformities. This includes symptoms, treatment alternatives, drug properties and interactions, and preventive health-care measures. Biology: Plant and animal living tissue, cells, organisms, and entities, including their functions, interdependencies, and interactions with each other and the environment. Chemistry: The composition, structure, and properties of substances and of the chemical processes and transformations that they undergo. This includes uses of chemicals and their interactions, danger signs, production techniques, and disposal methods. Psychology: Human behavior and performance, mental processes, psychological research methods, and the assessment and treatment of behavioral and affective disorders. Engineering and Technology: Equipment, tools, and mechanical devices and their uses to produce motion, light, power, technology, and other applications. Sales and Marketing: Principles and methods involved in showing, promoting, and selling products or services. This includes marketing strategies and tactics, product demonstration and sales techniques, and sales control systems.

Work Environment: Indoors; noisy; contaminants; disease or infections; hazardous equipment; using hands on objects, tools, or controls.

Psychiatrists

- ❋ Education/Training Required: First professional degree
- ❋ Annual Earnings: More than $145,600
- ❋ Beginning Wage: $59,090
- ❋ Earnings Growth Potential: Cannot be calculated
- ❋ Growth: 14.2%
- ❋ Annual Job Openings: 38,027
- ❋ Self-Employed: 14.7%
- ❋ Part-Time: 8.1%

The job openings listed here are shared with Anesthesiologists; Family and General Practitioners; Internists, General; Obstetricians and Gynecologists; Pediatricians, General; and Surgeons.

Diagnose, treat, and help prevent disorders of the mind. Prescribe, direct, and administer psychotherapeutic treatments or medications to treat mental, emotional, or behavioral disorders. Analyze and evaluate patient data and test findings to diagnose nature and extent of mental disorders. Collaborate with physicians, psychologists, social workers, psychiatric nurses, or other professionals to discuss treatment plans and progress. Gather and maintain patient information and records, including social and medical histories obtained from patients, relatives, and other professionals. Design individualized care plans, using a variety of treatments. Counsel outpatients and other patients during office visits. Examine or conduct laboratory or diagnostic tests on patients to provide information on general physical conditions and mental disorders. Advise and inform guardians, relatives, and significant others of patients' conditions and treatments. Teach, take continuing education classes, attend conferences and seminars, and conduct research and publish findings to increase understanding of mental, emotional, and behavioral states and disorders. Review and evaluate treatment procedures and outcomes of other psychiatrists and medical professionals. Prepare and submit case reports and summaries to government and mental health agencies. Serve on committees to promote and maintain community mental health services and delivery systems.

Personality Type: Investigative. These occupations frequently involve working with ideas and require an extensive amount of thinking. They can involve searching for facts and figuring out problems mentally.

GOE—Interest Area/Cluster: 08. Health Science. Work Group: 08.02. Medicine and Surgery. Other Jobs in This

Work Group: Anesthesiologists; Family and General Practitioners; Internists, General; Medical Assistants; Medical Transcriptionists; Obstetricians and Gynecologists; Pediatricians, General; Pharmacists; Pharmacy Aides; Pharmacy Technicians; Physician Assistants; Registered Nurses; Surgeons; Surgical Technologists.

Skills—Social Perceptiveness: Being aware of others' reactions and understanding why they react the way they do. **Systems Evaluation:** Looking at many indicators of system performance and taking into account their accuracy. **Systems Analysis:** Determining how a system should work and how changes will affect outcomes. **Active Listening:** Listening to what other people are saying and asking questions as appropriate. **Writing:** Communicating effectively with others in writing as indicated by the needs of the audience. **Speaking:** Talking to others to effectively convey information. **Reading Comprehension:** Understanding written sentences and paragraphs in work-related documents. **Judgment and Decision Making:** Weighing the relative costs and benefits of a potential action.

Education and Training Programs: Child Psychiatry; Physical Medical and Rehabilitation/Psychiatry; Psychiatry. **Related Knowledge/Courses—Therapy and Counseling:** Information and techniques needed to rehabilitate physical and mental ailments and to provide career guidance, including alternative treatments, rehabilitation equipment and its proper use, and methods to evaluate treatment effects. **Medicine and Dentistry:** The information and techniques needed to diagnose and treat injuries, diseases, and deformities. This includes symptoms, treatment alternatives, drug properties and interactions, and preventive healthcare measures. **Psychology:** Human behavior and performance, mental processes, psychological research methods, and the assessment and treatment of behavioral and affective disorders. **Biology:** Plant and animal living tissue, cells, organisms, and entities, including their functions, interdependencies, and interactions with each other and the environment. **Sociology and Anthropology:** Group behavior and dynamics; societal trends and influences; and cultures and their history, migrations, ethnicity, and origins. **Philosophy and Theology:** Different philosophical systems and religions, including their basic principles, values, ethics, ways of thinking, customs, and practices and their impact on human culture.

Work Environment: Indoors; disease or infections; sitting.

Psychology Teachers, Postsecondary

- ✸ Education/Training Required: Doctoral degree
- ✸ Annual Earnings: $60,610
- ✸ Beginning Wage: $34,030
- ✸ Earnings Growth Potential: High
- ✸ Growth: 22.9%
- ✸ Annual Job Openings: 5,261
- ✸ Self-Employed: 0.4%
- ✸ Part-Time: 27.8%

Teach courses in psychology, such as child, clinical, and developmental psychology, and psychological counseling. Prepare and deliver lectures to undergraduate and/or graduate students on topics such as abnormal psychology, cognitive processes, and work motivation. Evaluate and grade students' classwork, laboratory work, assignments, and papers. Initiate, facilitate, and moderate classroom discussions. Compile, administer, and grade examinations or assign this work to others. Keep abreast of developments in their field by reading current literature, talking with colleagues, and participating in professional conferences. Prepare course materials such as syllabi, homework assignments, and handouts. Plan, evaluate, and revise curricula, course content, and course materials and methods of instruction. Maintain student attendance records, grades, and other required records. Supervise undergraduate and/or graduate teaching, internship, and research work. Maintain regularly scheduled office hours to advise and assist students. Conduct research in a particular field of knowledge and publish findings in professional journals, books, and electronic media. Advise students on academic and vocational curricula and on career issues. Select and obtain materials and supplies such as textbooks. Collaborate with colleagues to address teaching and research issues. Serve on academic or administrative committees that deal with institutional policies, departmental matters, and academic issues. Compile bibliographies of specialized materials for outside reading assignments. Participate in student recruitment, registration, and placement activities. Supervise students' laboratory work. Perform administrative duties such as serving as department head. Act as advisers to student organizations. Write grant proposals to procure external research funding. Participate in campus and community events. Provide professional consulting services to government and industry.

Personality Type: Social. These occupations frequently involve working with, communicating with, and teaching people and often involve helping or providing service to others.

GOE—Interest Area/Cluster: 05. Education and Training. **Work Group:** 05.03. Postsecondary and Adult Teaching and Instructing. **Other Jobs in This Work Group:** Adult Literacy, Remedial Education, and GED Teachers and Instructors; Agricultural Sciences Teachers, Postsecondary; Anthropology and Archeology Teachers, Postsecondary; Architecture Teachers, Postsecondary; Area, Ethnic, and Cultural Studies Teachers, Postsecondary; Art, Drama, and Music Teachers, Postsecondary; Atmospheric, Earth, Marine, and Space Sciences Teachers, Postsecondary; Biological Science Teachers, Postsecondary; Business Teachers, Postsecondary; Chemistry Teachers, Postsecondary; Communications Teachers, Postsecondary; Computer Science Teachers, Postsecondary; Criminal Justice and Law Enforcement Teachers, Postsecondary; Economics Teachers, Postsecondary; Education Teachers, Postsecondary; Engineering Teachers, Postsecondary; English Language and Literature Teachers, Postsecondary; Environmental Science Teachers, Postsecondary; Farm and Home Management Advisors; Foreign Language and Literature Teachers, Postsecondary; Forestry and Conservation Science Teachers, Postsecondary; Geography Teachers, Postsecondary; Graduate Teaching Assistants; Health Specialties Teachers, Postsecondary; History Teachers, Postsecondary; Home Economics Teachers, Postsecondary; Law Teachers, Postsecondary; Library Science Teachers, Postsecondary; Mathematical Science Teachers, Postsecondary; Nursing Instructors and Teachers, Postsecondary; Philosophy and Religion Teachers, Postsecondary; Physics Teachers, Postsecondary; Political Science Teachers, Postsecondary; Recreation and Fitness Studies Teachers, Postsecondary; Self-Enrichment Education Teachers; Social Work Teachers, Postsecondary; Sociology Teachers, Postsecondary; Vocational Education Teachers, Postsecondary.

Skills—Science: Using scientific methods to solve problems. **Learning Strategies:** Using multiple approaches when learning or teaching new things. **Instructing:** Teaching others how to do something. **Social Perceptiveness:** Being aware of others' reactions and understanding why they react the way they do. **Writing:** Communicating effectively with others in writing as indicated by the needs of the audience. **Reading Comprehension:** Understanding written sentences and paragraphs in work-related documents. **Critical Thinking:** Using logic and analysis to identify the strengths and weaknesses of different approaches. **Active**

Learning: Working with new material or information to grasp its implications.

Education and Training Programs: Clinical Psychology; Cognitive Psychology and Psycholinguistics; Community Psychology; Comparative Psychology; Counseling Psychology; Developmental and Child Psychology; Educational Psychology; Experimental Psychology; Industrial and Organizational Psychology; Marriage and Family Therapy; Personality Psychology; Physiological Psychology/Psychobiology; Psychology Teacher Education; Psychology, General; Psychometrics and Quantitative Psychology; School Psychology; Social Psychology; others. **Related Knowledge/Courses—Therapy and Counseling:** Information and techniques needed to rehabilitate physical and mental ailments and to provide career guidance, including alternative treatments, rehabilitation equipment and its proper use, and methods to evaluate treatment effects. **Psychology:** Human behavior and performance, mental processes, psychological research methods, and the assessment and treatment of behavioral and affective disorders. **Sociology and Anthropology:** Group behavior and dynamics; societal trends and influences; and cultures and their history, migrations, ethnicity, and origins. **Philosophy and Theology:** Different philosophical systems and religions, including their basic principles, values, ethics, ways of thinking, customs, and practices and their impact on human culture. **Education and Training:** Instructional methods and training techniques, including curriculum design principles, learning theory, group and individual teaching techniques, design of individual development plans, and test design principles. **English Language:** The structure and content of the English language, including the meaning and spelling of words, rules of composition, and grammar.

Work Environment: Indoors; sitting.

Public Relations Managers

- ❋ Education/Training Required: Work experience plus degree
- ❋ Annual Earnings: $86,470
- ❋ Beginning Wage: $44,870
- ❋ Earnings Growth Potential: High
- ❋ Growth: 16.9%
- ❋ Annual Job Openings: 5,781
- ❋ Self-Employed: 1.7%
- ❋ Part-Time: 5.4%

Plan and direct public relations programs designed to create and maintain a favorable public image for employer or client or, if engaged in fundraising, plan and direct activities to solicit and maintain funds for special projects and nonprofit organizations. Identify main client groups and audiences and determine the best way to communicate publicity information to them. Write interesting and effective press releases, prepare information for media kits, and develop and maintain company Internet or intranet Web pages. Develop and maintain the company's corporate image and identity, which includes the use of logos and signage. Manage communications budgets. Manage special events such as sponsorship of races, parties introducing new products, or other activities the firm supports to gain public attention through the media without advertising directly. Draft speeches for company executives and arrange interviews and other forms of contact for them. Assign, supervise, and review the activities of public relations staff. Evaluate advertising and promotion programs for compatibility with public relations efforts. Establish and maintain effective working relationships with local and municipal government officials and media representatives. Confer with labor relations managers to develop internal communications that keep employees informed of company activities. Direct activities of external agencies, establishments, and departments that develop and implement communication strategies and information programs. Formulate policies and procedures related to public information programs, working with public relations executives. Respond to requests for information about employers' activities or status. Establish goals for soliciting funds, develop policies for collection and safeguarding of contributions, and coordinate disbursement of funds. Facilitate consumer relations or the relationship between parts of the company such as the managers and employees or different branch offices. Maintain company archives. Manage in-house communication courses. Produce films and other video products, regulate their distribution, and operate film library. Observe and report on social, economic, and political trends that might affect employers.

Personality Type: Enterprising. These occupations frequently involve starting up and carrying out projects and can involve leading people and making many decisions. They sometimes require risk taking and often deal with business.

GOE—Interest Area/Cluster: 03. Arts and Communication. **Work Group:** 03.01. Managerial Work in Arts and Communication. **Other Jobs in This Work Group:** Agents and Business Managers of Artists, Performers, and Athletes;

Art Directors; Producers; Producers and Directors; Program Directors; Technical Directors/Managers.

Skills—Management of Financial Resources: Determining how money will be spent to get the work done and accounting for these expenditures. **Monitoring:** Assessing how well one is doing when learning or doing something. **Social Perceptiveness:** Being aware of others' reactions and understanding why they react the way they do. **Writing:** Communicating effectively with others in writing as indicated by the needs of the audience. **Service Orientation:** Actively looking for ways to help people. **Operations Analysis:** Analyzing needs and product requirements to create a design. **Speaking:** Talking to others to effectively convey information. **Persuasion:** Persuading others to approach things differently.

Education and Training Program: Public Relations/Image Management. **Related Knowledge/Courses—Sales and Marketing:** Principles and methods involved in showing, promoting, and selling products or services. This includes marketing strategies and tactics, product demonstration and sales techniques, and sales control systems. **Economics and Accounting:** Economic and accounting principles and practices, the financial markets, banking, and the analysis and reporting of financial data. **Foreign Language:** The structure and content of a foreign (non-English) language, including the meaning and spelling of words, rules of composition and grammar, and pronunciation. **Law and Government:** Laws, legal codes, court procedures, precedents, government regulations, executive orders, agency rules, and the democratic political process. **Education and Training:** Instructional methods and training techniques, including curriculum design principles, learning theory, group and individual teaching techniques, design of individual development plans, and test design principles. **English Language:** The structure and content of the English language, including the meaning and spelling of words, rules of composition, and grammar.

Work Environment: Indoors; sitting.

Public Relations Specialists

* ❋ Education/Training Required: Bachelor's degree
* ❋ Annual Earnings: $49,800
* ❋ Beginning Wage: $29,580
* ❋ Earnings Growth Potential: High
* ❋ Growth: 17.6%
* ❋ Annual Job Openings: 51,216
* ❋ Self-Employed: 4.9%
* ❋ Part-Time: 13.9%

Engage in promoting or creating good will for individuals, groups, or organizations by writing or selecting favorable publicity material and releasing it through various communications media. May prepare and arrange displays and make speeches. Prepare or edit organizational publications for internal and external audiences, including employee newsletters and stockholders' reports. Respond to requests for information from the media or designate another appropriate spokesperson or information source. Establish and maintain cooperative relationships with representatives of community, consumer, employee, and public interest groups. Plan and direct development and communication of informational programs to maintain favorable public and stockholder perceptions of an organization's accomplishments and agenda. Confer with production and support personnel to produce or coordinate production of advertisements and promotions. Arrange public appearances, lectures, contests, or exhibits for clients to increase product and service awareness and to promote goodwill. Study the objectives, promotional policies, and needs of organizations to develop public relations strategies that will influence public opinion or promote ideas, products, and services. Consult with advertising agencies or staff to arrange promotional campaigns in all types of media for products, organizations, or individuals. Confer with other managers to identify trends and key group interests and concerns or to provide advice on business decisions. Coach client representatives in effective communication with the public and with employees. Prepare and deliver speeches to further public relations objectives. Purchase advertising space and time as required to promote client's product or agenda. Plan and conduct market and public opinion research to test products or determine potential for product success, communicating results to client or management.

Personality Type: Enterprising. These occupations frequently involve starting up and carrying out projects and can involve leading people and making many decisions. They sometimes require risk taking and often deal with business.

GOE—Interest Area/Cluster: 03. Arts and Communication. **Work Group:** 03.03. News, Broadcasting, and Public Relations. **Other Jobs in This Work Group:** Broadcast News Analysts; Interpreters and Translators; Reporters and Correspondents.

Skills—Service Orientation: Actively looking for ways to help people. **Management of Financial Resources:** Determining how money will be spent to get the work done and accounting for these expenditures. **Persuasion:** Persuading others to approach things differently. **Writing:** Communicating effectively with others in writing as indicated by the needs of the audience. **Negotiation:** Bringing others together and trying to reconcile differences. **Social Perceptiveness:** Being aware of others' reactions and understanding why they react the way they do. **Judgment and Decision Making:** Weighing the relative costs and benefits of a potential action. **Monitoring:** Assessing how well one is doing when learning or doing something.

Education and Training Programs: Communication Studies/Speech Communication and Rhetoric; Family and Consumer Sciences/Human Sciences Communication; Health Communication; Political Communication; Public Relations/Image Management. **Related Knowledge/Courses—Sales and Marketing:** Principles and methods involved in showing, promoting, and selling products or services. This includes marketing strategies and tactics, product demonstration and sales techniques, and sales control systems. **Communications and Media:** Media production, communication, and dissemination techniques and methods, including alternative ways to inform and entertain via written, oral, and visual media. **Customer and Personal Service:** Principles and processes for providing customer and personal services, including needs assessment techniques, quality service standards, alternative delivery systems, and customer satisfaction evaluation techniques. **Sociology and Anthropology:** Group behavior and dynamics; societal trends and influences; and cultures and their history, migrations, ethnicity, and origins. **Clerical Practices:** Administrative and clerical procedures and systems such as word-processing systems, filing and records management systems, stenography and transcription, forms, design principles, and other office procedures and terminology. **Administration and Management:** Principles and processes involved in business and organizational planning, coordination, and execution. This includes strategic planning, resource allocation, manpower modeling, leadership techniques, and production methods.

Work Environment: Indoors; sitting.

Purchasing Agents, Except Wholesale, Retail, and Farm Products

- ❋ Education/Training Required: Long-term on-the-job training
- ❋ Annual Earnings: $52,460
- ❋ Beginning Wage: $32,580
- ❋ Earnings Growth Potential: Medium
- ❋ Growth: 0.1%
- ❋ Annual Job Openings: 22,349
- ❋ Self-Employed: 1.6%
- ❋ Part-Time: 3.8%

Purchase machinery, equipment, tools, parts, supplies, or services necessary for the operation of an establishment. Purchase raw or semi-finished materials for manufacturing. Purchase the highest-quality merchandise at the lowest possible price and in correct amounts. Prepare purchase orders, solicit bid proposals, and review requisitions for goods and services. Research and evaluate suppliers based on price, quality, selection, service, support, availability, reliability, production and distribution capabilities, and the supplier's reputation and history. Analyze price proposals, financial reports, and other data and information to determine reasonable prices. Monitor and follow applicable laws and regulations. Negotiate, or renegotiate, and administer contracts with suppliers, vendors, and other representatives. Monitor shipments to ensure that goods come in on time and trace shipments and follow up undelivered goods in the event of problems. Confer with staff, users, and vendors to discuss defective or unacceptable goods or services and determine corrective action. Evaluate and monitor contract performance to ensure compliance with contractual obligations and to determine need for changes. Maintain and review computerized or manual records of items purchased, costs, delivery, product performance, and inventories. Review catalogs, industry periodicals, directories, trade journals, and Internet sites and consult with other department personnel to locate necessary goods and services. Study sales records and inventory levels of current stock to develop strategic purchasing programs that facilitate employee access to supplies. Interview vendors and visit suppliers' plants and distribution centers to examine and learn about products, services, and prices. Arrange the payment of duty and freight charges. Hire, train, and/or supervise purchasing clerks, buyers, and expediters. Write and review product specifications, maintaining a working technical knowledge of the goods or services to be purchased. Monitor changes affecting supply and demand, tracking market conditions, price trends, or futures markets. Formulate policies and procedures for bid proposals and procurement of goods and services. Attend meetings, trade shows, conferences, conventions, and seminars to network with people in other purchasing departments.

Personality Type: Conventional. These occupations frequently involve following set procedures and routines and can include working with data and details more than with ideas. Usually there is a clear line of authority to follow.

GOE—Interest Area/Cluster: 14. Retail and Wholesale Sales and Service. **Work Group:** 14.05. Purchasing. **Other Jobs in This Work Group:** Wholesale and Retail Buyers, Except Farm Products.

Skills—Operations Analysis: Analyzing needs and product requirements to create a design. **Management of Financial Resources:** Determining how money will be spent to get the work done and accounting for these expenditures. **Management of Material Resources:** Obtaining and seeing to the appropriate use of equipment, facilities, and materials needed to do certain work. **Mathematics:** Using mathematics to solve problems. **Writing:** Communicating effectively with others in writing as indicated by the needs of the audience. **Management of Personnel Resources:** Motivating, developing, and directing people as they work; identifying the best people for the job. **Speaking:** Talking to others to effectively convey information. **Judgment and Decision Making:** Weighing the relative costs and benefits of a potential action.

Education and Training Programs: Merchandising and Buying Operations; Sales, Distribution, and Marketing Operations, General. **Related Knowledge/Courses—Clerical Practices:** Administrative and clerical procedures and systems such as word-processing systems, filing and records management systems, stenography and transcription, forms, design principles, and other office procedures and terminology. **Economics and Accounting:** Economic and accounting principles and practices, the financial markets, banking, and the analysis and reporting of financial data. **Production**

and **Processing:** Inputs, outputs, raw materials, waste, quality control, costs, and techniques for maximizing the manufacture and distribution of goods. **Administration and Management:** Principles and processes involved in business and organizational planning, coordination, and execution. This includes strategic planning, resource allocation, manpower modeling, leadership techniques, and production methods. **Computers and Electronics:** Electric circuit boards, processors, chips, and computer hardware and software, including applications and programming. **Communications and Media:** Media production, communication, and dissemination techniques and methods, including alternative ways to inform and entertain via written, oral, and visual media.

Work Environment: Indoors; sitting; using hands on objects, tools, or controls; repetitive motions.

Purchasing Managers

- ❈ Education/Training Required: Work experience plus degree
- ❈ Annual Earnings: $85,440
- ❈ Beginning Wage: $48,480
- ❈ Earnings Growth Potential: High
- ❈ Growth: 3.4%
- ❈ Annual Job Openings: 7,243
- ❈ Self-Employed: 2.7%
- ❈ Part-Time: 1.9%

Plan, direct, or coordinate the activities of buyers, purchasing officers, and related workers involved in purchasing materials, products, and services. Maintain records of goods ordered and received. Locate vendors of materials, equipment, or supplies and interview them to determine product availability and terms of sales. Prepare and process requisitions and purchase orders for supplies and equipment. Control purchasing department budgets. Interview and hire staff and oversee staff training. Review purchase order claims and contracts for conformance to company policy. Analyze market and delivery systems to assess present and future material availability. Develop and implement purchasing and contract management instructions, policies, and procedures. Participate in the development of specifications for equipment, products, or substitute materials. Resolve vendor or contractor grievances and claims against suppliers. Represent companies in negotiating contracts and formulating policies with suppliers. Review, evaluate, and approve specifications for issuing and awarding bids. Direct

and coordinate activities of personnel engaged in buying, selling, and distributing materials, equipment, machinery, and supplies. Prepare bid awards requiring board approval. Prepare reports regarding market conditions and merchandise costs. Administer online purchasing systems. Arrange for disposal of surplus materials.

Personality Type: Enterprising. These occupations frequently involve starting up and carrying out projects and can involve leading people and making many decisions. They sometimes require risk taking and often deal with business.

GOE—Interest Area/Cluster: 14. Retail and Wholesale Sales and Service. **Work Group:** 14.01. Managerial Work in Retail/Wholesale Sales and Service. **Other Jobs in This Work Group:** Advertising and Promotions Managers; First-Line Supervisors/Managers of Non-Retail Sales Workers; First-Line Supervisors/Managers of Retail Sales Workers; Funeral Directors; Marketing Managers; Property, Real Estate, and Community Association Managers; Sales Managers.

Skills—Management of Material Resources: Obtaining and seeing to the appropriate use of equipment, facilities, and materials needed to do certain work. **Management of Financial Resources:** Determining how money will be spent to get the work done and accounting for these expenditures. **Negotiation:** Bringing others together and trying to reconcile differences. **Operations Analysis:** Analyzing needs and product requirements to create a design. **Mathematics:** Using mathematics to solve problems. **Systems Evaluation:** Looking at many indicators of system performance and taking into account their accuracy. **Operation Monitoring:** Watching gauges, dials, or other indicators to make sure a machine is working properly. **Operation and Control:** Controlling operations of equipment or systems.

Education and Training Program: Purchasing, Procurement/Acquisitions and Contracts Management.

Related Knowledge/Courses—Economics and Accounting: Economic and accounting principles and practices, the financial markets, banking, and the analysis and reporting of financial data. **Personnel and Human Resources:** Principles and procedures for personnel recruitment; selection; training; compensation and benefits; labor relations and negotiation; and personnel information systems. **Production and Processing:** Inputs, outputs, raw materials, waste, quality control, costs, and techniques for maximizing the manufacture and distribution of goods. **Administration and Management:** Principles and processes involved in business and organizational planning, coordination, and execution. This includes strategic planning, resource allocation, manpower modeling, leadership techniques, and production methods. **Mathematics:** Numbers and their operations and interrelationships, including arithmetic, algebra, geometry, calculus, and statistics and their applications. **Transportation:** Principles and methods for moving people or goods by air, rail, sea, or road, including their relative costs, advantages, and limitations.

Work Environment: Indoors; noisy; sitting.

Radiation Therapists

- ❋ Education/Training Required: Associate degree
- ❋ Annual Earnings: $70,010
- ❋ Beginning Wage: $46,580
- ❋ Earnings Growth Potential: Low
- ❋ Growth: 24.8%
- ❋ Annual Job Openings: 1,461
- ❋ Self-Employed: 0.0%
- ❋ Part-Time: 10.3%

Provide radiation therapy to patients as prescribed by radiologists according to established practices and standards. Duties may include reviewing prescriptions and diagnoses; acting as liaisons with physicians and supportive care personnel; preparing equipment such as immobilization, treatment, and protection devices; and maintaining records, reports, and files. May assist in dosimetry procedures and tumor localization. Position patients for treatment with accuracy according to prescription. Administer prescribed doses of radiation to specific body parts, using radiation therapy equipment according to established practices and standards. Check radiation therapy equipment to ensure proper operation. Review prescriptions, diagnoses, patient charts, and identification. Follow principles of radiation protection for patients, radiation therapists, and others. Maintain records, reports, and files as required, including such information as radiation dosages, equipment settings, and patients' reactions. Conduct most treatment sessions independently, in accordance with long-term treatment plans and under the general direction of patients' physicians. Enter data into computers and set controls to operate and adjust equipment and regulate dosages. Observe and reassure patients during treatments and report unusual reactions to physicians or turn equipment off if unexpected adverse reactions occur. Calculate actual treatment dosages delivered during each session. Check for side effects such as skin irritation, nausea, and hair loss to assess patients' reaction to treatment. Prepare and construct equipment such as immobilization, treatment, and protection devices. Educate, prepare, and reassure patients and their families by answering questions, providing physical assistance, and reinforcing physicians' advice regarding treatment reactions and post-treatment care. Provide assistance to other health-care personnel during dosimetry procedures and tumor localization. Help physicians, radiation oncologists, and clinical physicists to prepare physical and technical aspects of radiation treatment plans, using information about patient conditions and anatomies. Photograph treated areas of patients and process film. Act as liaisons with medical physicists and supportive care personnel. Train and supervise student or subordinate radiotherapy technologists. Implement appropriate follow-up care plans. Assist in the preparation of sealed radioactive materials such as cobalt, radium, cesium, and isotopes for use in radiation treatments. Store, sterilize, or prepare the special applicators containing the radioactive substances implanted by physicians.

Personality Type: Social. These occupations frequently involve working with, communicating with, and teaching people and often involve helping or providing service to others.

GOE—Interest Area/Cluster: 08. Health Science. **Work Group:** 08.07. Medical Therapy. **Other Jobs in This Work Group:** Audiologists; Massage Therapists; Occupational Therapist Aides; Occupational Therapist Assistants; Occupational Therapists; Physical Therapist Aides; Physical Therapist Assistants; Physical Therapists; Recreational Therapists; Respiratory Therapists; Respiratory Therapy Technicians; Speech-Language Pathologists.

Skills—Operation Monitoring: Watching gauges, dials, or other indicators to make sure a machine is working properly. **Operation and Control:** Controlling operations of equipment or systems. **Quality Control Analysis:** Evaluating the quality or performance of products, services, or processes.

Education and Training Program: Medical Radiologic Technology/Science—Radiation Therapist Training. **Related Knowledge/Courses—Medicine and Dentistry:** The information and techniques needed to diagnose and treat injuries, diseases, and deformities. This includes symptoms, treatment alternatives, drug properties and interactions, and preventive health-care measures. **Biology:** Plant and animal living tissue, cells, organisms, and entities, including their functions, interdependencies, and interactions with each other and the environment. **Physics:** Physical principles, laws, and applications, including air, water, material dynamics, light, atomic principles, heat, electric theory, earth formations, and meteorological and related natural phenomena. **Psychology:** Human behavior and performance, mental processes, psychological research methods, and the assessment and treatment of behavioral and affective disorders. **Philosophy and Theology:** Different philosophical systems and religions, including their basic principles, values, ethics, ways of thinking, customs, and practices and their impact on human culture. **Therapy and Counseling:** Information and techniques needed to rehabilitate physical and mental ailments and to provide career guidance, including alternative treatments, rehabilitation equipment and its proper use, and methods to evaluate treatment effects.

Work Environment: Indoors; radiation; disease or infections; standing; walking and running; using hands on objects, tools, or controls.

Radiologic Technicians

- ❀ Education/Training Required: Associate degree
- ❀ Annual Earnings: $50,260
- ❀ Beginning Wage: $33,910
- ❀ Earnings Growth Potential: Low
- ❀ Growth: 15.1%
- ❀ Annual Job Openings: 12,836
- ❀ Self-Employed: 1.1%
- ❀ Part-Time: 17.3%

The job openings listed here are shared with Radiologic Technologists.

Maintain and use equipment and supplies necessary to demonstrate portions of the human body on X-ray film or fluoroscopic screen for diagnostic purposes. Use beam-restrictive devices and patient-shielding techniques to minimize radiation exposure to patient and staff. Position X-ray equipment and adjust controls to set exposure factors, such as time and distance. Position patient on examining table and set up and adjust equipment to obtain optimum view of specific body area as requested by physician. Determine patients' X-ray needs by reading requests or instructions from physicians. Make exposures necessary for the requested procedures, rejecting and repeating work that does not meet established standards. Process exposed radiographs, using film processors or computer-generated methods. Explain

procedures to patients to reduce anxieties and obtain cooperation. Perform procedures such as linear tomography; mammography; sonograms; joint and cyst aspirations; routine contrast studies; routine fluoroscopy; and examinations of the head, trunk, and extremities under supervision of physician. Prepare and set up X-ray room for patient. Assure that sterile supplies, contrast materials, catheters, and other required equipment are present and in working order, requisitioning materials as necessary. Maintain records of patients examined, examinations performed, views taken, and technical factors used. Provide assistance to physicians or other technologists in the performance of more complex procedures. Monitor equipment operation and report malfunctioning equipment to supervisor. Provide students and other technologists with suggestions of additional views, alternate positioning, or improved techniques to ensure the images produced are of the highest quality. Coordinate work of other technicians or technologists when procedures require more than one person. Assist with on-the-job training of new employees and students and provide input to supervisors regarding training performance. Maintain a current file of examination protocols. Operate mobile X-ray equipment in operating room, in emergency room, or at patient's bedside. Provide assistance in radiopharmaceutical administration, monitoring patients' vital signs and notifying the radiologist of any relevant changes.

Personality Type: Realistic. These occupations frequently involve work activities that include practical, hands-on problems and solutions. They often deal with plants; animals; and real-world materials such as wood, tools, and machinery. Many of the occupations require working outside and don't involve a lot of paperwork or working closely with others.

GOE—Interest Area/Cluster: 08. Health Science. **Work Group:** 08.06. Medical Technology. **Other Jobs in This Work Group:** Biological Technicians; Cardiovascular Technologists and Technicians; Diagnostic Medical Sonographers; Medical and Clinical Laboratory Technicians; Medical and Clinical Laboratory Technologists; Medical Equipment Preparers; Medical Records and Health Information Technicians; Nuclear Medicine Technologists; Opticians, Dispensing; Orthotists and Prosthetists; Radiologic Technologists; Radiologic Technologists and Technicians.

Skills—Science: Using scientific methods to solve problems. **Operation Monitoring:** Watching gauges, dials, or other indicators to make sure a machine is working properly. **Equipment Selection:** Determining the kind of tools and equipment needed to do a job. **Operation and Control:**

Controlling operations of equipment or systems. **Service Orientation:** Actively looking for ways to help people. **Active Listening:** Listening to what other people are saying and asking questions as appropriate. **Negotiation:** Bringing others together and trying to reconcile differences. **Writing:** Communicating effectively with others in writing as indicated by the needs of the audience.

Education and Training Programs: Allied Health Diagnostic, Intervention, and Treatment Professions, Other; Medical Radiologic Technology/Science—Radiation Therapist Training; Radiologic Technology/Science—Radiographer Training. **Related Knowledge/Courses—Medicine and Dentistry:** The information and techniques needed to diagnose and treat injuries, diseases, and deformities. This includes symptoms, treatment alternatives, drug properties and interactions, and preventive health-care measures. **Clerical Practices:** Administrative and clerical procedures and systems such as word-processing systems, filing and records management systems, stenography and transcription, forms, design principles, and other office procedures and terminology. **Psychology:** Human behavior and performance, mental processes, psychological research methods, and the assessment and treatment of behavioral and affective disorders. **Physics:** Physical principles, laws, and applications, including air, water, material dynamics, light, atomic principles, heat, electric theory, earth formations, and meteorological and related natural phenomena. **Biology:** Plant and animal living tissue, cells, organisms, and entities, including their functions, interdependencies, and interactions with each other and the environment. **Chemistry:** The composition, structure, and properties of substances and of the chemical processes and transformations that they undergo. This includes uses of chemicals and their interactions, danger signs, production techniques, and disposal methods.

Work Environment: Indoors; radiation; disease or infections; standing; walking and running; using hands on objects, tools, or controls.

Radiologic Technologists

- ❋ Education/Training Required: Associate degree
- ❋ Annual Earnings: $50,260
- ❋ Beginning Wage: $33,910
- ❋ Earnings Growth Potential: Low
- ❋ Growth: 15.1%
- ❋ Annual Job Openings: 12,836
- ❋ Self-Employed: 1.1%
- ❋ Part-Time: 17.3%

The job openings listed here are shared with Radiologic Technicians.

Take X rays and Computerized Axial Tomography (CAT or CT) scans or administer nonradioactive materials into patient's bloodstream for diagnostic purposes. Includes technologists who specialize in other modalities, such as computed tomography, ultrasound, and magnetic resonance. Use radiation safety measures and protection devices to comply with government regulations and to ensure safety of patients and staff. Review and evaluate developed X rays, video tape, or computer-generated information to determine if images are satisfactory for diagnostic purposes. Position imaging equipment and adjust controls to set exposure times and distances, according to specification of examinations. Explain procedures and observe patients to ensure safety and comfort during scans. Key commands and data into computers to document and specify scan sequences, adjust transmitters and receivers, or photograph certain images. Operate or oversee operation of radiologic and magnetic imaging equipment to produce images of the body for diagnostic purposes. Position and immobilize patients on examining tables. Record, process, and maintain patient data and treatment records and prepare reports. Take thorough and accurate patient medical histories. Remove and process film. Set up examination rooms, ensuring that all necessary equipment is ready. Monitor patients' conditions and reactions, reporting abnormal signs to physicians. Coordinate work with clerical personnel or other technologists. Provide assistance in dressing or changing seriously ill, injured, or disabled patients. Demonstrate new equipment, procedures, and techniques to staff and provide technical assistance. Collaborate with other medical team members such as physicians and nurses to conduct angiography or special vascular procedures. Prepare and administer oral or injected contrast media to patients. Monitor video displays of areas being scanned and adjust density or contrast to improve picture quality. Operate fluoroscope to aid physicians to view and guide wires or catheters through blood vessels to areas of interest. Assign duties to radiologic staffs to maintain patient flows and achieve production goals. Perform scheduled maintenance and minor emergency repairs on radiographic equipment. Perform administrative duties such as developing departmental operating budgets, coordinating purchases of supplies and equipment, and preparing work schedules.

Personality Type: Realistic. These occupations frequently involve work activities that include practical, hands-on problems and solutions. They often deal with plants; animals; and real-world materials such as wood, tools, and machinery. Many of the occupations require working outside and don't involve a lot of paperwork or working closely with others.

GOE—Interest Area/Cluster: 08. Health Science. **Work Group:** 08.06. Medical Technology. **Other Jobs in This Work Group:** Biological Technicians; Cardiovascular Technologists and Technicians; Diagnostic Medical Sonographers; Medical and Clinical Laboratory Technicians; Medical and Clinical Laboratory Technologists; Medical Equipment Preparers; Medical Records and Health Information Technicians; Nuclear Medicine Technologists; Opticians, Dispensing; Orthotists and Prosthetists; Radiologic Technicians; Radiologic Technologists and Technicians.

Skills—Operation Monitoring: Watching gauges, dials, or other indicators to make sure a machine is working properly. **Operation and Control:** Controlling operations of equipment or systems.

Education and Training Programs: Allied Health Diagnostic, Intervention, and Treatment Professions, Other; Medical Radiologic Technology/Science—Radiation Therapist Training; Radiologic Technology/Science—Radiographer Training. **Related Knowledge/Courses—Medicine and Dentistry:** The information and techniques needed to diagnose and treat injuries, diseases, and deformities. This includes symptoms, treatment alternatives, drug properties and interactions, and preventive health-care measures. **Physics:** Physical principles, laws, and applications, including air, water, material dynamics, light, atomic principles, heat, electric theory, earth formations, and meteorological and related natural phenomena. **Customer and Personal Service:** Principles and processes for providing customer and personal services, including needs assessment techniques, quality service standards, alternative delivery systems, and customer satisfaction evaluation techniques. **Biology:** Plant and animal living tissue, cells, organisms, and entities, including their

functions, interdependencies, and interactions with each other and the environment. **Psychology:** Human behavior and performance, mental processes, psychological research methods, and the assessment and treatment of behavioral and affective disorders. **Chemistry:** The composition, structure, and properties of substances and of the chemical processes and transformations that they undergo. This includes uses of chemicals and their interactions, danger signs, production techniques, and disposal methods.

Work Environment: Indoors; radiation; disease or infections; standing; using hands on objects, tools, or controls; repetitive motions.

Railroad Conductors and Yardmasters

- ❈ Education/Training Required: Moderate-term on-the-job training
- ❈ Annual Earnings: $58,650
- ❈ Beginning Wage: $37,490
- ❈ Earnings Growth Potential: Medium
- ❈ Growth: 9.1%
- ❈ Annual Job Openings: 3,235
- ❈ Self-Employed: 0.0%
- ❈ Part-Time: 0.3%

Conductors coordinate activities of train crew on passenger or freight train. Coordinate activities of switch-engine crew within yard of railroad, industrial plant, or similar location. Yardmasters coordinate activities of workers engaged in railroad traffic operations, such as the makeup or breakup of trains; yard switching; and review train schedules and switching orders. Signal engineers to begin train runs, stop trains, or change speed, using telecommunications equipment or hand signals. Receive information regarding train or rail problems from dispatchers or from electronic monitoring devices. Direct and instruct workers engaged in yard activities, such as switching tracks, coupling and uncoupling cars, and routing inbound and outbound traffic. Keep records of the contents and destination of each train car and make sure that cars are added or removed at proper points on routes. Operate controls to activate track switches and traffic signals. Instruct workers to set warning signals in front and at rear of trains during emergency stops. Direct engineers to move cars to fit planned train configurations, combining or separating cars to make up or break up trains. Receive instructions from dispatchers regarding trains' routes, timetables, and cargoes. Review schedules, switching orders, way bills, and shipping records to obtain cargo loading and unloading information and to plan work. Confer with engineers regarding train routes, timetables, and cargoes and to discuss alternative routes when there are rail defects or obstructions. Arrange for the removal of defective cars from trains at stations or stops. Inspect each car periodically during runs. Observe yard traffic to determine tracks available to accommodate inbound and outbound traffic. Document and prepare reports of accidents, unscheduled stops, or delays. Confirm routes and destination information for freight cars. Supervise and coordinate crew activities to transport freight and passengers and to provide boarding, porter, maid, and meal services to passengers. Supervise workers in the inspection and maintenance of mechanical equipment to ensure efficient and safe train operation. Record departure and arrival times, messages, tickets and revenue collected, and passenger accommodations and destinations. Inspect freight cars for compliance with sealing procedures and record car numbers and seal numbers. Collect tickets, fares, or passes from passengers. Verify accuracy of timekeeping instruments with engineers to ensure that trains depart on time.

Personality Type: Enterprising. These occupations frequently involve starting up and carrying out projects and can involve leading people and making many decisions. They sometimes require risk taking and often deal with business.

GOE—Interest Area/Cluster: 16. Transportation, Distribution, and Logistics. **Work Group:** 16.01. Managerial Work in Transportation. **Other Jobs in This Work Group:** Aircraft Cargo Handling Supervisors; First-Line Supervisors/Managers of Transportation and Material-Moving Machine and Vehicle Operators; Postmasters and Mail Superintendents; Storage and Distribution Managers; Transportation Managers; Transportation, Storage, and Distribution Managers.

Skills—Operation and Control: Controlling operations of equipment or systems. **Operation Monitoring:** Watching gauges, dials, or other indicators to make sure a machine is working properly. **Coordination:** Adjusting actions in relation to others' actions. **Equipment Maintenance:** Performing routine maintenance and determining when and what kind of maintenance is needed. **Troubleshooting:** Determining what is causing an operating error and deciding what to do about it. **Instructing:** Teaching others how to do something.

Education and Training Program: Truck and Bus Driver Training/Commercial Vehicle Operation. **Related Knowledge/Courses—Transportation:** Principles and methods for moving people or goods by air, rail, sea, or road, including their relative costs, advantages, and limitations. **Public Safety and Security:** Weaponry; public safety; security operations, rules, regulations, precautions, and prevention; and the protection of people, data, and property. **Mechanical Devices:** Machines and tools, including their designs, uses, benefits, repair, and maintenance.

Work Environment: Outdoors; noisy; very hot or cold; very bright or dim lighting; contaminants; hazardous equipment.

Real Estate Brokers

- ❋ Education/Training Required: Work experience in a related occupation
- ❋ Annual Earnings: $58,860
- ❋ Beginning Wage: $25,990
- ❋ Earnings Growth Potential: Very high
- ❋ Growth: 11.1%
- ❋ Annual Job Openings: 18,689
- ❋ Self-Employed: 63.5%
- ❋ Part-Time: 15.5%

Operate real estate office or work for commercial real estate firm, overseeing real estate transactions. Other duties usually include selling real estate or renting properties and arranging loans. Sell, for a fee, real estate owned by others. Obtain agreements from property owners to place properties for sale with real estate firms. Monitor fulfillment of purchase contract terms to ensure that they are handled in a timely manner. Compare a property with similar properties that have recently sold to determine its competitive market price. Act as an intermediary in negotiations between buyers and sellers over property prices and settlement details and during the closing of sales. Generate lists of properties for sale, their locations and descriptions, and available financing options, using computers. Maintain knowledge of real estate law; local economies; fair housing laws; and types of available mortgages, financing options, and government programs. Check work completed by loan officers, attorneys, and other professionals to ensure that it is performed properly. Arrange for financing of property purchases. Appraise property values, assessing income potential when relevant. Maintain awareness of current income tax regulations, local zoning, building and tax laws, and growth possibilities of the area where a property is located. Manage and operate real estate offices, handling associated business details. Supervise agents who handle real estate transactions. Rent properties or manage rental properties. Arrange for title searches of properties being sold. Give buyers virtual tours of properties in which they are interested, using computers. Review property details to ensure that environmental regulations are met. Develop, sell, or lease property used for industry or manufacturing. Maintain working knowledge of various factors that determine a farm's capacity to produce, including agricultural variables and proximity to market centers and transportation facilities.

Personality Type: Enterprising. These occupations frequently involve starting up and carrying out projects and can involve leading people and making many decisions. They sometimes require risk taking and often deal with business.

GOE—Interest Area/Cluster: 14. Retail and Wholesale Sales and Service. **Work Group:** 14.03. General Sales. **Other Jobs in This Work Group:** Parts Salespersons; Real Estate Sales Agents; Retail Salespersons; Sales Representatives, Wholesale and Manufacturing, Except Technical and Scientific Products; Service Station Attendants.

Skills—Management of Financial Resources: Determining how money will be spent to get the work done and accounting for these expenditures. **Negotiation:** Bringing others together and trying to reconcile differences. **Mathematics:** Using mathematics to solve problems. **Judgment and Decision Making:** Weighing the relative costs and benefits of a potential action. **Active Listening:** Listening to what other people are saying and asking questions as appropriate. **Persuasion:** Persuading others to approach things differently. **Service Orientation:** Actively looking for ways to help people. **Complex Problem Solving:** Identifying complex problems, reviewing the options, and implementing solutions.

Education and Training Program: Real Estate. **Related Knowledge/Courses—Sales and Marketing:** Principles and methods involved in showing, promoting, and selling products or services. This includes marketing strategies and tactics, product demonstration and sales techniques, and sales control systems. **Law and Government:** Laws, legal codes, court procedures, precedents, government regulations, executive orders, agency rules, and the democratic political process. **Building and Construction:** Materials, methods, and the appropriate tools to construct objects, structures, and buildings. **Customer and Personal Service:** Principles

and processes for providing customer and personal services, including needs assessment techniques, quality service standards, alternative delivery systems, and customer satisfaction evaluation techniques. **Personnel and Human Resources:** Principles and procedures for personnel recruitment; selection; training; compensation and benefits; labor relations and negotiation; and personnel information systems. **Economics and Accounting:** Economic and accounting principles and practices, the financial markets, banking, and the analysis and reporting of financial data.

Work Environment: More often indoors than outdoors; sitting.

Real Estate Sales Agents

- ❋ Education/Training Required: Postsecondary vocational training
- ❋ Annual Earnings: $40,600
- ❋ Beginning Wage: $20,930
- ❋ Earnings Growth Potential: High
- ❋ Growth: 10.6%
- ❋ Annual Job Openings: 61,232
- ❋ Self-Employed: 60.2%
- ❋ Part-Time: 15.5%

Rent, buy, or sell property for clients. Perform duties such as studying property listings, interviewing prospective clients, accompanying clients to property site, discussing conditions of sale, and drawing up real estate contracts. Includes agents who represent buyer. Present purchase offers to sellers for consideration. Confer with escrow companies, lenders, home inspectors, and pest control operators to ensure that terms and conditions of purchase agreements are met before closing dates. Interview clients to determine what kinds of properties they are seeking. Prepare documents such as representation contracts, purchase agreements, closing statements, deeds, and leases. Coordinate property closings, overseeing signing of documents and disbursement of funds. Act as an intermediary in negotiations between buyers and sellers, generally representing one or the other. Promote sales of properties through advertisements, open houses, and participation in multiple listing services. Compare a property with similar properties that have recently sold to determine its competitive market price. Coordinate appointments to show homes to prospective buyers. Generate lists of properties that are compatible with buyers' needs and financial resources. Display commercial, industrial, agricultural, and residential properties to clients and explain their features. Arrange for title searches to determine whether clients have clear property titles. Review plans for new construction with clients, enumerating and recommending available options and features. Answer clients' questions regarding construction work, financing, maintenance, repairs, and appraisals. Accompany buyers during visits to and inspections of property, advising them on the suitability and value of the homes they are visiting. Inspect condition of premises and arrange for necessary maintenance or notify owners of maintenance needs. Advise sellers on how to make homes more appealing to potential buyers. Arrange meetings between buyers and sellers when details of transactions need to be negotiated. Advise clients on market conditions, prices, mortgages, legal requirements, and related matters. Evaluate mortgage options to help clients obtain financing at the best prevailing rates and terms. Review property listings, trade journals, and relevant literature and attend conventions, seminars, and staff and association meetings to remain knowledgeable about real estate markets.

Personality Type: Enterprising. These occupations frequently involve starting up and carrying out projects and can involve leading people and making many decisions. They sometimes require risk taking and often deal with business.

GOE—Interest Area/Cluster: 14. Retail and Wholesale Sales and Service. **Work Group:** 14.03. General Sales. **Other Jobs in This Work Group:** Parts Salespersons; Real Estate Brokers; Retail Salespersons; Sales Representatives, Wholesale and Manufacturing, Except Technical and Scientific Products; Service Station Attendants.

Skills—Negotiation: Bringing others together and trying to reconcile differences. **Service Orientation:** Actively looking for ways to help people. **Coordination:** Adjusting actions in relation to others' actions. **Speaking:** Talking to others to effectively convey information. **Management of Financial Resources:** Determining how money will be spent to get the work done and accounting for these expenditures. **Writing:** Communicating effectively with others in writing as indicated by the needs of the audience. **Time Management:** Managing one's own time and the time of others. **Mathematics:** Using mathematics to solve problems.

Education and Training Program: Real Estate. **Related Knowledge/Courses—Sales and Marketing:** Principles and methods involved in showing, promoting, and selling products or services. This includes marketing strategies and tactics, product demonstration and sales techniques, and

sales control systems. **Clerical Practices:** Administrative and clerical procedures and systems such as word-processing systems, filing and records management systems, stenography and transcription, forms, design principles, and other office procedures and terminology. **Law and Government:** Laws, legal codes, court procedures, precedents, government regulations, executive orders, agency rules, and the democratic political process. **Customer and Personal Service:** Principles and processes for providing customer and personal services, including needs assessment techniques, quality service standards, alternative delivery systems, and customer satisfaction evaluation techniques. **Economics and Accounting:** Economic and accounting principles and practices, the financial markets, banking, and the analysis and reporting of financial data. **Building and Construction:** Materials, methods, and the appropriate tools to construct objects, structures, and buildings.

Work Environment: More often indoors than outdoors; sitting.

Receptionists and Information Clerks

❋ Education/Training Required: Short-term on-the-job training

❋ Annual Earnings: $23,710

❋ Beginning Wage: $16,290

❋ Earnings Growth Potential: Low

❋ Growth: 17.2%

❋ Annual Job Openings: 334,124

❋ Self-Employed: 1.4%

❋ Part-Time: 31.7%

Answer inquiries and obtain information for general public, customers, visitors, and other interested parties. Provide information regarding activities conducted at establishment and location of departments, offices, and employees within organization. Operate telephone switchboard to answer, screen, and forward calls, providing information, taking messages, and scheduling appointments. Receive payment and record receipts for services. Perform administrative support tasks such as proofreading, transcribing handwritten information, and operating calculators or computers to work with pay records, invoices, balance sheets, and other documents. Greet persons entering establishment, determine nature and purpose of visit, and direct or escort them to specific destinations. Hear and resolve complaints from customers and public. File and maintain records. Transmit information or documents to customers, using computer, mail, or facsimile machine. Schedule appointments and maintain and update appointment calendars. Analyze data to determine answers to questions from customers or members of the public. Provide information about establishment such as location of departments or offices, employees within the organization, or services provided. Keep a current record of staff members' whereabouts and availability. Collect, sort, distribute, and prepare mail, messages, and courier deliveries. Calculate and quote rates for tours, stocks, insurance policies, or other products and services. Take orders for merchandise or materials and send them to the proper departments to be filled. Process and prepare memos, correspondence, travel vouchers, or other documents. Schedule space and equipment for special programs and prepare lists of participants. Enroll individuals to participate in programs and notify them of their acceptance. Conduct tours or deliver talks describing features of public facility such as a historic site or national park. Perform duties such as taking care of plants and straightening magazines to maintain lobby or reception area.

Personality Type: Conventional. These occupations frequently involve following set procedures and routines and can include working with data and details more than with ideas. Usually there is a clear line of authority to follow.

GOE—Interest Area/Cluster: 14. Retail and Wholesale Sales and Service. **Work Group:** 14.06. Customer Service. **Other Jobs in This Work Group:** Cashiers; Counter and Rental Clerks; Customer Service Representatives; Gaming Cage Workers; Gaming Change Persons and Booth Cashiers; Order Clerks.

Skills—Active Listening: Listening to what other people are saying and asking questions as appropriate. **Service Orientation:** Actively looking for ways to help people. **Writing:** Communicating effectively with others in writing as indicated by the needs of the audience. **Social Perceptiveness:** Being aware of others' reactions and understanding why they react the way they do. **Reading Comprehension:** Understanding written sentences and paragraphs in work-related documents.

Education and Training Programs: General Office Occupations and Clerical Services; Health Unit Coordinator/Ward Clerk Training; Medical Reception/Receptionist Training; Receptionist Training. **Related Knowledge/Courses—Clerical Practices:** Administrative and clerical procedures and systems such as word-processing systems,

filing and records management systems, stenography and transcription, forms, design principles, and other office procedures and terminology. **Customer and Personal Service:** Principles and processes for providing customer and personal services, including needs assessment techniques, quality service standards, alternative delivery systems, and customer satisfaction evaluation techniques. **Computers and Electronics:** Electric circuit boards, processors, chips, and computer hardware and software, including applications and programming.

Work Environment: Indoors; sitting; repetitive motions.

Recreation and Fitness Studies Teachers, Postsecondary

- ❋ Education/Training Required: Doctoral degree
- ❋ Annual Earnings: $52,170
- ❋ Beginning Wage: $26,790
- ❋ Earnings Growth Potential: High
- ❋ Growth: 22.9%
- ❋ Annual Job Openings: 3,010
- ❋ Self-Employed: 0.4%
- ❋ Part-Time: 27.8%

Teach courses pertaining to recreation, leisure, and fitness studies, including exercise physiology and facilities management. Evaluate and grade students' classwork, assignments, and papers. Maintain student attendance records, grades, and other required records. Prepare and deliver lectures to undergraduate and graduate students on topics such as anatomy, therapeutic recreation, and conditioning theory. Prepare course materials such as syllabi, homework assignments, and handouts. Maintain regularly scheduled office hours to advise and assist students. Compile, administer, and grade examinations or assign this work to others. Plan, evaluate, and revise curricula, course content, and course materials and methods of instruction. Initiate, facilitate, and moderate classroom discussions. Keep abreast of developments in their field by reading current literature, talking with colleagues, and participating in professional conferences. Advise students on academic and vocational curricula and on career issues. Participate in student recruitment, registration, and placement activities. Collaborate with colleagues to address teaching and research issues. Select and obtain materials and supplies such as textbooks. Participate in campus and community events. Serve on academic or administrative committees that deal with institutional policies, departmental matters, and academic issues. Compile bibliographies of specialized materials for outside reading assignments. Supervise undergraduate or graduate teaching, internship, and research work. Perform administrative duties such as serving as department heads. Prepare students to act as sports coaches. Conduct research in a particular field of knowledge and publish findings in professional journals, books, or electronic media. Act as advisers to student organizations. Write grant proposals to procure external research funding. Provide professional consulting services to government or industry.

Personality Type: Social. These occupations frequently involve working with, communicating with, and teaching people and often involve helping or providing service to others.

GOE—Interest Area/Cluster: 05. Education and Training. **Work Group:** 05.03. Postsecondary and Adult Teaching and Instructing. **Other Jobs in This Work Group:** Adult Literacy, Remedial Education, and GED Teachers and Instructors; Agricultural Sciences Teachers, Postsecondary; Anthropology and Archeology Teachers, Postsecondary; Architecture Teachers, Postsecondary; Area, Ethnic, and Cultural Studies Teachers, Postsecondary; Art, Drama, and Music Teachers, Postsecondary; Atmospheric, Earth, Marine, and Space Sciences Teachers, Postsecondary; Biological Science Teachers, Postsecondary; Business Teachers, Postsecondary; Chemistry Teachers, Postsecondary; Communications Teachers, Postsecondary; Computer Science Teachers, Postsecondary; Criminal Justice and Law Enforcement Teachers, Postsecondary; Economics Teachers, Postsecondary; Education Teachers, Postsecondary; Engineering Teachers, Postsecondary; English Language and Literature Teachers, Postsecondary; Environmental Science Teachers, Postsecondary; Farm and Home Management Advisors; Foreign Language and Literature Teachers, Postsecondary; Forestry and Conservation Science Teachers, Postsecondary; Geography Teachers, Postsecondary; Graduate Teaching Assistants; Health Specialties Teachers, Postsecondary; History Teachers, Postsecondary; Home Economics Teachers, Postsecondary; Law Teachers, Postsecondary; Library Science Teachers, Postsecondary; Mathematical Science Teachers, Postsecondary; Nursing Instructors and Teachers, Postsecondary; Philosophy and Religion Teachers, Postsecondary; Physics Teachers, Postsecondary; Political Science Teachers, Postsecondary; Psychology Teachers, Postsecondary; Self-Enrichment Education Teachers; Social Work Teachers, Postsecondary; Sociology Teachers, Postsecondary; Vocational Education Teachers, Postsecondary.

Skills—Instructing: Teaching others how to do something. **Learning Strategies:** Using multiple approaches when learning or teaching new things. **Science:** Using scientific methods to solve problems. **Social Perceptiveness:** Being aware of others' reactions and understanding why they react the way they do. **Persuasion:** Persuading others to approach things differently. **Time Management:** Managing one's own time and the time of others. **Management of Financial Resources:** Determining how money will be spent to get the work done and accounting for these expenditures. **Writing:** Communicating effectively with others in writing as indicated by the needs of the audience.

Education and Training Programs: Health and Physical Education, General; Parks, Recreation and Leisure Studies; Sport and Fitness Administration/Management. **Related Knowledge/Courses—Education and Training:** Instructional methods and training techniques, including curriculum design principles, learning theory, group and individual teaching techniques, design of individual development plans, and test design principles. **Philosophy and Theology:** Different philosophical systems and religions, including their basic principles, values, ethics, ways of thinking, customs, and practices and their impact on human culture. **Psychology:** Human behavior and performance, mental processes, psychological research methods, and the assessment and treatment of behavioral and affective disorders. **Therapy and Counseling:** Information and techniques needed to rehabilitate physical and mental ailments and to provide career guidance, including alternative treatments, rehabilitation equipment and its proper use, and methods to evaluate treatment effects. **Medicine and Dentistry:** The information and techniques needed to diagnose and treat injuries, diseases, and deformities. This includes symptoms, treatment alternatives, drug properties and interactions, and preventive health-care measures. **Sociology and Anthropology:** Group behavior and dynamics; societal trends and influences; and cultures and their history, migrations, ethnicity, and origins.

Work Environment: More often indoors than outdoors; standing.

Recreation Workers

- ❋ Education/Training Required: Bachelor's degree
- ❋ Annual Earnings: $21,220
- ❋ Beginning Wage: $14,980
- ❋ Earnings Growth Potential: Low
- ❋ Growth: 12.7%
- ❋ Annual Job Openings: 61,454
- ❋ Self-Employed: 8.5%
- ❋ Part-Time: 38.2%

Conduct recreation activities with groups in public, private, or volunteer agencies or recreation facilities. Organize and promote activities such as arts and crafts, sports, games, music, dramatics, social recreation, camping, and hobbies, taking into account the needs and interests of individual members. Enforce rules and regulations of recreational facilities to maintain discipline and ensure safety. Organize, lead, and promote interest in recreational activities such as arts, crafts, sports, games, camping, and hobbies. Manage the daily operations of recreational facilities. Administer first aid according to prescribed procedures and notify emergency medical personnel when necessary. Ascertain and interpret group interests, evaluate equipment and facilities, and adapt activities to meet participant needs. Greet new arrivals to activities, introducing them to other participants, explaining facility rules, and encouraging participation. Complete and maintain time and attendance forms and inventory lists. Explain principles, techniques, and safety procedures to participants in recreational activities and demonstrate use of materials and equipment. Evaluate recreation areas, facilities, and services to determine if they are producing desired results. Confer with management to discuss and resolve participant complaints. Supervise and coordinate the work activities of personnel, such as training staff members and assigning work duties. Meet and collaborate with agency personnel, community organizations, and other professional personnel to plan balanced recreational programs for participants. Schedule maintenance and use of facilities. Direct special activities or events such as aquatics, gymnastics, or performing arts. Meet with staff to discuss rules, regulations, and work-related problems. Provide for entertainment and set up related decorations and equipment. Encourage participants to develop their own activities and leadership skills through group discussions. Serve as liaison between park or recreation administrators and activity instructors. Evaluate staff performance, recording evaluations on appropriate forms. Oversee the purchase, planning, design, construction, and upkeep of recreation facilities and areas.

Personality Type: Social. These occupations frequently involve working with, communicating with, and teaching people and often involve helping or providing service to others.

GOE—Interest Area/Cluster: 09. Hospitality, Tourism, and Recreation. **Work Group:** 09.02. Recreational Services. **Other Jobs in This Work Group:** Amusement and Recreation Attendants; Gaming and Sports Book Writers and Runners; Gaming Dealers; Locker Room, Coatroom, and Dressing Room Attendants; Motion Picture Projectionists; Slot Key Persons; Ushers, Lobby Attendants, and Ticket Takers.

Skills—Management of Financial Resources: Determining how money will be spent to get the work done and accounting for these expenditures. **Management of Personnel Resources:** Motivating, developing, and directing people as they work; identifying the best people for the job. **Service Orientation:** Actively looking for ways to help people. **Management of Material Resources:** Obtaining and seeing to the appropriate use of equipment, facilities, and materials needed to do certain work. **Social Perceptiveness:** Being aware of others' reactions and understanding why they react the way they do. **Writing:** Communicating effectively with others in writing as indicated by the needs of the audience. **Equipment Selection:** Determining the kind of tools and equipment needed to do a job. **Systems Evaluation:** Looking at many indicators of system performance and taking into account their accuracy.

Education and Training Programs: Health and Physical Education/Fitness, Other; Parks, Recreation and Leisure Facilities Management; Parks, Recreation and Leisure Studies; Parks, Recreation, Leisure and Fitness Studies, Other; Sport and Fitness Administration/Management. **Related Knowledge/Courses—Psychology:** Human behavior and performance, mental processes, psychological research methods, and the assessment and treatment of behavioral and affective disorders. **Therapy and Counseling:** Information and techniques needed to rehabilitate physical and mental ailments and to provide career guidance, including alternative treatments, rehabilitation equipment and its proper use, and methods to evaluate treatment effects. **Customer and Personal Service:** Principles and processes for providing customer and personal services, including needs assessment techniques, quality service standards, alternative delivery systems, and customer satisfaction evaluation techniques. **Sociology and Anthropology:** Group behavior and dynamics; societal trends and influences; and cultures and their history, migrations, ethnicity, and origins. **Sales and Marketing:** Principles and methods involved in showing, promoting, and selling products or services. This includes marketing strategies and tactics, product demonstration and sales techniques, and sales control systems. **Clerical Practices:** Administrative and clerical procedures and systems such as word-processing systems, filing and records management systems, stenography and transcription, forms, design principles, and other office procedures and terminology.

Work Environment: Indoors; noisy; more often standing than sitting; using hands on objects, tools, or controls.

Recreational Vehicle Service Technicians

- ❋ Education/Training Required: Long-term on-the-job training
- ❋ Annual Earnings: $31,760
- ❋ Beginning Wage: $20,460
- ❋ Earnings Growth Potential: Medium
- ❋ Growth: 18.2%
- ❋ Annual Job Openings: 2,442
- ❋ Self-Employed: 3.5%
- ❋ Part-Time: 14.6%

Diagnose, inspect, adjust, repair, or overhaul recreational vehicles, including travel trailers. May specialize in maintaining gas, electrical, hydraulic, plumbing, or chassis/towing systems as well as repairing generators, appliances, and interior components. Examine or test operation of parts or systems that have been repaired to ensure completeness of repairs. Repair plumbing and propane gas lines, using caulking compounds and plastic or copper pipe. Inspect recreational vehicles to diagnose problems; then perform necessary adjustment, repair, or overhaul. Locate and repair frayed wiring, broken connections, or incorrect wiring, using ohmmeters, soldering irons, tape, and hand tools. Confer with customers, read work orders, and examine vehicles needing repair to determine the nature and extent of damage. List parts needed, estimate costs, and plan work procedures, using parts lists, technical manuals, and diagrams. Connect electrical systems to outside power sources and activate switches to test the operation of appliances and light fixtures. Connect water hoses to inlet pipes

of plumbing systems and test operation of toilets and sinks. Remove damaged exterior panels and repair and replace structural frame members. Open and close doors, windows, and drawers to test their operation, trimming edges to fit as necessary. Repair leaks with caulking compound or replace pipes, using pipe wrenches. Refinish wood surfaces on cabinets, doors, moldings, and floors, using power sanders, putty, spray equipment, brushes, paints, or varnishes. Reset hardware, using chisels, mallets, and screwdrivers. Seal open sides of modular units to prepare them for shipment, using polyethylene sheets, nails, and hammers.

Personality Type: Realistic. These occupations frequently involve work activities that include practical, hands-on problems and solutions. They often deal with plants; animals; and real-world materials such as wood, tools, and machinery. Many of the occupations require working outside and don't involve a lot of paperwork or working closely with others.

GOE—Interest Area/Cluster: 13. Manufacturing. **Work Group:** 13.14. Vehicle and Facility Mechanical Work. **Other Jobs in This Work Group:** Aircraft Mechanics and Service Technicians; Aircraft Structure, Surfaces, Rigging, and Systems Assemblers; Automotive Body and Related Repairers; Automotive Glass Installers and Repairers; Automotive Master Mechanics; Automotive Service Technicians and Mechanics; Automotive Specialty Technicians; Bus and Truck Mechanics and Diesel Engine Specialists; Farm Equipment Mechanics; Fiberglass Laminators and Fabricators; Mobile Heavy Equipment Mechanics, Except Engines; Motorboat Mechanics; Motorcycle Mechanics; Outdoor Power Equipment and Other Small Engine Mechanics; Rail Car Repairers; Tire Repairers and Changers.

Skills—Repairing: Repairing machines or systems, using the needed tools. **Installation:** Installing equipment, machines, wiring, or programs to meet specifications. **Troubleshooting:** Determining what is causing an operating error and deciding what to do about it. **Equipment Maintenance:** Performing routine maintenance and determining when and what kind of maintenance is needed. **Technology Design:** Generating or adapting equipment and technology to serve user needs. **Operation Monitoring:** Watching gauges, dials, or other indicators to make sure a machine is working properly. **Equipment Selection:** Determining the kind of tools and equipment needed to do a job. **Systems Evaluation:** Looking at many indicators of system performance and taking into account their accuracy.

Education and Training Program: Vehicle Maintenance and Repair Technologies, Other. **Related Knowledge/Courses—Mechanical Devices:** Machines and tools, including their designs, uses, benefits, repair, and maintenance. **Building and Construction:** Materials, methods, and the appropriate tools to construct objects, structures, and buildings. **Chemistry:** The composition, structure, and properties of substances and of the chemical processes and transformations that they undergo. This includes uses of chemicals and their interactions, danger signs, production techniques, and disposal methods. **Physics:** Physical principles, laws, and applications, including air, water, material dynamics, light, atomic principles, heat, electric theory, earth formations, and meteorological and related natural phenomena. **Engineering and Technology:** Equipment, tools, and mechanical devices and their uses to produce motion, light, power, technology, and other applications. **Design:** Design techniques, principles, tools, and instruments involved in the production and use of precision technical plans, blueprints, drawings, and models.

Work Environment: Noisy; contaminants; cramped work space, awkward positions; hazardous equipment; standing; using hands on objects, tools, or controls.

Refrigeration Mechanics and Installers

- ❋ Education/Training Required: Long-term on-the-job training
- ❋ Annual Earnings: $38,360
- ❋ Beginning Wage: $24,240
- ❋ Earnings Growth Potential: Medium
- ❋ Growth: 8.7%
- ❋ Annual Job Openings: 29,719
- ❋ Self-Employed: 12.7%
- ❋ Part-Time: 3.6%

The job openings listed here are shared with Heating and Air Conditioning Mechanics and Installers.

Install and repair industrial and commercial refrigerating systems. Braze or solder parts to repair defective joints and leaks. Observe and test system operation, using gauges and instruments. Test lines, components, and connections for leaks. Dismantle malfunctioning systems and test components, using electrical, mechanical, and pneumatic testing equipment. Adjust or replace worn or defective mechanisms and parts and reassemble repaired systems. Read blueprints

to determine location, size, capacity, and type of components needed to build refrigeration system. Supervise and instruct assistants. Perform mechanical overhauls and refrigerant reclaiming. Install wiring to connect components to an electric power source. Cut, bend, thread, and connect pipe to functional components and water, power, or refrigeration system. Adjust valves according to specifications and charge system with proper type of refrigerant by pumping the specified gas or fluid into the system. Estimate, order, pick up, deliver, and install materials and supplies needed to maintain equipment in good working condition. Install expansion and control valves, using acetylene torches and wrenches. Mount compressor, condenser, and other components in specified locations on frames, using hand tools and acetylene welding equipment. Keep records of repairs and replacements made and causes of malfunctions. Schedule work with customers and initiate work orders, house requisitions, and orders from stock. Lay out reference points for installation of structural and functional components, using measuring instruments. Fabricate and assemble structural and functional components of refrigeration system, using hand tools, power tools, and welding equipment. Lift and align components into position, using hoist or block and tackle. Drill holes and install mounting brackets and hangers into floor and walls of building. Insulate shells and cabinets of systems.

Personality Type: Realistic. These occupations frequently involve work activities that include practical, hands-on problems and solutions. They often deal with plants; animals; and real-world materials such as wood, tools, and machinery. Many of the occupations require working outside and don't involve a lot of paperwork or working closely with others.

GOE—Interest Area/Cluster: 02. Architecture and Construction. **Work Group:** 02.05. Systems and Equipment Installation, Maintenance, and Repair. **Other Jobs in This Work Group:** Electrical and Electronics Repairers, Powerhouse, Substation, and Relay; Electrical Power-Line Installers and Repairers; Elevator Installers and Repairers; Heating and Air Conditioning Mechanics and Installers; Maintenance and Repair Workers, General; Telecommunications Equipment Installers and Repairers, Except Line Installers; Telecommunications Line Installers and Repairers.

Skills—Installation: Installing equipment, machines, wiring, or programs to meet specifications. **Repairing:** Repairing machines or systems, using the needed tools. **Equipment Maintenance:** Performing routine maintenance and determining when and what kind of maintenance is needed.

Operation Monitoring: Watching gauges, dials, or other indicators to make sure a machine is working properly. **Science:** Using scientific methods to solve problems. **Systems Evaluation:** Looking at many indicators of system performance and taking into account their accuracy. **Systems Analysis:** Determining how a system should work and how changes will affect outcomes. **Troubleshooting:** Determining what is causing an operating error and deciding what to do about it.

Education and Training Programs: Heating, Air Conditioning and Refrigeration Technology/Technician Training (ACH/ACR/ACHR/HRAC/HVAC/; Heating, Air Conditioning, Ventilation and Refrigeration Maintenance Technology/Technician Training; Solar Energy Technology/Technician Training. **Related Knowledge/Courses— Building and Construction:** Materials, methods, and the appropriate tools to construct objects, structures, and buildings. **Mechanical Devices:** Machines and tools, including their designs, uses, benefits, repair, and maintenance. **Engineering and Technology:** Equipment, tools, and mechanical devices and their uses to produce motion, light, power, technology, and other applications. **Physics:** Physical principles, laws, and applications, including air, water, material dynamics, light, atomic principles, heat, electric theory, earth formations, and meteorological and related natural phenomena. **Chemistry:** The composition, structure, and properties of substances and of the chemical processes and transformations that they undergo. This includes uses of chemicals and their interactions, danger signs, production techniques, and disposal methods. **Design:** Design techniques, principles, tools, and instruments involved in the production and use of precision technical plans, blueprints, drawings, and models.

Work Environment: Outdoors; very hot or cold; cramped work space, awkward positions; minor burns, cuts, bites, or stings; standing; using hands on objects, tools, or controls.

Refuse and Recyclable Material Collectors

❋ Education/Training Required: Short-term on-the-job training
❋ Annual Earnings: $29,420
❋ Beginning Wage: $17,070
❋ Earnings Growth Potential: High
❋ Growth: 7.4%
❋ Annual Job Openings: 37,785
❋ Self-Employed: 6.1%
❋ Part-Time: 13.4%

Collect and dump refuse or recyclable materials from containers into truck. May drive truck. Inspect trucks prior to beginning routes to ensure safe operating condition. Refuel trucks and add other necessary fluids, such as oil. Fill out any needed reports for defective equipment. Drive to disposal sites to empty trucks that have been filled. Drive trucks along established routes through residential streets and alleys or through business and industrial areas. Operate equipment that compresses the collected refuse. Operate automated or semi-automated hoisting devices that raise refuse bins and dump contents into openings in truck bodies. Dismount garbage trucks to collect garbage and remount trucks to ride to the next collection point. Communicate with dispatchers concerning delays, unsafe sites, accidents, equipment breakdowns, and other maintenance problems. Keep informed of road and weather conditions to determine how routes will be affected. Tag garbage or recycling containers to inform customers of problems such as excess garbage or inclusion of items that are not permitted. Clean trucks and compactor bodies after routes have been completed. Sort items set out for recycling and throw materials into designated truck compartments. Organize schedules for refuse collection. Provide quotes for refuse collection contracts.

Personality Type: Realistic. These occupations frequently involve work activities that include practical, hands-on problems and solutions. They often deal with plants; animals; and real-world materials such as wood, tools, and machinery. Many of the occupations require working outside and don't involve a lot of paperwork or working closely with others.

GOE—Interest Area/Cluster: 13. Manufacturing. **Work Group:** 13.17. Loading, Moving, Hoisting, and Conveying. **Other Jobs in This Work Group:** Conveyor Operators and

Tenders; Hoist and Winch Operators; Industrial Truck and Tractor Operators; Machine Feeders and Offbearers; Packers and Packagers, Hand; Pump Operators, Except Wellhead Pumpers; Tank Car, Truck, and Ship Loaders.

Skills—Equipment Maintenance: Performing routine maintenance and determining when and what kind of maintenance is needed. **Operation and Control:** Controlling operations of equipment or systems. **Operation Monitoring:** Watching gauges, dials, or other indicators to make sure a machine is working properly. **Repairing:** Repairing machines or systems, using the needed tools.

Education and Training Programs: No related CIP programs; this job is learned through informal short-term on-the-job training. **Related Knowledge/Courses—Transportation:** Principles and methods for moving people or goods by air, rail, sea, or road, including their relative costs, advantages, and limitations. **Customer and Personal Service:** Principles and processes for providing customer and personal services, including needs assessment techniques, quality service standards, alternative delivery systems, and customer satisfaction evaluation techniques.

Work Environment: Outdoors; noisy; contaminants; using hands on objects, tools, or controls; bending or twisting the body; repetitive motions.

Registered Nurses

- Education/Training Required: Associate degree
- Annual Earnings: $60,010
- Beginning Wage: $42,020
- Earnings Growth Potential: Low
- Growth: 23.5%
- Annual Job Openings: 233,499
- Self-Employed: 0.8%
- Part-Time: 21.8%

Assess patient health problems and needs, develop and implement nursing care plans, and maintain medical records. Administer nursing care to ill, injured, convalescent, or disabled patients. May advise patients on health maintenance and disease prevention or provide case management. Licensing or registration required. Includes advance practice nurses such as nurse practitioners, clinical nurse specialists, certified nurse midwives, and certified registered nurse anesthetists. Advanced practice nursing is practiced by RNs who have specialized formal, post-basic education and who function in highly autonomous and specialized roles. Monitor, record, and report symptoms and changes in patients' conditions. Maintain accurate, detailed reports and records. Record patients' medical information and vital signs. Order, interpret, and evaluate diagnostic tests to identify and assess patients' conditions. Modify patient treatment plans as indicated by patients' responses and conditions. Direct and supervise less-skilled nursing or health-care personnel or supervise particular units. Consult and coordinate with health-care team members to assess, plan, implement, and evaluate patient care plans. Monitor all aspects of patient care, including diet and physical activity. Instruct individuals, families, and other groups on topics such as health education, disease prevention, and childbirth and develop health improvement programs. Prepare patients for, and assist with, examinations and treatments. Assess the needs of individuals, families, or communities, including assessment of individuals' home or work environments, to identify potential health or safety problems. Provide health care, first aid, immunizations, and assistance in convalescence and rehabilitation in locations such as schools, hospitals, and industry. Prepare rooms, sterile instruments, equipment, and supplies and ensure that stock of supplies is maintained. Inform physicians of patients' conditions during anesthesia. Administer local, inhalation, intravenous, and other anesthetics. Perform physical examinations, make tentative diagnoses, and treat patients en route to hospitals or at disaster site triage centers. Observe nurses and visit patients to ensure proper nursing care. Conduct specified laboratory tests. Direct and coordinate infection control programs, advising and consulting with specified personnel about necessary precautions. Prescribe or recommend drugs; medical devices; or other forms of treatment such as physical therapy, inhalation therapy, or related therapeutic procedures. Perform administrative and managerial functions such as taking responsibility for a unit's staff, budget, planning, and long-range goals. Hand items to surgeons during operations.

Personality Type: Social. These occupations frequently involve working with, communicating with, and teaching people and often involve helping or providing service to others.

GOE—Interest Area/Cluster: 08. Health Science. **Work Group:** 08.02. Medicine and Surgery. **Other Jobs in This Work Group:** Anesthesiologists; Family and General Practitioners; Internists, General; Medical Assistants; Medical Transcriptionists; Obstetricians and Gynecologists; Pediatricians, General; Pharmacists; Pharmacy Aides; Pharmacy

Technicians; Physician Assistants; Psychiatrists; Surgeons; Surgical Technologists.

Skills—Negotiation: Bringing others together and trying to reconcile differences. **Systems Analysis:** Determining how a system should work and how changes will affect outcomes. **Operation Monitoring:** Watching gauges, dials, or other indicators to make sure a machine is working properly. **Service Orientation:** Actively looking for ways to help people. **Systems Evaluation:** Looking at many indicators of system performance and taking into account their accuracy.

Education and Training Programs: Adult Health Nurse Training/Nursing; Clinical Nurse Specialist Training; Critical Care Nursing; Maternal/Child Health and Neonatal Nursing; Nurse Anesthetist Training; Nurse Practitioner Training; Nursing Midwifery; Nursing Science (MS, PhD); Nursing/Registered Nurse Training (RN, ASN, BSN, MSN); Occupational and Environmental Health Nursing; Pediatric Nursing; Perioperative/Operating Room and Surgical Nurse Training/Nursing; Psychiatric/Mental Health Nurse Training/Nursing; Public Health/Community Nurse Training/Nursing; others. **Related Knowledge/Courses—Medicine and Dentistry:** The information and techniques needed to diagnose and treat injuries, diseases, and deformities. This includes symptoms, treatment alternatives, drug properties and interactions, and preventive health-care measures. **Psychology:** Human behavior and performance, mental processes, psychological research methods, and the assessment and treatment of behavioral and affective disorders. **Therapy and Counseling:** Information and techniques needed to rehabilitate physical and mental ailments and to provide career guidance, including alternative treatments, rehabilitation equipment and its proper use, and methods to evaluate treatment effects. **Biology:** Plant and animal living tissue, cells, organisms, and entities, including their functions, interdependencies, and interactions with each other and the environment. **Philosophy and Theology:** Different philosophical systems and religions, including their basic principles, values, ethics, ways of thinking, customs, and practices and their impact on human culture. **Sociology and Anthropology:** Group behavior and dynamics; societal trends and influences; and cultures and their history, migrations, ethnicity, and origins.

Work Environment: Indoors; disease or infections; standing; walking and running; using hands on objects, tools, or controls.

Rehabilitation Counselors

- Education/Training Required: Master's degree
- Annual Earnings: $29,630
- Beginning Wage: $19,610
- Earnings Growth Potential: Low
- Growth: 23.0%
- Annual Job Openings: 32,081
- Self-Employed: 5.9%
- Part-Time: 15.4%

Counsel individuals to maximize the independence and employability of persons coping with personal, social, and vocational difficulties that result from birth defects, illness, disease, accidents, or the stress of daily life. Coordinate activities for residents of care and treatment facilities. Assess client needs and design and implement rehabilitation programs that may include personal and vocational counseling, training, and job placement. Monitor and record clients' progress in order to ensure that goals and objectives are met. Confer with clients to discuss their options and goals so that rehabilitation programs and plans for accessing needed services can be developed. Prepare and maintain records and case files, including documentation such as clients' personal and eligibility information, services provided, narratives of client contacts, and relevant correspondence. Arrange for physical, mental, academic, vocational, and other evaluations to obtain information for assessing clients' needs and developing rehabilitation plans. Analyze information from interviews, educational and medical records, consultation with other professionals, and diagnostic evaluations to assess clients' abilities, needs, and eligibility for services. Develop rehabilitation plans that fit clients' aptitudes, education levels, physical abilities, and career goals. Maintain close contact with clients during job training and placements to resolve problems and evaluate placement adequacy. Locate barriers to client employment, such as inaccessible work sites, inflexible schedules, and transportation problems, and work with clients to develop strategies for overcoming these barriers. Develop and maintain relationships with community referral sources such as schools and community groups. Arrange for on-site job coaching or assistive devices such as specially equipped wheelchairs in order to help clients adapt to work or school environments. Confer with physicians, psychologists, occupational therapists, and other professionals to develop and implement client rehabilitation programs. Develop diagnostic procedures for determining clients' needs. Participate in job development and placement programs, contacting prospective employers, placing clients in jobs, and evaluating the success of placements. Collaborate with clients' families to implement rehabilitation plans that include behavioral, residential, social, and/or employment goals. Collaborate with community agencies to establish facilities and programs to assist persons with disabilities.

Personality Type: Social. These occupations frequently involve working with, communicating with, and teaching people and often involve helping or providing service to others.

GOE—Interest Area/Cluster: 10. Human Service. **Work Group:** 10.01. Counseling and Social Work. **Other Jobs in This Work Group:** Child, Family, and School Social Workers; Clinical Psychologists; Clinical, Counseling, and School Psychologists; Counseling Psychologists; Marriage and Family Therapists; Medical and Public Health Social Workers; Mental Health and Substance Abuse Social Workers; Mental Health Counselors; Probation Officers and Correctional Treatment Specialists; Residential Advisors; Social and Human Service Assistants; Substance Abuse and Behavioral Disorder Counselors.

Skills—Management of Financial Resources: Determining how money will be spent to get the work done and accounting for these expenditures. **Social Perceptiveness:** Being aware of others' reactions and understanding why they react the way they do. **Writing:** Communicating effectively with others in writing as indicated by the needs of the audience. **Service Orientation:** Actively looking for ways to help people. **Monitoring:** Assessing how well one is doing when learning or doing something. **Coordination:** Adjusting actions in relation to others' actions. **Speaking:** Talking to others to effectively convey information. **Judgment and Decision Making:** Weighing the relative costs and benefits of a potential action.

Education and Training Programs: Assistive/Augmentative Technology and Rehabilitation Engineering; Vocational Rehabilitation Counseling/Counselor Training. **Related Knowledge/Courses—Therapy and Counseling:** Information and techniques needed to rehabilitate physical and mental ailments and to provide career guidance, including alternative treatments, rehabilitation equipment and its proper use, and methods to evaluate treatment effects. **Psychology:** Human behavior and performance, mental processes, psychological research methods, and the assessment and treatment of behavioral and affective disorders. **Philosophy and Theology:** Different philosophical

systems and religions, including their basic principles, values, ethics, ways of thinking, customs, and practices and their impact on human culture. **Education and Training:** Instructional methods and training techniques, including curriculum design principles, learning theory, group and individual teaching techniques, design of individual development plans, and test design principles. **Personnel and Human Resources:** Principles and procedures for personnel recruitment; selection; training; compensation and benefits; labor relations and negotiation; and personnel information systems. **Sociology and Anthropology:** Group behavior and dynamics; societal trends and influences; and cultures and their history, migrations, ethnicity, and origins.

Work Environment: More often indoors than outdoors; sitting; walking and running.

Reinforcing Iron and Rebar Workers

* Education/Training Required: Long-term on-the-job training
* Annual Earnings: $37,890
* Beginning Wage: $23,010
* Earnings Growth Potential: Medium
* Growth: 11.5%
* Annual Job Openings: 4,502
* Self-Employed: 0.0%
* Part-Time: 5.8%

Position and secure steel bars or mesh in concrete forms to reinforce concrete. Use a variety of fasteners, rod-bending machines, blowtorches, and hand tools. Cut rods to required lengths, using metal shears, hacksaws, bar cutters, or acetylene torches. Determine quantities, sizes, shapes, and locations of reinforcing rods from blueprints, sketches, or oral instructions. Space and fasten together rods in forms according to blueprints, using wire and pliers. Place blocks under rebar to hold the bars off the deck when reinforcing floors. Bend steel rods with hand tools and rodbending machines and weld them with arc-welding equipment. Cut and fit wire mesh or fabric, using hooked rods, and position fabric or mesh in concrete to reinforce concrete. Position and secure steel bars, rods, cables, or mesh in concrete forms, using fasteners, rod-bending machines, blowtorches, and hand tools.

Personality Type: Realistic. These occupations frequently involve work activities that include practical, hands-on problems and solutions. They often deal with plants;

animals; and real-world materials such as wood, tools, and machinery. Many of the occupations require working outside and don't involve a lot of paperwork or working closely with others.

GOE—Interest Area/Cluster: 02. Architecture and Construction. **Work Group:** 02.04. Construction Crafts. **Other Jobs in This Work Group:** Boilermakers; Brickmasons and Blockmasons; Carpet Installers; Cement Masons and Concrete Finishers; Commercial Divers; Construction Carpenters; Crane and Tower Operators; Drywall and Ceiling Tile Installers; Electricians; Fence Erectors; Floor Layers, Except Carpet, Wood, and Hard Tiles; Floor Sanders and Finishers; Glaziers; Hazardous Materials Removal Workers; Insulation Workers, Floor, Ceiling, and Wall; Insulation Workers, Mechanical; Manufactured Building and Mobile Home Installers; Operating Engineers and Other Construction Equipment Operators; Painters, Construction and Maintenance; Paperhangers; Paving, Surfacing, and Tamping Equipment Operators; Pile-Driver Operators; Pipe Fitters and Steamfitters; Pipelayers; Plasterers and Stucco Masons; Plumbers; Plumbers, Pipefitters, and Steamfitters; Rail-Track Laying and Maintenance Equipment Operators; Refractory Materials Repairers, Except Brickmasons; Riggers; Roofers; Rough Carpenters; Security and Fire Alarm Systems Installers; Segmental Pavers; Sheet Metal Workers; Stone Cutters and Carvers, Manufacturing; Stonemasons; Structural Iron and Steel Workers; Tapers; Terrazzo Workers and Finishers; Tile and Marble Setters.

Skills—Installation: Installing equipment, machines, wiring, or programs to meet specifications. **Equipment Selection:** Determining the kind of tools and equipment needed to do a job. **Coordination:** Adjusting actions in relation to others' actions. **Management of Material Resources:** Obtaining and seeing to the appropriate use of equipment, facilities, and materials needed to do certain work. **Mathematics:** Using mathematics to solve problems. **Operation and Control:** Controlling operations of equipment or systems. **Monitoring:** Assessing how well one is doing when learning or doing something. **Management of Personnel Resources:** Motivating, developing, and directing people as they work; identifying the best people for the job.

Education and Training Program: Construction Trades, Other. **Related Knowledge/Courses—Building and Construction:** Materials, methods, and the appropriate tools to construct objects, structures, and buildings. **Mechanical Devices:** Machines and tools, including their designs, uses, benefits, repair, and maintenance. **Public Safety and Security:** Weaponry; public safety; security operations, rules,

regulations, precautions, and prevention; and the protection of people, data, and property. **Transportation:** Principles and methods for moving people or goods by air, rail, sea, or road, including their relative costs, advantages, and limitations.

Work Environment: Outdoors; contaminants; standing; walking and running; using hands on objects, tools, or controls; repetitive motions.

Reservation and Transportation Ticket Agents and Travel Clerks

- ✳ Education/Training Required: Short-term on-the-job training
- ✳ Annual Earnings: $29,820
- ✳ Beginning Wage: $18,290
- ✳ Earnings Growth Potential: Medium
- ✳ Growth: 1.1%
- ✳ Annual Job Openings: 30,754
- ✳ Self-Employed: 3.7%
- ✳ Part-Time: 15.9%

Make and confirm reservations and sell tickets to passengers and for large hotel or motel chains. May check baggage and direct passengers to designated concourse, pier, or track; make reservations; deliver tickets; arrange for visas; contact individuals and groups to inform them of package tours; or provide tourists with travel information, such as points of interest, restaurants, rates, and emergency service. Plan routes, itineraries, and accommodation details and compute fares and fees, using schedules, rate books, and computers. Make and confirm reservations for transportation and accommodations, using telephones, faxes, mail, and computers. Prepare customer invoices and accept payment. Answer inquiries regarding such information as schedules, accommodations, procedures, and policies. Assemble and issue required documentation such as tickets, travel insurance policies, and itineraries. Determine whether space is available on travel dates requested by customers and assign requested spaces when available. Inform clients of essential travel information such as travel times, transportation connections, and medical and visa requirements. Maintain computerized inventories of available passenger space and provide information on space reserved or available. Confer with customers to determine their service requirements and travel preferences. Examine passenger documentation to determine destinations and to assign boarding passes. Provide boarding or disembarking assistance to passengers needing special assistance. Check baggage and cargo and direct passengers to designated locations for loading. Announce arrival and departure information, using public-address systems. Trace lost, delayed, or misdirected baggage for customers. Promote particular destinations, tour packages, and other travel services. Provide clients with assistance in preparing required travel documents and forms. Open and close information facilities and keep them clean during operation. Provide customers with travel suggestions and information such as guides, directories, brochures, and maps. Contact customers or travel agents to advise them of travel conveyance changes or to confirm reservations. Contact motel, hotel, resort, and travel operators to obtain current advertising literature.

Personality Type: Conventional. These occupations frequently involve following set procedures and routines and can include working with data and details more than with ideas. Usually there is a clear line of authority to follow.

GOE—Interest Area/Cluster: 09. Hospitality, Tourism, and Recreation. **Work Group:** 09.03. Hospitality and Travel Services. **Other Jobs in This Work Group:** Baggage Porters and Bellhops; Concierges; Flight Attendants; Hotel, Motel, and Resort Desk Clerks; Janitors and Cleaners, Except Maids and Housekeeping Cleaners; Maids and Housekeeping Cleaners; Tour Guides and Escorts; Transportation Attendants, Except Flight Attendants and Baggage Porters; Travel Agents; Travel Guides.

Skills—Service Orientation: Actively looking for ways to help people. **Operation and Control:** Controlling operations of equipment or systems. **Instructing:** Teaching others how to do something. **Operations Analysis:** Analyzing needs and product requirements to create a design. **Operation Monitoring:** Watching gauges, dials, or other indicators to make sure a machine is working properly. **Active Listening:** Listening to what other people are saying and asking questions as appropriate. **Speaking:** Talking to others to effectively convey information.

Education and Training Programs: Hospitality/Travel Services Sales Operations; Selling Skills and Sales Operations; Tourism and Travel Services Marketing Operations; Tourism Promotion Operations. **Related Knowledge/Courses— Customer and Personal Service:** Principles and processes for providing customer and personal services, including needs assessment techniques, quality service standards, alternative delivery systems, and customer satisfaction evaluation techniques. **Transportation:** Principles and methods for

moving people or goods by air, rail, sea, or road, including their relative costs, advantages, and limitations. **Sales and Marketing:** Principles and methods involved in showing, promoting, and selling products or services. This includes marketing strategies and tactics, product demonstration and sales techniques, and sales control systems. **Clerical Practices:** Administrative and clerical procedures and systems such as word-processing systems, filing and records management systems, stenography and transcription, forms, design principles, and other office procedures and terminology.

Work Environment: Indoors; noisy; sitting; using hands on objects, tools, or controls; repetitive motions.

Residential Advisors

- Education/Training Required: Short-term on-the-job training
- Annual Earnings: $23,050
- Beginning Wage: $15,560
- Earnings Growth Potential: Low
- Growth: 18.5%
- Annual Job Openings: 8,053
- Self-Employed: 4.9%
- Part-Time: 21.3%

Coordinate activities for residents of boarding schools, college fraternities or sororities, college dormitories, or similar establishments. Order supplies and determine need for maintenance, repairs, and furnishings. May maintain household records and assign rooms. May refer residents to counseling resources if needed. Enforce rules and regulations to ensure the smooth and orderly operation of dormitory programs. Provide emergency first aid and summon medical assistance when necessary. Mediate interpersonal problems between residents. Administer, coordinate, or recommend disciplinary and corrective actions. Communicate with other staff to resolve problems with individual students. Counsel students in the handling of issues such as family, financial, and educational problems. Make regular rounds to ensure that residents and areas are safe and secure. Observe students to detect and report unusual behavior. Determine the need for facility maintenance and repair and notify appropriate personnel. Collaborate with counselors to develop counseling programs that address the needs of individual students. Develop program plans for individuals or assist in plan development. Hold regular meetings with each assigned unit. Direct and participate in on- and off-campus recreational activities for residents of institutions, boarding schools, fraternities or sororities, children's homes, or similar establishments. Assign rooms to students. Provide requested information on students' progress and the development of case plans. Confer with medical personnel to better understand the backgrounds and needs of individual residents. Answer telephones and route calls or deliver messages. Supervise participants in work-study programs. Process contract cancellations for students who are unable to follow residence hall policies and procedures. Sort and distribute mail. Supervise the activities of housekeeping personnel. Order supplies for facilities. Supervise students' housekeeping work to ensure that it is done properly. Chaperone group-sponsored trips and social functions. Compile information such as residents' daily activities and the quantities of supplies used to prepare required reports. Accompany and supervise students during meals. Provide transportation or escort for expeditions such as shopping trips or visits to doctors or dentists. Inventory, pack, and remove items left behind by former residents.

Personality Type: Social. These occupations frequently involve working with, communicating with, and teaching people and often involve helping or providing service to others.

GOE—Interest Area/Cluster: 10. Human Service. **Work Group:** 10.01. Counseling and Social Work. **Other Jobs in This Work Group:** Child, Family, and School Social Workers; Clinical Psychologists; Clinical, Counseling, and School Psychologists; Counseling Psychologists; Marriage and Family Therapists; Medical and Public Health Social Workers; Mental Health and Substance Abuse Social Workers; Mental Health Counselors; Probation Officers and Correctional Treatment Specialists; Rehabilitation Counselors; Social and Human Service Assistants; Substance Abuse and Behavioral Disorder Counselors.

Skills—Social Perceptiveness: Being aware of others' reactions and understanding why they react the way they do. **Monitoring:** Assessing how well one is doing when learning or doing something. **Management of Personnel Resources:** Motivating, developing, and directing people as they work; identifying the best people for the job. **Time Management:** Managing one's own time and the time of others. **Persuasion:** Persuading others to approach things differently. **Service Orientation:** Actively looking for ways to help people. **Management of Financial Resources:** Determining how money will be spent to get the work done and accounting for these expenditures. **Negotiation:** Bringing others together and trying to reconcile differences.

Education and Training Program: Hotel/Motel Administration/Management. **Related Knowledge/Courses—Therapy and Counseling:** Information and techniques needed to rehabilitate physical and mental ailments and to provide career guidance, including alternative treatments, rehabilitation equipment and its proper use, and methods to evaluate treatment effects. **Philosophy and Theology:** Different philosophical systems and religions, including their basic principles, values, ethics, ways of thinking, customs, and practices and their impact on human culture. **Sociology and Anthropology:** Group behavior and dynamics; societal trends and influences; and cultures and their history, migrations, ethnicity, and origins. **Psychology:** Human behavior and performance, mental processes, psychological research methods, and the assessment and treatment of behavioral and affective disorders. **Personnel and Human Resources:** Principles and procedures for personnel recruitment; selection; training; compensation and benefits; labor relations and negotiation; and personnel information systems. **Public Safety and Security:** Weaponry; public safety; security operations, rules, regulations, precautions, and prevention; and the protection of people, data, and property.

Work Environment: Indoors; noisy; sitting.

Respiratory Therapists

- ❋ Education/Training Required: Associate degree
- ❋ Annual Earnings: $50,070
- ❋ Beginning Wage: $36,650
- ❋ Earnings Growth Potential: Low
- ❋ Growth: 22.6%
- ❋ Annual Job Openings: 5,563
- ❋ Self-Employed: 1.1%
- ❋ Part-Time: 15.0%

Assess, treat, and care for patients with breathing disorders. Assume primary responsibility for all respiratory care modalities, including the supervision of respiratory therapy technicians. Initiate and conduct therapeutic procedures; maintain patient records; and select, assemble, check, and operate equipment. Set up and operate devices such as mechanical ventilators, therapeutic gas administration apparatus, environmental control systems, and aerosol generators, following specified parameters of treatment. Provide emergency care, including artificial respiration, external cardiac massage, and assistance with cardiopulmonary resuscitation. Determine requirements for treatment, such as type, method, and duration of therapy; precautions to be taken; and medication and dosages, compatible with physicians' orders. Monitor patient's physiological responses to therapy, such as vital signs, arterial blood gases, and blood chemistry changes, and consult with physician if adverse reactions occur. Read prescription, measure arterial blood gases, and review patient information to assess patient condition. Work as part of a team of physicians, nurses, and other health-care professionals to manage patient care. Enforce safety rules and ensure careful adherence to physicians' orders. Maintain charts that contain patients' pertinent identification and therapy information. Inspect, clean, test, and maintain respiratory therapy equipment to ensure equipment is functioning safely and efficiently, ordering repairs when necessary. Educate patients and their families about their conditions and teach appropriate disease management techniques, such as breathing exercises and the use of medications and respiratory equipment. Explain treatment procedures to patients to gain cooperation and allay fears. Relay blood analysis results to a physician. Perform pulmonary function and adjust equipment to obtain optimum results in therapy. Perform bronchopulmonary drainage and assist or instruct patients in performance of breathing exercises. Demonstrate respiratory care procedures to trainees and other health-care personnel. Teach, train, supervise, and utilize the assistance of students, respiratory therapy technicians, and assistants. Make emergency visits to resolve equipment problems. Use a variety of testing techniques to assist doctors in cardiac and pulmonary research and to diagnose disorders. Conduct tests, such as electrocardiograms (EKGs), stress testing, and lung capacity tests, to evaluate patients' cardiopulmonary functions.

Personality Type: Social. These occupations frequently involve working with, communicating with, and teaching people and often involve helping or providing service to others.

GOE—Interest Area/Cluster: 08. Health Science. **Work Group:** 08.07. Medical Therapy. **Other Jobs in This Work Group:** Audiologists; Massage Therapists; Occupational Therapist Aides; Occupational Therapist Assistants; Occupational Therapists; Physical Therapist Aides; Physical Therapist Assistants; Physical Therapists; Radiation Therapists; Recreational Therapists; Respiratory Therapy Technicians; Speech-Language Pathologists.

Skills—Science: Using scientific methods to solve problems. **Mathematics:** Using mathematics to solve problems. **Operation Monitoring:** Watching gauges, dials, or other indicators to make sure a machine is working properly.

Reading Comprehension: Understanding written sentences and paragraphs in work-related documents. **Active Learning:** Working with new material or information to grasp its implications. **Troubleshooting:** Determining what is causing an operating error and deciding what to do about it. **Instructing:** Teaching others how to do something. **Service Orientation:** Actively looking for ways to help people.

Education and Training Program: Respiratory Care Therapy/Therapist Training. **Related Knowledge/Courses—Medicine and Dentistry:** The information and techniques needed to diagnose and treat injuries, diseases, and deformities. This includes symptoms, treatment alternatives, drug properties and interactions, and preventive health-care measures. **Biology:** Plant and animal living tissue, cells, organisms, and entities, including their functions, interdependencies, and interactions with each other and the environment. **Psychology:** Human behavior and performance, mental processes, psychological research methods, and the assessment and treatment of behavioral and affective disorders. **Customer and Personal Service:** Principles and processes for providing customer and personal services, including needs assessment techniques, quality service standards, alternative delivery systems, and customer satisfaction evaluation techniques. **Therapy and Counseling:** Information and techniques needed to rehabilitate physical and mental ailments and to provide career guidance, including alternative treatments, rehabilitation equipment and its proper use, and methods to evaluate treatment effects. **Chemistry:** The composition, structure, and properties of substances and of the chemical processes and transformations that they undergo. This includes uses of chemicals and their interactions, danger signs, production techniques, and disposal methods.

Work Environment: Indoors; disease or infections; standing.

Roofers

* Education/Training Required: Moderate-term on-the-job training
* Annual Earnings: $33,240
* Beginning Wage: $21,290
* Earnings Growth Potential: Medium
* Growth: 14.3%
* Annual Job Openings: 38,398
* Self-Employed: 20.1%
* Part-Time: 7.6%

Cover roofs of structures with shingles, slate, asphalt, aluminum, wood, and related materials. May spray roofs, sidings, and walls with material to bind, seal, insulate, or soundproof sections of structures. Install, repair, or replace single-ply roofing systems, using waterproof sheet materials such as modified plastics, elastomeric, or other asphaltic compositions. Apply alternate layers of hot asphalt or tar and roofing paper to roofs according to specification. Apply gravel or pebbles over top layers of roofs, using rakes or stiff-bristled brooms. Cement or nail flashing-strips of metal or shingle over joints to make them watertight. Punch holes in slate, tile, terra cotta, or wooden shingles, using punches and hammers. Hammer and chisel away rough spots or remove them with rubbing bricks to prepare surfaces for waterproofing. Align roofing materials with edges of roofs. Mop or pour hot asphalt or tar onto roof bases. Apply plastic coatings and membranes, fiberglass, or felt over sloped roofs before applying shingles. Install vapor barriers and/or layers of insulation on the roof decks of flat roofs and seal the seams. Install partially overlapping layers of material over roof insulation surfaces, determining distance of roofing material overlap by using chalk lines, gauges on shingling hatchets, or lines on shingles. Inspect problem roofs to determine the best procedures for repairing them. Glaze top layers to make a smooth finish or embed gravel in the bitumen for rough surfaces. Cut roofing paper to size, using knives, and nail or staple roofing paper to roofs in overlapping strips to form bases for other materials. Cut felt, shingles, and strips of flashing and fit them into angles formed by walls, vents, and intersecting roof surfaces. Cover roofs and exterior walls of structures with slate, asphalt, aluminum, wood, gravel, gypsum, and/or related materials, using brushes, knives, punches, hammers, and other tools. Clean and maintain equipment. Cover exposed nailheads with roofing cement or caulking to prevent water leakage and rust. Waterproof and damp-proof walls, floors, roofs, foundations, and basements by painting or spraying surfaces with waterproof coatings or by attaching waterproofing membranes to surfaces. Spray roofs, sidings, and walls with material to bind, seal, insulate, or soundproof sections of structures, using spray guns, air compressors, and heaters.

Personality Type: Realistic. These occupations frequently involve work activities that include practical, hands-on problems and solutions. They often deal with plants; animals; and real-world materials such as wood, tools, and machinery. Many of the occupations require working outside and don't involve a lot of paperwork or working closely with others.

GOE—Interest Area/Cluster: 02. Architecture and Construction. **Work Group:** 02.04. Construction Crafts. **Other Jobs in This Work Group:** Boilermakers; Brickmasons and Blockmasons; Carpet Installers; Cement Masons and Concrete Finishers; Commercial Divers; Construction Carpenters; Crane and Tower Operators; Drywall and Ceiling Tile Installers; Electricians; Fence Erectors; Floor Layers, Except Carpet, Wood, and Hard Tiles; Floor Sanders and Finishers; Glaziers; Hazardous Materials Removal Workers; Insulation Workers, Floor, Ceiling, and Wall; Insulation Workers, Mechanical; Manufactured Building and Mobile Home Installers; Operating Engineers and Other Construction Equipment Operators; Painters, Construction and Maintenance; Paperhangers; Paving, Surfacing, and Tamping Equipment Operators; Pile-Driver Operators; Pipe Fitters and Steamfitters; Pipelayers; Plasterers and Stucco Masons; Plumbers; Plumbers, Pipefitters, and Steamfitters; Rail-Track Laying and Maintenance Equipment Operators; Refractory Materials Repairers, Except Brickmasons; Reinforcing Iron and Rebar Workers; Riggers; Rough Carpenters; Security and Fire Alarm Systems Installers; Segmental Pavers; Sheet Metal Workers; Stone Cutters and Carvers, Manufacturing; Stonemasons; Structural Iron and Steel Workers; Tapers; Terrazzo Workers and Finishers; Tile and Marble Setters.

Skills—Repairing: Repairing machines or systems, using the needed tools. **Installation:** Installing equipment, machines, wiring, or programs to meet specifications. **Equipment Maintenance:** Performing routine maintenance and determining when and what kind of maintenance is needed. **Operations Analysis:** Analyzing needs and product requirements to create a design. **Technology Design:** Generating or adapting equipment and technology to serve user needs. **Mathematics:** Using mathematics to solve problems. **Management of Personnel Resources:** Motivating, developing, and directing people as they work; identifying the best people for the job. **Coordination:** Adjusting actions in relation to others' actions.

Education and Training Program: Roofer Training. **Related Knowledge/Courses—Building and Construction:** Materials, methods, and the appropriate tools to construct objects, structures, and buildings. **Design:** Design techniques, principles, tools, and instruments involved in the production and use of precision technical plans, blueprints, drawings, and models. **Engineering and Technology:** Equipment, tools, and mechanical devices and their uses to produce motion, light, power, technology, and other applications. **Transportation:** Principles and methods for moving people or goods by air, rail, sea, or road, including their relative costs, advantages, and limitations.

Work Environment: Outdoors; very hot or cold; high places; standing; walking and running; using hands on objects, tools, or controls.

Rough Carpenters

- ❋ Education/Training Required: Long-term on-the-job training
- ❋ Annual Earnings: $37,660
- ❋ Beginning Wage: $23,370
- ❋ Earnings Growth Potential: Medium
- ❋ Growth: 10.3%
- ❋ Annual Job Openings: 223,225
- ❋ Self-Employed: 31.8%
- ❋ Part-Time: 6.1%

The job openings listed here are shared with Construction Carpenters.

Build rough wooden structures, such as concrete forms, scaffolds, tunnel, bridge, or sewer supports, billboard signs, and temporary frame shelters, according to sketches, blueprints, or oral instructions. Study blueprints and diagrams to determine dimensions of structure or form to be constructed. Measure materials or distances, using square, measuring tape, or rule to lay out work. Cut or saw boards, timbers, or plywood to required size, using handsaw, power saw, or woodworking machine. Assemble and fasten material together to construct wood or metal framework of structure, using bolts, nails, or screws. Anchor and brace forms and other structures in place, using nails, bolts, anchor rods, steel cables, planks, wedges, and timbers. Mark cutting lines on materials, using pencil and scriber. Erect forms, framework, scaffolds, hoists, roof supports, or chutes, using hand tools, plumb rule, and level. Install rough door and window frames, subflooring, fixtures, or temporary supports in structures undergoing construction or repair. Examine structural timbers and supports to detect decay and replace timbers as required, using hand tools, nuts, and bolts. Bore boltholes in timber, masonry, or concrete walls, using power drill. Fabricate parts, using woodworking and metalworking machines. Dig or direct digging of post holes and set poles to support structures. Build sleds from logs and timbers for use in hauling camp buildings and machinery through wooded areas. Build chutes for pouring concrete.

Personality Type: Realistic. These occupations frequently involve work activities that include practical, hands-on problems and solutions. They often deal with plants; animals; and real-world materials such as wood, tools, and machinery. Many of the occupations require working outside and don't involve a lot of paperwork or working closely with others.

GOE—Interest Area/Cluster: 02. Architecture and Construction. **Work Group:** 02.04. Construction Crafts. **Other Jobs in This Work Group:** Boilermakers; Brickmasons and Blockmasons; Carpet Installers; Cement Masons and Concrete Finishers; Commercial Divers; Construction Carpenters; Crane and Tower Operators; Drywall and Ceiling Tile Installers; Electricians; Fence Erectors; Floor Layers, Except Carpet, Wood, and Hard Tiles; Floor Sanders and Finishers; Glaziers; Hazardous Materials Removal Workers; Insulation Workers, Floor, Ceiling, and Wall; Insulation Workers, Mechanical; Manufactured Building and Mobile Home Installers; Operating Engineers and Other Construction Equipment Operators; Painters, Construction and Maintenance; Paperhangers; Paving, Surfacing, and Tamping Equipment Operators; Pile-Driver Operators; Pipe Fitters and Steamfitters; Pipelayers; Plasterers and Stucco Masons; Plumbers; Plumbers, Pipefitters, and Steamfitters; Rail-Track Laying and Maintenance Equipment Operators; Refractory Materials Repairers, Except Brickmasons; Reinforcing Iron and Rebar Workers; Riggers; Roofers; Security and Fire Alarm Systems Installers; Segmental Pavers; Sheet Metal Workers; Stone Cutters and Carvers, Manufacturing; Stonemasons; Structural Iron and Steel Workers; Tapers; Terrazzo Workers and Finishers; Tile and Marble Setters.

Skills—Repairing: Repairing machines or systems, using the needed tools. **Installation:** Installing equipment, machines, wiring, or programs to meet specifications. **Management of Personnel Resources:** Motivating, developing, and directing people as they work; identifying the best people for the job. **Equipment Selection:** Determining the kind of tools and equipment needed to do a job. **Mathematics:** Using mathematics to solve problems. **Technology Design:** Generating or adapting equipment and technology to serve user needs. **Equipment Maintenance:** Performing routine maintenance and determining when and what kind of maintenance is needed. **Coordination:** Adjusting actions in relation to others' actions.

Education and Training Program: Carpentry/Carpenter Training. **Related Knowledge/Courses—Building and Construction:** Materials, methods, and the appropriate tools to construct objects, structures, and buildings. **Design:** Design techniques, principles, tools, and instruments involved in the production and use of precision technical plans, blueprints, drawings, and models. **Engineering**

and **Technology:** Equipment, tools, and mechanical devices and their uses to produce motion, light, power, technology, and other applications. **Mechanical Devices:** Machines and tools, including their designs, uses, benefits, repair, and maintenance. **Production and Processing:** Inputs, outputs, raw materials, waste, quality control, costs, and techniques for maximizing the manufacture and distribution of goods. **Physics:** Physical principles, laws, and applications, including air, water, material dynamics, light, atomic principles, heat, electric theory, earth formations, and meteorological and related natural phenomena.

Work Environment: Outdoors; noisy; very hot or cold; contaminants; standing; using hands on objects, tools, or controls.

Sailors and Marine Oilers

- ❊ Education/Training Required: Short-term on-the-job training
- ❊ Annual Earnings: $32,570
- ❊ Beginning Wage: $19,500
- ❊ Earnings Growth Potential: High
- ❊ Growth: 15.7%
- ❊ Annual Job Openings: 8,600
- ❊ Self-Employed: 0.1%
- ❊ Part-Time: 5.7%

Stand watch to look for obstructions in path of vessels; measure water depths; turn wheels on bridges; or use emergency equipment as directed by captains, mates, or pilots. Break out, rig, overhaul, and store cargo-handling gear, stationary rigging, and running gear. Perform a variety of maintenance tasks to preserve the painted surface of ships and to maintain line and ship equipment. Must hold government-issued certification and tankerman certification when working aboard liquid-carrying vessels. Provide engineers with assistance in repairing and adjusting machinery. Attach hoses and operate pumps in order to transfer substances to and from liquid cargo tanks. Give directions to crew members engaged in cleaning wheelhouses and quarterdecks. Load or unload materials from vessels. Lower and man lifeboats when emergencies occur. Participate in shore patrols. Read pressure and temperature gauges or displays and record data in engineering logs. Record in ships' logs data such as weather conditions and distances traveled. Stand by wheels when ships are on automatic pilot and verify accuracy of courses, using magnetic compasses. Steer ships under the direction of commanders or navigating officers or direct helmsmen to steer, following designated courses. Chip and clean rust spots on decks, superstructures, and sides of ships, using wire brushes and hand or air chipping machines. Relay specified signals to other ships, using visual signaling devices such as blinker lights and semaphores. Splice and repair ropes, wire cables, and cordage, using marlinespikes, wirecutters, twine, and hand tools. Paint or varnish decks, superstructures, lifeboats, or sides of ships. Overhaul lifeboats and lifeboat gear and lower or raise lifeboats with winches or falls. Operate, maintain, and repair ship equipment such as winches, cranes, derricks, and weapons systems. Measure depths of water in shallow or unfamiliar waters, using leadlines, and telephone or shout depth information to vessel bridges. Maintain ships' engines under direction of ships' engineering officers. Lubricate machinery; equipment; and engine parts such as gears, shafts, and bearings. Handle lines to moor vessels to wharfs, to tie up vessels to other vessels, or to rig towing lines. Examine machinery to verify specified pressures and lubricant flows. Clean and polish wood trim, brass, and other metal parts. Break out, rig, and stow cargo-handling gear, stationary rigging, and running gear. Stand gangway watches to prevent unauthorized persons from boarding ships while they are in port. Tie barges together into tow units for tugboats to handle, inspecting barges periodically during voyages and disconnecting them when destinations are reached.

Personality Type: Realistic. These occupations frequently involve work activities that include practical, hands-on problems and solutions. They often deal with plants; animals; and real-world materials such as wood, tools, and machinery. Many of the occupations require working outside and don't involve a lot of paperwork or working closely with others.

GOE—Interest Area/Cluster: 16. Transportation, Distribution, and Logistics. **Work Group:** 16.05. Water Vehicle Operation. **Other Jobs in This Work Group:** Captains, Mates, and Pilots of Water Vessels; Dredge Operators; Mates—Ship, Boat, and Barge; Motorboat Operators; Pilots, Ship; Ship and Boat Captains.

Skills—Repairing: Repairing machines or systems, using the needed tools. **Equipment Maintenance:** Performing routine maintenance and determining when and what kind of maintenance is needed.

Education and Training Program: Marine Transportation Services, Other. **Related Knowledge/Courses—Mechanical Devices:** Machines and tools, including their designs, uses, benefits, repair, and maintenance. **Transportation:** Principles and methods for moving people or goods by air, rail, sea, or road, including their relative costs, advantages, and limitations. **Engineering and Technology:** Equipment, tools, and mechanical devices and their uses to produce motion, light, power, technology, and other applications. **Public Safety and Security:** Weaponry; public safety; security operations, rules, regulations, precautions, and prevention; and the protection of people, data, and property. **Geography:** Various methods for describing the location and distribution of land, sea, and air masses, including their physical locations, relationships, and characteristics. **Production and Processing:** Inputs, outputs, raw materials, waste, quality control, costs, and techniques for maximizing the manufacture and distribution of goods.

Work Environment: More often outdoors than indoors; noisy; very hot or cold; contaminants; standing.

Sales Agents, Financial Services

- ❋ Education/Training Required: Bachelor's degree
- ❋ Annual Earnings: $68,430
- ❋ Beginning Wage: $30,890
- ❋ Earnings Growth Potential: Very high
- ❋ Growth: 24.8%
- ❋ Annual Job Openings: 47,750
- ❋ Self-Employed: 17.7%
- ❋ Part-Time: 6.9%

The job openings listed here are shared with Sales Agents, Securities and Commodities.

Sell financial services such as loan, tax, and securities counseling to customers of financial institutions and business establishments. Determine customers' financial services needs and prepare proposals to sell services that address these needs. Contact prospective customers to present information and explain available services. Sell services and equipment, such as trusts, investments, and check processing services. Prepare forms or agreements to complete sales. Develop prospects from current commercial customers, referral leads, and sales and trade meetings. Review business trends in order to advise customers regarding expected fluctuations. Make presentations on financial services to groups to attract new clients. Evaluate costs and revenue of agreements to determine continued profitability.

Personality Type: Enterprising. These occupations frequently involve starting up and carrying out projects and can involve leading people and making many decisions. They sometimes require risk taking and often deal with business.

GOE—Interest Area/Cluster: 06. Finance and Insurance. **Work Group:** 06.05. Finance/Insurance Sales and Support. **Other Jobs in This Work Group:** Advertising Sales Agents; Insurance Sales Agents; Personal Financial Advisors; Sales Agents, Securities and Commodities; Securities, Commodities, and Financial Services Sales Agents.

Skills—Persuasion: Persuading others to approach things differently. **Management of Financial Resources:** Determining how money will be spent to get the work done and accounting for these expenditures. **Service Orientation:** Actively looking for ways to help people. **Negotiation:** Bringing others together and trying to reconcile differences. **Operations Analysis:** Analyzing needs and product requirements to create a design. **Monitoring:** Assessing how well one is doing when learning or doing something. **Speaking:** Talking to others to effectively convey information. **Judgment and Decision Making:** Weighing the relative costs and benefits of a potential action.

Education and Training Programs: Business and Personal/Financial Services Marketing Operations; Financial Planning and Services; Investments and Securities. **Related Knowledge/Courses—Sales and Marketing:** Principles and methods involved in showing, promoting, and selling products or services. This includes marketing strategies and tactics, product demonstration and sales techniques, and sales control systems. **Economics and Accounting:** Economic and accounting principles and practices, the financial markets, banking, and the analysis and reporting of financial data. **Customer and Personal Service:** Principles and processes for providing customer and personal services, including needs assessment techniques, quality service standards, alternative delivery systems, and customer satisfaction evaluation techniques. **Law and Government:** Laws, legal codes, court procedures, precedents, government regulations, executive orders, agency rules, and the democratic political process. **Mathematics:** Numbers and their operations and interrelationships, including arithmetic, algebra, geometry, calculus, and statistics and their applications. **Personnel and Human Resources:** Principles and procedures for personnel recruitment; selection; training; compensation and benefits; labor relations and negotiation; and personnel information systems.

Work Environment: Indoors; sitting.

Sales Agents, Securities and Commodities

- ❋ Education/Training Required: Bachelor's degree
- ❋ Annual Earnings: $68,430
- ❋ Beginning Wage: $30,890
- ❋ Earnings Growth Potential: Very high
- ❋ Growth: 24.8%
- ❋ Annual Job Openings: 47,750
- ❋ Self-Employed: 17.7%
- ❋ Part-Time: 6.9%

The job openings listed here are shared with Sales Agents, Financial Services.

Buy and sell securities in investment and trading firms and develop and implement financial plans for individuals, businesses, and organizations. Complete sales order tickets and submit for processing of client requested transactions. Interview clients to determine clients' assets, liabilities, cash flow, insurance coverage, tax status, and financial objectives. Record transactions accurately and keep clients informed about transactions. Develop financial plans based on analysis of clients' financial status and discuss financial options with clients. Review all securities transactions to ensure accuracy of information and ensure that trades conform to regulations of governing agencies. Offer advice on the purchase or sale of particular securities. Relay buy or sell orders to securities exchanges or to firm trading departments. Identify potential clients, using advertising campaigns, mailing lists, and personal contacts. Review financial periodicals, stock and bond reports, business publications, and other material to identify potential investments for clients and to keep abreast of trends affecting market conditions. Contact prospective customers to determine customer needs, present information, and explain available services. Prepare documents needed to implement plans selected by clients. Analyze market conditions to determine optimum times to execute securities transactions. Explain stock market terms and trading practices to clients. Inform and advise concerned parties regarding fluctuations and securities transactions affecting plans or accounts. Calculate costs for billings and commissions purposes. Supply the latest price quotes on any security, as well as information on the activities and financial positions of the corporations issuing these securities. Prepare financial reports to monitor client or corporate finances. Read corporate reports and calculate ratios to determine best prospects for profit on stock purchases and to monitor client accounts.

Personality Type: Enterprising. These occupations frequently involve starting up and carrying out projects and can involve leading people and making many decisions. They sometimes require risk taking and often deal with business.

GOE—Interest Area/Cluster: 06. Finance and Insurance. **Work Group:** 06.05. Finance/Insurance Sales and Support. **Other Jobs in This Work Group:** Advertising Sales Agents; Insurance Sales Agents; Personal Financial Advisors; Sales Agents, Financial Services; Securities, Commodities, and Financial Services Sales Agents.

Skills—Management of Financial Resources: Determining how money will be spent to get the work done and accounting for these expenditures. **Persuasion:** Persuading others to approach things differently. **Social Perceptiveness:** Being aware of others' reactions and understanding why they react the way they do. **Negotiation:** Bringing others together and trying to reconcile differences. **Judgment and Decision Making:** Weighing the relative costs and benefits of a potential action. **Service Orientation:** Actively looking for ways to help people. **Speaking:** Talking to others to effectively convey information. **Time Management:** Managing one's own time and the time of others.

Education and Training Programs: Financial Planning and Services; Investments and Securities. **Related Knowledge/Courses—Economics and Accounting:** Economic and accounting principles and practices, the financial markets, banking, and the analysis and reporting of financial data. **Customer and Personal Service:** Principles and processes for providing customer and personal services, including needs assessment techniques, quality service standards, alternative delivery systems, and customer satisfaction evaluation techniques. **Sales and Marketing:** Principles and methods involved in showing, promoting, and selling products or services. This includes marketing strategies and tactics, product demonstration and sales techniques, and sales control systems. **Clerical Practices:** Administrative and clerical procedures and systems such as word-processing systems, filing and records management systems, stenography and transcription, forms, design principles, and other office procedures and terminology. **Law and Government:** Laws, legal codes, court procedures, precedents, government regulations, executive orders, agency rules, and the democratic political process. **Mathematics:** Numbers and their operations and interrelationships, including arithmetic, algebra, geometry, calculus, and statistics and their applications.

Work Environment: Indoors; sitting.

Sales Engineers

- ❁ Education/Training Required: Bachelor's degree
- ❁ Annual Earnings: $80,270
- ❁ Beginning Wage: $48,290
- ❁ Earnings Growth Potential: Medium
- ❁ Growth: 8.5%
- ❁ Annual Job Openings: 7,371
- ❁ Self-Employed: 0.0%
- ❁ Part-Time: 2.0%

Sell business goods or services, the selling of which requires a technical background equivalent to a baccalaureate degree in engineering. Plan and modify product configurations to meet customer needs. Confer with customers and engineers to assess equipment needs and to determine system requirements. Collaborate with sales teams to understand customer requirements, to promote the sale of company products, and to provide sales support. Secure and renew orders and arrange delivery. Develop, present, or respond to proposals for specific customer requirements, including request for proposal responses and industry-specific solutions. Sell products requiring extensive technical expertise and support for installation and use, such as material handling equipment, numerical-control machinery, and computer systems. Diagnose problems with installed equipment. Prepare and deliver technical presentations that explain products or services to customers and prospective customers. Recommend improved materials or machinery to customers, documenting how such changes will lower costs or increase production. Provide technical and non-technical support and services to clients or other staff members regarding the use, operation, and maintenance of equipment. Research and identify potential customers for products or services. Visit prospective buyers at commercial, industrial, or other establishments to show samples or catalogs and to inform them about product pricing, availability, and advantages. Create sales or service contracts for products or services. Arrange for demonstrations or trial installations of equipment. Keep informed on industry news and trends; products; services; competitors; relevant information about legacy, existing, and emerging technologies; and the latest product-line developments. Attend company training seminars to become familiar with product lines. Provide information needed for the development of custom-made machinery. Develop sales plans to introduce products in new markets. Write technical documentation for products. Identify resale opportunities and support them to achieve sales plans. Document account activities, generate reports, and keep records of business transactions with customers and suppliers.

Personality Type: Enterprising. These occupations frequently involve starting up and carrying out projects and can involve leading people and making many decisions. They sometimes require risk taking and often deal with business.

GOE—Interest Area/Cluster: 14. Retail and Wholesale Sales and Service. **Work Group:** 14.02. Technical Sales. **Other Jobs in This Work Group:** Sales Representatives, Wholesale and Manufacturing, Technical and Scientific Products.

Skills—Operations Analysis: Analyzing needs and product requirements to create a design. **Science:** Using scientific methods to solve problems. **Systems Evaluation:** Looking at many indicators of system performance and taking into account their accuracy. **Technology Design:** Generating or adapting equipment and technology to serve user needs. **Programming:** Writing computer programs for various purposes. **Installation:** Installing equipment, machines, wiring, or programs to meet specifications. **Equipment Selection:** Determining the kind of tools and equipment needed to do a job. **Mathematics:** Using mathematics to solve problems.

Education and Training Program: Selling Skills and Sales Operations. **Related Knowledge/Courses—Sales and Marketing:** Principles and methods involved in showing, promoting, and selling products or services. This includes marketing strategies and tactics, product demonstration and sales techniques, and sales control systems. **Engineering and Technology:** Equipment, tools, and mechanical devices and their uses to produce motion, light, power, technology, and other applications. **Design:** Design techniques, principles, tools, and instruments involved in the production and use of precision technical plans, blueprints, drawings, and models. **Physics:** Physical principles, laws, and applications, including air, water, material dynamics, light, atomic principles, heat, electric theory, earth formations, and meteorological and related natural phenomena. **Computers and Electronics:** Electric circuit boards, processors, chips, and computer hardware and software, including applications and programming. **Customer and Personal Service:** Principles and processes for providing customer and personal services, including needs assessment techniques, quality service standards, alternative delivery systems, and customer satisfaction evaluation techniques.

Work Environment: Indoors; sitting; repetitive motions.

Sales Managers

* Education/Training Required: Work experience plus degree
* Annual Earnings: $94,910
* Beginning Wage: $45,860
* Earnings Growth Potential: Very high
* Growth: 10.2%
* Annual Job Openings: 36,392
* Self-Employed: 2.2%
* Part-Time: 4.1%

Direct the actual distribution or movement of products or services to customers. Coordinate sales distribution by establishing sales territories, quotas, and goals; establish training programs for sales representatives. Analyze sales statistics gathered by staff to determine sales potential and inventory requirements and monitor the preferences of customers. Resolve customer complaints regarding sales and service. Oversee regional and local sales managers and their staffs. Plan and direct staffing, training, and performance evaluations to develop and control sales and service programs. Determine price schedules and discount rates. Review operational records and reports to project sales and determine profitability. Monitor customer preferences to determine focus of sales efforts. Prepare budgets and approve budget expenditures. Confer or consult with department heads to plan advertising services and to secure information on equipment and customer specifications. Direct and coordinate activities involving sales of manufactured products, services, commodities, real estate, or other subjects of sale. Confer with potential customers regarding equipment needs and advise customers on types of equipment to purchase. Direct foreign sales and service outlets of an organization. Advise dealers and distributors on policies and operating procedures to ensure functional effectiveness of businesses. Visit franchised dealers to stimulate interest in establishment or expansion of leasing programs. Direct clerical staff to keep records of export correspondence, bid requests, and credit collections and to maintain current information on tariffs, licenses, and restrictions. Direct, coordinate, and review activities in sales and service accounting and recordkeeping and in receiving and shipping operations. Assess marketing potential of new and existing store locations, considering statistics and expenditures. Represent company at trade association meetings to promote products.

Personality Type: Enterprising. These occupations frequently involve starting up and carrying out projects and can involve leading people and making many decisions. They sometimes require risk taking and often deal with business.

GOE—Interest Area/Cluster: 14. Retail and Wholesale Sales and Service. **Work Group:** 14.01. Managerial Work in Retail/Wholesale Sales and Service. **Other Jobs in This Work Group:** Advertising and Promotions Managers; First-Line Supervisors/Managers of Non-Retail Sales Workers; First-Line Supervisors/Managers of Retail Sales Workers; Funeral Directors; Marketing Managers; Property, Real Estate, and Community Association Managers; Purchasing Managers.

Skills—Management of Personnel Resources: Motivating, developing, and directing people as they work; identifying the best people for the job. **Systems Analysis:** Determining how a system should work and how changes will affect outcomes. **Management of Financial Resources:** Determining how money will be spent to get the work done and accounting for these expenditures. **Persuasion:** Persuading others to approach things differently. **Negotiation:** Bringing others together and trying to reconcile differences. **Systems Evaluation:** Looking at many indicators of system performance and taking into account their accuracy. **Social Perceptiveness:** Being aware of others' reactions and understanding why they react the way they do. **Speaking:** Talking to others to effectively convey information.

Education and Training Programs: Business Administration and Management, General; Business/Commerce, General; Consumer Merchandising/Retailing Management; Marketing, Other; Marketing/Marketing Management, General. **Related Knowledge/Courses—Sales and Marketing:** Principles and methods involved in showing, promoting, and selling products or services. This includes marketing strategies and tactics, product demonstration and sales techniques, and sales control systems. **Personnel and Human Resources:** Principles and procedures for personnel recruitment; selection; training; compensation and benefits; labor relations and negotiation; and personnel information systems. **Economics and Accounting:** Economic and accounting principles and practices, the financial markets, banking, and the analysis and reporting of financial data. **Administration and Management:** Principles and processes involved in business and organizational planning, coordination, and execution. This includes strategic planning, resource allocation, manpower modeling, leadership techniques, and production methods. **Customer and**

Personal Service: Principles and processes for providing customer and personal services, including needs assessment techniques, quality service standards, alternative delivery systems, and customer satisfaction evaluation techniques. **Psychology:** Human behavior and performance, mental processes, psychological research methods, and the assessment and treatment of behavioral and affective disorders.

Work Environment: Indoors; sitting.

Sales Representatives, Wholesale and Manufacturing, Except Technical and Scientific Products

* Education/Training Required: Work experience in a related occupation
* Annual Earnings: $50,750
* Beginning Wage: $26,490
* Earnings Growth Potential: High
* Growth: 8.4%
* Annual Job Openings: 156,215
* Self-Employed: 4.0%
* Part-Time: 6.7%

Sell goods for wholesalers or manufacturers to businesses or groups of individuals. Work requires substantial knowledge of items sold. Answer customers' questions about products, prices, availability, product uses, and credit terms. Recommend products to customers based on customers' needs and interests. Contact regular and prospective customers to demonstrate products, explain product features, and solicit orders. Estimate or quote prices, credit or contract terms, warranties, and delivery dates. Consult with clients after sales or contract signings to resolve problems and to provide ongoing support. Prepare drawings, estimates, and bids that meet specific customer needs. Provide customers with product samples and catalogs. Identify prospective customers by using business directories, following leads from existing clients, participating in organizations and clubs, and attending trade shows and conferences. Arrange and direct delivery and installation of products and equipment. Monitor market conditions; product innovations; and competitors' products, prices, and sales. Negotiate details of contracts and payments and prepare sales contracts and order forms. Perform administrative duties, such as preparing sales budgets and reports, keeping sales records, and filing expense account reports. Obtain credit information about prospective customers. Forward orders to manufacturers. Check stock levels and reorder merchandise as necessary. Plan, assemble, and stock product displays in retail stores or make recommendations to retailers regarding product displays, promotional programs, and advertising. Negotiate with retail merchants to improve product exposure such as shelf positioning and advertising. Train customers' employees to operate and maintain new equipment. Buy products from manufacturers or brokerage firms and distribute them to wholesale and retail clients.

Personality Type: Conventional. These occupations frequently involve following set procedures and routines and can include working with data and details more than with ideas. Usually there is a clear line of authority to follow.

GOE—Interest Area/Cluster: 14. Retail and Wholesale Sales and Service. **Work Group:** 14.03. General Sales. **Other Jobs in This Work Group:** Parts Salespersons; Real Estate Brokers; Real Estate Sales Agents; Retail Salespersons; Service Station Attendants.

Skills—Negotiation: Bringing others together and trying to reconcile differences. **Persuasion:** Persuading others to approach things differently. **Service Orientation:** Actively looking for ways to help people. **Management of Financial Resources:** Determining how money will be spent to get the work done and accounting for these expenditures. **Operations Analysis:** Analyzing needs and product requirements to create a design. **Time Management:** Managing one's own time and the time of others. **Speaking:** Talking to others to effectively convey information. **Installation:** Installing equipment, machines, wiring, or programs to meet specifications.

Education and Training Programs: Apparel and Accessories Marketing Operations; Business, Management, Marketing, and Related Support Services, Other; Fashion Merchandising; General Merchandising, Sales, and Related Marketing Operations, Other; Insurance; Sales, Distribution, and Marketing Operations, General; Special Products Marketing Operations; Specialized Merchandising, Sales, and Related Marketing Operations, Other. **Related Knowledge/Courses—Sales and Marketing:** Principles and methods involved in showing, promoting, and selling products or services. This includes marketing strategies and tactics, product demonstration and sales techniques, and sales control systems. **Economics and Accounting:** Economic and accounting principles and practices, the financial markets, banking, and the analysis and reporting of financial data. **Customer and Personal Service:** Principles and processes for providing customer and personal services, including needs assessment techniques, quality service standards, alternative delivery systems, and customer satisfaction evaluation techniques. **Transportation:** Principles and methods for moving people or goods by air, rail, sea, or road, including their relative costs, advantages, and limitations. **Mathematics:** Numbers and their operations and interrelationships, including arithmetic, algebra, geometry, calculus, and statistics and their applications. **Administration and Management:** Principles and processes involved in business and organizational planning, coordination, and execution. This includes strategic planning, resource allocation, manpower modeling, leadership techniques, and production methods.

Work Environment: Outdoors; noisy; contaminants; more often standing than sitting; walking and running.

Sales Representatives, Wholesale and Manufacturing, Technical and Scientific Products

- ❋ Education/Training Required: Work experience in a related occupation
- ❋ Annual Earnings: $68,270
- ❋ Beginning Wage: $35,090
- ❋ Earnings Growth Potential: High
- ❋ Growth: 12.4%
- ❋ Annual Job Openings: 43,469
- ❋ Self-Employed: 4.2%
- ❋ Part-Time: 6.7%

Sell goods for wholesalers or manufacturers where technical or scientific knowledge is required in such areas as biology, engineering, chemistry, and electronics, normally obtained from at least two years of postsecondary education. Contact new and existing customers to discuss their needs and to explain how these needs could be met by specific products and services. Answer customers' questions about products, prices, availability, product uses, and credit terms. Quote prices, credit terms, and other bid specifications. Emphasize product features based on analyses of customers' needs and on technical knowledge of product capabilities and limitations. Negotiate prices and terms of sales and service agreements. Maintain customer records, using automated systems. Identify prospective customers by using business directories, following leads from existing clients, participating in organizations and clubs, and attending trade shows and conferences. Prepare sales contracts for

orders obtained and submit orders for processing. Select the correct products or assist customers in making product selections based on customers' needs, product specifications, and applicable regulations. Collaborate with colleagues to exchange information such as selling strategies and marketing information. Prepare sales presentations and proposals that explain product specifications and applications. Provide customers with ongoing technical support. Demonstrate and explain the operation and use of products. Inform customers of estimated delivery schedules, service contracts, warranties, or other information pertaining to purchased products. Attend sales and trade meetings and read related publications in order to obtain information about market conditions, business trends, and industry developments. Visit establishments to evaluate needs and to promote product or service sales. Complete expense reports, sales reports, and other paperwork. Initiate sales campaigns and follow marketing plan guidelines in order to meet sales and production expectations. Recommend ways for customers to alter product usage in order to improve production. Complete product and development training as required. Provide feedback to companys' product design teams so that products can be tailored to clients' needs. Arrange for installation and test-operation of machinery.

Personality Type: Enterprising. These occupations frequently involve starting up and carrying out projects and can involve leading people and making many decisions. They sometimes require risk taking and often deal with business.

GOE—Interest Area/Cluster: 14. Retail and Wholesale Sales and Service. **Work Group:** 14.02. Technical Sales. **Other Jobs in This Work Group:** Sales Engineers.

Skills—Persuasion: Persuading others to approach things differently. **Negotiation:** Bringing others together and trying to reconcile differences. **Science:** Using scientific methods to solve problems. **Management of Financial Resources:** Determining how money will be spent to get the work done and accounting for these expenditures. **Service Orientation:** Actively looking for ways to help people. **Coordination:** Adjusting actions in relation to others' actions. **Operations Analysis:** Analyzing needs and product requirements to create a design. **Social Perceptiveness:** Being aware of others' reactions and understanding why they react the way they do.

Education and Training Programs: Business, Management, Marketing, and Related Support Services; Selling Skills and Sales Operations. **Related Knowledge/Courses—Sales and**

Marketing: Principles and methods involved in showing, promoting, and selling products or services. This includes marketing strategies and tactics, product demonstration and sales techniques, and sales control systems. **Customer and Personal Service:** Principles and processes for providing customer and personal services, including needs assessment techniques, quality service standards, alternative delivery systems, and customer satisfaction evaluation techniques. **Production and Processing:** Inputs, outputs, raw materials, waste, quality control, costs, and techniques for maximizing the manufacture and distribution of goods. **Administration and Management:** Principles and processes involved in business and organizational planning, coordination, and execution. This includes strategic planning, resource allocation, manpower modeling, leadership techniques, and production methods. **Computers and Electronics:** Electric circuit boards, processors, chips, and computer hardware and software, including applications and programming. **Transportation:** Principles and methods for moving people or goods by air, rail, sea, or road, including their relative costs, advantages, and limitations.

Work Environment: Indoors; sitting.

School Psychologists

- ❁ Education/Training Required: Doctoral degree
- ❁ Annual Earnings: $62,210
- ❁ Beginning Wage: $37,300
- ❁ Earnings Growth Potential: High
- ❁ Growth: 15.8%
- ❁ Annual Job Openings: 8,309
- ❁ Self-Employed: 34.2%
- ❁ Part-Time: 24.0%

The job openings listed here are shared with Clinical Psychologists and with Counseling Psychologists.

Investigate processes of learning and teaching and develop psychological principles and techniques applicable to educational problems. Compile and interpret students' test results, along with information from teachers and parents, to diagnose conditions and to help assess eligibility for special services. Report any pertinent information to the proper authorities in cases of child endangerment, neglect, or abuse. Assess an individual child's needs, limitations, and potential, using observation, review of school records, and consultation with parents and school personnel. Select, administer, and score psychological tests. Provide consultation to parents, teachers, administrators, and others on topics such as learning styles and behavior modification techniques. Promote an understanding of child development and its relationship to learning and behavior. Collaborate with other educational professionals to develop teaching strategies and school programs. Counsel children and families to help solve conflicts and problems in learning and adjustment. Develop individualized educational plans in collaboration with teachers and other staff members. Maintain student records, including special education reports, confidential records, records of services provided, and behavioral data. Serve as a resource to help families and schools deal with crises, such as separation and loss. Attend workshops, seminars, or professional meetings to remain informed of new developments in school psychology. Design classes and programs to meet the needs of special students. Refer students and their families to appropriate community agencies for medical, vocational, or social services. Initiate and direct efforts to foster tolerance, understanding, and appreciation of diversity in school communities. Collect and analyze data to evaluate the effectiveness of academic programs and other services, such as behavioral management systems. Provide educational programs on topics such as classroom management, teaching strategies, or parenting skills. Conduct research to generate new knowledge that can be used to address learning and behavior issues.

Personality Type: Investigative. These occupations frequently involve working with ideas and require an extensive amount of thinking. They can involve searching for facts and figuring out problems mentally.

GOE—Interest Area/Cluster: 15. Scientific Research, Engineering, and Mathematics. **Work Group:** 15.04. Social Sciences. **Other Jobs in This Work Group:** Anthropologists; Anthropologists and Archeologists; Archeologists; Economists; Historians; Industrial-Organizational Psychologists; Political Scientists; Sociologists.

Skills—Social Perceptiveness: Being aware of others' reactions and understanding why they react the way they do. **Negotiation:** Bringing others together and trying to reconcile differences. **Learning Strategies:** Using multiple approaches when learning or teaching new things. **Persuasion:** Persuading others to approach things differently. **Writing:** Communicating effectively with others in writing as indicated by the needs of the audience. **Active Listening:** Listening to what other people are saying and asking questions as appropriate. **Service Orientation:** Actively looking for ways to help people. **Active Learning:** Working with new material or information to grasp its implications.

Education and Training Programs: Clinical Psychology; Counseling Psychology; Developmental and Child Psychology; Educational Assessment, Testing, and Measurement; Psychoanalysis and Psychotherapy; Psychology, General; School Psychology. **Related Knowledge/Courses—Therapy and Counseling:** Information and techniques needed to rehabilitate physical and mental ailments and to provide career guidance, including alternative treatments, rehabilitation equipment and its proper use, and methods to evaluate treatment effects. **Psychology:** Human behavior and performance, mental processes, psychological research methods, and the assessment and treatment of behavioral and affective disorders. **Sociology and Anthropology:** Group behavior and dynamics; societal trends and influences; and cultures and their history, migrations, ethnicity, and origins. **Philosophy and Theology:** Different philosophical systems and religions, including their basic principles, values, ethics, ways of thinking, customs, and practices and their impact on human culture. **Education and Training:** Instructional methods and training techniques, including curriculum design principles, learning theory, group and individual teaching techniques, design of individual development plans, and test design principles. **Medicine and Dentistry:** The information and techniques needed to diagnose and treat injuries, diseases, and deformities. This includes symptoms, treatment alternatives, drug properties and interactions, and preventive health-care measures.

Work Environment: Indoors; sitting.

Secondary School Teachers, Except Special and Vocational Education

- ❋ Education/Training Required: Bachelor's degree
- ❋ Annual Earnings: $49,420
- ❋ Beginning Wage: $32,920
- ❋ Earnings Growth Potential: Low
- ❋ Growth: 5.6%
- ❋ Annual Job Openings: 93,166
- ❋ Self-Employed: 0.0%
- ❋ Part-Time: 7.8%

Instruct students in secondary public or private schools in one or more subjects at the secondary level, such as English, mathematics, or social studies. May be designated according to subject matter specialty, such as typing instructors, commercial teachers, or English teachers.

Establish and enforce rules for behavior and procedures for maintaining order among the students for whom they are responsible. Instruct through lectures, discussions, and demonstrations in one or more subjects such as English, mathematics, or social studies. Establish clear objectives for all lessons, units, and projects and communicate those objectives to students. Prepare, administer, and grade tests and assignments to evaluate students' progress. Prepare materials and classrooms for class activities. Adapt teaching methods and instructional materials to meet students' varying needs and interests. Assign and grade classwork and homework. Maintain accurate and complete student records as required by laws, district policies, and administrative regulations. Enforce all administration policies and rules governing students. Observe and evaluate students' performance, behavior, social development, and physical health. Plan and conduct activities for a balanced program of instruction, demonstration, and work time that provides students with opportunities to observe, question, and investigate. Prepare students for later grades by encouraging them to explore learning opportunities and to persevere with challenging tasks. Guide and counsel students with adjustment and/or academic problems or special academic interests. Instruct and monitor students in the use and care of equipment and materials to prevent injuries and damage. Prepare for assigned classes and show written evidence of preparation upon request of immediate supervisors. Meet with parents and guardians to discuss their children's progress and to determine their priorities for their children and their resource needs. Confer with parents or guardians, other teachers, counselors, and administrators in order to resolve students' behavioral and academic problems. Use computers, audiovisual aids, and other equipment and materials to supplement presentations. Prepare objectives and outlines for courses of study, following curriculum guidelines or requirements of states and schools. Meet with other professionals to discuss individual students' needs and progress.

Personality Type: Social. These occupations frequently involve working with, communicating with, and teaching people and often involve helping or providing service to others.

GOE—Interest Area/Cluster: 05. Education and Training. **Work Group:** 05.02. Preschool, Elementary, and Secondary Teaching and Instructing. **Other Jobs in This Work Group:** Elementary School Teachers, Except Special Education; Kindergarten Teachers, Except Special Education; Middle School Teachers, Except Special and Vocational Education; Preschool Teachers, Except Special Education;

Special Education Teachers, Middle School; Special Education Teachers, Preschool, Kindergarten, and Elementary School; Special Education Teachers, Secondary School; Teacher Assistants; Vocational Education Teachers, Middle School; Vocational Education Teachers, Secondary School.

Skills—Learning Strategies: Using multiple approaches when learning or teaching new things. **Social Perceptiveness:** Being aware of others' reactions and understanding why they react the way they do. **Persuasion:** Persuading others to approach things differently. **Monitoring:** Assessing how well one is doing when learning or doing something. **Instructing:** Teaching others how to do something. **Time Management:** Managing one's own time and the time of others. **Negotiation:** Bringing others together and trying to reconcile differences. **Service Orientation:** Actively looking for ways to help people.

Education and Training Programs: Art Teacher Education; Biology Teacher Education; Business Teacher Education; English/Language Arts Teacher Education; Family and Consumer Sciences Teacher Education; Foreign Language Teacher Education; Geography Teacher Education; History Teacher Education; Mathematics Teacher Education; Physical Education Teaching and Coaching; Science Teacher Education; Social Science Teacher Education; Social Studies Teacher Education; Spanish Language Teacher Education; Speech Teacher Education; others. **Related Knowledge/Courses—History and Archeology:** Historical events and their causes, indicators, and impact on particular civilizations and cultures. **Philosophy and Theology:** Different philosophical systems and religions, including their basic principles, values, ethics, ways of thinking, customs, and practices and their impact on human culture. **Sociology and Anthropology:** Group behavior and dynamics; societal trends and influences; and cultures and their history, migrations, ethnicity, and origins. **Education and Training:** Instructional methods and training techniques, including curriculum design principles, learning theory, group and individual teaching techniques, design of individual development plans, and test design principles. **Geography:** Various methods for describing the location and distribution of land, sea, and air masses, including their physical locations, relationships, and characteristics. **Therapy and Counseling:** Information and techniques needed to rehabilitate physical and mental ailments and to provide career guidance, including alternative treatments, rehabilitation equipment and its proper use, and methods to evaluate treatment effects.

Work Environment: Indoors; noisy; standing.

Secretaries, Except Legal, Medical, and Executive

- ❋ Education/Training Required: Moderate-term on-the-job training
- ❋ Annual Earnings: $28,220
- ❋ Beginning Wage: $17,920
- ❋ Earnings Growth Potential: Medium
- ❋ Growth: 1.2%
- ❋ Annual Job Openings: 239,630
- ❋ Self-Employed: 1.4%
- ❋ Part-Time: 18.9%

Perform routine clerical and administrative functions such as drafting correspondence, scheduling appointments, organizing and maintaining paper and electronic files, or providing information to callers. Operate office equipment such as fax machines, copiers, and phone systems and use computers for spreadsheet, word-processing, database management, and other applications. Answer telephones and give information to callers, take messages, or transfer calls to appropriate individuals. Greet visitors and callers, handle their inquiries, and direct them to the appropriate persons according to their needs. Set up and maintain paper and electronic filing systems for records, correspondence, and other material. Locate and attach appropriate files to incoming correspondence requiring replies. Open, read, route, and distribute incoming mail and other material and prepare answers to routine letters. Complete forms in accordance with company procedures. Make copies of correspondence and other printed material. Review work done by others to check for correct spelling and grammar, ensure that company format policies are followed, and recommend revisions. Compose, type, and distribute meeting notes, routine correspondence, and reports. Learn to operate new office technologies as they are developed and implemented. Maintain scheduling and event calendars. Schedule and confirm appointments for clients, customers, or supervisors. Manage projects and contribute to committee and team work. Mail newsletters, promotional material, and other information. Order and dispense supplies. Conduct searches to find needed information, using such sources as the Internet. Provide services to customers, such as order placement and account information. Collect and disburse funds from cash accounts and keep records of collections and disbursements. Prepare and mail checks. Establish work procedures and schedules and keep track of the daily work of clerical staff. Coordinate conferences and meetings. Take dictation in shorthand or by machine and transcribe information. Arrange conferences, meetings, and travel reservations for office personnel. Operate electronic mail systems and coordinate the flow of information both internally and with other organizations. Supervise other clerical staff and provide training and orientation to new staff.

Personality Type: Conventional. These occupations frequently involve following set procedures and routines and can include working with data and details more than with ideas. Usually there is a clear line of authority to follow.

GOE—Interest Area/Cluster: 04. Business and Administration. **Work Group:** 04.04. Secretarial Support. **Other Jobs in This Work Group:** Executive Secretaries and Administrative Assistants; Legal Secretaries; Medical Secretaries.

Skill—Writing: Communicating effectively with others in writing as indicated by the needs of the audience.

Education and Training Programs: Administrative Assistant and Secretarial Science, General; Executive Assistant/Executive Secretary Training. **Related Knowledge/Courses—Clerical Practices:** Administrative and clerical procedures and systems such as word-processing systems, filing and records management systems, stenography and transcription, forms, design principles, and other office procedures and terminology. **Customer and Personal Service:** Principles and processes for providing customer and personal services, including needs assessment techniques, quality service standards, alternative delivery systems, and customer satisfaction evaluation techniques. **Computers and Electronics:** Electric circuit boards, processors, chips, and computer hardware and software, including applications and programming. **Economics and Accounting:** Economic and accounting principles and practices, the financial markets, banking, and the analysis and reporting of financial data. **English Language:** The structure and content of the English language, including the meaning and spelling of words, rules of composition, and grammar. **Personnel and Human Resources:** Principles and procedures for personnel recruitment; selection; training; compensation and benefits; labor relations and negotiation; and personnel information systems.

Work Environment: Indoors; sitting; repetitive motions.

Security and Fire Alarm Systems Installers

* Education/Training Required: Postsecondary vocational training
* Annual Earnings: $35,390
* Beginning Wage: $22,800
* Earnings Growth Potential: Medium
* Growth: 20.2%
* Annual Job Openings: 5,729
* Self-Employed: 7.2%
* Part-Time: 2.7%

Install, program, maintain, and repair security and fire alarm wiring and equipment. Ensure that work is in accordance with relevant codes. Examine systems to locate problems such as loose connections or broken insulation. Test backup batteries, keypad programming, sirens, and all security features in order to ensure proper functioning and to diagnose malfunctions. Mount and fasten control panels, door and window contacts, sensors, and video cameras and attach electrical and telephone wiring in order to connect components. Install, maintain, or repair security systems, alarm devices, and related equipment, following blueprints of electrical layouts and building plans. Inspect installation sites and study work orders, building plans, and installation manuals in order to determine materials requirements and installation procedures. Feed cables through access holes, roof spaces, and cavity walls to reach fixture outlets; then position and terminate cables, wires, and strapping. Adjust sensitivity of units based on room structures and manufacturers' recommendations, using programming keypads. Test and repair circuits and sensors, following wiring and system specifications. Drill holes for wiring in wall studs, joists, ceilings, and floors. Demonstrate systems for customers and explain details such as the causes and consequences of false alarms. Consult with clients to assess risks and to determine security requirements. Keep informed of new products and developments. Mount raceways and conduits and fasten wires to wood framing, using staplers. Prepare documents such as invoices and warranties. Provide customers with cost estimates for equipment installation. Order replacement parts.

Personality Type: Realistic. These occupations frequently involve work activities that include practical, hands-on problems and solutions. They often deal with plants; animals; and real-world materials such as wood, tools, and machinery. Many of the occupations require working outside and don't involve a lot of paperwork or working closely with others.

GOE—Interest Area/Cluster: 02. Architecture and Construction. **Work Group:** 02.04. Construction Crafts. **Other Jobs in This Work Group:** Boilermakers; Brickmasons and Blockmasons; Carpet Installers; Cement Masons and Concrete Finishers; Commercial Divers; Construction Carpenters; Crane and Tower Operators; Drywall and Ceiling Tile Installers; Electricians; Fence Erectors; Floor Layers, Except Carpet, Wood, and Hard Tiles; Floor Sanders and Finishers; Glaziers; Hazardous Materials Removal Workers; Insulation Workers, Floor, Ceiling, and Wall; Insulation Workers, Mechanical; Manufactured Building and Mobile Home Installers; Operating Engineers and Other Construction Equipment Operators; Painters, Construction and Maintenance; Paperhangers; Paving, Surfacing, and Tamping Equipment Operators; Pile-Driver Operators; Pipe Fitters and Steamfitters; Pipelayers; Plasterers and Stucco Masons; Plumbers; Plumbers, Pipefitters, and Steamfitters; Rail-Track Laying and Maintenance Equipment Operators; Refractory Materials Repairers, Except Brickmasons; Reinforcing Iron and Rebar Workers; Riggers; Roofers; Rough Carpenters; Segmental Pavers; Sheet Metal Workers; Stone Cutters and Carvers, Manufacturing; Stonemasons; Structural Iron and Steel Workers; Tapers; Terrazzo Workers and Finishers; Tile and Marble Setters.

Skills—Installation: Installing equipment, machines, wiring, or programs to meet specifications. **Repairing:** Repairing machines or systems, using the needed tools. **Troubleshooting:** Determining what is causing an operating error and deciding what to do about it. **Equipment Maintenance:** Performing routine maintenance and determining when and what kind of maintenance is needed. **Systems Evaluation:** Looking at many indicators of system performance and taking into account their accuracy. **Technology Design:** Generating or adapting equipment and technology to serve user needs. **Operations Analysis:** Analyzing needs and product requirements to create a design. **Programming:** Writing computer programs for various purposes.

Education and Training Programs: Electrician Training; Security System Installation, Repair, and Inspection Technology/Technician Training. **Related Knowledge/Courses—Telecommunications:** Transmission, broadcasting, switching, control, and operation of telecommunications systems. **Building and Construction:** Materials, methods, and the appropriate tools to construct objects, structures, and buildings. **Mechanical Devices:** Machines and tools, including their designs, uses, benefits, repair, and

maintenance. **Computers and Electronics:** Electric circuit boards, processors, chips, and computer hardware and software, including applications and programming. **Public Safety and Security:** Weaponry; public safety; security operations, rules, regulations, precautions, and prevention; and the protection of people, data, and property. **Design:** Design techniques, principles, tools, and instruments involved in the production and use of precision technical plans, blueprints, drawings, and models.

Work Environment: More often indoors than outdoors; noisy; very hot or cold; standing; using hands on objects, tools, or controls.

Security Guards

- ❋ Education/Training Required: Short-term on-the-job training
- ❋ Annual Earnings: $22,570
- ❋ Beginning Wage: $15,880
- ❋ Earnings Growth Potential: Low
- ❋ Growth: 16.9%
- ❋ Annual Job Openings: 222,085
- ❋ Self-Employed: 0.7%
- ❋ Part-Time: 15.5%

Guard, patrol, or monitor premises to prevent theft, violence, or infractions of rules. Monitor and authorize entrance and departure of employees, visitors, and other persons to guard against theft and maintain security of premises. Write reports of daily activities and irregularities such as equipment or property damage, theft, presence of unauthorized persons, or unusual occurrences. Call police or fire departments in cases of emergency such as fire or presence of unauthorized persons. Answer alarms and investigate disturbances. Circulate among visitors, patrons, or employees to preserve order and protect property. Patrol industrial or commercial premises to prevent and detect signs of intrusion and ensure security of doors, windows, and gates. Escort or drive motor vehicle to transport individuals to specified locations or to provide personal protection. Operate detecting devices to screen individuals and prevent passage of prohibited articles into restricted areas. Answer telephone calls to take messages, answer questions, and provide information during non-business hours or when switchboard is closed. Warn persons of rule infractions or violations and apprehend or evict violators from premises, using force when necessary. Inspect and adjust security systems, equipment, or machinery to ensure operational use and to detect evidence of tampering. Monitor and adjust controls that regulate building systems such as air conditioning, furnace, or boiler.

Personality Type: Realistic. These occupations frequently involve work activities that include practical, hands-on problems and solutions. They often deal with plants; animals; and real-world materials such as wood, tools, and machinery. Many of the occupations require working outside and don't involve a lot of paperwork or working closely with others.

GOE—Interest Area/Cluster: 12. Law and Public Safety. **Work Group:** 12.05. Safety and Security. **Other Jobs in This Work Group:** Animal Control Workers; Crossing Guards; Gaming Surveillance Officers and Gaming Investigators; Lifeguards, Ski Patrol, and Other Recreational Protective Service Workers; Private Detectives and Investigators; Transportation Security Screeners.

Skill—None met the criteria.

Education and Training Programs: Securities Services Administration/Management; Security and Loss Prevention Services. **Related Knowledge/Course—Public Safety and Security:** Weaponry; public safety; security operations, rules, regulations, precautions, and prevention; and the protection of people, data, and property.

Work Environment: More often indoors than outdoors; noisy; standing; walking and running; using hands on objects, tools, or controls.

Self-Enrichment Education Teachers

- ❋ Education/Training Required: Work experience in a related occupation
- ❋ Annual Earnings: $34,580
- ❋ Beginning Wage: $18,530
- ❋ Earnings Growth Potential: High
- ❋ Growth: 23.1%
- ❋ Annual Job Openings: 64,449
- ❋ Self-Employed: 21.5%
- ❋ Part-Time: 41.3%

Teach or instruct courses other than those that normally lead to an occupational objective or degree. Courses may include self-improvement, nonvocational, and nonacademic subjects. Teaching may or may not take place in a traditional educational institution. Adapt teaching methods and instructional materials to meet students' varying needs and interests. Conduct classes, workshops, and demonstrations and provide individual instruction to teach topics and skills such as cooking, dancing, writing, physical fitness, photography, personal finance, and flying. Monitor students' performance to make suggestions for improvement and to ensure that they satisfy course standards, training requirements, and objectives. Observe students to determine qualifications, limitations, abilities, interests, and other individual characteristics. Instruct students individually and in groups, using various teaching methods such as lectures, discussions, and demonstrations. Establish clear objectives for all lessons, units, and projects and communicate those objectives to students. Instruct and monitor students in use and care of equipment and materials to prevent injury and damage. Prepare students for further development by encouraging them to explore learning opportunities and to persevere with challenging tasks. Prepare materials and classrooms for class activities. Enforce policies and rules governing students. Plan and conduct activities for a balanced program of instruction, demonstration, and work time that provides students with opportunities to observe, question, and investigate. Prepare instructional program objectives, outlines, and lesson plans. Maintain accurate and complete student records as required by administrative policy. Participate in publicity planning and student recruitment. Plan and supervise class projects, field trips, visits by guest speakers, contests, or other experiential activities and guide students in learning from those activities. Attend professional meetings, conferences, and workshops in order to maintain and improve professional competence. Meet with other instructors to discuss individual students and their progress. Confer with other teachers and professionals to plan and schedule lessons promoting learning and development. Attend staff meetings and serve on committees as required. Prepare and administer written, oral, and performance tests and issue grades in accordance with performance.

Personality Type: Social. These occupations frequently involve working with, communicating with, and teaching people and often involve helping or providing service to others.

GOE—Interest Area/Cluster: 05. Education and Training. **Work Group:** 05.03. Postsecondary and Adult Teaching and Instructing. **Other Jobs in This Work Group:** Adult Literacy, Remedial Education, and GED Teachers and Instructors; Agricultural Sciences Teachers, Postsecondary; Anthropology and Archeology Teachers, Postsecondary; Architecture

Teachers, Postsecondary; Area, Ethnic, and Cultural Studies Teachers, Postsecondary; Art, Drama, and Music Teachers, Postsecondary; Atmospheric, Earth, Marine, and Space Sciences Teachers, Postsecondary; Biological Science Teachers, Postsecondary; Business Teachers, Postsecondary; Chemistry Teachers, Postsecondary; Communications Teachers, Postsecondary; Computer Science Teachers, Postsecondary; Criminal Justice and Law Enforcement Teachers, Postsecondary; Economics Teachers, Postsecondary; Education Teachers, Postsecondary; Engineering Teachers, Postsecondary; English Language and Literature Teachers, Postsecondary; Environmental Science Teachers, Postsecondary; Farm and Home Management Advisors; Foreign Language and Literature Teachers, Postsecondary; Forestry and Conservation Science Teachers, Postsecondary; Geography Teachers, Postsecondary; Graduate Teaching Assistants; Health Specialties Teachers, Postsecondary; History Teachers, Postsecondary; Home Economics Teachers, Postsecondary; Law Teachers, Postsecondary; Library Science Teachers, Postsecondary; Mathematical Science Teachers, Postsecondary; Nursing Instructors and Teachers, Postsecondary; Philosophy and Religion Teachers, Postsecondary; Physics Teachers, Postsecondary; Political Science Teachers, Postsecondary; Psychology Teachers, Postsecondary; Recreation and Fitness Studies Teachers, Postsecondary; Social Work Teachers, Postsecondary; Sociology Teachers, Postsecondary; Vocational Education Teachers, Postsecondary.

Skills—Instructing: Teaching others how to do something. **Learning Strategies:** Using multiple approaches when learning or teaching new things. **Social Perceptiveness:** Being aware of others' reactions and understanding why they react the way they do. **Service Orientation:** Actively looking for ways to help people. **Monitoring:** Assessing how well one is doing when learning or doing something. **Speaking:** Talking to others to effectively convey information. **Persuasion:** Persuading others to approach things differently. **Time Management:** Managing one's own time and the time of others.

Education and Training Program: Adult and Continuing Education and Teaching. **Related Knowledge/Courses— Fine Arts:** Theory and techniques required to produce, compose, and perform works of music, dance, visual arts, drama, and sculpture. **Education and Training:** Instructional methods and training techniques, including curriculum design principles, learning theory, group and individual teaching techniques, design of individual development plans, and test design principles. **Psychology:** Human behavior and performance, mental processes, psychological research methods,

and the assessment and treatment of behavioral and affective disorders. **Customer and Personal Service:** Principles and processes for providing customer and personal services, including needs assessment techniques, quality service standards, alternative delivery systems, and customer satisfaction evaluation techniques. **Sales and Marketing:** Principles and methods involved in showing, promoting, and selling products or services. This includes marketing strategies and tactics, product demonstration and sales techniques, and sales control systems. **Administration and Management:** Principles and processes involved in business and organizational planning, coordination, and execution. This includes strategic planning, resource allocation, manpower modeling, leadership techniques, and production methods.

Work Environment: Indoors; standing.

Set and Exhibit Designers

- ✺ Education/Training Required: Bachelor's degree
- ✺ Annual Earnings: $43,220
- ✺ Beginning Wage: $23,600
- ✺ Earnings Growth Potential: High
- ✺ Growth: 17.8%
- ✺ Annual Job Openings: 1,402
- ✺ Self-Employed: 29.8%
- ✺ Part-Time: 16.7%

Design special exhibits and movie, television, and theater sets. May study scripts, confer with directors, and conduct research to determine appropriate architectural styles. Examine objects to be included in exhibits to plan where and how to display them. Acquire, or arrange for acquisition of, specimens or graphics required to complete exhibits. Prepare rough drafts and scale working drawings of sets, including floor plans, scenery, and properties to be constructed. Confer with clients and staff to gather information about exhibit space, proposed themes and content, timelines, budgets, materials, and promotion requirements. Estimate set- or exhibit-related costs, including materials, construction, and rental of props or locations. Develop set designs based on evaluation of scripts, budgets, research information, and available locations. Direct and coordinate construction, erection, or decoration activities to ensure that sets or exhibits meet design, budget, and schedule requirements. Inspect installed exhibits for conformance to specifications and satisfactory operation of special effects components. Plan for location-specific issues such as space limitations, traffic flow patterns, and safety concerns. Submit plans for approval and adapt plans to serve intended purposes or to conform to budget or fabrication restrictions. Prepare preliminary renderings of proposed exhibits, including detailed construction, layout, and material specifications and diagrams relating to aspects such as special effects and lighting. Select and purchase lumber and hardware necessary for set construction. Collaborate with those in charge of lighting and sound so that those production aspects can be coordinated with set designs or exhibit layouts. Research architectural and stylistic elements appropriate to the time period to be depicted, consulting experts for information as necessary. Design and produce displays and materials that can be used to decorate windows, interior displays, or event locations such as streets and fairgrounds. Coordinate the removal of sets, props, and exhibits after productions or events are complete. Select set props such as furniture, pictures, lamps, and rugs. Confer with conservators to determine how to handle an exhibit's environmental aspects, such as lighting, temperature, and humidity, so that objects will be protected and exhibits will be enhanced.

Personality Type: Artistic. These occupations frequently involve working with forms, designs, and patterns. They often require self-expression, and the work can be done without following a clear set of rules.

GOE—Interest Area/Cluster: 03. Arts and Communication. **Work Group:** 03.05. Design. **Other Jobs in This Work Group:** Commercial and Industrial Designers; Fashion Designers; Floral Designers; Graphic Designers; Interior Designers; Merchandise Displayers and Window Trimmers.

Skills—Installation: Installing equipment, machines, wiring, or programs to meet specifications. **Operations Analysis:** Analyzing needs and product requirements to create a design. **Persuasion:** Persuading others to approach things differently. **Management of Material Resources:** Obtaining and seeing to the appropriate use of equipment, facilities, and materials needed to do certain work. **Equipment Selection:** Determining the kind of tools and equipment needed to do a job. **Management of Personnel Resources:** Motivating, developing, and directing people as they work; identifying the best people for the job. **Management of Financial Resources:** Determining how money will be spent to get the work done and accounting for these expenditures. **Complex Problem Solving:** Identifying complex problems, reviewing the options, and implementing solutions.

Education and Training Programs: Design and Applied Arts, Other; Design and Visual Communications, General;

Illustration; Technical Theatre/Theatre Design and Technology. **Related Knowledge/Courses—Fine Arts:** Theory and techniques required to produce, compose, and perform works of music, dance, visual arts, drama, and sculpture. **Design:** Design techniques, principles, tools, and instruments involved in the production and use of precision technical plans, blueprints, drawings, and models. **History and Archeology:** Historical events and their causes, indicators, and impact on particular civilizations and cultures. **Communications and Media:** Media production, communication, and dissemination techniques and methods, including alternative ways to inform and entertain via written, oral, and visual media. **Sociology and Anthropology:** Group behavior and dynamics; societal trends and influences; and cultures and their history, migrations, ethnicity, and origins. **Computers and Electronics:** Electric circuit boards, processors, chips, and computer hardware and software, including applications and programming.

Work Environment: Indoors; sitting; using hands on objects, tools, or controls.

Sheet Metal Workers

* Education/Training Required: Long-term on-the-job training
* Annual Earnings: $39,210
* Beginning Wage: $22,820
* Earnings Growth Potential: High
* Growth: 6.7%
* Annual Job Openings: 31,677
* Self-Employed: 4.7%
* Part-Time: 4.2%

Fabricate, assemble, install, and repair sheet metal products and equipment, such as ducts, control boxes, drainpipes, and furnace casings. Work may involve any of the following: setting up and operating fabricating machines to cut, bend, and straighten sheet metal; shaping metal over anvils, blocks, or forms, using hammer; operating soldering and welding equipment to join sheet metal parts; and inspecting, assembling, and smoothing seams and joints of burred surfaces. Determine project requirements, including scope, assembly sequences, and required methods and materials, according to blueprints, drawings, and written or verbal instructions. Lay out, measure, and mark dimensions and reference lines on material such as roofing panels according to drawings or templates, using calculators, scribes, dividers, squares, and rulers. Maneuver completed units into position for installation and anchor the units. Convert blueprints into shop drawings to be followed in the construction and assembly of sheet metal products. Install assemblies such as flashing, pipes, tubes, heating and air conditioning ducts, furnace casings, rain gutters, and downspouts in supportive frameworks. Select gauges and types of sheet metal or non-metallic material according to product specifications. Drill and punch holes in metal for screws, bolts, and rivets. Fasten seams and joints together with welds, bolts, cement, rivets, solder, caulks, metal drive clips, and bonds to assemble components into products or to repair sheet metal items. Fabricate or alter parts at construction sites, using shears, hammers, punches, and drills. Finish parts, using hacksaws and hand, rotary, or squaring shears. Trim, file, grind, deburr, buff, and smooth surfaces, seams, and joints of assembled parts, using hand tools and portable power tools. Maintain equipment, making repairs and modifications when necessary. Shape metal material over anvils, blocks, or other forms, using hand tools. Transport prefabricated parts to construction sites for assembly and installation. Develop and lay out patterns that use materials most efficiently, using computerized metalworking equipment to experiment with different layouts. Inspect individual parts, assemblies, and installations for conformance to specifications and building codes, using measuring instruments such as calipers, scales, and micrometers. Secure metal roof panels in place and interlock and fasten grooved panel edges. Fasten roof panel edges and machine-made molding to structures, nailing or welding pieces into place.

Personality Type: Realistic. These occupations frequently involve work activities that include practical, hands-on problems and solutions. They often deal with plants; animals; and real-world materials such as wood, tools, and machinery. Many of the occupations require working outside and don't involve a lot of paperwork or working closely with others.

GOE—Interest Area/Cluster: 02. Architecture and Construction. **Work Group:** 02.04. Construction Crafts. **Other Jobs in This Work Group:** Boilermakers; Brickmasons and Blockmasons; Carpet Installers; Cement Masons and Concrete Finishers; Commercial Divers; Construction Carpenters; Crane and Tower Operators; Drywall and Ceiling Tile Installers; Electricians; Fence Erectors; Floor Layers, Except Carpet, Wood, and Hard Tiles; Floor Sanders and Finishers; Glaziers; Hazardous Materials Removal Workers; Insulation Workers, Floor, Ceiling, and Wall; Insulation Workers, Mechanical; Manufactured Building and Mobile Home Installers; Operating Engineers and Other Construction Equipment Operators; Painters, Construction and Maintenance; Paperhangers; Paving, Surfacing, and Tamping Equipment Operators; Pile-Driver Operators; Pipe Fitters and Steamfitters; Pipelayers; Plasterers and Stucco Masons; Plumbers; Plumbers, Pipefitters, and Steamfitters; Rail-Track Laying and Maintenance Equipment Operators; Refractory Materials Repairers, Except Brickmasons; Reinforcing Iron and Rebar Workers; Riggers; Roofers; Rough Carpenters; Security and Fire Alarm Systems Installers; Segmental Pavers; Stone Cutters and Carvers, Manufacturing; Stonemasons; Structural Iron and Steel Workers; Tapers; Terrazzo Workers and Finishers; Tile and Marble Setters.

Skills—Installation: Installing equipment, machines, wiring, or programs to meet specifications. **Repairing:** Repairing machines or systems, using the needed tools. **Equipment Maintenance:** Performing routine maintenance and determining when and what kind of maintenance is needed. **Mathematics:** Using mathematics to solve problems. **Technology Design:** Generating or adapting equipment and technology to serve user needs. **Equipment Selection:** Determining the kind of tools and equipment needed to do a job. **Troubleshooting:** Determining what is causing an operating error and deciding what to do about it. **Coordination:** Adjusting actions in relation to others' actions.

Education and Training Program: Sheet Metal Technology/Sheetworking. **Related Knowledge/Courses—Building and Construction:** Materials, methods, and the appropriate tools to construct objects, structures, and buildings. **Mechanical Devices:** Machines and tools, including their designs, uses, benefits, repair, and maintenance. **Physics:** Physical principles, laws, and applications, including air, water, material dynamics, light, atomic principles, heat, electric theory, earth formations, and meteorological and related natural phenomena. **Design:** Design techniques, principles, tools, and instruments involved in the production and use of precision technical plans, blueprints, drawings, and models. **Production and Processing:** Inputs, outputs, raw materials, waste, quality control, costs, and techniques for maximizing the manufacture and distribution of goods. **Mathematics:** Numbers and their operations and interrelationships, including arithmetic, algebra, geometry, calculus, and statistics and their applications.

Work Environment: Noisy; contaminants; hazardous equipment; minor burns, cuts, bites, or stings; standing; using hands on objects, tools, or controls.

Sheriffs and Deputy Sheriffs

- ❋ Education/Training Required: Long-term on-the-job training
- ❋ Annual Earnings: $49,630
- ❋ Beginning Wage: $28,820
- ❋ Earnings Growth Potential: High
- ❋ Growth: 10.8%
- ❋ Annual Job Openings: 37,842
- ❋ Self-Employed: 0.0%
- ❋ Part-Time: 1.1%

The job openings listed here are shared with Police Patrol Officers.

Enforce law and order in rural or unincorporated districts or serve legal processes of courts. May patrol courthouse, guard court or grand jury, or escort defendants. Drive vehicles or patrol specific areas to detect law violators, issue citations, and make arrests. Investigate illegal or suspicious activities. Verify that the proper legal charges have been made against law offenders. Execute arrest warrants, locating and taking persons into custody. Record daily activities and submit logs and other related reports and paperwork to appropriate authorities. Patrol and guard courthouses, grand jury rooms, or assigned areas to provide security, enforce laws, maintain order, and arrest violators. Notify patrol units to take violators into custody or to provide needed assistance or medical aid. Place people in protective custody. Serve statements of claims, subpoenas, summonses, jury summonses, orders to pay alimony, and other court orders. Take control of accident scenes to maintain traffic flow, to assist accident victims, and to investigate causes. Question individuals entering secured areas to determine their business, directing and rerouting individuals as necessary. Transport or escort prisoners and defendants en route to courtrooms, prisons or jails, attorneys' offices, or medical facilities. Locate and confiscate real or personal property, as directed by court order. Manage jail operations and tend to jail inmates.

Personality Type: Enterprising. These occupations frequently involve starting up and carrying out projects and can involve leading people and making many decisions. They sometimes require risk taking and often deal with business.

GOE—Interest Area/Cluster: 12. Law and Public Safety. **Work Group:** 12.04. Law Enforcement and Public Safety. **Other Jobs in This Work Group:** Bailiffs; Correctional Officers and Jailers; Criminal Investigators and Special Agents; Detectives and Criminal Investigators; Fire Investigators; Forensic Science Technicians; Parking Enforcement Workers; Police and Sheriff's Patrol Officers; Police Detectives; Police Identification and Records Officers; Police Patrol Officers; Transit and Railroad Police.

Skills—Negotiation: Bringing others together and trying to reconcile differences. **Persuasion:** Persuading others to approach things differently. **Social Perceptiveness:** Being aware of others' reactions and understanding why they react the way they do. **Service Orientation:** Actively looking for ways to help people. **Equipment Selection:** Determining the kind of tools and equipment needed to do a job. **Complex Problem Solving:** Identifying complex problems, reviewing the options, and implementing solutions. **Judgment and Decision Making:** Weighing the relative costs and benefits of a potential action. **Coordination:** Adjusting actions in relation to others' actions.

Education and Training Programs: Criminal Justice/Police Science; Criminalistics and Criminal Science. **Related Knowledge/Courses—Public Safety and Security:** Weaponry; public safety; security operations, rules, regulations, precautions, and prevention; and the protection of people, data, and property. **Law and Government:** Laws, legal codes, court procedures, precedents, government regulations, executive orders, agency rules, and the democratic political process. **Telecommunications:** Transmission, broadcasting, switching, control, and operation of telecommunications systems. **Psychology:** Human behavior and performance, mental processes, psychological research methods, and the assessment and treatment of behavioral and affective disorders. **Therapy and Counseling:** Information and techniques needed to rehabilitate physical and mental ailments and to provide career guidance, including alternative treatments, rehabilitation equipment and its proper use, and methods to evaluate treatment effects. **Philosophy and Theology:** Different philosophical systems and religions, including their basic principles, values, ethics, ways of thinking, customs, and practices and their impact on human culture.

Work Environment: More often outdoors than indoors; very hot or cold; contaminants; disease or infections; sitting.

Ship and Boat Captains

* Education/Training Required: Work experience in a related occupation
* Annual Earnings: $57,210
* Beginning Wage: $29,530
* Earnings Growth Potential: High
* Growth: 17.9%
* Annual Job Openings: 2,665
* Self-Employed: 6.8%
* Part-Time: 4.8%

The job openings listed here are shared with Mates—Ship, Boat, and Barge; and with Pilots, Ship.

Command vessels in oceans, bays, lakes, rivers, and coastal waters. Assign watches and living quarters to crew members. Sort logs, form log booms, and salvage lost logs. Perform various marine duties such as checking for oil spills or other pollutants around ports and harbors and patrolling beaches. Contact buyers to sell cargo such as fish. Tow and maneuver barges, or signal for tugboats to tow barges to destinations. Signal passing vessels, using whistles, flashing lights, flags, and radios. Resolve questions or problems with customs officials. Read gauges to verify sufficient levels of hydraulic fluid, air pressure, and oxygen. Purchase supplies and equipment. Measure depths of water, using depth-measuring equipment. Maintain boats and equipment on board, such as engines, winches, navigational systems, fire extinguishers, and life preservers. Collect fares from customers or signal ferryboat helpers to collect fares. Arrange for ships to be fueled, restocked with supplies, and/or repaired. Signal crew members or deckhands to rig tow lines, open or close gates and ramps, and pull guard chains across entries. Maintain records of daily activities, personnel reports, ship positions and movements, ports of call, weather and sea conditions, pollution control efforts, and/or cargo and passenger statuses. Inspect vessels to ensure efficient and safe operation of vessels and equipment and conformance to regulations. Direct and coordinate crew members or workers performing activities such as loading and unloading cargo; steering vessels; operating engines; and operating, maintaining, and repairing ship equipment. Compute positions, set courses, and determine speeds by using charts, area plotting sheets, compasses, sextants, and knowledge of local conditions. Calculate sightings of land, using electronic sounding devices and following contour lines on charts. Monitor the loading and discharging of cargo or passengers. Interview and hire crew members. Steer and operate vessels, using radios, depth finders, radars, lights, buoys, and lighthouses.

Personality Type: Enterprising. These occupations frequently involve starting up and carrying out projects and can involve leading people and making many decisions. They sometimes require risk taking and often deal with business.

GOE—Interest Area/Cluster: 16. Transportation, Distribution, and Logistics. **Work Group:** 16.05. Water Vehicle Operation. **Other Jobs in This Work Group:** Captains, Mates, and Pilots of Water Vessels; Dredge Operators; Mates—Ship, Boat, and Barge; Motorboat Operators; Pilots, Ship; Sailors and Marine Oilers.

Skills—Operation and Control: Controlling operations of equipment or systems. **Operation Monitoring:** Watching gauges, dials, or other indicators to make sure a machine is working properly. **Equipment Maintenance:** Performing routine maintenance and determining when and what kind of maintenance is needed. **Judgment and Decision Making:** Weighing the relative costs and benefits of a potential action. **Troubleshooting:** Determining what is causing an operating error and deciding what to do about it. **Management of Personnel Resources:** Motivating, developing, and directing people as they work; identifying the best people for the job. **Repairing:** Repairing machines or systems, using the needed tools. **Management of Material Resources:** Obtaining and seeing to the appropriate use of equipment, facilities, and materials needed to do certain work.

Education and Training Programs: Commercial Fishing; Marine Science/Merchant Marine Officer Training; Marine Transportation, Other. **Related Knowledge/Courses— Transportation:** Principles and methods for moving people or goods by air, rail, sea, or road, including their relative costs, advantages, and limitations. **Geography:** Various methods for describing the location and distribution of land, sea, and air masses, including their physical locations, relationships, and characteristics. **Public Safety and Security:** Weaponry; public safety; security operations, rules, regulations, precautions, and prevention; and the protection of people, data, and property. **Telecommunications:** Transmission, broadcasting, switching, control, and operation of telecommunications systems. **Psychology:** Human behavior and performance, mental processes, psychological research methods, and the assessment and treatment of behavioral and affective disorders. **Mechanical Devices:** Machines and tools, including their designs, uses, benefits, repair, and maintenance.

Work Environment: More often outdoors than indoors; noisy; very bright or dim lighting; contaminants; using hands on objects, tools, or controls.

Ship Engineers

- ❋ Education/Training Required: Work experience in a related occupation
- ❋ Annual Earnings: $56,090
- ❋ Beginning Wage: $34,450
- ❋ Earnings Growth Potential: Medium
- ❋ Growth: 14.1%
- ❋ Annual Job Openings: 1,102
- ❋ Self-Employed: 0.0%
- ❋ Part-Time: 5.7%

Supervise and coordinate activities of crew engaged in operating and maintaining engines; boilers; deck machinery; and electrical, sanitary, and refrigeration equipment aboard ship. Record orders for changes in ship speed and direction and note gauge readings and test data, such as revolutions per minute and voltage output, in engineering logs and bellbooks. Install engine controls, propeller shafts, and propellers. Perform and participate in emergency drills as required. Fabricate engine replacement parts such as valves, stay rods, and bolts, using metalworking machinery. Operate and maintain off-loading liquid pumps and valves. Maintain and repair engines, electric motors, pumps, winches and other mechanical and electrical equipment or assist other crew members with maintenance and repair duties. Maintain electrical power, heating, ventilation, refrigeration, water, and sewerage systems. Monitor and test operations of engines and other equipment so that malfunctions and their causes can be identified. Monitor engine, machinery, and equipment indicators when vessels are under way and report abnormalities to appropriate shipboard staff. Start engines to propel ships and regulate engines and power transmissions to control speeds of ships according to directions from captains or bridge computers. Order and receive engine rooms' stores such as oil and spare parts; maintain inventories and record usage of supplies. Act as liaisons between ships' captains and shore personnel to ensure that schedules and budgets are maintained and that ships are operated safely and efficiently. Clean engine parts and keep engine rooms clean. Supervise the activities of marine engine technicians engaged in the maintenance and repair of mechanical and electrical marine vessels and inspect their work to ensure that it is performed properly. Maintain complete records of engineering department activities, including machine operations. Perform general marine vessel maintenance and repair work such as repairing leaks, finishing interiors, refueling, and maintaining decks. Monitor the availability, use, and condition of lifesaving equipment

and pollution preventatives in order to ensure that international regulations are followed.

Personality Type: Realistic. These occupations frequently involve work activities that include practical, hands-on problems and solutions. They often deal with plants; animals; and real-world materials such as wood, tools, and machinery. Many of the occupations require working outside and don't involve a lot of paperwork or working closely with others.

GOE—Interest Area/Cluster: 13. Manufacturing. **Work Group:** 13.16. Utility Operation and Energy Distribution. **Other Jobs in This Work Group:** Chemical Plant and System Operators; Gas Compressor and Gas Pumping Station Operators; Gas Plant Operators; Nuclear Power Reactor Operators; Petroleum Pump System Operators, Refinery Operators, and Gaugers; Power Distributors and Dispatchers; Power Plant Operators; Stationary Engineers and Boiler Operators; Water and Liquid Waste Treatment Plant and System Operators.

Skills—Repairing: Repairing machines or systems, using the needed tools. **Installation:** Installing equipment, machines, wiring, or programs to meet specifications. **Equipment Maintenance:** Performing routine maintenance and determining when and what kind of maintenance is needed. **Operation Monitoring:** Watching gauges, dials, or other indicators to make sure a machine is working properly. **Operation and Control:** Controlling operations of equipment or systems. **Troubleshooting:** Determining what is causing an operating error and deciding what to do about it. **Systems Analysis:** Determining how a system should work and how changes will affect outcomes. **Science:** Using scientific methods to solve problems.

Education and Training Program: Marine Maintenance/Fitter and Ship Repair Technology/Technician Training. **Related Knowledge/Courses—Mechanical Devices:** Machines and tools, including their designs, uses, benefits, repair, and maintenance. **Engineering and Technology:** Equipment, tools, and mechanical devices and their uses to produce motion, light, power, technology, and other applications. **Building and Construction:** Materials, methods, and the appropriate tools to construct objects, structures, and buildings. **Transportation:** Principles and methods for moving people or goods by air, rail, sea, or road, including their relative costs, advantages, and limitations. **Chemistry:** The composition, structure, and properties of substances and of the chemical processes and transformations that they undergo. This includes uses of chemicals and their interactions, danger signs, production techniques, and disposal methods. **Public Safety and Security:** Weaponry; public safety; security operations, rules, regulations, precautions, and prevention; and the protection of people, data, and property.

Work Environment: Outdoors; noisy; very hot or cold; contaminants; hazardous equipment; using hands on objects, tools, or controls.

Shipping, Receiving, and Traffic Clerks

- ❋ Education/Training Required: Short-term on-the-job training
- ❋ Annual Earnings: $26,990
- ❋ Beginning Wage: $17,390
- ❋ Earnings Growth Potential: Medium
- ❋ Growth: 3.7%
- ❋ Annual Job Openings: 138,967
- ❋ Self-Employed: 0.2%
- ❋ Part-Time: 8.9%

Verify and keep records on incoming and outgoing shipments. Prepare items for shipment. Duties include assembling, addressing, stamping, and shipping merchandise or material; receiving, unpacking, verifying, and recording incoming merchandise or material; and arranging for the transportation of products. Examine contents and compare with records such as manifests, invoices, or orders to verify accuracy of incoming or outgoing shipment. Prepare documents such as work orders, bills of lading, and shipping orders to route materials. Determine shipping method for materials, using knowledge of shipping procedures, routes, and rates. Record shipment data such as weight, charges, space availability, and damages and discrepancies for reporting, accounting, and recordkeeping purposes. Contact carrier representative to make arrangements and to issue instructions for shipping and delivery of materials. Confer and correspond with establishment representatives to rectify problems such as damages, shortages, and nonconformance to specifications. Requisition and store shipping materials and supplies to maintain inventory of stock. Deliver or route materials to departments, using work devices such as handtruck, conveyor, or sorting bins. Compute amounts such as space available and shipping, storage, and demurrage charges, using calculator or price list. Pack, seal, label, and affix postage to prepare materials for shipping, using work devices such as hand tools, power tools, and postage meter.

Personality Type: Conventional. These occupations frequently involve following set procedures and routines and can include working with data and details more than with ideas. Usually there is a clear line of authority to follow.

GOE—Interest Area/Cluster: 04. Business and Administration. **Work Group:** 04.07. Records and Materials Processing. **Other Jobs in This Work Group:** Correspondence Clerks; File Clerks; Human Resources Assistants, Except Payroll and Timekeeping; Marking Clerks; Meter Readers, Utilities; Office Clerks, General; Order Fillers, Wholesale and Retail Sales; Postal Service Clerks; Postal Service Mail Sorters, Processors, and Processing Machine Operators; Procurement Clerks; Production, Planning, and Expediting Clerks; Stock Clerks and Order Fillers; Stock Clerks, Sales Floor; Stock Clerks—Stockroom, Warehouse, or Storage Yard; Weighers, Measurers, Checkers, and Samplers, Recordkeeping.

Skills—Mathematics: Using mathematics to solve problems. **Learning Strategies:** Using multiple approaches when learning or teaching new things. **Management of Financial Resources:** Determining how money will be spent to get the work done and accounting for these expenditures. **Writing:** Communicating effectively with others in writing as indicated by the needs of the audience. **Speaking:** Talking to others to effectively convey information. **Negotiation:** Bringing others together and trying to reconcile differences. **Social Perceptiveness:** Being aware of others' reactions and understanding why they react the way they do. **Time Management:** Managing one's own time and the time of others.

Education and Training Programs: General Office Occupations and Clerical Services; Traffic, Customs, and Transportation Clerk/Technician Training. **Related Knowledge/Courses—Clerical Practices:** Administrative and clerical procedures and systems such as word-processing systems, filing and records management systems, stenography and transcription, forms, design principles, and other office procedures and terminology. **Production and Processing:** Inputs, outputs, raw materials, waste, quality control, costs, and techniques for maximizing the manufacture and distribution of goods. **Transportation:** Principles and methods for moving people or goods by air, rail, sea, or road, including their relative costs, advantages, and limitations. **Computers and Electronics:** Electric circuit boards, processors, chips, and computer hardware and software, including applications and programming. **Education and Training:**

Instructional methods and training techniques, including curriculum design principles, learning theory, group and individual teaching techniques, design of individual development plans, and test design principles. **Public Safety and Security:** Weaponry; public safety; security operations, rules, regulations, precautions, and prevention; and the protection of people, data, and property.

Work Environment: Indoors; noisy; contaminants; sitting; walking and running; using hands on objects, tools, or controls.

Skin Care Specialists

- ❋ Education/Training Required: Postsecondary vocational training
- ❋ Annual Earnings: $27,190
- ❋ Beginning Wage: $15,230
- ❋ Earnings Growth Potential: High
- ❋ Growth: 34.3%
- ❋ Annual Job Openings: 6,643
- ❋ Self-Employed: 38.9%
- ❋ Part-Time: 26.3%

Provide skin care treatments to face and body to enhance an individual's appearance. Sterilize equipment and clean work areas. Keep records of client needs and preferences and the services provided. Demonstrate how to clean and care for skin properly and recommend skin-care regimens. Examine clients' skin, using magnifying lamps or visors when necessary, to evaluate skin condition and appearance. Select and apply cosmetic products such as creams, lotions, and tonics. Cleanse clients' skin with water, creams, or lotions. Treat the facial skin to maintain and improve its appearance, using specialized techniques and products such as peels and masks. Refer clients to medical personnel for treatment of serious skin problems. Determine which products or colors will improve clients' skin quality and appearance. Perform simple extractions to remove blackheads. Provide facial and body massages. Remove body and facial hair by applying wax. Apply chemical peels in order to reduce fine lines and age spots. Advise clients about colors and types of makeup and instruct them in makeup application techniques. Sell makeup to clients. Collaborate with plastic surgeons and dermatologists to provide patients with preoperative and postoperative skin care. Give manicures and pedicures and apply artificial nails. Tint eyelashes and eyebrows.

Personality Type: Enterprising. These occupations frequently involve starting up and carrying out projects and can involve leading people and making many decisions. They sometimes require risk taking and often deal with business.

GOE—Interest Area/Cluster: 09. Hospitality, Tourism, and Recreation. **Work Group:** 09.07. Barber and Beauty Services. **Other Jobs in This Work Group:** Barbers; Hairdressers, Hairstylists, and Cosmetologists; Manicurists and Pedicurists; Shampooers.

Skills—Equipment Selection: Determining the kind of tools and equipment needed to do a job. **Service Orientation:** Actively looking for ways to help people. **Science:** Using scientific methods to solve problems. **Equipment Maintenance:** Performing routine maintenance and determining when and what kind of maintenance is needed. **Time Management:** Managing one's own time and the time of others. **Social Perceptiveness:** Being aware of others' reactions and understanding why they react the way they do. **Technology Design:** Generating or adapting equipment and technology to serve user needs. **Active Learning:** Working with new material or information to grasp its implications.

Education and Training Programs: Aesthetician/Esthetician and Skin Care Specialist Training; Cosmetology/Cosmetologist Training, General; Facial Treatment Specialist/Facialist Training. **Related Knowledge/Courses—Sales and Marketing:** Principles and methods involved in showing, promoting, and selling products or services. This includes marketing strategies and tactics, product demonstration and sales techniques, and sales control systems. **Chemistry:** The composition, structure, and properties of substances and of the chemical processes and transformations that they undergo. This includes uses of chemicals and their interactions, danger signs, production techniques, and disposal methods. **Customer and Personal Service:** Principles and processes for providing customer and personal services, including needs assessment techniques, quality service standards, alternative delivery systems, and customer satisfaction evaluation techniques.

Work Environment: Indoors; standing; using hands on objects, tools, or controls; bending or twisting the body; repetitive motions.

Slaughterers and Meat Packers

- ❋ Education/Training Required: Moderate-term on-the-job training
- ❋ Annual Earnings: $22,500
- ❋ Beginning Wage: $16,510
- ❋ Earnings Growth Potential: Low
- ❋ Growth: 12.7%
- ❋ Annual Job Openings: 15,511
- ❋ Self-Employed: 1.2%
- ❋ Part-Time: 8.3%

Work in slaughtering, meat packing, or wholesale establishments performing precision functions involving the preparation of meat. Work may include specialized slaughtering tasks, cutting standard or premium cuts of meat for marketing, making sausage, or wrapping meat. Skin sections of animals or whole animals. Trim, clean, and/or cure animal hides. Cut, trim, skin, sort, and wash viscera of slaughtered animals to separate edible portions from offal. Shackle hind legs of animals to raise them for slaughtering or skinning. Slaughter animals in accordance with religious law, and determine that carcasses meet specified religious standards. Wrap dressed carcasses and/or meat cuts. Trim head meat and sever or remove parts of animals' heads or skulls. Stun animals prior to slaughtering. Slit open, eviscerate, and trim carcasses of slaughtered animals. Shave or singe and defeather carcasses and wash them in preparation for further processing or packaging. Sever jugular veins to drain blood and facilitate slaughtering. Saw, split, or scribe carcasses into smaller portions to facilitate handling. Remove bones and cut meat into standard cuts in preparation for marketing. Grind meat into hamburger and into trimmings used to prepare sausages, luncheon meats, and other meat products. Tend assembly lines, performing a few of the many cuts needed to process carcasses.

Personality Type: Realistic. These occupations frequently involve work activities that include practical, hands-on problems and solutions. They often deal with plants; animals; and real-world materials such as wood, tools, and machinery. Many of the occupations require working outside and don't involve a lot of paperwork or working closely with others.

GOE—Interest Area/Cluster: 13. Manufacturing. **Work Group:** 13.03. Production Work, Assorted Materials Processing. **Other Jobs in This Work Group:** Bakers; Cementing and Gluing Machine Operators and Tenders; Chemical Equipment Operators and Tenders; Cleaning, Washing, and Metal Pickling Equipment Operators and Tenders; Coating, Painting, and Spraying Machine Setters, Operators, and Tenders; Cooling and Freezing Equipment Operators and Tenders; Cutting and Slicing Machine Setters, Operators, and Tenders; Extruding and Forming Machine Setters, Operators, and Tenders, Synthetic and Glass Fibers; Extruding, Forming, Pressing, and Compacting Machine Setters, Operators, and Tenders; Food and Tobacco Roasting, Baking, and Drying Machine Operators and Tenders; Food Batchmakers; Food Cooking Machine Operators and Tenders; Furnace, Kiln, Oven, Drier, and Kettle Operators and Tenders; Heat Treating Equipment Setters, Operators, and Tenders, Metal and Plastic; Helpers—Production Workers; Meat, Poultry, and Fish Cutters and Trimmers; Metal-Refining Furnace Operators and Tenders; Mixing and Blending Machine Setters, Operators, and Tenders; Packaging and Filling Machine Operators and Tenders; Plating and Coating Machine Setters, Operators, and Tenders, Metal and Plastic; Pourers and Casters, Metal; Sawing Machine Setters, Operators, and Tenders, Wood; Separating, Filtering, Clarifying, Precipitating, and Still Machine Setters, Operators, and Tenders; Sewing Machine Operators; Shoe Machine Operators and Tenders; Team Assemblers; Textile Bleaching and Dyeing Machine Operators and Tenders; Tire Builders; Woodworking Machine Setters, Operators, and Tenders, Except Sawing.

Skills—Operation and Control: Controlling operations of equipment or systems. **Operation Monitoring:** Watching gauges, dials, or other indicators to make sure a machine is working properly. **Equipment Maintenance:** Performing routine maintenance and determining when and what kind of maintenance is needed. **Quality Control Analysis:** Evaluating the quality or performance of products, services, or processes. **Repairing:** Repairing machines or systems, using the needed tools. **Service Orientation:** Actively looking for ways to help people. **Monitoring:** Assessing how well one is doing when learning or doing something. **Management of Material Resources:** Obtaining and seeing to the appropriate use of equipment, facilities, and materials needed to do certain work.

Education and Training Program: Meat Cutting/Meat Cutter Training. **Related Knowledge/Courses—Food Production:** Techniques and equipment for planting, growing, and harvesting of food for consumption, including crop rotation methods, animal husbandry, and food storage/handling techniques. **Chemistry:** The composition, structure, and properties of substances and of the chemical processes and transformations that they undergo. This includes uses of chemicals and their interactions, danger signs, production techniques, and disposal methods. **Mechanical Devices:** Machines and tools, including their designs, uses, benefits, repair, and maintenance. **Production and Processing:** Inputs, outputs, raw materials, waste, quality control, costs, and techniques for maximizing the manufacture and distribution of goods.

Work Environment: Noisy; very hot or cold; minor burns, cuts, bites, or stings; standing; using hands on objects, tools, or controls; repetitive motions.

Social and Community Service Managers

- ❋ Education/Training Required: Bachelor's degree
- ❋ Annual Earnings: $54,530
- ❋ Beginning Wage: $32,480
- ❋ Earnings Growth Potential: High
- ❋ Growth: 24.7%
- ❋ Annual Job Openings: 23,788
- ❋ Self-Employed: 5.9%
- ❋ Part-Time: 11.6%

Plan, organize, or coordinate the activities of a social service program or community outreach organization. Oversee the program or organization's budget and policies regarding participant involvement, program requirements, and benefits. Work may involve directing social workers, counselors, or probation officers. Establish and maintain relationships with other agencies and organizations in community to meet community needs and to ensure that services are not duplicated. Prepare and maintain records and reports, such as budgets, personnel records, or training manuals. Direct activities of professional and technical staff members and volunteers. Evaluate the work of staff and volunteers to ensure that programs are of appropriate quality and that resources are used effectively. Establish and oversee administrative procedures to meet objectives set by boards of directors or senior management. Participate in the determination of organizational policies regarding such issues as participant eligibility, program requirements, and program benefits. Research and analyze member or community needs to determine program directions and goals. Speak to community groups to explain and interpret agency purposes, programs, and policies. Recruit, interview, and hire or sign up volunteers and staff. Represent organizations in relations with governmental and media institutions. Plan and administer budgets for programs, equipment, and support services. Analyze proposed legislation, regulations, or rule changes to determine how agency services could be impacted. Act as consultants to agency staff and other community programs regarding the interpretation of program-related federal, state, and county regulations and policies. Implement and evaluate staff training programs. Direct fundraising activities and the preparation of public relations materials.

Personality Type: Enterprising. These occupations frequently involve starting up and carrying out projects and can involve leading people and making many decisions. They sometimes require risk taking and often deal with business.

GOE—Interest Area/Cluster: 07. Government and Public Administration. **Work Group:** 07.01. Managerial Work in Government and Public Administration. **Other Jobs in This Work Group:** No other jobs in this group.

Skills—Social Perceptiveness: Being aware of others' reactions and understanding why they react the way they do. **Management of Personnel Resources:** Motivating, developing, and directing people as they work; identifying the best people for the job. **Service Orientation:** Actively looking for ways to help people. **Systems Evaluation:** Looking at many indicators of system performance and taking into account their accuracy. **Negotiation:** Bringing others together and trying to reconcile differences. **Persuasion:** Persuading others to approach things differently. **Monitoring:** Assessing how well one is doing when learning or doing something. **Writing:** Communicating effectively with others in writing as indicated by the needs of the audience.

Education and Training Programs: Business Administration and Management, General; Business, Management, Marketing, and Related Support Services, Other; Business/Commerce, General; Community Organization and Advocacy; Entrepreneurship/Entrepreneurial Studies; Human Services, General; Non-Profit/Public/Organizational Management; Public Administration. **Related Knowledge/Courses—Sociology and Anthropology:** Group behavior and dynamics; societal trends and influences; and cultures and their history, migrations, ethnicity, and origins. **Therapy and Counseling:** Information and techniques needed to rehabilitate physical and mental ailments and to provide career guidance, including alternative treatments, rehabilitation equipment and its proper use, and methods to evaluate treatment effects. **Psychology:** Human behavior and performance, mental processes, psychological research methods, and the assessment and treatment of behavioral and affective disorders. **Philosophy and Theology:** Different philosophical systems and religions, including their basic principles, values, ethics, ways of thinking, customs, and practices and their impact on human culture. **Clerical Practices:** Administrative and clerical procedures and systems such as word-processing systems, filing and records management systems, stenography and transcription, forms, design principles, and other office procedures and terminology. **Education and Training:** Instructional methods and training techniques, including curriculum design principles, learning theory, group and individual teaching techniques, design of individual development plans, and test design principles.

Work Environment: Indoors; noisy; sitting.

Social and Human Service Assistants

- ❋ Education/Training Required: Moderate-term on-the-job training
- ❋ Annual Earnings: $26,630
- ❋ Beginning Wage: $17,350
- ❋ Earnings Growth Potential: Low
- ❋ Growth: 33.6%
- ❋ Annual Job Openings: 80,142
- ❋ Self-Employed: 0.1%
- ❋ Part-Time: 12.0%

Assist professionals from a wide variety of fields, such as psychology, rehabilitation, or social work, to provide client services as well as support for families. May assist clients in identifying available benefits and social and community services and help clients obtain them. May assist social workers with developing, organizing, and conducting programs to prevent and resolve problems relevant to substance abuse, human relationships, rehabilitation, or adult daycare. Keep records and prepare reports for owner or management concerning visits with clients. Submit reports and review reports or problems with superior. Interview individuals and family members to compile information on social, educational, criminal, institutional, or drug histories. Provide information and refer individuals to public or private agencies or community services for assistance. Consult with supervisors concerning programs for individual families. Advise clients regarding

food stamps, child care, food, money management, sanitation, or housekeeping. Oversee day-to-day group activities of residents in institution. Visit individuals in homes or attend group meetings to provide information on agency services, requirements, and procedures. Monitor free, supplementary meal program to ensure cleanliness of facility and that eligibility guidelines are met for persons receiving meals. Meet with youth groups to acquaint them with consequences of delinquent acts. Assist in planning of food budgets, using charts and sample budgets. Transport and accompany clients to shopping areas or to appointments, using automobiles. Assist in locating housing for displaced individuals. Observe and discuss meal preparation and suggest alternate methods of food preparation. Observe clients' food selections and recommend alternate economical and nutritional food choices. Explain rules established by owner or management, such as sanitation and maintenance requirements and parking regulations. Care for children in clients' homes during clients' appointments. Inform tenants of facilities such as laundries and playgrounds. Assist clients with preparation of forms such as tax or rent forms. Demonstrate use and care of equipment for tenant use.

Personality Type: Conventional. These occupations frequently involve following set procedures and routines and can include working with data and details more than with ideas. Usually there is a clear line of authority to follow.

GOE—Interest Area/Cluster: 10. Human Service. **Work Group:** 10.01. Counseling and Social Work. **Other Jobs in This Work Group:** Child, Family, and School Social Workers; Clinical Psychologists; Clinical, Counseling, and School Psychologists; Counseling Psychologists; Marriage and Family Therapists; Medical and Public Health Social Workers; Mental Health and Substance Abuse Social Workers; Mental Health Counselors; Probation Officers and Correctional Treatment Specialists; Rehabilitation Counselors; Residential Advisors; Substance Abuse and Behavioral Disorder Counselors.

Skill—Negotiation: Bringing others together and trying to reconcile differences.

Education and Training Program: Mental and Social Health Services and Allied Professions, Other. **Related Knowledge/Courses—Therapy and Counseling:** Information and techniques needed to rehabilitate physical and mental ailments and to provide career guidance, including alternative treatments, rehabilitation equipment and its proper use, and methods to evaluate treatment effects. **Philosophy and Theology:** Different philosophical systems and religions, including their basic principles, values, ethics, ways of thinking, customs, and practices and their impact on human culture. **Psychology:** Human behavior and performance, mental processes, psychological research methods, and the assessment and treatment of behavioral and affective disorders. **Customer and Personal Service:** Principles and processes for providing customer and personal services, including needs assessment techniques, quality service standards, alternative delivery systems, and customer satisfaction evaluation techniques. **Sociology and Anthropology:** Group behavior and dynamics; societal trends and influences; and cultures and their history, migrations, ethnicity, and origins. **Clerical Practices:** Administrative and clerical procedures and systems such as word-processing systems, filing and records management systems, stenography and transcription, forms, design principles, and other office procedures and terminology.

Work Environment: Indoors; sitting.

Social Science Research Assistants

- ❋ Education/Training Required: Associate degree
- ❋ Annual Earnings: $35,870
- ❋ Beginning Wage: $21,940
- ❋ Earnings Growth Potential: Medium
- ❋ Growth: 12.4%
- ❋ Annual Job Openings: 3,571
- ❋ Self-Employed: 1.7%
- ❋ Part-Time: 19.4%

The job openings listed here are shared with City and Regional Planning Aides.

Assist social scientists in laboratory, survey, and other social research. May perform publication activities, laboratory analysis, quality control, or data management. Normally these individuals work under the direct supervision of social scientists and assist in those activities that are more routine. Code data in preparation for computer entry. Provide assistance in the design of survey instruments such as questionnaires. Prepare, manipulate, and manage extensive databases. Prepare tables, graphs, fact sheets, and written reports summarizing research results. Obtain informed consent of research subjects and/or their guardians. Edit and submit protocols and other required research documentation. Screen potential subjects in order

to determine their suitability as study participants. Conduct Internet-based and library research. Supervise the work of survey interviewers. Perform descriptive and multivariate statistical analyses of data, using computer software. Recruit and schedule research participants. Develop and implement research quality control procedures. Track research participants and perform any necessary follow-up tasks. Verify the accuracy and validity of data entered in databases; correct any errors. Track laboratory supplies and expenses such as participant reimbursement. Provide assistance with the preparation of project-related reports, manuscripts, and presentations. Present research findings to groups of people. Perform needs assessments and/or consult with clients in order to determine the types of research and information that are required. Allocate and manage laboratory space and resources. Design and create special programs for tasks such as statistical analysis and data entry and cleaning. Perform data entry and other clerical work as required for project completion. Administer standardized tests to research subjects and/or interview them in order to collect research data. Collect specimens such as blood samples as required by research projects.

Personality Type: Conventional. These occupations frequently involve following set procedures and routines and can include working with data and details more than with ideas. Usually there is a clear line of authority to follow.

GOE—Interest Area/Cluster: 15. Scientific Research, Engineering, and Mathematics. **Work Group:** 15.06. Mathematics and Data Analysis. **Other Jobs in This Work Group:** Actuaries; Mathematical Technicians; Mathematicians; Statistical Assistants; Statisticians.

Skills—Programming: Writing computer programs for various purposes. **Science:** Using scientific methods to solve problems. **Writing:** Communicating effectively with others in writing as indicated by the needs of the audience. **Mathematics:** Using mathematics to solve problems. **Active Learning:** Working with new material or information to grasp its implications. **Learning Strategies:** Using multiple approaches when learning or teaching new things. **Operations Analysis:** Analyzing needs and product requirements to create a design. **Time Management:** Managing one's own time and the time of others.

Education and Training Program: Social Sciences, General. **Related Knowledge/Courses—Psychology:** Human behavior and performance, mental processes, psychological research methods, and the assessment and treatment of behavioral and affective disorders. **Sociology and Anthropology:**

Group behavior and dynamics; societal trends and influences; and cultures and their history, migrations, ethnicity, and origins. **Clerical Practices:** Administrative and clerical procedures and systems such as word-processing systems, filing and records management systems, stenography and transcription, forms, design principles, and other office procedures and terminology. **Computers and Electronics:** Electric circuit boards, processors, chips, and computer hardware and software, including applications and programming. **English Language:** The structure and content of the English language, including the meaning and spelling of words, rules of composition, and grammar. **Communications and Media:** Media production, communication, and dissemination techniques and methods, including alternative ways to inform and entertain via written, oral, and visual media.

Work Environment: Indoors; sitting.

Social Work Teachers, Postsecondary

- ❋ Education/Training Required: Doctoral degree
- ❋ Annual Earnings: $56,240
- ❋ Beginning Wage: $33,840
- ❋ Earnings Growth Potential: Medium
- ❋ Growth: 22.9%
- ❋ Annual Job Openings: 1,292
- ❋ Self-Employed: 0.4%
- ❋ Part-Time: 27.8%

Teach courses in social work. Initiate, facilitate, and moderate classroom discussions. Evaluate and grade students' classwork, assignments, and papers. Prepare and deliver lectures to undergraduate or graduate students on topics such as family behavior, child and adolescent mental health, and social intervention evaluation. Keep abreast of developments in their field by reading current literature, talking with colleagues, and participating in professional conferences. Supervise students' laboratory work and fieldwork. Conduct research in a particular field of knowledge and publish findings in professional journals, books, or electronic media. Prepare course materials such as syllabi, homework assignments, and handouts. Maintain regularly scheduled office hours to advise and assist students. Supervise undergraduate or graduate teaching, internship, and research work. Plan, evaluate, and revise curricula, course content, and course materials and methods of instruction. Collaborate with colleagues and with community agencies to address teaching and research issues. Compile, administer, and grade examinations or assign this work to others. Advise students on academic and vocational curricula and on career issues. Maintain student attendance records, grades, and other required records. Write grant proposals to procure external research funding. Serve on academic or administrative committees that deal with institutional policies, departmental matters, and academic issues. Perform administrative duties such as serving as department head. Compile bibliographies of specialized materials for outside reading assignments. Select and obtain materials and supplies such as textbooks and laboratory equipment. Participate in student recruitment, registration, and placement activities. Participate in campus and community events. Provide professional consulting services to government and industry. Act as advisers to student organizations.

Personality Type: Social. These occupations frequently involve working with, communicating with, and teaching people and often involve helping or providing service to others.

GOE—Interest Area/Cluster: 05. Education and Training. **Work Group:** 05.03. Postsecondary and Adult Teaching and Instructing. **Other Jobs in This Work Group:** Adult Literacy, Remedial Education, and GED Teachers and Instructors; Agricultural Sciences Teachers, Postsecondary; Anthropology and Archeology Teachers, Postsecondary; Architecture Teachers, Postsecondary; Area, Ethnic, and Cultural Studies Teachers, Postsecondary; Art, Drama, and Music Teachers, Postsecondary; Atmospheric, Earth, Marine, and Space Sciences Teachers, Postsecondary; Biological Science Teachers, Postsecondary; Business Teachers, Postsecondary; Chemistry Teachers, Postsecondary; Communications Teachers, Postsecondary; Computer Science Teachers, Postsecondary; Criminal Justice and Law Enforcement Teachers, Postsecondary; Economics Teachers, Postsecondary; Education Teachers, Postsecondary; Engineering Teachers, Postsecondary; English Language and Literature Teachers, Postsecondary; Environmental Science Teachers, Postsecondary; Farm and Home Management Advisors; Foreign Language and Literature Teachers, Postsecondary; Forestry and Conservation Science Teachers, Postsecondary; Geography Teachers, Postsecondary; Graduate Teaching Assistants; Health Specialties Teachers, Postsecondary; History Teachers, Postsecondary; Home Economics Teachers, Postsecondary; Law Teachers, Postsecondary; Library Science Teachers, Postsecondary; Mathematical Science

Teachers, Postsecondary; Nursing Instructors and Teachers, Postsecondary; Philosophy and Religion Teachers, Postsecondary; Physics Teachers, Postsecondary; Political Science Teachers, Postsecondary; Psychology Teachers, Postsecondary; Recreation and Fitness Studies Teachers, Postsecondary; Self-Enrichment Education Teachers; Sociology Teachers, Postsecondary; Vocational Education Teachers, Postsecondary.

Skills—Social Perceptiveness: Being aware of others' reactions and understanding why they react the way they do. **Service Orientation:** Actively looking for ways to help people. **Instructing:** Teaching others how to do something. **Learning Strategies:** Using multiple approaches when learning or teaching new things. **Writing:** Communicating effectively with others in writing as indicated by the needs of the audience. **Complex Problem Solving:** Identifying complex problems, reviewing the options, and implementing solutions. **Critical Thinking:** Using logic and analysis to identify the strengths and weaknesses of different approaches. **Negotiation:** Bringing others together and trying to reconcile differences.

Education and Training Programs: Clinical/Medical Social Work; Social Work; Teacher Education and Professional Development, Specific Subject Areas, Other. **Related Knowledge/Courses—Therapy and Counseling:** Information and techniques needed to rehabilitate physical and mental ailments and to provide career guidance, including alternative treatments, rehabilitation equipment and its proper use, and methods to evaluate treatment effects. **Sociology and Anthropology:** Group behavior and dynamics; societal trends and influences; and cultures and their history, migrations, ethnicity, and origins. **Psychology:** Human behavior and performance, mental processes, psychological research methods, and the assessment and treatment of behavioral and affective disorders. **Philosophy and Theology:** Different philosophical systems and religions, including their basic principles, values, ethics, ways of thinking, customs, and practices and their impact on human culture. **Education and Training:** Instructional methods and training techniques, including curriculum design principles, learning theory, group and individual teaching techniques, design of individual development plans, and test design principles. **English Language:** The structure and content of the English language, including the meaning and spelling of words, rules of composition, and grammar.

Work Environment: Indoors; sitting.

Sociologists

* Education/Training Required: Master's degree
* Annual Earnings: $61,140
* Beginning Wage: $36,740
* Earnings Growth Potential: Medium
* Growth: 10.0%
* Annual Job Openings: 403
* Self-Employed: 0.0%
* Part-Time: 24.0%

Study human society and social behavior by examining the groups and social institutions that people form, as well as various social, religious, political, and business organizations. May study the behavior and interaction of groups, trace their origin and growth, and analyze the influence of group activities on individual members. Analyze and interpret data in order to increase the understanding of human social behavior. Prepare publications and reports containing research findings. Plan and conduct research to develop and test theories about societal issues such as crime, group relations, poverty, and aging. Collect data about the attitudes, values, and behaviors of people in groups, using observation, interviews, and review of documents. Develop, implement, and evaluate methods of data collection, such as questionnaires or interviews. Teach sociology. Direct work of statistical clerks, statisticians, and others who compile and evaluate research data. Consult with and advise individuals such as administrators, social workers, and legislators regarding social issues and policies, as well as the implications of research findings. Collaborate with research workers in other disciplines. Develop approaches to the solution of groups' problems based on research findings in sociology and related disciplines. Observe group interactions and role affiliations to collect data, identify problems, evaluate progress, and determine the need for additional change. Develop problem intervention procedures, utilizing techniques such as interviews, consultations, role-playing, and participant observation of group interactions.

Personality Type: Investigative. These occupations frequently involve working with ideas and require an extensive amount of thinking. They can involve searching for facts and figuring out problems mentally.

GOE—Interest Area/Cluster: 15. Scientific Research, Engineering, and Mathematics. **Work Group:** 15.04. Social Sciences. **Other Jobs in This Work Group:** Anthropologists;

Anthropologists and Archeologists; Archeologists; Economists; Historians; Industrial-Organizational Psychologists; Political Scientists; School Psychologists.

Skills—Science: Using scientific methods to solve problems. **Writing:** Communicating effectively with others in writing as indicated by the needs of the audience. **Management of Financial Resources:** Determining how money will be spent to get the work done and accounting for these expenditures. **Reading Comprehension:** Understanding written sentences and paragraphs in work-related documents. **Critical Thinking:** Using logic and analysis to identify the strengths and weaknesses of different approaches. **Complex Problem Solving:** Identifying complex problems, reviewing the options, and implementing solutions. **Mathematics:** Using mathematics to solve problems. **Active Learning:** Working with new material or information to grasp its implications.

Education and Training Programs: Criminology; Demography and Population Studies; Sociology; Urban Studies/Affairs. **Related Knowledge/Courses—Sociology and Anthropology:** Group behavior and dynamics; societal trends and influences; and cultures and their history, migrations, ethnicity, and origins. **Philosophy and Theology:** Different philosophical systems and religions, including their basic principles, values, ethics, ways of thinking, customs, and practices and their impact on human culture. **History and Archeology:** Historical events and their causes, indicators, and impact on particular civilizations and cultures. **Psychology:** Human behavior and performance, mental processes, psychological research methods, and the assessment and treatment of behavioral and affective disorders. **English Language:** The structure and content of the English language, including the meaning and spelling of words, rules of composition, and grammar. **Mathematics:** Numbers and their operations and interrelationships, including arithmetic, algebra, geometry, calculus, and statistics and their applications.

Work Environment: Indoors; sitting.

Sociology Teachers, Postsecondary

- ❋ Education/Training Required: Doctoral degree
- ❋ Annual Earnings: $58,160
- ❋ Beginning Wage: $31,310
- ❋ Earnings Growth Potential: High
- ❋ Growth: 22.9%
- ❋ Annual Job Openings: 2,774
- ❋ Self-Employed: 0.4%
- ❋ Part-Time: 27.8%

Teach courses in sociology. Evaluate and grade students' classwork, assignments, and papers. Prepare and deliver lectures to undergraduate and graduate students on topics such as race and ethnic relations, measurement and data collection, and workplace social relations. Initiate, facilitate, and moderate classroom discussions. Prepare course materials such as syllabi, homework assignments, and handouts. Compile, administer, and grade examinations or assign this work to others. Keep abreast of developments in their field by reading current literature, talking with colleagues, and participating in professional conferences. Maintain student attendance records, grades, and other required records. Maintain regularly scheduled office hours in order to advise and assist students. Plan, evaluate, and revise curricula, course content, and course materials and methods of instruction. Advise students on academic and vocational curricula and on career issues. Collaborate with colleagues to address teaching and research issues. Conduct research in a particular field of knowledge and publish findings in professional journals, books, or electronic media. Select and obtain materials and supplies such as textbooks and laboratory equipment. Supervise undergraduate and graduate teaching, internship, and research work. Serve on academic or administrative committees that deal with institutional policies, departmental matters, and academic issues. Participate in student recruitment, registration, and placement activities. Perform administrative duties such as serving as department head. Supervise students' laboratory work and fieldwork. Write grant proposals to procure external research funding. Act as advisers to student organizations. Compile bibliographies of specialized materials for outside reading assignments. Participate in campus and community events. Provide professional consulting services to government and industry.

Personality Type: Social. These occupations frequently involve working with, communicating with, and teaching people and often involve helping or providing service to others.

GOE—Interest Area/Cluster: 05. Education and Training. **Work Group:** 05.03. Postsecondary and Adult Teaching and Instructing. **Other Jobs in This Work Group:** Adult Literacy, Remedial Education, and GED Teachers and Instructors; Agricultural Sciences Teachers, Postsecondary; Anthropology and Archeology Teachers, Postsecondary; Architecture Teachers, Postsecondary; Area, Ethnic, and Cultural Studies Teachers, Postsecondary; Art, Drama, and Music Teachers, Postsecondary; Atmospheric, Earth, Marine, and Space Sciences Teachers, Postsecondary; Biological Science Teachers, Postsecondary; Business Teachers, Postsecondary; Chemistry Teachers, Postsecondary; Communications Teachers, Postsecondary; Computer Science Teachers, Postsecondary; Criminal Justice and Law Enforcement Teachers, Postsecondary; Economics Teachers, Postsecondary; Education Teachers, Postsecondary; Engineering Teachers, Postsecondary; English Language and Literature Teachers, Postsecondary; Environmental Science Teachers, Postsecondary; Farm and Home Management Advisors; Foreign Language and Literature Teachers, Postsecondary; Forestry and Conservation Science Teachers, Postsecondary; Geography Teachers, Postsecondary; Graduate Teaching Assistants; Health Specialties Teachers, Postsecondary; History Teachers, Postsecondary; Home Economics Teachers, Postsecondary; Law Teachers, Postsecondary; Library Science Teachers, Postsecondary; Mathematical Science Teachers, Postsecondary; Nursing Instructors and Teachers, Postsecondary; Philosophy and Religion Teachers, Postsecondary; Physics Teachers, Postsecondary; Political Science Teachers, Postsecondary; Psychology Teachers, Postsecondary; Recreation and Fitness Studies Teachers, Postsecondary; Self-Enrichment Education Teachers; Social Work Teachers, Postsecondary; Vocational Education Teachers, Postsecondary.

Skills—Science: Using scientific methods to solve problems. **Instructing:** Teaching others how to do something. **Writing:** Communicating effectively with others in writing as indicated by the needs of the audience. **Learning Strategies:** Using multiple approaches when learning or teaching new things. **Social Perceptiveness:** Being aware of others' reactions and understanding why they react the way they do. **Critical Thinking:** Using logic and analysis to identify the strengths and weaknesses of different approaches. **Reading Comprehension:** Understanding written sentences and paragraphs in work-related documents. **Speaking:** Talking to others to effectively convey information.

Education and Training Programs: Social Science Teacher Education; Sociology. **Related Knowledge/Courses—Sociology and Anthropology:** Group behavior and dynamics; societal trends and influences; and cultures and their history, migrations, ethnicity, and origins. **Philosophy and Theology:** Different philosophical systems and religions, including their basic principles, values, ethics, ways of thinking, customs, and practices and their impact on human culture. **History and Archeology:** Historical events and their causes, indicators, and impact on particular civilizations and cultures. **Education and Training:** Instructional methods and training techniques, including curriculum design principles, learning theory, group and individual teaching techniques, design of individual development plans, and test design principles. **English Language:** The structure and content of the English language, including the meaning and spelling of words, rules of composition, and grammar. **Geography:** Various methods for describing the location and distribution of land, sea, and air masses, including their physical locations, relationships, and characteristics.

Work Environment: Indoors; sitting.

Software Quality Assurance Engineers and Testers

- ❈ Education/Training Required: Associate degree
- ❈ Annual Earnings: $71,510
- ❈ Beginning Wage: $37,600
- ❈ Earnings Growth Potential: High
- ❈ Growth: 15.1%
- ❈ Annual Job Openings: 14,374
- ❈ Self-Employed: 6.6%
- ❈ Part-Time: 5.6%

The job openings listed here are shared with Computer Systems Engineers/Architects, Network Designers, Web Administrators, and Web Developers.

Develop and execute software test plans in order to identify software problems and their causes. Design test plans, scenarios, scripts, or procedures. Test system modifications to prepare for implementation. Document software defects, using a bug tracking system, and report defects to software developers. Develop testing programs that address areas such as database impacts, software scenarios, regression testing, negative testing, error or bug retests, or usability. Identify, analyze, and document problems with program function, output, online screens, or content. Monitor bug resolution efforts and track successes. Create or maintain databases of known test defects. Plan test schedules or strategies in accordance with project scope or delivery dates. Participate in product design reviews to provide input on functional requirements, product designs, schedules, or potential problems. Review software documentation to ensure technical accuracy, compliance, or completeness or to mitigate risks. Document test procedures to ensure replicability and compliance with standards. Develop or specify standards, methods, or procedures to determine product quality or release readiness. Update automated test scripts to ensure currency. Investigate customer problems referred by technical support. Install, maintain, or use software testing programs. Provide feedback and recommendations to developers on software usability and functionality. Monitor program performance to ensure efficient and problem-free operations. Install and configure recreations of software production environments to allow testing of software performance. Collaborate with field staff or customers to evaluate or diagnose problems and recommend possible solutions. Conduct software compatibility tests with programs, hardware, operating systems, or network environments. Identify program deviance from standards and suggest modifications to ensure compliance. Design or develop automated testing tools. Coordinate user or third-party testing. Perform initial debugging procedures by reviewing configuration files, logs, or code pieces to determine breakdown sources. Visit beta testing sites to evaluate software performance. Evaluate or recommend software for testing or bug tracking.

Personality Type: Investigative. These occupations frequently involve working with ideas and require an extensive amount of thinking. They can involve searching for facts and figuring out problems mentally.

GOE—Interest Area/Cluster: 11. Information Technology. **Work Group:** 11.02. Information Technology Specialties. **Other Jobs in This Work Group:** Computer and Information Scientists, Research; Computer Operators; Computer Programmers; Computer Security Specialists; Computer Software Engineers, Applications; Computer Software Engineers, Systems Software; Computer Support Specialists; Computer Systems Analysts; Computer Systems Engineers/Architects; Database Administrators; Network Designers; Network Systems and Data Communications Analysts; Web Administrators; Web Developers.

Skills—Quality Control Analysis: Evaluating the quality or performance of products, services, or processes. **Programming:** Writing computer programs for various purposes.

Systems Analysis: Determining how a system should work and how changes will affect outcomes. **Systems Evaluation:** Looking at many indicators of system performance and taking into account their accuracy. **Troubleshooting:** Determining what is causing an operating error and deciding what to do about it. **Technology Design:** Generating or adapting equipment and technology to serve user needs. **Operations Analysis:** Analyzing needs and product requirements to create a design. **Writing:** Communicating effectively with others in writing as indicated by the needs of the audience.

Education and Training Programs: Computer and Information Sciences and Support Services, Other; Computer and Information Sciences, General; Computer Engineering Technologies/Technicians, Other; Computer Engineering, General; Computer Science; Computer Software Engineering; Information Science/Studies; Information Technology. **Related Knowledge/Courses—Computers and Electronics:** Electric circuit boards, processors, chips, and computer hardware and software, including applications and programming. **Engineering and Technology:** Equipment, tools, and mechanical devices and their uses to produce motion, light, power, technology, and other applications. **Design:** Design techniques, principles, tools, and instruments involved in the production and use of precision technical plans, blueprints, drawings, and models. **English Language:** The structure and content of the English language, including the meaning and spelling of words, rules of composition, and grammar. **Mathematics:** Numbers and their operations and interrelationships, including arithmetic, algebra, geometry, calculus, and statistics and their applications. **Clerical Practices:** Administrative and clerical procedures and systems such as word-processing systems, filing and records management systems, stenography and transcription, forms, design principles, and other office procedures and terminology.

Work Environment: Indoors; sitting; using hands on objects, tools, or controls; repetitive motions.

Soil and Plant Scientists

* Education/Training Required: Bachelor's degree
* Annual Earnings: $58,000
* Beginning Wage: $34,620
* Earnings Growth Potential: High
* Growth: 8.4%
* Annual Job Openings: 850
* Self-Employed: 19.5%
* Part-Time: 11.4%

Conduct research in breeding, physiology, production, yield, and management of crops and agricultural plants, their growth in soils, and control of pests or study the chemical, physical, biological, and mineralogical composition of soils as they relate to plant or crop growth. May classify and map soils and investigate effects of alternative practices on soil and crop productivity. Communicate research and project results to other professionals and the public or teach related courses, seminars or workshops. Provide information and recommendations to farmers and other landowners regarding ways in which they can best use land, promote plant growth, and avoid or correct problems such as erosion. Investigate responses of soils to specific management practices to determine the use capabilities of soils and the effects of alternative practices on soil productivity. Develop methods of conserving and managing soil that can be applied by farmers and forestry companies. Conduct experiments to develop new or improved varieties of field crops, focusing on characteristics such as yield, quality, disease resistance, nutritional value, or adaptation to specific soils or climates. Investigate soil problems and poor water quality to determine sources and effects. Study soil characteristics to classify soils on the basis of factors such as geographic location, landscape position, and soil properties. Develop improved measurement techniques, soil conservation methods, soil sampling devices, and related technology. Conduct experiments investigating how soil forms and changes and how it interacts with land-based ecosystems and living organisms. Identify degraded or contaminated soils and develop plans to improve their chemical, biological, and physical characteristics. Survey undisturbed and disturbed lands for classification, inventory, mapping, environmental impact assessments, environmental protection planning, and conservation and reclamation planning. Plan and supervise land conservation and reclamation programs for industrial development projects and waste management programs for composting and farming. Perform chemical analyses of the microorganism content of soils to determine microbial reactions and chemical mineralogical relationships to plant growth. Provide advice regarding the development of regulatory standards for land reclamation and soil conservation. Develop new or improved methods and products for controlling and eliminating weeds, crop diseases, and insect pests.

Personality Type: Investigative. These occupations frequently involve working with ideas and require an extensive amount of thinking. They can involve searching for facts and figuring out problems mentally.

GOE—Interest Area/Cluster: 01. Agriculture and Natural Resources. **Work Group:** 01.02. Resource Science/Engineering for Plants, Animals, and the Environment. **Other Jobs in This Work Group:** Agricultural Engineers; Animal Scientists; Conservation Scientists; Environmental Engineers; Foresters; Mining and Geological Engineers, Including Mining Safety Engineers; Petroleum Engineers; Range Managers; Soil and Water Conservationists; Zoologists and Wildlife Biologists.

Skills—Science: Using scientific methods to solve problems. **Management of Financial Resources:** Determining how money will be spent to get the work done and accounting for these expenditures. **Writing:** Communicating effectively with others in writing as indicated by the needs of the audience. **Management of Material Resources:** Obtaining and seeing to the appropriate use of equipment, facilities, and materials needed to do certain work. **Reading Comprehension:** Understanding written sentences and paragraphs in work-related documents. **Management of Personnel Resources:** Motivating, developing, and directing people as they work; identifying the best people for the job. **Mathematics:** Using mathematics to solve problems. **Time Management:** Managing one's own time and the time of others.

Education and Training Programs: Soil Chemistry and Physics; Soil Microbiology; Soil Science and Agronomy, General. **Related Knowledge/Courses—Biology:** Plant and animal living tissue, cells, organisms, and entities, including their functions, interdependencies, and interactions with each other and the environment. **Food Production:** Techniques and equipment for planting, growing, and harvesting of food for consumption, including crop-rotation methods, animal husbandry, and food storage/handling techniques. **Geography:** Various methods for describing the location and distribution of land, sea, and air masses, including their physical locations, relationships, and characteristics. **Chemistry:** The composition, structure, and properties of substances and of the chemical processes and transformations that they undergo. This includes uses of chemicals and their interactions, danger signs, production techniques, and disposal methods. **Physics:** Physical principles, laws, and applications, including air, water, material dynamics, light, atomic principles, heat, electric theory, earth formations, and meteorological and related natural phenomena. **Communications and Media:** Media production, communication, and dissemination techniques and methods, including alternative ways to inform and entertain via written, oral, and visual media.

Work Environment: More often indoors than outdoors; sitting.

Solderers and Brazers

- ❋ Education/Training Required: Postsecondary vocational training
- ❋ Annual Earnings: $32,270
- ❋ Beginning Wage: $21,680
- ❋ Earnings Growth Potential: Low
- ❋ Growth: 5.1%
- ❋ Annual Job Openings: 61,125
- ❋ Self-Employed: 6.3%
- ❋ Part-Time: 1.9%

The job openings listed here are shared with Welders, Cutters, and Welder Fitters.

Braze or solder together components to assemble fabricated metal parts with soldering iron, torch, or welding machine and flux. Melt and apply solder along adjoining edges of workpieces to solder joints, using soldering irons, gas torches, or ultrasonic equipment. Heat soldering irons or workpieces to specified temperatures for soldering, using gas flames or electrical current. Examine seams for defects and rework defective joints or broken parts. Melt and separate brazed or soldered joints to remove and straighten damaged or misaligned components, using hand torches, irons, or furnaces. Melt and apply solder to fill holes, indentations, and seams of fabricated metal products, using soldering equipment. Clean workpieces to remove dirt and excess acid, using chemical solutions, files, wire brushes, or grinders. Guide torches and rods along joints of workpieces to heat them to brazing temperature, melt braze alloys, and bond workpieces together. Adjust electrical current and timing cycles of resistance welding machines to heat metals to bonding temperature. Clean equipment parts such as tips of soldering irons, using chemical solutions or cleaning compounds. Turn valves to start flow of gases and light flames and adjust valves to obtain desired colors and sizes of flames. Brush flux onto joints of workpieces or dip braze rods into flux to prevent oxidation of metal. Remove workpieces from fixtures, using tongs, and cool workpieces, using air or water. Align and clamp workpieces together, using rules, squares, or hand tools, or position items in fixtures, jigs, or vises. Sweat together workpieces coated with solder. Smooth soldered areas with alternate strokes of paddles and torches, leaving soldered sections slightly higher than surrounding areas for later filing. Remove workpieces from molten solder and hold parts together until color indicates that solder has set. Select torch tips, flux, and brazing alloys from data charts or work orders. Turn dials to set intensity and duration of ultrasonic impulses according to work order specifications. Dip workpieces into molten solder or place solder strips between seams and heat seams with irons to bond items together. Clean joints of workpieces with wire brushes or by dipping them into cleaning solutions.

Personality Type: Realistic. These occupations frequently involve work activities that include practical, hands-on problems and solutions. They often deal with plants; animals; and real-world materials such as wood, tools, and machinery. Many of the occupations require working outside and don't involve a lot of paperwork or working closely with others.

GOE—Interest Area/Cluster: 13. Manufacturing. **Work Group:** 13.04. Welding, Brazing, and Soldering. **Other Jobs in This Work Group:** Structural Metal Fabricators and Fitters; Welders, Cutters, and Welder Fitters; Welders, Cutters, Solderers, and Brazers; Welding, Soldering, and Brazing Machine Setters, Operators, and Tenders.

Skills—Quality Control Analysis: Evaluating the quality or performance of products, services, or processes. **Installation:** Installing equipment, machines, wiring, or programs to meet specifications. **Operation and Control:** Controlling operations of equipment or systems. **Equipment Selection:** Determining the kind of tools and equipment needed to do a job. **Troubleshooting:** Determining what is causing an operating error and deciding what to do about it. **Repairing:** Repairing machines or systems, using the needed tools. **Equipment Maintenance:** Performing routine maintenance and determining when and what kind of maintenance is needed. **Technology Design:** Generating or adapting equipment and technology to serve user needs.

Education and Training Program: Welding Technology/Welder Training. **Related Knowledge/Courses—Production and Processing:** Inputs, outputs, raw materials, waste, quality control, costs, and techniques for maximizing the manufacture and distribution of goods. **Mechanical Devices:** Machines and tools, including their designs, uses, benefits, repair, and maintenance. **Engineering and Technology:** Equipment, tools, and mechanical devices and their uses to produce motion, light, power, technology, and other applications.

Work Environment: Indoors; noisy; contaminants; minor burns, cuts, bites, or stings; using hands on objects, tools, or controls; repetitive motions.

Special Education Teachers, Middle School

* Education/Training Required: Bachelor's degree
* Annual Earnings: $48,940
* Beginning Wage: $33,690
* Earnings Growth Potential: Low
* Growth: 15.8%
* Annual Job Openings: 8,846
* Self-Employed: 0.3%
* Part-Time: 9.6%

Teach middle school subjects to educationally and physically handicapped students. Includes teachers who specialize and work with audibly and visually handicapped students and those who teach basic academic and life processes skills to the mentally impaired. Establish and enforce rules for behavior and policies and procedures to maintain order among students. Maintain accurate and complete student records and prepare reports on children and activities as required by laws, district policies, and administrative regulations. Prepare materials and classrooms for class activities. Confer with parents, administrators, testing specialists, social workers, and professionals to develop individual educational plans designed to promote students' educational, physical, and social development. Develop and implement strategies to meet the needs of students with a variety of handicapping conditions. Teach socially acceptable behavior, employing techniques such as behavior modification and positive reinforcement. Modify the general education curriculum for special-needs students based upon a variety of instructional techniques and instructional technology. Employ special educational strategies and techniques during instruction to improve the development of sensory- and perceptual-motor skills, language, cognition, and memory. Confer with parents or guardians, other teachers,

counselors, and administrators to resolve students' behavioral and academic problems. Instruct through lectures, discussions, and demonstrations in one or more subjects such as English, mathematics, or social studies. Coordinate placement of students with special needs into mainstream classes. Meet with parents and guardians to discuss their children's progress and to determine their priorities for their children and their resource needs. Guide and counsel students with adjustment or academic problems or special academic interests. Prepare, administer, and grade tests and assignments to evaluate students' progress. Observe and evaluate students' performance, behavior, social development, and physical health. Establish clear objectives for all lessons, units, and projects and communicate those objectives to students. Teach students personal development skills such as goal setting, independence, and self-advocacy. Plan and conduct activities for a balanced program of instruction, demonstration, and work time that provides students with opportunities to observe, question, and investigate.

Personality Type: Social. These occupations frequently involve working with, communicating with, and teaching people and often involve helping or providing service to others.

GOE—Interest Area/Cluster: 05. Education and Training. **Work Group:** 05.02. Preschool, Elementary, and Secondary Teaching and Instructing. **Other Jobs in This Work Group:** Elementary School Teachers, Except Special Education; Kindergarten Teachers, Except Special Education; Middle School Teachers, Except Special and Vocational Education; Preschool Teachers, Except Special Education; Secondary School Teachers, Except Special and Vocational Education; Special Education Teachers, Preschool, Kindergarten, and Elementary School; Special Education Teachers, Secondary School; Teacher Assistants; Vocational Education Teachers, Middle School; Vocational Education Teachers, Secondary School.

Skills—Learning Strategies: Using multiple approaches when learning or teaching new things. **Social Perceptiveness:** Being aware of others' reactions and understanding why they react the way they do. **Instructing:** Teaching others how to do something. **Monitoring:** Assessing how well one is doing when learning or doing something. **Persuasion:** Persuading others to approach things differently. **Writing:** Communicating effectively with others in writing as indicated by the needs of the audience. **Negotiation:** Bringing others together and trying to reconcile differences. **Time Management:** Managing one's own time and the time of others.

Education and Training Programs: Education/Teaching of Individuals in Early Childhood Special Education Programs; Education/Teaching of Individuals Who are Developmentally Delayed; Education/Teaching of the Gifted and Talented; Special Education and Teaching, General. **Related Knowledge/Courses—Geography:** Various methods for describing the location and distribution of land, sea, and air masses, including their physical locations, relationships, and characteristics. **History and Archeology:** Historical events and their causes, indicators, and impact on particular civilizations and cultures. **Psychology:** Human behavior and performance, mental processes, psychological research methods, and the assessment and treatment of behavioral and affective disorders. **Therapy and Counseling:** Information and techniques needed to rehabilitate physical and mental ailments and to provide career guidance, including alternative treatments, rehabilitation equipment and its proper use, and methods to evaluate treatment effects. **Sociology and Anthropology:** Group behavior and dynamics; societal trends and influences; and cultures and their history, migrations, ethnicity, and origins. **Education and Training:** Instructional methods and training techniques, including curriculum design principles, learning theory, group and individual teaching techniques, design of individual development plans, and test design principles.

Work Environment: Indoors; noisy; standing.

Special Education Teachers, Preschool, Kindergarten, and Elementary School

- ❊ Education/Training Required: Bachelor's degree
- ❊ Annual Earnings: $48,350
- ❊ Beginning Wage: $32,700
- ❊ Earnings Growth Potential: Low
- ❊ Growth: 19.6%
- ❊ Annual Job Openings: 20,049
- ❊ Self-Employed: 0.3%
- ❊ Part-Time: 9.6%

Teach elementary and preschool school subjects to educationally and physically handicapped students. Includes teachers who specialize and work with audibly and visually handicapped students and those who teach basic academic and life processes skills to the mentally impaired. Instruct students in academic subjects, using a variety of

techniques such as phonetics, multisensory learning, and repetition to reinforce learning and to meet students' varying needs and interests. Employ special educational strategies and techniques during instruction to improve the development of sensory- and perceptual-motor skills, language, cognition, and memory. Teach socially acceptable behavior, employing techniques such as behavior modification and positive reinforcement. Modify the general education curriculum for special-needs students based upon a variety of instructional techniques and technologies. Meet with parents and guardians to discuss their children's progress and to determine their priorities for their children and their resource needs. Plan and conduct activities for a balanced program of instruction, demonstration, and work time that provides students with opportunities to observe, question, and investigate. Establish and enforce rules for behavior and policies and procedures to maintain order among the students for whom they are responsible. Confer with parents, administrators, testing specialists, social workers, and professionals to develop individual educational plans designed to promote students' educational, physical, and social development. Maintain accurate and complete student records and prepare reports on children and activities as required by laws, district policies, and administrative regulations. Establish clear objectives for all lessons, units, and projects and communicate those objectives to students. Develop and implement strategies to meet the needs of students with a variety of handicapping conditions. Prepare classrooms for class activities and provide a variety of materials and resources for children to explore, manipulate, and use, both in learning activities and imaginative play. Confer with parents or guardians, teachers, counselors, and administrators to resolve students' behavioral and academic problems. Observe and evaluate students' performance, behavior, social development, and physical health. Teach students personal development skills such as goal setting, independence, and self-advocacy.

Personality Type: Social. These occupations frequently involve working with, communicating with, and teaching people and often involve helping or providing service to others.

GOE—Interest Area/Cluster: 05. Education and Training. **Work Group:** 05.02. Preschool, Elementary, and Secondary Teaching and Instructing. **Other Jobs in This Work Group:** Elementary School Teachers, Except Special Education; Kindergarten Teachers, Except Special Education; Middle School Teachers, Except Special and Vocational Education; Preschool Teachers, Except Special Education;

Secondary School Teachers, Except Special and Vocational Education; Special Education Teachers, Middle School; Special Education Teachers, Secondary School; Teacher Assistants; Vocational Education Teachers, Middle School; Vocational Education Teachers, Secondary School.

Skills—Learning Strategies: Using multiple approaches when learning or teaching new things. **Instructing:** Teaching others how to do something. **Social Perceptiveness:** Being aware of others' reactions and understanding why they react the way they do. **Monitoring:** Assessing how well one is doing when learning or doing something. **Negotiation:** Bringing others together and trying to reconcile differences. **Time Management:** Managing one's own time and the time of others. **Coordination:** Adjusting actions in relation to others' actions. **Writing:** Communicating effectively with others in writing as indicated by the needs of the audience.

Education and Training Programs: Education/Teaching of Individuals in Early Childhood Special Education Programs; Education/Teaching of Individuals with Autism; Education/Teaching of Individuals with Hearing Impairments; Education/Teaching of Individuals with Mental Retardation; Education/Teaching of Individuals with Multiple Disabilities; Education/Teaching of Individuals with Speech or Language Impairments; Education/Teaching of Individuals with Vision Impairments; Education/Teaching of the Gifted and Talented; others. **Related Knowledge/Courses—Psychology:** Human behavior and performance, mental processes, psychological research methods, and the assessment and treatment of behavioral and affective disorders. **History and Archeology:** Historical events and their causes, indicators, and impact on particular civilizations and cultures. **Therapy and Counseling:** Information and techniques needed to rehabilitate physical and mental ailments and to provide career guidance, including alternative treatments, rehabilitation equipment and its proper use, and methods to evaluate treatment effects. **Geography:** Various methods for describing the location and distribution of land, sea, and air masses, including their physical locations, relationships, and characteristics. **Philosophy and Theology:** Different philosophical systems and religions, including their basic principles, values, ethics, ways of thinking, customs, and practices and their impact on human culture. **Sociology and Anthropology:** Group behavior and dynamics; societal trends and influences; and cultures and their history, migrations, ethnicity, and origins.

Work Environment: Indoors; noisy; standing.

Special Education Teachers, Secondary School

- ❋ Education/Training Required: Bachelor's degree
- ❋ Annual Earnings: $49,640
- ❋ Beginning Wage: $33,930
- ❋ Earnings Growth Potential: Low
- ❋ Growth: 8.5%
- ❋ Annual Job Openings: 10,601
- ❋ Self-Employed: 0.3%
- ❋ Part-Time: 9.6%

Teach secondary school subjects to educationally and physically handicapped students. Includes teachers who specialize and work with audibly and visually handicapped students and those who teach basic academic and life processes skills to the mentally impaired. Maintain accurate and complete student records and prepare reports on children and activities as required by laws, district policies, and administrative regulations. Prepare materials and classrooms for class activities. Teach socially acceptable behavior, employing techniques such as behavior modification and positive reinforcement. Establish and enforce rules for behavior and policies and procedures to maintain order among students. Confer with parents, administrators, testing specialists, social workers, and professionals to develop individual educational plans designed to promote students' educational, physical, and social development. Instruct through lectures, discussions, and demonstrations in one or more subjects such as English, mathematics, or social studies. Employ special educational strategies and techniques during instruction to improve the development of sensory- and perceptual-motor skills, language, cognition, and memory. Plan and conduct activities for a balanced program of instruction, demonstration, and work time that provides students with opportunities to observe, question, and investigate. Prepare students for later grades by encouraging them to explore learning opportunities and to persevere with challenging tasks. Teach personal development skills such as goal setting, independence, and self-advocacy. Establish clear objectives for all lessons, units, and projects and communicate those objectives to students. Develop and implement strategies to meet the needs of students with a variety of handicapping conditions. Modify the general education curriculum for special-needs students based upon a variety of instructional techniques and technologies. Meet with other professionals to discuss individual students' needs and progress. Confer with parents or guardians, other teachers, counselors, and administrators to resolve students' behavioral and academic problems. Meet with parents and guardians to discuss their children's progress and to determine their priorities for their children and their resource needs. Guide and counsel students with adjustment or academic problems or special academic interests.

Personality Type: Social. These occupations frequently involve working with, communicating with, and teaching people and often involve helping or providing service to others.

GOE—Interest Area/Cluster: 05. Education and Training. **Work Group:** 05.02. Preschool, Elementary, and Secondary Teaching and Instructing. **Other Jobs in This Work Group:** Elementary School Teachers, Except Special Education; Kindergarten Teachers, Except Special Education; Middle School Teachers, Except Special and Vocational Education; Preschool Teachers, Except Special Education; Secondary School Teachers, Except Special and Vocational Education; Special Education Teachers, Middle School; Special Education Teachers, Preschool, Kindergarten, and Elementary School; Teacher Assistants; Vocational Education Teachers, Middle School; Vocational Education Teachers, Secondary School.

Skills—Learning Strategies: Using multiple approaches when learning or teaching new things. **Social Perceptiveness:** Being aware of others' reactions and understanding why they react the way they do. **Negotiation:** Bringing others together and trying to reconcile differences. **Instructing:** Teaching others how to do something. **Persuasion:** Persuading others to approach things differently. **Service Orientation:** Actively looking for ways to help people. **Time Management:** Managing one's own time and the time of others. **Monitoring:** Assessing how well one is doing when learning or doing something.

Education and Training Programs: Education/Teaching of Individuals in Early Childhood Special Education Programs; Education/Teaching of Individuals Who are Developmentally Delayed; Education/Teaching of the Gifted and Talented; Special Education and Teaching, General. **Related Knowledge/Courses—Therapy and Counseling:** Information and techniques needed to rehabilitate physical and mental ailments and to provide career guidance, including alternative treatments, rehabilitation equipment and its proper use, and methods to evaluate treatment effects. **History and Archeology:** Historical events and their causes, indicators, and impact on particular civilizations

and cultures. **Geography:** Various methods for describing the location and distribution of land, sea, and air masses, including their physical locations, relationships, and characteristics. **Psychology:** Human behavior and performance, mental processes, psychological research methods, and the assessment and treatment of behavioral and affective disorders. **Philosophy and Theology:** Different philosophical systems and religions, including their basic principles, values, ethics, ways of thinking, customs, and practices and their impact on human culture. **Sociology and Anthropology:** Group behavior and dynamics; societal trends and influences; and cultures and their history, migrations, ethnicity, and origins.

Work Environment: Indoors; noisy; standing.

Speech-Language Pathologists

- ❋ Education/Training Required: Master's degree
- ❋ Annual Earnings: $60,690
- ❋ Beginning Wage: $40,200
- ❋ Earnings Growth Potential: Low
- ❋ Growth: 10.6%
- ❋ Annual Job Openings: 11,160
- ❋ Self-Employed: 8.8%
- ❋ Part-Time: 24.6%

Assess and treat persons with speech, language, voice, and fluency disorders. May select alternative communication systems and teach their use. May perform research related to speech and language problems. Monitor patients' progress and adjust treatments accordingly. Evaluate hearing and speech/language test results and medical or background information to diagnose and plan treatment for speech, language, fluency, voice, and swallowing disorders. Administer hearing or speech and language evaluations, tests, or examinations to patients to collect information on type and degree of impairments, using written and oral tests and special instruments. Record information on the initial evaluation, treatment, progress, and discharge of clients. Develop and implement treatment plans for problems such as stuttering, delayed language, swallowing disorders, and inappropriate pitch or harsh voice problems, based on own assessments and recommendations of physicians, psychologists, or social workers. Develop individual or group programs in schools to deal with speech or language problems. Instruct clients in techniques for more effective communication, including sign language, lip reading, and voice improvement. Teach clients to control or strengthen tongue, jaw, face muscles, and breathing mechanisms. Develop speech exercise programs to reduce disabilities. Consult with and advise educators or medical staff on speech or hearing topics, such as communication strategies or speech and language stimulation. Instruct patients and family members in strategies to cope with or avoid communication-related misunderstandings. Design, develop, and employ alternative diagnostic or communication devices and strategies. Conduct lessons and direct educational or therapeutic games to assist teachers dealing with speech problems. Refer clients to additional medical or educational services if needed. Participate in conferences or training, or publish research results, to share knowledge of new hearing or speech disorder treatment methods or technologies. Communicate with non-speaking students, using sign language or computer technology. Provide communication instruction to dialect speakers or students with limited English proficiency. Use computer applications to identify and assist with communication disabilities.

Personality Type: Social. These occupations frequently involve working with, communicating with, and teaching people and often involve helping or providing service to others.

GOE—Interest Area/Cluster: 08. Health Science. **Work Group:** 08.07. Medical Therapy. **Other Jobs in This Work Group:** Audiologists; Massage Therapists; Occupational Therapist Aides; Occupational Therapist Assistants; Occupational Therapists; Physical Therapist Aides; Physical Therapist Assistants; Physical Therapists; Radiation Therapists; Recreational Therapists; Respiratory Therapists; Respiratory Therapy Technicians.

Skills—Learning Strategies: Using multiple approaches when learning or teaching new things. **Instructing:** Teaching others how to do something. **Social Perceptiveness:** Being aware of others' reactions and understanding why they react the way they do. **Speaking:** Talking to others to effectively convey information. **Monitoring:** Assessing how well one is doing when learning or doing something. **Service Orientation:** Actively looking for ways to help people. **Reading Comprehension:** Understanding written sentences and paragraphs in work-related documents. **Active Learning:** Working with new material or information to grasp its implications.

Education and Training Programs: Audiology/Audiologist and Speech-Language Pathology/Pathologist Training; Communication Disorders Sciences and Services,

Other; Communication Disorders, General; Speech-Language Pathology/Pathologist Training. **Related Knowledge/Courses—Therapy and Counseling:** Information and techniques needed to rehabilitate physical and mental ailments and to provide career guidance, including alternative treatments, rehabilitation equipment and its proper use, and methods to evaluate treatment effects. **Psychology:** Human behavior and performance, mental processes, psychological research methods, and the assessment and treatment of behavioral and affective disorders. **Sociology and Anthropology:** Group behavior and dynamics; societal trends and influences; and cultures and their history, migrations, ethnicity, and origins. **Medicine and Dentistry:** The information and techniques needed to diagnose and treat injuries, diseases, and deformities. This includes symptoms, treatment alternatives, drug properties and interactions, and preventive health-care measures. **Education and Training:** Instructional methods and training techniques, including curriculum design principles, learning theory, group and individual teaching techniques, design of individual development plans, and test design principles. **English Language:** The structure and content of the English language, including the meaning and spelling of words, rules of composition, and grammar.

Work Environment: Indoors; disease or infections; sitting.

Statement Clerks

- ❋ Education/Training Required: Moderate-term on-the-job training
- ❋ Annual Earnings: $29,970
- ❋ Beginning Wage: $20,930
- ❋ Earnings Growth Potential: Low
- ❋ Growth: 4.4%
- ❋ Annual Job Openings: 81,885
- ❋ Self-Employed: 1.6%
- ❋ Part-Time: 14.3%

The job openings listed here are shared with Billing, Cost, and Rate Clerks; and with Billing, Posting, and Calculating Machine Operators.

Prepare and distribute bank statements to customers, answer inquiries, and reconcile discrepancies in records and accounts. Encode and cancel checks, using bank machines. Take orders for imprinted checks. Compare previously prepared bank statements with canceled checks and reconcile discrepancies. Verify signatures and required information on checks. Post stop-payment notices to prevent payment of protested checks. Maintain files of canceled checks and customers' signatures. Match statements with batches of canceled checks by account numbers. Weigh envelopes containing statements to determine correct postage and affix postage, using stamps or metering equipment. Load machines with statements, cancelled checks, and envelopes to prepare statements for distribution to customers or stuff envelopes by hand. Retrieve checks returned to customers in error, adjusting customer accounts and answering inquiries about errors as necessary. Route statements for mailing or over-the-counter delivery to customers. Monitor equipment to ensure proper operation. Fix minor problems, such as equipment jams, and notify repair personnel of major equipment problems.

Personality Type: Conventional. These occupations frequently involve following set procedures and routines and can include working with data and details more than with ideas. Usually there is a clear line of authority to follow.

GOE—Interest Area/Cluster: 04. Business and Administration. **Work Group:** 04.06. Mathematical Clerical Support. **Other Jobs in This Work Group:** Billing and Posting Clerks and Machine Operators; Billing, Cost, and Rate Clerks; Bookkeeping, Accounting, and Auditing Clerks; Brokerage Clerks; Payroll and Timekeeping Clerks; Tax Preparers.

Skill—None met the criteria.

Education and Training Program: Accounting Technology/Technician Training and Bookkeeping. **Related Knowledge/Courses—Economics and Accounting:** Economic and accounting principles and practices, the financial markets, banking, and the analysis and reporting of financial data. **Clerical Practices:** Administrative and clerical procedures and systems such as word-processing systems, filing and records management systems, stenography and transcription, forms, design principles, and other office procedures and terminology. **Administration and Management:** Principles and processes involved in business and organizational planning, coordination, and execution. This includes strategic planning, resource allocation, manpower modeling, leadership techniques, and production methods.

Work Environment: Indoors; sitting; repetitive motions.

Statisticians

- Education/Training Required: Master's degree
- Annual Earnings: $69,900
- Beginning Wage: $38,140
- Earnings Growth Potential: High
- Growth: 8.5%
- Annual Job Openings: 3,433
- Self-Employed: 6.0%
- Part-Time: 13.1%

Engage in the development of mathematical theory or apply statistical theory and methods to collect, organize, interpret, and summarize numerical data to provide usable information. May specialize in fields such as bio-statistics, agricultural statistics, business statistics, economic statistics, or other fields. Report results of statistical analyses, including information in the form of graphs, charts, and tables. Process large amounts of data for statistical modeling and graphic analysis, using computers. Identify relationships and trends in data, as well as any factors that could affect the results of research. Analyze and interpret statistical data in order to identify significant differences in relationships among sources of information. Prepare data for processing by organizing information, checking for any inaccuracies, and adjusting and weighting the raw data. Evaluate the statistical methods and procedures used to obtain data in order to ensure validity, applicability, efficiency, and accuracy. Evaluate sources of information in order to determine any limitations in terms of reliability or usability. Plan data collection methods for specific projects and determine the types and sizes of sample groups to be used. Design research projects that apply valid scientific techniques and utilize information obtained from baselines or historical data in order to structure uncompromised and efficient analyses. Develop an understanding of fields to which statistical methods are to be applied in order to determine whether methods and results are appropriate. Supervise and provide instructions for workers collecting and tabulating data. Apply sampling techniques or utilize complete enumeration bases in order to determine and define groups to be surveyed. Adapt statistical methods in order to solve specific problems in many fields, such as economics, biology, and engineering. Develop and test experimental designs, sampling techniques, and analytical methods. Examine theories, such as those of probability and inference, in order to discover mathematical bases for new or improved methods of obtaining and evaluating numerical data.

Personality Type: Conventional. These occupations frequently involve following set procedures and routines and can include working with data and details more than with ideas. Usually there is a clear line of authority to follow.

GOE—Interest Area/Cluster: 15. Scientific Research, Engineering, and Mathematics. **Work Group:** 15.06. Mathematics and Data Analysis. **Other Jobs in This Work Group:** Actuaries; Mathematical Technicians; Mathematicians; Social Science Research Assistants; Statistical Assistants.

Skills—Programming: Writing computer programs for various purposes. **Science:** Using scientific methods to solve problems. **Mathematics:** Using mathematics to solve problems. **Writing:** Communicating effectively with others in writing as indicated by the needs of the audience. **Active Learning:** Working with new material or information to grasp its implications. **Negotiation:** Bringing others together and trying to reconcile differences. **Complex Problem Solving:** Identifying complex problems, reviewing the options, and implementing solutions. **Operations Analysis:** Analyzing needs and product requirements to create a design.

Education and Training Programs: Applied Mathematics; Biostatistics; Business Statistics; Mathematical Statistics and Probability; Mathematics, General; Statistics, General; Statistics, Other. **Related Knowledge/Courses—Mathematics:** Numbers and their operations and interrelationships, including arithmetic, algebra, geometry, calculus, and statistics and their applications. **Computers and Electronics:** Electric circuit boards, processors, chips, and computer hardware and software, including applications and programming. **English Language:** The structure and content of the English language, including the meaning and spelling of words, rules of composition, and grammar. **Law and Government:** Laws, legal codes, court procedures, precedents, government regulations, executive orders, agency rules, and the democratic political process. **Education and Training:** Instructional methods and training techniques, including curriculum design principles, learning theory, group and individual teaching techniques, design of individual development plans, and test design principles.

Work Environment: Indoors; sitting; using hands on objects, tools, or controls; repetitive motions.

Storage and Distribution Managers

- ❀ Education/Training Required: Work experience in a related occupation
- ❀ Annual Earnings: $76,310
- ❀ Beginning Wage: $44,900
- ❀ Earnings Growth Potential: High
- ❀ Growth: 8.3%
- ❀ Annual Job Openings: 6,994
- ❀ Self-Employed: 2.6%
- ❀ Part-Time: 2.3%

The job openings listed here are shared with Transportation Managers.

Plan, direct, and coordinate the storage and distribution operations within organizations or the activities of organizations that are engaged in storing and distributing materials and products. Prepare and manage departmental budgets. Supervise the activities of workers engaged in receiving, storing, testing, and shipping products or materials. Interview, select, and train warehouse and supervisory personnel. Plan, develop, and implement warehouse safety and security programs and activities. Prepare or direct preparation of correspondence; reports; and operations, maintenance, and safety manuals. Issue shipping instructions and provide routing information to ensure that delivery times and locations are coordinated. Review invoices, work orders, consumption reports, and demand forecasts to estimate peak delivery periods and to issue work assignments. Confer with department heads to coordinate warehouse activities such as production, sales, records control, and purchasing. Inspect physical conditions of warehouses, vehicle fleets, and equipment and order testing, maintenance, repair, or replacement as necessary. Schedule and monitor air or surface pickup, delivery, or distribution of products or materials. Respond to customers' or shippers' questions and complaints regarding storage and distribution services. Develop and document standard and emergency operating procedures for receiving, handling, storing, shipping, or salvaging products or materials. Develop and implement plans for facility modification or expansion such as equipment purchase or changes in space allocation or structural design. Track and trace goods while they are en route to their destinations, expediting orders when necessary. Negotiate with carriers, warehouse operators, and insurance company representatives for services and preferential rates. Arrange for necessary shipping documentation and contact customs officials to effect release of shipments. Evaluate freight costs and the inventory costs associated with transit times to ensure that costs are appropriate. Advise sales and billing departments of transportation charges for customers' accounts. Examine invoices and shipping manifests for conformity to tariff and customs regulations. Evaluate locations for new warehouses and distribution networks to determine their potential usefulness.

Personality Type: Enterprising. These occupations frequently involve starting up and carrying out projects and can involve leading people and making many decisions. They sometimes require risk taking and often deal with business.

GOE—Interest Area/Cluster: 16. Transportation, Distribution, and Logistics. **Work Group:** 16.01. Managerial Work in Transportation. **Other Jobs in This Work Group:** Aircraft Cargo Handling Supervisors; First-Line Supervisors/Managers of Transportation and Material-Moving Machine and Vehicle Operators; Postmasters and Mail Superintendents; Railroad Conductors and Yardmasters; Transportation Managers; Transportation, Storage, and Distribution Managers.

Skills—Management of Financial Resources: Determining how money will be spent to get the work done and accounting for these expenditures. **Systems Analysis:** Determining how a system should work and how changes will affect outcomes. **Management of Personnel Resources:** Motivating, developing, and directing people as they work; identifying the best people for the job. **Management of Material Resources:** Obtaining and seeing to the appropriate use of equipment, facilities, and materials needed to do certain work. **Systems Evaluation:** Looking at many indicators of system performance and taking into account their accuracy. **Negotiation:** Bringing others together and trying to reconcile differences. **Persuasion:** Persuading others to approach things differently.

Education and Training Programs: Aeronautics/Aviation/Aerospace Science and Technology, General; Aviation/Airway Management and Operations; Business Administration and Management, General; Logistics and Materials Management; Public Administration; Transportation/Transportation Management. **Related Knowledge/Courses—Transportation:** Principles and methods for moving people or goods by air, rail, sea, or road, including their relative costs, advantages, and limitations. **Personnel and Human Resources:** Principles and procedures for personnel recruitment; selection; training; compensation and benefits; labor relations and negotiation; and personnel information systems. **Production and Processing:** Inputs, outputs, raw materials, waste, quality control, costs, and techniques for maximizing the manufacture and distribution of goods. **Administration and Management:** Principles and processes involved in business and organizational planning, coordination, and execution. This includes strategic planning, resource allocation, manpower modeling, leadership techniques, and production methods. **Economics and Accounting:** Economic and accounting principles and practices, the financial markets, banking, and the analysis and reporting of financial data. **Psychology:** Human behavior and performance, mental processes, psychological research methods, and the assessment and treatment of behavioral and affective disorders.

Work Environment: Indoors; standing.

Structural Iron and Steel Workers

* Education/Training Required: Long-term on-the-job training
* Annual Earnings: $42,130
* Beginning Wage: $24,180
* Earnings Growth Potential: High
* Growth: 6.0%
* Annual Job Openings: 6,969
* Self-Employed: 5.3%
* Part-Time: 5.8%

Raise, place, and unite iron or steel girders, columns, and other structural members to form completed structures or structural frameworks. May erect metal storage tanks and assemble prefabricated metal buildings. Read specifications and blueprints to determine the locations, quantities, and sizes of materials required. Verify vertical and horizontal alignment of structural-steel members, using plumb bobs, laser equipment, transits, and/or levels. Connect columns, beams, and girders with bolts, following blueprints and instructions from supervisors. Hoist steel beams, girders, and columns into place, using cranes, or signal hoisting equipment operators to lift and position structural-steel members. Bolt aligned structural-steel members in position for permanent riveting, bolting, or welding into place. Ride on girders or other structural-steel members to position them or use rope to guide them into position. Fabricate metal parts such as steel frames, columns, beams, and girders according to blueprints or instructions from supervisors. Pull, push, or pry structural-steel members into approximate positions for bolting into place. Cut, bend, and weld steel pieces, using metal shears, torches, and welding equipment. Fasten structural-steel members to hoist cables, using chains, cables, or rope. Assemble hoisting equipment and rigging, such as cables, pulleys, and hooks, to move heavy equipment and materials. Force structural-steel members into final positions, using turnbuckles, crowbars, jacks, and hand tools. Erect metal and precast concrete components for structures such as buildings, bridges, dams, towers, storage tanks, fences, and highway guardrails. Unload and position prefabricated steel units for hoisting as needed. Drive drift pins through rivet holes in order to align rivet holes in structural-steel members with corresponding holes in previously placed members. Dismantle structures and equipment. Insert sealing strips, wiring, insulating material, ladders, flanges, gauges, and valves, depending on types of structures being assembled. Catch hot rivets in buckets and insert rivets in holes, using tongs. Place blocks under reinforcing bars used to reinforce floors. Hold rivets while riveters use air-hammers to form heads on rivets.

Personality Type: Realistic. These occupations frequently involve work activities that include practical, hands-on problems and solutions. They often deal with plants; animals; and real-world materials such as wood, tools, and machinery. Many of the occupations require working outside and don't involve a lot of paperwork or working closely with others.

GOE—Interest Area/Cluster: 02. Architecture and Construction. **Work Group:** 02.04. Construction Crafts. **Other Jobs in This Work Group:** Boilermakers; Brickmasons and Blockmasons; Carpet Installers; Cement Masons and Concrete Finishers; Commercial Divers; Construction Carpenters; Crane and Tower Operators; Drywall and Ceiling Tile Installers; Electricians; Fence Erectors; Floor Layers, Except Carpet, Wood, and Hard Tiles; Floor Sanders and Finishers; Glaziers; Hazardous Materials Removal Workers; Insulation Workers, Floor, Ceiling, and Wall; Insulation Workers, Mechanical; Manufactured Building and Mobile Home Installers; Operating Engineers and Other Construction Equipment Operators; Painters, Construction and Maintenance; Paperhangers; Paving, Surfacing, and Tamping Equipment Operators; Pile-Driver Operators; Pipe Fitters and Steamfitters; Pipelayers; Plasterers and Stucco Masons; Plumbers; Plumbers, Pipefitters, and Steamfitters; Rail-Track Laying and Maintenance Equipment Operators; Refractory Materials Repairers, Except Brickmasons; Reinforcing Iron and Rebar Workers; Riggers; Roofers; Rough Carpenters; Security and Fire Alarm Systems Installers; Segmental Pavers; Sheet Metal Workers; Stone Cutters and Carvers, Manufacturing; Stonemasons; Tapers; Terrazzo Workers and Finishers; Tile and Marble Setters.

Skills—Equipment Maintenance: Performing routine maintenance and determining when and what kind of maintenance is needed. **Installation:** Installing equipment, machines, wiring, or programs to meet specifications. **Troubleshooting:** Determining what is causing an operating error and deciding what to do about it. **Equipment Selection:** Determining the kind of tools and equipment needed to do a job. **Coordination:** Adjusting actions in relation to others' actions. **Technology Design:** Generating or adapting equipment and technology to serve user needs. **Operation Monitoring:** Watching gauges, dials, or other indicators to make sure a machine is working properly. **Repairing:** Repairing machines or systems, using the needed tools.

Education and Training Programs: Construction Trades, Other; Metal Building Assembly/Assembler Training. **Related Knowledge/Courses—Building and Construction:** Materials, methods, and the appropriate tools to construct objects, structures, and buildings. **Engineering and Technology:** Equipment, tools, and mechanical devices and their uses to produce motion, light, power, technology, and other applications. **Mechanical Devices:** Machines and tools, including their designs, uses, benefits, repair, and maintenance. **Production and Processing:** Inputs, outputs, raw materials, waste, quality control, costs, and techniques for maximizing the manufacture and distribution of goods. **Design:** Design techniques, principles, tools, and instruments involved in the production and use of precision technical plans, blueprints, drawings, and models. **Physics:** Physical principles, laws, and applications, including air, water, material dynamics, light, atomic principles, heat, electric theory, earth formations, and meteorological and related natural phenomena.

Work Environment: Outdoors; noisy; very hot or cold; high places; hazardous equipment; using hands on objects, tools, or controls.

Structural Metal Fabricators and Fitters

* ❀ Education/Training Required: Moderate-term on-the-job training
* ❀ Annual Earnings: $31,030
* ❀ Beginning Wage: $20,310
* ❀ Earnings Growth Potential: Low
* ❀ Growth: –0.2%
* ❀ Annual Job Openings: 20,746
* ❀ Self-Employed: 2.0%
* ❀ Part-Time: 2.4%

Fabricate, lay out, position, align, and fit parts of structural metal products. Position, align, fit, and weld parts to form complete units or subunits, following blueprints and layout specifications and using jigs, welding torches, and hand tools. Verify conformance of workpieces to specifications, using squares, rulers, and measuring tapes. Tack-weld fitted parts together. Lay out and examine metal stock or workpieces to be processed to ensure that specifications are met. Align and fit parts according to specifications, using jacks, turnbuckles, wedges, drift pins, pry bars, and hammers. Locate and mark workpiece bending and cutting lines, allowing for stock thickness, machine and welding shrinkage, and other component specifications. Position or tighten braces, jacks, clamps, ropes, or bolt straps or bolt parts in position for welding or riveting. Study engineering drawings and blueprints to determine materials requirements and task sequences. Move parts into position manually or by using hoists or cranes. Set up and operate fabricating machines such as brakes, rolls, shears, flame cutters, grinders, and drill presses to bend, cut, form, punch, drill, or otherwise form and assemble metal components. Hammer, chip, and grind workpieces to cut, bend, and straighten metal. Smooth workpiece edges and fix taps, tubes, and valves. Design and construct templates and fixtures, using hand tools. Straighten warped or bent parts, using sledges, hand torches, straightening presses, or bulldozers. Mark reference points onto floors or face blocks and transpose them to workpieces, using measuring devices, squares, chalk, and soapstone. Set up face blocks, jigs, and fixtures. Remove high spots and cut bevels, using hand files, portable grinders, and cutting torches. Direct welders to build up low spots or short pieces with weld. Lift or move materials and finished products, using large cranes. Heat-treat parts, using acetylene torches. Preheat workpieces to make them malleable, using hand torches or furnaces. Install boilers, containers, and other structures. Erect ladders and scaffolding to fit together large assemblies.

Personality Type: Realistic. These occupations frequently involve work activities that include practical, hands-on problems and solutions. They often deal with plants; animals; and real-world materials such as wood, tools, and machinery. Many of the occupations require working outside and don't involve a lot of paperwork or working closely with others.

GOE—Interest Area/Cluster: 13. Manufacturing. **Work Group:** 13.04. Welding, Brazing, and Soldering. **Other Jobs in This Work Group:** Solderers and Brazers; Welders, Cutters, and Welder Fitters; Welders, Cutters, Solderers, and Brazers; Welding, Soldering, and Brazing Machine Setters, Operators, and Tenders.

Skills—Quality Control Analysis: Evaluating the quality or performance of products, services, or processes. **Operation Monitoring:** Watching gauges, dials, or other indicators to make sure a machine is working properly. **Equipment Maintenance:** Performing routine maintenance and determining when and what kind of maintenance is needed. **Installation:** Installing equipment, machines, wiring, or programs to meet specifications. **Repairing:** Repairing machines or systems, using the needed tools. **Operation and Control:** Controlling operations of equipment or systems. **Technology Design:** Generating or adapting equipment and technology to serve user needs. **Equipment Selection:** Determining the kind of tools and equipment needed to do a job.

Education and Training Program: Machine Shop Technology/Assistant Training. **Related Knowledge/Courses—Design:** Design techniques, principles, tools, and instruments involved in the production and use of precision technical plans, blueprints, drawings, and models. **Building and Construction:** Materials, methods, and the appropriate tools to construct objects, structures, and buildings. **Mechanical Devices:** Machines and tools, including their designs, uses, benefits, repair, and maintenance. **Production and Processing:** Inputs, outputs, raw materials, waste, quality control, costs, and techniques for maximizing the manufacture and distribution of goods.

Work Environment: Noisy; contaminants; hazardous equipment; minor burns, cuts, bites, or stings; standing; using hands on objects, tools, or controls.

Substance Abuse and Behavioral Disorder Counselors

- ❋ Education/Training Required: Bachelor's degree
- ❋ Annual Earnings: $35,580
- ❋ Beginning Wage: $23,780
- ❋ Earnings Growth Potential: Low
- ❋ Growth: 34.3%
- ❋ Annual Job Openings: 20,821
- ❋ Self-Employed: 5.8%
- ❋ Part-Time: 15.4%

Counsel and advise individuals with alcohol; tobacco; drug; or other problems, such as gambling and eating disorders. May counsel individuals, families, or groups or engage in prevention programs. Counsel clients and patients individually and in group sessions to assist in overcoming dependencies, adjusting to life, and making changes. Complete and maintain accurate records and reports regarding the patients' histories and progress, services provided, and other required information. Develop client treatment plans based on research, clinical experience, and client histories. Review and evaluate clients' progress in relation to measurable goals described in treatment and care plans. Interview clients, review records, and confer with other professionals to evaluate individuals' mental and physical condition and to determine their suitability for participation in a specific program. Intervene as advocate for clients or patients to resolve emergency problems in crisis situations. Provide clients or family members with information about addiction issues and about available services and programs, making appropriate referrals when necessary. Modify treatment plans to comply with changes in client status. Coordinate counseling efforts with mental health professionals and other health professionals such as doctors, nurses, and social workers. Attend training sessions to increase knowledge and skills. Plan and implement follow-up and aftercare programs for clients to be discharged from treatment programs. Conduct chemical dependency program orientation sessions. Counsel family members to assist them in understanding, dealing with, and supporting clients or patients. Participate in case conferences and staff meetings. Act as liaisons between clients and medical staff. Coordinate activities with courts, probation officers, community services, and other post-treatment agencies. Confer with family members or others close to clients to keep them informed of treatment planning and progress. Instruct others in program methods, procedures, and functions. Follow progress of discharged patients to determine effectiveness of treatments. Develop, implement, and evaluate public education, prevention, and health promotion programs, working in collaboration with organizations, institutions, and communities.

Personality Type: Social. These occupations frequently involve working with, communicating with, and teaching people and often involve helping or providing service to others.

GOE—Interest Area/Cluster: 10. Human Service. **Work Group:** 10.01. Counseling and Social Work. **Other Jobs in This Work Group:** Child, Family, and School Social Workers; Clinical Psychologists; Clinical, Counseling, and School Psychologists; Counseling Psychologists; Marriage and Family Therapists; Medical and Public Health Social Workers; Mental Health and Substance Abuse Social Workers; Mental Health Counselors; Probation Officers and Correctional Treatment Specialists; Rehabilitation Counselors; Residential Advisors; Social and Human Service Assistants.

Skills—Social Perceptiveness: Being aware of others' reactions and understanding why they react the way they do. **Persuasion:** Persuading others to approach things differently. **Service Orientation:** Actively looking for ways to help people. **Negotiation:** Bringing others together and trying to reconcile differences. **Active Listening:** Listening to what other people are saying and asking questions as appropriate. **Learning Strategies:** Using multiple approaches when learning or teaching new things. **Writing:** Communicating effectively with others in writing as indicated by the needs of the audience. **Complex Problem Solving:** Identifying complex problems, reviewing the options, and implementing solutions.

Education and Training Programs: Clinical/Medical Social Work; Mental and Social Health Services and Allied Professions, Other; Substance Abuse/Addiction Counseling. **Related Knowledge/Courses—Therapy and Counseling:** Information and techniques needed to rehabilitate physical and mental ailments and to provide career guidance, including alternative treatments, rehabilitation equipment and its proper use, and methods to evaluate treatment effects. **Psychology:** Human behavior and performance, mental processes, psychological research methods, and the assessment and treatment of behavioral and affective disorders. **Sociology and Anthropology:** Group behavior and dynamics; societal trends and influences; and cultures and their history, migrations, ethnicity, and origins. **Philosophy and Theology:** Different philosophical systems and religions, including their basic principles, values, ethics, ways of thinking, customs, and practices and their impact on human culture. **Customer and Personal Service:** Principles and processes for providing customer and personal services, including needs assessment techniques, quality service standards, alternative delivery systems, and customer satisfaction evaluation techniques. **Education and Training:** Instructional methods and training techniques, including curriculum design principles, learning theory, group and individual teaching techniques, design of individual development plans, and test design principles.

Work Environment: Indoors; disease or infections; sitting.

Subway and Streetcar Operators

* Education/Training Required: Moderate-term on-the-job training
* Annual Earnings: $50,520
* Beginning Wage: $32,830
* Earnings Growth Potential: Medium
* Growth: 12.1%
* Annual Job Openings: 587
* Self-Employed: 0.0%
* Part-Time: 0.9%

Operate subway or elevated suburban train with no separate locomotive or electric-powered streetcar to transport passengers. May handle fares. Operate controls to open and close transit vehicle doors. Drive and control rail-guided public transportation such as subways; elevated trains; and electric-powered streetcars, trams, or trolleys in order to transport passengers. Monitor lights indicating obstructions or other trains ahead and watch for car and truck traffic at crossings to stay alert to potential hazards. Direct emergency evacuation procedures. Regulate vehicle speed and the time spent at each stop in order to maintain schedules. Report delays, mechanical problems, and emergencies to supervisors or dispatchers, using radios. Make announcements to passengers, such as notifications of upcoming stops or schedule delays. Complete reports, including shift summaries and incident or accident reports. Greet passengers; provide information; and answer questions concerning fares, schedules, transfers, and routings. Attend meetings on driver and passenger safety in order to learn ways in which job performance might be affected. Collect fares from passengers and issue change and transfers. Record transactions and coin receptor readings in order to verify the amount of money collected.

Personality Type: Realistic. These occupations frequently involve work activities that include practical, hands-on problems and solutions. They often deal with plants; animals; and real-world materials such as wood, tools, and machinery. Many of the occupations require working outside and don't involve a lot of paperwork or working closely with others.

GOE—Interest Area/Cluster: 16. Transportation, Distribution, and Logistics. **Work Group:** 16.04. Rail Vehicle Operation. **Other Jobs in This Work Group:** Locomotive Engineers; Locomotive Firers; Rail Yard Engineers, Dinkey Operators, and Hostlers.

Skills—Operation and Control: Controlling operations of equipment or systems. **Operation Monitoring:** Watching gauges, dials, or other indicators to make sure a machine is working properly. **Troubleshooting:** Determining what is causing an operating error and deciding what to do about it. **Active Listening:** Listening to what other people are saying and asking questions as appropriate. **Service Orientation:** Actively looking for ways to help people.

Education and Training Program: Truck and Bus Driver Training/Commercial Vehicle Operation. **Related Knowledge/Courses—Transportation:** Principles and methods for moving people or goods by air, rail, sea, or road, including their relative costs, advantages, and limitations. **Public Safety and Security:** Weaponry; public safety; security operations, rules, regulations, precautions, and prevention; and the protection of people, data, and property. **Customer and Personal Service:** Principles and processes for providing customer and personal services, including needs assessment techniques, quality service standards, alternative delivery systems, and customer satisfaction evaluation techniques. **Telecommunications:** Transmission, broadcasting, switching, control, and operation of telecommunications systems. **Mechanical Devices:** Machines and tools, including their designs, uses, benefits, repair, and maintenance. **Communications and Media:** Media production, communication, and dissemination techniques and methods, including alternative ways to inform and entertain via written, oral, and visual media.

Work Environment: Outdoors; noisy; contaminants; sitting; using hands on objects, tools, or controls; repetitive motions.

Surgeons

- ✳ Education/Training Required: First professional degree
- ✳ Annual Earnings: More than $145,600
- ✳ Beginning Wage: $104,410
- ✳ Earnings Growth Potential: Cannot be calculated
- ✳ Growth: 14.2%
- ✳ Annual Job Openings: 38,027
- ✳ Self-Employed: 14.7%
- ✳ Part-Time: 8.1%

The job openings listed here are shared with Anesthesiologists; Family and General Practitioners; Internists, General; Obstetricians and Gynecologists; Pediatricians, General; and Psychiatrists.

Treat diseases, injuries, and deformities by invasive methods, such as manual manipulation, or by using instruments and appliances. Analyze patient's medical history, medication allergies, physical condition, and examination results to verify operation's necessity and to determine best procedure. Operate on patients to correct deformities, repair injuries, prevent and treat diseases, or improve or restore patients' functions. Follow established surgical techniques during the operation. Prescribe preoperative and postoperative treatments and procedures, such as sedatives, diets, antibiotics, and preparation and treatment of the patient's operative area. Examine patient to provide information on medical condition and surgical risk. Diagnose bodily disorders and orthopedic conditions and provide treatments, such as medicines and surgeries, in clinics, hospital wards, and operating rooms. Direct and coordinate activities of nurses, assistants, specialists, residents, and other medical staff. Provide consultation and surgical assistance to other physicians and surgeons. Refer patient to medical specialist or other practitioners when necessary. Examine instruments, equipment, and operating room to ensure sterility. Prepare case histories. Manage surgery services, including planning, scheduling and coordination, determination of procedures, and procurement of supplies and equipment. Conduct research to develop and test surgical techniques that can improve operating procedures and outcomes.

Personality Type: Investigative. These occupations frequently involve working with ideas and require an extensive amount of thinking. They can involve searching for facts and figuring out problems mentally.

GOE—Interest Area/Cluster: 08. Health Science. **Work Group:** 08.02. Medicine and Surgery. **Other Jobs in This Work Group:** Anesthesiologists; Family and General Practitioners; Internists, General; Medical Assistants; Medical Transcriptionists; Obstetricians and Gynecologists; Pediatricians, General; Pharmacists; Pharmacy Aides; Pharmacy Technicians; Physician Assistants; Psychiatrists; Registered Nurses; Surgical Technologists.

Skills—Science: Using scientific methods to solve problems. **Reading Comprehension:** Understanding written sentences and paragraphs in work-related documents. **Judgment and Decision Making:** Weighing the relative costs and benefits of a potential action. **Complex Problem Solving:** Identifying complex problems, reviewing the options, and implementing solutions. **Management of Financial Resources:** Determining how money will be spent to get the work done and accounting for these expenditures. **Critical Thinking:** Using logic and analysis to identify the strengths and weaknesses of different approaches. **Equipment Selection:** Determining the kind of tools and equipment needed to do a job. **Technology Design:** Generating or adapting equipment and technology to serve user needs.

Education and Training Programs: Adult Reconstructive Orthopedics (Orthopedic Surgery); Colon and Rectal Surgery; Critical Care Surgery; General Surgery; Hand Surgery; Neurological Surgery/Neurosurgery; Orthopedic Surgery of the Spine; Orthopedics/Orthopedic Surgery; Otolaryngology; Pediatric Orthopedics; Pediatric Surgery; Plastic Surgery; Sports Medicine; Thoracic Surgery; Urology; Vascular Surgery. **Related Knowledge/Courses—Medicine and Dentistry:** The information and techniques needed to diagnose and treat injuries, diseases, and deformities. This includes symptoms, treatment alternatives, drug properties and interactions, and preventive health-care measures. **Biology:** Plant and animal living tissue, cells, organisms, and entities, including their functions, interdependencies, and interactions with each other and the environment. **Therapy and Counseling:** Information and techniques needed to rehabilitate physical and mental ailments and to provide career guidance, including alternative treatments, rehabilitation equipment and its proper use, and methods to evaluate treatment effects. **Psychology:** Human behavior and performance, mental processes, psychological research methods, and the assessment and treatment of behavioral and affective disorders. **Chemistry:** The composition, structure, and properties of substances and of the chemical processes and transformations that they undergo. This includes uses of chemicals and their interactions, danger signs, production techniques, and disposal methods. **Customer and Personal Service:** Principles and processes for providing customer and personal services, including needs assessment techniques, quality service standards, alternative delivery systems, and customer satisfaction evaluation techniques.

Work Environment: Indoors; contaminants; radiation; disease or infections; standing; using hands on objects, tools, or controls.

Surgical Technologists

- ❋ Education/Training Required: Postsecondary vocational training
- ❋ Annual Earnings: $37,540
- ❋ Beginning Wage: $26,650
- ❋ Earnings Growth Potential: Low
- ❋ Growth: 24.5%
- ❋ Annual Job Openings: 15,365
- ❋ Self-Employed: 0.2%
- ❋ Part-Time: 20.8%

Assist in operations under the supervision of surgeons, registered nurses, or other surgical personnel. May help set up operating rooms; prepare and transport patients for surgery; adjust lights and equipment; pass instruments and other supplies to surgeons and surgeons' assistants; hold retractors; cut sutures; and help count sponges, needles, supplies, and instruments. Count sponges, needles, and instruments before and after operations. Maintain a proper sterile field during surgical procedures. Hand instruments and supplies to surgeons and surgeons' assistants, hold retractors and cut sutures, and perform other tasks as directed by surgeons during operations. Prepare patients for surgery, including positioning patients on operating tables and covering them with sterile surgical drapes to prevent exposure. Scrub arms and hands and assist surgical teams to scrub and put on gloves, masks, and surgical clothing. Wash and sterilize equipment, using germicides and sterilizers. Monitor and continually assess operating room conditions, including patient and surgical team needs. Prepare dressings or bandages and apply or assist with their application following surgeries. Clean and restock operating rooms, gathering and placing equipment and supplies and arranging instruments according to instructions such as those found on a preference card. Operate, assemble, adjust, or monitor sterilizers, lights, suction machines, and diagnostic equipment to ensure proper operation. Prepare, care for, and dispose of tissue specimens taken for laboratory analysis. Provide technical assistance to surgeons, surgical nurses, and anesthesiologists. Maintain supply of fluids, such as plasma, saline, blood, and glucose, for use during operations. Maintain files and records of surgical procedures. Observe patients' vital signs to assess physical condition. Order surgical supplies.

Personality Type: Realistic. These occupations frequently involve work activities that include practical, hands-on problems and solutions. They often deal with plants; animals; and real-world materials such as wood, tools, and machinery. Many of the occupations require working outside and don't involve a lot of paperwork or working closely with others.

GOE—Interest Area/Cluster: 08. Health Science. **Work Group:** 08.02. Medicine and Surgery. **Other Jobs in This Work Group:** Anesthesiologists; Family and General Practitioners; Internists, General; Medical Assistants; Medical Transcriptionists; Obstetricians and Gynecologists; Pediatricians, General; Pharmacists; Pharmacy Aides; Pharmacy Technicians; Physician Assistants; Psychiatrists; Registered Nurses; Surgeons.

Skills—Operation Monitoring: Watching gauges, dials, or other indicators to make sure a machine is working properly. **Quality Control Analysis:** Evaluating the quality or performance of products, services, or processes.

Education and Training Programs: Pathology/Pathologist Assistant Training; Surgical Technology/Technologist Training. **Related Knowledge/Courses—Medicine and Dentistry:** The information and techniques needed to diagnose and treat injuries, diseases, and deformities. This includes symptoms, treatment alternatives, drug properties and interactions, and preventive health-care measures. **Biology:** Plant and animal living tissue, cells, organisms, and entities, including their functions, interdependencies, and interactions with each other and the environment. **Psychology:** Human behavior and performance, mental processes, psychological research methods, and the assessment and treatment of behavioral and affective disorders. **Chemistry:** The composition, structure, and properties of substances and of the chemical processes and transformations that they undergo. This includes uses of chemicals and their interactions, danger signs, production techniques, and disposal methods. **Therapy and Counseling:** Information and techniques needed to rehabilitate physical and mental ailments and to provide career guidance, including alternative treatments, rehabilitation equipment and its proper use, and methods to evaluate treatment effects. **Customer and**

Personal Service: Principles and processes for providing customer and personal services, including needs assessment techniques, quality service standards, alternative delivery systems, and customer satisfaction evaluation techniques.

Work Environment: Indoors; contaminants; radiation; disease or infections; standing; using hands on objects, tools, or controls.

Survey Researchers

- ❋ Education/Training Required: Bachelor's degree
- ❋ Annual Earnings: $36,820
- ❋ Beginning Wage: $17,240
- ❋ Earnings Growth Potential: Very high
- ❋ Growth: 15.9%
- ❋ Annual Job Openings: 4,959
- ❋ Self-Employed: 6.8%
- ❋ Part-Time: 12.5%

Design or conduct surveys. May supervise interviewers who conduct the survey in person or over the telephone. May present survey results to client. Prepare and present summaries and analyses of survey data, including tables, graphs, and fact sheets that describe survey techniques and results. Consult with clients in order to identify survey needs and any specific requirements, such as special samples. Analyze data from surveys, old records, and/or case studies, using statistical software programs. Review, classify, and record survey data in preparation for computer analysis. Conduct research in order to gather information about survey topics. Conduct surveys and collect data, using methods such as interviews, questionnaires, focus groups, market analysis surveys, public opinion polls, literature reviews, and file reviews. Collaborate with other researchers in the planning, implementation, and evaluation of surveys. Direct and review the work of staff members, including survey support staff and interviewers who gather survey data. Monitor and evaluate survey progress and performance, using sample disposition reports and response rate calculations. Produce documentation of the questionnaire development process, data collection methods, sampling designs, and decisions related to sample statistical weighting. Determine and specify details of survey projects, including sources of information, procedures to be used, and the design of survey instruments and materials. Support, plan, and coordinate operations for single or multiple surveys. Direct updates and changes in survey implementation and methods. Hire and

train recruiters and data collectors. Write training manuals to be used by survey interviewers. **Personality Type:** Investigative. These occupations frequently involve working with ideas and require an extensive amount of thinking. They can involve searching for facts and figuring out problems mentally. **GOE—Interest Area/Cluster:** 06. Finance and Insurance. **Work Group:** 06.02. Finance/Insurance Investigation and Analysis. **Other Jobs in This Work Group:** Appraisers and Assessors of Real Estate; Appraisers, Real Estate; Assessors; Claims Adjusters, Examiners, and Investigators; Claims Examiners, Property and Casualty Insurance; Cost Estimators; Credit Analysts; Financial Analysts; Insurance Adjusters, Examiners, and Investigators; Insurance Appraisers, Auto Damage; Insurance Underwriters; Loan Counselors; Loan Officers; Market Research Analysts. **Skills—Management of Financial Resources:** Determining how money will be spent to get the work done and accounting for these expenditures. **Management of Personnel Resources:** Motivating, developing, and directing people as they work; identifying the best people for the job. **Time Management:** Managing one's own time and the time of others. **Writing:** Communicating effectively with others in writing as indicated by the needs of the audience. **Persuasion:** Persuading others to approach things differently. **Mathematics:** Using mathematics to solve problems. **Complex Problem Solving:** Identifying complex problems, reviewing the options, and implementing solutions. **Active Learning:** Working with new material or information to grasp its implications.

Education and Training Programs: Applied Economics; Business/Managerial Economics; Economics, General; Marketing Research. **Related Knowledge/Courses—Administration and Management:** Principles and processes involved in business and organizational planning, coordination, and execution. This includes strategic planning, resource allocation, manpower modeling, leadership techniques, and production methods. **Sociology and Anthropology:** Group behavior and dynamics; societal trends and influences; and cultures and their history, migrations, ethnicity, and origins. **Mathematics:** Numbers and their operations and interrelationships, including arithmetic, algebra, geometry, calculus, and statistics and their applications. **Economics and Accounting:** Economic and accounting principles and practices, the financial markets, banking, and the analysis and reporting of financial data. **Personnel and Human Resources:** Principles and procedures for personnel recruitment; selection; training; compensation and benefits; labor relations and negotiation; and personnel information systems. **Clerical Practices:** Administrative and clerical procedures and systems such as word-processing systems, filing and records management systems, stenography and transcription, forms, design principles, and other office procedures and terminology.

Work Environment: Indoors; noisy; sitting.

Surveying Technicians

- ❋ Education/Training Required: Moderate-term on-the-job training
- ❋ Annual Earnings: $33,640
- ❋ Beginning Wage: $20,670
- ❋ Earnings Growth Potential: Medium
- ❋ Growth: 19.4%
- ❋ Annual Job Openings: 8,299
- ❋ Self-Employed: 4.2%
- ❋ Part-Time: 4.5%

The job openings listed here are shared with Mapping Technicians.

Adjust and operate surveying instruments, such as theodolite and electronic distance-measuring equipment, and compile notes, make sketches, and enter data into computers. Perform calculations to determine earth curvature corrections, atmospheric impacts on measurements, traverse closures and adjustments, azimuths, level runs, and placement of markers. Record survey measurements and descriptive data, using notes, drawings, sketches, and inked tracings. Search for section corners, property irons, and survey points. Position and hold the vertical rods, or targets, that theodolite operators use for sighting to measure angles, distances, and elevations. Lay out grids and determine horizontal and vertical controls. Compare survey computations with applicable standards to determine adequacy of data. Set out and recover stakes, marks, and other monumentation. Conduct surveys to ascertain the locations of natural features and man-made structures on the Earth's surface, underground, and underwater, using electronic distance-measuring equipment and other surveying instruments. Direct and supervise work of subordinate members of surveying parties. Compile information necessary to stake projects for construction, using engineering plans. Prepare topographic and contour maps of land surveyed, including site features and other relevant information such as charts, drawings, and survey notes. Place and hold measuring tapes when electronic distance-measuring equipment is not used. Collect information needed to carry out new surveys, using source maps, previous survey data, photographs, computer records, and other relevant information. Operate and manage land-information computer systems, performing tasks such as storing data, making inquiries, and producing plots and reports. Run rods for benches and cross-section elevations. Perform manual labor, such as cutting brush for lines; carrying stakes, rebar, and other heavy items; and stacking rods. Maintain equipment and vehicles used by surveying crews. Provide assistance in the development of methods and procedures for conducting field surveys.

Personality Type: Realistic. These occupations frequently involve work activities that include practical, hands-on problems and solutions. They often deal with plants; animals; and real-world materials such as wood, tools, and machinery. Many of the occupations require working outside and don't involve a lot of paperwork or working closely with others.

GOE—Interest Area/Cluster: 15. Scientific Research, Engineering, and Mathematics. **Work Group:** 15.09. Engineering Technology. **Other Jobs in This Work Group:** Aerospace Engineering and Operations Technicians; Cartographers and Photogrammetrists; Civil Engineering Technicians; Electrical and Electronic Engineering Technicians; Electrical and Electronics Drafters; Electrical Drafters; Electrical Engineering Technicians; Electro-Mechanical Technicians; Electronic Drafters; Electronics Engineering Technicians; Environmental Engineering Technicians; Mapping Technicians; Mechanical Drafters; Mechanical Engineering Technicians; Surveying and Mapping Technicians.

Skills—Mathematics: Using mathematics to solve problems. **Operation and Control:** Controlling operations of equipment or systems. **Management of Personnel Resources:** Motivating, developing, and directing people as they work; identifying the best people for the job. **Operation Monitoring:** Watching gauges, dials, or other indicators to make sure a machine is working properly. **Systems Analysis:** Determining how a system should work and how changes will affect outcomes.

Education and Training Programs: Cartography; Surveying Technology/Surveying. **Related Knowledge/Courses—Geography:** Various methods for describing the location and distribution of land, sea, and air masses, including their physical locations, relationships, and characteristics. **Design:** Design techniques, principles, tools, and instruments involved in the production and use of precision technical plans, blueprints, drawings, and models. **Building and Construction:** Materials, methods, and the appropriate tools to construct objects, structures, and buildings. **Mathematics:** Numbers and their operations and interrelationships, including arithmetic, algebra, geometry, calculus, and statistics and their applications. **Law and Government:** Laws, legal codes, court procedures, precedents, government regulations, executive orders, agency rules, and the democratic political process. **Engineering and Technology:** Equipment, tools, and mechanical devices and their uses to produce motion, light, power, technology, and other applications.

Work Environment: Outdoors; hazardous equipment; minor burns, cuts, bites, or stings; standing; walking and running; using hands on objects, tools, or controls.

Surveyors

- ❈ Education/Training Required: Bachelor's degree
- ❈ Annual Earnings: $51,630
- ❈ Beginning Wage: $28,590
- ❈ Earnings Growth Potential: High
- ❈ Growth: 23.7%
- ❈ Annual Job Openings: 14,305
- ❈ Self-Employed: 3.7%
- ❈ Part-Time: 4.6%

Make exact measurements and determine property boundaries. Provide data relevant to the shape, contour, gravitation, location, elevation, or dimension of land or land features on or near the Earth's surface for engineering, mapmaking, mining, land evaluation, construction, and other purposes. Verify the accuracy of survey data, including measurements and calculations conducted at survey sites. Calculate heights, depths, relative positions, property lines, and other characteristics of terrain. Search legal records, survey records, and land titles to obtain information about property boundaries in areas to be surveyed. Prepare and maintain sketches, maps, reports, and legal descriptions of surveys to describe, certify, and assume liability for work performed. Direct or conduct surveys to establish legal boundaries for properties, based on legal deeds and titles. Prepare or supervise preparation of all data, charts, plots, maps, records, and documents related to surveys. Write descriptions of property boundary surveys for use in deeds, leases, or other legal documents. Compute geodetic measurements and interpret survey data to determine positions,

shapes, and elevations of geomorphic and topographic features. Determine longitudes and latitudes of important features and boundaries in survey areas, using theodolites, transits, levels, and satellite-based global positioning systems (GPS). Record the results of surveys, including the shape, contour, location, elevation, and dimensions of land or land features. Coordinate findings with the work of engineering and architectural personnel, clients, and others concerned with projects. Establish fixed points for use in making maps, using geodetic and engineering instruments. Train assistants and helpers and direct their work in such activities as performing surveys or drafting maps. Plan and conduct ground surveys designed to establish baselines, elevations, and other geodetic measurements. Adjust surveying instruments to maintain their accuracy. Analyze survey objectives and specifications to prepare survey proposals or to direct others in survey proposal preparation. Develop criteria for survey methods and procedures. Survey bodies of water to determine navigable channels and to secure data for construction of breakwaters, piers, and other marine structures. Conduct research in surveying and mapping methods, using knowledge of techniques of photogrammetric map compilation and electronic data processing.

Personality Type: Realistic. These occupations frequently involve work activities that include practical, hands-on problems and solutions. They often deal with plants; animals; and real-world materials such as wood, tools, and machinery. Many of the occupations require working outside and don't involve a lot of paperwork or working closely with others.

GOE—Interest Area/Cluster: 02. Architecture and Construction. **Work Group:** 02.03. Architecture/Construction Engineering Technologies. **Other Jobs in This Work Group:** Architectural and Civil Drafters; Architectural Drafters; Civil Drafters.

Skills—Operation Monitoring: Watching gauges, dials, or other indicators to make sure a machine is working properly. **Management of Personnel Resources:** Motivating, developing, and directing people as they work; identifying the best people for the job. **Operation and Control:** Controlling operations of equipment or systems. **Repairing:** Repairing machines or systems, using the needed tools.

Education and Training Program: Surveying Technology/ Surveying. **Related Knowledge/Courses—Geography:** Various methods for describing the location and distribution of land, sea, and air masses, including their physical locations, relationships, and characteristics. **Design:** Design techniques, principles, tools, and instruments involved in the production and use of precision technical plans, blueprints, drawings, and models. **Building and Construction:** Materials, methods, and the appropriate tools to construct objects, structures, and buildings. **History and Archeology:** Historical events and their causes, indicators, and impact on particular civilizations and cultures. **Engineering and Technology:** Equipment, tools, and mechanical devices and their uses to produce motion, light, power, technology, and other applications. **Mathematics:** Numbers and their operations and interrelationships, including arithmetic, algebra, geometry, calculus, and statistics and their applications.

Work Environment: Outdoors; very hot or cold; hazardous equipment; minor burns, cuts, bites, or stings; standing; using hands on objects, tools, or controls.

Talent Directors

* Education/Training Required: Long-term on-the-job training
* Annual Earnings: $61,090
* Beginning Wage: $28,980
* Earnings Growth Potential: Very high
* Growth: 11.1%
* Annual Job Openings: 8,992
* Self-Employed: 29.5%
* Part-Time: 9.0%

The job openings listed here are shared with Directors—Stage, Motion Pictures, Television, and Radio; Producers; Program Directors; Technical Directors/Managers.

Audition and interview performers to select most appropriate talent for parts in stage, television, radio, or motion picture productions. Review performer information such as photos, resumes, voice tapes, videos, and union membership in order to decide whom to audition for parts. Read scripts and confer with producers in order to determine the types and numbers of performers required for a given production. Select performers for roles or submit lists of suitable performers to producers or directors for final selection. Audition and interview performers in order to match their attributes to specific roles or to increase the pool of available acting talent. Maintain talent files that include information such as performers' specialties, past performances, and availability. Prepare actors for auditions by providing scripts and information about roles and casting requirements. Serve as liaisons between directors, actors, and agents. Attend or view productions in order to maintain knowledge of available

actors. Negotiate contract agreements with performers, with agents, or between performers and agents or production companies. Contact agents and actors in order to provide notification of audition and performance opportunities and to set up audition times. Hire and supervise workers who help locate people with specified attributes and talents. Arrange for and/or design screen tests or auditions for prospective performers. Locate performers or extras for crowd and background scenes and stand-ins or photo doubles for actors by direct contact or through agents.

Personality Type: Enterprising. These occupations frequently involve starting up and carrying out projects and can involve leading people and making many decisions. They sometimes require risk taking and often deal with business.

GOE—Interest Area/Cluster: 03. Arts and Communication. **Work Group:** 03.07. Music. **Other Jobs in This Work Group:** Music Composers and Arrangers; Music Directors; Music Directors and Composers; Musicians and Singers; Musicians, Instrumental; Singers.

Skills—Management of Financial Resources: Determining how money will be spent to get the work done and accounting for these expenditures. **Management of Personnel Resources:** Motivating, developing, and directing people as they work; identifying the best people for the job. **Persuasion:** Persuading others to approach things differently. **Social Perceptiveness:** Being aware of others' reactions and understanding why they react the way they do. **Negotiation:** Bringing others together and trying to reconcile differences. **Judgment and Decision Making:** Weighing the relative costs and benefits of a potential action. **Time Management:** Managing one's own time and the time of others. **Management of Material Resources:** Obtaining and seeing to the appropriate use of equipment, facilities, and materials needed to do certain work.

Education and Training Programs: Cinematography and Film/Video Production; Directing and Theatrical Production; Drama and Dramatics/Theatre Arts, General; Dramatic/Theatre Arts and Stagecraft, Other; Film/Cinema Studies; Radio and Television; Theatre/Theatre Arts Management. **Related Knowledge/Courses—Fine Arts:** Theory and techniques required to produce, compose, and perform works of music, dance, visual arts, drama, and sculpture. **Communications and Media:** Media production, communication, and dissemination techniques and methods, including alternative ways to inform and entertain via written, oral, and visual media. **Clerical Practices:**

Administrative and clerical procedures and systems such as word-processing systems, filing and records management systems, stenography and transcription, forms, design principles, and other office procedures and terminology. **Computers and Electronics:** Electric circuit boards, processors, chips, and computer hardware and software, including applications and programming. **Sales and Marketing:** Principles and methods involved in showing, promoting, and selling products or services. This includes marketing strategies and tactics, product demonstration and sales techniques, and sales control systems. **Telecommunications:** Transmission, broadcasting, switching, control, and operation of telecommunications systems.

Work Environment: Indoors; noisy; sitting.

Tapers

* Education/Training Required: Moderate-term on-the-job training
* Annual Earnings: $42,050
* Beginning Wage: $25,310
* Earnings Growth Potential: Medium
* Growth: 7.1%
* Annual Job Openings: 9,026
* Self-Employed: 24.9%
* Part-Time: 6.1%

Seal joints between plasterboard or other wallboard to prepare wall surfaces for painting or papering. Sand rough spots of dried cement between applications of compounds. Remove extra compound after surfaces have been covered sufficiently. Press paper tape over joints to embed tape into sealing compound and to seal joints. Mix sealing compounds by hand or with portable electric mixers. Install metal molding at wall corners to secure wallboards. Seal joints between plasterboard or other wallboard in order to prepare wall surfaces for painting or papering. Check adhesives to ensure that they will work and will remain durable. Apply texturizing compounds and primers to walls and ceilings before final finishing, using trowels, brushes, rollers, or spray guns. Sand or patch nicks or cracks in plasterboard or wallboard. Apply additional coats to fill in holes and make surfaces smooth. Use mechanical applicators that spread compounds and embed tape in one operation. Spread sealing compound between boards or panels and over cracks, holes, and nail and screw heads, using trowels, broadknives, or spatulas. Spread and smooth cementing material over tape, using trowels or floating machines

to blend joints with wall surfaces. Select the correct sealing compound or tape. Countersink nails or screws below surfaces of walls before applying sealing compounds, using hammers or screwdrivers.

Personality Type: Realistic. These occupations frequently involve work activities that include practical, hands-on problems and solutions. They often deal with plants; animals; and real-world materials such as wood, tools, and machinery. Many of the occupations require working outside and don't involve a lot of paperwork or working closely with others.

GOE—Interest Area/Cluster: 02. Architecture and Construction. **Work Group:** 02.04. Construction Crafts. **Other Jobs in This Work Group:** Boilermakers; Brickmasons and Blockmasons; Carpet Installers; Cement Masons and Concrete Finishers; Commercial Divers; Construction Carpenters; Crane and Tower Operators; Drywall and Ceiling Tile Installers; Electricians; Fence Erectors; Floor Layers, Except Carpet, Wood, and Hard Tiles; Floor Sanders and Finishers; Glaziers; Hazardous Materials Removal Workers; Insulation Workers, Floor, Ceiling, and Wall; Insulation Workers, Mechanical; Manufactured Building and Mobile Home Installers; Operating Engineers and Other Construction Equipment Operators; Painters, Construction and Maintenance; Paperhangers; Paving, Surfacing, and Tamping Equipment Operators; Pile-Driver Operators; Pipe Fitters and Steamfitters; Pipelayers; Plasterers and Stucco Masons; Plumbers; Plumbers, Pipefitters, and Steamfitters; Rail-Track Laying and Maintenance Equipment Operators; Refractory Materials Repairers, Except Brickmasons; Reinforcing Iron and Rebar Workers; Riggers; Roofers; Rough Carpenters; Security and Fire Alarm Systems Installers; Segmental Pavers; Sheet Metal Workers; Stone Cutters and Carvers, Manufacturing; Stonemasons; Structural Iron and Steel Workers; Terrazzo Workers and Finishers; Tile and Marble Setters.

Skills—Installation: Installing equipment, machines, wiring, or programs to meet specifications. **Management of Personnel Resources:** Motivating, developing, and directing people as they work; identifying the best people for the job. **Management of Material Resources:** Obtaining and seeing to the appropriate use of equipment, facilities, and materials needed to do certain work. **Repairing:** Repairing machines or systems, using the needed tools. **Equipment Selection:** Determining the kind of tools and equipment needed to do a job. **Equipment Maintenance:** Performing routine maintenance and determining when and what kind of maintenance is needed.

Education and Training Program: Construction Trades, Other. **Related Knowledge/Courses—Building and Construction:** Materials, methods, and the appropriate tools to construct objects, structures, and buildings. **Design:** Design techniques, principles, tools, and instruments involved in the production and use of precision technical plans, blueprints, drawings, and models. **Public Safety and Security:** Weaponry; public safety; security operations, rules, regulations, precautions, and prevention; and the protection of people, data, and property.

Work Environment: Contaminants; standing; walking and running; using hands on objects, tools, or controls; bending or twisting the body; repetitive motions.

Tax Examiners, Collectors, and Revenue Agents

- ❀ Education/Training Required: Bachelor's degree
- ❀ Annual Earnings: $46,920
- ❀ Beginning Wage: $27,390
- ❀ Earnings Growth Potential: High
- ❀ Growth: 2.1%
- ❀ Annual Job Openings: 4,465
- ❀ Self-Employed: 0.0%
- ❀ Part-Time: 3.9%

Determine tax liability or collect taxes from individuals or business firms according to prescribed laws and regulations. Collect taxes from individuals or businesses according to prescribed laws and regulations. Maintain knowledge of tax code changes and of accounting procedures and theory to properly evaluate financial information. Maintain records for each case, including contacts, telephone numbers, and actions taken. Confer with taxpayers or their representatives to discuss the issues, laws, and regulations involved in returns and to resolve problems with returns. Contact taxpayers by mail or telephone to address discrepancies and to request supporting documentation. Send notices to taxpayers when accounts are delinquent. Notify taxpayers of any overpayment or underpayment and either issue a refund or request further payment. Conduct independent field audits and investigations of income tax returns to verify information or to amend tax liabilities. Review filed tax returns to determine whether claimed tax credits and deductions are allowed by law. Review selected tax returns to determine the nature and extent of audits to be performed on them.

Enter tax return information into computers for processing. Examine accounting systems and records to determine whether accounting methods used were appropriate and in compliance with statutory provisions. Process individual and corporate income tax returns and sales and excise tax returns. Impose payment deadlines on delinquent taxpayers and monitor payments to ensure that deadlines are met. Check tax forms to verify that names and taxpayer identification numbers are correct, that computations have been performed correctly, or that amounts match those on supporting documentation. Examine and analyze tax assets and liabilities to determine resolution of delinquent tax problems. Recommend criminal prosecutions or civil penalties. Determine appropriate methods of debt settlement, such as offers of compromise, wage garnishment, or seizure and sale of property. Secure a taxpayer's agreement to discharge a tax assessment or submit contested determinations to other administrative or judicial conferees for appeals hearings. Prepare briefs and assist in searching and seizing records to prepare charges and documentation for court cases.

Personality Type: Conventional. These occupations frequently involve following set procedures and routines and can include working with data and details more than with ideas. Usually there is a clear line of authority to follow.

GOE—Interest Area/Cluster: 07. Government and Public Administration. **Work Group:** 07.03. Regulations Enforcement. **Other Jobs in This Work Group:** Agricultural Inspectors; Aviation Inspectors; Compliance Officers, Except Agriculture, Construction, Health and Safety, and Transportation; Construction and Building Inspectors; Environmental Compliance Inspectors; Equal Opportunity Representatives and Officers; Financial Examiners; Fire Inspectors; Fish and Game Wardens; Forest Fire Inspectors and Prevention Specialists; Freight and Cargo Inspectors; Government Property Inspectors and Investigators; Immigration and Customs Inspectors; Licensing Examiners and Inspectors; Nuclear Monitoring Technicians; Occupational Health and Safety Specialists; Occupational Health and Safety Technicians; Transportation Vehicle, Equipment, and Systems Inspectors, Except Aviation.

Skills—Service Orientation: Actively looking for ways to help people. **Mathematics:** Using mathematics to solve problems. **Speaking:** Talking to others to effectively convey information. **Active Learning:** Working with new material or information to grasp its implications. **Complex Problem Solving:** Identifying complex problems, reviewing the options, and implementing solutions. **Instructing:** Teaching others how to do something. **Operations**

Analysis: Analyzing needs and product requirements to create a design. **Active Listening:** Listening to what other people are saying and asking questions as appropriate.

Education and Training Programs: Accounting; Taxation. **Related Knowledge/Courses—Law and Government:** Laws, legal codes, court procedures, precedents, government regulations, executive orders, agency rules, and the democratic political process. **Customer and Personal Service:** Principles and processes for providing customer and personal services, including needs assessment techniques, quality service standards, alternative delivery systems, and customer satisfaction evaluation techniques. **Economics and Accounting:** Economic and accounting principles and practices, the financial markets, banking, and the analysis and reporting of financial data. **Computers and Electronics:** Electric circuit boards, processors, chips, and computer hardware and software, including applications and programming. **Clerical Practices:** Administrative and clerical procedures and systems such as word-processing systems, filing and records management systems, stenography and transcription, forms, design principles, and other office procedures and terminology. **Mathematics:** Numbers and their operations and interrelationships, including arithmetic, algebra, geometry, calculus, and statistics and their applications.

Work Environment: Indoors; sitting; repetitive motions.

Teacher Assistants

- ❋ Education/Training Required: Short-term on-the-job training
- ❋ Annual Earnings: $21,580
- ❋ Beginning Wage: $14,650
- ❋ Earnings Growth Potential: Low
- ❋ Growth: 10.4%
- ❋ Annual Job Openings: 193,986
- ❋ Self-Employed: 0.2%
- ❋ Part-Time: 38.0%

Perform duties that are instructional in nature or deliver direct services to students or parents. Serve in a position for which a teacher or another professional has ultimate responsibility for the design and implementation of educational programs and services. Provide extra assistance to students with special needs, such as non-English-speaking students or those with physical and mental disabilities. Tutor and assist children individually or in small groups

to help them master assignments and to reinforce learning concepts presented by teachers. Supervise students in classrooms, halls, cafeterias, school yards, and gymnasiums or on field trips. Enforce administration policies and rules governing students. Observe students' performance and record relevant data to assess progress. Discuss assigned duties with classroom teachers to coordinate instructional efforts. Instruct and monitor students in the use and care of equipment and materials to prevent injuries and damage. Present subject matter to students under the direction and guidance of teachers, using lectures, discussions, or supervised role-playing methods. Organize and label materials and display students' work in a manner appropriate for their eye levels and perceptual skills. Distribute tests and homework assignments and collect them when they are completed. Type, file, and duplicate materials. Distribute teaching materials such as textbooks, workbooks, papers, and pencils to students. Use computers, audiovisual aids, and other equipment and materials to supplement presentations. Attend staff meetings and serve on committees as required. Prepare lesson materials, bulletin board displays, exhibits, equipment, and demonstrations. Carry out therapeutic regimens such as behavior modification and personal development programs under the supervision of special education instructors, psychologists, or speech-language pathologists. Provide disabled students with assistive devices, supportive technology, and assistance accessing facilities such as restrooms. Assist in bus loading and unloading. Take class attendance and maintain attendance records. Grade homework and tests, and compute and record results, using answer sheets or electronic marking devices. Organize and supervise games and other recreational activities to promote physical, mental, and social development.

Personality Type: Social. These occupations frequently involve working with, communicating with, and teaching people and often involve helping or providing service to others.

GOE—Interest Area/Cluster: 05. Education and Training. **Work Group:** 05.02. Preschool, Elementary, and Secondary Teaching and Instructing. **Other Jobs in This Work Group:** Elementary School Teachers, Except Special Education; Kindergarten Teachers, Except Special Education; Middle School Teachers, Except Special and Vocational Education; Preschool Teachers, Except Special Education; Secondary School Teachers, Except Special and Vocational Education; Special Education Teachers, Middle School; Special Education Teachers, Preschool, Kindergarten, and Elementary School; Special Education Teachers, Secondary

School; Vocational Education Teachers, Middle School; Vocational Education Teachers, Secondary School.

Skills—Social Perceptiveness: Being aware of others' reactions and understanding why they react the way they do. **Learning Strategies:** Using multiple approaches when learning or teaching new things. **Instructing:** Teaching others how to do something. **Active Listening:** Listening to what other people are saying and asking questions as appropriate. **Persuasion:** Persuading others to approach things differently. **Negotiation:** Bringing others together and trying to reconcile differences. **Service Orientation:** Actively looking for ways to help people. **Writing:** Communicating effectively with others in writing as indicated by the needs of the audience.

Education and Training Programs: Teacher Assistant/Aide Training; Teaching Assistants/Aide Training, Other. **Related Knowledge/Courses—Geography:** Various methods for describing the location and distribution of land, sea, and air masses, including their physical locations, relationships, and characteristics. **History and Archeology:** Historical events and their causes, indicators, and impact on particular civilizations and cultures. **Psychology:** Human behavior and performance, mental processes, psychological research methods, and the assessment and treatment of behavioral and affective disorders. **Therapy and Counseling:** Information and techniques needed to rehabilitate physical and mental ailments and to provide career guidance, including alternative treatments, rehabilitation equipment and its proper use, and methods to evaluate treatment effects. **Sociology and Anthropology:** Group behavior and dynamics; societal trends and influences; and cultures and their history, migrations, ethnicity, and origins. **English Language:** The structure and content of the English language, including the meaning and spelling of words, rules of composition, and grammar.

Work Environment: Indoors; noisy; standing.

Team Assemblers

- ❋ Education/Training Required: Moderate-term on-the-job training
- ❋ Annual Earnings: $24,630
- ❋ Beginning Wage: $16,450
- ❋ Earnings Growth Potential: Low
- ❋ Growth: 0.1%
- ❋ Annual Job Openings: 264,135
- ❋ Self-Employed: 1.7%
- ❋ Part-Time: 6.2%

Work as part of a team having responsibility for assembling an entire product or component of a product. Team assemblers can perform all tasks conducted by the team in the assembly process and rotate through all or most of them rather than being assigned to a specific task on a permanent basis. May participate in making management decisions affecting the work. Team leaders who work as part of the team should be included. Rotate through all the tasks required in a particular production process. Determine work assignments and procedures. Shovel and sweep work areas. Operate heavy equipment such as forklifts. Provide assistance in the production of wiring assemblies.

Personality Type: Realistic. These occupations frequently involve work activities that include practical, hands-on problems and solutions. They often deal with plants; animals; and real-world materials such as wood, tools, and machinery. Many of the occupations require working outside and don't involve a lot of paperwork or working closely with others.

GOE—Interest Area/Cluster: 13. Manufacturing. **Work Group:** 13.03. Production Work, Assorted Materials Processing. **Other Jobs in This Work Group:** Bakers; Cementing and Gluing Machine Operators and Tenders; Chemical Equipment Operators and Tenders; Cleaning, Washing, and Metal Pickling Equipment Operators and Tenders; Coating, Painting, and Spraying Machine Setters, Operators, and Tenders; Cooling and Freezing Equipment Operators and Tenders; Cutting and Slicing Machine Setters, Operators, and Tenders; Extruding and Forming Machine Setters, Operators, and Tenders, Synthetic and Glass Fibers; Extruding, Forming, Pressing, and Compacting Machine Setters, Operators, and Tenders; Food and Tobacco Roasting, Baking, and Drying Machine Operators and Tenders; Food Batchmakers; Food Cooking Machine Operators and Tenders; Furnace, Kiln, Oven, Drier, and Kettle Operators and

Tenders; Heat Treating Equipment Setters, Operators, and Tenders, Metal and Plastic; Helpers—Production Workers; Meat, Poultry, and Fish Cutters and Trimmers; Metal-Refining Furnace Operators and Tenders; Mixing and Blending Machine Setters, Operators, and Tenders; Packaging and Filling Machine Operators and Tenders; Plating and Coating Machine Setters, Operators, and Tenders, Metal and Plastic; Pourers and Casters, Metal; Sawing Machine Setters, Operators, and Tenders, Wood; Separating, Filtering, Clarifying, Precipitating, and Still Machine Setters, Operators, and Tenders; Sewing Machine Operators; Shoe Machine Operators and Tenders; Slaughterers and Meat Packers; Textile Bleaching and Dyeing Machine Operators and Tenders; Tire Builders; Woodworking Machine Setters, Operators, and Tenders, Except Sawing.

Skills—Operation Monitoring: Watching gauges, dials, or other indicators to make sure a machine is working properly. **Installation:** Installing equipment, machines, wiring, or programs to meet specifications. **Quality Control Analysis:** Evaluating the quality or performance of products, services, or processes. **Equipment Maintenance:** Performing routine maintenance and determining when and what kind of maintenance is needed. **Technology Design:** Generating or adapting equipment and technology to serve user needs. **Equipment Selection:** Determining the kind of tools and equipment needed to do a job. **Repairing:** Repairing machines or systems, using the needed tools. **Operation and Control:** Controlling operations of equipment or systems.

Education and Training Program: Precision Production, Other. **Related Knowledge/Courses—Production and Processing:** Inputs, outputs, raw materials, waste, quality control, costs, and techniques for maximizing the manufacture and distribution of goods. **Mechanical Devices:** Machines and tools, including their designs, uses, benefits, repair, and maintenance.

Work Environment: Indoors; noisy; contaminants; standing; using hands on objects, tools, or controls; repetitive motions.

Technical Directors/Managers

* Education/Training Required: Long-term on-the-job training
* Annual Earnings: $61,090
* Beginning Wage: $28,980
* Earnings Growth Potential: Very high
* Growth: 11.1%
* Annual Job Openings: 8,992
* Self-Employed: 29.5%
* Part-Time: 9.0%

The job openings listed here are shared with Directors—Stage, Motion Pictures, Television, and Radio; Producers; Program Directors; and Talent Directors.

Coordinate activities of technical departments, such as taping, editing, engineering, and maintenance, to produce radio or television programs. Direct technical aspects of newscasts and other productions, checking and switching between video sources and taking responsibility for the on-air product, including camera shots and graphics. Test equipment to ensure proper operation. Monitor broadcasts to ensure that programs conform to station or network policies and regulations. Observe pictures through monitors and direct camera and video staff concerning shading and composition. Act as liaisons between engineering and production departments. Supervise and assign duties to workers engaged in technical control and production of radio and television programs. Schedule use of studio and editing facilities for producers and engineering and maintenance staff. Confer with operations directors to formulate and maintain fair and attainable technical policies for programs. Operate equipment to produce programs or broadcast live programs from remote locations. Train workers in use of equipment such as switchers, cameras, monitors, microphones, and lights. Switch between video sources in a studio or on multi-camera remotes, using equipment such as switchers, video slide projectors, and video effects generators. Set up and execute video transitions and special effects such as fades, dissolves, cuts, keys, and supers, using computers to manipulate pictures as necessary. Collaborate with promotions directors to produce on-air station promotions. Discuss filter options, lens choices, and the visual effects of objects being filmed with photography directors and video operators. Follow instructions from production managers and directors during productions, such as commands for camera cuts, effects, graphics, and takes.

Personality Type: Enterprising. These occupations frequently involve starting up and carrying out projects and can involve leading people and making many decisions. They sometimes require risk taking and often deal with business.

GOE—Interest Area/Cluster: 03. Arts and Communication. **Work Group:** 03.01. Managerial Work in Arts and Communication. **Other Jobs in This Work Group:** Agents and Business Managers of Artists, Performers, and Athletes; Art Directors; Producers; Producers and Directors; Program Directors; Public Relations Managers.

Skills—Operation and Control: Controlling operations of equipment or systems. **Operation Monitoring:** Watching gauges, dials, or other indicators to make sure a machine is working properly. **Monitoring:** Assessing how well one is doing when learning or doing something. **Systems Analysis:** Determining how a system should work and how changes will affect outcomes. **Equipment Selection:** Determining the kind of tools and equipment needed to do a job. **Troubleshooting:** Determining what is causing an operating error and deciding what to do about it. **Installation:** Installing equipment, machines, wiring, or programs to meet specifications. **Time Management:** Managing one's own time and the time of others.

Education and Training Programs: Cinematography and Film/Video Production; Directing and Theatrical Production; Drama and Dramatics/Theatre Arts, General; Dramatic/Theatre Arts and Stagecraft, Other; Film/Cinema Studies; Radio and Television; Theatre/Theatre Arts Management. **Related Knowledge/Courses—Communications and Media:** Media production, communication, and dissemination techniques and methods, including alternative ways to inform and entertain via written, oral, and visual media. **Telecommunications:** Transmission, broadcasting, switching, control, and operation of telecommunications systems. **Computers and Electronics:** Electric circuit boards, processors, chips, and computer hardware and software, including applications and programming. **Philosophy and Theology:** Different philosophical systems and religions, including their basic principles, values, ethics, ways of thinking, customs, and practices and their impact on human culture. **Engineering and Technology:** Equipment, tools, and mechanical devices and their uses to produce motion, light, power, technology, and other applications. **Sales and Marketing:** Principles and methods involved in showing, promoting, and selling products or services. This includes marketing strategies and tactics, product demonstration and sales techniques, and sales control systems.

Work Environment: Indoors; noisy; sitting; using hands on objects, tools, or controls.

Technical Writers

- ❋ Education/Training Required: Bachelor's degree
- ❋ Annual Earnings: $60,390
- ❋ Beginning Wage: $36,490
- ❋ Earnings Growth Potential: Medium
- ❋ Growth: 19.5%
- ❋ Annual Job Openings: 7,498
- ❋ Self-Employed: 6.0%
- ❋ Part-Time: 6.5%

Write technical materials, such as equipment manuals, appendices, or operating and maintenance instructions. May assist in layout work. Organize material and complete writing assignment according to set standards regarding order, clarity, conciseness, style, and terminology. Maintain records and files of work and revisions. Edit, standardize, or make changes to material prepared by other writers or establishment personnel. Confer with customer representatives, vendors, plant executives, or publisher to establish technical specifications and to determine subject material to be developed for publication. Review published materials and recommend revisions or changes in scope, format, content, and methods of reproduction and binding. Select photographs, drawings, sketches, diagrams, and charts to illustrate material. Study drawings, specifications, mockups, and product samples to integrate and delineate technology, operating procedure, and production sequence and detail. Interview production and engineering personnel and read journals and other material to become familiar with product technologies and production methods. Observe production, developmental, and experimental activities to determine operating procedure and detail. Arrange for typing, duplication, and distribution of material. Assist in laying out material for publication. Analyze developments in specific field to determine need for revisions in previously published materials and development of new material. Review manufacturer's and trade catalogs, drawings, and other data relative to operation, maintenance, and service of equipment. Draw sketches to illustrate specified materials or assembly sequence.

Personality Type: Artistic. These occupations frequently involve working with forms, designs, and patterns. They often require self-expression, and the work can be done without following a clear set of rules.

GOE—Interest Area/Cluster: 03. Arts and Communication. **Work Group:** 03.02. Writing and Editing. **Other Jobs in This Work Group:** Copy Writers; Editors; Poets, Lyricists, and Creative Writers; Writers and Authors.

Skills—Writing: Communicating effectively with others in writing as indicated by the needs of the audience. **Technology Design:** Generating or adapting equipment and technology to serve user needs. **Quality Control Analysis:** Evaluating the quality or performance of products, services, or processes. **Active Listening:** Listening to what other people are saying and asking questions as appropriate. **Operations Analysis:** Analyzing needs and product requirements to create a design. **Reading Comprehension:** Understanding written sentences and paragraphs in work-related documents. **Coordination:** Adjusting actions in relation to others' actions. **Active Learning:** Working with new material or information to grasp its implications.

Education and Training Programs: Business/Corporate Communications; Communication Studies/Speech Communication and Rhetoric; Technical and Business Writing. **Related Knowledge/Courses—Communications and Media:** Media production, communication, and dissemination techniques and methods, including alternative ways to inform and entertain via written, oral, and visual media. **Clerical Practices:** Administrative and clerical procedures and systems such as word-processing systems, filing and records management systems, stenography and transcription, forms, design principles, and other office procedures and terminology. **English Language:** The structure and content of the English language, including the meaning and spelling of words, rules of composition, and grammar. **Computers and Electronics:** Electric circuit boards, processors, chips, and computer hardware and software, including applications and programming. **Education and Training:** Instructional methods and training techniques, including curriculum design principles, learning theory, group and individual teaching techniques, design of individual development plans, and test design principles. **Engineering and Technology:** Equipment, tools, and mechanical devices and their uses to produce motion, light, power, technology, and other applications.

Work Environment: Indoors; sitting; using hands on objects, tools, or controls; repetitive motions.

Telecommunications Equipment Installers and Repairers, Except Line Installers

* Education/Training Required: Postsecondary vocational training
* Annual Earnings: $54,070
* Beginning Wage: $31,520
* Earnings Growth Potential: High
* Growth: 2.5%
* Annual Job Openings: 13,541
* Self-Employed: 4.1%
* Part-Time: 3.1%

Set up, rearrange, or remove switching and dialing equipment used in central offices. Service or repair telephones and other communication equipment on customers' properties. May install equipment in new locations or install wiring and telephone jacks in buildings under construction. Note differences in wire and cable colors so that work can be performed correctly. Test circuits and components of malfunctioning telecommunications equipment to isolate sources of malfunctions, using test meters, circuit diagrams, polarity probes, and other hand tools. Test repaired, newly installed, or updated equipment to ensure that it functions properly and conforms to specifications, using test equipment and observation. Drive crew trucks to and from work areas. Inspect equipment on a regular basis in order to ensure proper functioning. Repair or replace faulty equipment such as defective and damaged telephones, wires, switching system components, and associated equipment. Remove and remake connections in order to change circuit layouts, following work orders or diagrams. Demonstrate equipment to customers, explain how it is to be used, and respond to any inquiries or complaints. Analyze test readings, computer printouts, and trouble reports to determine equipment repair needs and required repair methods. Adjust or modify equipment to enhance equipment performance or to respond to customer requests. Remove loose wires and other debris after work is completed. Request support from technical service centers when on-site procedures fail to solve installation or maintenance problems. Communicate with bases, using telephones or two-way radios to receive instructions or technical advice or to report equipment status. Assemble and install communication equipment such as data and telephone communication lines, wiring, switching equipment, wiring frames, power apparatus, computer systems, and networks. Collaborate with other workers in order to locate and correct malfunctions. Review manufacturers' instructions, manuals, technical specifications, building permits, and ordinances in order to determine communication equipment requirements and procedures. Test connections to ensure that power supplies are adequate and that communications links function. Refer to manufacturers' manuals to obtain maintenance instructions pertaining to specific malfunctions. Climb poles and ladders, use truck-mounted booms, and enter areas such as manholes and cable vaults in order to install, maintain, or inspect equipment.

Personality Type: Realistic. These occupations frequently involve work activities that include practical, hands-on problems and solutions. They often deal with plants; animals; and real-world materials such as wood, tools, and machinery. Many of the occupations require working outside and don't involve a lot of paperwork or working closely with others.

GOE—Interest Area/Cluster: 02. Architecture and Construction. **Work Group:** 02.05. Systems and Equipment Installation, Maintenance, and Repair. **Other Jobs in This Work Group:** Electrical and Electronics Repairers, Powerhouse, Substation, and Relay; Electrical Power-Line Installers and Repairers; Elevator Installers and Repairers; Heating and Air Conditioning Mechanics and Installers; Maintenance and Repair Workers, General; Refrigeration Mechanics and Installers; Telecommunications Line Installers and Repairers.

Skills—Installation: Installing equipment, machines, wiring, or programs to meet specifications. **Repairing:** Repairing machines or systems, using the needed tools. **Troubleshooting:** Determining what is causing an operating error and deciding what to do about it. **Technology Design:** Generating or adapting equipment and technology to serve user needs. **Equipment Selection:** Determining the kind of tools and equipment needed to do a job. **Systems Analysis:** Determining how a system should work and how changes will affect outcomes. **Quality Control Analysis:** Evaluating the quality or performance of products, services, or processes. **Equipment Maintenance:** Performing routine maintenance and determining when and what kind of maintenance is needed.

Education and Training Program: Communications Systems Installation and Repair Technology. **Related Knowledge/Courses—Telecommunications:** Transmission, broadcasting, switching, control, and operation of telecommnications systems. **Mechanical Devices:** Machines and tools, including their designs, uses, benefits, repair, and

maintenance. **Computers and Electronics:** Electric circuit boards, processors, chips, and computer hardware and software, including applications and programming. **Engineering and Technology:** Equipment, tools, and mechanical devices and their uses to produce motion, light, power, technology, and other applications. **Design:** Design techniques, principles, tools, and instruments involved in the production and use of precision technical plans, blueprints, drawings, and models. **Public Safety and Security:** Weaponry; public safety; security operations, rules, regulations, precautions, and prevention; and the protection of people, data, and property.

Work Environment: Outdoors; noisy; very hot or cold; contaminants; cramped work space, awkward positions; using hands on objects, tools, or controls.

Telecommunications Line Installers and Repairers

- ❋ Education/Training Required: Long-term on-the-job training
- ❋ Annual Earnings: $47,220
- ❋ Beginning Wage: $25,140
- ❋ Earnings Growth Potential: High
- ❋ Growth: 4.6%
- ❋ Annual Job Openings: 14,719
- ❋ Self-Employed: 3.3%
- ❋ Part-Time: 1.9%

String and repair telephone and television cable, including fiber optics and other equipment for transmitting messages or television programming. Travel to customers' premises to install, maintain, and repair audio and visual electronic reception equipment and accessories. Inspect and test lines and cables, recording and analyzing test results to assess transmission characteristics and locate faults and malfunctions. Splice cables, using hand tools, epoxy, or mechanical equipment. Measure signal strength at utility poles, using electronic test equipment. Set up service for customers, installing, connecting, testing, and adjusting equipment. Place insulation over conductors and seal splices with moisture-proof covering. Access specific areas to string lines and install terminal boxes, auxiliary equipment, and appliances, using bucket trucks or by climbing poles and ladders or entering tunnels, trenches, or crawl spaces. String cables between structures and lines from poles, towers, or trenches and pull lines to proper tension. Install equipment such as amplifiers and repeaters in order to maintain the strength of communications transmissions. Lay underground cable directly in trenches or string it through conduits running through trenches. Pull up cable by hand from large reels mounted on trucks; then pull lines through ducts by hand or with winches. Clean and maintain tools and test equipment. Explain cable service to subscribers after installation and collect any installation fees that are due. Compute impedance of wires from poles to houses in order to determine additional resistance needed for reducing signals to desired levels. Use a variety of construction equipment to complete installations, including digger derricks, trenchers, and cable plows. Dig trenches for underground wires and cables. Dig holes for power poles, using power augers or shovels; set poles in place with cranes; and hoist poles upright, using winches. Fill and tamp holes, using cement, earth, and tamping devices. Participate in the construction and removal of telecommunication towers and associated support structures.

Personality Type: Realistic. These occupations frequently involve work activities that include practical, hands-on problems and solutions. They often deal with plants; animals; and real-world materials such as wood, tools, and machinery. Many of the occupations require working outside and don't involve a lot of paperwork or working closely with others.

GOE—Interest Area/Cluster: 02. Architecture and Construction. **Work Group:** 02.05. Systems and Equipment Installation, Maintenance, and Repair. **Other Jobs in This Work Group:** Electrical and Electronics Repairers, Powerhouse, Substation, and Relay; Electrical Power-Line Installers and Repairers; Elevator Installers and Repairers; Heating and Air Conditioning Mechanics and Installers; Maintenance and Repair Workers, General; Refrigeration Mechanics and Installers; Telecommunications Equipment Installers and Repairers, Except Line Installers.

Skills—Installation: Installing equipment, machines, wiring, or programs to meet specifications. **Troubleshooting:** Determining what is causing an operating error and deciding what to do about it. **Repairing:** Repairing machines or systems, using the needed tools. **Equipment Maintenance:** Performing routine maintenance and determining when and what kind of maintenance is needed. **Programming:** Writing computer programs for various purposes. **Technology Design:** Generating or adapting equipment and technology to serve user needs. **Quality Control Analysis:** Evaluating the quality or performance of products, services, or processes. **Equipment Selection:** Determining the kind of tools and equipment needed to do a job.

Education and Training Program: Communications Systems Installation and Repair Technology. **Related Knowledge/Courses—Telecommunications:** Transmission, broadcasting, switching, control, and operation of telecommunications systems. **Engineering and Technology:** Equipment, tools, and mechanical devices and their uses to produce motion, light, power, technology, and other applications. **Building and Construction:** Materials, methods, and the appropriate tools to construct objects, structures, and buildings. **Customer and Personal Service:** Principles and processes for providing customer and personal services, including needs assessment techniques, quality service standards, alternative delivery systems, and customer satisfaction evaluation techniques. **Design:** Design techniques, principles, tools, and instruments involved in the production and use of precision technical plans, blueprints, drawings, and models. **Mechanical Devices:** Machines and tools, including their designs, uses, benefits, repair, and maintenance.

Work Environment: Outdoors; very hot or cold; contaminants; cramped work space, awkward positions; hazardous equipment; using hands on objects, tools, or controls.

Tellers

- ✳ Education/Training Required: Short-term on-the-job training
- ✳ Annual Earnings: $22,920
- ✳ Beginning Wage: $17,360
- ✳ Earnings Growth Potential: Very low
- ✳ Growth: 13.5%
- ✳ Annual Job Openings: 146,077
- ✳ Self-Employed: 0.0%
- ✳ Part-Time: 27.1%

Receive and pay out money. Keep records of money and negotiable instruments involved in a financial institution's various transactions. Balance currency, coin, and checks in cash drawers at ends of shifts and calculate daily transactions, using computers, calculators, or adding machines. Cash checks and pay out money after verifying that signatures are correct, that written and numerical amounts agree, and that accounts have sufficient funds. Receive checks and cash for deposit, verify amounts, and check accuracy of deposit slips. Examine checks for endorsements and to verify other information such as dates, bank names, identification of the persons receiving payments, and the legality of the documents. Enter customers' transactions into computers to record transactions and issue computer-generated receipts. Count currency, coins, and checks received, by hand or using currency-counting machine, to prepare them for deposit or shipment to branch banks or the Federal Reserve Bank. Identify transaction mistakes when debits and credits do not balance. Prepare and verify cashier's checks. Arrange monies received in cash boxes and coin dispensers according to denomination. Process transactions such as term deposits, retirement savings plan contributions, automated teller transactions, night deposits, and mail deposits. Receive mortgage, loan, or public utility bill payments, verifying payment dates and amounts due. Resolve problems or discrepancies concerning customers' accounts. Explain, promote, or sell products or services such as travelers' checks, savings bonds, money orders, and cashier's checks, using computerized information about customers to tailor recommendations. Perform clerical tasks such as typing, filing, and microfilm photography. Monitor bank vaults to ensure cash balances are correct. Order a supply of cash to meet daily needs. Sort and file deposit slips and checks. Receive and count daily inventories of cash, drafts, and travelers' checks. Process and maintain records of customer loans. Count, verify, and post armored car deposits. Carry out special services for customers, such as ordering bank cards and checks. Compute financial fees, interest, and service charges. Obtain and process information required for the provision of services, such as opening accounts, savings plans, and purchasing bonds.

Personality Type: Conventional. These occupations frequently involve following set procedures and routines and can include working with data and details more than with ideas. Usually there is a clear line of authority to follow.

GOE—Interest Area/Cluster: 06. Finance and Insurance. **Work Group:** 06.04. Finance/Insurance Customer Service. **Other Jobs in This Work Group:** Bill and Account Collectors; Loan Interviewers and Clerks; New Accounts Clerks.

Skills—Service Orientation: Actively looking for ways to help people. **Mathematics:** Using mathematics to solve problems.

Education and Training Program: Banking and Financial Support Services. **Related Knowledge/Courses—Customer and Personal Service:** Principles and processes for providing customer and personal services, including needs assessment techniques, quality service standards, alternative delivery systems, and customer satisfaction evaluation

techniques. **Sales and Marketing:** Principles and methods involved in showing, promoting, and selling products or services. This includes marketing strategies and tactics, product demonstration and sales techniques, and sales control systems. **English Language:** The structure and content of the English language, including the meaning and spelling of words, rules of composition, and grammar. **Clerical Practices:** Administrative and clerical procedures and systems such as word-processing systems, filing and records management systems, stenography and transcription, forms, design principles, and other office procedures and terminology.

Work Environment: Indoors; more often standing than sitting; using hands on objects, tools, or controls; repetitive motions.

Tile and Marble Setters

* Education/Training Required: Long-term on-the-job training
* Annual Earnings: $38,720
* Beginning Wage: $21,890
* Earnings Growth Potential: High
* Growth: 15.4%
* Annual Job Openings: 9,066
* Self-Employed: 33.8%
* Part-Time: 7.2%

Apply hard tile, marble, and wood tile to walls, floors, ceilings, and roof decks. Align and straighten tile, using levels, squares, and straightedges. Determine and implement the best layout to achieve a desired pattern. Cut and shape tile to fit around obstacles and into odd spaces and corners, using hand- and power-cutting tools. Finish and dress the joints and wipe excess grout from between tiles, using damp sponge. Apply mortar to tile back, position the tile, and press or tap with trowel handle to affix tile to base. Mix, apply, and spread plaster, concrete, mortar, cement, mastic, glue, or other adhesives to form a bed for the tiles, using brush, trowel, and screed. Prepare cost and labor estimates based on calculations of time and materials needed for project. Measure and mark surfaces to be tiled, following blueprints. Level concrete and allow to dry. Build underbeds and install anchor bolts, wires, and brackets. Prepare surfaces for tiling by attaching lath or waterproof paper or by applying a cement mortar coat onto a metal screen. Study blueprints and examine surface to be covered to determine amount of material needed. Cut, surface, polish, and install marble and granite or install pre-cast terrazzo, granite, or marble units. Install and anchor fixtures in designated positions, using hand tools. Cut tile backing to required size, using shears. Remove any old tile, grout, and adhesive, using chisels and scrapers, and clean the surface carefully. Lay and set mosaic tiles to create decorative wall, mural, and floor designs. Assist customers in selection of tile and grout. Remove and replace cracked or damaged tile. Measure and cut metal lath to size for walls and ceilings, using tin snips. Select and order tile and other items to be installed, such as bathroom accessories, walls, panels, and cabinets, according to specifications. Mix and apply mortar or cement to edges and ends of drain tiles to seal halves and joints. Spread mastic or other adhesive base on roof deck to form base for promenade tile, using serrated spreader. Apply a sealer to make grout stain- and water-resistant. Brush glue onto manila paper on which design has been drawn and position tiles, finished side down, onto paper.

Personality Type: Realistic. These occupations frequently involve work activities that include practical, hands-on problems and solutions. They often deal with plants; animals; and real-world materials such as wood, tools, and machinery. Many of the occupations require working outside and don't involve a lot of paperwork or working closely with others.

GOE—Interest Area/Cluster: 02. Architecture and Construction. **Work Group:** 02.04. Construction Crafts. **Other Jobs in This Work Group:** Boilermakers; Brickmasons and Blockmasons; Carpet Installers; Cement Masons and Concrete Finishers; Commercial Divers; Construction Carpenters; Crane and Tower Operators; Drywall and Ceiling Tile Installers; Electricians; Fence Erectors; Floor Layers, Except Carpet, Wood, and Hard Tiles; Floor Sanders and Finishers; Glaziers; Hazardous Materials Removal Workers; Insulation Workers, Floor, Ceiling, and Wall; Insulation Workers, Mechanical; Manufactured Building and Mobile Home Installers; Operating Engineers and Other Construction Equipment Operators; Painters, Construction and Maintenance; Paperhangers; Paving, Surfacing, and Tamping Equipment Operators; Pile-Driver Operators; Pipe Fitters and Steamfitters; Pipelayers; Plasterers and Stucco Masons; Plumbers; Plumbers, Pipefitters, and Steamfitters; Rail-Track Laying and Maintenance Equipment Operators; Refractory Materials Repairers, Except Brickmasons; Reinforcing Iron and Rebar Workers; Riggers; Roofers; Rough Carpenters; Security and Fire Alarm Systems Installers; Segmental Pavers; Sheet Metal Workers; Stone Cutters and Carvers, Manufacturing; Stonemasons; Structural Iron and Steel Workers; Tapers; Terrazzo Workers and Finishers.

Skills—Installation: Installing equipment, machines, wiring, or programs to meet specifications. **Management of Financial Resources:** Determining how money will be spent to get the work done and accounting for these expenditures. **Mathematics:** Using mathematics to solve problems. **Equipment Selection:** Determining the kind of tools and equipment needed to do a job. **Technology Design:** Generating or adapting equipment and technology to serve user needs. **Management of Material Resources:** Obtaining and seeing to the appropriate use of equipment, facilities, and materials needed to do certain work. **Social Perceptiveness:** Being aware of others' reactions and understanding why they react the way they do. **Equipment Maintenance:** Performing routine maintenance and determining when and what kind of maintenance is needed.

Education and Training Program: Mason Training/Masonry. **Related Knowledge/Courses—Building and Construction:** Materials, methods, and the appropriate tools to construct objects, structures, and buildings. **Design:** Design techniques, principles, tools, and instruments involved in the production and use of precision technical plans, blueprints, drawings, and models. **Production and Processing:** Inputs, outputs, raw materials, waste, quality control, costs, and techniques for maximizing the manufacture and distribution of goods. **Economics and Accounting:** Economic and accounting principles and practices, the financial markets, banking, and the analysis and reporting of financial data. **Administration and Management:** Principles and processes involved in business and organizational planning, coordination, and execution. This includes strategic planning, resource allocation, manpower modeling, leadership techniques, and production methods. **Transportation:** Principles and methods for moving people or goods by air, rail, sea, or road, including their relative costs, advantages, and limitations.

Work Environment: Noisy; contaminants; cramped work space, awkward positions; standing; using hands on objects, tools, or controls; bending or twisting the body.

Tire Repairers and Changers

* Education/Training Required: Short-term on-the-job training
* Annual Earnings: $21,880
* Beginning Wage: $15,890
* Earnings Growth Potential: Low
* Growth: 20.2%
* Annual Job Openings: 18,829
* Self-Employed: 3.3%
* Part-Time: 14.6%

Repair and replace tires. Identify and inflate tires correctly for the size and ply. Place wheels on balancing machines to determine counterweights required to balance wheels. Raise vehicles, using hydraulic jacks. Remount wheels onto vehicles. Locate punctures in tubeless tires by visual inspection or by immersing inflated tires in water baths and observing air bubbles. Unbolt wheels from vehicles and remove them, using lug wrenches and other hand and power tools. Reassemble tires onto wheels. Replace valve stems and remove puncturing objects. Hammer required counterweights onto rims of wheels. Rotate tires to different positions on vehicles, using hand tools. Inspect tire casings for defects, such as holes and tears. Seal punctures in tubeless tires by inserting adhesive material and expanding rubber plugs into punctures, using hand tools. Glue boots (tire patches) over ruptures in tire casings, using rubber cement. Assist mechanics and perform other duties as directed. Separate tubed tires from wheels, using rubber mallets and metal bars or mechanical tire changers. Patch tubes with adhesive rubber patches or seal rubber patches to tubes by using hot vulcanizing plates. Inflate innertubes and immerse them in water to locate leaks. Clean sides of whitewall tires. Apply rubber cement to buffed tire casings prior to vulcanization process. Drive automobile or service trucks to industrial sites to provide services and respond to emergency calls. Prepare rims and wheel drums for reassembly by scraping, grinding, or sandblasting. Order replacements for tires and tubes. Roll new rubber treads, known as camelbacks, over tire casings and mold the semi-raw rubber treads onto the buffed casings. Buff defective areas of innertubes, using scrapers. Place casing-camelback assemblies in tire molds for the vulcanization process and exert pressure on the camelbacks to ensure good adhesion.

Personality Type: Realistic. These occupations frequently involve work activities that include practical, hands-on problems and solutions. They often deal with plants; animals; and real-world materials such as wood, tools, and machinery. Many of the occupations require working outside and don't involve a lot of paperwork or working closely with others.

GOE—Interest Area/Cluster: 13. Manufacturing. **Work Group:** 13.14. Vehicle and Facility Mechanical Work. **Other Jobs in This Work Group:** Aircraft Mechanics and Service Technicians; Aircraft Structure, Surfaces, Rigging, and Systems Assemblers; Automotive Body and Related Repairers; Automotive Glass Installers and Repairers; Automotive Master Mechanics; Automotive Service Technicians and Mechanics; Automotive Specialty Technicians; Bus and Truck Mechanics and Diesel Engine Specialists; Farm Equipment Mechanics; Fiberglass Laminators and Fabricators; Mobile Heavy Equipment Mechanics, Except Engines; Motorboat Mechanics; Motorcycle Mechanics; Outdoor Power Equipment and Other Small Engine Mechanics; Rail Car Repairers; Recreational Vehicle Service Technicians.

Skills—Repairing: Repairing machines or systems, using the needed tools. **Installation:** Installing equipment, machines, wiring, or programs to meet specifications. **Equipment Maintenance:** Performing routine maintenance and determining when and what kind of maintenance is needed. **Troubleshooting:** Determining what is causing an operating error and deciding what to do about it. **Management of Material Resources:** Obtaining and seeing to the appropriate use of equipment, facilities, and materials needed to do certain work. **Operation and Control:** Controlling operations of equipment or systems.

Education and Training Programs: No related CIP programs; this job is learned through informal short-term on-the-job training. **Related Knowledge/Courses— Mechanical Devices:** Machines and tools, including their designs, uses, benefits, repair, and maintenance. **Transportation:** Principles and methods for moving people or goods by air, rail, sea, or road, including their relative costs, advantages, and limitations. **Engineering and Technology:** Equipment, tools, and mechanical devices and their uses to produce motion, light, power, technology, and other applications. **Sales and Marketing:** Principles and methods involved in showing, promoting, and selling products or services. This includes marketing strategies and tactics, product demonstration and sales techniques, and sales control systems.

Work Environment: Noisy; contaminants; standing; walking and running; using hands on objects, tools, or controls; repetitive motions.

Tour Guides and Escorts

- ❋ Education/Training Required: Moderate-term on-the-job training
- ❋ Annual Earnings: $22,110
- ❋ Beginning Wage: $14,820
- ❋ Earnings Growth Potential: Low
- ❋ Growth: 21.2%
- ❋ Annual Job Openings: 15,027
- ❋ Self-Employed: 20.1%
- ❋ Part-Time: 29.0%

Escort individuals or groups on sightseeing tours or through places of interest such as industrial establishments, public buildings, and art galleries. Conduct educational activities for schoolchildren. Escort individuals or groups on cruises; on sightseeing tours; or through places of interest such as industrial establishments, public buildings, and art galleries. Describe tour points of interest to group members and respond to questions. Monitor visitors' activities to ensure compliance with establishment or tour regulations and safety practices. Greet and register visitors and issue any required identification badges or safety devices. Distribute brochures, show audiovisual presentations, and explain establishment processes and operations at tour sites. Provide directions and other pertinent information to visitors. Provide for physical safety of groups, performing such activities as providing first aid and directing emergency evacuations. Research environmental conditions and clients' skill and ability levels to plan expeditions, instruction, and commentary that are appropriate. Provide information about wildlife varieties and habitats, as well as any relevant regulations, such as those pertaining to hunting and fishing. Collect fees and tickets from group members. Teach skills, such as proper climbing methods, and demonstrate and advise on the use of equipment. Select travel routes and sites to be visited based on knowledge of specific areas. Solicit tour patronage and sell souvenirs. Speak foreign languages to communicate with foreign visitors. Assemble and check the required supplies and equipment prior to departure. Perform clerical duties such as filing, typing, operating switchboards, and routing mail and messages. Drive motor vehicles to transport visitors to establishments and tour site locations.

Personality Type: Social. These occupations frequently involve working with, communicating with, and teaching people and often involve helping or providing service to others.

GOE—Interest Area/Cluster: 09. Hospitality, Tourism, and Recreation. **Work Group:** 09.03. Hospitality and Travel Services. **Other Jobs in This Work Group:** Baggage Porters and Bellhops; Concierges; Flight Attendants; Hotel, Motel, and Resort Desk Clerks; Janitors and Cleaners, Except Maids and Housekeeping Cleaners; Maids and Housekeeping Cleaners; Reservation and Transportation Ticket Agents and Travel Clerks; Transportation Attendants, Except Flight Attendants and Baggage Porters; Travel Agents; Travel Guides.

Skills—Reading Comprehension: Understanding written sentences and paragraphs in work-related documents. **Speaking:** Talking to others to effectively convey information.

Education and Training Program: Tourism and Travel Services Management. **Related Knowledge/Courses—History and Archeology:** Historical events and their causes, indicators, and impact on particular civilizations and cultures. **Fine Arts:** Theory and techniques required to produce, compose, and perform works of music, dance, visual arts, drama, and sculpture. **Philosophy and Theology:** Different philosophical systems and religions, including their basic principles, values, ethics, ways of thinking, customs, and practices and their impact on human culture. **Sociology and Anthropology:** Group behavior and dynamics; societal trends and influences; and cultures and their history, migrations, ethnicity, and origins. **Customer and Personal Service:** Principles and processes for providing customer and personal services, including needs assessment techniques, quality service standards, alternative delivery systems, and customer satisfaction evaluation techniques. **Communications and Media:** Media production, communication, and dissemination techniques and methods, including alternative ways to inform and entertain via written, oral, and visual media.

Work Environment: Standing.

Training and Development Managers

- ❋ Education/Training Required: Work experience plus degree
- ❋ Annual Earnings: $84,340
- ❋ Beginning Wage: $46,450
- ❋ Earnings Growth Potential: High
- ❋ Growth: 15.6%
- ❋ Annual Job Openings: 3,759
- ❋ Self-Employed: 1.6%
- ❋ Part-Time: 2.7%

Plan, direct, or coordinate the training and development activities and staff of organizations. Prepare training budgets for departments or organizations. Evaluate instructor performances and the effectiveness of training programs, providing recommendations for improvements. Analyze training needs to develop new training programs or modify and improve existing programs. Conduct or arrange for ongoing technical training and personal development classes for staff members. Plan, develop, and provide training and staff development programs, using knowledge of the effectiveness of methods such as classroom training, demonstrations, on-the-job training, meetings, conferences, and workshops. Conduct orientation sessions and arrange on-the-job training for new hires. Confer with management and conduct surveys to identify training needs based on projected production processes, changes, and other factors. Train instructors and supervisors in techniques and skills for training and dealing with employees. Develop and organize training manuals, multimedia visual aids, and other educational materials. Develop testing and evaluation procedures. Review and evaluate training and apprenticeship programs for compliance with government standards. Coordinate established courses with technical and professional courses provided by community schools and designate training procedures.

Personality Type: Enterprising. These occupations frequently involve starting up and carrying out projects and can involve leading people and making many decisions. They sometimes require risk taking and often deal with business.

GOE—Interest Area/Cluster: 04. Business and Administration. **Work Group:** 04.01. Managerial Work in General Business. **Other Jobs in This Work Group:** Chief Executives; Compensation and Benefits Managers; General and Operations Managers; Human Resources Managers.

Skills—Systems Evaluation: Looking at many indicators of system performance and taking into account their accuracy. **Management of Financial Resources:** Determining how money will be spent to get the work done and accounting for these expenditures. **Systems Analysis:** Determining how a system should work and how changes will affect outcomes. **Management of Personnel Resources:** Motivating, developing, and directing people as they work; identifying the best people for the job. **Negotiation:** Bringing others together and trying to reconcile differences. **Persuasion:** Persuading others to approach things differently. **Learning Strategies:** Using multiple approaches when learning or teaching new things. **Service Orientation:** Actively looking for ways to help people.

Education and Training Programs: Human Resources Development; Human Resources Management/Personnel Administration, General. **Related Knowledge/Courses— Education and Training:** Instructional methods and training techniques, including curriculum design principles, learning theory, group and individual teaching techniques, design of individual development plans, and test design principles. **Personnel and Human Resources:** Principles and procedures for personnel recruitment; selection; training; compensation and benefits; labor relations and negotiation; and personnel information systems. **Sociology and Anthropology:** Group behavior and dynamics; societal trends and influences; and cultures and their history, migrations, ethnicity, and origins. **Sales and Marketing:** Principles and methods involved in showing, promoting, and selling products or services. This includes marketing strategies and tactics, product demonstration and sales techniques, and sales control systems. **Therapy and Counseling:** Information and techniques needed to rehabilitate physical and mental ailments and to provide career guidance, including alternative treatments, rehabilitation equipment and its proper use, and methods to evaluate treatment effects. **English Language:** The structure and content of the English language, including the meaning and spelling of words, rules of composition, and grammar.

Work Environment: Indoors; sitting.

Training and Development Specialists

❋ Education/Training Required: Work experience plus degree
❋ Annual Earnings: $49,630
❋ Beginning Wage: $28,600
❋ Earnings Growth Potential: High
❋ Growth: 18.3%
❋ Annual Job Openings: 35,862
❋ Self-Employed: 2.3%
❋ Part-Time: 7.6%

Conduct training and development programs for employees. Monitor, evaluate, and record training activities and program effectiveness. Offer specific training programs to help workers maintain or improve job skills. Assess training needs through surveys; interviews with employees; focus groups; or consultation with managers, instructors, or customer representatives. Develop alternative training methods if expected improvements are not seen. Organize and develop, or obtain, training procedure manuals and guides and course materials such as handouts and visual materials. Present information, using a variety of instructional techniques and formats such as role playing, simulations, team exercises, group discussions, videos, and lectures. Evaluate training materials prepared by instructors, such as outlines, text, and handouts. Design, plan, organize, and direct orientation and training for employees or customers of industrial or commercial establishments. Monitor training costs to ensure budget is not exceeded and prepare budget reports to justify expenditures. Select and assign instructors to conduct training. Schedule classes based on availability of classrooms, equipment, and instructors. Keep up with developments in their individual areas of expertise by reading current journals, books, and magazine articles. Supervise instructors, evaluate instructor performances, and refer instructors to classes for skill development. Coordinate recruitment and placement of training program participants. Attend meetings and seminars to obtain information for use in training programs or to inform management of training program statuses. Negotiate contracts with clients, including desired training outcomes, fees, and expenses. Devise programs to develop executive potential among employees in lower-level positions. Screen, hire, and assign workers to positions based on qualifications. Refer trainees to employer relations representatives, to locations offering job placement assistance, or to appropriate social services agencies if warranted.

Personality Type: Social. These occupations frequently involve working with, communicating with, and teaching people and often involve helping or providing service to others.

GOE—Interest Area/Cluster: 04. Business and Administration. **Work Group:** 04.03. Human Resources Support. **Other Jobs in This Work Group:** Compensation, Benefits, and Job Analysis Specialists; Employment Interviewers; Employment, Recruitment, and Placement Specialists; Personnel Recruiters.

Skills—Systems Evaluation: Looking at many indicators of system performance and taking into account their accuracy. **Systems Analysis:** Determining how a system should work and how changes will affect outcomes. **Learning Strategies:** Using multiple approaches when learning or teaching new things. **Management of Personnel Resources:** Motivating, developing, and directing people as they work; identifying the best people for the job. **Management of Financial Resources:** Determining how money will be spent to get the work done and accounting for these expenditures. **Instructing:** Teaching others how to do something. **Negotiation:** Bringing others together and trying to reconcile differences. **Writing:** Communicating effectively with others in writing as indicated by the needs of the audience.

Education and Training Programs: Human Resources Management/Personnel Administration, General; Organizational Behavior Studies. **Related Knowledge/Courses— Education and Training:** Instructional methods and training techniques, including curriculum design principles, learning theory, group and individual teaching techniques, design of individual development plans, and test design principles. **Sociology and Anthropology:** Group behavior and dynamics; societal trends and influences; and cultures and their history, migrations, ethnicity, and origins. **Sales and Marketing:** Principles and methods involved in showing, promoting, and selling products or services. This includes marketing strategies and tactics, product demonstration and sales techniques, and sales control systems. **Clerical Practices:** Administrative and clerical procedures and systems such as word-processing systems, filing and records management systems, stenography and transcription, forms, design principles, and other office procedures and terminology. **Personnel and Human Resources:** Principles and procedures for personnel recruitment; selection; training; compensation and benefits; labor relations and negotiation; and personnel information systems. **Psychology:** Human behavior and performance, mental processes, psychological research methods, and the assessment and treatment of behavioral and affective disorders.

Work Environment: Indoors; sitting.

Transportation Managers

* ❋ Education/Training Required: Work experience in a related occupation
* ❋ Annual Earnings: $76,310
* ❋ Beginning Wage: $44,900
* ❋ Earnings Growth Potential: High
* ❋ Growth: 8.3%
* ❋ Annual Job Openings: 6,994
* ❋ Self-Employed: 2.6%
* ❋ Part-Time: 2.3%

The job openings listed here are shared with Storage and Distribution Managers.

Plan, direct, and coordinate the transportation operations within an organization or the activities of organizations that provide transportation services. Direct activities related to dispatching, routing, and tracking transportation vehicles such as aircraft and railroad cars. Plan, organize, and manage the work of subordinate staff to ensure that the work is accomplished in a manner consistent with organizational requirements. Direct investigations to verify and resolve customer or shipper complaints. Serve as contact persons for all workers within assigned territories. Implement schedule and policy changes. Collaborate with other managers and staff members to formulate and implement policies, procedures, goals, and objectives. Monitor operations to ensure that staff members comply with administrative policies and procedures, safety rules, union contracts, and government regulations. Promote safe work activities by conducting safety audits, attending company safety meetings, and meeting with individual staff members. Develop criteria, application instructions, procedural manuals, and contracts for federal and state public transportation programs. Monitor spending to ensure that expenses are consistent with approved budgets. Direct and coordinate, through subordinates, activities of operations department to obtain use of equipment, facilities, and human resources. Direct activities of staff performing repairs and maintenance to equipment, vehicles, and facilities. Conduct investigations in cooperation with government agencies to determine causes of transportation accidents and to improve safety procedures. Analyze expenditures and other financial information to develop plans, policies, and budgets for increasing profits and improving

services. Negotiate and authorize contracts with equipment and materials suppliers and monitor contract fulfillment. Supervise workers assigning tariff classifications and preparing billing. Set operations policies and standards, including determination of safety procedures for the handling of dangerous goods. Recommend or authorize capital expenditures for acquisition of new equipment or property to increase efficiency and services of operations department. Prepare management recommendations, such as proposed fee and tariff increases or schedule changes.

Personality Type: Enterprising. These occupations frequently involve starting up and carrying out projects and can involve leading people and making many decisions. They sometimes require risk taking and often deal with business.

GOE—Interest Area/Cluster: 16. Transportation, Distribution, and Logistics. **Work Group:** 16.01. Managerial Work in Transportation. **Other Jobs in This Work Group:** Aircraft Cargo Handling Supervisors; First-Line Supervisors/ Managers of Transportation and Material-Moving Machine and Vehicle Operators; Postmasters and Mail Superintendents; Railroad Conductors and Yardmasters; Storage and Distribution Managers; Transportation, Storage, and Distribution Managers.

Skills—Negotiation: Bringing others together and trying to reconcile differences. **Time Management:** Managing one's own time and the time of others. **Coordination:** Adjusting actions in relation to others' actions. **Management of Financial Resources:** Determining how money will be spent to get the work done and accounting for these expenditures. **Mathematics:** Using mathematics to solve problems. **Monitoring:** Assessing how well one is doing when learning or doing something. **Management of Material Resources:** Obtaining and seeing to the appropriate use of equipment, facilities, and materials needed to do certain work. **Writing:** Communicating effectively with others in writing as indicated by the needs of the audience.

Education and Training Programs: Aeronautics/Aviation/ Aerospace Science and Technology, General; Aviation/Airway Management and Operations; Business Administration and Management, General; Logistics and Materials Management; Public Administration; Transportation/Transportation Management. **Related Knowledge/Courses—Transportation:** Principles and methods for moving people or goods by air, rail, sea, or road, including their relative costs, advantages, and limitations. **Clerical Practices:** Administrative and clerical procedures and systems such as word-processing systems, filing and records management systems, stenography and transcription, forms, design principles, and other office procedures and terminology. **Customer and Personal Service:** Principles and processes for providing customer and personal services, including needs assessment techniques, quality service standards, alternative delivery systems, and customer satisfaction evaluation techniques. **Sales and Marketing:** Principles and methods involved in showing, promoting, and selling products or services. This includes marketing strategies and tactics, product demonstration and sales techniques, and sales control systems. **Production and Processing:** Inputs, outputs, raw materials, waste, quality control, costs, and techniques for maximizing the manufacture and distribution of goods. **Psychology:** Human behavior and performance, mental processes, psychological research methods, and the assessment and treatment of behavioral and affective disorders.

Work Environment: Indoors; noisy; sitting.

Transportation Security Screeners

- ❀ Education/Training Required: Short-term on-the-job training
- ❀ Annual Earnings: $28,240
- ❀ Beginning Wage: $16,870
- ❀ Earnings Growth Potential: High
- ❀ Growth: 12.6%
- ❀ Annual Job Openings: 29,298
- ❀ Self-Employed: 0.0%
- ❀ Part-Time: 55.3%

Inspect baggage or cargo and screen passengers to detect and prevent potentially dangerous objects from being transported into secure areas or onto aircraft. Watch for potentially dangerous persons whose pictures are posted at checkpoints. Locate suspicious bags pictured in printouts sent from remote monitoring areas and set these bags aside for inspection. Monitor passenger flow through screening checkpoints to ensure order and efficiency. Notify supervisors or other appropriate personnel when security breaches occur. Record information about any baggage that sets off alarms in monitoring equipment. Send checked baggage through automated screening machines and set bags aside for searching or rescreening as indicated by equipment. Ask passengers to remove shoes and divest themselves of metal objects prior to walking through metal detectors. View images of checked bags and cargo, using remote screening equipment, and alert baggage screeners or handlers to any

possible problems. Perform pat-down or hand-held wand searches of passengers who have triggered machine alarms, who are unable to pass through metal detectors, or who have been randomly identified for such searches. Search carry-on or checked baggage by hand when it is suspected to contain prohibited items such as weapons. Test baggage for any explosive materials, using equipment such as explosive detection machines or chemical swab systems. Challenge suspicious people, requesting their badges and asking what their business is in a particular areas. Follow those who breach security until police or other security personnel arrive to apprehend them. Patrol work areas to detect any suspicious items. Provide directions and respond to passenger inquiries. Contact police directly in cases of urgent security issues, using phones or two-way radios. Inspect checked baggage for signs of tampering. Close entry areas following security breaches or reopen areas after receiving notification that the airport is secure. Contact leads or supervisors to discuss objects of concern that are not on prohibited object lists. Check passengers' tickets to ensure that they are valid and to determine whether passengers have designations that require special handling, such as providing photo identification.

Personality Type: Realistic. These occupations frequently involve work activities that include practical, hands-on problems and solutions. They often deal with plants; animals; and real-world materials such as wood, tools, and machinery. Many of the occupations require working outside and don't involve a lot of paperwork or working closely with others.

GOE—Interest Area/Cluster: 12. Law and Public Safety. **Work Group:** 12.05. Safety and Security. **Other Jobs in This Work Group:** Animal Control Workers; Crossing Guards; Gaming Surveillance Officers and Gaming Investigators; Lifeguards, Ski Patrol, and Other Recreational Protective Service Workers; Private Detectives and Investigators; Security Guards.

Skills—No data available.

Education and Training Programs: No related CIP programs; this job is learned through work experience in a related occupation; this job is learned through work experience in a related occupation. **Related Knowledge/Courses**—No data available.

Work Environment: No data available.

Transportation Vehicle, Equipment, and Systems Inspectors, Except Aviation

- ❀ Education/Training Required: Work experience in a related occupation
- ❀ Annual Earnings: $51,440
- ❀ Beginning Wage: $27,340
- ❀ Earnings Growth Potential: High
- ❀ Growth: 16.4%
- ❀ Annual Job Openings: 2,122
- ❀ Self-Employed: 5.9%
- ❀ Part-Time: 3.7%

The job openings listed here are shared with Aviation Inspectors; and with Freight and Cargo Inspectors.

Inspect and monitor transportation equipment, vehicles, or systems to ensure compliance with regulations and safety standards. Conduct vehicle or transportation equipment tests, using diagnostic equipment. Investigate and make recommendations on carrier requests for waiver of federal standards. Prepare reports on investigations or inspections and actions taken. Issue notices and recommend corrective actions when infractions or problems are found. Investigate incidents or violations such as delays, accidents, and equipment failures. Investigate complaints regarding safety violations. Inspect repairs to transportation vehicles and equipment to ensure that repair work was performed properly. Examine transportation vehicles, equipment, or systems to detect damage, wear, or malfunction. Inspect vehicles and other equipment for evidence of abuse, damage, or mechanical malfunction. Examine carrier operating rules, employee qualification guidelines, and carrier training and testing programs for compliance with regulations or safety standards. Inspect vehicles or equipment to ensure compliance with rules, standards, or regulations.

Personality Type: Realistic. These occupations frequently involve work activities that include practical, hands-on problems and solutions. They often deal with plants; animals; and real-world materials such as wood, tools, and machinery. Many of the occupations require working outside and don't involve a lot of paperwork or working closely with others.

GOE—Interest Area/Cluster: 07. Government and Public Administration. **Work Group:** 07.03. Regulations Enforcement. **Other Jobs in This Work Group:** Agricultural Inspectors; Aviation Inspectors; Compliance Officers, Except Agriculture, Construction, Health and Safety, and Transportation; Construction and Building Inspectors; Environmental Compliance Inspectors; Equal Opportunity Representatives and Officers; Financial Examiners; Fire Inspectors; Fish and Game Wardens; Forest Fire Inspectors and Prevention Specialists; Freight and Cargo Inspectors; Government Property Inspectors and Investigators; Immigration and Customs Inspectors; Licensing Examiners and Inspectors; Nuclear Monitoring Technicians; Occupational Health and Safety Specialists; Occupational Health and Safety Technicians; Tax Examiners, Collectors, and Revenue Agents.

Skills—Repairing: Repairing machines or systems, using the needed tools. **Equipment Maintenance:** Performing routine maintenance and determining when and what kind of maintenance is needed. **Troubleshooting:** Determining what is causing an operating error and deciding what to do about it. **Installation:** Installing equipment, machines, wiring, or programs to meet specifications. **Quality Control Analysis:** Evaluating the quality or performance of products, services, or processes. **Operation Monitoring:** Watching gauges, dials, or other indicators to make sure a machine is working properly. **Systems Analysis:** Determining how a system should work and how changes will affect outcomes. **Systems Evaluation:** Looking at many indicators of system performance and taking into account their accuracy.

Education and Training Programs: No related CIP programs; this job is learned through work experience in a related occupation; this job is learned through work experience in a related occupation. **Related Knowledge/Courses—Mechanical Devices:** Machines and tools, including their designs, uses, benefits, repair, and maintenance. **Transportation:** Principles and methods for moving people or goods by air, rail, sea, or road, including their relative costs, advantages, and limitations. **Public Safety and Security:** Weaponry; public safety; security operations, rules, regulations, precautions, and prevention; and the protection of people, data, and property. **Engineering and Technology:** Equipment, tools, and mechanical devices and their uses to produce motion, light, power, technology, and other applications. **Administration and Management:** Principles and processes involved in business and organizational planning, coordination, and execution. This includes strategic planning, resource allocation, manpower modeling, leadership techniques, and production methods. **Physics:** Physical principles, laws, and applications, including air, water, material dynamics, light, atomic principles, heat, electric theory, earth formations, and meteorological and related natural phenomena.

Work Environment: Noisy; very hot or cold; contaminants; cramped work space, awkward positions; hazardous equipment; using hands on objects, tools, or controls.

Treasurers and Controllers

- ❋ Education/Training Required: Work experience plus degree
- ❋ Annual Earnings: $95,310
- ❋ Beginning Wage: $51,910
- ❋ Earnings Growth Potential: High
- ❋ Growth: 12.6%
- ❋ Annual Job Openings: 57,589
- ❋ Self-Employed: 4.6%
- ❋ Part-Time: 4.2%

The job openings listed here are shared with Financial Managers, Branch or Department.

Direct financial activities, such as planning, procurement, and investments, for all or part of an organization. Prepare and file annual tax returns or prepare financial information so that outside accountants can complete tax returns. Prepare or direct preparation of financial statements, business activity reports, financial position forecasts, annual budgets, and/or reports required by regulatory agencies. Supervise employees performing financial reporting, accounting, billing, collections, payroll, and budgeting duties. Delegate authority for the receipt, disbursement, banking, protection, and custody of funds, securities, and financial instruments. Maintain current knowledge of organizational policies and procedures, federal and state policies and directives, and current accounting standards. Conduct or coordinate audits of company accounts and financial transactions to ensure compliance with state and federal requirements and statutes. Receive and record requests for disbursements; authorize disbursements in accordance with policies and procedures. Monitor financial activities and details such as reserve levels to ensure that all legal and regulatory requirements are met. Monitor and evaluate the performance of accounting and other financial staff; recommend and implement personnel actions such as promotions and dismissals. Develop and maintain relationships with banking, insurance, and non-organizational accounting personnel in order to facilitate financial activities. Coordinate and direct the financial planning, budgeting, procurement, or investment activities of all or part of an organization.

Develop internal control policies, guidelines, and procedures for activities such as budget administration, cash and credit management, and accounting. Analyze the financial details of past, present, and expected operations in order to identify development opportunities and areas where improvement is needed. Advise management on short-term and long-term financial objectives, policies, and actions. Provide direction and assistance to other organizational units regarding accounting and budgeting policies and procedures and efficient control and utilization of financial resources. Evaluate needs for procurement of funds and investment of surpluses and make appropriate recommendations.

Personality Type: Conventional. These occupations frequently involve following set procedures and routines and can include working with data and details more than with ideas. Usually there is a clear line of authority to follow.

GOE—Interest Area/Cluster: 06. Finance and Insurance. **Work Group:** 06.01. Managerial Work in Finance and Insurance. **Other Jobs in This Work Group:** Financial Managers; Financial Managers, Branch or Department.

Skills—Management of Financial Resources: Determining how money will be spent to get the work done and accounting for these expenditures. **Management of Material Resources:** Obtaining and seeing to the appropriate use of equipment, facilities, and materials needed to do certain work. **Judgment and Decision Making:** Weighing the relative costs and benefits of a potential action. **Management of Personnel Resources:** Motivating, developing, and directing people as they work; identifying the best people for the job. **Mathematics:** Using mathematics to solve problems. **Negotiation:** Bringing others together and trying to reconcile differences. **Time Management:** Managing one's own time and the time of others. **Persuasion:** Persuading others to approach things differently.

Education and Training Programs: Accounting and Business/Management; Accounting and Finance; Credit Management; Finance and Financial Management Services, Other; Finance, General; International Finance; Public Finance. **Related Knowledge/Courses—Economics and Accounting:** Economic and accounting principles and practices, the financial markets, banking, and the analysis and reporting of financial data. **Administration and Management:** Principles and processes involved in business and organizational planning, coordination, and execution. This includes strategic planning, resource allocation, manpower modeling, leadership techniques, and production methods. **Personnel and Human Resources:** Principles and procedures for personnel recruitment; selection; training; compensation and benefits; labor relations and negotiation; and personnel information systems. **Law and Government:** Laws, legal codes, court procedures, precedents, government regulations, executive orders, agency rules, and the democratic political process. **Mathematics:** Numbers and their operations and interrelationships, including arithmetic, algebra, geometry, calculus, and statistics and their applications. **English Language:** The structure and content of the English language, including the meaning and spelling of words, rules of composition, and grammar.

Work Environment: Indoors; sitting.

Tree Trimmers and Pruners

- ❀ Education/Training Required: Short-term on-the-job training
- ❀ Annual Earnings: $29,800
- ❀ Beginning Wage: $19,370
- ❀ Earnings Growth Potential: Medium
- ❀ Growth: 11.1%
- ❀ Annual Job Openings: 9,621
- ❀ Self-Employed: 28.9%
- ❀ Part-Time: 14.6%

Cut away dead or excess branches from trees or shrubs to maintain right-of-way for roads, sidewalks, or utilities or to improve appearance, health, and value of trees. Prune or treat trees or shrubs, using handsaws, pruning hooks, shears, and clippers. May use truck-mounted lifts and power pruners. May fill cavities in trees to promote healing and prevent deterioration. Supervise others engaged in tree trimming work and train lower-level employees. Transplant and remove trees and shrubs and prepare trees for moving. Operate shredding and chipping equipment and feed limbs and brush into the machines. Remove broken limbs from wires, using hooked extension poles. Prune, cut down, fertilize, and spray trees as directed by tree surgeons. Spray trees to treat diseased or unhealthy trees, including mixing chemicals and calibrating spray equipment. Clean, sharpen, and lubricate tools and equipment. Clear sites, streets, and grounds of woody and herbaceous materials such as tree stumps and fallen trees and limbs. Load debris and refuse onto trucks and haul it away for disposal. Inspect trees to determine if they have diseases or pest problems. Cut away dead and excess branches from trees or clear branches around power lines, using climbing equipment or buckets of extended truck booms, chainsaws, hooks,

handsaws, shears, and clippers. Collect debris and refuse from tree trimming and removal operations into piles, using shovels, rakes, or other tools. Operate boom trucks, loaders, stump chippers, brush chippers, tractors, power saws, trucks, sprayers, and other equipment and tools. Apply tar or other protective substances to cut surfaces to seal surfaces and to protect them from fungi and insects. Climb trees, using climbing hooks and belts, or climb ladders to gain access to work areas. Split logs or wooden blocks into bolts, pickets, posts, or stakes, using hand tools such as ax wedges, sledgehammers, and mallets. Cable, brace, tie, bolt, stake, and guy trees and branches to provide support. Trim jagged stumps, using saws or pruning shears. Trim, top, and reshape trees to achieve attractive shapes or to remove low-hanging branches. Water, root-feed, and fertilize trees. Harvest tanbark by cutting rings and slits in bark and stripping bark from trees, using spuds or axes. Install lightning protection on trees. Plan and develop budgets for tree work and estimate the monetary value of trees. Provide information to the public regarding trees, such as advice on tree care.

Personality Type: Realistic. These occupations frequently involve work activities that include practical, hands-on problems and solutions. They often deal with plants; animals; and real-world materials such as wood, tools, and machinery. Many of the occupations require working outside and don't involve a lot of paperwork or working closely with others.

GOE—Interest Area/Cluster: 01. Agriculture and Natural Resources. **Work Group:** 01.05. Nursery, Groundskeeping, and Pest Control. **Other Jobs in This Work Group:** Landscaping and Groundskeeping Workers; Nursery Workers; Pest Control Workers; Pesticide Handlers, Sprayers, and Applicators, Vegetation.

Skills—Equipment Maintenance: Performing routine maintenance and determining when and what kind of maintenance is needed. **Equipment Selection:** Determining the kind of tools and equipment needed to do a job. **Repairing:** Repairing machines or systems, using the needed tools. **Operation and Control:** Controlling operations of equipment or systems. **Management of Personnel Resources:** Motivating, developing, and directing people as they work; identifying the best people for the job. **Science:** Using scientific methods to solve problems. **Operation Monitoring:** Watching gauges, dials, or other indicators to make sure a machine is working properly. **Installation:** Installing equipment, machines, wiring, or programs to meet specifications.

Education and Training Program: Applied Horticulture/ Horicultural Business Services, Other. **Related Knowledge/ Courses—Biology:** Plant and animal living tissue, cells, organisms, and entities, including their functions, interdependencies, and interactions with each other and the environment. **Mechanical Devices:** Machines and tools, including their designs, uses, benefits, repair, and maintenance. **Transportation:** Principles and methods for moving people or goods by air, rail, sea, or road, including their relative costs, advantages, and limitations. **Physics:** Physical principles, laws, and applications, including air, water, material dynamics, light, atomic principles, heat, electric theory, earth formations, and meteorological and related natural phenomena. **Public Safety and Security:** Weaponry; public safety; security operations, rules, regulations, precautions, and prevention; and the protection of people, data, and property. **Sales and Marketing:** Principles and methods involved in showing, promoting, and selling products or services. This includes marketing strategies and tactics, product demonstration and sales techniques, and sales control systems.

Work Environment: Outdoors; noisy; contaminants; hazardous equipment; minor burns, cuts, bites, or stings; using hands on objects, tools, or controls.

Truck Drivers, Heavy and Tractor-Trailer

- ❋ Education/Training Required: Moderate-term on-the-job training
- ❋ Annual Earnings: $36,220
- ❋ Beginning Wage: $23,380
- ❋ Earnings Growth Potential: Medium
- ❋ Growth: 10.4%
- ❋ Annual Job Openings: 279,032
- ❋ Self-Employed: 8.8%
- ❋ Part-Time: 7.2%

Drive a tractor-trailer combination or a truck with a capacity of at least 26,000 GVW to transport and deliver goods, livestock, or materials in liquid, loose, or packaged form. May be required to unload truck. May require use of automated routing equipment. Requires commercial drivers' license. Follow appropriate safety procedures when transporting dangerous goods. Check vehicles before driving them to ensure that mechanical, safety, and emergency equipment is in good working order. Maintain logs of working hours and of vehicle service and repair status, following applicable state and federal regulations. Obtain receipts or signatures when loads are delivered and collect payment for services when required. Check all load-related documentation to ensure that it is complete and accurate. Maneuver trucks into loading or unloading positions, following signals from loading crew as needed; check that vehicle position is correct and any special loading equipment is properly positioned. Drive trucks with capacities greater than 3 tons, including tractor-trailer combinations, to transport and deliver products, livestock, or other materials. Secure cargo for transport, using ropes, blocks, chain, binders, or covers. Read bills of lading to determine assignment details. Report vehicle defects, accidents, traffic violations, or damage to the vehicles. Read and interpret maps to determine vehicle routes. Couple and uncouple trailers by changing trailer jack positions, connecting or disconnecting air and electrical lines, and manipulating fifth-wheel locks. Collect delivery instructions from appropriate sources, verifying instructions and routes. Drive trucks to weigh stations before and after loading and along routes to document weights and to comply with state regulations. Operate equipment such as truck cab computers, CB radios, and telephones to exchange necessary information with bases, supervisors, or other drivers. Check conditions of trailers after contents have been unloaded to ensure that there has been no damage. Crank trailer landing gear up and down to safely secure vehicles. Wrap goods, using pads, packing paper, and containers, and secure loads to trailer walls, using straps. Perform basic vehicle maintenance tasks such as adding oil, fuel, and radiator fluid or performing minor repairs. Load and unload trucks or help others with loading and unloading, operating any special loading-related equipment on vehicles and using other equipment as necessary.

Personality Type: Realistic. These occupations frequently involve work activities that include practical, hands-on problems and solutions. They often deal with plants; animals; and real-world materials such as wood, tools, and machinery. Many of the occupations require working outside and don't involve a lot of paperwork or working closely with others.

GOE—Interest Area/Cluster: 16. Transportation, Distribution, and Logistics. **Work Group:** 16.03. Truck Driving. **Other Jobs in This Work Group:** Truck Drivers, Light or Delivery Services.

Skills—Equipment Maintenance: Performing routine maintenance and determining when and what kind of maintenance is needed. **Repairing:** Repairing machines or systems, using the needed tools. **Operation Monitoring:** Watching gauges, dials, or other indicators to make sure a machine is working properly. **Troubleshooting:** Determining what is causing an operating error and deciding what to do about it. **Operation and Control:** Controlling operations of equipment or systems.

Education and Training Program: Truck and Bus Driver Training/Commercial Vehicle Operation. **Related Knowledge/Courses—Transportation:** Principles and methods for moving people or goods by air, rail, sea, or road, including their relative costs, advantages, and limitations. **Geography:** Various methods for describing the location and distribution of land, sea, and air masses, including their physical locations, relationships, and characteristics. **Public Safety and Security:** Weaponry; public safety; security operations, rules, regulations, precautions, and prevention; and the protection of people, data, and property. **Law and Government:** Laws, legal codes, court procedures, precedents, government regulations, executive orders, agency rules, and the democratic political process. **Mechanical Devices:** Machines and tools, including their designs, uses, benefits, repair, and maintenance.

Work Environment: Outdoors; very hot or cold; contaminants; sitting; using hands on objects, tools, or controls; repetitive motions.

Truck Drivers, Light or Delivery Services

- ❋ Education/Training Required: Short-term on-the-job training
- ❋ Annual Earnings: $26,380
- ❋ Beginning Wage: $16,180
- ❋ Earnings Growth Potential: Medium
- ❋ Growth: 8.4%
- ❋ Annual Job Openings: 154,330
- ❋ Self-Employed: 9.3%
- ❋ Part-Time: 7.2%

Drive a truck or van with a capacity of under 26,000 GVW primarily to deliver or pick up merchandise or to deliver packages within a specified area. May require use of automatic routing or location software. May load and unload truck. Obey traffic laws and follow established traffic and transportation procedures. Inspect and maintain vehicle supplies and equipment such as gas, oil, water, tires, lights, and brakes to ensure that vehicles are in proper working condition. Report any mechanical problems encountered with vehicles. Present bills and receipts and collect payments for goods delivered or loaded. Load and unload trucks, vans, or automobiles. Turn in receipts and money received from deliveries. Verify the contents of inventory loads against shipping papers. Maintain records such as vehicle logs, records of cargo, or billing statements in accordance with regulations. Read maps and follow written and verbal geographic directions. Report delays, accidents, or other traffic and transportation situations to bases or other vehicles, using telephones or mobile two-way radios. Sell and keep records of sales for products from truck inventory. Drive vehicles with capacities under three tons to transport materials to and from specified destinations such as railroad stations, plants, residences, and offices or within industrial yards. Drive trucks equipped with public address systems through city streets to broadcast announcements for advertising or publicity purposes. Use and maintain the tools and equipment found on commercial vehicles, such as weighing and measuring devices. Perform emergency repairs such as changing tires or installing light bulbs, fuses, tire chains, and spark plugs.

Personality Type: Realistic. These occupations frequently involve work activities that include practical, hands-on problems and solutions. They often deal with plants; animals; and real-world materials such as wood, tools, and machinery. Many of the occupations require working outside and don't involve a lot of paperwork or working closely with others.

GOE—Interest Area/Cluster: 16. Transportation, Distribution, and Logistics. **Work Group:** 16.03. Truck Driving. **Other Jobs in This Work Group:** Truck Drivers, Heavy and Tractor-Trailer.

Skills—Equipment Maintenance: Performing routine maintenance and determining when and what kind of maintenance is needed. **Operation and Control:** Controlling operations of equipment or systems. **Operation Monitoring:** Watching gauges, dials, or other indicators to make sure a machine is working properly. **Social Perceptiveness:** Being aware of others' reactions and understanding why they react the way they do.

Education and Training Program: Truck and Bus Driver Training/Commercial Vehicle Operation. **Related Knowledge/Course—Transportation:** Principles and methods for moving people or goods by air, rail, sea, or road, including their relative costs, advantages, and limitations.

Work Environment: Outdoors; very hot or cold; contaminants; cramped work space, awkward positions; minor burns, cuts, bites, or stings; using hands on objects, tools, or controls.

Umpires, Referees, and Other Sports Officials

- ❈ Education/Training Required: Long-term on-the-job training
- ❈ Annual Earnings: $24,770
- ❈ Beginning Wage: $14,930
- ❈ Earnings Growth Potential: Medium
- ❈ Growth: 16.0%
- ❈ Annual Job Openings: 4,461
- ❈ Self-Employed: 24.0%
- ❈ Part-Time: 39.1%

Officiate at competitive athletic or sporting events. Detect infractions of rules and decide penalties according to established regulations. Officiate at sporting events, games, or competitions to maintain standards of play and to ensure that game rules are observed. Judge performances in sporting competitions in order to award points, impose scoring penalties, and determine results. Inspect sporting equipment and/or examine participants in order to ensure compliance with event and safety regulations. Keep track of event times, including race times and elapsed time during game segments, starting or stopping play when necessary. Signal participants or other officials to make them aware of infractions or to otherwise regulate play or competition. Verify scoring calculations before competition winners are announced. Resolve claims of rule infractions or complaints by participants and assess any necessary penalties according to regulations. Start races and competitions. Teach and explain the rules and regulations governing a specific sport. Confer with other sporting officials, coaches, players, and facility managers in order to provide information, coordinate activities, and discuss problems. Verify credentials of participants in sporting events and make other qualifying determinations such as starting order or handicap number. Report to regulating organizations regarding sporting activities; complaints made; and actions taken or needed, such as fines or other disciplinary actions. Compile scores and other athletic records. Direct participants to assigned areas such as starting blocks or penalty areas. Research and study players and teams in order to anticipate issues that might arise in future engagements.

Personality Type: Realistic. These occupations frequently involve work activities that include practical, hands-on problems and solutions. They often deal with plants; animals; and real-world materials such as wood, tools, and machinery. Many of the occupations require working outside and don't involve a lot of paperwork or working closely with others.

GOE—Interest Area/Cluster: 09. Hospitality, Tourism, and Recreation. **Work Group:** 09.06. Sports. **Other Jobs in This Work Group:** Athletes and Sports Competitors; Coaches and Scouts.

Skills—Judgment and Decision Making: Weighing the relative costs and benefits of a potential action. **Negotiation:** Bringing others together and trying to reconcile differences. **Persuasion:** Persuading others to approach things differently.

Education and Training Program: Personal and Culinary Services, Other. **Related Knowledge/Course—Psychology:** Human behavior and performance, mental processes, psychological research methods, and the assessment and treatment of behavioral and affective disorders.

Work Environment: Outdoors; noisy; standing; walking and running.

Urban and Regional Planners

- ❈ Education/Training Required: Master's degree
- ❈ Annual Earnings: $57,970
- ❈ Beginning Wage: $36,950
- ❈ Earnings Growth Potential: Medium
- ❈ Growth: 14.5%
- ❈ Annual Job Openings: 1,967
- ❈ Self-Employed: 0.2%
- ❈ Part-Time: 6.0%

Develop comprehensive plans and programs for use of land and physical facilities of local jurisdictions such as towns, cities, counties, and metropolitan areas. Design, promote, and administer government plans and policies affecting land use, zoning, public utilities, community facilities, housing, and transportation. Hold public meetings and confer with government, social scientists, lawyers, developers, the public, and special interest groups to formulate and develop land use or community plans. Recommend approval, denial, or conditional approval of proposals. Determine the effects of regulatory limitations on projects. Assess the feasibility of proposals and identify necessary changes. Create, prepare, or requisition graphic and narrative reports on land use data, including land area maps overlaid with geographic variables such as population density. Conduct field investigations, surveys, impact studies, or other research to compile and analyze data on economic, social, regulatory, and physical factors affecting land use. Advise planning officials on project feasibility, cost-effectiveness, regulatory conformance, and possible alternatives. Discuss with planning officials the purpose of land use projects such as transportation, conservation, residential, commercial, industrial, and community use. Keep informed about economic and legal issues involved in zoning codes, building codes, and environmental regulations. Mediate community disputes and assist in developing alternative plans and recommendations for programs or projects. Coordinate work with economic consultants and architects during the formulation of plans and the design of large pieces of infrastructure. Review and evaluate environmental impact reports pertaining to private and public planning projects and programs. Supervise and coordinate the work of urban planning technicians and technologists. Investigate property availability.

Personality Type: Investigative. These occupations frequently involve working with ideas and require an extensive amount of thinking. They can involve searching for facts and figuring out problems mentally.

GOE—Interest Area/Cluster: 07. Government and Public Administration. **Work Group:** 07.02. Public Planning. **Other Jobs in This Work Group:** City and Regional Planning Aides.

Skills—Complex Problem Solving: Identifying complex problems, reviewing the options, and implementing solutions. **Persuasion:** Persuading others to approach things differently. **Writing:** Communicating effectively with others in writing as indicated by the needs of the audience. **Coordination:** Adjusting actions in relation to others' actions. **Judgment and Decision Making:** Weighing the relative costs and benefits of a potential action. **Service Orientation:** Actively looking for ways to help people. **Speaking:** Talking to others to effectively convey information. **Social Perceptiveness:** Being aware of others' reactions and understanding why they react the way they do.

Education and Training Program: City/Urban, Community and Regional Planning. **Related Knowledge/Courses—Design:** Design techniques, principles, tools, and instruments involved in the production and use of precision technical plans, blueprints, drawings, and models. **Building and Construction:** Materials, methods, and the appropriate tools to construct objects, structures, and buildings. **Geography:** Various methods for describing the location and distribution of land, sea, and air masses, including their physical locations, relationships, and characteristics. **History and Archeology:** Historical events and their causes, indicators, and impact on particular civilizations and cultures. **Law and Government:** Laws, legal codes, court procedures, precedents, government regulations, executive orders, agency rules, and the democratic political process. **Customer and Personal Service:** Principles and processes for providing customer and personal services, including needs assessment techniques, quality service standards, alternative delivery systems, and customer satisfaction evaluation techniques.

Work Environment: Indoors; noisy; very bright or dim lighting; sitting; using hands on objects, tools, or controls; repetitive motions.

Veterinarians

- ❉ Education/Training Required: First professional degree
- ❉ Annual Earnings: $75,230
- ❉ Beginning Wage: $44,150
- ❉ Earnings Growth Potential: High
- ❉ Growth: 35.0%
- ❉ Annual Job Openings: 5,301
- ❉ Self-Employed: 17.1%
- ❉ Part-Time: 13.4%

Diagnose and treat diseases and dysfunctions of animals. May engage in a particular function, such as research and development, consultation, administration, technical writing, sale or production of commercial products, or rendering of technical services to commercial firms or other organizations. Includes veterinarians who inspect livestock. Examine animals to detect and determine the nature of diseases or injuries. Treat sick or injured animals by prescribing medication, setting bones, dressing wounds, or performing surgery. Inoculate animals against various diseases such as rabies and distemper. Collect body tissue, feces, blood, urine, or other body fluids for examination and analysis. Operate diagnostic equipment such as radiographic and ultrasound equipment and interpret the resulting images. Advise animal owners regarding sanitary measures, feeding, and general care necessary to promote health of animals.

Educate the public about diseases that can be spread from animals to humans. Train and supervise workers who handle and care for animals. Provide care to a wide range of animals or specialize in a particular species, such as horses or exotic birds. Euthanize animals. Establish and conduct quarantine and testing procedures that prevent the spread of diseases to other animals or to humans and that comply with applicable government regulations. Conduct postmortem studies and analyses to determine the causes of animals' deaths. Perform administrative duties such as scheduling appointments, accepting payments from clients, and maintaining business records. Drive mobile clinic vans to farms so that health problems can be treated or prevented. Direct the overall operations of animal hospitals, clinics, or mobile services to farms. Specialize in a particular type of treatment such as dentistry, pathology, nutrition, surgery, microbiology, or internal medicine. Inspect and test horses, sheep, poultry, and other animals to detect the presence of communicable diseases. Research diseases to which animals could be susceptible. Plan and execute animal nutrition and reproduction programs. Inspect animal housing facilities to determine their cleanliness and adequacy. Determine the effects of drug therapies, antibiotics, or new surgical techniques by testing them on animals.

Personality Type: Investigative. These occupations frequently involve working with ideas and require an extensive amount of thinking. They can involve searching for facts and figuring out problems mentally.

GOE—Interest Area/Cluster: 08. Health Science. **Work Group:** 08.05. Animal Care. **Other Jobs in This Work Group:** Animal Breeders; Animal Trainers; Nonfarm Animal Caretakers; Veterinary Assistants and Laboratory Animal Caretakers; Veterinary Technologists and Technicians.

Skills—Science: Using scientific methods to solve problems. **Management of Financial Resources:** Determining how money will be spent to get the work done and accounting for these expenditures. **Reading Comprehension:** Understanding written sentences and paragraphs in work-related documents. **Judgment and Decision Making:** Weighing the relative costs and benefits of a potential action. **Complex Problem Solving:** Identifying complex problems, reviewing the options, and implementing solutions. **Management of Personnel Resources:** Motivating, developing, and directing people as they work; identifying the best people for the job. **Equipment Selection:** Determining the kind of tools and equipment needed to do a job. **Management of Material Resources:** Obtaining and seeing

to the appropriate use of equipment, facilities, and materials needed to do certain work.

Education and Training Programs: Comparative and Laboratory Animal Medicine; Laboratory Animal Medicine; Veterinary Anatomy (Cert, MS, PhD); Veterinary Anesthesiology; Veterinary Dentistry; Veterinary Emergency and Critical Care Medicine; Veterinary Internal Medicine; Veterinary Medicine (DVM); Veterinary Nutrition; Veterinary Pathology; Veterinary Preventive Medicine; Veterinary Radiology; Veterinary Surgery; Veterinary Toxicology; Veterinary Toxicology and Pharmacology (Cert, MS, PhD); Zoological Medicine; others. **Related Knowledge/Courses—Biology:** Plant and animal living tissue, cells, organisms, and entities, including their functions, interdependencies, and interactions with each other and the environment. **Medicine and Dentistry:** The information and techniques needed to diagnose and treat injuries, diseases, and deformities. This includes symptoms, treatment alternatives, drug properties and interactions, and preventive health-care measures. **Chemistry:** The composition, structure, and properties of substances and of the chemical processes and transformations that they undergo. This includes uses of chemicals and their interactions, danger signs, production techniques, and disposal methods. **Therapy and Counseling:** Information and techniques needed to rehabilitate physical and mental ailments and to provide career guidance, including alternative treatments, rehabilitation equipment and its proper use, and methods to evaluate treatment effects. **Sales and Marketing:** Principles and methods involved in showing, promoting, and selling products or services. This includes marketing strategies and tactics, product demonstration and sales techniques, and sales control systems. **Customer and Personal Service:** Principles and processes for providing customer and personal services, including needs assessment techniques, quality service standards, alternative delivery systems, and customer satisfaction evaluation techniques.

Work Environment: Indoors; noisy; contaminants; disease or infections; standing; using hands on objects, tools, or controls.

Veterinary Technologists and Technicians

- ❋ Education/Training Required: Associate degree
- ❋ Annual Earnings: $27,970
- ❋ Beginning Wage: $18,840
- ❋ Earnings Growth Potential: Low
- ❋ Growth: 41.0%
- ❋ Annual Job Openings: 14,674
- ❋ Self-Employed: 0.2%
- ❋ Part-Time: 20.8%

Perform medical tests in a laboratory environment for use in the treatment and diagnosis of diseases in animals. Prepare vaccines and serums for prevention of diseases. Prepare tissue samples; take blood samples; and execute laboratory tests, such as urinalysis and blood counts. Clean and sterilize instruments and materials and maintain equipment and machines. Administer anesthesia to animals, under the direction of a veterinarian, and monitor animals' responses to anesthetics so that dosages can be adjusted. Care for and monitor the condition of animals recovering from surgery. Prepare and administer medications, vaccines, serums, and treatments as prescribed by veterinarians. Perform laboratory tests on blood, urine, and feces, such as urinalyses and blood counts, to assist in the diagnosis and treatment of animal health problems. Administer emergency first aid, such as performing emergency resuscitation or other life-saving procedures. Collect, prepare, and label samples for laboratory testing, culture, or microscopic examination. Clean and sterilize instruments, equipment, and materials. Provide veterinarians with the correct equipment and instruments as needed. Fill prescriptions, measuring medications and labeling containers. Prepare animals for surgery, performing such tasks as shaving surgical areas. Take animals into treatment areas and assist with physical examinations by performing such duties as obtaining temperature, pulse, and respiration data. Observe the behavior and condition of animals and monitor their clinical symptoms. Take and develop diagnostic radiographs, using X-ray equipment. Maintain laboratory, research, and treatment records, as well as inventories of pharmaceuticals, equipment, and supplies. Give enemas and perform catheterizations, ear flushes, intravenous feedings, and gavages. Prepare treatment rooms for surgery. Maintain instruments, equipment, and machinery to ensure proper working condition. Perform dental work such as cleaning, polishing, and extracting teeth. Clean kennels, animal holding areas, surgery suites, examination rooms, and animal loading/unloading facilities to control the spread of disease. Provide information and counseling regarding issues such as animal health care, behavior problems, and nutrition. Provide assistance with animal euthanasia and the disposal of remains. Dress and suture wounds and apply splints and other protective devices. Perform a variety of office, clerical, and accounting duties, such as reception, billing, bookkeeping, or selling products.

Personality Type: Realistic. These occupations frequently involve work activities that include practical, hands-on problems and solutions. They often deal with plants; animals; and real-world materials such as wood, tools, and machinery. Many of the occupations require working outside and don't involve a lot of paperwork or working closely with others.

GOE—Interest Area/Cluster: 08. Health Science. **Work Group:** 08.05. Animal Care. **Other Jobs in This Work Group:** Animal Breeders; Animal Trainers; Nonfarm Animal Caretakers; Veterinarians; Veterinary Assistants and Laboratory Animal Caretakers.

Skills—Science: Using scientific methods to solve problems. **Operation Monitoring:** Watching gauges, dials, or other indicators to make sure a machine is working properly. **Instructing:** Teaching others how to do something. **Equipment Maintenance:** Performing routine maintenance and determining when and what kind of maintenance is needed. **Social Perceptiveness:** Being aware of others' reactions and understanding why they react the way they do. **Operation and Control:** Controlling operations of equipment or systems. **Mathematics:** Using mathematics to solve problems. **Reading Comprehension:** Understanding written sentences and paragraphs in work-related documents.

Education and Training Program: Veterinary/Animal Health Technology/Technician and Veterinary Assistant Training. **Related Knowledge/Courses—Biology:** Plant and animal living tissue, cells, organisms, and entities, including their functions, interdependencies, and interactions with each other and the environment. **Medicine and Dentistry:** The information and techniques needed to diagnose and treat injuries, diseases, and deformities. This includes symptoms, treatment alternatives, drug properties and interactions, and preventive health-care measures. **Chemistry:** The composition, structure, and properties of substances and of the chemical processes and transformations that they undergo. This includes uses of chemicals and their interactions, danger signs, production techniques, and disposal methods. **Sales and Marketing:** Principles and methods involved in showing, promoting, and selling products or services. This includes marketing strategies and tactics, product demonstration and sales techniques, and sales control systems. **Customer and Personal Service:** Principles and processes for providing customer and personal services, including needs assessment techniques, quality service standards, alternative delivery systems, and customer satisfaction evaluation techniques. **Mathematics:** Numbers and their operations and interrelationships, including arithmetic, algebra, geometry, calculus, and statistics and their applications.

Work Environment: Indoors; contaminants; radiation; disease or infections; minor burns, cuts, bites, or stings; standing.

Vocational Education Teachers, Postsecondary

- ❋ Education/Training Required: Work experience in a related occupation
- ❋ Annual Earnings: $45,850
- ❋ Beginning Wage: $26,380
- ❋ Earnings Growth Potential: High
- ❋ Growth: 22.9%
- ❋ Annual Job Openings: 19,313
- ❋ Self-Employed: 0.4%
- ❋ Part-Time: 27.8%

Teach or instruct vocational or occupational subjects at the postsecondary level (but at less than the baccalaureate) to students who have graduated or left high school. Includes correspondence school instructors; industrial, commercial, and government training instructors; and adult education teachers and instructors who prepare persons to operate industrial machinery and equipment and transportation and communications equipment. Teaching may take place in public or private schools whose primary business is education or in a school associated with an organization whose primary business is other than education. Supervise and monitor students' use of tools and equipment. Observe and evaluate students' work to determine progress, provide feedback, and make suggestions for improvement. Present lectures and conduct discussions to increase students' knowledge and competence, using visual aids such as graphs, charts, videotapes,

and slides. Administer oral, written, or performance tests to measure progress and to evaluate training effectiveness. Prepare reports and maintain records such as student grades, attendance rolls, and training activity details. Supervise independent or group projects, field placements, laboratory work, or other training. Determine training needs of students or workers. Provide individualized instruction and tutorial or remedial instruction. Conduct on-the-job training, classes, or training sessions to teach and demonstrate principles, techniques, procedures, and methods of designated subjects. Develop curricula and plan course content and methods of instruction. Prepare outlines of instructional programs and training schedules and establish course goals. Integrate academic and vocational curricula so that students can obtain a variety of skills. Develop teaching aids such as instructional software, multimedia visual aids, or study materials. Select and assemble books, materials, supplies, and equipment for training, courses, or projects. Advise students on course selection, career decisions, and other academic and vocational concerns. Participate in conferences, seminars, and training sessions to keep abreast of developments in the field and integrate relevant information into training programs. Serve on faculty and school committees concerned with budgeting, curriculum revision, and course and diploma requirements. Review enrollment applications and correspond with applicants to obtain additional information. Arrange for lectures by experts in designated fields.

Personality Type: Social. These occupations frequently involve working with, communicating with, and teaching people and often involve helping or providing service to others.

GOE—Interest Area/Cluster: 05. Education and Training. **Work Group:** 05.03. Postsecondary and Adult Teaching and Instructing. **Other Jobs in This Work Group:** Adult Literacy, Remedial Education, and GED Teachers and Instructors; Agricultural Sciences Teachers, Postsecondary; Anthropology and Archeology Teachers, Postsecondary; Architecture Teachers, Postsecondary; Area, Ethnic, and Cultural Studies Teachers, Postsecondary; Art, Drama, and Music Teachers, Postsecondary; Atmospheric, Earth, Marine, and Space Sciences Teachers, Postsecondary; Biological Science Teachers, Postsecondary; Business Teachers, Postsecondary; Chemistry Teachers, Postsecondary; Communications Teachers, Postsecondary; Computer Science Teachers, Postsecondary; Criminal Justice and Law Enforcement Teachers, Postsecondary; Economics Teachers, Postsecondary; Education Teachers, Postsecondary; Engineering Teachers, Postsecondary; English Language and Literature

Teachers, Postsecondary; Environmental Science Teachers, Postsecondary; Farm and Home Management Advisors; Foreign Language and Literature Teachers, Postsecondary; Forestry and Conservation Science Teachers, Postsecondary; Geography Teachers, Postsecondary; Graduate Teaching Assistants; Health Specialties Teachers, Postsecondary; History Teachers, Postsecondary; Home Economics Teachers, Postsecondary; Law Teachers, Postsecondary; Library Science Teachers, Postsecondary; Mathematical Science Teachers, Postsecondary; Nursing Instructors and Teachers, Postsecondary; Philosophy and Religion Teachers, Postsecondary; Physics Teachers, Postsecondary; Political Science Teachers, Postsecondary; Psychology Teachers, Postsecondary; Recreation and Fitness Studies Teachers, Postsecondary; Self-Enrichment Education Teachers; Social Work Teachers, Postsecondary; Sociology Teachers, Postsecondary; Teachers, Postsecondary.

Skills—Instructing: Teaching others how to do something. **Learning Strategies:** Using multiple approaches when learning or teaching new things. **Social Perceptiveness:** Being aware of others' reactions and understanding why they react the way they do. **Service Orientation:** Actively looking for ways to help people. **Speaking:** Talking to others to effectively convey information. **Time Management:** Managing one's own time and the time of others. **Science:** Using scientific methods to solve problems. **Writing:** Communicating effectively with others in writing as indicated by the needs of the audience.

Education and Training Programs: Agricultural Teacher Education; Business Teacher Education; Health Occupations Teacher Education; Sales and Marketing Operations/Marketing and Distribution Teacher Education; Teacher Education and Professional Development, Specific Subject Areas, Other; Technical Teacher Education; Technology Teacher Education/Industrial Arts Teacher Education; Trade and Industrial Teacher Education. **Related Knowledge/Courses—Education and Training:** Instructional methods and training techniques, including curriculum design principles, learning theory, group and individual teaching techniques, design of individual development plans, and test design principles. **Psychology:** Human behavior and performance, mental processes, psychological research methods, and the assessment and treatment of behavioral and affective disorders. **Therapy and Counseling:** Information and techniques needed to rehabilitate physical and mental ailments and to provide career guidance, including alternative treatments, rehabilitation equipment and its proper use, and methods to evaluate treatment effects. **Computers and**

Electronics: Electric circuit boards, processors, chips, and computer hardware and software, including applications and programming. **Sales and Marketing:** Principles and methods involved in showing, promoting, and selling products or services. This includes marketing strategies and tactics, product demonstration and sales techniques, and sales control systems. **Design:** Design techniques, principles, tools, and instruments involved in the production and use of precision technical plans, blueprints, drawings, and models.

Work Environment: Indoors; standing; using hands on objects, tools, or controls.

Vocational Education Teachers, Secondary School

- ❋ Education/Training Required: Work experience plus degree
- ❋ Annual Earnings: $50,090
- ❋ Beginning Wage: $34,040
- ❋ Earnings Growth Potential: Low
- ❋ Growth: –4.6%
- ❋ Annual Job Openings: 7,639
- ❋ Self-Employed: 0.0%
- ❋ Part-Time: 7.8%

Teach or instruct vocational or occupational subjects at the secondary school level. Prepare materials and classroom for class activities. Maintain accurate and complete student records as required by law, district policy, and administrative regulations. Instruct students individually and in groups, using various teaching methods such as lectures, discussions, and demonstrations. Observe and evaluate students' performance, behavior, social development, and physical health. Establish and enforce rules for behavior and procedures for maintaining order among the students for whom they are responsible. Instruct and monitor students the in use and care of equipment and materials to prevent injury and damage. Plan and conduct activities for a balanced program of instruction, demonstration, and work time that provides students with opportunities to observe, question, and investigate. Prepare, administer, and grade tests and assignments to evaluate students' progress. Enforce all administration policies and rules governing students. Assign and grade classwork and homework. Instruct students in the knowledge and skills required in a specific occupation or occupational field, using a systematic plan of lectures; discussions; audio-visual presentations; and laboratory, shop, and field studies.

Establish clear objectives for all lessons, units, and projects and communicate those objectives to students. Use computers, audiovisual aids, and other equipment and materials to supplement presentations. Plan and supervise work-experience programs in businesses, industrial shops, and school laboratories. Prepare students for later grades by encouraging them to explore learning opportunities and to persevere with challenging tasks. Confer with parents or guardians, other teachers, counselors, and administrators in order to resolve students' behavioral and academic problems. Guide and counsel students with adjustment or academic problems or special academic interests. Prepare objectives and outlines for courses of study, following curriculum guidelines or requirements of states and schools. Keep informed about trends in education and subject matter specialties.

Personality Type: Social. These occupations frequently involve working with, communicating with, and teaching people and often involve helping or providing service to others.

GOE—Interest Area/Cluster: 05. Education and Training. **Work Group:** 05.02. Preschool, Elementary, and Secondary Teaching and Instructing. **Other Jobs in This Work Group:** Elementary School Teachers, Except Special Education; Kindergarten Teachers, Except Special Education; Middle School Teachers, Except Special and Vocational Education; Preschool Teachers, Except Special Education; Secondary School Teachers, Except Special and Vocational Education; Special Education Teachers, Middle School; Special Education Teachers, Preschool, Kindergarten, and Elementary School; Special Education Teachers, Secondary School; Teacher Assistants; Vocational Education Teachers, Middle School.

Skills—Management of Financial Resources: Determining how money will be spent to get the work done and accounting for these expenditures. **Learning Strategies:** Using multiple approaches when learning or teaching new things. **Management of Material Resources:** Obtaining and seeing to the appropriate use of equipment, facilities, and materials needed to do certain work. **Social Perceptiveness:** Being aware of others' reactions and understanding why they react the way they do. **Instructing:** Teaching others how to do something. **Persuasion:** Persuading others to approach things differently. **Monitoring:** Assessing how well one is doing when learning or doing something. **Management of Personnel Resources:** Motivating, developing, and directing people as they work; identifying the best people for the job.

Education and Training Program: Technology Teacher Education/Industrial Arts Teacher Education. **Related Knowledge/Courses—Education and Training:** Instructional methods and training techniques, including curriculum design principles, learning theory, group and individual teaching techniques, design of individual development plans, and test design principles. **Therapy and Counseling:** Information and techniques needed to rehabilitate physical and mental ailments and to provide career guidance, including alternative treatments, rehabilitation equipment and its proper use, and methods to evaluate treatment effects. **Sociology and Anthropology:** Group behavior and dynamics; societal trends and influences; and cultures and their history, migrations, ethnicity, and origins. **Psychology:** Human behavior and performance, mental processes, psychological research methods, and the assessment and treatment of behavioral and affective disorders. **Design:** Design techniques, principles, tools, and instruments involved in the production and use of precision technical plans, blueprints, drawings, and models. **Mechanical Devices:** Machines and tools, including their designs, uses, benefits, repair, and maintenance.

Work Environment: Indoors; noisy; standing; using hands on objects, tools, or controls.

Water and Liquid Waste Treatment Plant and System Operators

- ❋ Education/Training Required: Long-term on-the-job training
- ❋ Annual Earnings: $37,090
- ❋ Beginning Wage: $22,570
- ❋ Earnings Growth Potential: Medium
- ❋ Growth: 13.8%
- ❋ Annual Job Openings: 9,575
- ❋ Self-Employed: 1.3%
- ❋ Part-Time: 3.4%

Operate or control an entire process or system of machines, often through the use of control boards, to transfer or treat water or liquid waste. Add chemicals such as ammonia, chlorine, or lime to disinfect and deodorize water and other liquids. Operate and adjust controls on equipment to purify and clarify water, process or dispose of sewage, and generate power. Inspect equipment or monitor operating conditions, meters, and gauges to determine load requirements and detect malfunctions. Collect and test water and sewage samples, using test equipment and color analysis standards. Record operational data, personnel attendance, or meter and gauge readings on specified forms. Maintain, repair, and lubricate equipment, using hand tools and power tools. Clean and maintain tanks and filter beds, using hand tools and power tools. Direct and coordinate plant workers engaged in routine operations and maintenance activities.

Personality Type: Realistic. These occupations frequently involve work activities that include practical, hands-on problems and solutions. They often deal with plants; animals; and real-world materials such as wood, tools, and machinery. Many of the occupations require working outside and don't involve a lot of paperwork or working closely with others.

GOE—Interest Area/Cluster: 13. Manufacturing. **Work Group:** 13.16. Utility Operation and Energy Distribution. **Other Jobs in This Work Group:** Chemical Plant and System Operators; Gas Compressor and Gas Pumping Station Operators; Gas Plant Operators; Nuclear Power Reactor Operators; Petroleum Pump System Operators, Refinery Operators, and Gaugers; Power Distributors and Dispatchers; Power Plant Operators; Ship Engineers; Stationary Engineers and Boiler Operators.

Skills—Operation Monitoring: Watching gauges, dials, or other indicators to make sure a machine is working properly. **Operation and Control:** Controlling operations of equipment or systems. **Installation:** Installing equipment, machines, wiring, or programs to meet specifications. **Troubleshooting:** Determining what is causing an operating error and deciding what to do about it. **Operations Analysis:** Analyzing needs and product requirements to create a design. **Management of Material Resources:** Obtaining and seeing to the appropriate use of equipment, facilities, and materials needed to do certain work. **Equipment Maintenance:** Performing routine maintenance and determining when and what kind of maintenance is needed. **Science:** Using scientific methods to solve problems.

Education and Training Program: Water Quality and Wastewater Treatment Management and Recycling Technology/Technician Training. **Related Knowledge/Courses— Biology:** Plant and animal living tissue, cells, organisms, and entities, including their functions, interdependencies, and interactions with each other and the environment. **Chemistry:** The composition, structure, and properties of substances and of the chemical processes and transformations that they undergo. This includes uses of chemicals and

their interactions, danger signs, production techniques, and disposal methods. **Physics:** Physical principles, laws, and applications, including air, water, material dynamics, light, atomic principles, heat, electric theory, earth formations, and meteorological and related natural phenomena. **Public Safety and Security:** Weaponry; public safety; security operations, rules, regulations, precautions, and prevention; and the protection of people, data, and property. **Mechanical Devices:** Machines and tools, including their designs, uses, benefits, repair, and maintenance. **Law and Government:** Laws, legal codes, court procedures, precedents, government regulations, executive orders, agency rules, and the democratic political process.

Work Environment: More often outdoors than indoors; noisy; very hot or cold; contaminants; minor burns, cuts, bites, or stings.

Web Administrators

* Education/Training Required: Bachelor's degree
* Annual Earnings: $71,510
* Beginning Wage: $37,600
* Earnings Growth Potential: High
* Growth: 15.1%
* Annual Job Openings: 14,374
* Self-Employed: 6.6%
* Part-Time: 5.6%

The job openings listed here are shared with Computer Systems Engineers/Architects; Network Designers; Software Quality Assurance Engineers and Testers; and Web Developers.

Manage Web environment design, deployment, development, and maintenance activities. Perform testing and quality assurance of Web sites and Web applications. Back up or modify applications and related data to provide for disaster recovery. Determine sources of Web page or server problems and take action to correct such problems. Review or update Web page content or links in a timely manner, using appropriate tools. Monitor systems for intrusions or denial of service attacks and report security breaches to appropriate personnel. Implement Web site security measures, such as firewalls or message encryption. Administer Internet/intranet infrastructure, including components such as Web, file transfer protocol (FTP), news, and mail servers. Collaborate with development teams to discuss, analyze, or resolve usability issues. Test backup or recovery plans regularly and resolve any problems. Monitor Web developments through continuing education; reading; or participation in professional conferences, workshops, or groups. Implement updates, upgrades, and patches in a timely manner to limit loss of service. Identify or document backup or recovery plans. Collaborate with Web developers to create and operate internal and external Web sites or to manage projects such as e-marketing campaigns. Install or configure Web server software or hardware to ensure that directory structure is well-defined, logical, and secure and that files are named properly. Gather, analyze, or document user feedback to locate or resolve sources of problems. Develop Web site performance metrics. Identify or address interoperability requirements. Document installation or configuration procedures to allow maintenance and repetition. Identify, standardize, and communicate levels of access and security. Track, compile, and analyze Web site usage data. Test issues such as system integration, performance, and system security on a regular schedule or after any major program modifications. Recommend Web site improvements and develop budgets to support recommendations. Inform Web site users of problems, problem resolutions, or application changes and updates. Document application and Web site changes or change procedures. Develop or implement procedures for ongoing Web site revision.

Personality Type: Conventional. These occupations frequently involve following set procedures and routines and can include working with data and details more than with ideas. Usually there is a clear line of authority to follow.

GOE—Interest Area/Cluster: 11. Information Technology. **Work Group:** 11.02. Information Technology Specialties. **Other Jobs in This Work Group:** Computer and Information Scientists, Research; Computer Operators; Computer Programmers; Computer Security Specialists; Computer Software Engineers, Applications; Computer Software Engineers, Systems Software; Computer Support Specialists; Computer Systems Analysts; Computer Systems Engineers/Architects; Database Administrators; Network Designers; Network Systems and Data Communications Analysts; Software Quality Assurance Engineers and Testers; Web Developers.

Skills—Programming: Writing computer programs for various purposes. **Systems Evaluation:** Looking at many indicators of system performance and taking into account their accuracy. **Systems Analysis:** Determining how a system should work and how changes will affect outcomes. **Troubleshooting:** Determining what is causing an operating error and deciding what to do about it. **Operations Analysis:** Analyzing needs and product requirements to

create a design. **Technology Design:** Generating or adapting equipment and technology to serve user needs. **Installation:** Installing equipment, machines, wiring, or programs to meet specifications. **Equipment Selection:** Determining the kind of tools and equipment needed to do a job.

Education and Training Programs: Computer and Information Sciences and Support Services, Other; Computer and Information Sciences, General; Computer Science; Computer Systems Networking and Telecommunications; E-Commerce/Electronic Commerce; Information Science/Studies; Information Technology; System, Networking, and LAN/WAN Management/Manager; Web Page, Digital/Multimedia and Information Resources Design; Web/Multimedia Management and Webmaster. **Related Knowledge/Courses—Computers and Electronics:** Electric circuit boards, processors, chips, and computer hardware and software, including applications and programming. **Telecommunications:** Transmission, broadcasting, switching, control, and operation of telecommunications systems. **Design:** Design techniques, principles, tools, and instruments involved in the production and use of precision technical plans, blueprints, drawings, and models. **Communications and Media:** Media production, communication, and dissemination techniques and methods, including alternative ways to inform and entertain via written, oral, and visual media. **Sales and Marketing:** Principles and methods involved in showing, promoting, and selling products or services. This includes marketing strategies and tactics, product demonstration and sales techniques, and sales control systems. **Engineering and Technology:** Equipment, tools, and mechanical devices and their uses to produce motion, light, power, technology, and other applications.

Work Environment: Indoors; sitting; using hands on objects, tools, or controls; repetitive motions.

Web Developers

- ❋ Education/Training Required: Bachelor's degree
- ❋ Annual Earnings: $71,510
- ❋ Beginning Wage: $37,600
- ❋ Earnings Growth Potential: High
- ❋ Growth: 15.1%
- ❋ Annual Job Openings: 14,374
- ❋ Self-Employed: 6.6%
- ❋ Part-Time: 5.6%

The job openings listed here are shared with Computer Systems Engineers/Architects; Network Designers; Software Quality Assurance Engineers and Testers; and Web Administrators.

Develop and design Web applications and Web sites. Create and specify architectural and technical parameters. Direct Web site content creation, enhancement, and maintenance. Design, build, or maintain Web sites, using authoring or scripting languages, content creation tools, management tools, and digital media. Perform or direct Web site updates. Write, design, or edit Web page content or direct others producing content. Confer with management or development teams to prioritize needs, resolve conflicts, develop content criteria, or choose solutions. Back up files from Web sites to local directories for instant recovery in case of problems. Identify problems uncovered by testing or customer feedback and correct problems or refer problems to appropriate personnel for correction. Evaluate code to ensure that it is valid; is properly structured; meets industry standards; and is compatible with browsers, devices, or operating systems. Maintain understanding of current Web technologies or programming practices through continuing education, reading, or participation in professional conferences, workshops, or groups. Analyze user needs to determine technical requirements. Develop or validate test routines and schedules to ensure that test cases mimic external interfaces and address all browser and device types. Develop databases that support Web applications and Web sites. Renew domain name registrations. Collaborate with management or users to develop e-commerce strategies and to integrate these strategies with Web sites. Write supporting code for Web applications or Web sites. Communicate with network personnel or Web site hosting agencies to address hardware or software issues affecting Web sites. Design and implement Web site security measures such as firewalls or message encryption. Perform Web site tests according to planned schedules or after any Web site or product revisions. Select programming languages, design tools, or applications. Incorporate technical considerations into Web site design plans, such as budgets, equipment, performance requirements, or legal issues, including accessibility and privacy. Respond to user e-mail inquiries or set up automated systems to send responses. Develop or implement procedures for ongoing Web site revision.

Personality Type: Conventional. These occupations frequently involve following set procedures and routines and can include working with data and details more than with ideas. Usually there is a clear line of authority to follow.

GOE—Interest Area/Cluster: 11. Information Technology. **Work Group:** 11.02. Information Technology Specialties. **Other Jobs in This Work Group:** Computer and Information Scientists, Research; Computer Operators; Computer Programmers; Computer Security Specialists; Computer Software Engineers, Applications; Computer Software Engineers, Systems Software; Computer Support Specialists; Computer Systems Analysts; Computer Systems Engineers/Architects; Database Administrators; Network Designers; Network Systems and Data Communications Analysts; Software Quality Assurance Engineers and Testers; Web Administrators.

Skills—Programming: Writing computer programs for various purposes. **Troubleshooting:** Determining what is causing an operating error and deciding what to do about it. **Operations Analysis:** Analyzing needs and product requirements to create a design. **Technology Design:** Generating or adapting equipment and technology to serve user needs. **Systems Evaluation:** Looking at many indicators of system performance and taking into account their accuracy. **Quality Control Analysis:** Evaluating the quality or performance of products, services, or processes. **Systems Analysis:** Determining how a system should work and how changes will affect outcomes. **Complex Problem Solving:** Identifying complex problems, reviewing the options, and implementing solutions.

Education and Training Programs: Computer and Information Sciences and Support Services, Other; Computer and Information Sciences, General; Computer Science; Computer Systems Networking and Telecommunications; E-Commerce/Electronic Commerce; Information Science/Studies; Information Technology; System, Networking, and LAN/WAN Management/Manager; Web Page, Digital/Multimedia and Information Resources Design; Web/Multimedia Management and Webmaster. **Related Knowledge/Courses—Computers and Electronics:** Electric circuit boards, processors, chips, and computer hardware and software, including applications and programming. **Design:** Design techniques, principles, tools, and instruments involved in the production and use of precision technical plans, blueprints, drawings, and models. **Sales and Marketing:** Principles and methods involved in showing, promoting, and selling products or services. This includes marketing strategies and tactics, product demonstration and sales techniques, and sales control systems. **Communications and Media:** Media production, communication, and dissemination techniques and methods, including alternative ways to inform and entertain via written, oral, and visual media. **Telecommunications:** Transmission, broadcasting, switching, control, and operation of telecommunications systems. **Clerical Practices:** Administrative and clerical procedures and systems such as word-processing systems, filing and records management systems, stenography and transcription, forms, design principles, and other office procedures and terminology.

Work Environment: Indoors; sitting; using hands on objects, tools, or controls; repetitive motions.

Welders, Cutters, and Welder Fitters

* ❋ Education/Training Required: Postsecondary vocational training
* ❋ Annual Earnings: $32,270
* ❋ Beginning Wage: $21,680
* ❋ Earnings Growth Potential: Low
* ❋ Growth: 5.1%
* ❋ Annual Job Openings: 61,125
* ❋ Self-Employed: 6.3%
* ❋ Part-Time: 1.9%

The job openings listed here are shared with Solderers and Brazers.

Use hand-welding or flame-cutting equipment to weld or join metal components or to fill holes, indentations, or seams of fabricated metal products. Operate safety equipment and use safe work habits. Weld components in flat, vertical, or overhead positions. Ignite torches or start power supplies and strike arcs by touching electrodes to metals being welded, completing electrical circuits. Clamp, hold, tack-weld, heat-bend, grind, or bolt component parts to obtain required configurations and positions for welding. Detect faulty operation of equipment or defective materials and notify supervisors. Operate manual or semi-automatic welding equipment to fuse metal segments, using processes such as gas tungsten arc, gas metal arc, flux-cored arc, plasma arc, shielded metal arc, resistance welding, and submerged arc welding. Monitor the fitting, burning, and welding processes to avoid overheating of parts or warping, shrinking, distortion, or expansion of material. Examine workpieces for defects and measure workpieces with straightedges or templates to ensure conformance with specifications. Recognize, set up, and operate hand and power tools common to the welding trade, such as shielded metal arc and gas metal arc welding equipment. Lay out, position, align, and secure parts and assemblies prior to assembly, using straightedges,

combination squares, calipers, and rulers. Chip or grind off excess weld, slag, or spatter, using hand scrapers or power chippers, portable grinders, or arc-cutting equipment. Analyze engineering drawings, blueprints, specifications, sketches, work orders, and material safety data sheets to plan layout, assembly, and welding operations. Connect and turn regulator valves to activate and adjust gas flow and pressure so that desired flames are obtained. Weld separately or in combination, using aluminum, stainless steel, cast iron, and other alloys. Determine required equipment and welding methods, applying knowledge of metallurgy, geometry, and welding techniques. Mark or tag material with proper job number, piece marks, and other identifying marks as required. Prepare all material surfaces to be welded, ensuring that there is no loose or thick scale, slag, rust, moisture, grease, or other foreign matter.

Personality Type: Realistic. These occupations frequently involve work activities that include practical, hands-on problems and solutions. They often deal with plants; animals; and real-world materials such as wood, tools, and machinery. Many of the occupations require working outside and don't involve a lot of paperwork or working closely with others.

GOE—Interest Area/Cluster: 13. Manufacturing. **Work Group:** 13.04. Welding, Brazing, and Soldering. **Other Jobs in This Work Group:** Solderers and Brazers; Structural Metal Fabricators and Fitters; Welders, Cutters, Solderers, and Brazers; Welding, Soldering, and Brazing Machine Setters, Operators, and Tenders.

Skills—Repairing: Repairing machines or systems, using the needed tools. **Equipment Maintenance:** Performing routine maintenance and determining when and what kind of maintenance is needed. **Installation:** Installing equipment, machines, wiring, or programs to meet specifications. **Equipment Selection:** Determining the kind of tools and equipment needed to do a job. **Operation and Control:** Controlling operations of equipment or systems. **Quality Control Analysis:** Evaluating the quality or performance of products, services, or processes.

Education and Training Program: Welding Technology/Welder Training. **Related Knowledge/Courses—Building and Construction:** Materials, methods, and the appropriate tools to construct objects, structures, and buildings. **Mechanical Devices:** Machines and tools, including their designs, uses, benefits, repair, and maintenance. **Design:** Design techniques, principles, tools, and instruments involved in the production and use of precision technical plans, blueprints, drawings, and models. **Engineering and Technology:** Equipment, tools, and mechanical devices and their uses to produce motion, light, power, technology, and other applications.

Work Environment: Noisy; contaminants; minor burns, cuts, bites, or stings; standing; using hands on objects, tools, or controls; repetitive motions.

Wholesale and Retail Buyers, Except Farm Products

- ❋ Education/Training Required: Long-term on-the-job training
- ❋ Annual Earnings: $46,960
- ❋ Beginning Wage: $27,810
- ❋ Earnings Growth Potential: High
- ❋ Growth: –0.1%
- ❋ Annual Job Openings: 19,847
- ❋ Self-Employed: 12.0%
- ❋ Part-Time: 15.6%

Buy merchandise or commodities, other than farm products, for resale to consumers at the wholesale or retail level, including both durable and nondurable goods. Analyze past buying trends, sales records, price, and quality of merchandise to determine value and yield. Select, order, and authorize payment for merchandise according to contractual agreements. May conduct meetings with sales personnel and introduce new products. Examine, select, order, and purchase at the most favorable price merchandise consistent with quality, quantity, specification requirements, and other factors. Negotiate prices, discount terms, and transportation arrangements for merchandise. Analyze and monitor sales records, trends, and economic conditions to anticipate consumer buying patterns and determine what the company will sell and how much inventory is needed. Interview and work closely with vendors to obtain and develop desired products. Authorize payment of invoices or return of merchandise. Inspect merchandise or products to determine value or yield. Set or recommend markup rates, markdown rates, and selling prices for merchandise. Confer with sales and purchasing personnel to obtain information about customer needs and preferences. Consult with store or merchandise managers about budget and goods to be purchased. Conduct staff meetings with sales personnel to introduce new merchandise. Manage the department for which they buy. Use computers to organize and locate inventory and operate spreadsheet and word processing software. Provide clerks with information to print on price tags, such as price, markups or markdowns, manufacturer number, season code, and style number. Train and supervise sales and clerical staff. Determine which products should be featured in advertising, the advertising medium to be used, and when the ads should be run. Monitor competitors' sales activities by following their advertisements in newspapers and other media.

Personality Type: Enterprising. These occupations frequently involve starting up and carrying out projects and can involve leading people and making many decisions. They sometimes require risk taking and often deal with business.

GOE—Interest Area/Cluster: 14. Retail and Wholesale Sales and Service. **Work Group:** 14.05. Purchasing. **Other Jobs in This Work Group:** Purchasing Agents, Except Wholesale, Retail, and Farm Products.

Skills—Management of Financial Resources: Determining how money will be spent to get the work done and accounting for these expenditures. **Management of Material Resources:** Obtaining and seeing to the appropriate use of equipment, facilities, and materials needed to do certain work. **Operations Analysis:** Analyzing needs and product requirements to create a design. **Quality Control Analysis:** Evaluating the quality or performance of products, services, or processes. **Negotiation:** Bringing others together and trying to reconcile differences. **Service Orientation:** Actively looking for ways to help people. **Equipment Selection:** Determining the kind of tools and equipment needed to do a job. **Management of Personnel Resources:** Motivating, developing, and directing people as they work; identifying the best people for the job.

Education and Training Programs: Apparel and Accessories Marketing Operations; Apparel and Textile Marketing Management; Fashion Merchandising; Merchandising and Buying Operations; Sales, Distribution, and Marketing Operations, General. **Related Knowledge/Courses—Sales and Marketing:** Principles and methods involved in showing, promoting, and selling products or services. This includes marketing strategies and tactics, product demonstration and sales techniques, and sales control systems. **Economics and Accounting:** Economic and accounting principles and practices, the financial markets, banking, and the analysis and reporting of financial data. **Clerical Practices:** Administrative and clerical procedures and systems such as word-processing systems, filing and records management systems, stenography and transcription, forms, design principles, and other office procedures and terminology. **Customer and Personal Service:** Principles and processes for providing customer and personal services, including needs assessment techniques, quality service standards, alternative delivery systems, and customer satisfaction evaluation techniques. **Administration and Management:** Principles and processes involved in business and organizational planning, coordination, and execution. This includes strategic planning, resource allocation, manpower modeling, leadership techniques, and production methods. **Mathematics:** Numbers and their operations and interrelationships, including arithmetic, algebra, geometry, calculus, and statistics and their applications.

Work Environment: Indoors; sitting; repetitive motions.

Zoologists and Wildlife Biologists

- ✸ Education/Training Required: Bachelor's degree
- ✸ Annual Earnings: $55,100
- ✸ Beginning Wage: $34,500
- ✸ Earnings Growth Potential: Medium
- ✸ Growth: 8.7%
- ✸ Annual Job Openings: 1,444
- ✸ Self-Employed: 2.6%
- ✸ Part-Time: 7.3%

Study the origins, behavior, diseases, genetics, and life processes of animals and wildlife. May specialize in wildlife research and management, including the collection and analysis of biological data to determine the environmental effects of present and potential use of land and water areas. Study animals in their natural habitats, assessing effects of environment and industry on animals, interpreting findings, and recommending alternative operating conditions for industry. Inventory or estimate plant and wildlife populations. Analyze characteristics of animals to identify and classify them. Make recommendations on management systems and planning for wildlife populations and habitat, consulting with stakeholders and the public at large to explore options. Disseminate information by writing reports and scientific papers or journal articles and by making presentations and giving talks for schools, clubs, interest groups, and park interpretive programs. Study characteristics of animals such as origin, interrelationships, classification, life histories and diseases, development, genetics, and distribution. Perform administrative duties such as

fundraising, public relations, budgeting, and supervision of zoo staff. Organize and conduct experimental studies with live animals in controlled or natural surroundings. Oversee the care and distribution of zoo animals, working with curators and zoo directors to determine the best way to contain animals, maintain their habitats, and manage facilities. Coordinate preventive programs to control the outbreak of wildlife diseases. Prepare collections of preserved specimens or microscopic slides for species identification and study of development or disease. Raise specimens for study and observation or for use in experiments. Collect and dissect animal specimens and examine specimens under microscope.

Personality Type: Investigative. These occupations frequently involve working with ideas and require an extensive amount of thinking. They can involve searching for facts and figuring out problems mentally.

GOE—Interest Area/Cluster: 01. Agriculture and Natural Resources. **Work Group:** 01.02. Resource Science/Engineering for Plants, Animals, and the Environment. **Other Jobs in This Work Group:** Agricultural Engineers; Animal Scientists; Conservation Scientists; Environmental Engineers; Foresters; Mining and Geological Engineers, Including Mining Safety Engineers; Petroleum Engineers; Range Managers; Soil and Plant Scientists; Soil and Water Conservationists.

Skills—Science: Using scientific methods to solve problems. **Management of Financial Resources:** Determining how money will be spent to get the work done and accounting for these expenditures. **Writing:** Communicating effectively with others in writing as indicated by the needs of the audience. **Coordination:** Adjusting actions in relation to others' actions. **Persuasion:** Persuading others to approach things differently. **Operations Analysis:** Analyzing needs and product requirements to create a design. **Judgment and Decision Making:** Weighing the relative costs and benefits of a potential action. **Reading Comprehension:** Understanding written sentences and paragraphs in work-related documents.

Education and Training Programs: Animal Behavior and Ethology; Animal Physiology; Cell/Cellular Biology and Anatomical Sciences, Other; Ecology; Entomology; Wildlife and Wildlands Science and Management; Wildlife Biology; Zoology/Animal Biology; Zoology/Animal Biology, Other. **Related Knowledge/Courses—Biology:** Plant and animal living tissue, cells, organisms, and entities, including their functions, interdependencies, and interactions with each other and the environment. **Geography:**

Various methods for describing the location and distribution of land, sea, and air masses, including their physical locations, relationships, and characteristics. **Law and Government:** Laws, legal codes, court procedures, precedents, government regulations, executive orders, agency rules, and the democratic political process. **English Language:** The structure and content of the English language, including the meaning and spelling of words, rules of composition, and grammar. **Administration and Management:** Principles and processes involved in business and organizational planning, coordination, and execution. This includes strategic planning, resource allocation, manpower modeling, leadership techniques, and production methods. **Computers and Electronics:** Electric circuit boards, processors, chips, and computer hardware and software, including applications and programming.

Work Environment: More often indoors than outdoors; sitting.

Index